World Travel Atlas

The **Atlas for the Travel Industry**

ISBN: 1–902221–35–4

© 2000 Columbus Travel Guides, save where marked*

REFERENCE

Do not remove from Library

* *Maps on pages 1 to 54 supplied by ICA Bokförlag, AB, Sweden © 1998/9, and designed and produced by European Map Graphics Ltd*
* *Information for the skiing maps on pages 100 and 149 © 1999 Snow-Hunter, Inverness*
* *Maps on pages 164 to 172 supplied by Mountain High Maps © 1993 Digital Wisdom Inc.*
* *Information for the Human Rights map on page 68 © 1999 The Observer*

Columbus Travel Guides, Jordan House, 47 Brunswick Place, London N1 6EB, United Kingdom
Tel: **+44 (0)20 7608 6666** ◆ Fax: **+44 (0)20 7608 6569** ◆ E-mail: **booksales@columbus-group.co.uk**

original cartography David Burles.

design & production Space Design and Production Services Ltd, London N1.

researchers Patrick Fitzgerald, Jon Gillaspie, Ned Middleton, Tony Peisley, Patrick Thorne, Karen Wrack, Sachiko Burles, Penny Locke, Annelouise van der Sterre, Lynda Anderson.

sector booksales managers Matthew Roe, Keith Tennant, James MacPherson (*Columbus Travel Guides, London N1 6EB*). Gunter Knop, Michael Knop (*Columbus Travel Guides, 38618 Braunschweig*). David Frank, Amanda Betley (*SF Communications, Roanoke VA 24018*).

colour reproduction Kingswood-Steele, London N1.

printed & bound by Thanet Press Ltd, Margate.

founding editor Mike Taylor of the University of Brighton.

publisher Peter Korniczky.

◆ *The World Travel Atlas has been created from a wide range of sources, and where appropriate these have been credited on the relevant maps or charts. The publishers would like to thank all the tourist offices, embassies, high commissions, airlines, airports, cruise and ferry operators, travel industry associations, publishers, sporting bodies and other organisations and individuals who have assisted in the preparation of this edition, with particular thanks to UNESCO, the World Tourism Organisation, the British Tourism Authority, the English Tourist Board, The Observer, the World Health Organisation, European Map Graphics, Snow-Hunter, the Astronomy Information Service, Parks Canada, the United States National Parks Service, the Canadian Tourism Commission, ToerBoek and the Royal Greenwich Observatory.*

◆ *Whilst every effort is made by the publishers to ensure the accuracy of the information contained in this edition of the* World Travel Atlas, *the publishers can accept no responsibility for any loss occasioned to any person acting or refraining from acting as a result of the material contained in this publication, nor liability for any financial or other agreements which may be entered into with any organisations or individuals listed in the text.*

◆ *The publishers welcome comments from all users as to how future editions can be yet further improved. Please contact Columbus Travel Guides at the address above. Many of the improvements made to past editions of the title have been suggested by readers: your response will, therefore, be influential.*

COLUMBUS
TRAVEL GUIDES

CONTENTS

This atlas has been designed to give travellers, travel trade professionals, business people, teachers, students and researchers a clear and comprehensive overview of the world: many features are wholly new to this edition. It is divided into seven colour-coded sections (the black-boxed headings below). The **Statistics Section** provides information on a broad range of travel- and business-related topics. The **General Maps** are a conventional set of plates covering the entire world and featuring particularly detailed coverage of the USA. The **Specialist Maps**, the heart of the book, explore a large number of diverse themes and offer in-depth coverage of the most significant countries and regions, together with many supporting charts and tables. This section is sub-divided by continent. The **Relief Maps** provide physical imaging of the whole world. The **Appendices** provide much useful additional information, in particular the Country Statistics table which provides exact data for many of the maps which appear elsewhere in the book. The **Index** references every place name found in the Atlas to its largest-scale location. Finally, there is a set of **Outline Maps** designed for a wide range of teaching and training applications.

Statistics iv-x
Global Travel	iv-v
Business & Economic	vi-vii
USA & Canada	viii-ix
UK	x

General Maps 1-54
Key & Introduction	1
World Political	2-3
Europe	4
Benelux	5
British Isles	6-7
Germany	8-9
France	10
Spain & Portugal	11
Italy	12
Central Europe	13
The Balkans	14
Greece & Turkey	15
Scandinavia	16
European Russia	17
Middle East	18
Africa	19
Northwest Africa	20
Northeast Africa	21
West Africa	22
Central Africa	23
Southern Africa	24
Asia	25
Northwest Asia	26
Northeast Asia	27
South Asia	28
East Asia	29
Japan & Korea	30
Southeast Asia	31
Malaysia & Indonesia	32
Oceania	33
Australia	34
New Zealand & New Guinea	35
North America	36

Central America	37
Canada	38-39
USA	40-41
Northwest USA	42
Midwest USA	43
Northeast USA	44
Southwest USA	45
Central USA	46
Southern USA	47
Southeast USA	48
Florida & Alaska	49
South America	50
Northern South America	51
Central South America	52
Southern South America	53
Polar Regions	54

Specialist Maps 55-163
Key & Introduction	55

World
WTO Regions	55
Climate	56
Time	57
The Sun, Earth & Moon	57
Lithospheric Plates	58
Prevailing Winds	58
Ocean Surface Currents	58
Population Density	59
Urbanization	59
Tourist Receipts	60
Tourist Arrivals	60
Tourist Expenditure	60
Income	61
External Debt	61
Growth Rates	61
Economic Activity	62-63
Oil, Gas & Coal Deposits	64
Energy Production	64
Energy Consumption	65
Renewable Energy	65

Telecoms Subscribers	66
Submarine Cables	66
Telecoms Traffic	67
Internet Subscribers	67
Human Development	68
Human Rights	68
Military Spending	69
Military Strength	69
Weapons of Mass Destruction	69
International Organisations	70-71
Agriculture & Forests	72
Threatened Plant Species	72
Carbon Dioxide Emissions	72
Health	73
Sport	74
Driving	75
Airports	76-78
IATA Areas	76-78
International Flight Times	79
Cruising	80-81
Natural Heritage Sites	82-83
Cultural Heritage Sites	84-86

Europe
Climate	88
National Parks	89
Historical	90
Empires	91
The European Union	92-93
Railways	94-95
Ferries	94-95
Blue Flag Beaches	96-97
Leisure Parks	98
Museums & Art Galleries	99
Skiing	100
UK	101-107
UK Beaches	101
UK National Parks	101
UK Counties	102-103
UK Rail Operators	105
UK Motorways	106

UK Airports	106
UK Ferries	106
London Airport Connections	107
Ireland	108
Benelux	109
Netherlands Attractions	110
Germany	111-113
Berlin Airport Connections	111
German Castles	113
German Spas	113
France	114-115
France Wine Regions	114
Paris Airport Connections	114
Spain	116-117
Canary Islands	116-117
Balearic Islands	117
Portugal	118
Azores	118
Madeira	118
Switzerland	119
Austria	119
Italy	120-121
Greece	122-123
Turkey	122-123
Malta	123
Cyprus	123
Scandinavia	124-125
Former Soviet Union	126-127
Ancient Trade Routes	127
Central Europe	128

Africa & Indian Ocean

Climate	129
Languages	130
Tanzania	130
Zimbabwe	130
Morocco	131
Egypt	131
Tunisia	131
Kenya	131
Wildlife Parks & Reserves	132-133
Réunion	132
Mauritius	132
Seychelles	133
South Africa	134
Red Sea Diving	135

Asia

The Holy Land	135
Climate	136
India	137-138
Indian Hill Stations	138

Sri Lanka	138
Maldives	138
China	139
Hong Kong	139
Macau	139
Japan	140
Malaysia	141
Singapore	141
Vietnam	141
Thailand	142
Indonesia	143

Australasia

Australia	144-145
New Zealand	145

Canada & the USA

North America Climate	146
Railways	147
Airports	147
NYC Airport Connections	147
Museums & Art Galleries	148
Skiing	149
USA	150-154
US National Parks	150-151
US Theme Parks	150-151
Canada	155-156
Canadian National Parks	156
Canadian Theme Parks	156

The Rest of the Americas

Mexico	157
Caribbean Languages	158
The Bahamas	158
Turks & Caicos Islands	158
Cuba	158
Haiti	159
Dominican Republic	159
Cayman Islands	159
Jamaica	159
Puerto Rico	159
Bermuda	159
Caribbean Diving	160-161
British Virgin Islands	160
US Virgin Islands	160
Anguilla	160
St Maarten	160
St Martin	160
St Barthélemy	160
Aruba	160
Curaçao	160
Bonaire	160
Isla de Margarita	160

Trinidad	160
Tobago	160
Grenada	160
Saba	161
St Eustatius	161
St Kitts & Nevis	161
Montserrat	161
Antigua	161
Barbuda	161
Guadeloupe	161
Martinique	161
Dominica	161
St Lucia	161
Barbados	161
St Vincent	161
The Grenadines	161
South America Climate	162
South America	163

Relief Maps 164-172

World	164
Europe	165
Africa	166
Asia	167
North America	168
South America	169
Australia & New Zealand	170
The Arctic	171
The Antarctic	171
Pacific Ocean	172
Atlantic Ocean	172

Appendices 173-182

1	Geographical Definitions	173
2	Highest & Lowest	173
3	World's Longest Rivers	173
4	Conversion Chart	173
5	Foreign Terms	174-175
6	Climate Terms	175
7	US States	176
8	Canadian Prov's/Terr's	176
9	Australian Prov's/Terr's	176
10	French Départements	176
11	World Fed. of Gt Towers	177
12	World Monuments Watch	177
13	Country Statistics	178-182

Index 183-230

Outline Maps X1-X16

GLOBAL TRAVEL

Figure W1

TRAVEL PAYMENTS – RECEIPTS AND EXPENDITURE, 1998
Source: World Tourism Organization

Income from travel (excluding transport), US$m
– money received from foreigners visiting that country

Expenditure on travel (excluding transport), US$m
– money spent abroad by nationals of that country

Countries (x-axis): USA, Italy, France, Spain, UK, China, Germany, Austria, Canada, Turkey, Switzerland, Poland, Mexico, Russia, Netherlands, Thailand, Korea, Rep., Australia, Belgium, Argentina

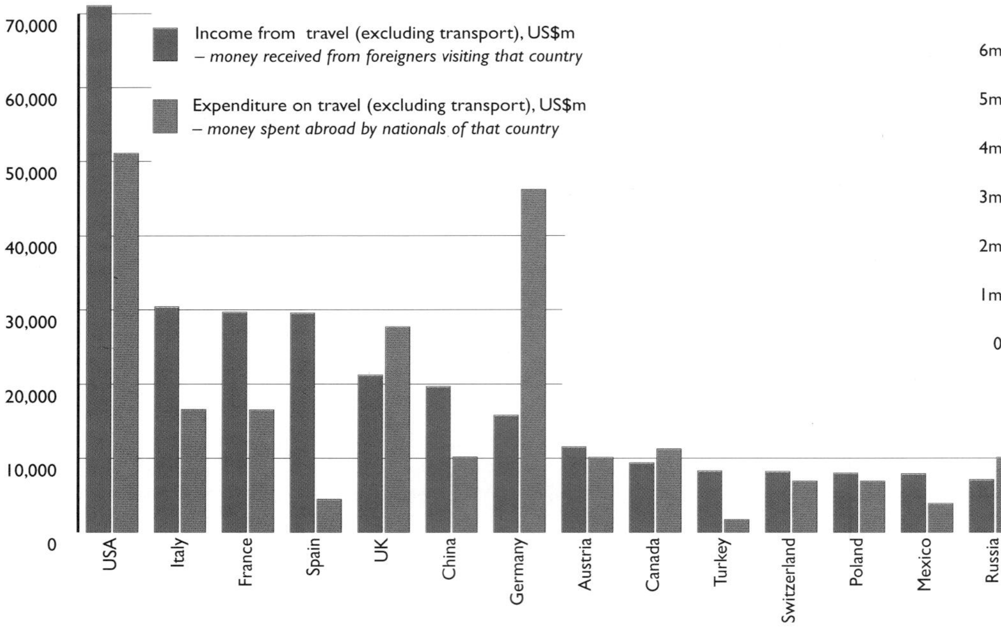

Figure W4

NUMBER OF BED-PLACES IN HOTELS AND SIMILAR ESTABLISHMENTS
Source: World Tourism Organization

Countries: USA, Japan, Italy, Germany, China, France, Spain, UK, Mexico, Canada

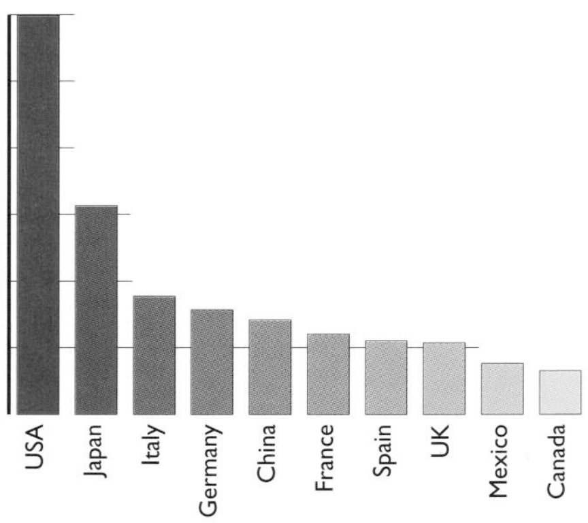

Figure W2

THE WORLD'S TOP 50 AIRPORTS, 1996
Source: Annual Airport Traffic Statistics, Airports Council International

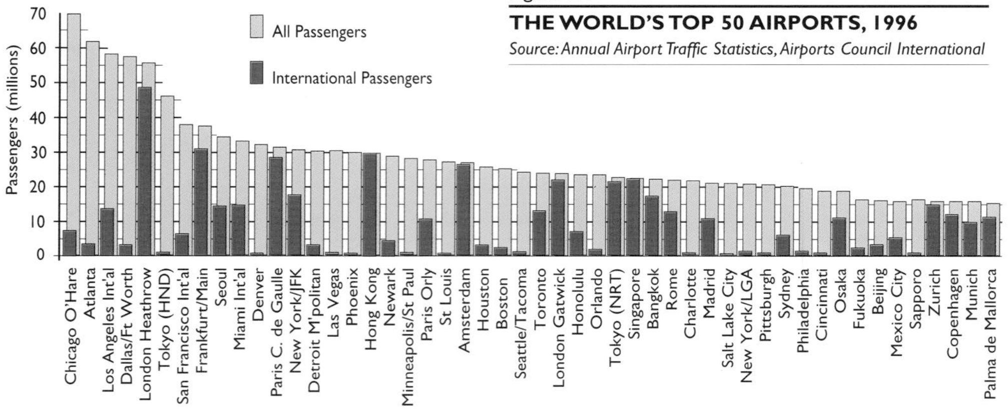

All Passengers

International Passengers

Airports: Chicago O'Hare, Atlanta, Los Angeles Int'l, Dallas/Ft Worth, London Heathrow, Tokyo (HND), San Francisco Int'l, Frankfurt/Main, Seoul, Miami Int'l, Denver, Paris C. de Gaulle, New York/JFK, Detroit M'politan, Las Vegas, Phoenix, Hong Kong, Newark, Minneapolis/St Paul, Paris Orly, St Louis, Amsterdam, Houston, Boston, Seattle/Tacoma, Toronto, London Gatwick, Honolulu, Orlando, Tokyo (NRT), Singapore, Bangkok, Rome, Charlotte, Madrid, Salt Lake City, New York/LGA, Pittsburgh, Sydney, Philadelphia, Cincinnati, Osaka, Fukuoka, Mexico City, Sapporo, Zurich, Beijing, Copenhagen, Munich, Palma de Mallorca

Figure W5

WORLD TOURISM RECEIPTS
Source: World Tourism Organisation

Receipts (US$ Billions). Years: 1988, 1989, 1990, 1991, 1992, 1993, 1994, 1995, 1996, 1997

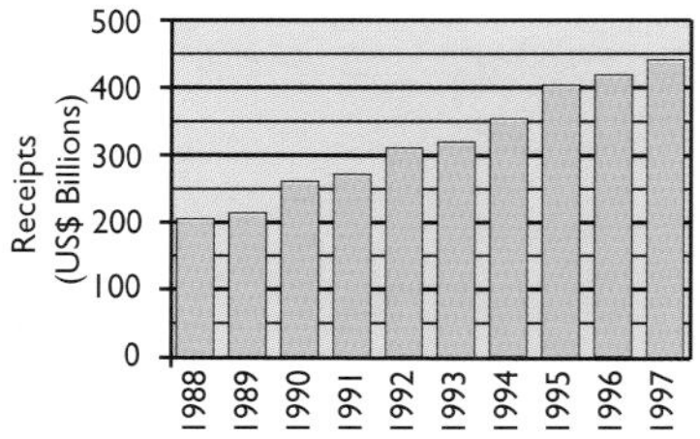

Figure W6

AVERAGE VACATION DAYS
Source: World Tourism Organisation

Italy 42, France 37, Germany 35, Brazil 34, UK 28, Canada 26, Korea 25, Japan 25, USA 13

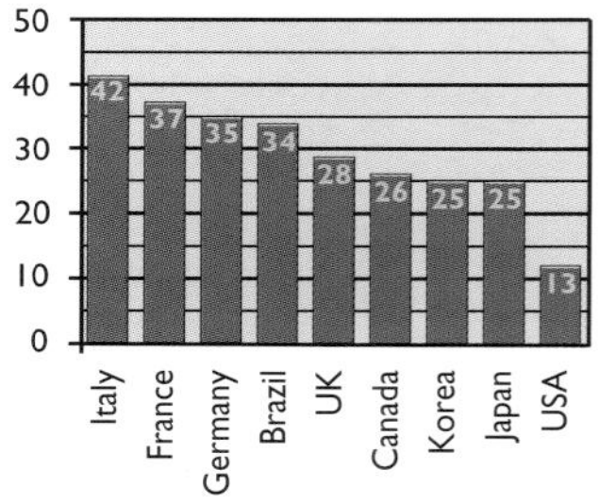

Figure W3

THE TOP 25 TRAVEL DESTINATIONS, 1998
Source: World Tourism Organization

The chart below shows tourism arrival figures (excluding same-day visitors) for 1998. Figures for China, Hong Kong and Macau have been shown separately. For exact totals, please consult the Countries A-Z section on pages 178–182.

The figures above each chart show the world ranking in 1990, coloured in red if the ranking has fallen since that time, in blue if it has risen and in black if it has remained the same. The 1990 ranking for Russia relates to the whole of the old USSR. 1990 figures for Ukraine and Croatia are not available as the countries did not exist as independent states at that time.

The pie-chart to the right shows the figures for the top ten destinations expressed as a percentage of all tourist arrivals. Thus it can be seen that these countries accounted for over half of all arrivals; France, the USA and Spain for over a quarter; and France alone for almost one in nine.

Eleven other countries had tourist arrivals in excess of 2,000,000 in 1998: Bulgaria, Romania, Norway, Sweden, India, Dominican Rep., Taiwan, Cyprus, Uruguay, Philippines and Denmark.

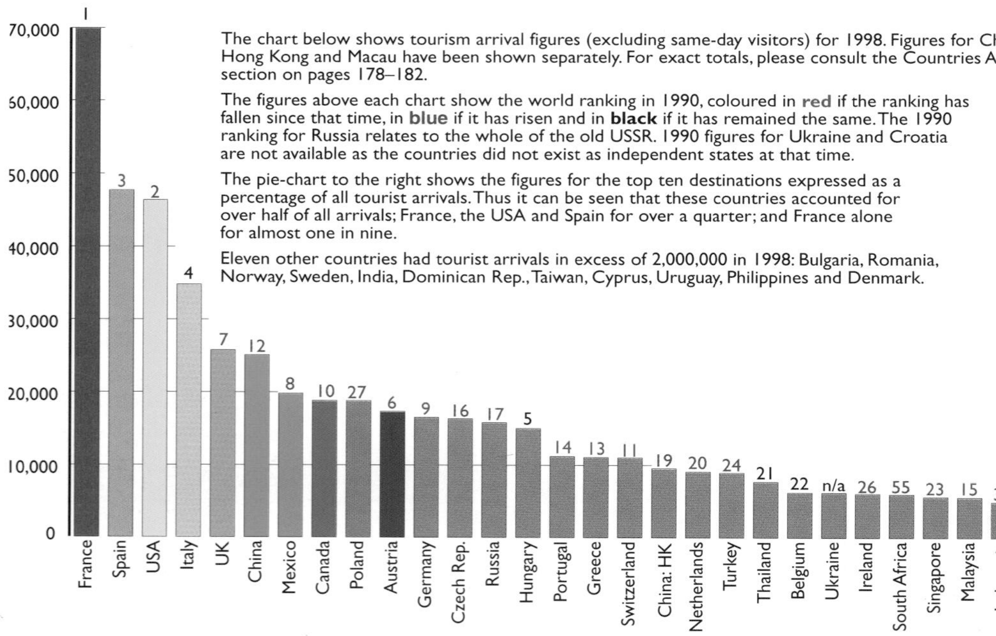

Bar chart rankings and countries: France 1, Spain 3, USA 2, Italy 4, UK 7, China 12, Mexico 8, Canada 10, Poland 27, Austria 6, Germany 9, Czech Rep. 16, Russia 17, Hungary 5, Portugal 14, Greece 13, Switzerland 11, China: HK 19, Netherlands 20, Turkey 24, Thailand 21, Belgium 22, Ukraine n/a, Ireland 26, South Africa 55, Singapore 23, Malaysia 15, Indonesia 38, Argentina 32, Brazil 53, Tunisia 29, Korea, Rep. 31, Australia 36, Croatia n/a, Japan 28, Saudi Arabia 37, China: Macau 34, Puerto Rico 33, Morocco 25, Egypt 35

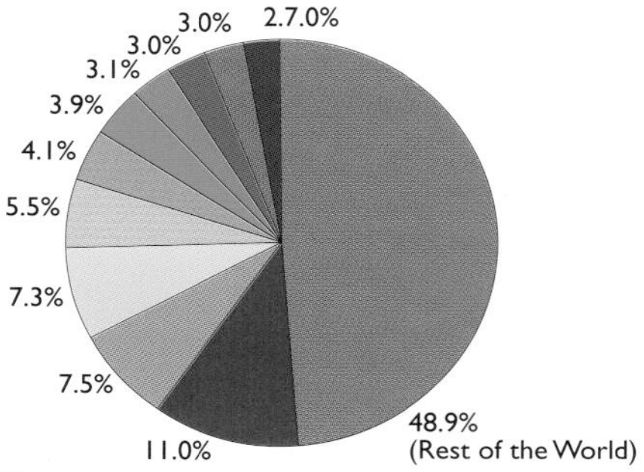

Pie chart: 48.9% (Rest of the World), 11.0%, 7.5%, 7.3%, 5.5%, 4.1%, 3.9%, 3.1%, 3.0%, 3.0%, 2.7%

GLOBAL TRAVEL

Figure W6

WORLDWIDE DESTINATIONS – WHO GOES WHERE, 1998
Source: World Tourism Organization

The large charts show the regions visited by nationals of each country in 1998. The small charts show the average number of trips abroad made by nationals of that country in 1998 – the total number of foreign visits divided by the population of the country.

United States of America

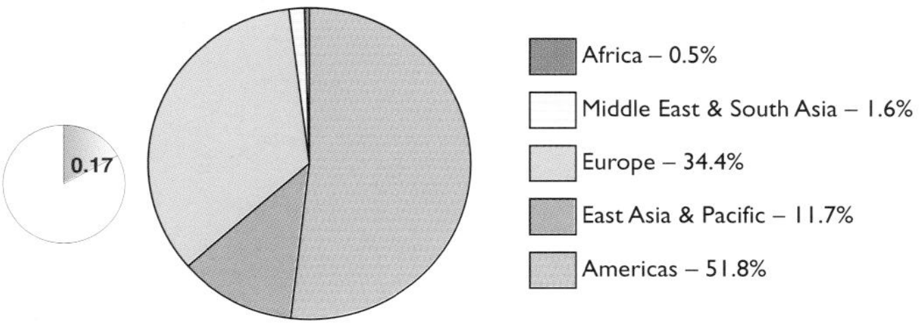

0.17

- Africa – 0.5%
- Middle East & South Asia – 1.6%
- Europe – 34.4%
- East Asia & Pacific – 11.7%
- Americas – 51.8%

Australia

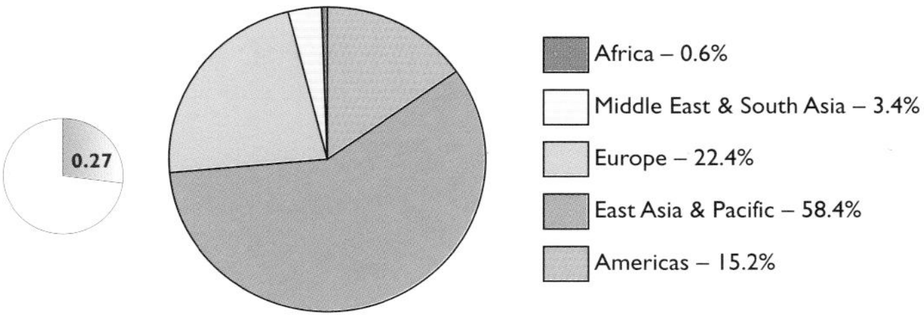

0.27

- Africa – 0.6%
- Middle East & South Asia – 3.4%
- Europe – 22.4%
- East Asia & Pacific – 58.4%
- Americas – 15.2%

Canada

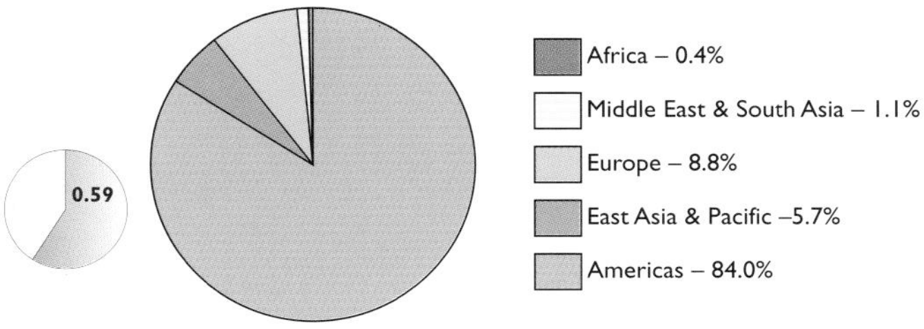

0.59

- Africa – 0.4%
- Middle East & South Asia – 1.1%
- Europe – 8.8%
- East Asia & Pacific – 5.7%
- Americas – 84.0%

Netherlands

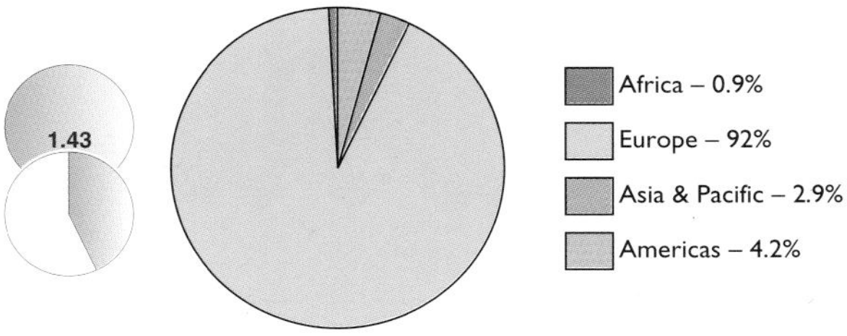

1.43

- Africa – 0.9%
- Europe – 92%
- Asia & Pacific – 2.9%
- Americas – 4.2%

United Kingdom

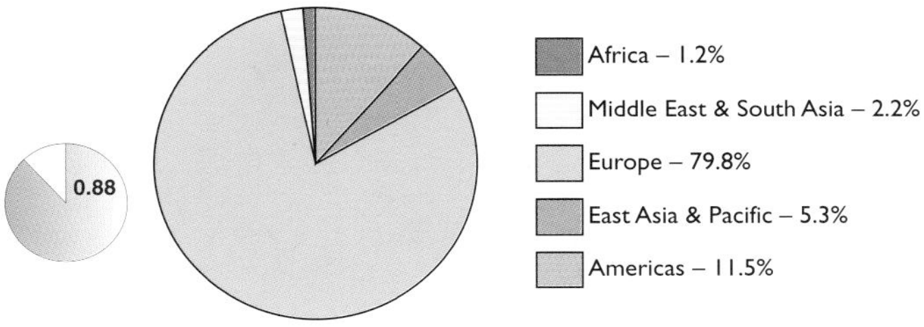

0.88

- Africa – 1.2%
- Middle East & South Asia – 2.2%
- Europe – 79.8%
- East Asia & Pacific – 5.3%
- Americas – 11.5%

France

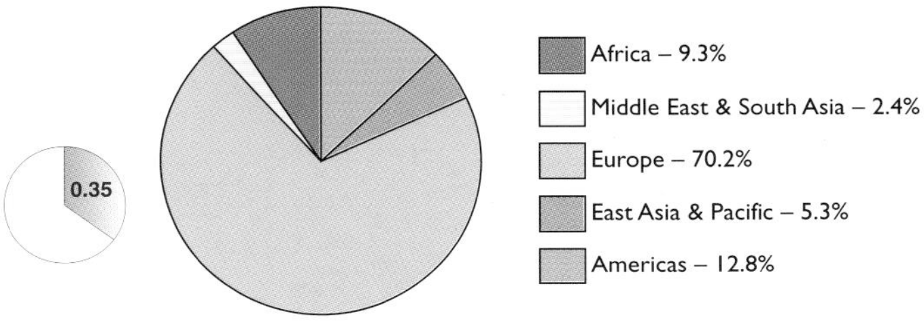

0.35

- Africa – 9.3%
- Middle East & South Asia – 2.4%
- Europe – 70.2%
- East Asia & Pacific – 5.3%
- Americas – 12.8%

Germany

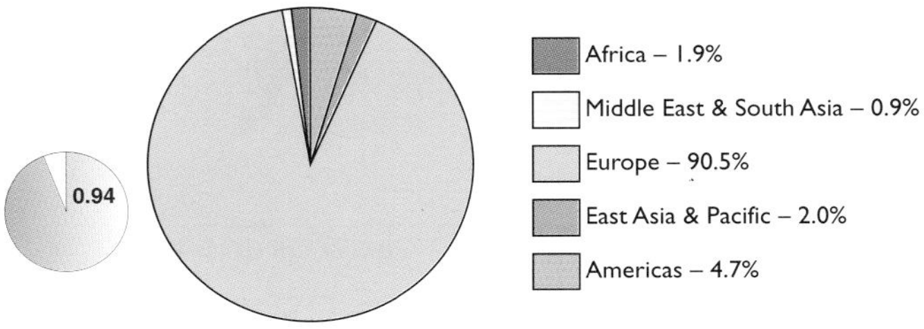

0.94

- Africa – 1.9%
- Middle East & South Asia – 0.9%
- Europe – 90.5%
- East Asia & Pacific – 2.0%
- Americas – 4.7%

Spain

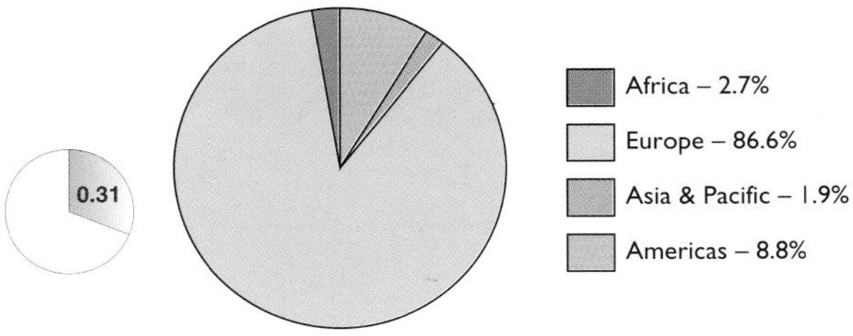

0.31

- Africa – 2.7%
- Europe – 86.6%
- Asia & Pacific – 1.9%
- Americas – 8.8%

Japan

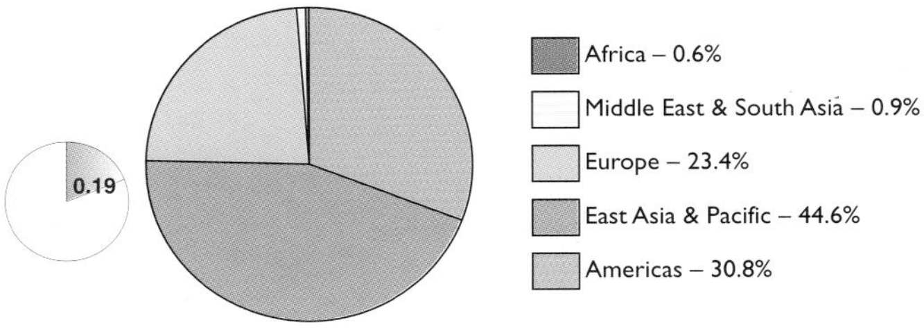

0.19

- Africa – 0.6%
- Middle East & South Asia – 0.9%
- Europe – 23.4%
- East Asia & Pacific – 44.6%
- Americas – 30.8%

Sweden

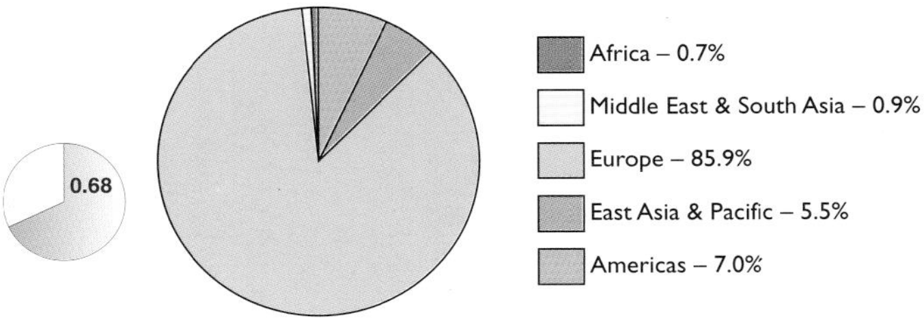

0.68

- Africa – 0.7%
- Middle East & South Asia – 0.9%
- Europe – 85.9%
- East Asia & Pacific – 5.5%
- Americas – 7.0%

BUSINESS & ECONOMIC

Figure E1

THE WORLD'S LARGEST COMPANIES, BY MARKET CAP, 1998
Source: Financial Times

These figures show the world's largest companies ranked by their market capital as at 28th January 1999. Although this measure is volatile as it is affected by the number of issued shares and their price, it is a good yardstick of the value of the company in the eyes of the world's stock markets.

65 other companies had market capital in excess of £30,000 million on this day: the chart below ranks all 100 of these companies by country.

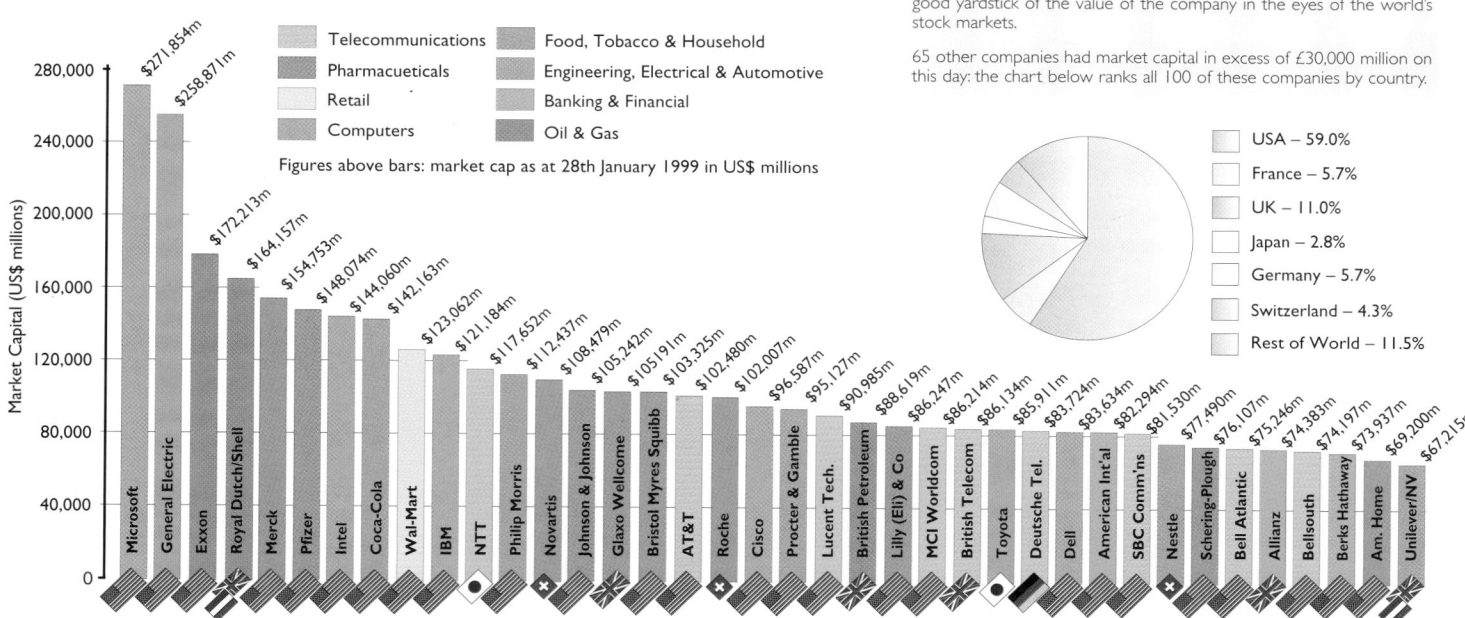

Telecommunications
Pharmaceuticals
Retail
Computers
Food, Tobacco & Household
Engineering, Electrical & Automotive
Banking & Financial
Oil & Gas

Figures above bars: market cap as at 28th January 1999 in US$ millions

USA – 59.0%
France – 5.7%
UK – 11.0%
Japan – 2.8%
Germany – 5.7%
Switzerland – 4.3%
Rest of World – 11.5%

Figure E2

EUROPE'S LARGEST CORPORATE EMPLOYERS, 1998
Source: Finacial Times

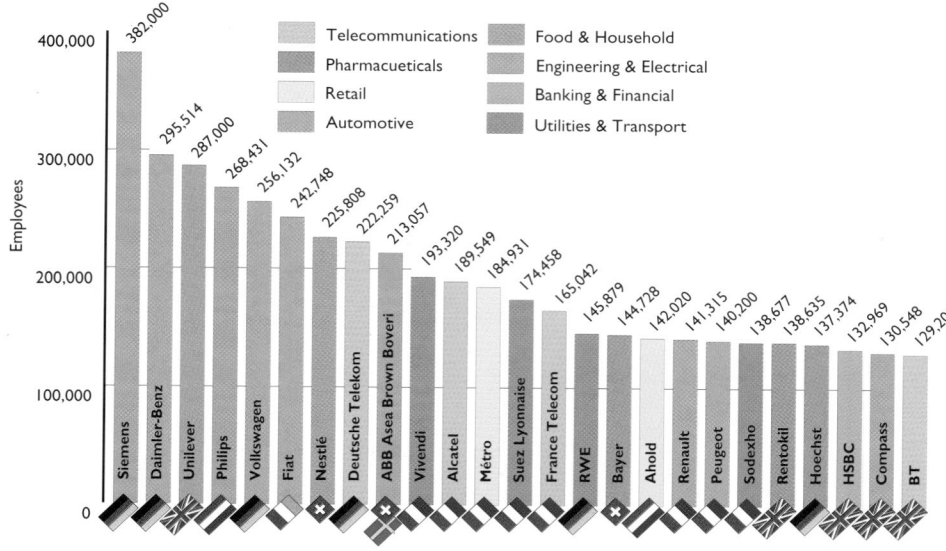

Telecommunications
Pharmacueticals
Retail
Automotive
Food & Household
Engineering & Electrical
Banking & Financial
Utilities & Transport

Figure E3

GOVERNMENT SPENDING, 1997
Source: Economist Diary/OECD/World Bank

These figures show the government spending for the world's 16 largest economies, expressed (in orange) as a percentage of the country's national income. Countries are ranked in descending order of size of national income reading from the top left.

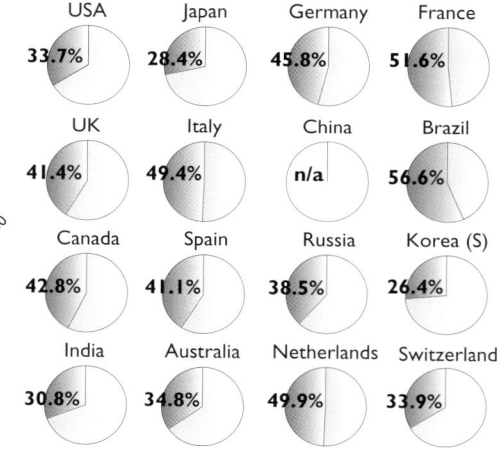

USA 33.7%	Japan 28.4%	Germany 45.8%	France 51.6%
UK 41.4%	Italy 49.4%	China n/a	Brazil 56.6%
Canada 42.8%	Spain 41.1%	Russia 38.5%	Korea (S) 26.4%
India 30.8%	Australia 34.8%	Netherlands 49.9%	Switzerland 33.9%

Figure E4

MOTHER-TONGUE SPEAKERS, c.1992
Source: Cambridge Factfinder

Figures given below are estimates of mother-tongue speakers in the early 1990s. They do not include second-language speakers.

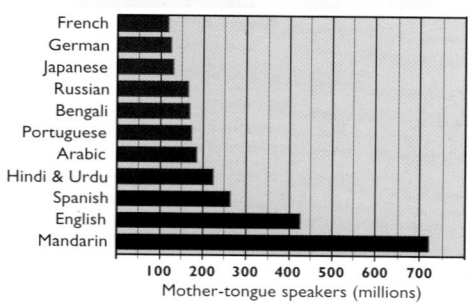

French
German
Japanese
Russian
Bengali
Portuguese
Arabic
Hindi & Urdu
Spanish
English
Mandarin

100 200 300 400 500 600 700
Mother-tongue speakers (millions)

Figure E5

ONLINE SALES
Source: The Economist/Jupiter

Actual European and North American online retail sales for 1998 and predictions for 2002.

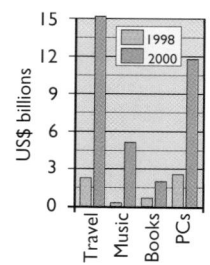

1998
2000

Travel Music Books PCs

Figure E6

GROSS DOMESTIC PROUCT GROWTH AND INFLATION
Source: The Economist

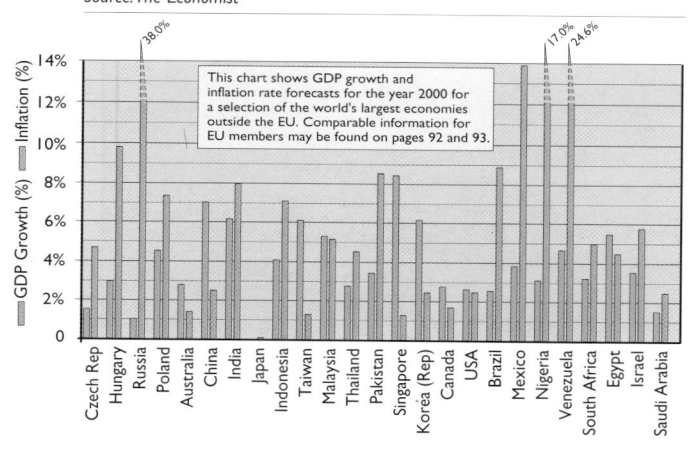

This chart shows GDP growth and inflation rate forecasts for the year 2000 for a selection of the world's largest economies outside the EU. Comparable information for EU members may be found on pages 92 and 93.

Czech Rep, Hungary, Russia, Poland, Australia, China, India, Japan, Indonesia, Taiwan, Malaysia, Thailand, Pakistan, Singapore, Korea (Rep), Canada, USA, Brazil, Mexico, Nigeria, Venezuela, South Africa, Egypt, Israel, Saudi Arabia

BUSINESS & ECONOMIC

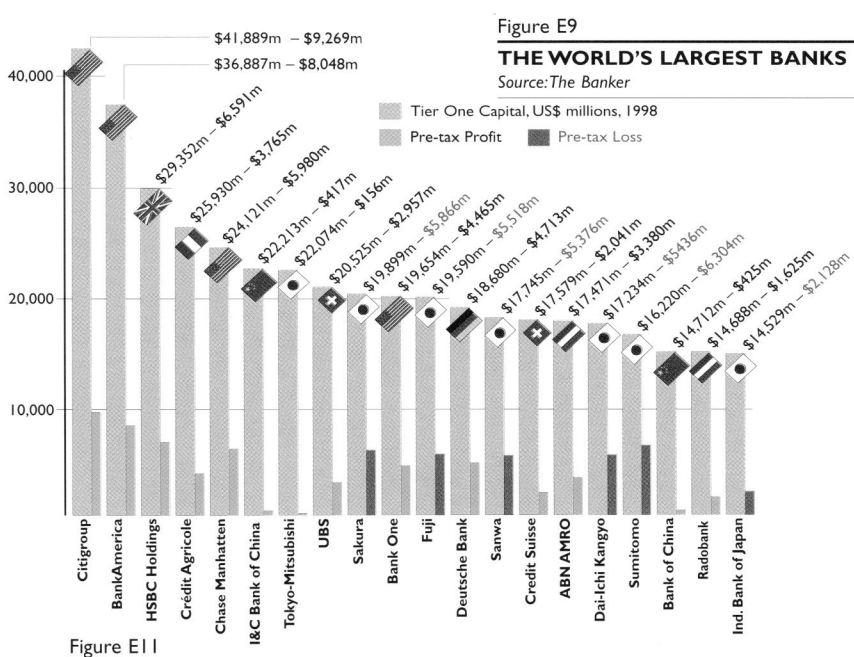

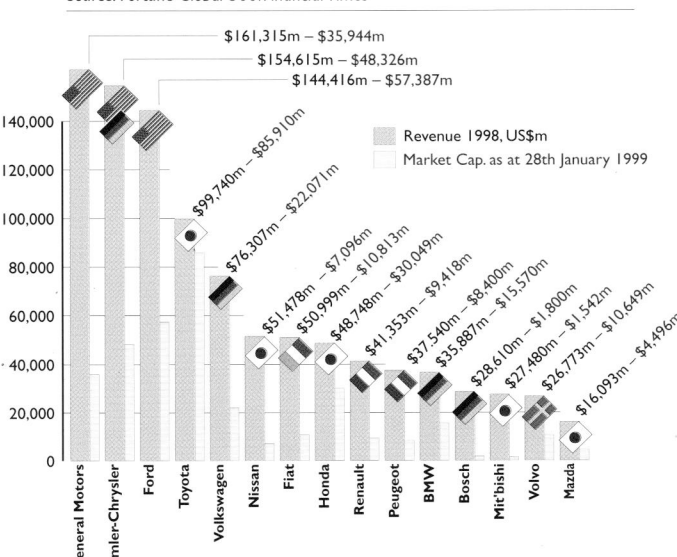

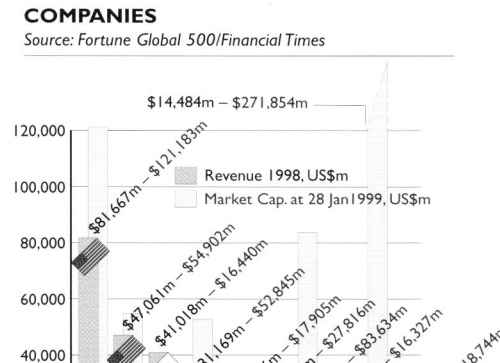

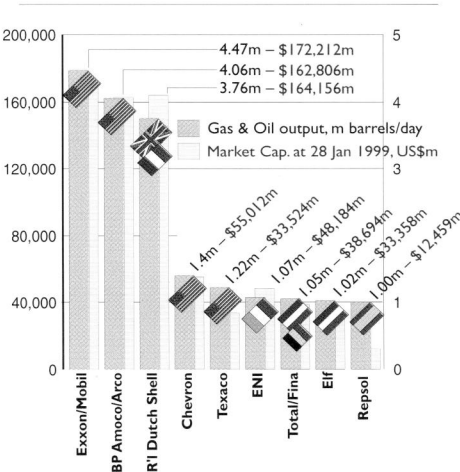

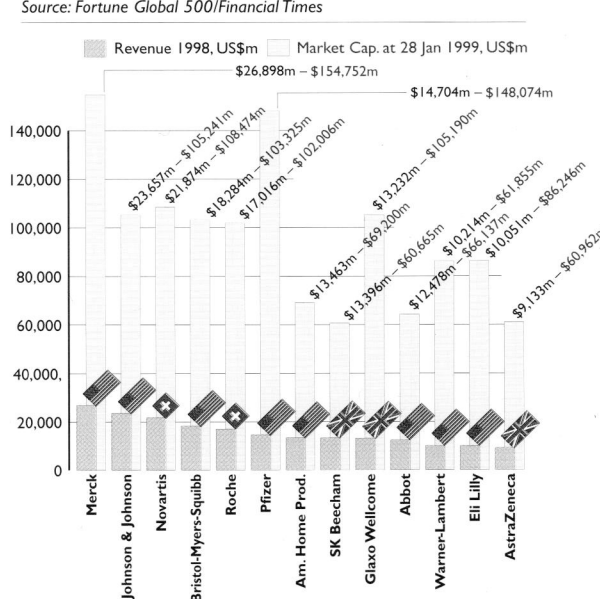

Figure E7
THE WORLD'S LARGEST TELECOM CARRIERS
Source: ITU

- Million International Telecom Traffic (MITT) minutes, 1998
- Million US$ of revenue derived from this traffic

14,529 – $9,555m
10,747 – $3,357m
10,058 – $4,743m
7,300 – $1,859m
6,350 – $924m
5,289 – $1,438m
4,470 – $1,820m
4,212 – $2,200m
3,818 – $1,1995m
3,704 – $813m
3,680 – $1,379m
3,286 – $879m
3,243 – $847m
2,670 – $477m
2,622 – $548m
2,251 – $1,267m
2,200 – $1,903m
1,954 – $492m
1,905 – $631m
1,679 – $1,600m

AT&T, Deutsche Telekom, MCI-Worldcom, France Télécom, British Telecom, Telecom Italia, Sprint, DGT, Hong Kong Tel., Telefonica, Swisscom, Telmex, KPN, C&W, Belgacom, S'pore Tel., KDD, PTA, Teleglobe, VSNL

Figure E8
THE WORLD'S LARGEST COMPUTING COMPANIES
Source: Fortune Global 500/Financial Times

- Revenue 1998, US$m
- Market Cap. at 28 Jan 1999, US$m

$14,484m – $271,854m
$81,667m – $121,183m
$47,061m – $54,902m
$41,018m – $16,440m
$31,169m – $52,845m
$21,616m – $17,905m
$20,019m – $27,816m
$18,243m – $83,634m
$16,891m – $16,327m
$9,791m – $18,744m

IBM, H-Packard, Fujitsu, Compaq, Canon, Xerox, Dell, EDS, Microsoft, Sun

Figure E9
THE WORLD'S LARGEST BANKS
Source: The Banker

- Tier One Capital, US$ millions, 1998
- Pre-tax Profit
- Pre-tax Loss

$41,889m – $9,269m
$36,887m – $8,048m
$29,352m – $6,591m
$25,930m – $3,765m
$24,121m – $5,980m
$22,213m – $417m
$22,074m – $156m
$20,525m – $2,957m
$19,899m – $5,866m
$19,654m – $4,465m
$19,590m – $5,518m
$18,680m – $4,713m
$17,745m – $5,376m
$17,579m – $2,041m
$17,471m – $3,380m
$17,234m – $436m
$16,220m – $6,304m
$14,712m – $425m
$14,688m – $1,625m
$14,529m – $2,128m

Citigroup, BankAmerica, HSBC Holdings, Crédit Agricole, Chase Manhattan, I&C Bank of China, Tokyo-Mitsubishi, UBS, Sakura, Bank One, Fuji, Deutsche Bank, Sanwa, Credit Suisse, ABN AMRO, Dai-Ichi Kangyo, Sumitomo, Bank of China, Radobank, Ind. Bank of Japan

Figure E10
THE WORLD'S MOST PRODUCTIVE OIL & GAS COMPANIES
Source: Alexander's Gas & Oil Connections/Financial Times

- Gas & Oil output, m barrels/day
- Market Cap. at 28 Jan 1999, US$m

4.47m – $172,212m
4.06m – $162,806m
3.76m – $164,156m
1.4m – $55,012m
1.22m – $33,524m
1.07m – $48,184m
1.05m – $38,694m
1.02m – $33,358m
1.00m – $12,459m

Exxon/Mobil, BP Amoco/Arco, R'l Dutch Shell, Chevron, Texaco, ENI, Total/Fina, Elf, Repsol

Figure E11
THE WORLD'S LARGEST AUTOMOTIVE COMPANIES
Source: Fortune Global 500/Financial Times

- Revenue 1998, US$m
- Market Cap. as at 28th January 1999

$161,315m – $35,944m
$154,615m – $48,326m
$144,416m – $57,387m
$99,740m – $85,910m
$76,307m – $22,071m
$51,478m – $7,096m
$50,999m – $10,813m
$48,748m – $30,049m
$41,353m – $9,418m
$37,540m – $8,400m
$35,887m – $15,570m
$28,610m – $1,800m
$27,480m – $1,542m
$26,773m – $10,649m
$16,093m – $4,496m

General Motors, Daimler-Chrysler, Ford, Toyota, Volkswagen, Nissan, Fiat, Honda, Renault, Peugeot, BMW, Bosch, Mit'bishi, Volvo, Mazda

Figure E12
THE WORLD'S LARGEST PHARMACEUTICALS COMPANIES
Source: Fortune Global 500/Financial Times

- Revenue 1998, US$m
- Market Cap. at 28 Jan 1999, US$m

$26,898m – $154,752m
$14,704m – $148,074m
$23,657m – $105,241m
$21,874m – $108,474m
$18,284m – $103,325m
$17,016m – $102,006m
$13,463m – $69,200m
$13,396m – $60,665m
$13,232m – $105,190m
$12,478m – $66,137m
$10,214m – $61,855m
$10,051m – $86,246m
$9,133m – $60,962m

Merck, Johnson & Johnson, Novartis, Bristol-Myers-Squibb, Roche, Pfizer, Am. Home Prod., SK Beecham, Glaxo Wellcome, Abbot, Warner-Lambert, Eli Lilly, AstraZeneca

UNITED STATES

Figure U1

INTERNATIONAL TRAVEL TO THE USA, 1989-98

Source: Travel Industry Association of America

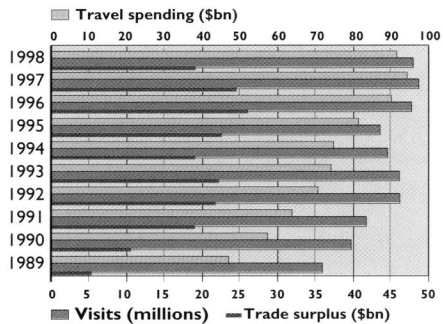

Figure U2

OVERSEAS VISITORS TO US STATES, TERRITORIES & CITIES, 1998

Source: Tourism Industries/International Trade Administration, Dept of Commerce

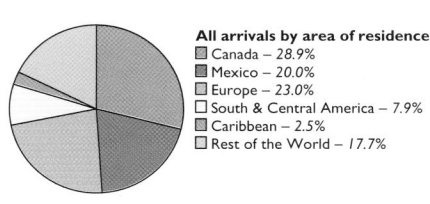

This chart shows the number of overseas visitors (excluding those from Canada and Mexico) to the principal states and cities in the USA in 1998. The arrows indicate an increase or decrease in arrivals compared to 1997. The % figures above each column show the total market share for that category: thus it can be seen that 73% of all overseas visitors went to at least one of Florida, California and New York, while the six most-visited cities accounted for 82% of all urban stays.

Figure U3

INTERNATIONAL VISITS TO THE USA, 1987 AND 1998

Sources: Tourism Industries, Bureau of Economic Analysis

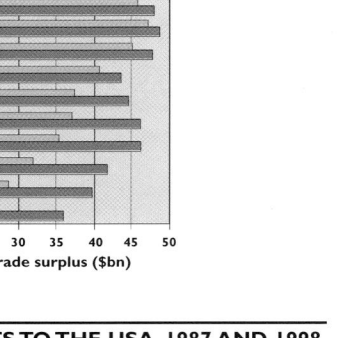

Residents of Japan, Canada and the UK accounted for 29% of all air arrivals into the USA in 1998. Over 200,000 residents of each of the following countries also visited the USA in 1998: Spain, Sweden, Israel, Bahamas, Ireland, Belgium, Jamaica and India.

Air arrivals by area of residence
- Africa – 0.9%
- Canada – 15.4%
- Asia – 26.8%
- South & Central America – 12.3%
- Caribbean – 3.9%
- Europe – 35.9%
- Mexico – 4.8%

Air arrivals by country of residence
- 1998
- 1987

All arrivals by area of residence
- Canada – 28.9%
- Mexico – 20.0%
- Europe – 23.0%
- South & Central America – 7.9%
- Caribbean – 2.5%
- Rest of the World – 17.7%

Figure U4

ON-LINE TRAVEL BUYERS IN THE USA

Source: Travel Industries of America

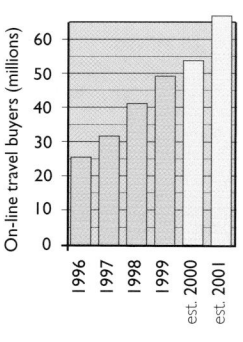

Figure U5

TOP 10 STATES BY TRAVELLER SPENDING, 1998

Source: Tourism Works for America Report

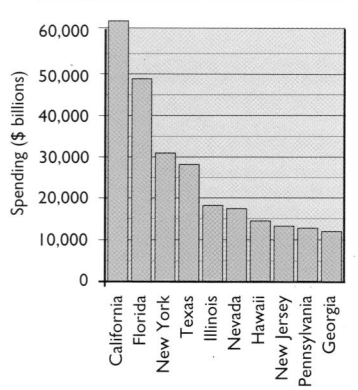

Figure U6

STATE SPENDING ON TOURISM PROMOTION, 1998

Source: Travel Industries of America

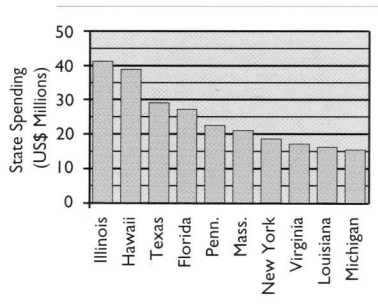

Figure U7

DEPARTURES & PAYMENTS BY US TRAVELLERS ABROAD, 1997

Source: Tourism Industries, International Trade Administration

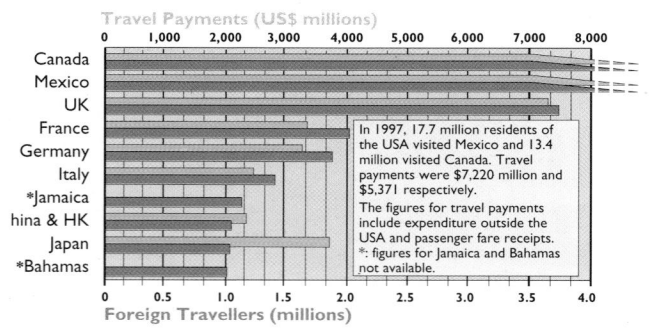

In 1997, 17.7 million residents of the USA visited Mexico and 13.4 million visited Canada. Travel payments were $7,220 million and $5,371 respectively.

The figures for travel payments include expenditure outside the USA and passenger fare receipts.
*: figures for Jamaica and Bahamas not available.

Figure U8

TYPES OF LODGING (US RESIDENTS), 1998

Source: National Travel Survey

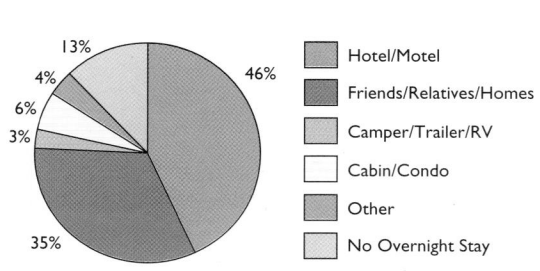

- Hotel/Motel
- Friends/Relatives/Homes
- Camper/Trailer/RV
- Cabin/Condo
- Other
- No Overnight Stay

UNITED STATES & CANADA

Figure U9
MARKET SHARE INDICATOR FOR LONG-HAUL VISITORS TO THE USA, 1998
Source: Tourism Industries of America/International Trade Administration and World Tourism Organisation

These charts represent the share of long-haul travellers who visit the USA. 'Long haul' is for this purpose defined as any journey outside the appropriate country's World Tourism Organisation region – see the map on page 55 for details of these. Canadian and Mexican shares are calculated on all departures as these countries are in the same WTO region as the USA.

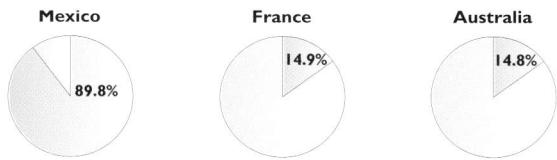

Mexico — 89.8%   France — 14.9%   Australia — 14.8%

Netherlands — 23.7%   Germany — 24.7%   Brazil — 43.1%

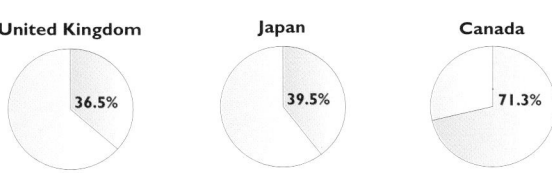

United Kingdom — 36.5%   Japan — 39.5%   Canada — 71.3%

Figure U10
TRAVEL SPENDING BY US RESIDENTS
Source: Travel Industries Association of America/ITA

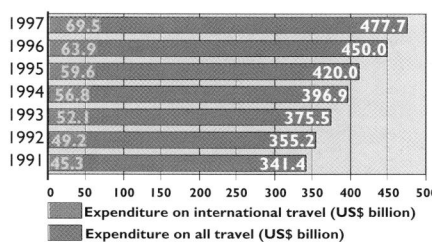

Year	Expenditure on international travel (US$ billion)	Expenditure on all travel (US$ billion)
1997	69.5	477.7
1996	63.9	450.0
1995	59.6	420.0
1994	56.8	396.9
1993	52.1	375.5
1992	49.2	355.2
1991	45.3	341.4

Figure U11
PROFILE OF OVERSEAS BUSINESS & LEISURE TRAVELLERS TO THE USA, 1998
Source: Tourism Industries, ITA, US Dept of Commerce

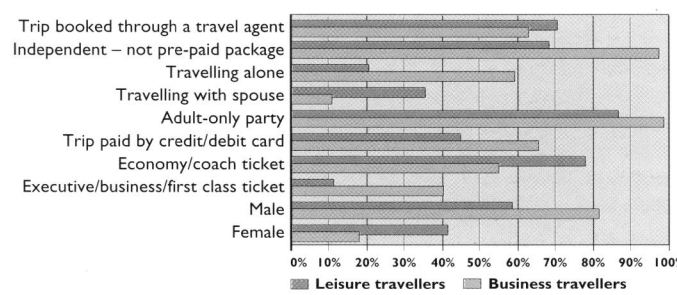

Trip booked through a travel agent
Independent – not pre-paid package
Travelling alone
Travelling with spouse
Adult-only party
Trip paid by credit/debit card
Economy/coach ticket
Executive/business/first class ticket
Male
Female

Leisure travellers   Business travellers

Figure U12
AVERAGE SPENDING AND LENGTH OF STAY BY VISITORS TO THE USA
Source: Tourism Industries, Bureau of Economic Analysis

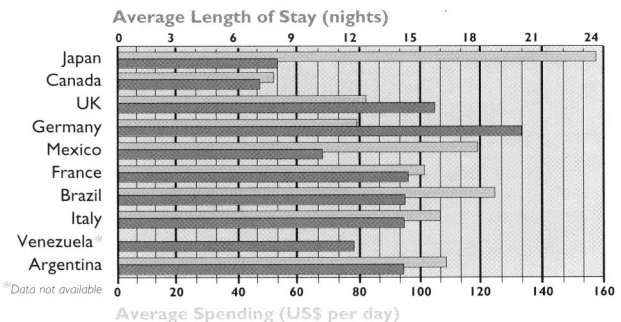

Average Length of Stay (nights)

Japan
Canada
UK
Germany
Mexico
France
Brazil
Italy
Venezuela*
Argentina

*Data not available

Average Spending (US$ per day)

Figure U13
WORLDWIDE VISITORS TO CANADA – ARRIVALS BY REGION, 1998
Source: Canadian Tourism Commission

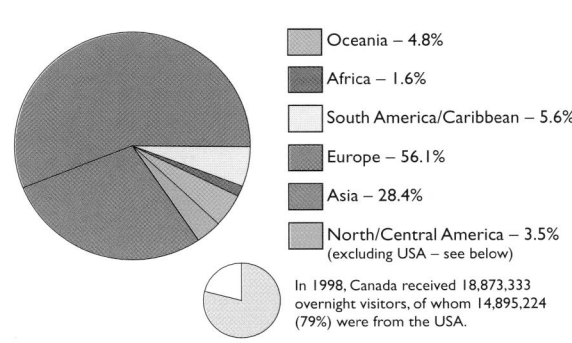

- Oceania – 4.8%
- Africa – 1.6%
- South America/Caribbean – 5.6%
- Europe – 56.1%
- Asia – 28.4%
- North/Central America – 3.5% (excluding USA – see below)

In 1998, Canada received 18,873,333 overnight visitors, of whom 14,895,224 (79%) were from the USA.

Figure U14
CANADIAN VISITORS TO THE USA, 1991-97
Source: Travel Industries Association of America

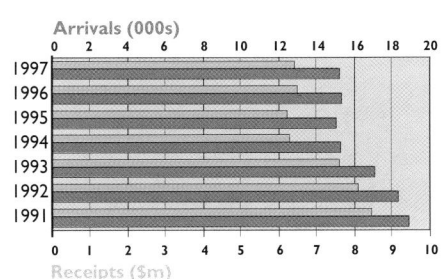

Arrivals (000s)

1997
1996
1995
1994
1993
1992
1991

Receipts ($m)

Figure U15
VISITORS TO CANADA – THE TOP TEN COUNTRIES, 1998
Source: Canadian Tourism Commission

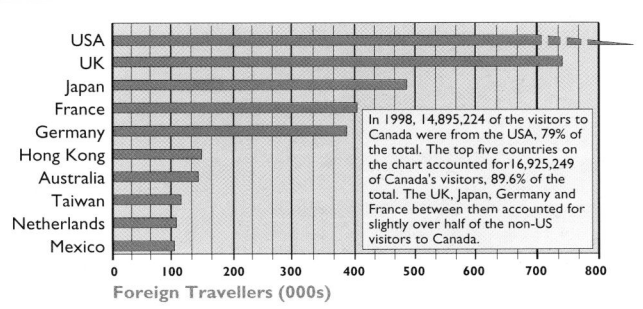

USA
UK
Japan
France
Germany
Hong Kong
Australia
Taiwan
Netherlands
Mexico

In 1998, 14,895,224 of the visitors to Canada were from the USA, 79% of the total. The top five countries on the chart accounted for 16,925,249 of Canada's visitors, 89.6% of the total. The UK, Japan, Germany and France between them accounted for slightly over half of the non-US visitors to Canada.

Foreign Travellers (000s)

UNITED KINGDOM

Figure BI
NUMBER OF OVERSEAS VISITORS & NIGHTS SPENT, 1998
Source: British Tourist Authority

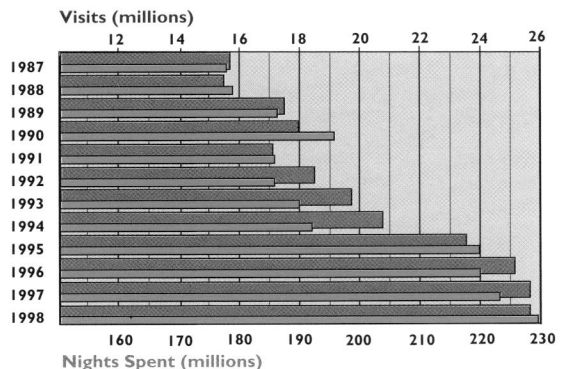

Figure B3
VISITORS TO THE UK BY COUNTRY OF ORIGIN, 1998
Source: British Tourist Authority

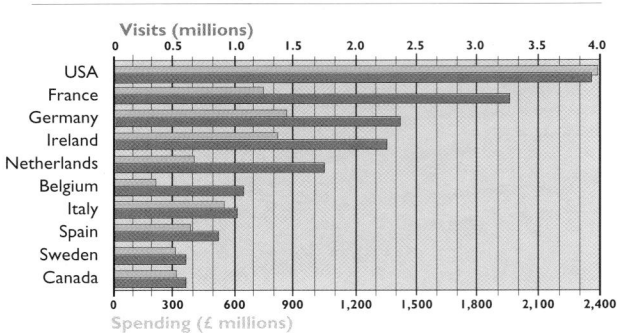

Figure B5
DISTRIBUTION OF OVERSEAS TOURISM, 1998
Source: British Tourist Authority

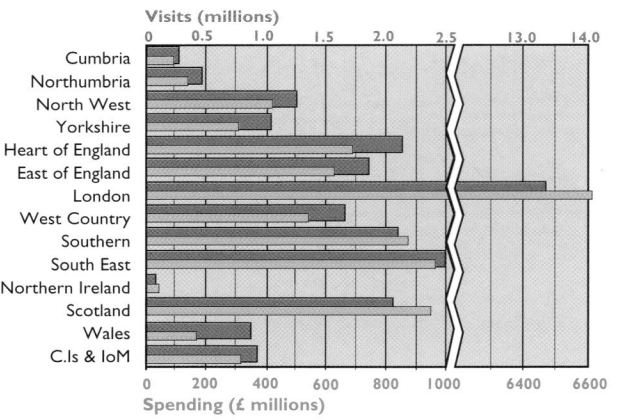

Figure B7
OVERSEAS SPENDING IN THE UK, 1988-1998
Source: British Tourist Authority 1998

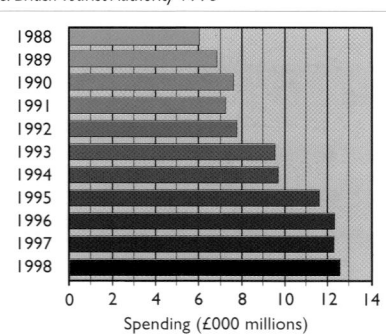

Figure B2
OVERSEAS VISITS TO THE UK BY PURPOSE OF VISIT, 1998
Source: British Tourist Authority

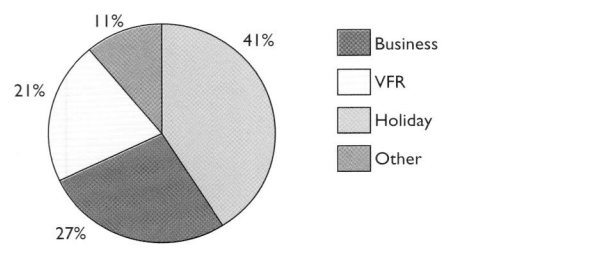

Figure B4
VISITS TO ATTRACTIONS 1998
Source: British Tourist Authority

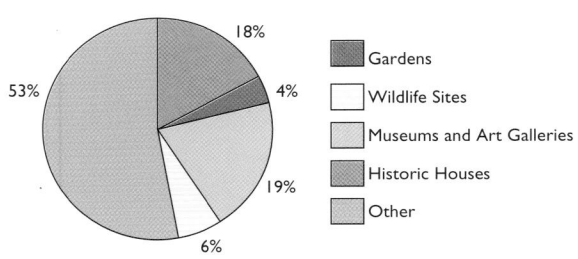

Figure B6
TOURISM SPENDING BREAKDOWN, 1998
Source: British Tourist Authority

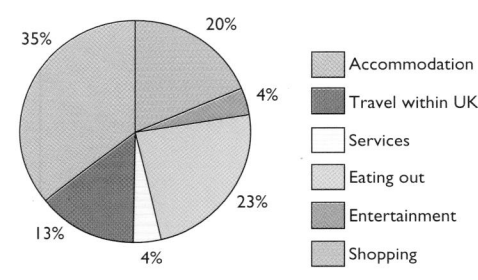

Figure B8
VISITS TO TOP 20 ATTRACTIONS CHARGING ADMISSIONS
Source: British Tourist Authority

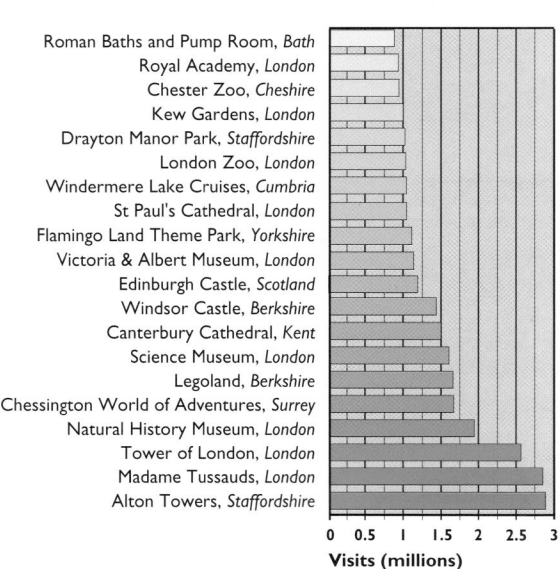

GENERAL MAP SECTION

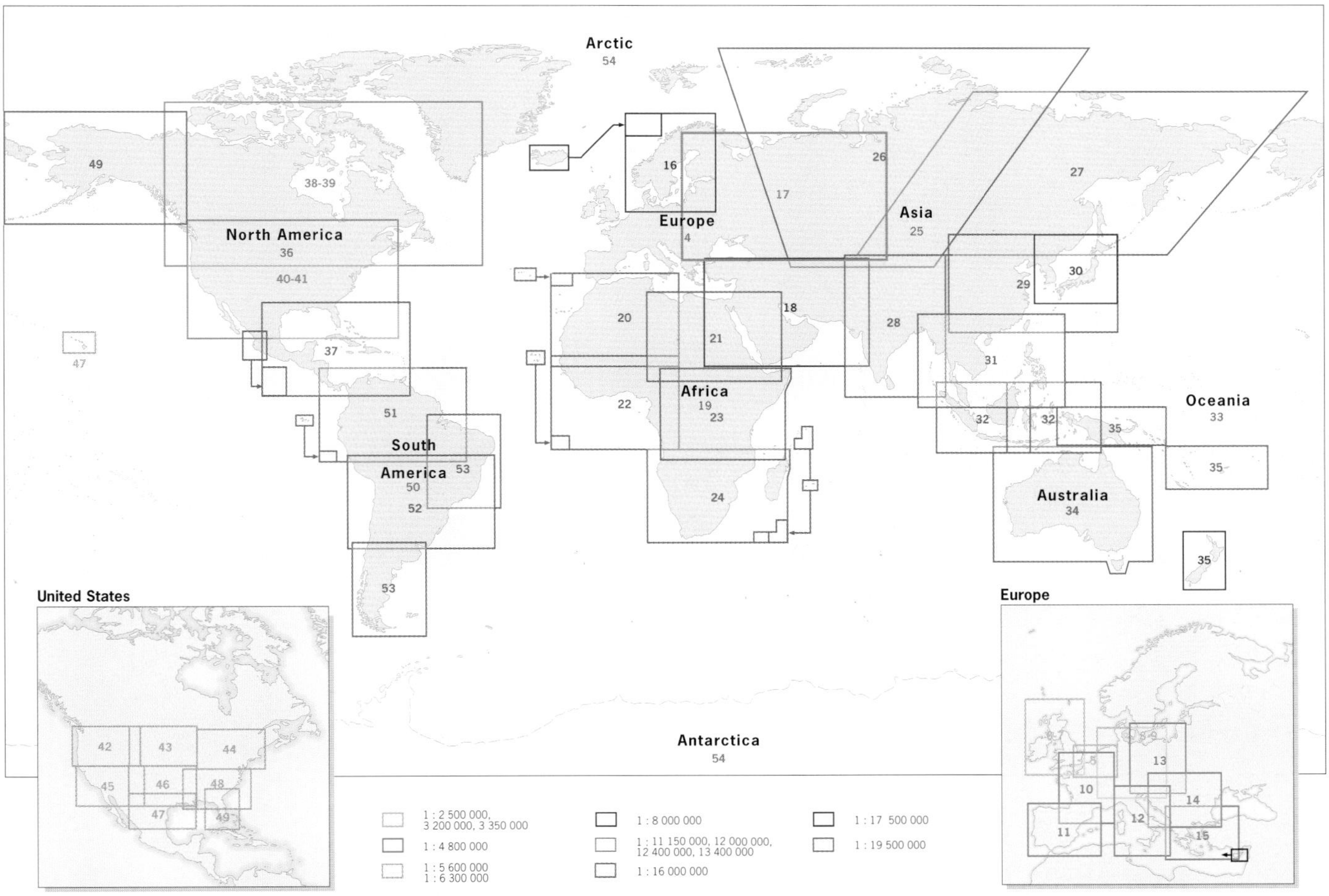

Arctic
54

49

38-39

North America
36

40-41

47

37

Arctic
54

16

Europe
4

17

26

27

Asia
25

29

30

20

18

31

22

21

Africa
19
23

28

32

32

35

Oceania
33

35

51

South America 53
50

52

24

Australia
34

35

53

United States

42   43   44

45   46   48

47   49

Europe

8

13

10

14

11   12

15

1 : 2 500 000, 3 200 000, 3 350 000	
1 : 4 800 000	
1 : 5 600 000 1 : 6 300 000	

1 : 8 000 000	
1 : 11 150 000, 12 000 000, 12 400 000, 13 400 000	
1 : 16 000 000	

1 : 17 500 000	
1 : 19 500 000	

Antarctica
54

KEY TO MAP SYMBOLS

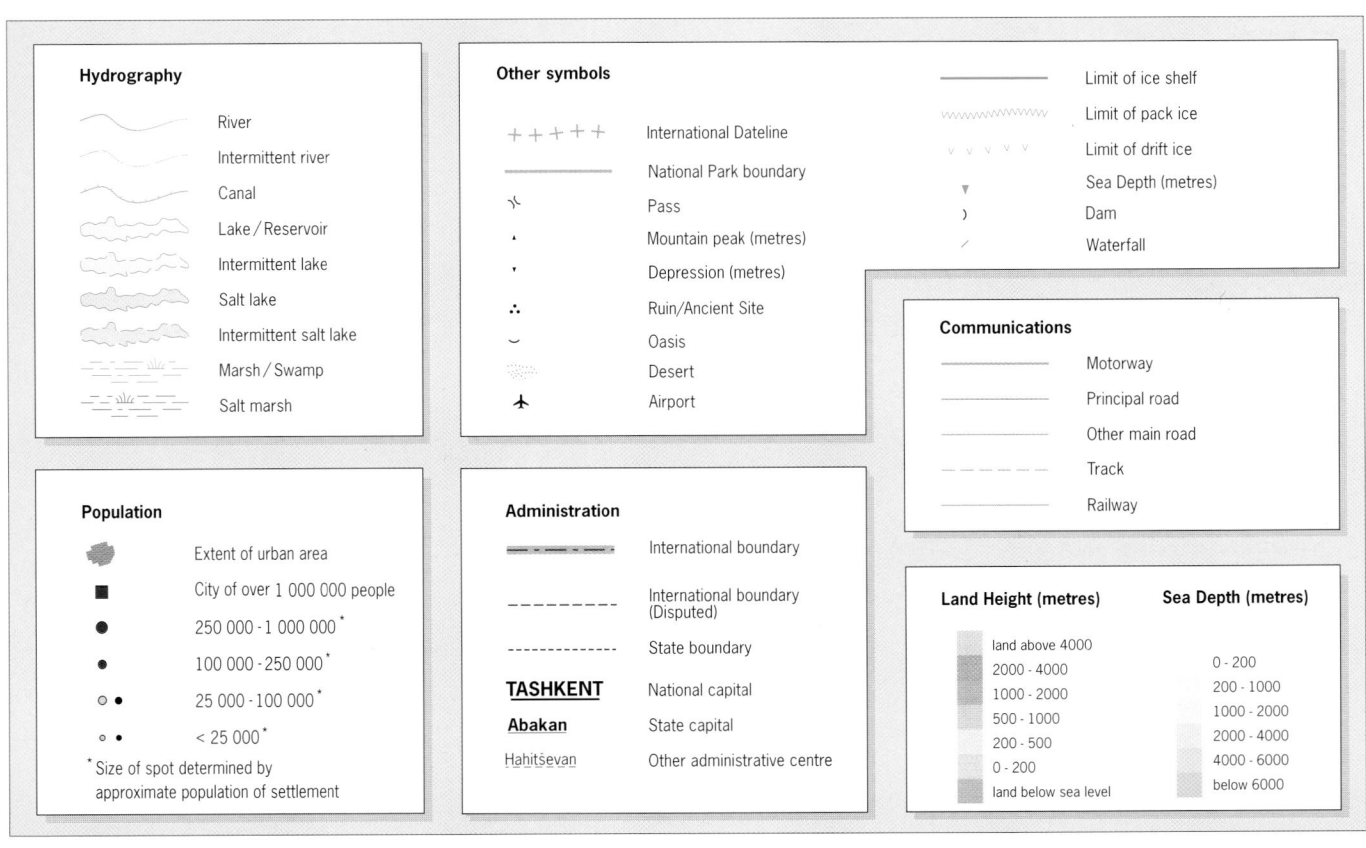

Hydrography

River
Intermittent river
Canal
Lake / Reservoir
Intermittent lake
Salt lake
Intermittent salt lake
Marsh / Swamp
Salt marsh

Other symbols

+ + + + +   International Dateline
National Park boundary
Pass
Mountain peak (metres)
Depression (metres)
Ruin/Ancient Site
Oasis
Desert
Airport

Limit of ice shelf
Limit of pack ice
Limit of drift ice
Sea Depth (metres)
Dam
Waterfall

Communications

Motorway
Principal road
Other main road
Track
Railway

Population

Extent of urban area
City of over 1 000 000 people
250 000 - 1 000 000 *
100 000 - 250 000 *
25 000 - 100 000 *
< 25 000 *

* Size of spot determined by approximate population of settlement

Administration

International boundary
International boundary (Disputed)
State boundary
TASHKENT   National capital
Abakan   State capital
Hahitševan   Other administrative centre

Land Height (metres)

land above 4000
2000 - 4000
1000 - 2000
500 - 1000
200 - 500
0 - 200
land below sea level

Sea Depth (metres)

0 - 200
200 - 1000
1000 - 2000
2000 - 4000
4000 - 6000
below 6000

WORLD - POLITICAL

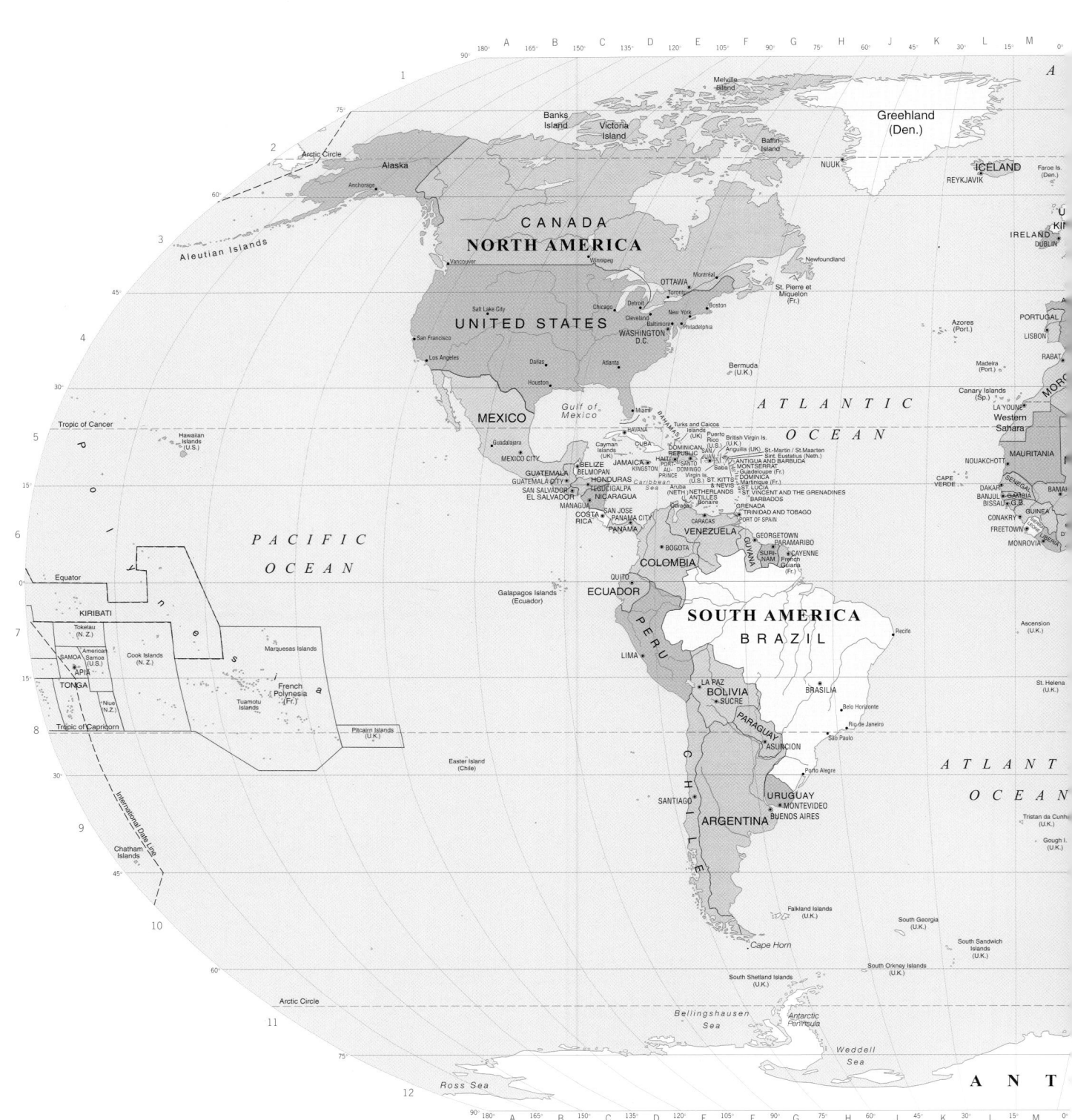

ICA Förlaget AB

WORLD - POLITICAL

ALB. - Albania
AR. - Armenia
AZ. - Azerbaijan
B. - Burundi
B.H. - Bosnia-Herzegovina
BEL. - Belgium
BH. - Bhutan
BULG. - Bulgaria
CR. - Czech Republic
CZ. - Croatia
EQ.G. - Equatorial Guinea
G.B. - Guinea-Bissau
GE. - Georgia
HGY. - Hungary
L. - Lesotho
LEB. - Lebanon
LIE. - Liechtenstein
LUX. - Luxembourg
MA. - Former Yugoslav Republic of Macedonia
NETH. - The Netherlands
R. - Rwanda
S.M. - San Marino
S. - Swaziland
SL. - Slovenia
SLO. - Slovak Republic
U.A.E. - United Arab Emirates
YUG. - Federal Republic of Yugoslavia

Robinson Projection

0   1000   2000   3000 km

0   1000   2000   3000 miles

EUROPE

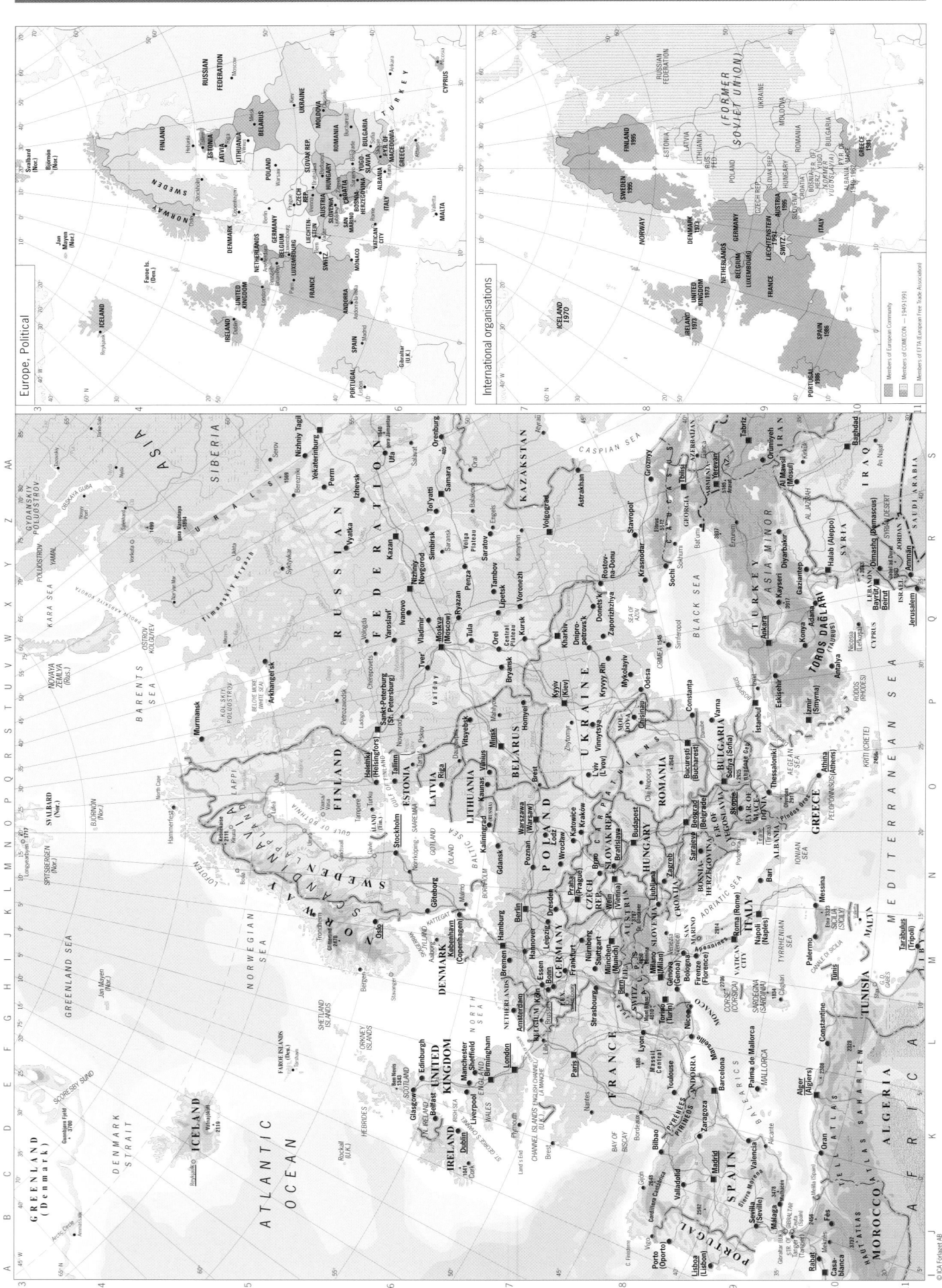

Europe, Political

International organisations

Members of European Community — 1949-1991
Members of EFTA (European Free Trade Association)

Scale 1 : 20 000 000

© ICA Förlaget AB

BENELUX AND SURROUNDING AREA

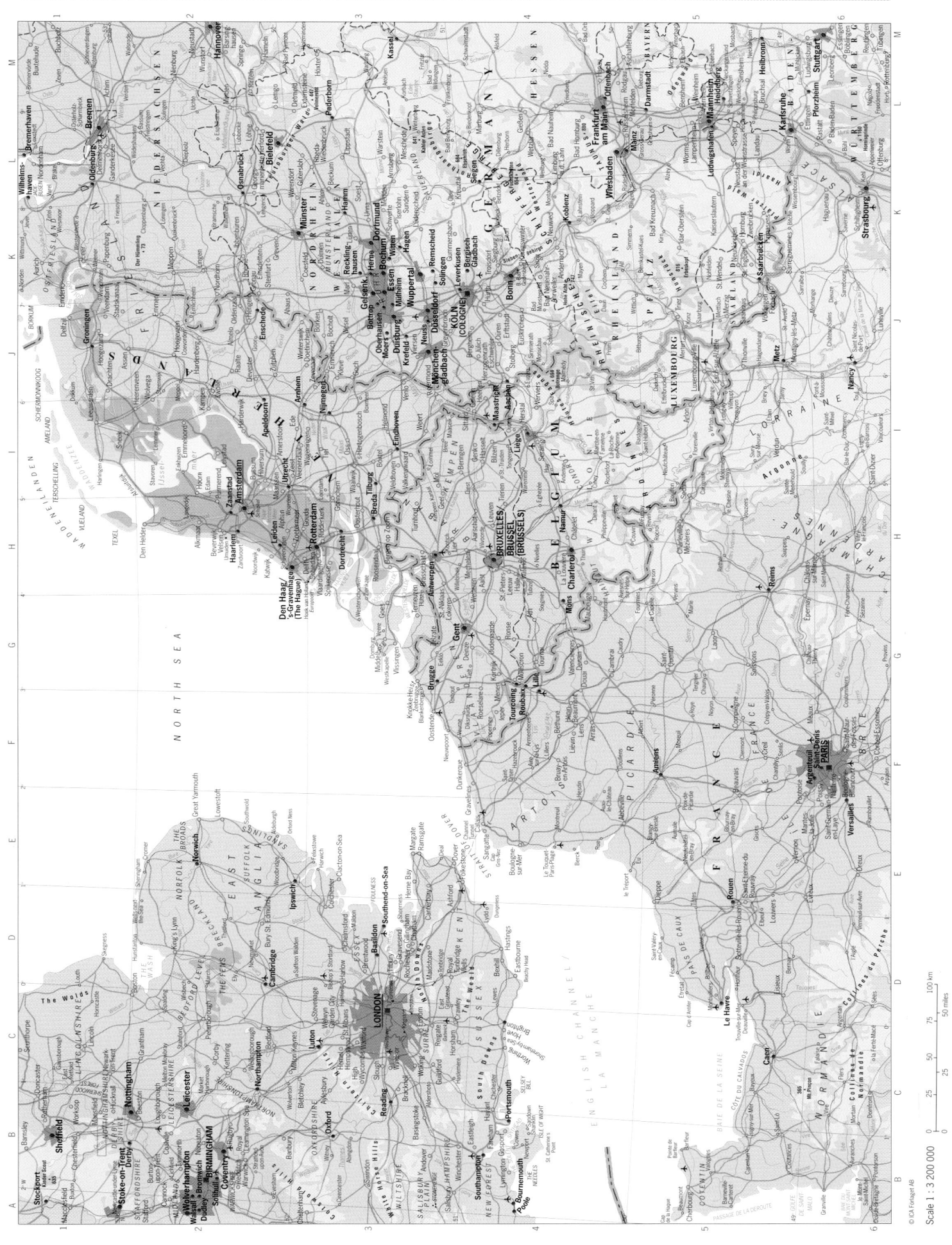

Scale 1 : 3 200 000

© ICA Förlaget AB

BRITISH ISLES

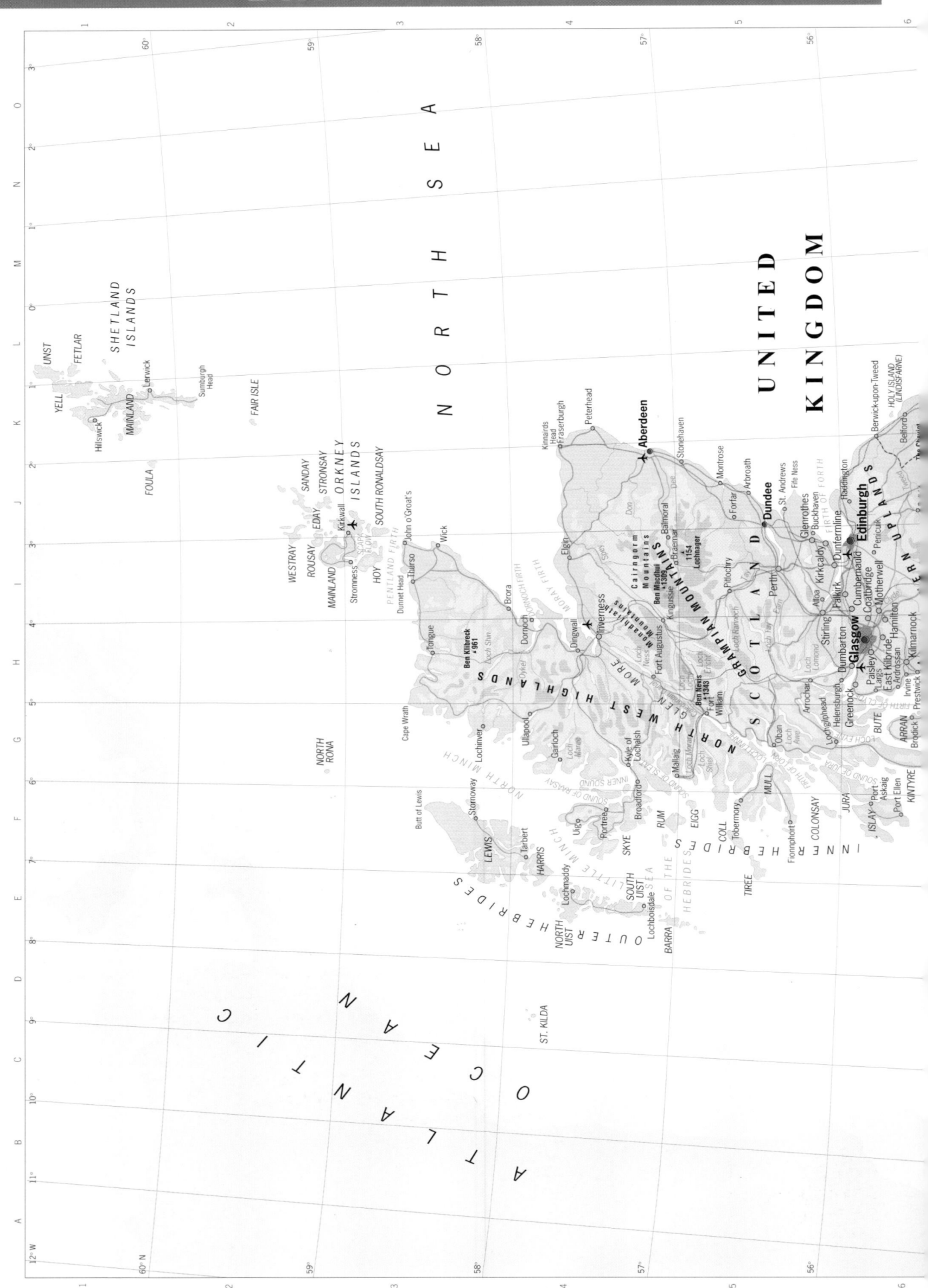

BRITISH ISLES

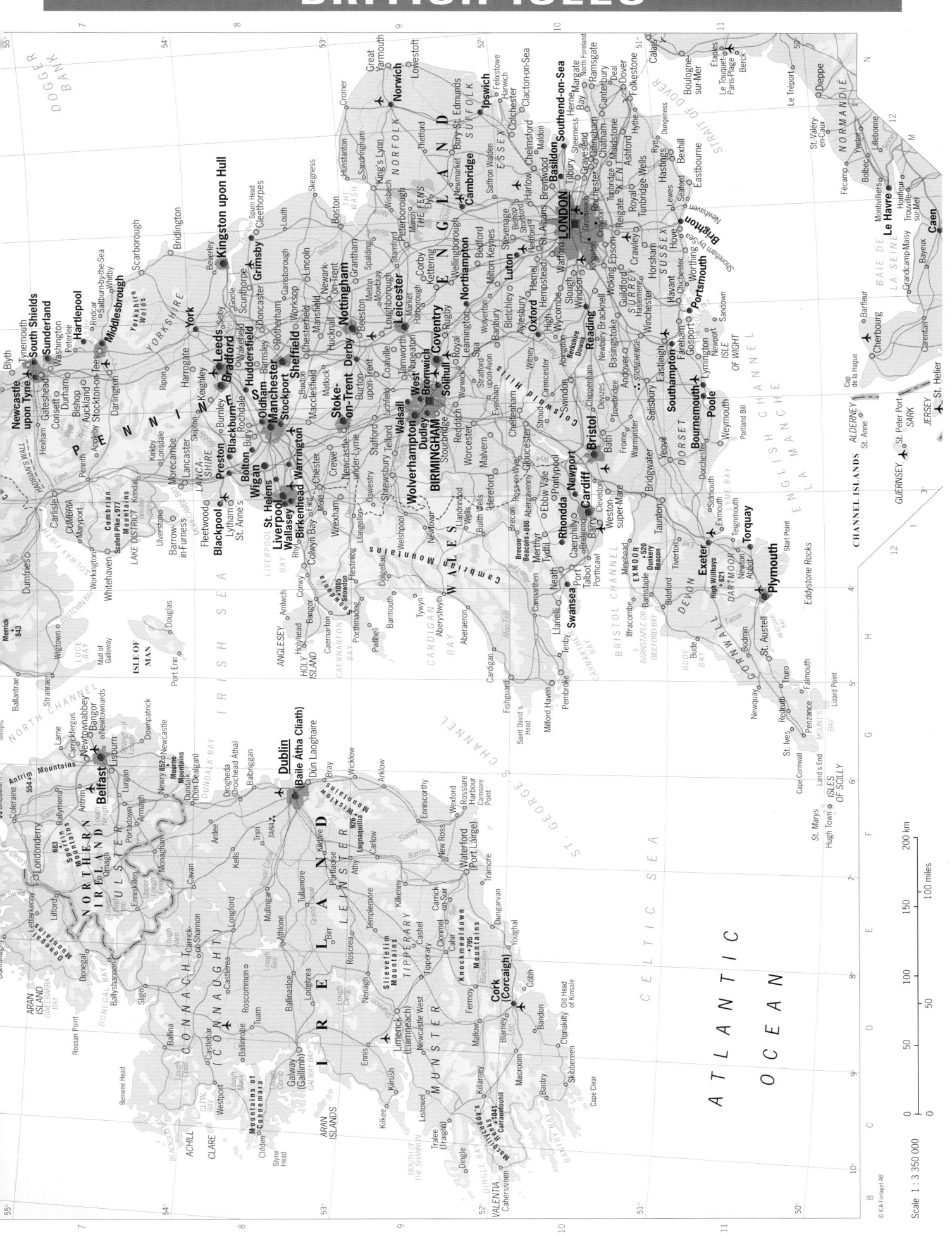

Scale 1 : 3 350 000

© ICA Förlaget AB

GERMANY

GERMANY

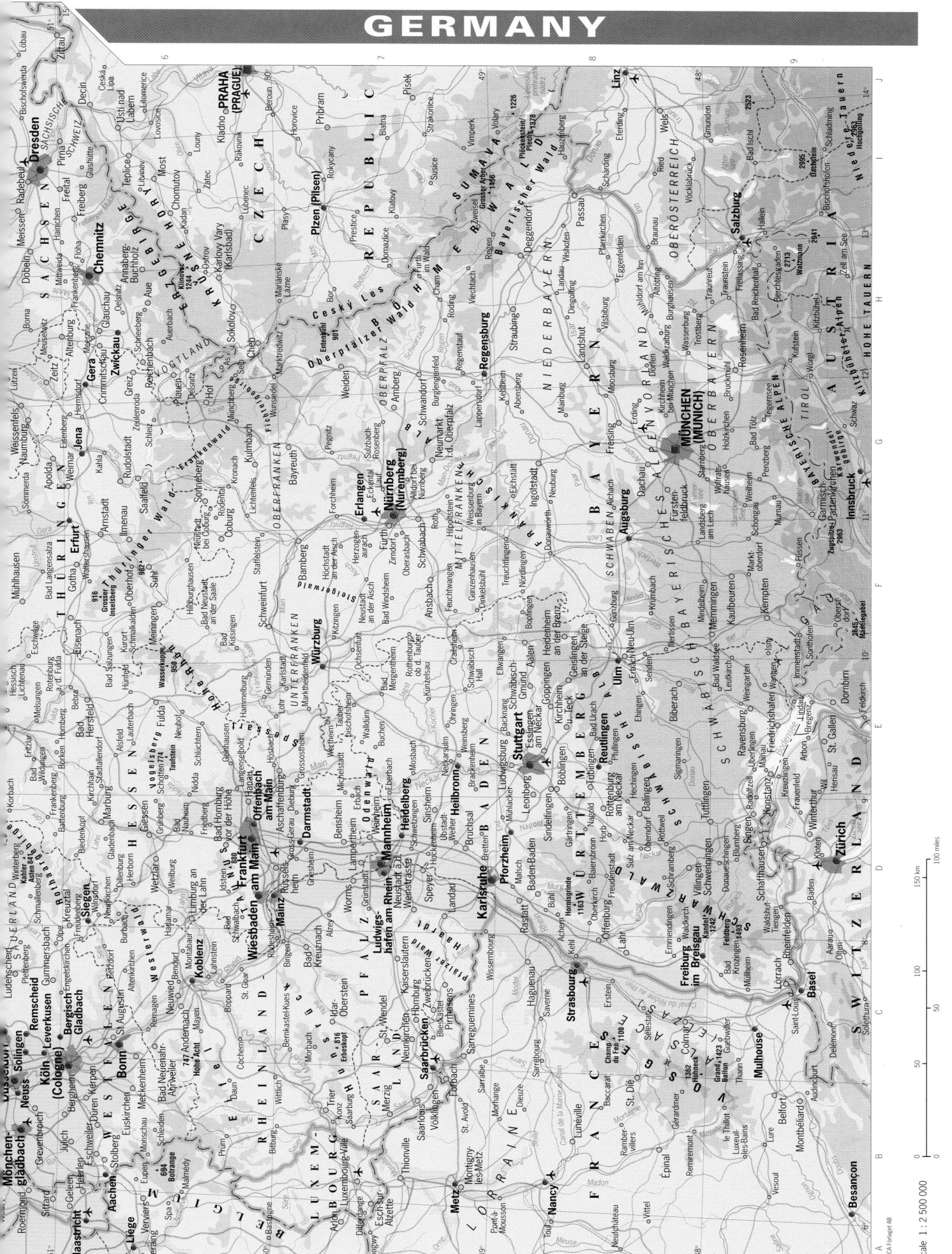

Scale 1 : 2 500 000

FRANCE

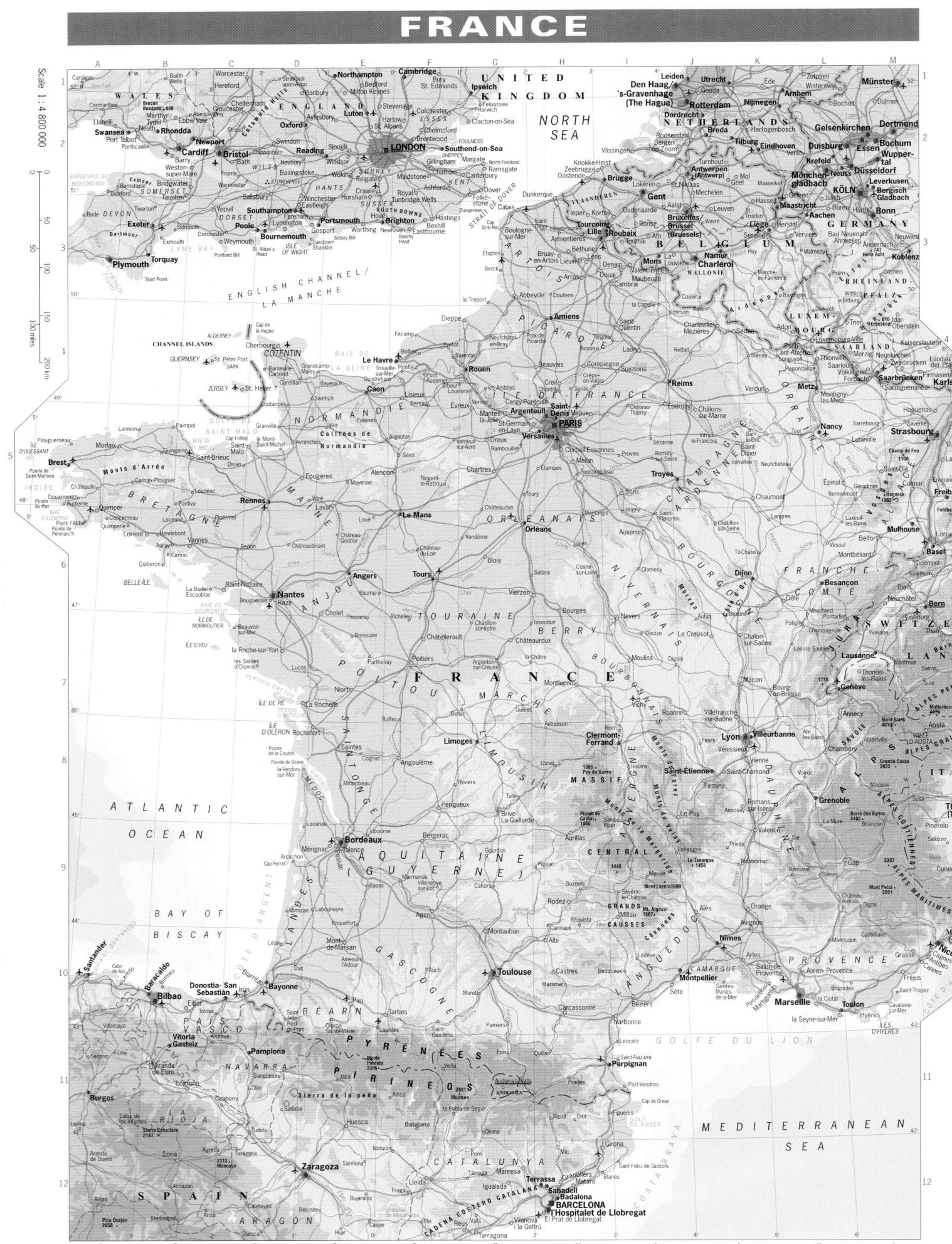

Scale 1 : 4 800 000

© ICA Förlaget AB

SPAIN AND PORTUGAL

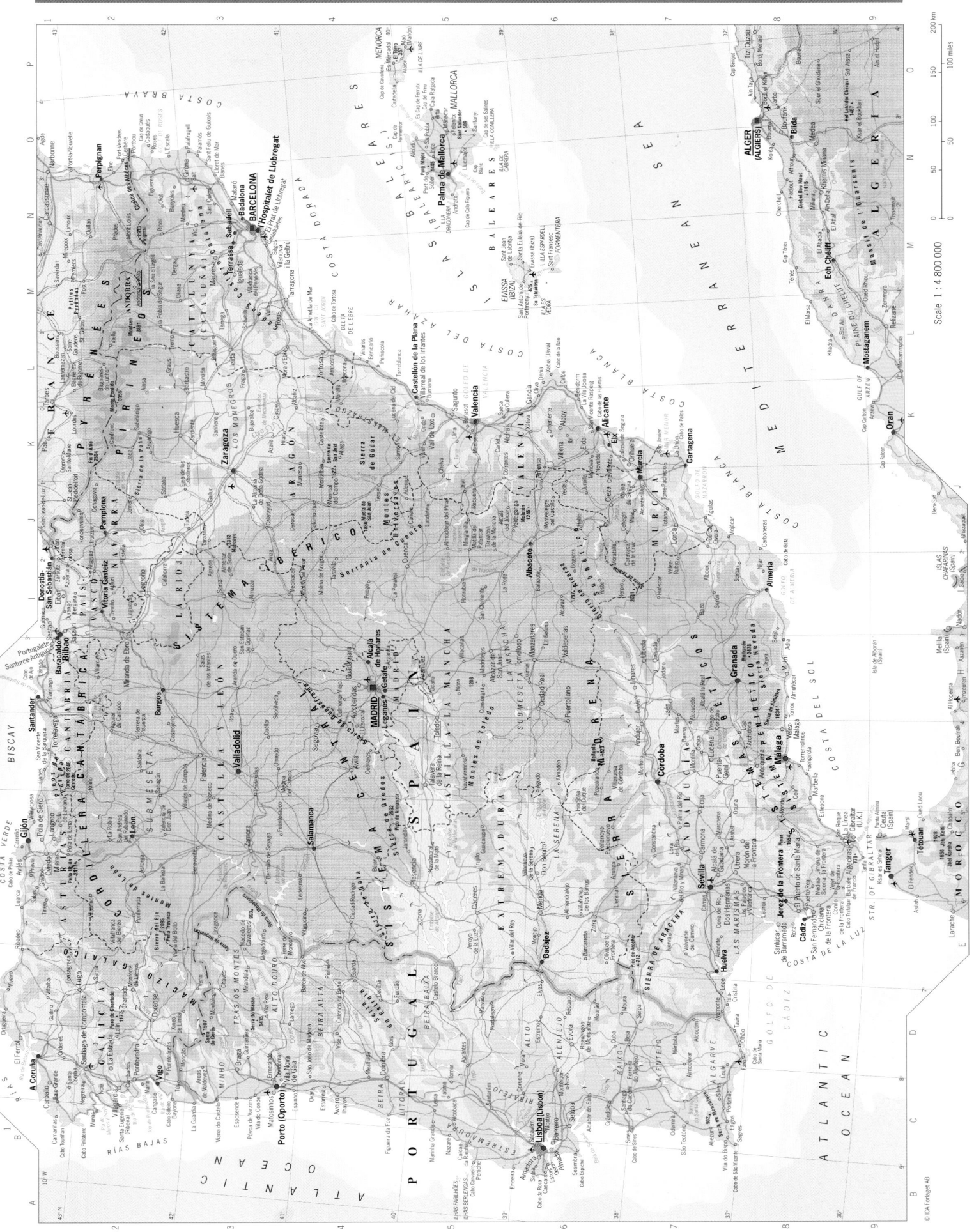

Scale 1 : 4 800 000

ITALY

Scale 1 : 4 800 000

© ICA Förlaget AB

CENTRAL EUROPE

Scale 1 : 4 800 000

© ICA Förlaget AB

THE BALKANS

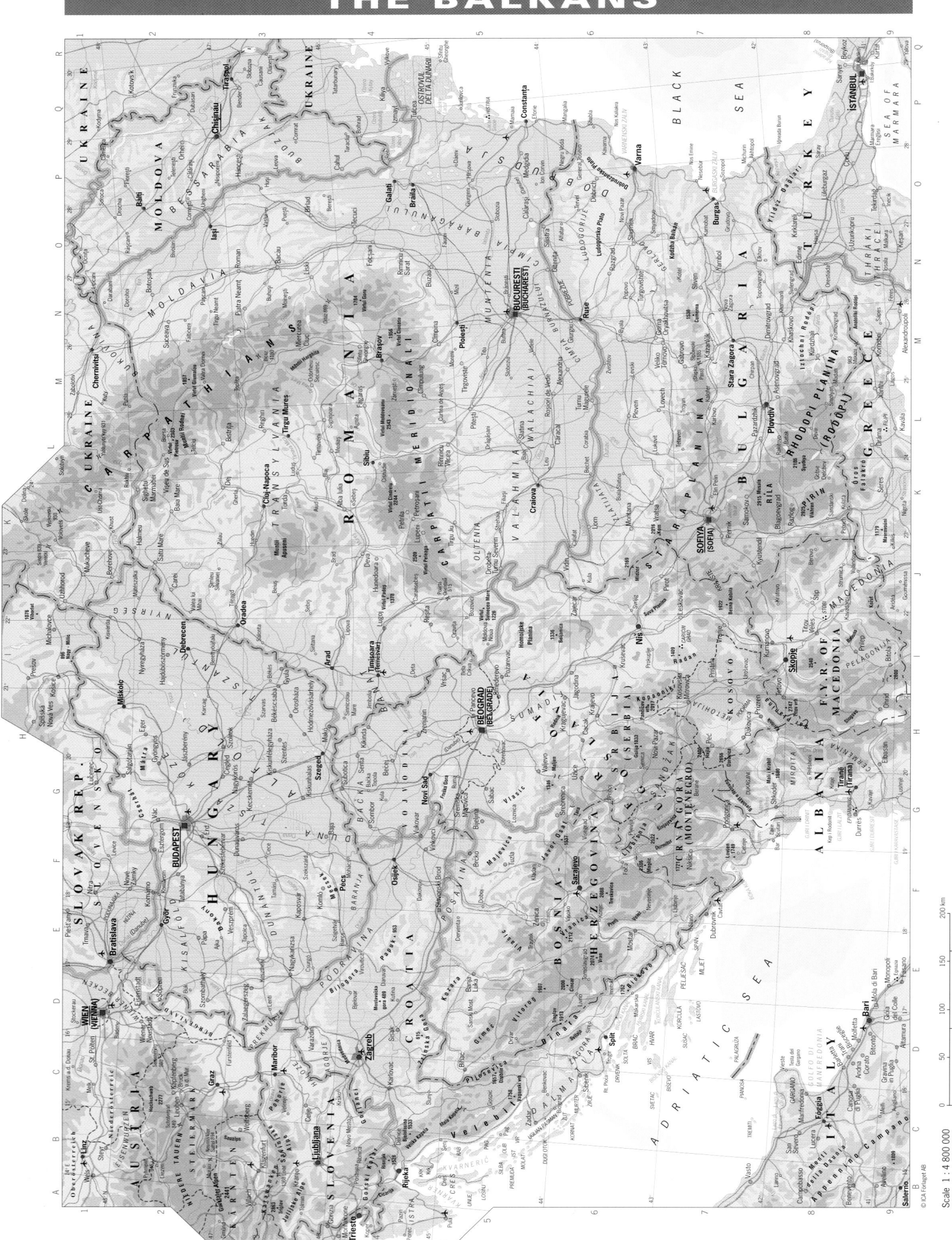

Scale 1 : 4 800 000

GREECE AND TURKEY

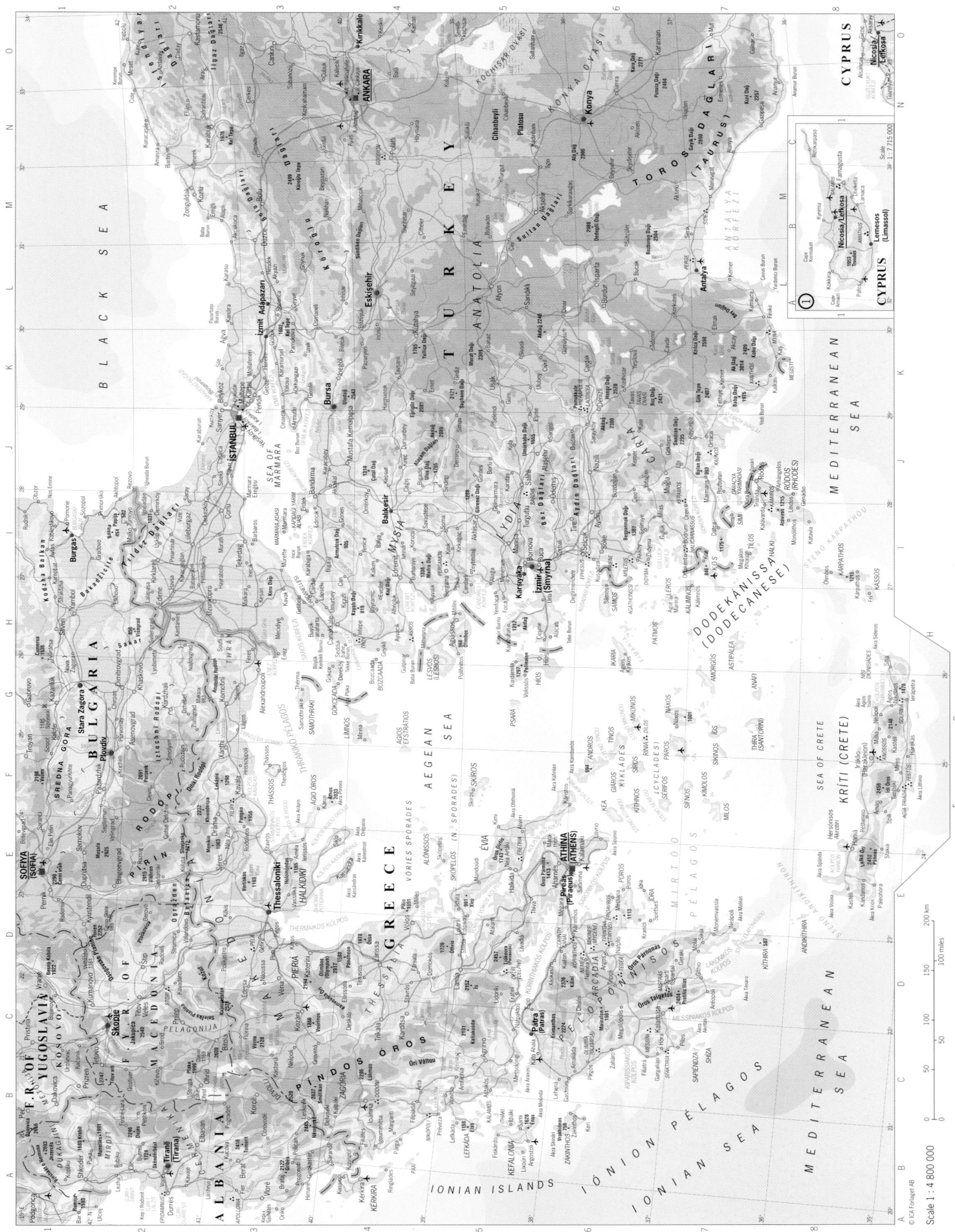

SCANDINAVIA AND THE BALTIC STATES

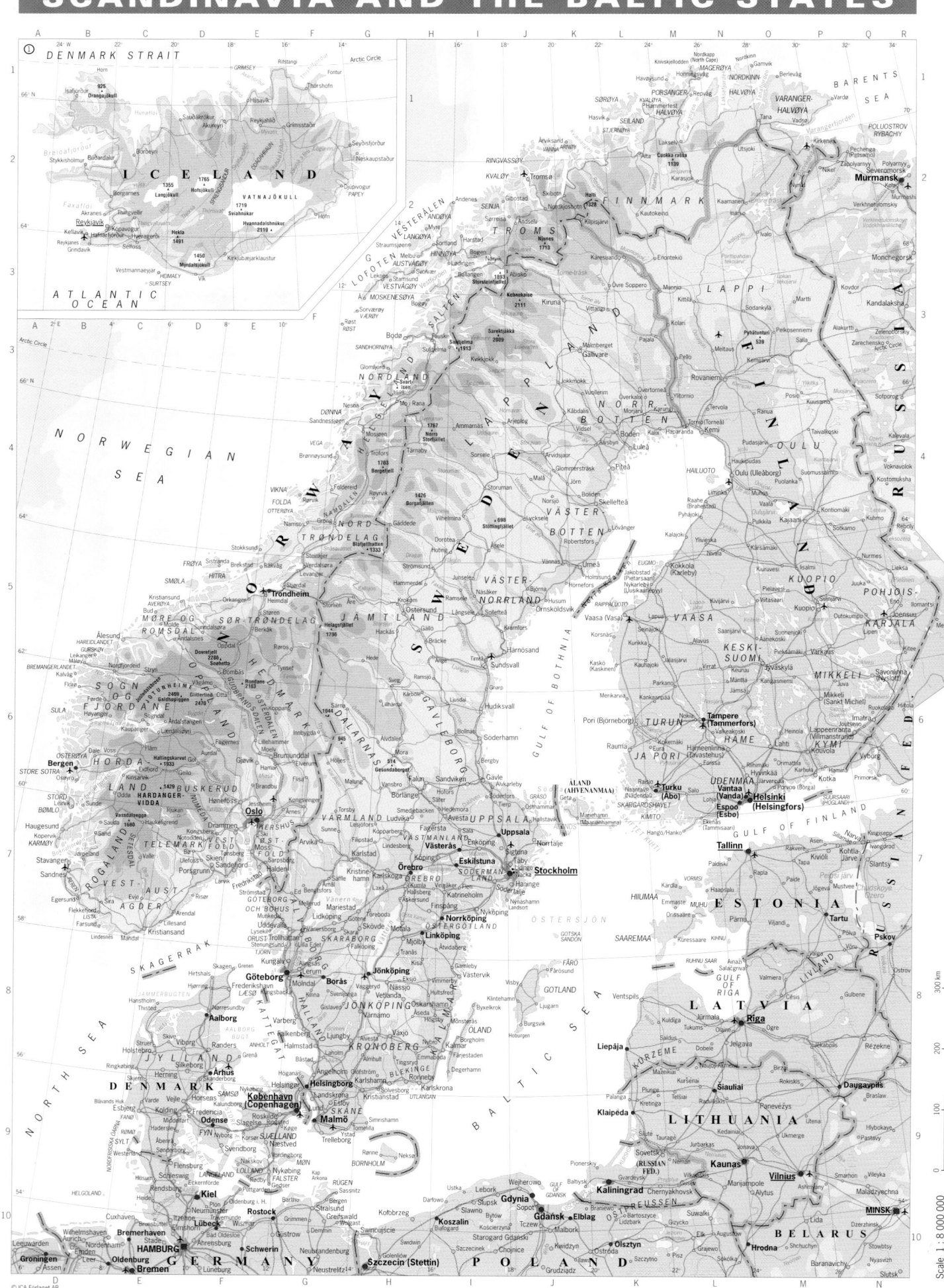

Scale 1 : 8 000 000

© ICA Förlaget AB

EUROPEAN RUSSIA

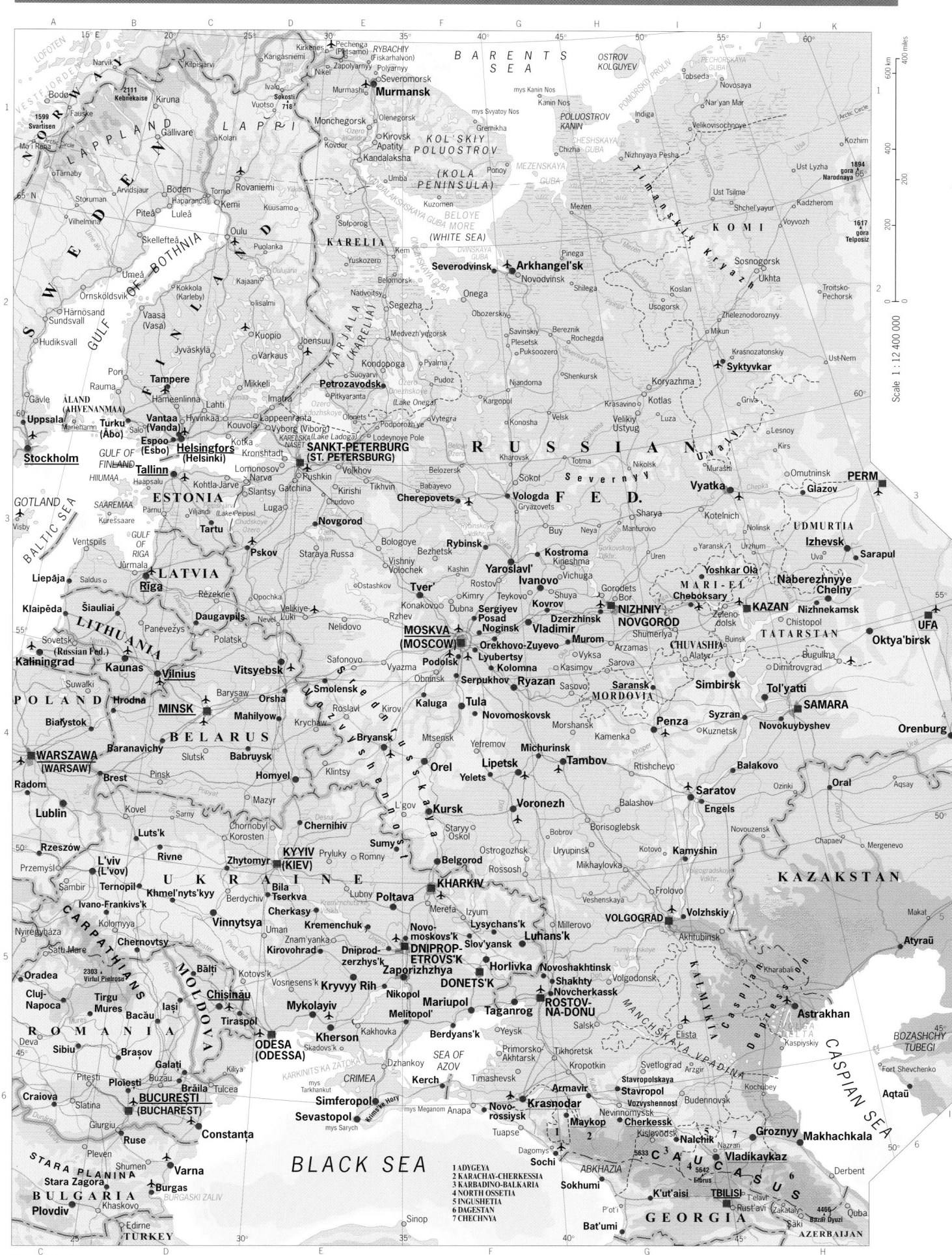

BARENTS SEA

OSTROV KOLGUYEV

NORWAY

LOFOTEN

Narvik
Bodø
1599 Svartisen
Mo i Rana
Fauske

Kilpisjärvi
Kirkenes
Pechenga (Petsamo)
RYBACHIY (Fiskarhalvon)
mys Kanin Nos
Kanin Nos

Murmansk
Severomorsk
Monchegorsk
Olenegorsk

Kebnekaise 2111
Kiruna
Gällivare
Sokosti 718

Severodvinsk
Arkhangel'sk
Novodvinsk

KOL'SKIY POLUOSTROV (KOLA PENINSULA)

KOMI

BELOYE MORE (WHITE SEA)

KARELIA

R U S S I A N   F E D.

Syktyvkar

Tampere
Petrozavodsk

Vologda
Cherepovets
Vyatka
PERM

Uppsala
Turku (Åbo)
Espoo (Esbo)
Helsingfors (Helsinki)
Tallinn
SANKT-PETERBURG (ST. PETERSBURG)

Stockholm

BALTIC SEA

ESTONIA
Tartu
Pskov
Novgorod

LATVIA
Riga

Yaroslavl'
Ivanovo
Kostroma

Yoshkar Ola
MARI-EL
Cheboksary
Naberezhnyye Chelny

Izhevsk
UDMURTIA
Sarapul

KAZAN
Nizhnekamsk
TATARSTAN
UFA
Oktya'birsk

LITHUANIA
Vilnius
Vitsyebsk

Tver'
MOSKVA (MOSCOW)

CHUVASHIA
Simbirsk
SAMARA
Tol'yatti

Kaliningrad
Kaunas

POLAND
MINSK
BELARUS

WARSZAWA (WARSAW)

Tula
Kaluga

Ryazan
MORDOVIA
Saransk
Penza
Syzran

Orenburg

Lublin

Bryansk
Orel
Lipetsk
Tambov

Saratov
Engels

Rzeszów
L'viv (L'vov)

Kursk
Voronezh

Kamyshin

UKRAINE
KYIV (KIEV)

Belgorod

KHARKIV

Poltava

VOLGOGRAD
Volzhskiy

KAZAKSTAN

DNIPROP-ETROVS'K
Zaporizhzhya
Kryvyy Rih

DONETS'K
ROSTOV-NA-DONU

Astrakhan

MOLDOVA
Chişinău

Mykolayiv
ODESA (ODESSA)
Kherson

Mariupol
Taganrog

CASPIAN SEA

ROMANIA

CRIMEA
Simferopol
Sevastopol

SEA OF AZOV
Kerch

Krasnodar
Novorossiysk
Sochi

BUCUREŞTI (BUCHAREST)

Stavropol
Cherkessk
Maykop
Groznyy
Makhachkala
Nalchik
Vladikavkaz

BULGARIA
Plovdiv

BLACK SEA

1 Adygeya
2 Karachay-Cherkessia
3 Karbadino-Balkaria
4 North Ossetia
5 Ingushetia
6 Dagestan
7 Chechnya

C A U C A S U S

GEORGIA
TBILISI

AZERBAIJAN

TURKEY

Scale 1 : 12 400 000

© European Map Graphics Ltd.

MIDDLE EAST

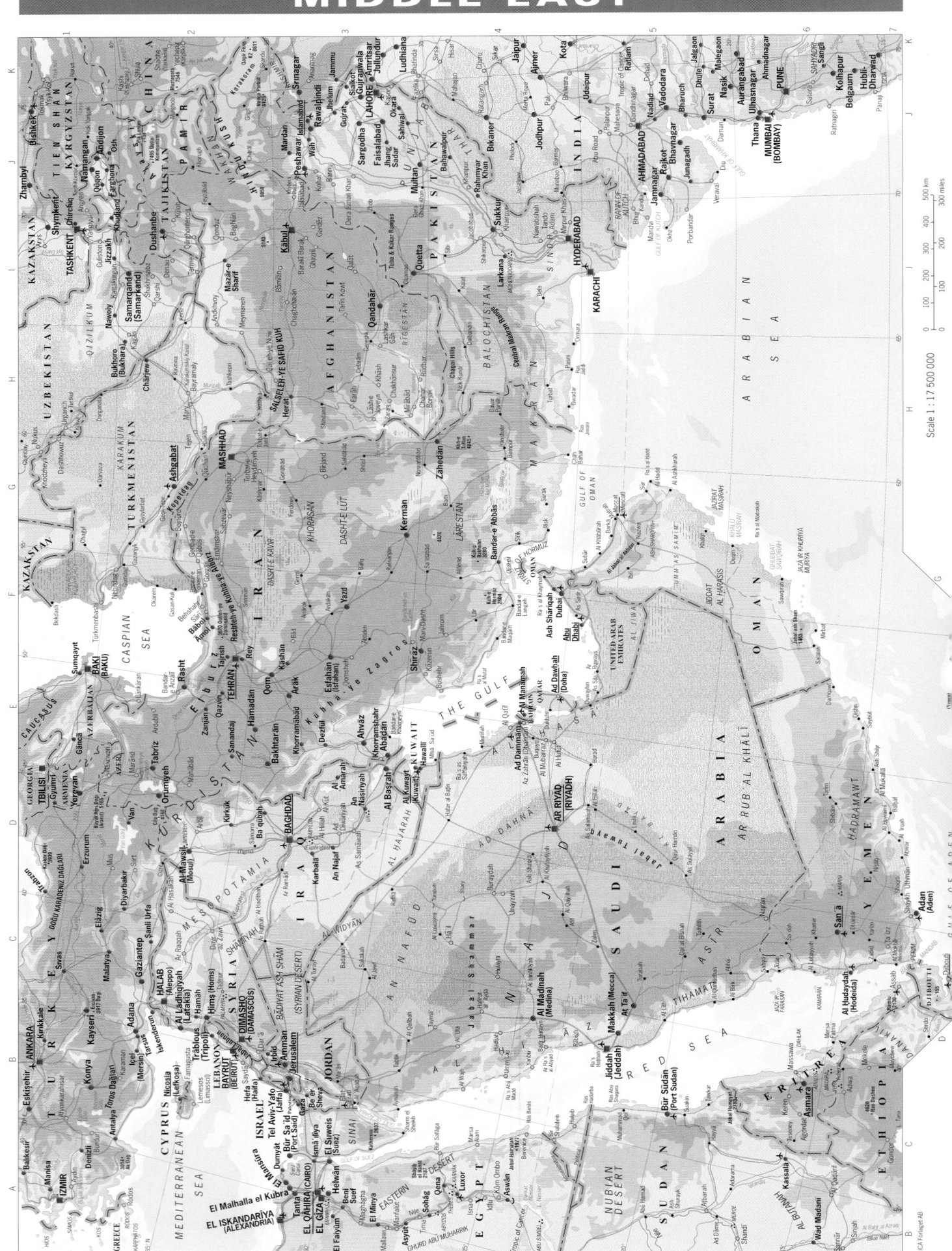

Scale 1 : 17 500 000

AFRICA

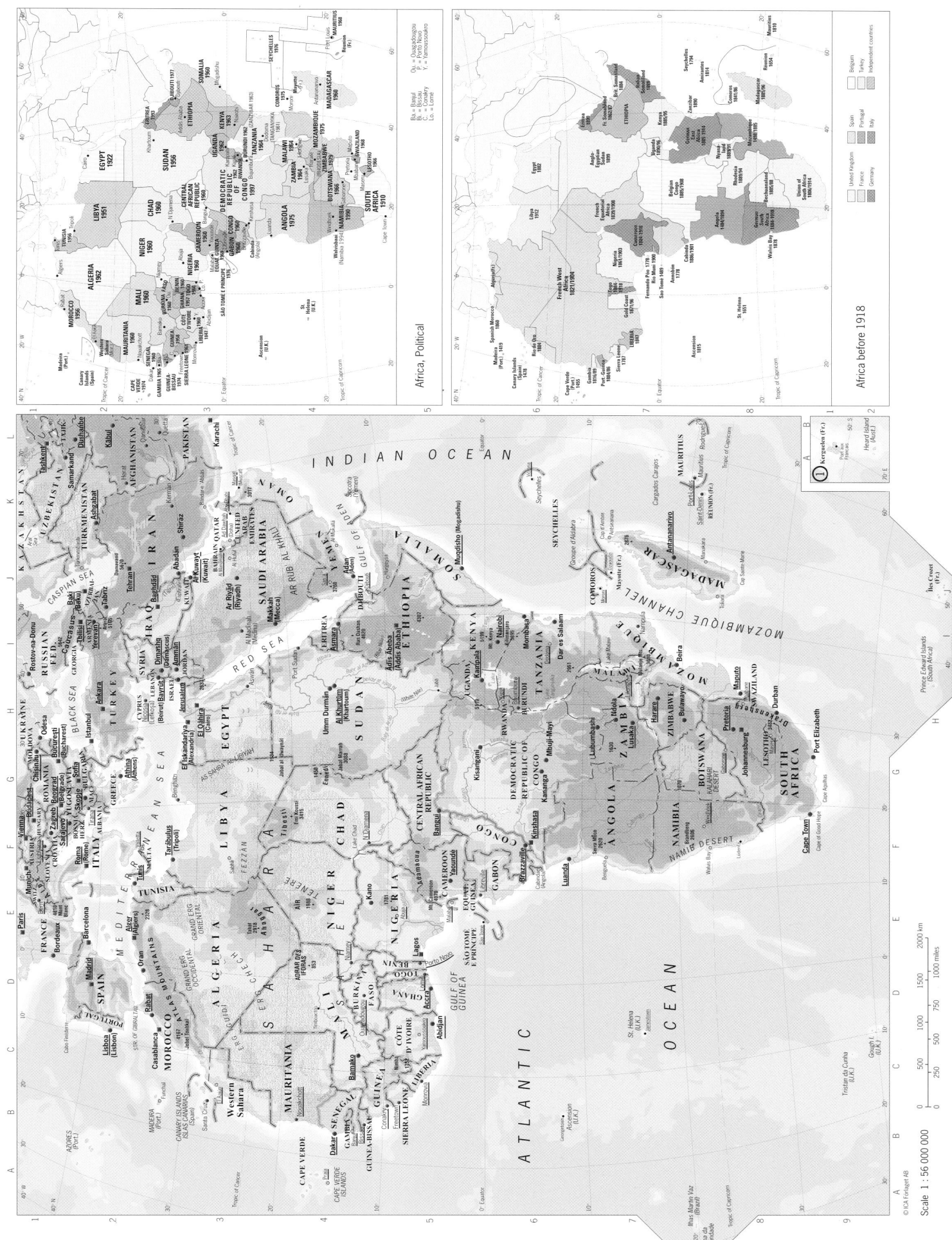

Africa, Political

Africa before 1918

Scale 1 : 56 000 000

© ICA Förlaget AB

NORTHWEST AFRICA

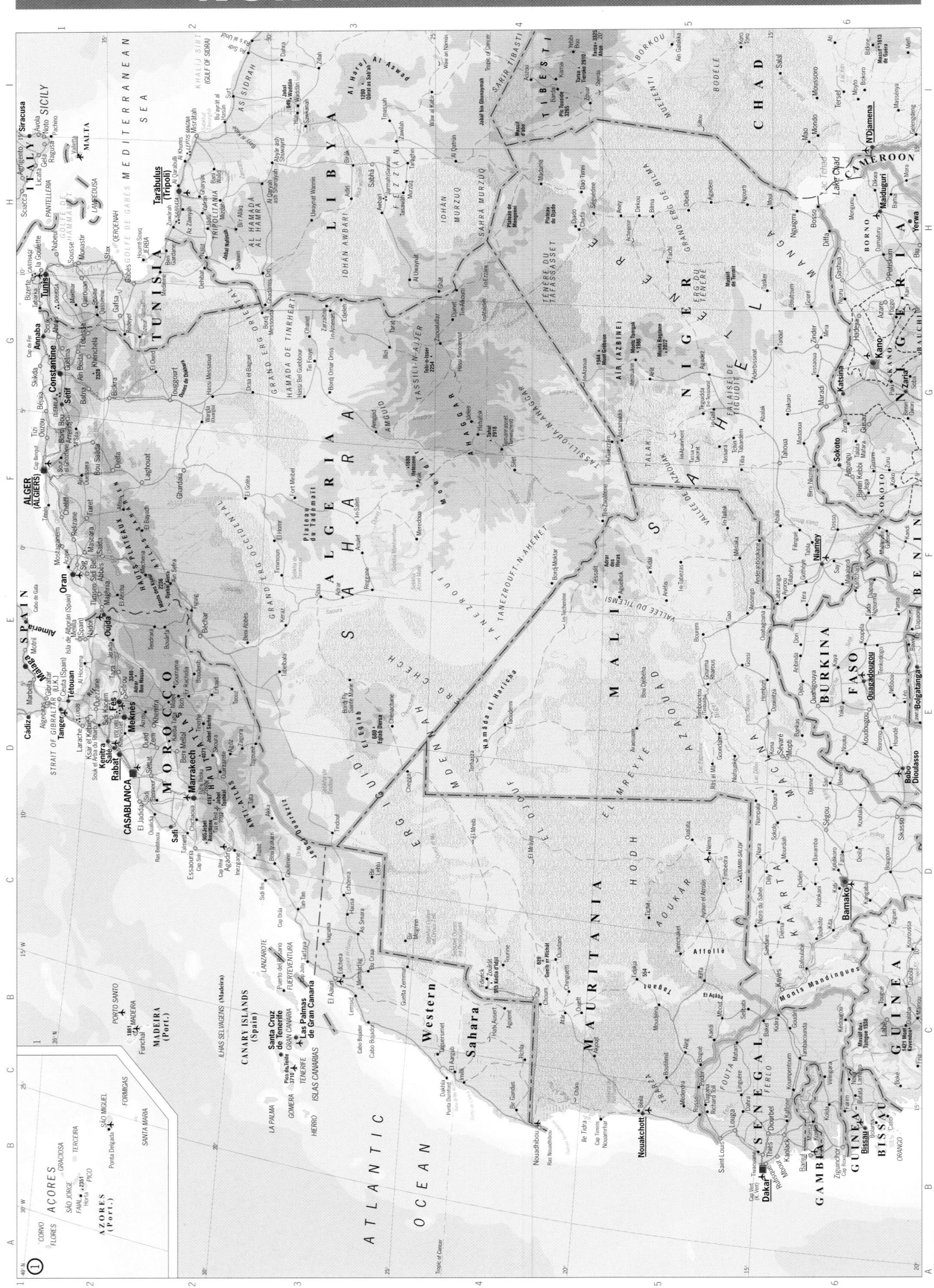

Scale 1 : 16 000 000

© ICA Förlaget AB

NORTHEAST AFRICA

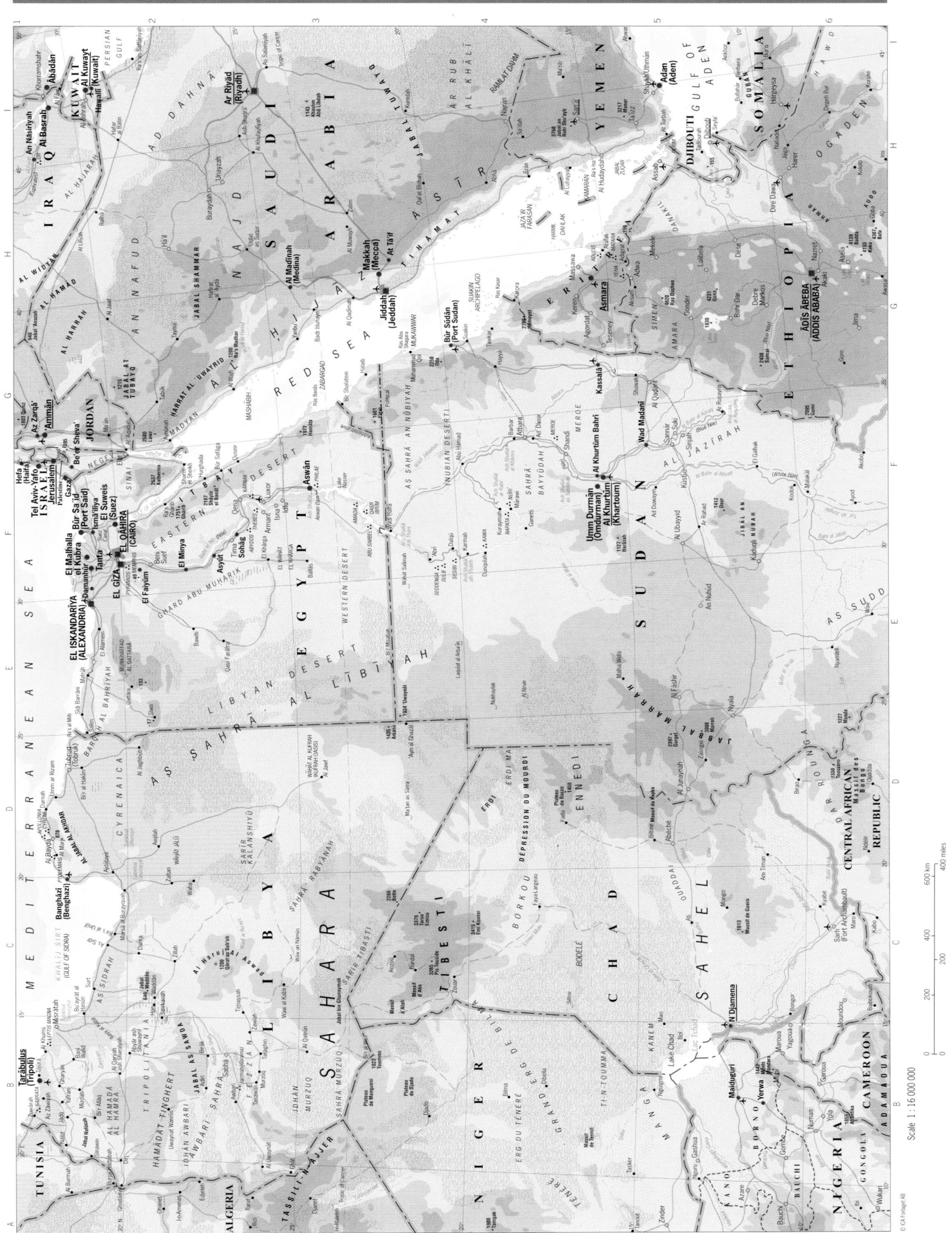

Scale 1 : 16 000 000

© CA Fricke! IB

WEST AFRICA

Scale 1 : 16 000 000

CENTRAL AFRICA

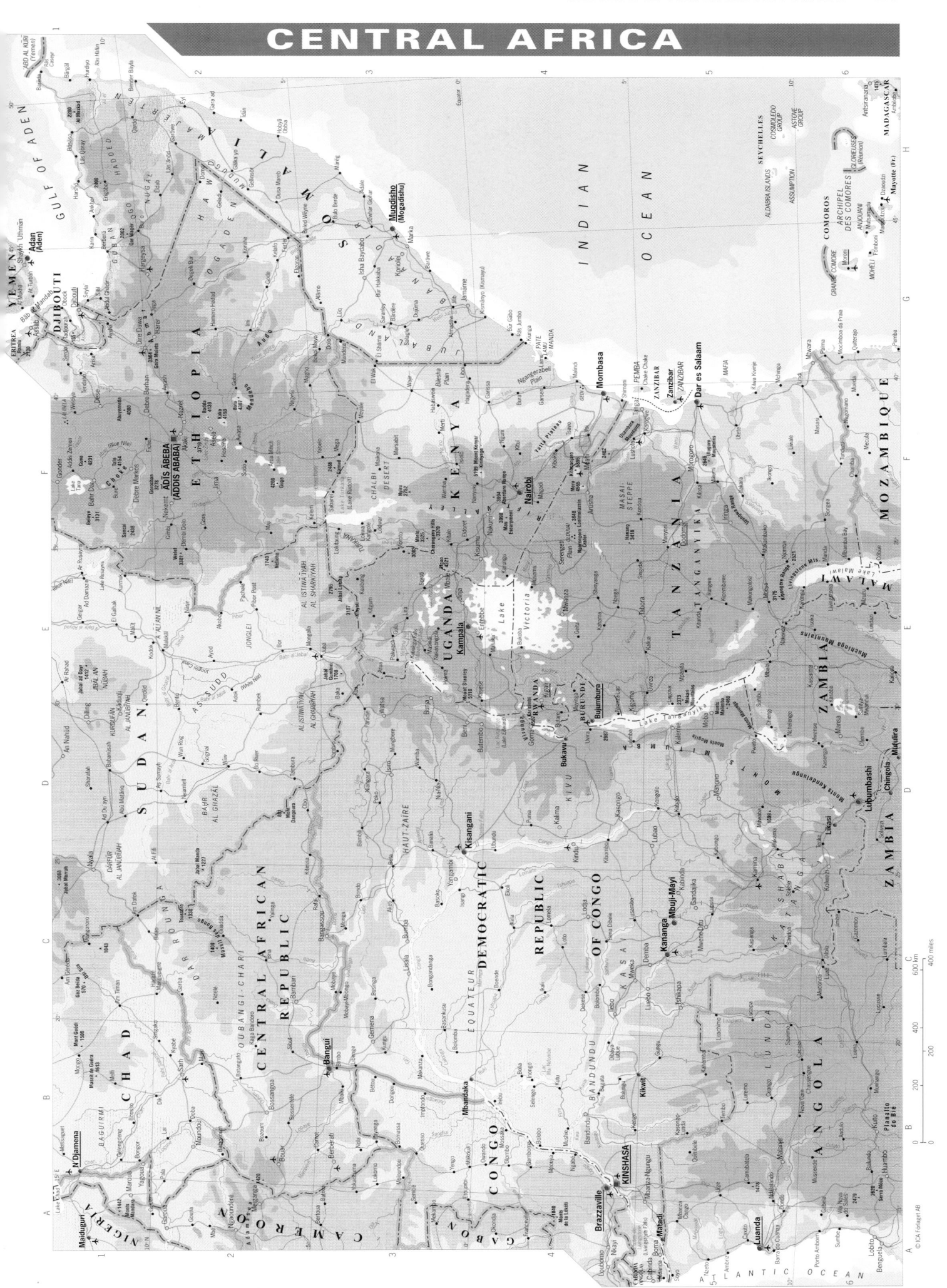

SOUTHERN AFRICA

DEMOCRATIC REPUBLIC OF CONGO

KATANGA

TANZANIA

ANGOLA

ZAMBIA

MALAWI

MOZAMBIQUE

ZIMBABWE

NAMIBIA

BOTSWANA

SOUTH AFRICA

LESOTHO

SWAZILAND

MADAGASCAR

SEYCHELLES

COMOROS

KALAHARI DESERT

NAMIB DESERT

SKELETON COAST

CAPRIVI STRIP

OVAMBOLAND

NGAMILAND

KAOKOVELD

NORTH WEST

NORTHERN PROVINCE

MPUMALANGA

FREE STATE

NORTHERN CAPE

EASTERN CAPE

WESTERN CAPE

GREAT KARROO

DRAKENSBERG

INDIAN OCEAN

ATLANTIC OCEAN

CANAL DE MOZAMBIQUE / MOZAMBIQUE CHANNEL

Luanda
Lubumbashi
Ndola
Kitwe-Nkana
Lusaka
Harare
Bulawayo
Blantyre
Lilongwe
Nampula
Quelimane
Beira
Maputo
Antananarivo
Pretoria
JOHANNESBURG
Vereeniging
Springs
Benoni
Krugersdorp
Bloemfontein
Kimberley
Welkom
Durban
Pietermaritzburg
East London
Port Elizabeth
Cape Town
Windhoek
Walvis Bay
Richard's Bay
Maseru
Mbabane

Cape of Good Hope
Cape Agulhas

Tropic of Capricorn

MAURITIUS
Port Louis
Curepipe
RÉUNION (France)
Saint-Denis
Saint-Pierre
Saint-Paul
Saint Joseph

SEYCHELLES
Victoria
PRASLIN
SILHOUETTE
LA DIGUE
ILE PLATE

COMOROS
GRANDE COMORE
MOHÉLI
ANJOUAN
Mayotte (France)
Moroni

Scale 1 : 16 000 000

0   200   400   600 km
0   200   400 miles

© ICA Forlaget AB

ASIA

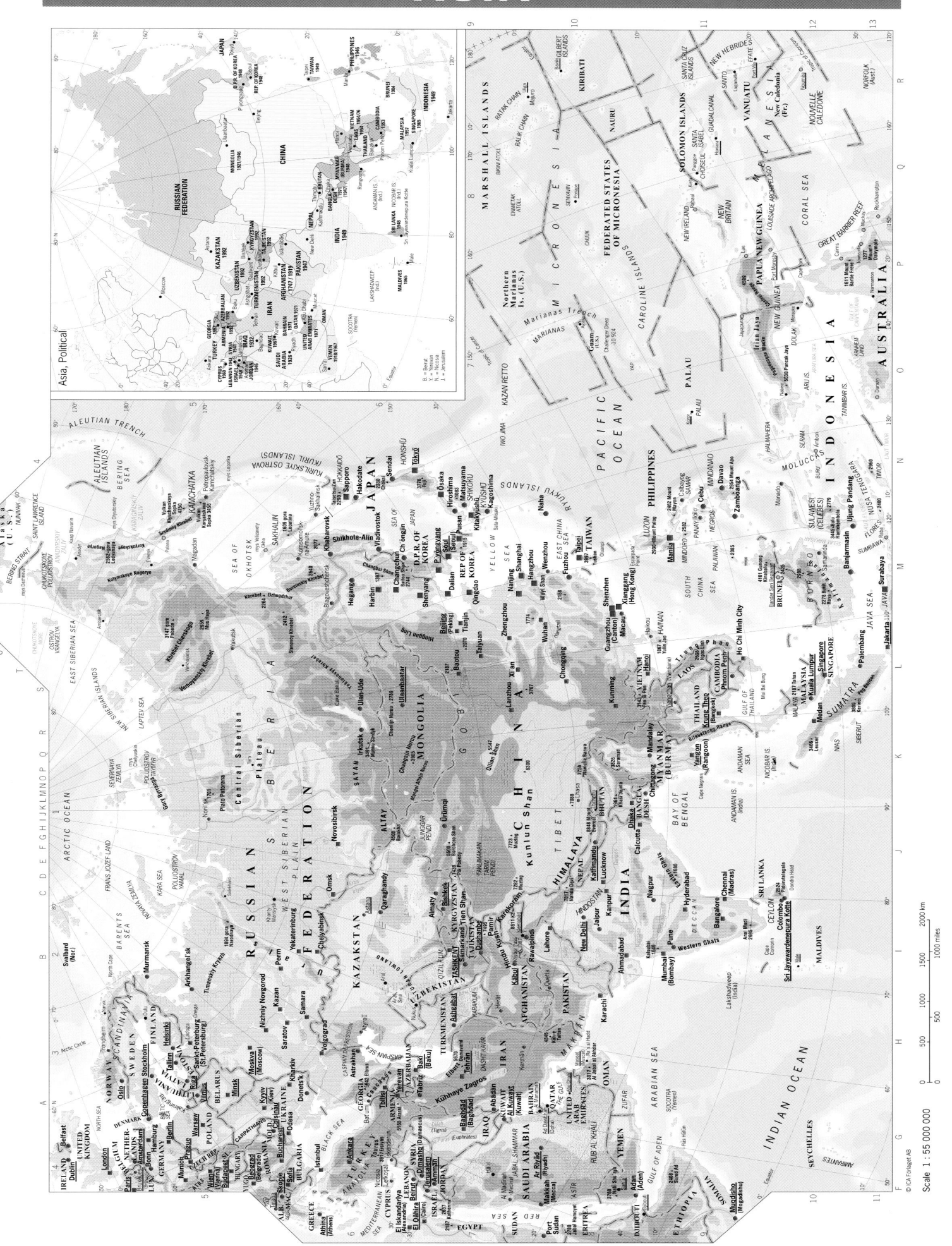

Asia, Political

Scale 1 : 55 000 000

© ICA Förlaget AB

Scale 1 : 19 150 000

© ICA Förlaget AB

NORTHEAST ASIA

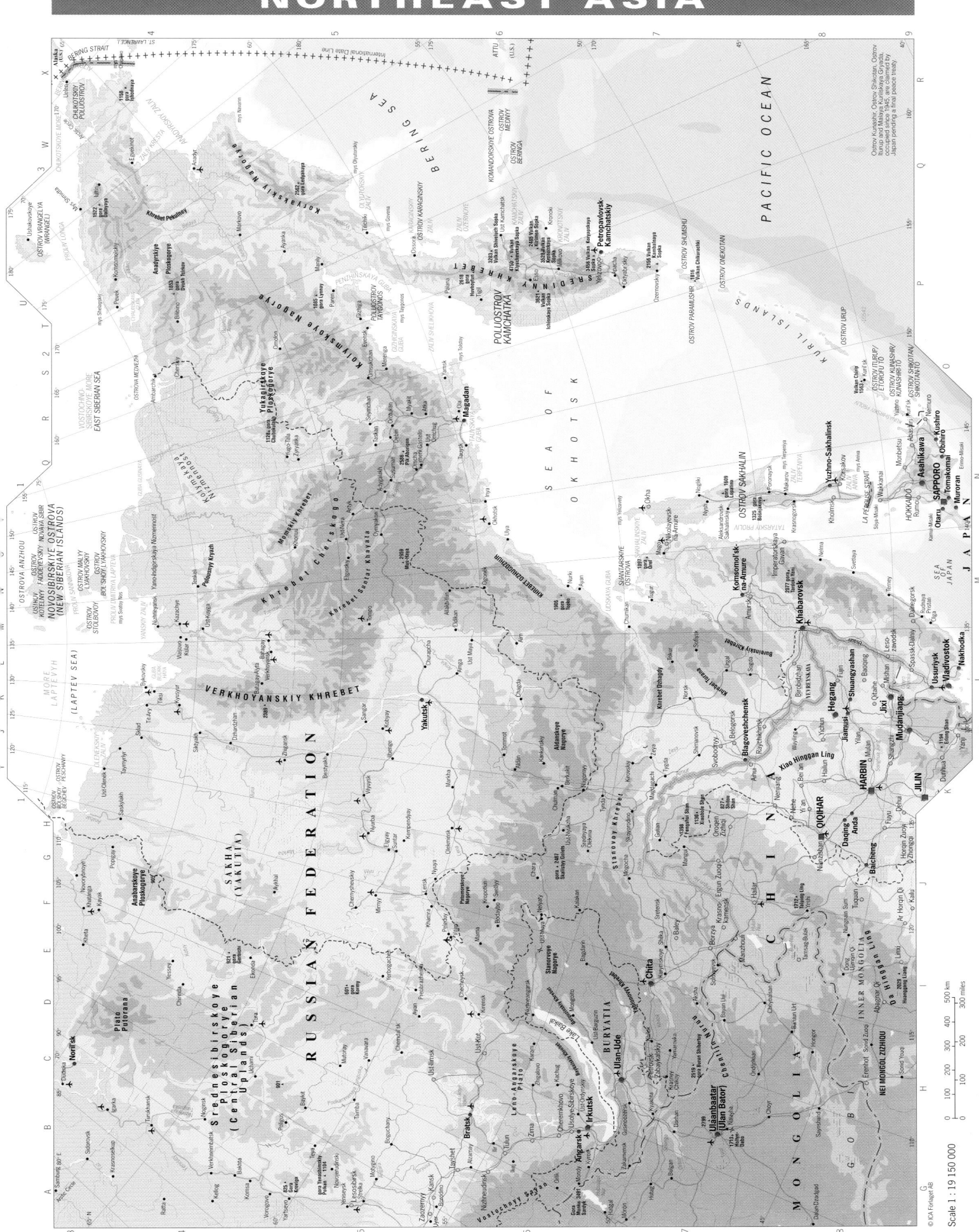

Ostrov Kunashir, Ostrov Shikotan, Ostrov Iturup and Malaya Kurilskaya Gryada, occupied since 1945, are claimed by Japan pending a final peace treaty.

Scale 1 : 19 150 000

0 100 200 300 400 500 km
0 100 200 300 miles

© ICA Förlaget AB

SOUTH ASIA

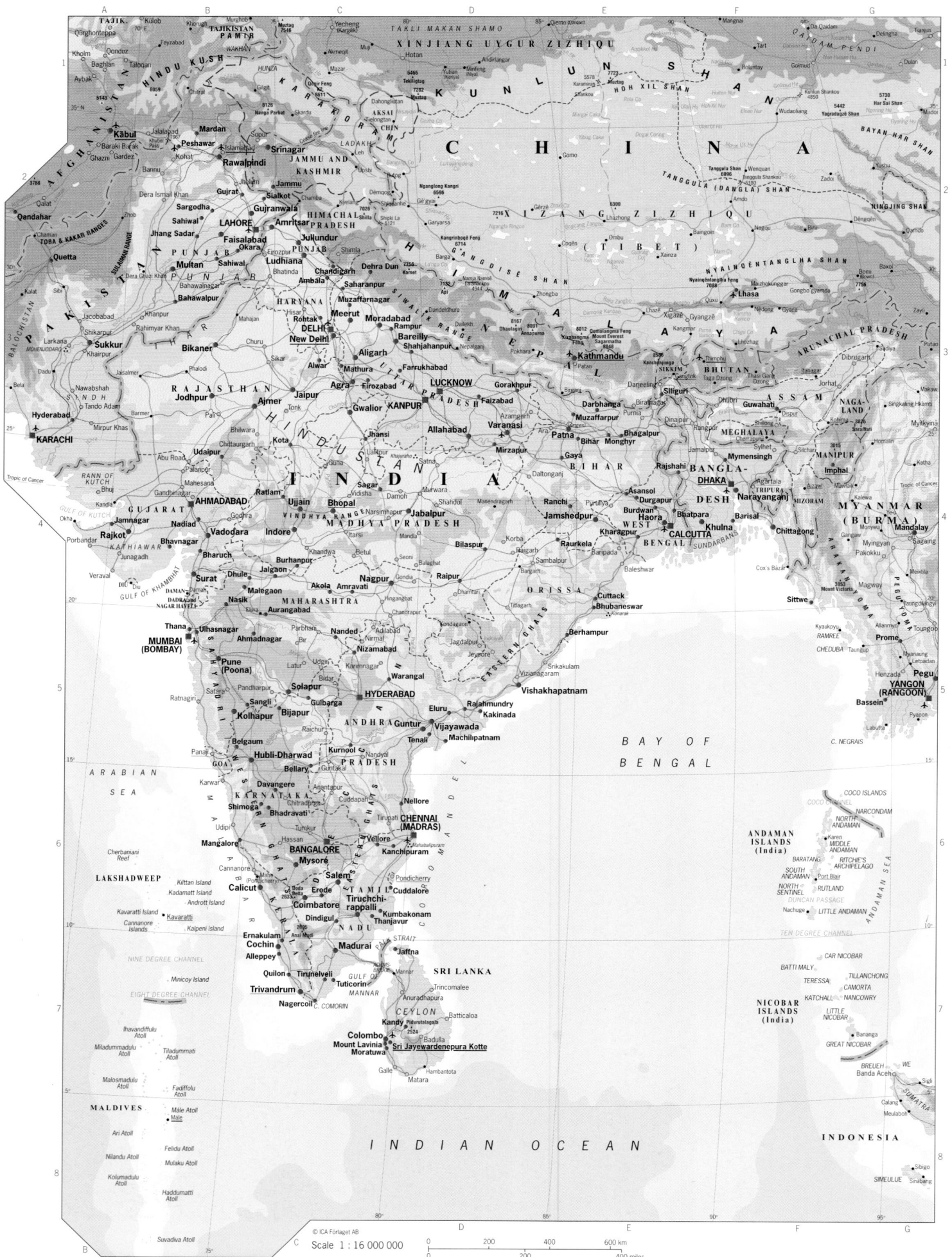

Scale 1 : 16 000 000

0   200   400   600 km

0   200   400 miles

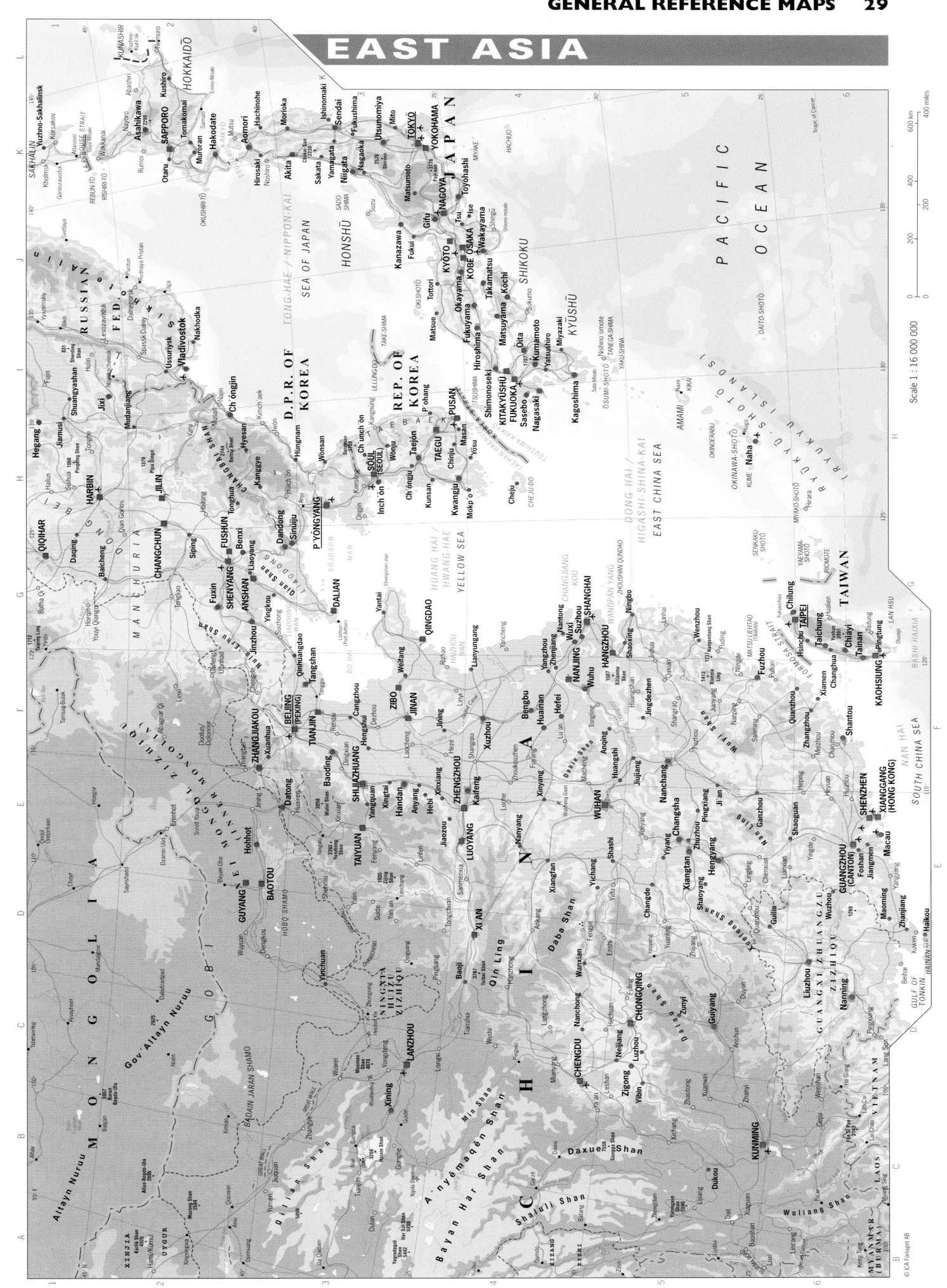

EAST ASIA

JAPAN AND KOREA

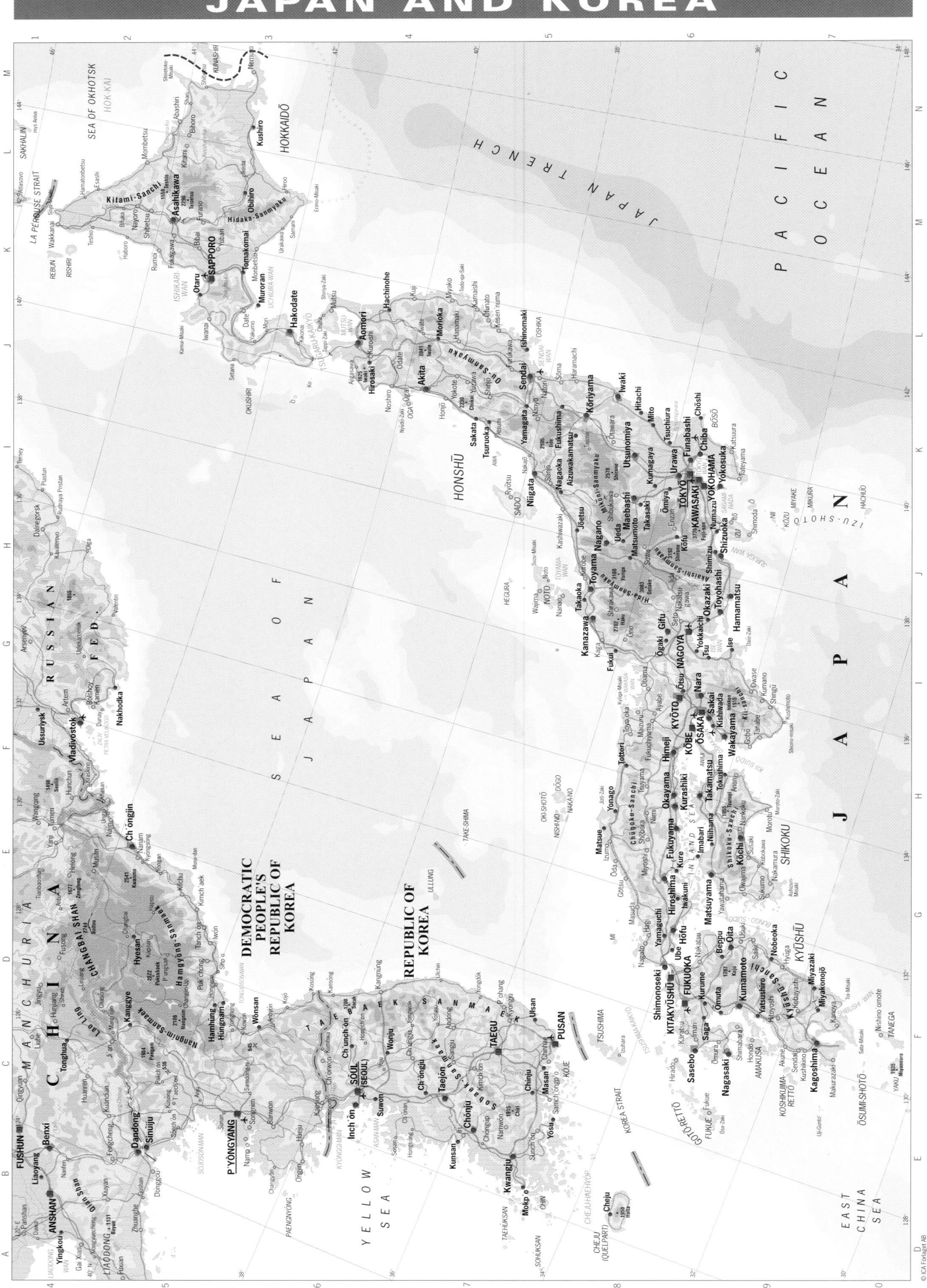

Scale 1 : 8 000 000

© ICA Förlaget AB

SOUTH-EAST ASIA

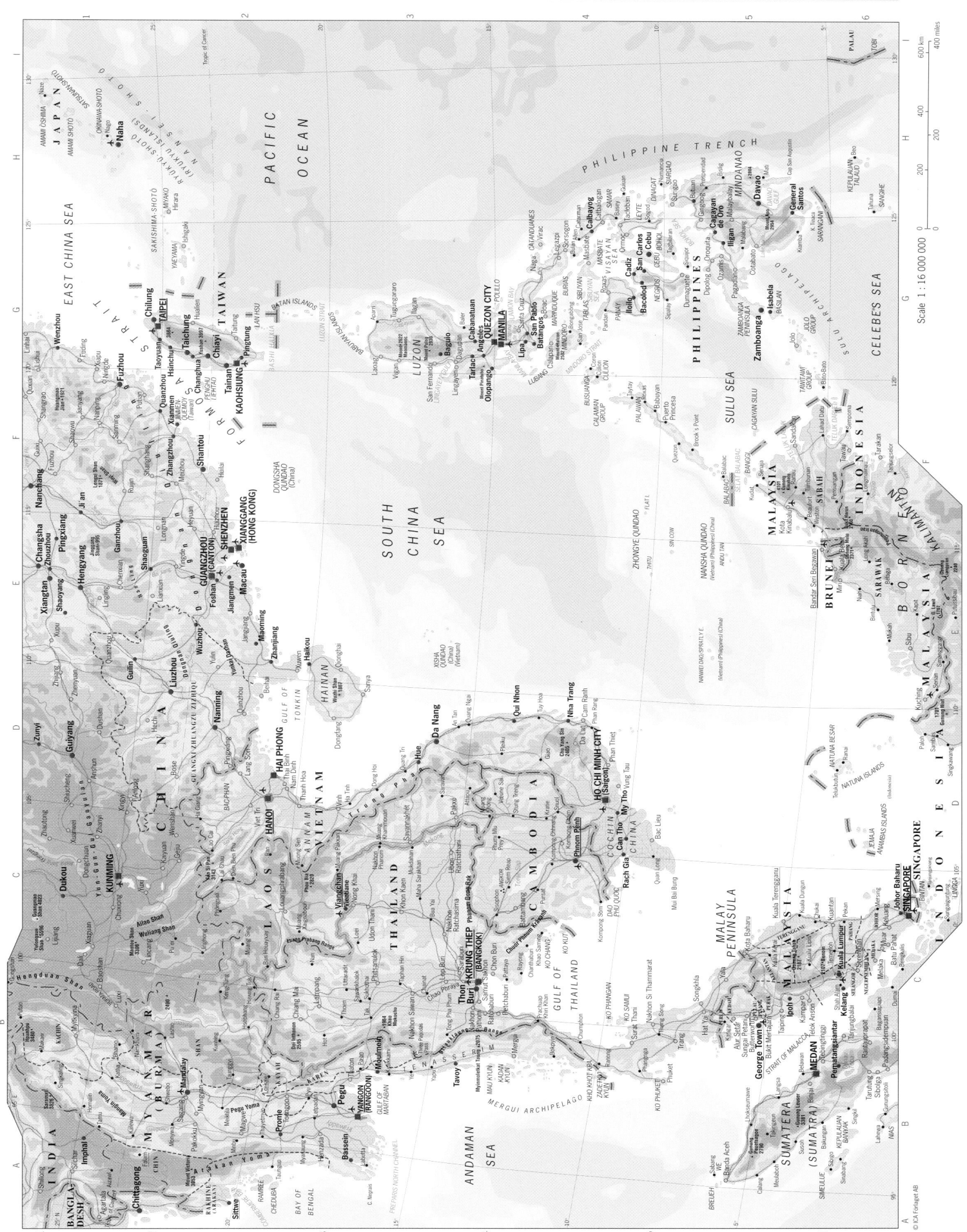

Scale 1 : 16 000 000

© ICA Förlaget AB

MALAYSIA AND INDONESIA

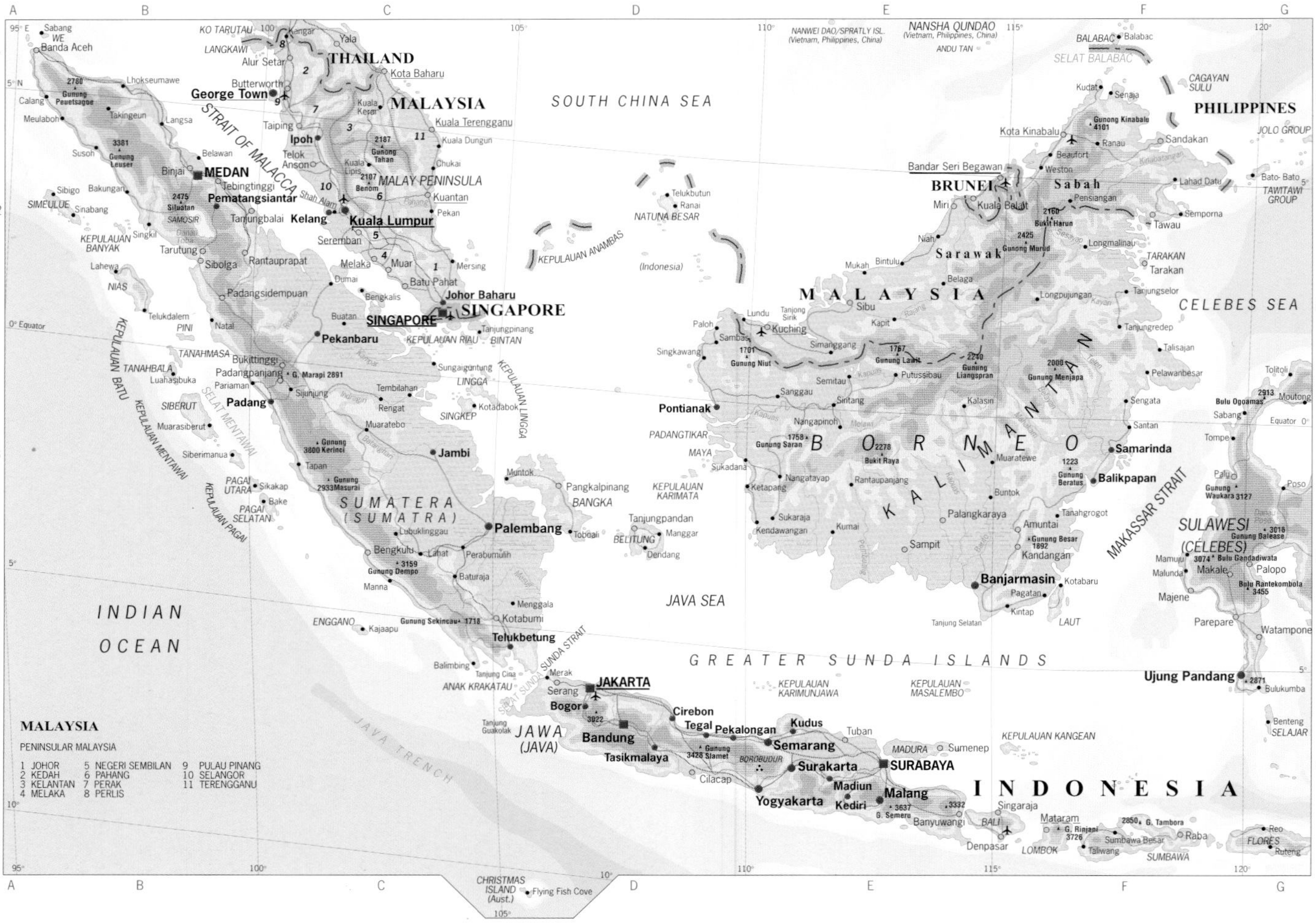

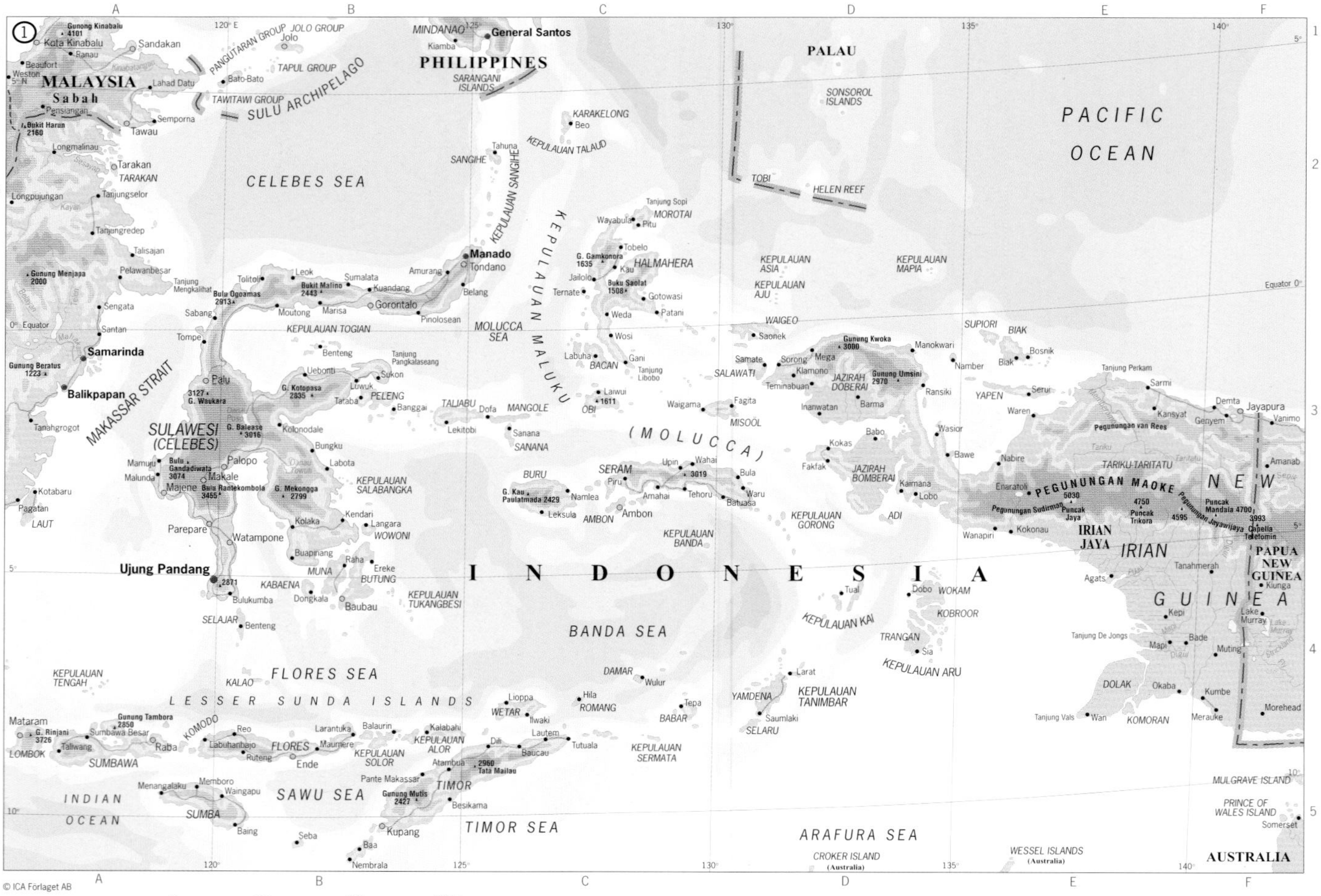

A B C D E F G

THAILAND
MALAYSIA
SOUTH CHINA SEA
PHILIPPINES

Sabang
WE
Banda Aceh
KO TARUTAU
LANGKAWI
Kangar
Yala
Kota Baharu
NANWEI DAO/SPRATLY ISL. (Vietnam, Philippines, China)
NANSHA QUNDAO (Vietnam, Philippines, China)
ANDU TAN
BALABAC
Balabac
SELAT BALABAC
CAGAYAN SULU
JOLO GROUP

Calang
Lhokseumawe
Alur Setar
Butterworth
George Town
Kuala Terengganu
Kudat
Senaja
Gunong Kinabalu 4101
Kota Kinabalu
Sandakan
TAWITAWI GROUP

Meulaboh
Gunung Leuser
Takengeun
Taiping
Ipoh
Gunung Tahan 2187
Kuala Dungun
Chukai
Kota Kinabalu
Beaufort
Ranau
Lahad Datu
Bato-Bato

Susoh
3381
Langsa
Belawan
MEDAN
Tebingtinggi
Telok Anson
Benom 2107
MALAY PENINSULA
Kuantan
BRUNEI
Bandar Seri Begawan
Sabah
Semporna
Tawau

Sibigo
Gunung Leuser
Binjai
Pematangsiantar
Pekan
Miri
Kuala Belit
Longmalinau
Tarakan
Tarakan

SIMEULUE
2475 Siluatan
Tanjungbalai
Kelang
Seremban
MALAYSIA
Gunung Murid
2425
Longbujungan
Tanjungselor

KEPULAUAN BANYAK
Lahewa
Tarutung
Rantauprapat
Melaka
Muar
Mersing
Sarawak
Sibu
Kapit
CELEBES SEA

NIAS
Sibolga
Padangsidempuan
Johor Baharu
Mukah
Bintulu
Belaga
Tanjungredeb

SINGAPORE
SINGAPORE
Paloh
Lundu
Kuching
Singkawang

Padang
Bukittinggi
Pekanbaru
KEPULAUAN RIAU
BINTAN
Gunung Niut 1701
Gunong Liangsaran 2240
Gunong Menjapa 2000

G. Marapi 2891
Padangpanjang
Sungaiguntung
Sanggau
Sintang
Putussibau
Samarinda

Pariaman
Sijunjung
Tembilahan
LINGGA
SINGKEP
Nangapinoh
Kalasin

TANAHMASA
Muarasiberut
Rengat
Muaratebo
PADANGTIKAR
MAYA
BORNEO
Gunung Besar 2278
Muaratewob
Gunung Beratus 1223
Balikpapan

SIBERUT
Siberimanua
Jambi
Muntok
Pangkalpinang
KALIMANTAN
Bukit Raya
Rantaupanjang

PAGAI UTARA
Tapan
Gunung Kerinci 3800
BANGKA
Sukadana
Ketapang
Palangkaraya
Amuntai
SULAWESI (CELEBES)

PAGAI SELATAN
Sikakap
Bangko
SUMATERA (SUMATRA)
Palembang
BELITUNG
Kendawangan
Kumai
Buntok
Gunung Besar 1892
Makale
Bulu Rantekombola 3455

KEPULAUAN MENTAWAI
Bengkulu
Lahat
Peraburulih
Dandang
Sampit
Kandangan
Banjarmasin
Kotabaru
Majene

3159
Gunung Dempo
Baturaja
Tanjungpandan
Manggar
JAVA SEA
Pagatan
Parepare

Manna
Menggala
Kotabumi
Tanjung Selatan
LAUT
Watampone

INDIAN OCEAN
Gunung Sekincau 1718
Kajaapu
Telukbetung
GREATER SUNDA ISLANDS
KEPULAUAN MASALEMBO
Ujung Pandang
2871

ENGGANO
Balimbing
SUNDA STRAIT
Merak
KEPULAUAN KARIMUNJAWA
KEPULAUAN KANGEAN
Benteng
SELAJAR

ANAK KRAKATAU
Serang
JAKARTA
Bogor
Cirebon
Tegal
Pekalongan
Kudus
Tuban
MADURA
Sumenep

JAVA TRENCH
Tanjung Guakolak
JAWA (JAVA)
Bandung
Tasikmalaya
Gunung Slamet 3428
Semarang
Surakarta
SURABAYA

MALAYSIA
PENINSULAR MALAYSIA
1 JOHOR 5 NEGERI SEMBILAN 9 PULAU PINANG
2 KEDAH 6 PAHANG 10 SELANGOR
3 KELANTAN 7 PERAK 11 TERENGGANU
4 MELAKA 8 PERLIS

Cilacap
Yogyakarta
Madiun
Kediri
Malang 3637 3332
Singaraja
INDONESIA

Mataram
G. Semeru
Banyuwangi
BALI
G. Rinjani 3726
Sumbawa Besar
G. Tambora 2850
Raba
Reo
FLORES

Denpasar
LOMBOK
Taliwang
SUMBAWA

CHRISTMAS ISLAND (Aust.)
Flying Fish Cove

---

① Gunung Kinabalu 4101
Kota Kinabalu
Sandakan
PANGUTARAN GROUP
JOLO GROUP
Jolo
MINDANAO
General Santos
PALAU
PACIFIC OCEAN

Beaufort
Banau
Weston
Bato-Bato
TAPUL GROUP
Kiamba
SARANGANI ISLANDS
SONSOROL ISLANDS

MALAYSIA
Sabah
Lahad Datu
TAWITAWI GROUP
SULU ARCHIPELAGO
PHILIPPINES

Pensiangan
Bukit Harun 2160
Tawau
Semporna
KARAKELONG
Beo
TOBI
HELEN REEF

Longmalinau
Tarakan
TARAKAN
CELEBES SEA
Tahuna
KEPULAUAN TALAUD
KEPULAUAN MAPIA

Longpujungan
Kayu
Tanjungselor
SANGIHE
MOROTAI
WAIGEO
Equator 0°

Tanjungredeb
Talisajan
Pelawanbesar
Tanjung Sopi
Pitu
KEPULAUAN ASIA

Gunung Menjapa 2000
Sengata
Tompe
KEPULAUAN SANGIHE
Wayabula
Tobelo
KEPULAUAN AJU
SUPIORI
BIAK

Samarinda
Santan
Manado
Tondano
HALMAHERA
Ternate
WAIGEO
Manokwari
Bosnik

Balikpapan
MAKASSAR STRAIT
Leok
Sumalata
Amurang
Belang
Jailolo
Weda
Sorong
Nabire

Tanahgrogot
SULAWESI (CELEBES)
Palu
G. Waskura 3127
Gorontalo
Marisa
MOLUCCA SEA
Patani
MALUKU (MOLUCCA)
Fakfak

Kotabaru
Palopo
Makale
Kolonodale
PELENG
Banggai
TALIABU
MANGOLE
OBI
BURU
SERAM
AMBON
KEPULAUAN GORONG
PEGUNUNGAN MAOKE
IRIAN JAYA
PAPUA NEW GUINEA

Ujung Pandang
KABAENA
MUNA
BUTUNG
KEPULAUAN TUKANGBESI
INDONESIA
BANDA SEA
KEPULAUAN KAI
KEPULAUAN ARU
NEW GUINEA

FLORES SEA
LESSER SUNDA ISLANDS
WETAR
ROMANG
BABAR
YAMDENA
KEPULAUAN TANIMBAR
DOLAK
AUSTRALIA

Mataram
G. Rinjani 3726
KOMODO
FLORES
KEPULAUAN SOLOR
KEPULAUAN ALOR
TIMOR
SAWU SEA
TIMOR SEA
ARAFURA SEA

INDIAN OCEAN
SUMBA
SUMBAWA
Kupang
CROKER ISLAND (Australia)
WESSEL ISLANDS (Australia)
PRINCE OF WALES ISLAND
Somerset

© ICA Förlaget AB

Scale 1 : 16 000 000

0 200 400 600 km
0 200 400 miles

OCEANIA

Oceania, Political

AUSTRALIA

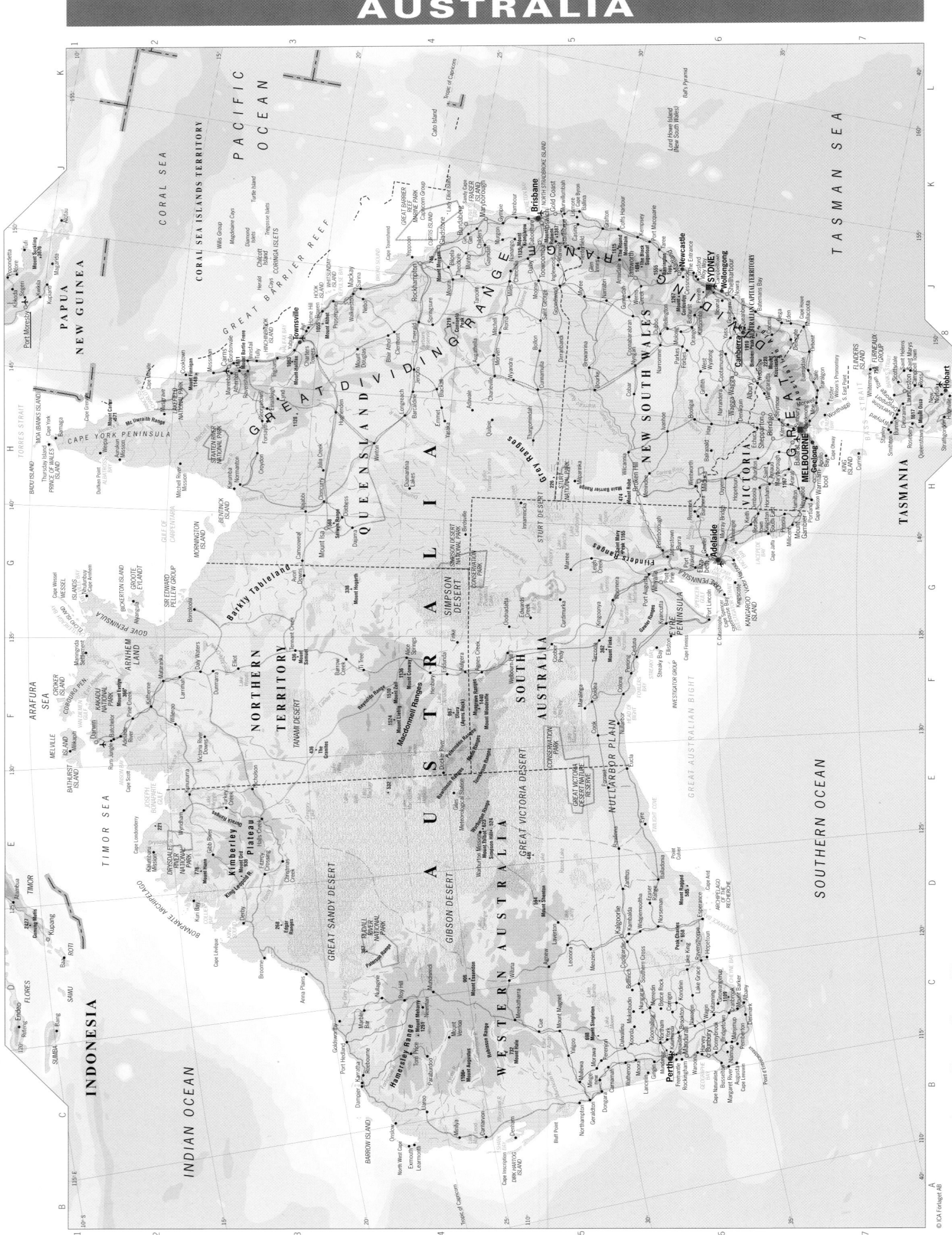

Scale 1 : 19 150 000

NEW ZEALAND AND NEW GUINEA

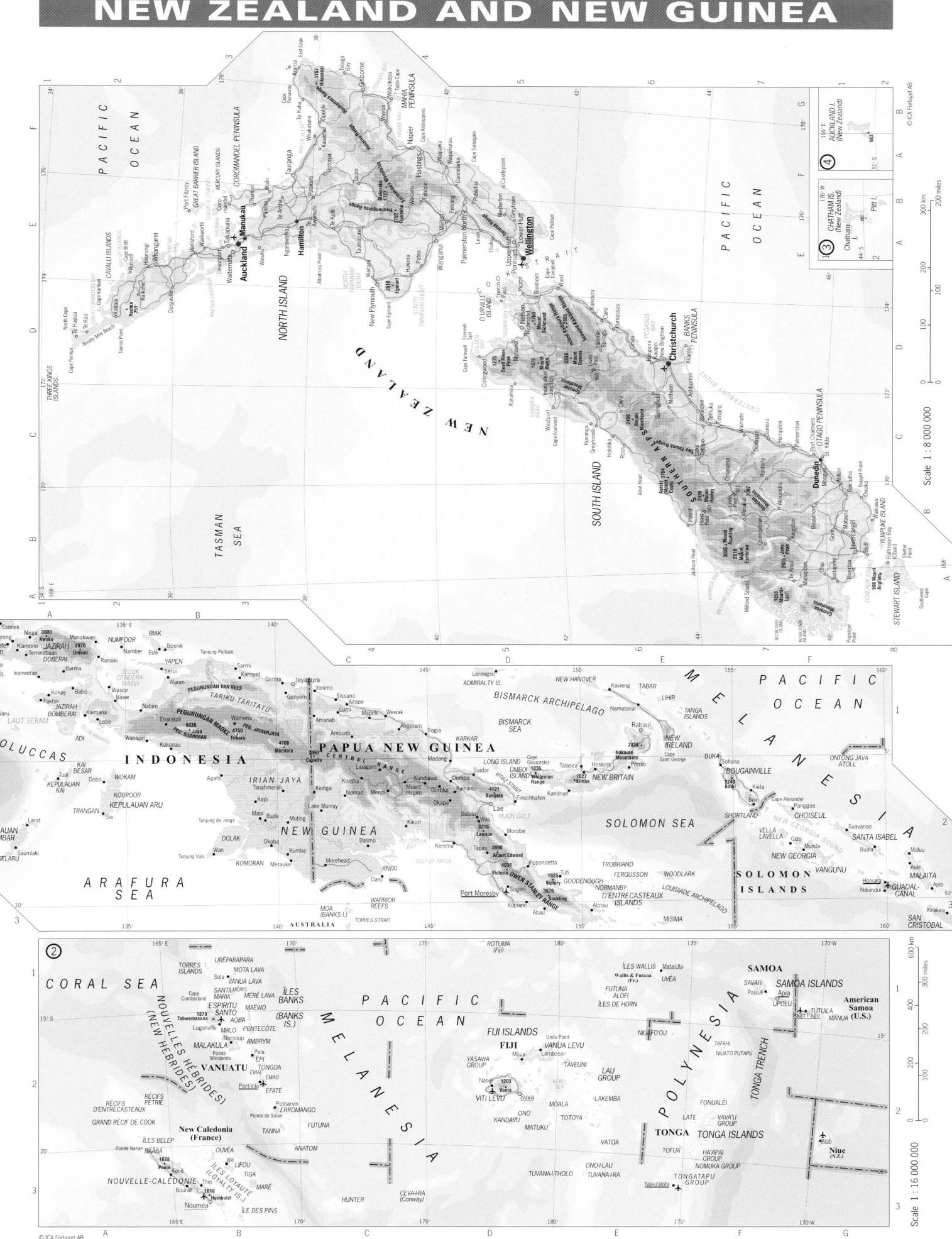

Scale 1 : 8 000 000

Scale 1 : 16 000 000

© ICA Förlaget AB

NORTH AMERICA

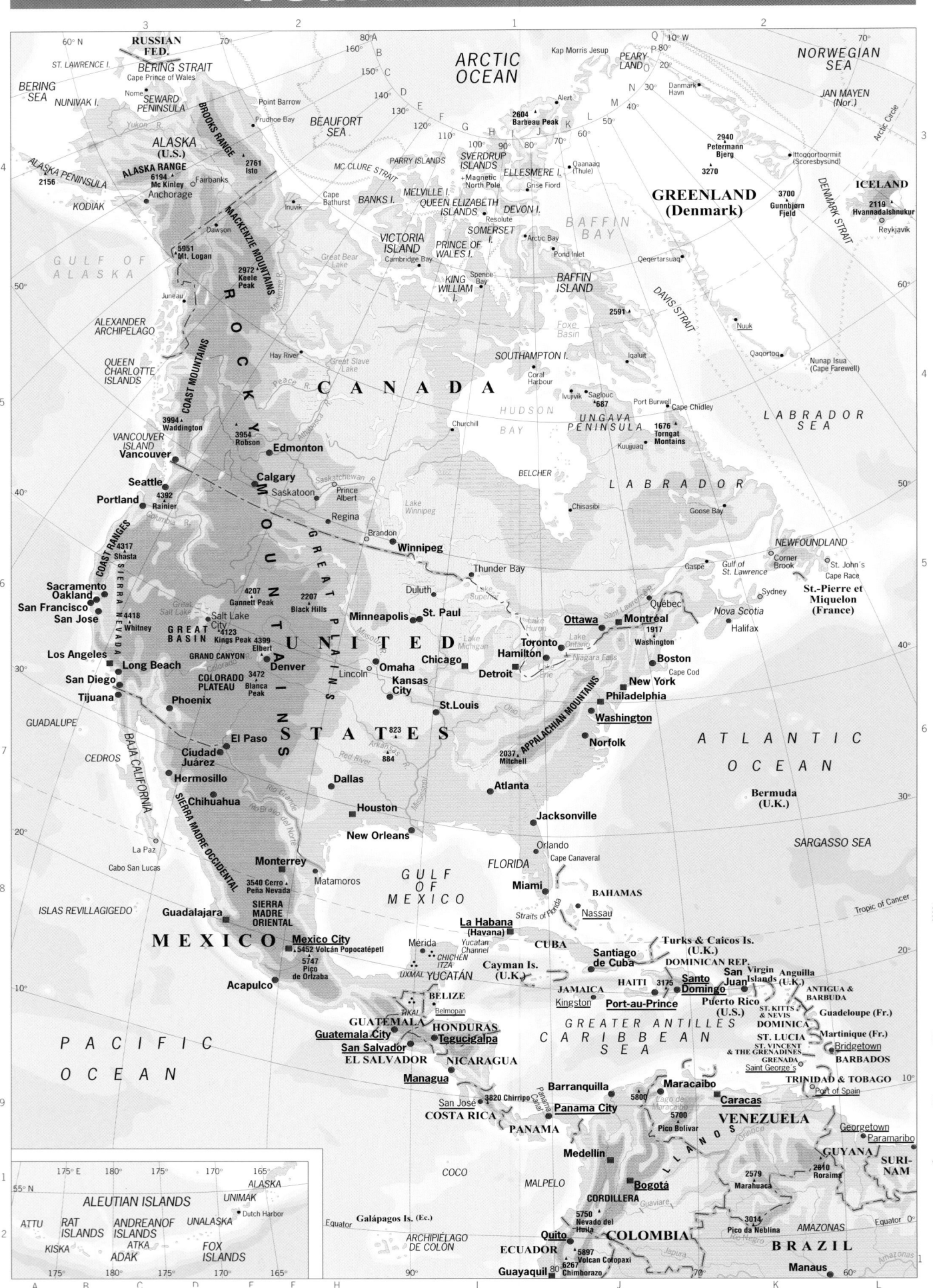

RUSSIAN FED.
ST. LAWRENCE I.
BERING STRAIT
Cape Prince of Wales
BERING SEA
NUNIVAK I.
Nome
SEWARD PENINSULA
Point Barrow
Prudhoe Bay
ALASKA (U.S.)
ALASKA RANGE
6194 Mc Kinley
2761 Isto
2156
Fairbanks
Anchorage
KODIAK
ALASKA PENINSULA
GULF OF ALASKA
Yukon
Dawson
Inuvik
Cape Bathurst
BEAUFORT SEA
MC CLURE STRAIT
BANKS I.
BROOKS RANGE
MACKENZIE MOUNTAINS
5951 Mt. Logan
2072 Keele Peak
ALEXANDER ARCHIPELAGO
Juneau
QUEEN CHARLOTTE ISLANDS
COAST MOUNTAINS
ROCKY
3994 Waddington
3954 Robson
VANCOUVER ISLAND
Vancouver
Seattle
Portland
4392 Rainier
4317 Shasta
COAST RANGES
SIERRA NEVADA
Sacramento
Oakland
San Francisco
San Jose
4418 Whitney
Los Angeles
Long Beach
San Diego
Tijuana
GUADALUPE
CEDROS
BAJA CALIFORNIA
La Paz
Cabo San Lucas
ISLAS REVILLAGIGEDO
GREAT BASIN
Salt Lake City
4123 Kings Peak
GRAND CANYON
COLORADO PLATEAU
Phoenix
El Paso
Ciudad Juárez
Hermosillo
Chihuahua
SIERRA MADRE OCCIDENTAL
3540 Cerro Peña Nevada
Monterrey
Matamoros
Guadalajara
SIERRA MADRE ORIENTAL
MEXICO
Mexico City
5452 Volcán Popocatépetl
5747 Pico de Orizaba
Acapulco
4207 Gannett Peak
2207 Black Hills
GREAT PLAINS
4399 Elbert
3472 Blanca Peak
Denver
Lincoln
Omaha
Kansas City
UNITED STATES
Minneapolis
St. Paul
Chicago
St.Louis
Dallas
Houston
New Orleans
823
884
Red River
Rio Grande
Rio Bravo del Norte
GULF OF MEXICO
Mérida
Yucatan Channel
CHICHEN ITZA
UXMAL
YUCATÁN
TIKAL
BELIZE
Belmopan
GUATEMALA
Guatemala City
San Salvador
EL SALVADOR
HONDURAS
Tegucigalpa
NICARAGUA
Managua
San José
3820 Chirripó
COSTA RICA
Panama Canal
PANAMA
Panama City
PACIFIC OCEAN
COCO
MALPELO
Galápagos Is. (Ec.)
ARCHIPIÉLAGO DE COLÓN
Equator
ECUADOR
Quito
Guayaquil
5897 Volcán Cotopaxi
6267 Chimborazo
5750 Nevado del Huila
Pico da Neblina
COLOMBIA
CORDILLERA
Medellín
Bogotá
Guaviare
ARCTIC OCEAN
Kap Morris Jesup
PEARY-LAND
Alert
2604 Barbeau Peak
SVERDRUP ISLANDS
Magnetic North Pole
ELLESMERE I.
Qaanaaq (Thule)
Grise Fiord
PARRY ISLANDS
MELVILLE I.
QUEEN ELIZABETH ISLANDS
DEVON I.
Resolute
Arctic Bay
Pond Inlet
Cape Bathurst
VICTORIA ISLAND
SOMERSET I.
PRINCE OF WALES I.
Cambridge Bay
KING WILLIAM I.
Spence Bay
BAFFIN BAY
2591
Qeqertarsuaq
GREENLAND (Denmark)
3700 Gunnbjørn Fjeld
2940 Petermann Bjerg
3270
Danmark Havn
NORWEGIAN SEA
JAN MAYEN (Nor.)
Arctic Circle
Ittoqqortoormiit (Scoresbysund)
DENMARK STRAIT
ICELAND
2119 Hvannadalshnukur
Reykjavik
Nuuk
Qaqortoq
Nunap Isua (Cape Farewell)
DAVIS STRAIT
Iqaluit
SOUTHAMPTON I.
Coral Harbour
FOXE BASIN
BAFFIN ISLAND
HUDSON BAY
Churchill
Great Bear Lake
Great Slave Lake
Hay River
Peace R.
CANADA
Lake Athabasca
Edmonton
Calgary
Saskatoon
Prince Albert
Regina
Brandon
Saskatchewan R.
Lake Winnipeg
Winnipeg
Thunder Bay
Duluth
Lake Superior
Lake Huron
Lake Michigan
Lake Erie
Lake Ontario
Niagara Falls
Ottawa
Montréal
1917
Toronto
Hamilton
Detroit
Washington
Boston
Cape Cod
New York
Philadelphia
Washington
Norfolk
APPALACHIAN MOUNTAINS
2037 Mitchell
Atlanta
Jacksonville
Orlando
Cape Canaveral
FLORIDA
Miami
Ohio
Mississippi
Ivujivik
Saglouc
687
Port Burwell
Cape Chidley
UNGAVA PENINSULA
Kuujjuaq
1676 Torngat Mountains
LABRADOR SEA
LABRADOR
Chisasibi
Goose Bay
BELCHER
NEWFOUNDLAND
Gaspe
Gulf of St. Lawrence
Corner Brook
St. John's
Cape Race
Sydney
Nova Scotia
Halifax
St.-Pierre et Miquelon (France)
Saint Lawrence R.
Québec
ATLANTIC OCEAN
Bermuda (U.K.)
SARGASSO SEA
Tropic of Cancer
BAHAMAS
Nassau
Straits of Florida
La Habana (Havana)
CUBA
Santiago de Cuba
Turks & Caicos Is. (U.K.)
Cayman Is. (U.K.)
JAMAICA
Kingston
HAITI
Port-au-Prince
DOMINICAN REP.
Santo Domingo
3175
PUERTO RICO (U.S.)
San Juan
Virgin Islands (U.K.)
Anguilla (U.K.)
ST. KITTS & NEVIS
ANTIGUA & BARBUDA
Guadeloupe (Fr.)
DOMINICA
Martinique (Fr.)
ST. LUCIA
ST. VINCENT & THE GRENADINES
Bridgetown
BARBADOS
GRENADA
Saint George's
TRINIDAD & TOBAGO
Port of Spain
GREATER ANTILLES
CARIBBEAN SEA
Barranquilla
Maracaibo
Caracas
5800
5700 Pico Bolívar
LLANOS
VENEZUELA
Georgetown
Paramaribo
GUYANA
SURINAM
2579 Marahuaca
2810 Roraima
3014 Pico da Neblina
AMAZONAS
BRAZIL
Manaus
Amazonas
Japura
NORWEGIAN SEA

Scale 1 : 36 000 000

2000 km
1000 miles
1500
1000
500
0

ALEUTIAN ISLANDS
ALASKA
UNIMAK
Dutch Harbor
UNALASKA
FOX ISLANDS
ANDREANOF ISLANDS
ATKA
ADAK
RAT ISLANDS
KISKA
ATTU

CENTRAL AMERICA

Scale 1 : 16 000 000

© ICA Förlaget AB

CANADA

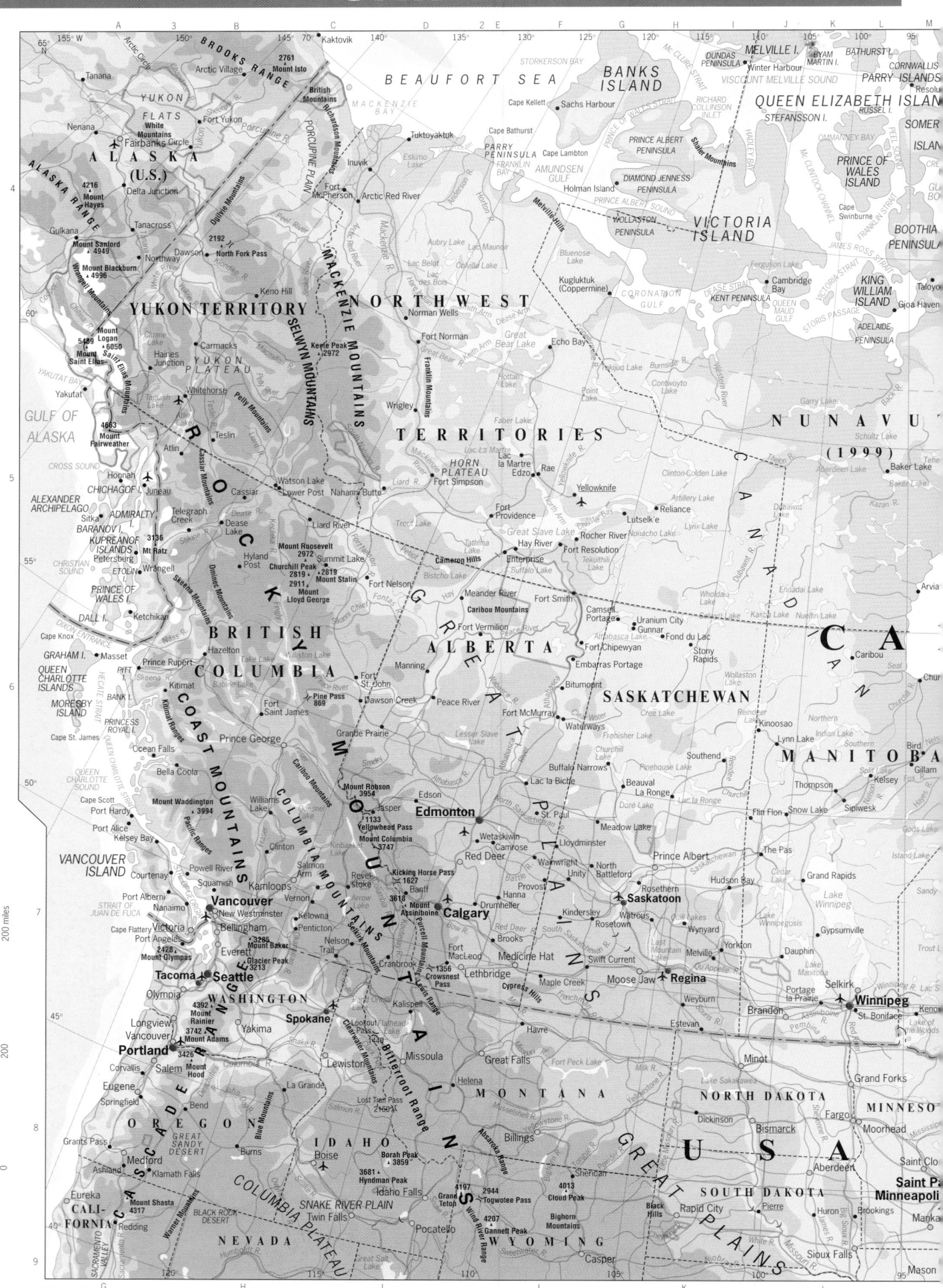

Scale 1 : 12 000 000

© ICA Förlaget AB

CANADA

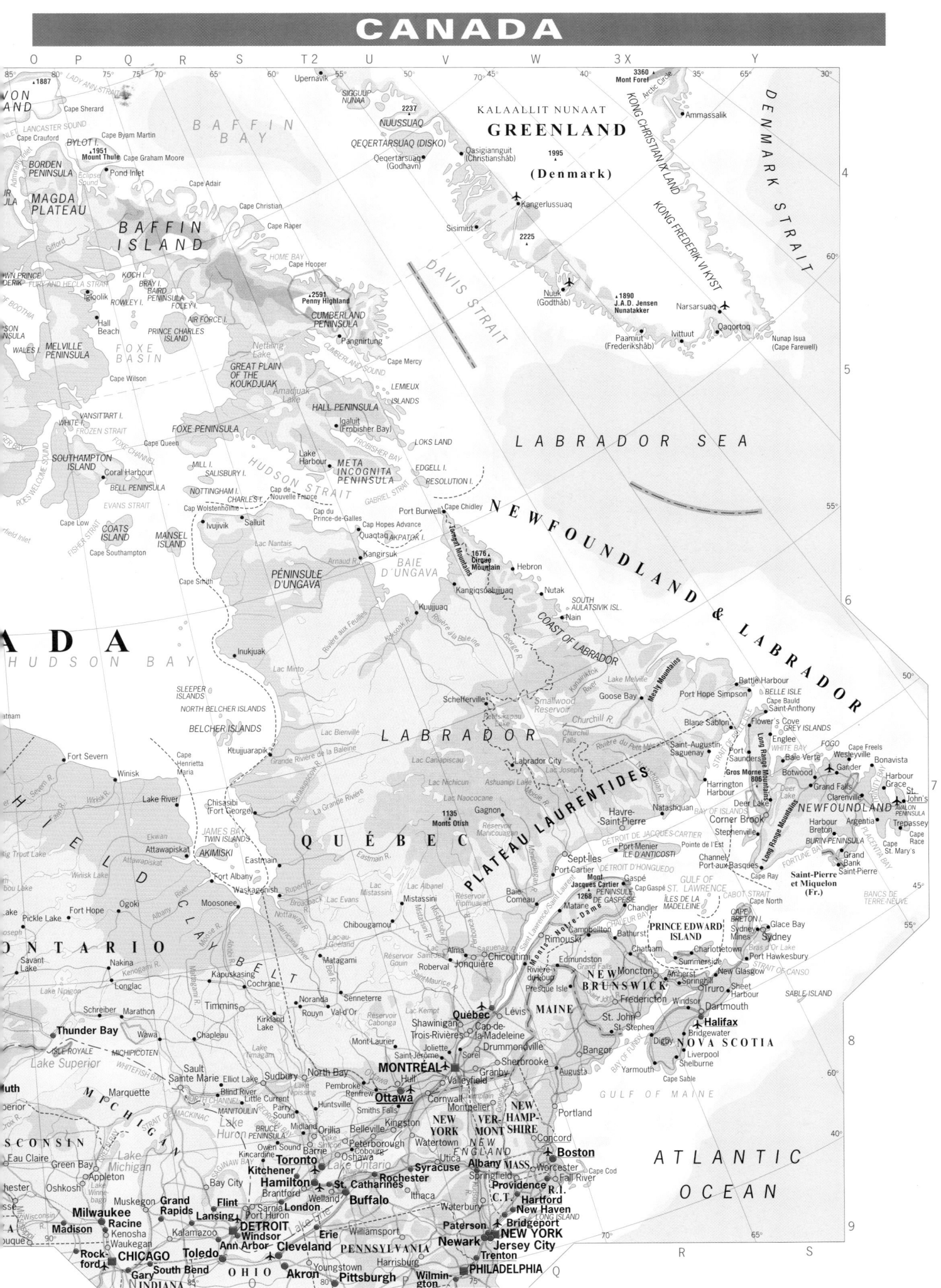

O P Q R S T2 U V W 3X Y

GREENLAND
KALAALLIT NUNAAT
(Denmark)

BAFFIN BAY

BAFFIN ISLAND

DAVIS STRAIT

LABRADOR SEA

DENMARK STRAIT

NEWFOUNDLAND & LABRADOR

HUDSON BAY

LABRADOR

QUÉBEC

PLATEAU LAURENTIDES

ONTARIO

NEWFOUNDLAND

PRINCE EDWARD ISLAND

NEW BRUNSWICK

NOVA SCOTIA

GULF OF ST. LAWRENCE

MAINE

Thunder Bay

MONTRÉAL
Ottawa
Québec

Halifax

NEW YORK
VERMONT
NEW HAMPSHIRE

Toronto
Hamilton
Buffalo

Boston
MASS.
Albany

ATLANTIC OCEAN

GULF OF MAINE

DETROIT
Cleveland
CHICAGO

NEW YORK
Newark
Jersey City
PHILADELPHIA

PENNSYLVANIA

OHIO

Pittsburgh

UNITED STATES

© ICA Förlaget AB

Scale 1 : 13 400 000

| 0 | 200 | 400 | 600 km |
| 0 | 200 | 400 miles |

Map of the western United States, southwestern Canada, and northern Mexico, with inset maps of Hawaii and Alaska. Major labeled features include:

Canada: British Columbia, Alberta, Saskatchewan, Vancouver Island, Vancouver, Victoria, Kamloops, Kelowna, Calgary, Banff, Lethbridge, Medicine Hat, Red Deer, Saskatoon, Regina, Moose Jaw, Prince Albert

United States (Pacific Northwest): Washington, Oregon, Seattle, Tacoma, Olympia, Portland, Salem, Spokane, Yakima, Eugene, Bend, Mount Rainier, Mount Olympus, Cascade Range, Coast Ranges

California: Sacramento, San Francisco, Oakland, Berkeley, San Jose, Stockton, Fresno, Los Angeles, Long Beach, San Diego, Santa Ana, San Bernardino, Riverside, Bakersfield, Sierra Nevada, Death Valley, Mojave Desert, Mount Whitney 4418, Golden Gate, San Joaquin Valley, Central Valley

Nevada/Utah: Nevada, Utah, Great Basin, Great Salt Lake Desert, Carson City, Las Vegas, Salt Lake City, Provo, Grand Canyon, Colorado Plateau

Idaho/Montana/Wyoming: Idaho, Montana, Wyoming, Boise, Idaho Falls, Pocatello, Missoula, Helena, Great Falls, Butte, Billings, Bozeman, Casper, Cheyenne, Rocky Mountains, Bighorn Mountains, Gannett Peak 4207, Borah Peak 3859, Grand Teton 4197

North Dakota/Nebraska/Colorado: North Dakota, Nebraska, Colorado, Denver, Colorado Springs, Pueblo, Boulder, Aurora, Fort Collins, Rapid City, Mandan, Bismarck, Mount Elbert 4399

Arizona/New Mexico/Texas: Arizona, New Mexico, Texas, Phoenix, Tucson, Mesa, Scottsdale, Flagstaff, Albuquerque, Santa Fe, Las Cruces, El Paso, Lubbock, Amarillo, Roswell, Carlsbad, Wichita Falls, San Antonio, Llano Estacado

Mexico: Baja California, Baja California Sur, Sonora, Chihuahua, Coahuila, Durango, Sinaloa, Nuevo León, Nayarit, Zacatecas, San Luis Potosí, Tijuana, Mexicali, Ensenada, La Paz, Hermosillo, Ciudad Obregón, Chihuahua, Ciudad Juárez, Culiacán, Mazatlán, Durango, Torreón, Monterrey, Saltillo, Monclova, Nuevo Laredo, Reynosa, Golfo de California, Sierra Madre Occidental, Sierra Madre Oriental, Altiplanicie Mexicana, Bolsón de Mapimí

Hawaii inset: Kauai, Oahu, Molokai, Maui, Lanai, Kahoolawe, Hawaii, Honolulu, Hilo, Kaneohe, Wahiawa, Waimea, Mauna Kea 4205, Mauna Loa 4170, Pacific Ocean, Kaiwi Channel, Kauai Channel, Alenuihaha Channel, Pailolo Channel

Alaska inset: Russian Fed., Alaska U.S., Canada, Anchorage, Fairbanks, Juneau, Nome, Bethel, Prudhoe Bay, Mt McKinley 6194, Mt Logan 6050, Mt Wrangell 4317, Mt Isto 2761, Chukchi Sea, Bering Sea, Bering Strait, Gulf of Alaska, Pacific Ocean, Aleutian Islands, Alaska Peninsula, Kodiak I., St. Lawrence I., Nunivak I., Norton Sound, Yukon, Arctic Circle

UNITED STATES

CANADA

ONTARIO

QUÉBEC

MINNESOTA

WISCONSIN

MICHIGAN

NEW YORK

MAINE

NEW BRUNSWICK

NEW HAMPSHIRE

VERMONT

MASSACHUSETTS

CONNECTICUT

RHODE ISLAND

NEW JERSEY

PENNSYLVANIA

OHIO

INDIANA

ILLINOIS

IOWA

MISSOURI

KENTUCKY

TENNESSEE

ARKANSAS

OKLAHOMA

LOUISIANA

MISSISSIPPI

ALABAMA

GEORGIA

FLORIDA

NORTH CAROLINA

SOUTH CAROLINA

VIRGINIA

WEST VIRGINIA

MARYLAND

DELAWARE

APPALACHIANS

ATLANTIC OCEAN

GULF OF MEXICO

BAHAMAS

CUBA

LA HABANA (HAVANA)

Lake Superior

Lake Michigan

Lake Huron

Lake Erie

Lake Ontario

Lake Winnipeg

CENTRAL LOWLAND

Winnipeg, Thunder Bay, Duluth, Saint Paul, Minneapolis, Madison, Milwaukee, Chicago, Rockford, Des Moines, Omaha, Kansas City, St. Louis, Topeka, Wichita, Tulsa, Oklahoma City, Dallas, Houston, Shreveport, Little Rock, Memphis, Nashville, Birmingham, Jackson, Montgomery, Baton Rouge, New Orleans, Mobile, Jacksonville, Orlando, Tampa, St. Petersburg, Fort Lauderdale, Miami, Nassau, Atlanta, Columbus, Macon, Savannah, Columbia, Charlotte, Charleston, Greensboro, Winston-Salem, Raleigh, Richmond, Norfolk, Virginia Beach, Washington, Baltimore, Philadelphia, Trenton, New York, Jersey City, Newark, New Haven, Bridgeport, Hartford, Providence, Boston, Worcester, Springfield, Albany, Syracuse, Rochester, Buffalo, Pittsburgh, Cleveland, Akron, Columbus, Cincinnati, Indianapolis, Detroit, Toledo, Fort Wayne, Louisville, Lexington, Knoxville, Chattanooga, Huntsville, Montréal, Ottawa, Québec, Toronto, Hamilton

NORTHWEST USA

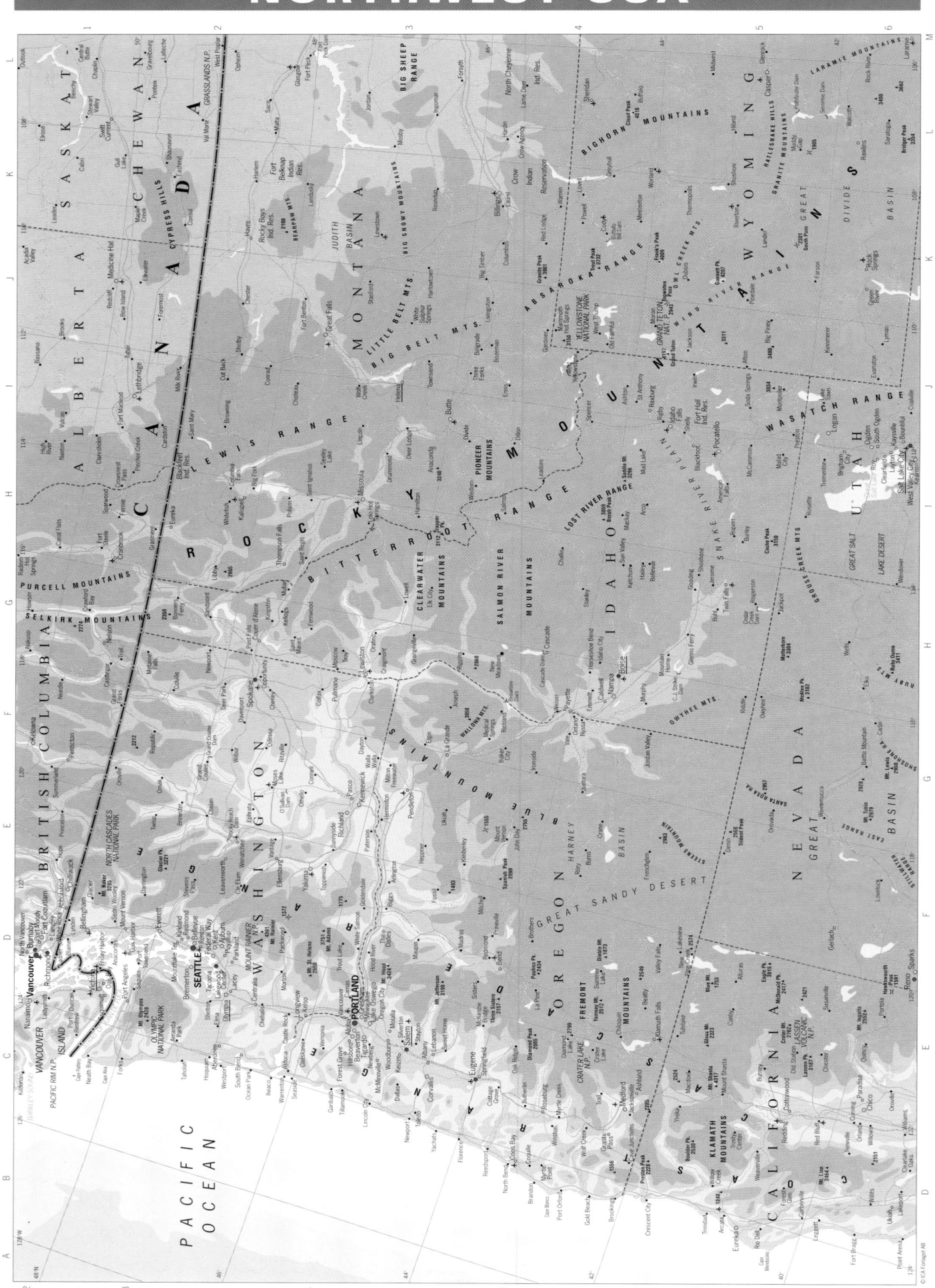

Scale 1 : 6 300 000

© ICA Förlaget AB

MIDWEST USA

Scale 1 : 6 300 000

©ICA Förlaget AB

NORTHEAST USA

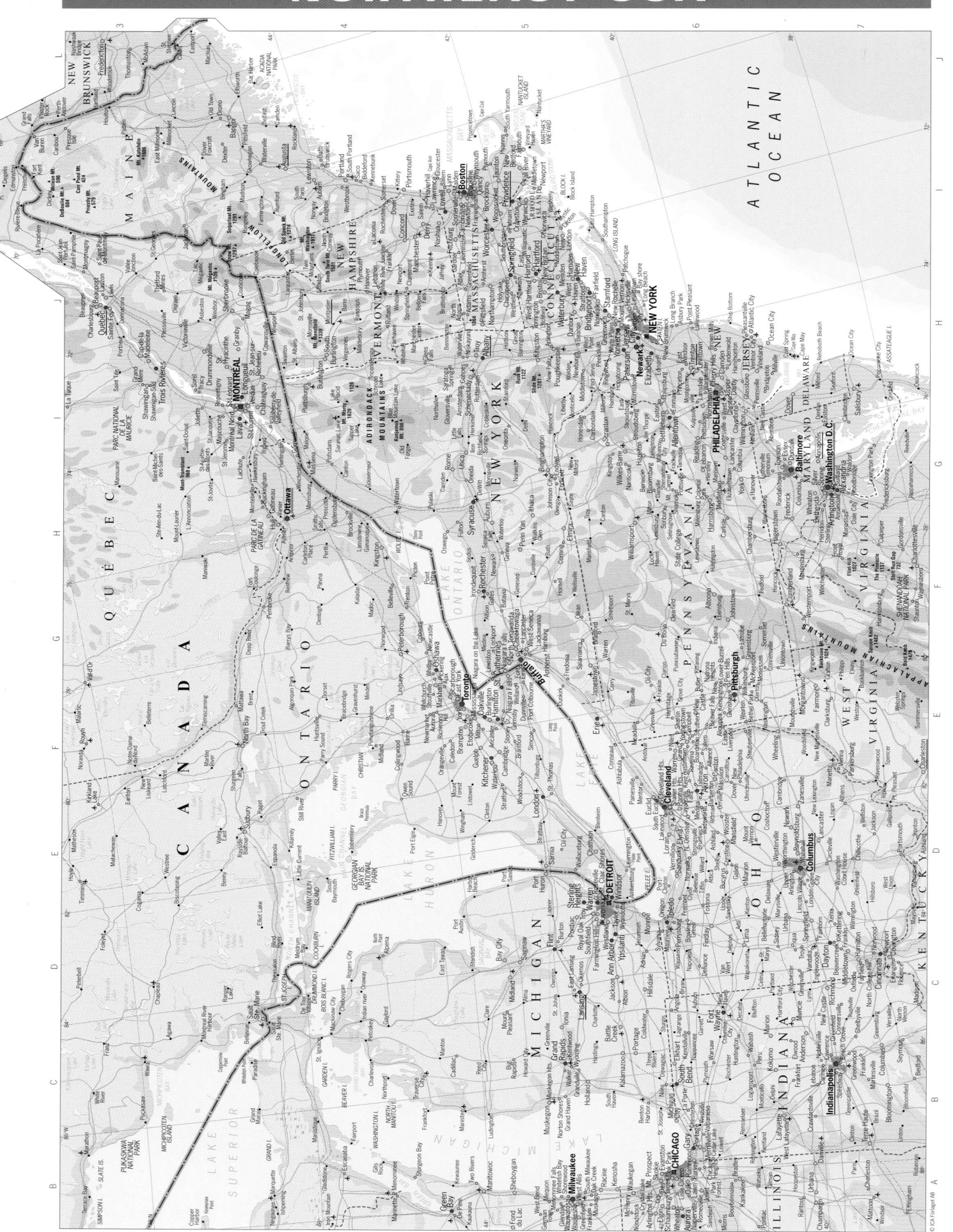

SOUTHWEST USA

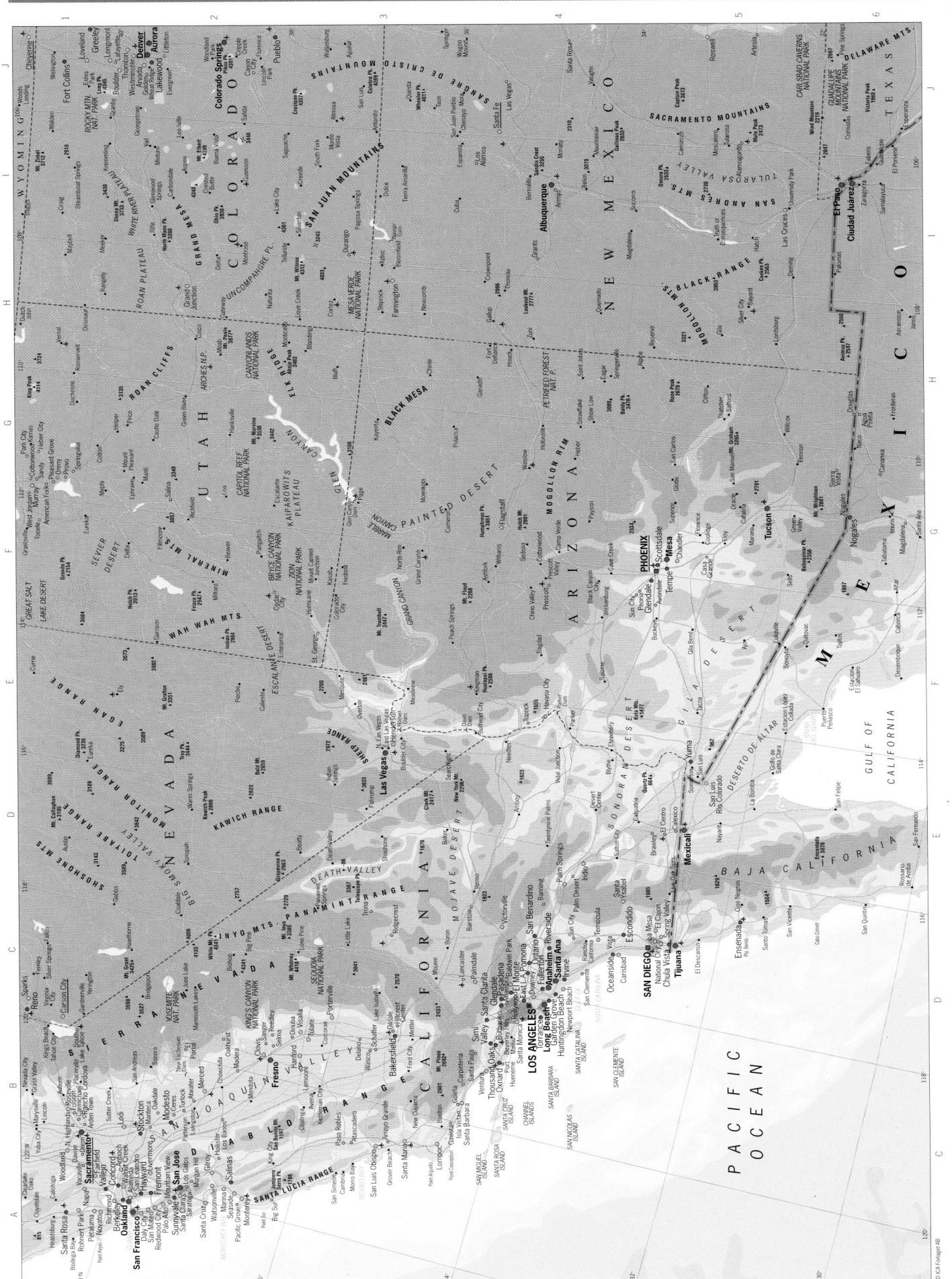

Scale 1 : 6 300 000

© LA Forlaget AB

CENTRAL USA

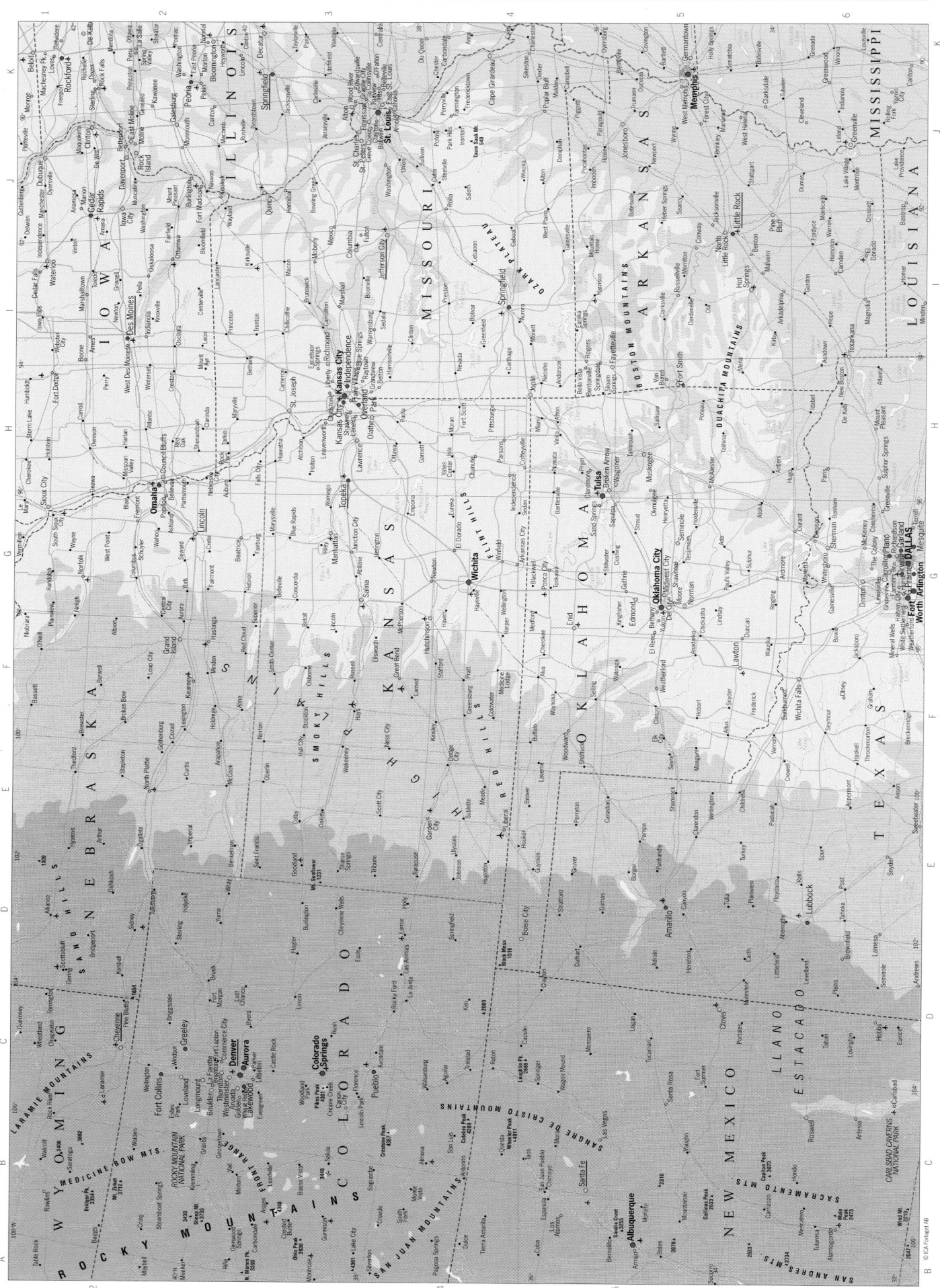

SOUTHERN USA

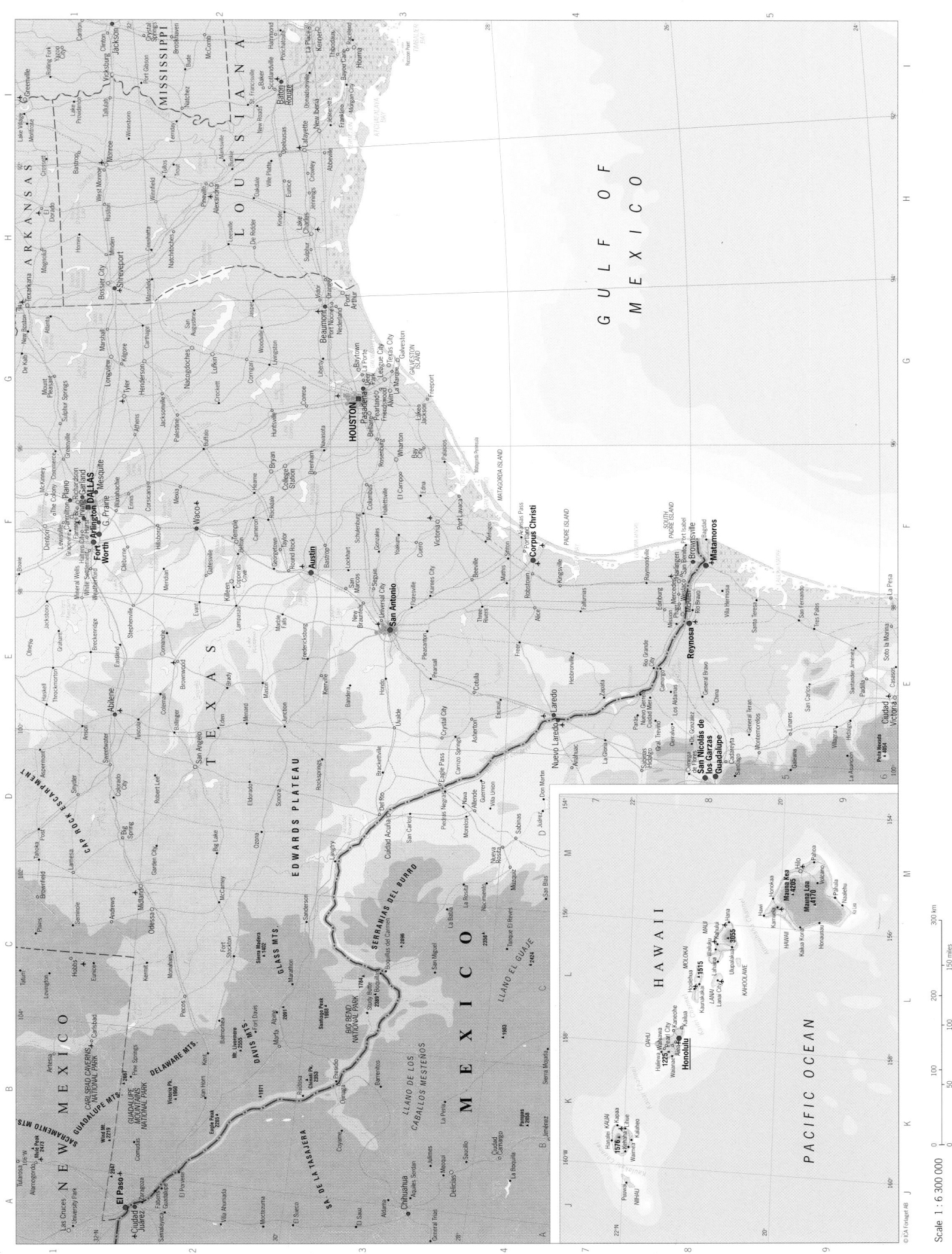

Scale 1 : 6 300 000

© IGA Förlaget AB

SOUTHEAST USA

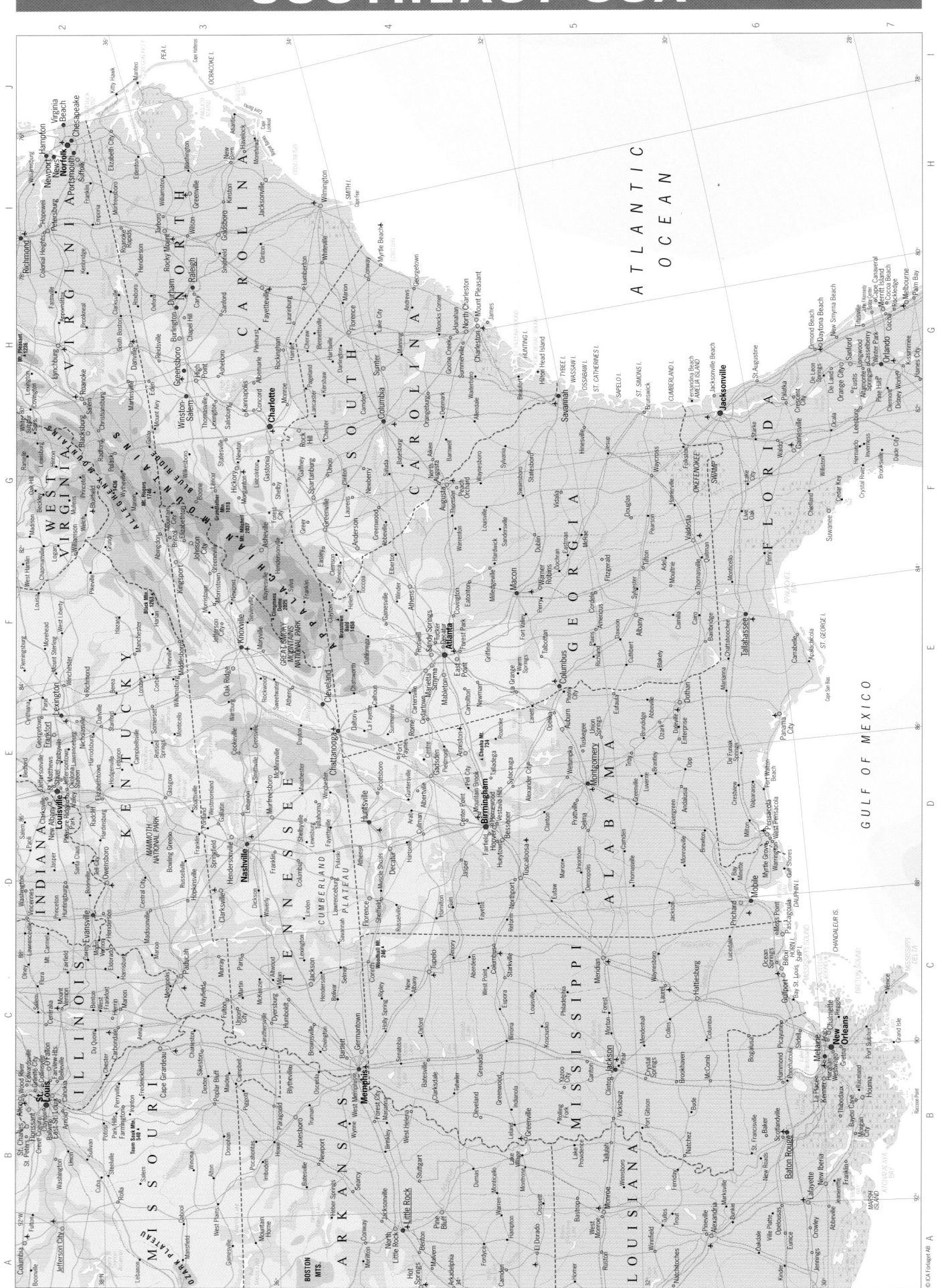

FLORIDA AND ALASKA

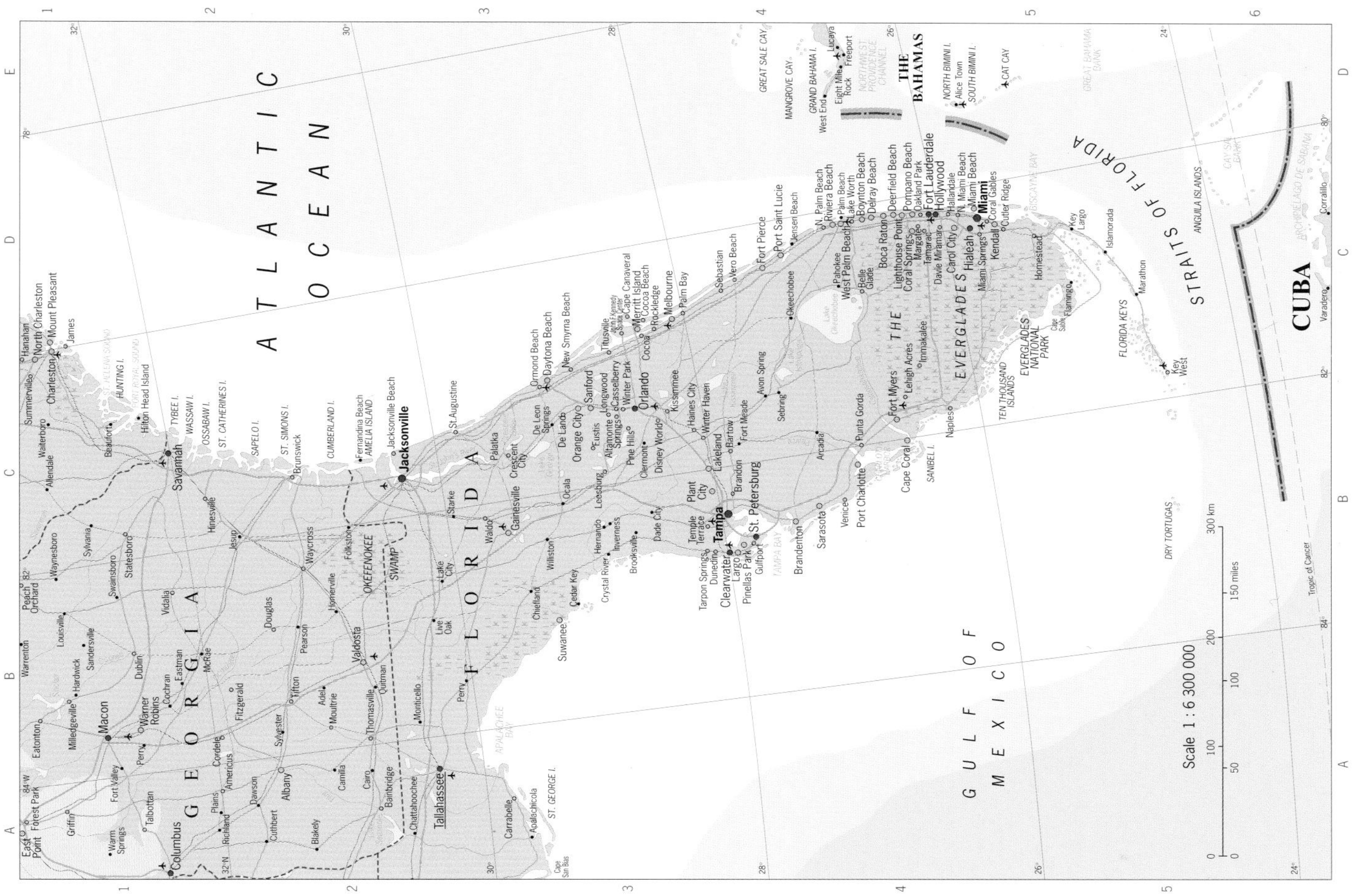

Florida map

ATLANTIC OCEAN

GULF OF MEXICO

STRAITS OF FLORIDA

CUBA

THE BAHAMAS

GEORGIA

FLORIDA

OKEEFENOKEE SWAMP

EVERGLADES NATIONAL PARK

TEN THOUSAND ISLANDS

FLORIDA KEYS

DRY TORTUGAS

Jacksonville, Tallahassee, Tampa, St. Petersburg, Clearwater, Orlando, Miami, Hialeah, Fort Lauderdale, Hollywood, Miami Beach, Coral Gables, Kendall, Homestead, Key West, Key Largo, Marathon, Naples, Fort Myers, Cape Coral, Port Charlotte, Punta Gorda, Sarasota, Venice, Arcadia, Sebring, Avon Park, Lakeland, Plant City, Winter Haven, Bartow, Kissimmee, Winter Park, Sanford, De Land, Daytona Beach, Ormond Beach, New Smyrna Beach, Titusville, Cocoa Beach, Cape Canaveral, Merritt Island, Melbourne, Palm Bay, Vero Beach, Sebastian, Fort Pierce, Port Saint Lucie, Jensen Beach, Stuart, Jupiter, West Palm Beach, Lake Worth, Boynton Beach, Delray Beach, Boca Raton, Deerfield Beach, Pompano Beach, Coral Springs, Pembroke Pines, Carol City, North Miami Beach, Immokalee, Belle Glade, Clewiston, Okeechobee, Lake Okeechobee

Savannah, Charleston, North Charleston, Mount Pleasant, Hilton Head Island, Brunswick, Waycross, Valdosta, Douglas, Tifton, Moultrie, Thomasville, Albany, Americus, Cordele, Fitzgerald, Macon, Warner Robins, Columbus, Fort Valley, Perry, Dublin, Statesboro, Hinesville, Jesup

TYBEE I., WASSAW I., OSSABAW I., ST. CATHERINES I., SAPELO I., ST. SIMONS I., CUMBERLAND I., AMELIA ISLAND, ANGUILLA ISLANDS

Scale 1 : 6 300 000

300 km
150 miles

Alaska map

RUSSIAN FEDERATION

ALASKA

CANADA

YUKON

NORTHWEST TERRITORIES

BRITISH COLUMBIA

CHUKCHI SEA

BEAUFORT SEA

BERING SEA

GULF OF ALASKA

PACIFIC OCEAN

NORTH SLOPE

BROOKS RANGE

ALASKA RANGE

ALEUTIAN ISLANDS

FOX ISLANDS

ANDREANOF ISLANDS

RAT ISLANDS

ISLANDS OF FOUR MTS.

SHUMAGIN IS.

KODIAK I.

NUNIVAK I.

ST. LAWRENCE I.

ST. MATTHEW I.

PRIBILOF IS.

BRISTOL BAY

NORTON SOUND

SEWARD PENINSULA

KUSKOKWIM MTS.

KILBUCK MTS.

COAST MOUNTAINS

CHUGACH MOUNTAINS

WRANGELL MTS.

ST. ELIAS MTS.

MACKENZIE MOUNTAINS

SELWYN MOUNTAINS

RICHARDSON MTS.

KORJAKSKOE NAGORE

OLOJSKIJ HREBET

ANJUJSKIJ HREBET

ČUKOTSKOE NAG.

INTERNATIONAL DATE LINE

GATES OF THE ARCTIC NATIONAL PARK

KOBUK VALLEY N.P.

DENALI N.P.

LAKE CLARK N.P.

KATMAI N.P.

KENAI FJORDS N. MON.

ANIAKCHAK N. MON.

WRANGELL-ST. ELIAS N.P.

KLUANE N.P.

GLACIER BAY N.P.

CAPE KRUSENSTERN N. MON.

NORTH YUKON N.P.

Anchorage, Fairbanks, Juneau, Nome, Barrow, Kotzebue, Bethel, Dillingham, Kodiak, Sitka, Ketchikan, Valdez, Cordova, Seward, Kenai, Homer, Palmer, Wasilla, Whitehorse, Dawson, Fort Yukon, Galena, McGrath, Unalaska, Dutch Harbor, Prince Rupert, Petersburg, Wrangell, Haines, Skagway, Tok, Delta Junction, Nenana, Tanana, Eagle, Circle, Coldfoot, Wiseman, Prudhoe Bay

Mt. McKinley 6194, Mt. Logan 6050, Mt. St. Elias 5489, Mt. Foraker 5304, Mt. Hayes 4216, Mt. Sanford 4317, Mt. Wrangell, Mt. Michelson 2699

ATTU I., AGATTU, KISKA, AMCHITKA, ADAK I., ATKA I., UMNAK I., UNALASKA I., UNIMAK I., NUNIVAK I., PRINCE OF WALES I., ADMIRALTY I., BARANOF I., CHICAGOF I., QUEEN CHARLOTTE IS.

Scale 1 : 19 500 000

500 km
300 miles

SOUTH AMERICA

UNITED STATES
New Orleans
Atlanta
Jacksonville
Cape Canaveral
Tampa
FLORIDA
Miami
GULF OF MEXICO
Bermuda (U.K.)
SARGASSO SEA

BAHAMAS
Nassau
La Habana (Havana)
CUBA
Turks & Caicos Is. (U.K.)
Mérida
CHICHÉN-ITZÁ
UXMAL
YUCATÁN
Santiago de Cuba
Sierra 1994 Maestra
DOMINICAN REP.
Virgin Is. (U.S./U.K.)
Anguilla (U.K.)
ATLANTIC OCEAN
MEXICO
Belmopan
NKAL
BELIZE
GUATEMALA 2590
Guatemala City
HONDURAS
Tegucigalpa
EL SALVADOR
San Salvador
NICARAGUA
Managua
HISPANIOLA
3175 Pico Duarte
JAMAICA
HAITI
Kingston
Port-au-Prince
Santo Domingo
San Juan
Puerto Rico (U.S.)
ST. KITTS & NEVIS
Montserrat
ANTIGUA
Guadeloupe (Fr.)
DOMINICA
Martinique (Fr.)
ST. LUCIA
ST. VINCENT AND THE GRENADINES
BARBADOS
GREATER ANTILLES
CARIBBEAN SEA
LESSER ANTILLES
Neth. Antilles
TRINIDAD AND TOBAGO
Port of Spain

COSTA RICA
San José
3820 Chirripó
PANAMA
Panama City
Panama Canal
Barranquilla
5800
Maracaibo
Caracas
5007 Pico Bolívar
LLANOS
Orinoco
VENEZUELA
Georgetown
Paramaribo
GUYANA
2810 Roraima
SURINAME
French Guiana (Fr.)
Cayenne
COCO (C. Rica)
Medellín
Bogotá
5750 Huila
COLOMBIA
2579 Marahuaca
GUIANA HIGHLANDS
Boa Vista
MALPELO (Col.)
Galápagos Islands (Ecuador)
ECUADOR
Quito
5897 Volcán Cotopaxi
6267 Chimborazo
Guayaquil
Puntta Parinas
Iquitos
3014 Neblina
Japurá
Equator
Amazon
Manaus
Santarém
Belém
São Luís
TERRITÓRIO DE FERNANDO DE NORONHA (Braz.)
Fortaleza
Tefé
Amazonas
SELVAS
CATINGAS
Teresina
Cabo de São Roque
Natal
PERU
6768 Huascarán
BRAZIL
Pucallpa
Rio Branco
Porto Velho
Madeira
Carolina
Planalto 1123 da Borborema
Recife
Callao
Lima
6425 Coropuna
Lago Titicaca
Xingu
PLANALTO DO MATO GROSSO
Cuiabá
Tocantins
PLANALTO
Salvador de Bahia
Arequipa
La Paz
6682 Illimani
6520 Sajama
Sucre
BOLIVIA
DO BRASIL
Brasília
PERU-CHILE TRENCH
ALTIPLANO DE BOLIVIA
Transp. Rway
São Francisco
Belo Horizonte
2890 Pico da Bandeira
Golfo de Arica
ATACAMA
PARAGUAY
São Paulo
1898
Río de Janeiro
TRINDADE (Braz.)
Antofagasta
6723 Llullaillaco
San Miguel de Tucumán
Asunción
SERRA DO MAR
1889
Tropic of Capricorn
CHILE
6863 Ojos del Salado
GRAN CHACO
Pôrto Alegre
SAN FELIX
SAN AMBROSIO (Chile)
Córdoba
2884 Champaqui
Santa Fe
URUGUAY
EMILY ROCK
6960 Aconcagua
ARGENTINA
Montevideo
ARCHIPIÉLAGO JUAN-FERNÁNDEZ (Chile)
Santiago
Volcán Maipo 5323
Buenos Aires
Mar del Plata
PAMPAS
Punta Lavapié
Colorado
Bahía Blanca
Valdivia
3776 Volcán Lanin
Golfo San Matías
PENÍNSULA VALDÉS
PACIFIC OCEAN
ATLANTIC OCEAN
PATAGONIA
Comodoro Rivadavia
Cabo Tres Puntas
4058 San Valentín
Falkland Islands (U.K.)
WEST FALKLAND
Stanley
EAST FALKLAND
Strait of Magellan
Punta Arenas
Cabo San Diego
SOUTH GEORGIA (U.K.)
2469 Yogan
TIERRA DEL FUEGO
Cape Horn

© ICA Förlaget AB
Scale 1 : 39 000 000
0 500 1000 1500 2000 km
0 500 1000 miles

NORTHERN SOUTH AMERICA

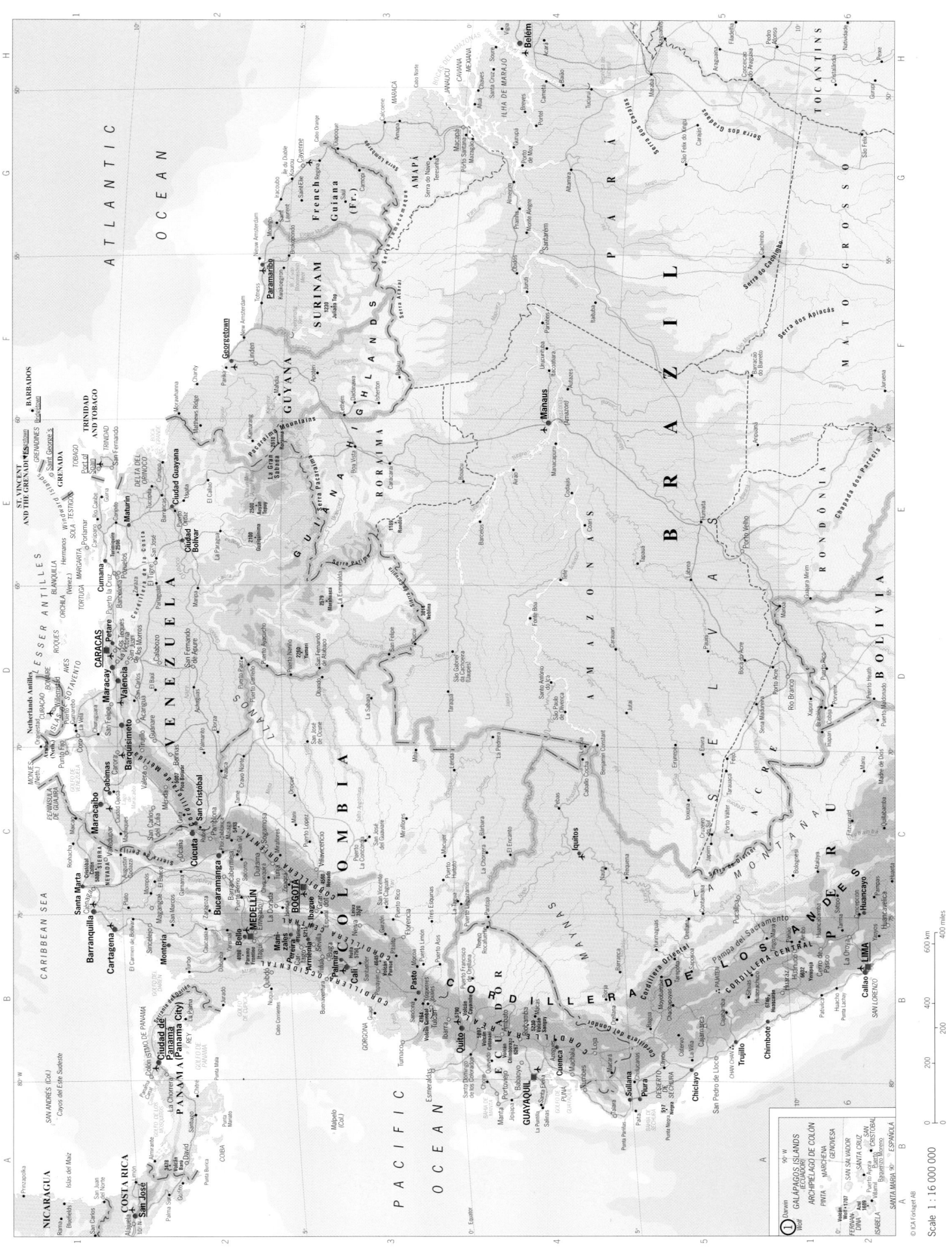

Scale 1 : 16 000 000

© IGA Forlaget AB

CENTRAL SOUTH AMERICA

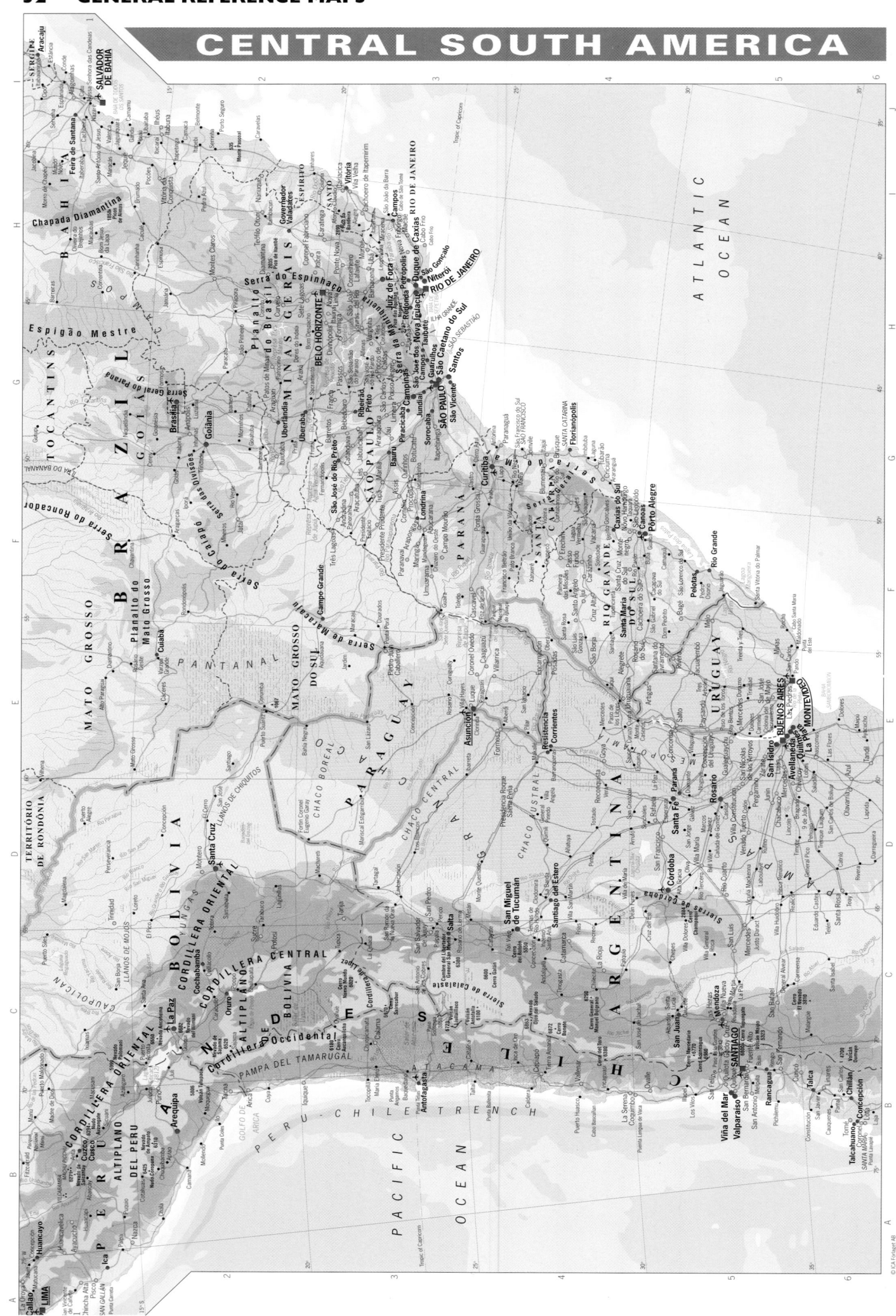

ATLANTIC OCEAN

PACIFIC OCEAN

Scale 1 : 16 000 000

0   200   400   600 km

EAST BRAZIL AND SOUTHERN SOUTH AMERICA

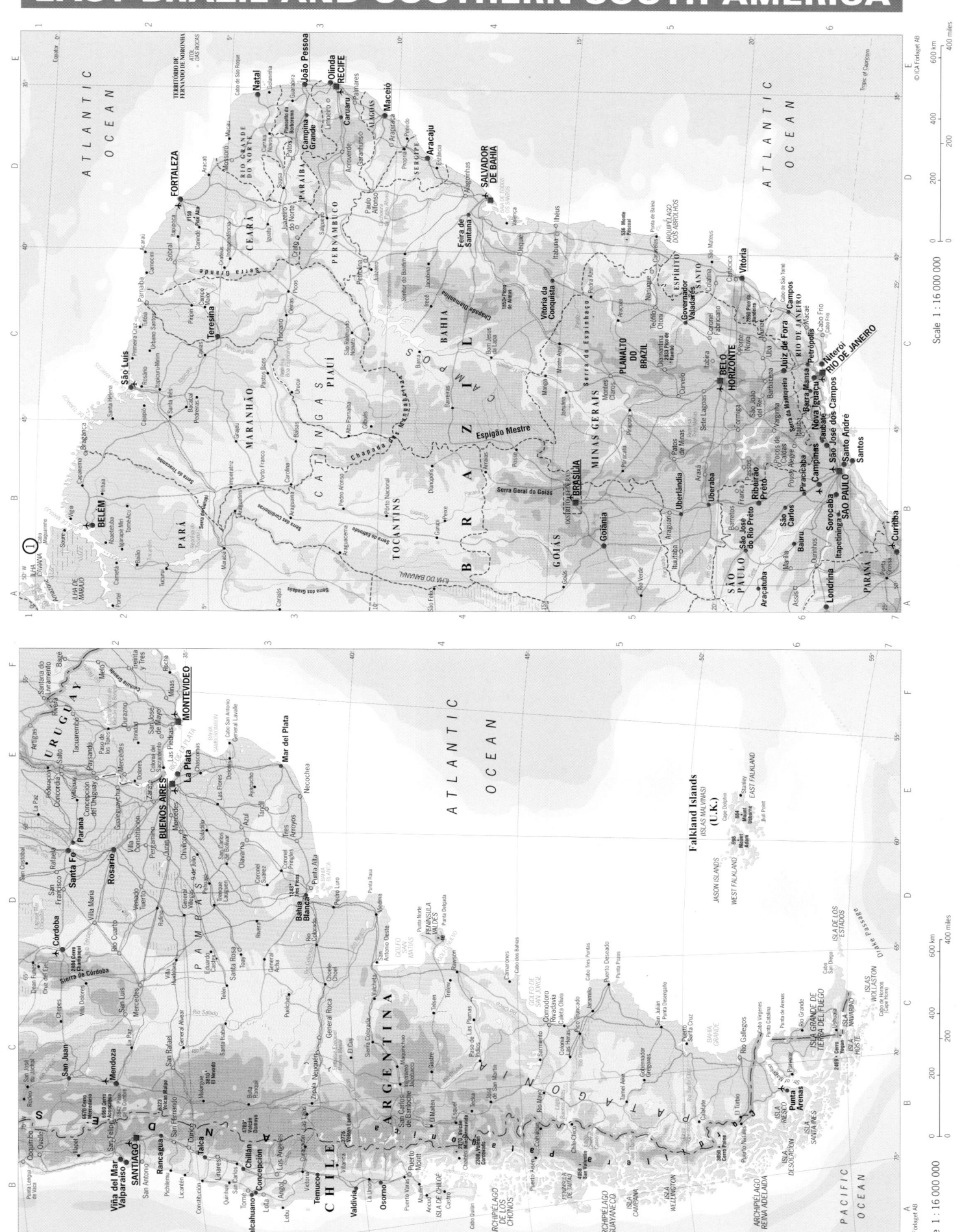

Scale 1 : 16 000 000

POLAR REGIONS

Scale 1 : 49 000 000

© ICA Förlaget AB

SPECIALIST MAP SECTION

World

Climate	56
Time, eclipses & hours of daylight	57
Natural world	58
Population & urbanization	59
Tourism	60
Income & growth	61
External debt	61
Economic activity	62-63
Oil, gas & coal deposits	64
Energy production	64
Energy consumption	65

Renewable & nuclear energy	65
Telecommunications	66-67
The internet	67
Human Development Index	68
Human rights	68
Arms & defence	69
International organisations	70-71
Environment	72

Health	73
Sport	74
Driving	75
Airports & IATA codes	76-78
Flight times	79
Cruising & bad weather areas	80-81
Unesco world heritage sites	82-87
World heritage cities	84-87

Europe and the Former Soviet Union

Climate	88
National parks	89
Historical	90-91
European Union	92-93
Railways & ferries	94-95
Blue Flag beaches	96-97
Leisure parks	98
Museums & galleries	99

Skiing	100
United Kingdom	101-107
Ireland	108
Belgium & Luxembourg	109
The Netherlands	109-110
Germany	111-113
France	114-115
Spain	116-117

Portugal	118
Switzerland	119
Austria	119
Italy	120-121
Greece	122-123
Turkey	122-123
Malta & Cyprus	123
Scandinavia	124-125
Former Soviet Union	126-127
Ancient trade routes	127
Central Europe	128

Canada and United States

Climate	146
Railways & airports	147
Skiing	148
Museums & galleries	149
United States	150-154
Canada	155-156

Mexico, Central America and Caribbean

Climate	146
Mexico	157
Languages	158-159
West Indies	158-161
Caribbean dive sites	160-161

South America

Climate	162
Languages	163
South America	163

Asia

Holy Land	135
Climate	136
India	137-138
Sri Lanka	138
Maldives	138
China	139
Japan	140
Malaysia	141
Vietnam	141
Thailand	142
Indonesia	143

Relief maps	164-172
Appendices	173-182
Index	183-230
Outline maps	X1-X16

Africa

Climate	129	Tunisia	131
Languages	130	Parks & reserves	132-133
Tanzania	130	Mauritius	132
Zimbabwe	130	Réunion	132
Egypt	131	Seychelles	133
Kenya	131	South Africa	134
Morocco	131	Red Sea dive sites	135

Australasia

Australia	144-145
New Zealand	145

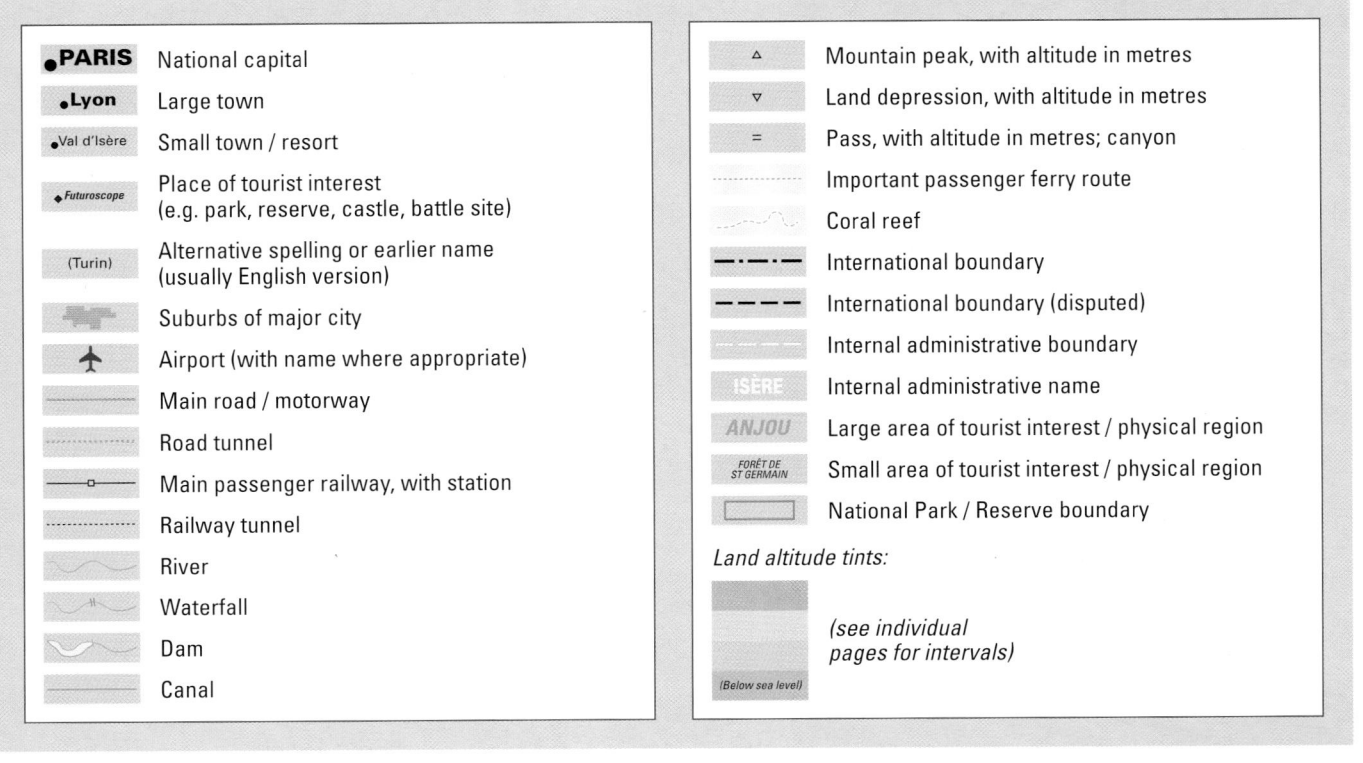

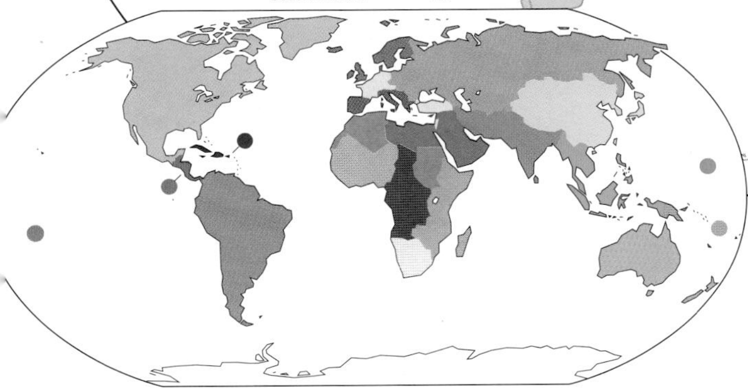

WORLD TOURISM ORGANISATION (WTO) REGIONS

01 Africa:
- Northern Africa
- Western Africa
- Middle Africa
- Eastern Africa
- Southern Africa

02 Americas:
- Northern America
- Central America
- Caribbean
- Southern America

03 East Asia & the Pacific:
- Northeastern Asia
- Southeastern Asia
- Australasia
- Melanesia } Oceania
- Micronesia
- Polynesia

04 Europe:
- Northern Europe
- Western Europe
- Southern Europe
- Central / East Europe
- East Mediterranean Europe

05 Middle East:
- Middle East

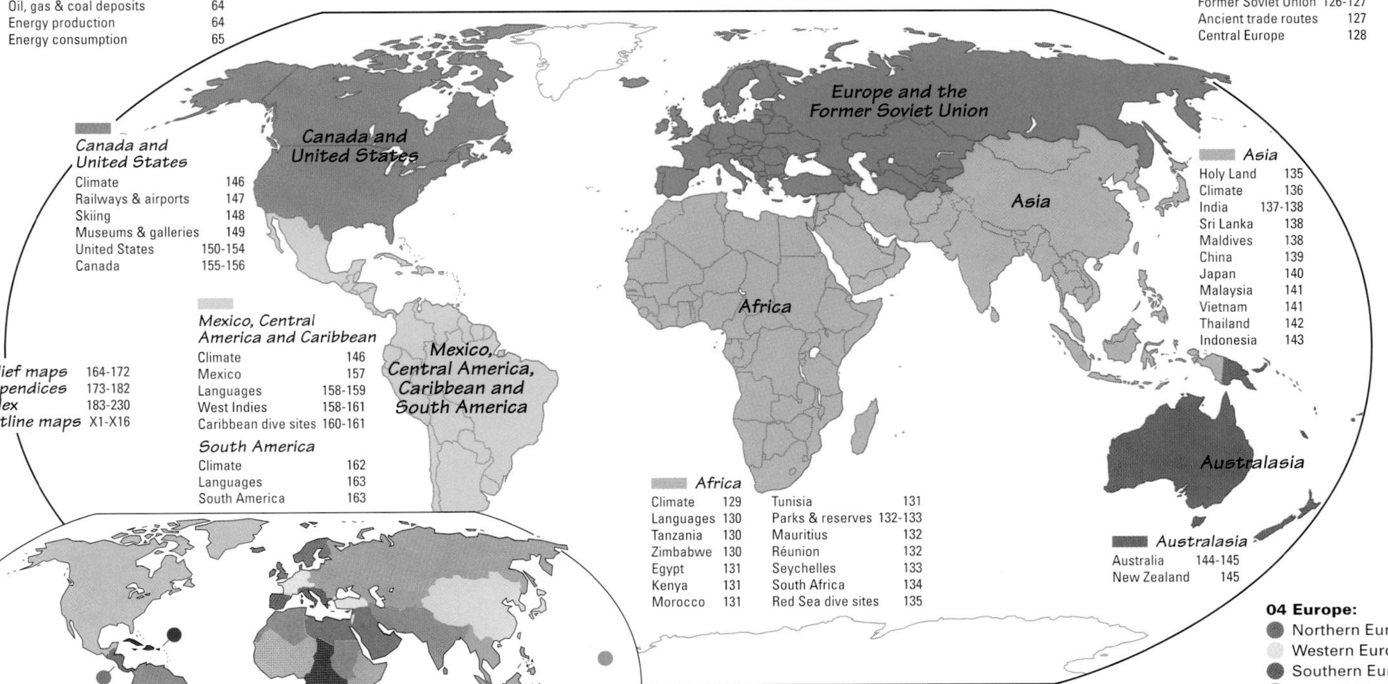

06 South Asia:
- South Asia

MAP LEGEND

●PARIS	National capital
●Lyon	Large town
●Val d'Isère	Small town / resort
◆Futuroscope	Place of tourist interest (e.g. park, reserve, castle, battle site)
(Turin)	Alternative spelling or earlier name (usually English version)
	Suburbs of major city
✈	Airport (with name where appropriate)
	Main road / motorway
	Road tunnel
	Main passenger railway, with station
	Railway tunnel
	River
	Waterfall
	Dam
	Canal

△	Mountain peak, with altitude in metres
▽	Land depression, with altitude in metres
=	Pass, with altitude in metres; canyon
	Important passenger ferry route
	Coral reef
— · — · —	International boundary
— — —	International boundary (disputed)
	Internal administrative boundary
ISÈRE	Internal administrative name
ANJOU	Large area of tourist interest / physical region
FORÊT DE ST GERMAIN	Small area of tourist interest / physical region
	National Park / Reserve boundary

Land altitude tints:

(see individual pages for intervals)

(Below sea level)

CLIMATE

Climate Legend

Polar: no warm season (warmest month below 10°C)
Ice cap (perpetual frost: all months below 0°C) and tundra (warmest month between 0°C and 10°C)

Cooler humid: rainy climates with severe winters (coldest month below 0°C, warmest month above 10°C)
Subarctic (less than four months over 10°C), continental cool summer (warmest month below 22°C) and continental warm summer (warmest month above 22°C)

Warmer humid: rainy climates with mild winters (coolest month between 0°C and 18°C, warmest month above 10°C)
Marine west coast (warmest month below 22°C), humid subtropical (warmest month above 22°C) and mediterranean (dry season in summer)

Dry Steppe/semi-arid and desert/arid

Tropical humid: rainy climates with no winter (coolest month above 18°C)
Savannah (dry season in either summer or winter) and rainforest (constantly moist or monsoon rain with only a short dry season)

WEATHER EXTREMES

Highest temperature in the shade: Al' Aziziyah, Libya
57.8°C (136.0°F) on 13th Sept 1922

Hottest place: Dalol, Ethiopia
average annual temperature of 34.4°C (94.0°F)

Lowest temperature: Vostok Base, Antarctica
-89.2°C (-128.6°F) on 21st July 1983

Coldest place: Plateau Base, Antarctica
average annual temperature of -56.6°C (-69.9°F)

Coldest inhabited place: Noril'sk, Russian Federation
average annual temperature of -10.9°C (12.4°F)

Greatest snowfall: Mt Rainier, Washington, USA
31,102 mm (1,224.5 inches) over a 12-month period, 1972-73

Most sunshine: Yuma, Arizona, USA
averages 4,127 hours of sunshine per year

Least sunshine: South Pole
no sunshine for 182 days a year

Driest place: Atacama Desert, Chile
virtually no rain throughout the year

Wettest place: Mawsynram, Meghalaya, India
11,873 mm (467.4 inches) during a 12-month period

Most rainy days: Mt Waialeale, Hawaii
up to 350 rainy days per year

Most thunder days: Tororo, Uganda
up to 251 days per year

Highest surface wind speed
• Tornado: Oklahoma City, Oklahoma, USA
512 km per hour (318 miles per hour) on 3rd May 1999
• High altitude: Mt Washington, New Hampshire, USA
372 km per hour (231 miles per hour) on 12th Apr 1934
• Low altitude: Qaanaaq (Thule), Greenland
333 km per hour (207 miles per hour) on 8th Mar 1972

Windiest place: Commonwealth Bay, Antarctica
322 km per hour (200 miles per hour) in gales

Heaviest hailstones: Gopalganj, Bangladesh
weighing up to one kilogram (2.2 lb) on 14th Apr 1986

TEMPERATURE CONVERSION

Celsius	-10	0	10	20	30	40
Fahrenheit	14	32	50	68	86	104

RAINFALL CONVERSION

Millimetres	102	203	305	406	508	610
Inches	4	8	12	16	20	24

Map annotation boxes

The Tropics of Cancer and Capricorn are lines of latitude, 23° 28' N and S, where the sun appears directly overhead at noon during the summer solstice in the respective northern and southern hemispheres.

The Arctic Circle marks the northernmost point at which the sun can be seen during the northern hemisphere's winter solstice. Positioned at 66° 30' N.

The Antarctic Circle marks the southernmost point at which the sun can be seen during the southern hemisphere's winter solstice. Positioned at 66° 30' S.

TIME

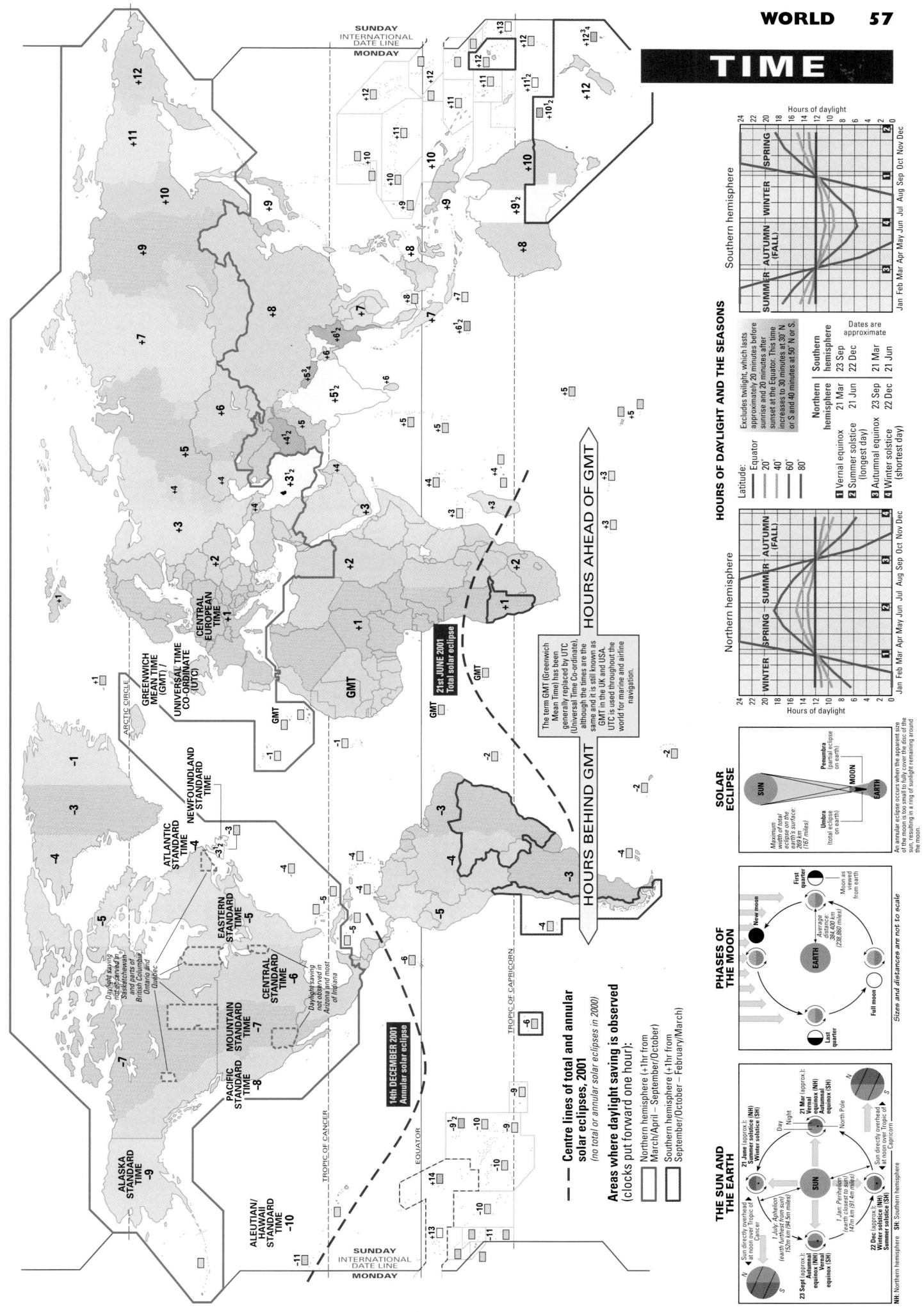

LITHOSPHERIC PLATES

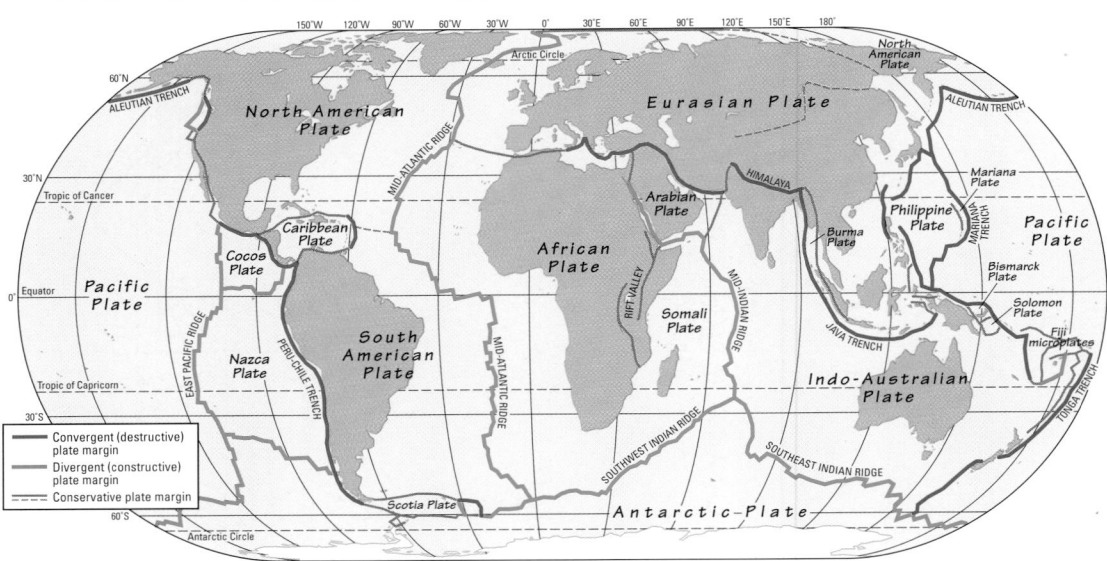

The Earth's crust is a layer averaging 33km under the continents and approximately 10km under the oceans. It is broken into large fragments which move relative to each other, a process known as continental drift. Most volcanic and earthquake activity is concentrated at the margins of these plates.

EARTHQUAKES WITH THE HIGHEST DEATH TOLLS SINCE 1900

		Magnitude	Deaths
July 1976	Tangshan, China	8.0	255,000
Dec 1920	Gansu, China	8.6	200,000
May 1927	Xining, China	8.3	200,000
Sept 1923	Tokyo-Yokohama, Japan	8.3	143,000
Oct 1948	Ashgabat, Turkmenistan	7.3	110,000
Dec 1908	Messina, Italy	7.5	110,000
Dec 1932	Gansu, China	7.6	70,000
May 1970	Chimbote, Peru	7.8	66,000
June 1990	Manjil, Iran	7.7	50,000
May 1935	Quetta, Pakistan	7.5	30,000
Dec 1939	Erzincan, Turkey	8.0	30,000
Jan 1915	Avezzano, Italy	7.5	29,980
Jan 1939	Chillán, Chile	7.5	28,000
Dec 1988	Spitak, Armenia	7.0	25,000
Feb 1976	Central Guatemala	8.3	23,000
Aug 1906	Santiago, Chile	8.6	20,000
May 1974	Yunnan/Sichuan, China	6.8	20,000

Earthquakes are measured by two different scales. The Richter Scale measures magnitude (the size of the shock wave and the energy it produces). Each number in the scale is ten times greater than the previous one. A figure of two or less is barely perceptible, while seven or more is a major earthquake. The Modified Mercalli Scale measures how much an earthquake shakes the ground at a particular place and ranges from one to twelve.

PREVAILING WINDS

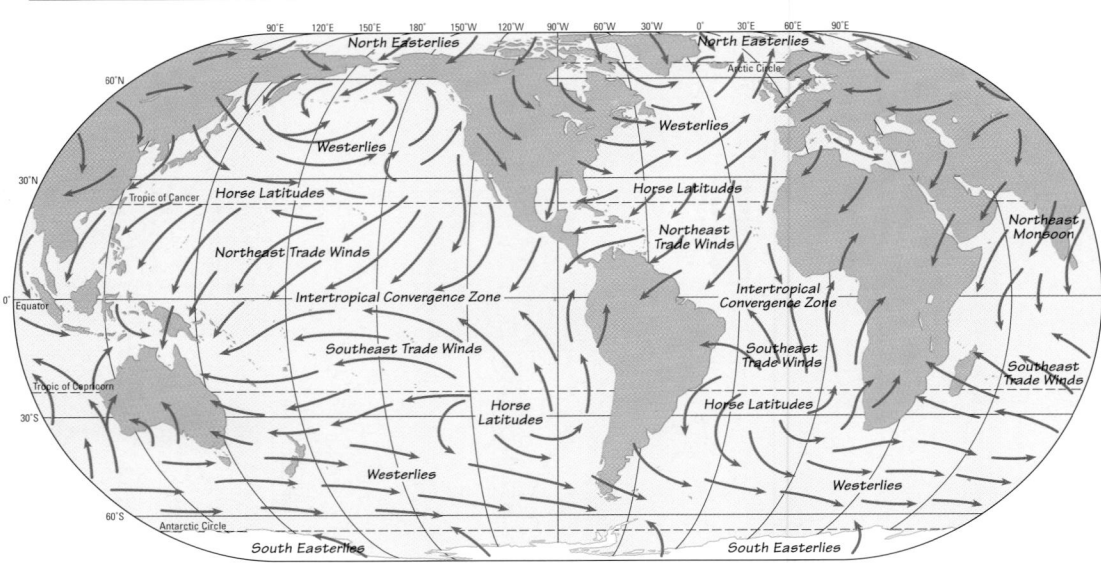

Variations in air pressure are created by the unequal heating or cooling of layers of atmosphere. Air moves from areas of high to low pressure and its direction and strength is the result of four factors: the steepness of the pressure gradient; the Coriolis Force (the deflecting component produced by the rotation of the earth); centrifugal force and the effect of friction caused by the earth's surface. In the northern hemisphere air moves clockwise around areas of high pressure and anticlockwise around the lows, with the opposite occurring in the southern hemisphere. At higher altitudes in both hemispheres there is a general movement of air eastward, with a number of powerful currents known as jet streams.

The map shows prevailing winds during northern hemisphere winter. The monsoon winds of the northern Indian Ocean and neighbouring areas reverse direction in the summer.

The Beaufort Scale measures wind speed and is used worldwide in weather reports and shipping forecasts.

BEAUFORT SCALE

Force		km/hr			km/hr
0	Calm	<1	7	Near gale	50-61
1	Light air	1-5	8	Gale	62-74
2	Light breeze	6-11	9	Strong gale	75-88
3	Gentle breeze	12-19	10	Storm	89-102
4	Moderate breeze	20-28	11	Violent storm	103-117
5	Fresh breeze	29-38	12-17	Hurricane	>117
6	Strong breeze	39-49			

Tropical storms are known by different names around the world – hurricanes in the north Atlantic and eastern Pacific, typhoons in the northwestern Pacific, cyclones in the Indian Ocean and willy-willies in northwest Australia.

OCEAN SURFACE CURRENTS

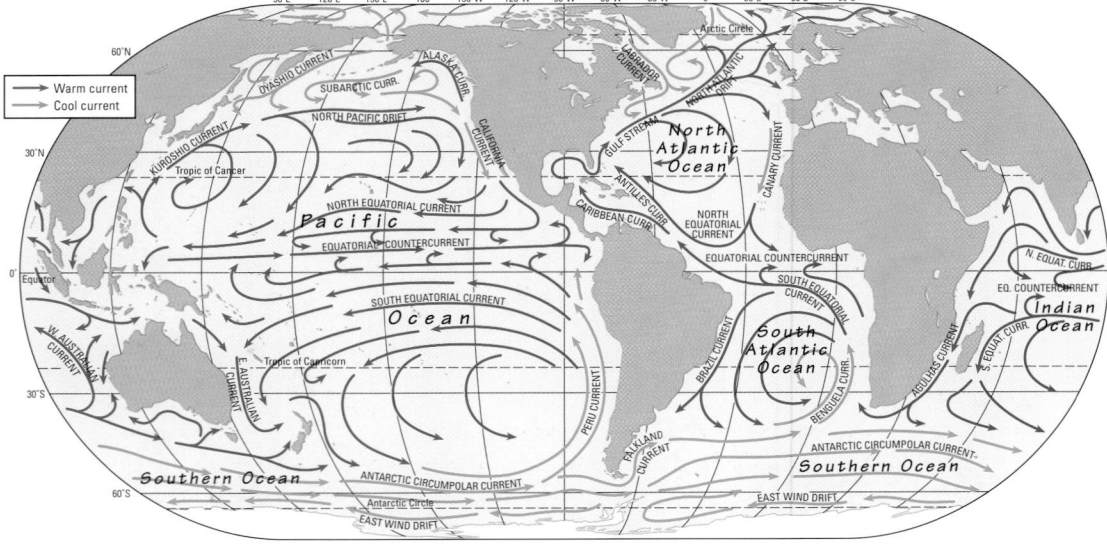

Ocean surface currents are driven primarily by the prevailing winds, and influenced by other factors including sub-surface movements, differences in density and the rotation of the earth. The persistent trade winds of both hemispheres produce westward-flowing equatorial currents, which are then deflected by continents to flow either north or south as boundary currents, the most well-known being the poleward flows of the Gulf Stream, the Kuroshio Current and the Brazil Current. These flows then return to the equator which complete a gyre in each hemisphere basin. The systems are separated at the equator by an eastward-flowing equatorial counter-current, developed at the Intertropical Convergence Zone, the area of weak winds known as the doldrums.

The map shows currents during northern hemisphere winter. Seasonal changes affect the Atlantic and Pacific systems only slightly, but in the Indian Ocean there is a complete reversal as a result of the monsoonal change of air-streams – the North Equatorial Current changes direction to flow north as the Somali Current.

Sea disturbance is measured on a scale which corresponds to the Beaufort Scale of wind speed.

SEA DISTURBANCE NUMBERS

	Beaufort scale		Average wave height (m)
0	0-1	(Calm-light air)	0
1	2	(Light breeze)	0.3
2	3	(Gentle breeze)	0.3-0.6
3	4	(Moderate breeze)	0.6-1.2
4	5	(Fresh breeze)	1.2-2.4
5	6	(Strong breeze)	2.4-4.0
6	7-9	(Gale)	4-6
7	10	(Storm)	6-9
8	11	(Violent storm)	9-14
9	12-17	(Hurricane)	14+

POPULATION

The Azores and Madeira are treated separately from mainland Portugal; the Canary Islands separately from mainland Spain; and Alaska and Hawaii separately from the conterminous 48 states of the USA

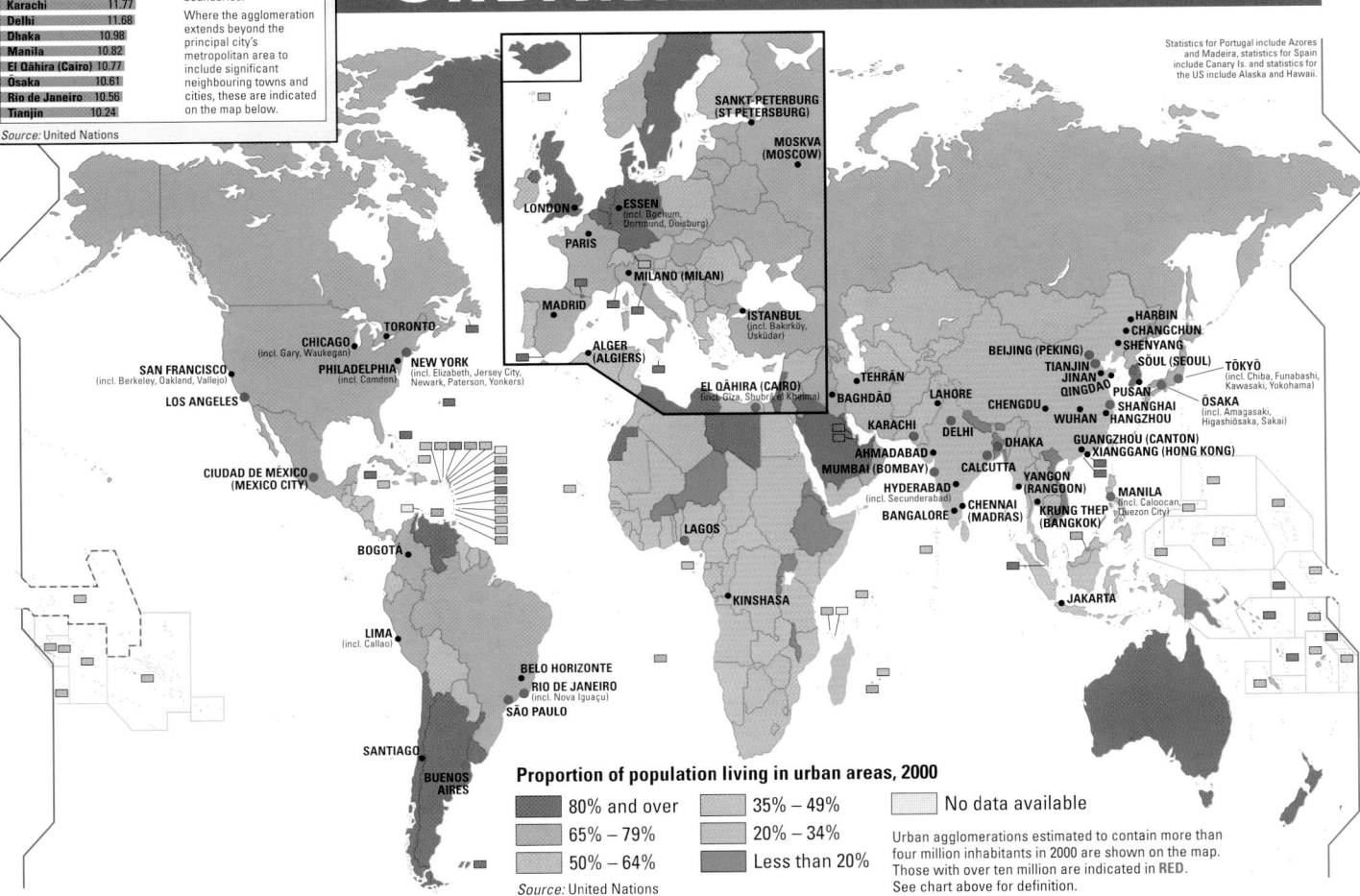

Urban agglomerations over ten million, 2000

Tōkyō	28.03 million
Ciudad de México (Mexico City)	18.13
Mumbai (Bombay)	18.04
São Paulo	17.71
New York	16.63
Shanghai	14.17
Lagos	13.49
Los Angeles	13.13
Calcutta	12.90
Buenos Aires	12.43
Sŏul (Seoul)	12.22
Beijing (Peking)	12.03
Karachi	11.77
Delhi	11.68
Dhaka	10.98
Manila	10.82
El Qâhira (Cairo)	10.77
Ōsaka	10.61
Rio de Janeiro	10.56
Tianjin	10.24

Source: United Nations

The UN defines the term 'urban agglomeration' as a contiguous area inhabited at a density regarded as urban, ignoring administrative boundaries.

Where the agglomeration extends beyond the principal city's metropolitan area to include significant neighbouring towns and cities, these are indicated on the map below.

Population density, 1997
(people per square kilometre)

- 250 and over
- 100 – 249
- 50 – 99
- 20 – 49
- 5 – 19
- Less than 5

Population growth rate, 1995 – 2000 (annual average)

- 3.0% and over
- Population decrease
- No data available

Sources: World Bank Atlas; Statesman's Yearbook; United Nations

Countries with a total population of more than two million in 1997 are named on the map. Those with an population of over 50 million are shown in **BOLD CAPITALS**.

URBANIZATION

Statistics for Portugal include Azores and Madeira, statistics for Spain include Canary Is. and statistics for the US include Alaska and Hawaii.

Proportion of population living in urban areas, 2000

- 80% and over
- 65% – 79%
- 50% – 64%
- 35% – 49%
- 20% – 34%
- Less than 20%
- No data available

Source: United Nations

Urban agglomerations estimated to contain more than four million inhabitants in 2000 are shown on the map. Those with over ten million are indicated in **RED**. See chart above for definition.

TOURIST RECEIPTS

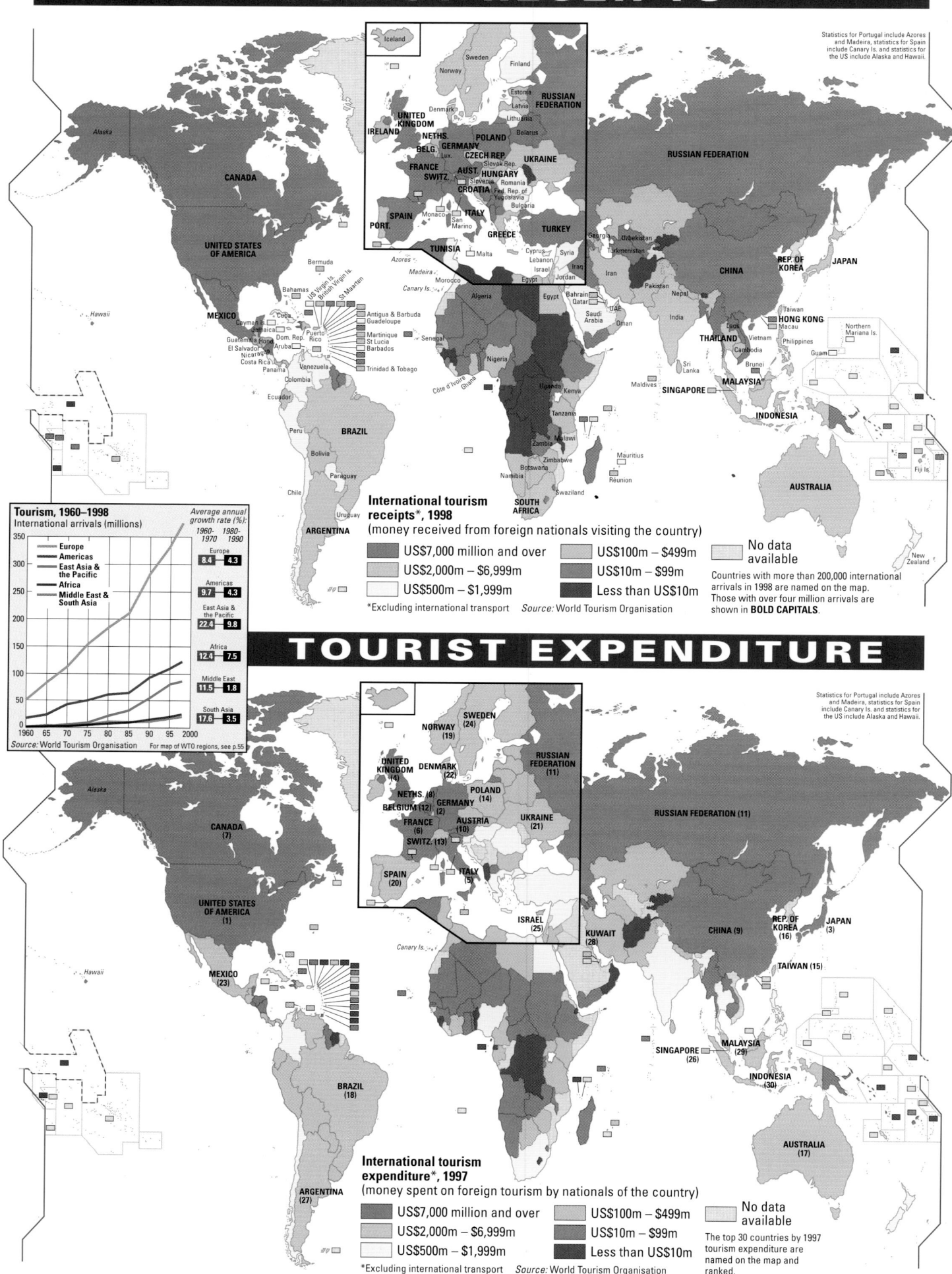

Statistics for Portugal include Azores and Madeira, statistics for Spain include Canary Is. and statistics for the US include Alaska and Hawaii.

International tourism receipts*, 1998
(money received from foreign nationals visiting the country)

- US$7,000 million and over
- US$2,000m – $6,999m
- US$500m – $1,999m
- US$100m – $499m
- US$10m – $99m
- Less than US$10m
- No data available

*Excluding international transport   Source: World Tourism Organisation

Countries with more than 200,000 international arrivals in 1998 are named on the map. Those with over four million arrivals are shown in **BOLD CAPITALS**.

Tourism, 1960–1998
International arrivals (millions)

Average annual growth rate (%):

	1960–1970	1980–1990
Europe	8.4	4.3
Americas	9.7	4.3
East Asia & the Pacific	22.4	9.8
Africa	12.4	7.5
Middle East	11.5	1.8
South Asia	17.6	3.5

Source: World Tourism Organisation   For map of WTO regions, see p.55

TOURIST EXPENDITURE

Statistics for Portugal include Azores and Madeira, statistics for Spain include Canary Is. and statistics for the US include Alaska and Hawaii.

International tourism expenditure*, 1997
(money spent on foreign tourism by nationals of the country)

- US$7,000 million and over
- US$2,000m – $6,999m
- US$500m – $1,999m
- US$100m – $499m
- US$10m – $99m
- Less than US$10m
- No data available

*Excluding international transport   Source: World Tourism Organisation

The top 30 countries by 1997 tourism expenditure are named on the map and ranked.

INCOME

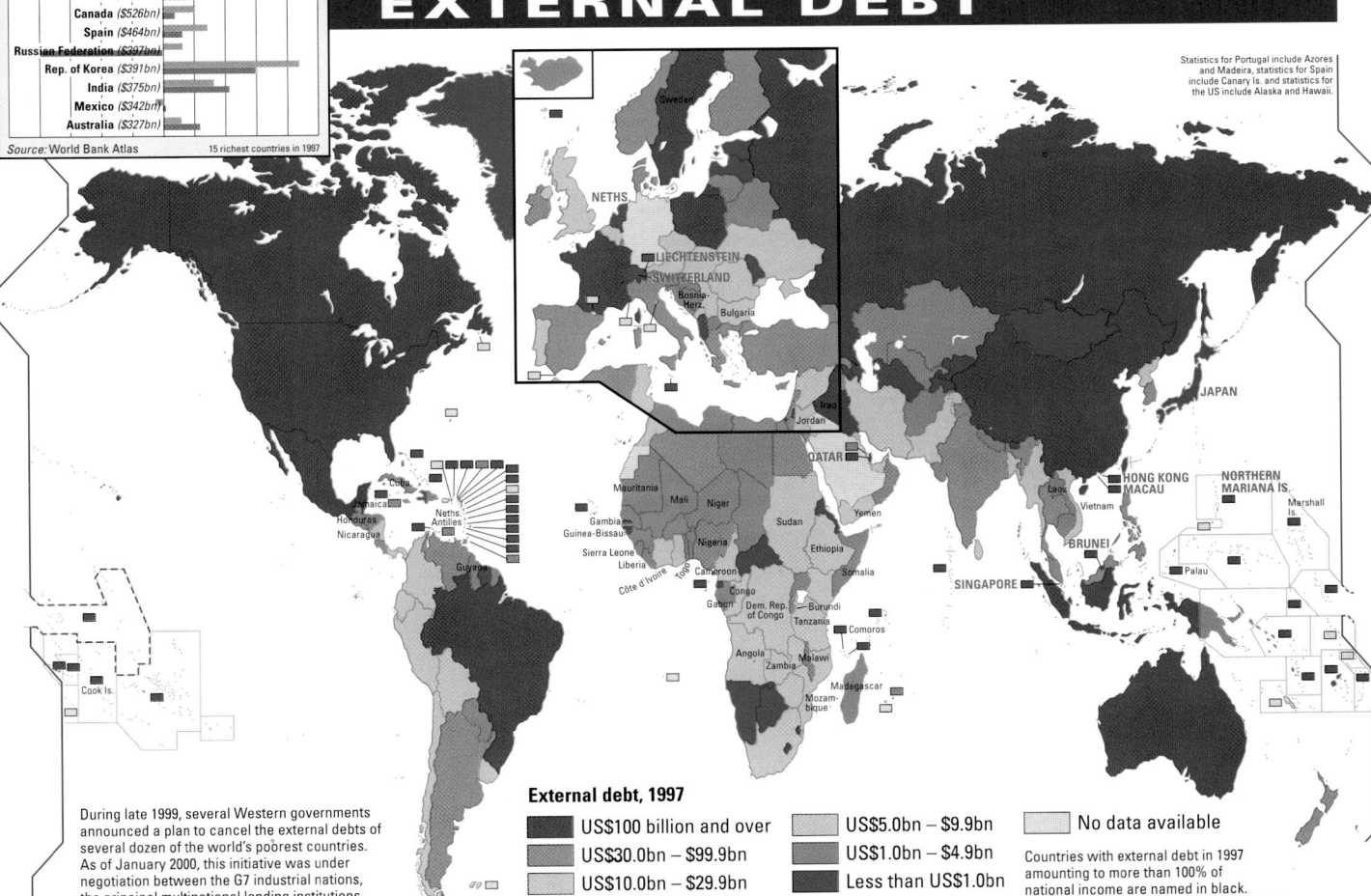

Statistics for Portugal include Azores and Madeira, statistics for Spain include Canary Is. and statistics for the US include Alaska and Hawaii.

Growth rates, 1980–1997
Average annual real growth in GNP per person (%)

	1980-90	1990-97
USA (nat. income: $7,231bn)		
Japan ($3,586bn)		
Germany ($1,804bn)		
France ($1,219bn)		
United Kingdom ($1,184bn)		
Italy ($993bn)		
China ($871bn)		
Brazil ($686bn)		
Canada ($526bn)		
Spain ($464bn)		
Russian Federation ($397bn)		
Rep. of Korea ($391bn)		
India ($375bn)		
Mexico ($342bn)		
Australia ($327bn)		

Source: World Bank Atlas   15 richest countries in 1997

Income per person, 1997

- US$17,000 and over
- US$9,000 – $16,999
- US$3,500 – $8,999
- US$1,500 – $3,499
- US$700 – $1,499
- Less than US$700
- No data available

Source: The Economist Diary 2000 edition

Countries with a total income of more than $4 billion in 1997 are named on the map. Those with an income of over $100bn are shown in **BOLD CAPITALS**.

EXTERNAL DEBT

Statistics for Portugal include Azores and Madeira, statistics for Spain include Canary Is. and statistics for the US include Alaska and Hawaii.

During late 1999, several Western governments announced a plan to cancel the external debts of several dozen of the world's poorest countries. As of January 2000, this initiative was under negotiation between the G7 industrial nations, the principal multinational lending institutions and the debtor nations.

External debt, 1997

- US$100 billion and over
- US$30.0bn – $99.9bn
- US$10.0bn – $29.9bn
- US$5.0bn – $9.9bn
- US$1.0bn – $4.9bn
- Less than US$1.0bn
- No data available

Sources: IMF International Financial Statistics; Europa World Yearbook; World Bank

Countries with external debt in 1997 amounting to more than 100% of national income are named in black. Net creditors in 1997 are named in GREEN.

ECONOMIC ACTIVITY

Income from each sector as a percentage of national income, 1997

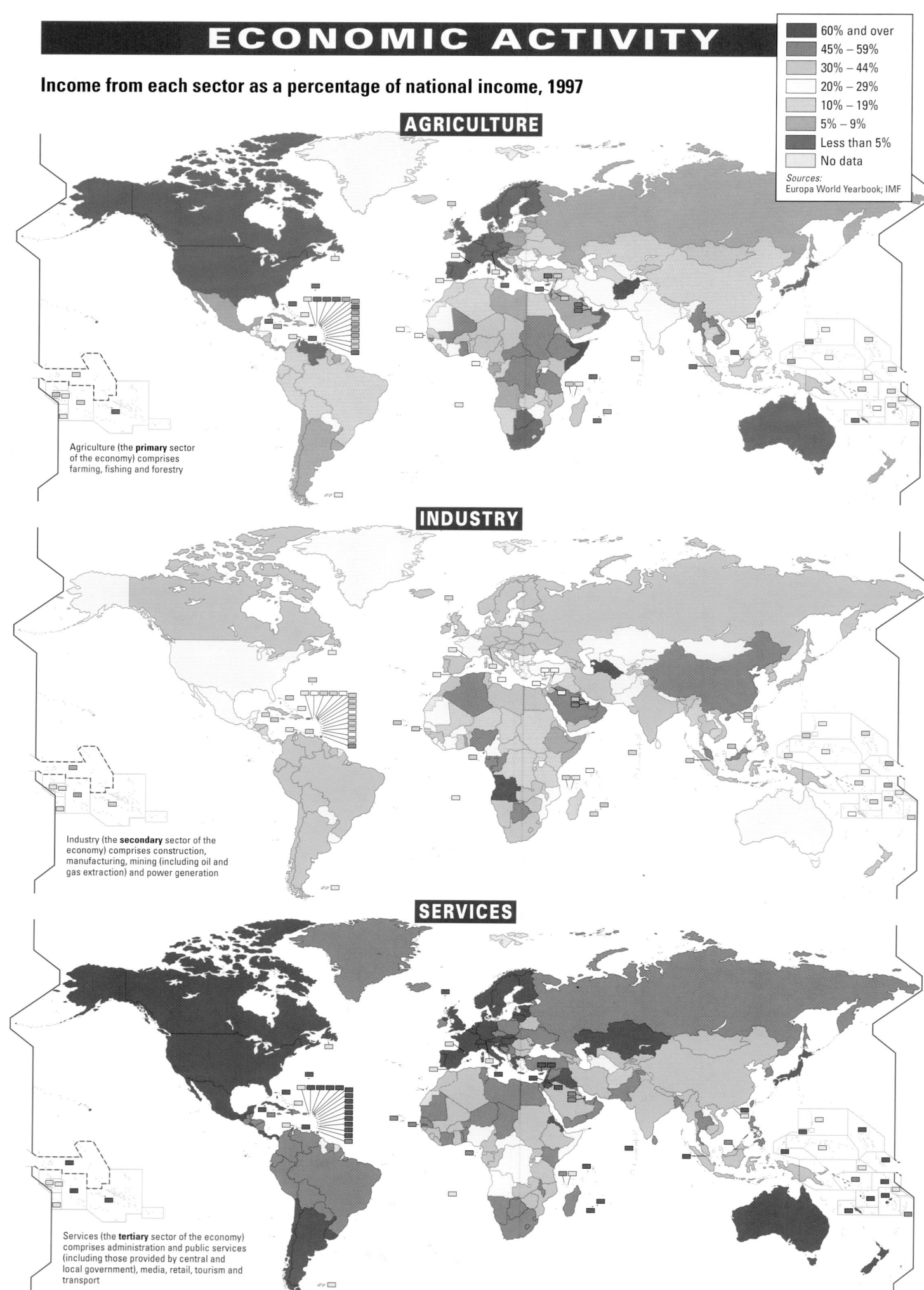

	60% and over
	45% – 59%
	30% – 44%
	20% – 29%
	10% – 19%
	5% – 9%
	Less than 5%
	No data

Sources:
Europa World Yearbook; IMF

AGRICULTURE

Agriculture (the **primary** sector of the economy) comprises farming, fishing and forestry

INDUSTRY

Industry (the **secondary** sector of the economy) comprises construction, manufacturing, mining (including oil and gas extraction) and power generation

SERVICES

Services (the **tertiary** sector of the economy) comprises administration and public services (including those provided by central and local government), media, retail, tourism and transport

ECONOMIC ACTIVITY

Employment in each sector as a percentage of national workforce, 1997

Legend:
- 60% and over
- 45% – 59%
- 30% – 44%
- 20% – 29%
- 10% – 19%
- 5% – 9%
- Less than 5%
- No data

Sources:
Europa World Yearbook; IMF

AGRICULTURE

Agriculture (the **primary** sector of the economy) comprises farming, fishing and forestry

INDUSTRY

Industry (the **secondary** sector of the economy) comprises construction, manufacturing, mining (including oil and gas extraction) and power generation

SERVICES

Services (the **tertiary** sector of the economy) comprises administration and public services (including those provided by central and local government), media, retail, tourism and transport

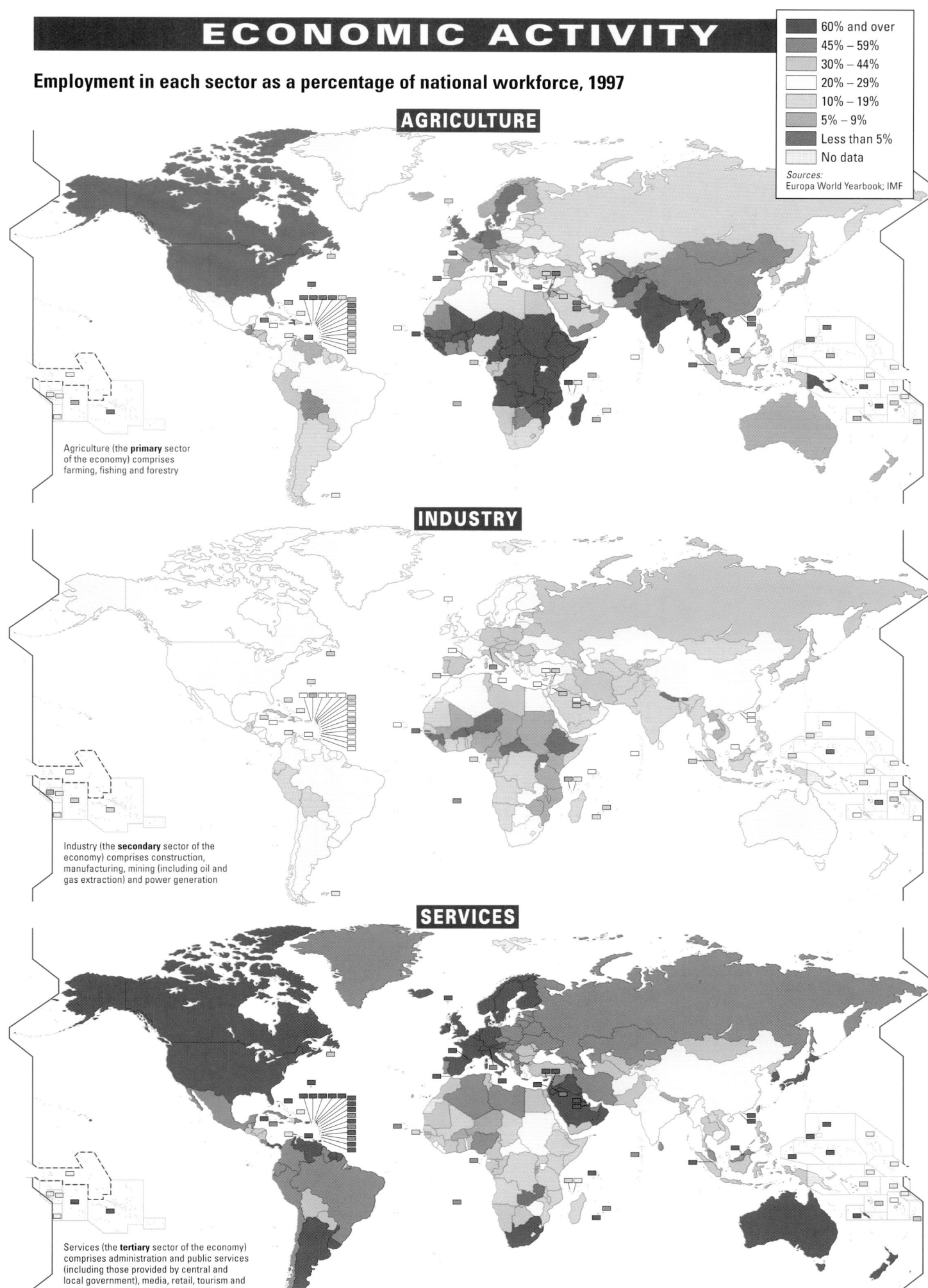

OIL, GAS AND COAL DEPOSITS

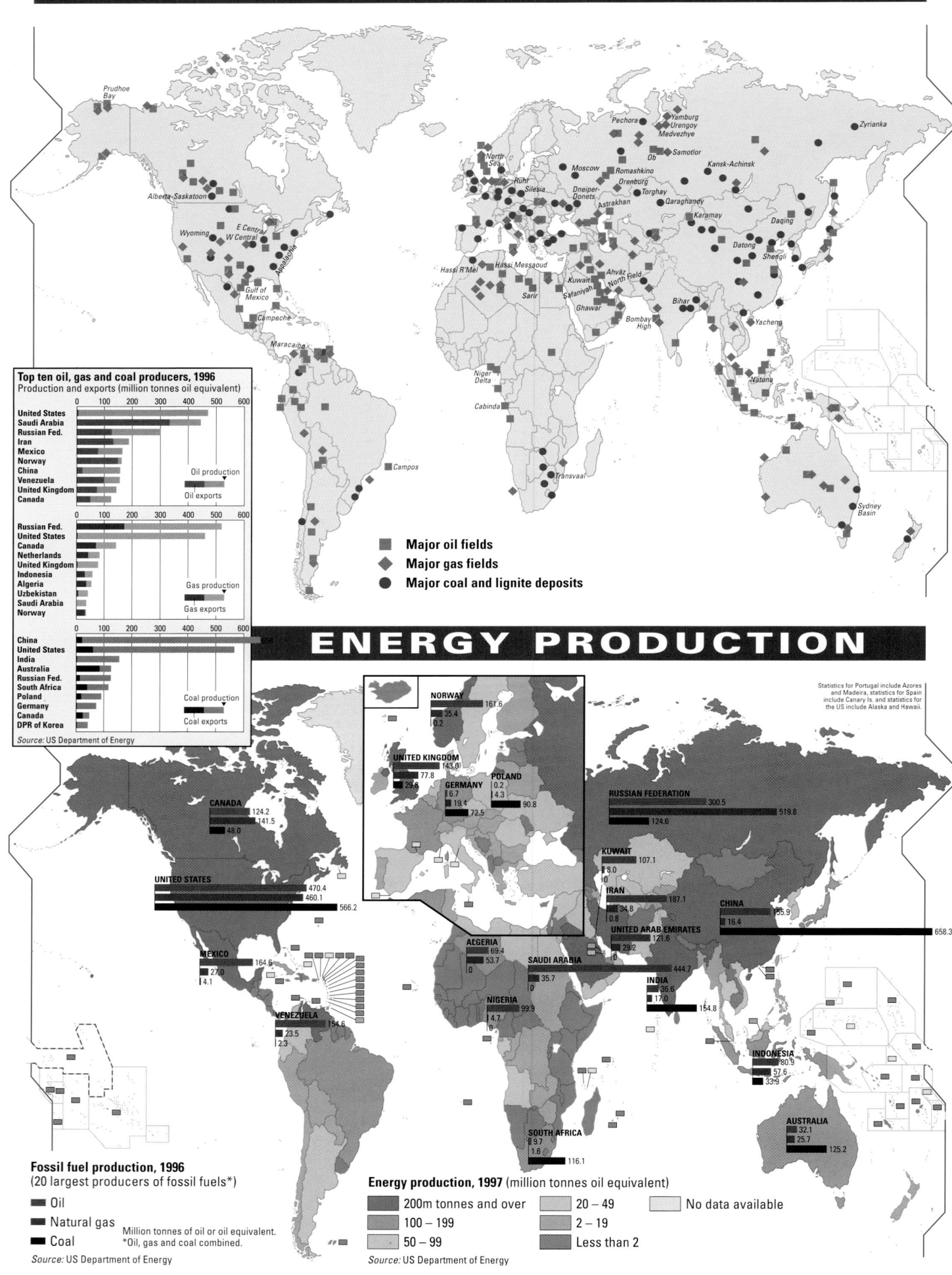

Top ten oil, gas and coal producers, 1996
Production and exports (million tonnes oil equivalent)

Oil production / Oil exports:
United States
Saudi Arabia
Russian Fed.
Iran
Mexico
Norway
China
Venezuela
United Kingdom
Canada

Gas production / Gas exports:
Russian Fed.
United States
Canada
Netherlands
United Kingdom
Indonesia
Algeria
Uzbekistan
Saudi Arabia
Norway

Coal production / Coal exports:
China
United States
India
Australia
Russian Fed.
South Africa
Poland
Germany
Canada
DPR of Korea

Source: US Department of Energy

- ■ Major oil fields
- ◆ Major gas fields
- ● Major coal and lignite deposits

ENERGY PRODUCTION

Statistics for Portugal include Azores and Madeira, statistics for Spain include Canary Is. and statistics for the US include Alaska and Hawaii.

NORWAY 161.6 / 35.4 / 0.2

UNITED KINGDOM 143.0 / 77.8 / 29.6

GERMANY 6.7 / 19.4 / 72.5

POLAND 0.2 / 4.3 / 90.8

RUSSIAN FEDERATION 300.5 / 519.8 / 124.6

CANADA 124.2 / 141.5 / 48.0

UNITED STATES 470.4 / 460.1 / 566.2

KUWAIT 107.1 / 8.0 / 0

IRAN 187.1 / 34.8 / 0.8

CHINA 135.9 / 16.4 / 658.3

MEXICO 164.6 / 27.0 / 4.1

UNITED ARAB EMIRATES 121.6 / 29.2 / 0

ALGERIA 69.4 / 53.7 / 0

SAUDI ARABIA 444.7 / 35.7 / 0

INDIA 36.6 / 17.0 / 154.8

VENEZUELA 154.6 / 23.5 / 2.3

NIGERIA 99.9 / 4.7 / 0

INDONESIA 80.9 / 57.6 / 33.9

SOUTH AFRICA 9.7 / 1.6 / 116.1

AUSTRALIA 32.1 / 25.7 / 125.2

Fossil fuel production, 1996
(20 largest producers of fossil fuels*)

- ■ Oil
- ■ Natural gas
- ■ Coal

Million tonnes of oil or oil equivalent.
*Oil, gas and coal combined.

Source: US Department of Energy

Energy production, 1997 (million tonnes oil equivalent)

- 200m tonnes and over
- 100 – 199
- 50 – 99
- 20 – 49
- 2 – 19
- Less than 2
- No data available

Source: US Department of Energy

ENERGY CONSUMPTION

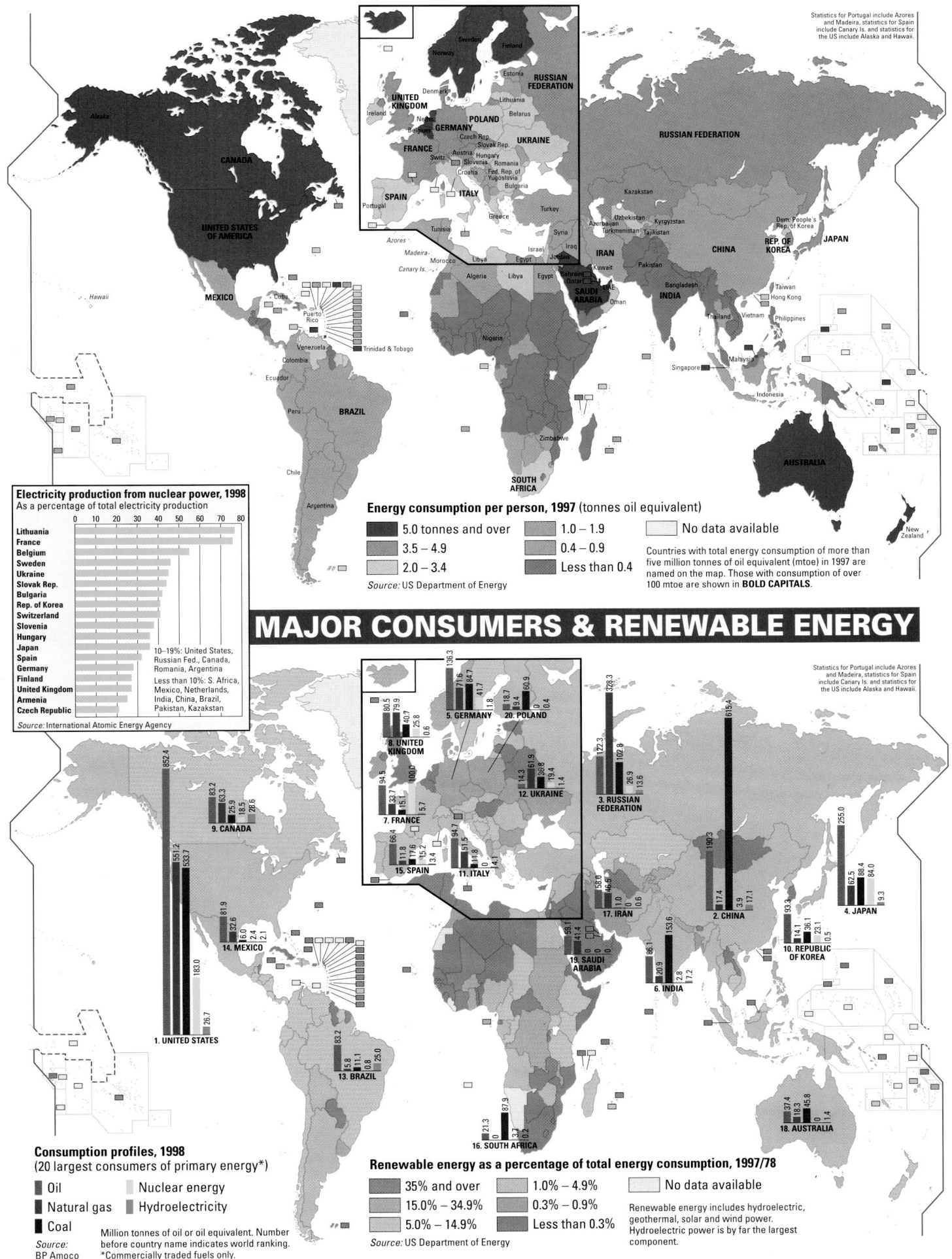

Statistics for Portugal include Azores and Madeira, statistics for Spain include Canary Is. and statistics for the US include Alaska and Hawaii.

Electricity production from nuclear power, 1998
As a percentage of total electricity production

Lithuania
France
Belgium
Sweden
Ukraine
Slovak Rep.
Bulgaria
Rep. of Korea
Switzerland
Slovenia
Hungary
Japan
Spain
Germany
Finland
United Kingdom
Armenia
Czech Republic

10–19%: United States, Russian Fed., Canada, Romania, Argentina
Less than 10%: S. Africa, Mexico, Netherlands, India, China, Brazil, Pakistan, Kazakstan

Source: International Atomic Energy Agency

Energy consumption per person, 1997 (tonnes oil equivalent)

5.0 tonnes and over	1.0 – 1.9	No data available
3.5 – 4.9	0.4 – 0.9	
2.0 – 3.4	Less than 0.4	

Source: US Department of Energy

Countries with total energy consumption of more than five million tonnes of oil equivalent (mtoe) in 1997 are named on the map. Those with consumption of over 100 mtoe are shown in **BOLD CAPITALS**.

MAJOR CONSUMERS & RENEWABLE ENERGY

Statistics for Portugal include Azores and Madeira, statistics for Spain include Canary Is. and statistics for the US include Alaska and Hawaii.

Consumption profiles, 1998
(20 largest consumers of primary energy*)

- Oil
- Natural gas
- Coal
- Nuclear energy
- Hydroelectricity

Million tonnes of oil or oil equivalent. Number before country name indicates world ranking.
*Commercially traded fuels only.

Source: BP Amoco

Renewable energy as a percentage of total energy consumption, 1997/78

35% and over	1.0% – 4.9%	No data available
15.0% – 34.9%	0.3% – 0.9%	
5.0% – 14.9%	Less than 0.3%	

Source: US Department of Energy

Renewable energy includes hydroelectric, geothermal, solar and wind power. Hydroelectric power is by far the largest component.

TELECOMMUNICATIONS: a. LAND

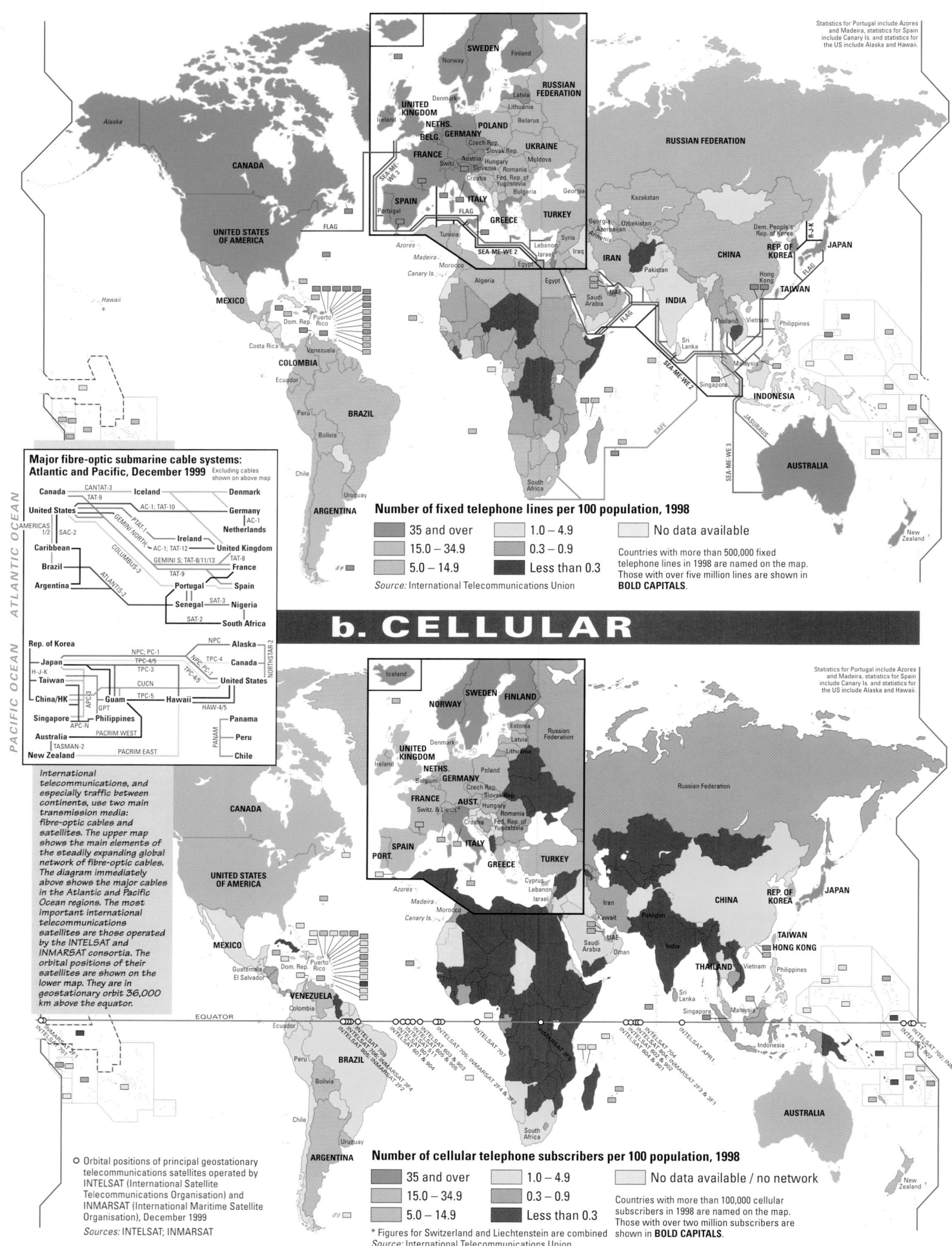

Statistics for Portugal include Azores and Madeira, statistics for Spain include Canary Is. and statistics for the US include Alaska and Hawaii.

Major fibre-optic submarine cable systems: Atlantic and Pacific, December 1999

Excluding cables shown on above map

ATLANTIC OCEAN

Canada — CANTAT-3 — Iceland — Denmark
United States — AC-1; TAT-10 — Germany
— AC-1 — Netherlands
AMERICAS 1/2
SAC-2 — PTAT-1 — GEMINI NORTH — Ireland
Caribbean — AC-1; TAT-12 — United Kingdom
COLUMBUS-3 — GEMINI S; TAT-8/11/13
Brazil — TAT-8 — France
ATLANTIS-2 — TAT-9 — Spain
Argentina — Portugal
Senegal — SAT-3 — Nigeria
SAT-2 — South Africa

PACIFIC OCEAN

Rep. of Korea — NPC; PC-1 — NPC — Alaska
Japan — TPC-4/5 — NPC; PC-1 — Canada
H-J-K — TPC-3 — NORTHSTAR-2
Taiwan — TPC-4/5 — United States
China/HK — CUCN
APC3 — TPC-5 — Hawaii
Singapore — GPT — Guam — Philippines — HAW-4/5
APC-N — PACRIM WEST
Australia — TASMAN-2 — PANAM — Panama
New Zealand — PACRIM EAST — Peru
— Chile

Number of fixed telephone lines per 100 population, 1998

35 and over	1.0 – 4.9	No data available
15.0 – 34.9	0.3 – 0.9	
5.0 – 14.9	Less than 0.3	

Source: International Telecommunications Union

Countries with more than 500,000 fixed telephone lines in 1998 are named on the map. Those with over five million lines are shown in **BOLD CAPITALS**.

b. CELLULAR

Statistics for Portugal include Azores and Madeira, statistics for Spain include Canary Is. and statistics for the US include Alaska and Hawaii.

International telecommunications, and especially traffic between continents, use two main transmission media: fibre-optic cables and satellites. The upper map shows the main elements of the steadily expanding global network of fibre-optic cables. The diagram immediately above shows the major cables in the Atlantic and Pacific Ocean regions. The most important international telecommunications satellites are those operated by the INTELSAT and INMARSAT consortia. The orbital positions of their satellites are shown on the lower map. They are in geostationary orbit 36,000 km above the equator.

○ Orbital positions of principal geostationary telecommunications satellites operated by INTELSAT (International Satellite Telecommunications Organisation) and INMARSAT (International Maritime Satellite Organisation), December 1999

Sources: INTELSAT; INMARSAT

Number of cellular telephone subscribers per 100 population, 1998

35 and over	1.0 – 4.9	No data available / no network
15.0 – 34.9	0.3 – 0.9	
5.0 – 14.9	Less than 0.3	

* Figures for Switzerland and Liechtenstein are combined
Source: International Telecommunications Union

Countries with more than 100,000 cellular subscribers in 1998 are named on the map. Those with over two million subscribers are shown in **BOLD CAPITALS**.

TELECOMMUNICATIONS TRAFFIC

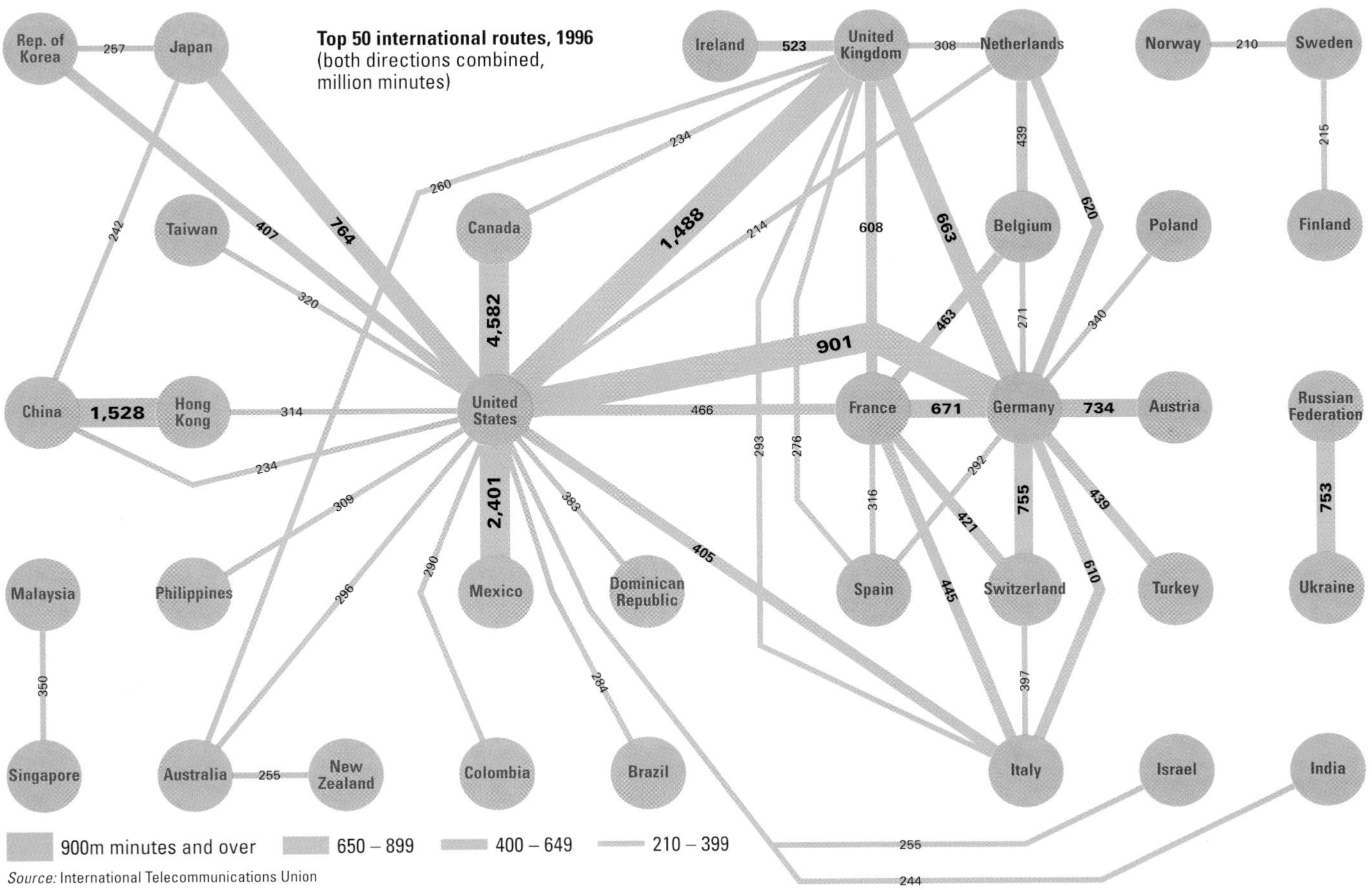

Top 50 international routes, 1996
(both directions combined, million minutes)

Rep. of Korea — 257 — Japan

Ireland — 523 — United Kingdom — 308 — Netherlands

Norway — 210 — Sweden

Japan: 242, 407, 764

Taiwan 320

Canada 234, 260

United Kingdom: 1,488, 214, 608, 663

Belgium 439, 620

Poland

Sweden 215

Finland

China — 1,528 — Hong Kong — 314

United States 4,582

901, 463

France 671 — Germany 734 — Austria

Russian Federation

234

466

297, 276, 293

Spain 316

755, 421, 439, 610

Turkey

Ukraine 753

Malaysia

Philippines

Mexico 2,401

383, 309, 296, 290

405

Dominican Republic

284

445, 397

Switzerland

Israel

India

Malaysia — 350 — Singapore

Australia — 255 — New Zealand

Colombia

Brazil

Italy

255

244

900m minutes and over | **650 – 899** | **400 – 649** | **210 – 399**

Source: International Telecommunications Union

INTERNET SUBSCRIBERS

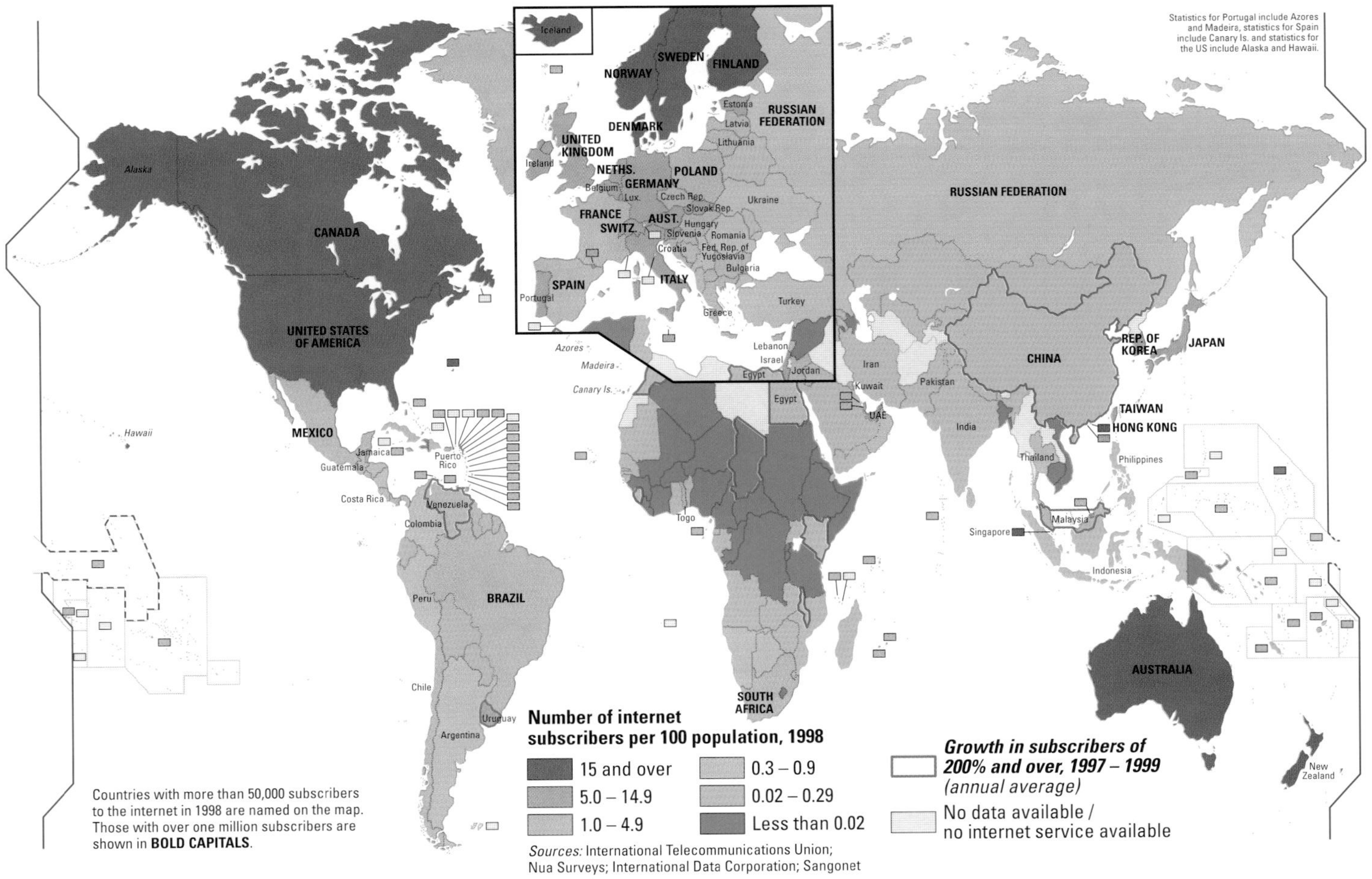

Statistics for Portugal include Azores and Madeira, statistics for Spain include Canary Is. and statistics for the US include Alaska and Hawaii.

Number of internet subscribers per 100 population, 1998

- 15 and over
- 5.0 – 14.9
- 1.0 – 4.9
- 0.3 – 0.9
- 0.02 – 0.29
- Less than 0.02

Growth in subscribers of 200% and over, 1997 – 1999 (annual average)

No data available / no internet service available

Countries with more than 50,000 subscribers to the internet in 1998 are named on the map. Those with over one million subscribers are shown in **BOLD CAPITALS**.

Sources: International Telecommunications Union; Nua Surveys; International Data Corporation; Sangonet

HUMAN DEVELOPMENT INDEX

Statistics for Portugal include Azores and Madeira, statistics for Spain include Canary Is. and statistics for the US include Alaska and Hawaii.

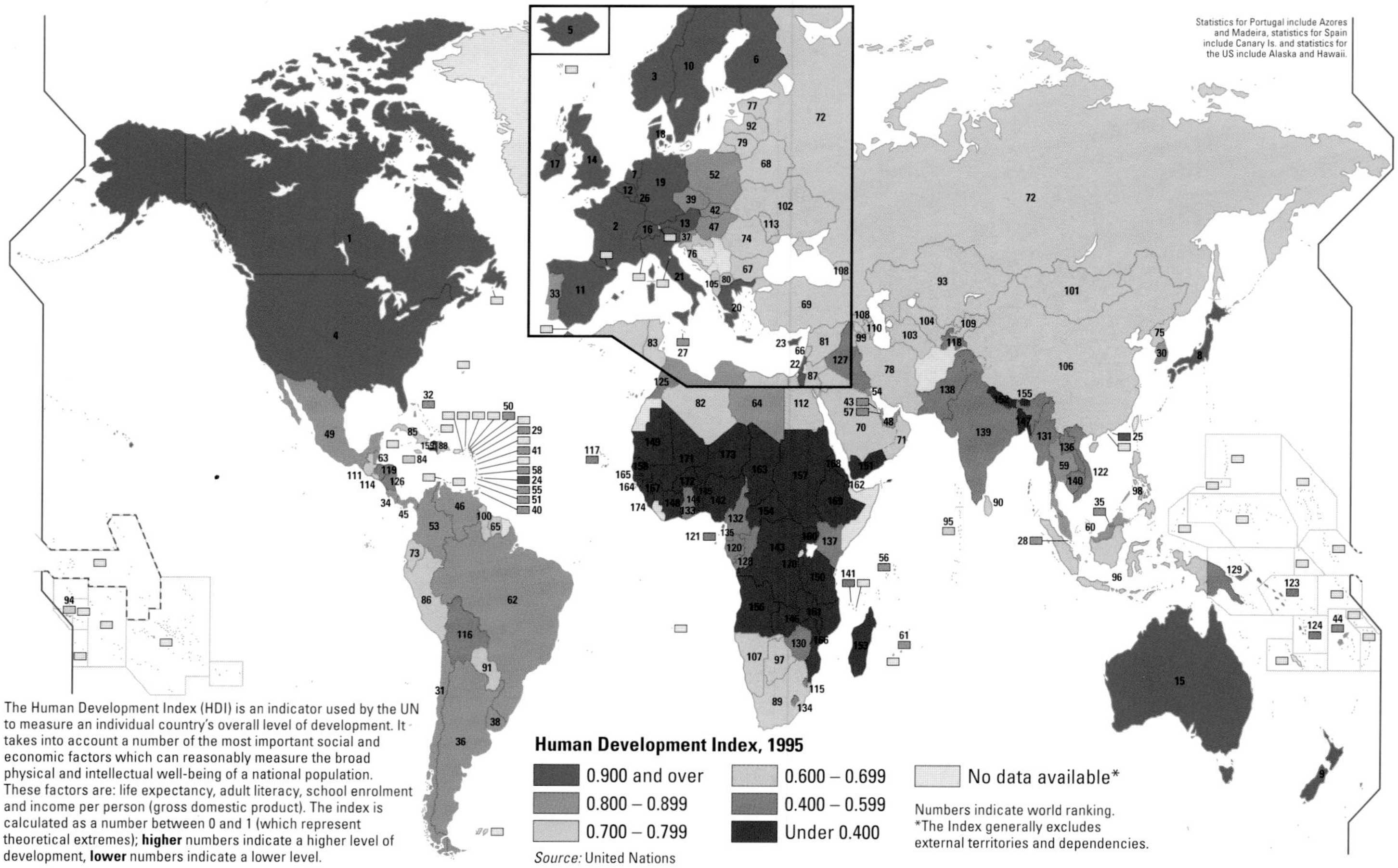

The Human Development Index (HDI) is an indicator used by the UN to measure an individual country's overall level of development. It takes into account a number of the most important social and economic factors which can reasonably measure the broad physical and intellectual well-being of a national population. These factors are: life expectancy, adult literacy, school enrolment and income per person (gross domestic product). The index is calculated as a number between 0 and 1 (which represent theoretical extremes); **higher** numbers indicate a higher level of development, **lower** numbers indicate a lower level.

Human Development Index, 1995

0.900 and over	0.600 – 0.699
0.800 – 0.899	0.400 – 0.599
0.700 – 0.799	Under 0.400

No data available*

Source: United Nations

Numbers indicate world ranking.
*The Index generally excludes external territories and dependencies.

HUMAN RIGHTS INDEX

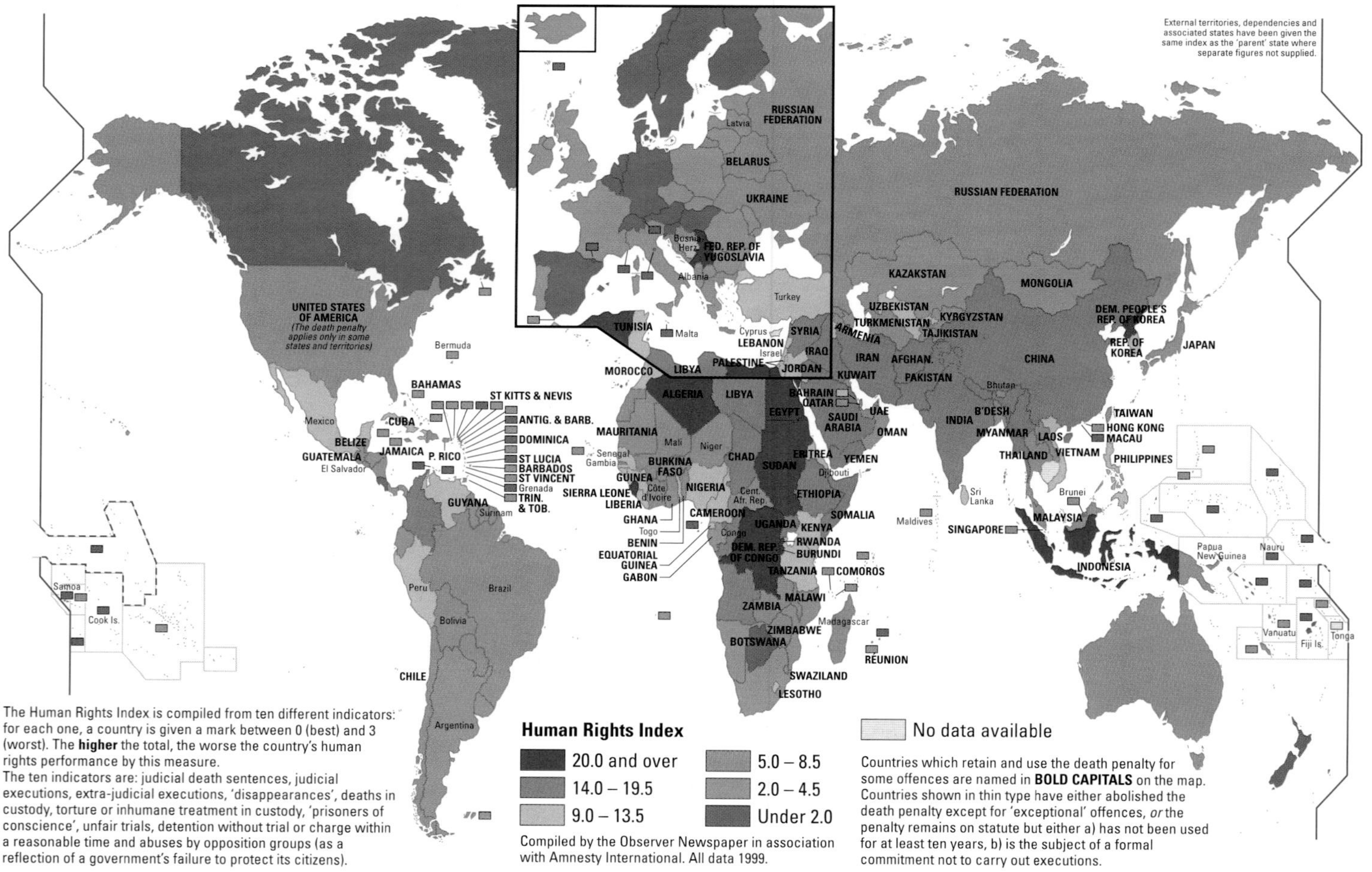

External territories, dependencies and associated states have been given the same index as the 'parent' state where separate figures not supplied.

RUSSIAN FEDERATION
Latvia
BELARUS
UKRAINE
Bosnia Herz.
FED. REP. OF YUGOSLAVIA
Albania
Turkey
KAZAKSTAN
MONGOLIA
UZBEKISTAN
KYRGYZSTAN
TURKMENISTAN
TAJIKISTAN
DEM. PEOPLE'S REP. OF KOREA
Cyprus
SYRIA
ARMENIA
TUNISIA
Malta
LEBANON
IRAQ
IRAN
AFGHAN.
CHINA
REP. OF KOREA
JAPAN
MOROCCO
PALESTINE
JORDAN
KUWAIT
PAKISTAN
Bhutan
TAIWAN
LIBYA
LIBYA
BAHRAIN
QATAR
EGYPT
UAE
SAUDI ARABIA
OMAN
B'DESH
INDIA
MYANMAR
LAOS
HONG KONG
MACAU
ALGERIA
YEMEN
THAILAND
VIETNAM
MAURITANIA
Mali
Niger
CHAD
SUDAN
ERITREA
Sri Lanka
PHILIPPINES
Brunei
UNITED STATES OF AMERICA (The death penalty applies only in some states and territories)
Bermuda
BAHAMAS
ST KITTS & NEVIS
Mexico
ANTIG. & BARB.
CUBA
DOMINICA
BELIZE
JAMAICA
P. RICO
GUATEMALA
El Salvador
ST LUCIA
BARBADOS
ST VINCENT
Grenada
TRIN. & TOB.
GUYANA
Surinam
GUINEA
SIERRA LEONE
LIBERIA
Senegal
Gambia
BURKINA FASO
NIGERIA
Côte d'Ivoire
Cent. Afr. Rep.
ETHIOPIA
SOMALIA
Maldives
MALAYSIA
SINGAPORE
GHANA
Togo
CAMEROON
Congo
UGANDA
KENYA
RWANDA
BURUNDI
INDONESIA
Papua New Guinea
Nauru
BENIN
EQUATORIAL GUINEA
GABON
DEM. REP. OF CONGO
TANZANIA
COMOROS
Peru
Brazil
ZAMBIA
MALAWI
Madagascar
REUNION
Vanuatu
Fiji Is.
Tonga
Bolivia
ZIMBABWE
BOTSWANA
Samoa
Cook Is.
SWAZILAND
CHILE
LESOTHO
Argentina

The Human Rights Index is compiled from ten different indicators: for each one, a country is given a mark between 0 (best) and 3 (worst). The **higher** the total, the worse the country's human rights performance by this measure.

The ten indicators are: judicial death sentences, judicial executions, extra-judicial executions, 'disappearances', deaths in custody, torture or inhumane treatment in custody, 'prisoners of conscience', unfair trials, detention without trial or charge within a reasonable time and abuses by opposition groups (as a reflection of a government's failure to protect its citizens).

Human Rights Index

20.0 and over	5.0 – 8.5
14.0 – 19.5	2.0 – 4.5
9.0 – 13.5	Under 2.0

No data available

Compiled by the Observer Newspaper in association with Amnesty International. All data 1999.

Countries which retain and use the death penalty for some offences are named in **BOLD CAPITALS** on the map. Countries shown in thin type have either abolished the death penalty except for 'exceptional' offences, *or* the penalty remains on statute but either a) has not been used for at least ten years, b) is the subject of a formal commitment not to carry out executions.

MILITARY SPENDING

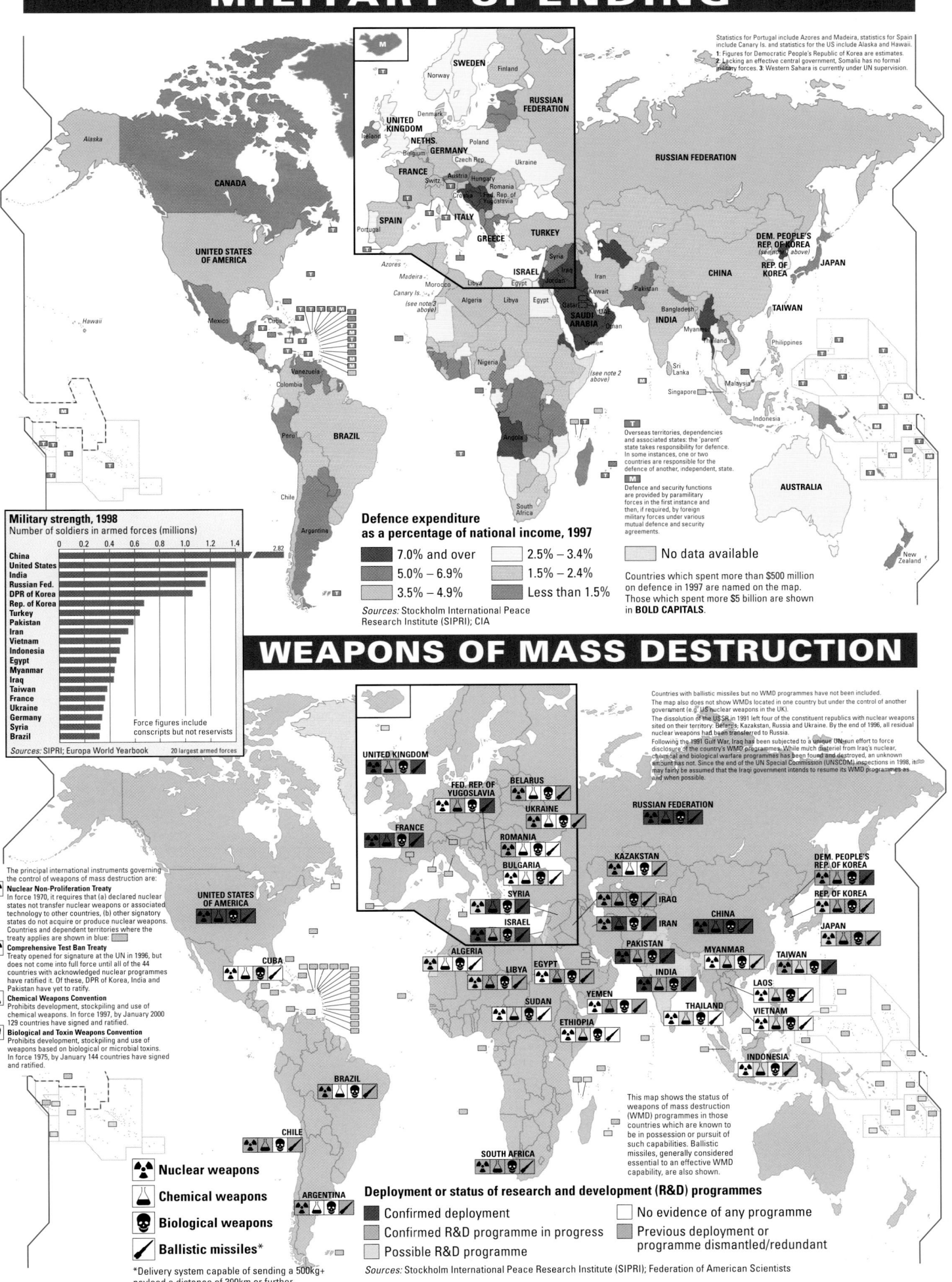

Statistics for Portugal include Azores and Madeira, statistics for Spain include Canary Is. and statistics for the US include Alaska and Hawaii.
1: Figures for Democratic People's Republic of Korea are estimates.
2: Lacking an effective central government, Somalia has no formal military forces. **3**: Western Sahara is currently under UN supervision.

T Overseas territories, dependencies and associated states: the 'parent' state takes responsibility for defence. In some instances, one or two countries are responsible for the defence of another, independent, state.

M Defence and security functions are provided by paramilitary forces in the first instance and then, if required, by foreign military forces under various mutual defence and security agreements.

Military strength, 1998
Number of soldiers in armed forces (millions)

	0	0.2	0.4	0.6	0.8	1.0	1.2	1.4
China									2.82
United States								
India								
Russian Fed.								
DPR of Korea							
Rep. of Korea						
Turkey					
Pakistan					
Iran				
Vietnam				
Indonesia				
Egypt			
Myanmar			
Iraq			
Taiwan			
France			
Ukraine			
Germany			
Syria		
Brazil		

Force figures include conscripts but not reservists

Sources: SIPRI; Europa World Yearbook   20 largest armed forces

Defence expenditure as a percentage of national income, 1997

- 7.0% and over
- 5.0% – 6.9%
- 3.5% – 4.9%
- 2.5% – 3.4%
- 1.5% – 2.4%
- Less than 1.5%
- No data available

Sources: Stockholm International Peace Research Institute (SIPRI); CIA

Countries which spent more than $500 million on defence in 1997 are named on the map. Those which spent more $5 billion are shown in **BOLD CAPITALS**.

WEAPONS OF MASS DESTRUCTION

Countries with ballistic missiles but no WMD programmes have not been included.
The map also does not show WMDs located in one country but under the control of another government (e.g. US nuclear weapons in the UK).
The dissolution of the USSR in 1991 left four of the constituent republics with nuclear weapons sited on their territory: Belarus, Kazakstan, Russia and Ukraine. By the end of 1996, all residual nuclear weapons had been transferred to Russia.
Following the 1991 Gulf War, Iraq has been subjected to a unique UN-run effort to force disclosure of the country's WMD programmes. While much material from Iraq's nuclear, chemical and biological warfare programmes has been found and destroyed, an unknown amount has not. Since the end of the UN Special Commission (UNSCOM) inspections in 1998, it may fairly be assumed that the Iraqi government intends to resume its WMD programmes as and when possible.

The principal international instruments governing the control of weapons of mass destruction are:

Nuclear Non-Proliferation Treaty
In force 1970, it requires that (a) declared nuclear states not transfer nuclear weapons or associated technology to other countries, (b) other signatory states do not acquire or produce nuclear weapons. Countries and dependent territories where the treaty applies are shown in blue:

Comprehensive Test Ban Treaty
Treaty opened for signature at the UN in 1996, but does not come into full force until all of the 44 countries with acknowledged nuclear programmes have ratified it. Of these, DPR of Korea, India and Pakistan have yet to ratify.

Chemical Weapons Convention
Prohibits development, stockpiling and use of chemical weapons. In force 1997, by January 2000 129 countries have signed and ratified.

Biological and Toxin Weapons Convention
Prohibits development, stockpiling and use of weapons based on biological or microbial toxins. In force 1975, by January 144 countries have signed and ratified.

This map shows the status of weapons of mass destruction (WMD) programmes in those countries which are known to be in possession or pursuit of such capabilities. Ballistic missiles, generally considered essential to an effective WMD capability, are also shown.

Legend
- Nuclear weapons
- Chemical weapons
- Biological weapons
- Ballistic missiles*

Deployment or status of research and development (R&D) programmes
- Confirmed deployment
- Confirmed R&D programme in progress
- Possible R&D programme
- No evidence of any programme
- Previous deployment or programme dismantled/redundant

*Delivery system capable of sending a 500kg+ payload a distance of 300km or further

Sources: Stockholm International Peace Research Institute (SIPRI); Federation of American Scientists

INTERNATIONAL ORGANISATIONS

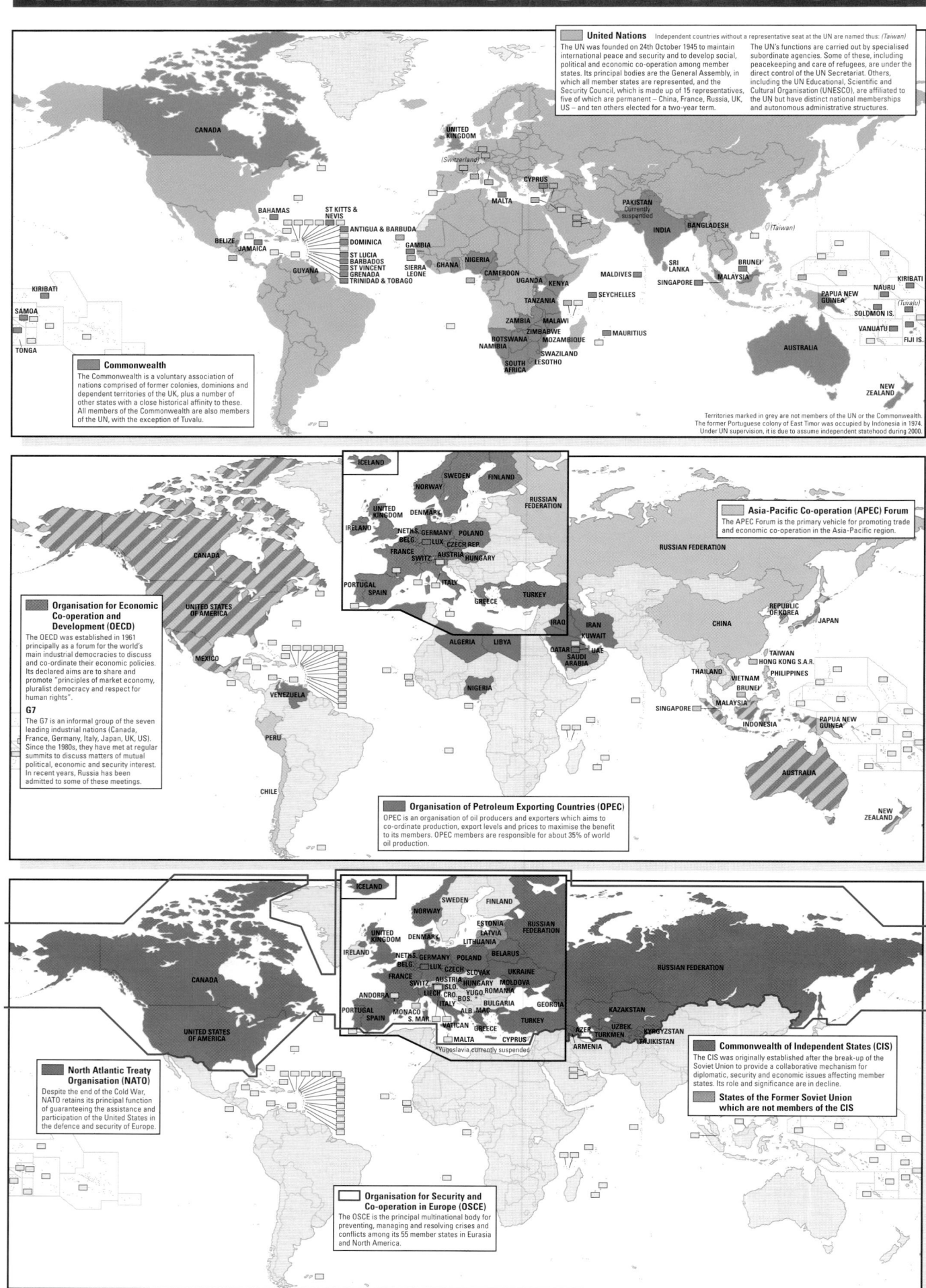

United Nations Independent countries without a representative seat at the UN are named thus: *(Taiwan)*

The UN was founded on 24th October 1945 to maintain international peace and security and to develop social, political and economic co-operation among member states. Its principal bodies are the General Assembly, in which all member states are represented, and the Security Council, which is made up of 15 representatives, five of which are permanent – China, France, Russia, UK, US – and ten others elected for a two-year term.

The UN's functions are carried out by specialised subordinate agencies. Some of these, including peacekeeping and care of refugees, are under the direct control of the UN Secretariat. Others, including the UN Educational, Scientific and Cultural Organisation (UNESCO), are affiliated to the UN but have distinct national memberships and autonomous administrative structures.

Commonwealth

The Commonwealth is a voluntary association of nations comprised of former colonies, dominions and dependent territories of the UK, plus a number of other states with a close historical affinity to these. All members of the Commonwealth are also members of the UN, with the exception of Tuvalu.

Territories marked in grey are not members of the UN or the Commonwealth. The former Portuguese colony of East Timor was occupied by Indonesia in 1974. Under UN supervision, it is due to assume independent statehood during 2000.

Organisation for Economic Co-operation and Development (OECD)

The OECD was established in 1961 principally as a forum for the world's main industrial democracies to discuss and co-ordinate their economic policies. Its declared aims are to share and promote "principles of market economy, pluralist democracy and respect for human rights".

G7

The G7 is an informal group of the seven leading industrial nations (Canada, France, Germany, Italy, Japan, UK, US). Since the 1980s, they have met at regular summits to discuss matters of mutual political, economic and security interest. In recent years, Russia has been admitted to some of these meetings.

Asia-Pacific Co-operation (APEC) Forum

The APEC Forum is the primary vehicle for promoting trade and economic co-operation in the Asia-Pacific region.

Organisation of Petroleum Exporting Countries (OPEC)

OPEC is an organisation of oil producers and exporters which aims to co-ordinate production, export levels and prices to maximise the benefit to its members. OPEC members are responsible for about 35% of world oil production.

North Atlantic Treaty Organisation (NATO)

Despite the end of the Cold War, NATO retains its principal function of guaranteeing the assistance and participation of the United States in the defence and security of Europe.

Commonwealth of Independent States (CIS)

The CIS was originally established after the break-up of the Soviet Union to provide a collaborative mechanism for diplomatic, security and economic issues affecting member states. Its role and significance are in decline.

States of the Former Soviet Union which are not members of the CIS

Organisation for Security and Co-operation in Europe (OSCE)

The OSCE is the principal multinational body for preventing, managing and resolving crises and conflicts among its 55 member states in Eurasia and North America.

*Yugoslavia currently suspended

INTERNATIONAL ORGANISATIONS

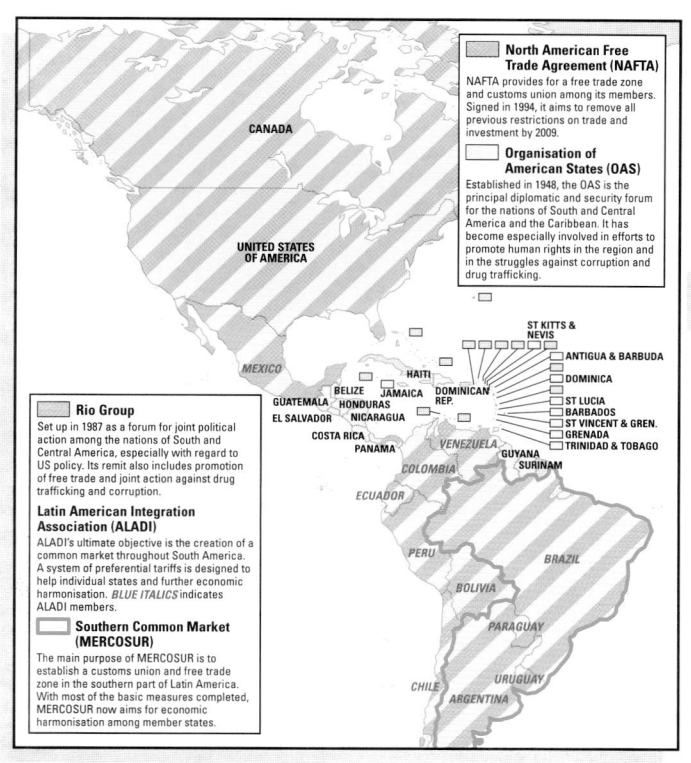

North American Free Trade Agreement (NAFTA)
NAFTA provides for a free trade zone and customs union among its members. Signed in 1994, it aims to remove all previous restrictions on trade and investment by 2009.

Organisation of American States (OAS)
Established in 1948, the OAS is the principal diplomatic and security forum for the nations of South and Central America and the Caribbean. It has become especially involved in efforts to promote human rights in the region and in the struggles against corruption and drug trafficking.

Rio Group
Set up in 1987 as a forum for joint political action among the nations of South and Central America, especially with regard to US policy. Its remit also includes promotion of free trade and joint action against drug trafficking and corruption.

Latin American Integration Association (ALADI)
ALADI's ultimate objective is the creation of a common market throughout South America. A system of preferential tariffs is designed to help individual states and further economic harmonisation. BLUE ITALICS indicates ALADI members.

Southern Common Market (MERCOSUR)
The main purpose of MERCOSUR is to establish a customs union and free trade zone in the southern part of Latin America. With most of the basic measures completed, MERCOSUR now aims for economic harmonisation among member states.

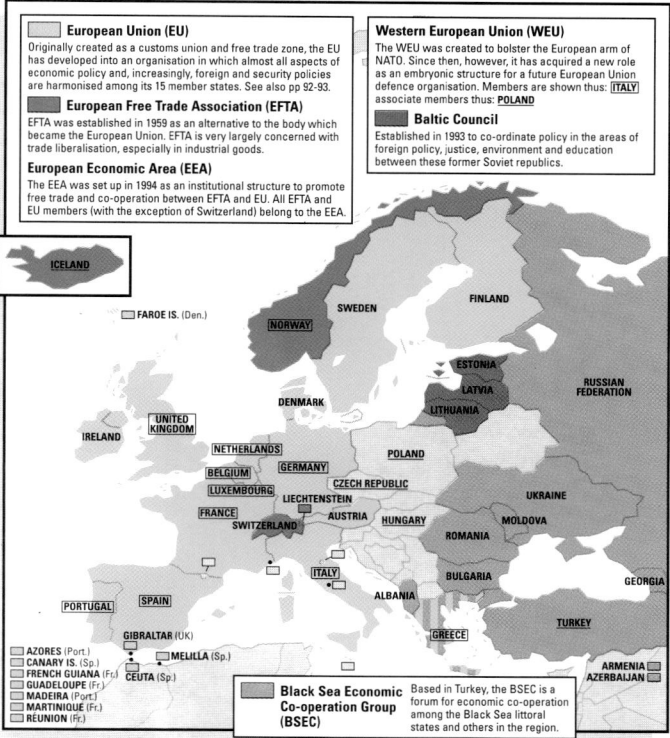

European Union (EU)
Originally created as a customs union and free trade zone, the EU has developed into an organisation in which almost all aspects of economic policy and, increasingly, foreign and security policies are harmonised among its 15 member states. See also pp 92-93.

European Free Trade Association (EFTA)
EFTA was established in 1959 as an alternative to the body which became the European Union. EFTA is very largely concerned with trade liberalisation, especially in industrial goods.

European Economic Area (EEA)
The EEA was set up in 1994 as an institutional structure to promote free trade and co-operation between EFTA and EU. All EFTA and EU members (with the exception of Switzerland) belong to the EEA.

Western European Union (WEU)
The WEU was created to bolster the European arm of NATO. Since then, however, it has acquired a new role as an embryonic structure for a future European Union defence organisation. Members are shown thus: ITALY associate members thus: POLAND

Baltic Council
Established in 1993 to co-ordinate policy in the areas of foreign policy, justice, environment and education between these former Soviet republics.

Black Sea Economic Co-operation Group (BSEC)
Based in Turkey, the BSEC is a forum for economic co-operation among the Black Sea littoral states and others in the region.

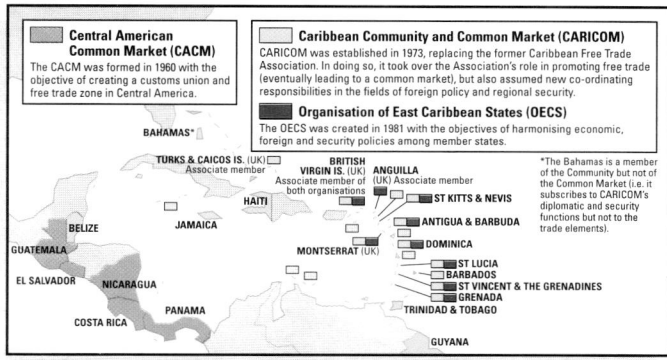

Central American Common Market (CACM)
The CACM was formed in 1960 with the objective of creating a customs union and free trade zone in Central America.

Caribbean Community and Common Market (CARICOM)
CARICOM was established in 1973, replacing the former Caribbean Free Trade Association. In doing so, it took over the Association's role in promoting free trade (eventually leading to a common market), but also assumed new co-ordinating responsibilities in the fields of foreign policy and regional security.

Organisation of East Caribbean States (OECS)
The OECS was created in 1981 with the objectives of harmonising economic, foreign and security policies among member states.

*The Bahamas is a member of the Community but not of the Common Market (i.e. it subscribes to CARICOM's diplomatic and security functions but not to the trade elements).

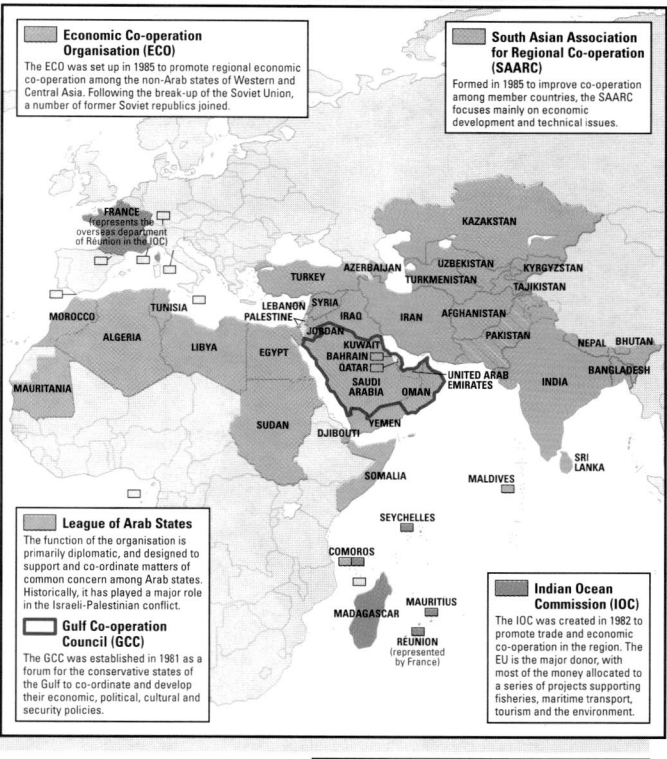

Economic Co-operation Organisation (ECO)
The ECO was set up in 1985 to promote regional economic co-operation among the non-Arab states of Western and Central Asia. Following the break-up of the Soviet Union, a number of former Soviet republics joined.

South Asian Association for Regional Co-operation (SAARC)
Formed in 1985 to improve co-operation among member countries, the SAARC focuses mainly on economic development and technical issues.

FRANCE represents the overseas department of Réunion in the IOC.

League of Arab States
The function of the organisation is primarily diplomatic and designed to support and co-ordinate matters of common concern among Arab states. Historically, it has played a major role in the Israeli-Palestinian conflict.

Gulf Co-operation Council (GCC)
The GCC was established in 1981 as a forum for the conservative states of the Gulf to co-ordinate and develop their economic, political, cultural and security policies.

Indian Ocean Commission (IOC)
The IOC was created in 1982 to promote trade and economic co-operation in the region. The EU is the major donor, with most of the money allocated to a series of projects supporting fisheries, maritime transport, tourism and the environment.

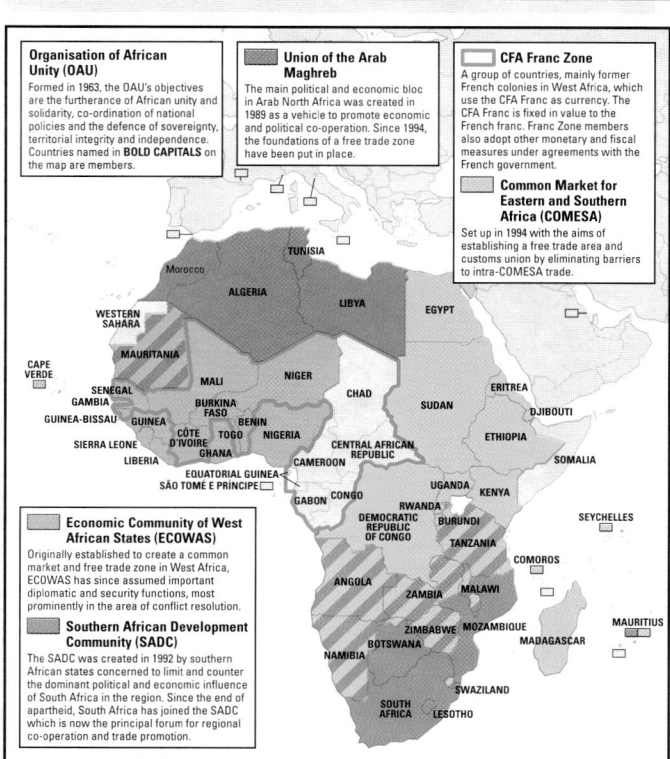

Organisation of African Unity (OAU)
Formed in 1963, the OAU's objectives are the furtherance of African unity and solidarity, co-ordination of national policies and the defence of sovereignty, territorial integrity and independence. Countries named in BOLD CAPITALS on the map are members.

Union of the Arab Maghreb
The main political and economic bloc in Arab North Africa was created in 1989 as a vehicle to promote economic and political co-operation. Since 1994, the foundations of a free trade zone have been put in place.

Common Market for Eastern and Southern Africa (COMESA)
Set up in 1994 with the aims of establishing a free trade area and customs union by eliminating barriers to intra-COMESA trade.

CFA Franc Zone
A group of countries, mainly former French colonies in West Africa, which use the CFA Franc as currency. The CFA Franc is fixed in value to the French franc. Franc Zone members also adopt other monetary and fiscal measures under agreements with the French government.

Economic Community of West African States (ECOWAS)
Originally established to create a common market and free trade zone in West Africa, ECOWAS has since assumed important diplomatic and security functions, most prominently in the area of conflict resolution.

Southern African Development Community (SADC)
The SADC was created in 1992 by southern African states concerned to limit and counter the dominant political and economic influence of South Africa in the region. Since the end of apartheid, South Africa has joined the SADC which is now the principal forum for regional co-operation and trade promotion.

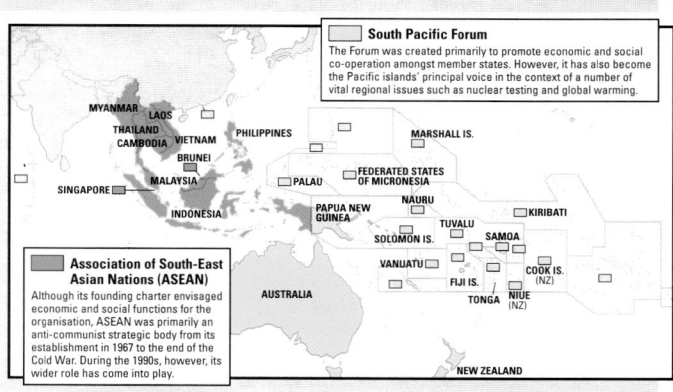

South Pacific Forum
The Forum was created primarily to promote economic and social co-operation amongst member states. However, it has become the Pacific islands' principal voice in the context of a number of vital regional issues such as nuclear testing and global warming.

Association of South-East Asian Nations (ASEAN)
Although its founding charter envisaged economic and social functions for the organisation, ASEAN was primarily an anti-communist strategic body from its establishment in 1967 to the end of the Cold War. During the 1990s, however, its wider role has come into play.

AGRICULTURAL LAND AND FORESTS

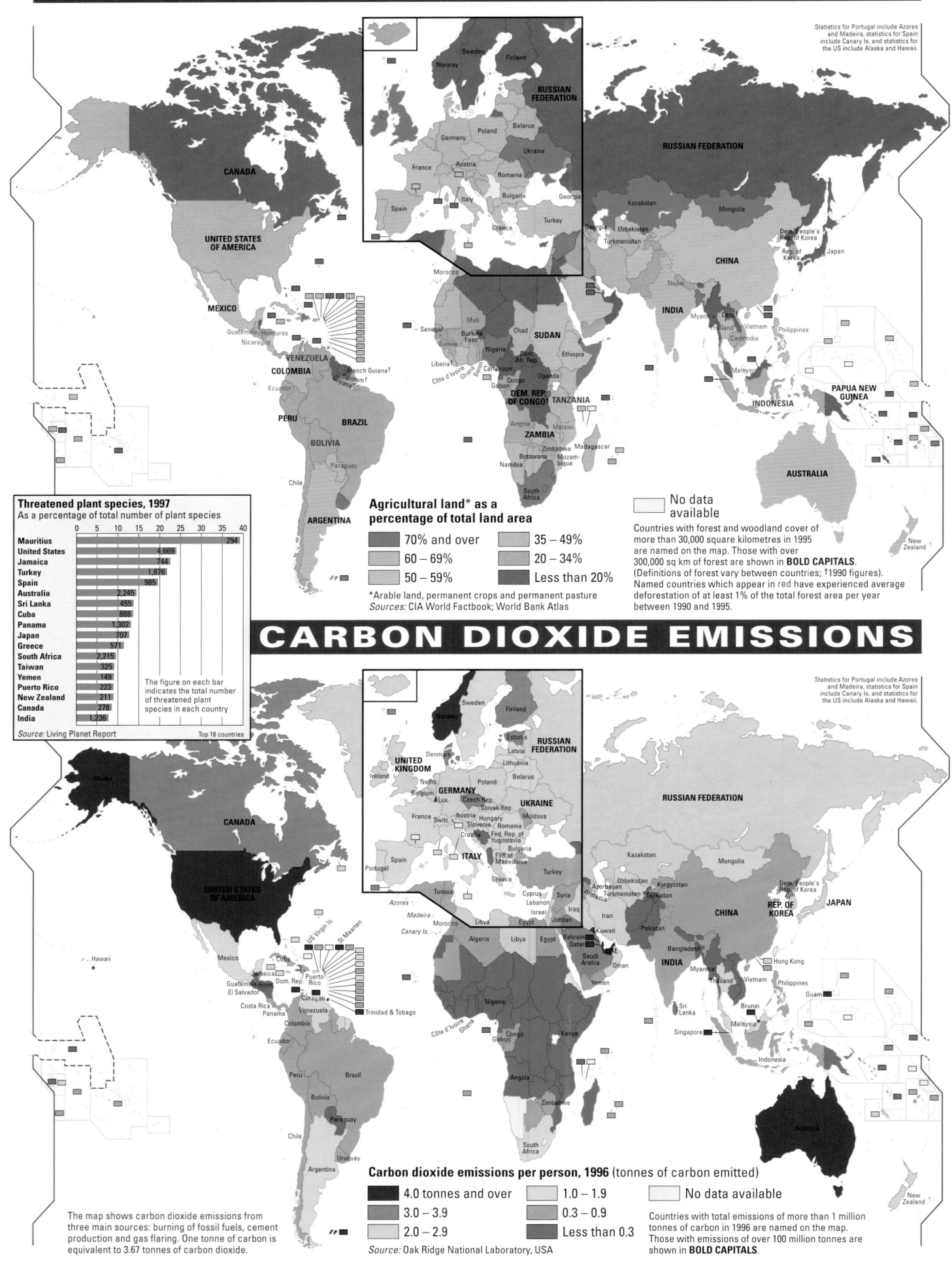

Statistics for Portugal include Azores and Madeira, statistics for Spain include Canary Is. and statistics for the US include Alaska and Hawaii.

Threatened plant species, 1997
As a percentage of total number of plant species

	0	5	10	15	20	25	30	35	40

Mauritius — 294
United States — 4,669
Jamaica — 744
Turkey — 1,876
Spain — 985
Australia — 2,245
Sri Lanka — 455
Cuba — 888
Panama — 1,302
Japan — 707
Greece — 571
South Africa — 2,215
Taiwan — 325
Yemen — 149
Puerto Rico — 223
New Zealand — 211
Canada — 278
India — 1,236

The figure on each bar indicates the total number of threatened plant species in each country

Source: Living Planet Report   Top 18 countries

Agricultural land* as a percentage of total land area

- 70% and over
- 60 – 69%
- 50 – 59%
- 35 – 49%
- 20 – 34%
- Less than 20%

*Arable land, permanent crops and permanent pasture
Sources: CIA World Factbook; World Bank Atlas

No data available

Countries with forest and woodland cover of more than 30,000 square kilometres in 1995 are named on the map. Those with over 300,000 sq km of forest are shown in **BOLD CAPITALS**. (Definitions of forest vary between countries; †1990 figures). Named countries which appear in red have experienced average deforestation of at least 1% of the total forest area per year between 1990 and 1995.

CARBON DIOXIDE EMISSIONS

Statistics for Portugal include Azores and Madeira, statistics for Spain include Canary Is. and statistics for the US include Alaska and Hawaii.

Carbon dioxide emissions per person, 1996 (tonnes of carbon emitted)

- 4.0 tonnes and over
- 3.0 – 3.9
- 2.0 – 2.9
- 1.0 – 1.9
- 0.3 – 0.9
- Less than 0.3
- No data available

The map shows carbon dioxide emissions from three main sources: burning of fossil fuels, cement production and gas flaring. One tonne of carbon is equivalent to 3.67 tonnes of carbon dioxide.

Source: Oak Ridge National Laboratory, USA

Countries with total emissions of more than 1 million tonnes of carbon in 1996 are named on the map. Those with emissions of over 100 million tonnes are shown in **BOLD CAPITALS**.

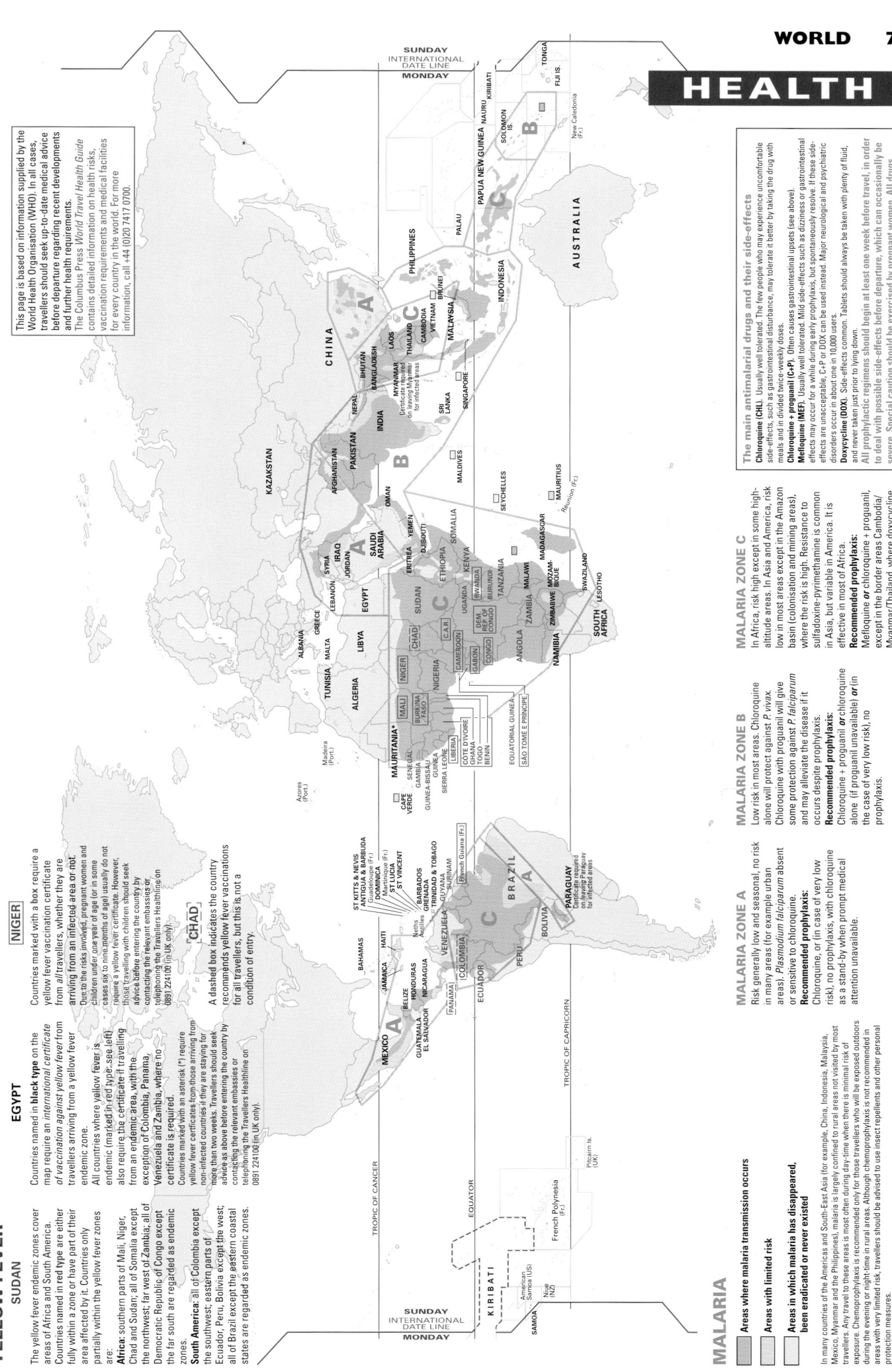

HEALTH

YELLOW FEVER

The yellow fever endemic zones cover areas of Africa and South America. Countries named in red type are either fully within a zone or have part of their area affected by it. Countries only partially within the yellow fever zones are:

Africa: southern parts of Mali, Niger, Chad and Sudan; all of Somalia except the northwest; far west of Zambia; all of Democratic Republic of Congo except the far south are regarded as endemic zones.

South America: all of Colombia except the southwest; eastern parts of Ecuador, Peru, Bolivia except the west; all of Brazil except the eastern coastal states are regarded as endemic zones.

Countries named in **black type** on the map require an *international certificate of vaccination against yellow fever* from travellers arriving from a yellow fever endemic zone.

All countries where yellow fever is endemic (marked in red type: see left) also require the certificate if travelling from an endemic area, with the exception of Colombia, Panama, Venezuela and Zambia, where no certificate is required.

Countries marked with an asterisk (*) require yellow fever certificates from those arriving from non-infected countries if they are staying for more than two weeks. Travellers should seek advice as above before entering the country by contacting the relevant embassies or telephoning the Travellers Healthline on 0891 224100 (in UK only).

A dashed box indicates the country recommends yellow fever vaccinations for all travellers, but this is not a condition of entry.

This page is based on information supplied by the World Health Organisation (WHO). In all cases, travellers should seek up-to-date medical advice before departure regarding recent developments and further health requirements.
The Columbus Press *World Travel Health Guide* contains detailed information on health risks, vaccination requirements and medical facilities for every country in the world. For more information, call +44 (0)20 7417 0700.

MALARIA

Areas where malaria transmission occurs

Areas with limited risk

Areas in which malaria has disappeared, been eradicated or never existed

In many countries in the Americas and South-East Asia (for example, China, Indonesia, Malaysia, Mexico, Myanmar and the Philippines), malaria is largely confined to rural areas not visited by most travellers. Any travel to these areas is most often made during day-time when there is minimal risk of exposure. Chemoprophylaxis is recommended only for those travellers who will be exposed outdoors during the evening or night-time in rural areas. Although chemoprophylaxis is not recommended in areas with very limited risk, travellers should be advised to use insect repellents and other personal protection measures.
Travellers are reminded that protection from biting mosquitoes is the first line of defence against malaria, and no antimalarial prophylactic regimen gives complete protection.

MALARIA ZONE A

Risk generally low and seasonal, no risk in many areas (for example urban areas). *Plasmodium falciparum* absent or sensitive to chloroquine.
Recommended prophylaxis:
Chloroquine, or (in case of very low risk), no prophylaxis, with chloroquine as a stand-by when prompt medical attention unavailable.

MALARIA ZONE B

Low risk in most areas. Chloroquine alone will protect against *P. vivax*. Chloroquine with proguanil will give some protection against *P. falciparum* and may alleviate the disease if it occurs despite prophylaxis.
Recommended prophylaxis:
Chloroquine + proguanil *or* chloroquine alone (if proguanil unavailable) *or* (in the case of very low risk), no prophylaxis.

MALARIA ZONE C

In Africa, risk high except in some high-altitude areas. In Asia and America, risk low in most areas except in the Amazon basin (colonisation and mining areas), where the risk is high. Resistance to sulfadoxine-pyrimethamine is common in Asia, but variable in America. It is effective in most of Africa.
Recommended prophylaxis:
Mefloquine *or* chloroquine + proguanil, except in the border areas Cambodia/Myanmar/Thailand, where doxycycline is recommended.

The main antimalarial drugs and their side-effects

Chloroquine (CHL). Usually well tolerated. The few people who may experience uncomfortable side-effects, such as gastrointestinal disturbance, may tolerate it better by taking the drug with meals and in divided twice-weekly doses.
Chloroquine + proguanil (C+P). Often causes gastrointestinal upsets (see above).
Mefloquine (MEF). Usually well tolerated. Mild side-effects such as dizziness or gastrointestinal effects may occur for a while during early prophylaxis, but spontaneously resolve. If these side-effects are unacceptable, C+P or DOX can be used instead. Major neurological and psychiatric disorders occur in about one in 10,000 users.
Doxycycline (DOX). Side-effects common. Tablets should always be taken with plenty of fluid, and never taken just prior to lying down.
All prophylactic regimens should begin at least one week before travel, in order to deal with possible side-effects before departure, which can occasionally be severe. Special caution should be exercised by pregnant women. All drugs should be continued for four weeks after the last possible exposure to infection.

SPORT

SUMMER OLYMPICS

The first modern Olympic Games, founded by Frenchman Baron de Coubertin, were held at Athens in 1896. They are held every four years. An extra Olympics were held in 1906 to celebrate the tenth anniversary of the 1896 games. The next Games are due to be held at Sydney in the year 2000 and at Athens in 2004.

WINTER OLYMPICS

The first separate Winter Games took place in 1924 at Chamonix, France. The games originally took place in the same year as the Summer Games, but beginning in 1994, are now held in between the Summer Games. The next Winter Olympics are due to be held at Salt Lake City, Utah in 2002 and at Turin in 2006.

COMMONWEALTH GAMES

Originally the British Empire Games and first held in 1930 at Hamilton, Ontario. Renamed the British Empire and Commonwealth Games in 1954, the British Commonwealth Games in 1970 and the Commonwealth Games in 1978. Held every four years, the next Games are due to be held at Manchester, England in 2002.

WORLD ATHLETICS CHAMPIONSHIPS

The World Athletics Championships were first held in Helsinki in 1983, and at four-year intervals until 1991. They are now held every two years. The next Championships are due to be held at Edmonton in 2001.

FOOTBALL WORLD CUP

Association Football's premier event. Brazil kept the Jules Rimet Trophy after winning it for the third time in 1970. The teams now compete for the FIFA World Cup. Held every four years, the next competition is due to be co-hosted by Japan and the Republic of Korea in 2002.

RUGBY UNION WORLD CUP

The first Rugby Union World Cup was held in 1987 and is now held every four years, with the next competition in Australia and New Zealand in 2003.

CRICKET WORLD CUP

The venue of the first Cricket World Cup in 1975 was England. Played every 3–5 years, it was not until 1987 that the competition was held outside England. The next World Cup is due to be held in South Africa in 2002/03.

CYCLING annual events

Major tours:
Giro d'Italia (Tour of Italy)
Tour de France
Tour DuPont, USA
Vuelta d'España (Tour of Spain)

Classics:
Fléche Wallonne, Belgium
Grand Prix des Nations, France
Liège-Bastogne-Liège, Belgium
Milan-San Remo, Italy
Paris-Brussels, France/Belgium
Paris-Nice, France
Paris-Roubaix, France
Tour of Flanders, Belgium
Tour of Lombardy, Italy

GOLF annual events

Major tournaments:
British Open
US Masters
US Open
US PGA Championship

Principal international tournament:
Ryder Cup (every 2 yrs)

HORSE RACING annual events

The English Classics:
1,000 Guineas, Newmarket
2,000 Guineas, Newmarket
St Leger, Doncaster

The Derby, Epsom
The Oaks, Epsom
The Triple Crown, USA:
Belmont Stakes, New York
Kentucky Derby, Louisville
Preakness Stakes, Baltimore
Other major races:
Cheltenham Gold Cup, UK
Dubai World Cup
Grand National, Aintree, UK
Irish Derby, The Curragh
Japan Cup, Tokyo
Melbourne Cup, Australia
Prix de l'Arc de Triomphe, Paris, France
Royal Ascot, UK

MARATHON

Major marathons are marked on the map: **M**
Boston, Chicago, London, New York, Rotterdam

MOTOR RACING

All circuits which have held a Formula One race since 1990 are shown on the map: **F1**

TENNIS annual events

Grand Slam tournaments:
Australian Open, Melbourne
French Open, Stade Roland Garros, Paris, France
US Open, Flushing Meadow, New York
Wimbledon, UK
Principal international tournament:
Davis Cup

WORLD CUP FINALS: RESULTS

FOOTBALL

1930	Uruguay 4		Argentina 2	
1934	Italy 2		Czechoslovakia 1	
1938	Italy 4		Hungary 2	
1950	Uruguay 2		Brazil 1	
1954	F.R. of Germany 3		Hungary 2	
1958	Brazil 5		Sweden 2	
1962	Brazil 3		Czechoslovakia 1	
1966	England 4		F.R. of Germany 2	
1970	Brazil 4		Italy 1	
1974	F.R. of Germany 2		Netherlands 1	
1978	Argentina 3		Netherlands 1	
1982	Italy 3		F.R. of Germany 1	
1986	Argentina 3		F.R. of Germany 2	
1990	F.R. of Germany 1		Argentina 0	
1994	Brazil 0		Italy 0	
	(Brazil won 3–2 on penalties)			
1998	France 3		Brazil 0	

RUGBY UNION

1987	New Zealand 29	France 9
1991	Australia 12	England 6
1995	South Africa 15	New Zealand 12
1999	Australia 35	France 12

CRICKET

1975	West Indies (291–8) beat	Australia (274) by 17 runs
1979	West Indies (286–9) beat	England (194) by 92 runs
1983	India (183) beat	West Indies (140) by 43 runs
1987	Australia (253–5) beat	England (246–8) by 7 runs
1992	Pakistan (249–6) beat	England (227) by 22 runs
1996	Sri Lanka (245–3) beat	Australia (241) by 7 wickets
1999	Australia (133–2) beat	Pakistan (132) by 8 wickets

ASIA

Asian Cup (football)
Held every 4 years
Last held: United Arab Emirates, 1996
Next: Lebanon, 2000

Asian Games
Held every 4 years
Last held: Bangkok, Thailand, 1998
Next: Pusan, Republic of Korea, 2002

WORLDWIDE

Goodwill Games
Held every 3–4 years
Last held: New York, USA, 1998
Next: Brisbane, Australia, 2001

World Student Games
("Universiade")
Held every 2 years
Last held: Majorca, 1999
Next: Beijing, China, 2001

AFRICA

African Cup of Nations (football)
Held every 2 years
Last held: Ghana & Nigeria, 2000
Next venue: to be confirmed, 2002

All-Africa Games
Held every 4 years
Last held: Johannesburg, South Africa, 1999
Next: Nigeria, 2003

EUROPE

European Championships (athletics)
Held every 4 years
Last held: Budapest, Hungary, 1998
Next: Munich, Germany, 2002

European Championships (football)
Held every 4 years
Last held: England, 1996
Next: Belgium & Netherlands, 2000

AMERICAS

Copa America (football)
Held every 2 years
Last held: Paraguay, 1999
Next: Colombia, 2001

Pan-American Games
Held every 4 years
Last held: Winnipeg, Canada, 1999
Next: Santo Domingo, Dominican Rep., 2003

Map labels

SUNDAY INTERNATIONAL DATE LINE MONDAY

Auckland 1950 1990
Christchurch 1974
Brisbane 1982
Sydney 2000 1938
AUSTRALIA & NEW ZEALAND 1987 Final: Auckland 2003
(Equestrian events held in Stockholm due to Australian quarantine regulations)
Adelaide
Melbourne 1956
Perth 1962

Sapporo 1972
Nagano 1998
Aida
Tokyo 1964 1991
Suzuka
JAPAN & REP. OF KOREA 2002
Seoul 1988

Kuala Lumpur 1998
Sepang

INDIA & PAKISTAN 1987 Final: Calcutta, India
INDIA, PAKISTAN & SRI LANKA 1996 Final: Lahore, Pakistan

Kyalami, Johannesburg
SOUTH AFRICA 2002/03 Final: Johannesburg

Moscow 1980
A1 Ring, Spielberg, Austria
Spa-Francorchamps, Belgium
Le Castellet, France
Magny Cours, France
New Nürburgring, Germany
Hockenheim, Germany
Budapest, Hungary
Imola, Italy
Monza, Italy
Monte Carlo, Monaco
Estoril, Portugal
Barcelona, Spain
Jerez de la Frontera, Spain
Silverstone, UK

Helsinki 1952 1983
Stockholm 1912 Final: Stockholm
SWEDEN 1958 Final: Stockholm
Gothenburg 1995
Lillehammer 1994
Oslo 1952
Berlin 1936
GERMANY 1974 Final: Munich
Stuttgart 1993
Munich 1972
Cortina 1956
Sarajevo 1984
Athens 1896 1997 1906 2004
Innsbruck 1964 1976
Rome 1960 1987 Final: Rome
ITALY 1934 1990 Final: Rome
Garmisch Partenkirchen 1936
Turin 2006
St Moritz 1928 1948
Antwerp 1920
Amsterdam 1928
R'dam
ENGLAND 1966 1975 1979 1999 Final: London
Manchester 2002
Edinburgh 1970 1986
WALES 1958 1999 Final: Cardiff
Cardiff 1958
London 1908 1934 1948
Paris 1900 1924
FRANCE 1938 1998 Final: Paris
SWITZ. 1954
Chamonix 1924
Grenoble 1968
Albertville 1992
SPAIN 1982 Final: Madrid
Barcelona 1992
Seville 1999
Madrid
Interlagos, São Paulo
BRAZIL 1950 Final: Rio de Janeiro
URUGUAY 1930 Final: Montevideo
Buenos Aires
ARGENTINA 1978 Final: Buenos Aires
CHILE 1962 Final: Santiago

Edmonton 1978 2001
Calgary 1988
Vancouver
Victoria 1994
Squaw Valley 1960
Salt Lake City 2002
Los Angeles 1932 1984
Phoenix
UNITED STATES 1994 Final: Los Angeles
St Louis 1904
Chicago
Indianapolis
Lake Placid 1932 1980
Hamilton 1930
Montreal 1976
Boston
New York
Atlanta 1996
MEXICO 1970 1986 Final: Mexico City
Mexico City 1968
Kingston 1966

SUNDAY INTERNATIONAL DATE LINE MONDAY

DRIVING

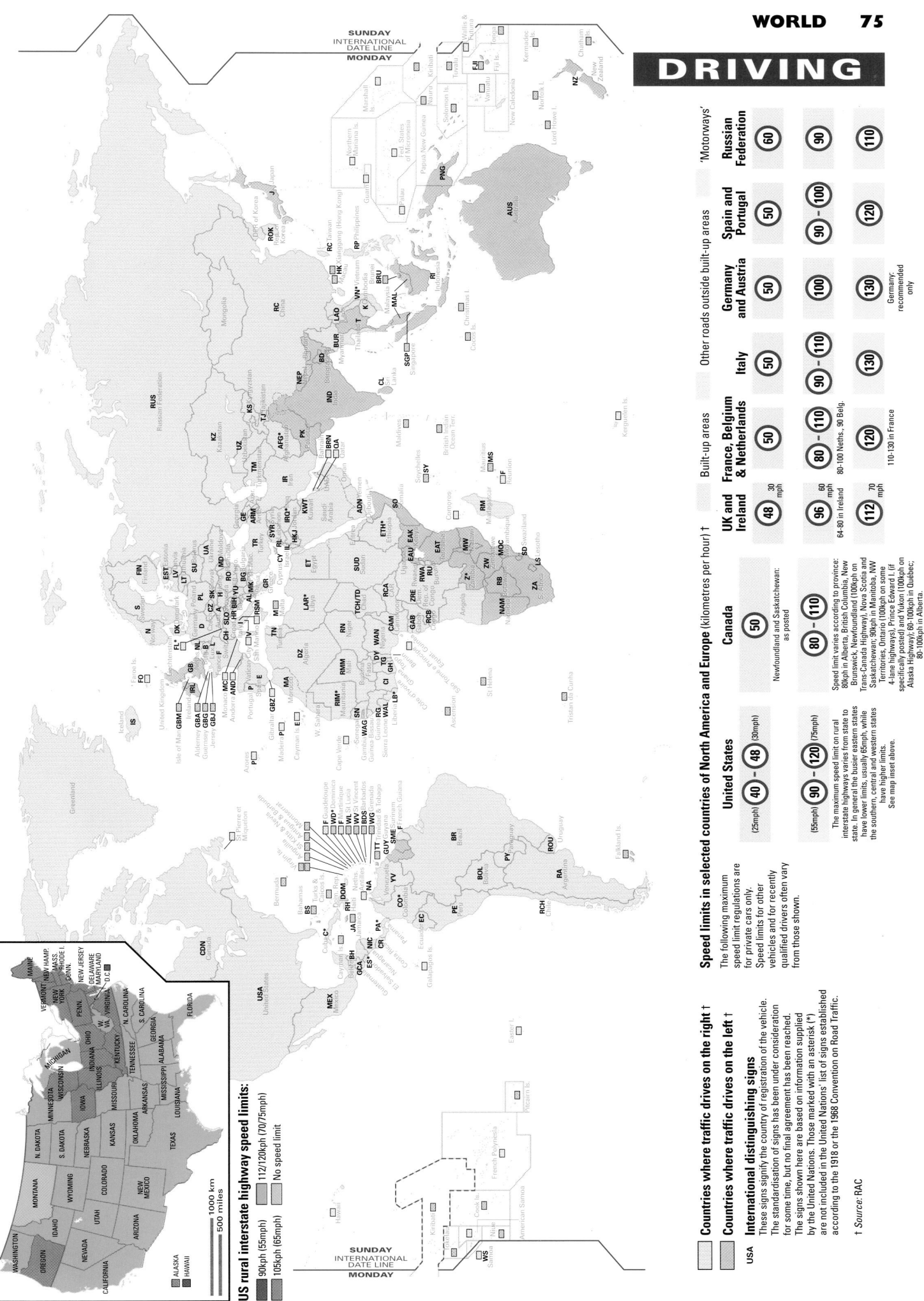

Speed limits in selected countries of North America and Europe (kilometres per hour) †

The following maximum speed limit regulations are for private cars only. Speed limits for other vehicles and for recently qualified drivers often vary from those shown.

	Built-up areas	Other roads outside built-up areas	'Motorways'
United States	(25mph) 40 – 48 (30mph)	(55mph) 90 – 120 (75mph)	

The maximum speed limit on rural interstate highways varies from state to state. In general the busier eastern states have lower limits, usually 65mph; while the southern, central and western states have higher limits. See map inset above.

Canada	50	80 – 110	

Newfoundland and Saskatchewan: as posted

Speed limit varies according to province: 80kph in Alberta, British Columbia, New Brunswick, Newfoundland (100kph on Trans-Canada Highway), Nova Scotia and Saskatchewan; 90kph in Manitoba, NW Territories, Ontario (100kph on some 4-lane highways), Prince Edward I. (if specifically posted) and Yukon (100kph on Alaska Highway); 60-100kph in Québec; 80-100kph in Alberta.

UK and Ireland	48 / 30 mph	96 / 60 mph	112 / 70 mph
France, Belgium & Netherlands	50	80 – 110	120
Italy	50	90 – 110	130
Germany and Austria	50	100	130
Spain and Portugal	50	90 – 100	120
Russian Federation	60	90	110

64-80 in Ireland

80-100 Neths, 90 Belg.

110-130 in France

Germany: recommended only

US rural interstate highway speed limits:

- 90kph (55mph)
- 105kph (65mph)
- 112/120kph (70/75mph)
- No speed limit

1000 km
500 miles

ALASKA
HAWAII

Countries where traffic drives on the right †

Countries where traffic drives on the left †

International distinguishing signs

These signs signify the country of registration of the vehicle. The standardisation of signs has been under consideration for some time, but no final agreement has been reached. The signs shown here are based on information supplied by the United Nations. Those marked with an asterisk (*) are not included in the United Nations' list of signs established according to the 1918 or the 1968 Convention on Road Traffic.

USA

† Source: RAC

AIRPORTS

MAP A

The world's main airports are shown here, together with their international three-letter code.

In some cases the city itself may have its own code in addition to those used by the airport or airports that serve it; these city codes are not included here.

International Air Transport Association (IATA) Conference Areas

Area 1:
- North Atlantic
- Mid Atlantic
- South Atlantic

Area 2:
- Europe
- Middle East
- Africa
- East Africa

Area 3:
- Asia
- SW Pacific

AREA 1, NORTH ATLANTIC

ACA	Acapulco, Mexico
ALB	Albany, NY, USA
ANC	Anchorage, AK, USA
ATL	Atlanta, GA, USA
BDL	Hartford, CT, USA
BIL	Billings, MT, USA
BNA	Nashville, TN, USA
BOI	Boise, ID, USA
BOS	Boston, MA, USA
BUF	Buffalo, NY, USA
BWI	Baltimore-Washington International, MD, USA
CLE	Cleveland, OH, USA
CLT	Charlotte, NC, USA
CVG	Cincinnati, OH, USA
CUU	Chihuahua, Mexico
DCA	Washington National, VA, USA
DEN	Denver, CO, USA
DFW	Dallas-Fort Worth, TX, USA
DTW	Detroit, MI, USA
EWR	New York Newark, NJ, USA
FLL	Fort Lauderdale-Hollywood, FL, USA
GDL	Guadalajara, Mexico
GEG	Spokane, WA, USA
GOH	Nuuk (Godthåb), Greenland
HNL	Honolulu, HI, USA
IAD	Washington Dulles, VA, USA
IAH	Houston, TX, USA
IND	Indianapolis, IN, USA
JAX	Jacksonville, FL, USA
JFK	New York John F. Kennedy, NY, USA
LAS	Las Vegas, NV, USA
LAX	Los Angeles, CA, USA
LGA	New York LaGuardia, NY, USA
MCI	Kansas City, MO, USA
MCO	Orlando, FL, USA
MEM	Memphis, TN, USA
MEX	Ciudad de México (Mexico City), Mexico
MIA	Miami, FL, USA
MKE	Milwaukee, WI, USA
MSP	Minneapolis-St Paul, MN, USA
MSY	New Orleans, LA, USA
MTY	Monterrey, Mexico
ORD	Chicago, IL, USA
PDX	Portland, OR, USA
PHL	Philadelphia, PA, USA
PHX	Phoenix, AZ, USA
PIT	Pittsburgh, PA, USA
PWM	Portland, ME, USA
RDU	Raleigh-Durham, NC, USA
RSW	Southwest Florida, FL, USA
SAN	San Diego, CA, USA
SEA	Seattle, WA, USA
SFJ	Kangerlussaq, Greenland
SFO	San Francisco, CA, USA
SJD	San José del Cabo, Mexico
SLC	Salt Lake City, UT, USA
STL	St Louis, MO, USA
SYR	Syracuse, NY, USA
TPA	Tampa, FL, USA
UAK	Narsarsuaq, Greenland
YEG	Edmonton, AL, Canada
YFB	Iqaluit, NU, Canada
YHM	Hamilton, OT, Canada
YHZ	Halifax, NS, Canada
YMX	Montréal Mirabel, QU, Canada
YOW	Ottawa, OT, Canada
YQB	Québec, QU, Canada
YQX	Gander, NF, Canada
YUL	Montréal Dorval, QU, Canada
YVR	Vancouver, BC, Canada
YWG	Winnipeg, MN, Canada
YXE	Saskatoon, SA, Canada
YYC	Calgary, AL, Canada
YYT	St John's, NF, Canada
YYZ	Toronto, OT, Canada
YZF	Yellowknife, NT, Canada

AREA 1, MID ATLANTIC

ANU	Antigua
BAQ	Barranquilla, Colombia
BDA	Bermuda
BGI	Barbados
BOG	Bogotá, Colombia
BZE	Belize City, Belize
CAY	Cayenne, French Guiana
CCS	Caracas, Venezuela
FPO	Freeport, Bahamas
GEO	Georgetown, Guyana
GND	Grenada
GUA	Ciudad de Guatemala (Guatemala City), Guatemala
GYE	Guayaquil, Ecuador
HAV	La Habana (Havana), Cuba
KIN	Kingston, Jamaica
LIM	Lima, Peru
LPB	La Paz, Bolivia
MGA	Managua, Nicaragua
NAS	Nassau, Bahamas
PAP	Port-au-Prince, Haiti
PBM	Paramaribo, Surinam
POP	Puerto Plata, Dominican Republic
POS	Port of Spain, Trinidad
PTY	Ciudad de Panamá (Panama City), Panama
SAL	San Salvador, El Salvador
SDQ	Santo Domingo, Dominican Republic
SJO	San José, Costa Rica
SJU	San Juan, Puerto Rico
SKB	St Kitts
SRZ	Santa Cruz, Bolivia
SVD	St Vincent
TGU	Tegucigalpa, Honduras
UIO	Quito, Ecuador
UVF	Hewanorra, St Lucia

AREA 1, SOUTH ATLANTIC

ARI	Arica, Chile
ASU	Asunción, Paraguay
BSB	Brasília, Brazil
EZE	Buenos Aires, Argentina
GIG	Rio de Janeiro, Brazil
GRU	São Paulo, Brazil
IPC	Easter Island
MAO	Manaus, Brazil
MVD	Montevideo, Uruguay
REC	Recife, Brazil
SCL	Santiago, Chile
SSA	Salvador, Brazil

AREA 2, EUROPE*

BAK	Baki (Baku), Azerbaijan
EVN	Yerevan, Armenia
FNC	Funchal, Madeira
KEF	Reykjavík, Iceland
KUF	Samara, Russian Federation
LPA	Las Palmas de Gran Canaria, Canary Is.
OUL	Oulu, Finland
PDL	Ponta Delgada, São Miguel, Azores
PXO	Porto Santo, Madeira
SMA	Vila do Porto, Santa Maria, Azores
TBS	Tbilisi, Georgia
TER	Terceira, Azores
TFN	Tenerife North, Canary Is.
TFS	Tenerife South, Canary Is.
TOS	Tromsø, Norway
VOG	Volgograd, Russian Federation

AREA 2, MIDDLE EAST*

ADE	Adan (Aden), Yemen
AUH	Abu Dhabi, UAE
BAH	Bahrain
BGW	Baghdad, Iraq
DHA	Dhahran, Saudi Arabia
DOH	Ad Dawhah (Doha), Qatar
DXB	Dubai, UAE
JED	Jiddah (Jeddah), Saudi Arabia
KRT	Al Khurtum (Khartoum), Sudan
KWI	Al Kuwayt (Kuwait)
LXR	Luxor, Egypt
MCT	Masqat (Muscat), Oman
RUH	Ar Riyad (Riyadh), Saudi Arabia
SAH	San'a, Yemen
THR	Tehran, Iran

AREA 2, AFRICA*

ABJ	Abidjan, Côte d'Ivoire
ABV	Abuja, Nigeria
ACC	Accra, Ghana
ADD	Adis Abeba (Addis Ababa), Ethiopia
ASM	Asmara, Eritrea
BEW	Beira, Mozambique
BGF	Bangui, Central African Republic
BJL	Banjul, The Gambia
BJM	Bujumbura, Burundi
BKO	Bamako, Mali
BZV	Brazzaville, Congo
CKY	Conakry, Guinea
COO	Cotonou, Benin
CPT	Cape Town, South Africa
DKR	Dakar, Senegal

AIRPORTS

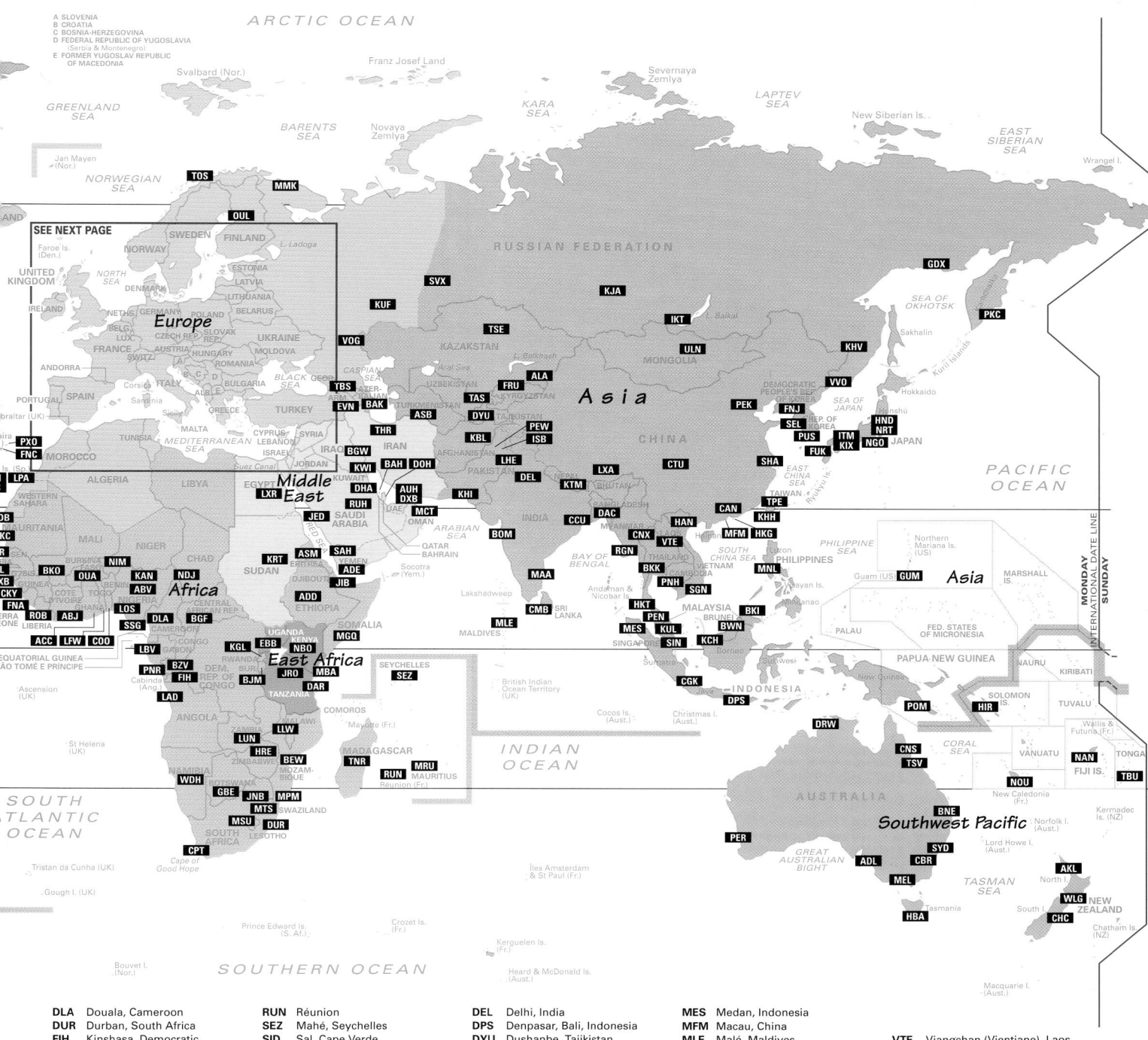

A SLOVENIA
B CROATIA
C BOSNIA-HERZEGOVINA
D FEDERAL REPUBLIC OF YUGOSLAVIA
(Serbia & Montenegro)
E FORMER YUGOSLAV REPUBLIC
OF MACEDONIA

DLA	Douala, Cameroon	RUN	Réunion	DEL	Delhi, India
DUR	Durban, South Africa	SEZ	Mahé, Seychelles	DPS	Denpasar, Bali, Indonesia
FIH	Kinshasa, Democratic Republic of Congo	SID	Sal, Cape Verde	DYU	Dushanbe, Tajikistan

DLA Douala, Cameroon
DUR Durban, South Africa
FIH Kinshasa, Democratic Republic of Congo
FNA Freetown, Sierra Leone
GBE Gaborone, Botswana
HRE Harare, Zimbabwe
JIB Djibouti
JNB Johannesburg, South Africa
KAN Kano, Nigeria
KGL Kigali, Rwanda
LAD Luanda, Angola
LBV Libreville, Gabon
LFW Lomé, Togo
LLW Lilongwe, Malawi
LOS Lagos, Nigeria
LUN Lusaka, Zambia
MGQ Muqdisho (Mogadishu), Somalia
MPM Maputo, Mozambique
MRU Mauritius
MSU Maseru, Lesotho
MTS Manzini, Swaziland
NDB Nouadhibou, Mauritania
NDJ N'Djamena, Chad
NIM Niamey, Niger
NKC Nouakchott, Mauritania
OUA Ouagadougou, Burkina Faso
OXB Bissau, Guinea-Bissau
PNR Pointe-Noire, Congo
ROB Monrovia, Liberia

RUN Réunion
SEZ Mahé, Seychelles
SID Sal, Cape Verde
SSG Malabo, Equatorial Guinea
TNR Antananarivo, Madagascar
WDH Windhoek, Namibia

AREA 2, EAST AFRICA
DAR Dar es Salaam, Tanzania
EBB Entebbe, Uganda
JRO Kilimanjaro, Tanzania
MBA Mombasa, Kenya
NBO Nairobi, Kenya

AREA 3, ASIA
ALA Almaty, Kazakstan
ASB Ashgabat, Turkmenistan
BKI Kota Kinabalu, Malaysia
BKK Krung Thep (Bangkok), Thailand
BOM Mumbai (Bombay), India
BWN Bandar Seri Begawan, Brunei
CAN Guangzhou (Canton), China
CCU Calcutta, India
CGK Jakarta, Indonesia
CNX Chiang Mai, Thailand
CTU Chengdu, China
DAC Dhaka, Bangladesh

DEL Delhi, India
DPS Denpasar, Bali, Indonesia
DYU Dushanbe, Tajikistan
FNJ P'yongyang, Democratic People's Republic of Korea
FRU Bishkek, Kyrgyzstan
FUK Fukuoka, Japan
GDX Magadan, Russian Federation
GUM Guam
HAN Hanoi, Vietnam
HKG Xianggang (Hong Kong), China
HKT Phuket, Thailand
HND Tokyo Haneda, Japan
IKT Irkutsk, Russian Federation
ISB Islamabad, Pakistan
ITM Osaka Itami, Japan
KBL Kabul, Afghanistan
KCH Kuching, Malaysia
KHH Kaohsiung, Taiwan
KHI Karachi, Pakistan
KHV Khabarovsk, Russian Federation
KIX Osaka Kansai, Japan
KJA Krasnoyarsk, Russian Federation
KTM Kathmandu, Nepal
KUL Kuala Lumpur, Malaysia
LHE Lahore, Pakistan
LXA Lhasa, China
MAA Chennai (Madras), India

MES Medan, Indonesia
MFM Macau, China
MLE Malé, Maldives
MMK Murmansk, Russian Federation
MNL Manila, the Philippines
NGO Nagoya, Japan
NRT Tokyo Narita, Japan
PEK Beijing (Peking), China
PEN Pinang (Penang), Malaysia
PEW Peshawar, Pakistan
PKC Petropavlovsk Kamchatskiy, Russian Federation
PNH Phnom Penh, Cambodia
POM Port Moresby, Papua New Guinea
PUS Pusan, Republic of Korea
RGN Yangon (Rangoon), Myanmar
SEL Soul (Seoul), Republic of Korea
SGN Ho Chi Minh City (Saigon), Vietnam
SHA Shanghai, China
SIN Singapore
SVX Yekaterinburg, Russian Federation
TAS Tashkent, Uzbekistan
TPE Taipei, Taiwan
TSE Astana, Kazakstan
ULN Ulaanbaatar (Ulan Bator), Mongolia

VTE Viangchan (Vientiane), Laos
VVO Vladivostok, Russian Federation

AREA 3, SOUTHWEST PACIFIC
ADL Adelaide, Australia
AKL Auckland, New Zealand
APW Apia, Samoa
BNE Brisbane, Australia
CBR Canberra, Australia
CHC Christchurch, New Zealand
CNS Cairns, Australia
DRW Darwin, Australia
HBA Hobart, Tasmania, Australia
HIR Honiara, Solomon Is.
MEL Melbourne, Australia
NAN Nadi, Fiji Is.
NOU Nouméa, New Caledonia
PER Perth, Australia
PPT Papeete, Tahiti, French Polynesia
RAR Rarotonga, Cook Is.
SYD Sydney, Australia
TBU Tongatapu, Tonga
TSV Townsville, Australia
WLG Wellington, New Zealand
* See next page for other airports in these areas

AIRPORTS

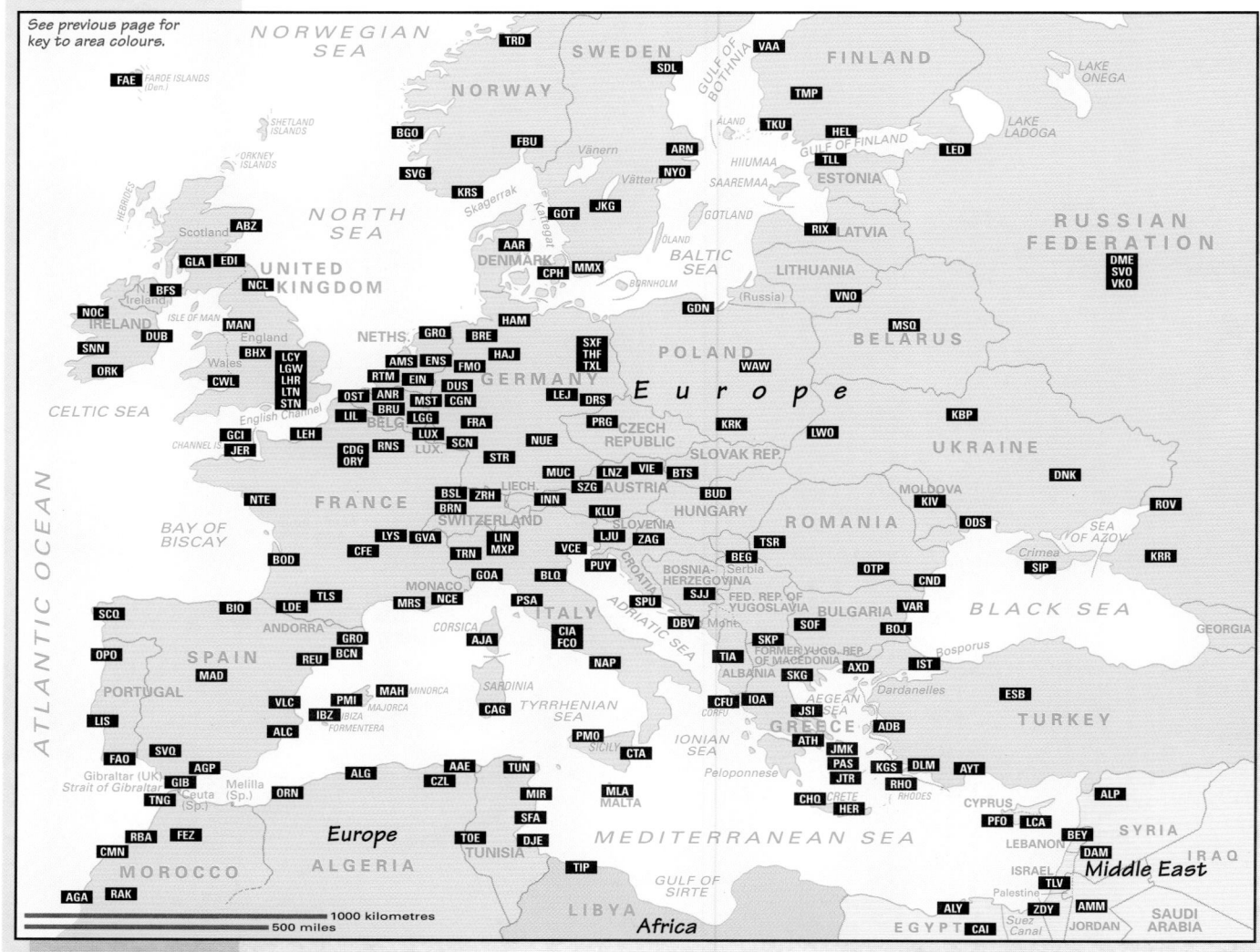

See previous page for key to area colours.

Europe and North Africa's main airports are shown here, together with their international three-letter code.

In some cases the city itself may have its own code in addition to those used by the airport or airports that serve it; these city codes are not included here.

AREA 2, EUROPE

AAE	Annaba, Algeria
AAR	Århus, Denmark
ABZ	Aberdeen, Scotland
ADB	Izmir (Smyrna), Turkey
AGA	Agadir, Morocco
AGP	Málaga, Spain
AJA	Ajaccio, France
ALC	Alicante, Spain
ALG	Alger (Algiers), Algeria
AMS	Amsterdam, The Netherlands
ANR	Antwerpen (Antwerp), Belgium
ARN	Stockholm Arlanda, Sweden
ATH	Athína (Athens), Greece
AXD	Alexandroúpoli, Greece
AYT	Antalya, Turkey
BCN	Barcelona, Spain
BEG	Beograd (Belgrade), Federal Republic of Yugoslavia
BFS	Belfast, Northern Ireland
BGO	Bergen, Norway
BHX	Birmingham, England
BIO	Bilbao, Spain
BLQ	Bologna, Italy
BOD	Bordeaux, France
BOJ	Burgas, Bulgaria
BRE	Bremen, Germany
BRN	Bern (Berne), Switzerland
BRU	Bruxelles/Brussel (Brussels), Belgium
BSL	Basel (Basle), Switzerland
BTS	Bratislava, Slovak Republic

BUD	Budapest, Hungary
CAG	Cágliari, Italy
CDG	Paris Charles de Gaulle, France
CFE	Clermont-Ferrand, France
CFU	Kérkira (Corfu), Greece
CGN	Köln (Cologne)-Bonn, Germany
CHQ	Haniá (Canea), Greece
CIA	Roma (Rome) Ciampino, Italy
CMN	Casablanca, Morocco
CND	Constanta, Romania
CPH	København (Copenhagen), Denmark
CTA	Catánia, Italy
CWL	Cardiff, Wales
CZL	Constantine, Algeria
DBV	Dubrovnik, Croatia
DJE	Jerba, Tunisia
DLM	Dalaman, Turkey
DME	Moskva (Moscow) Domodedovo, Russian Federation
DNK	Dnipropetrovs'k, Ukraine
DRS	Dresden, Germany
DUB	Dublin, Ireland
DUS	Düsseldorf, Germany
EDI	Edinburgh, Scotland
EIN	Eindhoven, The Netherlands
ENS	Enschede, The Netherlands
ESB	Ankara, Turkey
FAE	Vágar, Faroe Islands
FAO	Faro, Portugal
FBU	Oslo, Norway
FCO	Roma (Rome) Fiumicino/ Leonardo da Vinci, Italy
FEZ	Fès, Morocco
FMO	Münster-Osnabrück, Germany
FRA	Frankfurt am Main, Germany
GCI	Guernsey
GDN	Gdansk, Poland
GIB	Gibraltar
GLA	Glasgow, Scotland
GOA	Génova (Genoa), Italy
GOT	Göteborg (Gothenburg), Sweden
GRO	Girona, Spain
GRQ	Groningen, The Netherlands
GVA	Genève (Geneva), Switzerland
HAJ	Hannover, Germany

HAM	Hamburg, Germany
HEL	Helsinki (Helsingfors), Finland
HER	Iráklio (Herakleion), Greece
IBZ	Eivissa (Ibiza), Spain
INN	Innsbruck, Austria
IOA	Ioánina, Greece
IST	Istanbul, Turkey
JER	Jersey
JKG	Jönköping, Sweden
JMK	Míkonos, Greece
JSI	Skiathos, Greece
JTR	Thíra, Greece
KBP	Kyyiv (Kiev), Ukraine
KGS	Kos (Cos), Greece
KIV	Chisinau (Kishinev), Moldova
KLU	Klagenfurt, Austria
KRK	Kraków (Cracow), Poland
KRR	Krasnodar, Russian Federation
KRS	Kristiansand, Norway
LCY	London City, England
LDE	Lourdes, France
LED	Sankt-Peterburg (St Petersburg), Russian Federation
LEH	Le Havre, France
LEJ	Leipzig-Halle, Germany
LGG	Liège, Belgium
LGW	London Gatwick, England
LHR	London Heathrow, England
LIL	Lille, France
LIN	Milano (Milan) Linate, Italy
LIS	Lisboa (Lisbon), Portugal
LJU	Ljubljana, Slovenia
LNZ	Linz, Austria
LTN	London Luton, England
LUX	Luxembourg
LWO	L'viv (L'vov), Ukraine
LYS	Lyon, France
MAD	Madrid, Spain
MAH	Maó (Mahón), Spain
MAN	Manchester, England
MIR	Monastir, Tunisia
MLA	Malta
MMX	Malmö, Sweden
MRS	Marseille, France
MSQ	Minsk, Belarus
MST	Maastricht, The Netherlands

MUC	München (Munich), Germany
MXP	Milano (Milan) Malpensa, Italy
NAP	Nápoli (Naples), Italy
NCE	Nice, France
NCL	Newcastle, England
NOC	Horan (Knock), Ireland
NTE	Nantes, France
NUE	Nürnberg (Nuremberg), Germany
NYO	Stockholm Skavsta, Sweden
ODS	Odesa (Odessa), Ukraine
OPO	Porto (Oporto), Portugal
ORK	Cork, Ireland
ORN	Oran, Algeria
ORY	Paris: Orly, France
OST	Oostende (Ostend), Belgium
OTP	Bucuresti (Bucharest), Romania
PAS	Páros, Greece
PMI	Palma de Mallorca, Spain
PMO	Palermo, Italy
PRG	Praha (Prague), Czech Republic
PSA	Pisa, Italy
PUY	Pula, Croatia
RAK	Marrakech, Morocco
RBA	Rabat, Morocco
REU	Reus, Spain
RHO	Ródos (Rhodes), Greece
RIX	Riga, Latvia
RNS	Reims, France
ROV	Rostov-na-Donu, Russian Federation
RTM	Rotterdam, The Netherlands
SCN	Saarbrücken, Germany
SCQ	Santiago de Compostela, Spain
SDL	Sundsvall, Sweden
SFA	Sfax, Tunisia
SIP	Simferopol, Ukraine
SJJ	Sarajevo, Bosnia-Herzegovina
SKG	Thessaloníki, Greece
SKP	Skopje, Former Yugoslav Republic of Macedonia
SNN	Shannon, Ireland
SOF	Sofiya (Sofia), Bulgaria
SPU	Split, Croatia
STN	London Stansted, England
STR	Stuttgart, Germany
SVG	Stavanger, Norway
SVO	Moskva (Moscow) Sheremetyevo,

	Russian Federation
SVQ	Sevilla (Seville), Spain
SXF	Berlin Schönefeld, Germany
SZG	Salzburg, Austria
THF	Berlin Tempelhof, Germany
TIA	Tiranë (Tirana), Albania
TKU	Turku (Åbo), Finland
TLL	Tallinn, Estonia
TLS	Toulouse, France
TMP	Tampere, Finland
TNG	Tanger (Tangier), Morocco
TOE	Tozeur, Tunisia
TRD	Trondheim, Norway
TRN	Torino (Turin), Italy
TSR	Timisoara, Romania
TUN	Tunis, Tunisia
TXL	Berlin Tegel, Germany
VAA	Vaasa (Vasa), Finland
VAR	Varna, Bulgaria
VCE	Venézia (Venice), Italy
VIE	Wien (Vienna), Austria
VKO	Moskva (Moscow) Vnukovo, Russian Federation
VLC	Valencia, Spain
VNO	Vilnius, Lithuania
WAW	Warszawa (Warsaw), Poland
ZAG	Zagreb, Croatia
ZRH	Zürich, Switzerland

AREA 2, MIDDLE EAST

ALP	Halab (Aleppo), Syria
ALY	El Iskandarîya (Alexandria), Egypt
AMM	Amman, Jordan
BEY	Bayrut (Beirut), Lebanon
CAI	El Qâhira (Cairo), Egypt
DAM	Dimashq (Damascus), Syria
LCA	Larnaca, Cyprus
PFO	Pafos, Cyprus
TLV	Tel Aviv-Yafo, Israel
ZDY	Gaza, Palestine National Authority Region

AREA 2, AFRICA

TIP	Tarabulus (Tripoli), Libya

FLIGHT TIMES

Average flight times from London, New York and Singapore to other major destinations. Hours do not include stopover time, when necessary, from one destination to another.

▢ Less than 2 hours	▢ 5 hours – 8 hours 59 mins
▢ 2 hours – 4 hours 59 mins	▢ 9 hours – 14 hours 59 mins

▢ 15 hours – 24 hours 59 mins	
▢ 25 hours and over	

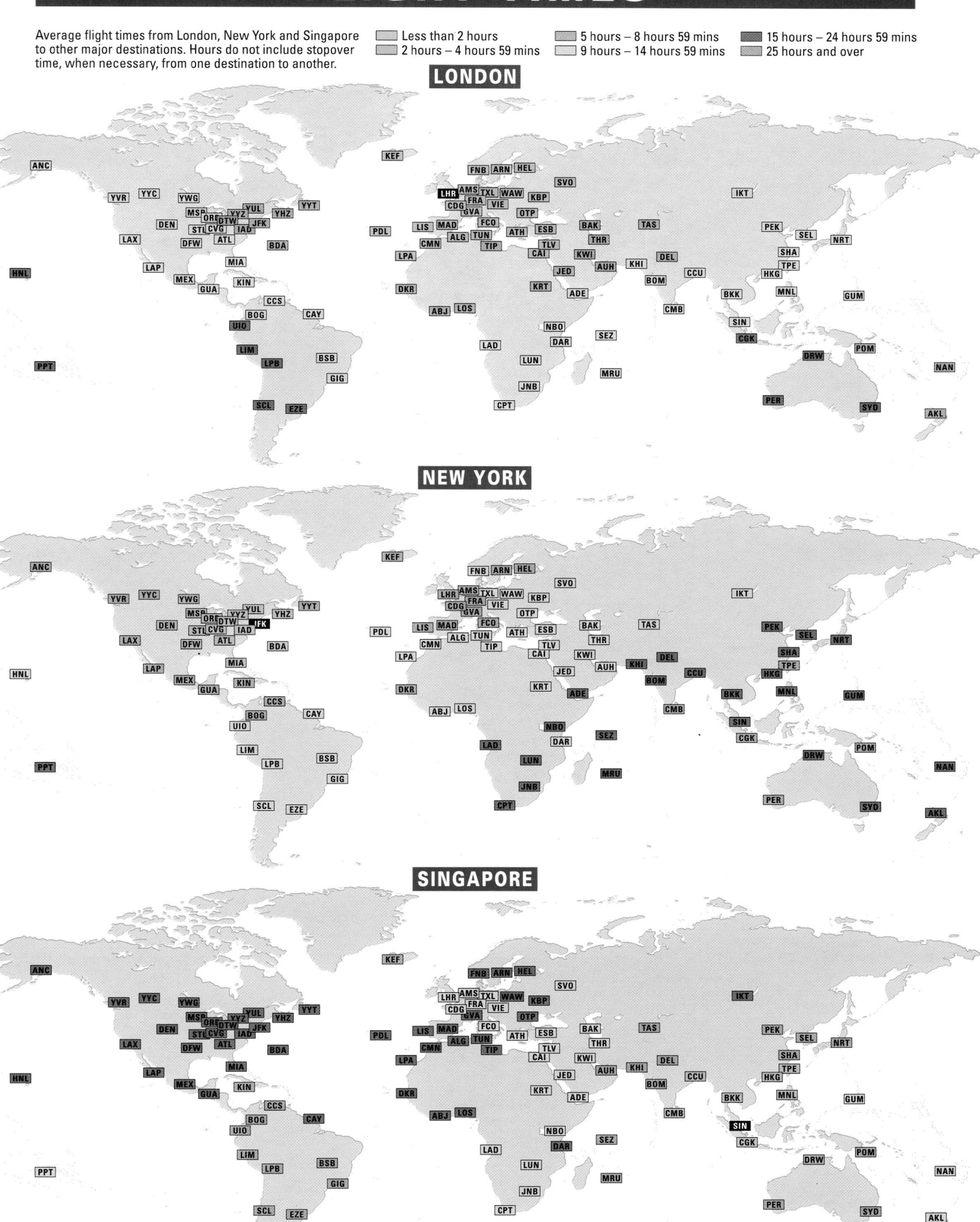

LONDON

NEW YORK

SINGAPORE

CRUISING

Cruising is one of the fastest-growing holiday choices in the world and, as new ships are built and new lines created, there is a continuing search for new ports of call. This map includes ports that are now beginning to be visited for the first time along with those which have featured in cruise brochures for decades. Key ports on the most popular river itineraries are also shown.

The main cruising areas are shown, as well as ports outside these areas that appear only on the schedules of world cruises.

Some of the places marked are accessable only by tender or, in some cases (notably Antarctica) by zodiac or other powered inflatable boat from the ship which will be anchored offshore.

The 'Round-the-World' cruise routes shown on the map are examples used by some passenger shipping companies. There are considerable variations, but cruise programmes offering 'Round-the-World' trips will call at many of the ports marked. Route variations might be caused due to size of ship, port-berthing facilities, weather conditions at particular times of year or marketing considerations.

Areas where the risk of bad weather is greatest are shaded different tints of *mauve*. Those areas experiencing bad weather throughout the year are shown in the darkest tint. Areas with shorter seasons of bad weather are in lighter tints.

Period of bad weather risk

JFMAMJJASOND

Maximum frequency of bad weather

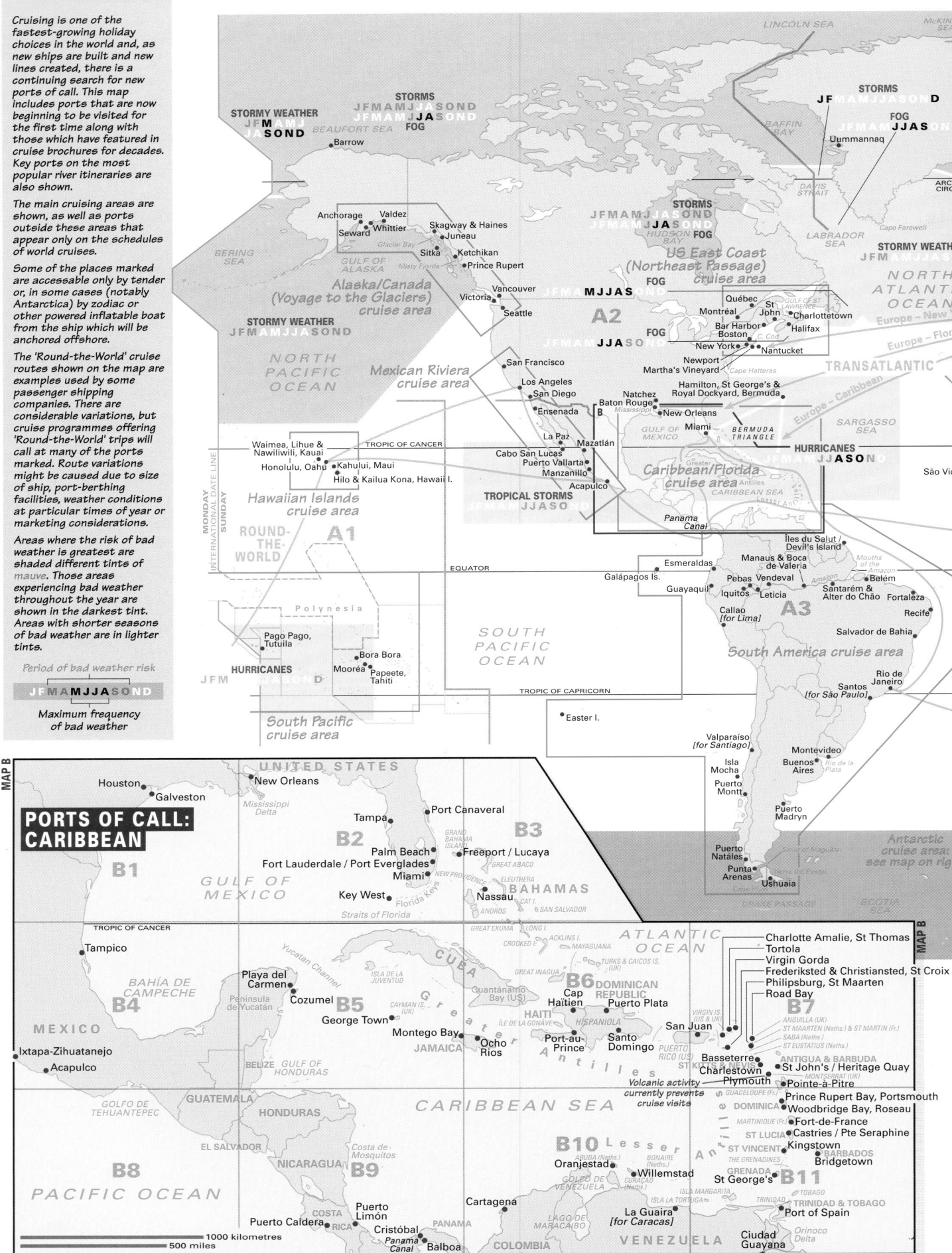

PORTS OF CALL: CARIBBEAN

CRUISING

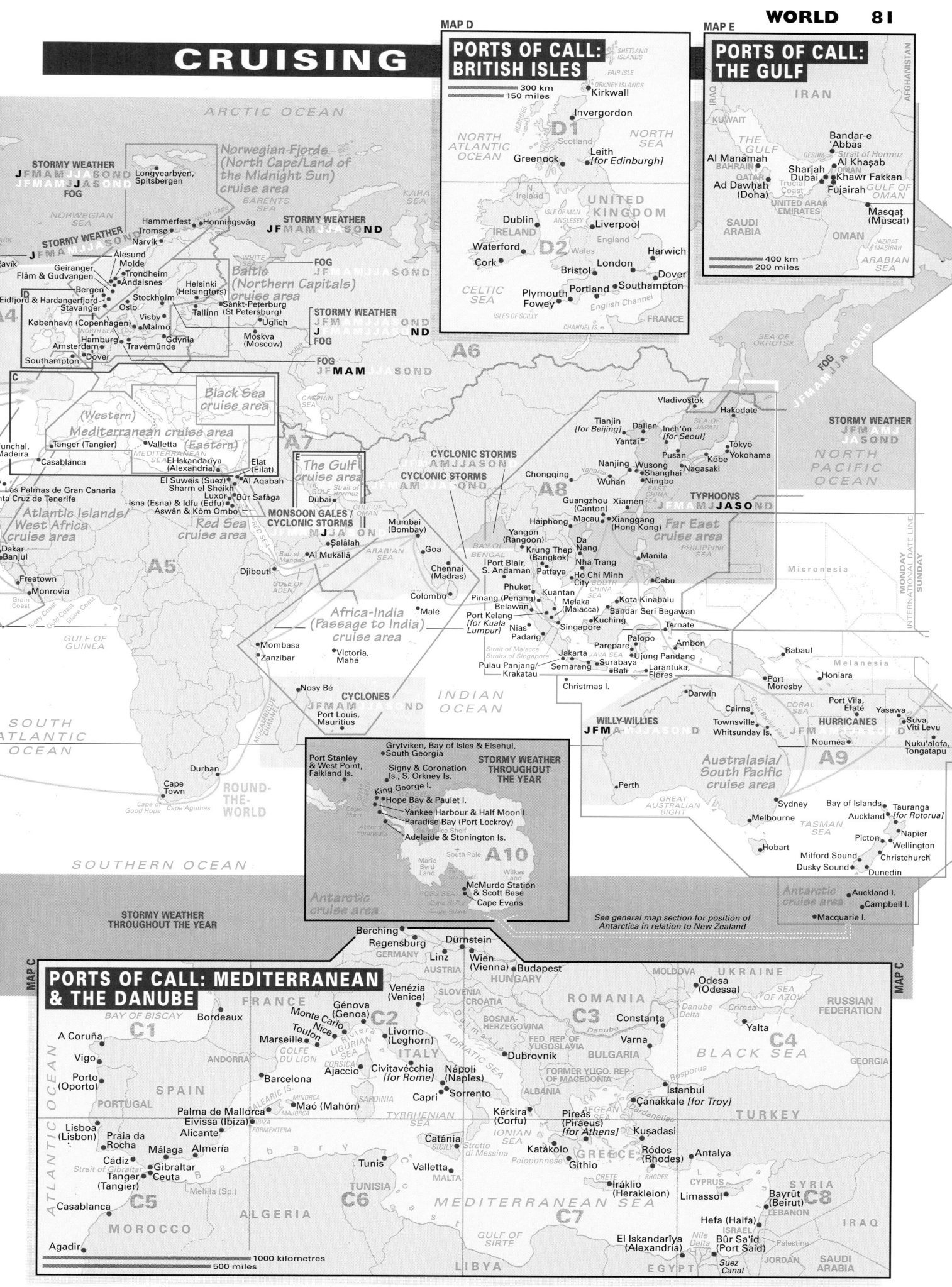

UNESCO NATURAL HERITAGE SITES

All properties which belong to the UNESCO World Heritage List are considered to be of world importance either because of their natural features or their significant man-made contribution to world culture. Sites for consideration of heritage status are submitted by the appropriate government ministry. UNESCO then considers each proposal under strict criteria and designates sites where appropriate.

Some countries are not signatories to the World Heritage Convention; sites in these countries cannot be considered for the World Heritage List.

There are two main categories of property: natural and cultural.

NATURAL SITES.
(i) Natural features: physical and biological formations of scientific importance;
(ii) Geological and physiographical formations: delineated areas which constitute the habitat of threatened species of animals or plants;
(iii) Natural sites: areas of universal value in terms of natural beauty and conservation.

Properties named in red are included on the list of World Heritage in Danger.

For further information, contact:

The World Heritage Centre, UNESCO, 7 place de Fontenoy, 75352 Paris 07, France.

Tel: +33 1 45 68 10 00.

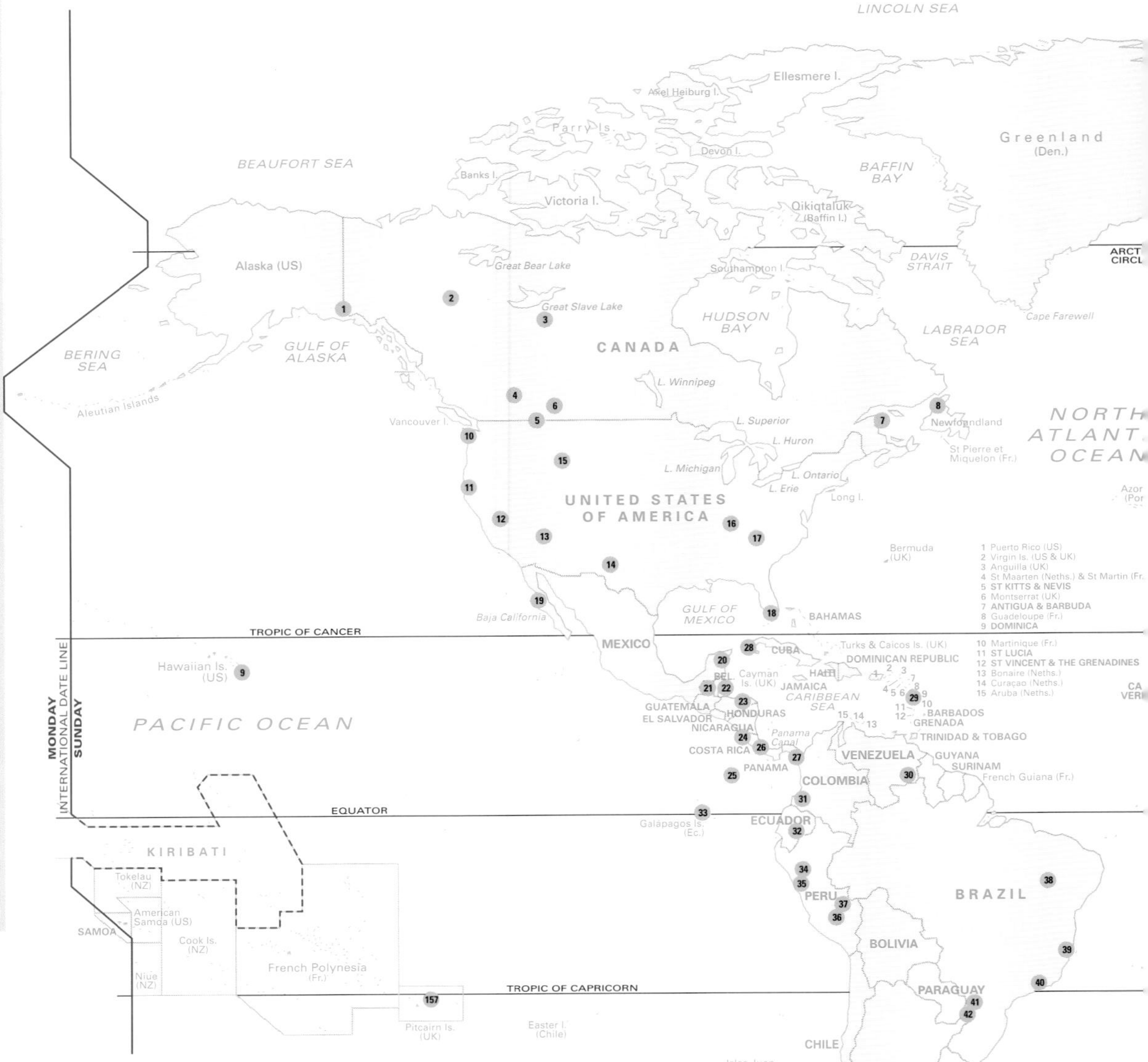

CHILE
Islas Juan Fernández (Chile)
URUGUAY
ARGENTINA
Falkland Is. (UK)
Tierra del Fuego
South Georgia (UK)
Cape Horn
DRAKE PASSAGE
SCOTIA SEA

CANADA & UNITED STATES
1 Kluane National Park, Glacier Bay National Park & Preserve, Wrangell-St Elias National Park & Preserve and Tatshenshini-Alsek Provincial Wilderness Park, Alaska/Yukon
2 Nahanni National Park, Northwest Territories
3 Wood Buffalo National Park, Northwest Territories/Alberta
4 Canadian Rocky Mountains Parks, British Columbia/Alberta
5 Waterton-Glacier International Peace Park, Alberta/Montana
6 Dinosaur Provincial Park, Alberta
7 Miquasha Park, Québec
8 Gros Morne National Park, Newfoundland
9 Hawaii Volcanoes National Park, Hawaii
10 Olympic National Park, Washington
11 Redwood National Park, California
12 Yosemite National Park, California
13 Grand Canyon National Park, Arizona
14 Carlsbad Caverns National Park, New Mexico
15 **Yellowstone National Park**, Wyoming
16 Mammoth Cave National Park, Kentucky
17 Great Smoky Mountains National Park, Tennessee/North Carolina
18 **Everglades National Park**, Florida

MEXICO, CENTRAL AMERICA & CARIBBEAN
19 El Vizcaíno whale sanctuary, Mexico
20 Reserva Biósfera Sian Ka'an, Mexico
21 Parque Nacional Tikal, Guatemala
22 Barrier Reef Reserve System, Belize
23 **Reserva Biósfera Río Plátano**, Honduras
24 Area de Conservácion Guanacaste, Costa Rica
25 Parque Nacional Isla del Coco, Costa Rica
26 Cordillera de Talamanca and Parque Internacional La Amistad, Costa Rica/Panama
27 Parque Nacional del Darién, Panama
28 Parque Nacional Desembarco del Granma, Cuba
29 Morne Trois Pitons National Park, Dominica

SOUTH AMERICA
30 Parque Nacional Canaima, Venezuela
31 Parque Nacional Los Katios, Colombia
32 **Parque Nacional Sangay**, Ecuador
33 Parque Nacional Galápagos
34 Parque Nacional Río Abiseo, Peru
35 Parque Nacional Huascarán, Peru
36 Santuario histórico Machu Picchu, Peru
37 Parque Nacional Manú, Peru
38 Parque Nacional Serra da Capivara, Brazil
39 Discovery Coast Atlantic forest reserves, Brazil
40 Southeast Atlantic forest reserves, Brazil
41 **Parque Nacional do Iguaçu**, Brazil
42 Parque Nacional de Iguazú, Argentina
43 Península Valdés, Argentina
44 Parque Nacional Los Glaciares, Argentina

EUROPE (including Atlantic islands and Turkey)
45 Lapponian area, Sweden
46 St Kilda, Scotland
47 Giant's Causeway and its coast, Northern Ireland
48 Messel Pit fossil site, Germany
49 Paris: banks of the Seine, France
50 Mont St Michel and its bay, France
51 Golfe de Girolata, Golfe de Porto, les Calanche and Réserve Naturelle Scandola, Corsica, France
52 Mont Perdu/Monte Perdido, France/Spain
53 Ibiza: biodiversity and culture, Spain
54 Parque Nacional Coto de Doñana, Spain
55 Laurisilva of Madeira
56 Parque Nacional de Garajonay, Gomera, Canary Is.
57 Bialowieza Forest & Belovezhskaya Pushcha, Poland/Belarus
58 Aggtelek Caves anzd the Slovak karst, Hungary/Slovak Republic
59 Skocjan Caves, Slovenia
60 Plitvice Lakes National Park, Croatia
61 Durmitor National Park, Federal Republic of Yugoslavia
62 **Kotor and its gulf**, Federal Republic of Yugoslavia
63 Ohrid Lake and its region, Former Yugoslav Republic of Macedonia
64 Danube Delta, Romania
65 **Srebarna Nature Reserve**, Bulgaria
66 Pirin National Park, Bulgaria
67 Metéora, Greece
68 Olimbía (Olympía): archaeological site, Greece
69 Áthos, Greece
70 Hierapolis-Pamukkale, Turkey
71 Göreme National Park and Cappadocia rock sites, Turkey

FORMER SOVIET UNION
72 Western Caucasus, Russian Federation
73 Komi virgin forests, Russian Federation
74 Golden Mountains of Altay, Russian Federation
75 Lake Baikal, Russian Federation
76 Kamchatka volcanoes, Russian Federation

AFRICA
77 **Ichkeul National Park**, Tunisia
78 Tassili n'Ajjer, Algeria
79 Bandiagara Cliffs: Land of the Dogon, Mali
80 Banc d'Arguin National Park, Mauritania
81 Parc national des Oiseaux du Djoudj (Djoudj National Bird Sanctuary), Senegal
82 Parc national du Niokolo Koba, Senegal
83 **Mount Nimba Nature Reserve** Guinea/Côte d'Ivoire
84 Parc national de la Komoé, Côte d'Ivoire
85 Parc national de Taï, Côte d'Ivoire
86 Parc national du "W", Niger
87 **Aïr and Ténéré Natural Reserves**, Niger
88 **Simien National Park**, Ethiopia

UNESCO NATURAL HERITAGE SITES

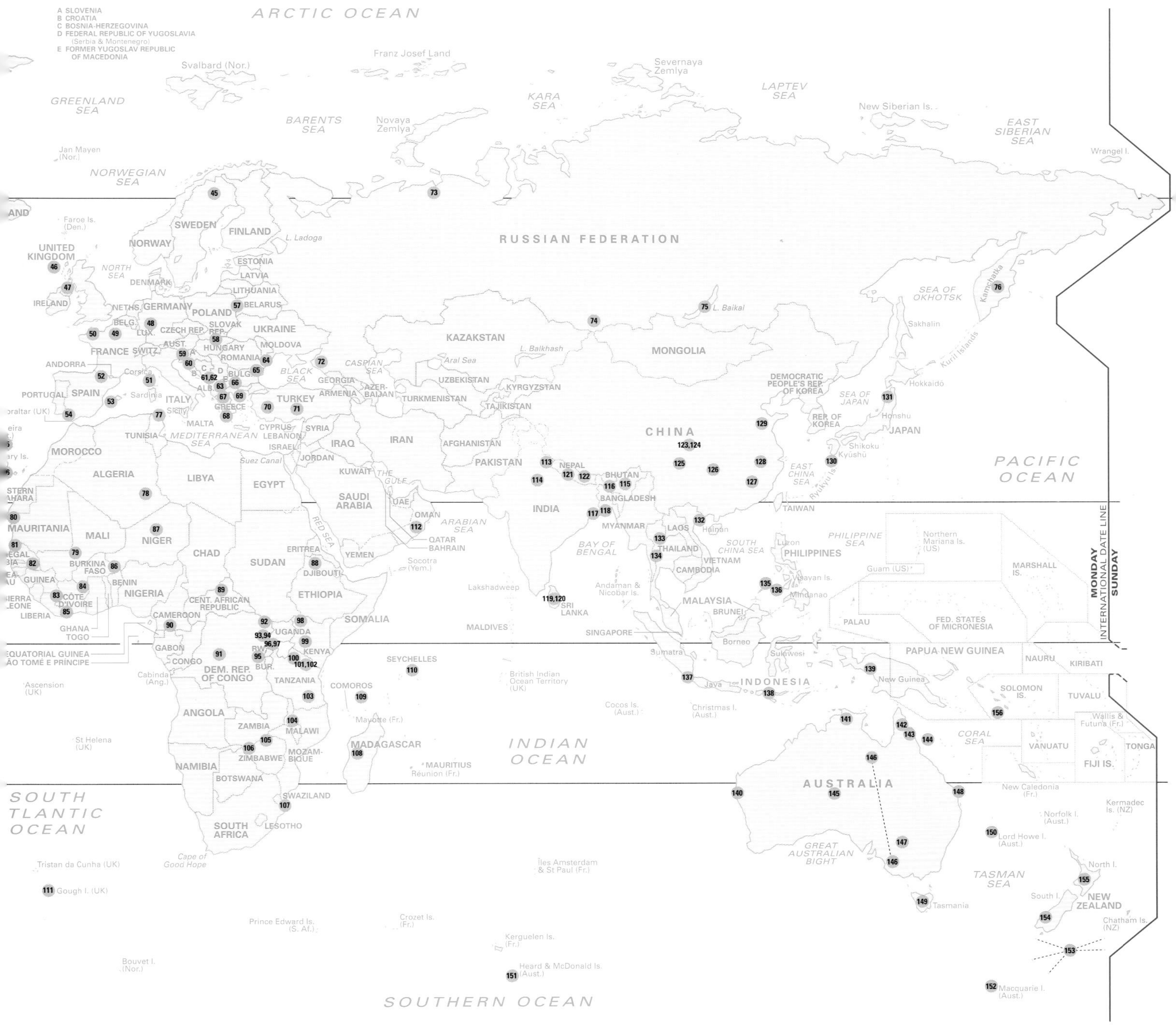

A SLOVENIA
B CROATIA
C BOSNIA-HERZEGOVINA
D FEDERAL REPUBLIC OF YUGOSLAVIA
  (Serbia & Montenegro)
E FORMER YUGOSLAV REPUBLIC
  OF MACEDONIA

[World map with numbered site locations]

89 Parc national de Manovo-Gounda-St Floris
Central African Republic
90 Réserve du Dja, Cameroon
91 Parc national de la Salonga, Dem. Rep. of Congo
92 Parc national de la Garamba, Dem. Rep. of Congo
93 Réserve du Okapi, Dem. Rep. of Congo
94 Parc national des Virunga, Dem. Rep. of Congo
95 Parc national du Kahuzi-Biega, Dem. Rep. of Congo
96 Ruwenzori Mountains National Park, Uganda
97 Bwindi National Park, Uganda
98 Sibiloi and Central Island National Parks, Kenya
99 Mount Kenya National Park and forest, Kenya
100 Serengeti National Park, Tanzania
101 Ngorongoro Conservation Area, Tanzania
102 Kilimanjaro National Park, Tanzania
103 Selous Game Reserve, Tanzania
104 Lake Malawi National Park, Malawi
105 Mana Pools National Park and Sapi & Chewore
safari areas, Zimbabwe
106 Victoria Falls (Mosi-oa-Tunya), Zambia/Zimbabwe
107 Greater St Lucia Wetland Park, South Africa
108 Réserve du Tsingy Bemaraha, Madagascar
109 Groupe d'Aldabra, Seychelles
110 Vallée de Mai Nature Reserve, Seychelles
111 Gough Island Wildlife Reserve

MIDDLE EAST
112 Arabian Oryx Sanctuary, Oman

SOUTH, EAST & SE ASIA
113 Nanda Devi National Park, India
114 Keoladeo National Park, India
115 Manas Wildlife Sanctuary, India
116 Kaziranga National Park, India
117 Sundarbans National Park, India
118 Sundarbans, Bangladesh
119 Dambulla Golden Rock Temple, Sri Lanka
120 Sinharaja Forest Reserve, Sri Lanka
121 Royal Chitwan National Park, Nepal
122 Sagarmatha National Park, Nepal
123 Jiuzhaigou Valley Scenic and Historic Interest
Area, Sichuan, China
124 Huanglong Scenic and Historic Interest Area,
Sichuan, China
125 Emei Shan and Leshan Giant Buddha, Sichuan,
China
126 Wulingyuan Scenic and Historic Interest Area,
Hunan, China
127 Wuyi Shan, Fujian, China
128 Huang Shan, Anhui, China
129 Tai Shan, Shandong, China
130 Yaku-shima, Japan
131 Shirakami-Sanchi, Japan
132 Ha Long Bay, Vietnam
133 Sukhothai and its region: historic towns, Thailand
134 Thung Yai-Huai Kha Khaeng Wildlife Sanctuaries,
Thailand

135 Puerto-Princesa Subterranean River National Park,
the Philippines
136 Tubbataha Reef Marine Park, the Philippines
137 Ujung Kulon National Park and Krakatau Nature
Reserve, Indonesia
138 Komodo National Park, Indonesia
139 Lorentz National Park, Indonesia

AUSTRALASIA & PACIFIC
140 Shark Bay, Australia
141 Kakadu National Park, Australia
142 Queensland wet tropics, Australia
143 Central eastern rainforest reserves, Australia
144 Great Barrier Reef, Australia
145 Uluru-Kata Tjuta National Park, Australia
146 Naracoorte & Riversleigh: fossil mammal sites,
Australia
147 Willandra Lakes region, Australia
148 Fraser Island, Australia
149 Tasmanian wilderness, Australia
150 Lord Howe island group, Australia
151 Heard and McDonald Islands
152 Macquarie Island
153 New Zealand Sub-Antarctic islands
154 Te Wahipounamu-Southwest New Zealand
155 Tongariro National Park, New Zealand
156 East Rennell, Solomon Islands
157 Henderson Island

UNESCO CULTURAL HERITAGE SITES

All properties which belong to the UNESCO World Heritage List are considered to be of world importance either because of their natural features or their significant man-made contribution to world culture. Sites for consideration of heritage status are submitted by the appropriate government ministry. UNESCO then considers each proposal under strict criteria and designates sites where appropriate.

Some countries are not signatories to the World Heritage Convention; sites in these countries cannot be considered for the World Heritage List.

There are two main categories of property: natural and cultural.

CULTURAL SITES.
(i) Monuments: including sculptures, memorial stones, obelisks, cave paintings and inscriptions;
(ii) Groups of buildings: these can be separated or connected but are usually set in a unique landscape;
(iii) Sites of anthropological or archaeological importance.

Properties named in red are included on the list of World Heritage in Danger.

The Organisation of World Heritage Cities (OWHC) was established in 1993, with the aim of assisting member cities in adapting and improving their management methods in relation to any site included as a cultural property on the UNESCO World Heritage List located within the city.

World Heritage Cities are named on the map.

For further information, contact:

The World Heritage Centre, UNESCO,
7 place de Fontenoy,
75352 Paris 07,
France.

Tel: +33 1 45 68 10 00.

CANADA & UNITED STATES
1 Anthony Island, British Columbia
2 Head-Smashed-In Buffalo Jump, Alberta
3 Québec: historic area
4 Lunenburg: old city, Nova Scotia
5 L'Anse aux Meadows Historic Park, Newfoundland
6 Mesa Verde National Park, Colorado
7 Chaco Culture National Historical Park, New Mexico
8 Pueblo de Taos, New Mexico
9 Cahokia Mounds State Historic Site, Illinois
10 Charlottesville: Monticello and University of Virginia, Virginia
11 Philadelphia: Independence Hall, Pennsylvania
12 Statue of Liberty, New Jersey

MEXICO, CENTRAL AMERICA & CARIBBEAN
13 Sierra de la San Francisco: rock paintings, Mexico
14 Paquimé Casas Grandes: archaeological site, Mexico
15 Zacatecas: historic centre, Mexico
16 Guadalajara: Hospicio Cabañas, Mexico
17 Guanajuato: historic town and adjacent mines, Mexico
18 Querétaro: historic monuments, Mexico
19 Teotihuacán: pre-Hispanic city, Mexico
20 El Tajín: pre-Hispanic city, Mexico
21 Morelia: historic centre, Mexico
22 Ciudad de México (Mexico City): historic centre and Xochimilco, Mexico
23 Xochicalco: archaeological site, Mexico
24 Popocatépetl: monasteries, Mexico
25 Puebla: historic centre, Mexico
26 Tlacotalpan: historic monuments, Mexico
27 Oaxaca: historic centre and Monte Albán: archaeological site, Mexico
28 Palenque: pre-Hispanic city and National Park, Mexico
29 Campeche: historic fortified town, Mexico

30 Uxmal: pre-Hispanic city, Mexico
31 Chichén-Itzá: pre-Hispanic city, Mexico
32 Antigua, Guatemala
33 Quiriguá: archaeological park and ruins, Guatemala
34 Copán: Maya site, Honduras
35 Joya de Cerén: archaeological site, El Salvador
36 Portobelo and San Lorenzo: fortifications, Panama
37 Ciudad de Panamá (Panama City): historic district and the Salón Bolívar, Panama
38 Viñales valley, Cuba
39 La Habana (Havana): old town and its fortifications, Cuba
40 Trinidad and Valley de los Ingenios, Cuba
41 Santiago de Cuba: San Pedro de la Roca Castle, Cuba
42 Sans-Souci citadel and Ramiers Historic Park, Haiti
43 Santo Domingo: colonial city, Dominican Republic
44 La Fortaleza and San Juan: historic sites, Puerto Rico
45 Brimstone Hill Fortress National Park, St Kitts and Nevis
46 Willemstad: historic area, inner city and harbour, Curaçao

SOUTH AMERICA
47 Coro: town and its port, Venezuela
48 Cartagena: port, fortress and monuments, Colombia
49 Mompós: historic centre, Colombia
50 Parque Arqueológico Nacional Tierradentro, Colombia
51 Parque Arqueológico San Agustín, Colombia
52 Quito: old city, Ecuador
53 Cuenca: historic centre, Ecuador
54 Parque Nacional Río Abiseo, Peru
55 Chan Chan: archaeological area, Peru
56 Chavin: archaeological site, Peru
57 Lima: historic centre, Peru

58 Santuario histórico Machu Picchu, Peru
59 Cuzco: old city, Peru
60 Nazca: geoglyphs and Pampas de Juma, Peru
61 Potosí, Bolivia
62 Sucre: historic city, Bolivia
63 El Fuerte de Samaipata, Bolivia
64 Chiquitos Jesuit missions, Bolivia
65 Jesús and Trinidad: Jesuit missions, Paraguay
66 Brasília, Brazil
67 Parque Nacional Serra da Capivara, Brazil
68 São Luís: historic centre, Brazil
69 Olinda: historic centre, Brazil
70 Salvador de Bahia: historic centre, Brazil
71 Diamantina: historic centre, Brazil
72 Ouro Prêto: historic town, Brazil
73 Congonhas: Sanctuary of Bom Jesus, Brazil
74 São Miguel: Jesuit mission ruins, Brazil; Loreto, San Ignacio Miní, Santa Ana & Santa Maria Mayor: Guaraní Jesuit missions, Argentina
75 Colonia del Sacramento: historic quarter, Uruguay
76 Cueva de las Manos, Río Pinturas, Argentina
77 Parque Nacional Rapa Nui, Easter Island

EUROPE* (including Atlantic islands)
78 San Cristóbal de la Laguna, Tenerife, Canary Is.
79 Angra do Heroísmo: central area, Terceira, Azores
80 Urnes: stave church, Norway
81 Røros: mining town, Norway
82 Alta: rock drawings, Norway
83 Lapponian area, Sweden
84 Luleå: Gammelstad church town, Sweden
85 Rauma: old town, Finland
86 Sammallahdenmäki: Bronze Age burial site, Finland
87 Petäjävesi: old church, Finland
88 Verla: groundwood and board mill, Finland

FORMER SOVIET UNION*
89 Solovetskiye Ostrova: cultural and historic

ensemble, Russian Federation
90 Khizi Pogost, Russian Federation
91 Mtskheta: historic church, Georgia
92 Haghpat: monastery, Armenia
93 Mary: Merv State Historical and Cultural Park, Turkmenistan
94 Itchan Kala, Uzbekistan
95 Bukhoro (Bukhara): historic centre, Uzbekistan

AFRICA*
96 Thebes: ancient city and necropolis, Egypt
97 Abu Simbel to Philae: Nubian monuments, Egypt
98 Aksum: archaeological site, Ethiopia
99 Fasil Ghebbi & Gonder monuments, Ethiopia
100 Lalibela: rock-hewn churches, Ethiopia
101 Awash Lower Valley, Ethiopia
102 Tiya: carved steles, Ethiopia
103 Omo Lower Valley, Ethiopia
104 Tadrart Acacus: rock-art sites, Libya
105 Tassili n'Ajjer, Algeria
106 Chinguetti, Ouadane, Oualata and Tichitt: trading and religious centres, Mauritania
107 Timbuktu, Mali
108 Djenne: old towns, Mali
109 Île de Gorée, Senegal
110 Ashante traditional buildings, Ghana
111 Accra and Volta areas: forts and castles, Ghana
112 Abomey: royal palaces, Benin
113 Sukur: cultural landscape, Nigeria

Map labels:
LINCOLN SEA
Ellesmere I.
Axel Heiburg I.
Greenland (Den.)
Parry Is.
Devon I.
BEAUFORT SEA
Banks I.
BAFFIN BAY
Qikiqtaluk (Baffin I.)
Victoria I.
Great Bear Lake
DAVIS STRAIT
Alaska (US)
Southampton I.
ARCTIC CIRC.
Great Slave Lake
BERING SEA
GULF OF ALASKA
HUDSON BAY
CANADA
Cape Farewell
LABRADOR SEA
Aleutian Islands
L. Winnipeg
NORTH ATLANTIC OCEAN
Vancouver I.
L. Superior
Québec
Newfoundland
St Pierre et Miquelon (Fr.)
UNITED STATES OF AMERICA
L. Michigan
L. Huron
L. Ontario
Lunenburg
Angra do Heroísmo
Azores (Por.)
L. Erie
Long I.
Bermuda (UK)

1 DOMINICAN REPUBLIC
2 Puerto Rico (US)
3 Virgin Is. (US & UK)
4 Anguilla (UK)
5 St Maarten (Neths.) I & St Martin (Fr.)
6 ST KITTS & NEVIS
7 Montserrat (UK)
8 ANTIGUA & BARBUDA
9 Guadeloupe (Fr.)
10 DOMINICA
11 Martinique (Fr.)
12 ST LUCIA
13 ST VINCENT & THE GRENADINES
14 Bonaire (Neths.)
15 Curaçao (Neths.)
16 Aruba (Neths.)

MONDAY / INTERNATIONAL DATE LINE / SUNDAY
Hawaiian Is. (US)
PACIFIC OCEAN
TROPIC OF CANCER
Baja California
MEXICO
Zacatecas
GULF OF MEXICO
La Habana (Havana)
BAHAMAS
CUBA
HAITI
Turks & Caicos Is. (UK)
Cayman Is. (UK)
Trinidad
San Juan
Sto. Domingo
JAMAICA
BELIZE
GUATEMALA
HONDURAS
EL SALVADOR
NICARAGUA
Willemstad
Cartagena
Coro & La Vela
BARBADOS
GRENADA
TRINIDAD & TOBAGO
COSTA RICA
PANAMA
Ciudad de Panamá (Panama City)
Mompós
VENEZUELA
GUYANA
SURINAM
French Guiana (Fr.)
COLOMBIA
Galápagos Is. (Ec.)
Quito
ECUADOR
São Luís
Olinda
BRAZIL
Salvador de Bahia
Lima
Cuzco
PERU
Brasília
BOLIVIA
Sucre
Potosí
Ouro Prêto
PARAGUAY
KIRIBATI
Tokelau (NZ)
American Samoa (US)
SAMOA
Cook Is. (NZ)
Niue (NZ)
French Polynesia (Fr.)
TROPIC OF CAPRICORN
Pitcairn Is. (UK)
Easter I. (Chile)
Islas Juan Fernández (Chile)
CHILE
URUGUAY
Colonia del Sacramento
ARGENTINA
Falkland Is. (UK)
Tierra del Fuego
Cape Horn
DRAKE PASSAGE
South Georgia (UK)
SCOTIA SEA

MAP A
Guanajuato
Querétaro
BAHÍA DE CAMPECHE
Morelia
Cd. de México (Mexico City)
Puebla
MEXICO
Yucatán Peninsula
Tlacotalpan
Oaxaca
BELIZE
PACIFIC OCEAN
GUATEMALA
HONDURAS
Antigua
EL SALVADOR
NICARAG.
EQUATOR
1000 km
500 miles

UNESCO CULTURAL HERITAGE SITES

A SLOVENIA
B CROATIA
C BOSNIA-HERZEGOVINA
D FEDERAL REPUBLIC OF YUGOSLAVIA
   (Serbia & Montenegro)
E FORMER YUGOSLAV REPUBLIC
   OF MACEDONIA

Map with numbered UNESCO Cultural Heritage Sites across the world, including inset Map B of South Asia

---

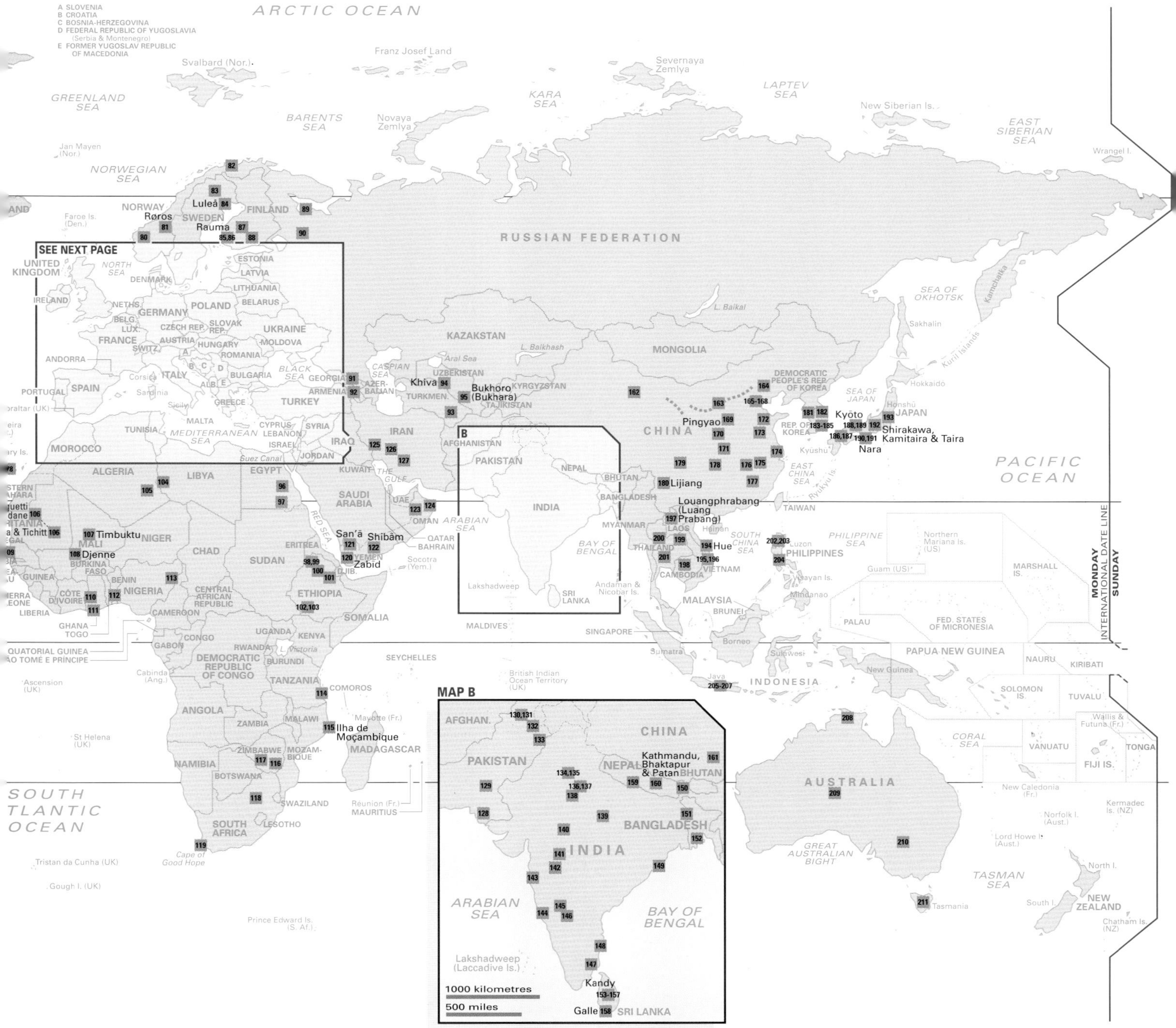

114 Kilwa Kisiwani and Songo Mnara: ruins, Tanzania
115 Ilha de Moçambique, Mozambique
116 Great Zimbabwe National Monument, Zimbabwe
117 Khami Ruins National Monument, Zimbabwe
118 Sterkfontein, Swartkrans, Kromdraai and environs: fossil hominid sites, South Africa
119 Robben Island, South Africa

MIDDLE EAST*
120 Zabid: historic town, Yemen
121 San'a: old city, Yemen
122 Shibam: old walled city, Yemen
123 Bahla: fort, Oman
124 Bat, Al-Khutm and Al-Ayn: archaeological sites, Oman
125 Tchogha Zanbil: ziggurat and complex, Iran
126 Esfahan (Isfahan): Meidam Emam, Iran
127 Persepolis: ancient city, Iran

SOUTH, EAST & SE ASIA
128 Thatta: historical monuments, Pakistan
129 Mohenjodaro: archaeological site, Pakistan
130 Takht-i-Bakhi: Buddhist ruins; and Sahr-i-Bahlol: remains of city, Pakistan
131 Taxila: archaeological site, Pakistan
132 Rohtas: fort, Pakistan
133 Lahore: fort and Shalimar Gardens, Pakistan
134 Delhi: Humayun's Tomb, India
135 Delhi: Qutb Minar and its monuments, India
136 Agra Fort, India

137 Taj Mahal, Agra, India
138 Fatehpur Sikri: Mongol city, India
139 Khajuraho: group of monuments, India
140 Sanchi: Buddhist monastery, India
141 Ajanta Caves, India
142 Ellora Caves, India
143 Elephanta Caves, India
144 Goa: churches and convents, India
145 Pattadakal: group of monuments, India
146 **Hampi: group of monuments**, India
147 Thanjavur: Brihadisvara Temple, India
148 Mahabalipuram (Mamallapuram): group of monuments, India
149 Konarak: Sun Temple, India
150 Darjeeling Himalayan Railway, India
151 Paharpur: ruins of the Buddhist Vihara, Bangladesh
152 Bagerhat: historic city, Bangladesh
153 Anuradhapura: sacred city, Sri Lanka
154 Sigiriya: ancient city, Sri Lanka
155 Polonnaruwa: ancient city, Sri Lanka
156 Dambulla Golden Rock Temple, Sri Lanka
157 Kandy: sacred city, Sri Lanka
158 Galle: old town and its fortifications, Sri Lanka
159 Lumbini: birthplace of Lord Buddha, Nepal
160 Kathmandu valley, Nepal
161 Lhasa: Potala Palace, Tibet, China
162 Mogao Caves, Gansu, China
163 Great Wall, China
164 Chengde: mountain resort and outlying temples, Hebei, China
165 Beijing (Peking): Imperial Palace of the Ming

and Qing Dynasties, China
166 Beijing (Peking): Imperial Summer Palace, China
167 Beijing (Peking): Temple of Heaven, China
168 Zhoukoudian: Peking Man site, China
169 Pingyao: ancient city, Shanxi, China
170 Xi'an area: Mausoleum of the first Qin Emperor, Shaanxi, China
171 Wudangshan: ancient building complex, Hubei, China
172 Tai Shan, Shandong, China
173 Qufu: temple & cemetery of Confucius and Kong family mansion, Shandong, China
174 Suzhou: classical gardens, Jiangsu, China
175 Huang Shan, Anhui, China
176 Lu Shan, Jiangxi, China
177 Wuyi Shan, Fujian, China
178 Dazu rock carvings, Chongqing, China
179 Emei Shan and Leshan Giant Buddha, Sichuan, China
180 Lijiang: old town, Yunnan, China
181 Soul (Seoul): Ch'angdokkung Palace Complex, Republic of Korea
182 Chongmyo Shrine, Republic of Korea
183 Haeinsa Temple, Republic of Korea
184 Kyongju: Hwasong Fortress, Republic of Korea
185 Sokkuram Grotto and Pulguksa Temple, Republic of Korea
186 Hiroshima: Peace Memorial, Japan
187 Itsukushima Shrine, Japan
188 Himeji, Japan

189 Kyoto: ancient city monuments, Japan
190 Horyu-ji: Buddhist monuments, Japan
191 Nara: historic monuments, Japan
192 Shirakawa-Go and Gokayama: historic villages, Japan
193 Nikko: shrines and temples, Japan
194 Hue: monuments complex, Vietnam
195 Hoi An: ancient town, Vietnam
196 My Son Sanctuary, Vietnam
197 Louangphrabang (Luang Prabang), Laos
198 **Angkor**, Cambodia
199 Ban Chiang: archaeological site, Thailand
200 Sukhothai and its region: historic towns, Thailand
201 Ayutthaya and its region: historic towns, Thailand
202 Vigan: historic town, the Philippines
203 Cordillera Central: rice terraces, the Philippines
204 Manila: Baroque churches, the Philippines
205 Borobodur: temple compound, Indonesia
206 Prambanan: temple compound, Indonesia
207 Sangiran: early man site, Indonesia

AUSTRALASIA & PACIFIC
208 Kakadu National Park, Australia
209 Uluru National Park, Australia
210 Willandra Lakes region, Australia
211 Tasmanian wilderness, Australia

* See next page for other sites in these areas

UNESCO CULTURAL HERITAGE SITES

THE SEVEN WONDERS OF THE ANCIENT WORLD

A **Statue of Zeus, Olympia** 9-metre statue of the Greek god covered in gold and ivory

B **Temple of Artemis, Ephesus** Marble temple in honour of goddess of hunting and the moon

C **Mausoleum, Halikarnassos** Tomb of Mausolus built by his widow

D **Colossus of Rhodes** 32-metre high bronze statue of the sun god Helios

E **Pharos of Alexandria** World's first known lighthouse, 122 metres high

F **Egyptian Pyramids** Oldest of the ancient wonders and the only one surviving today

G **Hanging Gardens of Babylon** Series of terraces of trees and flowers along the banks of the Euphrates

---

ATLANTIC OCEAN

NORTH SEA

BALTIC SEA

BLACK SEA

MEDITERRANEAN SEA

TYRRHENIAN SEA

ADRIATIC SEA

IONIAN SEA

AEGEAN SEA

CELTIC SEA

BAY OF BISCAY

GULF OF SIRTE

SEA OF AZOV

RUSSIAN FEDERATION

UKRAINE

BELARUS

POLAND

GERMANY

FRANCE

SPAIN

PORTUGAL

ITALY

GREECE

TURKEY

NORWAY

SWEDEN

FINLAND

DENMARK

NETHERLANDS

BELGIUM

UNITED KINGDOM

IRELAND

ESTONIA

LATVIA

LITHUANIA

ROMANIA

MOLDOVA

BULGARIA

HUNGARY

AUSTRIA

SWITZERLAND

CZECH REP.

SLOVAK REP.

SLOVENIA

CROATIA

BOSNIA-HERZEGOVINA

FEDERAL REPUBLIC OF YUGOSLAVIA

FORMER YUGOSLAV REPUBLIC OF MACEDONIA

ALBANIA

SYRIA

IRAQ

SAUDI ARABIA

JORDAN

LEBANON

ISRAEL

CYPRUS

EGYPT

LIBYA

TUNISIA

ALGERIA

MOROCCO

GEORGIA

LUX.

UNESCO CULTURAL HERITAGE SITES

Properties named in red are included on the list of World Heritage in Danger.

Cities named on the map are members of the Organisation of World Heritage Cities (OWHC). See previous page for explanation.

EUROPE (including Turkey)

1 Bergen: Bryggen area, Norway
2 Tanum: rock carvings, Sweden
3 Karlskrona: naval city, Sweden
4 Engelsberg: ironworks, Sweden
5 Birka and Hovgården: archaeological sites, Sweden
6 Drottningholm Palace, Sweden
7 Stockholm: Skogskyrkogarden, Sweden
8 Visby: Hanseatic town and former Viking site, Sweden
9 Helsinki (Helsingfors): Suomenlinna Fortress, Finland
10 Roskilde: cathedral, Denmark
11 Jelling: mounds, runic stones and church, Denmark
12 Skellig Michael: monastic complex, Ireland
13 Brú Na Bóinne: archaeological ensemble at the bend of the Boyne, Ireland
14 Neolithic Orkney, Scotland
15 Edinburgh: old and new towns, Scotland
16 Castles and town walls of King Edward, northwest Wales
17 Hadrian's Wall, England
18 Durham: castle and cathedral, England
19 Studley Royal Park and Fountains Abbey ruins, England
20 Ironbridge Gorge, England
21 Bath, England
22 Stonehenge, Avebury and associated megalithic sites, England
23 Blenheim Palace, England
24 London: Tower of London, England
25 London: Westminster Palace, Abbey of Westminster and St Margaret's Church, England
26 London: Maritime Greenwich, England
27 Canterbury: cathedral, St Augustine's Abbey and St Martin's Church, England
28 D.F. Wouda steam pumping station, The Netherlands
29 Schokland: prehistoric settlements, The Netherlands
30 Droogmakerij de Beemster (Beemster Polder), The Netherlands
31 Amsterdam: defence line, The Netherlands
32 Kinderdijk-Elshout: mill network, The Netherlands
33 Belfries of Flanders and Wallonia, Belgium
34 Flemish Béguinages, Belgium
35 Bruxelles/Brussel (Brussels): Grand-Place, Belgium
36 Canal du Centre: four boat-lifts and environs, La Louvière and La Rœulx, Belgium
37 Luxembourg-Ville: old quarters and fortifications
38 Lübeck: Hanseatic city, Germany
39 Berlin: Museumsinsel, Berlin
40 Berlin and Potsdam: palaces and parks, Germany
41 Eisleben and Wittenberg: Luther memorials, Germany
42 Dessau and Weimar: Bauhaus buildings, Germany
43 Weimar: classical city, Germany
44 Wartburg: castle, Germany
45 Quedlinburg: Collegiate church, castle and old town, Germany
46 Goslar: historic town and Rammelsberg mines, Germany
47 Hildesheim: St Mary's Cathedral and St Michael's Church, Germany
48 Aachen (Aix-la-Chapelle): cathedral, Germany
49 Köln (Cologne): cathedral, Germany
50 Brühl: Augustusburg and Falkenlust Castles, Germany
51 Trier: Roman monuments, cathedral and Liebfrauen Church, Germany
52 Völklingen: ironworks, Germany
53 Lorsch: abbey and Altenmünster, Germany
54 Speyer: cathedral, Germany
55 Maulbronn: Cistercian monastery complex, Germany
56 Würzburg: Residence with the Court Gardens and Residence Square, Germany
57 Bamberg, Germany
58 Wies: pilgrimage church, Germany
59 Strasbourg: Grand Île, France
60 Nancy: Place Stanislas, Place de la Carrière and Place d'Alliance, France
61 Reims: Notre-Dame Cathedral, former Abbey of St Remi and Tau Palace, France
62 Amiens: cathedral, France
63 Mont-St Michel and its bay, France
64 Chartres: cathedral, France
65 Versailles: palace and park, France
66 Paris: banks of the Seine, France
67 Fontainebleau: palace and park, France
68 Fontenay: Cistercian abbey, France
69 Vézelay: basilica and hill, France
70 Bourges: cathedral, France
71 Chambord: château and estate, France
72 St Savin-sur-Gartempe: church, France
73 Arc-et-Senans: royal saltworks, France
74 Lyon: historic city, France
75 Orange: Roman theatre and its surroundings and the triumphal arch, France
76 Avignon: historic centre, France
77 Arles: Roman and Romanesque monuments, France
78 Remoulins: Pont du Gard Roman aqueduct, France
79 Carcassonne: historic fortified city, France
80 Canal du Midi, France
81 Vallée du Vézère: Lascaux and other decorated grottoes, France
82 St Emilion: vineyard landscape, France
83 The Way of St James pilgrimage route: four routes through France
84 Mont Perdu/Monte Perdido, France/Spain
85 Barcelona: Parque and Palacio Güell and Casa Milá, Spain
86 Barcelona: Palau de la Música Catalaña and the Hospital de Sant Pau, Spain
87 Poblet: monastery, Spain
88 Ibiza: biodiversity and culture, Spain
89 Valencia: La Lonja de la Sada, Spain
90 Teruel: Mujedar architecture, Spain
91 Cuenca: historic walled town, Spain
92 San Millán and Suso: monasteries, Spain
93 Burgos: cathedral, Spain
94 Las Médulas, Spain
95 Camino de Santiago: The Way of St James pilgrimage route, Spain
96 Altamira Cave, Spain
97 Oviedo: churches of the Asturias Kingdom, Spain
98 Santiago de Compostela: old town, Spain
99 Salamanca: old city, Spain
100 Ávila: old town with extra-muros churches, Spain
101 Segovia: old town and aqueduct, Spain
102 El Escorial: monastery, Spain
103 Alcalá de Henares: university and historic precinct, Spain
104 Toledo: historic city, Spain
105 Guadalupe: Royal Monastery of Santa Maria, Spain
106 Cáceres: old town, Spain
107 Mérida: archaeological ensemble, Spain
108 Sevilla (Seville): cathedral, Alcazar and Archivo de Indias, Spain
109 Córdoba: mosque and historic centre, Spain
110 Granada: Alhambra, Generalife & Albaicín quarter, Spain
111 Mediterranean seaboard prehistoric rock-art sites, Spain
112 Porto (Oporto): historic centre, Portugal
113 Vale do Côa: prehistoric rock-art sites, Portugal
114 Tomar: Convent of Christ, Portugal
115 Batalha: monastery, Portugal
116 Alcobaça: monastery, Portugal
117 Sintra: historic city, Portugal
118 Lisboa (Lisbon): Mosteiro dos Jeronimos and Torre de Belém, Portugal
119 Évora: historic centre, Portugal
120 Bern (Berne): old city, Switzerland
121 St Gallen: convent, Switzerland
122 Müstair: Benedictine Convent of St John, Switzerland
123 Salzburg: historic centre, Austria
124 Hallstatt-Dachstein-Salzkammergut: cultural landscape, Austria
125 Graz: historic centre, Austria
126 Semmering Railway, Austria
127 Wien (Vienna): Schönbrunn Palace and Gardens, Austria
128 Torino (Turin): Residences of the Royal House of Savoy, Italy
129 Milano (Milan): Church and Dominican Convent of Santa Maria delle Grazie with 'The Last Supper' by Leonardo da Vinci, Italy
130 Crespi d'Adda, Italy
131 Val Camónica: rock drawings, Italy
132 Vicenza: city and the Palladian Villas of the Veneto, Italy
133 Pádova (Padua): botanical garden, Italy
134 Venézia (Venice) and its lagoon, Italy
135 Aquileia: archaeological site including Patriarchal Basilica, Italy
136 Ferrara, Renaissance city and Po delta, Italy
137 Ravenna: early Christian monuments and mosaics, Italy
138 Modena: cathedral, Torre Civica and Piazza Grande, Italy
139 Portovénere, Cinque Terre, Ísola Palmária, Ísola del Tino and Ísola del Tinetto, Italy
140 Firenze (Florence): historic centre, Italy
141 Pisa: Piazza del Duomo, Italy
142 San Gimignano: historic centre, Italy
143 Siena: historic centre, Italy
144 Pienza: historic centre, Italy
145 Urbino: historic centre, Italy
146 Villa Adriana, Italy
147 Vatican City
148 Roma (Rome): historic centre, incl. extraterritorial properties of the Holy See & San Paolo fuori le Mura, Italy
149 Caserta: royal palace with park, Vanvitelli Aqueduct and San Leucio complex, Italy
150 Nápoli (Naples): historic centre, Italy
151 Herculaneum, Pompei and Torre Annunziata: archaeological areas, Italy
152 Costiera Amalfitana, Italy
153 Cilento area: cultural landscape including Vallo di Diano National Park, Certosa di Padula and the archaeological sites of Paestum and Vélia, Italy
154 Castel del Monte: medieval castle, Italy
155 Matera: I Sassi di Matera, Italy
156 Alberobello: Trulli houses, Italy
157 Villa Romana del Casale, Sicily, Italy
158 Agrigento: archaeological area, Sicily, Italy
159 Su Nuraxi di Barúmini, Sardinia, Italy
160 Malbork: Teutonic castle, Poland
161 Torun: medieval town, Poland
162 Warszawa (Warsaw): historic centre, Poland
163 Zamosc: old city, Poland
164 Wieliczka: salt mines, Poland
165 Kraków (Cracow): historic centre, Poland
166 Kalwaria Zebrzydowska: Mannerist architectural and park landscape complex and pilgrimage park, Poland
167 Oswiecim (Auschwitz): concentration camp, Poland
168 Praha (Prague): historic centre, Czech Republic
169 Kutná Hora: historical centre, Church of Santa Barbara and Cathedral of Our Lady at Sedlec, Czech Republic
170 Litomysl Castle, Czech Republic
171 Holasovice: historical village reservation, Czech Republic
172 Cesky Krumlov: historic centre, Czech Republic
173 Telc: historic centre, Czech Republic
174 Lednice-Valtice: cultural landscape, Czech Republic
175 Zelená Hora: St John of Nepomuk, Czech Republic
176 Kromeríz: castle and gardens, Czech Republic
177 Banská Stiavnica, Slovak Republic
178 Vlkolínec, Slovak Republic
179 Spisské Pohradie: Spissky Hrad and associated monuments, Slovak Republic
180 Hortobágyi National Park, Hungary
181 Hollokö: traditional village, Hungary
182 Budapest: including the banks of the Danube and Buda Castle area, Hungary
183 Pannonhalma: Millenary Benedictine Abbey and its natural environment, Hungary
184 Porec: Episcopal complex, Croatia
185 Trogir: historic city, Croatia
186 Split: historic centre with Diocletian palace, Croatia
187 Dubrovnik: old city, Croatia
188 Kotor and its gulf, Federal Republic of Yugoslavia
189 Studenica: monastery, Federal Republic of Yugoslavia
190 Stari Ras and Sopocani Monastery, Federal Republic of Yugoslavia
191 Ohrid Lake and its region, Former Yugoslav Republic of Macedonia
192 Butrinti (Buthrotum): archaeological site, Albania
193 Horezu: monastery, Romania
194 Orastie Mountains: Dacian fortresses, Romania
195 Biertan: town and fortified church, Romania
196 Sighisoara: historic centre, Romania
197 Maramures: wooden churches, Romania
198 Moldavian churches, Romania
199 Boyana: church, Bulgaria
200 Sveshtari: Thracian tomb, Bulgaria
201 Ivanovo: rock chapels, Bulgaria
202 Madara: horseman stone relief, Bulgaria
203 Nesebur (Nessebar): ancient city, Bulgaria
204 Kazanluk: Thracian tomb, Bulgaria
205 Rila: monastery, Bulgaria
206 Áthos, Greece
207 Thessaloníki: Palaeochristian and Byzantine monuments, Greece
208 Vergina: archaeological site, Greece
209 Metéora, Greece
210 Delfí (Delphi): archaeological site, Greece
211 Olimbía (Olympía): archaeological site, Greece
212 Bassae: Temple of Apollo Epicurius, Greece
213 Mistrás, Greece
214 Mycenae and Tiryns; archaeological sites, Greece
215 Epídavros (Epidaurus): archaeological site, Greece
216 Athína (Athens): Acropolis, Greece
217 Dílos, Greece
218 Híos (Chios): Daphni, Hossios, Luckas and Néa Moni monasteries, Greece
219 Sámos: Pythagoreion and Heraion, Greece
220 Pátmos: historic centre (chorá) with the monastery of St John the Theologian and the Cave of the Apocalypse, Greece
221 Ródos (Rhodes): medieval city, Greece
222 Xanthos-Letoon, Turkey
223 Hierapolis-Pamukkale, Turkey
224 Troy: archaeological site, Turkey
225 Istanbul: historic areas, Turkey
226 Safranbolu, Turkey
227 Hattusha: Hittite city, Turkey
228 Göreme National Park and Cappadocia rock sites, Turkey
229 Divrigi: Great Mosque and hospital, Turkey
230 Nemrut Dagi: archaeological site, Turkey
231 Ggantija: megalithic temples, Malta
232 Hal Saflieni Hypogeum, Malta
233 Valletta: old city, Malta
234 Pafos: archaeological site, Cyprus
235 Troodos region: painted churches, Cyprus
236 Choirokoitia: archaeological site, Cyprus

FORMER SOVIET UNION

237 Tallinn: historic centre, Estonia
238 Riga: historic centre, Latvia
239 Vilnius: old city, Lithuania
240 L'viv (L'vov): historic centre, Ukraine
241 Kyyiv (Kiev): St Sophia Cathedral, related monastic buildings and Lavra of Kyyiv-Pechersk, Ukraine
242 Sankt-Peterburg (St Petersburg): historic centre and related monuments, Russian Federation
243 Novgorod: historic monuments and surroundings, Russian Federation
244 Moskva (Moscow): Kremlin & Red Square, Russian Federation
245 Moskva (Moscow): Church of the Ascension at Kolomenskoye, Russian Federation
246 Sergiyev Posad: architectural ensemble of the Trinity Sergius Lavra, Russian Federation
247 Vladimir and Suzdal: White Monuments, Russian Federation
248 Upper Svaneti area, Georgia
249 Kutaisi: Bagrati Cathedral and Gelati Monastery, Georgia

AFRICA

250 Tétouan: medina, Morocco
251 Fès: medina, Morocco
252 Volubilis: archaeological site, Morocco
253 Meknès: historic city, Morocco
254 Marrakech: medina, Morocco
255 Aït Benhaddou: fortified village, Morocco
256 Tipasa: archaeological park, Algeria
257 Alger (Algiers): kasbah, Algeria
258 Benî Hammâd: Al Qal'a, Algeria
259 Djemila: Roman ruins, Algeria
260 Timgad: Roman ruins, Algeria
261 M'Zab valley, Algeria
262 Dougga, Tunisia
263 Tunis: medina, Tunisia
264 Carthage: archaeological site, Tunisia
265 Kerkouane: Punic town and its necropolis, Tunisia
266 Sousse: medina, Tunisia
267 Qairouan (Kairouan), Tunisia
268 El Jem: amphitheatre, Tunisia
269 Ghadamis: old town, Libya
270 Sabratha: archaeological site, Libya
271 Leptis Magna: archaeological site, Libya
272 Cyrene: archaeological site, Libya
273 Abu Mena: Christian ruins, Egypt
274 Memphis: Pyramid fields from Giza to Dahshur and its necropolis, Egypt
275 El Qâhira (Cairo): Islamic city, Egypt

MIDDLE EAST

276 Halab: ancient city of Aleppo, Syria
277 Tadmur: archaeological site of Palmyra, Syria
278 Dimashq (Damascus): ancient city, Syria
279 Bosra: ancient city, Syria
280 Anjar: archaeological site, Lebanon
281 Baalbek, Lebanon
282 Ouadi Qadisha (the Holy Valley) and Horsh Arz el-Rab (Forest of the Cedars of God), Lebanon
283 Byblos, Lebanon
284 Soûr: archaeological site of Tyre, Lebanon
285 Jerusalem: old city and its walls (site proposed by Jordan)
286 Qasr Amra, Jordan
287 Petra, Jordan
288 Hatra, Iraq

CLIMATE

The Columbus Press *World Travel Guide* contains detailed climate charts for every country in the world, including temperature, rainfall, sunshine and humidity. For more information, call +44 (0)20 7417 0700.

TEMPERATURE CONVERSION

°Celsius	−10	0	10	20	30	40
°Fahrenheit	14	32	50	68	86	104

RAINFALL CONVERSION

Millimetres	102	203	305	406	508	610
Inches	4	8	12	16	20	24

WINTER

TEMPERATURE (January average, degrees Celsius)
- 10° – 19°
- 0° – 9°
- Minus 10° – minus 1°
- Below minus 10°

RAINFALL (November to April total)
- 500mm and over
- 250 – 499mm
- Less than 250mm

PREVAILING WIND shown as white arrows

NORTH ATLANTIC DRIFT
An extension of the Gulf Stream which helps to maintain relatively mild winters in the British Isles and along the coast of Norway

FÖHN
A wind which blows down Alpine valleys, warming as it descends, and melts snow rapidly

MISTRAL
A strong cold dry wind from the north

BORA
A cold dry wind which blows from the N and NE, affecting the Adriatic coastline

LEVECHE
A hot, dry and dusty wind which blows from the Sahara

SUMMER

TEMPERATURE (July average, degrees Celsius)
- 30° and over
- 20° – 29°
- 10° – 19°
- 0° – 9°

RAINFALL (May to October total)
- 500mm and over
- 250 – 499mm
- Less than 250mm

PREVAILING WIND shown as white arrows

SIROCCO
A hot dusty wind which blows from north Africa; after crossing the Mediterranean the wind is often very humid

ETESIAN WIND / MELTEMI
A wind blowing from the N and NW, often creating rough seas

NATIONAL PARKS

Europe has a large variety of scenery, habitats and fauna, and most countries have set aside areas of natural beauty in order to preserve the landscape and wildlife. This map shows the most important areas designated as National Parks throughout Europe except for the former Soviet Union, but including the Baltic states. The best period for visiting each park is shown in blue (no date: all year / information not available).

Iceland
1 **Jokulsargljufur**
Spectacular gorges
2 **Skaftafell**
Glacial country with icecap & sand plain

Norway
3 **Øvre Pasvik** May–Sep
Forest & tundra
4 **Stabbursdalen** May–Sep
Arctic landscape with tundra, lakes, gravel plains & forest
5 **Øvre Anarjokka** May–Sep
Undulating tundra with woodland & lakes
6 **Reisa** May–Oct
Mixed mountain country
7 **Øvre Dividal** May–Sep
Mountainous country with tundra & woodland
8 **Ånderdalen** May–Oct
Mixed mountain country
9 **Saltfjellet-Svartisen** May–Sep Varied landscape; fjords, mountains & glacier
10 **Børgefjell** May–Oct
Remote mountain area with varied habitats
11 **Gressåmoen** May–Oct
Mountainous country & spruce forest
12 **Dovrefjell** May–Aug
Mountainous tundra & permanent snowfields; famous for its flora
13 **Rondane** May–Sep
Mountain country with varied landscapes
14 **Jotunheimen** May–Sep
Mountainous area with tundra, bogs & forest
15 **Hardangervidda** May–Oct Large mountain plateau, a popular walking area

Sweden
16 **Vadvetjåkka** May–Sep
Mountainous country
17 **Abisko** May–Sep
Mountain & forest with tundra, lakes & rivers
18 **Muddus** May–Sep
Forest, tundra & bog
19 **Padjelanta, Sarek and Stora Sjöfallet** May–Sep
3 parks protect Europe's largest wilderness area; mixed landscape
20 **Pieljekaise** May–Sep
Wooded mountainous country with tundra, open water & bogs
21 **Skuleskogen** Apr–Oct
Forested hill country
22 **Töfsingdalen** May–Sep
Woodland, tundra & bog
23 **Sånfjället** May–Oct
Woodland, tundra & bog
24 **Hamra** May–Oct
Woodland, tundra & bog, noted for its insects
25 **Garphyttan** Apr–Oct
Forest & meadows
26 **Tiveden** May–Sep
Hilly forest, lakes & bogs
27 **Store Mosse** Apr–Jul
Predominantly boggy, with lakes & forest

Finland
28 **Pallas-Ounastunturi** May–Sep Upland plateau & taiga, with lakes, tundra, gorges & forest
29 **Lemmenjoki** May–Sep
Wilderness mountain area; gold rush in 1940's
30 **Urho Kekkonen** May–Sep
Large wilderness area; fells and pine moors
31 **Pyhätunturi** May–Sep
Mountainous area with tundra, bogs & forest
32 **Oulanka** May–Sep
Varied tundra landscape
33 **Petkeljärvi** May–Oct
Typical Finnish lakeland scenery, with lakes, bogs, forest & moorland
34 **Linnansaari** May–Oct
Mainly lake with some islands
35 **Pyhä-Häkki** May–Sep
Mainly forest & bog
36 **Liesjärvi** May–Sep
Lakes, previously cultivated land & forest

37 **Saaristomeri** May–Sep
Extensive island group with mixed habitats

Ireland
38 **Glenveagh** Apr–Jul
Mixed upland area
39 **Connemara** Apr–Sep
Typical western Ireland mountain area
40 **Killarney** May–Oct
Ancient woodland with moorland, lakes, bogs, wetland & mountains
41 **Wicklow Mountains** May–Aug Partly wooded mountains with upland moorland & grassland

United Kingdom
42 **Northumberland** Apr–Oct
Mainly upland grassy moorland; Hadrian's Wall in the south
43 **Lake District** Apr–Nov
Mountain & lakeland; very popular all year
44 **Yorkshire Dales** May–Jul
Varied upland country
45 **North York Moors** Apr–Sep Hilly uplands with heather moorland
46 **Peak District** May–Jul
Limestone in the south, with many caves; high peat moors in the north
47 **Snowdonia** May–Aug
Mountain country with lakes, moorland, grassland & woodland
48 **Pembrokeshire Coast** Apr–Jul Scenic coastline; varied seabird habitats
49 **Brecon Beacons** May–Oct Mainly grass-covered mountain area
50 **Exmoor** May–Jul
High heather moorland & wooded valleys, with dramatic coastline
51 **Dartmoor** May–Sep
Granite uplands with heather & grassland

Netherlands
52 **Dwingelderveld** May–Sep Heathland, fen & woodland with lakes
53 **De Hoge Veluwe** Apr–Oct
Variety of habitats: heathland, dunes, fens, wet heath & woodland
54 **Veluwezoom** Apr–Oct
Heath & mixed woodland

Germany
55 **Niedersächsisches Wattenmeer**
East Frisian Islands; mudflats & saltmarsh
56 **Hamburgisches W'meer**
Mudflats & saltmarsh
57 **Schleswig-Holsteinisches W'meer**
Mudflats & saltmarsh
58 **Vorpommersche Boddenlandschaft**
Mudflats & saltmarsh with dunes, lagoons, lakes & woodland
59 **Jasmund** May–Nov
Varied landscape with cliffs, lakes & woodland
60 **Müritz** Apr–Nov
Woodland & lakes with heath, marsh & pasture
61 **Unteres Odertal** Apr–Jun, Sep–Nov
Floodplain of the Oder; park shared with Poland
62 **Sächsische Schweiz** Apr–Oct Numerous rock towers; lower slopes wooded; deep valleys
63 **Hoch Harz** May–Oct
Wooded mountains with moorland, bogs & lakes; affected by acid rain
64 **Bayerischer Wald** May–Aug
Wooded mountain area
65 **Berchtesgaden** May–Sep
Mountain landscape with Alpine pastures, small glaciers, cliffs, lakes & varied woodland

France
66 **Vanoise** Jun–Sep
High mountain scenery
67 **Écrins** Apr–Sep
High mountain scenery with many glaciers

68 **Mercantour** Apr–Sep
Some of the best parts of the Maritime Alps
69 **Port-Cros** Mar–Sep
Small wooded island
70 **Cévennes** May–Sep
Varied mountain & forest
71 **Pyrénées Occidentales** May–Sep, Oct
Diverse mountain landscape; snowfields, pastures & woodland

Spain
72 **Ordesa** May–Jul
Spectacular mountain & gorge scenery; forests & Alpine pastures
73 **Covadonga** May–Sep
Mountain area with mixed woodlands, pasture & glacial lakes
74 **Tablas de Daimiel** Apr–Jul Small wetland
75 **Coto de Doñana** Feb–Jun
Guadalquivir delta; important wildlife site
76 **Caldera de Taburiente**
Volcanic landscape
77 **Garajonay**
Heavily wooded area
78 **Cañadas del Teide**
Volcanic landscapes
79 **Timanfaya**
Volcanic landscapes

Portugal
80 **Peneda-Gerês** Apr–Oct
Mountain & forest area; cliffs & rock formations

Switzerland
81 **The Swiss National Park** May–Oct Strictly controlled mountainous area; forests, pastures, lakes, cliffs & snowfields

Austria
82 **Hohe Tauern** May–Sep
High Alpine scenery; forests in lower areas
83 **Nockberge** Apr–Oct
Forested mountain area with bogs & moors

Italy
84 **Stelvio** Apr–Oct
Typical Alpine scenery & Italy's largest glacier
85 **Gran Paradiso** Apr–Oct
High Alpine country; famous for the Ibex
86 **Abruzzo** Apr–Oct
Wooded mountainous area
87 **Circeo** Mar–Jun
Coastal marsh & rocky promontory near Rome
88 **Calábria** Apr–Jul
Three areas of wooded mountainous landscape

Poland
89 **Wolinski** Apr–Oct
Woodland, lakes and sea cliffs; white-tailed sea eagle the main attraction
90 **Slowinski** Apr–Jul
Coastal landscape with shifting sand dunes
91 **Kampinoski** May–Jul
Varied landscape close to Warsaw
92 **Mazurski and Wigierski**
Numerous lakes and extensive forests
93 **Biebrzanski** Apr–Jul
Central Europe's largest area of natural peat bogs
94 **Bialowieski** Apr–Jul
Europe's largest original lowland forest; European bison the main attraction

95 **Bieszczadzki** May–Sep
Remote wooded mountain area in E. Carpathians
96 **Babiogórski, Tatrzanski, Gorczanski & Pieninski** May–Oct Four parks in the spectacular High Tatra mountains
97 **Ojcówski** May–Sep
Hilly landscape with many rock pinnacles
98 **Gory Stolowe and Karkonoski** May–Sep
Dramatic mountain scenery of the Sudeten Mountains

Czech Republic
99 **Krkonose** May–Oct
Wooded mountain area with Alpine pastures, meadows, bogs & lakes

Slovak Republic
100 **Vysoké Tatry** May–Oct
Spectacular mountain area with forests, lakes, grassland & bogs
101 **Nizke Tatry** Apr–Jul
Mountainous country with varied woodland, pastures, bogs & lakes
102 **Pieninsky** May–Jul
Limestone mountains with mixed forests

Hungary
103 **Aggtelek** Apr–Oct
Important karst scenery
104 **Bukk** Apr–Jul
Hilly forested region
105 **Hortobágyi**
Varied steppe landscape good for birdwatching
106 **Kiskunság** Apr–Jul
Wide range of lowland habitats

Slovenia
107 **Triglav** May–Oct
Limestone mountain scenery & mixed forest
108 **Krka**
Follows the Krka river; lakes, dams, gorges, falls & woodland

Croatia
109 **Risnjak** May–Sep
Limestone mountain scenery & mixed forest
110 **Plitvice Lakes** May–Sep
Scenic lakes linked by waterfalls
111 **Paklenica** May–Sep
Limestone peaks, gorges & mixed forest
112 **Kornati** May–Sep
Limestone islands with karst scenery
113 **Mljet** May–Sep
Western part of island

Bosnia-Herzegovina
114 **Sutjeska** May–Sep
Wooded mountainous area; mixed landscape & reserve of virgin forest

Federal Republic of Yugoslavia
115 **Fruska Gora** May–Sep
Wooded hilly valley
116 **Djerdap**
Gorge of the Danube; dam has created a long thin lake
117 **Tara**
Mixed upland scenery
118 **Durmitor** May–Sep
Mountain area in the west, Tara Gorge in east; mixed landscape & karst

119 **Biogradska Gora** May–Sep
Mountain area with high grasslands & five lakes
120 **Lovcen**
Wooded limestone mountains
121 **Skadarsko jezero** May–Sep
Yugoslav part of Lake Scutari

Former Yugoslav Rep. of Macedonia
122 **Mavrovo** May–Sep
Mountain area, partly wooded
123 **Galicica**
S. end of Dinaric Alps; mostly natural forest
124 **Pelister**
Wooded mountain area with Alpine pastures

Albania
125 **Dajtit, Lura and Thethi**
Three separate parks; forested mountain areas
126 **Divjaka**
Dunes & coastal woodland
127 **Tomorri**
Mountainous landscape with forests & pastures
128 **Llogara**
Woodland & pastures

Romania
129 **Retezat** May–Sep
Mountain country with extensive forests

Bulgaria
130 **Rusenski Lom** May–Oct
Deciduous woodland
131 **Vitosa** May–Oct
Varied mountain area
132 **Pirin** Apr–Oct
High mountains; forest & mixed woodland

Greece
133 **Préspa** Apr–Jul
Shallow lakes with reed- & sedge-beds
134 **Olimbos (Olympus)** Apr–Oct Mountain area with maquis & forest
135 **Pindos** May–Jul
Wooded mountain area
136 **Vikos-Aóos** May–Jun
Wooded mountain area; Vikos & Aóos gorges
137 **Ainos** Mar–Jul
Area around Mt Aínos
138 **Iti Óros** May–Oct
Wooded mountain area
139 **Parnassós** Apr–Nov
Wilderness mountain area; mixed habitats
140 **Párnitha** Apr–Jul
Limestone area; maquis
141 **Soúnion** Mar–May
Typical Greek coast

Turkey
142 **Manyas-Kuscenneti**
Part of large lake

Estonia
143 **Lahemaa**
Wooded area & scenic coast

Latvia
144 **Gauja**
River & gorge scenery

Lithuania
145 **Zemaitija**
Lakeland area
146 **Aukstaitija (Ignalina)**
Forest & lakes; great diversity of wildlife
147 **Trakai**
Five lakes with Trakai Castle as centrepiece
148 **Dzukija**
Confluence of Nemunas & Merkys rivers

HISTORICAL

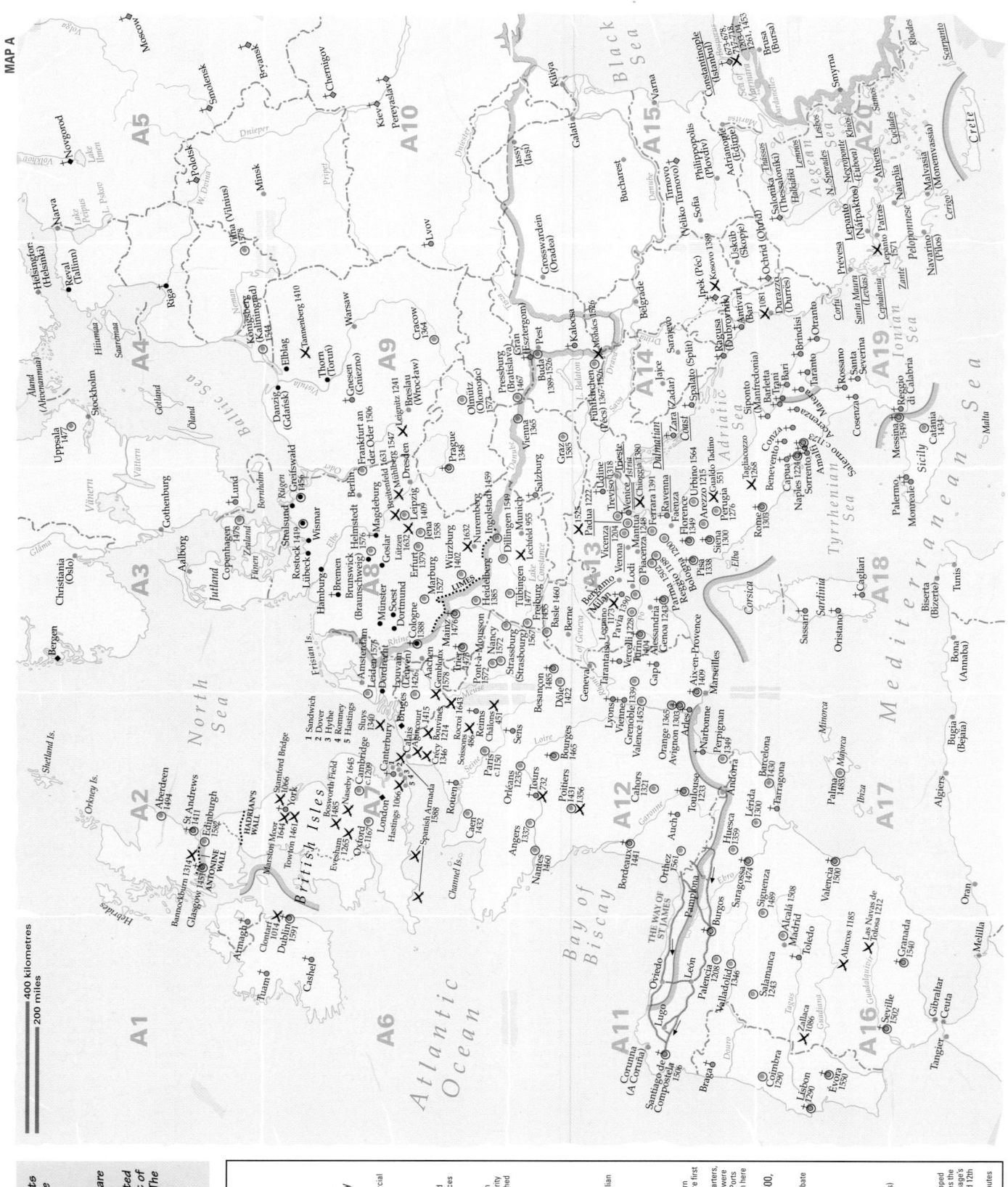

MAP A

This map shows selected aspects of European history between the end of the Roman Empire in the 5th century and the Peace of Westphalia in 1648. Modern equivalents of important cities are included in parentheses. No historical boundaries are indicated apart from the maximum extent of Roman and Islamic conquests. The present-day coastline is shown and current international boundaries marked in grey.

Northern limit of the Roman Empire at its greatest extent

Northern limit of Islamic conquests in Europe between the 7th and 11th centuries

Trieste Cities and regions which came under Venetian influence in any period prior to 1648. Venice acquired many trading posts at various times during this period of commercial expansion in the late Middle Ages

X Sites of major battles in the period 476–1648, with date. In general, battles have only been marked which had important political consequences

The Hanseatic League
A commercial union of northern European cities, designed to create economic security in an age of political chaos, which flourished in the 14th and 15th centuries

● Principal cities

● ◆ Principal foreign trading posts (kontore)

Principal cities of the Lombard League
A shifting political alliance of northern Italian cities designed to combat the territorial ambitions of the Holy Roman Emperors (principally Frederick I and Frederick II) between 1152 and 1288

The Cinque Ports
A loose confederation of towns in southern England whose defensive obligations were first established in the 11th century and subsequently redefined by many royal charters, principally in the 11th century and subsequently redefined by many royal charters. At one time there were over 30 towns and villages in the Cinque Ports Confederation; the original five are shown here

○ Universities founded prior to 1600, with year of foundation. In some cases, particularly for the oldest universities, precise dates are open to debate

Major ecclesiastical centres, 16th century:
✝ Roman Catholic (Patriarchal and Archiepiscopal Sees)
✝ Orthodox (Patriarchal Sees and other major centres)

Camino de Santiago (The Way of St James)
A medieval pilgrimage route which developed after the discovery of the tomb of St James the Apostle in Galicia in about 812; the pilgrimage's popularity was at its height in the 11th and 12th centuries, resulting in the legacy of many churches and chapels along its various routes

HISTORICAL

VIKING AND ISLAMIC CONQUESTS AND THE CAROLINGIAN EMPIRE

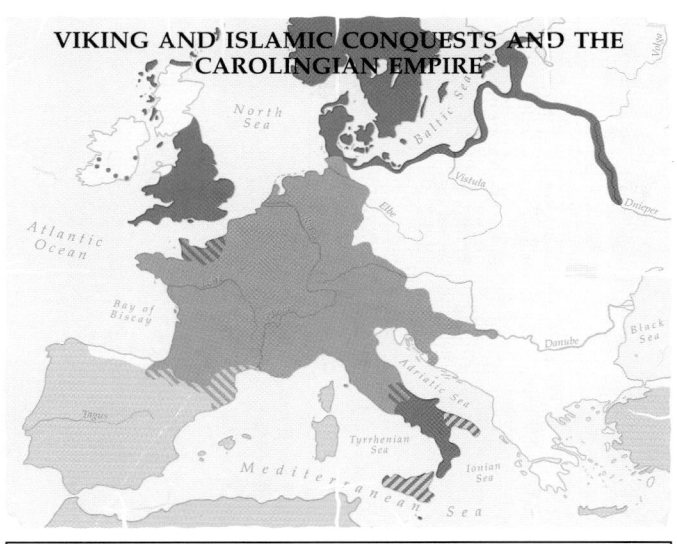

Maximum extent of Islamic conquests, 7th – 11th centuries	Areas ruled by the Vikings or Normans, 9th – 12th centuries	Carolingian Empire at the death of Charlemagne in 814

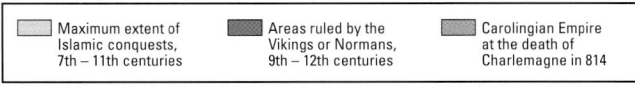

THE ANGEVIN AND HOHENSTAUFEN EMPIRES

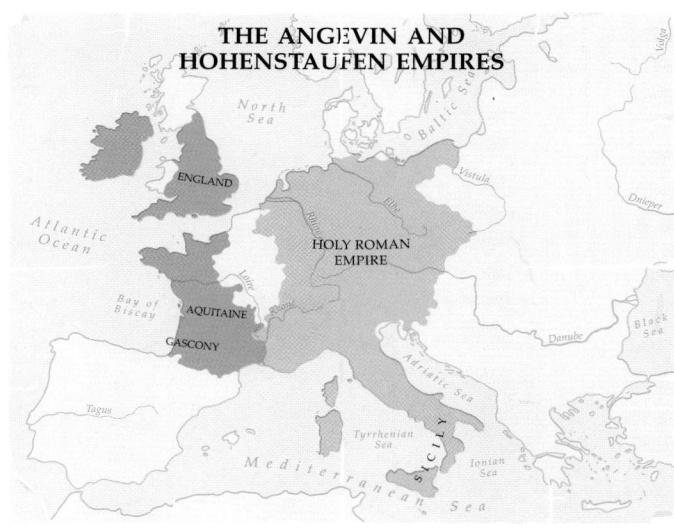

The Angevin Empire at the death of Henry II in 1189

The Hohenstaufen Empire at the death of Frederick II in 1250

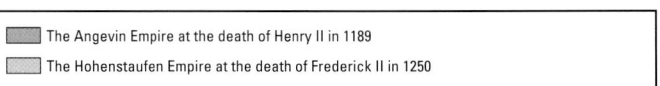

THE EMPIRE OF CHARLES V

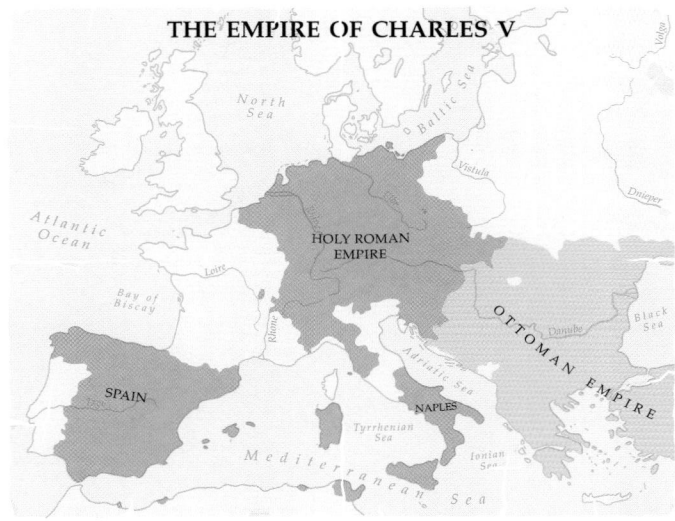

The European Habsburg Empire at the abdication of Charles V in 1556

The Ottoman Empire, c1560

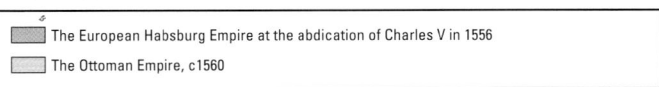

THE EMPIRE OF NAPOLEON

Area under direct rule of Napoleon in 1812

Dependent states in 1812

EVE OF WORLD WAR ONE

Triple Alliance, 1914 (Austria-Hungary, Germany, Italy)

Triple Entente, 1914 (France, Russia, United Kingdom)

THE COLD WAR

North Atlantic Treaty Organisation (NATO), 1962 *[other members: Iceland, Canada, USA]*

Warsaw Pact, 1962

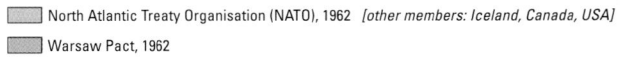

EUROPEAN UNION

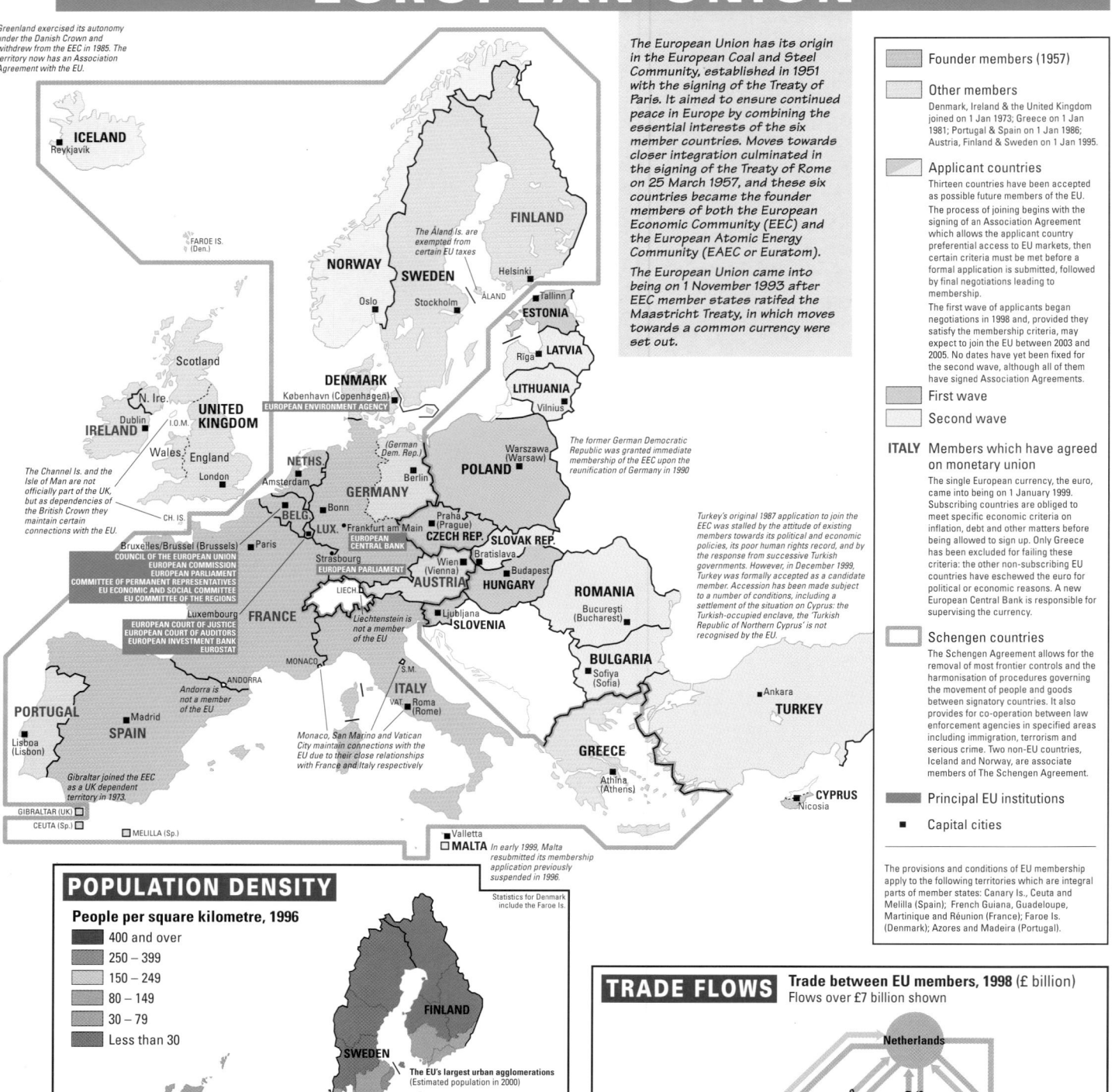

Greenland exercised its autonomy under the Danish Crown and withdrew from the EEC in 1985. The territory now has an Association Agreement with the EU.

The European Union has its origin in the European Coal and Steel Community, established in 1951 with the signing of the Treaty of Paris. It aimed to ensure continued peace in Europe by combining the essential interests of the six member countries. Moves towards closer integration culminated in the signing of the Treaty of Rome on 25 March 1957, and these six countries became the founder members of both the European Economic Community (EEC) and the European Atomic Energy Community (EAEC or Euratom).

The European Union came into being on 1 November 1993 after EEC member states ratified the Maastricht Treaty, in which moves towards a common currency were set out.

The Åland Is. are exempted from certain EU taxes.

The former German Democratic Republic was granted immediate membership of the EEC upon the reunification of Germany in 1990

Turkey's original 1987 application to join the EEC was stalled by the attitude of existing members towards its political and economic policies, its poor human rights record, and by the response from successive Turkish governments. However, in December 1999, Turkey was formally accepted as a candidate member. Accession has been made subject to a number of conditions, including a settlement of the situation on Cyprus: the Turkish-occupied enclave, the 'Turkish Republic of Northern Cyprus' is not recognised by the EU.

The Channel Is. and the Isle of Man are not officially part of the UK, but as dependencies of the British Crown they maintain certain connections with the EU.

Liechtenstein is not a member of the EU

Andorra is not a member of the EU

Monaco, San Marino and Vatican City maintain connections with the EU due to their close relationships with France and Italy respectively

Gibraltar joined the EEC as a UK dependent territory in 1973.

In early 1999, Malta resubmitted its membership application previously suspended in 1996.

Statistics for Denmark include the Faroe Is.

Legend:
- Founder members (1957)
- Other members
  Denmark, Ireland & the United Kingdom joined on 1 Jan 1973; Greece on 1 Jan 1981; Portugal & Spain on 1 Jan 1986; Austria, Finland & Sweden on 1 Jan 1995.
- Applicant countries
  Thirteen countries have been accepted as possible future members of the EU.
  The process of joining begins with the signing of an Association Agreement which allows the applicant country preferential access to EU markets, then certain criteria must be met before a formal application is submitted, followed by final negotiations leading to membership.
  The first wave of applicants began negotiations in 1998 and, provided they satisfy the membership criteria, may expect to join the EU between 2003 and 2005. No dates have yet been fixed for the second wave, although all of them have signed Association Agreements.
- First wave
- Second wave
- ITALY Members which have agreed on monetary union
  The single European currency, the euro, came into being on 1 January 1999. Subscribing countries are obliged to meet specific economic criteria on inflation, debt and other matters before being allowed to sign up. Only Greece has been excluded for failing these criteria: the other non-subscribing EU countries have eschewed the euro for political or economic reasons. A new European Central Bank is responsible for supervising the currency.
- Schengen countries
  The Schengen Agreement allows for the removal of most frontier controls and the harmonisation of procedures governing the movement of people and goods between signatory countries. It also provides for co-operation between law enforcement agencies in specified areas including immigration, terrorism and serious crime. Two non-EU countries, Iceland and Norway, are associate members of The Schengen Agreement.
- Principal EU institutions
- ■ Capital cities

The provisions and conditions of EU membership apply to the following territories which are integral parts of member states: Canary Is., Ceuta and Melilla (Spain); French Guiana, Guadeloupe, Martinique and Réunion (France); Faroe Is. (Denmark); Azores and Madeira (Portugal).

POPULATION DENSITY

People per square kilometre, 1996
- 400 and over
- 250 – 399
- 150 – 249
- 80 – 149
- 30 – 79
- Less than 30

The EU's largest urban agglomerations
(Estimated population in 2000)
1. Paris 9.64 million
2. Greater London 7.64m
3. Essen 6.56m [incl. Bochum, Dortmund and Duisburg]
4. Milano (Milan) 4.25m
5. Madrid 4.07m
6. Frankfurt am Main 3.70m [incl. Darmstadt and Wiesbaden]
7. Berlin 3.34m
8. Düsseldorf 3.25m [incl. Mönchengladbach and Wuppertal]
9. Athina (Athens) 3.10m
10. Köln (Cologne) 3.07m [incl. Bonn and Leverkusen]
11. Nápoli (Naples) 3.01m
12. Barcelona 2.82m
13. Roma (Rome) 2.69m
14. Stuttgart 2.69m
15. Hamburg 2.68m
16. München (Munich) 2.31m
17. West Midlands 2.27m [Birmingham area]
18. Greater Manchester 2.25m
19. Wien (Vienna) 2.07m

The UN defines the term 'urban agglomeration' as a contiguous area inhabited at a density regarded as urban, ignoring administrative boundaries. Source: United Nations

French Guiana (Fr.)*
Guadeloupe (Fr.)*
Martinique (Fr.)*
Réunion (Fr.)*

Azores (Port.)
Madeira (Port.)
Canary Is. (Sp.)
Ceuta & Melilla (Sp.)

Source: Eurostat   *1994 figures

TRADE FLOWS

Trade between EU members, 1998 (£ billion)
Flows over £7 billion shown

Denmark, Finland, Greece and Portugal are not shown here as their trade with any other single EU country did not exceed £7bn in 1998

Source: The Economist Diary 2000 edition   *Estimate

EUROPEAN UNION

TRADE

EU countries' external trade, 1998
(ECU billion)

◀ Total trade

Trade with other EU countries
(for details of principal trade flows between EU states, see diagram on previous page)

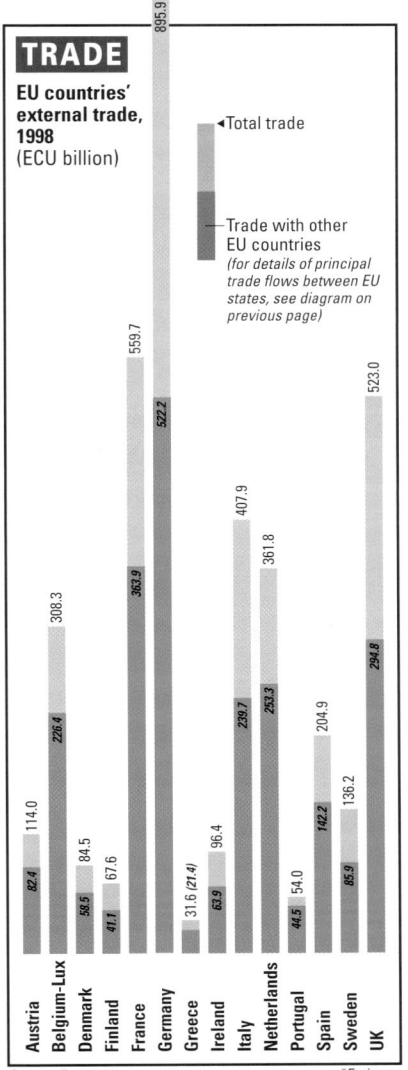

Country	Total trade	Trade with other EU countries
Austria	114.0	82.4
Belgium-Lux	308.3	226.4
Denmark	84.5	58.5
Finland	67.6	41.1
France	559.7	363.9
Germany	895.9 / 522.2	
Greece	31.6	(21.4)
Ireland	96.4	63.9
Italy	407.9	239.7
Netherlands	361.8	253.3
Portugal	54.0	44.5
Spain	204.9	142.2
Sweden	136.2	85.9
UK	523.0	294.8

Source: Eurostat   *Estimate

THE EU BUDGET

Contributions by member states to the EU, 1997
(Total: ECU 80,311 million)

- Germany **ECU 24,173m** (30.1%)
- France **13,974m** (17.4%)
- Italy **9,557m** (11.9%)
- UK **9,075m** (11.3%)
- Spain **5,060m** (6.3%)
- Netherlands **4,738m** (5.9%)
- Belgium **3,132m** (3.9%)
- Austria **2,329m** (2.9%)
- Sweden **2,329m** (2.9%)
- Denmark **1,526m** (1.9%)
- Finland **1,205m** (1.5%)
- Greece **1,205m** (1.5%)
- Portugal **1,124m** (1.4%)
- Ireland **723m** (0.9%)
- Luxembourg **161m** (0.2%)

EU budget allocations, 1997
(Total: ECU 87,652 million)

- Agriculture (including Common Agricultural Policy) **ECU 41,305m** (47.1%)
- Regional operations, transport, fisheries and other structural operations **31,838m** (36.3%)
- Aid and co-operation with developing countries **5,900m** (6.7%)
- Research and development **3,500m** (4.0%)
- Administration **2,798m** (3.2%)
- Consumer protection, internal market and industry **887m** (1.0%)
- Training, culture, media and information **793m** (0.9%)
- Energy and environment **186m** (0.2%)
- Common foreign and security policy **30m** (0.03%)
- Other **415m** (0.5%)

SUMMARY TABLE

Country	Exchange rate, 1 Jan 2000 One euro equals:	Central Bank interest rate, 1 Jan 2000 (%)	Normal VAT rate (%)	Inflation, 1999 (%)	Unemployment, 1999 (% of work-force)	Balance of payments, 1997 (US$m)	Budget surplus/ deficit, 1998 (% of GDP)	Government debt, 1998 (% of GDP)
Austria	Schilling 13.76	5.5	20	1.0	4.2	–3,053	–2.2	63.0
Belgium	Belgian franc 40.34	5.5	20.5	1.6	8.9	+1,056	–0.9	118.2
Denmark	Krone 7.44	5.2	25	2.7	5.6	+6,478	+1.0	58.0
Finland	Markka 5.95	5.5	22	1.9	10.0	+2,305	+0.9	49.7
France	French franc 6.56	5.5	18.6	1.0	10.6	+5,940	–2.9	58.8
Germany	Deutschmark 1.96	5.5	14	1.1	9.1	–3,760	–2.0	61.1
Greece	Drachma 329.95	9.8	18*	2.2	10.0††	–4,515	–2.5	106.3
Ireland	Punt 0.79	5.5	21	3.0	6.2	–1,109	+2.4	49.5
Italy	Lira 1936.3	5.5	19	2.0	12.0	+13,150	–2.7	118.7
Luxembourg	Lux. franc 40.34	5.5	12	1.9	2.7	+73	+2.5	6.9
Netherlands	Guilder 2.20	5.5	17.5	2.0	3.1	–2,707	–0.7	67.5
Portugal	Escudo 200.48	5.5	16	1.9	4.6	–407	–2.2	57.8
Spain	Peseta 166.39	5.5	16**	2.7	15.3	–11,775	–1.7	65.1
Sweden	Krona 8.56	5.2	25	0.8	6.6	–6,712	+1.9	74.2
UK	Pound Sterling (£) 0.62	5.5	17.5†	1.3	5.9	–2,357	+0.5	48.7

Countries in red have agreed to monetary union. Their currency rates were set with the creation of the euro on 1st Jan 1999, and interest rates are set by the European Central Bank.   *12.5% in certain islands of the Dodecanese.   **Excluding the Canary Is., Ceuta and Melilla.   †Excluding the Channel Is., but including the Isle of Man.   ††1998.

Source: Eurostat

INCOME

Gross domestic product per person, 1994-96*

- ECU 23,000 and over
- ECU 18,000 – 22,999
- ECU 14,000 – 17,999
- ECU 11,000 – 13,999
- ECU 9,000 – 10,999
- Less than ECU 9,000

Statistics for Denmark include the Faroe Is.

Prior to the introduction of the euro, the European Currency Unit (ECU) was used as a common financial instrument within the EU. The value of the ECU was calculated as a weighted average of participating national currencies. Sterling equivalents since 1991 are shown below:

1 Jan,	One ECU equals:
1991	£0.71
1992	£0.72
1993	£0.80
1994	£0.75
1995	£0.78
1996	£0.83
1997	£0.73
1998	£0.67

1 Jan,	One euro equals:
1999	£0.71
2000	£0.62

French Guiana (Fr.)†
Guadeloupe (Fr.)†
Martinique (Fr.)†
Réunion (Fr.)†

Azores (Port.)
Madeira (Port.)
Canary Is. (Sp.)
Ceuta & Melilla (Sp.)

Source: Eurostat   *Annual average   †1995 figures

UNEMPLOYMENT

Unemployed as a percentage of the workforce, April 1998

- 20% and over
- 15.0% – 19.9%
- 11.0% – 14.9%
- 8.0% – 10.9%
- 5.0% – 7.9%
- Less than 5.0%

Statistics for Denmark include the Faroe Is.

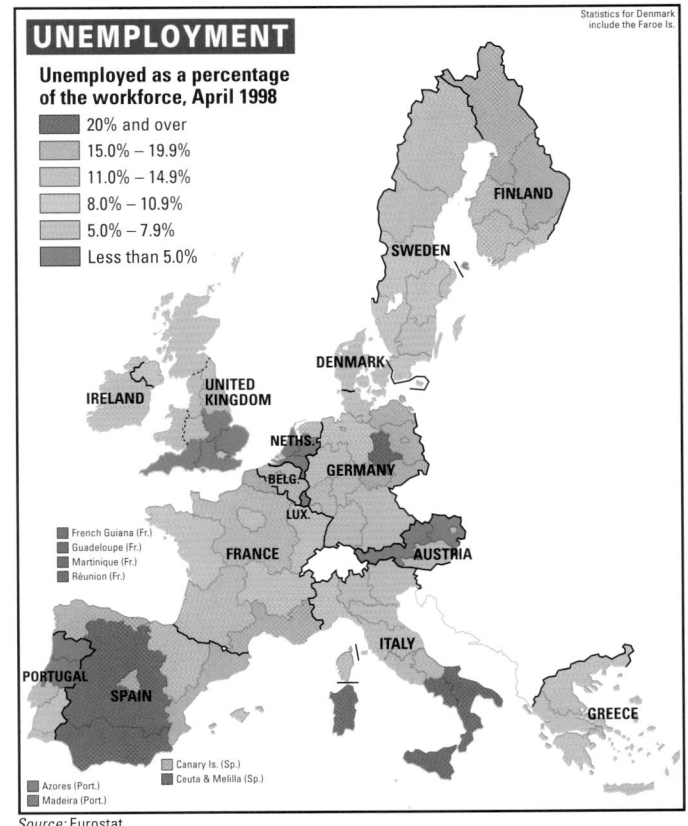

French Guiana (Fr.)
Guadeloupe (Fr.)
Martinique (Fr.)
Réunion (Fr.)

Azores (Port.)
Madeira (Port.)
Canary Is. (Sp.)
Ceuta & Melilla (Sp.)

Source: Eurostat

RAILWAYS AND FERRIES

This map shows principal rail and shipping routes in Europe. Some of the railways marked have limited services but are included because of their significance (such as connection to resort or international crossing).

A number of European rail passes are available, offering free travel on many rail and ferry services.

The Eurail pass is valid for first-class rail travel in the countries shown on the map. For those under 26, the Eurail Youthpass is valid in the same countries for second-class rail travel. The pass is not available to European residents or to visitors from Algeria, Morocco, Tunisia, Turkey or the former Soviet Union.

European residents are eligible for the Inter-Rail pass, offering train travel in the area shown on the map, excluding the country of purchase. Passes are available for one or more zones within the validity area.

CHANNEL TUNNEL
Eurostar: Direct railway services between London (Waterloo International) and Paris (Gare du Nord), Disneyland Paris and Brussels (Gare du Midi / Zuidstation) via Ashford International, Calais-Fréthun and Lille-Europe. Services from Scotland and the north of England are planned.
Le Shuttle: Cars, coaches and motorcycles, together with their passengers, are carried on shuttles operating 24 hours a day throughout the year. Loading/unloading takes place at the Folkestone and Calais Coquelles terminals.

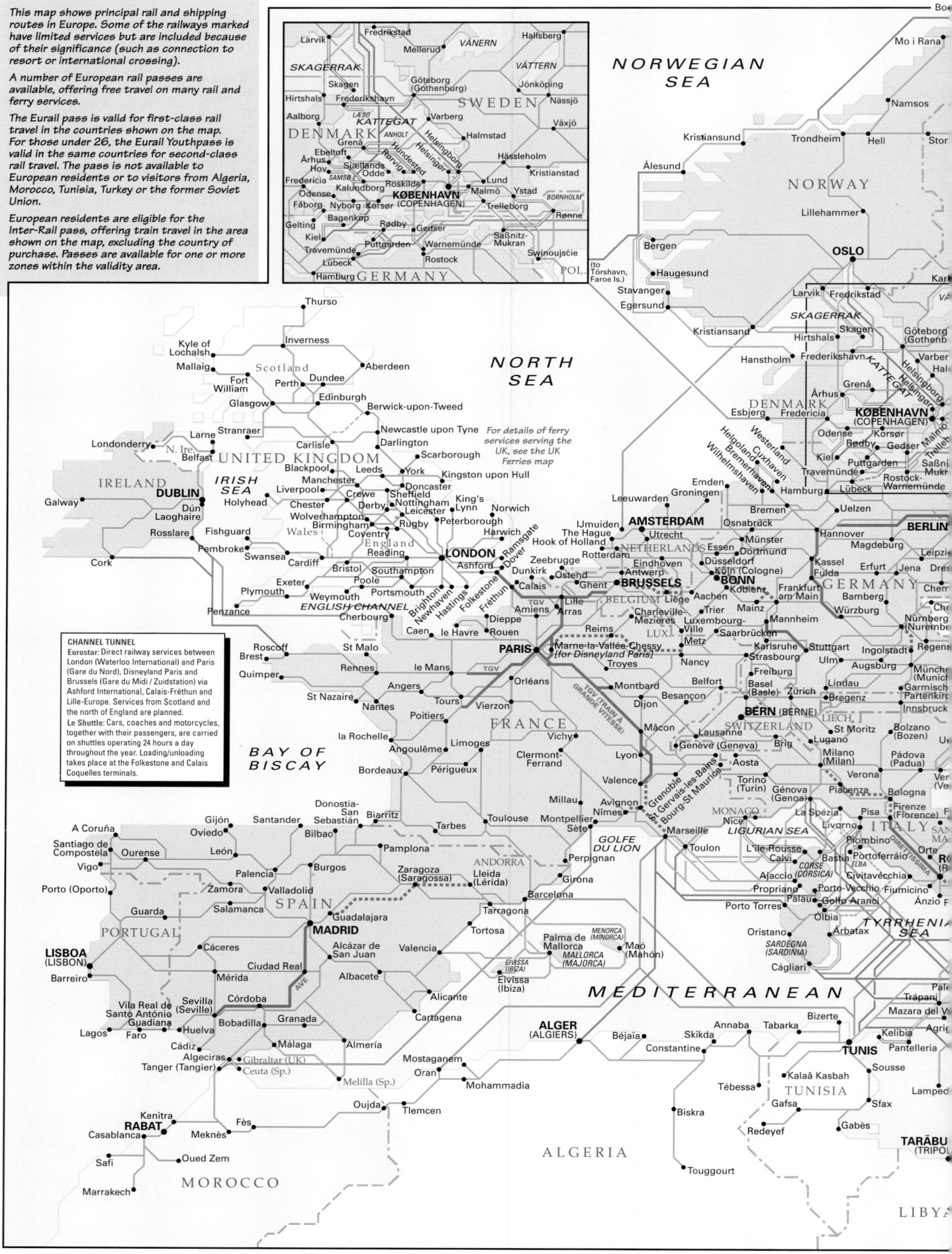

RAILWAYS AND FERRIES

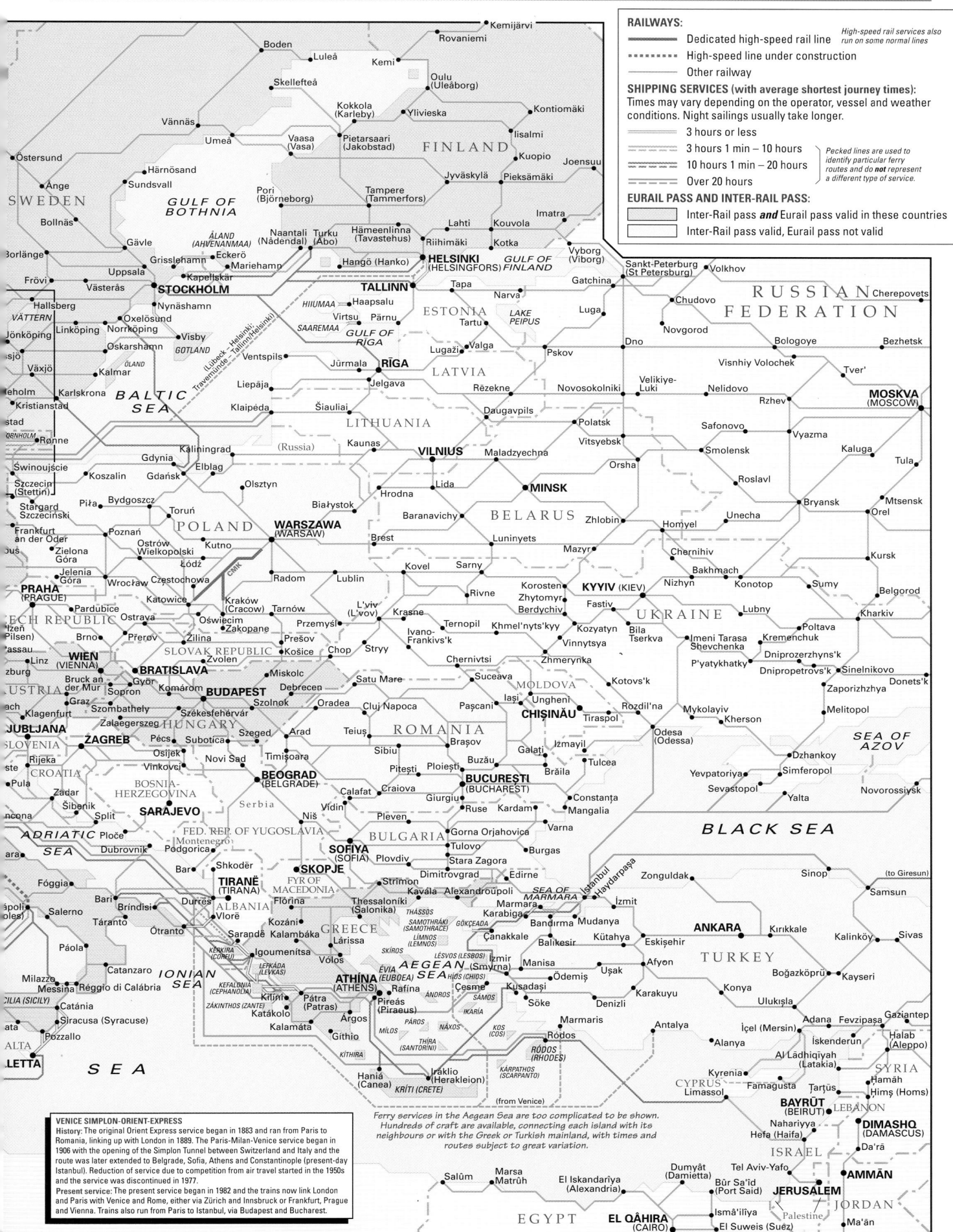

RAILWAYS:

─────── Dedicated high-speed rail line   *High-speed rail services also run on some normal lines*

- - - - - - High-speed line under construction

─────── Other railway

SHIPPING SERVICES (with average shortest journey times):
Times may vary depending on the operator, vessel and weather conditions. Night sailings usually take longer.

─────── 3 hours or less
─────── 3 hours 1 min – 10 hours   *Pecked lines are used to identify particular ferry routes and do not represent a different type of service.*
─────── 10 hours 1 min – 20 hours
─────── Over 20 hours

EURAIL PASS AND INTER-RAIL PASS:

Inter-Rail pass *and* Eurail pass valid in these countries

Inter-Rail pass valid, Eurail pass not valid

VENICE SIMPLON-ORIENT-EXPRESS

History: The original Orient Express service began in 1883 and ran from Paris to Romania, linking up with London in 1889. The Paris-Milan-Venice service began in 1906 with the opening of the Simplon Tunnel between Switzerland and Italy and the route was later extended to Belgrade, Sofia, Athens and Constantinople (present-day Istanbul). Reduction of service due to competition from air travel started in the 1950s and the service was discontinued in 1977.

Present service: The present service began in 1982 and the trains now link London and Paris with Venice and Rome, either via Zürich and Innsbruck or Frankfurt, Prague and Vienna. Trains also run from Paris to Istanbul, via Budapest and Bucharest.

Ferry services in the Aegean Sea are too complicated to be shown. Hundreds of craft are available, connecting each island with its neighbours or with the Greek or Turkish mainland, with times and routes subject to great variation.

BLUE FLAG BEACHES

The European Blue Flag Campaign is an environmental awareness raising activity by the Foundation for Environmental Education in Europe (FEEE).

To qualify for a Blue Flag, a beach has to fulfil a number of strict criteria regarding water quality (compliance with the EU Bathing Water Directive), environmental education and information, environmental management and safety and services. The Blue Flag is awarded annually and is valid for one year.

1,927 resort beaches in 17 countries were awarded Blue Flags for 1998. In addition, Blue Flags, based on slightly different criteria, were awarded to 572 marinas.

For further information, contact any of the national Blue Flag operator organisations.

Countries where the Blue Flag Campaign is operational

NORWEGIAN SEA

NORWA

IRELAND

Blue Flags awarded to 74 beaches and four marinas

An Taisce, Blue Flag Office, State Apartments, Dublin Castle, Dublin 2.

Figures in brackets after the name indicate the number of Blue Flag beaches in each municipality

Leinster

53 **Louth:** Shelling Hill / Templetown (1), Clogherhead (1)
54 **Dublin:** Donabate (1), Seapoint (1), Killiney (1)
55 **Wicklow:** Greystones (1), Arklow (2)
56 **Wexford:** Courtown (1), Curracloe (1), Rosslare (1), Duncannon (1)
57 **Westmeath:** Collinstown (1), Mullingar (1)

Munster

58 **Waterford:** Dunmore East (1), Bunmahon (1), Clonea (1)
59 **Cork:** Youghal (2), Shanagarry (1), Old Head of Kinsale (1), Clonakilty (1),

Ross Carbery (2), Skibbereen (1)
60 **Kerry:** Caherdaniel (1), Ballinskelligs (1), Caherciveen (2), Glenbeigh (1), Anascaul (1), Ventry (1), Castlegregory (1), Fenit (1), Ardfert (1), Ballyheige (1), Ballybunion (2)

Connacht (Connaught)

61 **Clare:** Kilrush (1), Milltown-Malbay (1), Lehinch (1), Ballyvaughan (1)
62 **Galway:** Kilronan, Inishmore (1), Kinvarra (1), Loughrea (1), Galway City (1), Spiddal (2), Carraroe (1)
63 **Mayo:** Louisburgh (2), Clare Island (1), Murrisk (1), Mulranny (1), Achill (5), Belmullet (2), Killala (1)
64 **Sligo:** Inishcrone (1), Rosses Point (1), Mullaghmore (1)

Ulster

65 **Donegal:** Bundoran (1), Rossnowlagh (1), Laghy (1), Killybegs (1), Portnoo (1), Creeslough (1), Downings (1), Kerrykeel (1), Culdaff (1), Fahan (1)

DENMARK

Blue Flags awarded to 185 beaches and 81 marinas

Friluftsrådet, Scandiagade 13, DK-2450 København

Figures in brackets after the name indicate the number of Blue Flag beaches in each municipality

Sjælland (Zealand), Falster, Lolland, Møn

37 **Storstrøm:** Næstved (1), Vordingborg (2), Nakskov (1), Rudbjerg (4), Rødby (3), Holeby (1), Sydfalster (2)
38 **Roskilde (east coast):** Greve (1)
39 **Københavns Amt (Copenhagen County):** Ishøj (1), Vallensbæk (1), Brøndby (1), Værløse (1)
40 **København (Copenhagen City):** København (Copenhagen) (1)

Fyn (Fünen), Ærø, Langeland

41 **Frederiksborg:** Græsted-Gilleleje (4), Helsinge (1), Frederiksværk (1), Hundested (2), Jægerspris (1)
42 **Roskilde (west coast):** Roskilde (1), Lejre (1)
43 **Vestsjælland:** Holbæk (2), Nykøbing Rørvig (4), Trundholm (1), Dragsholm (4), Bjergsted (1), Kalundborg (1), Gørlev (3), Slagelse (2), Korsør (3), Skælskør (2), Ringsted (1), Sorø (1)
44 **Fyn:** Marstal (1), Sydlangeland (2), Rudkøbing (1), Svendborg (3), Middelfart (3), Norre Åby (2), Fåborg (1)
45 **Sønderjylland (east coast):** Sønderborg (1), Sydals (2), Nordborg (2), Åbenrå (5), Haderslev (2)
46 **Vejle:** Kolding (1), Fredericia (2), Børkop (2), Vejle (1), Juelsminde (1),

Horsens (1)
47 **Århus:** Odder (5), Ry (2), Ebeltoft (4), Grenå (2), Nørre Djurs (4), Rougsø (3)
48 **Nordjylland:** Hadsund (2), Sejlflod (1), Hals (5), Dronninglund (1), Sæby (2), Læsø (1), Frederikshavn (3), Skagen (5), Hirtshals (5), Hjørring (3), Løkken-Vrå (2), Pandrup (4), Brovst (1), Fjerritslev (2), Aalborg (1), Løgstør (2), Farsø (2)
49 **Viborg:** Sallingsund (1), Spøttrup (1), Mors (1), Thisted (3), Sydthy (1)
50 **Ringkøbing:** Struer (1), Thyborøn-Harboør (2), Lemvig (4), Ulfborg-Vemb (3), Ringkøbing (3), Holmsland (2)
51 **Ribe:** Blåbjerg (3), Blåvands Huk (4), Fanø (1)
52 **Sønderjylland (west coast):** Skærbæk (1)

Jylland (Jutland)

THE NETHERLANDS

Blue Flags awarded to 19 beaches and 10 marinas

Secretariat Blauwe Vlag, P.A. ANWB (ALB/PTGR), Wassenaarseweg 220, NL-2596 EC Den Haag.

Figures in brackets after the name indicate the number of Blue Flag beaches in each municipality

66 **Friesland:** Ameland (2), Terschelling (1)
67 **Noord-Holland:** Den Helder (1), Zijpe (4)
68 **Zuid-Holland:** Noordwijk (1), Voorne (1), Goeree (2)
69 **Zeeland:** Schouwen-Duiveland (1), Veere (6)

BELGIUM

Blue Flags awarded to nine beaches and four marinas

Bond Beter Leefmilieu, Tweekerkenstraat 47, B-1000 Brussel.

Figures in brackets after the name indicate the number of Blue Flag beaches in each municipality

70 **West-Vlaanderen:** Jabbeke (1)
71 **Antwerpen:** Lille (1), Kasterlee (1), Dessel (1)
72 **Limburg:** Zonhoven (1)
73 **Vlaams-Brabant:** Zemst (1), Londerzeel (1), Averbode (1)

GERMANY

Blue Flags awarded to 15 beaches and 156 marinas

Deutsche Gesellschaft für Umwelterziehung, Frauental 25, D-20149 Hamburg.

Figures in brackets after the name indicate the number of Blue Flag beaches in each municipality

Mecklenburg-Vorpommern

30 **Wolgast:** Ahlbeck (1), Heringsdorf (1), Bansin (1), Zinnowitz (1)
31 **Rügen:** Binz (1)
32 **Ribnitz-Damgarten:** Zingst (1), Prerow (1), Ahrenshoop (1), Dierhagen (1)
33 **Rostock:** Graal-Müritz (1), Warnemünde (1)
34 **Bad Doberan:** Heiligendamm (1), Kühlungsborn (1)
35 **Grevesmühlen:** Boltenhagen (1)

Nordrhein-Westfalen

36 **Kleve:** Wisseler See (1)

PORTUGAL

Blue Flags awarded to 117 beaches and four marinas

Associacao Bandeira Azul da Europa (ABAE), Edifício Bartolomeu Dias, no. 11-1, Gab. 8, Doca de Alcântara, P-1350 Lisboa.

Figures in brackets after the name indicate the number of Blue Flag beaches in each municipality

94 **Viana do Castelo:** Caminha (1), Viana do Castelo (5), Ponte de Lima (1)
95 **Aveiro:** Espinho (1), Ovar (2), Murtosa (1), Ílhavo (2), Vagos (1)
96 **Coimbra:** Mira (1), Cantanhede (1), Figueira da Foz (2)
97 **Leiria:** Leiria (1), Marinha Grande (2), Alcobaça (3), Nazaré (1), Peniche (4)
98 **Lisboa (Lisbon):** Torres Vedras (3),

Sintra (3), Cascais (4)
99 **Setúbal:** Almada (3), Sesimbra (1), Grândola (2)
100 **Faro:** Aljezur (2), Vila do Bispo (1), Lagos (3), Portimão (5), Lagoa (1), Silves (2), Albufeira (14), Loulé (5), Tavira (3), Castro Marim (3), Vila Real de Santo António (2)

Açores (Azores)

101 **Faial** (2)
102 **Pico** (1)
103 **Graciosa** (4)
104 **Terceira:** Vila Praia da Vitória (3), Angra do Heroísmo (3)
105 **São Miguel:** Nordeste (1), Vila Franca do Campo (4), Lagoa (1), Ponta Delgada (3)
106 **Santa Maria** (2)

Madeira

107 **Porto Santo** (2)
108 **Madeira:** Porto Moniz (1), Santa Cruz (1), Funchal (4)

For Blue Flag and Seaside Award beaches in the UK, see UK beaches map

SPAIN

Blue Flags awarded to 370 beaches and 88 marinas

Asociación de Educación Ambiental y del Consumidor (A.D.E.A.C.), Salustiano Olozaga 5, 4 derecha, 28001 Madrid.

Figures in brackets after the name indicate the number of Blue Flag beaches in each municipality

País Vasco

87 **Guipúzcoa:** Getaria (1), Zumaia (1)
88 **Vizcaya:** Ibarrangelua (1), Bermeo (1), Sopelana (2), Getxo (1)

Cantabria

89 **Castro-Urdiales (1), Laredo (1), Santoña (1), Noja (2), Arnuero (1), Santander (5), Comillas (1), San Vicente de la Barquera (1)

Principado de Asturias

90 **Llanes** (2)

Galicia

91 **Lugo:** Ribadeo (2), Barreiros (2), Foz (4), Burela (1), Cervo (2), Viveiro (2), Vicedo (1)
92 **A Coruña:** Mañón (2), Valdoviño (1), Miño (1), Oleiros (2), A Coruña (2), Carballo (1), Malpica (1), Laxe (1), Fisterra (1), Muros (2), A Pobra do Caramiñal (1)
93 **Pontevedra:** Vilagarcía (1), O Grove (1), Sanxenxo (1), Marín (2), Bueu (1), Cangas (1), Vigo (2), Nigrán (1)

Canarias (Canary Islands)

109 **Tenerife:** Adeje (1), Puerto del Santiago (1), Icod de los Vinos (1), Puerto de la Cruz (1), Tacoronte (1)
110 **Gran Canaria:** Las Palmas de Gran Canaria (1), San Bartolomé de Tirajana (3), Mogán (1)
111 **Lanzarote:** Haría (1), Teguise (3), Arrecife (1), Tías (1), Yaiza (2)

Andalucia

112 **Huelva:** Isla Cristina (1), Islantilla (1), Punta Umbría (3), Moguer (1), Almonte (1)
113 **Cádiz:** Chipiona (2), Rota (2), San Fernando (1), Cádiz (2), Chiclana de la Frontera (2), Conil de la Frontera (1), Algeciras (1), La Línea de la Concepción (1)
114 **Málaga:** Manilva (1), Estepona (1), Marbella (5), Mijas (2), Fuengirola (2), Benalmádena (1), Torremolinos (4), Málaga (1), Vélez-Málaga (1), Nerja (1)
115 **Granada:** Almuñécar (2)
116 **Almería:** Adra (2), El Ejido (3), Roquetas de Mar (3), Almería (5), Níjar (2), Carboneras (1), Mojácar (2), Vera (2), Cuevas de Almanzora (1), Pulpí (1)

Región de Murcia

117 **Águilas (4), Mazarrón (4), Cartagena (7), Los Alcázares (4), San Javier (4)

Comunidad Valenciana

118 **Alicante:** Pilar de la Horadada (3), Orihuela (4), Torrevieja (3), Guardamar del Segura (3), Santa Pola (3), Elx (Elche) (2), Alicante (4), Campello (3), La Vila Joiosa (2), Finestrat (1), Benidorm (3), Alfaz del Pi (1), Altea (1), Calpe (3), Benissa (1), Teulada (1), Xabia (Jávea) (2), Denia (3)
119 **Valencia:** Oliva (1), Gandía (5), Xeraco (1), Tavernes de la Valldigna (2), Cullera (4), Sueca (1), Valencia (1), Sagunto (2), Canet d'En Berenguer (1)
120 **Castellón:** Xilxes (1), Moncófar (1), Benicàsim (5), Oropesa (2),

Torreblanca (2), Alcalá de Chivert (4), Peñíscola (1), Benicarló (1), Vinaròs (1)

Catalunya (Catalonia)

121 **Tarragona:** Alcanar (1), Sant Carles de la Ràpita (1), Deltebre (1), l'Ampolla (2), l'Ametlla de Mar (4), Vandellòs i l'Hospitalet de l'Infant (3), Mont-roig del Camp (2), Cambrils (2), Salou (2), Tarragona (3), Altafulla (1), Torredembarra (2), El Vendrell (3), Calafell (3), Cunit (1)
122 **Barcelona:** Cubelles (1), Vilanova i la Geltrú (2), Sitges (5), Barcelona (4), El Masnou (1), Canet de Mar (1), Calella (1), Pineda de Mar (1), Malgrat de Mar (1)
123 **Girona:** Blanes (3), Lloret de Mar (3), Tossa de Mar (2), Sant Feliu de Guíxols (1), Castell-Platja d'Aro (3),

Calonge (2), Palamós (3), Palafrugell (4), Begur (2), l'Escala (3), Castelló d'Empúries (1), Roses (4), El Port de la Selva (2), Llançà (2), Portbou (1)

Islas Baleares (Balearic Islands)

124 **Formentera** (2)
125 **Eivissa (Ibiza):** Sant Josep (3), Sant Joan de Labritja (2), Santa Eulalia del Río (3)
126 **Mallorca (Majorca):** Palma de Mallorca (1), Calvià (6), Alcúdia (1), Muro (1), Santa Margalida (1), Capdepera (4), Son Servera (2), Sant Llorenç des Cardassar (2), Manacor (6), Felanitx (2), Santanyí (4), Ses Salines (1)
127 **Menorca (Minorca):** Es Mercadal (2), Maó (Mahón) (2), Alaior (1), Ferreries (1)

Not to scale

BLUE FLAG BEACHES

SWEDEN
Blue Flags awarded to 37 beaches and 44 marinas

Keep Sweden Tidy Foundation,
Kapellgränd 7,
PO Box 4155,
S-102 64 Stockholm.
Figures in brackets after the name indicate the number of Blue Flag beaches in each municipality

Göteborg och Bohus
1 Göteborg (3)
Halland
2 Varberg (4)
3 Träslövsläge (1)
4 Falkenberg (3)
5 Halmstad (2)
6 Laholm (4)
7 Hyltebruk (1)
Skåne
8 Båstad (1)
9 Ängelholm (1)
10 Helsingborg (1)
11 Malmö (1)
12 Vellinge (1)
13 Ystad (1)
14 Kristianstad (3)
Blekinge
15 Sölvesborg (1)
Kalmar
16 Torsås (1)
17 Borgholm (1)
18 Västervik (1)
Östergötland
19 Motala (2)
Stockholm
20 Södertälje (1)
21 Skärholmen (1)
22 Stockholm (1)
23 Norrtälje (1)
Västernorrland
24 Ånge (1)

FINLAND
Blue Flags awarded to five beaches and 40 marinas
Pidä Saaristo Siistinä ry,
PO Box 826,
FIN-20101 Turku.
25 Kalajoki: Camping Hiekkasärkät
26 Vaasa: Paradise Beach
27 Helsinki: Hietaranta
28 Heinola: Kylpylän Uimaranta
29 Kuopio: Rauhalahti

ESTONIA
Blue Flags awarded to seven marinas
Hoia Eesti Merd,
Regati Boulevard 1 6K/238,
EE-0019 Tallinn.

FRANCE
Blue Flags awarded to beaches in 102 municipalities and to 63 individual marinas
of - F.E.E.E.,
6, avenue du Maine,
75015 Paris.
Certain criteria are examined at the municipal level as well as for individual beaches.
Figures in brackets after the name indicate the number of Blue Flag beaches in each municipality. The municipalities where all the beaches satisfied Blue Flag criteria are identified with an asterisk: *.
Nord-Pas-de-Calais
74 Nord: Flandre-Zuydcoote*
75 Pas-de-Calais: le Portel*, Cucq*, Merlimont*, Berck-sur-Mer*
Picardie
76 Somme: Ault (2)
Haute-Normandie
77 Seine-Maritime: Dieppe*, Hautot-sur-Mer*, le Tilleul*
Basse-Normandie
78 Manche: St Vaast-la-Hougue*, Siouville-Hague*, Barneville-Carteret*, St Georges-de-la-Rivière*
Bretagne (Brittany)
79 Ille-et-Vilaine: Cancale (4)
80 Côtes d'Armor: Etables-sur-Mer (1), St Quay-Portrieux (1), Trévou-Treguignec (3), Trégastel (1), Trébeurden (3), Trédrez (1)
81 Morbihan: Guidel (2), Étel*, Erdeven*, Vannes*, Locmariaquer*
Pays de la Loire
82 Loire-Atlantique: Mesquer (3), Piriac-sur-Mer (3), la Turballe (3), St Brévin-les-Pins (4), St Michel-Chef-Chef (2), Pornic (4)
83 Vendée: Noirmoutier-en-l'Île (4), St Hilaire-de-Riez (4), St Gilles-Croix-de-Vie (1), Brétignolles-sur-Mer*, Olonne-sur-Mer*, Jard-sur-Mer*, St Vincent-sur-Jard (1),

Longeville-sur-Mer*, la Faute-sur-Mer*, l'Aiguillon-sur-Mer*
Poitou-Charentes
84 Charente-Maritime: la Rochelle (2), Fouras (3), Port-des-Barques (1), la Tremblade (1), Meschers-sur-Gironde (1), Île de Ré: Loix*, le Bois-Plage-en-Ré*, Île d'Oléron: St Denis d'Oléron*, Dolus-d'Oleron (1), le Grand-Village-Plage*, St Trojan-les-Bains*
Aquitaine
85 Gironde: Soulac-sur-Mer (1), Vendays-Montalivet*, Hourtin (1), Carcans (2), Lège-Cap-Ferret*, Arès (1), Andernos-les-Bains*, Lanton*, Arcachon (1), la Teste-de-Buch*
86 Landes: Seignosse (2)
Languedoc-Roussillon
128 Pyrénées-Orientales: Cerbère (2), Banyuls-sur-Mer*, Port-Vendres (2), Collioure (3), Argelès-sur-Mer*, St Cyprien*, Canet en Roussillon*, Torreilles (2), le Barcarès*
129 Aude: Leucate*, Port-la-Nouvelle*, Peyriac-de-Mer*, Gruissan (6), Narbonne*
130 Hérault: Sète (3), Frontignan (2), Villeneuve-les-Maguelonne (1), Mauguio (3), la Grand-Motte (3)
131 Gard: le Grau-du-Roi (7)
Provence-Alpes-Côte d'Azur
132 Bouches-du-Rhône: Fos-sur-Mer*, Martigues*, la Ciotat (2)
133 Var: St Cyr-sur-Mer (2), Bandol (3), Hyères (11), la Londe-les-Maures*, Bormes-les-Mimosas (2), le Lavandou (6), la Croix-Valmer (2), Cogolin*, Grimaud (2), Fréjus (4)
134 Alpes-Maritimes: Mandelieu (4), Cannes (10), Antibes (21), Cap d'Ail*, Menton (6)
Corse (Corsica)
135 Corse-du-Sud: Grosseto-Prugna (1)

SLOVENIA
Blue Flags awarded to three beaches and one marina
Figures in brackets after the name indicate the number of Blue Flag beaches in each municipality
DOVES,
C. Solinarjev 4,
6320 Portoroz.
168 Piran (1)
169 Portoroz (2)

CROATIA
Blue Flag awarded to one marina
Pokret Prijatelja Prirode -
"Lijepa Nasa",
Demetrova 11,
HR-1000 Zagreb.

GREECE
Blue Flags awarded to 326 beaches and seven marinas
Hellenic Society for the Protection of Nature,
24, Nikis Str.,
GR-105 57 Athens.
Figures in brackets after the name indicate the number of Blue Flag beaches in each municipality
Ionian Islands
170 Kérkira (Corfu): Kassiópi (5), Spartilas (1), Káto Korakiana (2), Kérkira (Corfu) (2), Lefkimi (2), Pélekas (2), Gianades (1), Thinalio (2), Pági (1), Magoulades (1), Avliótes (1), Peroulades (1), Sidári (1)
171 Kefalonía (Cephalonia): Póros (1), Skála (1), Argostóli (2), Mandzavinata (1)
172 Zákinthos (Zante): Meso Gerakari (1), Plános (1), Zákinthos (Zante) (1), Tragaki (2)
Epirus
173 Thesprotia: Igoumenitsa (2)
174 Préveza: Mitikas (1)
Western Greece (north)
175 Etolia Akarnania: Mitikas (1), Messolóngi (1), Náfpaktos (2)
Central Greece (southwest)
176 Fokida: Itéa (1)
177 Viotia: Antikira (1)

Peloponnese (north)
178 Kórinthia (north): Loutráki (2), Vraháti (1), Kokkoni (1), Xilókastro (1)
Western Greece (south)
179 Ahaia: Lakópetra (1), Metóhi (1)
180 Ilia: Kástro (1), Amaliáda (1), Zaháro (1)
Peloponnese (south)
181 Messinia: Methóni (2), Finikoúndas (3), Messini (1), Kalamáta (1)
182 Lakonia: Néo Itilo (1), Githio (1), Mólai/Elaea (1), Neápoli (2)
183 Arkadia: Leonídio (1), Parálio Ástros (1)
184 Argolida: Kivéri (1), Náfplio (2), Toló (1), Portohéli (1), Thermisia (1)
Attica
185 Atiki: Alimos (1), Vouliagméni (2), Anávissos (1), Markópoulo (1)
Central Greece (northeast)
186 Evia (Euboea): Erétria (4)
187 Pefkohória: Atalánti (1), Livanates (2), Kaména Voúrla (1), Ráhes (1)
Thessaly
188 Magnissia: Almirós (1), Efxinoúpolis (1), Vólos (3), Afétes (1), Tsangaráda (1), Mourési (2), Agios Dimitrios (1), Zagorá (1), Skiathos (8), Skópelos (5)
189 Lárissa: Skiti (1)
Central Macedonia
190 Pieria: Néa Póri (1), Platamónas (2), Pandeleimónas (2), Skotína (1), Litohóro (2), Peristasi (1), Kateríni (1),

Korinós (1), Makrigialós (2)
191 Thessaloniki (west): Peréa (1), Agia Triáda (2), Epanomi (1)
192 Halkidiki: Kassándria (2), Kalándra (2), Foúrka (1), Néa Skióni (1), Pefkohóri (1), Haniótis (2), Políhrono (2), Kriopigí (4), Kalithéa (1), Néa Fókea (1), Gerakiní (1), Ormília (1), Metamórfossi (1), Nikitas (4), Néos Marmarás (5), Sikia (2), Sárti (1), Ágios Nikólaos (5), Ouranópoli (2), Néa Róda (2), Olimbiáda (3)
193 Thessaloniki (east): Káto Stavrós (1), Vrassná (1), Asproválta (2)
Eastern Macedonia & Thrace
194 Kavála: Kariani (1), Kavála (3), Thassos: Prínos (1), Panagiá (1), Thassos (1)
195 Xánthi: Mángana (1)
196 Rodópi: Fanári (1)
197 Évros: Alexandroúpoli (1)
Northern Aegean
198 Limnos (Lemnos): Mirina (1)
199 Lésvos (Lesbos): Pétra (2), Mithimna (2), Klió (1), Mitilíni (1), Paleókipos (1), Skópelos (1), Plomári (1), Vrissa (1), Polihnitos (1), Kalloni (1), Messótopos (1), Eressós (1)
200 Hios (Chios): Neohóri (1), Kardámila (1), Omiroúpoli (1)
201 Sámos: Sámos (1), Pithagório (1)

Southern Aegean
202 Tinos: Ktikados (1)
203 Siros: Ano Síros (1)
204 Mikonos: Mikonos (1), Áno Merá (1)
205 Páros: Márpissa (3)
206 Náxos: Koronída (1)
207 Milos: Adamandás (1), Milos (1)
208 Ios: Íos (3)
209 Thira (Santorini): Kamári (1)
210 Kos (Cos): Asfendíoú (1), Kos (Cos) (4), Kardámena (1)
211 Ródos (Rhodes): Theológos (1), Ialisos (1), Ródos (Rhodes) (2), Koskinoú (6), Kalithiés (6), Afándou (4), Kálathos (2), Líndos (1), Lárdos (2), Asklipío (2), Genádio (1)
Crete
212 Haniá (Canea): Paleohóra (2), Máleme (1), Platanias (1), Geraniou (1), Néa Kidonia (4), Stérnes (1), Kalives (1), Pláka (1)
213 Réthimno (north coast): Réthimno (6), Adéle (1), Pigi (1), Prínos (1)
214 Iráklio (Herakleion) (north coast): Ahlada (4), Rodiá (1), Gázi (2), Elia (1), Anópolis (1), Goúves (2), Limenas Hersonissou (4), Mália (1)
215 Lassithi: Vrahási (1), Eloúnda (6), Ágios Nikólaos (12), Kató Horió (1), Sitia (2), Palékastro (3), Péfki (3), Ágios Ioánnni (1), Ierápetra (1)
216 Iráklio (Herakleion) (south coast): Pitsidía (1)

BULGARIA
Blue Flags awarded to nine beaches
Bulgarian Blue Flag Movement,
Slantchev Briag - 8240.
Figures in brackets after the name indicate the number of Blue Flag beaches in each municipality
242 Burgas: Primorsko (1), Sozopol (1), Nesebur (Nessebar) (2)
243 Varna: Varna (3), Balchik (1), Kavarna (1)

TURKEY
Blue Flags awarded to 43 beaches and ten marinas
Türkiye Çevre Egitim Vakfi,
Gazi Mustafa Kemal Bulvari No. 121/22,
06570 Tandogan-Ankara.
Figures in brackets after the name indicate the number of Blue Flag beaches in each municipality

Antalya		Bolu
221 Kestel (1)	227 Beldibi (1)	233 Turunç (1)	238 Akçakoca (1)
222 Manavgat (4)	228 Göynük (1)	234 Datça (1)	Sinop
223 Çolakli (1)	229 Kemer (2)	235 Bodrum (9)	239 Sinop (3)
224 Belek (4)	230 Tekirova (2)	Izmir	Isparta
225 Muratpasa (1)	231 Kas (1)	236 Foça (1)	240 Egirdir (1)
226 Konyaalti (4)	232 Marmaris (1)	Balikesir	Elazig
		237 Ayvalik (2)	241 Sivrice (1)

Mugla
232 Marmaris (1)

ITALY
Blue Flags awarded to beaches in 58 municipalities and to 44 marinas
FEEE-Italia,
Via della Guglia, 69b,
00186 Roma.
The Blue Flag is awarded, in most cases, to the local administrations and not to individual beaches. The municipal authority is then responsible for ensuring that the Blue Flag flies only on those beaches which fulfil the criteria relating to beach management and provision of environmental

information. The following municipalities have been awarded Blue Flags or contain individual Blue Flag beaches.
Sardegna (Sardinia)
136 Nuoro (west coast): Bosa
137 Sassari: Castelsardo, Santa Teresa di Gallura, La Maddalena, Golfo Aranci
138 Nuoro (east coast): Siniscóla
139 Cagliari: Quartu San'Elena
Liguria
140 Imperia: Bordighera, Taggia, Diano Marina, San

Bartolomeo al Mare, Cervo
141 Savona: Andora, Laiguéglia, Finale Ligure, Noli, Bergeggi, Albisola Marina, Celle Ligure
142 Génova (Genoa): Portofino, Lavagna, Sestri Levante
143 La Spézia: Déiva Marina, Framura, Monterosso
Toscana (Tuscany)
144 Lucca: Forte dei Marmi, Camaiore, Viaréggio
145 Pisa: Tirrénia
146 Livorno: Rosignano

Marittimo, Castagneto Carducci
Lazio
147 Latina: Sperlonga
Campania
148 Nápoli (Naples): Anacapri
149 Salerno: Positano, Agrópoli, Póllica, Centola
Basilicata (west coast)
150 Potenza: Maratea
Sicilia (Sicily)
151 Palermo: Ustica

152 Agrigento: Menfi
153 Messina: Taormina
Calábria (east coast)
154 Cosenza: Roseto Capo
Basilicata (east coast)
155 Matera: Policoro
Puglia
156 Taranto: Ginosa
157 Brindisi: Ostuni
158 Fóggia: Vieste, Rodi Gargánico, Chiéuti
Molise
159 Campobasso: Térmoli

Abruzzo
160 Chieti: Vasto
161 Téramo: Tortoreto
Marche
162 Ascoli Piscenо: Cupra Marittima
163 Ancona: Sirolo, Senigállia
Veneto
164 Venézia (Venice): Bibione
Friuli-Venézia Giulia
165 Udine: Lignano Sabbiadoro
166 Gorizia: Grado
167 Trieste: Trieste

CYPRUS
Blue Flags awarded to 25 beaches
CYMEPA,
Irinis Square & Navarinou Str.,
P.O. Box 6671,
3309 Limassol.
Figures in brackets after the name indicate the number of Blue Flag beaches in each municipality.
217 Paphos: Pólis (2), Péyia (2), Paphos (5), Geroskipou (1)
218 Lemesos (Limassol): Pissoúri (1), Yermasóyia (1), Áyios Tychon (1), Pyrgos (1)
219 Larnaca: Larnaca (2)
220 Famagusta: Ayía Nápa (4), Paralimni (1)

LEISURE PARKS

This map shows major theme parks and amusement parks in Europe. Most of those shown are members of either the International Association of Amusement Parks and Attractions (IAAPA) or the European Federation of Amusement and Leisure Parks (Europark). Most parks which primarily attract visitors from the local area have been excluded. A number of zoos, waterparks and museums are also members of IAAPA or Europark.

For more information, contact:

IAAPA,
1448 Duke Street,
Alexandria,
Virginia 22314,
USA.

Tel. +1 703 836 4800.

Europark,
Floralaan West 143,
NL-5644 BH Eindhoven,
The Netherlands.

Tel. +31 40 212 8526.

EUROPE'S MOST POPULAR PARKS IN 1998
Number of visitors (world ranking in brackets)
Disneyland Paris France: 12.5 million (4th)
Blackpool Pleasure Beach UK: 6.6 million (9th)
Gardaland Italy: 2.9 million (30th)
Tivoli Denmark: 2.8 million (34th)
De Efteling The Netherlands: 2.7 million (=35th)
Port Aventura Spain: 2.7 million (=35th)
Europa-Park Germany: 2.7 million (=35th)
Alton Towers UK: 2.5 million (=41st)
Liseberg Sweden: 2.5 million (=41st)
Source: Amusement Business

Norway

1 Kristiansand Dyrepark
Combined animal park and entertainment park
2 Telemark Sommerland, Bø
Combined theme park and waterpark
3 Lunds Tivoli, Oslo
Amusement park
4 TusenFryd & VikingLandet, Vinterbru
Theme park with many rides and large Viking Land

Sweden

5 Liseberg, Gothenburg
Large theme park with convention facilities, exhibition hall and sports stadium
6 Parken Zoo i Eskilstuna
Theme park, waterpark and zoo
7 Gröna Lunds Tivoli, Stockholm
Amusement park in the centre of Stockholm
8 Furuviksparken, Gavle
Amusement park and zoo
9 Jamtli Historieland, Östersund
Historical theme park

Finland

10 Wasalandia, Vaasa
Amusement park; Tropical Spa Tropiclandia nearby
11 Tampereen Sarkanniemi Oy, Tampere
City-centre amusement park and entertainment centre; also includes an art museum
12 Linnanmäki, Helsinki
Finland's most popular amusement park

Denmark

13 Jesperhus Blomstherpark, Nykøbing, Mors
Amusement park, family entertainment centre and zoo
14 Fårup Aquapark & Sommerland, Saltum
Amusement park with more than 30 activities and Scandinavia's largest waterpark
15 Djurs Sommerland, Nimtofte
Amusement park with more than 50 activities in six attractions: Summerland, Waterland, Africa Land, Mexico Land, Cowboy Village and Lillensland; plus Grand Prix Land and Laredo Theatre
16 Legoland, Billund
Theme park based on Lego toy products; 22 family rides plus 75,000 square metres of Lego brick replicas of world monuments
17 Dyrehavsbakken ('Bakken'), Klampenborg
The world's oldest amusement park, with 24 rides
18 Tivoli, Copenhagen
Large amusement park in the centre of Copenhagen

Ireland

19 Perks Pleasure Park, Youghal
Major rides include Vampire Ghost Train, Trabant and a giant big wheel supported by Perkie Bear
20 Clara Lara Fun Park, Wicklow
Park and amusement centre including Aqua Shuttle and Pirate Galleon plus a junior playground

United Kingdom

21 Barry's Amusement Park, Portrush
Star rides include Looping Dipper and Music Express
22 Blackpool Pleasure Beach
150 attractions including The Avalanche, Blackhole, Tagada, Nicky's Circus Ride, Beaver Creek, Believe It Or Not, Haunted Crypt, five wooden rollercoasters and a bobsleigh run; Ocean Boulevard shopping centre
23 Camelot Theme Park, Chorley, Lancashire
A medieval world with over 100 attractions and rides including Excalibur, a 360° rotation swing ride
24 Lightwater Valley, Ripon
Theme park with unique attractions including the world's first suspended hang-glider ride and the world's longest rollercoaster
25 Flamingo Land, Malton
Popular holiday village and zoo with many rides
26 Alton Towers, near Stoke-on-Trent
One of the UK's most popular theme parks with 125 rides and attractions including Nemesis, Oblivion vertical-drop rollercoaster and Storybook Land
27 Gullivers Kingdom, Matlock Bath
Family theme park with over 40 rides, hot-air balloon flights and chair lift
28 American Adventure World, Ilkeston
Theme park with Nightmare Niagara log flume
29 Magical World of Fantasy Island, Ingoldmells
Themed indoor family resort; based on Jules Verne
30 Drayton Manor Park, Tamworth
Theme park and zoo; over 100 rides and attractions including Paratower, Jungle Cruise, Pirate's Adventure, Splash Canyon and The Haunting
31 Pleasurewood Hills, Lowestoft
50 rides including Pirate Ship, Cannonball Express rollercoaster and the Log Flume

32 Oakwood Adventure, Narberth
Amusement park with over 40 attractions including Megafobia rollercoaster, The Bounce, Snake River Falls flume and a bobsleigh run
33 Legoland, Windsor
Children's theme park divided into five areas: The Beginning, The Imaginative Centre, Miniland, Duplo Gardens & Lego Traffic, My Town & The Wild Woods
34 Thorpe Park, Chertsey
Theme park with many rides including Canada Creek, Carousel Kingdom, A Drive in the Country, Flying Fish, Depth Charge and No Way Out, a backwards dark ride
35 Chessington World of Adventures
Zoo and amusement park with rides including Samurai, Dragon River and Rameses Revenge
36 Fun Acres, Southsea
Seaside park with boat trips and 10 major rides
37 Harbour Park, Littlehampton
Seaside amusement park

The Netherlands

38 Attractiepark Slagharen, Slagharen
Theme park with Wild West shows and over 40 rides
39 Avonturenpark Hellendoorn
Amusement park with many rides and animal attractions
40 Six Flags, Dronten
Family amusement park with El Condor rollercoaster and Crazy River water flume
41 Dolfinarium Harderwijk
Europe's largest marine park, with a research department; six different shows with animals and an open-air dolphin lagoon
42 Duinrell, Wassenaar
Theme park close to the beach with over 50 rides and attractions, including Splash and Waterspin
43 Drievliet, Rijswijk
More than 20 major attractions, including Coppermine rollercoaster
44 De Efteling, Kaatsheuvel
Family leisure park with a full range of attractions including a golf course, Dreamflight dark ride, Fata Morgana, Inca City and two rollercoasters

Belgium

45 Meli Park, De Panne
Attractions and rides plus a bird and animal park
46 Bellewaerde Park, Ypres
Exotic animals on display; six areas: Canada, Far West, India, Jungle, Mexico and Pepinoland; over 30 rides
47 Action Planet, Antwerp
Indoor adventure sports park
48 Bobbejaanland, Lichtaart
Amusement park with many rides with 45 major rides, including The Revolution and Arcade 2000; also includes Kinderland, a covered children's play area with 20 rides
49 Walibi, Wavre
Amusement park and waterpark with 40 rides including Rapid River, Shuttle Loop, Corkscrew and Jumbo Jet

Germany

50 Familien-Freizeitpark Tolk-Schau, Tolk
Amusement park situated in a scenic landscape
51 Hansapark, Neustadt in Holstein
Theme park with rides and attractions including an Aqua Stadium, a water circus and Adventureland
52 Ferienzentrum Schloss Dankern, Haren
Family entertainment centre with many water facilities
53 Heide-Park, Soltau
Amusement park with 36 major rides including a rapids ride, two monorails, a looping rollercoaster with four 360° turns and a bobsleigh ride
54 Serengeti Safaripark, Hodenhagen
Animal park with leisure attractions
55 Dinosaurier Park Münchehagen, Rehburg-Loccum
Dinosaur park
56 Warner Brothers Movie World, Bottrop
A unique movie theme park
57 Hollywood-Park, Stukenbrock
Combined safari park and amusement park, with attractions including Hollywood Theatre, a circus and a western show, a monkey area, Disco Round, Flying Carpet, a steam carousel and rollercoasters
58 Fort Fun Abenteuerland, Bestwig
Amusement park with a Western town
59 Panoramapark Sauerland, Kirchhundem
Wild animal park and amusement park with its own 500-kilowatt windpower station
60 Phantasialand, Brühl
Theme park divided into five areas: China Town, Old Berlin, Mexico, Petite Paris and Future World; many rides including Mystery Castle, Colorado Adventure-The Michael Jackson Thrill Ride and Galaxy
61 Eifelpark, Gondorf bei Bitburg
Wild animal park and amusement park, includes the Eifel Express
62 Holiday-Park, Hassloch
Theme park with many attractions including Thunder River, The Barrels of The Devil, Lilliput-Express, Aquascope, Stormship, a 180° cinema, Falkenstein Castle, Pfalz village and a looping rollercoaster
63 Erlebnispark Tripsdrill, Cleebronn
Germany's oldest amusement park
64 Freizeit-Land, Geiselwind
Theme park with many attractions including Cinema 2000, a Viking ship, a space adventure area, prehistoric world, Enterprise ride, Shuttle ride and a rollercoaster
65 Freizeit- und Miniaturpark Allgäu, Weitnau
Adventure park with many miniature buildings and trains; includes a large children's park with Nautic Jet, Luna Loop and Butterfly
66 Europa-Park, Rust
Large theme park with many rides

France

67 Mirapolis, Cergy-Pontoise
Large amusement park with activities related to legends and epics, includes Gargantua statue
68 Jardin d'Acclimation, Paris
Amusement park with family rides and a zoo
69 Parc Floral, Paris
Amusement park set within a large garden area
70 La Mer de Sable, Ermenonville
Amusement park developed into themed areas: China, Wild West and Morocco; includes Babagattau Village
71 Parc Astérix, Plailly
Theme park based on comic strip hero Asterix with star rides Descent of the Styx, Big Splash and Goudume
72 Disneyland Paris, Marne-la-Vallée
Divided into five 'lands': Main Street USA, Frontierland, Adventureland, Fantasyland and Discoveryland; attractions include Space Mountain, Raiders of The Lost Ark and Honey I Shrunk The Audience
73 Futuroscope, Poitiers
Advanced visual-image technology in cinemas and leisure complexes; Showscan has a double-3D screen

Spain

74 Parc d'Atraccions Tibidabo, Barcelona
Urban amusement park, founded 1899, renovated 1988
75 Port Aventura, Salou
Spain's largest theme park with five areas: Mediterrania, Polynesia, China, Mexico and Far West
76 Txiki Park, Pamplona
Family entertainment centre designed for children
77 Parque de Atracciones Casa de Campo, Madrid
Urban amusement park, Madrid's principal entertainment centre
78 Sioux City, San Agustin
Theme park with stage shows and concerts

Portugal

79 Zoomarine, Albufeira
Zoo and marine theme park

Switzerland

80 Conny-Land, Lipperswil
Amusement park with underwater and animal shows

Austria

81 Safari- und Abenteuerpark, Gänserndorf
Adventure park and drive-through safari park

Italy

82 Gardaland, Castelnuovo del Garda
Large amusement park with 25 different attractions, eleven entertainments and four themed villages
83 Mirabilandia, Savio
30 attractions including two 60m twin towers called the Turbo Drop, plus River Rapid water ride
84 Fiabilandia, Rímini
Amusement park and funfair
85 Luneur, Rome
Amusement park and funfair
86 Edenlandia, Naples
Amusement/theme park

Turkey

87 Tatilya Turizm, Avcilar, Istanbul
World's fourth largest indoor entertainment centre

MUSEUMS AND ART GALLERIES

EUROPEAN CITIES OF CULTURE

1985	Athens
1986	Florence
1987	Amsterdam
1988	Berlin
1989	Paris
1990	Glasgow
1991	Dublin
1992	Madrid
1993	Antwerp
1994	Lisbon
1995	Luxembourg
1996	Copenhagen
1997	Thessaloniki
1998	Stockholm
1999	Weimar
2000	Avignon, Bergen, Bologna, Brussels, Cracow, Helsinki, Prague, Reykjavik, Santiago de Compostela
2001	Oporto, Rotterdam
2002	Bruges, Salamanca
2003	Graz
2004	Genoa, Lille

The number and thematic range of European institutions of cultural heritage is extraordinary. This map shows the principal museums and art galleries selected accorded to the following criteria: international importance and size of the collection(s); depth and quality of the displays; accessibility from cities with international airports; and a general demographic spread across Europe based on the demands of tourism.

Most cities named will also offer the visitor a number of smaller museums of specialist interest. Many single great works of art may also be housed in local cathedrals and churches.

Data compiled by Jon A. Gillaspie.
Fax: +44 (0)20 8780 2427.
email: let@sarastro.com

Principal contents of institution:

AA Applied & decorative art
AR Archaeology / ancient art
FA Fine art (paintings, sculpture)
FO Folk art & culture / ethnology
NH Natural history
ST Science / technology
W Wide range of subjects

Opening times:

Days or months preceded by a red circle (●) indicate when the institution is closed.
Many close on national holidays and other special days. Some museums and galleries have shorter opening hours at certain days of the week or in certain months.

Admission charges:

All charge for admission except those shown in *italics*, where entry is free (although charges for special exhibitions may apply).
Some institutions allow free entry or reduce their admission charges on certain days.

Amsterdam THE NETHERLANDS
W Rijksmuseum
FA Stedelijk Museum; Van Gogh Museum
Ankara TURKEY
AR Museum of Anatolian Civilizations ● Mon
Antalya TURKEY
AR Archaeological Museum ● Mon
Antibes FRANCE
FA Musée Picasso ● Mon
Antwerpen (Antwerp) BELGIUM
FA Museum voor Schone Kunsten ● Mon
Athína (Athens) GREECE
AR Acropolis Museum; Nat. Archaeological Mus.
W Benáki Museum ● Tue
AR Museum of Cycladic and Ancient Greek Art ● Tue & Sun
Avignon FRANCE
W Musée Calvet ● Tue
FA Musée du Petit Palais ● Tue
Barcelona SPAIN
AR Museu Arqueològic ● Mon
FA Museu d'Art Contemporani; Museu N. d'Art de Catalunya; Museu Picasso ● all Mon
Bath ENGLAND
AA Museum of Costume
AA Roman Baths and Museum
Bayeux FRANCE
AA Bayeux Tapestry
Bérgamo ITALY
FA Accademia Carrara ● Mon
Bergen NORWAY
AR Bryggens Museum
FA Rasmus Meyer Collection ● Mon (Sep-May)
Berlin GERMANY
AR Ägyptisches Museum ● Mon; Antiken Museum ● Fri
W Dahlem museums ● Mon
ST Deutsches Teknikmuseum ● Mon
W Kulturforum ● Mon includes:
FA Gemäldegalerie
AA Kunstgewerbemuseum
NH Museum für Naturkunde ● Mon
W Museumsinsel ● Mon includes:
FA Alte Nationalgalerie
AR Bodemuseum; Pergamonmuseum
Bern (Berne) SWITZERLAND
FA Kunstmuseum ● Mon
Bilbao SPAIN
FA Mus. de Bellas Arte; Mus. Guggenheim ● Mon
Bologna ITALY
AR Museo Civico Archeologico ● Mon
Bonn GERMANY
NH Alexander-Koenig-Museum ● Mon
FA Kunstmuseum ● Mon
Brugge (Bruges) BELGIUM
FA Groeningemuseum ● Tue (Oct-Mar)
Bruxelles/Brussel (Brussels) BELGIUM
FA Musées Royaux des Beaux-Arts ● Mon
Budapest HUNGARY
FA National Gall.; Mus. of Fine Arts ● both Mon
AA National Jewish Museum ● Sat
W National Museum ● Mon
Cágliari SARDINIA, ITALY
AR Museo Nazionale Archeologico
Cambridge ENGLAND
W Fitzwilliam Museum ● Mon

Cardiff WALES
W National Museum and Gallery ● Mon
Den Haag (The Hague) THE NETHERLANDS
W Gemeentemuseum ● Mon
FA Mauritshuis ● Mon
Dresden GERMANY
AA Gemäldegalerie Alte Meister ● Mon
FO Museum of Ethnography ● Thu
Dublin IRELAND
FA National Gallery
AR National Museum ● Mon
Düsseldorf GERMANY
FA Kunstmuseum ● Mon
FA Kunstsammlung Nordrhein-Westfalen ● Mon
Edinburgh SCOTLAND
W Museum of Scotland
FA Nat. Gall. of Scot.; Royal Mus. of Scot.; Scot. Gall. of Modern Art; Scot. Nat. Port. Gall.
El Escorial SPAIN
FA Monasterio de El Escorial ● Mon
Les Eyzies-de-Tayac FRANCE
AR Musée National de Préhistoire ● Tue
Figueres SPAIN
FA Teatre-Museu Dalí ● Mon (Oct-Jun)
Firenze (Florence) ITALY
FA Uffizi ● Mon; Bargello ● Mon (& 1st+3rd Sun)
AR Museo Archeologico ● Mon
Frankfurt am Main GERMANY
FA Museum für Moderne Kunst ● Mon
W Museumsufer ● Mon & Thu includes:
AA Städel; Museum für Kunsthandwerk
Gdansk POLAND
W National Art Museum ● Mon
Gent (Ghent) BELGIUM
FA Museum voor Schone Kunsten
Glasgow SCOTLAND
FA Art Gallery and Museum, Kelvingrove
W Burrell Collection
FA Hunterian Art Gallery and Museum ● Sun
Göteborg (Gothenburg) SWEDEN
FA Konstmuseet ● Mon (Sep-Apr)
AA Röhsska Konstlöjdmuseet ● Mon (Sep-Apr)
Guimarães PORTUGAL
AA Museu Alberto Sampaio ● Mon
AR Museu Martins Sarmiento ● Mon
AA Sé (Cathedral museum), Braga
Hamburg GERMANY
FA Kunsthalle ● Mon
AA Museum für Kunst und Gewerbe ● Mon
Hannover GERMANY
FA Sprengel Museum ● Mon
Hildesheim GERMANY
AR Roemer-Pelizaeus Museum ● Mon
Helsinki (Helsingfors) FINLAND
FA Helsinki kaupingin museo ● Mon & Tue
W Kansallismuseo; Kiasma
Iráklio (Herakleion) CRETE, GREECE
AR Archaeological Museum
Istanbul TURKEY
AR Museum of Turkish and Islamic Art ● Mon
København (Copenhagen) DENMARK
AR Nationalmuseet ● Mon
FA Ny Carlsberg Glyptotek ● Mon
FA Statens Museum for Kunst ● Mon
Köln (Cologne) GERMANY
AR Römisch-Germanisches Museum ● Mon
FA Wallraf-Richartz/Ludwig Museum ● Mon

Kraków (Cracow) POLAND
W Czartoryski Museum ● Mon
FO Museum of Ethnography ● Tue
Kyyiv (Kiev) UKRAINE
W Historical Treasures Museum
FA Russian Art Museum ● Thu
Lisboa (Lisbon) PORTUGAL
FA Museu Nacional de Arte Antiga ● Mon
W Museu Calouste Gulbenkian ● Mon
Liverpool ENGLAND
FA Walker Art Gallery
London ENGLAND
W British Museum; Museum of London
FA Nat. Gallery; Nat. Portrait Gallery; Tate Gallery; Tate Gallery of Modern Art
NH Natural History Museum
ST Science Museum
AA Victoria and Albert Museum
Luxembourg-Ville LUXEMBOURG
FA Musée national ● Mon
Madrid SPAIN
FA Centro de Arte Reina Sofia ● Tue; Mus. del Prado; Mus. Thyssen-Bornemisza ● both Mon
AR Museo Arqueológico Nacional ● Mon
W Museo de América ● Mon
Minsk BELARUS
AR Nat. Museum of History and Culture ● Wed
Milano (Milan) ITALY
FA Civico Mus. di Arte Contemporanea; Pinacoteca Ambrosiana; Pin. di Brera ● all Mon
AR Museo Civico di Archeologico ● Mon
Moskva (Moscow) RUSSIAN FEDERATION
AA Kremlin ● Thu
FA Museum of Private Collections ● Mon & Tue; Tretyakov Gallery ● Mon
W Pushkin Museum of Fine Arts ● Mon
München (Munich) GERMANY
FA Alte und Neue Pinakothek ● Mon
AR Bayerisches Nationalmuseum ● Mon
ST Deutsches Museum
FA Glyptothek und Antikensammlungen ● Mon
Nápoli (Naples) ITALY
AR Museo Archeologico Nazionale
Nice FRANCE
FA Musée Marc-Chagall; Mus. Matisse ● both Tue
Novgorod RUSSIAN FEDERATION
AA Museum of History, Architecture and Art ● Tue
Nuoro SARDINIA, ITALY
FO Museo Etnografico ● Mon (Oct-Easter)
Oslo NORWAY
FA Nasjonalgalleriet
FO Norsk Folkemuseum
W Vikingskiphuset ● Mon (Sep-May)
Oxford ENGLAND
W Ashmolean Museum ● Mon
FA Museum of Modern Art (MOMA) ● Mon
Palermo SICILY, ITALY
AR Museo Archeologico Regionale
FO Museo Etnografico Pitrè ● Fri
Paris FRANCE
ST Cité des Sciences et de l'Industrie ● Mon
W Inst. du Monde Arabe ● Mon; Louvre ● Tue
FA Musée d'Orsay; Mus. Marmottan; Mus. Rodin ● all Mon; Musée nat. d'art moderne (Centre Georges Pompidou); Musée nat. du Moyen-Âge; Musée nat. Picasso ● all Tue

Perúgia ITALY
AR Museu Archeologico Naz. dell'Umbria ● Mon
Porto (Oporto) PORTUGAL
AA FA Museu Nacional Soares dos Reis ● Mon
Praha (Prague) CZECH REPUBLIC
AA Museum of Decorative Arts (UPM) ● Mon
FA Mus. of Mod. and Cont. Czech Art; Mucha Mus.; Mus.of Modern Czech Sculpture (Zbraslav); Nat. Gall. of Old Boh. Art (St George Conv.) ● all Mon
NH National Museum ● Tue
ST National Museum of Technology ● Mon
Reykjavík ICELAND
W Thjódminjasafn Íslands (National Museum)
Riga LATVIA
AA Museum of Decorative and Applied Arts ● Mon
Roma (Rome) ITALY
W Capitoline museums ● Mon includes:
AR Museo Capitolino
W Museo del Palazzo del Conservatori
AR Mus. Naz. di Villa Giulia; Mus. Naz. Romano ● Mon
FA Galleria Borghese; Palazzo Barberini ● both Mon Galleria Doria Pamphili ● Mon
W Musei Vaticani, Vatican City ● Sun
Rotterdam THE NETHERLANDS
FA Museum Boymans-van Beuningen ● Mon
Sankt-Peterburg (St Petersburg) RUSSIAN FED.
W Hermitage ● Mon
FO Museum of Anthropology and Ethnography ● Thu
FA Russian Museum ● Mon
Santiago de Compostela SPAIN
AA Catedral
Selçuk TURKEY
AR Archaeological Museum
Stockholm SWEDEN
FA Modernamuséet ● Mon
AA Nationalmuseum ● Mon
AR Vasamuseet
Stuttgart GERMANY
FA Staatsgalerie ● Mon
Tallinn ESTONIA
FA National Art Museum ● Mon
Thessaloníki GREECE
AR Archaeological Museum
FO Folklore Mus. ● Tue (summer), Thu (winter)
Toledo SPAIN
FA Museo de Arte Visigótico ● Mon
FA Museo de Santa Cruz
Venézia (Venice) ITALY
FA Coll. Guggenheim ● Tue; Gall. dell'Accademia
W Museo Correr
AA Museo Vitrario di Murano ● Wed
Vilnius LITHUANIA
AA Lith. Hist. and Ethnographic Mus. ● Mon & Tue
Warszawa (Warsaw) POLAND
W National Museum ● Mon
Weimar GERMANY
FA Schlossmuseum ● Mon
Wien (Vienna) AUSTRIA
FA Albertina (Hofburg) ● both Mon; Österreichische Galerie, Belvedere ● Tue
FA Kunsthistorisches Museum ● Mon
NH Naturhistorisches Museum ● Tue
Zürich SWITZERLAND
FA Kunsthaus ● Mon
W Schweizerisches Landesmuseum ● Mon

SKIING

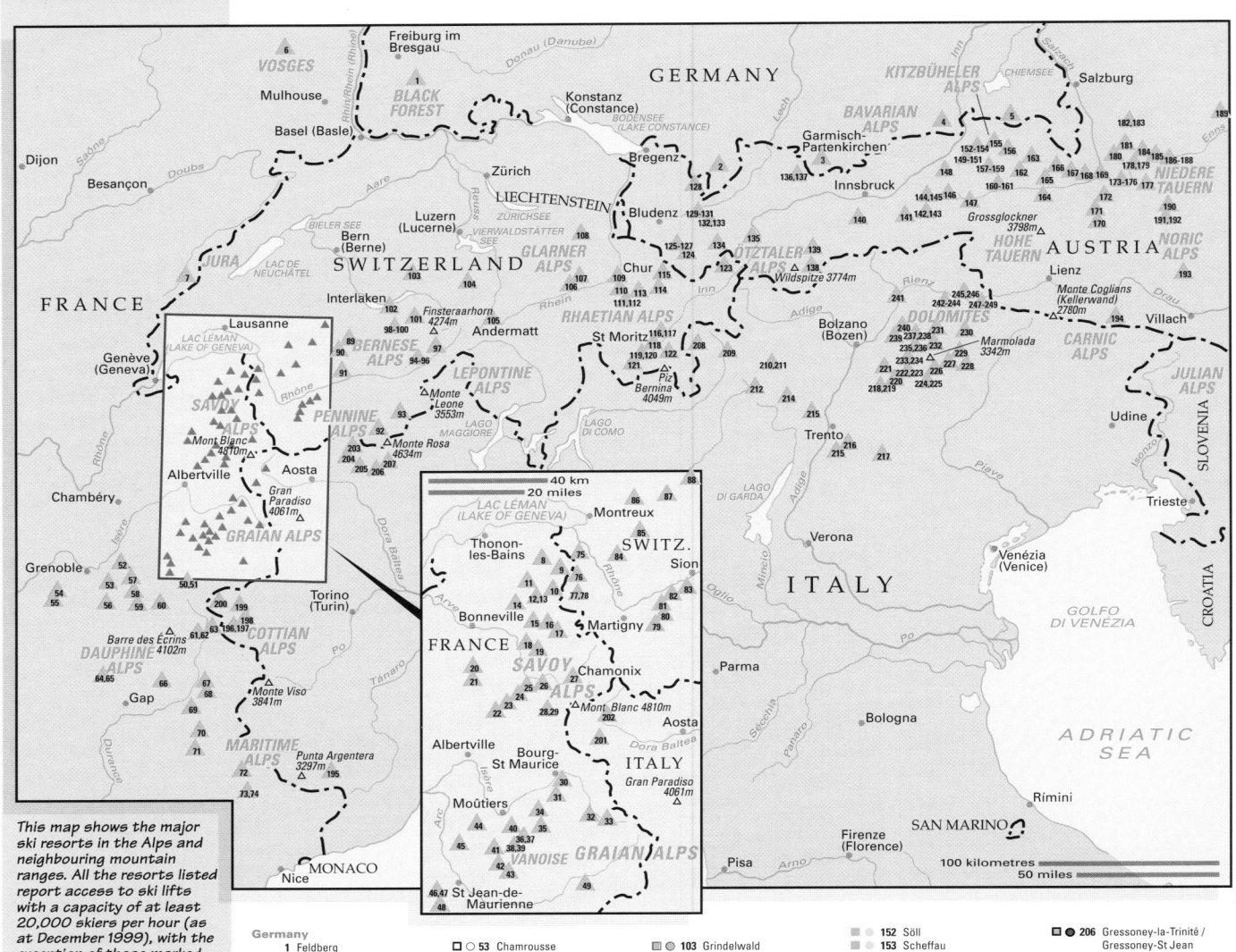

This map shows the major ski resorts in the Alps and neighbouring mountain ranges. All the resorts listed report access to ski lifts with a capacity of at least 20,000 skiers per hour (as at December 1999), with the exception of those marked with an asterisk (*), which are included because of their significance.

Resorts based on traditional villages are shown in normal type; modern-style purpose-built resorts in bold italics.

The classifications include facilities and slopes of neighbouring resorts where lift access is shared.

Data compiled by Snow-Hunter Ltd., all rights reserved.

Fax: +44 (0) 1463 741273.

email: info@snowhunter.co.uk

http://www.snowhunter.co.uk

Resort altitude:

☐ 1,500 metres or above

☐ 1,000 – 1,499 metres

No black square: under 1,000 metres

Skier uplift:

■ 100,000 skiers per hour or more

■ 50,000 – 99,999 skiers per hour

■ 30,000 – 49,999 skiers per hour

No colour: Less than 30,000

Altitude at top of highest ski run:

○ 3,000 metres or above

○ 2,000 – 2,999 metres

No black circle: under 2,000 metres

Maximum vertical drop:

● 2,000 metres or more

● 1,500 – 1,999 metres

● 1,000 – 1,499 metres

No colour: Less than 1,000 metres

Germany
1 Feldberg
2 Oberstdorf
3 Garmisch-Partenkirchen
4 Bayrischzell
5 Reit im Winkl

France
6 la Bresse-Hohneck
7 Métabief / le Mont d'Or
8 Abondance / la Chapelle d'A.
9 Châtel
10 *Avoriaz*
11 St Jean d'Aulps
12 Morzine
13 les Gets
14 *le Praz de Lys**
15 Morillon les Essert
16 Samoëns
17 Sixt
18 les Carroz
19 *Flaine*
20 le Grand-Bornand
21 la Clusaz
22 Notre-Dame-de-Bellecombe
23 Praz-sur-Arly
24 Megève
25 Combloux
26 St Gervais / *le Bettex*
27 Chamonix-Mont Blanc
28 St Nicolas-de-Véroce
29 les Contamines-Montjoie
30 *les Arcs*
31 Peisey-Nancroix-Vallandry
32 *Tignes*
33 Val d'Isère
34 *la Plagne / les Coches /*
   Montchavin / Pl. Montalbert
35 Champagny-en-Vanoise
36 *la Tania*
37 Courchevel
38 *la Rosière*
39 Méribel
40 Brides-les-Bains
41 St Martin-de-Belleville
42 *les Menuires*
43 *Val Thorens*
44 *Valmorel*
45 *St François-Longchamp*
46 la Toussuire
47 le Corbier
48 St Jean d'Arves
49 Val Cenis
50 Valmeinier
51 Valloire
52 *les Sept Laux*
   (*le Pleiney / Prapoutel*)

53 Chamrousse
54 Villard-de-Lans / *Cote 2000*
55 Corrençon-en-Vercors
56 *Alpe du Grand Serre*
57 Vaujany / Oz-en-Oisans
58 *Alpe d'Huez* / Auris-en-
   Oisans / Villard-Reculas
59 *les Deux Alpes*
60 la Grave
61 Serre-Chevalier
62 Briançon
63 la Joue du Loup
64 *Superdévoluy*
65 *Orcières-Merlette*
66 *Risoul*
67 Vars
68 *les Orres*
69 *Pra-Loup*
70 Val d'Allos-La Foux*
71 *Val d'Allos-La Foux*
72 Auron / St Étienne-de-Tinée
73 Valberg
74 Beuil-les-Launes

Switzerland
75 Torgon
76 Morgins
77 *Champoussin*
78 Champéry-Planachaux /
   Val-d'Illiez / Les Crosets
79 Le Châble / Bruson
80 Verbier
81 La Tzoumas (Mayens-de-
   Riddes)
82 Nendaz
83 Mayens-de-l'Ours /
   Veysonnaz / Les Collons
84 Villars-sur-Ollon / Gryon
85 Les Diablerets
86 Château-d'Oex*
87 Gstaad-Saanenland
88 Zweisimmen
89 Adelboden
90 Lenk
91 Crans-Montana
92 Zermatt
93 Saas Fee
94 Bettmeralp
95 Mörel-Breiten
96 Fiesch
97 Sörenberg
98 Lauterbrunnen
99 Wengen
100 Mürren* / Stechelberg*
101 Riederalp
102 Interlaken / Wilderswil bei I.

103 Grindelwald
104 Engelberg
105 Andermatt*
106 Laax
107 Flims
108 Flumserberg
109 Chur*
110 Churwalden
111 Lenzerheide-Valbella
112 Parpan
113 Arosa
114 Davos
115 Klosters / Fideris
116 Celerina
117 Samedan*
118 St Moritz
119 Sils-Maria*
120 Silvaplana-Surlej*
121 Maloja*
122 Pontresina*
123 Samnaun

Austria
124 Partenen
125 Gaschurn
126 Gortipohl
127 St Gallenkirch
128 Kleinwalsertal [Hirschegg /
   Mittelberg / Riezlern]
129 Lech / Oberlech
130 Zug
131 Zürs
132 St Anton am Arlberg /
   St Jakob am Arlberg
133 St Christoph am Arlberg
134 Ischgl / Silvretta
135 Serfaus
136 Lermoos
137 Ehrwald
138 Obergurgl / Hochgurgl
139 Sölden
140 Neustift im Stubaital
141 Hintertux
142 Finkenberg
143 Mayrhofen
144 Zell am Ziller
145 Kaltenbach
146 Gerlos
147 Wald im Oberpinzgau /
   Königsleiten
148 Wildschönau [Auffach /
   Mühltal / Niederau /
   Oberau / Thierbach]
149 Brixen im Thale
150 Hopfgarten im Brixental
151 Westendorf*

152 Söll
153 Scheffau
154 Ellmau / Going
155 St Johann in Tirol
156 Fieberbrunn*
157 Kirchberg in Tirol /
   Aschau in Tirol
158 Kitzbühel
159 Aurach
160 Mittersill / Pass Thurn
161 Jochberg / Pass Thurn
162 Saalbach Hinterglemm
163 Leogang
164 Kaprun
165 Zell am See
166 Maria Alm
167 Dienten am Hochkönig
168 Mühlbach am Hochkönig
169 St Johann im Pongau
170 Badgastein
171 Bad Hofgastein
172 Grossarl
173 Flachauwinkel
174 Kleinarl
175 Flachau
176 Wagrain
177 Obertauern
178 Altenmarkt-Zauchensee
179 Radstadt
180 Werfenweng
181 Annaberg
182 Gosau
183 Russbach
184 Filzmoos
185 Pichl-Mandling
186 Haus in Ennstal
187 Ramsau am Dachstein*
188 Schladming
189 Tauplitz
190 Mauterndorf / Mariapfarr
191 St Margarethen im Lungau
192 St Michael im Lungau
193 Bad Kleinkirchheim
194 Karnische Skiregion

Italy
195 Limone Piemonte
196 *San Sicário* / Cesana
197 Clavière
198 *Sestriere*
199 Sàuze d'Oulx
200 Bardonécchia
201 la Thuile
202 Courmayeur*
203 *Breuil-Cervinia*
204 Valtournenche
205 Champoluc / Antagnod

206 Gressoney-la-Trinité /
   Gressoney-St Jean
207 Alagna-Valsésia
208 Livigno
209 Bormio*
210 *Folgàrida*
211 *Marilléva*
212 Passo Tonale
213 Madonna di Campíglio
214 Andalo
215 Folgària
216 Lavarone / Luserna
217 Asiago / Canove
218 Alpe di Pampeago / Tésero
219 Cavalese*
220 Predazzo
221 *Obereggen*
222 Moena di Fassa
223 Bellamonte
224 San Martino di Castrozza
225 *Passo Rolle*
226 Falcade
227 Alleghe
228 Zoldo Alto / Valzoldana
229 Selva di Cadore
230 Cortina
231 Alta Badia [Colfosco /
   Corvara / la Villa (Stern) /
   San Cassiano (St Kassian) /
   Pedráces / San Leonardo
   (St Leonhard)]
232 Arabba
233 Pozza di Fassa*
234 Vigo di Fassa*
235 Campitello di Fassa*
236 Canazei*
237 Santa Cristina / Pranauron
238 Selva Gardena
   (Wolkenstein)
239 Castelrotto (Kastelruth)
240 Ortisei (St Ulrich)
241 Bressanone (Brixen)
242 San Vigilio di Marebbe
243 Riscone (Reischach)
244 Valdàora (Olang)
245 Dobiaco (Toblach)
246 Villabassa (Niederdorf)
247 San Cándido (Innichen)
248 Sesto (Sexten)
249 Versciaco (Vierschach)

The World Ski and Snowboarding Guide, published by Columbus Press, is a comprehensive guide to the world's ski resorts. For more information, call +44 (0)20 7417 0700.

UK BEACHES AND NATIONAL PARKS

The European Blue Flag Campaign is an environmental awareness raising activity by the Foundation for Environmental Education in Europe (FEEE).

To qualify for a Blue Flag, a beach has to fulfil a number of strict criteria regarding water quality (compliance with the EU Bathing Water Directive), environment, education and information, beach area management and safety. The Blue Flag is awarded annually and is valid for one year.

41 beaches in the UK were awarded Blue Flags for 1999.

For further information, contact:

Tidy Britain Group, Seymour House, Muspole Street, Norwich, NR3 1DJ.

Tel. +44 (0) 1603 766076.

The Seaside Award is awarded annually by the Tidy Britain Group to resort and rural beaches in the UK and Channel Is.

Resort beaches: busy beaches in or close to towns are assessed on 29 criteria including general cleanliness, water quality, safety provisions, beach facilities and provision for the disabled.

Rural beaches: usually in more remote locations, they are assessed on 13 similar key issues but are not expected to maintain the same standard of supervision or facilities as resort beaches.

259 beaches qualified for the Award for 1999.

Key

1999 European Blue Flag:
○ Blue Flag beach

1999 Seaside Award:
● Resort beach
● Rural beach

Water quality results for the current season are updated weekly and are displayed at all Seaside Award beaches. All Award beaches have reached the 'Mandatory' standard of the EU bathing water directive the previous year. Beaches shown in **bold** have achieved the higher 'Guideline' standard for the previous five years (1994-98).

Beach character:
s Sandy
h Shingle
r Rocky
m Mud flats

Tourism, 1980–1998

International arrivals to the UK (millions)

Source: World Tourism Organisation

Scotland
- sh 1 Troon South
- shr 2 Lunderston Bay
- s 3 Dornoch
- shr 4 Nairn Central
- sr 5 St Andrews: West Sands
- s 6 St Andrews: East Sands
- s 7 Kingsbarns
- s 8 Crail: Roome Bay
- sr 9 Anstruther: Billow Ness
- sr 10 Elie: Ruby Bay
- sr 11 Elie
- sr 12 Shell Bay
- sr 13 Aberdour: Silver Sands
- s 14 Aberdour Harbour
- s 15 Gullane Bents
- sh 16 North Berwick: Milsey Bay
- s 17 Belhaven Bay

Northumbria
- s 18 Low Newton
- sr 19 Warkworth
- sr 20 Amble Links
- s 21 Tynemouth: Cullercoats
- s 22 Tynemouth: Longsands South
- sh 23 Whitburn North: Seaburn
- s 24 Whitburn South: Roker
- s 25 Seaton Carew: Foreshore
- sh 26 Redcar Lifeboat Station

Yorkshire
- s 27 Sandsend
- s 28 Whitby: West Cliff
- srm 29 Robin Hood's Bay
- sm 30 Scarborough: North Bay
- s 31 Scarborough: South Bay
- s 32 Cayton Bay
- sm 33 Filey
- shr 34 Flamborough: South Landing
- sh 35 Bridlington North
- sh 36 Bridlington South
- sh 37 Cleethorpes North

East of England
- s 38 Mablethorpe Central
- s 39 Sutton on Sea Central
- sh 40 Skegness: Tower Esplanade
- shm 41 Snettisham
- sh 42 Heacham North
- sh 43 Heacham South
- sh 44 Hunstanton
- sh 45 **Sheringham**
- s 46 Cromer
- sh 47 Mundesley
- sh 48 Sea Palling
- sh 49 Great Yarmouth Central
- s 50 Great Yarmouth: Gorleston
- s 51 Lowestoft: Gunton
- s 52 Lowestoft South
- s 53 Lowestoft: Victoria
- s 54 Kessingland
- s 55 Southwold
- s 56 Southwold: The Denes
- s 57 Sizewell
- sh 58 Thorpeness
- sh 59 **Aldeburgh**
- s 60 Dovercourt
- s 61 Clacton-on-Sea West
- s 62 Brightlingsea
- sm 63 Shoeburyness East
- sm 64 Shoebury Common
- sm 65 Southend-on-Sea: Three Shells
- s 66 Leigh-on-Sea: Bell Wharf

South East England
- shm 67 **Sheerness: Beach Street**
- hm 68 Sheerness: Minster Leas
- h 69 Leysdown-on-Sea: Grove Avenue
- h 70 Herne Bay West
- shm 71 Herne Bay Central
- shrm 72 Birchington: Minnis Bay
- sr 73 Margate: Main Sands
- sr 74 Broadstairs: Joss Bay
- s 75 Broadstairs: Viking Bay
- ○ s 76 Ramsgate: Main Sands
- h 77 Dymchurch
- sh 78 Greatstone-on-Sea: Romney Sands
- h 79 Camber
- h 80 Winchelsea
- sh 81 Bexhill-on-Sea
- sh 82 Pevensey Bay
- h 83 Eastbourne: pier to Wish Tower
- shr 84 Birling Gap
- sh 85 Seaford
- sh 86 Worthing Town
- sh 87 Littlehampton: Coastguards
- sh 88 Bognor Regis: east of the pier
- sh 89 West Wittering

Southern England
- sh 90 **Hayling Island: Beachlands Central**
- s 91 **Hayling Island: Beachlands West**
- shm 92 Lepe Country Park
- sh 93 **Bournemouth: Fisherman's Walk**
- s 94 **Bournemouth: Durley**
- s 95 Poole: Sandbanks
- s 96 Swanage Central

Isle of Wight
- sh 97 Totland Bay
- s 98 Colwell Bay
- h 99 Cowes West
- h 100 Cowes East
- s 101 Ryde East
- s 102 Springvale
- sr 103 Seagrove Bay
- s 104 St Helens: Duver
- s 105 Sandown: Yaverland
- s 106 Sandown
- s 107 Shanklin
- h 108 Ventnor

West Country
- s 109 Weymouth Central
- sr 110 Charmouth West
- sr 111 Charmouth East
- sr 112 Dawlish Warren
- sr 113 Dawlish: Coryton Cove
- s 114 Teignmouth Town
- sr 114 **Sheldon: Ness Cove**
- hr 115 **Torquay: Oddicombe**
- h 116 Torquay: Meadfoot
- r 117 Torquay: Corbyn's Head
- h 118 Paignton Sands
- s 119 Paignton: Goodrington Sands South
- s 120 Broadsands
- s 121 Brixham: Shoalstone Breakwater
- sh 122 **Blackpool Sands**
- s 123 Strete Gate
- h 124 Torcross: Slapton Sands
- h 125 Beesands
- s 126 Salcombe: North Sands
- s 127 Salcombe: South Sands
- s 128 Thurlestone: South Milton Sands
- sr 129 Bigbury-on-Sea
- sh 130 Challaborough
- s 131 Fowey: Readymoney
- s 132 Par
- s 133 **Porthpean**
- s 134 Kennack Sands West
- s 135 Sennen Cove
- s 136 St Ives: Porthmeor
- s 137 St Ives: Porthminster
- s 138 Newquay: Fistral
- s 139 Newquay: Porth
- s 140 Mawgan Porth
- shr 141 **Treyarnon Bay**
- s 142 **Constantine Bay**
- shr 143 Trevone
- s 144 Polzeath
- ○ sh 145 **Bude: Widemouth Sands**
- s 146 Bude: Crooklets
- s 147 Bude: Sandymouth
- s 148 Bude: Summerleaze
- s 149 Croyde Bay
- s 150 Putsborough Sands
- s 151 Woolacombe
- sh 152 Combe Martin
- sm 153 Berrow
- sm 154 Brean
- ○ s 155 Weston-super-Mare

Wales
- s 156 Porthcawl: Rest Bay
- s 157 Caswell Bay
- ○ s 158 Port-Eynon
- s 159 Pembrey Country Park: Cefn Sidan
- sr 160 Amroth
- s 161 Wiseman's Bridge
- s 162 Saundersfoot
- shr 163 Saundersfoot: Coppet Hall
- sr 164 Tenby North
- s 165 Tenby Castle
- s 166 Tenby South
- sr 167 Lydstep
- sh 168 Manorbier
- sr 169 Freshwater East
- s 170 **Barafundle Bay**
- sh 171 **Bosherston: Broadhaven**
- sr 172 West Angle Bay
- s 173 Gelliswick
- s 174 Dale
- sr 175 Marloes
- h 176 **Martin's Haven**
- s 177 St Brides Haven
- s 178 Little Haven
- sr 179 Broad Haven
- shr 180 Nolton Haven
- ○ sr 181 Newgale
- ○ s 182 **St David's: Caerfai**
- ○ sr 183 St David's: Whitesands
- h 184 **Abereiddy**
- s 185 Goodwick Sands
- s 186 Dinas Cross: Cwm-yr-Eglwys
- s 187 Newport Sands
- s 188 Mwnt
- s 189 Aberporth
- sr 190 Tresaith
- sr 191 Penbryn
- s 192 Llangrannog
- s 193 Llangrannog: Cilborth
- s 194 Cwmtydu
- ○ s 195 New Quay: Traeth yr Harbwr
- r 196 New Quay: Traeth y Dolau
- s 197 Aberaeron South: Traeth y De
- r 198 Llanrhystud
- s 199 Aberystwyth South: Traeth y De
- s 200 Aberystwyth North: Traeth y Gogledd
- hr 201 Clarach
- s 202 Borth
- s 203 Tywyn
- s 204 Llanenddwyn: Bennar-Morfa Dyffryn
- s 205 Llandanwg
- sh 206 Aberdaron
- sr 207 Penmaenmawr
- s 208 Llandudno: North Shore
- s 209 Rhos-on-Sea
- s 210 Old Colwyn
- s 211 Abergele: Pensarn
- s 212 Rhyl
- s 213 Prestatyn Central
- s 214 Talacre/Gronant

Anglesey
- s 215 **Newborough: Llanddwyn**
- s 216 Aberffraw: Traeth Mawr
- s 217 Llanfaelog: Porth Trecastell
- s 218 Llanfaelog: Porth Nobla
- s 219 Llanfaelog: Porth Tyn Tywyn
- s 220 **Rhosneigr: Traeth Llydan (Broad Beach)**
- s 221 Rhosneigr: Traeth Crigyll
- s 222 Holy Island: Traeth Llydan (Silver Bay)
- s 223 Holy Island: Borth Wen
- ○ s 224 Holy Island: Trearddur Bay
- s 225 Holy Island: Porth Dafarch
- s 226 Llanfwrog: Porth Tywyn Mawr (Sandy Beach)
- s 227 Llanfaethlu: Porth Trwyn
- s 228 Church Bay: Porth Swtan
- s 229 Cemlyn
- s 230 Cemaes Bay: Traeth Bach
- s 231 Cemaes Bay: Traeth Mawr
- s 232 Benllech
- s 233 Red Wharf Bay
- s 234 Llanddona
- s 235 Penmon
- s 236 Beaumaris

North West
- s 237 West Kirby
- s 238 Wallasey: New Brighton
- s 239 Formby: Lifeboat Road
- s 240 Ainsdale-on-Sea
- s 241 Southport

Cumbria
- s 242 Walney Island: Biggar Bank
- h 243 Silecroft
- s 244 St Bees
- s 245 Allonby
- s 246 Silloth West

Northern Ireland
- ○ s 247 **Benone Strand**
- ○ s 248 Portstewart Strand
- ○ s 249 **Portrush West Strand**
- s 250 Ballycastle
- s 251 **Millisle Lagoon**
- s 252 **Tyrella**
- s 253 Cranfield West

Channel Islands
Guernsey
- sr 254 L'Erée Bay
- shr 255 **Vazon Bay**
- sr 256 Cobo Bay
- s 257 Port Soif Bay
- s 258 **Pembroke/L'Ancresse Bay**
- s 259 Fermain Bay
- shr 260 Petit Bot Bay
- s 261 Portelet Bay

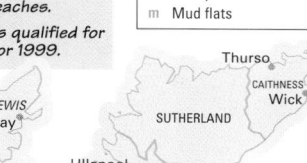
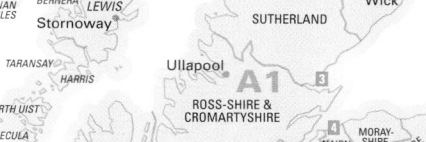
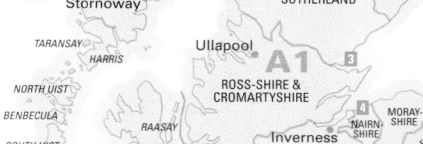

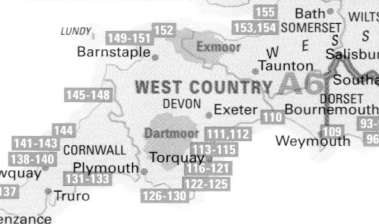
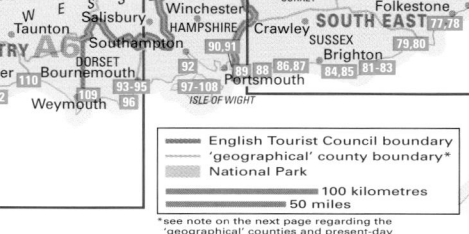
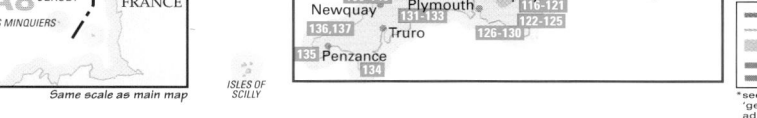

English Tourist Council boundary
'geographical' county boundary*
National Park

100 kilometres
50 miles

*see note on the next page regarding the 'geographical' counties and present-day administrative divisions

UK GEOGRAPHICAL AND...

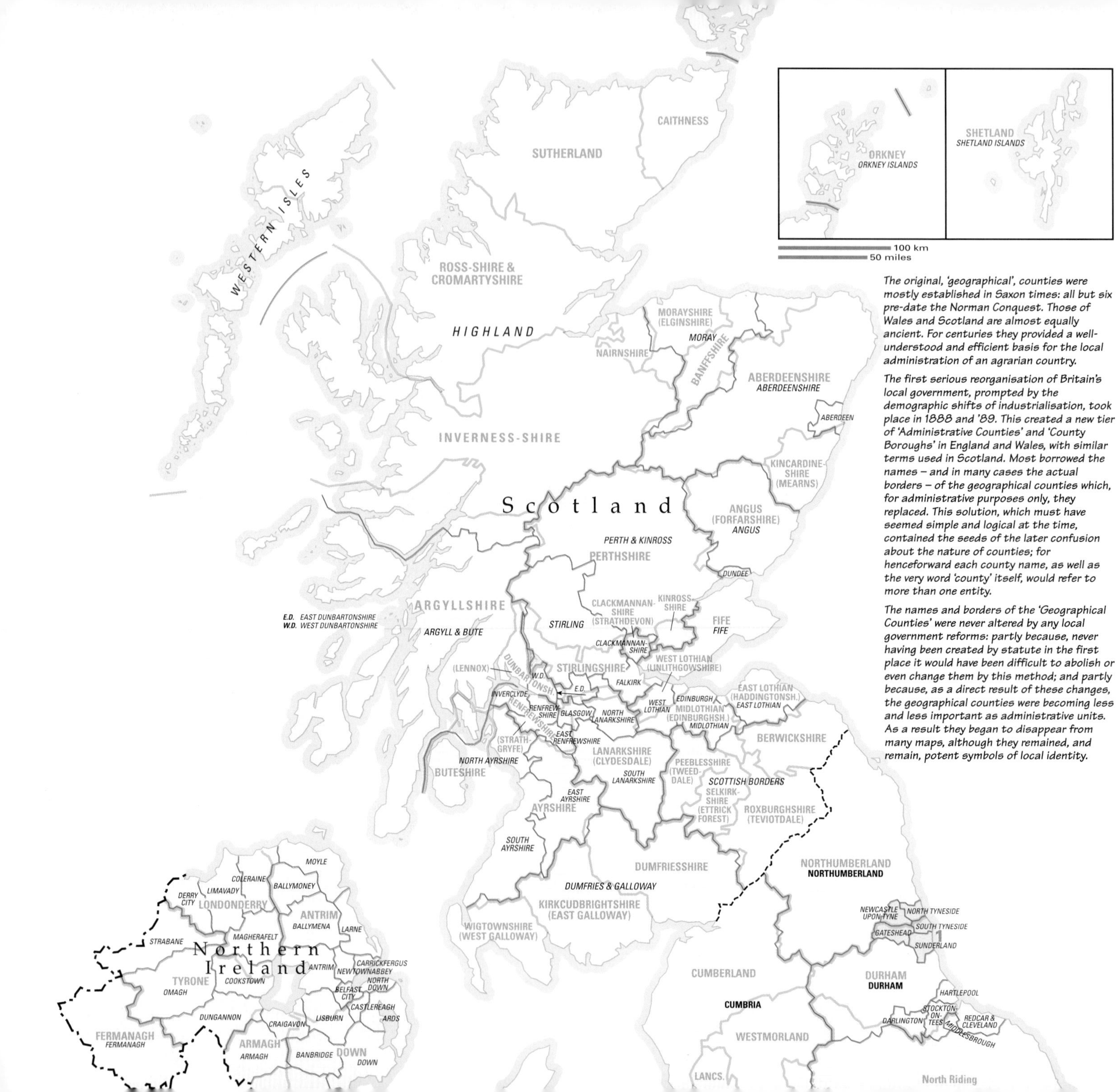

The next major change was the Local Government Act of 1972. Its most dramatic provision was the creation of six Metropolitan Counties and Greater London; more insidious was the abolition of the terms 'County Borough' and 'Administrative Counties' in favour of the simpler, but ambiguous, 'County' as the top tier of all the non-Metropolitan administrative units. Subsequent reorganisations have led to the situation displayed on the map – 46 'Unitary Authorities' with control over all aspects of local government, with the rest of the country divided into 'Administrative Counties' with some functions handled by a second tier of Borough or District Councils. Many of these Counties have the same names as their Geographical forebears, although rarely exactly the same borders. Ironically, one of the few which does is Rutland, which became a potent symbol of this issue after its administrative demise in 1972 – a reaction against the successive waves of new administrative names which were often short-lived, generally unloved and at times virtually impossible to locate.

The original, 'geographical', counties were mostly established in Saxon times: all but six pre-date the Norman Conquest. Those of Wales and Scotland are almost equally ancient. For centuries they provided a well-understood and efficient basis for the local administration of an agrarian country.

The first serious reorganisation of Britain's local government, prompted by the demographic shifts of industrialisation, took place in 1888 and '89. This created a new tier of 'Administrative Counties' and 'County Boroughs' in England and Wales, with similar terms used in Scotland. Most borrowed the names – and in many cases the actual borders – of the geographical counties which, for administrative purposes only, they replaced. This solution, which must have seemed simple and logical at the time, contained the seeds of the later confusion about the nature of counties; for henceforward each county name, as well as the very word 'county' itself, would refer to more than one entity.

The names and borders of the 'Geographical Counties' were never altered by any local government reforms; partly because, never having been created by statute in the first place it would have been difficult to abolish or even change them by this method; and partly because, as a direct result of these changes, the geographical counties were becoming less and less important as administrative units. As a result they began to disappear from many maps, although they remained, and remain, potent symbols of local identity.

Because of its distinct legal system, acts pertaining to Scotland were passed separately and so some different terms were used. In Wales, the position was rendered, to non-Welsh speakers, wholly opaque by the bilingualism of the newly created names. The confusions caused by these overlapping and shifting tiers are, however, broadly common to the whole of Great Britain.

Several other points are worthy of note. In 1997, 'Ceremonial Counties' were established, dividing up Britain roughly (but by no means exactly) according to the 'Geographical Counties'. Although based on no exact historical, or useful administrative, logic, they perhaps correspond closely with most people's mental map of Britain; for they include the Metropolitan Authorities, abolished as units in 1986 but still alive as useful descriptions of large urban areas. Secondly, many other structures such as parliamentary constituencies, health authorities, police forces and sporting organisations have borrowed names from all kinds of local divisions – including some, such as Mercia and Wessex, which pre-date even the 'Geographical Counties' – thus creating new and specific regional associations. Thirdly, there are the so-called 'Postal Counties' of the Royal Mail and as post-codes have overtaken county names of whatever kind as the key ingredient of an address, so the distinction between the various kinds of counties have blurred yet further. Fourthly, there are the regions of Britain as defined by the EU, as well as possible changes resulting from regional devolution, the long-term impact of which is still uncertain. Finally, in this as in other aspects of British tradition, old usages survive in cricket. Here one will still find Middlesex and Huntingdonshire and the undivided Sussex, Yorkshire and Glamorgan.

For further information on Britain's Geographical Counties, see: http://www.abcounties.co.uk/index.htm

SHETLAND
SHETLAND ISLANDS

ORKNEY
ORKNEY ISLANDS

100 km
50 miles

CAITHNESS

SUTHERLAND

ROSS-SHIRE & CROMARTYSHIRE

HIGHLAND

INVERNESS-SHIRE

WESTERN ISLES

ABERDEENSHIRE
ABERDEENSHIRE

ABERDEEN

KINCARDINE-SHIRE (MEARNS)

MORAYSHIRE (ELGINSHIRE)
MORAY

BANFFSHIRE

NAIRNSHIRE

ANGUS (FORFARSHIRE)
ANGUS

DUNDEE

FIFE
FIFE

Scotland

PERTH & KINROSS
PERTHSHIRE

KINROSS-SHIRE

CLACKMANNAN-SHIRE (STRATHDEVON)
CLACKMANNAN-SHIRE

WEST LOTHIAN (LINLITHGOWSHIRE)

EAST LOTHIAN (HADDINGTONSH)
EAST LOTHIAN

EDINBURGH

MIDLOTHIAN (EDINBURGH)
MIDLOTHIAN

WEST LOTHIAN

BERWICKSHIRE

SCOTTISH BORDERS

ROXBURGHSHIRE (TEVIOTDALE)

PEEBLESSHIRE (TWEED DALE)

SELKIRK-SHIRE (ETTRICK FOREST)

STIRLING

STIRLINGSHIRE

FALKIRK

E.D.

N.D.

DUNBARTONSHIRE

(LENNOX)

RENFREWSHIRE

GLASGOW

NORTH LANARKSHIRE

EAST RENFREWSHIRE

LANARKSHIRE (CLYDESDALE)

SOUTH LANARKSHIRE

INVERCLYDE

(STRATH GRYFE)

EAST AYRSHIRE

NORTH AYRSHIRE

AYRSHIRE

(STRATH)

BUTESHIRE

SOUTH AYRSHIRE

DUMFRIESSHIRE

DUMFRIES & GALLOWAY

KIRKCUDBRIGHTSHIRE (EAST GALLOWAY)

WIGTOWNSHIRE (WEST GALLOWAY)

ARGYLLSHIRE

ARGYLL & BUTE

E.D. EAST DUNBARTONSHIRE
W.D. WEST DUNBARTONSHIRE

NEWCASTLE UPON TYNE

NORTH TYNESIDE

SOUTH TYNESIDE

GATESHEAD

SUNDERLAND

NORTHUMBERLAND
NORTHUMBERLAND

DURHAM
DURHAM

HARTLEPOOL

STOCKTON-ON-TEES

DARLINGTON

MIDDLESBROUGH

REDCAR & CLEVELAND

North Riding

CUMBERLAND

CUMBRIA

WESTMORLAND

LANCS.

Northern Ireland

ANTRIM
ANTRIM

MOYLE

BALLYMONEY

BALLYMENA

LARNE

CARRICKFERGUS

NEWTOWNABBEY

BELFAST CITY

LISBURN

CASTLEREAGH

NORTH DOWN

ARDS

DOWN
DOWN

BANBRIDGE

CRAIGAVON

ARMAGH
ARMAGH

DUNGANNON

COOKSTOWN

MAGHERAFELT

COLERAINE

LIMAVADY

DERRY

LONDONDERRY

STRABANE

OMAGH

TYRONE
TYRONE

FERMANAGH
FERMANAGH

...ADMINISTRATIVE DIVISIONS

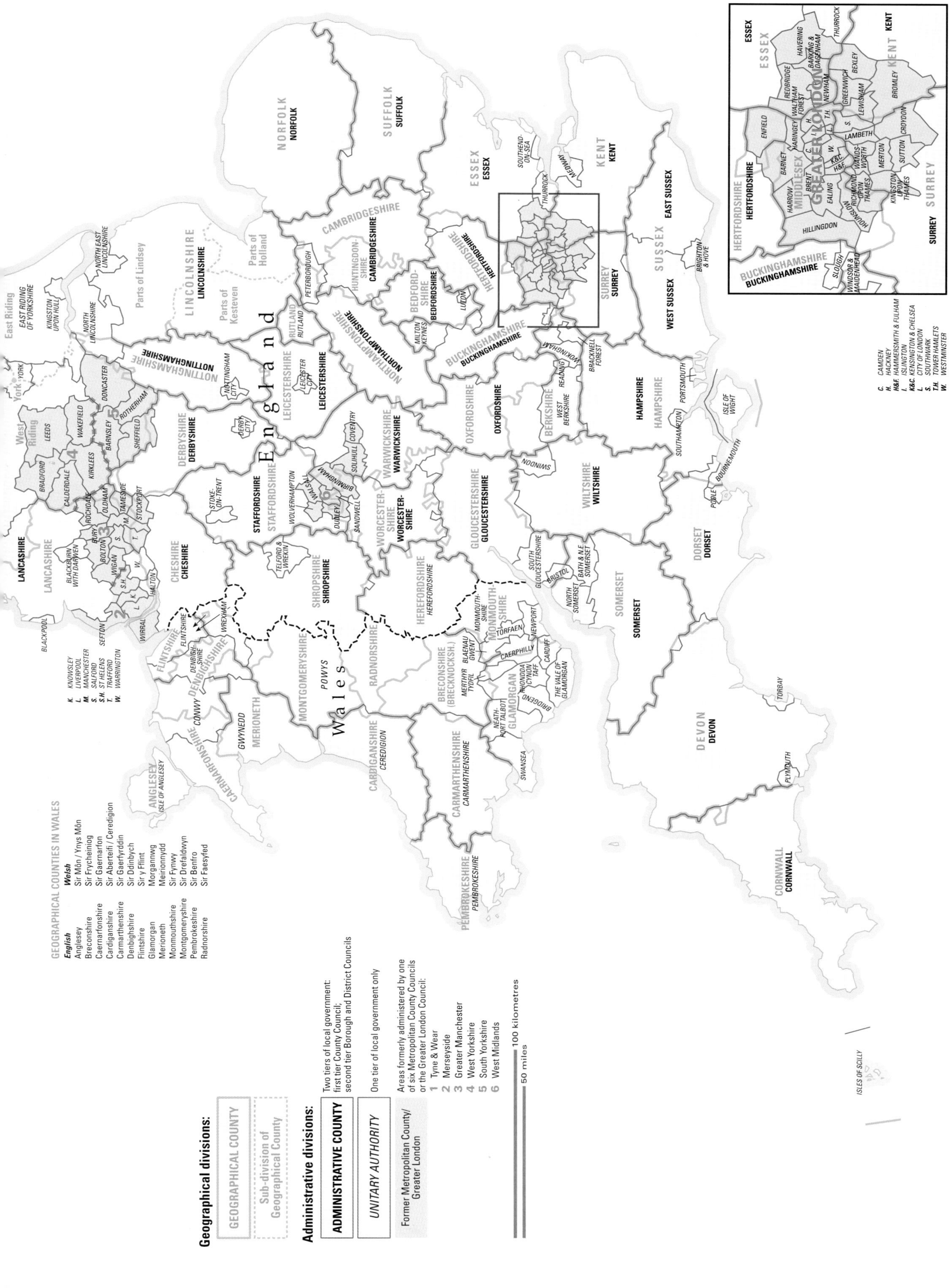
Geographical divisions:
GEOGRAPHICAL COUNTY
Sub-division of Geographical County
Administrative divisions:
ADMINISTRATIVE COUNTY
Two tiers of local government: first tier County Council; second tier Borough and District Councils
UNITARY AUTHORITY
One tier of local government only
Former Metropolitan County/ Greater London
Areas formerly administered by one of six Metropolitan County Councils or the Greater London Council:
1 Tyne & Wear
2 Merseyside
3 Greater Manchester
4 West Yorkshire
5 South Yorkshire
6 West Midlands
50 miles
100 kilometres
GEOGRAPHICAL COUNTIES IN WALES
English
Welsh
Anglesey
Sir Môn / Ynys Môn
Breconshire
Sir Frycheiniog
Caernarfonshire
Sir Gaernarfon
Cardiganshire
Sir Aberteifi / Ceredigion
Carmarthenshire
Sir Gaerfyrddin
Denbighshire
Sir Ddinbych
Flintshire
Sir y Fflint
Glamorgan
Morgannwg
Merioneth
Meirionnydd
Monmouthshire
Sir Fynwy
Montgomeryshire
Sir Drefaldwyn
Pembrokeshire
Sir Benfro
Radnorshire
Sir Faesyfed
K. KNOWSLEY
L. LIVERPOOL
M. MANCHESTER
S. SALFORD
S.H. ST HELENS
T. TRAFFORD
W. WARRINGTON
C. CAMDEN
H. HACKNEY
H&F. HAMMERSMITH & FULHAM
I. ISLINGTON
K&C. KENSINGTON & CHELSEA
L. CITY OF LONDON
S. SOUTHWARK
T.H. TOWER HAMLETS
W. WESTMINSTER
England
Wales
NORFOLK
SUFFOLK
ESSEX
KENT
EAST SUSSEX
WEST SUSSEX
SUSSEX
SURREY
HAMPSHIRE
ISLE OF WIGHT
DORSET
DEVON
CORNWALL
ISLES OF SCILLY
SOMERSET
WILTSHIRE
GLOUCESTERSHIRE
OXFORDSHIRE
BERKSHIRE
WEST BERKSHIRE
BUCKINGHAMSHIRE
HERTFORDSHIRE
BEDFORDSHIRE
CAMBRIDGESHIRE
HUNTINGDONSHIRE
NORTHAMPTONSHIRE
RUTLAND
LEICESTERSHIRE
LINCOLNSHIRE
Parts of Lindsey
Parts of Kesteven
Parts of Holland
NOTTINGHAMSHIRE
DERBYSHIRE
STAFFORDSHIRE
WARWICKSHIRE
WORCESTERSHIRE
HEREFORDSHIRE
SHROPSHIRE
CHESHIRE
LANCASHIRE
West Riding
East Riding
EAST RIDING OF YORKSHIRE
KINGSTON UPON HULL
NORTH LINCOLNSHIRE
NORTH EAST LINCOLNSHIRE
YORK
LEEDS
BRADFORD
CALDERDALE
KIRKLEES
WAKEFIELD
BARNSLEY
DONCASTER
ROTHERHAM
SHEFFIELD
ROCHDALE
OLDHAM
TAMESIDE
STOCKPORT
BURY
BOLTON
WIGAN
BLACKBURN WITH DARWEN
BLACKPOOL
SEFTON
WIRRAL
HALTON
STOKE-ON-TRENT
TELFORD & WREKIN
WOLVERHAMPTON
WALSALL
BIRMINGHAM
SOLIHULL
COVENTRY
DUDLEY
SANDWELL
NOTTINGHAM CITY
DERBY CITY
LEICESTER CITY
PETERBOROUGH
LUTON
MILTON KEYNES
SOUTHEND-ON-SEA
THURROCK
MEDWAY
READING
WOKINGHAM
BRACKNELL FOREST
SWINDON
PORTSMOUTH
SOUTHAMPTON
BOURNEMOUTH
POOLE
BRIGHTON & HOVE
SOUTH GLOUCESTERSHIRE
BRISTOL
BATH & N.E. SOMERSET
NORTH SOMERSET
TORBAY
PLYMOUTH
FLINTSHIRE
DENBIGHSHIRE
WREXHAM
CONWY
GWYNEDD
MERIONETH
CAERNARFONSHIRE
ANGLESEY
ISLE OF ANGLESEY
MONTGOMERYSHIRE
POWYS
RADNORSHIRE
BRECONSHIRE (BRECKNOCKSH.)
CARDIGANSHIRE
CEREDIGION
CARMARTHENSHIRE
PEMBROKESHIRE
GLAMORGAN
SWANSEA
NEATH-PORT TALBOT
BRIDGEND
RHONDDA CYNON TAFF
MERTHYR TYDFIL
CAERPHILLY
BLAENAU GWENT
TORFAEN
MONMOUTHSHIRE
NEWPORT
CARDIFF
THE VALE OF GLAMORGAN
GREATER LONDON
MIDDLESEX
ENFIELD
BARNET
HARROW
BRENT
EALING
HILLINGDON
HOUNSLOW
RICHMOND UPON THAMES
KINGSTON UPON THAMES
SUTTON
MERTON
WANDSWORTH
LAMBETH
CROYDON
BROMLEY
LEWISHAM
GREENWICH
BEXLEY
HAVERING
BARKING & DAGENHAM
REDBRIDGE
WALTHAM FOREST
HARINGEY
NEWHAM
SLOUGH
WINDSOR & MAIDENHEAD
20 miles
40 km

UNITED KINGDOM

See pages 6-7 for general map

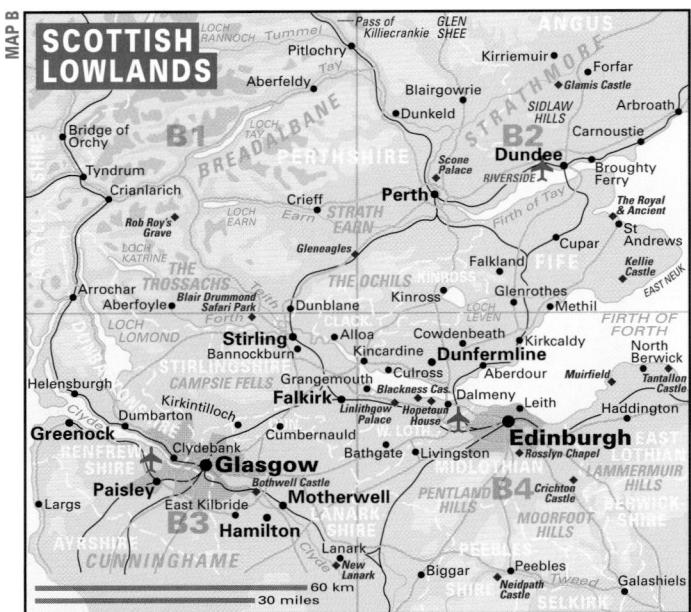

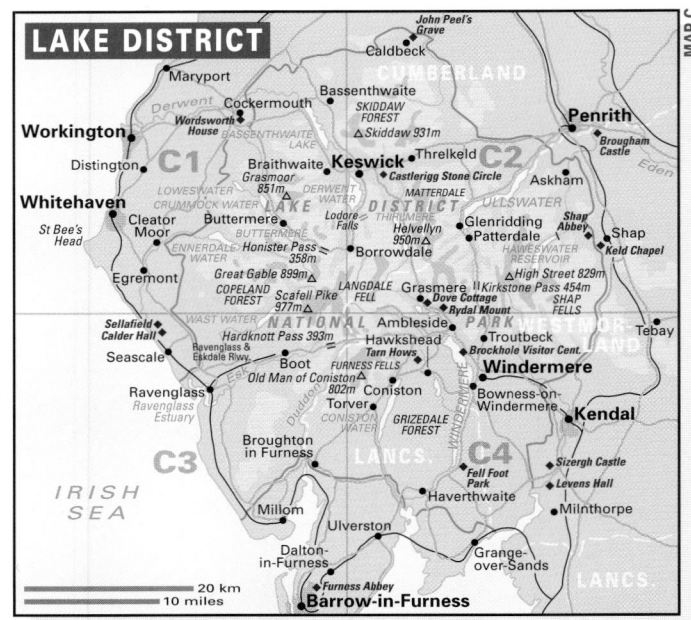

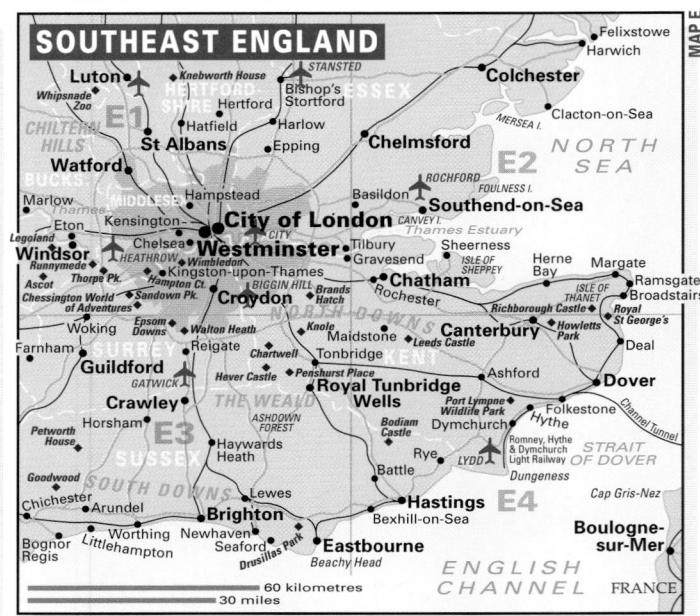

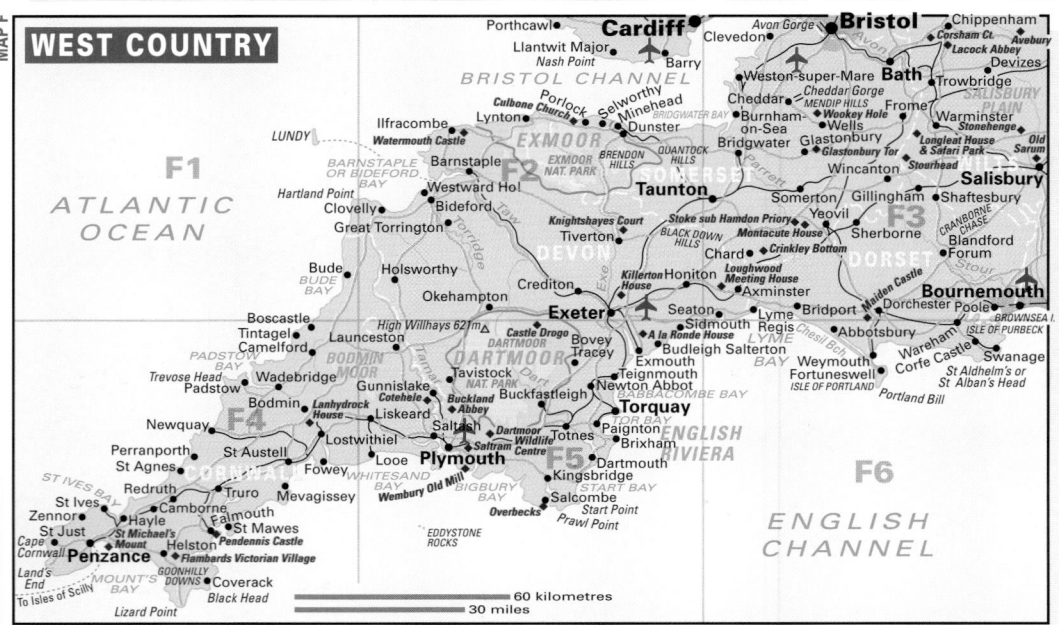

JAN 1st New Year's Day Parade (London)
JAN Up Helly Aa (Lerwick, Shetland)
APR Oxford-Cambridge Boat Race (River Thames, London)
MAY 1st 'Obby 'Oss: May Day celebrations (Padstow)
MAY Flora Day Furry Dance (Helston)
MAY Chelsea Flower Show (London)
MAY-AUG Glyndebourne Music Festival
JUN Trooping The Colour (London)
JUN-JUL York Mystery Plays; 2000 and every four years
JUL Henley Royal Regatta
JUL International Eisteddfod (Llangollen)
JUL-SEP Promenade Concerts 'Proms' (London)
AUG Highland Games (Aboyne)
AUG Three Choirs Festival (Gloucester; Hereford or Worcester); every three years
AUG Edinburgh Festival
AUG Bank Holiday Notting Hill Carnival (London)
SEP Royal Highland Gathering (Braemar)
NOV 5th Guy Fawkes Night: Bonfire Night
NOV London Film Festival
NOV State Opening of Parliament (London)
NOV Lord Mayor's Procession and Show (London)

UK RAILWAYS

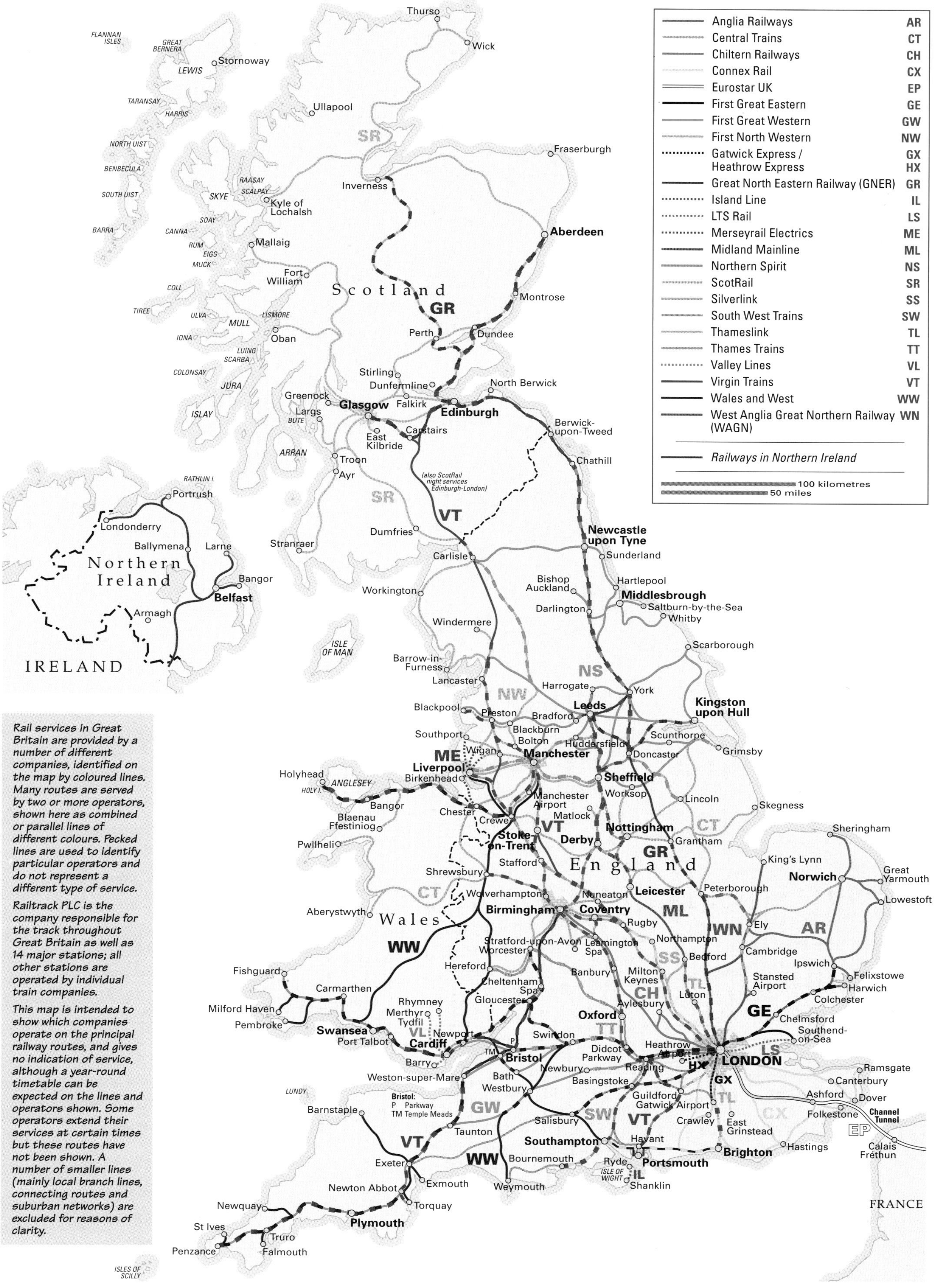

Legend

Anglia Railways	AR
Central Trains	CT
Chiltern Railways	CH
Connex Rail	CX
Eurostar UK	EP
First Great Eastern	GE
First Great Western	GW
First North Western	NW
Gatwick Express /	GX
Heathrow Express	HX
Great North Eastern Railway (GNER)	GR
Island Line	IL
LTS Rail	LS
Merseyrail Electrics	ME
Midland Mainline	ML
Northern Spirit	NS
ScotRail	SR
Silverlink	SS
South West Trains	SW
Thameslink	TL
Thames Trains	TT
Valley Lines	VL
Virgin Trains	VT
Wales and West	WW
West Anglia Great Northern Railway (WAGN)	WN

Railways in Northern Ireland

100 kilometres
50 miles

Sidebar note

Rail services in Great Britain are provided by a number of different companies, identified on the map by coloured lines. Many routes are served by two or more operators, shown here as combined or parallel lines of different colours. Pecked lines are used to identify particular operators and do not represent a different type of service.

Railtrack PLC is the company responsible for the track throughout Great Britain as well as 14 major stations; all other stations are operated by individual train companies.

This map is intended to show which companies operate on the principal railway routes, and gives no indication of service, although a year-round timetable can be expected on the lines and operators shown. Some operators extend their services at certain times but these routes have not been shown. A number of smaller lines (mainly local branch lines, connecting routes and suburban networks) are excluded for reasons of clarity.

Map labels

FLANNAN ISLES, GREAT BERNERA, LEWIS, Stornoway, TARANSAY, HARRIS, NORTH UIST, BENBECULA, SOUTH UIST, BARRA, RAASAY, SCALPAY, SKYE, SOAY, CANNA, RUM, EIGG, MUCK, COLL, TIREE, ULVA, MULL, LISMORE, IONA, LUING, SCARBA, COLONSAY, JURA, ISLAY, BUTE, ARRAN, RATHLIN I.

Thurso, Wick, Ullapool, Inverness, Fraserburgh, Kyle of Lochalsh, Mallaig, Fort William, **Aberdeen**, Montrose, Perth, Dundee, Oban, Stirling, Dunfermline, North Berwick, Greenock, Largs, **Glasgow**, Falkirk, **Edinburgh**, Berwick-upon-Tweed, East Kilbride, Carstairs, Chathill, Troon, Ayr, Dumfries, Carlisle, **Newcastle upon Tyne**, Sunderland, Stranraer, Workington, Bishop Auckland, Hartlepool, **Middlesbrough**, Saltburn-by-the-Sea, Whitby, Darlington, Windermere, Scarborough, Barrow-in-Furness, Lancaster, Harrogate, York, **Kingston upon Hull**, Blackpool, Preston, Bradford, **Leeds**, Scunthorpe, Grimsby, Southport, Blackburn, Bolton, Huddersfield, Doncaster, Wigan, **Manchester**, Holyhead, ANGLESEY, HOLY I., **Liverpool**, Birkenhead, Manchester Airport, **Sheffield**, Worksop, Lincoln, Skegness, Bangor, Blaenau Ffestiniog, Chester, Crewe, Matlock, **Nottingham**, Sheringham, Pwllheli, **Stoke-on-Trent**, **Derby**, Grantham, Shrewsbury, Stafford, King's Lynn, **Norwich**, Great Yarmouth, Lowestoft, Aberystwyth, Wolverhampton, Nuneaton, **Leicester**, Peterborough, **Birmingham**, **Coventry**, Ely, Rugby, Stratford-upon-Avon, Leamington Spa, Northampton, Cambridge, Ipswich, Fishguard, Hereford, Banbury, Milton Keynes, Bedford, Stansted Airport, Harwich, Felixstowe, Colchester, Carmarthen, Cheltenham Spa, Worcester, Aylesbury, Luton, Chelmsford, Milford Haven, Pembroke, Rhymney, Merthyr Tydfil, Gloucester, **Oxford**, **LONDON**, Southend-on-Sea, **Swansea**, Port Talbot, Newport, Swindon, Heathrow, Ramsgate, Barry, **Cardiff**, **Bristol**, Didcot Parkway, Reading, Canterbury, Weston-super-Mare, Bath, Newbury, Basingstoke, Gatwick Airport, Ashford, Dover, LUNDY, Westbury, Guildford, Crawley, East Grinstead, Folkestone, Barnstaple, Salisbury, Hastings, Calais Fréthun, Taunton, **Southampton**, Havant, **Brighton**, Exeter, **Portsmouth**, Ryde, Exmouth, **Bournemouth**, Weymouth, ISLE OF WIGHT, Shanklin, Newton Abbot, Torquay, Newquay, St Ives, **Plymouth**, Truro, Penzance, Falmouth, ISLES OF SCILLY

Channel Tunnel, FRANCE

Scotland, England, Wales, Northern Ireland, IRELAND

Portrush, Londonderry, Ballymena, Larne, Bangor, **Belfast**, Armagh

Bristol: P Parkway, TM Temple Meads

(also ScotRail night services Edinburgh-London)

UK AIRPORTS, MOTORWAYS AND FERRIES

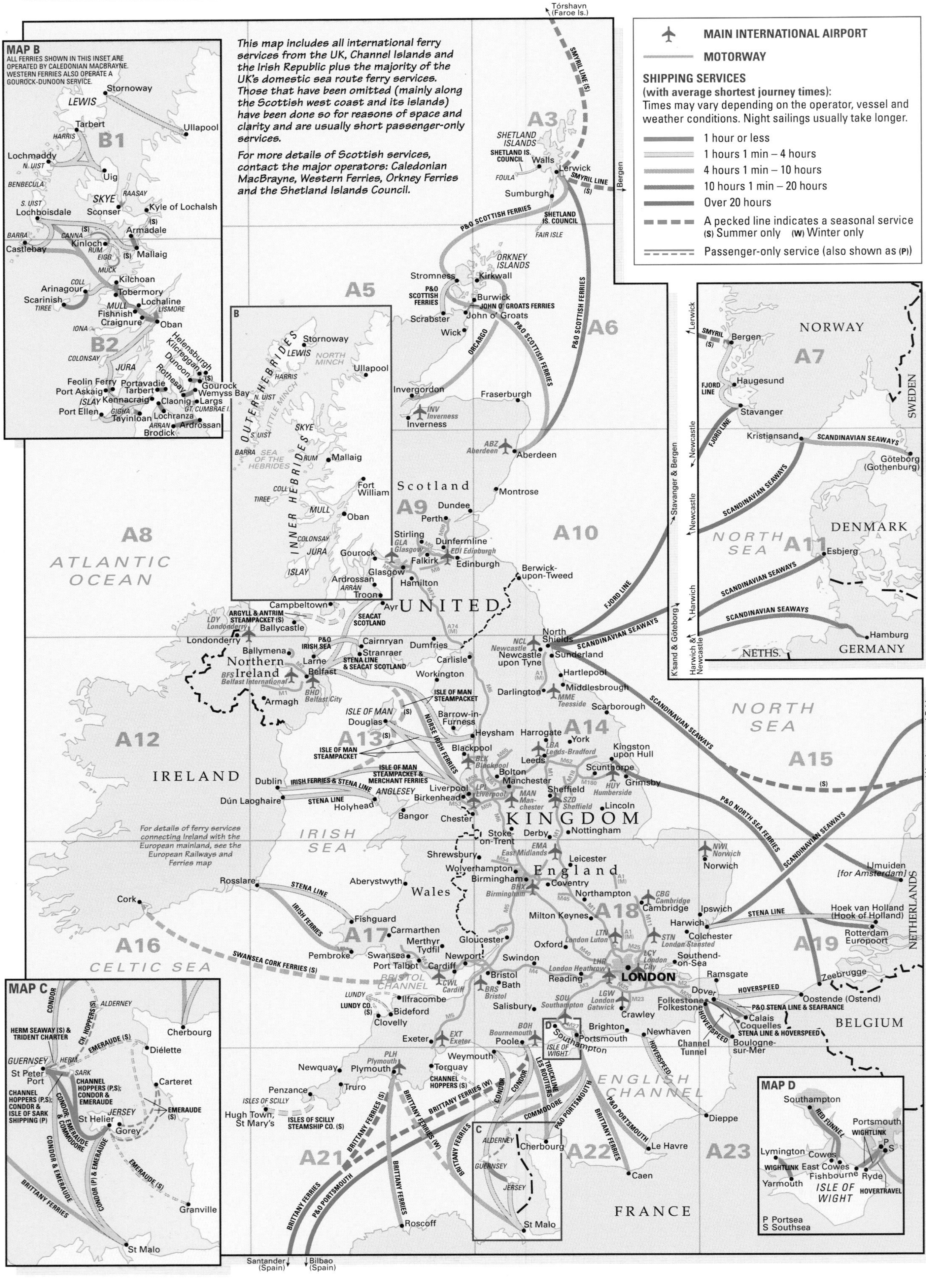

MAP B
ALL FERRIES SHOWN IN THIS INSET ARE OPERATED BY CALEDONIAN MACBRAYNE. WESTERN FERRIES ALSO OPERATE A GOUROCK-DUNOON SERVICE.

This map includes all international ferry services from the UK, Channel Islands and the Irish Republic plus the majority of the UK's domestic sea route ferry services. Those that have been omitted (mainly along the Scottish west coast and its islands) have been done so for reasons of space and clarity and are usually short passenger-only services.

For more details of Scottish services, contact the major operators: Caledonian MacBrayne, Western Ferries, Orkney Ferries and the Shetland Islands Council.

Legend

✈ **MAIN INTERNATIONAL AIRPORT**
MOTORWAY

SHIPPING SERVICES
(with average shortest journey times):
Times may vary depending on the operator, vessel and weather conditions. Night sailings usually take longer.

- 1 hour or less
- 1 hours 1 min – 4 hours
- 4 hours 1 min – 10 hours
- 10 hours 1 min – 20 hours
- Over 20 hours
- A pecked line indicates a seasonal service
  (S) Summer only (W) Winter only
- Passenger-only service (also shown as (P))

Map B (Scotland — Western Isles)

LEWIS — Stornoway, Tarbert, Ullapool
HARRIS
Lochmaddy, N. UIST, Uig
BENBECULA
RAASAY, SKYE
S. UIST — Lochboisdale, Sconser, Kyle of Lochalsh
BARRA, CANNA, RUM, Armadale (S)
Castlebay, Kinloch, EIGG (S) Mallaig
MUCK
COLL — Arinagour, Kilchoan, Tobermory, Lochaline, LISMORE
Scarinish, TIREE, Fishnish, Craignure, Oban
IONA, MULL
Helensburgh, Kilcreggan
COLONSAY — Rothesay, Dunoon (S), Gourock
JURA — Portavadie, Wemyss Bay, Largs, GT. CUMBRAE I.
Feolin Ferry, Port Askaig, Tarbert, Claonig, Lochranza
ISLAY — Kennacraig, GIGHA, ARRAN
Port Ellen, Tayinloan, Brodick, Ardrossan

Map A5 / A9 inset (B)

OUTER HEBRIDES — LEWIS, Stornoway
NORTH MINCH
HARRIS, Ullapool
LITTLE MINCH, N. UIST
S. UIST, SKYE, RUM, Mallaig
BARRA, SEA OF THE HEBRIDES
COLL, TIREE, Fort William
INNER HEBRIDES, MULL, Oban
COLONSAY, JURA, Gourock
ISLAY, Glasgow, Ardrossan, ARRAN, Troon

Map A7 / A11 (Norway / Denmark)

NORWAY
SMYRIL (S) Bergen
FJORD LINE — Haugesund
Stavanger
Kristiansand — SCANDINAVIAN SEAWAYS — Göteborg (Gothenburg)
NORTH SEA
DENMARK
Esbjerg
NETHS.
Hamburg
GERMANY
SWEDEN

Main map labels

Tórshavn (Faroe Is.)
SMYRIL LINE (S)
SHETLAND ISLANDS
SHETLAND IS. COUNCIL — Walls, Lerwick
FOULA
SMYRIL LINE (S) — Bergen
Sumburgh
P&O SCOTTISH FERRIES
FAIR ISLE
ORKNEY ISLANDS
Stromness, Kirkwall
P&O SCOTTISH FERRIES — Burwick
JOHN O' GROATS FERRIES — John o' Groats
Scrabster, Wick
ORCADIA
Invergordon, Fraserburgh
INV Inverness, Inverness
ABZ Aberdeen, Aberdeen
Scotland
Montrose
Dundee, Perth
Stirling, Dunfermline
GLA Glasgow, EDI Edinburgh
Falkirk, Edinburgh
Gourock, Glasgow, Hamilton
Ardrossan, Troon, Ayr
Berwick-upon-Tweed

Lerwick, SMYRIL (S), Bergen
FJORD LINE
Newcastle, Stavanger & Bergen
K'sand & Göteborg
Harwich & Newcastle
Harwich
SCANDINAVIAN SEAWAYS

UNITED KINGDOM
Campbeltown
ARGYLL & ANTRIM STEAMPACKET (S)
LDY Londonderry, Ballycastle
Londonderry, Ballymena
P&O IRISH SEA
Northern Ireland
BFS Belfast International
Armagh, BHD Belfast City
Cairnryan, Stranraer
STENA LINE & SEACAT SCOTLAND
Larne, Belfast
Dumfries, Carlisle
Workington
SEACAT SCOTLAND
NCL Newcastle, Newcastle upon Tyne
North Shields, Sunderland
Hartlepool
Darlington, Middlesbrough
MME Teesside, Scarborough

ISLE OF MAN STEAMPACKET
ISLE OF MAN, Douglas
Barrow-in-Furness
IRELAND
A12
Dublin
Dún Laoghaire
IRISH FERRIES & STENA LINE ANGLESEY
ISLE OF MAN STEAMPACKET & MERCHANT FERRIES
STENA LINE, Holyhead
NORSE IRISH FERRIES
Heysham, Harrogate, York
IBA Leeds-Bradford
Blackpool, BLK Blackpool
Leeds
Bolton, Manchester
MAN Manchester
Liverpool, LPL Liverpool
Birkenhead, Sheffield, SZD Sheffield
Bangor, Chester
Stoke-on-Trent
Derby, Nottingham
Kingston upon Hull
HUY Humberside
Scunthorpe, Grimsby
Lincoln

ENGLAND
Shrewsbury
Wolverhampton, Birmingham, BHX Birmingham
Coventry, Leicester
Northampton
Milton Keynes
EMA East Midlands
Aberystwyth
Wales
Fishguard
Carmarthen, Merthyr Tydfil
Gloucester
Oxford
CBG Cambridge, Cambridge
Ipswich
NWI Norwich, Norwich
STENA LINE
Hoek van Holland (Hook of Holland)
IJmuiden [for Amsterdam]
NETHERLANDS
Rotterdam Europoort

STENA LINE
IRISH FERRIES
Rosslare
Cork
A16 CELTIC SEA
SWANSEA CORK FERRIES (S)
Pembroke, Swansea, Port Talbot, Cardiff, CWL Cardiff
Newport, Swindon
Reading
LTN London Luton
STN London Stansted
Harwich, Colchester
Southend-on-Sea
LCY London City
LHR London Heathrow
LGW London Gatwick
LONDON
Ramsgate
HOVERSPEED
Dover, Calais
Folkestone, Coquelles
Boulogne-sur-Mer
P&O STENA LINE & SEAFRANCE
STENA LINE & HOVERSPEED
Oostende (Ostend), Zeebrugge
BELGIUM
Channel Tunnel
Newhaven, Dieppe

BRISTOL CHANNEL
LUNDY, LUNDY CO. (S)
Ilfracombe, Bideford, Clovelly
Bristol, BRS Bristol, Bath, Salisbury
EXT Exeter, Exeter
BOH Bournemouth, Bournemouth, Poole
SOU Southampton, Southampton, Portsmouth
ISLE OF WIGHT
Brighton, Crawley
HOVERSPEED
English Channel
Le Havre, Caen
Dieppe
FRANCE
P&O PORTSMOUTH, BRITTANY FERRIES

PLH Plymouth, Plymouth, Weymouth, Torquay
Newquay, Truro
Penzance
ISLES OF SCILLY
Hugh Town, St Mary's
ISLES OF SCILLY STEAMSHIP CO. (S)
CHANNEL HOPPERS (W)
BRITTANY FERRIES (W)
COMMODORE, COMMANDORE
TRUCKLINE
LES ROUTIERS
CONDOR
ALDERNEY, GUERNSEY, JERSEY
Cherbourg, St Malo
A21, A22
Santander (Spain), Bilbao (Spain)
Roscoff

Map C (Channel Islands)

CONDOR, CH. HOPPERS (S), ALDERNEY
HERM SEAWAY (S) & TRIDENT CHARTER
HERM, Cherbourg, Diélette
GUERNSEY, St Peter Port
SARK, Carteret
CHANNEL HOPPERS (P,S), CONDOR & ISLE OF SARK SHIPPING (P)
EMERAUDE (S)
JERSEY, St Helier, Gorey
CONDOR, EMERAUDE & COMMANDORE
COMMODORE (P) & EMERAUDE (S)
BRITTANY FERRIES
Granville, St Malo

Map D (Isle of Wight)

MAP D
Southampton
RED FUNNEL
Portsmouth, WIGHTLINK
Lymington, Cowes, WIGHTLINK
East Cowes, Ryde
WIGHTLINK, Fishbourne, HOVERTRAVEL
Yarmouth
ISLE OF WIGHT
P Portsea S Southsea

Ocean / Sea labels

ATLANTIC OCEAN
IRISH SEA
NORTH SEA
ENGLISH CHANNEL
CELTIC SEA

LONDON AIRPORTS AND CONNECTIONS

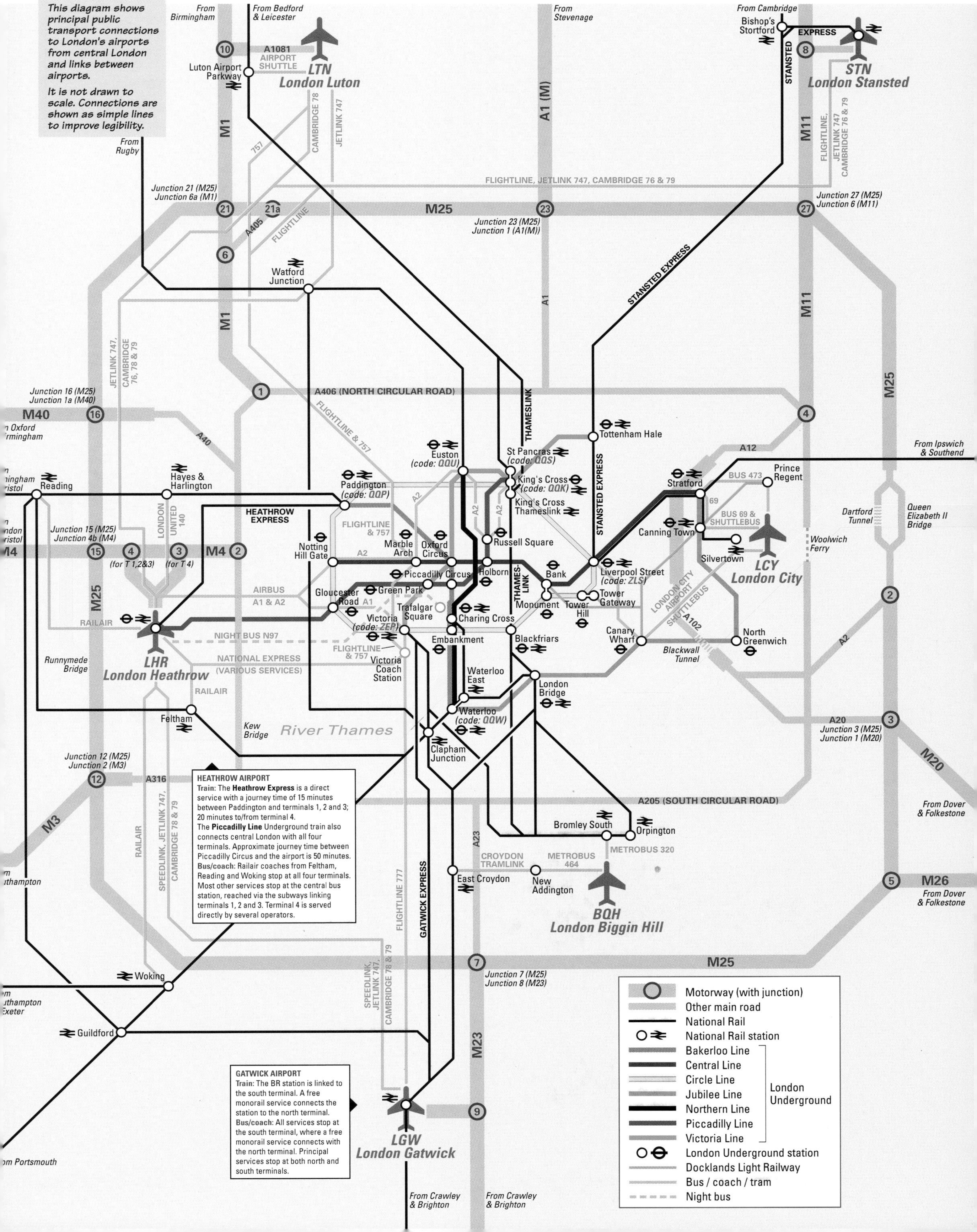

This diagram shows principal public transport connections to London's airports from central London and links between airports.

It is not drawn to scale. Connections are shown as simple lines to improve legibility.

HEATHROW AIRPORT
Train: The **Heathrow Express** is a direct service with a journey time of 15 minutes between Paddington and terminals 1, 2 and 3; 20 minutes to/from terminal 4.
The **Piccadilly Line** Underground train also connects central London with all four terminals. Approximate journey time between Piccadilly Circus and the airport is 50 minutes.
Bus/coach: Railair coaches from Feltham, Reading and Woking stop at all four terminals. Most other services stop at the central bus station, reached via the subways linking terminals 1, 2 and 3. Terminal 4 is served directly by several operators.

GATWICK AIRPORT
Train: The BR station is linked to the south terminal. A free monorail service connects the station to the north terminal.
Bus/coach: All services stop at the south terminal, where a free monorail service connects with the north terminal. Principal services stop at both north and south terminals.

Legend

- ⊙ Motorway (with junction)
- Other main road
- National Rail
- National Rail station
- Bakerloo Line
- Central Line
- Circle Line
- Jubilee Line — London Underground
- Northern Line
- Piccadilly Line
- Victoria Line
- London Underground station
- Docklands Light Railway
- Bus / coach / tram
- Night bus

IRELAND

See page 7 for general map

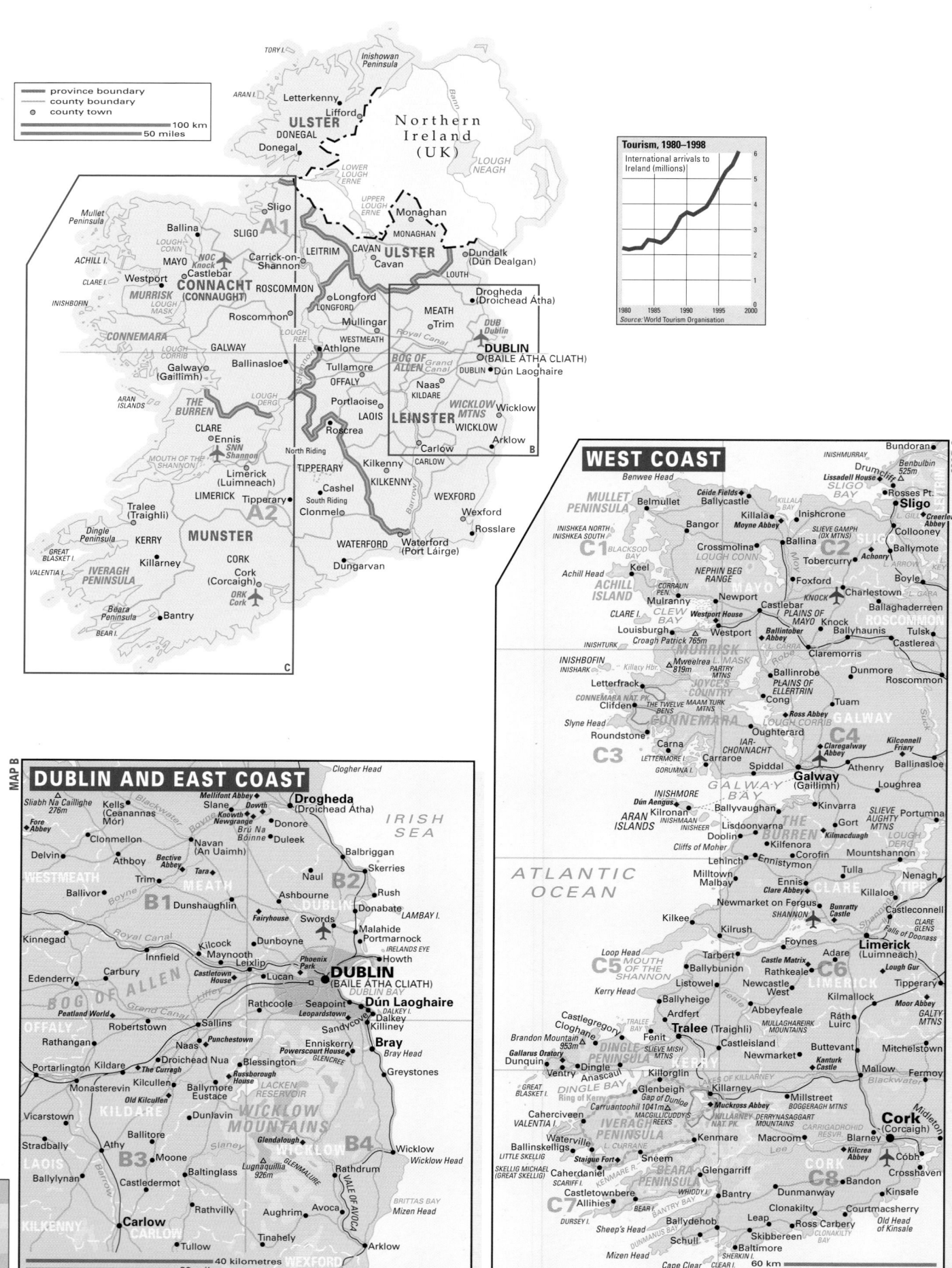

BELGIUM LUXEMBOURG NETHERLANDS

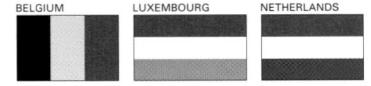

BENELUX

See page 5 for general map

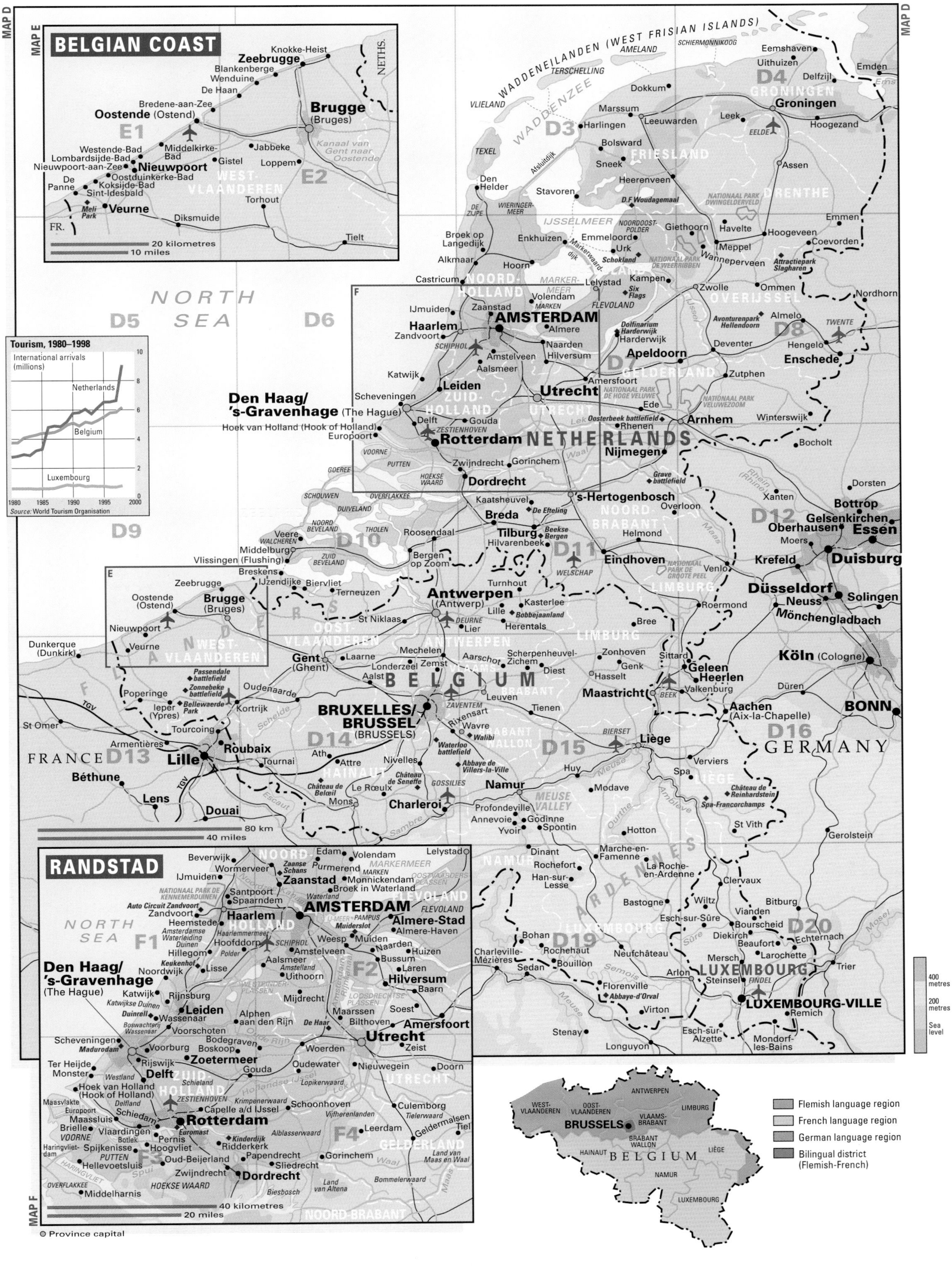

BELGIAN COAST

E1 · E2

Knokke-Heist
Zeebrugge
Blankenberge
Wenduine
De Haan
Bredene-aan-Zee
Brugge (Bruges)
Oostende (Ostend)
Westende-Bad
Middelkirke-Bad
Jabbeke
Lombardsijde-Bad
Loppem
Nieuwpoort-aan-Zee
Nieuwpoort
Oostduinkerke-Bad
Gistel
De Panne
Koksijde-Bad
Sint-Idesbald
Meli Park
Veurne
WEST-VLAANDEREN
Diksmuide
Torhout
Tielt
FR.
Kanaal van Gent naar Oostende

20 kilometres
10 miles

Tourism, 1980–1998
International arrivals (millions)
Netherlands
Belgium
Luxembourg
1980 1985 1990 1995 2000
Source: World Tourism Organisation

NORTH SEA

WADDENEILANDEN (WEST FRISIAN ISLANDS)
AMELAND
SCHIERMONNIKOOG
TERSCHELLING
VLIELAND
WADDENZEE
TEXEL
DE ZIJPE
WIERINGER-MEER
IJSSELMEER
Eemshaven
Uithuizen
Delfzijl
Emden
Groningen
GRONINGEN
Hoogezand
Dokkum
Marssum
Leek
Delfzijl
Harlingen
Leeuwarden
Assen
DRENTHE
Bolsward
FRIESLAND
Sneek
Heerenveen
NATIONAAL PARK DWINGELDERVELD
Den Helder
Stavoren
D.F. Woudagemaal
Giethoorn
Havelte
Emmen
Coevorden
Hoogeveen
Broek op Langedijk
Enkhuizen
Emmeloord
Urk
NATIONAAL PARK DE WEERRIBBEN
Meppel
Wanneperveen
Attractiepark Slagharen
Alkmaar
Hoorn
Schokland
NOORDOOST-POLDER
Zwolle
Ommen
Nordhorn
Castricum
NOORD-HOLLAND
Volendam
Lelystad
Six Flags
OVERIJSSEL
MARKEN
FLEVOLAND
Kampen
IJmuiden
Zaanstad
AMSTERDAM
MARKER-MEER
Almere
Dolfinarium Harderwijk
Avonturenpark Hellendoorn
Almelo
Haarlem
Zandvoort
Amstelveen
Naarden
Hilversum
Harderwijk
Deventer
Hengelo
TWENTE
Enschede
Katwijk
SCHIPHOL
Aalsmeer
Amersfoort
GELDERLAND
Zutphen
Leiden
Utrecht
NATIONAAL PARK DE HOGE VELUWE
Ede
NATIONAAL PARK VELUWEZOOM
Winterswijk
Scheveningen
ZUID-HOLLAND
Delft
Gouda
UTRECHT
Lek
Oosterbeek battlefield
Arnhem
Den Haag/'s-Gravenhage (The Hague)
Rhenen
Bocholt
Hoek van Holland (Hook of Holland)
ZESTIENHOVEN
Rotterdam
Waal
NETHERLANDS
Nijmegen
Dorsten
Europoort
VOORNE
Zwijndrecht
Gorinchem
Grave battlefield
Xanten
Bottrop
GOEREE
PUTTEN
Dordrecht
's-Hertogenbosch
Gelsenkirchen
Essen
HOEKSE WAARD
Kaatsheuvel
NOORD-BRABANT
Overloon
D12
Oberhausen
Moers
SCHOUWEN
DUIVELAND
OVERFLAKKEE
De Efteling
Breda
Helmond
Krefeld
Duisburg
DUIVELAND
Tilburg
Beekse Bergen
NOORD BEVELAND
Roosendaal
Hilvarenbeek
Venlo
Düsseldorf
Veere
WALCHEREN
THOLEN
Bergen op Zoom
Eindhoven
NATIONAAL PARK DE GROOTE PEEL
Roermond
Neuss
Solingen
Middelburg
ZUID BEVELAND
WELSCHAP
Mönchengladbach
Vlissingen (Flushing)
Breskens
Turnhout
LIMBURG
Köln (Cologne)
Zeebrugge
IJzendijke
Biervliet
Antwerpen (Antwerp)
Kasterlee
Bobbejaanland
Bree
Brugge (Bruges)
Terneuzen
DEURNE
Lille
Herentals
Sittard
Oostende (Ostend)
St Niklaas
Zonhoven
Geleen
Heerlen
Nieuwpoort
Mechelen
Aarschot
Scherpenheuvel-Zichem
Genk
Valkenburg
Veurne
WEST-VLAANDEREN
Gent (Ghent)
Laarne
Lier
Diest
Hasselt
LIMBURG
Maastricht
BEEK
Aachen (Aix-la-Chapelle)
BONN
Passendale battlefield
VLAANDEREN
OOST-VLAANDEREN
Londerzeel
Zemst
Leuven
Tienen
Düren
Poperinge
Zonnebeke battlefield
Oudenaarde
Aalst
ANTWERPEN
GERMANY
Ieper (Ypres)
Bellewaerde Park
Kortrijk
BRUXELLES/BRUSSEL (BRUSSELS)
ZAVENTEM
Rixensart
Wavre
BRABANT WALLON
Liège
D16
St Omer
Tourcoing
Roubaix
Walibi
BIERSET
Dunkerque (Dunkirk)
FRANCE
Lille
Ath
Nivelles
Waterloo battlefield
D15
Huy
Verviers
Spa
Béthune
Armentières
Tournai
Attre
Abbaye de Villers-la-Ville
Modave
Château de Reinhardstein
Lens
Mons
Le Rœulx
Namur
GOSSILIES
Profondeville
MEUSE VALLEY
Spa-Francorchamps
Douai
Château de Belœil
Charleroi
Annevoie
Godinne
Hotton
St Vith
Abbaye de Seneffe
Yvoir
Spontin
Gerolstein
HAINAUT
D13
D14
Dinant
Rochefort
Marche-en-Famenne
Han-sur-Lesse
La Roche-en-Ardenne
Clervaux
RANDSTAD
Beverwijk
Edam
Volendam
Lelystad
NAMUR
Rochehaut
Bohan
Wiltz
Bitburg
Wormerveer
Purmerend
MARKERMEER
Bastogne
Vianden
IJmuiden
Zaanse Schans
MARKEN
OOSTVAARDERSPLASSEN
Diekirch
Bourscheid
D20
NATIONAAL PARK DE KENNEMERDUINEN
Zaanstad
Monnickendam
FLEVOLAND
Esch-sur-Sûre
Beaufort
Echternach
Auto Circuit Zandvoort
Santpoort
Spaarndam
Broek in Waterland
Charleville-Mézières
Sedan
Bouillon
Neufchâteau
Larochette
Trier
Zandvoort
Waterland
Muiderslot
Almere-Haven
Florenville
Mersch
FINDEL
Haarlem
Amsterdamse Waterleiding Duinen
Heemstede
Haarlemmermeer
PAMPUS
Muiden
Almere-Stad
LUXEMBOURG
Steinsel
Amsterdam
Hillegom
Hoofddorp
SCHIPHOL
Polder
Weesp
Naarden
Huizen
Laren
Virton
400 metres
Keukenhof
Aalsmeer
Amstelveen
Bussum
Hilversum
Abbaye-d'Orval
Arlon
LUXEMBOURG-VILLE
200 metres
Lisse
De Haar
Mijdrecht
Uithoorn
Amstelland
Baarn
Esch-sur-Alzette
Remich
Sea level
Den Haag/'s-Gravenhage (The Hague)
Rijnsburg
Alphen aan den Rijn
Maarssen
Soest
Amersfoort
Longuyon
Mondorf-les-Bains
Katwijk
Leiden
Wassenaar
Voorschoten
Bodegraven
Boskoop
Utrecht
Zeist
Stenay
Scheveningen
Madurodam
Voorburg
Rijswijk
Zoetermeer
Gouda
Woerden
Oudewater
Nieuwegein
Doorn
Ter Heijde
Monster
Westland
Delft
ZUID-HOLLAND
Schieland
Krimpenerwaard
Lopikerwaard
Vijfherenlanden
Culemborg
Tielerwaard
Geldermalsen
Tiel
Maasvlakte
Europoort
Hoek van Holland (Hook of Holland)
Delfland
ZESTIENHOVEN
Capelle a/d IJssel
Schoonhoven
GELDERLAND
Maassluis
Schiedam
Rotterdam
Leerdam
Brielle
VOORNE
Vlaardingen
Pernis
Hoogvliet
Botlek
Euromast
Ridderkerk
Alblasserwaard
Land van Maas en Waal
Haringvliet-dam
Spijkenisse
Oud-Beijerland
Papendrecht
Waal
Hellevoetsluis
HOEKSE WAARD
Kinderdijk
Sliedrecht
Gorinchem
OVERFLAKKEE
Zwijndrecht
Dordrecht
Land van Altena
Bommelerwaard
Middelharnis
Biesbosch
NOORD-BRABANT
40 kilometres
20 miles

F1 · F2 · F3 · F4

© Province capital

Belgium language regions
WEST-VLAANDEREN
OOST-VLAANDEREN
ANTWERPEN
LIMBURG
VLAAMS-BRABANT
BRABANT WALLON
BRUSSELS
HAINAUT
NAMUR
LIÈGE
LUXEMBOURG
BELGIUM

Flemish language region
French language region
German language region
Bilingual district (Flemish-French)

NORTH SEA
WADDENZEE
MAP D · MAP E · MAP F
NETHS.
D3 D4 D5 D6 D7 D8 D9 D10 D11 D12 D13 D14 D15 D16 D19 D20

THE NETHERLANDS

GERMANY

See pages 8-9 for general map

FEB Berliner Filmfestspiele: Berlin Film Festival
before LENT Fasching: Carnival, especially Weiberfastnacht and Rosenmontag
APR Walpurgisnacht: witches' sabbath festival (Harz region)
MAY-SEP Rattenfängerspiele: Ratcatcher's Play (Hameln)
MAY-SEP Passionsspiele: Passion Play (Oberammergau); 2000 and every ten years
JUN Corpus Christi Procession (Hüfingen; Cologne and Munich)
JUN Kieler Woche: regatta (Kiel)
JUN-JUL Fürstenhochzeit: royal marriage (Landshut); 2001 and every four years
JUN-AUG Meistertrunk: 'Long Drink' history play (Rothenburg ob der Tauber)
JUL Love Parade (Berlin)
JUL-AUG Bayreuther Festspiele: Wagner opera festival (Bayreuth)
AUG Der Rhein in Flammen: The Rhine in Flames (Braubach to Koblenz)
AUG Schlossfest: castle festival (Heidelberg)
SEP Dürkheimer Wurstmarkt: sausage and wine festival (Bad Dürkheim)
SEP-OCT Oktoberfest (Munich)
OCT Weinlesefest: wine fair and Queen of Wine (Neustadt an der Weinstrasse)
OCT Frankfurt Book Fair
NOV Hamburger Dom: festival (Hamburg)
NOV-DEC Christkindelsmarkt/Weihnachtsmarkt: Christmas markets (Nuremberg and countrywide)

Tourism, 1980–1998 
International arrivals to Germany (millions)
Unified Germany
West Germany
East Germany
Source: World Tourism Organisation

BERLIN AIRPORTS

Principal public transport connections between Berlin's three airports and the city centre

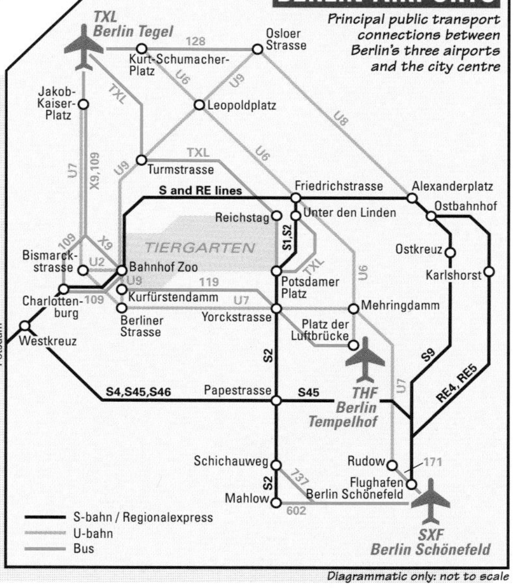

S-bahn / Regionalexpress
U-bahn
Bus

Diagrammatic only: not to scale

Map legend
— Land boundary
○ Land capital
100 km
50 miles

RUHRGEBIET

BERLIN

GERMANY

See pages 8-9 for general map

Germany tourist routes

Germany has a well-developed network of tourist routes passing through areas of scenic or historic interest. Some of the most well-known are:

Romantische Strasse (Romantic Road). Established in 1950, the route runs for 350 kilometres from northern Bavaria to the Austrian border. See panel for the route.

Strasse der Kaiser und Könige (Route of Emperors and Kings). One of Germany's oldest transit routes, running from Frankfurt am Main in the west, following the Main and Danube rivers to Passau and then continuing to Vienna.

Weinstrasse (Wine Road). Germany's oldest designated tourist route, passing through the vineyards of the Pfalz.

Mosel Weinstrasse (Mosel Wine Road). Follows the Mosel from Trier to Koblenz. Boat cruises are popular along this stretch of river.

Deutsche Märchenstrasse (German Fairy-Tale Road). This route runs from Bremen to the River Main through many places connected with fairy tales.

Burgenstrasse (Castle Road). Passes many fortifications in the Neckar valley between Mannheim and Heilbronn, then continues east to Nuremberg.

Schwarzwald-Hochstrasse (Black Forest Scenic Route). One of Germany's most famous roads, linking Baden-Baden with Freudenstadt.

ROMANTIC ROAD

- **Würzburg**
- Tauberbischofsheim
- Bad Mergentheim
- Weikersheim
- Röttingen
- Creglingen
- **Rothenburg ob der Tauber**
- Schillingsfürst
- Feuchtwangen
- Dinkelsbühl
- Wallerstein
- **Nördlingen im Ries**
- Harburg
- **Donauwörth**
- **Augsburg**
- Friedberg
- **Landsberg am Lech**
- Hohenfurch
- Schongau
- Peiting
- Rottenbuch
- Wildsteig
- Wieskirche
- Steingaden
- Schwangau
- **Füssen**

Diagrammatic only: not to scale

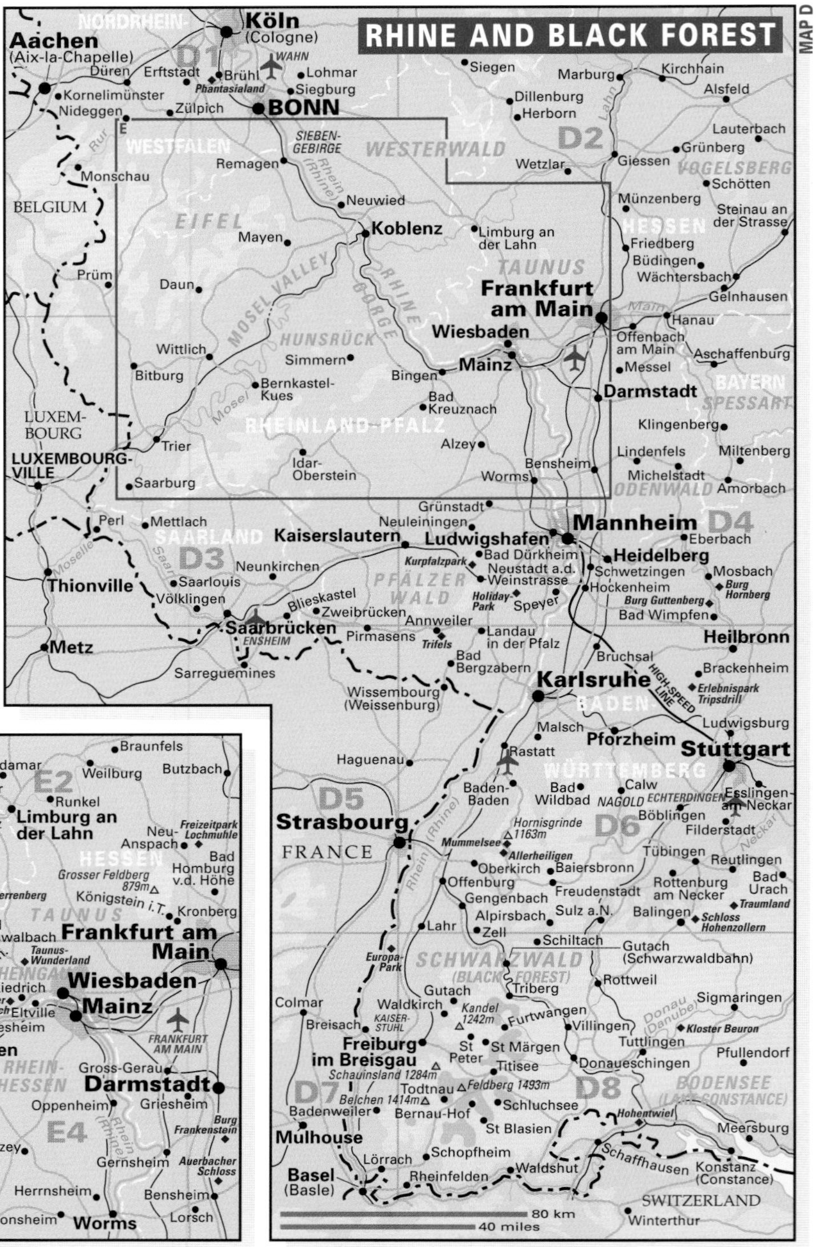

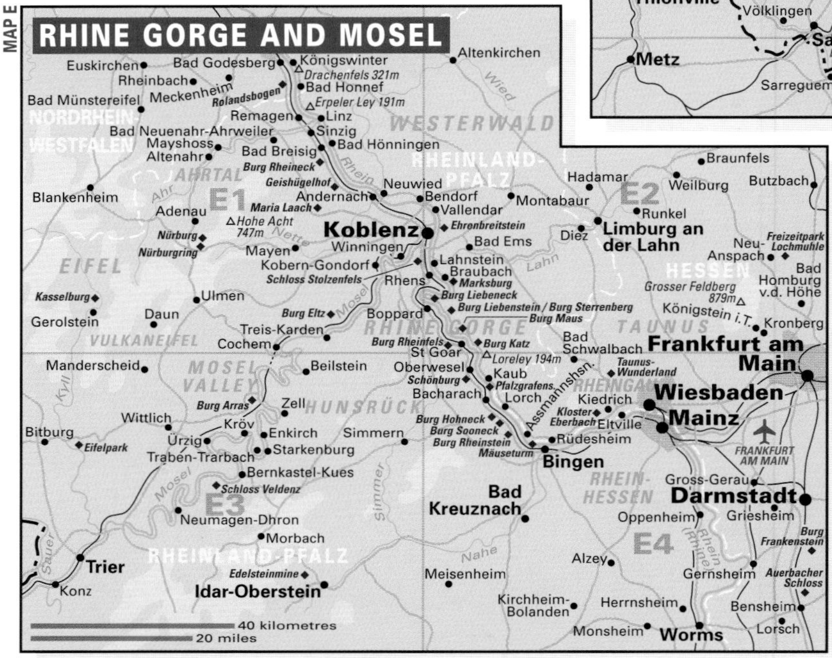

RHINE AND BLACK FOREST (MAP D)

RHINE GORGE AND MOSEL (MAP E)

SOUTHERN BAVARIA (MAP F)

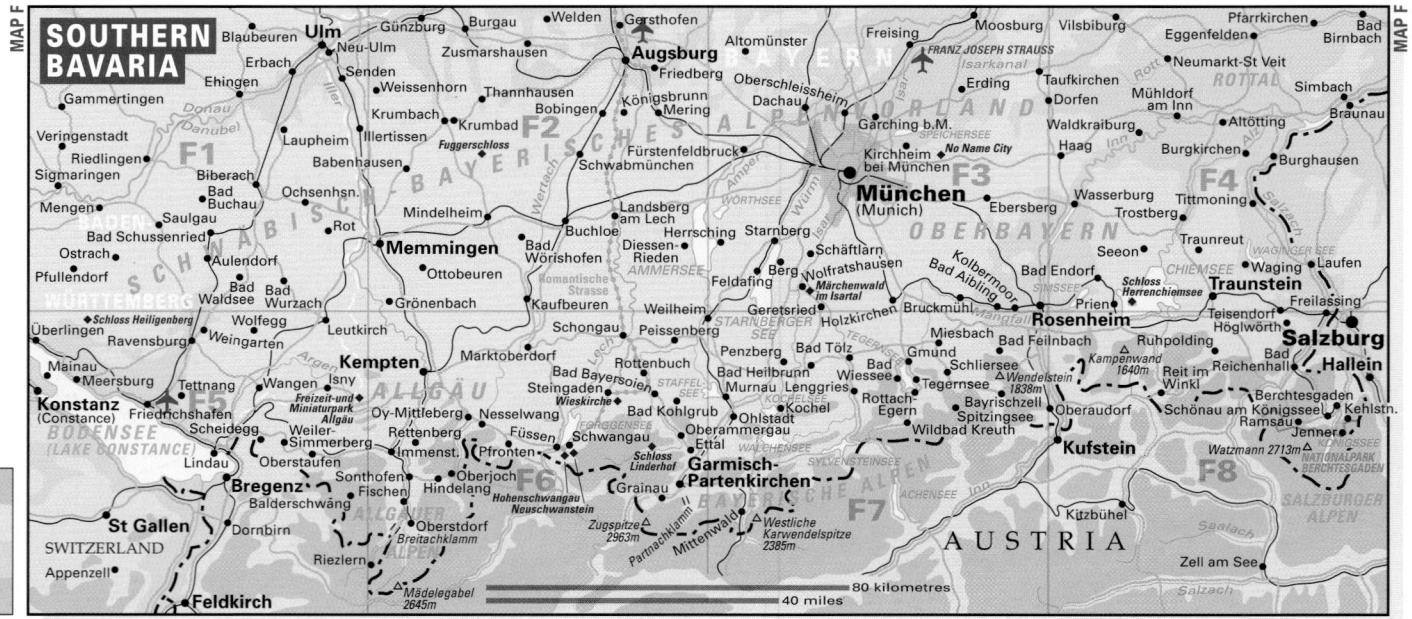

GERMAN CASTLES AND SPAS

This map represents the finest achievements of nine centuries of castle building, from the functional fortresses of the early middle ages to the highly elaborate palaces of the 19th century. The selection has been based on historical, architectural and aesthetic considerations. In general, the castles have been referred to by their original names.

Map legend:
- Land boundary
- castle
- spa / health resort
- 100 km
- 50 miles

Schloss (palace, important residence):
- ○ Schloss
- ○ Schloss with moat
- ○ Schloss ruin
- ○ Schloss ruin with moat

Burg (fortified, often in a strategic location):
- ■ Burg
- ■ Burg with moat
- ■ Burg ruin
- ■ Burg ruin with moat

Other fortifications:
- ■ Former military fortress
- ■ Historic walls / city defences
- ■ Fortified church or cemetery

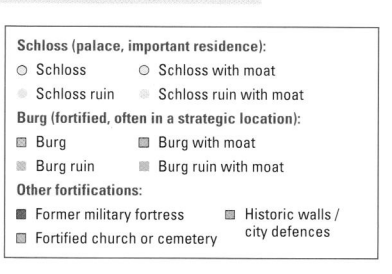

Schleswig-Holstein
- ○ 1 Glücksburg
- ○ 2 Gottorf
- ○ 3 Emkendorf

Niedersachsen (Lower Saxony)
- ○ 4 Clemenswerth
- ○ 5 Celle
- ○ 6 Gifhorn
- ○ 7 Wolfenbüttel
- ○ 8 Herrenhausen, Hannover
- ○ 9 Marienburg
- ○ 10 Hämelschenburg
- ○ 11 Bückeburg

Nordrhein-Westfalen (North Rhine-Westphalia)
Münsterländer Wasserburgen (Water Castles of Münsterland):
- ○ 12 • Burgsteinfurt
- ○ 13 • Hülshoff
- ○ 14 • Gemen
- ○ 15 • Anholt
- ○ 16 • Raesfeld
- ○ 17 • Lembeck
- ○ 18 • Vischering
- ○ 19 • Nordkirchen
- ○ 20 • Westerwinkel
- ○ 21 • Vornholz
- ○ 22 • Rheda
- ○ 23 Schwarzenraben
- ○ 24 Detmold
- ○ 25 Corvey
- ○ 26 Rhedyt
- ○ 27 Dyck
- ○ 28 Benrath
- ○ 29 Nideggen
- ■ 30 Konradsheim
- ○ 31 Augustusburg, Brühl

Hessen (Hesse)
- ■ 32 Krukenburg
- ○ 33 Wilhelmsthal
- ○ 34 Wilhelmshöhe, Kassel
- ○ 35 Arolsen
- ■ 36 Weidelsburg
- ■ 37 Felsberg
- ■ 38 Spangenberg
- ○ 39 Marburg
- ■ 40 Greifenstein
- ■ 41 Braunfels
- ○ 42 Weilburg
- ○ 43 Runkel
- ■ 44 Hohenstein
- ○ 45 Biebrich
- ■ 46 Eppstein
- ■ 47 Königstein im Taunus
- ○ 48 Kronberg
- ○ 49 Friedberg
- ○ 50 Münzenberg
- ○ 51 Fulda
- ○ 52 Eichenzell [Fasanerie]
- ○ 53 Steinau
- ○ 54 Kaiserpfalz, Gelnhausen
- ○ 55 Philippsruhe
- ■ 56 Kaiserpfalz, Seligenstadt
- ■ 57 Breuberg
- ■ 58 Auerbacher Schloss

Rheinland-Pfalz (Rhineland-Palatinate)
- ○ 59 Kasselburg
Moseltal (Mosel Valley):
- ■ 60 • Arras
- ■ 61 • Cochem
- ■ 62 • Eltz
- ■ 63 • Oberburg, Kobern-Gondorf
- ■ 64 Ehrenbreitstein
Rhine Gorge:
- ■ 65 • Marksburg
- ■ 66 • Stolzenfels
- ■ 67 • Rheinfels
- ■ 68 • Schönburg
- ■ 69 • Pfalzgrafenstein
- ■ 70 • Bacharach
- ■ 71 • Rheinstein
- ○ 72 Lichtenberg
- ■ 73 Hardenburg
- ■ 74 Dahner 'Schlosser'
- ■ 75 Trifels

Baden-Württemberg
- ○ 76 Mannheim
- ○ 77 Heidelberg
- ○ 78 Schwetzingen
- ○ 79 Bruchsal
- ○ 80 Karlsruhe
Neckartal (Neckar Valley):
- ■ 81 • Minneburg
- ■ 82 • Guttenberg
- ○ 83 • Zwingenberg
- ○ 84 • Hornberg
- ○ 85 • Horneck
- ○ 86 • Kaiserpfalz, Bad Wimpfen
- ■ 87 Neipperg
- ○ 88 Steinsberg
- ○ 89 Wertheim
- ○ 90 Bad Mergentheim
- ○ 91 Weikersheim
- ○ 92 Krautheim
- ○ 93 Stetten
- ○ 94 Leofels
- ○ 95 Neuenstein
- ■ 96 Lichtenberg
- ○ 97 Ludwigsburg
- ○ 98 Solitude
- ○ 99 Hirsau
- ○ 100 Rastatt
- ○ 101 Favorite
- ■ 102 Hohenbaden
- ○ 103 Hohengeroldseck
- ○ 104 Landeck
- ○ 105 Hochburg
- ○ 106 Hohenzollern
- ○ 107 Hohentübingen
- ■ 108 Hoheneuffen
- ■ 109 Hohenrechberg
- ■ 110 Hohentwiel
- ■ 111 Wildenstein
- ○ 112 Sigmaringen
- ○ 113 Heiligenberg
- ○ 114 Meersburg

Bayern (Bavaria)
- ○ 115 Hohes Schloss, Füssen
'Königsschlosser':
- ○ 116 • Hohenschwangau
- ○ 117 • Neuschwanstein
- ○ 118 Linderhof
- ○ 119 Hohenaschau
- ○ 120 Herrenchiemsee
- ■ 121 Stein
- ■ 122 Burghausen
- ○ 123 Neuburg
- ○ 124 Alte Bischöflicher Residenz, Passau
- ■ 125 Neue Bischöflicher Residenz, Passau
- ■ 126 Oberhaus, Passau
- ■ 127 Trausnitz
- ○ 128 Stadtresidenz, Landshut
- ○ 129 Neues Schloss, Oberschleissheim
- ○ 130 Lustheim
- ○ 131 Residenz, München
- ○ 132 Nymphenburg
- ○ 133 Fuggerschloss
- ○ 134 Dillingen
- ○ 135 Nördlingen
- ○ 136 Harburg
- ○ 137 Leitheim
- ○ 138 Neues Schloss, Ingolstadt
- ■ 139 Prunn
- ○ 140 Hirschberg
- ○ 141 Fürstbischöflicher Residenz, Eichstätt
- ○ 142 Sommerresidenz, Eichstätt
- ○ 143 Wülzburg
- ○ 144 Weissenburg
- ○ 145 Ellingen
- ○ 146 Dinkelsbühl
- ○ 147 Rothenburg on der Tauber
- ○ 148 Ansbach
- ■ 149 Lichtenau
- ○ 150 Cadolzburg
- ■ 151 Nürnberg (Nuremberg)
- ■ 152 Rothenberg
- ■ 153 Leuchtenburg
- ■ 154 Flossenbürg
- ○ 155 Eremitage, Bayreuth
- ○ 156 Neues Schloss, Bayreuth
- ○ 157 Plassenburg
- ■ 158 Rosenberg
- ■ 159 Veste Coburg
- ○ 160 Aufsess
- ○ 161 Seehof
- ○ 162 Alte Hofhaltung, Bamberg
- ○ 163 Neue Residenz, Bamberg
- ○ 164 Weissenstein
- ○ 165 Johanniterkastell Biebelried
- ○ 166 Marienberg, Würzburg
- ○ 167 Residenz, Würzburg
- ○ 168 Veitshöchheim
- ○ 169 Rothenfels
- ○ 170 Henneburg
- ○ 171 Kleinheubach
- ○ 172 Wildenburg
- ○ 173 Johannisburg
- ○ 174 Mespelbrunn
- ○ 175 Homburg
- ○ 176 Werneck
- ○ 177 Trimburg
- ○ 178 Salzburg
- ○ 179 Ostheim

Thüringen (Thuringia)
- ○ 180 Hanstein
- ○ 181 Wartburg
- ○ 182 Friedenstein
- ○ 183 Molsdorf
- ○ 184 Grünes Schloss, Weimar
- ○ 185 Heidecksburg
- ○ 186 Gnandstein

Sachsen (Saxony)
- ○ 187 Augustusburg
- ○ 188 Weesenstein
- ○ 189 Grosssedlitz
- ○ 190 Königstein
- ○ 191 Ortenburg
- ○ 192 Rammenau
- ○ 193 Stolpen
- ○ 194 Pillnitz
- ○ 195 Zwinger
- ○ 196 Moritzburg
- ○ 197 Albrechtsburg
- ■ 198 Kriebstein
- ○ 199 Bochsburg
- ○ 200 Rochlitz
- ○ 201 Colditz
- ○ 202 Mildenstein
- ○ 203 Hubertusburg
- ○ 204 Hartenfels

Sachsen-Anhalt
- ○ 205 Rudelsburg
- ○ 206 Neuenburg
- ○ 207 Querfurt
- ○ 208 Allstedt
- ○ 209 Falkenstein
- ○ 210 Regenstein
- ○ 211 Wettin
- ○ 212 Bernburg
- ○ 213 Mosigkau
- ○ 214 Wörlitz
- ○ 215 Leitzkau

Brandenburg
- ○ 216 Neues Palais, Potsdam
- ○ 217 Sanssouci
- ○ 218 Rheinsberg

Berlin
- ○ 219 Charlottenburg
- ○ 220 Spandau

Mecklenburg-Vorpommern
- ○ 221 Ludwigslust
- ○ 222 Schwerin
- ○ 223 Fürstenhof
- ○ 224 Güstrow [Renaissanceschloss]
- ○ 225 Ivenack
- ○ 226 Friedland
- ○ 227 Granitz

Spa holidays are first and foremost to improve or restore one's health, but patients also have a chance to meet people and get to know a different culture. There are nearly 400 recognised spas and health resorts in Germany, shown as blue symbols on the map.

For further information, contact:

Deutscher Bäderverband, Schumannstrasse 111, D-53113 Bonn. Tel. +49 (0) 228 201200.

Principal German spa towns
- s1 Bad Pyrmont
- s2 Bad Wildungen
- s3 Bad Orb
- s4 Bad Vilbel
- s5 Bad Homburg
- s6 Bad Ems
- s7 Bad Kreuznach
- s8 Baden-Baden
- s9 Bad Wildbad
- s10 Badenweiler
- s11 Bad Tölz
- s12 Bad Wiessee
- s13 Bad Reichenhall
- s14 Bad Kissingen
- s15 Bad Brückenau
- s16 Bad Langensalza
- s17 Bad Düben
- s18 Bad Doberan

Principal climatic health resorts
- h1 Hahenklee
- h2 Braunlage
- h3 Königstein im Taunus
- h4 Bad Bergzabern
- h5 Bad Herrenalb
- h6 Freudenstadt
- h7 Schönwald
- h8 Titisee
- h9 St Blasien
- h10 Isny
- h11 Oberstdorf
- h12 Garmisch-Partenkirchen
- h13 Rottach-Egern
- h14 Bayrischzell
- h15 Bad Suderode
- h16 Rheinsberg

Coastal health resorts include–
North Sea coast:
- c1 Helgoland
- c2 Westerland, Sylt
- c3 Wyk, Föhr
- c4 St Peter Ording
- c5 Cuxhaven
- c6 Wilhelmshaven
- c7 Horumersiel
- c8 Norden
- c9 Borkum
- c10 Juist
- c11 Norderney
- c12 Wangerooge

Baltic coast:
- c13 Damp
- c14 Eckernförde
- c15 Heiligenhafen
- c16 Grömitz
- c17 Neustadt in Holstein
- c18 Scharbeutz-Haffkrug
- c19 Timmendorfer Strand
- c20 Kühlungsborn
- c21 Heiligendamm
- c22 Graal-Müritz
- c23 Zingst
- c24 Binz
- c25 Heringsdorf

Kneipp spas
(offering treatments developed by Sebastian Kneipp in the 19th century; includes baths, warm & cold showers, strict diet, plenty of walking, herbal medication)

Selected Kneipp spas:
- k1 Bad Bevensen
- k2 Fallingbostel
- k3 Oberharz
- k4 Willingen
- k5 Daun
- k6 Manderscheid
- k7 Kyllburg
- k8 Schömberg
- k9 Königsfeld
- k10 St Blasien
- k11 Hindelang
- k12 Oberstdorf

FRANCE

See page 10 for general map

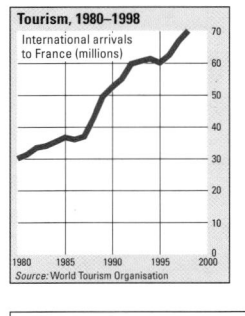

Tourism, 1980–1998

International arrivals to France (millions)

Source: World Tourism Organisation

JAN 1st La Grande Parade de Montmartre (Paris)
JAN Internat. Circus Festival (Monaco)
JAN 22nd St Vincent Festival: patron saint of wine
FEB La Fête de Citron: Lemon Festival (Menton)
before LENT Carnaval de Nice
MAY Cannes Film Festival
MAY Annual Gypsy gathering (les Saintes-Maries-de-la-Mer)
JUN Paris Air Show
JUN-JUL Aix en Musique (Aix-en-Provence)
JUL Festival of the Giants (Douai)
JUL Carnaval and arts festival (Nantes)
JUL 14th Bastille Day

JUL La Festival de Cornouaille: folklore festival (Quimper)
JUL Tour de France
JUL Festival d'Avignon: drama festival
JUL-AUG International Fireworks Festival (Monaco)
AUG Celtic Festival (Lorient)
AUG Haute-Provence Festival (Forcalquier)
SEP Festival du Livre Vivant: historical pageant (Fougères)
SEP German-French Festival (Strasbourg and Germany)
SEP Coupe Icarus: unpowered flight festival (St Hilaire-du-Touvet)
NOV Mondial du Snowboard (les Deux Alpes)
NOV Les Trois Glorieuses: wine festival (Côte d'Or)
NOV Les Sarmentelles: Beaujolais Nouveau
DEC Marché de Noël: Christmas market (Strasbourg)

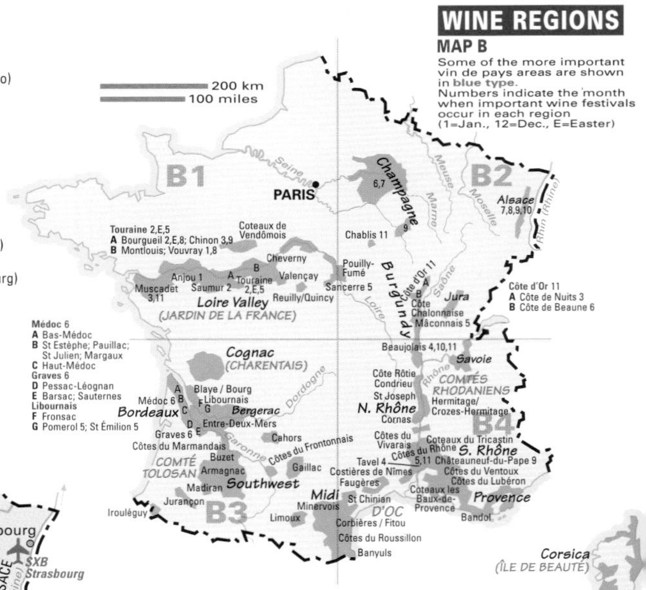

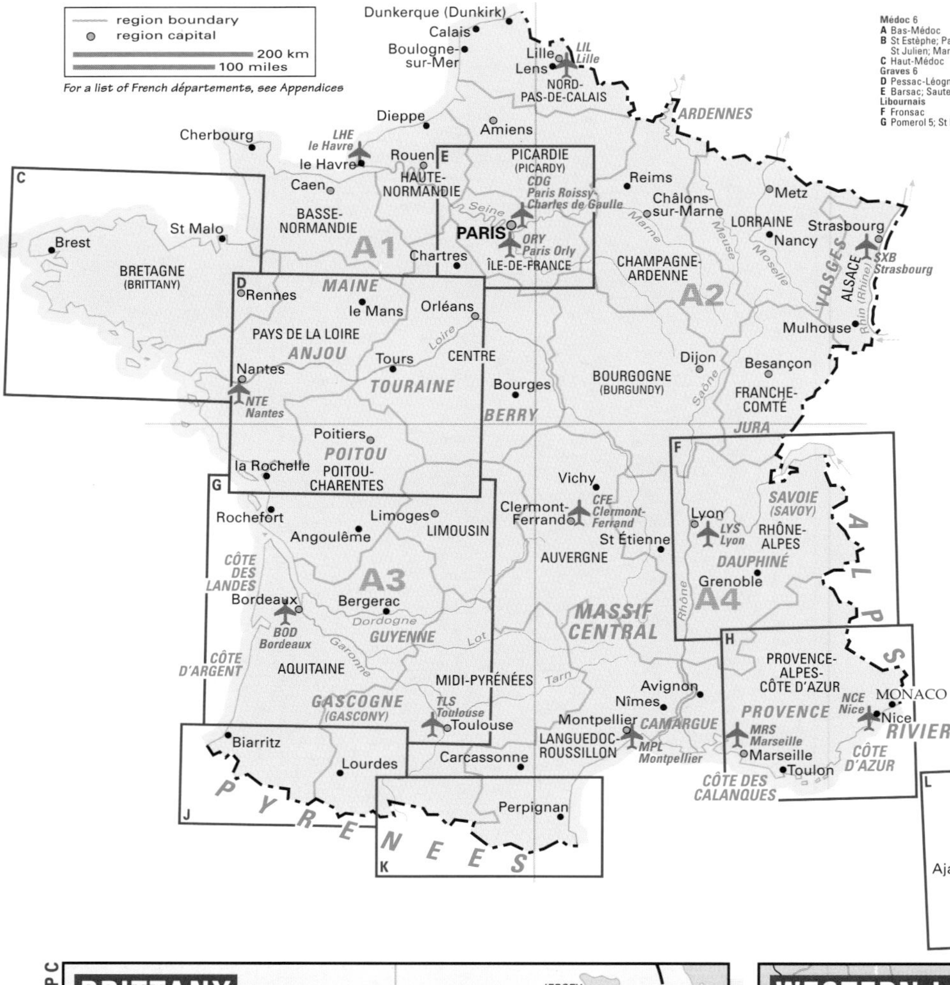

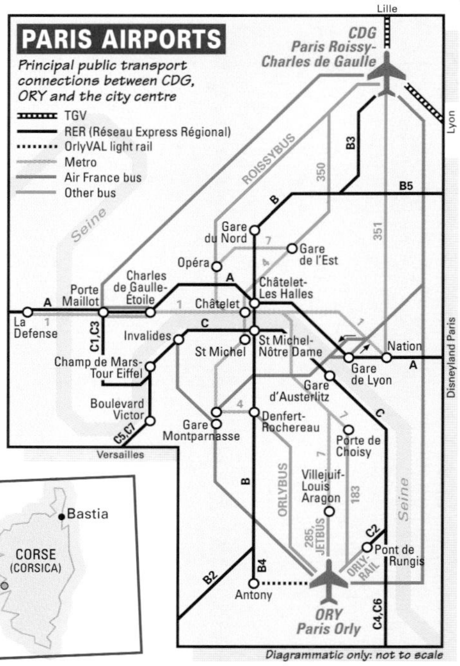

WINE REGIONS

MAP B

Some of the more important vin de pays areas are shown in blue type. Numbers indicate the month when important wine festivals occur in each region (1=Jan., 12=Dec., E=Easter).

PARIS AIRPORTS

Principal public transport connections between CDG, ORY and the city centre

- TGV
- RER (Réseau Express Régional)
- OrlyVAL light rail
- Metro
- Air France bus
- Other bus

Diagrammatic only: not to scale

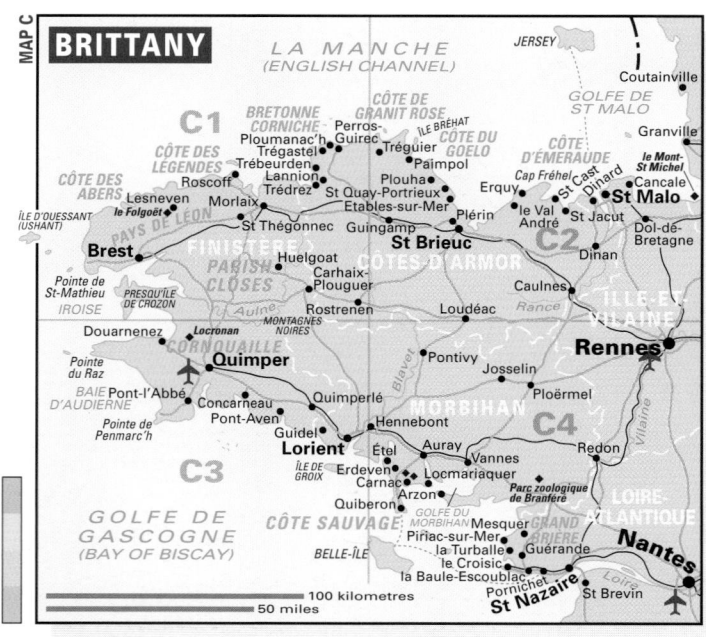

BRITTANY

LA MANCHE (ENGLISH CHANNEL)

GOLFE DE GASCOGNE (BAY OF BISCAY)

2000 metres
1000 metres
Sea level

100 kilometres
50 miles

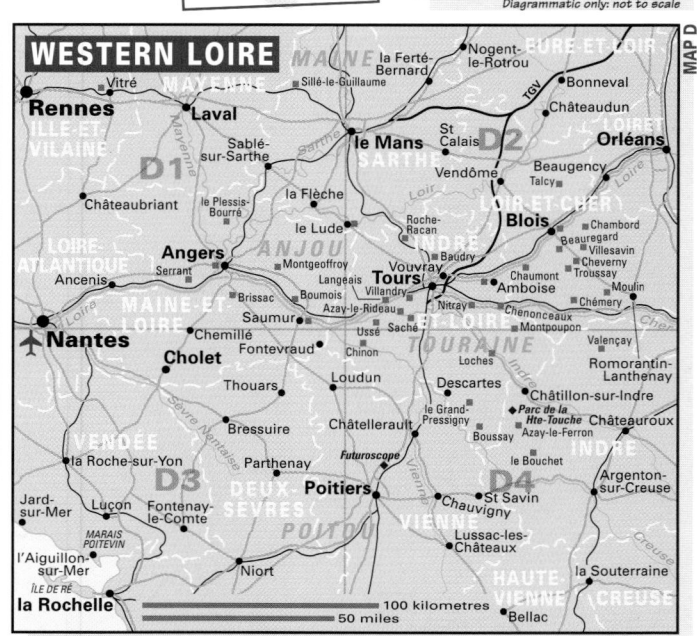

WESTERN LOIRE

■ château

100 kilometres
50 miles

FRANCE

See page 10 for general map

PARIS

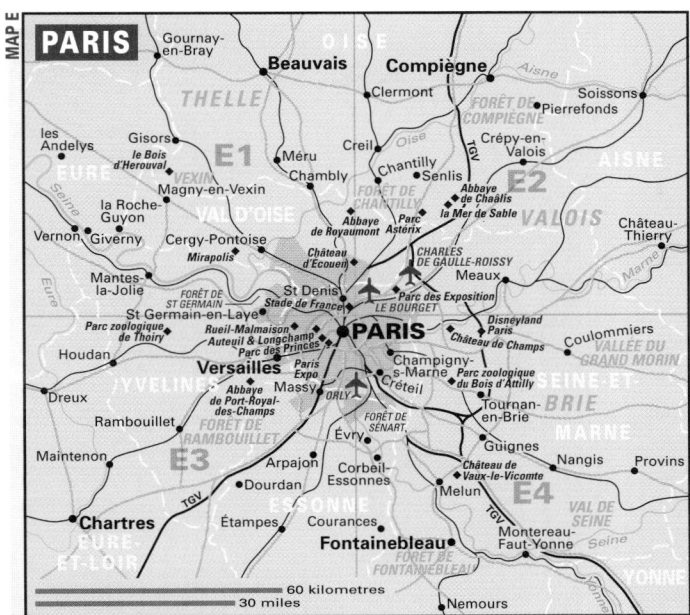

FRENCH ALPS

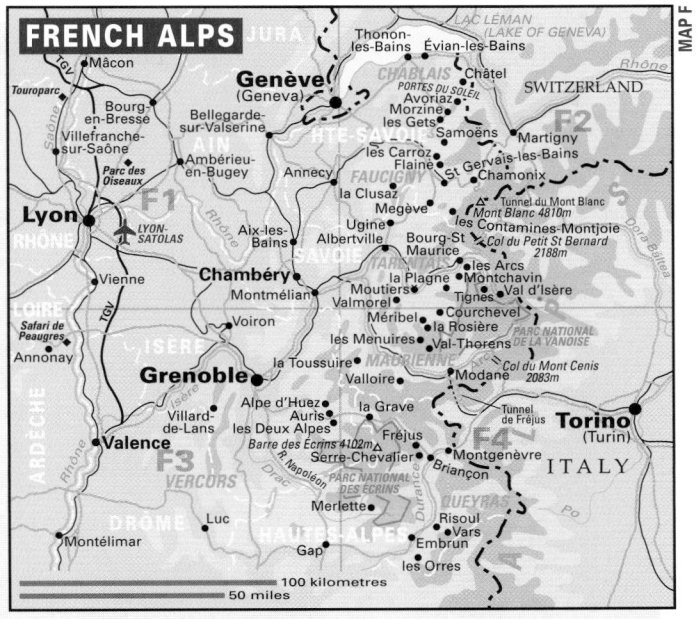

SOUTHWEST FRANCE

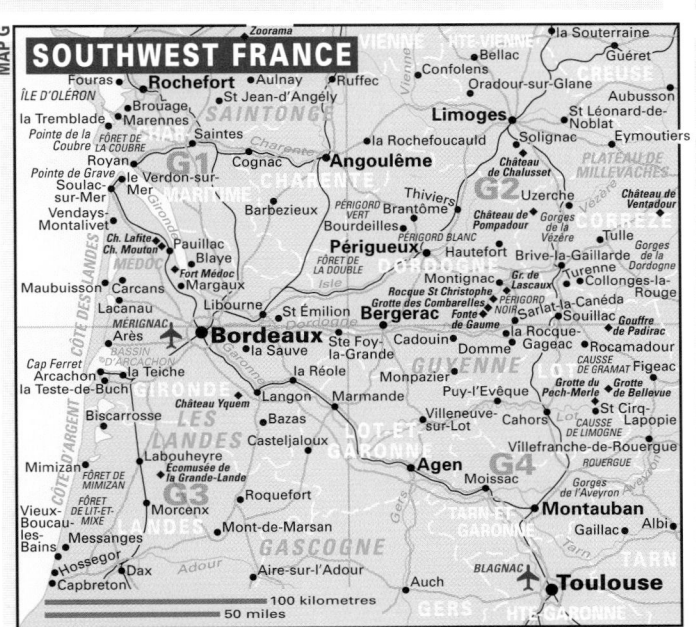

CÔTE D'AZUR

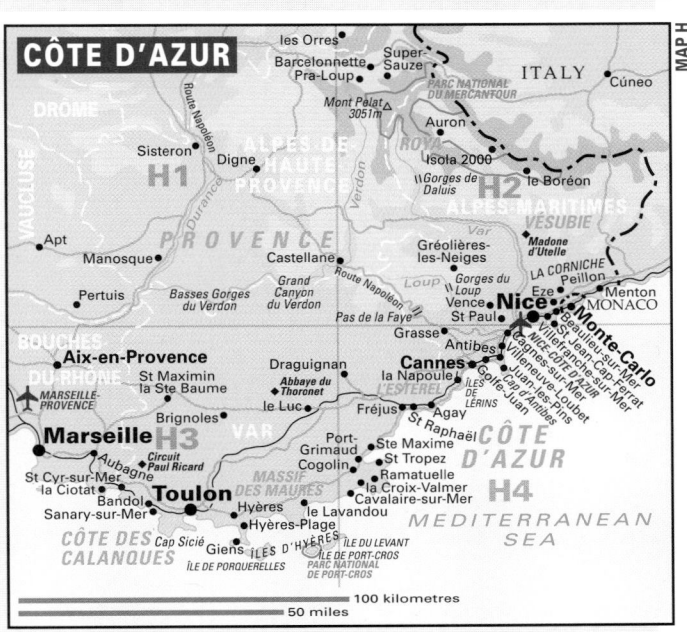

PYRENEES (WEST)

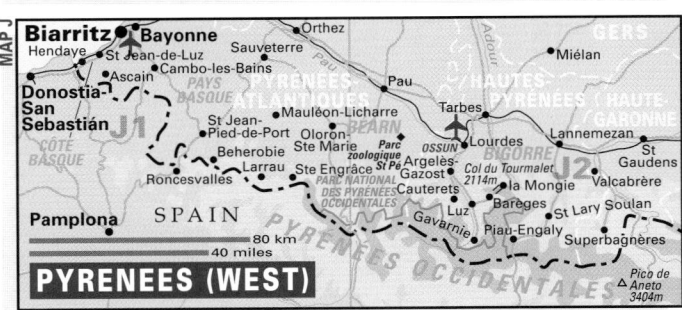

PYRENEES (EAST)

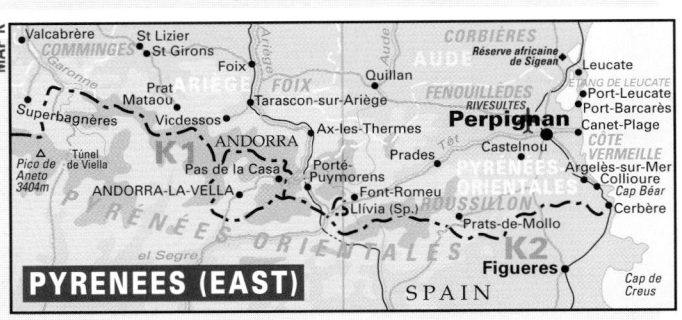

CORSICA

SPAIN

See page 11 for general map

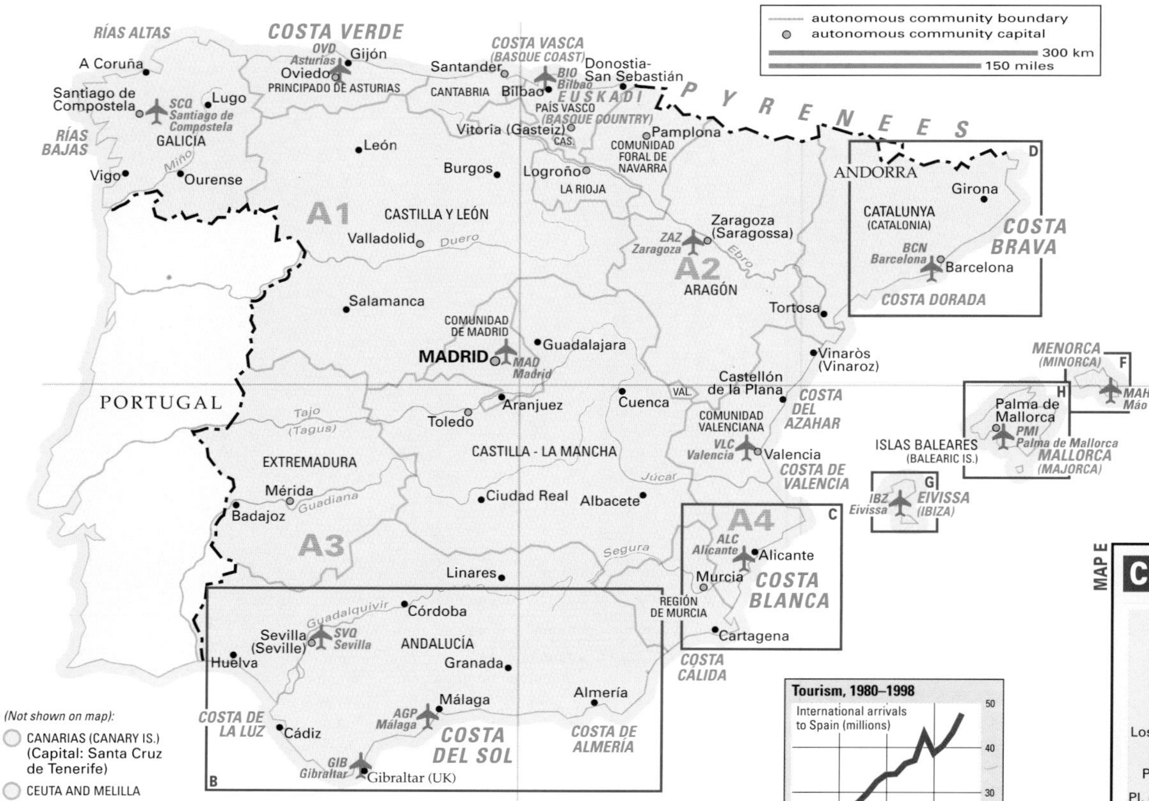

--- autonomous community boundary
○ autonomous community capital
▬▬▬ 300 km
▬▬▬ 150 miles

JAN Festividad de San Sebastián: drum parades
before Lent Carnaval (Cádiz and countrywide)
MAR Las Fallas de San José (Valencia)
EASTER Semana Santa: Holy Week
APR Feria de Abril: April Fair (Seville)
APR Moros y Cristanos mock battle: St George's Festival (Alcoy)
MAY Cruces de Mayo and national flamenco competition (Córdoba)
MAY Feria del Caballo: horse fair (Jeréz de la Frontera)
MAY Fiestas de San Isidro (Madrid)
MAY Romería del Rocío: pilgrimage (near Huelva)
MAY/JUN Corpus Christi
JUN Haro: Wine war (La Rioja)
JUN 23-24th Festes de Sant Joan (Barcelona and Catalonia)
JUN 24th Xiquets de Valls: human towers (Valls)
JUN-JUL International Festival of Music and Dance (Granada)
JUL Fiesta de San Fermín: bull-running (Pamplona)
JUL 22nd Cuesta de los Danzadores: stilt dancers (Anguiano, La Rioja)
JUL 25th Feast of St James (Santiago de Compostela)
AUG Semana Grande: Basque sports (Euskadi)
AUG Moros y Cristanos mock battle and mystery play (Elche)
AUG La Tomatina: Tomato Battle (Buñol)
SEP 19th Americas Day (Oviedo)
SEP 24th Festa de la Mercè (Barcelona)

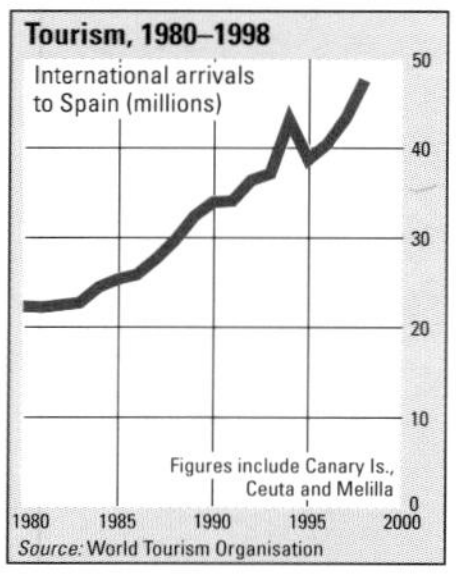

Main map labels

RÍAS ALTAS
COSTA VERDE
COSTA VASCA (BASQUE COAST)
PYRENEES
A Coruña · Santiago de Compostela · Lugo
SCQ Santiago de Compostela
GALICIA
RÍAS BAJAS
Vigo · Ourense
Miño
OVD Asturias Oviedo · Gijón
PRINCIPADO DE ASTURIAS
CANTABRIA · Santander
BIO Bilbao
Donostia-San Sebastián
EUSKADI PAÍS VASCO (BASQUE COUNTRY)
Vitoria (Gasteiz)
CAS. · Pamplona
COMUNIDAD FORAL DE NAVARRA
ANDORRA
Girona
CATALUNYA (CATALONIA)
COSTA BRAVA
León
Burgos · Logroño
LA RIOJA
A1
CASTILLA Y LEÓN
Valladolid
Duero
Zaragoza (Saragossa) ZAZ Zaragoza
A2
ARAGÓN
BCN Barcelona · Barcelona
COSTA DORADA
Salamanca
Tortosa
COMUNIDAD DE MADRID
MADRID MAD Madrid
Guadalajara
Vinaròs (Vinaroz)
MENORCA (MINORCA)
MAH Máo
F
PORTUGAL
Tajo (Tagus)
Toledo · Aranjuez
Cuenca
Castellón de la Plana
VAL
COSTA DEL AZAHAR
Palma de Mallorca PMI Palma de Mallorca
MALLORCA (MAJORCA)
H
EXTREMADURA
CASTILLA - LA MANCHA
VLC Valencia · Valencia
COSTA DE VALENCIA
ISLAS BALEARES (BALEARIC IS.)
Mérida · Badajoz
Guadiana
Ciudad Real · Albacete
Júcar
IBZ Eivissa · EIVISSA (IBIZA)
G
Linares
Segura
ALC Alicante · Alicante
A4
C
Córdoba
REGIÓN DE MURCIA
COSTA BLANCA
Sevilla (Seville) SVQ Sevilla
ANDALUCÍA
Guadalquivir
Granada
Murcia
COSTA CALIDA
Huelva
Málaga AGP Málaga
Almería
COSTA DE LA LUZ
Cádiz
GIB Gibraltar · Gibraltar (UK)
COSTA DEL SOL
COSTA DE ALMERÍA
B

(Not shown on map):
○ CANARIAS (CANARY IS.) (Capital: Santa Cruz de Tenerife)
○ CEUTA AND MELILLA

Tourism chart

Tourism, 1980–1998
International arrivals to Spain (millions)
50 / 40 / 30 / 20 / 10
1980 1985 1990 1995 2000
Figures include Canary Is., Ceuta and Melilla
Source: World Tourism Organisation

Camino text

The 'Camino de Santiago' or 'Way of St James' leads to the tomb of St James the Apostle in Santiago de Compostela. From the four traditional gathering places in France (Paris, Vézelay, Le Puy and Arles), pilgrims would travel over the Pyrenees and continue through northern Spain on two routes. The 'French Route' is shown here. The northern or coastal route, used less by travellers, passes Hondarribia, Santillana (and Altamira Cave), Avilés and Mondoñedo.

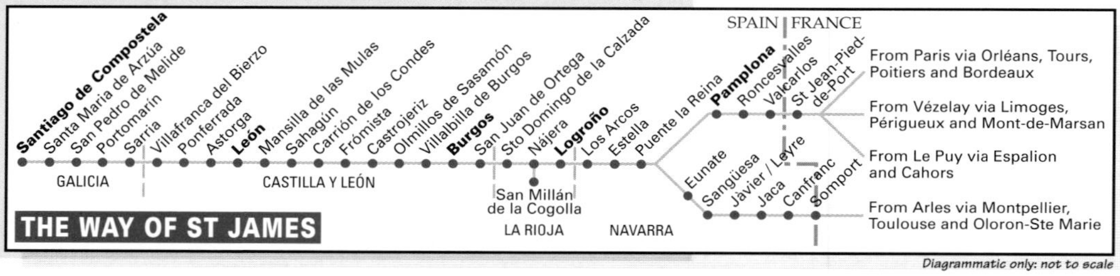

THE WAY OF ST JAMES

Santiago de Compostela · Santa María de Arzúa · San Pedro de Melide · Portomarín · Sarria · Villafranca del Bierzo · Ponferrada · Astorga · León · Mansilla de las Mulas · Sahagún · Carrión de los Condes · Frómista · Castrojeriz · Olmillos de Sasamón · Villabilla de Burgos · Burgos · San Juan de Ortega · Sto Domingo de la Calzada · Nájera · Logroño · Los Arcos · Estella · Puente la Reina · Pamplona · Roncesvalles · Valcarlos · St Jean-Pied-de-Port

GALICIA · CASTILLA Y LEÓN · LA RIOJA · NAVARRA
SPAIN | FRANCE

Eunate · Sangüesa · Javier / Leyre · Jaca · Canfranc · Somport
San Millán de la Cogolla

From Paris via Orléans, Tours, Poitiers and Bordeaux
From Vézelay via Limoges, Périgueux and Mont-de-Marsan
From Le Puy via Espalion and Cahors
From Arles via Montpellier, Toulouse and Oloron-Ste Marie

Diagrammatic only: not to scale

CANARY ISLANDS (MAP E)

San Cristóbal de la Laguna
Tacoronte · Puerto de la Cruz
Icod de los Vinos · Garachico · La Orotava · Candelaria · Güimar
LOS RODEOS · Santa Cruz de Tenerife
PARQUE NACIONAL DE LAS CAÑADAS DEL TEIDE
Los Gigantes
Puerto de Santiago · Playa de la Arena
Playa Paraíso · Adeje
La Caleta · Pico de Teide 3715m
E1
TENERIFE
Pl. de las Américas · REINA SOFIA · El Médano
Los Cristianos · Las Galletas · El Abrigo
COSTA DEL SILENCIO
40 kilometres / 20 miles
ATLANTIC OCEAN

GRAN CANARIA Las Palmas Gran Canaria
Arucas
San Nicolás de Tolentino · Bandama 574m
Tejeda · Telde
Pico de las Nieves 1949m · Ingenio
Mogán · San Bartolomé de Tirajana
La Playa de Mogán · San Agustín Sioux City
La Playa de Tauro · Puerto Rico · Playa del Inglés
Playa de la Balita · Maspalomas
Arguineguín
COSTA CANARIA
E4
40 kilometres / 20 miles

For location see general map section

COSTA DEL SOL (MAP B)

Aracena
Almodóvar del Río · **Córdoba**
Constantina
AVE Guadalquivir
Palma del Río
Torredonjimeno · **Jaén**
Huéscar
B1
Montilla
Baena
Vélez-Rubio
Huelva
Cartaya · Moguer · Almonte
Lepe · El Rompido · Punta Umbría · Mazagón
Isla Antilla · Isla Cristina
PARQUE NACIONAL COTO DE DOÑANA
Carmona · Écija
Sevilla (Seville)
Estepa
Alcalá la Real
Baza
B2
Guadix
B3
B4
Huércal-Overa
Playa de Castilla
Playa de Matalascañas
LAS MARISMAS
Bobadilla
Loja
Granada
SIERRA NEVADA
Sierra Nevada (Sol y Nieve)
Pico de Veleta 3392m · Mulhacén 3478m
Capileira
Vera · Mojácar
Sanlúcar de Barrameda · Chipiona
Algodonales
Antequera
ANDALUCÍA
SIERRA DE ALMIJARA
Carboneras
Costa DE LA LUZ · Rota
Jeréz de la Frontera
SERRANÍA DE RONDA
Vélez-Málaga
Nerja · Salobreña · Motril
Almería
Níjar
El Cabo de Gata
El Puerto de Santa María
Ronda
Málaga
El Palo · Torre del Mar · Torrox · Almuñécar · Calahonda
Adra · El Ejido · Almerimar · Roquetas de Mar · Aguadulce
Cabo de Gata
San José
BAHÍA DE CÁDIZ
San Fernando · Chiclana de la Frontera
Puerto Banús · Torremolinos · Benalmádena Costa · Fuengirola
COSTA TROPICAL
B5
Cádiz
San Pedro Alcántara · Marbella · Mijas Costa
COSTA DEL SOL
B7
B8
GOLFO DE CÁDIZ
Casares · Estepona
Manilva
B6
Conil de la Frontera · Barbate de Franco
Valderrama
San Roque · La Línea
Algeciras · **Gibraltar (UK)**
Cabo Trafalgar
Punta de Europa
MEDITERRANEAN SEA
Tarifa
Punta de Tarifa o Marroquí

1000 metres / 500 metres / Sea level
100 km / 50 miles

SPAIN

See page 11 for general map

COSTA BLANCA

Denia
Xabia (Jávea)
Alcoy
Guadaleste
Benissa
Teulada
Cabo de la Nao
Yecla
Villena
Calpe
Moraira
Peñon de Ifach
C1
Elda
Finestrat
Altea
Alfaz del Pi
COMUNIDAD VALENCIANA
Jumilla
Benidorm
La Vila Joiosa
C2
Novelda
Campello
COSTA
Cieza
Elx (Elche)
Alicante
ALTET
Los Arenales del Sol
Crevillente
Santa Pola
BLANCA
Orihuela
ISLOTE DE LA CANTERA
Guardamar
del Segura
Segura
Murcia
Torrevieja
MEDITERRANEAN SEA
Pilar de la Horadada
Campoamor
MURCIA
Santiago de la Ribera
San Pedro del Pinatar
C3
San Javier
Los Alcázares
C4
MAR MENOR
La Manga del Mar Menor
Mazarrón
La Unión
Cabo de Palos
Puerto de Mazarrón
Cartagena
COSTA CÁLIDA

100 kilometres
50 miles

COSTA BRAVA

Llívia (Sp.)
FRANCE
ANDORRA
Puigcerdà
la Jonquera
Llançà
Portbou
Sant Pere de Rodes
la Seu d'Urgell
Figueres
Roses
Cadaqués
Cap de Creus
D1
Ripoll
Olot
EMPORDÀ
GOLF DE ROSES
Berga
Sant Pere Pescador
Empúries
l'Escala
El Llobregat
Vic
Girona
l'Estartit
COSTA DE LA MORT
Ter
Palafrugell
Aiguablava
CATALUNYA
Llafranc
Palamós
Manresa
Maçanet
Platja d'Aro
S.Feliu d.Guíxols
Igualada
Montserrat
Granollers
Blanes
Tossa de Mar
COSTA DE LLEVANT
Reial Monestir de Poblet
Terrassa
Pineda de Mar
Lloret de Mar
Montblanc
Sabadell
Calella
Malgrat de Mar
Santa Susanna
D2
Martorell
Arenys de Mar
COSTA BRAVA
Monestir de Santes Creus
Vilafranca del Penedès
El Masnou
Mataró
Reial Monestir de Poblet
Valls
Badalona
COSTA DEL MARESME
Tibidabo
El Vendrell
Comaruga
Calafell
Barcelona
EL PRAT DE LLOBREGAT
D3
Reus
Sitges
Castelldefels
D4
Torredembarra
Vilanova i la Geltrú
Tarragona
MEDITERRANEAN SEA
la Pineda
COSTA DORADA
Salou *Port Aventura*
Cambrils de Mar

100 kilometres
50 miles

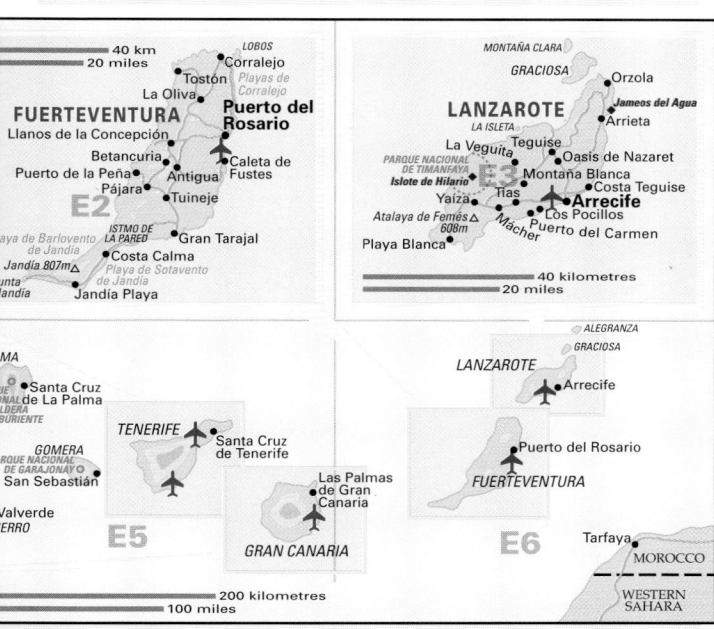

40 km
20 miles
LOBOS
Corralejo
Tostón
Playas de Corralejo
La Oliva
MONTAÑA CLARA
GRACIOSA
Orzola
FUERTEVENTURA
Puerto del Rosario
LANZAROTE
Jameos del Agua
Llanos de la Concepción
LA ISLETA
Arrieta
Betancuria
PARQUE NACIONAL DE TIMANFAYA
La Veguita
Teguise
Oasis de Nazaret
Puerto de la Peña
Antigua
Caleta de Fustes
Islote de Hilario
Montaña Blanca
E3
Costa Teguise
Pájara
Tuineje
E2
Yaiza
Atalaya de Femés
Tías
Arrecife
Gran Tarajal
Playa de Sotavento de Jandía
608m
Los Pocillos
Puerto del Carmen
Mácher
ISTMO DE LA PARED
Playa de Barlovento de Jandía
Costa Calma
Playa Blanca
Jandía 807m△
Punta de Jandía
Jandía Playa

ALEGRANZA
GRACIOSA
LANZAROTE
LMA
Santa Cruz de La Palma
Arrecife
QUE NACIONAL CALDERA BURIENTE
GOMERA
TENERIFE
Santa Cruz de Tenerife
ARQUE NACIONAL DE GARAJONAY
San Sebastián
Puerto del Rosario
FUERTEVENTURA
Valverde
IERRO
Las Palmas de Gran Canaria
E5
GRAN CANARIA
E6
Tarfaya
MOROCCO
WESTERN SAHARA

200 kilometres
100 miles

MINORCA

MEDITERRANEAN SEA
Cap de Cavalleria
F1
Cala Morell
Cala Tirant
Fornells
F2
Es Delfins
Cala Forcat
S'Albufeira
Son Parc
Cala Blanes
Arenal d'en Castell
Port d'Addaia
Ciutadella
Es Mercadal
El Torro
Cap de Favàritx
△357m
Cala de Santandria
Naveta d'Es Tudons
Ferreries
ILLA D'EN COLOM
Cala Blanca
Es Migjorn Redones
Es Grau
Gran Sant Cristóbal
Shangri-La
Tamarinda
Cala Santa
Galdana
Alaior
Cala En Bosc
San Xoriguer
Platja de Son Bou
Sant Tomàs
Maó (Mahón)
Cala Llonga
Cap d'Artrutx
Sant Jaume Mediterrani
Son Bou de Baix
Villa Carlos
Sant Climent
Trebaluger
F3
Cala En Porter
Cales Coves
Es Canutells
Sant Lluís
S'Algar
F4
Binissafúller
Binibequer Vell
Punta Prima
Cala Torret
Biniancolla
ILLA DE L'AIRE

20 kilometres
10 miles

IBIZA

Portinatx
Port de Sant Miquel
Sant Joan de Labritja
Cala de Sant Vicenç
Sant Miquel de Balansat
ILLA DE TAGOMAGO
Sant Carles de Peralta
Cala Salada
EIVISSA (IBIZA)
G1
Cala Gració
Sant Antoni de Portmany
Cala Llenya
G2
Es Canyar
SA CONILLERA
Cala Bassa
S'Argamassa
ILLES BLEDES
Port d'es Torrent
Sant Rafael de Forca
Santa Eulalia del Río
Fantasylandia
Cala Conta
Sant Josep
Cala Llonga
Cala Tarida
Platja Talamanca
Cala Vadella
△ Sa Talaiassa de Sant Josep 475m
Eivissa (Ibiza)
Ses Figueretes
Cubells
Platja d'En Bossa
ILLA ES VEDRA
La Canal
Punta de ses Portes
ILLA DES PENJAT
MEDITERRANEAN SEA
G3
ILLA ESPARDELL
ILLA ESPALMADOR
G4
Es Savina
ESTANY PUDENT
Es Pujols
Cala Sahona
FORMENTERA
Sant Fransesc de Formentera
Platja de Migjorn
El Pilar

20 km
10 miles

MAJORCA

Cap de Formentor
Cala de Sant Vicenç
Formentor
MEDITERRANEAN SEA
S'Horta
Port de Pollença
Pollença
Cap d'es Pinar
Sa Calobra
Alcúdia
Monestir de Lluc
Port d'Alcúdia
BADIA D'ALCÚDIA
Puig Major 1445m
Platja de Muro
Sa Mesquida de Baix
Port de Sóller
S'ALBUFERA
Can Picafort
Lluc Alcari
Sóller
Sa Pobla
H1
Deià
Muro
Capdepera
Cala Ratjada
Banyalbufar
Orient
Son Moll
Mirador de Ses Animas
Valldemossa
Inca
Coves d'Artà
Estellencs
Sineu
Santa Margalida
Artà
SERRA DE TRAMUNTANA
Sant Llorenç des Cardassar
H2
ES PLA
Sant Sa Millor
ILLA SANT DRAGONERA
Sant Telm
Calvià
Castell de Bendinat
Palma de Mallorca
SON SANT JOAN
Manacor
Reserva Africana
Andratx
Randa
Porto Cristo
S'Illot / Sa Coma
13
Playa de Palma
Llucmajor
Coves del Drac
COSTA DE LA CALMA
2 1
5 6 3
4
11
10
9
Felanitx
Cales de Mallorca
16
8 17
7
12
14
Santuari de Nostra Senyora de Cura
Cala Antena
15
18
Cales de Mallorca
Cala Murada
Santuari de Sant Salvador
Cap de Cala Figuera
BADIA DE PALMA
Cas Concos
Porto Colom
Cala Marçal
Bahía Grande
Campos
Alqueria Blanca
Cala d'Or
H3
Santanyí
Cala Llonga / Cala Egos
La Rapita
Porto Petro
Cala Pi
Ses Salines
Cala Mondragó
ILLA CONILLERA
Colònia de Sant Jordi
Platja dels Dols
Cala Figuera
Cala Santanyí
H4
ILLA DE CABRERA
Cala Llombarts

1 Cala Blava
2 Cala Egos
3 Cala Fornells
4 Cala Major / Sant Agusti
5 Cala Vinyes
6 Camp de Mar
7 Can Pastilla
8 Costa d'en Blanes
9 El Molinar
10 Illetes
11 Magalluf
12 Palma Nova
13 Peguera
14 Portals Nous / Puerto Portals
15 Portals Vells
16 Port de Andratx
17 Santa Ponça
18 S'Arenal

40 kilometres
20 miles

1000 metres
500 metres
Sea level

PORTUGAL

See page 11 for general map

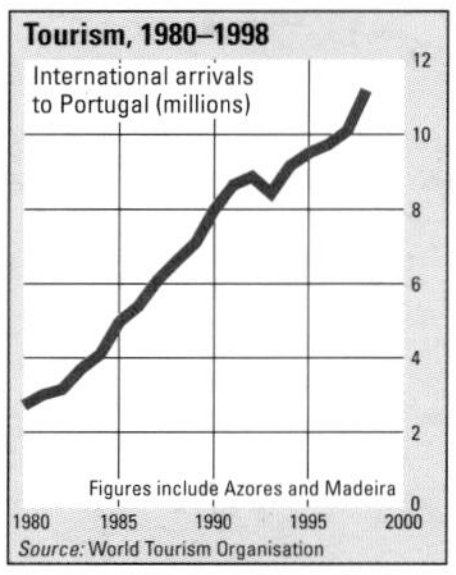

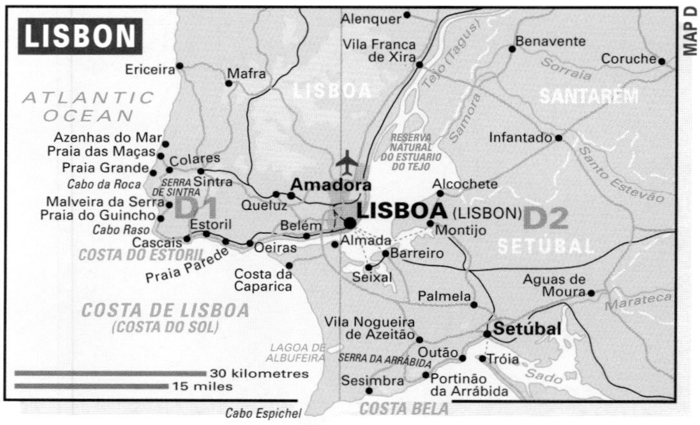

district boundary
district capital

100 km
50 miles

Tourism, 1980–1998
International arrivals to Portugal (millions)

Figures include Azores and Madeira

1980 1985 1990 1995 2000

Source: World Tourism Organisation

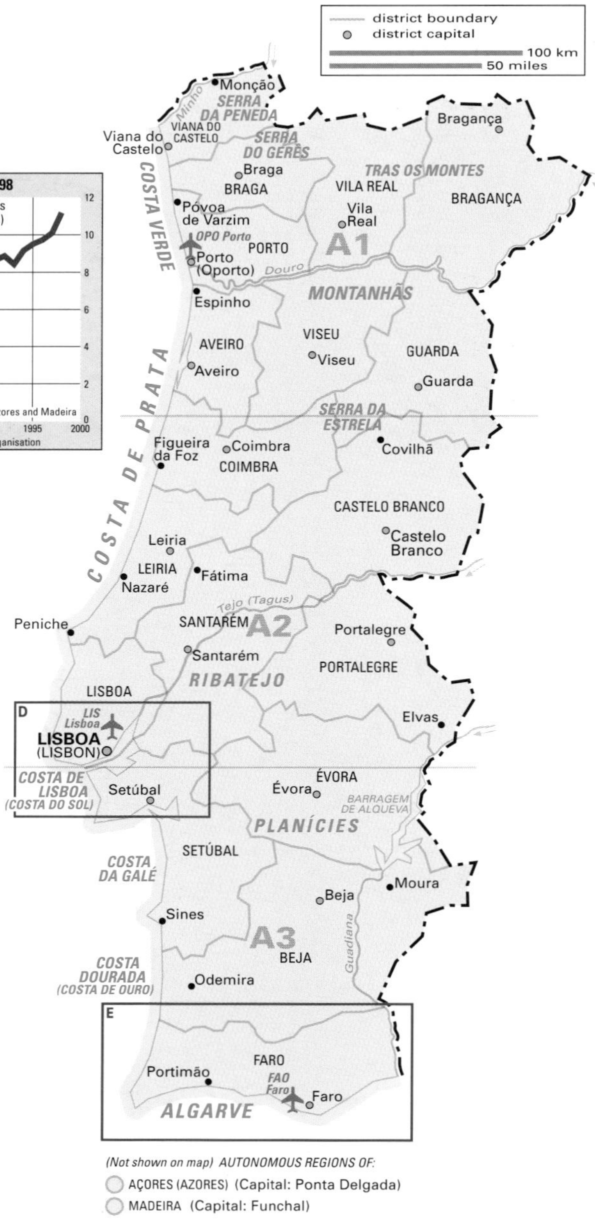

12
10
8
6
4
2
0

Monção
SERRA DA PENEDA
Viana do Castelo
VIANA DO CASTELO
SERRA DO GERÊS
Bragança
Braga
BRAGA
TRÁS OS MONTES
VILA REAL
BRAGANÇA
Póvoa de Varzim
Vila Real
OPORTO Porto
Porto (Oporto)
PORTO
Douro
Espinho
MONTANHAS
A1
VISEU
AVEIRO
Aveiro
Viseu
GUARDA
Guarda
SERRA DA ESTRELA
Figueira da Foz
Coimbra
COIMBRA
Covilhã
CASTELO BRANCO
Leiria
LEIRIA
Fátima
Nazaré
Castelo Branco
Peniche
SANTARÉM
A2
Santarém
Portalegre
PORTALEGRE
RIBATEJO
COSTA DE PRATA
COSTA VERDE
LISBOA
LIS Lisboa
LISBOA (LISBON)
Elvas
COSTA DE LISBOA (COSTA DO SOL)
Setúbal
ÉVORA
Évora
PLANÍCIES
BARRAGEM DE ALQUEVA
SETÚBAL
COSTA DA GALÉ
Beja
Moura
Sines
A3
BEJA
Guadiana
COSTA DOURADA (COSTA DE OURO)
Odemira
Portimão
FARO
FAO Faro
Faro
ALGARVE

(Not shown on map) AUTONOMOUS REGIONS OF:
AÇORES (AZORES) (Capital: Ponta Delgada)
MADEIRA (Capital: Funchal)

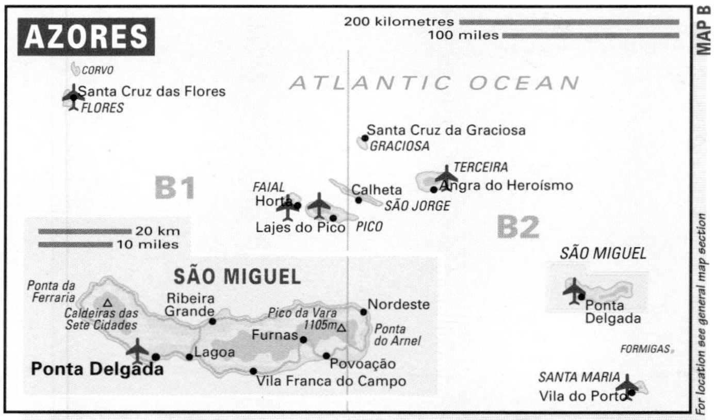

AZORES

200 kilometres
100 miles

CORVO
Santa Cruz das Flores
FLORES
ATLANTIC OCEAN
Santa Cruz da Graciosa
GRACIOSA
B1
TERCEIRA
FAIAL
Horta
Calheta
Angra do Heroísmo
SÃO JORGE
Lajes do Pico
PICO
B2
SÃO MIGUEL

20 km
10 miles

Ponta da Ferraria
Ribeira Grande
Nordeste
SÃO MIGUEL
Caldeiras das Sete Cidades
Pico da Vara 1105m
Ponta do Arnel
FORMIGAS
Ponta Delgada
Furnas
Lagoa
Povoação
SANTA MARIA
Vila Franca do Campo
Vila do Porto

MADEIRA

ATLANTIC OCEAN
Porto Moniz
São Jorge
Santana
Seixal
Boaventura
Faial
C2
BAIA DE ZARCO
São Vicente
Porto da Cruz
Ponta do Pargo
Prazeres
PAUL DA SERRA
Pico Ruivo 1862m
Ponta do Castelo
ILHÉU DE AGOSTINHO
ILHÉU DE FORA
C1
Curral das Freiras
Pico de Arieiro 1818m
Portela
Canical
Prainha
Calheta
Santo da Serra
Machico
Agua de Pena
Terreiro da Luta
Santa Cruz
Ponta do Sol
Cabo Girão
Quinta do Palheiro Ferreiro
Câmara de Lobos
Caniço
Funchal

30 kilometres
15 miles

LISBON

Alenquer
Ericeira
Mafra
Vila Franca de Xira
Benavente
Coruche
ATLANTIC OCEAN
LISBOA
SANTARÉM
Azenhas do Mar
Praia das Maçãs
Colares
Infantado
Praia Grande
Cabo da Roca
SERRA DE SINTRA
Sintra
RESERVA NATURAL DO ESTUÁRIO DO TEJO
Malveira da Serra
Amadora
Alcochete
Praia do Guincho
Queluz
D1
LISBOA (LISBON)
D2
Cabo Raso
Estoril
Belém
Almada
Montijo
SETÚBAL
Cascais
Oeiras
Barreiro
COSTA DO ESTORIL
Costa da Caparica
Seixal
Aguas de Moura
Praia Parede
Palmela
COSTA DE LISBOA (COSTA DO SOL)
Vila Nogueira de Azeitão
Setúbal
LAGOA DE ALBUFEIRA
SERRA DA ARRÁBIDA
Outão
Tróia
Sesimbra
Portinho da Arrábida
COSTA BELA
Cabo Espichel

30 kilometres
15 miles

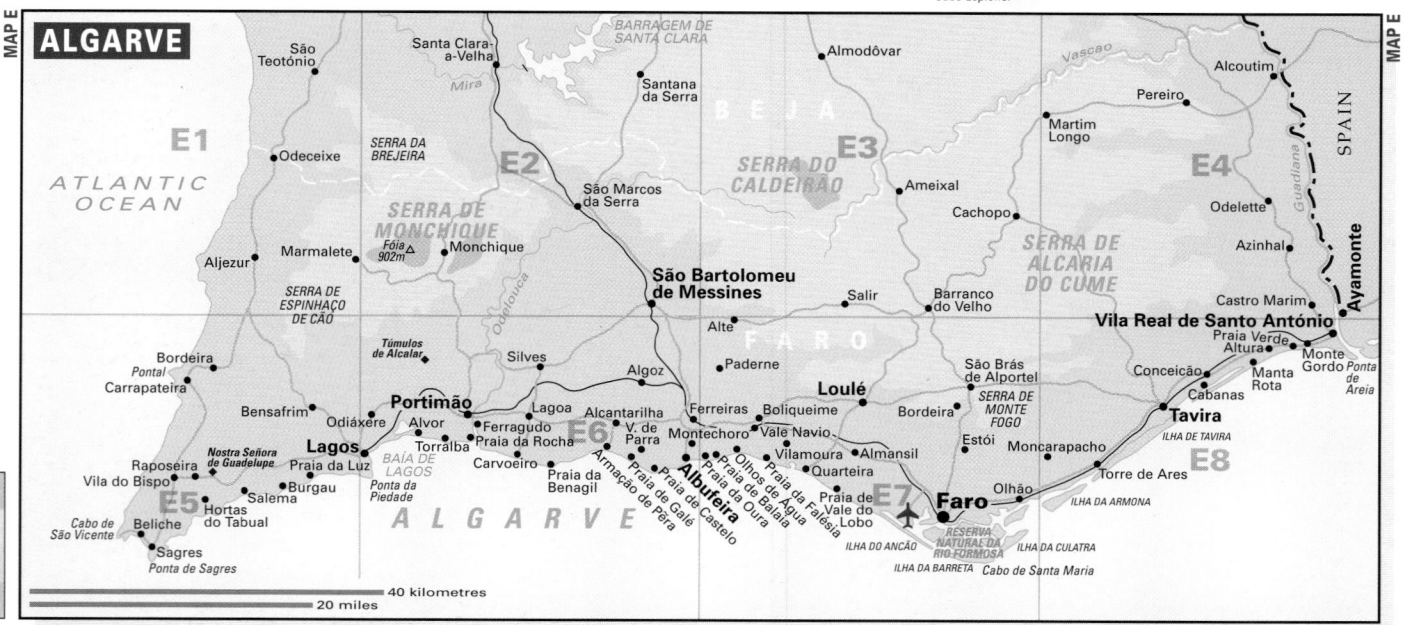

ALGARVE

BARRAGEM DE SANTA CLARA
São Teotónio
Santa Clara-a-Velha
Almodôvar
Alcoutim
E1
Odeceixe
SERRA DA BREJEIRA
Mira
Santana da Serra
BEJA
Pereiro
ATLANTIC OCEAN
E2
São Marcos da Serra
E3
SERRA DO CALDEIRÃO
Martim Longo
E4
Aljezur
Marmalete
Foia 902m
Monchique
SERRA DE MONCHIQUE
Ameixal
Cachopo
SERRA DE ALCARIA DO CUME
Odelette
Azinhal
SERRA DE ESPINHAÇO DE CÃO
São Bartolomeu de Messines
Salir
Barranco do Velho
Ayamonte
SPAIN
Bordeira
Pontal
Carrapateira
Túmulos de Alcalar
Silves
Algoz
Alte
Paderne
Castro Marim
Vila Real de Santo António
Bensafrim
Odiáxere
Lagoa
Alcantarilha
Ferreiras
Boliqueime
São Brás de Alportel
Praia Verde
Altura
Conceição
Monte Gordo
Manta Rota
Ponta de Areia
Portimão
Alvor
Ferragudo
V. de Parra
Montechoro
Vale Navio
Bordeira
Estói
Cabanas
Tavira
E8
Lagos
Torralba
Praia da Rocha
Carvoeiro
Praia de Benagil
Armação de Pêra
Praia da Galé
Albufeira
Olhos de Água
Praia da Falésia
Vilamoura
Almancil
Moncarapacho
ILHA DE TAVIRA
Raposeira
Nostra Señora de Guadelupe
Praia da Luz
Ponta da Piedade
BAÍA DE LAGOS
Praia de Castelo
Praia da Oura
Quarteira
Estói
Torre de Ares
Vila do Bispo
Burgau
Praia do Vale do Lobo
ALGARVE
Olhão
Hortas do Tabual
Beliche
Salema
Faro
ILHA DA ARMONA
E5
Cabo de São Vicente
Sagres
Ponta de Sagres
RESERVA NATURAL DA RIA FORMOSA
ILHA DO ANCÃO
ILHA DA CULATRA
ILHA DA BARRETA
Cabo de Santa Maria
E7

40 kilometres
20 miles

500 metres
200 metres
Sea level

SWITZERLAND AND AUSTRIA

See pages 9, 10, 12 & 13 for general maps

Cantons where the majority of the population speak:

French   German   Italian

AG	AARGAU	NW	NIDWALDEN
AI	APPENZELL-INNER RHODEN	OW	OBWALDEN
AR	APPENZELL-AUSSER RHODEN	SG	ST GALLEN
BE	BERN	SH	SCHAFFHAUSEN
BL	BASEL-LAND	SO	SOLOTHURN
BS	BASEL-STADT	SZ	SCHWYZ
FR	FRIBOURG	TG	THURGAU
GE	GENÈVE	TI	TICINO
GL	GLARUS	UR	URI
GR	GRAUBÜNDEN	VD	VAUD
JU	JURA	VS	VALAIS
LU	LUZERN	ZG	ZUG
NE	NEUCHÂTEL	ZH	ZÜRICH

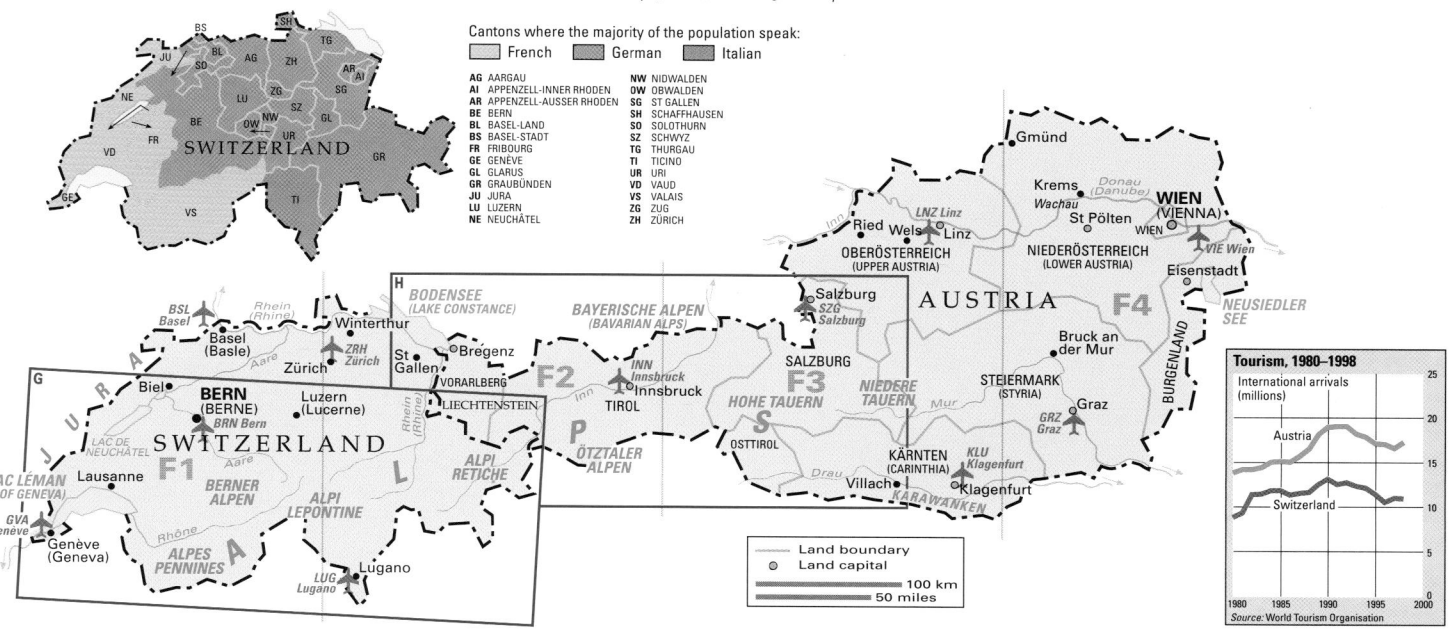

Land boundary
Land capital

100 km
50 miles

Tourism, 1980–1998

International arrivals (millions)

Austria

Switzerland

Source: World Tourism Organisation

SWISS ALPS

100 kilometres
50 miles

AUSTRIAN ALPS

100 kilometres
50 miles

2000 metres
1000 metres
Sea level

ITALY

See page 12 for general map

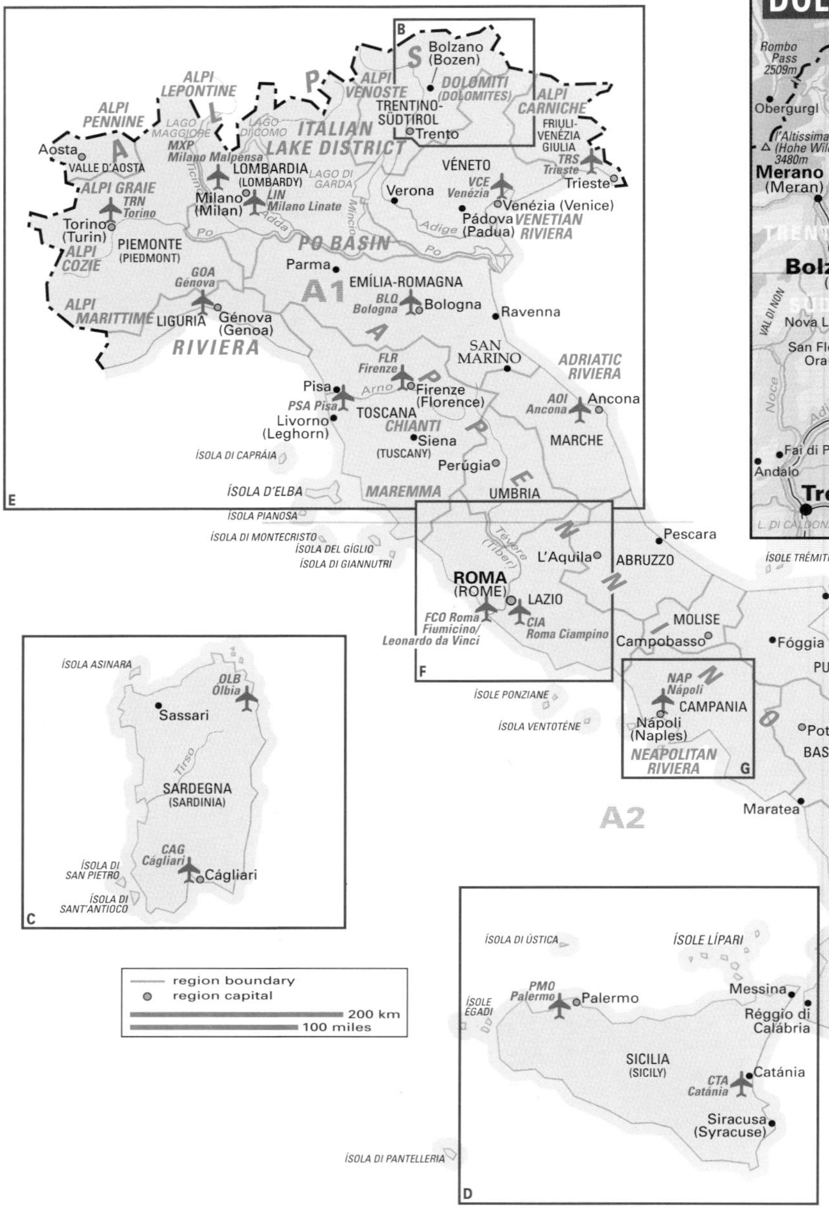

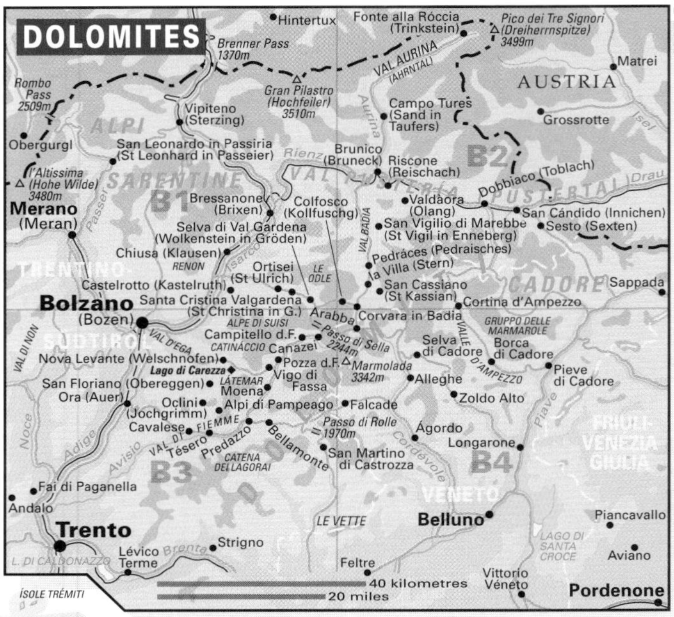

DOLOMITES

MAP B

Hintertux · Fonte alla Róccia (Trinkstein) · Pico dei Tre Signori (Dreiherrnspitze) △ 3499m · Matrei
Brenner Pass 1370m
△ Gran Pilastro (Hochfeiler) 3510m
Rombo Pass 2509m
Vipiteno (Sterzing)
Campo Tures (Sand in Taufers)
Grossrotte
AUSTRIA
Obergurgl · San Leonardo in Passiria (St Leonhard in Passeier)
Brunico (Bruneck)
Riscone (Reischach)
B2
△ Altissima (Hohe Wilde) 3480m
Bressanone (Brixen)
Colfosco (Kollfuschg)
San Cándido (Innichen)
Sesto (Sexten)
B1
Selva di Val Gardena (Wolkenstein in Gröden)
San Vigílio di Marebbe (St Vigil in Enneberg)
Dobbiaco (Toblach)
Chiusa (Klausen)
Ortisei (St Ulrich)
Pedráces (Pedraisches)
Sappada
Merano (Meran)
Castelrotto (Kastelruth)
Santa Cristina Valgardena (St Christina in G.)
a Villa (Stern)
San Cassiano (St Kassian)
Cortina d'Ampezzo
Bolzano (Bozen)
Alpe di Suisi
Corvara in Badia
Selva di Cadore
Borca di Cadore
GRUPPO DELLE MARMAROLE
TRENTINO-SÜDTIROL
Campitello d.F.
Passo di Sella 2244m
Arabba
Pieve di Cadore
Nova Levante (Welschnofen)
Lago di Carezza
Pozza d.F.
Marmolada 3342m
Alleghe
Zoldo Alto
Ágordo
San Floriano (Obereggen)
Vigo di Fassa
CATINACCIO Canazei
Oclini (Jochgrimm)
LATEMAR
Moena
Longarone
FRIULI-VENEZIA GIULIA
Ora (Auer)
Alpi di Pampeago
Falcade
Cavalese
FIEMME
Predazzo
Passo di Rolle 1970m
San Martino di Castrozza
Bellamonte
CATENA DELLA GORAI
VENETO
Fai di Paganella
B3
Tésero
Andalo
Belluno
LE VETTE
Piancavallo
Trento
Lévico Terme
L. DI CALDONAZZO
Strigno
Feltre
Vittório Véneto
Aviano
Pordenone
40 kilometres
20 miles

Festival Calendar

JAN Fiera di Sant'Orso (Aosta)
FEB Festa del Mandorlo in fiore: almond blossom festival (Agrigento)
before LENT Carnevale (Venice; Verona; Viaréggio and countrywide)
ASH WEDNESDAY Il Pranzo del Purgatori: Purgatory Dinner (Grádoli, Lazio)
GOOD FRIDAY Processions (Southern Italy and Sicily)
EASTER SUNDAY Il Scoppio del Carro: fireworks (Florence)
MAR-APR La Festa di Primavera: Spring Festival (Rome)
MAY 1st Festa di Sant'Efisio (Cágliari)
MAY Festa di San Domenico Abate (Cocullo, L'Aquila)
MAY Festa di San Gennaro (Naples); also Sep 19th and Dec 16th
MAY Sagra di San Nicola (Bari)
MAY 15th Corso dei Ceri: 'candle' race (Gúbbio)
MAY Cavalcata Sarda: Sardinian Cavalcade (Sassari)
MAY La Festa della Sensa: Wedding to the Sea (Venice)
JUN Luminaria: Festival of Lights; Gioco del Ponte: tug-of-war; historical regatta (Pisa)
JUN Corpus Christi Procession (Orvieto)
JUN La Festa di San Giovanni and Gioco di Calcio Storico: football match in medieval costume (Florence)
JUN-JUL Festival dei Due Mondi: arts festival (Spoleto)
JUN-SEP Biennale (Venice); 2001 and every two years
JUL 2nd Palio delle Contrade: horse races (Siena); also Aug 16th
JUL La Festa del Redentore: Feast of the Redeemer (Venice)
JUL-AUG International Opera Festival (Verona)
AUG La Festa del Redentore: Feast of the Redeemer (Nuoro)
AUG-SEP International Film Festival (Venice Lido)
SEP La Giostra del Saracine: jousting tournament (Arezzo)
SEP La Festa della Madonna di Piedigrotta (Naples)
SEP La Regatta Storico: historical regatta (Venice)
SEP Douja d'Or: wine festival; Festival delle Sagre; Palio (Asti)
SEP La Partita a Scacchi: living chess (Maróstica); 2000 and every two years
OCT Festa dell'uva: Grape Festival (Merano)
NOV La Festa della Madonna della Salute (Venice)

Italy (main map)

B · Bolzano (Bozen)
ALPI LEPONTINE · ALPI PENNINE · ALPI GRAIE · ALPI COZIE · ALPI MARITTIME
LAGO MAGGIORE · LAGO DI COMO · LAGO DI GARDA
TRENTINO-SÜDTIROL · DOLOMITI (DOLOMITES) · ALPI CARNICHE · FRIULI-VENEZIA GIULIA
Trento · Trieste (TRS)
ITALIAN LAKE DISTRICT
VÉNETO
Aosta · VALLE D'AOSTA
LOMBARDIA (LOMBARDY)
Milano Malpensa (MXP)
Milano (Milan) · Milano Linate (LIN)
Verona · Venézia (Venice) (VCE)
Pádova (Padua) · VENETIAN RIVIERA
Torino (Turin) (TRN)
PIEMONTE (PIEDMONT)
Génova (Genoa) (GOA)
EMÍLIA-ROMAGNA
Parma
Bologna (BLQ)
Ravenna
LIGURIA
RIVIERA
A1
SAN MARINO
ADRIATIC RIVIERA
Pisa (PSA) · Firenze (Florence) (FLR)
Ancona (AOI)
Livorno (Leghorn)
TOSCANA (TUSCANY) · CHIANTI
Siena
MARCHE
Perúgia
UMBRIA
ÍSOLA DI CAPRÁIA
MAREMMA
ÍSOLA D'ELBA
ÍSOLA PIANOSA
ÍSOLA DI MONTECRISTO
ÍSOLA DEL GIGLIO
ÍSOLA DI GIANNUTRI
Pescara
L'Aquila · ABRUZZO
ROMA (ROME)
FCO Roma Fiumicino/Leonardo da Vinci
CIA Roma Ciampino
LAZIO
MOLISE
Campobasso
Vieste
Fóggia
BRI Bari · Bari
PUGLIA
Ostuni
Bríndisi
NAP Nápoli
CAMPANIA
Nápoli (Naples)
NEAPOLITAN RIVIERA
BASILICATA
Potenza
Táranto
Lecce
ÍSOLE TRÉMITI
ÍSOLE PONZIANE
ÍSOLA VENTOTÉNE
Scanzano Iónico
A2
Maratea
Cosenza
CALÁBRIA
Catanzaro

ÍSOLA ASINARA
OLB Ólbia
Sassari
SARDEGNA (SARDINIA)
CAG Cágliari · Cágliari
ÍSOLA DI SAN PIETRO
ÍSOLA DI SANT'ANTIOCO
C

region boundary
region capital
200 km
100 miles

ÍSOLA DI ÚSTICA
ÍSOLE LÍPARI
ÍSOLE EGADI
PMO Palermo · Palermo
Messina
Réggio di Calábria
SICILIA (SICILY)
CTA Catánia · Catánia
Siracusa (Syracuse)
ÍSOLA DI PANTELLERIA
D

SARDINIA

MAP C

STRAIT OF BONIFACIO
Capo Testa · Santa Teresa di Gallura · ÍSOLA MADDALENA · ÍSOLA CADDALENA
Porto Rafael · Palau · ÍSOLA CAPRERA
Porto Cervo
GOLFO DELL'ASINARA
Báia Sardinia · Porto Rotondo · COSTA SMERALDA
Golfo Aranci
ÍSOLA ASINARA
Capo del Falcone
Castelsardo
Ólbia
GOLFO DI MARINELLA · ÍSOLA TAVOLARA · ÍSOLA MOLARA
Porto Tórres
C1
Porto Conte
Grotta di Nettuno
FERTILIA
Alghero
LA NURRA
Sassari
Santissima Trinitá di Saccargia
COSTA SMERALDA
Posada
C2
la Caletta
RIVIERA DEL CORALLO
Bosa
Necropoli di S. Andria Priu
BARONIA
Monte Ferru 1050m △
Macomér
Nuoro · Orosei
Cala Liberotto
Villaggio nuragico di Serra Orrios
GOLFO DI OROSEI
Oliena
MEDITERRANEAN SEA
Santa Caterina di Pittinuri
MONTI DEL GENNARGENTU
SARDEGNA
SINIS
Tharros
Oristano
△ Punta La Mármora 1834m
Árbatax
GOLFO DI ORISTANO
Su Nuraxi di Barúmini
Ulássai
Barúmini
COSTA VERDE
C3
Iglesias
C4
COSTA REI
Cágliari
ÍSOLA DI SAN PIETRO
Portoscuso
ELMAS
Capo Boi · Villasimíus
Sant'Antíoco
Pula · Nora · Capo Carbonara
ÍSOLA DI SANT'ANTIOCO
Chia · Santa Margherita di Pula
Bithia
GOLFO DI CÁGLIARI
GOLFO DI PALMAS
Capo Spartivento
COSTA DEL SUD
2000 metres / 1000 metres / Sea level
100 km
50 miles

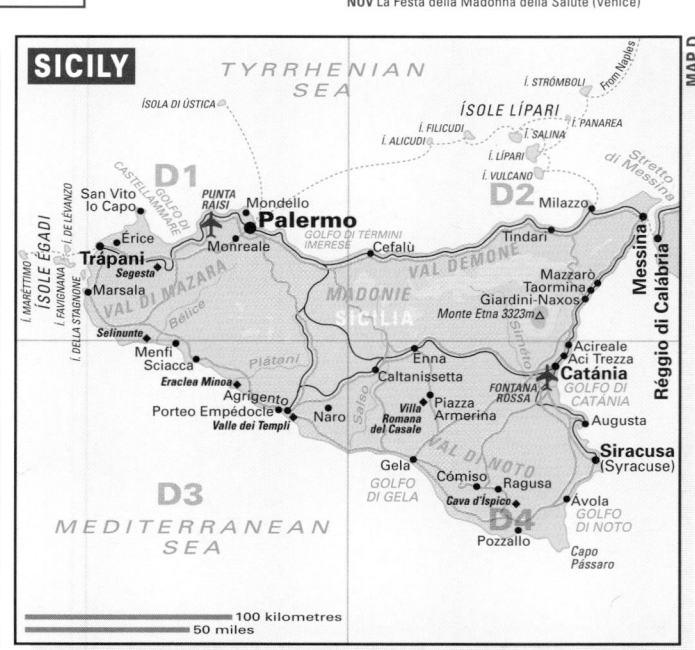

SICILY

MAP D

TYRRHENIAN SEA
From Naples
i. STRÓMBOLI
ÍSOLE LÍPARI
ÍSOLA DI ÚSTICA
i. PANAREA
i. FILICUDI · i. SALINA
i. ALICUDI · i. LÍPARI
i. VULCANO
Stretto di Messina
D1
PUNTA RAISI
Mondello
San Vito lo Capo
CASTELLAMMARE DEL GOLFO
Palermo
GOLFO DI TÉRMINI IMERESE
Milazzo
D2
ÍSOLE ÉGADI
Érice · Monreale · Cefalù
Trápani
Tindari
i. MARETTIMO · FAVIGNANA · DI LÉVANZO
VAL DI MAZARA
Mazzarò · Taormina
Messina
Marsala · Segesta
MADONIE
Giardini-Naxos
Selinunte
VAL DÉMONE
SICILIA
Monte Etna 3323m △
Réggio di Calábria
Menfi
Enna
Aci Trezza
Sciacca
Caltanissetta
Aci reale
Catánia
Eraclea Minoa
Piazza Armerina
FONTANA ROSSA
Agrigento
Villa Romana del Casale
GOLFO DI CATÁNIA
Pórteo Empédocle
Náro
Augusta
Valle dei Templi
Caltagirone
VAL DI NOTO
Gela
Cómiso
Ragusa
Siracusa (Syracuse)
GOLFO DI GELA
Cava d'Ispica
D4
D3
Ávola
GOLFO DI NOTO
MEDITERRANEAN SEA
Pozzallo
Capo Pássaro
100 kilometres
50 miles

ITALY

See page 12 for general map

NORTH ITALY

(Selected labels)

SWITZERLAND · LIECHTENSTEIN · AUSTRIA · SLOVENIA · CROATIA · FRANCE · MONACO

BERN (BERNE) · Lausanne · Montreux · Luzern · Chur · Davos · Andermatt · Bellinzona · Locarno · Bormio · Bolzano (Bozen) · Merano (Meran) · Bressanone (Brixen) · Brunico (Bruneck) · Cortina d'Ampezzo · Lienz · Spittal · Villach

Torino (Turin) · Milano (Milan) · Novara · Monza · Bérgamo · Bréscia · Verona · Vicenza · Pádova (Padua) · Venézia (Venice) · Trento · Trieste · Udine · Gorizia

Alessándria · Piacenza · Parma · Réggio nell'Emília · Modena · Bologna · Ferrara · Mantova (Mantua) · Cremona · Pavia

Génova (Genoa) · La Spézia · Carrara · Pisa · Livorno (Leghorn) · Firenze (Florence) · Prato · Siena · Arezzo · Perúgia · Ancona · Rímini · Ravenna · Forlì · SAN MARINO

Nice · Cannes · San Remo · Ventimiglia · Imperia · Savona

Seas / regions: LIGURIAN SEA · ADRIATIC SEA · GOLFO DI VENÉZIA · GOLFO DI GENOVA · TYRRHENIAN SEA · CORSICA (France) · ÍSOLA D'ELBA

Grid: E1 E2 E3 E4 E5 E6 E7 E8 E9 E10 E11 E12

Scale: 100 kilometres / 50 miles

MAP E · MAP F · MAP G

ROME

Orvieto · Spoleto · Terni · Rieti · L'Aquila · Viterbo · Civitavécchia · Bracciano · ROMA (ROME) · VATICAN CITY · FIUMICINO / LEONARDO DA VINCI · CIAMPINO · Ostia Antica · Lido di Óstia · Frascati · Tivoli · Avezzano · Sulmona · Anagni · Frosinone · Latina · Ánzio · Nettuno · Aprilia · Terracina · Formia · Gaeta

TYRRHENIAN SEA · GOLFO DI GAETA

Grid: F1 F2 F3 F4

Scale: 60 km / 30 miles

Tourism, 1980–1998

International arrivals to Italy (millions)

(graph, values 0–35 against years 1980, 1985, 1990, 1995, 2000)

Source: World Tourism Organisation

NAPLES

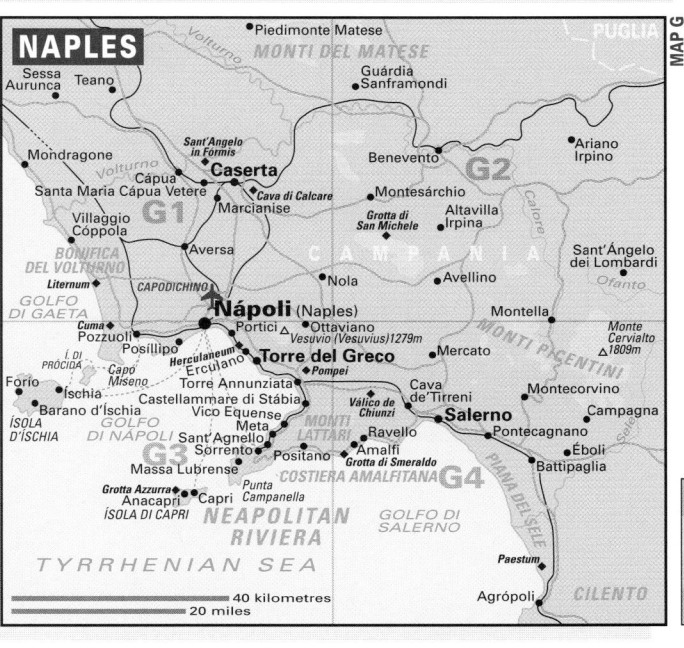

Caserta · Benevento · Ariano Irpino · Santa Maria Cápua Vetere · Cápua · Aversa · Nápoli (Naples) · Pozzuoli · Vesuvio (Vesuvius) 1279m · Torre del Greco · Pompei · Ercolano · Castellammare di Stábia · Sorrento · Positano · Amalfi · Salerno · Avellino · Agrópoli · Paestum

ÍSOLA D'ÍSCHIA · ÍSOLA DI CAPRI · Capri · Anacapri

GOLFO DI GAETA · GOLFO DI NÁPOLI · GOLFO DI SALERNO · TYRRHENIAN SEA · NEAPOLITAN RIVIERA · COSTIERA AMALFITANA · CILENTO · CAMPANIA · PUGLIA

Grid: G1 G2 G3 G4

Scale: 40 kilometres / 20 miles

Elevation key: 2000 metres · 1000 metres · Sea level

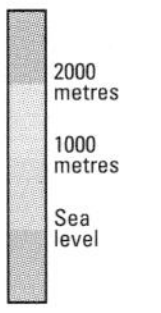

GREECE AND TURKEY

See page 15 for general map

IONIAN ISLANDS

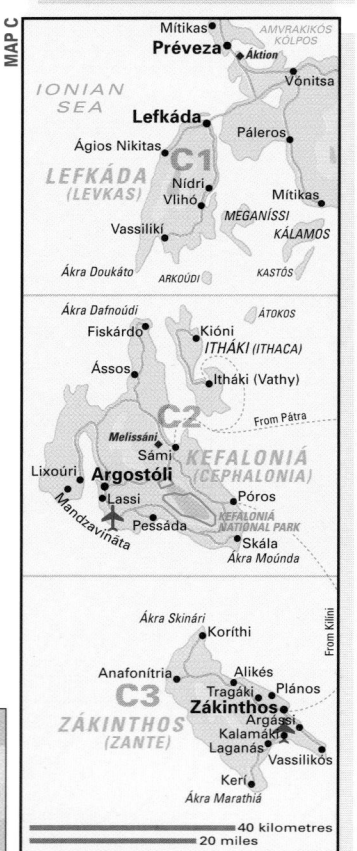

AEGEAN, CRETE & TURKISH COAST

Tourism, 1980–1998

International arrivals (millions)

Greece

Turkey

Cyprus

Malta

1980 1985 1990 1995 2000

Source: World Tourism Organisation

APOLLO BEACH resorts
(from north to south)

Paleo Faliro — Vouliagméni
Alimós — Varkiza
Glifáda — Lagoníssi
Voúla — Anávissos
Kavoúri — Cape Soúnio

1000 metres
500 metres
Sea level

40 kilometres
20 miles

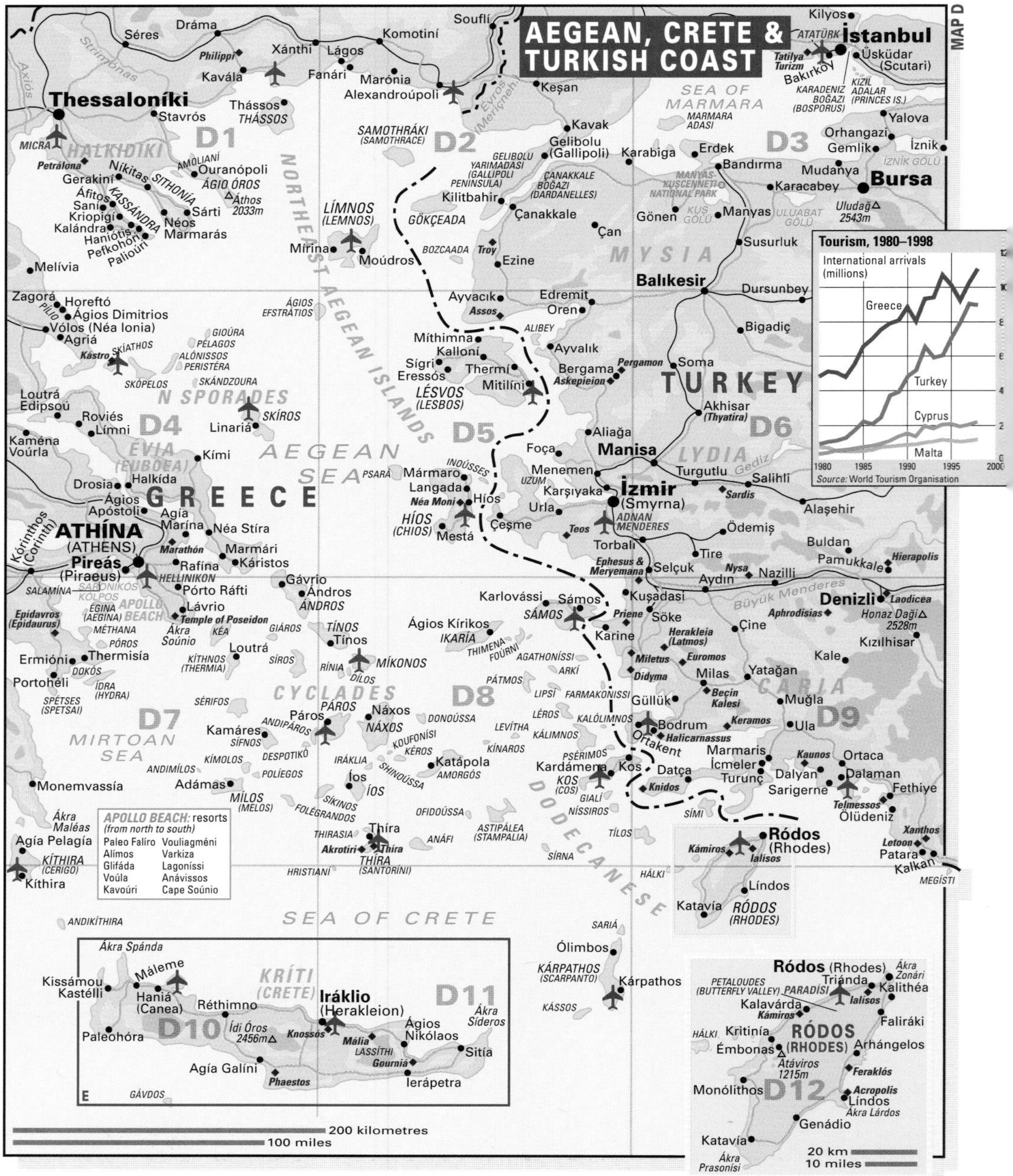

200 kilometres
100 miles

20 km
10 miles

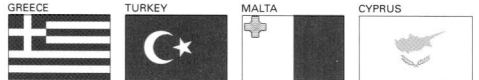

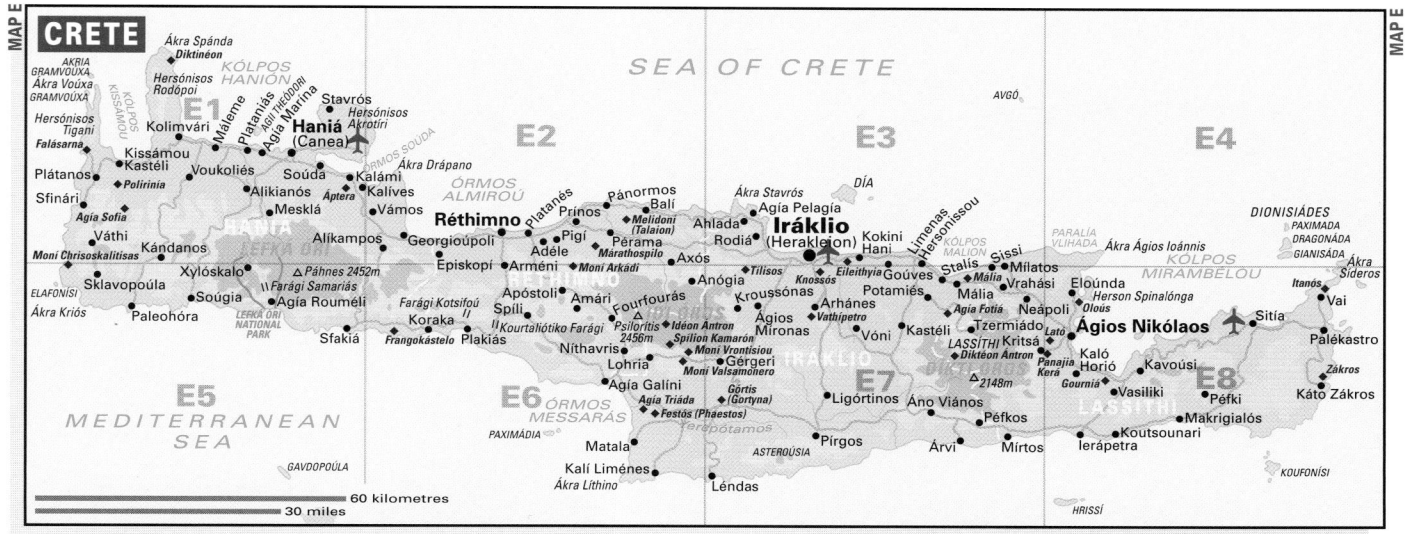

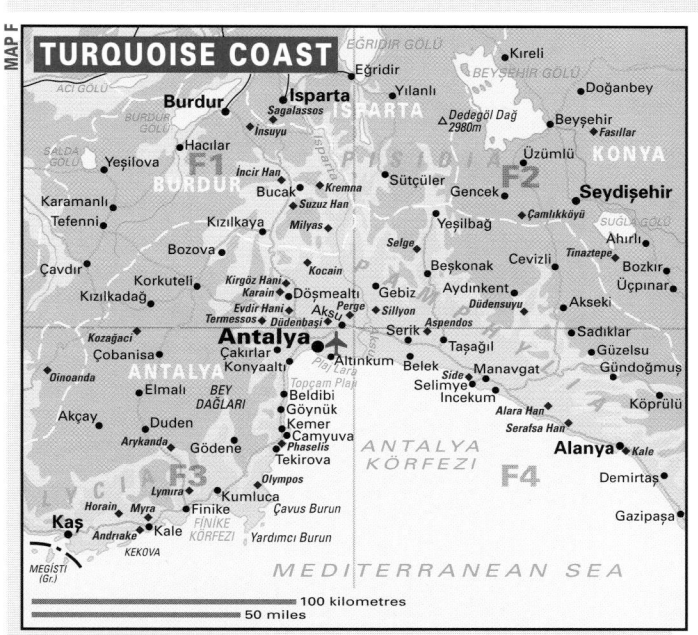

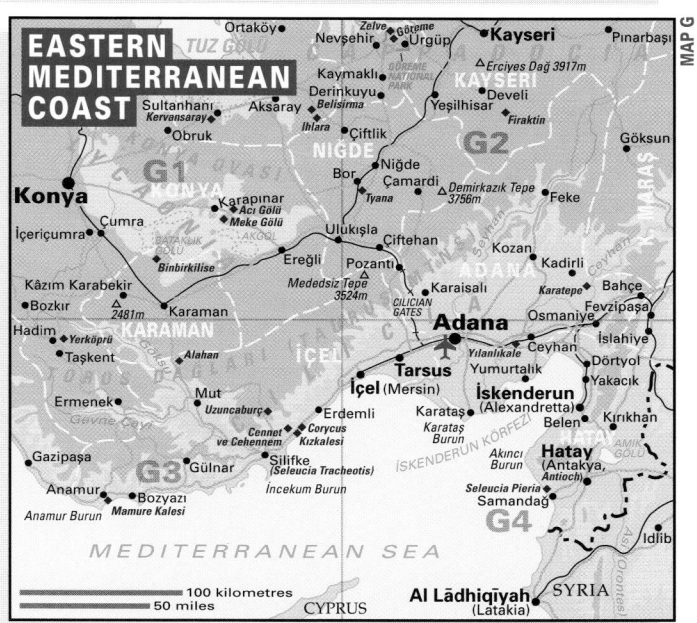

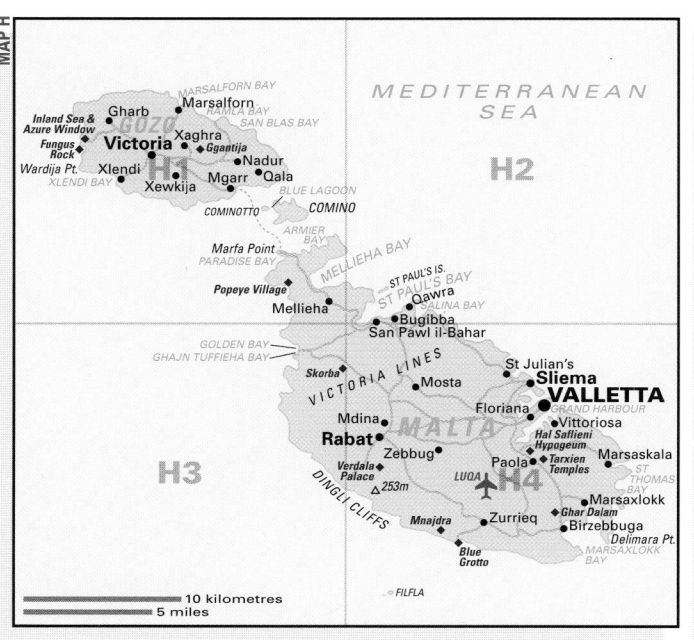

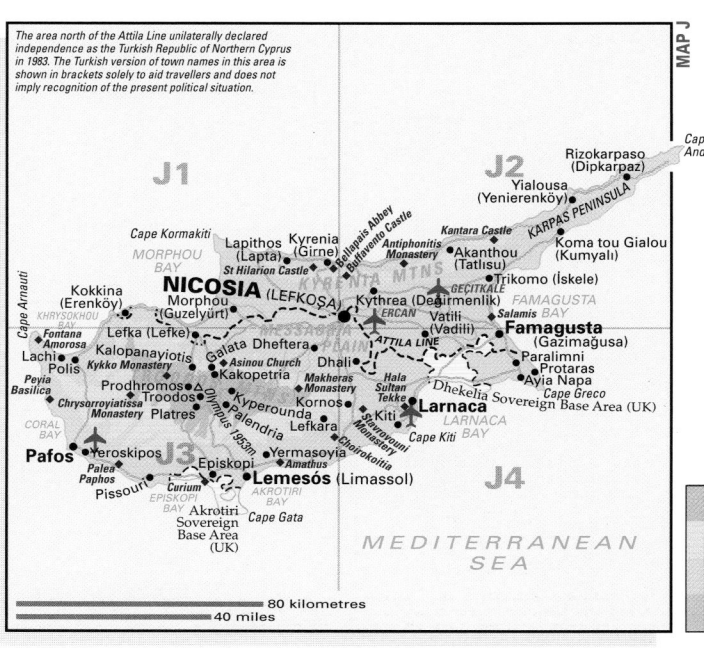

SCANDINAVIA

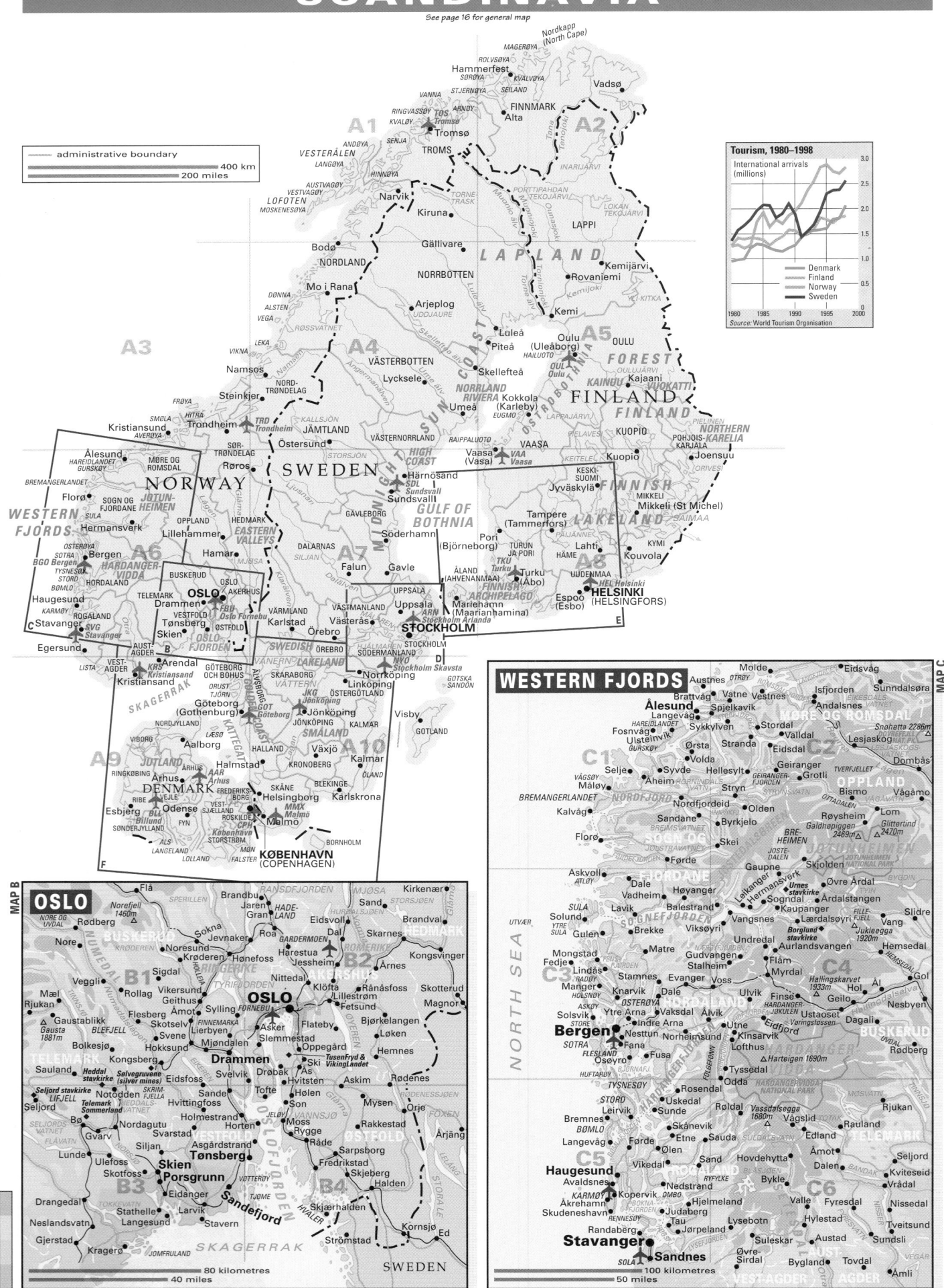

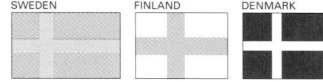

SWEDEN FINLAND DENMARK

SCANDINAVIA

See page 16 for general map

STOCKHOLM

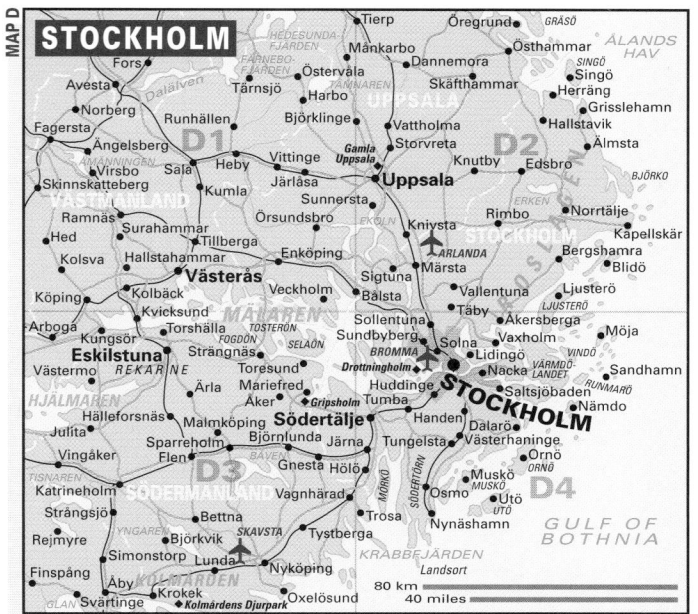

SOUTHWEST FINLAND

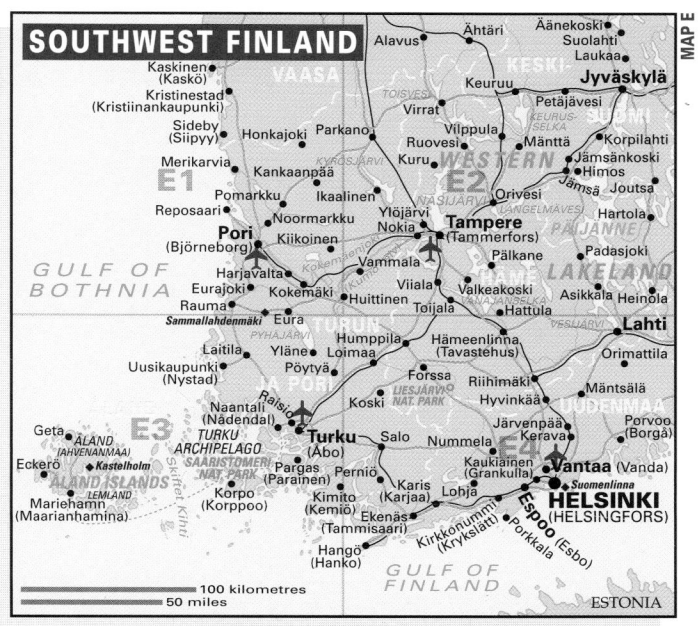

DENMARK AND SOUTHERN SWEDEN

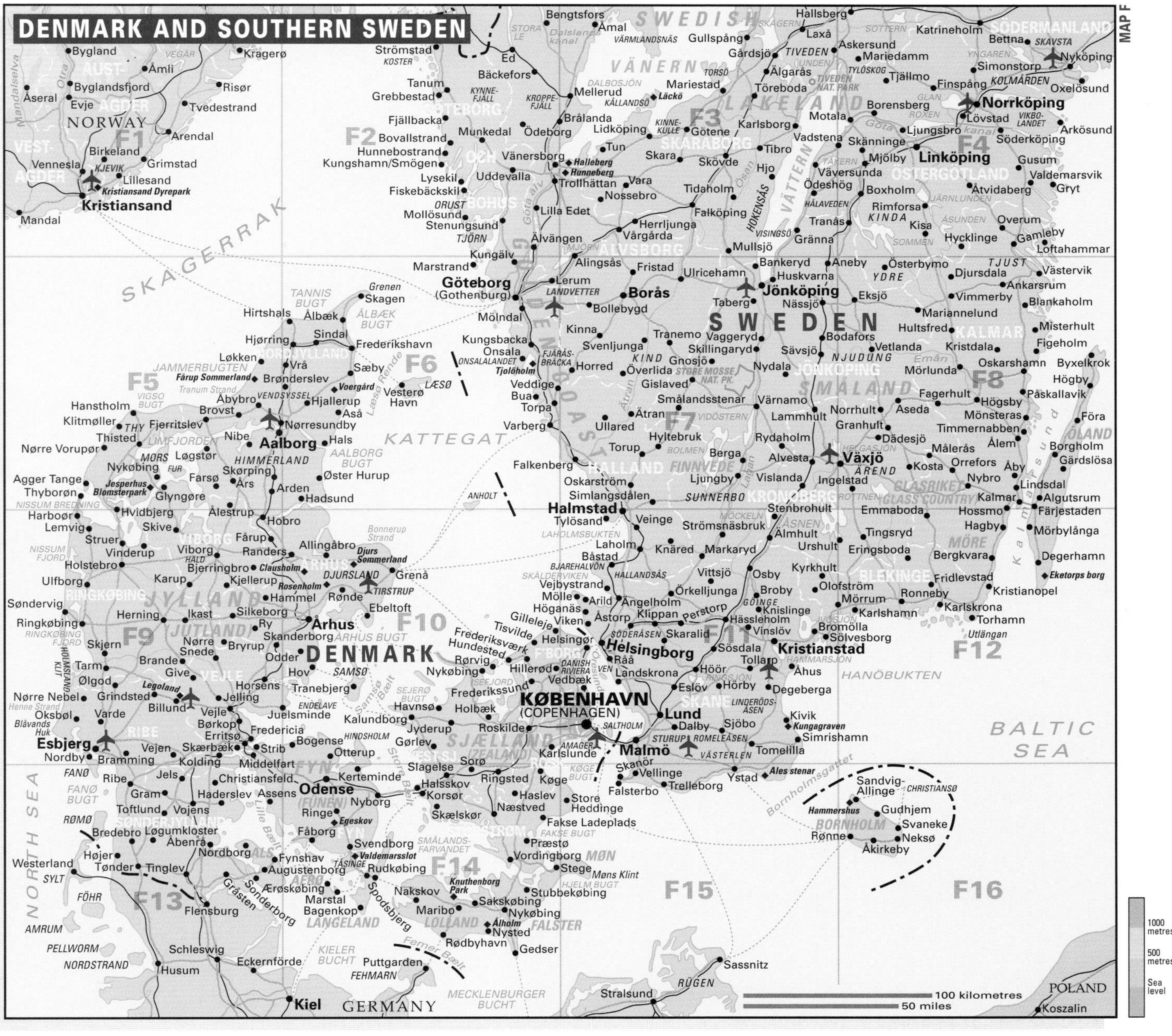

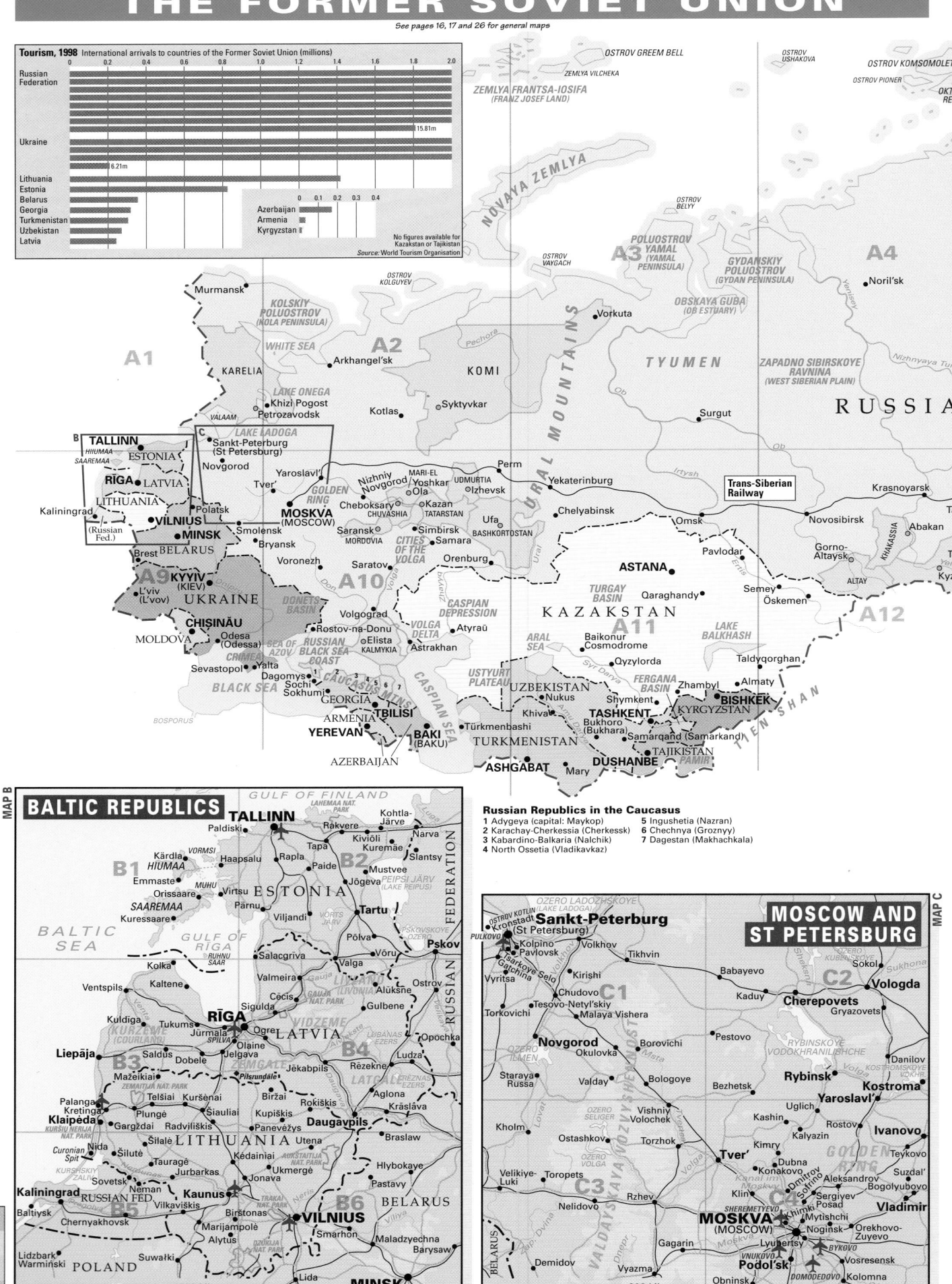

THE FORMER SOVIET UNION

See page 27 for general map

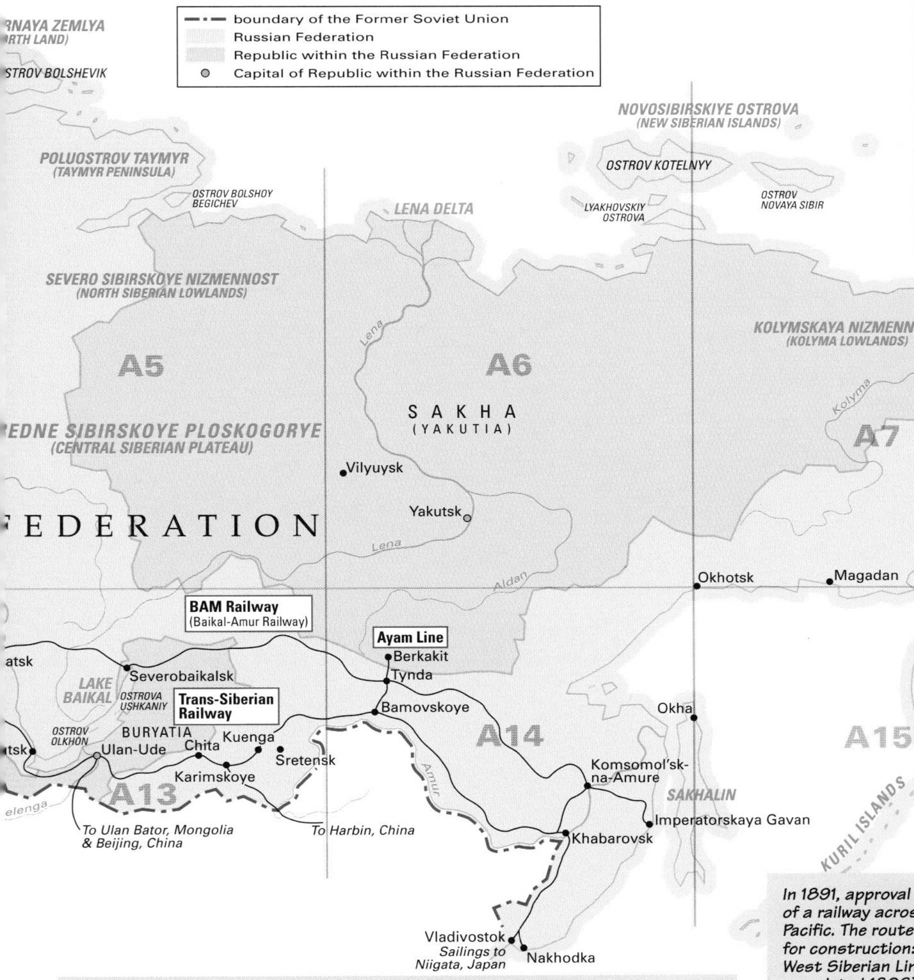

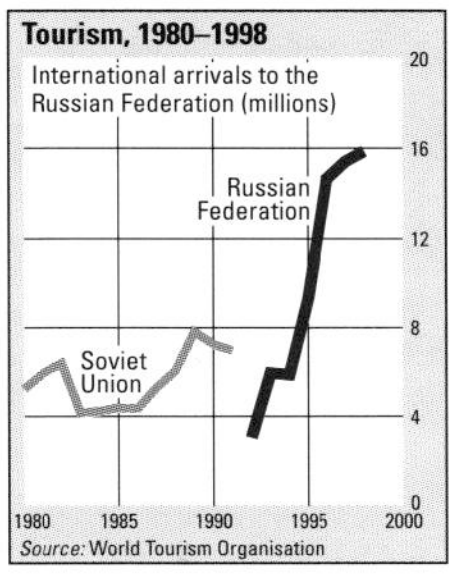

boundary of the Former Soviet Union
Russian Federation
Republic within the Russian Federation
○ Capital of Republic within the Russian Federation

Tourism, 1980–1998
International arrivals to the
Russian Federation (millions)

Russian Federation

Soviet Union

1980 1985 1990 1995 2000

Source: World Tourism Organisation

TRANS-SIBERIAN RAILWAY

Distance from Moscow

	Kilometres	Miles
Moscow ●	0	0
Alexandrov ●	112	70
Yaroslavl' ●	282	175
Danilov ●	357	222
Buy ●	450	280
Kotelnich ●	870	541
Kirov ●	957	595
Perm ●	1437	893
Yekaterinburg ●	1818	1130
Tyumen ●	2144	1332
Ishim ●	2433	1512
Omsk ●	2716	1688
Tatarsk ●	2585	1606
Novosibirsk ●	3343	2077
Yurga ●	3498	2174
Tayga ●	3571	2219
Achinsk ●	3920	2436
Krasnoyarsk ●	4104	2550
Uyar ●	4235	2632
Kansk ●	4351	2704
Tayshet ●	4522	2810
Irkutsk ●	5191	3226
Slyudyanka ●	5317	3304
Ulan-Ude ●	5647	3509
Ulan Bator ●	6304	3917
Beijing ●	7865	4887
Khilok ●	5940	3691
Chita ●	6204	3855
Karimskoye ●	6300	3915
Harbin ●	7610	4729
Bamovskoye ●	7281	4524
Skovorodino ●	7313	4544
Belogorsk ●	7873	4892
Izvestkovyy ●	8242	5121
Khabarovsk ●	8531	5301
Bikin ●	8764	5446
Spassk Dalny ●	9057	5628
Ussuriysk ●	9185	5707
Nakhodka ●	9446	5869
Ugolnaya ●	9264	5756
Vladivostok ●	9297	5777

In 1891, approval was given to begin construction of a railway across Siberia, linking Moscow to the Pacific. The route was divided into six sections for construction:
West Siberian Line (Yekaterinburg to Novosibirsk, completed 1896); Mid-Siberian Line (Novosibirsk to Irkutsk, 1899); Circum-Baikal Loop (1904); Trans-Baikal Line (Lake Baikal to Sretensk, 1900); Amur Line (Kuenga to Khabarovsk, 1916); Ussuri Line (Khabarovsk to Vladivostok, 1897).

Prior to the completion of the Circum-Baikal Loop, a ferry service was introduced to cross Lake Baikal. The ferry 'Baikal' was able to carry the complete train on its deck. The original rail link from Chita to Vladivostok, the Chinese Eastern Railway, ran through Manchuria, with steamer services on the Amur linking Sretensk with Khabarovsk. The Amur Line was only constructed when the Manchurian connection became vulnerable after the Russo-Japanese war.

Three long-distance services currently run from Moscow: Trans-Siberian (Moscow to Vladivostok); Trans-Manchurian (Moscow to Beijing via Chita and Harbin); Trans-Mongolian (Moscow to Beijing via Ulan-Ude and Ulan Bator).

The ancient trade routes between Europe and the Far East have been used for many centuries, but the Central Asian region has been virtually closed to travellers for the last 70 years. With the recent independence of the former Soviet republics and the opening up of tourism in China, fabled cities like Bukhara, Kashgar and Samarkand are now once again accessible to travellers and tourists.

The famous Silk Road, once linking China with Europe, is in fact not one road, but a number of different routes depending on the season and local conditions. With the opening of the borders between China and the Central Asian republics, together with improved road and rail links, it is possible to visit many ancient sites associated with the Silk Road and package tours are available linking many of these places.

The modern Karakoram Highway crosses the Khunjerab Pass, one of the chief routes over the Himalayas between Jammu and Kashmir and China. The road is still vulnerable to closure along its 1200 km length.

ANCIENT TRADE ROUTES

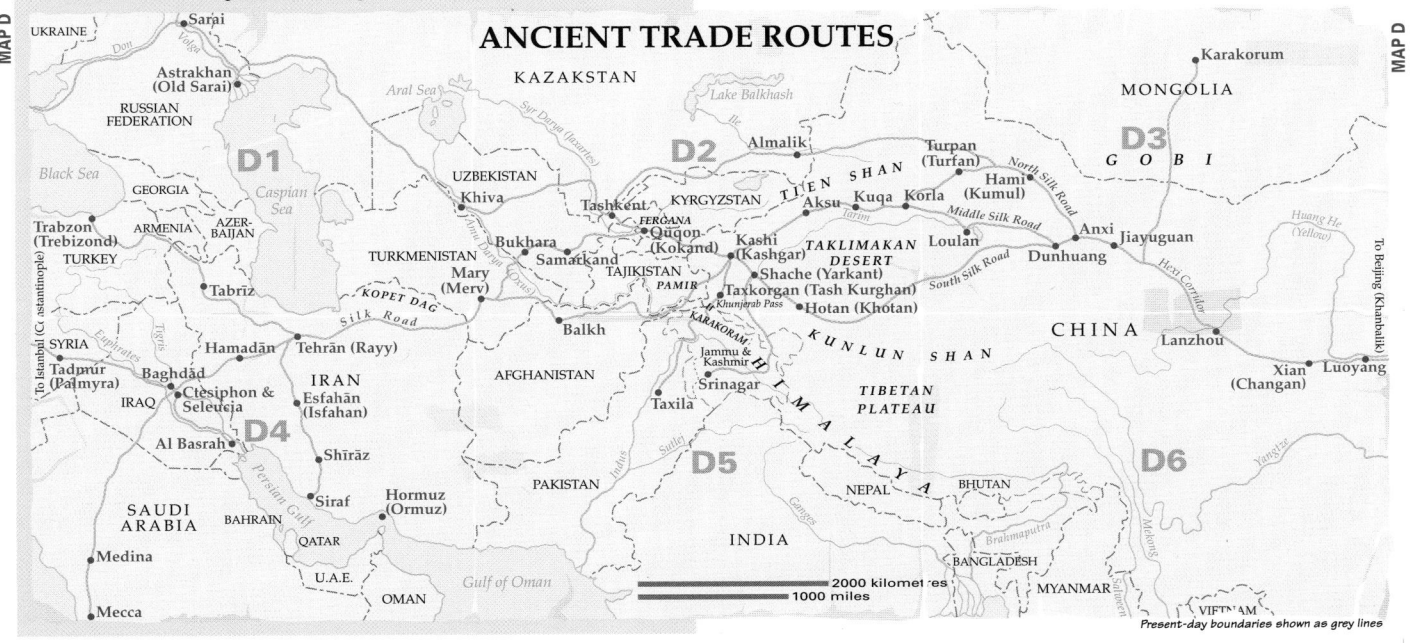

MAP D

2000 kilometres
1000 miles

Present-day boundaries shown as grey lines

BULGARIA   CROATIA   CZECH REPUBLIC   POLAND   ROMANIA   SLOVENIA

CENTRAL EUROPE

See pages 13 & 14 for general maps

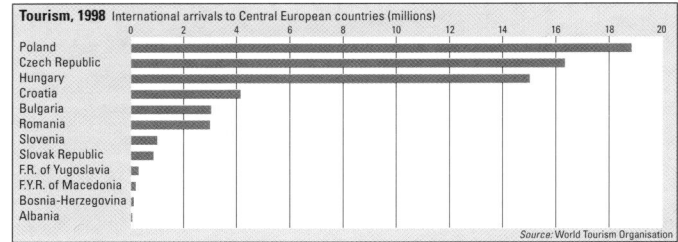

Tourism, 1998 International arrivals to Central European countries (millions)

Poland
Czech Republic
Hungary
Croatia
Bulgaria
Romania
Slovenia
Slovak Republic
F.R. of Yugoslavia
F.Y.R. of Macedonia
Bosnia-Herzegovina
Albania

0   2   4   6   8   10   12   14   16   18   20

Source: World Tourism Organisation

--- boundary of the Socialist Federal
Republic of Yugoslavia (1945–1992)

400 km
200 miles

BOHEMIA

CENTRAL SOUTHERN POLAND

SLOVENIA AND THE CROATIAN COAST

ROMANIAN AND BULGARIAN COAST

CLIMATE

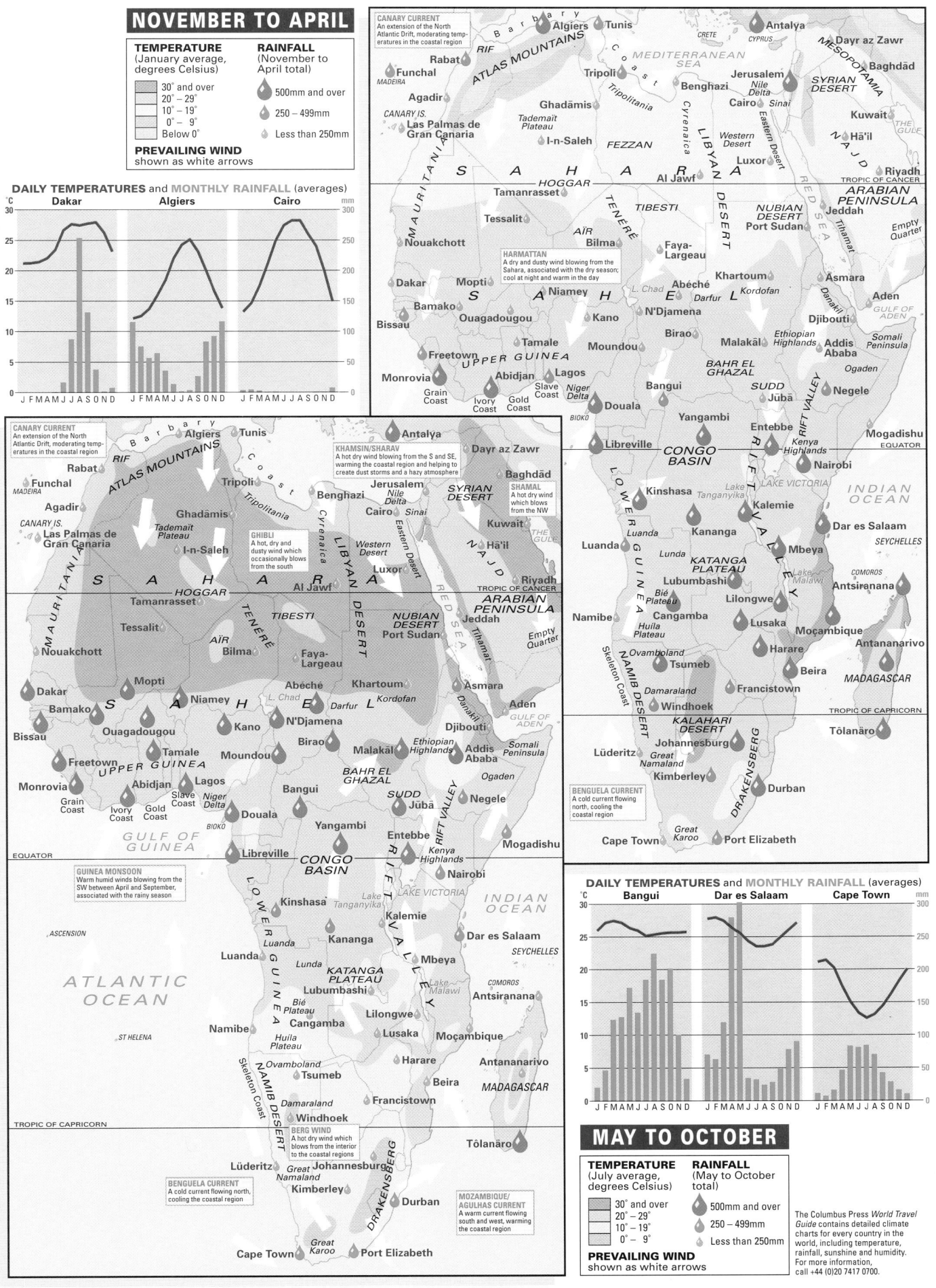

TEMPERATURE CONVERSION

°Celsius	−10	0	10	20	30	40
°Fahrenheit	14	32	50	68	86	104

RAINFALL CONVERSION

Millimetres	102	203	305	406	508	610
Inches	4	8	12	16	20	24

NOVEMBER TO APRIL

TEMPERATURE
(January average, degrees Celsius)

- 30° and over
- 20° – 29°
- 10° – 19°
- 0° – 9°
- Below 0°

RAINFALL
(November to April total)

- 500mm and over
- 250 – 499mm
- Less than 250mm

PREVAILING WIND
shown as white arrows

DAILY TEMPERATURES and MONTHLY RAINFALL (averages)

Dakar   Algiers   Cairo

CANARY CURRENT
An extension of the North Atlantic Drift, moderating temperatures in the coastal region

HARMATTAN
A dry and dusty wind blowing from the Sahara, associated with the dry season; cool at night and warm in the day

CANARY CURRENT
An extension of the North Atlantic Drift, moderating temperatures in the coastal region

KHAMSIN/SHARAV
A hot dry wind blowing from the S and SE, warming the coastal region and helping to create dust storms and a hazy atmosphere

SHAMAL
A hot dry wind which blows from the NW

GHIBLI
A hot, dry and dusty wind which occasionally blows from the south

GUINEA MONSOON
Warm humid winds blowing from the SW between April and September, associated with the rainy season

BERG WIND
A hot dry wind which blows from the interior to the coastal regions

BENGUELA CURRENT
A cold current flowing north, cooling the coastal region

MOZAMBIQUE/AGULHAS CURRENT
A warm current flowing south and west, warming the coastal region

BENGUELA CURRENT
A cold current flowing north, cooling the coastal region

DAILY TEMPERATURES and MONTHLY RAINFALL (averages)

Bangui   Dar es Salaam   Cape Town

MAY TO OCTOBER

TEMPERATURE
(July average, degrees Celsius)

- 30° and over
- 20° – 29°
- 10° – 19°
- 0° – 9°

RAINFALL
(May to October total)

- 500mm and over
- 250 – 499mm
- Less than 250mm

PREVAILING WIND
shown as white arrows

The Columbus Press *World Travel Guide* contains detailed climate charts for every country in the world, including temperature, rainfall, sunshine and humidity. For more information, call +44 (0)20 7417 0700.

AFRICA

See page 19 for general map

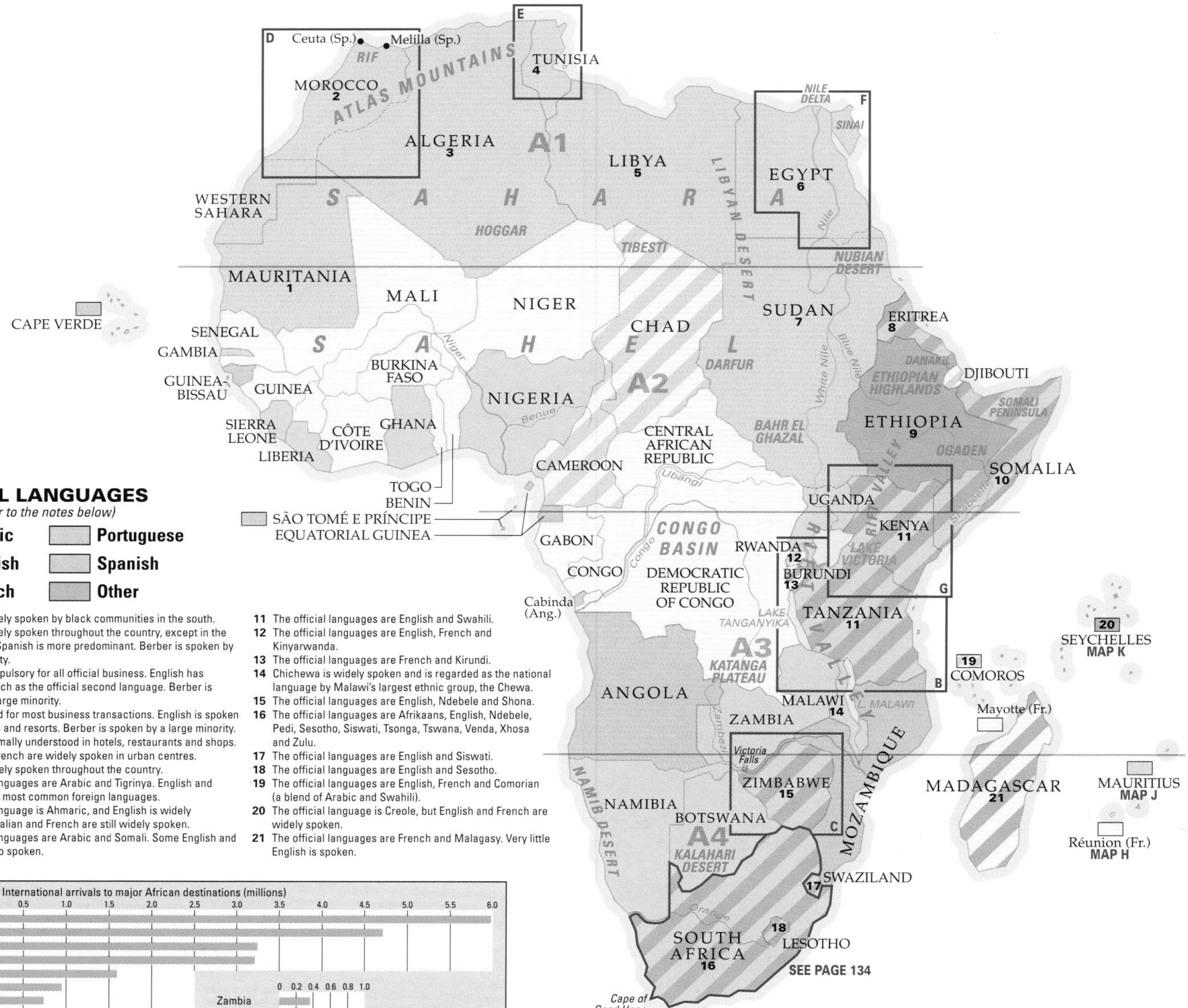

(map labels)

Ceuta (Sp.)   Melilla (Sp.)
D   RIF   E
MOROCCO   ATLAS MOUNTAINS   TUNISIA
2   4
ALGERIA   A1
3
WESTERN   LIBYA   EGYPT
SAHARA   5   6   NILE DELTA   F
SAHARA   SINAI   A
HOGGAR   LIBYAN DESERT   NUBIAN DESERT
MAURITANIA   TIBESTI   SUDAN
1   MALI   NIGER   CHAD   7   ERITREA
8   DANAKIL   DJIBOUTI
CAPE VERDE   SAHEL   DARFUR   ETHIOPIAN   SOMALI
SENEGAL   BURKINA   A2   BAHR EL   HIGHLANDS   PENINSULA
GAMBIA   FASO   GHAZAL   ETHIOPIA   OGADEN
GUINEA-   GUINEA   NIGERIA   9
BISSAU   CENTRAL   SOMALIA
SIERRA   CÔTE   AFRICAN   10
LEONE   D'IVOIRE   GHANA   CAMEROON   REPUBLIC   UGANDA   KENYA
LIBERIA   TOGO   Ubangi   11
BENIN   CONGO   RWANDA   LAKE   G
SÃO TOMÉ E PRÍNCIPE   BASIN   Congo   12   VICTORIA   20
EQUATORIAL GUINEA   GABON   BURUNDI   SEYCHELLES
CONGO   DEMOCRATIC   13   MAP K
Cabinda   REPUBLIC   LAKE   TANZANIA   19
(Ang.)   OF CONGO   TANGANYIKA   11   COMOROS
A3   B   Mayotte (Fr.)
KATANGA   MALAWI   LAKE MALAWI
PLATEAU   14
ANGOLA   ZAMBIA   MADAGASCAR   MAURITIUS
Victoria   MOZAMBIQUE   21   MAP J
Falls   ZIMBABWE
NAMIB DESERT   15   Réunion (Fr.)
NAMIBIA   BOTSWANA   C   MAP H
A4   17
KALAHARI   SWAZILAND
DESERT   18
SOUTH   LESOTHO
AFRICA   SEE PAGE 134
16
Cape of
Good Hope

OFFICIAL LANGUAGES
(Numbers refer to the notes below)

Arabic   Portuguese
English   Spanish
French   Other

1 French is widely spoken by black communities in the south.
2 French is widely spoken throughout the country, except in the north where Spanish is more predominant. Berber is spoken by a large minority.
3 Arabic is compulsory for all official business. English has replaced French as the official second language. Berber is spoken by a large minority.
4 French is used for most business transactions. English is spoken in major cities and resorts. Berber is spoken by a large minority.
5 English is normally understood in hotels, restaurants and shops.
6 English and French are widely spoken in urban centres.
7 English is widely spoken throughout the country.
8 The official languages are Arabic and Tigrinya. English and Italian are the most common foreign languages.
9 The official language is Ahmaric, and English is widely understood. Italian and French are still widely spoken.
10 The official languages are Arabic and Somali. Some English and Italian are also spoken.

11 The official languages are English and Swahili.
12 The official languages are English, French and Kinyarwanda.
13 The official languages are French and Kirundi.
14 Chichewa is widely spoken and is regarded as the national language by Malawi's largest ethnic group, the Chewa.
15 The official languages are English, Ndebele and Shona.
16 The official languages are Afrikaans, English, Ndebele, Pedi, Sesotho, Siswati, Tsonga, Tswana, Venda, Xhosa and Zulu.
17 The official languages are English and Siswati.
18 The official languages are English and Sesotho.
19 The official languages are English, French and Comorian (a blend of Arabic and Swahili).
20 The official language is Creole, but English and French are widely spoken.
21 The official languages are French and Malagasy. Very little English is spoken.

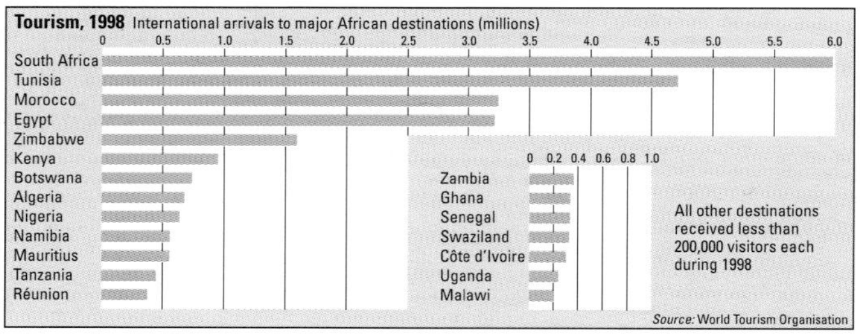

Tourism, 1998 — International arrivals to major African destinations (millions)

Scale: 0 0.5 1.0 1.5 2.0 2.5 3.0 3.5 4.0 4.5 5.0 5.5 6.0

South Africa
Tunisia
Morocco
Egypt
Zimbabwe
Kenya
Botswana
Algeria
Nigeria
Namibia
Mauritius
Tanzania
Réunion

(inset scale: 0 0.2 0.4 0.6 0.8 1.0)

Zambia
Ghana
Senegal
Swaziland
Côte d'Ivoire
Uganda
Malawi

All other destinations received less than 200,000 visitors each during 1998

Source: World Tourism Organisation

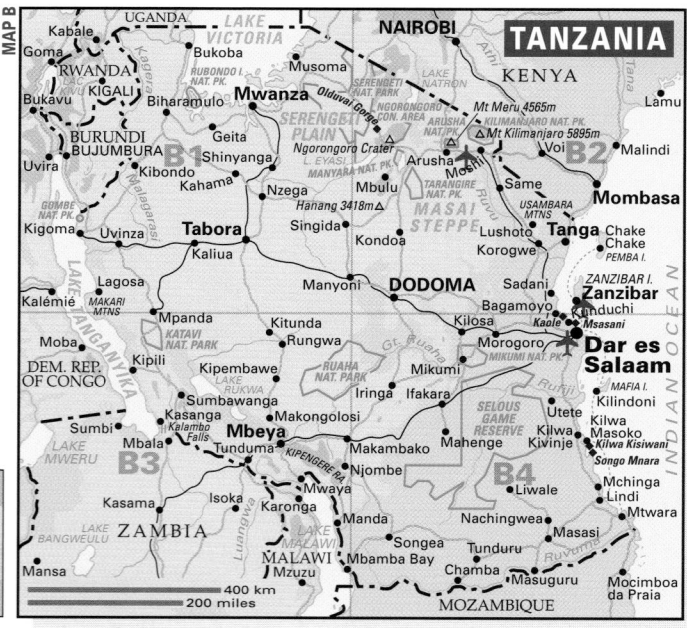

TANZANIA

MAP B

UGANDA   LAKE VICTORIA   NAIROBI
Kabale   Bukoba   Musoma   KENYA
Goma   RWANDA   RUBONDO I.   SERENGETI NAT. PARK   LAKE NATRON
Bukavu   KIGALI   Biharamulo   Mwanza   NAT. PARK   Lamu
Uvira   BURUNDI   Geita   NGORONGORO   Mt Meru 4565m
BUJUMBURA   Shinyanga   CON. AREA   ARUSHA NAT. PK.   Mt Kilimanjaro 5895m   KILIMANJARO NAT. PK.
Kibondo   Nzega   SERENGETI   Ngorongoro Crater   Arusha   Voi   Malindi
Kigoma   Kahama   PLAIN   MANYARA   Mbulu   Same   USAMBARA MTS.
B1   Hanang 3418m   TARANGIRE   B2
Uvinza   Singida   NAT. PK.   Mombasa
Tabora   Kondoa   Lushoto   Tanga   Chake Chake
Kalémié   Kaliua   MASAI   Korogwe   PEMBA I.
Lagosa   STEPPE
Mpanda   Manyoni   Sadani   ZANZIBAR I.
Moba   KATAVI   Kitunda   DODOMA   Bagamoyo   Zanzibar
Kipili   NAT. PARK   Rungwa   Kilosa   Kaole   Unduchi   Msasani
DEM. REP.   Kipembawe   Morogoro   Dar es Salaam
OF CONGO   Mikumi   MIKUMI NAT. PK.
Sumbawanga   RUAHA   Iringa   Ifakara   Utete
Sumbi   Makongolosi   NAT. PARK   Kilindoni   MAFIA I.
B3   Mbeya   Mahenge   Kilwa   Masoko
Kasama   Tunduma   SELOUS   Kivinje   Kilwa Kisiwani
Kambala   KIPENGERE RA.   GAME RESERVE   Songo Mnara
Isoka   Njombe   B4   Mchinga
Mbala   Mwaya   Karonga   Manda   Liwale   Lindi
Mansa   Kasanga   Masasi   Mtwara
ZAMBIA   LAKE MALAWI   Songea   Nachingwea
LAKE BANGWEULU   MALAWI   Tunduru   Masuguru   Mocimboa da Praia
Mzuzu   Mbamba Bay   Chamba
400 km   MOZAMBIQUE
200 miles

2000 metres
1000 metres
Sea level

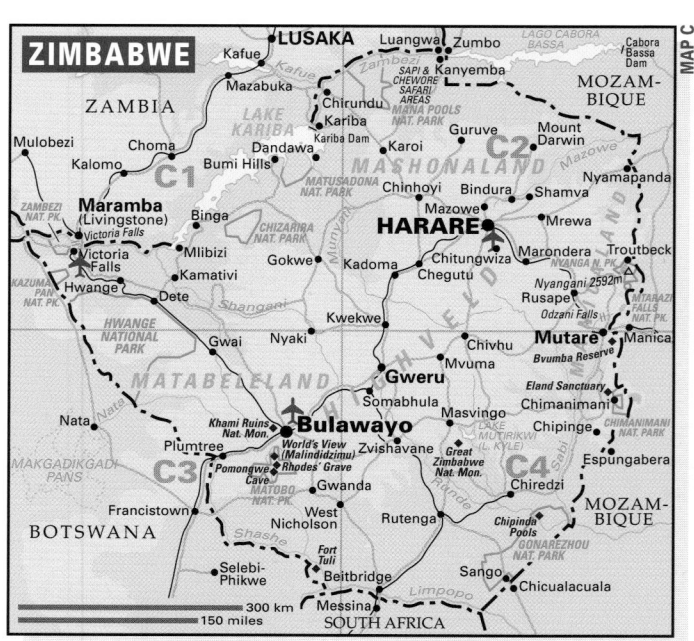

ZIMBABWE

MAP C

LUSAKA   Luangwa   Zumbo   LAGO CABORA BASSA   Cabora Bassa Dam
Kafue   Zambezi
ZAMBIA   Mazabuka   Chirundu   SAPI & KANYEMBA   MOZAMBIQUE
Choma   Kariba   CHEWORE SAFARI AREAS   Mount Darwin
Mulobezi   Kalomo   LAKE KARIBA   Kariba Dam   MANA POOLS NAT. PARK   Guruve   C2
Dandawa   Karoi   MASHONALAND   Nyamapanda
Bumi Hills   Mazowe
Maramba   Binga   CHIZARIRA   Chinhoyi   Bindura   Shamva
(Livingstone)   NAT. PARK   C1   Gokwe   Chegutu   HARARE   Mrewa
Victoria Falls   Mlibizi   Kadoma   Chitungwiza   Marondera   Troutbeck
KAZUMA   Kamativi   Nyangani 2592m
PAN NAT. PK.   Hwange   Dete   Kwekwe   Rusape   Odzani Falls
ZAMBEZI   HWANGE   Gwai   Chivhu   Mutare   Manica
NAT. PARK   NATIONAL   Nyaki   Gweru   Mvuma   Bvumba Reserve
PARK   Somabhula   Eland Sanctuary
MATABELELAND   Chimanimani
Nata   Khami Ruins Nat. Mon.   Masvingo   Chipinge
World's View   Bulawayo   Zvishavane   Great Zimbabwe Nat. Mon.
(Malindidzimu)   Rhodes' Grave   Chiredzi
Plumtree   Pomongwe Cave   MATOBO NAT. PK.   Gwanda   Espungabera
Francistown   West Nicholson   Rutenga   MOZAMBIQUE
BOTSWANA   MAKGADIKGADI PANS   Chicualacuala
Selebi-Phikwe   Fort Tuli   GONAREZHOU NAT. PARK   Sango
Beitbridge   Limpopo
Messina   SOUTH AFRICA
300 km
150 miles

INDIAN OCEAN

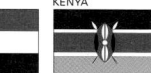

MOROCCO TUNISIA EGYPT KENYA

AFRICA

See pages 20-23 for general maps

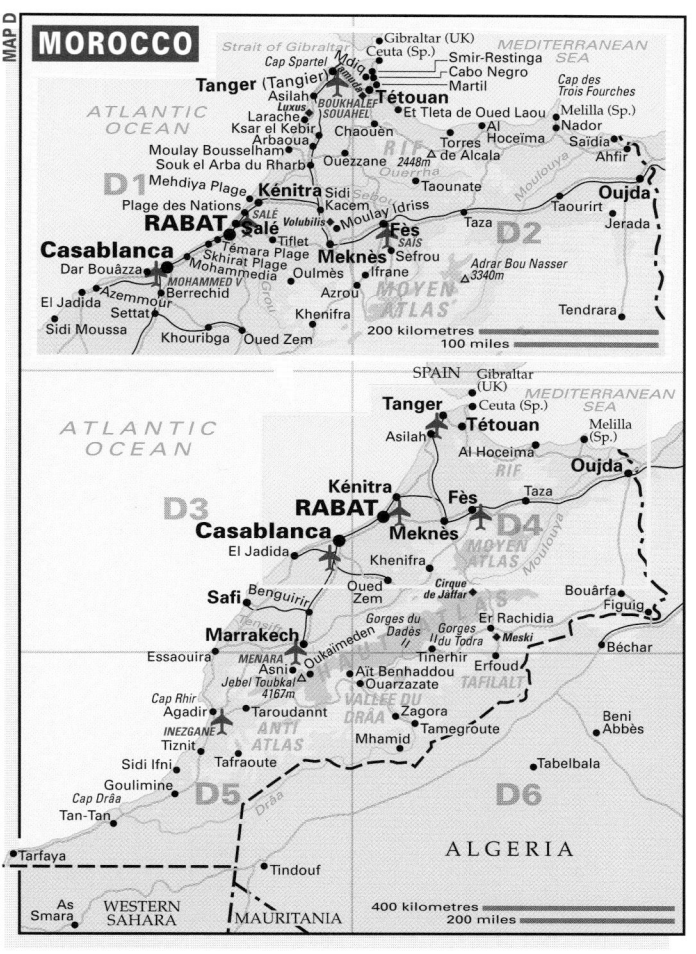

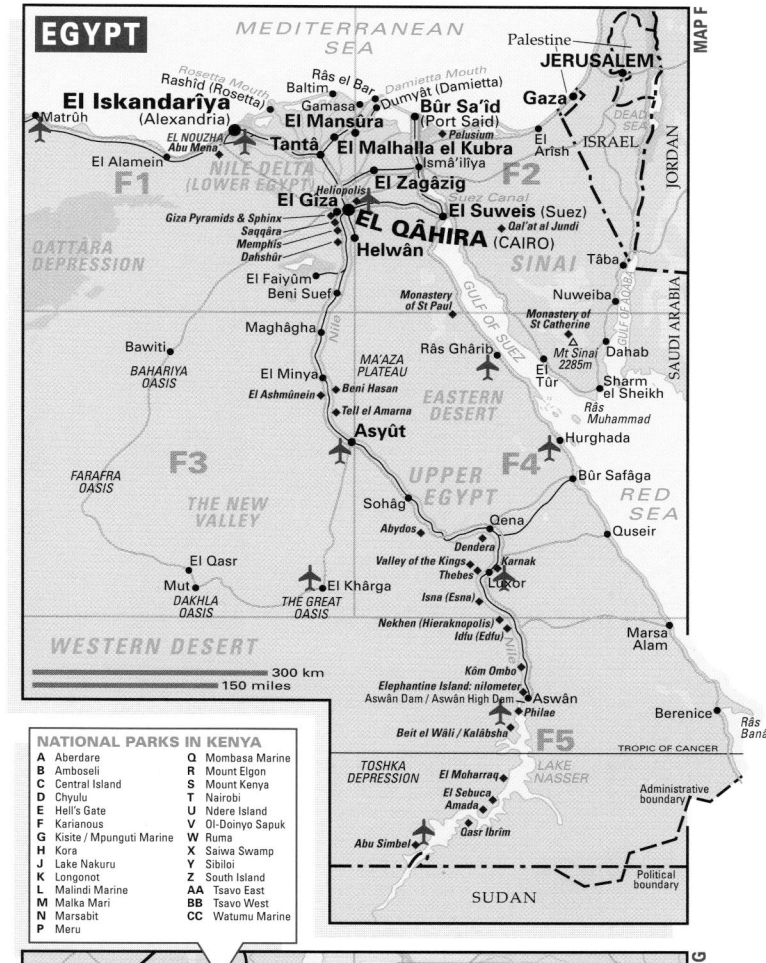

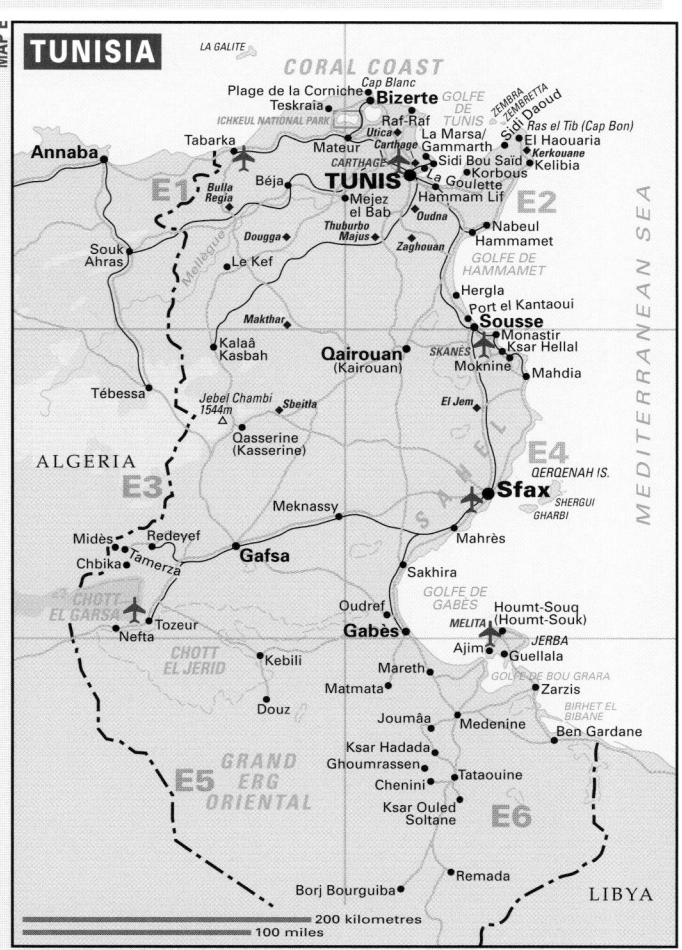

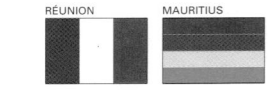

RÉUNION   MAURITIUS

Animal columns (left to right): ELEPHANT · RHINOCEROS · HIPPOPOTAMUS · BUFFALO · ZEBRA · GIRAFFE · ANTELOPE · LION · LEOPARD · CHEETAH · HYENA · WARTHOG · GORILLA · CHIMPANZEE · MONKEY

#	Country	Park/Reserve	Notes
1	Mauritania	Banc d'Arguin National Park	MIGRATING BIRDS
2	Mali	Lac Faguibine	MIGRATING BIRDS
3	Niger	Parc national du "W"	
4	Niger	Aïr and Ténéré Natural Reserves	
5	Senegal	Parc national des Oiseaux du Djoudj	MIGRATING BIRDS
6	Senegal	Parc national de la Langue de Barbarie	WATERFOWL (FLAMINGOS ETC)
7	Senegal	Parc national du Delta du Saloum	SMALL MAMMALS & MIGRATING BIRDS
8	Senegal	Parc national de Basse-Casamance	
9	Senegal	Parc national de Niokolo Koba	
10	The Gambia	Abuko Nature Reserve	BUDGERIGARS
11	The Gambia	Kiang West National Park	
12	Sierra Leone	Outamba-Kilimi National Park	
13	Sierra Leone	Mount Bintumani	
14	Sierra Leone	Mamunta-Mayoso Wildlife Sanctuary	BIRDS & SMALL MAMMALS
15	Sierra Leone	Gola Forest Reserve	BUDGERIGARS
16	Sierra Leone	Tiwai Island Wildlife Sanctuary	BUTTERFLIES & BUDGERIGARS
17	Liberia	Sapo National Park	
18	Côte d'Ivoire	Parc national de Taï	
19	Côte d'Ivoire	Parc national de la Marahoué	
20	Côte d'Ivoire	Parc national de la Komoé	
21	Ghana	Mole National Park	
22	Ghana	Bui National Park	
23	Ghana	Kujani Game Reserve	
24	Ghana	Owabi Wildlife Sanctuary	BIRDS & SMALL MAMMALS
25	Ghana	Bia National Park	
26	Ghana	Kakum Nature Park	
27	Burkina Faso	Parc national d'Arly	
28	Togo	Parc national de la Kéran	
29	Togo	Parc national de Fazao-Malfakassa	
30	Benin	Parc national de la Pendjari	
31	Nigeria	Kamuku Wildlife Reserve	BUDGERIGARS
32	Nigeria	Hadejia-Nguru Wetlands	WETLAND BIRDS
33	Nigeria	Yankari National Park	
34	Nigeria	Gashaka Game Reserve	
35	Nigeria	Okomo Sanctuary	
36	Nigeria	Cross River National Park	BUDGERIGARS & RAINFOREST BIRDS
37	Cameroon	Parc national du Korup	
38	Cameroon	Réserve du Dja	
39	Cameroon	Parc national de la Bénoué	
40	Cameroon	Parc national de Bouba Ndjida	
41	Cameroon	Parc national de Waza	
42	Chad	Parc national de Zakouma	(Widespread poaching; greatly depleted stocks)
43	Central African Rep.	Parc national Manovo-Gounda-St Floris	
44	Central African Rep.	Parc national du Bamingui-Bangoran	
45	Central African Rep.	Réserve de Dzanga-Sangha	
46	Gabon	Réserve de Lopé	OKAPI
47	Gabon	Parc national de l'Okanda	
48	Gabon	Réserve d'Iguéla	LEATHERBACK SEA TURTLE
49	Gabon	Réserve de Petit-Loango	LEATHERBACK SEA TURTLE
50	Gabon	Réserve de la Moukalaba	
51	Gabon	Réserve de Ndendé	
52	Congo, Dem. Rep.	Parc national de la Salonga	
53	Congo, Dem. Rep.	Parc national de la Garamba	
54	Congo, Dem. Rep.	Réserve du Okapi	OKAPI
55	Congo, Dem. Rep.	Parc national des Virunga	
56	Congo, Dem. Rep.	Parc national de la Maiko	
57	Congo, Dem. Rep.	Parc national du Kahuzi-Biega	
58	Congo, Dem. Rep.	Parc national de l'Upemba	
59	Congo, Dem. Rep.	Parc national de Kundelungu	
60	Sudan	Dinder National Park	(Data unavailable)
61	Ethiopia	Simien National Park	
62	Ethiopia	Awash National Park	
63	Ethiopia	Langano & Shala-Abiyata Lakes Nat. Park	(Data unavailable)
64	Ethiopia	Bale Mountains National Park	
65	Ethiopia	Omo and Mago National Parks	
66	Somalia	Hargeysa National Park	(Data unavailable)
67	Somalia	Kismayo National Park	(Data unavailable)
68	Uganda	Ruwenzori National Park	
69	Uganda	Queen Elizabeth National Park	
70	Uganda	Bwindi National Park	
71	Rwanda	Parc des Volcans	
72	Rwanda	Parc national de l'Akagera	BIRDS
73	Kenya	Sibiloi National Park	
74	Kenya	Marsabit National Park	
75	Kenya	Mount Elgon National Park	
76	Kenya	Samburu National Reserve	
77	Kenya	Meru National Park	
78	Kenya	Mount Kenya National Park	
79	Kenya	Aberdare National Park	
80	Kenya	Lake Nakuru National Park	FLAMINGOS
81	Kenya	Masai Mara National Reserve	
82	Kenya	Nairobi National Park	
83	Kenya	Amboseli National Park	
84	Kenya	Tsavo National Park	
85	Kenya	Shimba Hills National Reserve	SABLE ANTELOPE
86	Tanzania	Rubondo Island National Park	WETLAND BIRDS
87	Tanzania	Serengeti National Park	
88	Tanzania	Ngorongoro Conservation Area	
89	Tanzania	Kilimanjaro National Park	
90	Tanzania	Arusha National Park	
91	Tanzania	Tarangire National Park	
92	Tanzania	Gombe National Park	
93	Tanzania	Ruaha National Park	
94	Tanzania	Selous Game Reserve	
95	Malawi	Nyika National Park	BUTTERFLIES & BIRDS
96	Malawi	Kasungu National Park	
97	Malawi	Lake Malawi National Park	
98	Malawi	Liwonde National Park	
99	Malawi	Majete Game Reserve	
100	Malawi	Lengwe National Park	
101	Malawi	Mwabvi National Park	
102	Zambia	Sumbu National Park	Heavily poached in 1980's; lodges re-opened 1997
103	Zambia	North Luangwa National Park	
104	Zambia	South Luangwa National Park	
105	Zambia	Kasanka National Park	
106	Zambia	Kafue National Park	
107	Zambia	Lochinvar National Park	
108	Zambia	Lower Zambezi National Park	
109	Zimbabwe	Mana Pools National Park	
110	Zimbabwe	Matsudona National Park	
111	Zimbabwe	Zambezi National Park	
112	Zimbabwe	Hwange National Park	
113	Zimbabwe	Matobo National Park	
114	Zimbabwe	Gonarezhou National Park	
115	Botswana	Chobe National Park	
116	Botswana	Moremi Wildlife Reserve	
117	Botswana	Makgadikgadi Pans Game Reserve	FLAMINGOS
118	Botswana / S. Africa	Kalahari Gemsbok National Park	
119	Namibia	Etosha National Park	
120	Namibia	Cape Cross Reserve	SEALS
121	Namibia	Namib-Naukluft National Park	
122	South Africa	Cape of Good Hope Nature Reserve	
123	South Africa	Bontebok National Park	BONTEBOK
124	South Africa	Karoo National Park	
125	South Africa	Mountain Zebra National Park	MOUNTAIN ZEBRA
126	South Africa	Addo Elephant National Park	
127	South Africa	Willem Pretorius Game Reserve	
128	South Africa	Pilanesberg National Park	
129	South Africa	Kruger National Park	
130	South Africa	Ndumo Game Reserve	
131	South Africa	Mkuzi Game Reserve	
132	South Africa	Greater St Lucia Wetland Park	
133	South Africa	Hluhluwe-Umfolozi Game Reserve	
134	South Africa	Giant's Castle Game Reserve	
135	Lesotho	Sehlabathebe National Park	BABOONS & BIRDS
136	Swaziland	Hlane Game Sanctuary	(Wide range of habitats; small mammals most likely to be seen but larger game being reintroduced into the country)
137	Swaziland	Malolotja Nature Reserve	
138	Swaziland	Mkhaya Nature Reserve	
139	Mozambique	Maputo Elephant Reserve	
140	Mozambique	Parque Nacional da Gorongosa	(Data unavailable)
141	Mozambique	Reserve de Marromeu	(Data unavailable)
142	Madagascar	Réserve de Perinet	
143	Madagascar	Parc national de Ranomafana	
144	Madagascar	Parc national de l'Isalo	
145	Seychelles	Cousin Island Nature Reserve	BIRDS

INDIAN OCEAN

See pages 19 & 24 for general maps

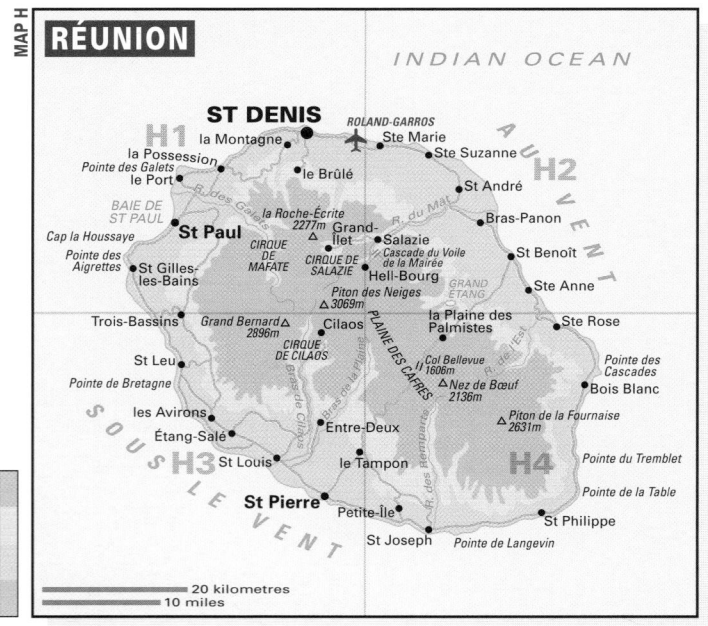

RÉUNION

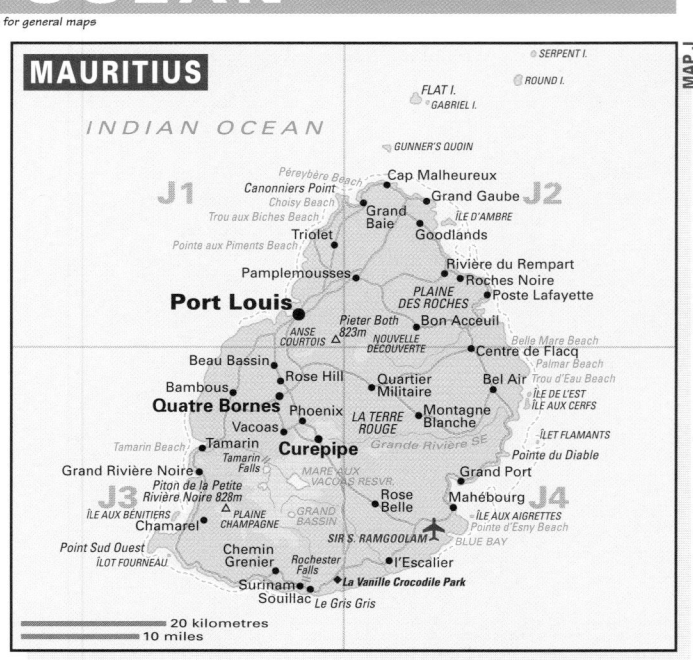

MAURITIUS

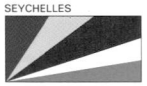

WILDLIFE PARKS AND RESERVES

Africa is a prime destination for wildlife holidays: its national parks, game reserves and wildlife sanctuaries feature prominently in package holidays and tourist itineraries. Many parks, such as the Masai Mara, Serengeti and Kruger, are well-known throughout the world and some have been recognised by both UNESCO and the WWF for their unique and important character (UNESCO's World Heritage list is featured elsewhere in this atlas).

The area of Africa south of the Sahara is featured here. Although there are areas of wildlife interest in northern Africa, particularly on the Mediterranean coast, these are generally on a much smaller scale and do not usually provide the primary motivation for travel to these countries.

The map and table features the major parks and reserves used by tour operators and visited by overseas tourists. Some lesser-known parks are also included to give a broader geographical spread; access to many of these may be difficult due to poor infrastructure or political problems.

The table lists the major species most likely to be seen while visiting each park or those animals for which the park is famous, according to government literature and independent reports. Quality of information varies considerably from country to country and the following table should be regarded as a rough guide only; in some cases no species information is currently available. Poaching is a serious problem in some countries, particularly where wildlife tourism is less developed.

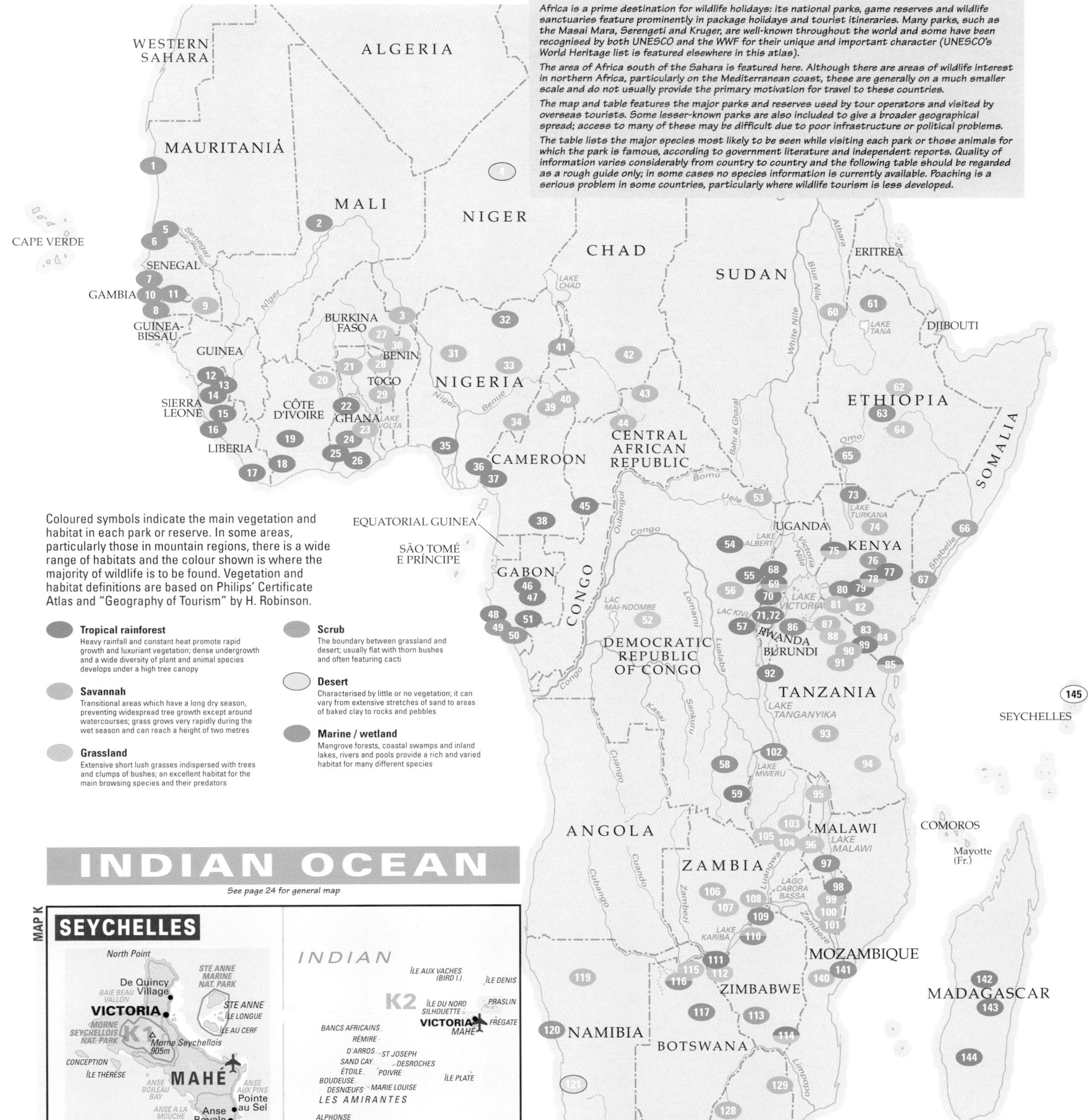
WESTERN SAHARA
ALGERIA
MAURITANIA
MALI
NIGER
CHAD
SUDAN
ERITREA
DJIBOUTI
CAPE VERDE
SENEGAL
GAMBIA
GUINEA-BISSAU
GUINEA
SIERRA LEONE
LIBERIA
CÔTE D'IVOIRE
BURKINA FASO
GHANA
TOGO
BENIN
NIGERIA
LAKE CHAD
LAKE TANA
ETHIOPIA
SOMALIA
CENTRAL AFRICAN REPUBLIC
CAMEROON
EQUATORIAL GUINEA
SÃO TOMÉ E PRÍNCIPE
GABON
CONGO
DEMOCRATIC REPUBLIC OF CONGO
UGANDA
KENYA
RWANDA
BURUNDI
TANZANIA
LAKE TURKANA
LAKE ALBERT
LAKE VICTORIA
LAC KIVU
LAC MAI-NDOMBE
LAKE TANGANYIKA
LAKE MWERU
LAKE MALAWI
LAGO CABORA BASSA
LAKE KARIBA
ANGOLA
ZAMBIA
MALAWI
MOZAMBIQUE
ZIMBABWE
NAMIBIA
BOTSWANA
SWAZILAND
LESOTHO
SOUTH AFRICA
MADAGASCAR
COMOROS
Mayotte (Fr.)
SEYCHELLES
145
Senegal
Niger
Benue
Volta
Bomu
Uele
Congo
Oubangui
Lomami
Lualaba
Kasai
Sankuru
Cuango
Cubango
Cuando
Zambezi
Luangwa
Limpopo
Vaal
Orange
Fish
Shabelle
Omo
Athbara
Blue Nile
White Nile
Bahr al Ghazal
Victoria Nile

Coloured symbols indicate the main vegetation and habitat in each park or reserve. In some areas, particularly those in mountain regions, there is a wide range of habitats and the colour shown is where the majority of wildlife is to be found. Vegetation and habitat definitions are based on Philips' Certificate Atlas and "Geography of Tourism" by H. Robinson.

Tropical rainforest
Heavy rainfall and constant heat promote rapid growth and luxuriant vegetation; dense undergrowth and a wide diversity of plant and animal species develops under a high tree canopy

Savannah
Transitional areas which have a long dry season, preventing widespread tree growth except around watercourses; grass grows very rapidly during the wet season and can reach a height of two metres

Grassland
Extensive short lush grasses indispersed with trees and clumps of bushes; an excellent habitat for the main browsing species and their predators

Scrub
The boundary between grassland and desert; usually flat with thorn bushes and often featuring cacti

Desert
Characterised by little or no vegetation; it can vary from extensive stretches of sand to areas of baked clay to rocks and pebbles

Marine / wetland
Mangrove forests, coastal swamps and inland lakes, rivers and pools provide a rich and varied habitat for many different species

INDIAN OCEAN

See page 24 for general map

MAP K

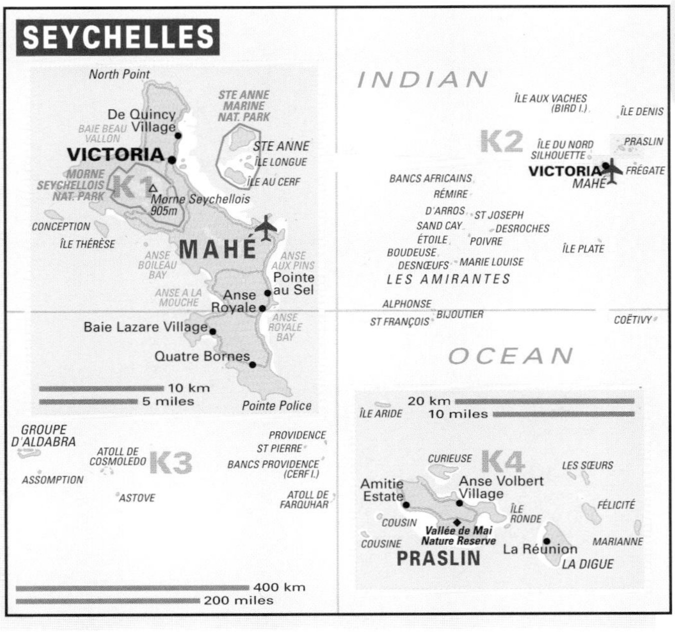
SEYCHELLES
North Point
De Quincy Village
BAIE BEAU VALLON
VICTORIA
STE ANNE MARINE NAT. PARK
STE ANNE
ÎLE LONGUE
ÎLE AU CERF
MORNE SEYCHELLOIS NAT. PARK
K1
Morne Seychellois 905m
CONCEPTION
ÎLE THÉRÈSE
ANSE BOILEAU BAY
MAHÉ
ANSE AUX PINS
Pointe au Sel
ANSE A LA MOUCHE
Anse Royale
ANSE ROYALE BAY
Baie Lazare Village
Quatre Bornes
Pointe Police
10 km
5 miles
INDIAN
OCEAN
ÎLE AUX VACHES (BIRD I.)
ÎLE DENIS
K2
ÎLE DU NORD
SILHOUETTE
PRASLIN
VICTORIA
MAHÉ
FRÉGATE
BANCS AFRICAINS
RÉMIRE
D'ARROS
ST JOSEPH
SAND CAY
DESROCHES
ÉTOILE
POIVRE
BOUDEUSE
DESNŒUFS
MARIE LOUISE
ÎLE PLATE
LES AMIRANTES
ALPHONSE
BIJOUTIER
ST FRANÇOIS
COËTIVY
GROUPE D'ALDABRA
ATOLL DE COSMOLEDO
K3
ASSOMPTION
ASTOVE
PROVIDENCE
ST PIERRE
BANCS PROVIDENCE (CERF I.)
ATOLL DE FARQUHAR
400 km
200 miles
20 km
10 miles
ÎLE ARIDE
CURIEUSE
K4
LES SŒURS
Amitie Estate
Anse Volbert Village
FÉLICITÉ
ÎLE RONDE
COUSIN
Vallée de Mai Nature Reserve
COUSINE
PRASLIN
La Réunion
MARIANNE
LA DIGUE

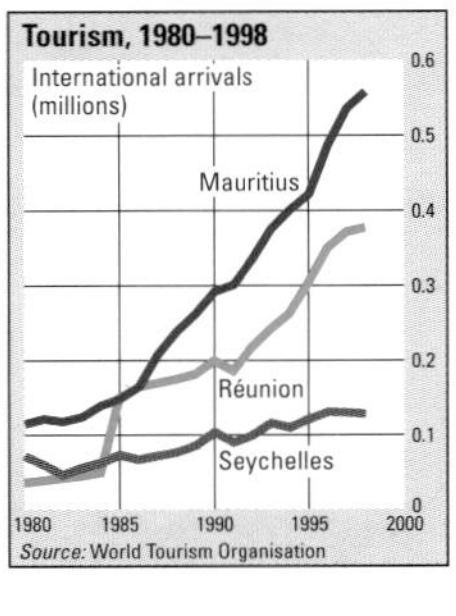
Tourism, 1980–1998
International arrivals (millions)
0.6
0.5
0.4
0.3
0.2
0.1
0
Mauritius
Réunion
Seychelles
1980
1985
1990
1995
2000
Source: World Tourism Organisation

SOUTH AFRICA

See page 24 for general map

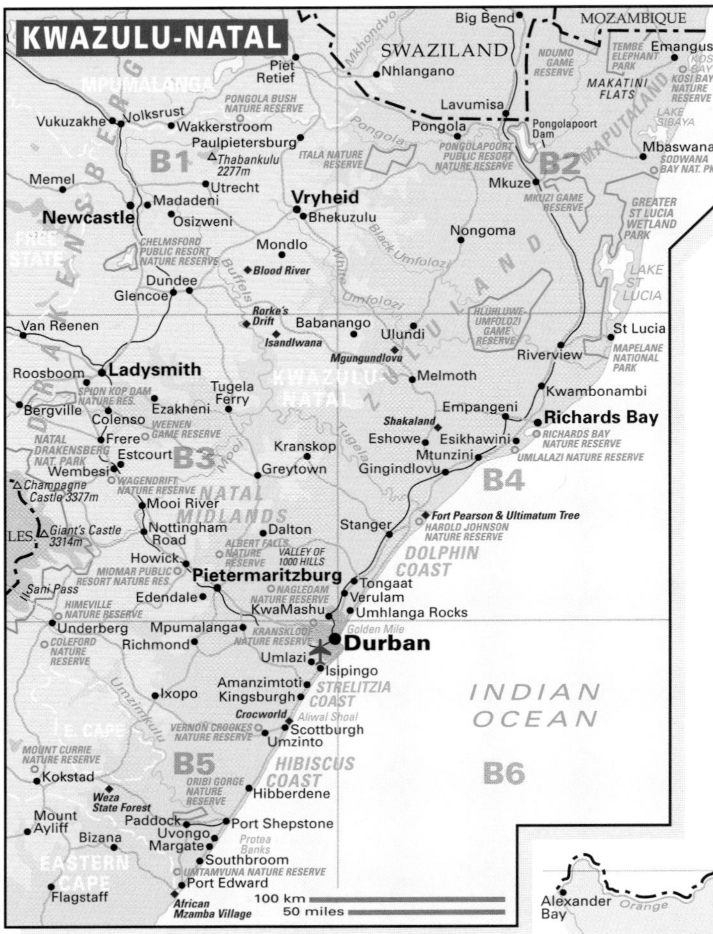

KWAZULU-NATAL (MAP B)

SWAZILAND
MOZAMBIQUE

Big Bend
Emangusi
Piet Retief
Nhlangano
TEMBE ELEPHANT PARK
NDUMO GAME RESERVE
KOSI BAY
KOSI BAY NATURE RESERVE

MPUMALANGA
Vukuzakhe
Volksrust
Wakkerstroom
Paulpietersburg
Lavumisa
Pongola
Pongolapoort Dam
MAKATINI FLATS
SODWANA BAY NAT. PK.

B1
Memel
Madadeni
Utrecht
Thabankulu 2277m
ITALA NATURE RESERVE
PONGOLA BUSH NATURE RESERVE
PONGOLAPOORT PUBLIC RESORT NATURE RESERVE
B2
Mbaswana

Newcastle
Osizweni
Vryheid
Bhekuzulu
Mkuze
MKUZI GAME RESERVE
GREATER ST LUCIA WETLAND PARK
LAKE SIBAYA

FREE STATE
Dundee
Mondlo
CHELMSFORD PUBLIC RESORT NATURE RESERVE
Nongoma
LAKE ST LUCIA

Glencoe
Blood River
Rorke's Drift
Babanango
Ulundi
St Lucia
MAPELANE NATURE RESERVE

Van Reenen
Isandlwana
Mgungundlovu
Riverview

Roosboom
Ladysmith
Tugela Ferry
Melmoth
Kwambonambi

Bergville
Colenso
Ezakheni
Shakaland
Empangeni
Richards Bay
RICHARDS BAY NATURE RESERVE

Frere
Estcourt
WEENEN GAME RESERVE
Greytown
Eshowe
Esikhawini
Mtunzini
UMLALAZI NATURE RESERVE
B4

Wembesi
WAGENDRIFT NATURE RESERVE
Kranskop
Gingindlovu

Champagne Castle 3377m
Mooi River
NATAL MIDLANDS
Dalton
Stanger
DOLPHIN COAST

Giant's Castle 3314m
Nottingham Road
ALBERT FALLS NATURE RESERVE
Fort Pearson & Ultimatum Tree
HAROLD JOHNSON NATURE RESERVE

LES.
Howick
MIDMAR PUBLIC RESORT NATURE RES.
Pietermaritzburg
VALLEY OF 1000 HILLS

Sani Pass
HIMEVILLE NATURE RESERVE
Edendale
NAGLEDAM NATURE RESERVE
Tongaat
Verulam

Underberg
Mpumalanga
KRANSKLOOF NATURE RESERVE
Umhlanga Rocks
Durban
Golden Mile

COLEFORD NATURE RESERVE
Richmond
Umlazi
Isipingo
INDIAN OCEAN

E. CAPE
Ixopo
Amanzimtoti
Kingsburgh
STRELITZIA COAST

MOUNT CURRIE NATURE RESERVE
Crocworld
Aliwal Shoal
VERNON CROOKES NATURE RESERVE
Scottburgh
B6

Kokstad
Umzinto
HIBISCUS COAST
B5

Mount Ayliff
Weza State Forest
Paddock
ORIBI GORGE NATURE RESERVE
Hibberdene

Bizana
Uvongo
Margate
Protea Banks
Port Shepstone

UMTAMVUNA NATURE RESERVE
Southbroom
Flagstaff
Port Edward
African Mzamba Village

100 km
50 miles

The Blue Train is a luxury train service which connects Cape Town and Pretoria – a 25-hour journey – at regular intervals throughout the year. The Blue Train's other services (to Victoria Falls, the Valley of the Olifants and the Garden Route) run less frequently.

Rovos Rail also runs services on similar routes and include guided tours and excursions: Pretoria-Cape Town; Pretoria-Victoria Falls; Pretoria-Komatipoort and Cape Town-Knysna. The company also operates annual rail safaris to Swakopmund (Namibia) and Dar-es-Salaam (Tanzania).

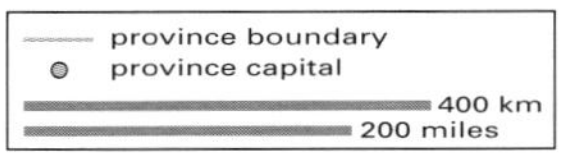

BLUE TRAIN

- Victoria Falls
- Hwange (Wankie)
- Dete
- **Bulawayo**
- Somabhula
- Rutenga
- Beitbridge
- **Messina**
- Pietersburg
- Hoedspruit

Victoria Falls
ZIMBABWE
SOUTH AFRICA

Pretoria
Nelspruit
Johannesburg
Valley of the Olifants
Klerksdorp
Kimberley
De Aar
Cape Route
Beaufort West
Worcester
Wellington
Garden Route
Cape Town
Port Elizabeth

Diagrammatic only: not to scale

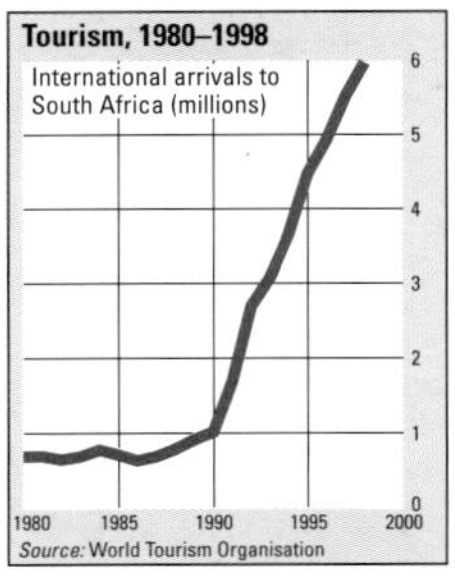

Tourism, 1980–1998

International arrivals to South Africa (millions)

1980 1985 1990 1995 2000

Source: World Tourism Organisation

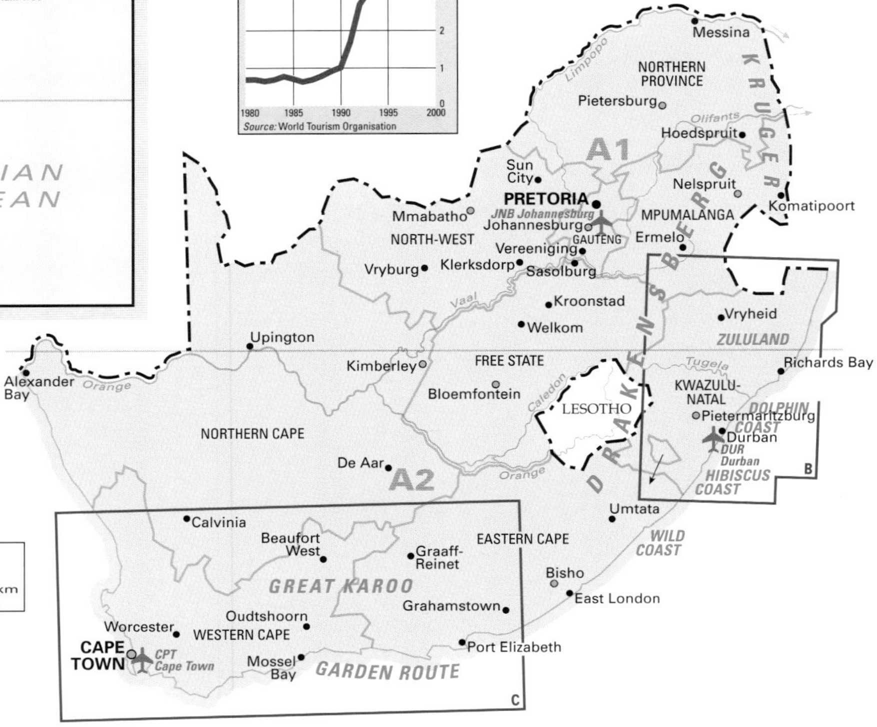

Messina
NORTHERN PROVINCE
Limpopo
KRUGER
Pietersburg
Olifants
Hoedspruit
A1
Sun City
Nelspruit
PRETORIA
Komatipoort
Mmabatho
JNB Johannesburg
Johannesburg
MPUMALANGA
NORTH-WEST
Vereeniging
GAUTENG
Ermelo
Vryburg
Klerksdorp
Sasolburg
Kroonstad
Vryheid
ZULULAND
Welkom
Upington
Richards Bay
FREE STATE
KWAZULU-NATAL
Kimberley
Pietermaritzburg
Alexander Bay
Orange
Bloemfontein
DOLPHIN COAST
LESOTHO
DUR Durban
NORTHERN CAPE
Caledon
DRAKENSBERG
HIBISCUS COAST
De Aar
Umtata
WILD COAST
A2
Orange
Calvinia
Beaufort West
Graaff-Reinet
EASTERN CAPE
Bisho
GREAT KAROO
Grahamstown
East London
Worcester
Oudtshoorn
WESTERN CAPE
CAPE TOWN
CPT Cape Town
Mossel Bay
Port Elizabeth
GARDEN ROUTE
C

— province boundary
● province capital

400 km
200 miles

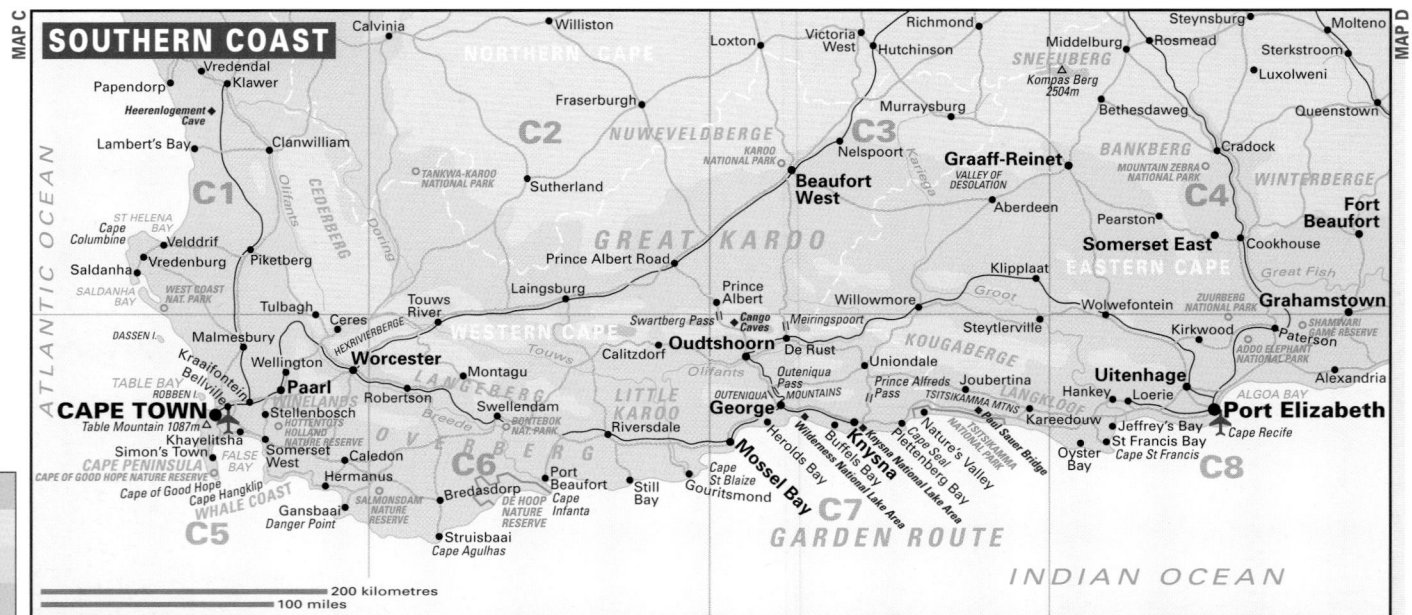

SOUTHERN COAST (MAP C)

ATLANTIC OCEAN

Calvinia
Williston
Loxton
Victoria West
Richmond
Steynsburg
Molteno

Vredendal
Klawer
NORTHERN CAPE
Hutchinson
Middelburg
Rosmead
Sterkstroom
Luxolweni

Papendorp
Heerenlogement Cave
Clanwilliam
Fraserburg
Murraysburg
SNEEUBERG
Kompas Berg 2504m
Queenstown

Lambert's Bay
C1
CEDERBERG
NUWEVELDBERGE
Nelspoort
BANKBERG
Cradock
WINTERBERG

St Helena Bay
Cape Columbine
Velddrif
TANKWA-KAROO NATIONAL PARK
Sutherland
KAROO NATIONAL PARK
Graaff-Reinet
VALLEY OF DESOLATION
MOUNTAIN ZEBRA NATIONAL PARK
Fort Beaufort

Saldanha
Vredenburg
Piketberg
Beaufort West
Aberdeen
Pearston
Somerset East
Cookhouse

SALDANHA BAY
WEST COAST NAT. PARK
C2
GREAT KAROO
Prince Albert Road
Klipplaat
EASTERN CAPE
Grahamstown
C4

DASSEN I.
Malmesbury
Tulbagh
Laingsburg
Prince Albert
Willowmore
Wolwefontein
ZUURBERG NATIONAL PARK
SHAMWARI GAME RESERVE

Kraaifontein
Ceres
HEXRIVIERBERGE
Swartberg Pass
Cango Caves
Meiringspoort
Steytlerville
Kirkwood
Paterson
ADDO ELEPHANT NATIONAL PARK

CAPE TOWN
Bellville
Worcester
Montagu
Calitzdorp
Oudtshoorn
De Rust
Olifants
KOUGABERG
LANGKLOOF
Uitenhage
Alexandria

Table Mountain 1087m
Paarl
Robertson
WESTERN CAPE
Prince Alberts Pass
Joubertina
Hankey
Loerie
Port Elizabeth
ALGOA BAY

ROBBEN I.
Stellenbosch
Swellendam
Riversdale
Outeniqua Pass
George
OUTENIQUA MOUNTAINS
TSITSIKAMMA MTNS
Nature's Valley
Cape Seal Bay
Paul Sauer Bridge
Kareedouw
Cape Recife

Khayelitsha
CAPE PENINSULA
Somerset West
Caledon
LITTLE KAROO
BONTEBOK NAT. PARK
Herolds Bay
Knysna
Plettenberg Bay
Buffels Bay
Jeffrey's Bay
St Francis Bay

Simon's Town
FALSE BAY
OVERBERG
C6
Bredasdorp
Port Beaufort
Mossel Bay
Knysna National Lake Area
TSITSIKAMMA NATIONAL PARK
Oyster Bay
Cape St Francis

Cape of Good Hope
Hangklip
Hermanus
DE HOOP NATURE RESERVE
Still Bay
Cape St Blaize
Gouritsmond
C7
WILD COAST
C8

WHALE COAST
Gansbaai
Danger Point
SALMONSDAM NATURE RESERVE
Cape Infanta
GARDEN ROUTE
Cape Agulhas
Struisbaai

2000 metres
1000 metres
Sea level

INDIAN OCEAN

200 kilometres
100 miles

THE HOLY LAND

See page 18 for general map

Crucible of ancient civilizations, harsh landscape of the Prophets of the Old Testament revered by Jew, Muslim and Christian alike, and dramatic setting for the story of Christ from his birth in Bethlehem to his crucifixion outside Jerusalem, the Holy Land is a region of monumental and complex significance – as Promised Land, place of pilgrimage and miracles and the setting for the rise and fall of empires and kingdoms.

No city symbolises this rich heritage more than Jerusalem. As the site of the ancient Temples of Judaism, so central to the ancient Jewish state, Jerusalem is the region's spiritual heart. For Christians, Jerusalem is the site of the Crucifixion, the culmination of the life of Christ. The city is also an integral part of the sacred geography of Islam, which also reveres the Old Testament Patriarchs, and is the third most sacred site in Islam after Mecca and Medina. In addition to sites of great spiritual significance, the Holy Land contains archaeological and architectural sites of immense importance.

Since the proclamation of the state of Israel in 1948, the politics of the area have been dominated by conflict between Israel and surrounding Arab states. Recent developments have offered some hope of future peace, which should herald a significant rise in the number of visitors to the region.

✡	Site significant in Judaism
✝	Site significant in Christianity
☪	Site significant in Islam
◉	Important location relating to the life of Jesus
⌂	Crusader castle or fortifications
⚜	Other important historical site
•	City of the Decapolis
DAN	The Twelve Tribes of Israel

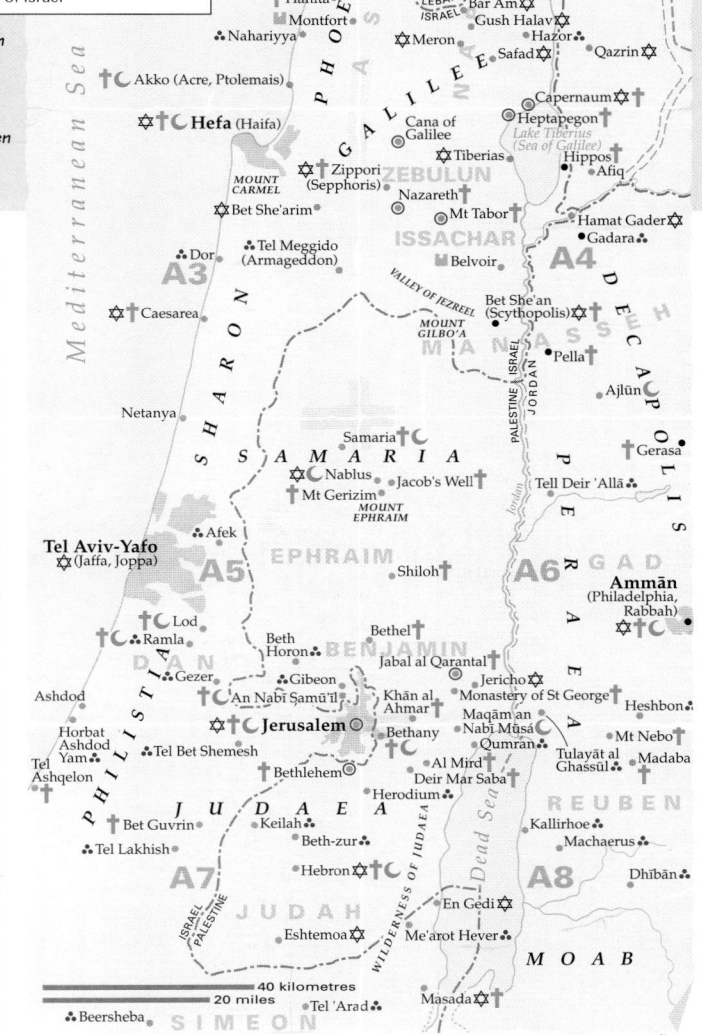

THE HOLY LAND

Present-day boundaries shown as grey lines

RED SEA DIVING

See page 18 for general map

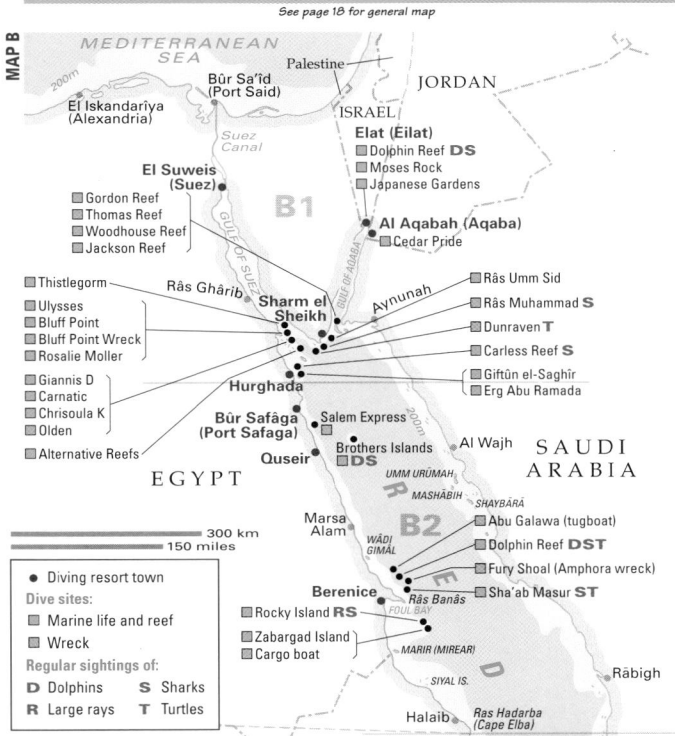

300 km
150 miles

Diving resort town (●)

Dive sites:
- ☐ Marine life and reef
- ☐ Wreck

Regular sightings of:
- **D** Dolphins
- **S** Sharks
- **R** Large rays
- **T** Turtles

This map shows the principal dive sites in the Red Sea and highlights the main diving resort towns. The three sites close to Eilat are shore dives: all other sites can be visited from the many day boats or 'live-aboard' boats which regularly ply these waters. All the resort towns marked act as bases for these boats and have equipment for hire, but most have few specialist facilities at present.

The dives are divided into those which feature an underwater wreck and those where the main focus is on the prolific marine life and the reef.

The sharks of Râs Muhammad are legendary; professional photographers and film makers travel to this site just to photograph them. Hammerheads, Reef Sharks and Oceanic White Tip Sharks are regularly sighted in the Red Sea. Manta Ray, Eagle Ray and various species of dolphin and turtle are also quite common. Whilst any of these may be seen at any time, the sites where this is a regular occurrence have been marked.

The table on the right gives the depths that divers must reach to achieve a reasonable exploration of each site: this will determine the equipment and level of experience required.

Data compiled by Ned Middleton, all rights reserved. Fax +44 (0) 1227 741819.

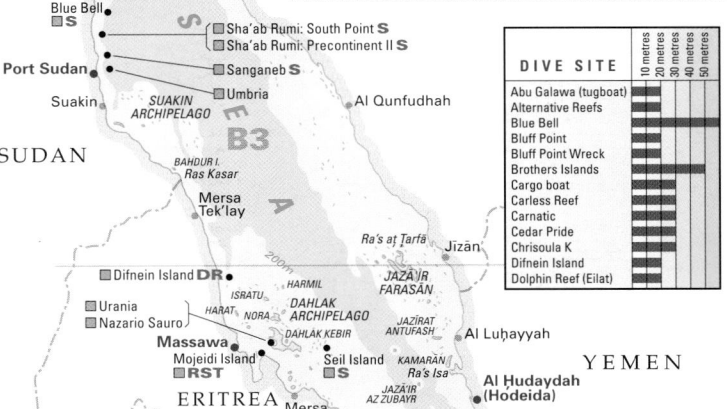

DIVE SITE	10 metres	20 metres	30 metres	40 metres	50 metres
Abu Galawa (tugboat)					
Alternative Reefs					
Blue Bell					
Bluff Point					
Bluff Point Wreck					
Brothers Islands					
Cargo boat					
Carless Reef					
Carnatic					
Cedar Pride					
Chrisoula K					
Difnein Island					
Dolphin Reef (Eilat)					

DIVE SITE	10 metres	20 metres	30 metres	40 metres	50 metres
Dolphin Reef (Berenice)					
Dunraven					
Erg Abu Ramada					
Fury Shoal (Amphora wreck)					
Giannis D					
Giftûn el-Saghîr					
Gordon Reef					
Jackson Reef					
Japanese Gardens					
Mojeidi Island					
Moses Rock					
Nazario Sauro					
Kimon M					
Râs Muhammad					
Râs Umm Sid					
Rocky Island					
Rosalie Moller					
Salem Express					
Sanganeb					
Seil Island					
Sha'ab Masur					
Sha'ab Rumi: Precontinent II					
Sha'ab Rumi: South Point					
Thistlegorm					
Thomas Reef					
Ulysses					
Umbria					
Urania					
Woodhouse Reef					
Zabargad Island					

CLIMATE

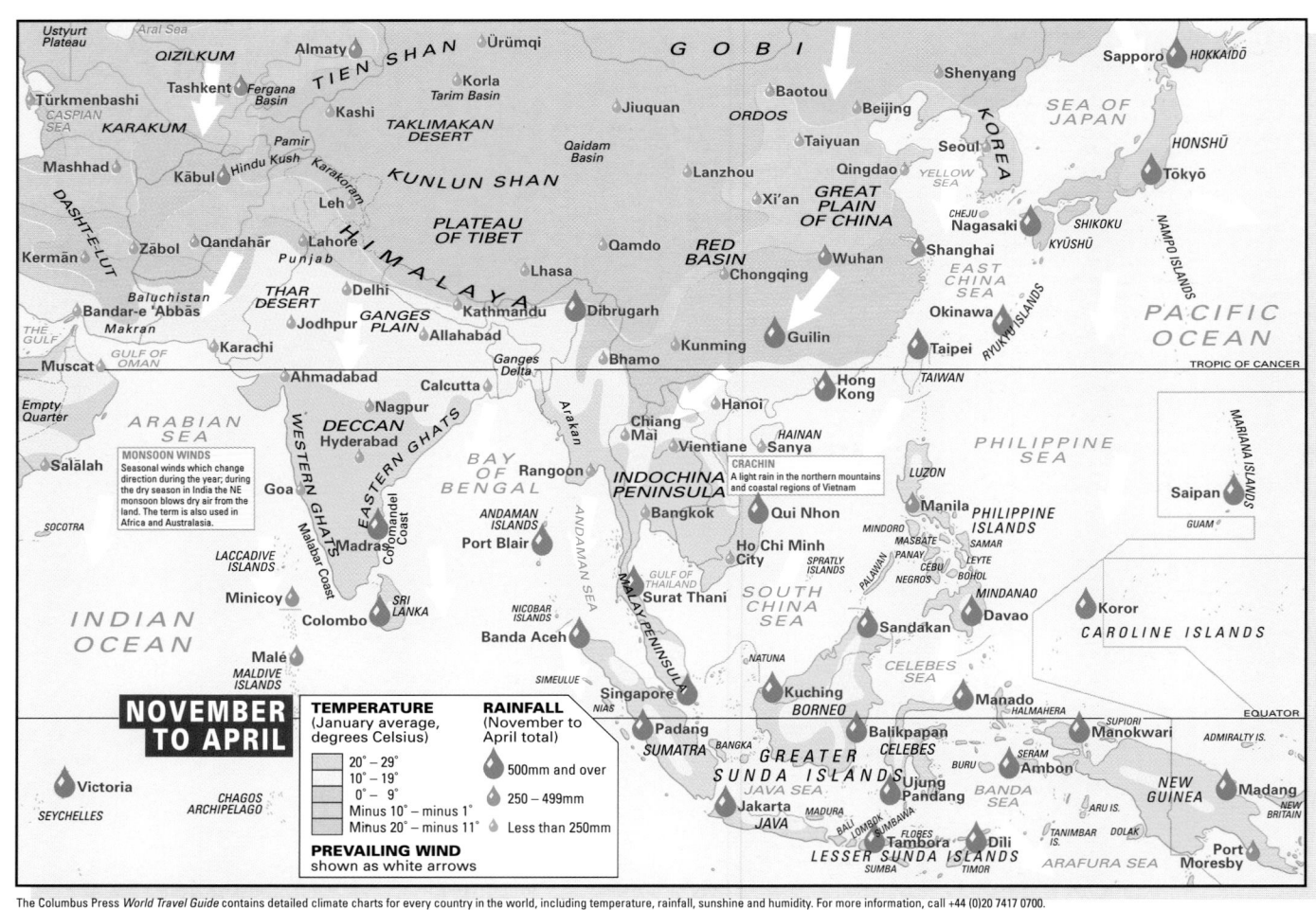

NOVEMBER TO APRIL

TEMPERATURE (January average, degrees Celsius)
- 20° – 29°
- 10° – 19°
- 0° – 9°
- Minus 10° – minus 1°
- Minus 20° – minus 11°

RAINFALL (November to April total)
- 500mm and over
- 250 – 499mm
- Less than 250mm

PREVAILING WIND shown as white arrows

MONSOON WINDS
Seasonal winds which change direction during the year; during the dry season in India the NE monsoon blows dry air from the land. The term is also used in Africa and Australasia.

CRACHIN
A light rain in the northern mountains and coastal regions of Vietnam

The Columbus Press *World Travel Guide* contains detailed climate charts for every country in the world, including temperature, rainfall, sunshine and humidity. For more information, call +44 (0)20 7417 0700.

MAY TO OCTOBER

TEMPERATURE (July average, degrees Celsius)
- 30° and over
- 20° – 29°
- 10° – 19°
- 0° – 9°
- Minus 10° – minus 1°

RAINFALL (May to October total)
- 500mm and over
- 250 – 499mm
- Less than 250mm

PREVAILING WIND shown as white arrows

MONSOON WINDS
Seasonal winds which change direction during the year; during the wet season in India the SW monsoon blows humid air from the ocean. The term is also used in Africa and Australasia.

KHARIF
The rainy season in northern India and Arab countries

INDIA

See page 28 for general map

PALACE ON WHEELS

The Palace on Wheels is a luxury train service linking Delhi and Agra with a number of historic cities in Rajasthan. Following its success, a number of other similar services are now in preparation. The first of these, the Royal Orient, entered service in 1995.

Delhi • Jaipur • Agra • Bharatpur • Jaisalmer • Jodhpur • Sawai Madhopur • Udaipur • Chittaurgarh

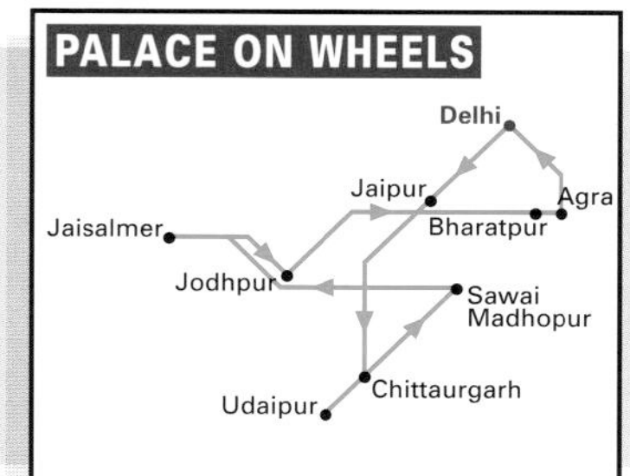

ROYAL ORIENT

Delhi • Jaipur • Chittaurgarh • Udaipur • Ahmadabad • Sarkhej • Junagadh • Palitana • Sasan Gir • Veraval & Somnath • Ahmedpur-Mandvi & Diu

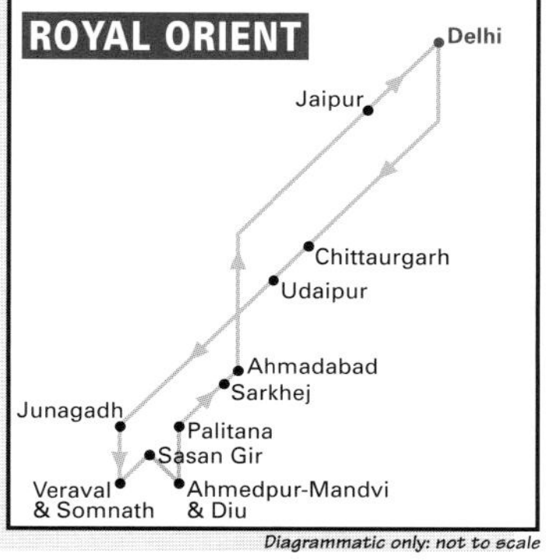

Diagrammatic only: not to scale

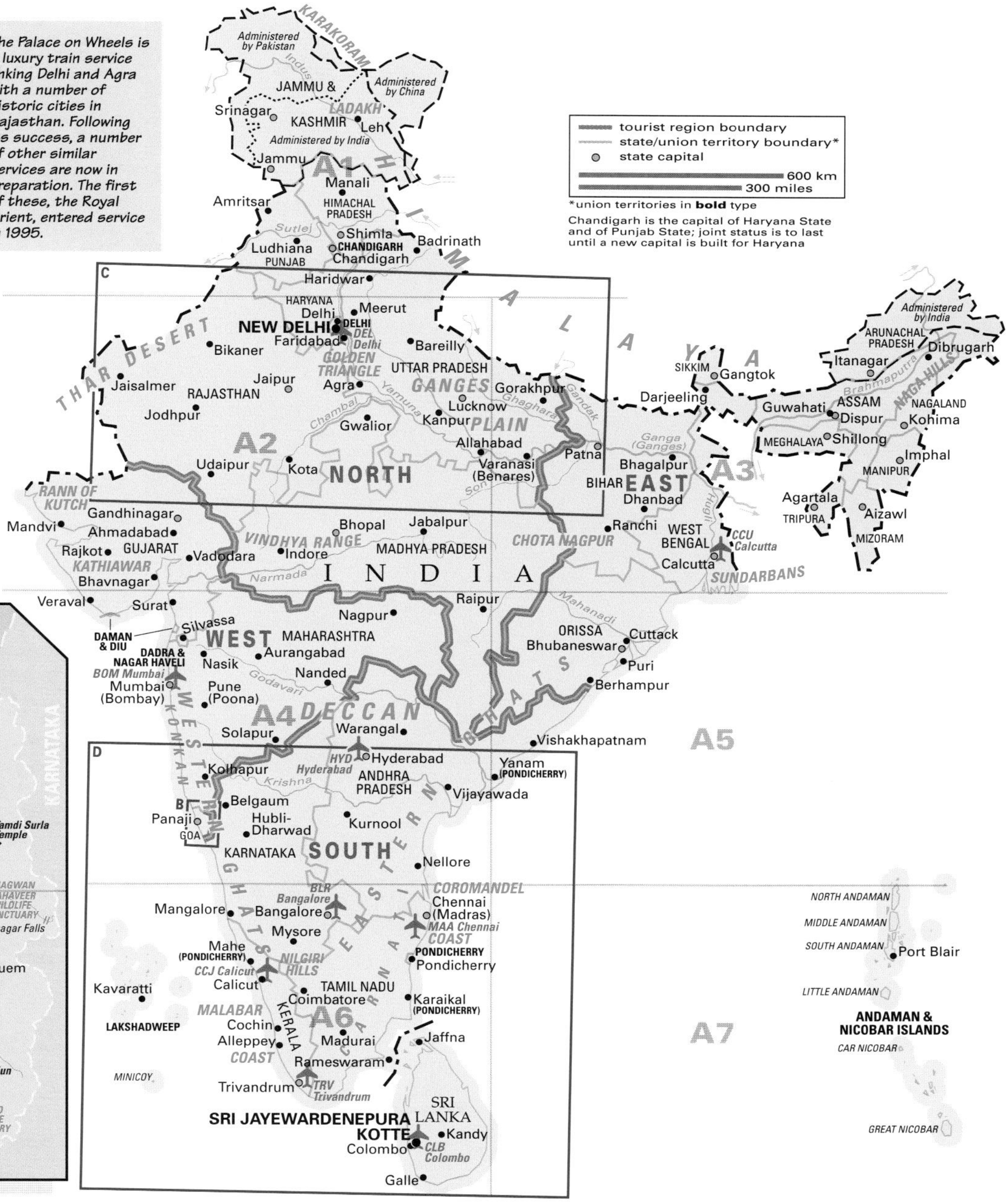

GOA BEACHES

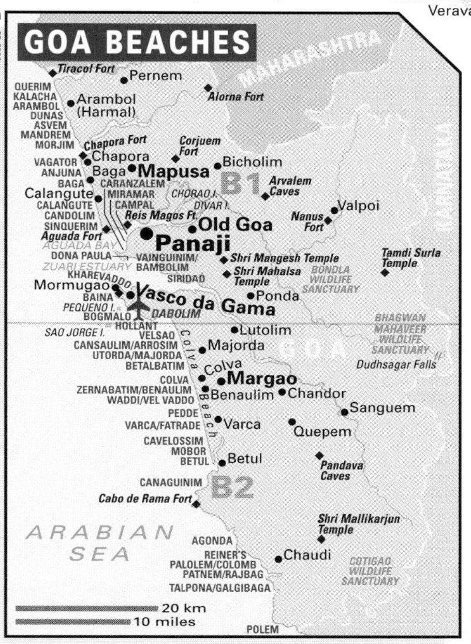

MAHARASHTRA · KARNATAKA · GOA · ARABIAN SEA

Tiracol Fort, Pernem, Querim, Kalacha, Arambol (Harmal), Dunas, Asvem, Mandrem, Morjim, Chapora Fort, Corjuem Fort, Alorna Fort, Vagator, Anjuna, Baga, Chapora, Mapusa, Bicholim, Calangute, Candolim, Sinquerim, Arvalem Caves, Valpoi, Miramar, Campal, Reis Magos Ft., Aguada Fort, Aguada Bay, Dona Paula, Old Goa, Panaji, Shri Mangesh Temple, Shri Mahalsa Temple, Ponda, Mormugao, Vasco da Gama, Dabolim, Bhagwan Mahaveer Wildlife Sanctuary, Bondla Wildlife Sanctuary, Tamdi Surla Temple, Dudhsagar Falls, Lutolim, Majorda, Colva, Margao, Benaulim, Chandor, Sanguem, Varca, Quepem, Betul, Pandava Caves, Cabo de Rama Fort, Chaudi, Shri Mallikarjun Temple, Agonda, Reiner's, Palolem/Colomb, Patnem/Rajbag, Talpona/Galgibaga, Cotigao Wildlife Sanctuary, Polem

ARABIAN SEA

20 km / 10 miles

CENTRAL NORTH INDIA

PAKISTAN · THAR DESERT · RAJASTHAN · HARYANA · UTTAR PRADESH · NEPAL · CHINA · BIHAR · MADHYA PRADESH

Selected cities: Delhi, NEW DELHI, Faridabad, Meerut, Jaipur, Jodhpur, Agra, Gwalior, Kanpur (Cawnpore), Lucknow, Allahabad, Varanasi (Benares), Gorakhpur, Patna, KATHMANDU

300 kilometres / 150 miles

1000 metres / 500 metres / Sea level

Legend

— tourist region boundary
— state/union territory boundary*
○ state capital

600 km / 300 miles

*union territories in **bold** type
Chandigarh is the capital of Haryana State and of Punjab State; joint status is to last until a new capital is built for Haryana

Main map labels

KARAKORAM, Administered by Pakistan, JAMMU & KASHMIR, LADAKH, Administered by China, Srinagar, Leh, Administered by India, Jammu, HIMALAYA, Manali, Amritsar, HIMACHAL PRADESH, Ludhiana, CHANDIGARH, Badrinath, PUNJAB, Haridwar, HARYANA, Meerut, NEW DELHI, DELHI, Bareilly, Bikaner, Faridabad, GOLDEN TRIANGLE, UTTAR PRADESH, Gorakhpur, Jaisalmer, Jaipur, Agra, Lucknow, RAJASTHAN, Kanpur, GANGES PLAIN, Jodhpur, Gwalior, Allahabad, Varanasi (Benares), Patna, BIHAR, EAST, Darjeeling, SIKKIM, Gangtok, ARUNACHAL PRADESH, Itanagar, Dibrugarh, NAGA HILLS, Guwahati, ASSAM, Dispur, NAGALAND, Kohima, MEGHALAYA, Shillong, Imphal, MANIPUR, TRIPURA, Agartala, Aizawl, MIZORAM, Udaipur, Kota, NORTH, Bhagalpur, Dhanbad, WEST BENGAL, Calcutta, CHOTA NAGPUR, Ranchi, SUNDARBANS, Gandhinagar, Ahmadabad, Mandvi, Bhopal, Jabalpur, Rajkot, Indore, MADHYA PRADESH, Cuttack, Vadodara, GUJARAT, KATHIAWAR, Bhavnagar, Surat, VINDHYA RANGE, Narmada, Raipur, ORISSA, Bhubaneswar, Puri, Veraval, DAMAN & DIU, DADRA & NAGAR HAVELI, Silvassa, WEST, Nagpur, Berhampur, Mumbai (Bombay), MAHARASHTRA, Aurangabad, Nanded, Vishakhapatnam, Nasik, Pune (Poona), DECCAN, Warangal, Solapur, Kolhapur, HYDERABAD, ANDHRA PRADESH, Yanam (PONDICHERRY), Belgaum, Hubli-Dharwad, Vijayawada, Kurnool, Nellore, KARNATAKA, SOUTH, Panaji, GOA, Mangalore, Bangalore, Chennai (Madras), COROMANDEL COAST, Mysore, PONDICHERRY, Kavaratti, LAKSHADWEEP, Mahe (PONDICHERRY), Calicut, NILGIRI HILLS, Coimbatore, TAMIL NADU, Karaikal (PONDICHERRY), MALABAR COAST, Cochin, KERALA, Madurai, Jaffna, MINICOY, Alleppey, Rameswaram, Trivandrum, SRI LANKA, SRI JAYEWARDENEPURA KOTTE, Colombo, Kandy, Galle

ANDAMAN & NICOBAR ISLANDS: NORTH ANDAMAN, MIDDLE ANDAMAN, SOUTH ANDAMAN, Port Blair, LITTLE ANDAMAN, CAR NICOBAR, GREAT NICOBAR

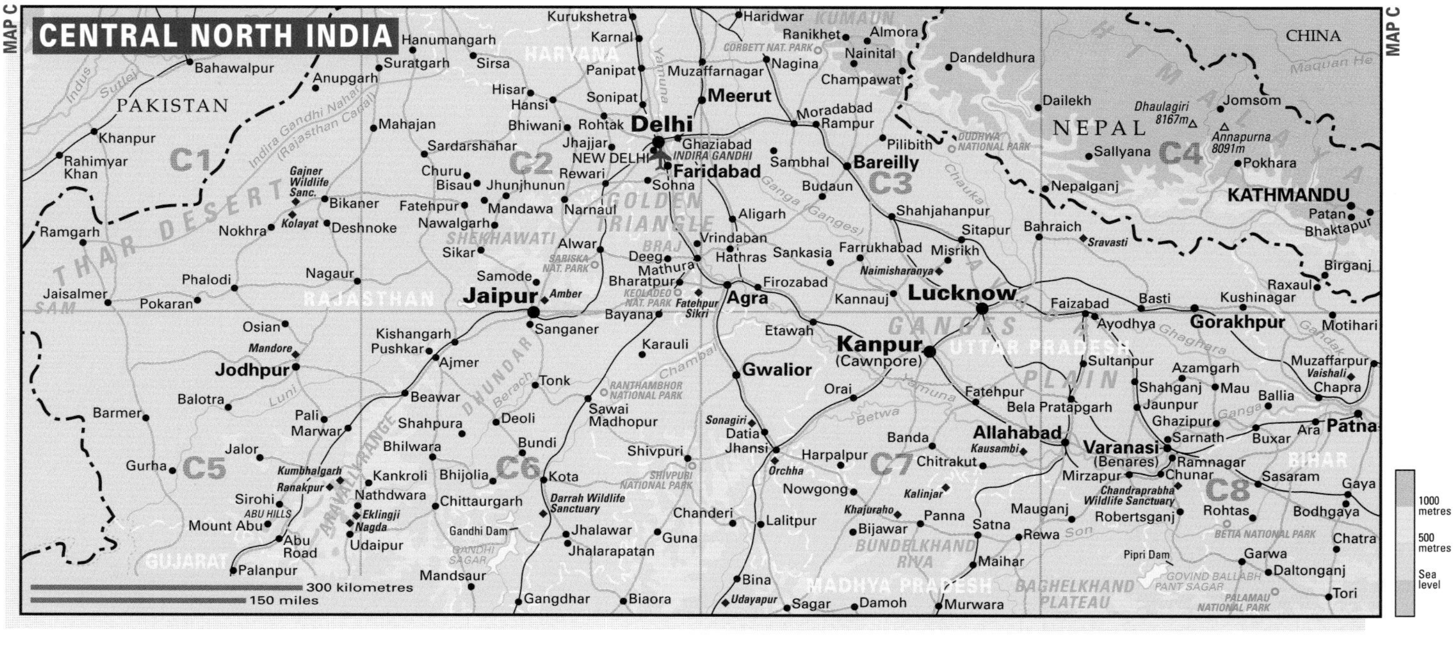

INDIA SRI LANKA MALDIVES
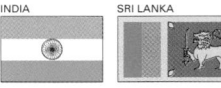

INDIA AND SRI LANKA

See page 28 for general map

SOUTH INDIA AND SRI LANKA

MAP D   MAP D

D1   D2   D3   D4

D5   D6   D7   D8

D9   D10   D11   D12

D13   D14   D15   D16

ARABIAN SEA

BAY OF BENGAL

INDIAN OCEAN

Selected labels

Ratnagiri, Panhala, Vijayadurg, Kolhapur, Sangli, Miraj, Malwan, Sawantwadi, Panaji, Margao, GOA, Karwar, Gokarn, Honavar, Kundapura, Udupi, Mangalore, Kasaragod, Bekal, Cannanore, Mahe, Calicut, Guruvayur, Trichur, Kodungallur, Ernakulam, **Cochin**, Mattancheri, Kottayam, Alleppey, Quilon, Varkala, **Trivandrum**, Kovalam, Ponmudi

Bijapur, Belgaum, Dharwad, **Hubli**, Gadag, Savanur, Badami, Pattadakal, Aihole, Hospet, Hampi (Vijayanagar), Sandur, Bellary, Anantapur, Davangere, Chitradurga, Shimoga, Bhadravati, Halebid, Belur, Hassan, Sravanabelgola, **Bangalore**, Mysore, Srirangapatnam, Somnathpur, Madikeri, KODAGU (COORG)

Secunderabad, **Hyderabad**, Gulbarga, Wadi, Mahbubnagar, Raichur, Lingsugur, Kurnool, Nandyal, Adoni, Guntakal, Gooty, Banaganapalle, Penukonda, Hindupur, Tumkur, Kolar, Kolar Gold Fields, Puttaparthy, Cuddapah, Nellore, Gudur

Sangareddy, Nalgonda, Kammam, Vijayavada, Guntur, Tenali, Machilipatnam, Eluru, Rajahmundry, Kakinada, Yanam, Bheemavaram, Amaravati, Srisailam, Vinukonda, Ongole, Kavali, Srikalahasti, Tirupati, Tirumala, Chandragiri, Chittoor, Vellore, **Chennai** (Madras), Kanchipuram, Mahabalipuram (Mamallapuram)

Horsley Hills, Tirupati, Auroville, Pondicherry, Cuddalore, Chidambaram, Gangaikondacholapuram, Neyveli, Salem, Yercaud, Erode, Tiruppur, **Coimbatore**, Pollachi, Palani, Dindigul, Kodaikanal, Munnar, **Madurai**, Rajapalaiyam, Tuticorin, Tirunelveli, Cape Comorin, Kanniyakumari, Nagercoil, Padmanabhapuram

Rameswaram, Mannar, Vavuniya, Jaffna, Kankesanturai, Mullaittivu, Nilaveli, Trincomalee, **SRI LANKA**, Anuradhapura, Puttalam, Habarane, Sigiriya, Polonnaruwa, Kalkudah, Batticaloa, Kurunegala, Matale, Kandy, Dambulla Golden Rock Temple, Pidurutalagala 2524m, Negombo, Hendala, Adam's Peak 2243m, Nuwara Eliya, Badulla, Pottuvil, **Colombo**, Dehiwala-Mount Lavinia, Moratuwa, Kalutara, Beruwala, Bentota, Ahungalla & Induruwa, Hikkaduwa, Galle, Dondra Head, Matara, Tangalla, Hambantota, **SRI JAYEWARDENEPURA KOTTE**

PALK STRAIT, PALK BAY, ADAM'S BRIDGE, GULF OF MANNAR, NINE DEGREE CHANNEL, EIGHT DEGREE CHANNEL, LAKSHADWEEP SEA, LAKSHADWEEP, Kavaratti, MINICOY I.

Tourism chart

Tourism, 1980–1998
International arrivals (millions)
India, Sri Lanka, Maldives
2.5, 2.0, 1.5, 1.0, 0.5, 0
1980, 1985, 1990, 1995, 2000
Source: World Tourism Organisation

Scale

1000 metres, 500 metres, Sea level
400 kilometres / 200 miles

HILL STATIONS AND BEACH RESORTS

MAP E

▲ hill station
● beach resort

600 km / 300 miles

JAMMU & KASHMIR, Srinagar, Sonamarg, Gulmarg, Leh, Pahalgam, KASH., Batote, Chamba, Dalhousie, Keylong, Manali, Dharamsala, Kangra, Kulu, H. PRAD., Kufri, Shimla, Nahan, Paonta Sahib, PUNJAB, CHANDIGARH, Dehra Dun, Mussoorie, HARYANA, Lansdowne, Almora, Nainital, Ranikhet, DELHI, RAJASTHAN, UTTAR PRADESH, Mount Abu, GUJARAT, Dwarka, Porbandar, Chorwad, Somnath, Veraval, Diu, Ahmedpur-Mandvi, Champaner, Dumas, Hajira, Ubarat, DAMAN & DIU, Saputara, DADRA & NAGAR HAVELI, MAHARASHTRA, MADHYA PRADESH, Pachmarhi, Netarhat, BIHAR, Juhu Beach, Manori, Marve, Murud, Matheran, Lonavala, Mahabaleshwar, Panchgani, Panhala, Goa, GOA, KARNATAKA, ANDHRA PRADESH, Puri, Gopalpur-on-Sea, Bheemunipatnam, ORISSA, WEST BENGAL, Darjeeling, Kalimpong, Mirik, SIKKIM, Gangtok, Shillong, ASSAM, MEGHALAYA, NAGALAND, MANIPUR, TRIPURA, MIZORAM, ARUNACHAL PRADESH, Digha, Machilipatnam, Manginipudi, Maipadu, Covelong, Mahabalipuram (Mamallapuram), Horsley Hills, Mangalore, Ullal, Mercara, Yercaud, PONDICHERRY, Cannanore, Mahe, Udagamandalam (Ootacamund Ooty), Coonoor, Kotagiri, Kodaikanal, Munnar, LAKSHADWEEP, KERALA, TAMIL NADU, Quilon, Varkala, Ponmudi, Kovalam, Tiruchendur, Rameswaram, Kanniyakumari, ANDAMAN & NICOBAR IS.

E1, E2, E3, E4

INDIAN OCEAN

See page 28 for general map

MAP F

MALDIVES

IHAVANDIFFULU ATOLL, TILADUMMATI-MILADUMMADULU ATOLL, MAKUNUDU ATOLL, FADIFFOLU ATOLL, MALOSMADULU ATOLL NORTH, MALOSMADULU ATOLL SOUTH, GOIFULHA FEHENDHU, KARIDU ATOLL, RASDHU ATOLL, MALÉ ATOLL, **MALÉ**, ARI ATOLL, Kuramathi, Nika, Fesdu Fun I., Angaga, Alimatha, FELIDU ATOLL, NILANDU ATOLL NORTH, NILANDU ATOLL SOUTH, MULAKU ATOLL, KOLUMADULU ATOLL, HADDUMMATI ATOLL, SUVADIVA ATOLL, EQUATORIAL CHANNEL, FUAH MULAH ATOLL, Gan, ADDU ATOLL

GAAFARU ATOLL, Helengeli, Eriyadu, Makunudhoo, Ziyaaraiyfushi, Reethi Rah, Asdhu Sun I., Meerufenfushi, Hembadoo, Dhiffushi, Boduhithi Coral Isle, Kudahithi, Thulusdhu, Nakatchafushi, Gasfinolhu, Lhohifushi, Hura, Kanifinolhu, Vabbinfaru, Thulhagiri, Little Hura & Leisure I., Ihuru, Hudhuveli & Lankanfinolhu, Baros, Bandos, Furana (Full Moon), Farukolhufushi, NORTH MALÉ ATOLL, Kurumba, **HUDHUVELI**, **MALÉ ATOLL**, Giravaru, Villingili Beach, Vaadhu Diving Paradise, Velassaru, Bolifushi, Embudhu, Embudhu Finolhu, Dhigufinolhu, Veligandu Huraa, Biyadoo, Villivaru, Cocoa I., Guradu & Kandooma, SOUTH MALÉ ATOLL, Gulhi, **Maafushi**, Rannalhi, Fihalhohi, Olhuveli, Bodufinolhu (Fun I.), Rihiveli Beach

F1, F2, F3, F4

200 km / 100 miles
30 km / 15 miles

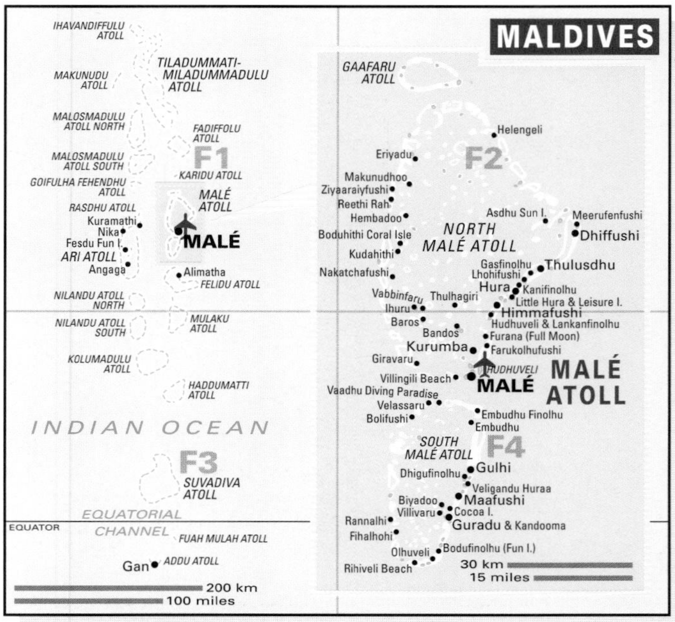

CHINA

See pages 28, 29 & 31 for general maps

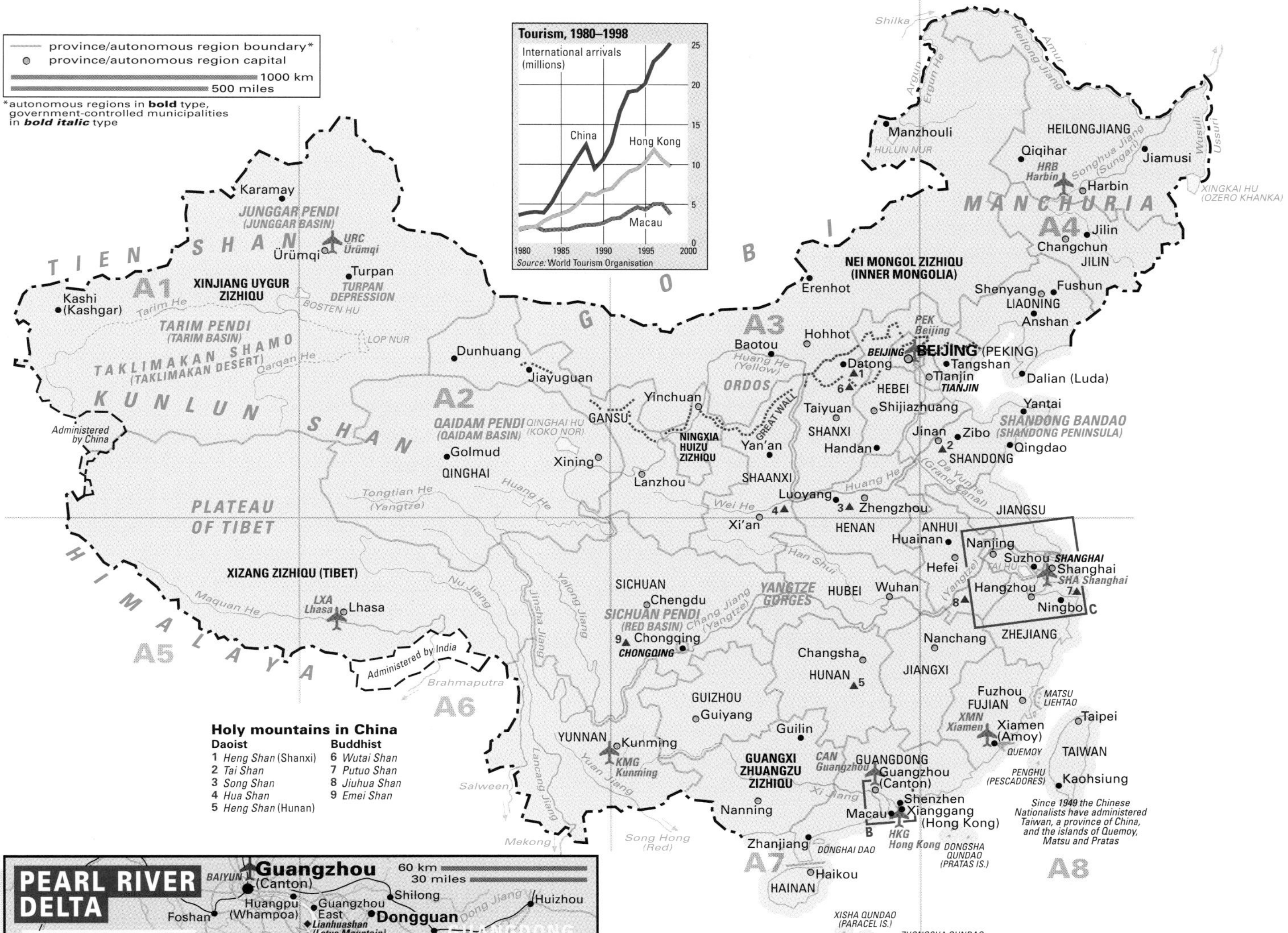

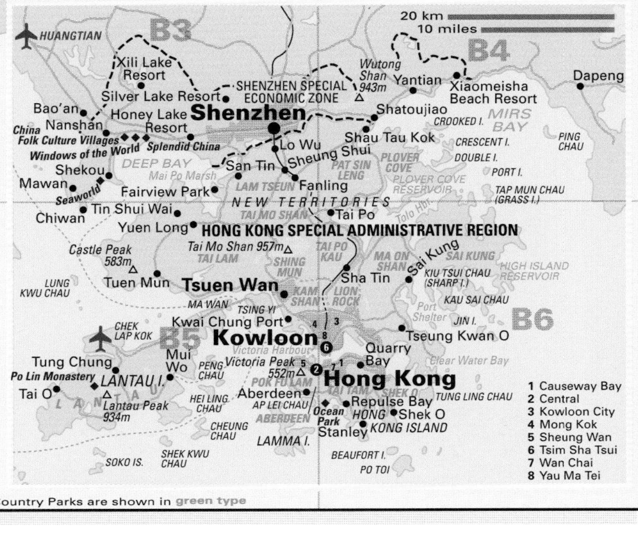

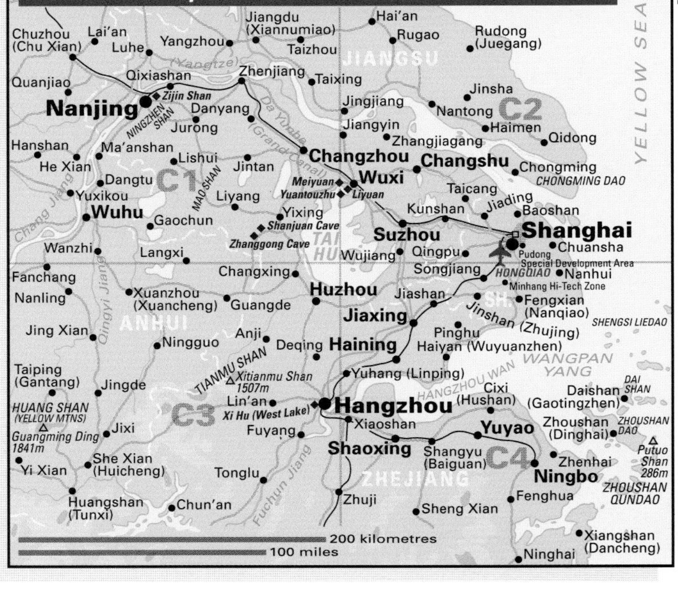

JAPAN

See page 30 for general map

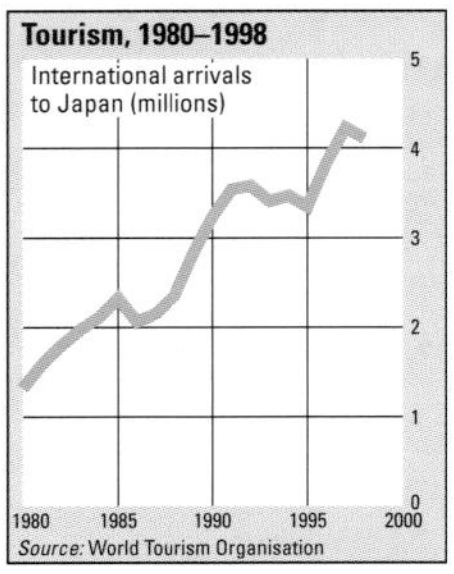

Tourism, 1980–1998

International arrivals to Japan (millions)

Source: World Tourism Organisation

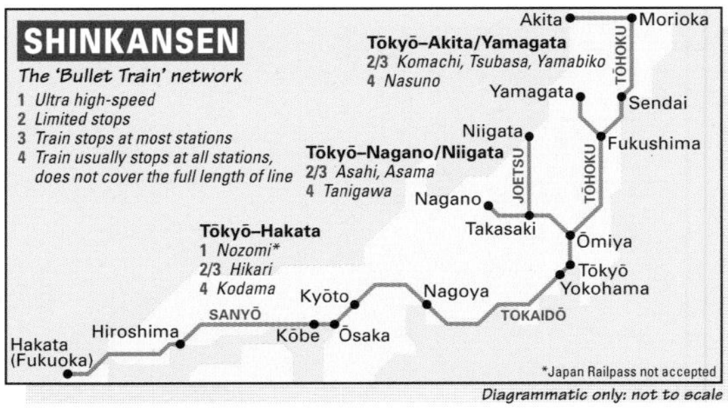

SHINKANSEN

The 'Bullet Train' network
1 Ultra high-speed
2 Limited stops
3 Train stops at most stations
4 Train usually stops at all stations, does not cover the full length of line

Tōkyō–Akita/Yamagata
2/3 Komachi, Tsubasa, Yamabiko
4 Nasuno

Tōkyō–Nagano/Niigata
2/3 Asahi, Asama
4 Tanigawa

Tōkyō–Hakata
1 Nozomi*
2/3 Hikari
4 Kodama

*Japan Railpass not accepted

Diagrammatic only: not to scale

Akita · Morioka · Yamagata · Sendai · Fukushima · Niigata · Nagano · Takasaki · Ōmiya · Tōkyō · Yokohama · Nagoya · Kyōto · Ōsaka · Kōbe · Hiroshima · Hakata (Fukuoka)

TOHOKU · JOETSU · TOKAIDO · SANYO

TOP JAPANESE THEME PARKS IN 1998

Number of visitors (world ranking in brackets)
Tokyo Disneyland Chiba: 16.7 million (1st)
Yokohama Hakkeijima Sea Paradise Kanagawa: 5.7 million (12th)
Huis ten Bosch Sasebo, Nagasaki: 4.1 million (16th)
Suzuka Circuit Mie: 3.2 million (22nd)
Nagashima Spa Land Mie: 3.2 million (23rd)
Toshimaen Tokyo: 2.5 million (40th)
Parque Espana Shima, Mie: 2.5 million (43rd)
Takarazuka Family Land Hyogo: 2.4 million (46th)
Space World Fukuoka: 2.2 million (50th)

Source: Amusement Business

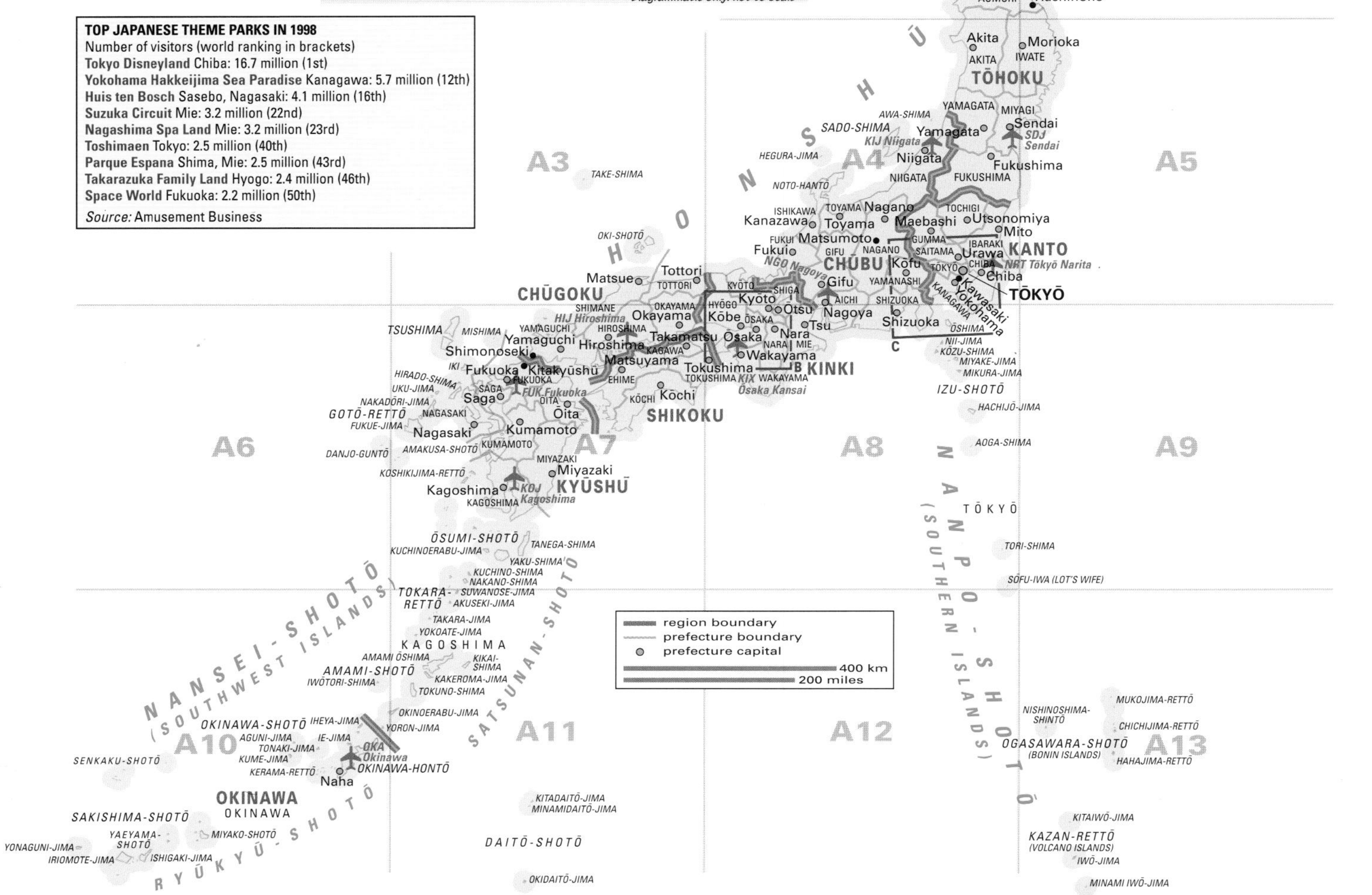

HOKKAIDŌ · Asahikawa · Sapporo · Muroran · Hakodate · Aomori · Hachinohe · Akita · Morioka · Yamagata · Sendai · Niigata · Fukushima · Kanazawa · Toyama · Nagano · Maebashi · Utsunomiya · Mito · Matsumoto · Fukui · Kōfu · Urawa · Chiba · TŌKYŌ · Kawasaki · Yokohama · Gifu · Nagoya · Shizuoka · Matsue · Tottori · Okayama · Kyōto · Kōbe · Ōsaka · Ōtsu · Nara · Wakayama · Yamaguchi · Hiroshima · Takamatsu · Tokushima · Matsuyama · Kōchi · Kitakyūshū · Fukuoka · Saga · Ōita · Nagasaki · Kumamoto · Miyazaki · Kagoshima · Naha

REBUN-TŌ · RISHIRI-TŌ · ETOROFU-TŌ · *Administered by Russian Federation* · KUNASHIRI-TŌ · SHIKOTAN-TŌ · HABOMAI-SHOTŌ · OKUSHIRI-TŌ · ŌSHIMA · SHIMOKITA-HANTŌ

HOKKAIDŌ · TŌHOKU · HONSHŪ · CHŪBU · KANTŌ · KINKI · CHŪGOKU · SHIKOKU · KYŪSHŪ

PACIFIC OCEAN · NANPŌ-SHOTŌ (SOUTHERN ISLANDS) · IZU-SHOTŌ · OGASAWARA-SHOTŌ (BONIN ISLANDS) · KAZAN-RETTŌ (VOLCANO ISLANDS)

NANSEI-SHOTŌ (SOUTHWEST ISLANDS) · SATSUNAN-SHOTŌ · RYŪKYŪ-SHOTŌ · OKINAWA · SAKISHIMA-SHOTŌ · YAEYAMA-SHOTŌ

region boundary
prefecture boundary
○ prefecture capital
400 km
200 miles

ŌSAKA–KYŌTO–KŌBE

MAP B

Kyoto · Ōtsu · Kōbe · Ōsaka · Higashi-ōsaka · Sakai · Amagasaki · Himeji · Wakayama · Kyoto · Otsu · Kusatsu · Moriyama · Uji · Hirakata · Nara · Tenri · Kashihara · Tondabayashi · Kaizuka · Izumi · Izumiōtsu · Kishiwada · Misaki · Sumoto · Naruto · Tokushima · Komatsushima · Kainan · Arida · Shimizu

HYOGO · KYOTO · SHIGA · OSAKA · NARA · WAKAYAMA

1000 metres · 500 metres · Sea level

40 km
20 miles

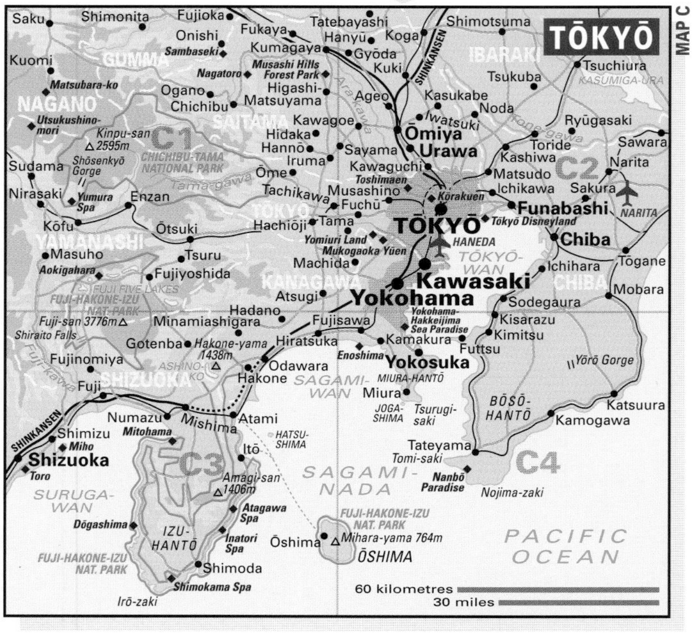

TŌKYŌ

MAP C

TŌKYŌ · Omiya · Urawa · Funabashi · Chiba · Kawasaki · Yokohama · Yokosuka · Shizuoka · Numazu · Mishima · Atami · Ito · Odawara · Hiratsuka · Fujisawa · Kamakura · Hachiōji · Hanno · Kawagoe · Ageo · Kasukabe · Noda · Narita · Sakura · Kisarazu

GUMMA · NAGANO · SAITAMA · IBARAKI · YAMANASHI · TŌKYŌ · KANAGAWA · SHIZUOKA · CHIBA

Tōkyō Disneyland · Yomiuri Land · Toshimaen · Korakuen · Yokohama Hakkeijima Sea Paradise · Nara Dreamland · Expoland · Takarazuka Family Land · Kobe Portopia Land

PACIFIC OCEAN · SAGAMI-NADA · SAGAMI-WAN · TŌKYŌ-WAN · BŌSŌ-HANTŌ · MIURA-HANTŌ · IZU-HANTŌ · ŌSHIMA

Fuji-san 3776m △ · Mihara-yama 764m △ · Amagi-san 1406m △

FUJI-HAKONE-IZU NAT. PARK · CHICHIBU-TAMA NATIONAL PARK

60 kilometres
30 miles

INDOCHINA

See page 31 for general map

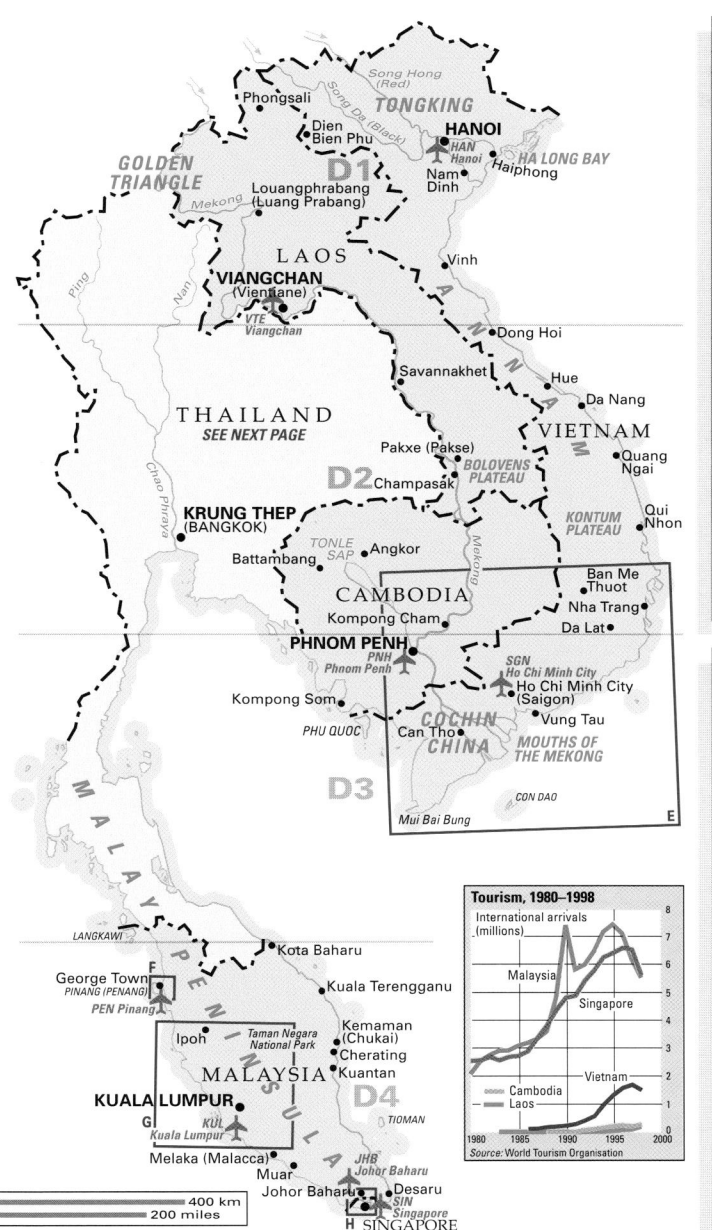

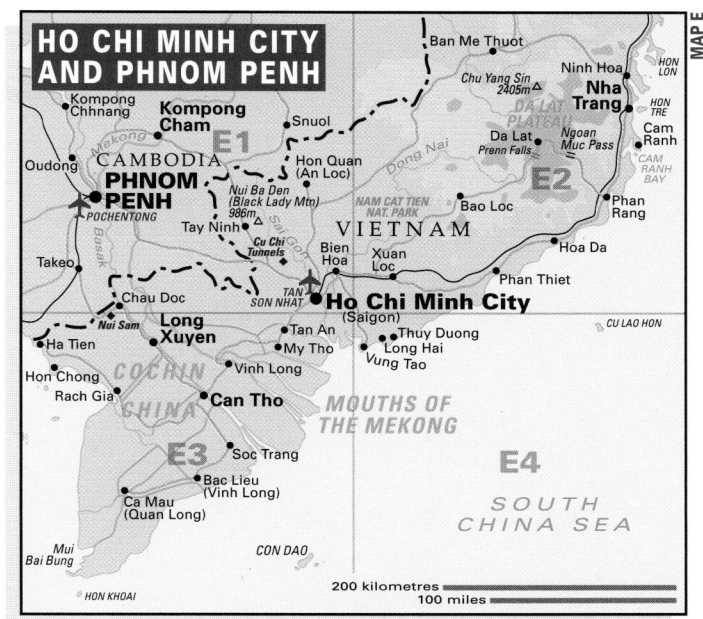

HO CHI MINH CITY AND PHNOM PENH

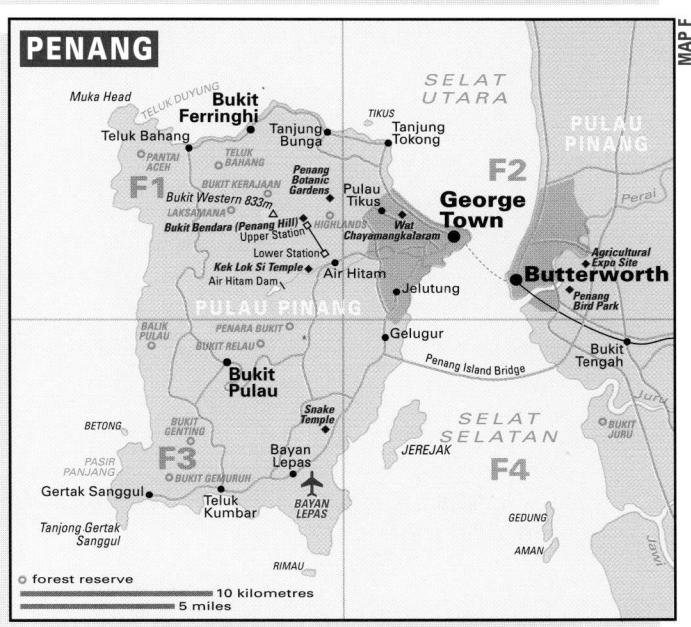

PENANG

KUALA LUMPUR

SINGAPORE

THAILAND

See page 31 for general map

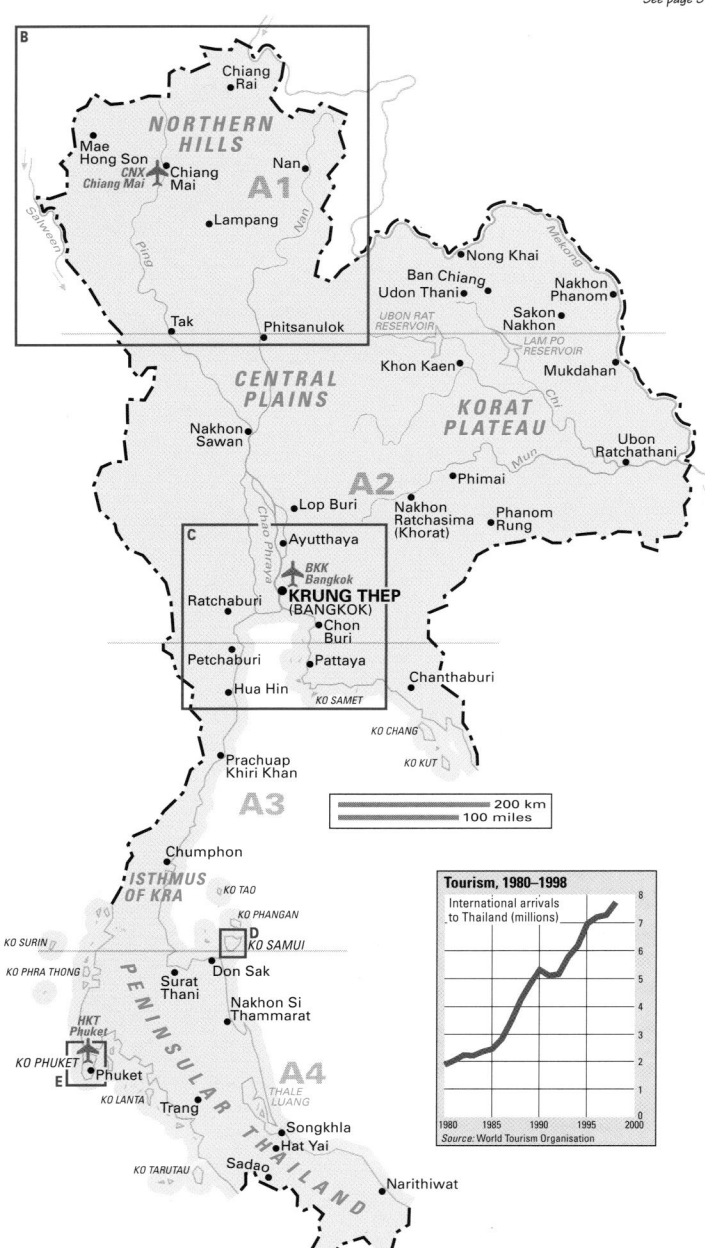

Tourism, 1980–1998

International arrivals to Thailand (millions)

Source: World Tourism Organisation

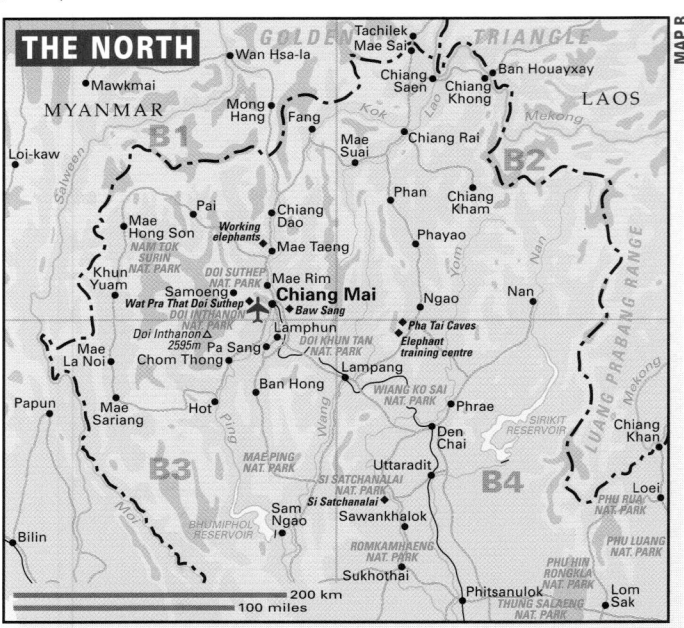

THE NORTH

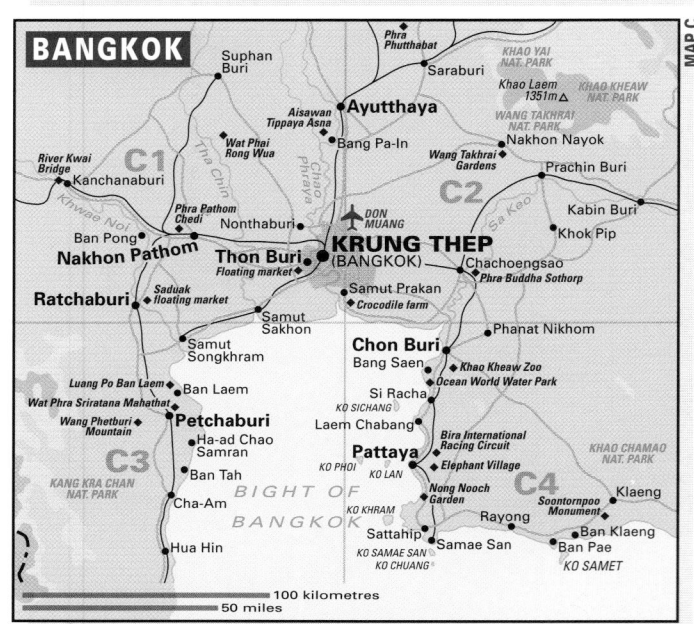

BANGKOK

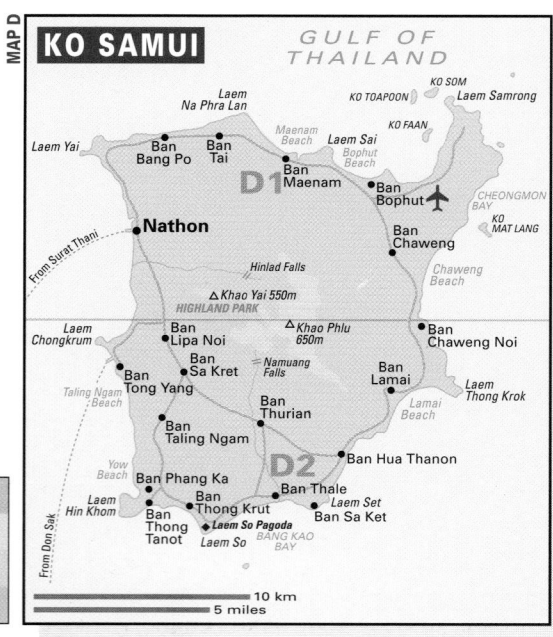

KO SAMUI

EASTERN & ORIENTAL EXPRESS

	Distance from Bangkok	
	Kilometres	Miles
Chiang Mai	751	467
Lampang	642	390
Phitsanulok	389	242
Ayutthaya	71	44
Bangkok	0	0
Kanchanaburi	(138)	(86)
Hua Hin	229	142
Hat Yai	945	587
Butterworth	1161	721
Kuala Lumpur	1552	964
Singapore	1946	1209

The Eastern & Oriental Express is a luxury train service operating on two routes. The service from Bangkok to Singapore runs twice a week throughout the year; the journey takes three days and includes guided tours of Kwai and Penang. The Bangkok–Chiang Mai overnight service operates twice a week from September to April.

KO PHUKET

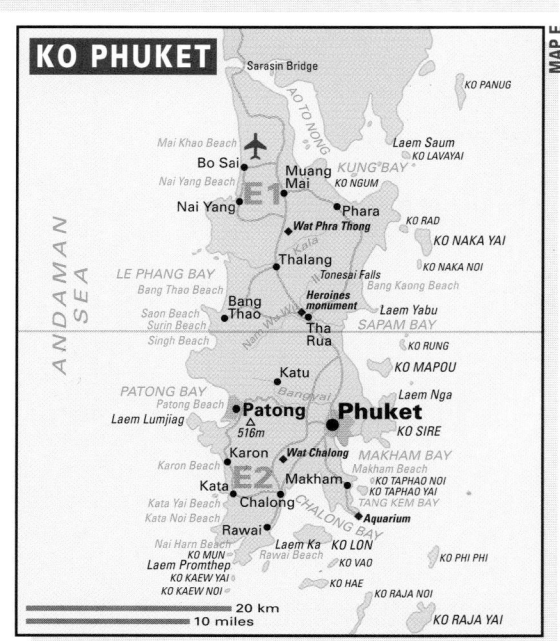

INDONESIA

See page 32 for general maps

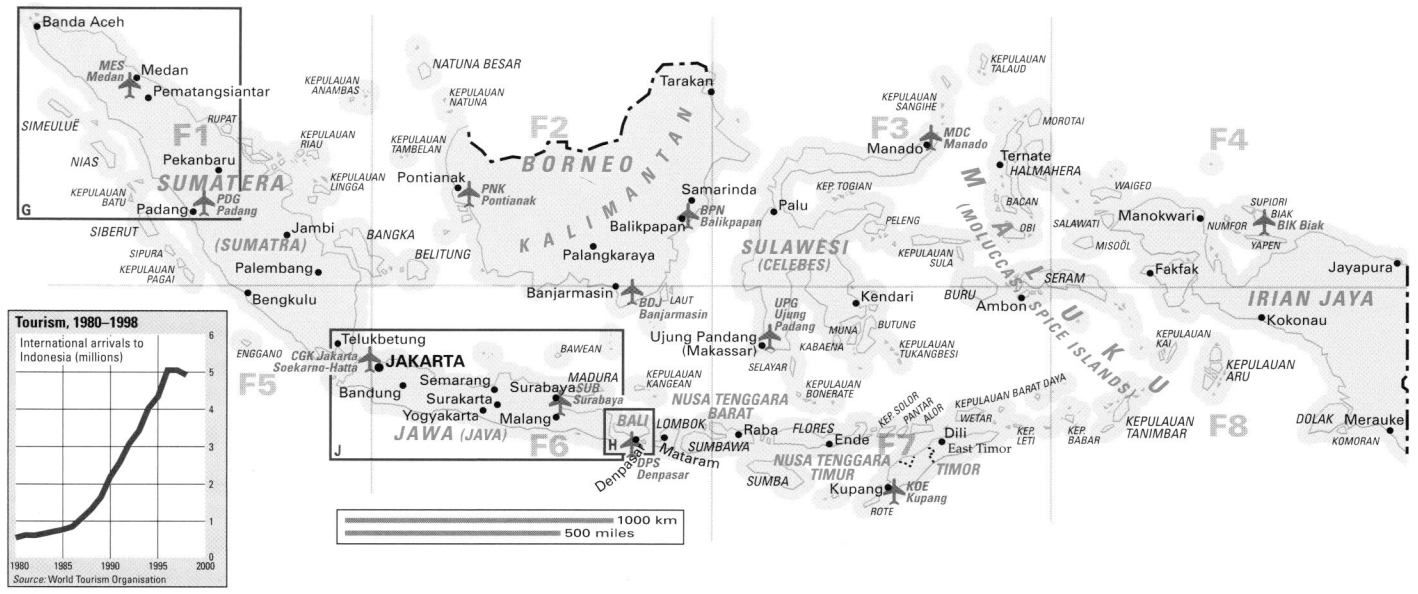

Tourism, 1980–1998
International arrivals to Indonesia (millions)
Source: World Tourism Organisation

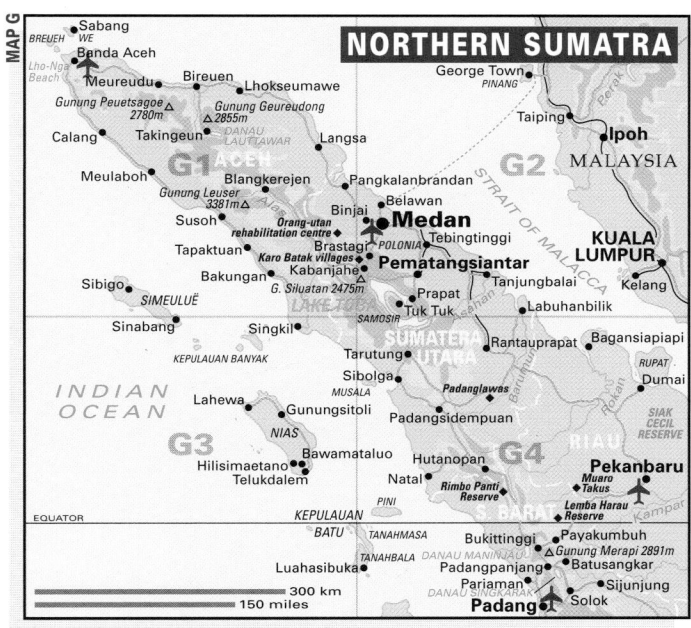

NORTHERN SUMATRA

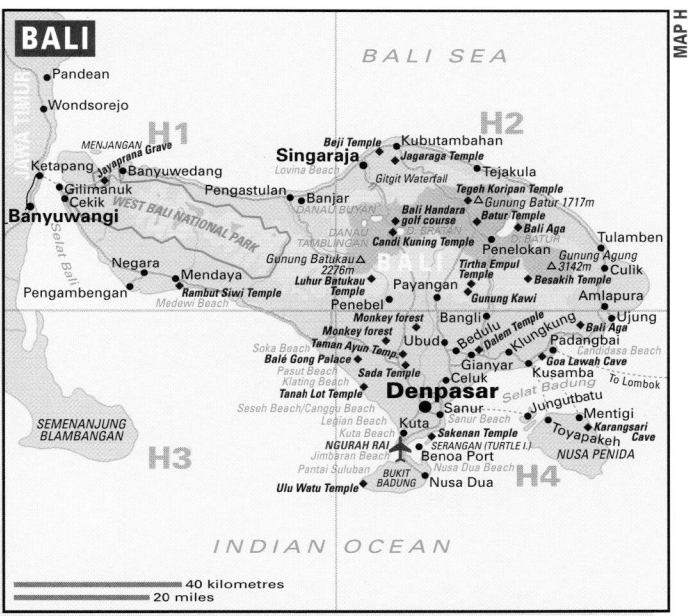

BALI

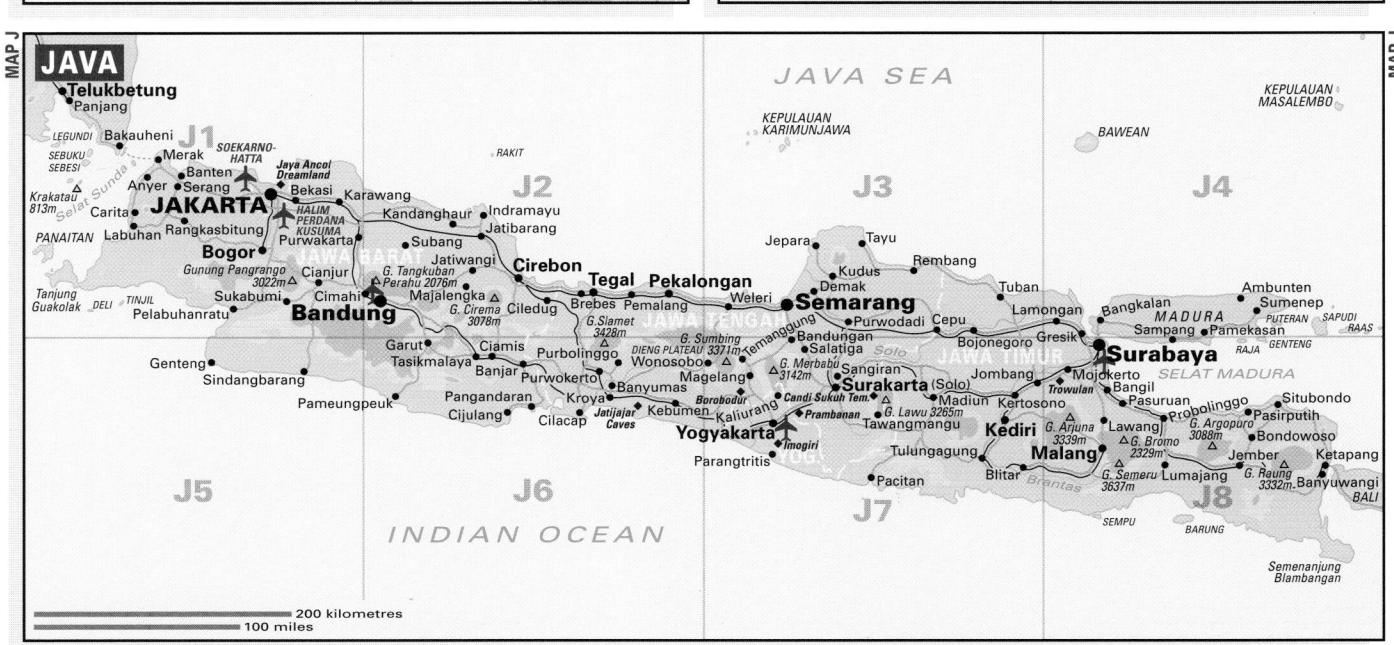

JAVA

AUSTRALIA

See page 34 for general map

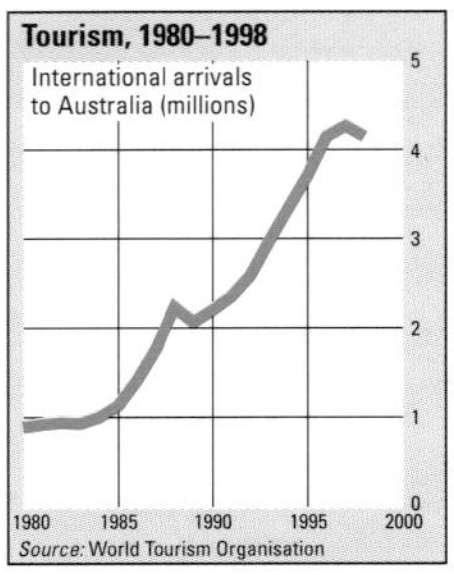

Tourism, 1980–1998
International arrivals to Australia (millions)

5
4
3
2
1
0

1980 1985 1990 1995 2000
Source: World Tourism Organisation

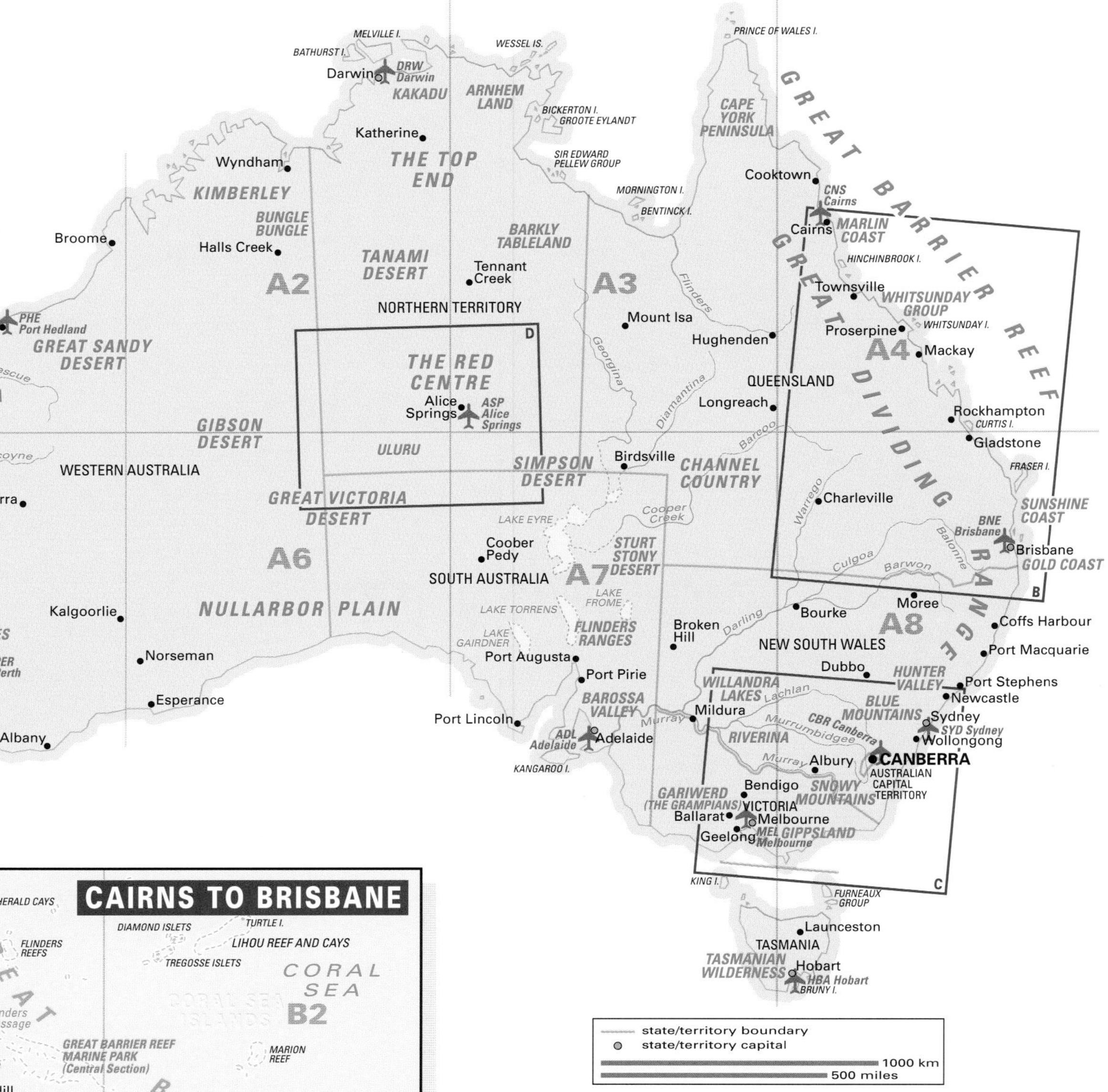

MELVILLE I.
BATHURST I.
WESSEL IS.
PRINCE OF WALES I.

Darwin
DRW *Darwin*
KAKADU
ARNHEM LAND
BICKERTON I.
GROOTE EYLANDT
SIR EDWARD PELLEW GROUP
CAPE YORK PENINSULA

Katherine
THE TOP END
MORNINGTON I.
BENTINCK I.
Cooktown
CNS *Cairns*
Cairns
MARLIN COAST

Wyndham
KIMBERLEY
BUNGLE BUNGLE
TANAMI DESERT
BARKLY TABLELAND
Townsville
HINCHINBROOK I.
WHITSUNDAY GROUP
WHITSUNDAY I.

Broome
Halls Creek
Tennant Creek
Proserpine
Mackay
A2
A3
A4

NORTHERN TERRITORY
Mount Isa
Hughenden
QUEENSLAND

Port Hedland
PHE *Port Hedland*
Dampier
BARROW I.
GREAT SANDY DESERT
D
THE RED CENTRE
Alice Springs
ASP *Alice Springs*
Longreach
Rockhampton
CURTIS I.
Gladstone
FRASER I.

A1
NINGALOO REEF
PILBARA
GIBSON DESERT
ULURU
Birdsville
CHANNEL COUNTRY

Carnarvon
DIRK HARTOG I.
Meekatharra
WESTERN AUSTRALIA
GREAT VICTORIA DESERT
SIMPSON DESERT
Charleville
SUNSHINE COAST
BNE *Brisbane*
Brisbane
GOLD COAST

A5
Geraldton
Coober Pedy
LAKE EYRE
STURT STONY DESERT
SOUTH AUSTRALIA
A7
Moree
Bourke
A8
Coffs Harbour

THE PINNACLES
Kalgoorlie
NULLARBOR PLAIN
LAKE TORRENS
LAKE GAIRDNER
FLINDERS RANGES
Broken Hill
NEW SOUTH WALES
Port Macquarie
Port Stephens

Perth
PER *Perth*
Fremantle
Norseman
Port Augusta
Port Pirie
BAROSSA VALLEY
Dubbo
HUNTER VALLEY
Newcastle

Bunbury
Esperance
Port Lincoln
ADL *Adelaide*
Adelaide
Mildura
WILLANDRA LAKES
CBR *Canberra*
BLUE MOUNTAINS
Sydney
SYD *Sydney*
Wollongong

Albany
KANGAROO I.
RIVERINA
Albury
CANBERRA
AUSTRALIAN CAPITAL TERRITORY

GARIWERD (THE GRAMPIANS)
Bendigo
SNOWY MOUNTAINS
Ballarat
VICTORIA
Melbourne
MEL *Melbourne*
GIPPSLAND
Geelong

KING I.
FURNEAUX GROUP
Launceston
TASMANIA
TASMANIAN WILDERNESS
Hobart
HBA *Hobart*
BRUNY I.

— state/territory boundary
⊙ state/territory capital

1000 km
500 miles

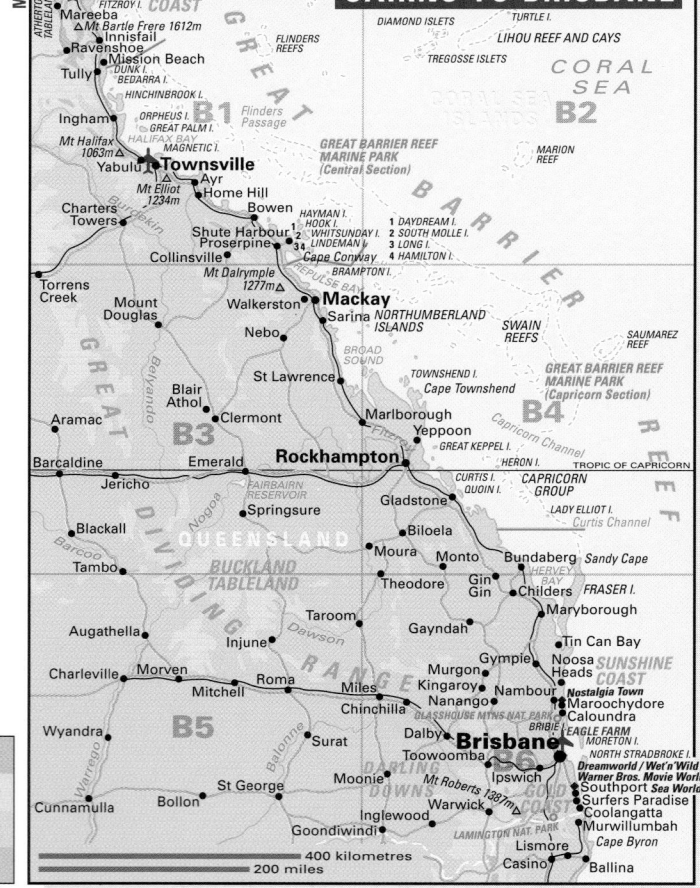

CAIRNS TO BRISBANE

Kuranda
GREEN I.
(Cairns Section)
Cairns
MARLIN COAST
FITZROY I.
HERALD CAYS
DIAMOND ISLETS
TURTLE I.

Mareeba
Mt Bartle Frere 1612m
Innisfail
FLINDERS REEFS
LIHOU REEF AND CAYS
Ravenshoe
Mission Beach
TREGOSSE ISLETS

Tully
DUNK I.
BEDARRA I.
CORAL SEA
HINCHINBROOK I.
B1
B2

Ingham
ORPHEUS I.
GREAT PALM I.
MAGNETIC I.
Flinders Passage
Mt Halifax 1063m
HALIFAX BAY
GREAT BARRIER REEF MARINE PARK (Central Section)
MARION REEF

Yabulu
Townsville
Ayr
Home Hill
1 DAYDREAM I.
2 SOUTH MOLLE I.

Mt Elliot 1234m
Bowen
HAYMAN I.
HOOK I.
WHITSUNDAY I.
LINDEMAN I.
3 LONG I.
4 HAMILTON I.

Charters Towers
Shute Harbour
Proserpine
Cape Conway
BRAMPTON I.
SWAIN REEFS

Collinsville
REPULSE BAY
Mt Dalrymple 1277m
SAUMAREZ REEF

Torrens Creek
Mount Douglas
Walkerston
Mackay
Sarina
NORTHUMBERLAND ISLANDS
TOWNSHEND I.
Cape Townshend

Aramac
Blair Athol
Nebo
St Lawrence
BROAD SOUND
GREAT BARRIER REEF MARINE PARK (Capricorn Section)
B4

Clermont
Marlborough
Yeppoon
Capricorn Channel
GREAT KEPPEL I.
HERON I.
TROPIC OF CAPRICORN

Barcaldine
B3
Emerald
Rockhampton
FAIRBAIRN RESERVOIR
CURTIS I.
QUOIN I.
CAPRICORN GROUP

Jericho
Springsure
Gladstone
LADY ELLIOT I.
Curtis Channel

Blackall
Biloela
Moura
Bundaberg
Sandy Cape

Tambo
QUEENSLAND
BUCKLAND TABLELAND
Monto
Gin Gin
Childers
FRASER I.
HERVEY BAY

Augathella
Taroom
Theodore
Maryborough

Injune
Gayndah
Tin Can Bay

Charleville
Morven
Mitchell
Roma
Miles
Murgon
Kingaroy
Nanango
Gympie
Noosa Heads
SUNSHINE COAST

Wyandra
B5
Chinchilla
Nambour
Nostalgia Town
Maroochydore
Caloundra

Cunnamulla
Surat
Dalby
Toowoomba
GLASSHOUSE MTNS NAT. PARK
BRIBIE I.
EAGLE FARM
MORETON I.

St George
Moonie
Ipswich
Mt Roberts 1187m
Brisbane
B6
Dreamworld / Wet'n'Wild / Warner Bros. Movie World
Southport
Sea World

Bollon
Inglewood
Warwick
NORTH STRADBROKE I.
Surfers Paradise
Coolangatta

Goondiwindi
LAMINGTON NAT. PARK
Murwillumbah
Cape Byron

DARLING DOWNS
Lismore
Casino
Ballina

1000 metres
500 metres
Sea level

400 kilometres
200 miles

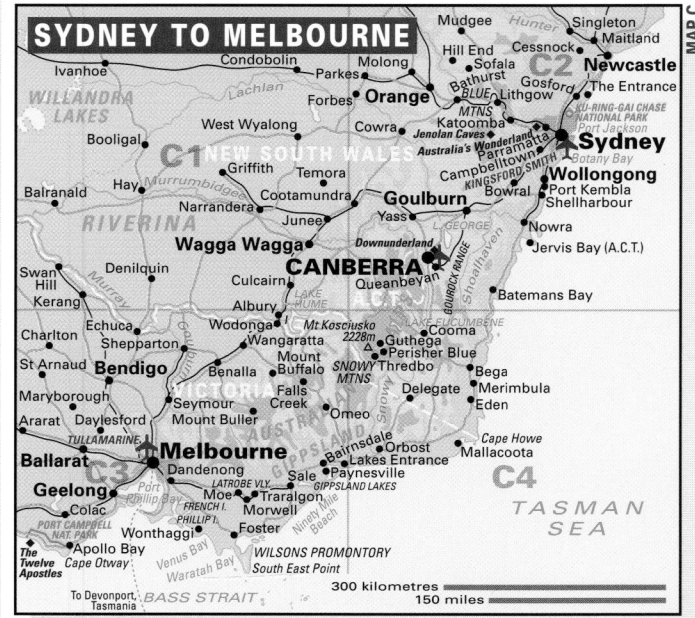

SYDNEY TO MELBOURNE

MAP C

Mudgee
HUNTER
Singleton
Ivanhoe
Condobolin
Molong
Hill End
Cessnock
Maitland

WILLANDRA LAKES
Parkes
Bathurst
Gosford
Newcastle
The Entrance

Booligal
Forbes
Orange
Lithgow
KU-RING-GAI CHASE NATIONAL PARK
Port Jackson

West Wyalong
Cowra
BLUE MTNS
Katoomba
Jenolan Caves
Australia's Wonderland
Parramatta
Sydney

C1
NEW SOUTH WALES
Griffith
Temora
Campbelltown
KINGSFORD SMITH
Botany Bay

Balranald
Hay
Cootamundra
Goulburn
Wollongong
Port Kembla
Shellharbour

RIVERINA
Narrandera
Junee
Yass
Nowra
Jervis Bay (A.C.T.)

Swan Hill
Deniliquin
Wagga Wagga
Downunderland
CANBERRA
Queanbeyan
A.C.T.
Batemans Bay

Kerang
Culcairn
Albury
Mt Kosciusko 2228m
Cooma
Echuca
Wodonga
SNOWY MTNS
Perisher Blue
Bega
Merimbula
Eden

Charlton
Shepparton
Wangaratta
Guthega
Thredbo
Delegate

St Arnaud
Benalla
Mount Buffalo
Falls Creek
Omeo
Cape Howe
Mallacoota

Maryborough
Bendigo
VICTORIA
Seymour
Mount Buller
C4
TASMAN SEA

Ararat
Daylesford
Benalla
Bairnsdale
Lakes Entrance

Ballarat
TULLAMARINE
Melbourne
Dandenong
LATROBE VLY
Sale
Paynesville
GIPPSLAND LAKES

Geelong
C3
Port Phillip
FRENCH I.
Moe
Morwell
Traralgon
Ninety Mile Beach

Colac
PHILLIP I.
Wonthaggi
Foster
WILSONS PROMONTORY

The Twelve Apostles
Apollo Bay
Cape Otway
Venus Bay
Waratah Bay
South East Point

To Devonport, Tasmania
BASS STRAIT

300 kilometres
150 miles

AUSTRALIA

See page 34 for general map

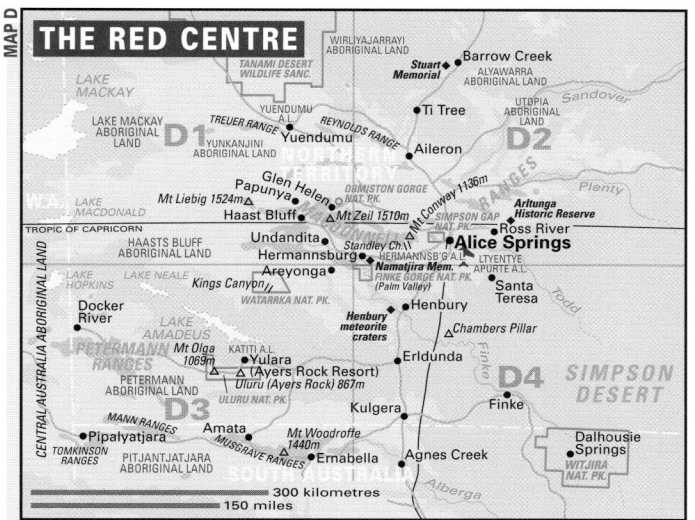

THE RED CENTRE

MAP D

D1
D2
D3
D4

LAKE MACKAY
TANAMI DESERT WILDLIFE SANC.
WIRLIYAJARRAYI ABORIGINAL LAND
Stuart Memorial
Barrow Creek
ALYAWARRA ABORIGINAL LAND
Sandover
LAKE MACKAY ABORIGINAL LAND
YUENDUMU
TREUER RANGE
REYNOLDS RANGE
Ti Tree
UTOPIA ABORIGINAL LAND
W.A.
YUNKANJINI ABORIGINAL LAND
Yuendumu
Aileron
LAKE MACDONALD
Glen Helen
Papunya
OMISTON GORGE NAT. PK.
Plenty
TROPIC OF CAPRICORN
Mt Liebig 1524m△
△Mt Zeil 1510m
SIMPSON GAP NAT. PK.
Arltunga Historic Reserve
Haast Bluff
HERMANNSBG G.A.L.
Mt Conway 1136m
Ross River
HAASTS BLUFF ABORIGINAL LAND
Undandita
Standley Ch.△
Alice Springs
APURTE A.L.
LAKE NEALE
Hermannsburg
Namatjira Mem.
LYENTYE
Santa Teresa
LAKE HOPKINS
Areyonga
FINKE GORGE NAT. PK. (Palm Valley)
Todd
Kings Canyon
WATARRKA NAT. PK.
Henbury meteorite craters
Henbury
CENTRAL AUSTRALIA ABORIGINAL LAND
Docker River
LAKE AMADEUS
KATITI A.L.
△Chambers Pillar
PETERMANN RANGES
Mt Olga 1069m△
Yulara
Erldunda
SIMPSON DESERT
PETERMANN ABORIGINAL LAND
△(Ayers Rock Resort)
Uluru (Ayers Rock) 867m
ULURU NAT. PK.
Finke
MANN RANGES
Kulgera
D4
Pipalyatjara
Amata
MUSGRAVE RANGES
Mt Woodroffe 1440m△
Agnes Creek
Dalhousie Springs
TOMKINSON RANGES
PITJANTJATJARA ABORIGINAL LAND
Ernabella
WITJIRA NAT. PK.
SOUTH AUSTRALIA
Alberga

300 kilometres
150 miles

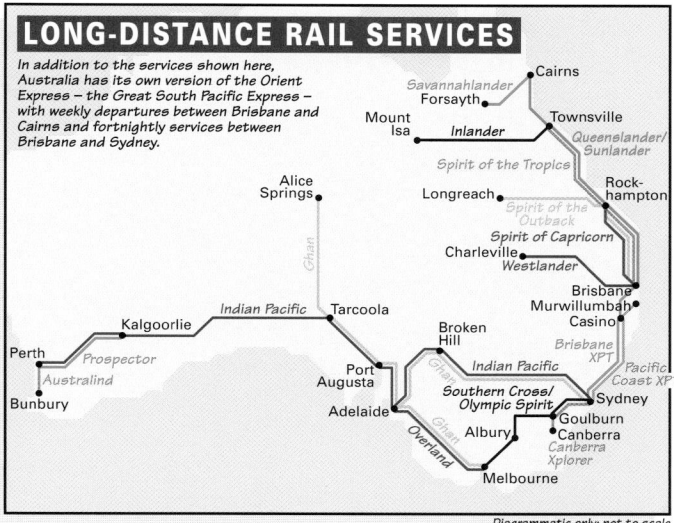

LONG-DISTANCE RAIL SERVICES

In addition to the services shown here, Australia has its own version of the Orient Express – the Great South Pacific Express – with weekly departures between Brisbane and Cairns and fortnightly services between Brisbane and Sydney.

Cairns
Savannahlander
Forsayth
Mount Isa
Townsville
Inlander
Queenslander/ Sunlander
Spirit of the Tropics
Alice Springs
Longreach
Rockhampton
Spirit of the Outback
Charleville
Spirit of Capricorn
Westlander
Brisbane
Murwillumbah
Casino
Indian Pacific
Tarcoola
Broken Hill
Brisbane XPT
Perth
Kalgoorlie
Prospector
Australind
Port Augusta
Indian Pacific
Pacific Coast XPT
Bunbury
Adelaide
Southern Cross/ Olympic Spirit
Sydney
Goulburn
Canberra
Albury
Canberra Xplorer
Overland
Melbourne

Diagrammatic only: not to scale

NEW ZEALAND

See page 35 for general map

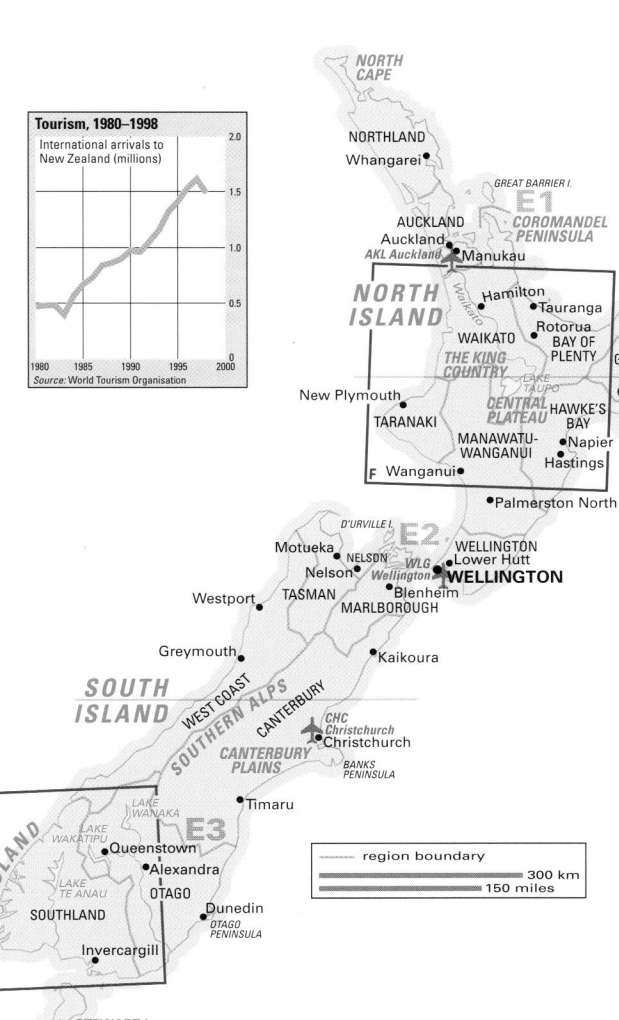

Tourism, 1980–1998

International arrivals to New Zealand (millions)

Source: World Tourism Organisation

NORTH CAPE
NORTHLAND
Whangarei
GREAT BARRIER I.
E1
COROMANDEL PENINSULA
AUCKLAND
Auckland
AKL Auckland
Manukau
NORTH ISLAND
Hamilton
Tauranga
Rotorua
WAIKATO
BAY OF PLENTY
THE KING COUNTRY
GISBORNE
New Plymouth
LAKE TAUPO
Gisborne
TARANAKI
CENTRAL PLATEAU
HAWKE'S BAY
MAHIA PENINSULA
F
Wanganui
MANAWATU-WANGANUI
Napier
Hastings
Palmerston North
D'URVILLE I.
E2
WELLINGTON
Motueka
NELSON
Lower Hutt
Nelson
WLG
Wellington
Westport
TASMAN
Blenheim
WELLINGTON
MARLBOROUGH
Greymouth
Kaikoura
SOUTH ISLAND
WEST COAST
SOUTHERN ALPS
CANTERBURY
CHC Christchurch
Christchurch
CANTERBURY PLAINS
BANKS PENINSULA
FIORDLAND
LAKE WAKATIPU
Timaru
LAKE WANAKA
E3
Queenstown
Alexandra
LAKE TE ANAU
OTAGO
Dunedin
SOUTHLAND
OTAGO PENINSULA
Invercargill
G
STEWART I.

region boundary
300 km
150 miles

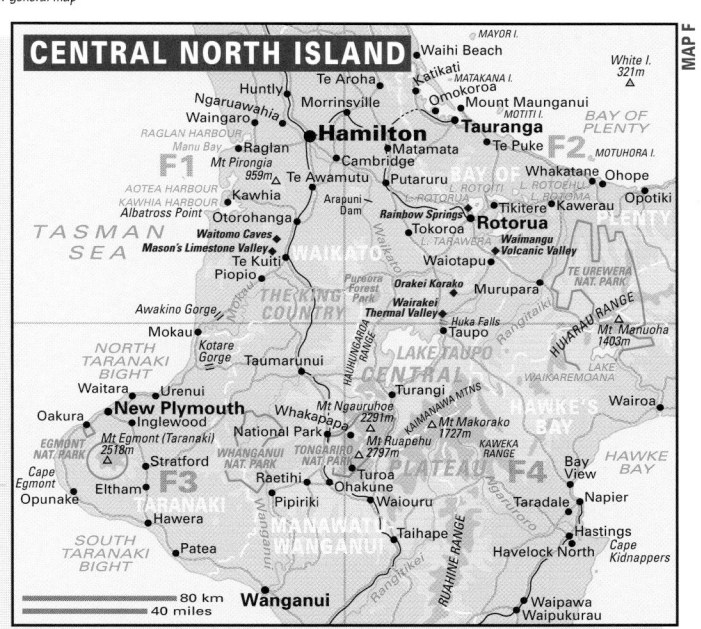

CENTRAL NORTH ISLAND

MAP F

MAYOR I.
Waihi Beach
White I. 321m
Te Aroha
Katikati
MATAKANA I.
Huntly
Omokoroa
Mount Maunganui
MOTITI I.
Ngaruawahia
Morrinsville
Tauranga
BAY OF PLENTY
Waingaro
Hamilton
Te Puke
F2
MOTUHORA I.
RAGLAN HARBOUR
Raglan
Matamata
Whakatane
Ohope
Manu Bay
Mt Pirongia 959m
Cambridge
L. ROTOEHU
Opotiki
AOTEA HARBOUR
Te Awamutu
Putaruru
L. ROTOITI
F1
KAWHIA HARBOUR
Kawhia
Arapuni Dam
Rainbow Springs
Tikitere
Kawerau
Albatross Point
Otorohanga
ROTORUA
Rotorua
TASMAN SEA
Waitomo Caves
Tokoroa
Waimangu Volcanic Valley
TE UREWERA NAT. PARK
Mason's Limestone Valley
Te Kuiti
WAIKATO
L. TARAWERA
Waiotapu
Piopio
Pureora Forest Park
Orakei Korako
Murupara
Awakino Gorge
THE KING COUNTRY
Wairakei Thermal Valley
Huka Falls
HUIARAU RANGE
Mokau
Kotare Gorge
Taupo
Mt Manuoha 1403m
NORTH TARANAKI BIGHT
Taumarunui
LAKE TAUPO
Waitara
Urenui
CENTRAL
RANGITAIKI
WAIKAREMOANA
Oakura
New Plymouth
Whakapapa
Turangi
KAIMANAWA MTNS
Wairoa
Inglewood
Mt Ngauruhoe 2291m
△Mt Makorako 1727m
HAWKE'S BAY
EGMONT NAT. PARK
National Park
△Mt Ruapehu 2797m
KAWEKA RANGE
Cape Egmont
Mt Egmont (Taranaki) 2518m△
TONGARIRO NAT. PARK
Bay View
HAWKE BAY
Opunake
Stratford
PLATEAU
Turoa
Waiouru
Taradale
Napier
Eltham
Raetihi
Ohakune
F4
Hawera
Pipiriki
F3
Taihape
Havelock North
Cape Kidnappers
TARANAKI
Patea
RUAHINE RANGE
SOUTH TARANAKI BIGHT
MANAWATU WANGANUI
Waipawa
Waipukurau
Wanganui

80 km
40 miles

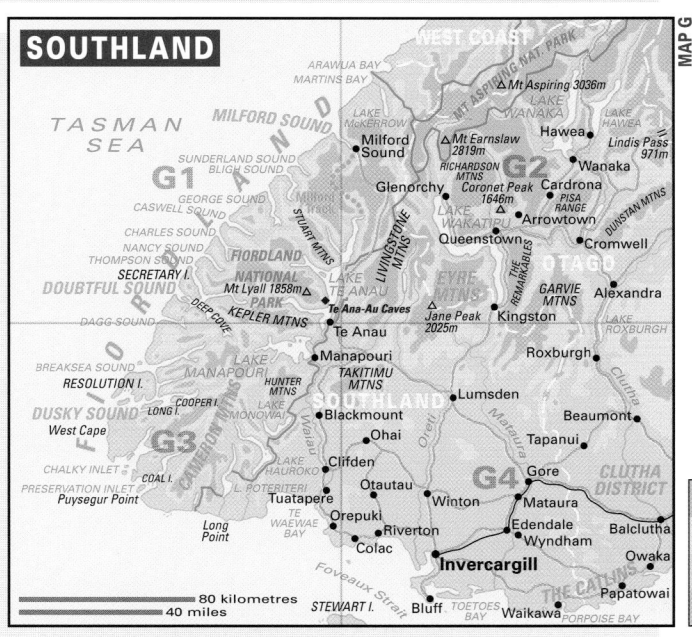

SOUTHLAND

MAP G

ARAWIA BAY
WEST COAST NAT. PARK
MARTINS BAY
△Mt Aspiring 3036m
MILFORD SOUND
LAKE McKERROW
MT ASPIRING NAT. PARK
LAKE WANAKA
LAKE HAWEA
TASMAN SEA
Milford Sound
Hawea
Lindis Pass 971m
G1
SUNDERLAND SOUND
BLIGH SOUND
△Mt Earnslaw 2819m
RICHARDSON MTNS
G2
Wanaka
CASWELL SOUND
Glenorchy
Coronet Peak 1646m
Cardrona
PISA RANGE
GEORGE SOUND
Arrowtown
DURSTAN MTNS
CHARLES SOUND
FIORDLAND
LIVINGSTONE MTNS
Queenstown
Cromwell
NANCY SOUND
THOMPSON SOUND
LAKE WAKATIPU
EYRE MTNS
OTAGO
SECRETARY I.
NATIONAL
Mt Lyall 1858m△
THE REMARKABLES
GARVIE MTNS
Alexandra
DOUBTFUL SOUND
PARK
Te Ana-Au Caves
Jane Peak 2025m
Kingston
LAKE ROXBURGH
DAGG SOUND
DEEP COVE
KEPLER MTNS
Te Anau
Roxburgh
BREAKSEA SOUND
LAKE MANAPOURI
Manapouri
Clutha
RESOLUTION I.
HUNTER MTNS
TAKITIMU MTNS
Lumsden
Beaumont
DUSKY SOUND
LONG I.
LAKE MONOWAI
SOUTHLAND
Blackmount
Tapanui
West Cape
COOPER I.
Ohai
CLUTHA DISTRICT
G3
CAMERON MTNS
Clifden
Otautau
Winton
Mataura
Gore
G4
CHALKY INLET
COAL I.
LAKE HAUROKO
Tuatapere
Orepuki
Riverton
Edendale
Wyndham
Balclutha
PRESERVATION INLET
L. POTERITERI
Colac
Owaka
Puysegur Point
TE WAEWAE BAY
Invercargill
THE CATLINS
Long Point
Bluff
TOETOES BAY
Waikawa
Papatowai
STEWART I.
FOVEAUX STRAIT
PORPOISE BAY

80 kilometres
40 miles

1000 metres
500 metres
Sea level

CLIMATE

TEMPERATURE CONVERSION						
°Celsius	−10	0	10	20	30	40
°Fahrenheit	14	32	50	68	86	104

RAINFALL CONVERSION						
Millimetres	102	203	305	406	508	610
Inches	4	8	12	16	20	24

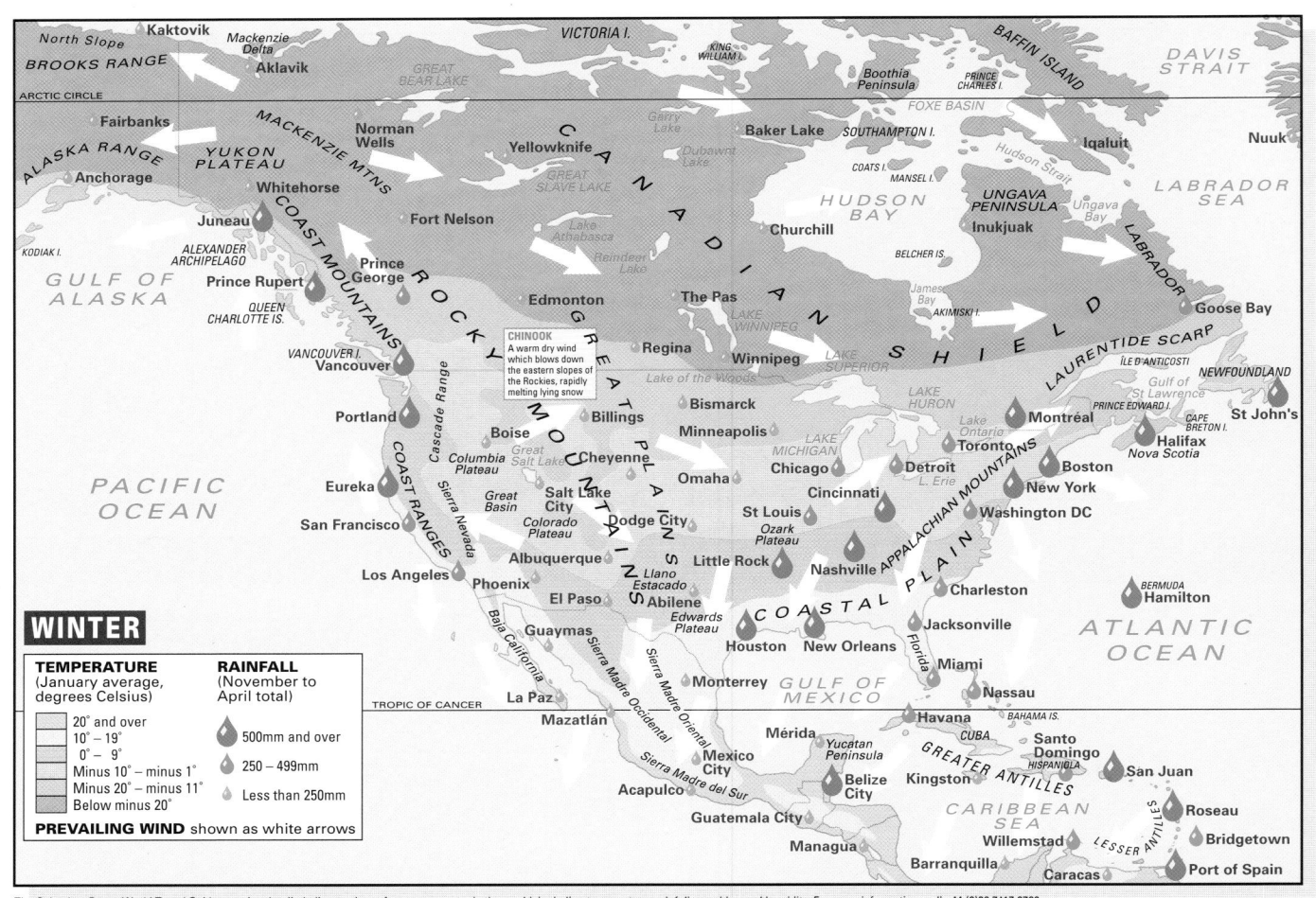

WINTER

TEMPERATURE
(January average, degrees Celsius)

- 20° and over
- 10° – 19°
- 0° – 9°
- Minus 10° – minus 1°
- Minus 20° – minus 11°
- Below minus 20°

RAINFALL
(November to April total)

- 500mm and over
- 250 – 499mm
- Less than 250mm

PREVAILING WIND shown as white arrows

CHINOOK
A warm dry wind which blows down the eastern slopes of the Rockies, rapidly melting lying snow

The Columbus Press *World Travel Guide* contains detailed climate charts for every country in the world, including temperature, rainfall, sunshine and humidity. For more information, call +44 (0)20 7417 0700.

SUMMER

TEMPERATURE
(July average, degrees Celsius)

- 30° and over
- 20° – 29°
- 10° – 19°
- 0° – 9°
- Minus 10° – minus 1°

RAINFALL
(May to October total)

- 500mm and over
- 250 – 499mm
- Less than 250mm

PREVAILING WIND shown as white arrows

LABRADOR CURRENT
A cold current flowing south, carrying icebergs and keeping the coastal region relatively cool during the summer; fogs are caused off the Newfoundland coast where the current meets the warmer Gulf Stream flowing NE from the Gulf of Mexico

CALIFORNIA CURRENT
A cold current which flows south, cooling the coastal region, and responsible for the frequent sea fogs particularly during the summer

AIRPORTS AND RAILWAYS

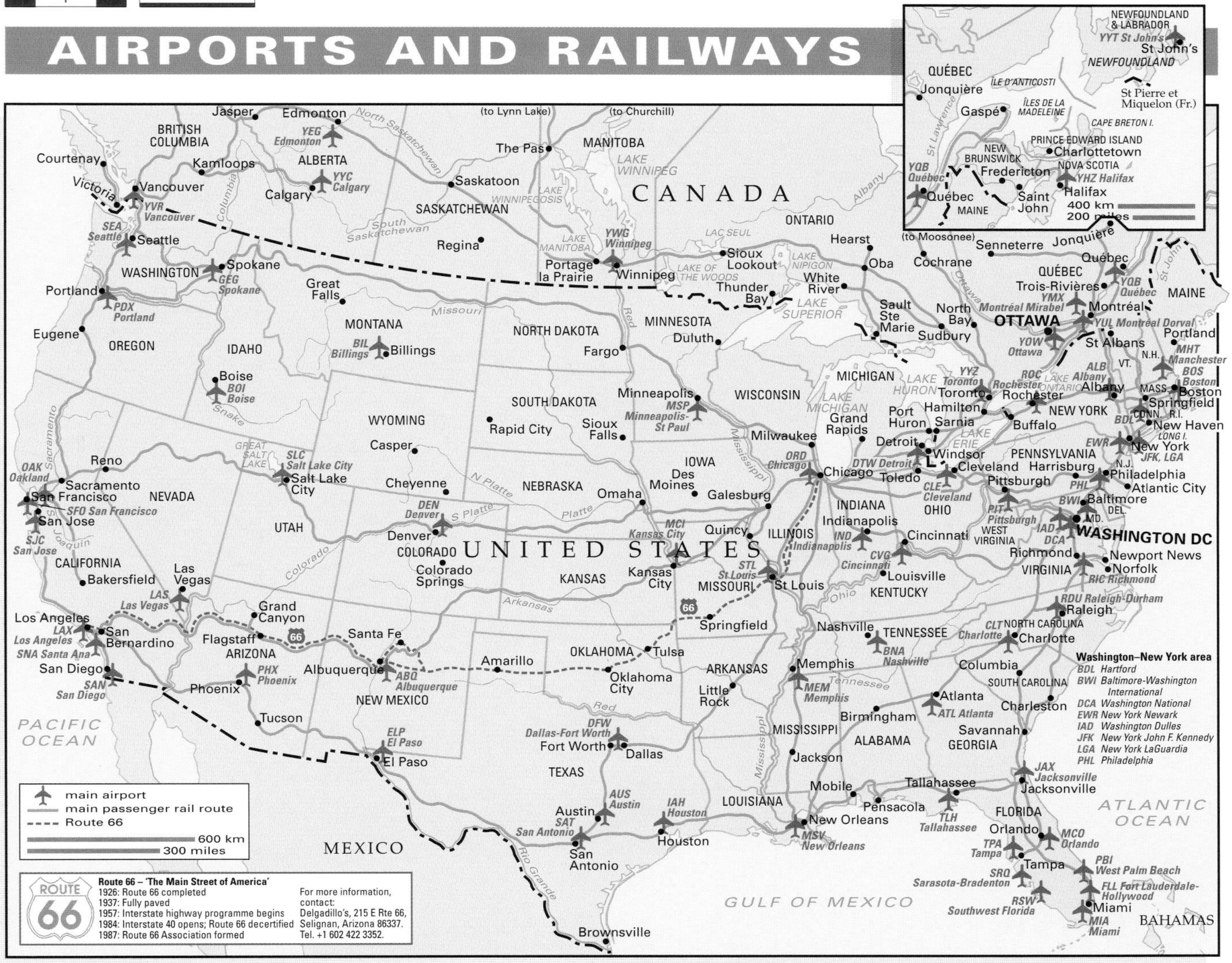

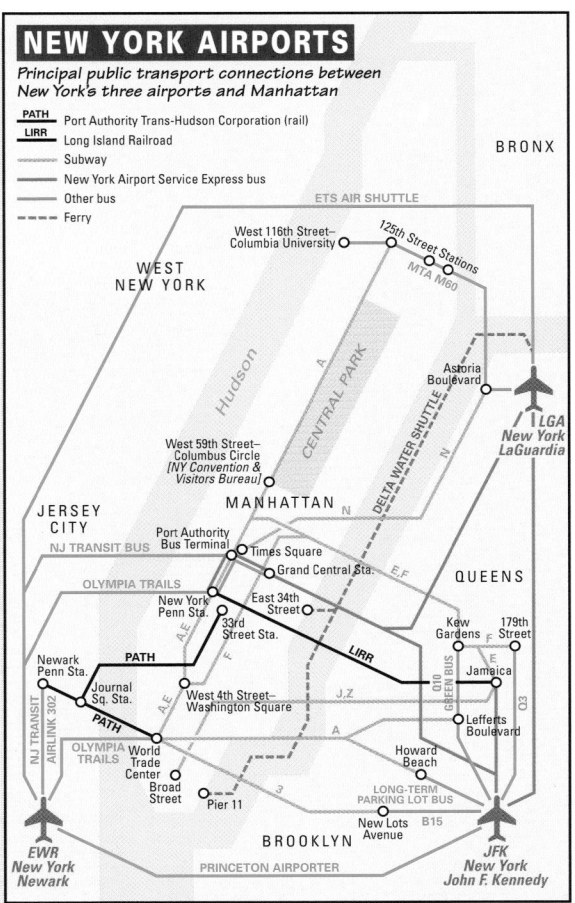

NEW YORK AIRPORTS

Principal public transport connections between New York's three airports and Manhattan

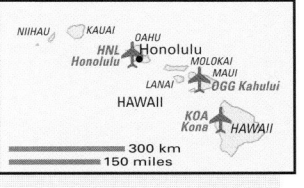

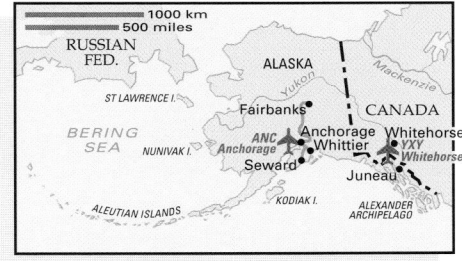

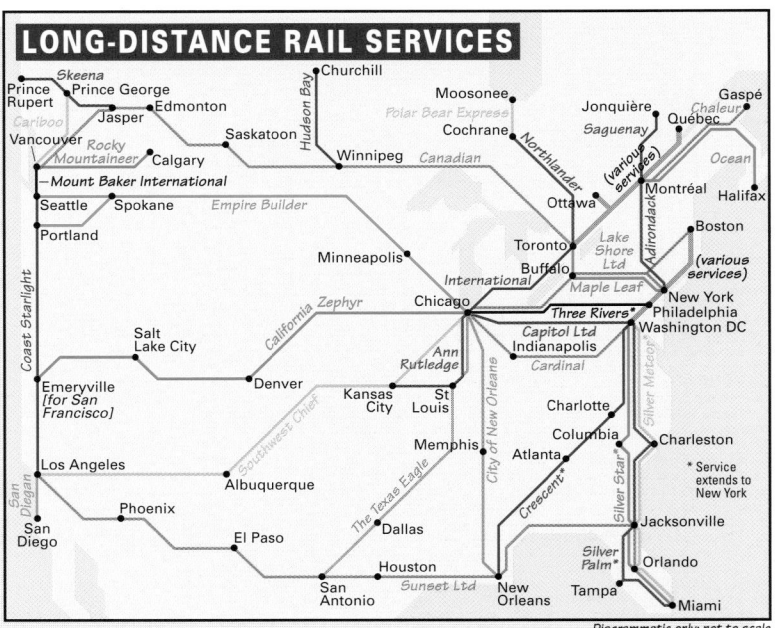

LONG-DISTANCE RAIL SERVICES

CANADA UNITED STATES

MUSEUMS AND ART GALLERIES

NEWFOUNDLAND & LABRADOR

QUÉBEC
ÎLE D'ANTICOSTI
NEWFOUNDLAND
St Pierre et Miquelon (Fr.)
ÎLES DE LA MADELEINE
CAPE BRETON I.
PRINCE EDWARD ISLAND
NEW BRUNSWICK
NOVA SCOTIA
Fredericton
Québec Saint John Halifax
MAINE
400 km
200 miles

The thousands of museums and galleries in the United States and Canada reflect both national and ethnic concerns and a broader world perspective. Major institutions can be found in virtually every state and province, along with countless smaller ones.

This selection is based on importance and depth of the collection and its cultural diversity within a demographic spread.

Data compiled by Jon A. Gillaspie.
Fax: +44 (0)20 8780 2427. email: let@sarastro.com

Principal contents of institution:

AA Applied & decorative art
AR Archaeology / ancient art
FA Fine art (paintings, sculpture)
FO Folk art & culture / ethnology
H   History / historical site / reconstruction
NH Natural history
ST Science / technology
W   Wide range of subjects

Opening times:

Days or months preceded by a red circle (●) indicate when the institution is closed. Many close on national holidays and other special days. Some institutions have shorter opening hours at certain days of the week or in certain months.

Admission charges:

All charge for admission except those shown in *italics*, where entry is free (although charges for special exhibitions may apply). Some institutions allow free entry or reduce their admission charges on certain days.

Albuquerque NEW MEXICO
W Indian Pueblo Cultural Center
Atlanta GEORGIA
FA High Museum of Art ● Mon
W Michael C. Carlos Museum (Emory Univ.)
Baltimore MARYLAND
FA Baltimore Museum of Art ● Mon & Tue
W Walters Art Gallery ● Mon
Banff ALBERTA
NH Whyte Museum of Rockies ● Mon (Oct-May)
Baraboo WISCONSIN
H Circus World Museum ● Oct-Apr, no shows
Baton Rouge LOUISIANA
W LSU Rural Life Museum
Boston MASSACHUSETTS
FA Isabella Stewart Gardner Museum ● Mon
W Museum of Fine Arts
Bozeman MONTANA
W Museum of the Rockies
Buffalo NEW YORK
FA Albright-Knox Art Gallery ● Mon
Burlington VERMONT
W Shelburne Museum ● Nov-May, tours only
Calgary ALBERTA
W Glenbow Museum ● Mon (Sep-May)
Chicago ILLINOIS
FA Art Inst. of Chic.; Mus. of Contem. Art ● Mon
W Field Museum of Chicago
ST Museum of Science and Technology
Cincinnati OHIO
FA Cincinnati Art Museum ● Mon; Contem-porary Arts Center ● Sun; Taft Museum
Cleveland OHIO
ST Great Lakes Science Center
FA Museum of Art ● Mon
NH Museum of Natural History
H Rock and Roll Hall of Fame and Museum
Cody WYOMING
H Buffalo Bill Hist. Center ● Tue & Wed (Nov-Apr) includes: Plains Ind. Mus., Witney Gall.
Columbus OHIO
FA Columbus Museum of Art ● Mon
Corpus Christi TEXAS
FA Art Museum of South Texas ● Mon
Dallas TEXAS
FO African-American Museum ● Mon

AR FA *Dallas Museum of Art* ● Mon
NH Dallas Museum of Natural History
Denver COLORADO
H Black Amer. West Mus. ● Mon & Tue (winter)
W Denver Art Museum ● Mon; Denver Museum of Natural History
Des Moines IOWA
FA Des Moines Art Center ● Mon
H Museum of Afro-American History ● Mon
Detroit OHIO
W Detroit Institute of Art ● Mon & Tue
Drumheller ALBERTA
NH Royal Tyrrell Museum of Paleontology ● Mon (Oct-May)
Edmonton ALBERTA
ST Edmonton Space and Science Cent. ● Mon
Flagstaff ARIZONA
FO Museum of Northern Arizona
Fort Steele BRITISH COLUMBIA
H Fort Steele Heritage Town
Fort Worth TEXAS
FA *Amon Carter Museum*; Kimbell Art Museum; Modern Art Museum; Sid Richardson Coll. of Western Art ● Mon
W Museum of Science and History ● Mon
Fredericton NEW BRUNSWICK
FA Beaverbrook Art Gallery ● Mon (winter)
Halifax NOVA SCOTIA
H Atlantic Maritime Mus. ● Mon (Oct-May)
NH NS Natural History Mus. ● Mon (Oct-May)
Houston TEXAS
FA Museum of Fine Arts ● Mon
NH Museum of Natural Science
ST Space Center Houston
Huntsville ALABAMA
ST Space and Rocket Center
Indianapolis INDIANA
FO Eiteljorg Museum ● Mon (Sep-Jun)
FA Indianapolis Museum of Art ● Sun & Mon
W Children's Mus. of Indianap. ● Mon (winter)
Kansas City MISSOURI
W Nelson-Atkins Museum of Art ● Mon
Kingston ONTARIO
W Agnes Ethrington Art Center ● Mon
Los Angeles CALIFORNIA
AA *J. Paul Getty Center* ● Mon

FA Armand Hammer Museum of Art; Museum of Contemporary Art (MOCA) ● Mon
AR FA LA County Museum of Art (LACMA)
W Natural History Museum of LA County ● Mon
H Simon Weisenthal Cent. (Beit Hashoa Mus.)
Louisville KENTUCKY
FA *J.B. Speed Art Museum* ● Mon
Macon GEORGIA
W Tubman African-American Museum
Manchester NEW HAMPSHIRE
AA FA Currier Gallery of Art ● Tue
Memphis TENNESSEE
W National Civil Rights Museum ● Tue
Merritt Island FLORIDA
ST John F. Kennedy Space Center
Mesa Verde National Park COLORADO
AR Archaeological Museum
Miami FLORIDA
FA Bass Mus.; Center for Fine Arts ● both Mon
W Lowe Art Museum (Univ. of Miami) ● Mon
AA Wolfsonian Museum ● Mon
Milwaukee WISCONSIN
FA Milwaukee Art Gallery ● Mon
W Museum Center
Minneapolis and St Paul MINNESOTA
W Minneapolis Institute of Arts ● Mon; Minnesota Children's Mus. ● Mon (winter)
ST Science Museum of Minnesota
FA Walker Art Cent. and Sculpture Gdn. ● Mon
Montréal QUÉBEC
NH Biodôme
AA Canadian Cent. for Architecture ● Mon & Tue (Oct-May); Chât. Ramezay ● Mon (Oct-May)
AR Mont. Mus. of Archaeology & History ● Mon
FA Montréal Museum of Fine Arts; Montréal Contemporary Art Museum ● both Mon
H McCord Museum of Canadian History
Morrisburg ONTARIO
FO Upper Canada Village ● Oct-May
Nashville TENNESSEE
H Country Museum Hall of Fame
W Tennessee State Museum ● Mon
New Haven CONNECTICUT
FA Center for British Art ● Mon; Yale University Library ● Mon, July-Aug
NH Peabody Museum of Natural History
New Orleans LOUISIANA
W Louisiana State Museum ● Mon includes: Cabildo; Presbytere; 1850 House; Jazz Mus.
FA New Orleans Museum of Art ● Mon
New York NEW YORK
W American Mus. of Natural History; Brooklyn Mus. ● Mon & Tue; Metropolitan Mus. of Art ● Mon; NY Historical Society ● Mon
AA Cooper-Hewitt National Design Mus. ● Mon
FA Guggenheim Museum ● Thu; Whitney Museum of American Art ● Mon & Tue
AA Museum of Modern Art (MoMA) ● Wed
FO *National Museum of the American Indian*

Norfolk VIRGINIA
FA Chrysler Museum ● Mon
Oberlin OHIO
W Allen Memorial Art Museum ● Mon
Omaha NEBRASKA
H Great Plains Black Museum ● Sat & Sun
Ottawa QUÉBEC
NH Canadian Museum of Nature
FA Can. Mus. of Civilization ● Mon (Oct-Apr)
FA FO National Gallery ● Mon & Tue (Sep-Apr)
ST National Aviation Museum ● Mon (Sep-Apr)
ST National Mus. of Science ● Mon (Sep-Apr)
Pasadena CALIFORNIA
FA Huntington Museum and Library ● Mon; Norton Simon Museum ● Mon-Wed
Philadelphia PENNSYLVANIA
H Afro-American Hist. & Cultural Mus. ● Mon
AR FO Museum of Archaeology and Anthro-pology (University of Pennsylvania) ● Mon
FA Philadelphia Museum of Art; Rodin Museum ● both Mon
Phoenix ARIZONA
FO Heard Museum
Pittsburgh PENNSYLVANIA
FA Andy Warhol Museum ● Mon; Museum of Art (Carnegie Center) ● Mon (Sep-Jun)
AA FA Frick Art Museum ● Mon
Portland OREGON
ST Oregon Museum of Science and Industry ● Mon (winter)
W Portland Art Museum ● Mon
Princeton NEW JERSEY
ST Carnegie Science Center
NH Natural History Museum ● Mon (Sep-Jun)
FA *University Art Museum* ● Mon
Québec QUÉBEC
W Museum of Civilization ● Mon (Sep-Jun)
FA Québec Museum ● Mon (Sep-May)
Raleigh NORTH CAROLINA
FA North Carolina Museum of Art ● Mon
ST North Carolina Museum of Natural Sciences
Rapid City SOUTH DAKOTA
H Sioux Indian Museum ● Mon
Richmond VIRGINIA
W Virginia Museum of Fine Arts ● Mon
Rochester NEW YORK
AA International Mus. of Photography ● Mon
Saint John NEW BRUNSWICK
W New Brunswick Museum
St Louis MISSOURI
H Museum of Western Expansion
W *St Louis Art Museum* ● Mon
St Petersburg FLORIDA
FA Museum of Fine Arts ● Mon
FA Salvador Dali Museum
Salem MASSACHUSETTS
W Peabody Essex Museum
San Diego CALIFORNIA
FA Mus. of Contemporary Art, La Jolla ● Mon

San Francisco CALIFORNIA
FA California Palace of the Legion of Honor; Yerba Buena Gardens; SF Art Institute ● all Mon; SF Museum of Modern Art ● Wed
Santa Fe NEW MEXICO
W Museum of New Mexico ● Mon includes: Georgia O'Keeffe Mus.; Mus. of Fine Arts
FO Mus. of Indian Arts; Mus. of Int. Folk Art
Sarasota FLORIDA
FA Ringling Museum Complex
Saskatoon SASKATCHEWAN
FA Mendel Art Gallery
Seattle WASHINGTON
ST Museum of Flight; Pacific Science Center
Sudbury ONTARIO
ST Science North
Tallahassee FLORIDA
W Black Archives Research Center ● Sat & Sun
Tampa FLORIDA
ST Museum of Science and Industry ● varies
Toronto ONTARIO
FA Art Gall. of Ontario (AGO) ● Mon & Tue (Oct-May), Mon (summer); Thomson Gall. ● Sun
FO Gallery of Inuit Art
FA McMichael Can. Art Coll. ● Mon (Oct-May)
ST Ontario Science Centre
W Royal Ontario Museum (ROM)
Tucson ARIZONA
NH Arizona-Sonora Desert Museum
FO Arizona State Museum
AR FA Tucson Museum of Art ● Mon (Jun-Aug)
Vancouver BRITISH COLUMBIA
FO UBC Mus. of Anthropology ● Mon (Sep-May)
Victoria BRITISH COLUMBIA
W Royal British Columbia Museum
Washington DC
FA Corcoran Gall. ● Tue; Nat. Gall. of Art; Nat. Mus. of Women in the Arts; Phillips Coll.
H US Holocaust Memorial Museum
W Smithsonian Institution includes:
AR FA Freer Gallery of Art
FA Hirshhorn Museum; National Museum of American Art; National Portrait Gallery
ST National Air and Space Museum
FO Nat. Mus. of African Art; Sackler Gallery
H National Museum of American History
NH National Museum of Natural History
Williamsburg VIRGINIA
H Colonial Williamsburg; Jamestown Settlement
Wilmington DELAWARE
AA Nemours Mansion
AA FO Winterthur Museum
Winnipeg MANITOBA
NH Manit. Mus. of Man & Nature ● Mon (Sep-Jun)
W Winnipeg Art Gallery ● Mon (Sep-May)
Winston-Salem NORTH CAROLINA
FA Reynolda House Mus. of American Art ● Mon
Wichita KANSAS
W Wichita Art Museum ● Mon

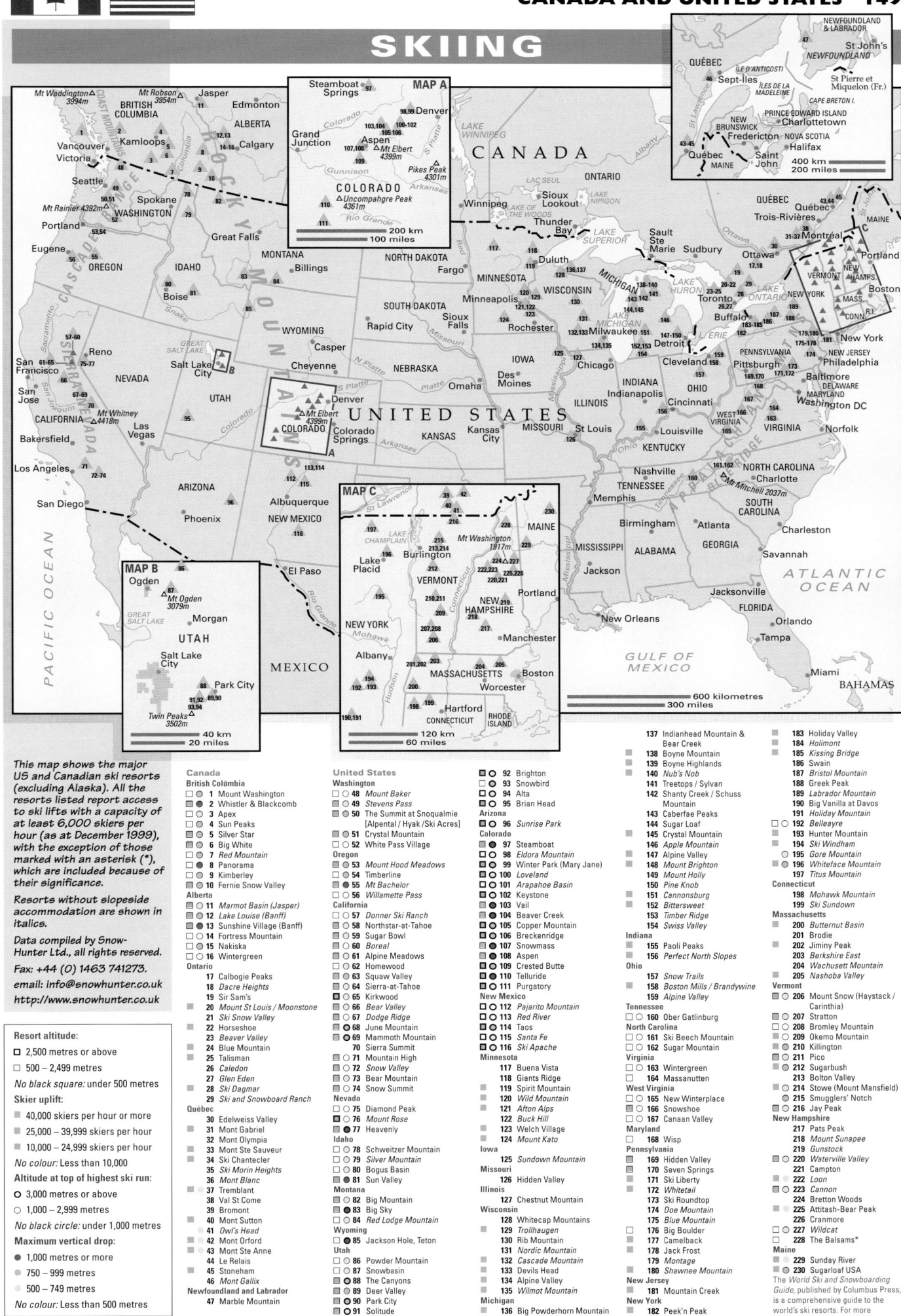

SKIING

Steamboat Springs 97
MAP A
98,99 Denver
Grand Junction
103,104 100-102
105 106
107,108
109
△Mt Elbert 4399m
Pikes Peak 4301m
COLORADO
△Uncompahgre Peak 4361m
110
Rio Grande
111
200 km
100 miles

NEWFOUNDLAND & LABRADOR
47
St John's
NEWFOUNDLAND
QUÉBEC
ÎLE D'ANTICOSTI
46 Sept-Îles
ÎLES DE LA MADELEINE
St Pierre et Miquelon (Fr.)
CAPE BRETON I.
NEW BRUNSWICK
PRINCE EDWARD ISLAND
43-45 Fredericton
Charlottetown
NOVA SCOTIA
Québec
MAINE
Saint John
Halifax
400 km
200 miles

Mt Waddington △ 3994m
COAST MOUNTAINS
Mt Robson △ 3954m
Jasper
Edmonton
11
BRITISH COLUMBIA
ALBERTA
1
Vancouver
Kamloops
4
2
12,13
8
14-16 Calgary
Victoria
48
Seattle
49
Spokane
78
Portland
Mt Rainier 4392m△
50,51
52
53,54
WASHINGTON
82
79
Great Falls
Eugene
56
55
OREGON
IDAHO
MONTANA
Billings
Boise
80
81
85
83
Reno
57-60
San Francisco
61-65
66
75-77
NEVADA
67-69
70
71
Mt Whitney △4418m
CALIFORNIA
Bakersfield
GREAT SALT LAKE
B
Salt Lake City
UTAH
95
WYOMING
Casper
Cheyenne
S Platte
Denver
△Mt Elbert 4399m
COLORADO
A
Colorado Springs
72-74
Las Vegas
Los Angeles
San Diego
ARIZONA
Phoenix
96
Albuquerque
NEW MEXICO
112 113,114
115
116
El Paso

CANADA
Winnipeg
LAKE WINNIPEG
Sioux Lookout
ONTARIO
117
118
Thunder Bay
LAKE SUPERIOR
Sault Ste Marie
Sudbury
Ottawa
17,18
QUÉBEC
Trois-Rivières
Québec
43,44
31-37 Montréal
38
MAINE
Portland
LAC SEUL
LAKE NIPIGON
Duluth
136,137
128
MINNESOTA
120
WISCONSIN
130
MICHIGAN
138-140
143 142
141
144,145
LAKE HURON
20-22
Toronto
23-25
26,27
LAKE ONTARIO
28
Buffalo
VERMONT
187
NEW HAMPS.
189
MASS.
Boston
CONN. R.I.
Minneapolis
121,122
123
Rochester
131
132,133 Milwaukee 151
134,135
Chicago
LAKE MICHIGAN
152,153 Detroit
154
147-150
159
Cleveland 158
ERIE
182
179,180
185
NEW YORK
175-178
174
New York
NEW JERSEY
Philadelphia
SOUTH DAKOTA
Rapid City
Sioux Falls
IOWA
125
NEBRASKA
Omaha
Des Moines
127
ILLINOIS
Indianapolis
INDIANA
126
Cincinnati
156
PENNSYLVANIA
169,170
171,172
173
Pittsburgh
168
OHIO
WEST VIRGINIA
167
166
163
164
Baltimore
DELAWARE
MARYLAND
Washington DC
Kansas City
KANSAS
MISSOURI
St Louis
Louisville
165
KENTUCKY
VIRGINIA
Norfolk

MAP C
39 42
40
41
216
197
LAKE CHAMPLAIN
215
213,214
Mt Washington 1917m
224△227
222,223
225,226
220,221
228
229
230
MAINE
Lake Placid
Burlington
212
VERMONT
210,211
NEW HAMPSHIRE
218
217
Portland
195
209
207,208
206
NEW YORK
Mohawk
Albany
201,202
203
MASSACHUSETTS
204 205
Boston
194
192 193
200
Worcester
198 199
Hartford
CONNECTICUT
RHODE ISLAND
190,191

Memphis
TENNESSEE
160
161,162
△Mt Mitchell 2037m
NORTH CAROLINA
Charlotte
SOUTH CAROLINA
Charleston
Nashville
Birmingham
MISSISSIPPI
ALABAMA
GEORGIA
Atlanta
Savannah
Jackson
New Orleans
Jacksonville
FLORIDA
Orlando
Tampa
GULF OF MEXICO
ATLANTIC OCEAN
Miami
BAHAMAS
600 kilometres
300 miles

PACIFIC OCEAN

MAP B
86
Ogden
87
Mt Ogden 3079m
Morgan
GREAT SALT LAKE
UTAH
Salt Lake City
88 Park City
91,92 89,90
93,94
Twin Peaks △ 3502m
40 km
20 miles

MEXICO

Rio Grande

This map shows the major US and Canadian ski resorts (excluding Alaska). All the resorts listed report access to ski lifts with a capacity of at least 6,000 skiers per hour (as at December 1999), with the exception of those marked with an asterisk (*), which are included because of their significance.

Resorts without slopeside accommodation are shown in italics.

Data compiled by Snow-Hunter Ltd., all rights reserved.

Fax: +44 (0) 1463 741273.

email: info@snowhunter.co.uk

http://www.snowhunter.co.uk

Resort altitude:
☐ 2,500 metres or above
☐ 500 – 2,499 metres
No black square: under 500 metres

Skier uplift:
■ 40,000 skiers per hour or more
■ 25,000 – 39,999 skiers per hour
■ 10,000 – 24,999 skiers per hour
No colour: Less than 10,000

Altitude at top of highest ski run:
○ 3,000 metres or above
○ 1,000 – 2,999 metres
No black circle: under 1,000 metres

Maximum vertical drop:
● 1,000 metres or more
● 750 – 999 metres
● 500 – 749 metres
No colour: Less than 500 metres

Canada
British Columbia
1 Mount Washington
2 Whistler & Blackcomb
3 Apex
4 Sun Peaks
5 Silver Star
6 Big White
7 Red Mountain
8 Panorama
9 Kimberley
10 Fernie Snow Valley
Alberta
11 Marmot Basin (Jasper)
12 Lake Louise (Banff)
13 Sunshine Village (Banff)
14 Fortress Mountain
15 Nakiska
16 Wintergreen
Ontario
17 Calbogie Peaks
18 Dacre Heights
19 Sir Sam's
20 Mount St Louis / Moonstone
21 Ski Snow Valley
22 Horseshoe
23 Beaver Valley
24 Blue Mountain
25 Talisman
26 Caledon
27 Glen Eden
28 Ski Dagmar
29 Ski and Snowboard Ranch
Québec
30 Edelweiss Valley
31 Mont Gabriel
32 Mont Olympia
33 Mont Ste Sauveur
34 Ski Chantecler
35 Ski Morin Heights
36 Mont Blanc
37 Tremblant
38 Val St Come
39 Bromont
40 Mont Sutton
41 Owl's Head
42 Mont Orford
43 Mont Ste Anne
44 Le Relais
45 Stoneham
46 Mont Gallix
Newfoundland and Labrador
47 Marble Mountain

United States
Washington
48 Mount Baker
49 Stevens Pass
50 The Summit at Snoqualmie [Alpental / Hyak /Ski Acres]
51 Crystal Mountain
52 White Pass Village
Oregon
53 Mount Hood Meadows
54 Timberline
55 Mt Bachelor
56 Willamette Pass
California
57 Donner Ski Ranch
58 Northstar-at-Tahoe
59 Sugar Bowl
60 Boreal
61 Alpine Meadows
62 Homewood
63 Squaw Valley
64 Sierra-at-Tahoe
65 Kirkwood
66 Bear Valley
67 Dodge Ridge
68 June Mountain
69 Mammoth Mountain
70 Sierra Summit
71 Mountain High
72 Snow Valley
73 Bear Mountain
74 Snow Summit
Nevada
75 Diamond Peak
76 Mount Rose
77 Heavenly
Idaho
78 Schweitzer Mountain
79 Silver Mountain
80 Bogus Basin
81 Sun Valley
Montana
82 Big Mountain
83 Big Sky
84 Red Lodge Mountain
Wyoming
85 Jackson Hole, Teton
Utah
86 Powder Mountain
87 Snowbasin
88 The Canyons
89 Deer Valley
90 Park City
91 Solitude
92 Brighton
93 Snowbird
94 Alta
95 Brian Head
Arizona
96 Sunrise Park
Colorado
97 Steamboat
98 Eldora Mountain
99 Winter Park (Mary Jane)
100 Loveland
101 Arapahoe Basin
102 Keystone
103 Vail
104 Beaver Creek
105 Copper Mountain
106 Breckenridge
107 Snowmass
108 Aspen
109 Crested Butte
110 Telluride
111 Purgatory
New Mexico
112 Pajarito Mountain
113 Red River
114 Taos
115 Santa Fe
116 Ski Apache
Minnesota
117 Buena Vista
118 Giants Ridge
119 Spirit Mountain
120 Wild Mountain
121 Afton Alps
122 Buck Hill
123 Welch Village
124 Mount Kato
Iowa
125 Sundown Mountain
Missouri
126 Hidden Valley
Illinois
127 Chestnut Mountain
Wisconsin
128 Whitecap Mountains
129 Trollhaugen
130 Rib Mountain
131 Nordic Mountain
132 Cascade Mountain
133 Devils Head
134 Alpine Valley
135 Wilmot Hills
Michigan
136 Big Powderhorn Mountain
137 Indianhead Mountain & Bear Creek
138 Boyne Mountain
139 Boyne Highlands
140 Nub's Nob
141 Treetops / Sylvan
142 Shanty Creek / Schuss Mountain
143 Caberfae Peaks
144 Sugar Loaf
145 Crystal Mountain
146 Apple Mountain
147 Alpine Valley
148 Mount Brighton
149 Mount Holly
150 Pine Knob
151 Cannonsburg
152 Bittersweet
153 Timber Ridge
154 Swiss Valley
Indiana
155 Paoli Peaks
156 Perfect North Slopes
Ohio
157 Snow Trails
158 Boston Mills / Brandywine
159 Alpine Valley
Tennessee
160 Ober Gatlinburg
North Carolina
161 Ski Beech Mountain
162 Sugar Mountain
Virginia
163 Wintergreen
164 Massanutten
West Virginia
165 New Winterplace
166 Snowshoe
167 Canaan Valley
Maryland
168 Wisp
Pennsylvania
169 Hidden Valley
170 Seven Springs
171 Ski Liberty
172 Whitetail
173 Ski Roundtop
174 Doe Mountain
175 Blue Mountain
176 Big Boulder
177 Camelback
178 Jack Frost
179 Montage
180 Shawnee Mountain
New Jersey
181 Mountain Creek
New York
182 Peek'n Peak
183 Holiday Valley
184 Holimont
185 Kissing Bridge
186 Swain
187 Bristol Mountain
188 Greek Peak
189 Labrador Mountain
190 Big Vanilla at Davos
191 Holiday Mountain
192 Belleayre
193 Hunter Mountain
194 Ski Windham
195 Gore Mountain
196 Whiteface Mountain
197 Titus Mountain
Connecticut
198 Mohawk Mountain
199 Ski Sundown
Massachusetts
200 Butternut Basin
201 Brodie
202 Jiminy Peak
203 Berkshire East
204 Wachusett Mountain
205 Nashoba Valley
Vermont
206 Mount Snow (Haystack / Carinthia)
207 Stratton
208 Bromley Mountain
209 Okemo Mountain
210 Killington
211 Pico
212 Sugarbush
213 Bolton Valley
214 Stowe (Mount Mansfield)
215 Smugglers' Notch
216 Jay Peak
New Hampshire
217 Pats Peak
218 Mount Sunapee
219 Gunstock
220 Waterville Valley
221 Campton
222 Loon
223 Cannon
224 Bretton Woods
225 Attitash-Bear Peak
226 Cranmore
227 Wildcat
228 The Balsams*
Maine
229 Sunday River
230 Sugarloaf USA

The World Ski and Snowboarding Guide, published by Columbus Press, is a comprehensive guide to the world's ski resorts. For more information, call +44 (0)20 7417 0700.

NATIONAL PARKS...

National Park Service:

● **National Park / Preserve**
National Parks contain a variety of resources protected by large areas of land or water; National Preserves permit activities not permitted in National Parks, such as hunting, fishing and mineral extraction

○ **National Memorial**
Commemorate a historical subject or person

● **National Monument**
Generally smaller than National Parks, they tend to focus on one site or feature of national significance

○ **National Recreation Area / Seashore / Lakeshore**
National Recreation Areas are set aside for purely recreational use and are often near major cities; National Seashores and Lakeshores provide water-oriented recreation whilst preserving shorelines and islands

● **National Battlefield / Battlefield Park / Battlefield Site / Military Park**
All associated with US military history

○ **National Historic Site / Historical Park**
National Historic Sites preserve locations and commemorate persons or events important in the nation's history; National Historical Parks are similar but larger and more complex

● **National Parkways**
Roadways that have been preserved for their scenic value.

Other areas (not included here) include National Rivers, and Wild and Scenic Riverways; areas under the protection of the National Trails System – established to preserve and maintain a wide variety of public footpaths; and affiliated areas including National Heritage Areas which are managed by government-private partnerships.

● **Theme park**

The National Park Service is responsible for over 370 sites set aside to preserve the natural, historical and cultural heritage of the United States. For further information, contact:

National Park Service,
1849 C Street Northwest,
Washington DC, 20240.
Tel. +1 202 208 4747.

The map also shows some of the more well-known theme parks, from Disneyland in California to Sea World of Florida.
For further information, contact:

International Association of Amusement Parks and Attractions (IAAPA),
1448 Duke Street,
Alexandria, Virginia 22314.
Tel. +1 703 836 4800.

TOP US THEME PARKS IN 1998
Number of visitors in millions
(world ranking in brackets)
Magic Kingdom FL: 15.6 (2nd)
Disneyland CA: 13.7 (3rd)
EPCOT Center FL: 10.6 (5th)
Disney-MGM Studios FL: 9.5 (6th)
Universal Studios FL: 8.9 (7th)
Animal Kingdom FL: 6.0 (10th)
Universal Studios CA: 5.1 (13th)
Sea World FL: 4.9 (14th)
Busch Gardens FL: 4.2 (15th)
Sea World CA: 3.7 (17th)
Great Adventure NJ: 3.4 (18th)
Berry Farm CA: 3.4 (=19th)
Kings Island OH: 3.4 (=19th)
Cedar Point OH: 3.4 (=19th)
Santa Cruz Beach CA: 3.2 (=23rd)
Magic Mountain CA: 3.1 (25th)
Morey's Pier NJ: 3.0 (27th)
Great America IL: 2.9 (29th)
Six Flags over Texas: 2.8 (31st)
Circus Circus NV: 2.8 (=32nd)
Camp Snoopy MN: 2.6 (39th)
Hersheypark PA: 2.4 (=44th)
Busch Gardens VA: 2.4 (=44th)
Kings Dominion VA: 2.3 (47th)
Six Flags over Georgia: 2.3 (48th)
Dollywood TN: 2.2 (49th)
Source: Amusement Business

Alaska
● 1 Bering Land Bridge National Preserve
● 2 Cape Krusenstern National Monument
● 3 Kobuk Valley National Park
● 4 Noatak National Preserve
● 5 Gates of the Arctic National Park and Preserve
● 6 Yukon-Charley Rivers National Preserve
● 7 Denali National Park and Preserve
● 8 Lake Clark National Park and Preserve
● 9 Katmai National Park and Preserve
● 10 Aniakchak National Monument and Preserve
● 11 Kenai Fjords National Park
● 12 Wrangell-St Elias National Park and Preserve
○ 13 Klondike Gold Rush National Historical Park
● 14 Glacier Bay National Park and Preserve
○ 15 Sitka National Historical Park

Hawaii
○ 16 USS Arizona Memorial
○ 17 Kalaupapa National Historical Park
● 18 Haleakala National Park
○ 19 Puukohola Heiau National Historic Site
○ 20 Kaloko-Honokohau National Historical Park
○ 21 Pu'uhonua o Honaunau National Historical Park
● 22 Hawaii Volcanoes National Park

Washington
● 23 San Juan Island National Historical Park
● 24 Olympic National Park
○ 25 Ebey's Landing National Historical Reserve
● 26 North Cascades National Park
○ 27 Ross Lake National Recreation Area
○ 28 Lake Chelan National Recreation Area
○ 29 Lake Roosevelt National Recreation Area
○ 30 Whitman Mission National Historic Site
● 31 Mount Rainier National Park
○ 32 Fort Vancouver National Historic Site

Oregon
○ 33 Fort Clatsop National Memorial
● 34 John Day Fossil Beds National Monument
● 35 Crater Lake National Park
○ 36 Oregon Caves National Monument

California
● 37 Redwood National Park
● 38 Lava Beds National Monument
○ 39 Whiskeytown-Shasta-Trinity National Recreation Area
● 40 Lassen Volcanic National Park
○ 41 Point Reyes National Seashore
● 42 Muir Woods National Monument
○ 43 Fort Point National Historic Site
○ 44 Golden Gate National Recreation Area
○ 45 San Francisco Maritime National Historical Park
○ 46 John Muir National Historic Site
○ 47 Eugene O'Neill National Historic Site
● 48 Pinnacles National Monument
● 49 Yosemite National Park
● 50 Devils Postpile National Monument
● 51 Sequoia and Kings Canyon National Parks
○ 52 Manzanar National Historic Site
● 53 Death Valley National Park
● 54 Channel Islands National Park
○ 55 Santa Monica Mountains National Recreation Area
● 56 Cabrillo National Monument
● 57 Joshua Tree National Park
● 58 Mojave National Preserve

Nevada
○ 59 Lake Mead National Recreation Area (also in Arizona)
● 60 Great Basin National Park

Idaho
● 61 City of Rocks National Reserve
● 62 Hagerman Fossil Beds National Monument
● 63 Craters of the Moon National Monument
○ 64 Nez Perce National Historical Park

Montana
● 65 Glacier National Park
○ 66 Grant-Kohrs Ranch National Historic Site
● 67 Big Hole National Battlefield
○ 68 Bighorn Canyon National Recreation Area

● 69 Little Bighorn Battlefield National Monument

Wyoming
● 70 Devils Tower National Monument
○ 71 Fort Laramie National Historic Site
● 72 Yellowstone National Park
● 73 John D. Rockefeller, Jr. Memorial Parkway
● 74 Grand Teton National Park
● 75 Fossil Butte National Monument

Utah
○ 76 Golden Spike National Historic Site
● 77 Timpanogos Cave National Monument
● 78 Zion National Park
● 79 Cedar Breaks National Monument
● 80 Bryce Canyon National Park
● 81 Capitol Reef National Park
● 82 Rainbow Bridge National Monument
● 83 Natural Bridges National Monument
● 84 Canyonlands National Park
● 85 Arches National Park

Colorado
● 86 Dinosaur National Monument
● 87 Rocky Mountain National Park
● 88 Colorado National Monument
● 89 Black Canyon of the Gunnison National Monument
○ 90 Curecanti National Recreation Area
● 91 Hovenweep National Monument
● 92 Yucca House National Monument
● 93 Mesa Verde National Park
● 94 Great Sand Dunes National Monument
● 95 Florissant Fossil Beds National Monument
○ 96 Bent's Old Fort National Historic Site

Arizona
● 97 Pipe Spring National Monument
● 98 Grand Canyon National Park
○ 99 Glen Canyon National Recreation Area (also in Utah)
● 100 Navajo National Monument
● 101 Canyon de Chelly National Monument
○ 102 Hubbell Trading Post National Historic Site
● 103 Petrified Forest National Park
● 104 Wupatki National Monument
● 105 Sunset Crater Volcano National Monument
● 106 Walnut Canyon National Monument
● 107 Tuzigoot National Monument
● 108 Montezuma Castle National Monument
● 109 Tonto National Monument
● 110 Hohokam Pima National Monument

● 111 Casa Grande Ruins National Monument
● 112 Organ Pipe Cactus National Monument
○ 113 Tumacacori National Historical Park
● 114 Coronado National Memorial
● 115 Saguaro National Park
○ 116 Fort Bowie National Historic Site
● 117 Chiricahua National Monument

New Mexico
● 118 Gila Cliff Dwellings National Monument
● 119 White Sands National Monument
● 120 Carlsbad Caverns National Park
● 121 Salinas Pueblo Missions National Monument
● 122 Aztec Ruins National Monument
○ 123 Chaco Culture National Historical Park
● 124 El Morro National Monument
● 125 El Malpais National Monument
● 126 Petroglyph National Monument
● 127 Bandelier National Monument
● 128 Pecos National Historical Park
● 129 Fort Union National Monument
● 130 Capulin Volcano National Monument

Texas
○ 131 Lake Meredith National Recreation Area
● 132 Alibates Flint Quarries National Monument
● 133 Chamizal National Memorial
● 134 Guadalupe Mountains National Park
○ 135 Fort Davis National Historic Site
● 136 Big Bend National Park
○ 137 Amistad National Recreation Area
● 138 Lyndon B. Johnson National Historical Park
○ 139 San Antonio Missions National Historical Park
○ 140 Palo Alto Battlefield National Historic Site
○ 141 Padre Island National Seashore
● 142 Big Thicket National Preserve

Oklahoma
○ 143 Chickasaw National Recreation Area
○ 144 Oklahoma City National Memorial
● 145 Washita Battlefield National Historic Site

North Dakota
○ 146 Fort Union Trading Post National Historic Site
● 147 Theodore Roosevelt National Park
○ 148 Knife River Indian Villages National Historic Site

South Dakota
● 149 Jewel Cave National Monument
○ 150 Mount Rushmore National Memorial
● 151 Wind Cave National Park
● 152 Badlands National Park

Minnesota
● 153 Pipestone National Monument
● 154 Voyageurs National Park
● 155 Grand Portage National Monument

Wisconsin
○ 156 Apostle Islands National Lakeshore

Michigan
● 157 Isle Royale National Park
○ 158 Keweenaw National Historical Park
○ 159 Pictured Rocks National Lakeshore
○ 160 Sleeping Bear Dunes National Lakeshore

Nebraska
● 161 Agate Fossil Beds National Monument
● 162 Scotts Bluff National Monument
● 163 Homestead National Monument of America

Iowa
● 164 Effigy Mounds National Monument
○ 165 Herbert Hoover National Historic Site

Kansas
○ 166 Nicodemus National Historic Site
○ 167 Fort Larned National Historic Site
○ 168 Tallgrass Prairie National Preserve
○ 169 Brown v. Board of Education National Historic Site
○ 170 Fort Scott National Historic Site

Missouri
○ 171 Harry S. Truman National Historic Site
● 172 George Washington Carver National Monument
● 173 Wilson's Creek National Battlefield
○ 174 Ulysses S. Grant National Historic Site
○ 175 Jefferson National Expansion Memorial

Illinois
○ 176 Lincoln Home National Historic Site

Indiana
○ 177 Indiana Dunes National Lakeshore
○ 178 George Rogers Clark National Historical Park
● 179 Lincoln Boyhood National Memorial

Ohio
○ 180 William Howard Taft National Historic Site
○ 181 Dayton Aviation National Historical Park
○ 182 Hopewell Culture National Historical Park
● 183 Perry's Victory and International Peace Memorial
○ 184 James A. Garfield National Historic Site
○ 185 Cuyahoga Valley National Recreation Area

Arkansas
● 186 Pea Ridge National Military Park
○ 187 Fort Smith National Historic Site
● 188 Hot Springs National Park

...AND THEME PARKS

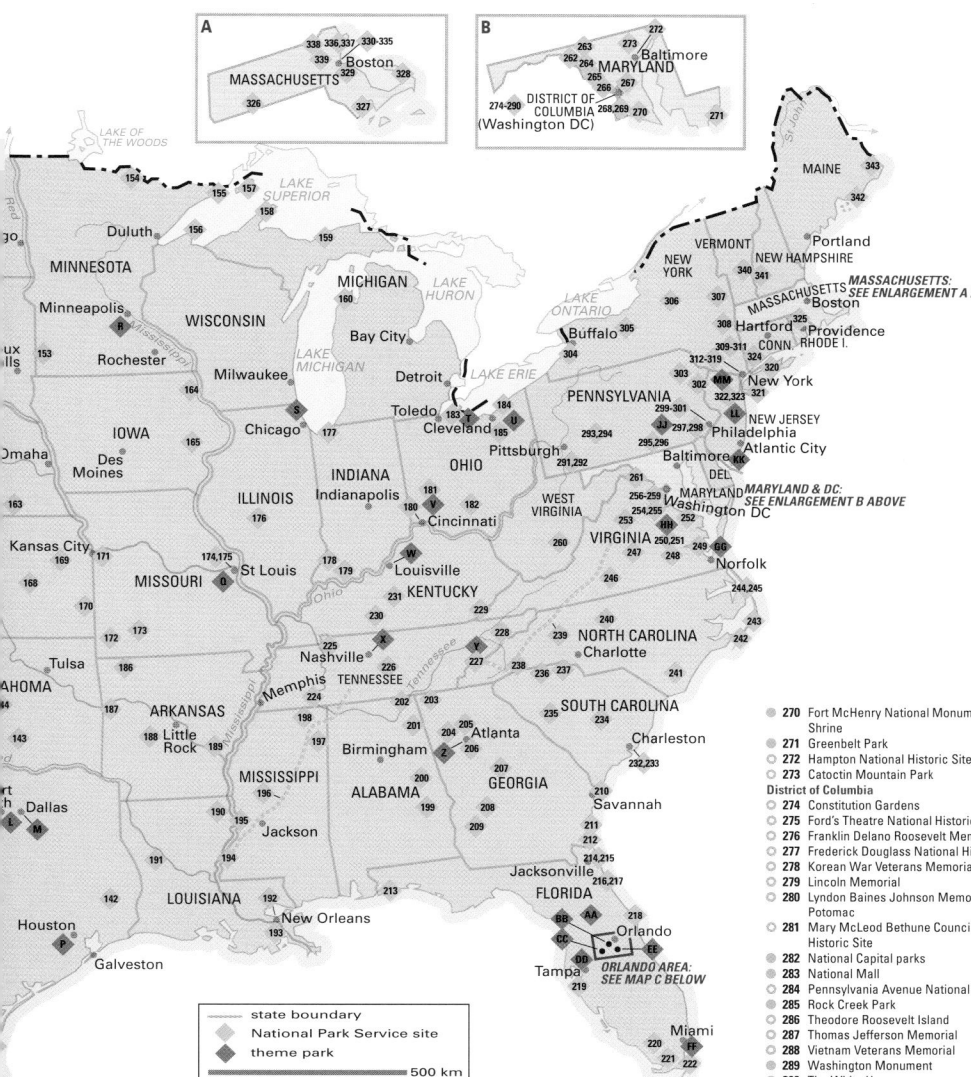

MASSACHUSETTS: SEE ENLARGEMENT A ABOVE

MARYLAND & DC: SEE ENLARGEMENT B ABOVE

- 314 Gateway National Recreation Area (also in New Jersey)
- 315 General Grant National Memorial
- 316 Hamilton Grange National Memorial
- 317 St Paul's Church National Historic Site
- 318 Statue of Liberty National Monument
- 319 Theodore Roosevelt Birthplace National Historic Site
- 320 Sagamore Hill National Historic Site
- 321 Fire Island National Seashore

New Jersey
- 322 Edison National Historic Site
- 323 Morristown National Historical Park

Connecticut
- 324 Weir Farm National Historic Site

Rhode Island
- 325 Roger Williams National Memorial

Massachusetts
- 326 Springfield Armory National Historic Site
- 327 New Bedford Whaling National Historical Park
- 328 Cape Cod National Seashore
- 329 Adams National Historic Site
- 330 Boston African American National Historical Site
- 331 Boston Harbor Islands National Recreation Area
- 332 Boston National Historical Park
- 333 Frederick Law Olmsted National Historic Site
- 334 John F. Kennedy National Historic Site
- 335 Longfellow National Historic Site
- 336 Saugus Iron Works National Historic Site
- 337 Salem Maritime National Historic Site
- 338 Lowell National Historical Park
- 339 Minute Man National Historical Park

Vermont
- 340 Marsh-Billings National Historical Park

New Hampshire
- 341 St-Gaudens National Historic Site

Maine
- 342 Acadia National Park
- 343 St Croix Island International Historic Site

(Not shown on map):

Puerto Rico
- San Juan National Historic Site

US Virgin Islands
- Buck Island Reef National Monument
- Christiansted National Historic Site
- Salt River Bay National Historical Park and Ecological Preserve
- Virgin Islands National Park

American Samoa
- National Park of American Samoa

Northern Mariana Islands
- War in the Pacific National Historical Park

THEME PARKS
- A Marine World Africa USA, Vallejo, California
- B Paramount's Great America, Santa Clara, California
- C Santa Cruz Beach Boardwalk, Santa Cruz, California
- D Six Flags Magic Mountain, Valencia, California
- E Universal Studios Hollywood, Universal City, Los Angeles, California
- F Raging Waters, San Dimas, Los Angeles, California
- G Knott's Berry Farm, Buena Park, Los Angeles, California
- H Disneyland, Anaheim, Los Angeles, California
- J Sea World of California, San Diego, California
- K Circus Circus, Las Vegas, Nevada
- L Six Flags over Texas, Arlington, Texas
- M Fair Park, Dallas, Texas
- N Six Flags Fiesta, San Antonio, Texas
- O Sea World of Texas, San Antonio, Texas
- P Six Flags AstroWorld / Six Flags WaterWorld, Houston, Texas
- Q Six Flags over Mid-America, Eureka, Missouri
- R Knott's Camp Snoopy, Bloomington, Minnesota
- S Six Flags Great America, Gurnee, Illinois
- T Cedar Point, Sandusky, Ohio
- U Sea World of Ohio, Aurora, Ohio
- V Paramount's Kings Island, Kings Mills, Ohio
- W Kentucky Kingdom – The Thrill Park, Louisville, Kentucky
- X Opryland USA, Nashville, Tennessee
- Y Dollywood, Pigeon Forge, Tennessee
- Z Six Flags over Georgia, Atlanta, Georgia
- AA Florida's Silver Springs, Silver Springs, Florida
- BB Universal Studios Florida, Orlando, Florida
- CC Walt Disney World Resort Complex (including the Magic Kingdom theme park, EPCOT Center, Disney-MGM Studios theme park, Animal Kingdom), Lake Buena Vista, Florida
- DD Busch Gardens Tampa Bay, Florida
- EE Sea World of Florida, Orlando, Florida
- FF Miami Seaquarium, Miami, Florida
- GG Busch Gardens the Old Country, Williamsburg, Virginia
- HH Paramount's Kings Dominion, Doswell, Virginia
- JJ Hersheypark, Hershey, Pennsylvania
- KK Morey's Pier, Wildwood, New Jersey
- LL Six Flags Great Adventure, Jackson, New Jersey
- MM Great Gorge Resort Action Park, McAfee, New Jersey

- 189 Arkansas Post National Memorial

Louisiana
- 190 Poverty Point National Monument
- 191 Cane River Creole National Historical Park
- 192 New Orleans Jazz National Historical Park
- 193 Jean Lafitte National Historical Park and Preserve

Mississippi
- 194 Natchez National Historical Park
- 195 Vicksburg National Military Park
- 196 Natchez Trace Parkway (also in Alabama and Tennessee)
- 197 Tupelo National Battlefield
- 198 Brices Cross Roads National Battlefield Site

Alabama
- 199 Tuskegee Institute National Historic Site
- 200 Horseshoe Bend National Military Park
- 201 Little River Canyon National Preserve
- 202 Russell Cave National Monument

Georgia
- 203 Chickamauga and Chattanooga National Military Park
- 204 Kennesaw Mountain National Battlefield Park
- 205 Chattahoochee River National Recreation Area
- 206 Martin Luther King Jr. National Historic Site
- 207 Ocmulgee National Monument
- 208 Andersonville National Historic Site
- 209 Jimmy Carter National Historic Site
- 210 Fort Pulaski National Monument
- 211 Fort Frederica National Monument
- 212 Cumberland Island National Seashore

Florida
- 213 Gulf Islands National Seashore (also in Mississippi)
- 214 Timucuan Ecological and Historic Preserve
- 215 Fort Caroline National Memorial
- 216 Castillo de San Marcos National Monument
- 217 Fort Matanzas National Monument
- 218 Canaveral National Seashore
- 219 De Soto National Memorial
- 220 Big Cypress National Preserve
- 221 Everglades National Park
- 222 Biscayne National Park
- 223 Dry Tortugas National Park

Tennessee
- 224 Shiloh National Military Park
- 225 Fort Donelson National Battlefield
- 226 Stones River National Battlefield and Cemetery
- 227 Great Smoky Mountains National Park (also in North Carolina)
- 228 Andrew Johnson National Historic Site

Kentucky
- 229 Cumberland Gap National Historical Park
- 230 Mammoth Cave National Park
- 231 Abraham Lincoln Birthplace National Historic Site

South Carolina
- 232 Fort Sumter National Monument
- 233 Charles Pinckney National Historic Site
- 234 Congaree Swamp National Monument
- 235 Ninety Six National Historic Site
- 236 Kings Mountain National Military Park
- 237 Cowpens National Battlefield

North Carolina
- 238 Carl Sandburg Home National Historic Site
- 239 Blue Ridge Parkway (also in Virginia)
- 240 Guilford Courthouse National Military Park
- 241 Moores Creek National Battlefield
- 242 Cape Lookout National Seashore
- 243 Cape Hatteras National Seashore
- 244 Fort Raleigh National Historic Site
- 245 Wright Brothers National Memorial

Virginia
- 246 Booker T. Washington National Monument
- 247 Appomattox Court House National Historical Park
- 248 Petersburg National Battlefield
- 249 Colonial National Historical Park
- 250 Maggie L. Walker National Historic Site
- 251 Richmond National Battlefield Park
- 252 George Washington Birthplace National Monument
- 253 Shenandoah National Park
- 254 Fredericksburg and Spotsylvania County Battlefields Memorial National Military Park
- 255 Prince William Forest Park
- 256 Manassas National Battlefield Park
- 257 Wolf Trap Farm Park for the Performing Arts
- 258 George Washington National Parkway
- 259 Arlington House, The Robert E. Lee Memorial

West Virginia
- 260 Gauley River National Recreation Area
- 261 Harpers Ferry National Historical Park

Maryland
- 262 Antietam National Battlefield
- 263 Monocacy National Battlefield
- 264 Chesapeake and Ohio Canal National Historical Park
- 265 Clara Barton National Historic Site
- 266 Fort Washington Park
- 267 Piscataway Park
- 268 Thomas Stone National Historic Site
- 269 Assateague Island National Seashore

- 270 Fort McHenry National Monument and Historic Shrine
- 271 Greenbelt Park
- 272 Hampton National Historic Site
- 273 Catoctin Mountain Park

District of Columbia
- 274 Constitution Gardens
- 275 Ford's Theatre National Historic Site
- 276 Franklin Delano Roosevelt Memorial
- 277 Frederick Douglass National Historic Site
- 278 Korean War Veterans Memorial
- 279 Lincoln Memorial
- 280 Lyndon Baines Johnson Memorial Grove on the Potomac
- 281 Mary McLeod Bethune Council House National Historic Site
- 282 National Capital parks
- 283 National Mall
- 284 Pennsylvania Avenue National Historic Site
- 285 Rock Creek Park
- 286 Theodore Roosevelt Island
- 287 Thomas Jefferson Memorial
- 288 Vietnam Veterans Memorial
- 289 Washington Monument
- 290 The White House

Pennsylvania
- 291 Friendship Hill National Historic Site
- 292 Fort Necessity National Battlefield
- 293 Johnstown Flood National Memorial
- 294 Allegheny Portage Railroad National Historic Site
- 295 Eisenhower National Historic Site
- 296 Gettysburg National Military Park
- 297 Hopewell Furnace National Historic Site
- 298 Valley Forge National Historical Park
- 299 Edgar Allen Poe National Historic Site
- 300 Independence National Historical Park
- 301 Thaddeus Kosciuszko National Memorial
- 302 Delaware Water Gap National Recreation Area
- 303 Steamtown National Historic Site

New York
- 304 Theodore Roosevelt Inaugural National Historic Site
- 305 Women's Rights National Historical Park
- 306 Fort Stanwix National Monument
- 307 Saratoga National Historical Park
- 308 Martin Van Buren National Historic Site
- 309 Eleanor Roosevelt National Historic Site
- 310 Vanderbilt Mansion National Historic Site
- 311 Home of Franklin Delano Roosevelt National Historic Site
- 312 Castle Clinton National Monument
- 313 Federal Hall National Memorial

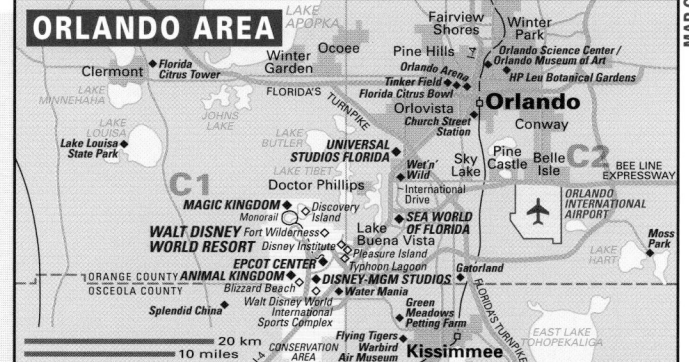

ORLANDO AREA

MAP C

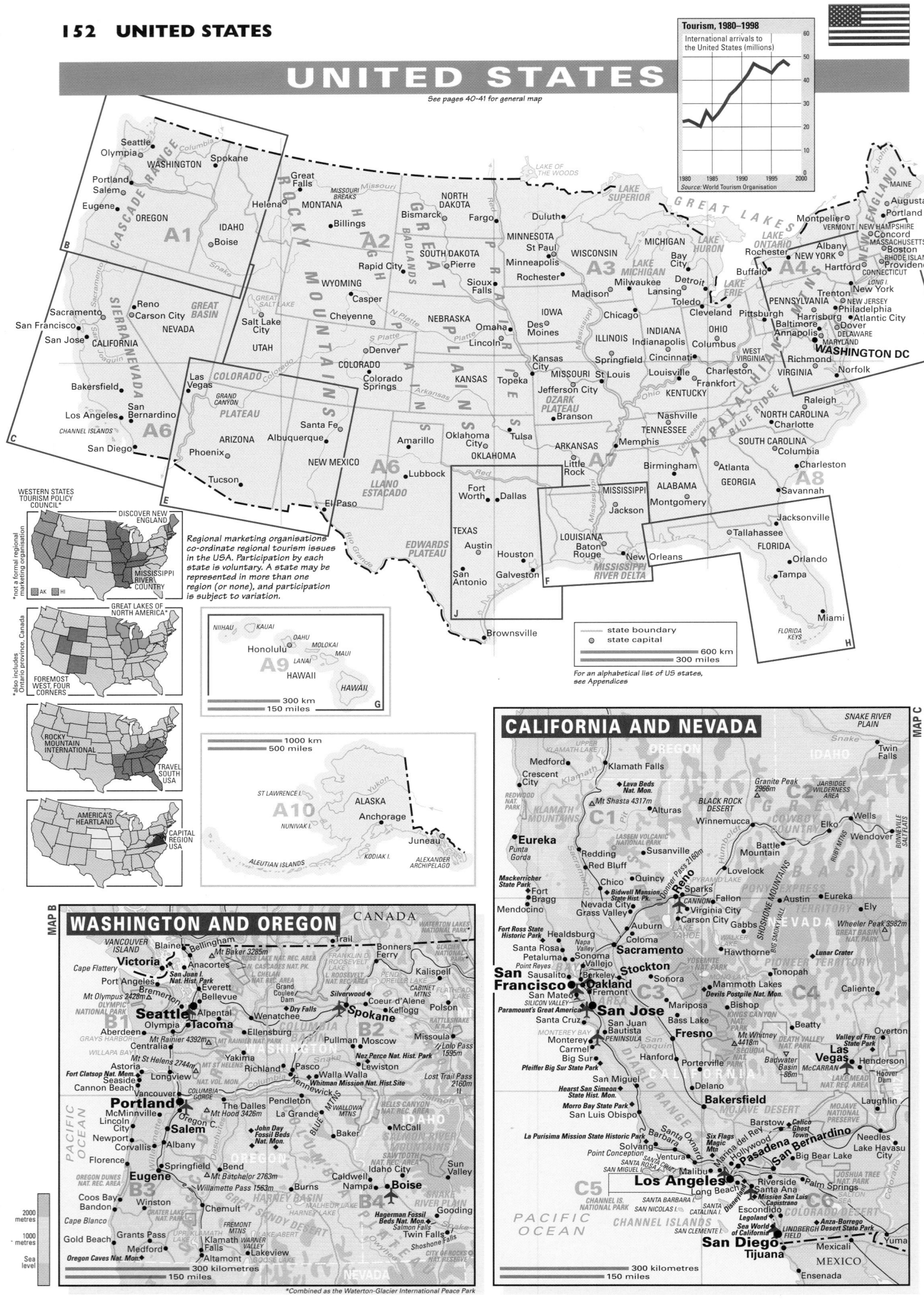

UNITED STATES

See pages 40-41 for general map

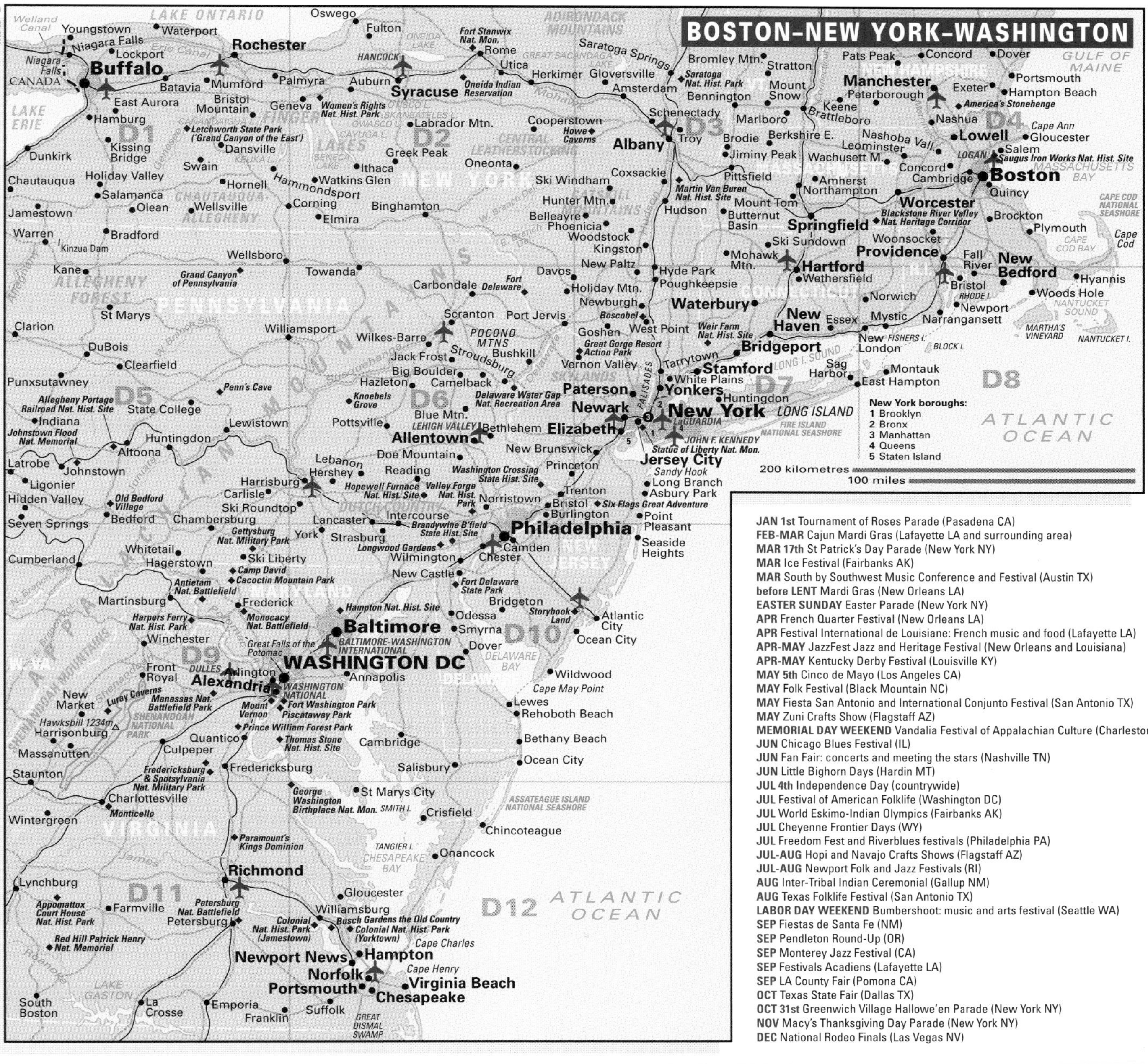

BOSTON-NEW YORK-WASHINGTON

200 kilometres
100 miles

New York boroughs:
1 Brooklyn
2 Bronx
3 Manhattan
4 Queens
5 Staten Island

JAN 1st Tournament of Roses Parade (Pasadena CA)
FEB-MAR Cajun Mardi Gras (Lafayette LA and surrounding area)
MAR 17th St Patrick's Day Parade (New York NY)
MAR Ice Festival (Fairbanks AK)
MAR South by Southwest Music Conference and Festival (Austin TX)
before LENT Mardi Gras (New Orleans LA)
EASTER SUNDAY Easter Parade (New York NY)
APR French Quarter Festival (New Orleans LA)
APR Festival International de Louisiane: French music and food (Lafayette LA)
APR-MAY JazzFest Jazz and Heritage Festival (New Orleans and Louisiana)
APR-MAY Kentucky Derby Festival (Louisville KY)
MAY 5th Cinco de Mayo (Los Angeles CA)
MAY Folk Festival (Black Mountain NC)
MAY Fiesta San Antonio and International Conjunto Festival (San Antonio TX)
MAY Zuni Crafts Show (Flagstaff AZ)
MEMORIAL DAY WEEKEND Vandalia Festival of Appalachian Culture (Charleston WV)
JUN Chicago Blues Festival (IL)
JUN Fan Fair: concerts and meeting the stars (Nashville TN)
JUN Little Bighorn Days (Hardin MT)
JUL 4th Independence Day (countrywide)
JUL Festival of American Folklife (Washington DC)
JUL World Eskimo-Indian Olympics (Fairbanks AK)
JUL Cheyenne Frontier Days (WY)
JUL Freedom Fest and Riverblues festivals (Philadelphia PA)
JUL-AUG Hopi and Navajo Crafts Shows (Flagstaff AZ)
JUL-AUG Newport Folk and Jazz Festivals (RI)
AUG Inter-Tribal Indian Ceremonial (Gallup NM)
AUG Texas Folklife Festival (San Antonio TX)
LABOR DAY WEEKEND Bumbershoot: music and arts festival (Seattle WA)
SEP Fiestas de Santa Fe (NM)
SEP Pendleton Round-Up (OR)
SEP Monterey Jazz Festival (CA)
SEP Festivals Acadiens (Lafayette LA)
SEP LA County Fair (Pomona CA)
OCT Texas State Fair (Dallas TX)
OCT 31st Greenwich Village Hallowe'en Parade (New York NY)
NOV Macy's Thanksgiving Day Parade (New York NY)
DEC National Rodeo Finals (Las Vegas NV)

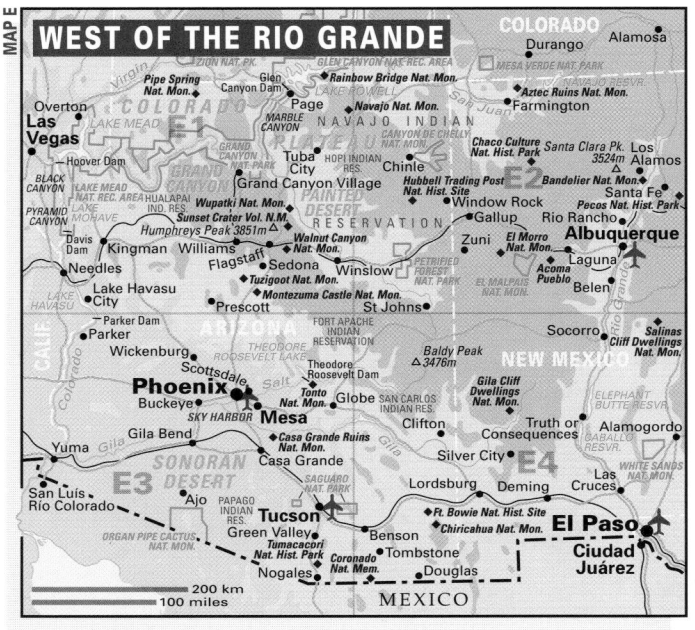

WEST OF THE RIO GRANDE

200 km
100 miles

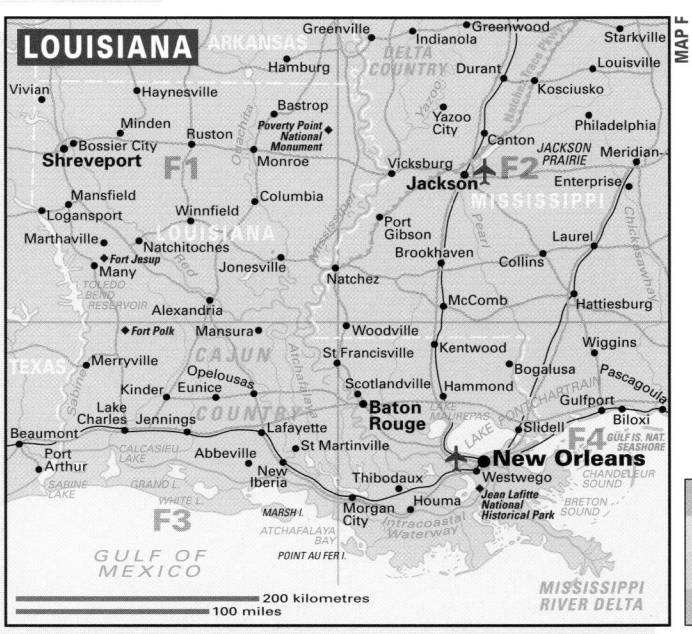

LOUISIANA

200 kilometres
100 miles

2000 metres
1000 metres
Sea level

UNITED STATES

See pages 40-41 for general map

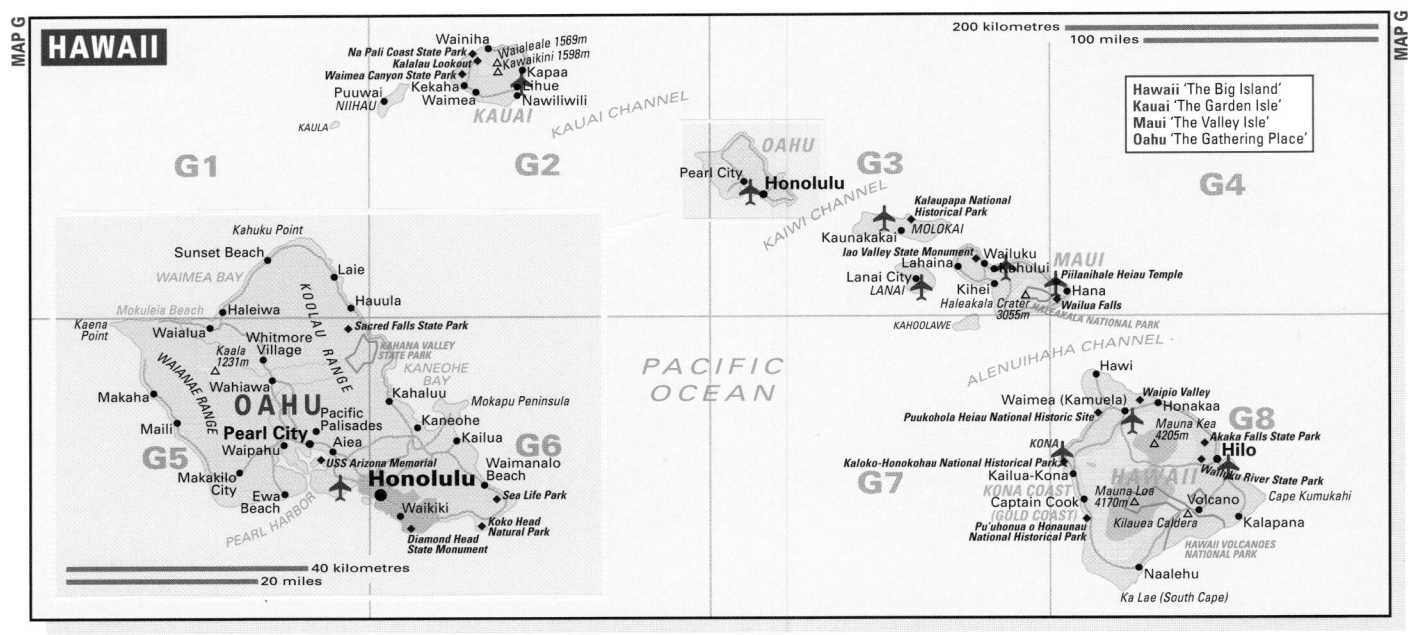

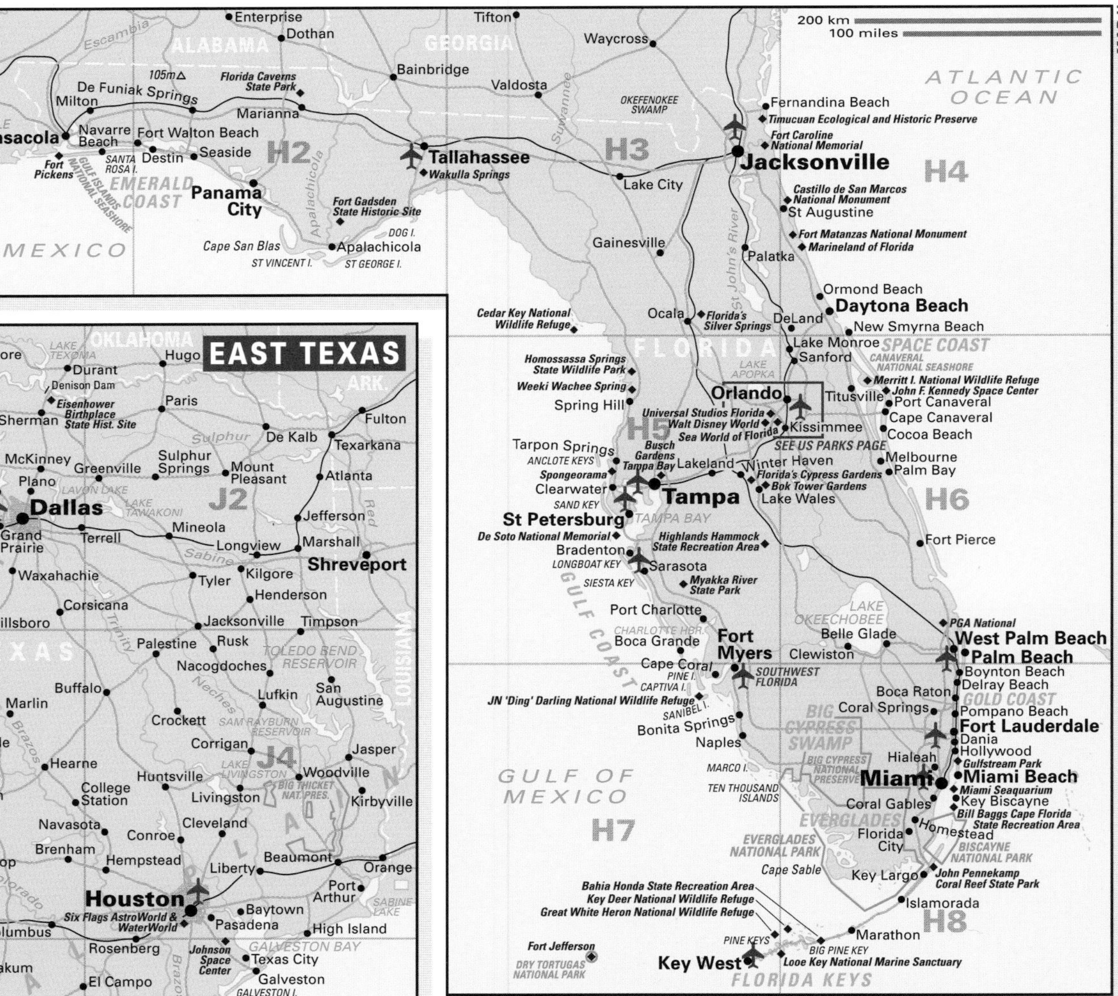

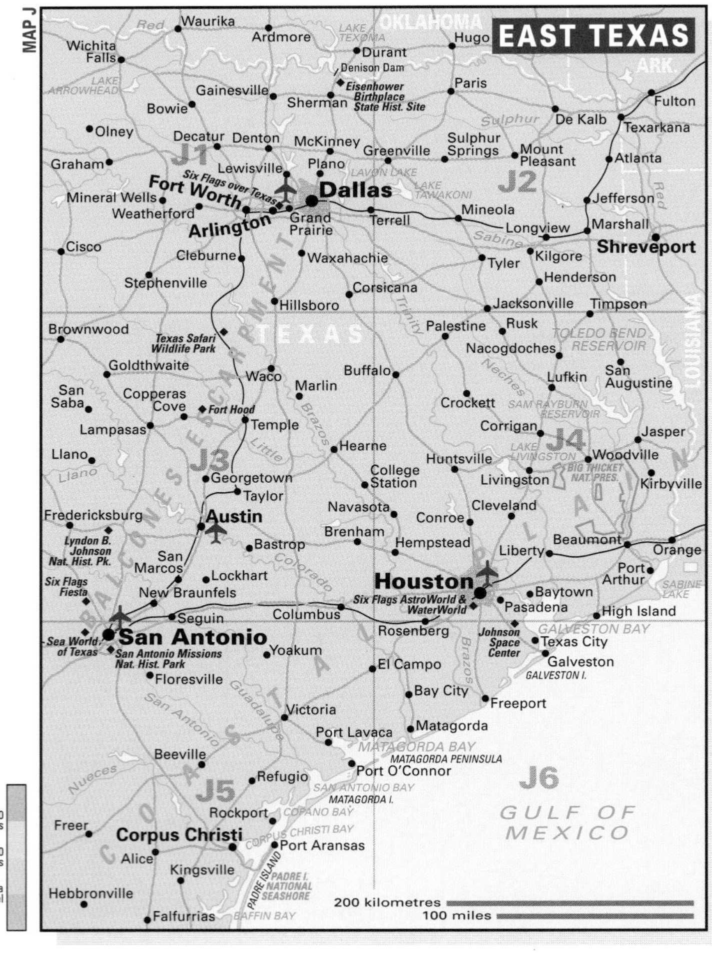

HAWAII

Hawaii 'The Big Island'
Kauai 'The Garden Isle'
Maui 'The Valley Isle'
Oahu 'The Gathering Place'

FLORIDA

EAST TEXAS

Income from tourism, 1997
Total spent by domestic and foreign tourists and travellers

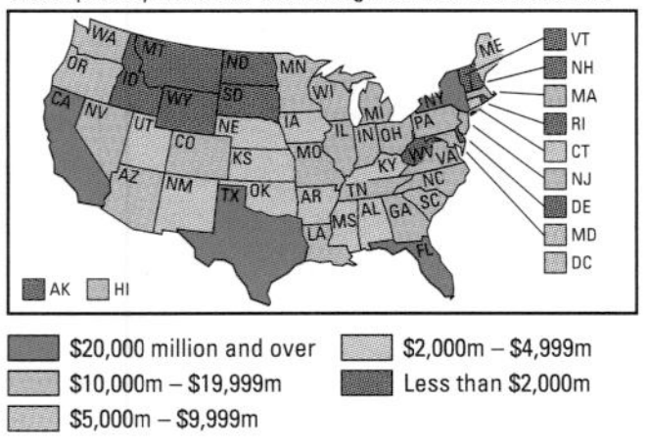

$20,000 million and over	$2,000m – $4,999m
$10,000m – $19,999m	Less than $2,000m
$5,000m – $9,999m	

Employment in tourism, 1996
Employment generated by travel and tourism as % of total state employee

7.0% and over	3.0 – 4.9%
5.0 – 6.9%	Less than 3.0%

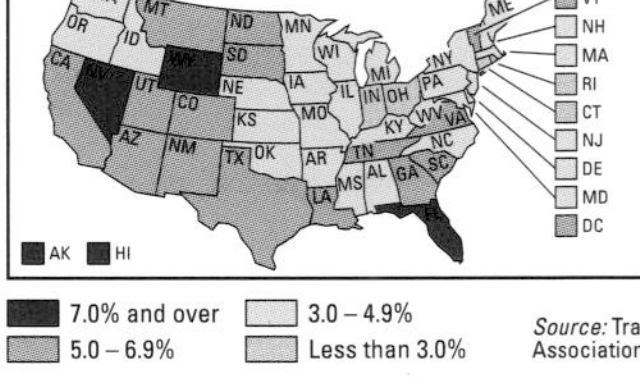

Source: Travel Industry Association of America

2000 metres
1000 metres
Sea level

CANADA

See pages 38–39 for general map

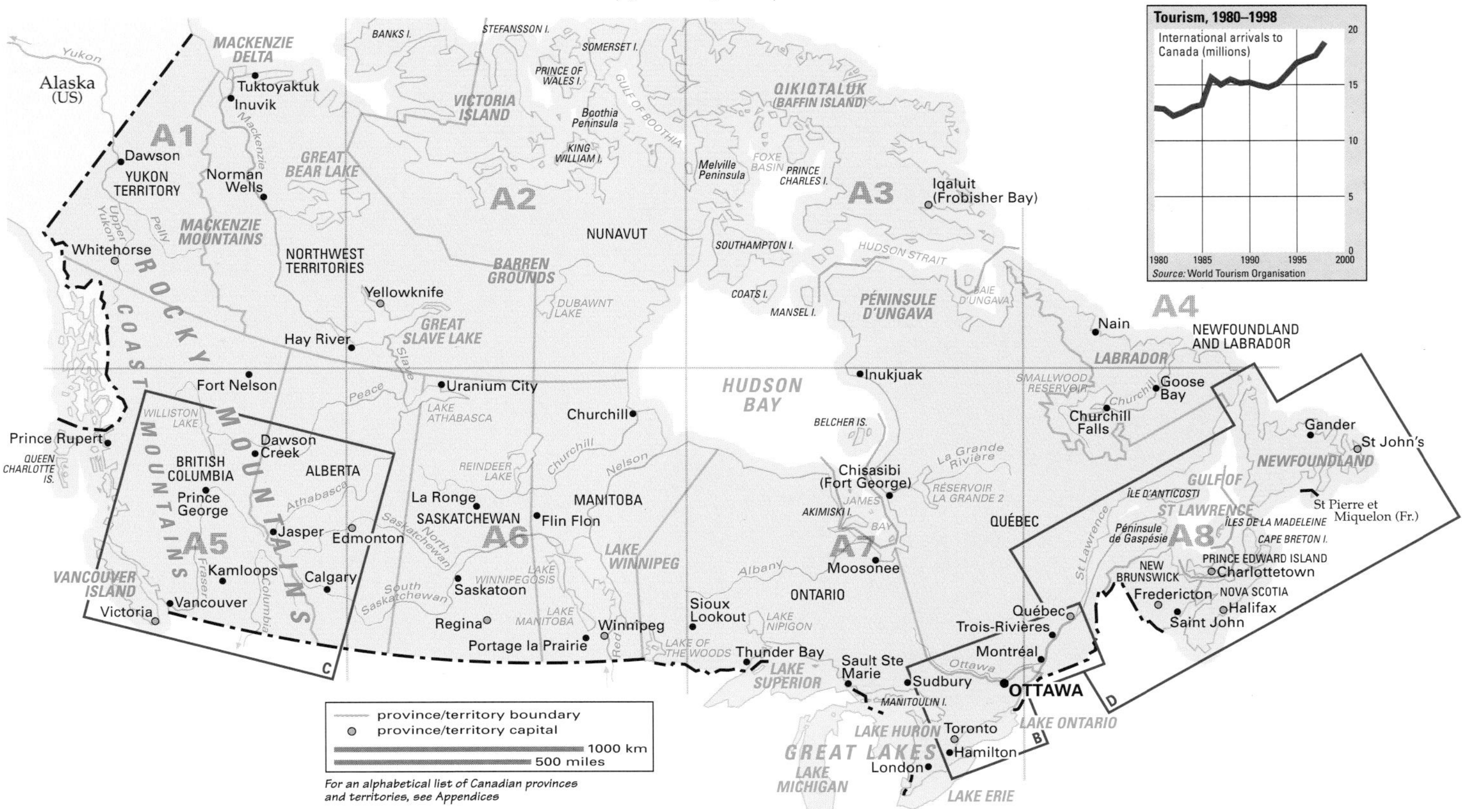

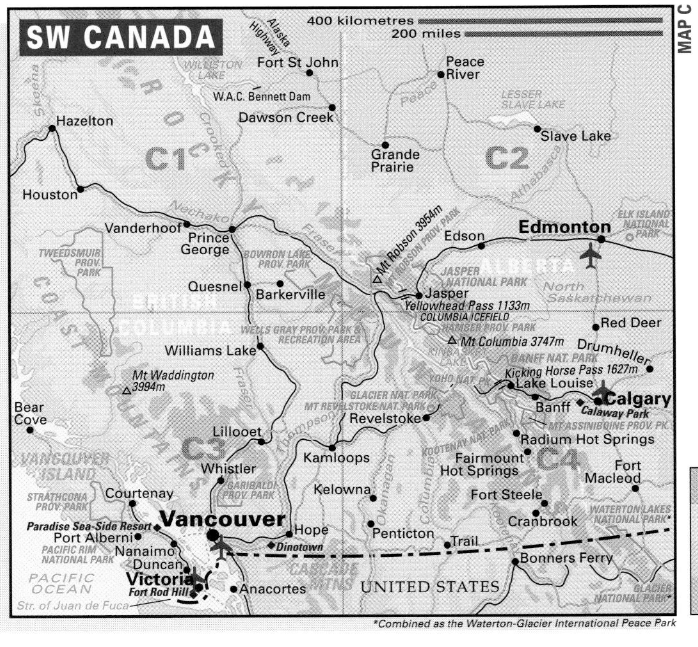

Tourism, 1980–1998
International arrivals to Canada (millions)
Source: World Tourism Organisation

province/territory boundary
province/territory capital

1000 km
500 miles

For an alphabetical list of Canadian provinces and territories, see Appendices

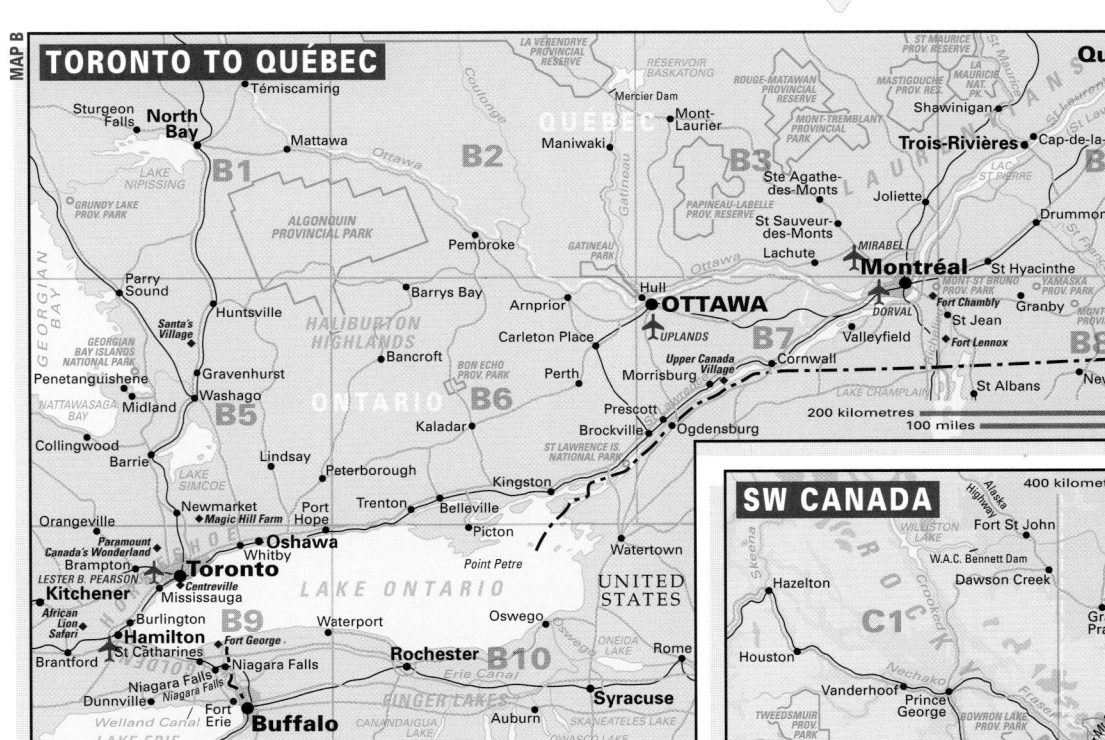

TORONTO TO QUÉBEC

SW CANADA

*Combined as the Waterton-Glacier International Peace Park

FEB Carnaval de Québec (QU)
FEB Winterlude (Ottawa OT)
FEB Sourdough Rendezvous (Whitehorse YT)
MAY Canadian Tulip Festival (Ottawa OT)
MAY-OCT Shakespeare Festival (Stratford OT)
JUN Festival d'Été (Québec City QU)
JUN Metro International Caravan (Toronto OT)
JUN Nova Scotia International Tattoo (Halifax NS)
JUN 24th St Jean Baptiste Day (Québec City QU)
JUN-JUL International Jazz Festival (Montréal OT)
JUN-SEP Harbourfront Centre Summerfete (Toronto OT)
JUL 1st Canada Day (Ottawa OT and countrywide)
JUL International Freedom Festival (Windsor OT)
JUL Stampede (Williams Lake BC)
JUL Sea Festival (Vancouver BC)
JUL Loyalist Days Festival (Saint John NB)
JUL Klondike Days (Edmonton AL)

JUL Calgary Stampede (AL)
JUL Folklorama (Winnipeg MN)
JUL Manitoba Stampede and Exhibition (Morris MN)
JUL Manitoba Threshermen's Reunion (Austin MN)
JUL New Brunswick Highland Games and Scottish Festival (Fredericton NB)
JUL-AUG Caribana (Toronto OT)
AUG Regatta Day (St John's NF)
AUG Gaelic Mod: Scottish festival (St Ann's NS)
AUG Fringe Festival (Edmonton AL)
AUG Six Nations Native Pageant (Brantford OT)
AUG Nova Scotia Fisheries Exhibition and Fishermen's Reunion (Lunenburg NS)
AUG Discovery Day (Dawson City YT)
AUG-SEP Canadian National Exhibition (Toronto OT)
OCT Oktoberfest (Kitchener-Waterloo OT)
NOV Canadian Rodeo Finals (Edmonton AL)

CANADA

See pages 38-39 for general map

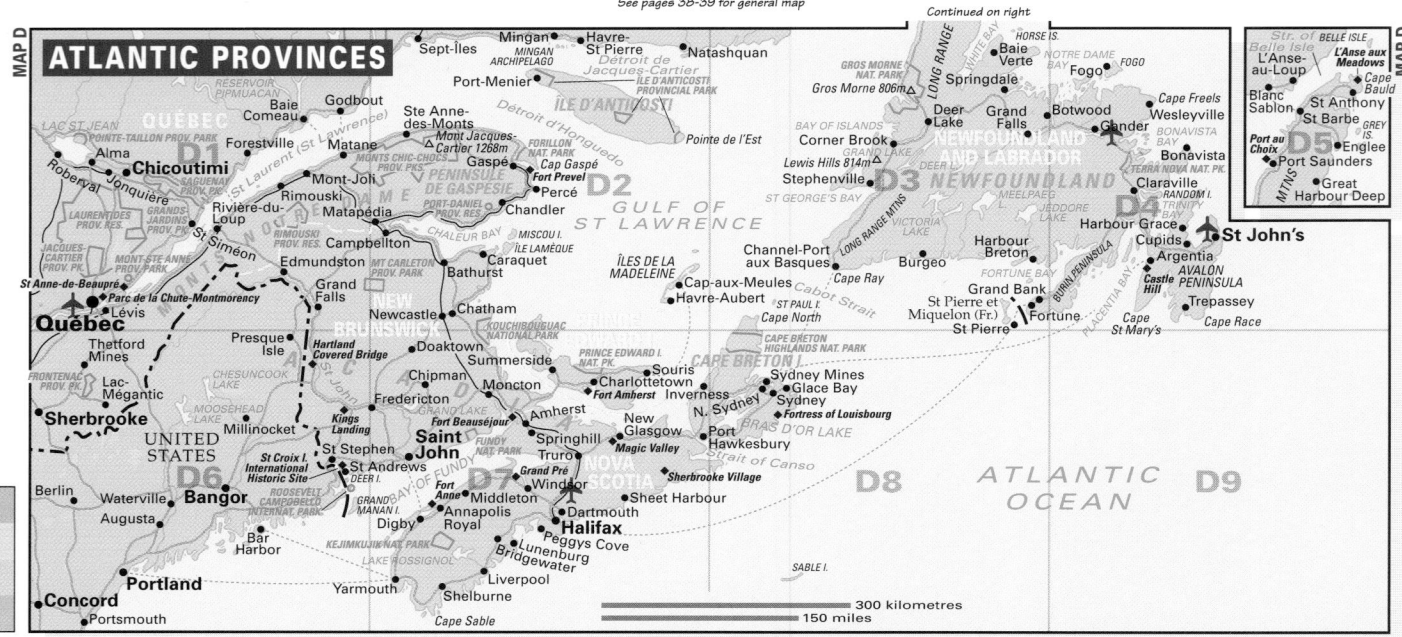

ATLANTIC PROVINCES

MAP D

Continued on right

Str. of BELLE ISLE

MAP D

2000 metres
1000 metres
Sea level

300 kilometres
150 miles

NATIONAL PARKS AND THEME PARKS

Parks Canada administers 36 National Parks and four National Marine Conservation Areas. There are also 800 National Historic Sites; most of these are privately owned but Parks Canada is responsible for 130.
For further information, contact:

Canadian Heritage Parks Canada, Room 10H2, 25 Eddy St., Hull, Québec, K1A 0M5. Tel. +1 819 997 0055.

The map also shows some of Canada's major theme parks.

For further information, contact the IAAPA at the address shown on the US parks map.

province/territory boundary
◇ Parks Canada site
◆ theme park

1000 km
500 miles

Yukon Territory
1 Ivvavik National Park
2 Vuntut National Park
3 Kluane National Park
Five National Historic Sites: four in Dawson, one in Whitehorse
Northwest Territories
4 Nahanni National Park
5 Aulavik National Park
Nunavut
6 Ellesmere Island National Park
7 Auyuittuq National Park
British Columbia
8 Gwaii Haanas National Park & National Marine Conservation Area
9 Pacific Rim National Park (including marine area)
10 Mount Revelstoke National Park
11 Glacier National Park
12 Yoho National Park
13 Kootenay National Park
13 National Historic Sites, including two in Victoria and four in the Vancouver area

British Columbia/Alberta
Kicking Horse Pass and Yellowhead Pass National Historic Sites
Alberta
14 Wood Buffalo National Park (also in Northwest Territories)
15 Elk Island National Park
16 Jasper National Park
17 Banff National Park
18 Waterton Lakes National Park
13 National Historic Sites, including three in Jasper National Park, six in Banff NP and one in Waterton Lakes NP
Saskatchewan
19 Prince Albert National Park
20 Grasslands National Park
Nine National Historic Sites, including Fort Battleford
Manitoba
21 Riding Mountain National Park
Eight National Historic Sites, including one in Riding Mountain National Park and four in the Winnipeg area

Ontario
22 Pukaskwa National Park
23 Fathom Five National Marine Conservation Area
24 Bruce Peninsula National Park
25 Georgian Bay Islands National Park
26 Point Pelee National Park
27 St Lawrence Islands National Park
Nine National Historic Sites, including Rideau Canal, Sault Ste Marie Canal, Trent-Severn Waterway, five sites in the St Catharines/Niagara Falls area and seven along the St Lawrence River
Québec
28 La Mauricie National Park
29 Saguenay-St Lawrence Marine Park
30 Mingan Archipelago National Park
31 Forillon National Park
27 National Historic Sites, predominantly along the St Lawrence and in the Montréal region; including Fort Chambly, Fort Lennox and four

canals; two sites in Québec City are included on the UNESCO World Heritage List
New Brunswick
32 Kouchibouguac National Park
33 Fundy National Park
Five National Historic Sites, including Fort Beauséjour
Prince Edward Island
34 Prince Edward Island National Park
Four National Historic Sites, including Province House, the 'Birthplace of Canada'
Nova Scotia
35 Cape Breton Highlands National Park
36 Kejimkujik National Park
14 National Historic Sites, including Fort Anne and Fortress of Louisbourg
Newfoundland and Labrador
37 Gros Morne National Park
38 Terra Nova National Park
Eight National Historic Sites, including L'Anse aux Meadows, a World Heritage Site

THEME PARKS AND AMUSEMENT PARKS
A Playland, Vancouver, British Columbia
B Calaway Park, Calgary, Alberta
C West Edmonton Mall, Edmonton, Alberta
D Santa's Village, Bracebridge, Ontario
E Fantasy Fair, Rexdale, Ontario
F Paramount Canada's Wonderland, Vaughan, Ontario
G Bingemans (Action Park), Kitchener, Ontario
H Sportsworld, Kitchener, Ontario
J African Lion Safari, Cambridge, Ontario
K Wild Zone, Chatham, Ontario
L Centreville, Toronto, Ontario
M Mont St Sauveur Waterpark, St Sauveur-des-Monts, Québec
N La Ronde, Montréal, Québec
O Parc Safari, Hemmingford, Québec
P Village des Sports, Valcartier, Québec
Q Rainbow Valley, Kensington, Prince Edward I.
R Sandspit, Hunter River, Prince Edward I.
S Magic Valley, Westville, Nova Scotia

MEXICO

See page 37 for general map

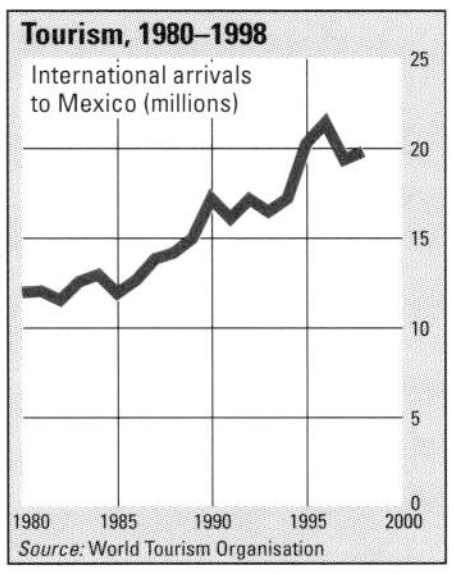

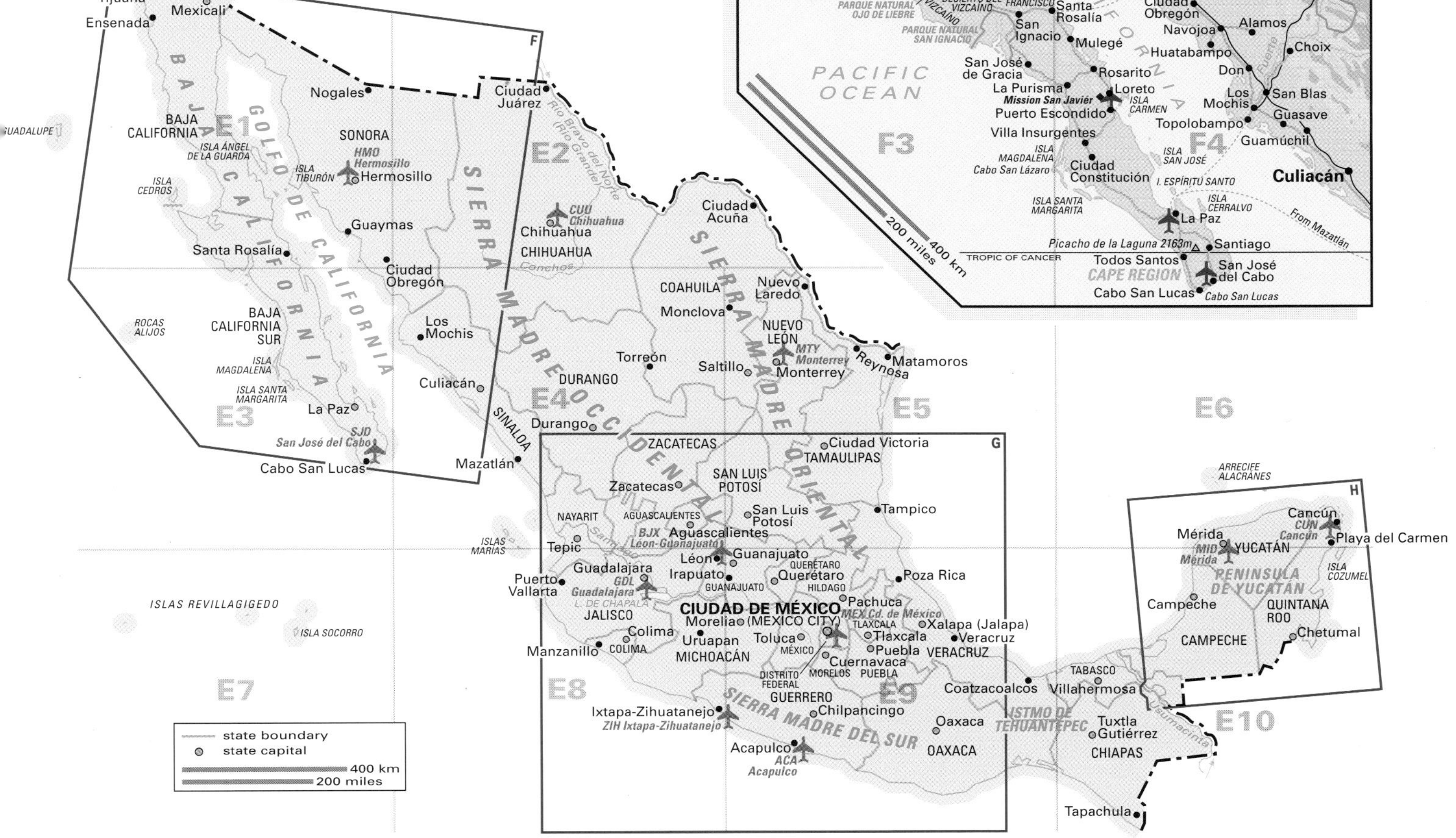

Tourism, 1980–1998
International arrivals to Mexico (millions)
Source: World Tourism Organisation

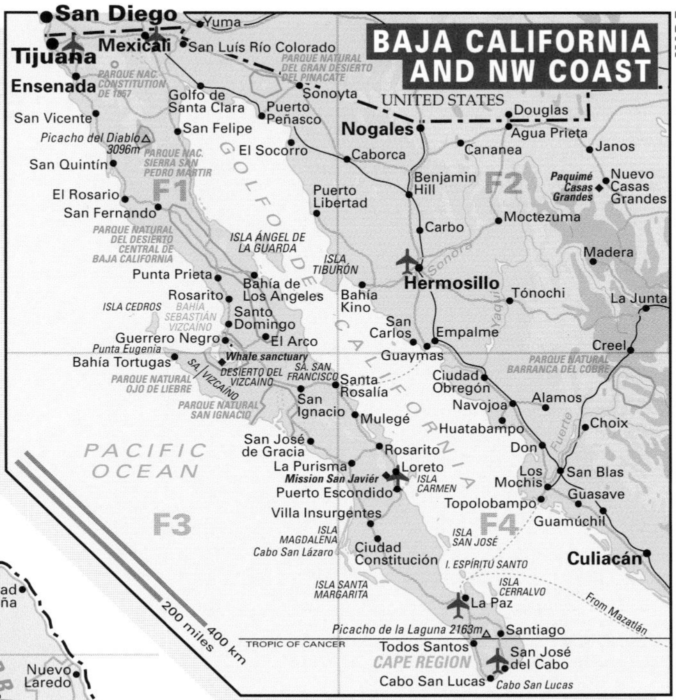

BAJA CALIFORNIA AND NW COAST

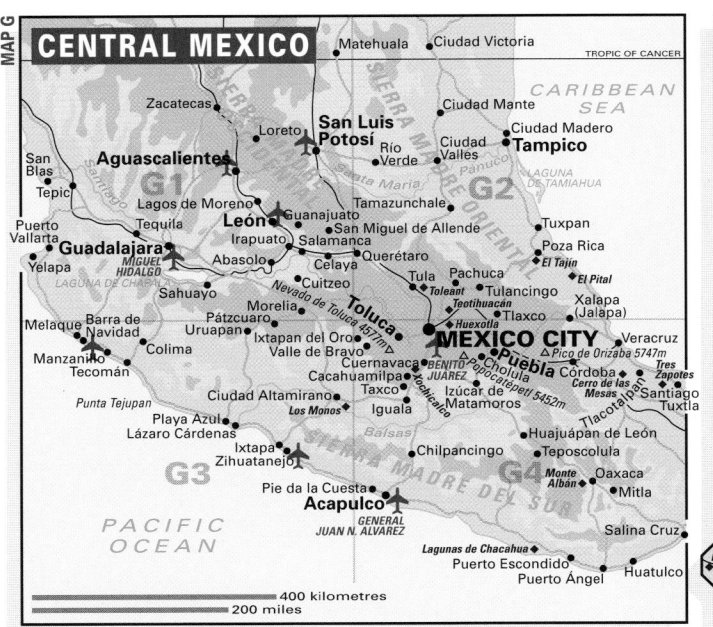

CENTRAL MEXICO

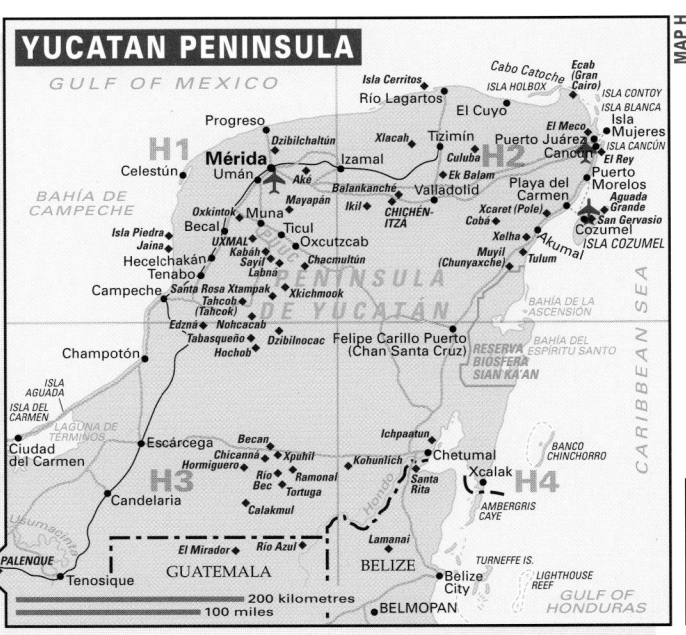

YUCATAN PENINSULA

BAHAMAS   CUBA   TURKS & CAICOS IS.

BAHAMA ISLANDS AND...

See page 37 for general map

See page 37 for general map

OFFICIAL LANGUAGES
(Numbers refer to the notes below)

- English
- Dutch
- French
- Other
- Spanish

1 English is widely spoken.
2 English is widely spoken by the West Indian settlers in the north and on the Bay Islands.
3 English-speaking communities are found on the Caribbean coast.
4 Local Indian dialects and some English, French, German and Italian are spoken
5 English, French, German and Portuguese are spoken by some sections of the community.
6 Some English and French are spoken. Some German, Italian and Russian are also spoken.
7 The official languages are French and Creole. English is widely spoken in tourist areas.
8 Some English and French is spoken.
9 Spanish and Creole are widely spoken.
10 The official language is Dutch. Papiamento (a combination of Dutch, English, Portuguese, Spanish and African languages) is the commonly used lingua franca. English and Spanish are also widely spoken.
11 The islanders speak Creole. Patois and English are also widely spoken.
12 English patois is widely spoken.
13 Creole French is the national language and is spoken by most of the population.
14 The main local dialect is Creole.
15 Local French patois is also spoken.
16 Local Bajan dialect is also spoken.
17 A French patois is spoken by a minority.
18 English and Spanish are also spoken. The islanders speak Papiamento (see 10).

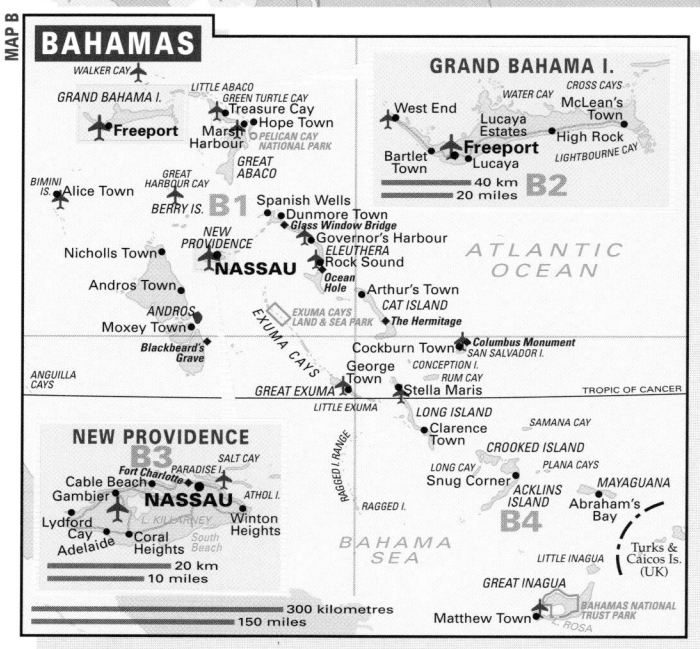

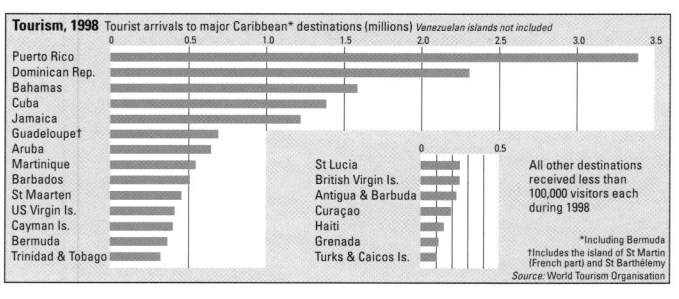

Tourism, 1998 Tourist arrivals to major Caribbean* destinations (millions) Venezuelan islands not included

Puerto Rico
Dominican Rep.
Bahamas
Cuba
Jamaica
Guadeloupe†
Aruba
Martinique
Barbados
St Maarten
US Virgin Is.
Cayman Is.
Bermuda
Trinidad & Tobago

St Lucia
British Virgin Is.
Antigua & Barbuda
Curaçao
Haiti
Grenada
Turks & Caicos Is.

All other destinations received less than 100,000 visitors each during 1998

*Including Bermuda
†Includes the island of St Martin (French part) and St Barthélemy
Source: World Tourism Organisation

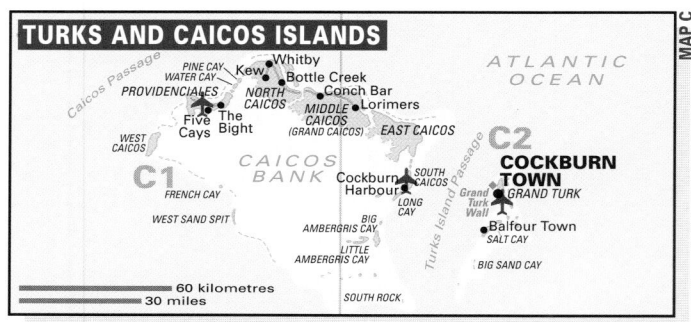

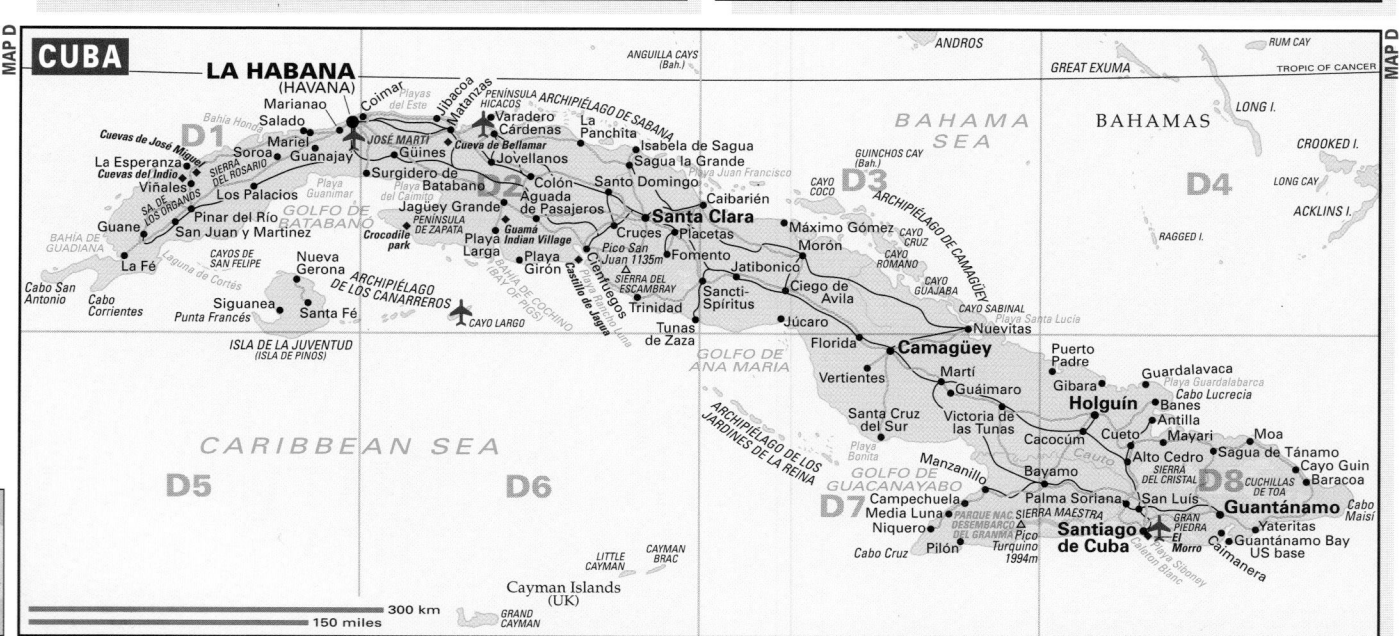

    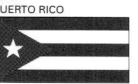
...THE GREATER ANTILLES

See page 37 for general map

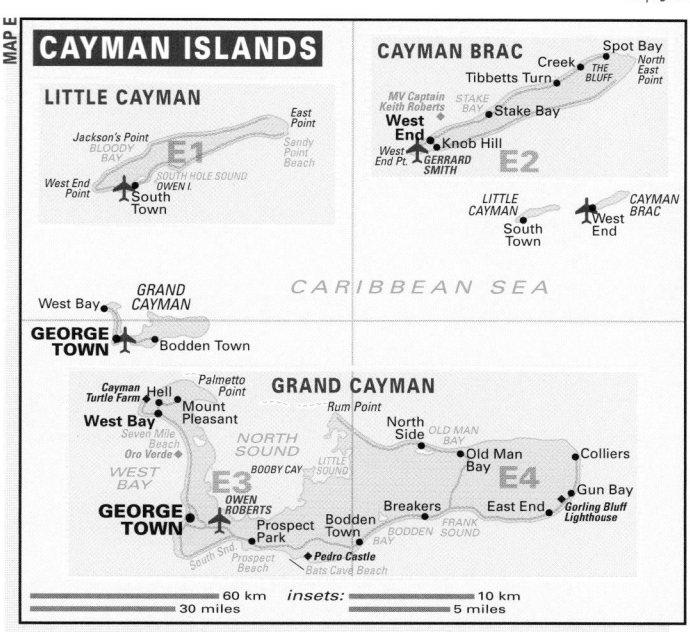

CAYMAN ISLANDS

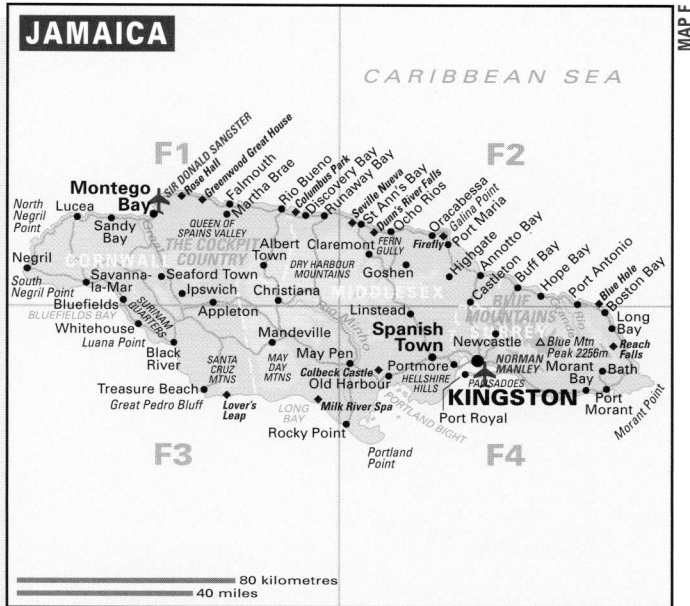

JAMAICA

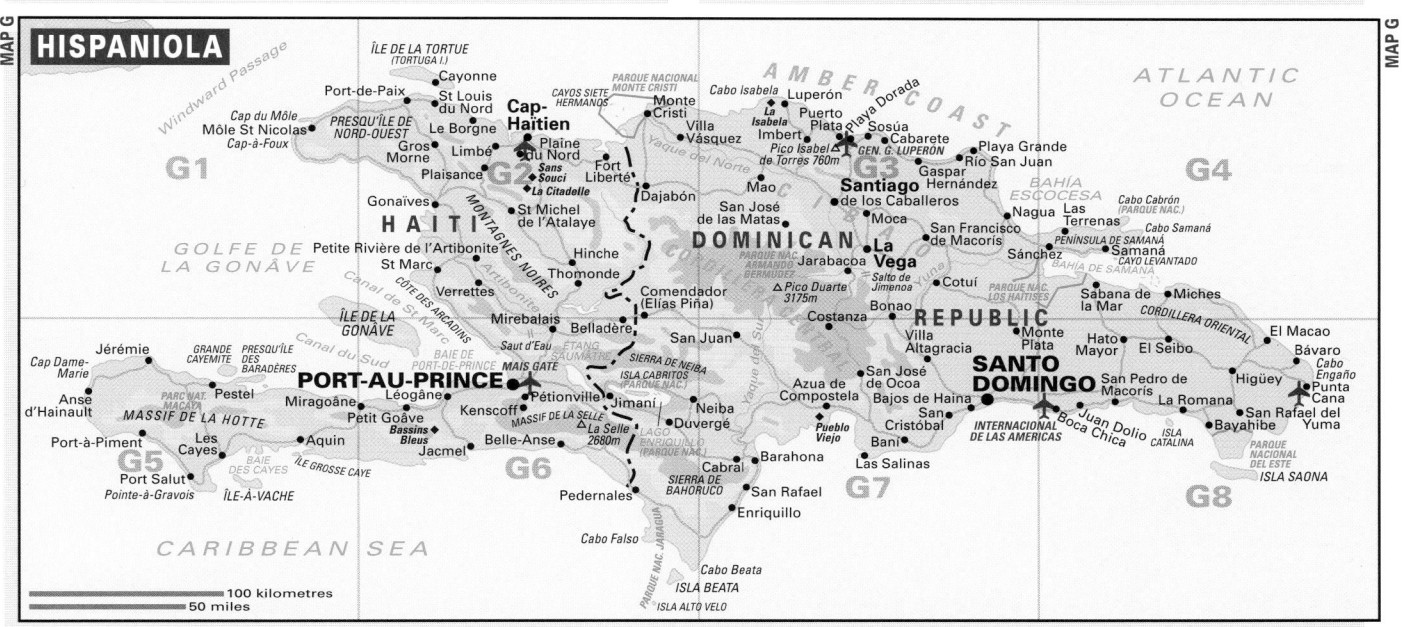

HISPANIOLA

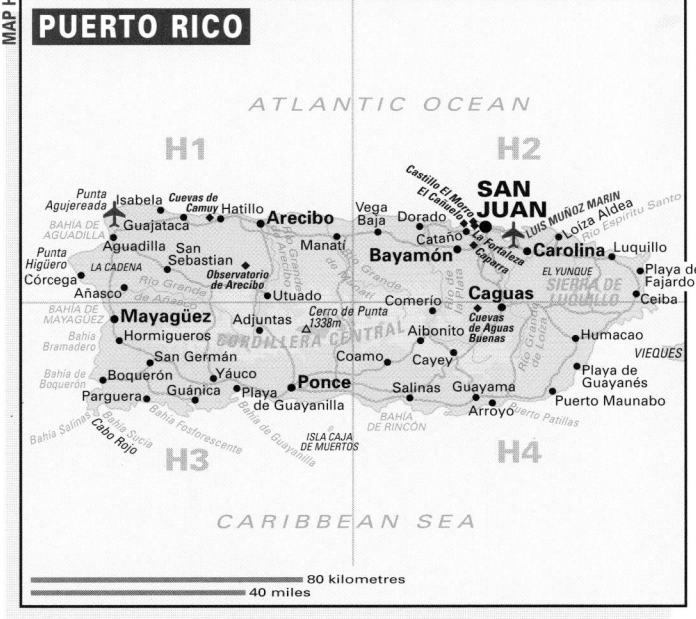

PUERTO RICO

ATLANTIC OCEAN

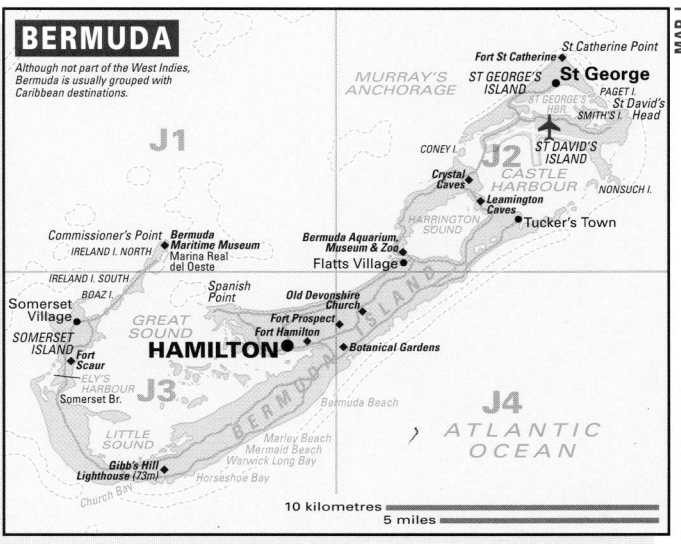

BERMUDA

Although not part of the West Indies, Bermuda is usually grouped with Caribbean destinations.

1000 metres	
500 metres	
Sea level	

ANGUILLA · ANTIGUA & BARBUDA · ARUBA · BARBADOS · BRITISH VIRGIN IS. · DOMINICA · GRENADA · GUADELOUPE & MARTINIQUE

160 WEST INDIES

DIVING SITES AND...

See page 37 for general map

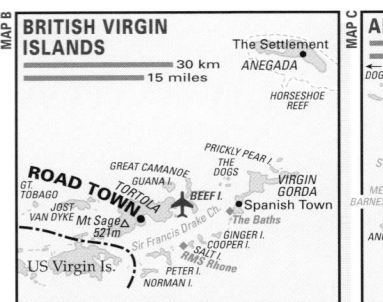

BRITISH VIRGIN ISLANDS
30 km / 15 miles
The Settlement, ANEGADA, HORSESHOE REEF, GT TOBAGO, JOST VAN DYKE, GREAT CAMANOE, GUANA I., TORTOLA, Mt Sage 521m, BEEF I., ROAD TOWN, Spanish Town, VIRGIN GORDA, GINGER I., COOPER I., The Baths, Sir Francis Drake Ch., RMS Rhone, PETER I., NORMAN I., US Virgin Is., THE DOGS, PRICKLY PEAR I., SALT I., DEAD CHEST I.

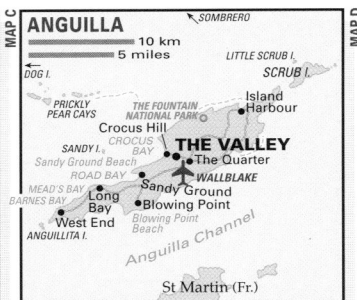

ANGUILLA
10 km / 5 miles
SOMBRERO, LITTLE SCRUB I., SCRUB I., DOG I., Island Harbour, PRICKLY PEAR CAYS, THE FOUNTAIN NATIONAL PARK, Crocus Hill, CROCUS BAY, THE VALLEY, The Quarter, SANDY I., WALLBLAKE, Sandy Ground, Blowing Point, MEAD'S BAY, BARNES BAY, Sandy Ground Beach, Long Bay, West End, Blowing Point Beach, ANGUILLITA I., Anguilla Channel, St Martin (Fr.)

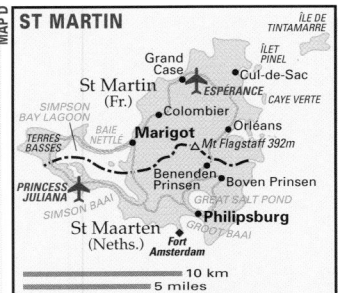

ST MARTIN
10 km / 5 miles
ÎLE DE TINTAMARRE, Grand Case, Cul-de-Sac, ÎLET PINEL, ESPÉRANCE, CAYE VERTE, St Martin (Fr.), Colombier, Orléans, SIMPSON BAY LAGOON, Marigot, Mt Flagstaff 392m, TERRES BASSES, Benenden Prinsen, Boven Prinsen, PRINCESS JULIANA, GREAT SALT POND, St Maarten (Neths.), GROOT BAAI, Philipsburg, SIMSON BAAI, Fort Amsterdam, St Martin (Fr.)

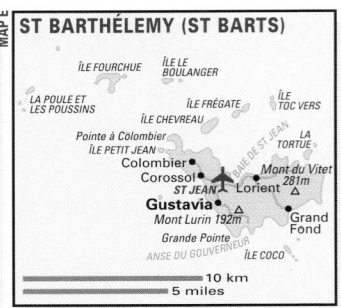

ST BARTHÉLEMY (ST BARTS)
10 km / 5 miles
ÎLE FOURCHUE, ÎLE LE BOULANGER, ÎLE FRÉGATE, ÎLE TOC VERS, LA POULE ET LES POUSSINS, ÎLE CHEVREAU, LA TORTUE, Pointe à Colombier, ÎLE PETIT JEAN, Colombier, Corossol, ST JEAN, Lorient, Mont du Vitet 281m, Gustavia, Mont Lurin 192m, Grand Fond, Grande Pointe, ANSE DU GOUVERNEUR, ÎLE COCO

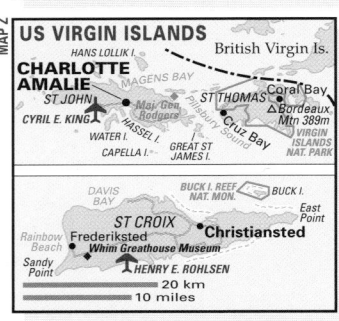

US VIRGIN ISLANDS
20 km / 10 miles
HANS LOLLIK I., British Virgin Is., CHARLOTTE AMALIE, MAGENS BAY, ST JOHN, ST THOMAS, Coral Bay, CYRIL E. KING, Maj. Gen. Rodgers, Cruz Bay, Bordeaux Mtn 389m, VIRGIN ISLANDS NAT. PARK, WATER I., HASSEL I., GREAT ST JAMES I., CAPELLA I., BUCK REEF NAT. MON., BUCK I., DAVIS BAY, ST CROIX, East Point, Rainbow Beach, Frederiksted, Christiansted, Whim Greathouse Museum, Sandy Point, HENRY E. ROHLSEN

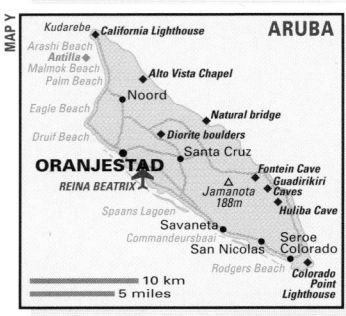

ARUBA
10 km / 5 miles
Kudarebe, California Lighthouse, Arashi Beach, Antilla, Malmok Beach, Palm Beach, Alto Vista Chapel, Eagle Beach, Noord, Natural bridge, Druif Beach, Diorite boulders, Santa Cruz, ORANJESTAD, REINA BEATRIX, Fontein Cave, Guadirikiri Caves, Jamanota 188m, Huliba Cave, Spaans Lagoen, Savaneta, San Nicolas, Seroe Colorado, Rodgers Beach, Colorado Point Lighthouse

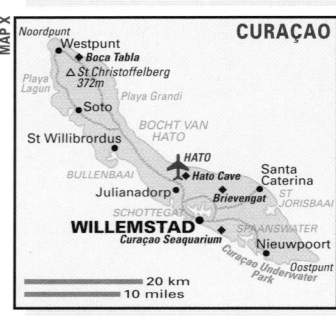

CURAÇAO
20 km / 10 miles
Noordpunt, Westpunt, Boca Tabla, St Christoffelberg 372m, Playa Lagun, Playa Grandi, BOCHT VAN HATO, Soto, St Willibrordus, HATO, Hato Cave, Julianadorp, Brievengat, Santa Caterina, ST JORISBAAI, BULLENBAAI, SCHOTTEGAT, WILLEMSTAD, Curaçao Seaquarium, SPAANSWATER, Nieuwpoort, Curaçao Underwater Park, Oostpunt

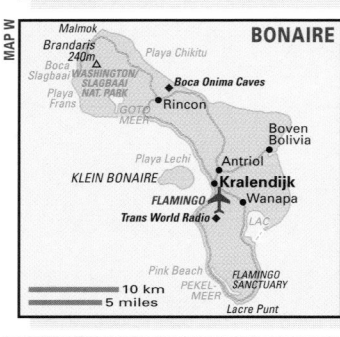

BONAIRE
10 km / 5 miles
Malmok, Brandaris 240m, WASHINGTON/SLAGBAAI NAT. PARK, Boca Slagbaai, Playa Frans, Boca Onima Caves, Rincon, Boven Bolivia, GOTO MEER, Playa Chikitu, Playa Lechi, Antriol, KLEIN BONAIRE, Kralendijk, FLAMINGO, Wanapa, Trans World Radio, LAC, Pink Beach, PEKEL MEER, FLAMINGO SANCTUARY, Lacre Punt

BAHAMAS 1 2 3 4 **DST W** ★★★
Dive sites off western (lee) shores of most islands and all around Andros and New Providence; facilities at Nassau and on individual islands
Blue Hole diving; 700 islands; shark feeding

GULF OF MEXICO, UNITED STATES, A1, A2, A3, GRAND BAHAMA I., GREAT ABACO, BIMINI IS., BERRY IS., NEW PROVIDENCE, ELEUTHERA, DRY TORTUGAS, FLORIDA KEYS, STRAITS OF FLORIDA, CAY SAL BANK, ANDROS, BAHAMAS, CAT I., SAN SALVADOR, RUM CAY, Varadero, ARCH. DE SABANA, GUINCHOS CAY, GREAT EXUMA, LONG I., CROOKED I., ACKLINS I., TROPIC OF CANCER

CANCÚN 1 2 3 4 **DST W** ★★
Main dive sites off eastern shore; facilities centred at Cancún
Eight main reef dives to 10m; more popular as a boat trip to Cozumel

COZUMEL 1 2 3 4 **DST W** ★★★
Main dive sites off western (lee) shore; facilities centred at San Miguel
Dramatic underwater vertical cliffs; diving with manatee and cave diving

ISLA CANCÚN, ISLA COZUMEL, A6, YUCATAN CHANNEL, YUCATAN BASIN, Maria la Gorda, GOLFO DE BATABANO, Isla de la Juventud (Isla de Pinos), Cayo Largo, Cienfuegos/Rancho Luna, CUBA, A7, Santa Lucia, Guardalavaca, ARCHIPIÉLAGO DE LOS JARDINES DE LA REINA, A8, GREAT INAGUA, Santiago de Cuba

CUBA 1 2 3 4 **DST W** ★
Several designated diving regions around the country (shown in red); limited facilities in most major coastal towns
96m frigate recently sunk off Varadero as a diving attraction

BANCO CHINCHORRO 1 2 3 4 **DST W** ★
Main dive sites off east coast of atoll; no facilities on atoll or nearby mainland
Atoll reef with numerous shipwrecks on east coast; large unidentified/intact freighter in north

CAYMAN ISLANDS 1 2 3 4 **DST W** ★★★
Dive sites all around the islands due to their sheltered location within the Caribbean; facilities at George Town and West Bay (Grand Cayman) and West End (Cayman Brac)
Grand Cayman: Stingray City, where many stingrays congregate and are fed by divers, and shipwreck Oro Verde – a 56m ship in 25m of water; Cayman Brac: wreck of Russian frigate – a 100m ship in 25m of water, renamed MV Captain Keith Tibbetts

BELIZE 1 2 3 4 **DST W** ★★★
Main dive sites Lighthouse and Turneffe atoll reefs; facilities centred at San Pedro (Ambergris Caye) and on all three atoll reefs
World's second largest barrier reef; three atoll reefs; the Great Blue Hole; exceptional corals and marine life; regular whale shark sightings

BAY ISLANDS 1 2 3 4 **DST W** ★★
Main dive sites mostly off southern shores; facilities centred at Roatán
Roatán: exceptional wall diving on north coast when sea is calm; Guanaja: 55m shipwreck 'Jado Trader' in 30m of water

MEXICO, BANCO CHINCHORRO, AMBERGRIS CAYE, TURNEFFE IS., LIGHTHOUSE REEF, GLOVER REEF, BELIZE, BARRIER REEF, ISLAS DE LA BAHIA (BAY IS.), ROATÁN, UTILA, GUANAJA, A11, ISLAS SANTANILLA (SWAN IS., Hon.), CAYOS CAJONES, A12, LITTLE CAYMAN, CAYMAN BRAC, GRAND CAYMAN, Cayman Is. (UK), CAYMAN TRENCH, JAMAICA, A13, NAVASSA I. (US), ÎLE DE LA GONÂVE, Windward Passage

JAMAICA 1 2 3 4 **D ST W** ★
Main dive sites off north coast (Negril, Montego Bay, Ocho Rios, Runaway Bay and Port Antonio), and Kingston (Port Royal); facilities centred at Ocho Rios, Port Royal and Montego Bay
Spectacular canyons and deep walls off the north coast; sunken city of Port Royal

ARUBA 1 2 3 4 **DST W** ★★★
Main dive sites off western (lee) shore; facilities centred at Oranjestad
121m shipwreck 'Antilla' – a large freighter scuttled at the outbreak of war

HONDURAS, EL SALVADOR, NICARAGUA, ARRECIFE DE LA MEDIA LUNA, CAYOS MISKITOS (Nic.), QUITA SUEÑO BANK (Col.), SERRANA BANK (Col.), CAYO DE RONCADOR (Col.), A17, A18, A19, ISLA DE PROVIDENCIA (Col.), ISLA DE SAN ANDRÉS (Col.), CAYOS DE ALBUQUERQUE (Col.), ISLAS DEL MAÍZ (CORN IS., Nic.), CARIBBEAN, COLOMBIAN BASIN, COLOMBIA, PACIFIC OCEAN, COSTA RICA

MARGARITA
30 km / 15 miles
LOS FRAILES, Cabo Negro, Manzanillo, Punta de Tigra, Altagracia, PENÍNSULA DE MACANAO, Robledal, Asunción, La Guardia, Playa Guacuco, Pampatar, Punta Arenas, Los Hernández, 900m, Porlamar, Punta de Piedra, Punta Mangle, GEN. SANTIAGO MARIÑO, ISLA DE CUBAGUA, Nueva Cádiz, ISLA DE COCHE, San Pedro de Coche, Caimancita, LAGUNA LA RESTINGA, ENSENADA LA GUARDIA

Depth scale:
1000 metres
500 metres
Sea level

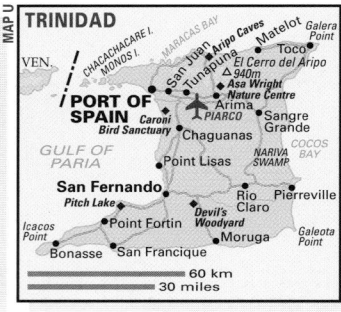

TRINIDAD
60 km / 30 miles
VEN., CHACACHACARE I., MONOS I., MARACAS BAY, Maracas Bay, Galera Point, San Juan, Tunapuna, Aripo Caves, Matelot, Toco, El Cerro del Aripo 940m, PORT OF SPAIN, Caroni, Arima, Nature Centre, PIARCO, Sangre Grande, Chaguanas, GULF OF PARIA, Caroni Bird Sanctuary, Point Lisas, NARIVA SWAMP, COCOS BAY, San Fernando, Rio Claro, Pierreville, Pitch Lake, Devil's Woodyard, Moruga, GALEOTA POINT, Icacos Point, Point Fortin, Bonasse, San Francique

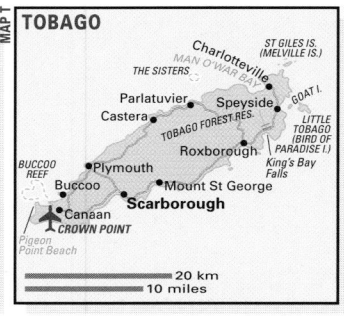

TOBAGO
20 km / 10 miles
ST GILES IS. (MELVILLE IS.), MAN O'WAR BAY, Charlotteville, THE SISTERS, Speyside, GOAT I., LITTLE TOBAGO (BIRD OF PARADISE I.), Parlatuvier, TOBAGO FOREST RES., Castera, Roxborough, King's Bay Falls, BUCCOO REEF, Plymouth, Mount St George, Buccoo, Scarborough, CROWN POINT, Canaan, PIGEON POINT BEACH

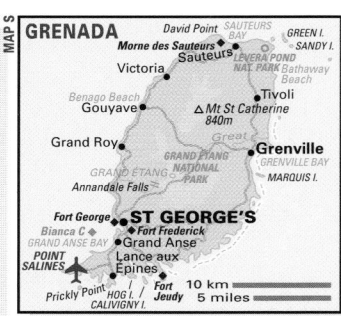

GRENADA
10 km / 5 miles
David Point, SAUTEURS BAY, GREEN I., SANDY I., Morne des Sauteurs, Sauteurs, LEVERA POND NAT. PARK, Sathaway Beach, Victoria, Tivoli, Benago Beach, Gouyave, Mt St Catherine 840m, GRAND ÉTANG NAT. PARK, GRAND PLANS NAT. PARK, Grand Roy, Grenville, GRENVILLE BAY, MARQUIS I., Annandale Falls, Fort George, Bianca C, ST GEORGE'S, GRAND MAL BAY, Fort Frederick, Grand Anse, POINT SALINES, Lance aux Epines, Prickly Point, Fort Jeudy, HOG I., CALIVIGNY I.

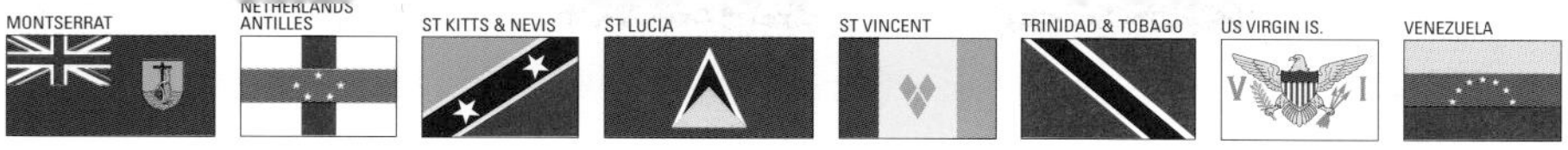
MONTSERRAT
NETHERLANDS ANTILLES
ST KITTS & NEVIS
ST LUCIA
ST VINCENT
TRINIDAD & TOBAGO
US VIRGIN IS.
VENEZUELA
V I

...THE LESSER ANTILLES

See page 37 for general map

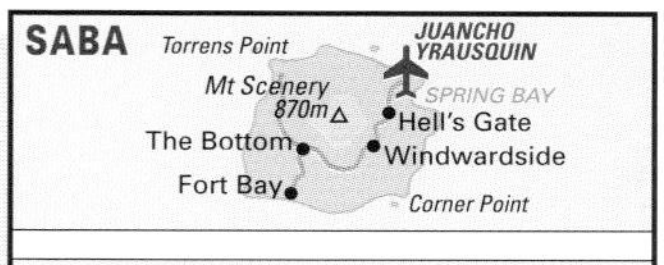
SABA
MAP F
Torrens Point
JUANCHO YRAUSQUIN
Mt Scenery 870m △
SPRING BAY
Hell's Gate
The Bottom
Windwardside
Fort Bay
Corner Point

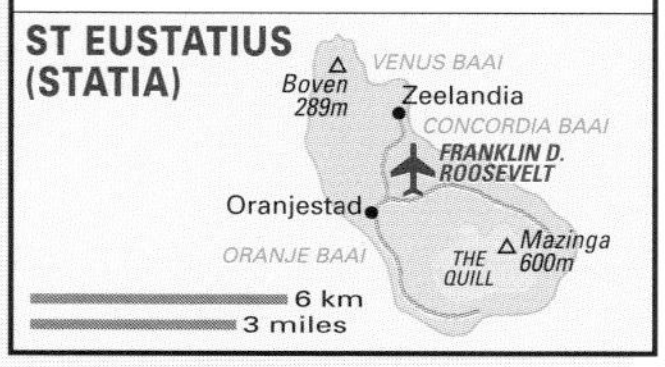
ST EUSTATIUS (STATIA)
VENUS BAAI
Boven 289m
Zeelandia
CONCORDIA BAAI
FRANKLIN D. ROOSEVELT
Oranjestad
ORANJE BAAI
THE QUILL
Mazinga 600m
6 km
3 miles

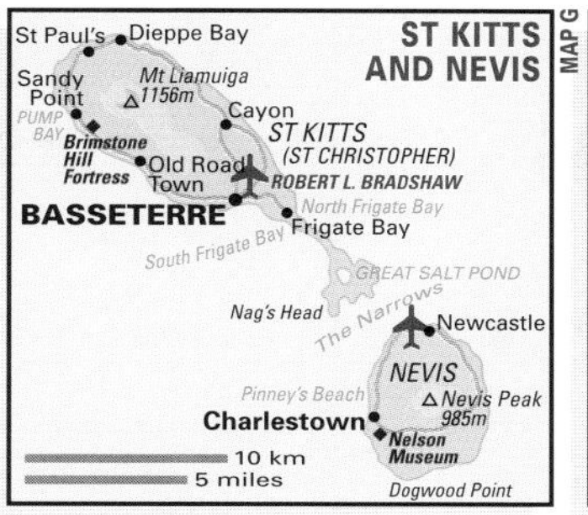
ST KITTS AND NEVIS
MAP G
St Paul's
Dieppe Bay
Sandy Point
Mt Liamuiga 1156m
PUMP BAY
Brimstone Hill Fortress
Cayon
ST KITTS (ST CHRISTOPHER)
Old Road Town
ROBERT L. BRADSHAW
BASSETERRE
North Frigate Bay
Frigate Bay
South Frigate Bay
GREAT SALT POND
Nag's Head
The Narrows
Newcastle
NEVIS
Pinney's Beach
Nevis Peak 985m
Charlestown
Nelson Museum
10 km
5 miles
Dogwood Point

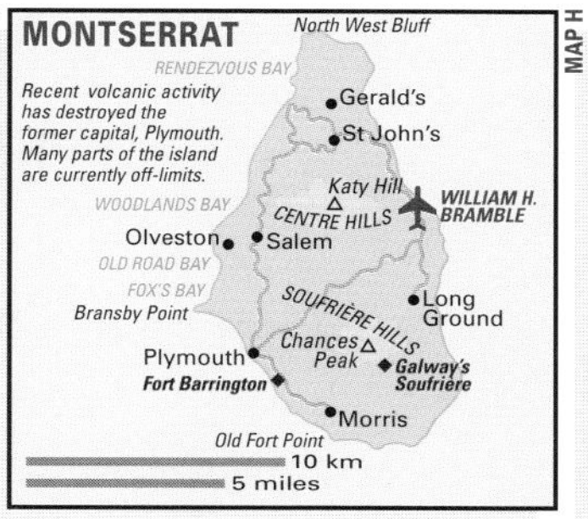
MONTSERRAT
MAP H
North West Bluff
RENDEZVOUS BAY
Gerald's
Recent volcanic activity has destroyed the former capital, Plymouth. Many parts of the island are currently off-limits.
St John's
Katy Hill
WOODLANDS BAY
CENTRE HILLS
WILLIAM H. BRAMBLE
Olveston
Salem
OLD ROAD BAY
FOX'S BAY
Bransby Point
SOUFRIERE HILLS
Long Ground
Chances Peak
Plymouth
Fort Barrington
Galway's Soufriere
Morris
Old Fort Point
10 km
5 miles

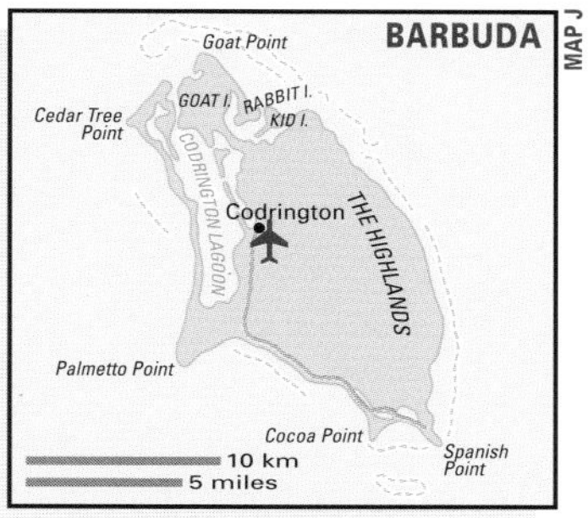
BARBUDA
MAP J
Goat Point
GOAT I.
RABBIT I.
KID I.
Cedar Tree Point
CODRINGTON LAGOON
Codrington
THE HIGHLANDS
Palmetto Point
Cocoa Point
Spanish Point
10 km
5 miles

This map shows the Caribbean's principal diving destinations and the main underwater attractions they have to offer. Details include the existence of coral reefs; atoll reefs (of which there are only four in the entire Caribbean); blue hole and cave diving plus the existence of shipwrecks (including wrecked aircraft). Whilst the diver may encounter turtle, shark, large rays and dolphin at any time – and whales occasionally – only those places where these are featured and regular sightings occur are indicated here.

Diving facilities for each destination, including availability of scuba diving equipment and related support services, are graded as limited, good or excellent. It must be emphasised that these grades are a general reflection on the overall availability of everything required by the visiting scuba diver and are not an interpretation of the standards found within any one facility or organisation.

Each diving destination provides every level of depth from the very shallow to the extremely deep.

Data compiled by Ned Middleton, all rights reserved. Fax +44 (0) 1227 741819.

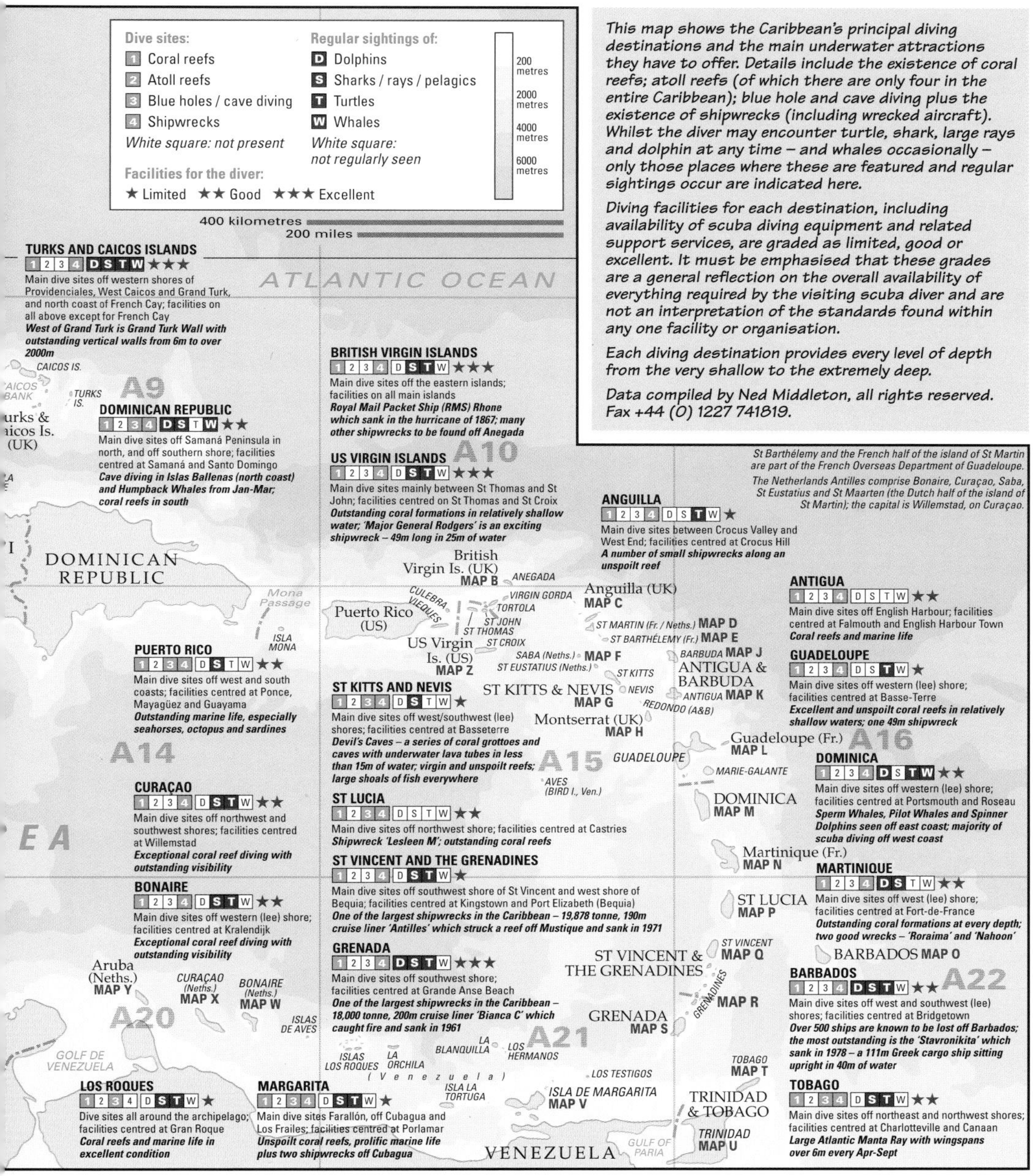
Dive sites:
1 Coral reefs
2 Atoll reefs
3 Blue holes / cave diving
4 Shipwrecks
White square: not present
Regular sightings of:
D Dolphins
S Sharks / rays / pelagics
T Turtles
W Whales
White square: not regularly seen
Facilities for the diver:
★ Limited ★★ Good ★★★ Excellent
200 metres
2000 metres
4000 metres
6000 metres
400 kilometres
200 miles
ATLANTIC OCEAN
TURKS AND CAICOS ISLANDS
■1 □2 □3 ■4 ■D ■S ■T ■W ★★★
Main dive sites off western shores of Providenciales, West Caicos and Grand Turk, and north coast of French Cay; facilities on all above except for French Cay
West of Grand Turk is Grand Turk Wall with outstanding vertical walls from 6m to over 2000m
CAICOS IS.
CAICOS BANK
TURKS IS.
Turks & Caicos Is. (UK)
A9
DOMINICAN REPUBLIC
■1 □2 ■3 ■4 ■D ■S □T ■W ★★
Main dive sites off Samaná Peninsula in north, and off southern shore; facilities centred at Samaná and Santo Domingo
Cave diving in Islas Ballenas (north coast) and Humpback Whales from Jan-Mar; coral reefs in south
DOMINICAN REPUBLIC
Mona Passage
ISLA MONA
PUERTO RICO
■1 □2 ■3 ■4 □D ■S □T □W ★★
Main dive sites off west and south coasts; facilities centred at Ponce, Mayagüez and Guayama
Outstanding marine life, especially seahorses, octopus and sardines
A14
CURAÇAO
■1 □2 □3 ■4 □D ■S ■T □W ★★
Main dive sites off northwest and southwest shores; facilities centred at Willemstad
Exceptional coral reef diving with outstanding visibility
BONAIRE
■1 □2 □3 ■4 □D ■S ■T □W ★★
Main dive sites off western (lee) shore; facilities centred at Kralendijk
Exceptional coral reef diving with outstanding visibility
Aruba (Neths.) MAP Y
CURAÇAO (Neths.) MAP X
BONAIRE (Neths.) MAP W
ISLAS DE AVES
A20
GOLF DE VENEZUELA
LOS ROQUES
■1 □2 ■3 □4 □D ■S ■T □W ★
Dive sites all around the archipelago; facilities centred at Gran Roque
Coral reefs and marine life in excellent condition
MARGARITA
■1 □2 ■3 ■4 □D ■S ■T □W ★
Main dive sites Farallón, off Cubagua and Los Frailes; facilities centred at Porlamar
Unspoilt coral reefs, prolific marine life plus two shipwrecks off Cubagua
BRITISH VIRGIN ISLANDS
■1 □2 □3 ■4 □D ■S ■T □W ★★★
Main dive sites off the eastern islands; facilities on all main islands
Royal Mail Packet Ship (RMS) Rhone which sank in the hurricane of 1867; many other shipwrecks to be found off Anegada
US VIRGIN ISLANDS
■1 □2 □3 ■4 □D ■S ■T □W ★★★
Main dive sites mainly between St Thomas and St John; facilities centred on St Thomas and St Croix
Outstanding coral formations in relatively shallow water; 'Major General Rodgers' is an exciting shipwreck – 49m long in 25m of water
A10
British Virgin Is. (UK) MAP B
ANEGADA
VIRGIN GORDA
TORTOLA
CULEBRA
VIEQUES
ST JOHN
ST THOMAS
ST CROIX
Puerto Rico (US)
US Virgin Is. (US) MAP Z
SABA (Neths.) MAP F
ST EUSTATIUS (Neths.)
ST KITTS
NEVIS
ST KITTS & NEVIS MAP G
REDONDO (A&B)
Montserrat (UK) MAP H
ST KITTS AND NEVIS
■1 □2 ■3 ■4 □D ■S □T □W ★
Main dive sites off west/southwest (lee) shores; facilities centred at Basseterre
Devil's Caves – a series of coral grottoes and caves with underwater lava tubes in less than 15m of water; virgin and unspoilt reefs; large shoals of fish everywhere
A15
GUADELOUPE
AVES (BIRD I., Ven.)
ST LUCIA
■1 □2 ■3 ■4 □D □S □T □W ★★
Main dive sites off northwest shore; facilities centred at Castries
Shipwreck 'Lesleen M'; outstanding coral reefs
ST VINCENT AND THE GRENADINES
■1 □2 □3 ■4 □D ■S ■T □W ★
Main dive sites off southwest shore of St Vincent and west shore of Bequia; facilities centred at Kingstown and Port Elizabeth (Bequia)
One of the largest shipwrecks in the Caribbean – 19,878 tonne, 190m cruise liner 'Antilles' which struck a reef off Mustique and sank in 1971
GRENADA
■1 □2 □3 ■4 ■D ■S ■T □W ★★★
Main dive sites off southwest shore; facilities centred at Grande Anse Beach
One of the largest shipwrecks in the Caribbean – 18,000 tonne, 200m cruise liner 'Bianca C' which caught fire and sank in 1961
A21
ISLAS LOS ROQUES
LA ORCHILA
LA BLANQUILLA
LOS HERMANOS
(V e n e z u e l a)
ISLA LA TORTUGA
LOS TESTIGOS
ISLA DE MARGARITA MAP V
VENEZUELA
GULF OF PARIA
ST VINCENT & THE GRENADINES
ST VINCENT MAP Q
GRENADINES MAP R
GRENADA MAP S
TOBAGO MAP T
TRINIDAD & TOBAGO
TRINIDAD MAP U
St Barthélemy and the French half of the island of St Martin are part of the French Overseas Department of Guadeloupe.
The Netherlands Antilles comprise Bonaire, Curaçao, Saba, St Eustatius and St Maarten (the Dutch half of the island of St Martin); the capital is Willemstad, on Curaçao.
ANGUILLA
■1 □2 □3 ■4 □D □S ■T □W ★
Main dive sites between Crocus Valley and West End; facilities centred at Crocus Hill
A number of small shipwrecks along an unspoilt reef
Anguilla (UK) MAP C
ST MARTIN (Fr. / Neths.) MAP D
ST BARTHÉLEMY (Fr.) MAP E
BARBUDA MAP J
ANTIGUA & BARBUDA
ANTIGUA MAP K
ANTIGUA
■1 □2 □3 ■4 □D □S □T □W ★★
Main dive sites off English Harbour; facilities centred at Falmouth and English Harbour Town
Coral reefs and marine life
GUADELOUPE
■1 □2 □3 ■4 □D □S ■T □W ★
Main dive sites off western (lee) shore; facilities centred at Basse-Terre
Excellent and unspoilt coral reefs in relatively shallow waters; one 49m shipwreck
Guadeloupe (Fr.) MAP L
A16
MARIE-GALANTE
DOMINICA MAP M
DOMINICA
■1 □2 □3 ■4 ■D □S ■T ■W ★★
Main dive sites off western (lee) shore; facilities centred at Portsmouth and Roseau
Sperm Whales, Pilot Whales and Spinner Dolphins seen off east coast; majority of scuba diving off west coast
Martinique (Fr.) MAP N
MARTINIQUE
■1 □2 □3 ■4 ■D ■S □T □W ★★
Main dive sites off west (lee) shore; facilities centred at Fort-de-France
Outstanding coral formations at every depth; two good wrecks – 'Roraima' and 'Nahoon'
ST LUCIA MAP P
BARBADOS MAP O
BARBADOS
■1 □2 □3 ■4 ■D ■S ■T □W ★★
Main dive sites off west and southwest (lee) shores; facilities centred at Bridgetown
Over 500 ships are known to be lost off Barbados; the most outstanding is the 'Stavronikita' which sank in 1978 – a 111m Greek cargo ship sitting upright in 40m of water
A22
TOBAGO
■1 □2 ■3 ■4 □D ■S ■T □W ★★
Main dive sites off northeast and northwest shores; facilities centred at Charlotteville and Canaan
Large Atlantic Manta Ray with wingspans over 6m every Apr-Sept

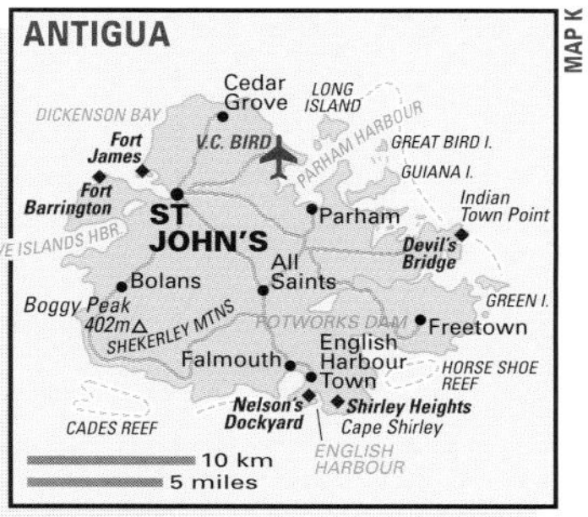
ANTIGUA
MAP K
Cedar Grove
LONG ISLAND
DICKENSON BAY
PARHAM HARBOUR
Fort James
V.C. BIRD
GREAT BIRD I.
GUIANA I.
Fort Barrington
ST JOHN'S
Parham
Indian Town Point
FIVE ISLANDS HBR.
Devil's Bridge
All Saints
Bolans
Boggy Peak 402m
SHEKERLEY MTNS
POTWORKS DAM
GREEN I.
Freetown
English Harbour Town
Falmouth
HORSE SHOE REEF
Nelson's Dockyard
Shirley Heights
CADES REEF
Cape Shirley
ENGLISH HARBOUR
10 km
5 miles

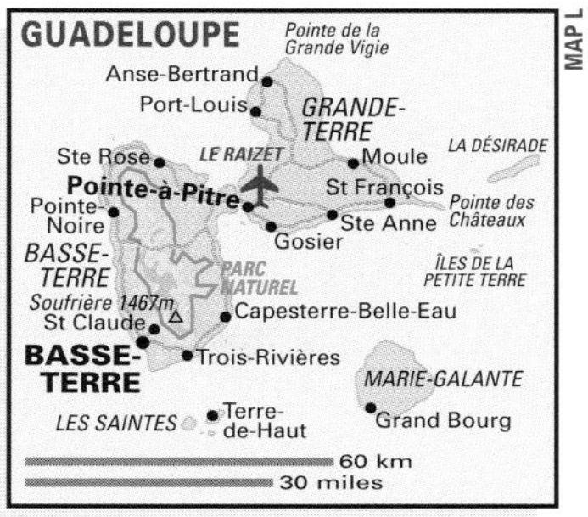
GUADELOUPE
MAP L
Pointe de la Grande Vigie
Anse-Bertrand
Port-Louis
GRANDE-TERRE
Ste Rose
LE RAIZET
Moule
LA DÉSIRADE
Pointe-à-Pitre
St François
Pointe-Noire
Pointe des Châteaux
Ste Anne
Gosier
BASSE-TERRE
PARC NATUREL
ÎLES DE LA PETITE TERRE
Soufrière 1467m
St Claude
Capesterre-Belle-Eau
BASSE-TERRE
Trois-Rivières
MARIE-GALANTE
LES SAINTES
Terre-de-Haut
Grand Bourg
60 km
30 miles

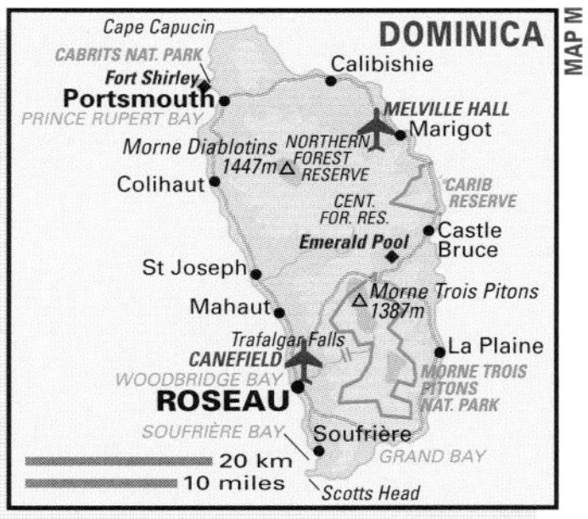
DOMINICA
MAP M
Cape Capucin
CABRITS NAT. PARK
Calibishie
Fort Shirley
Portsmouth
MELVILLE HALL
PRINCE RUPERT BAY
Marigot
Morne Diablotins 1447m
NORTHERN FOREST RESERVE
Colihaut
CARIB RESERVE
CENT. FOR. RES.
Castle Bruce
Emerald Pool
St Joseph
Morne Trois Pitons 1387m
Mahaut
Trafalgar Falls
La Plaine
CANEFIELD
WOODBRIDGE BAY
MORNE TROIS PITONS NAT. PARK
ROSEAU
SOUFRIÈRE BAY
Soufrière
GRAND BAY
20 km
10 miles
Scotts Head

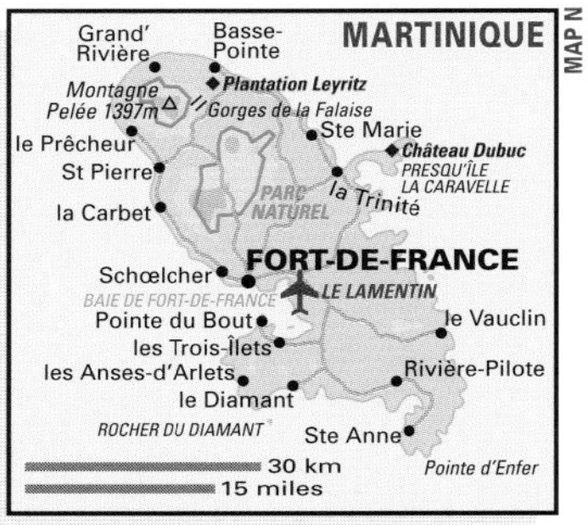
MARTINIQUE
MAP N
Grand' Rivière
Basse-Pointe
Montagne Pelée 1397m
Plantation Leyritz
Gorges de la Falaise
le Prêcheur
Ste Marie
Château Dubuc
St Pierre
PRESQU'ÎLE LA CARAVELLE
PARC NATUREL
la Trinité
la Carbet
Schœlcher
FORT-DE-FRANCE
LE LAMENTIN
BAIE DE FORT-DE-FRANCE
Pointe du Bout
le Vauclin
les Trois-Îlets
les Anses-d'Arlets
Rivière-Pilote
le Diamant
ROCHER DU DIAMANT
Ste Anne
Pointe d'Enfer
30 km
15 miles

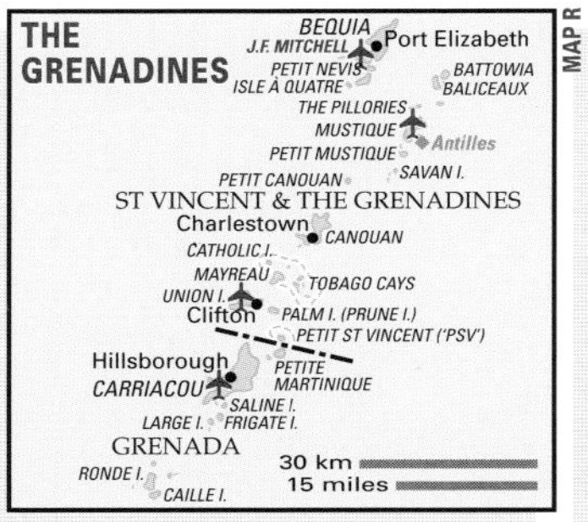
THE GRENADINES
MAP R
BEQUIA
J.F. MITCHELL
Port Elizabeth
PETIT NEVIS
ISLE À QUATRE
BATTOWIA
BALICEAUX
THE PILLORIES
MUSTIQUE
PETIT MUSTIQUE
Antilles
PETIT CANOUAN
SAVAN I.
ST VINCENT & THE GRENADINES
Charlestown
CANOUAN
CATHOLIC I.
MAYREAU
TOBAGO CAYS
UNION I.
PALM I. (PRUNE I.)
Clifton
PETIT ST VINCENT ('PSV')
Hillsborough
PETITE MARTINIQUE
CARRIACOU
SALINE I.
LARGE I.
FRIGATE I.
GRENADA
RONDE I.
CAILLE I.
30 km
15 miles

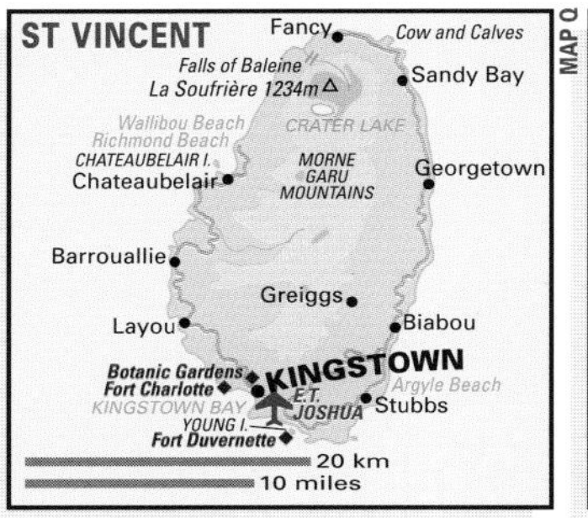
ST VINCENT
MAP Q
Fancy
Cow and Calves
Falls of Baleine
La Soufrière 1234m
Sandy Bay
Wallibou Beach
Richmond Beach
CRATER LAKE
CHATEAUBELAIR I.
Chateaubelair
MORNE GARU MOUNTAINS
Georgetown
Barrouallie
Greiggs
Layou
Biabou
Botanic Gardens
Fort Charlotte
KINGSTOWN
KINGSTOWN BAY
E.T. JOSHUA
Argyle Beach
Stubbs
YOUNG I.
Fort Duvernette
20 km
10 miles

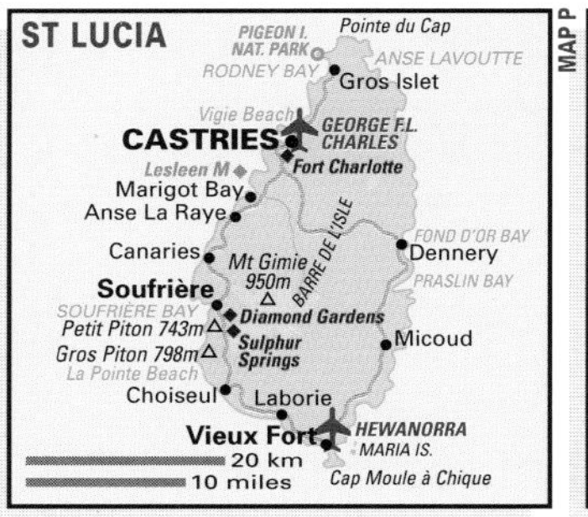
ST LUCIA
MAP P
PIGEON I. NAT. PARK
Pointe du Cap
ANSE LAVOUTTE
RODNEY BAY
Gros Islet
Vigie Beach
CASTRIES
GEORGE F.L. CHARLES
Fort Charlotte
Lesleen M
Marigot Bay
Anse La Raye
BARRE DE L'ISLE
Canaries
FOND D'OR BAY
Dennery
Mt Gimie 950m
PRASLIN BAY
Soufrière
SOUFRIERE BAY
Diamond Gardens
Petit Piton 743m
Micoud
Gros Piton 798m
Sulphur Springs
La Pointe Beach
Choiseul
Laborie
Vieux Fort
HEWANORRA
MARIA IS.
20 km
10 miles
Cap Moule à Chique

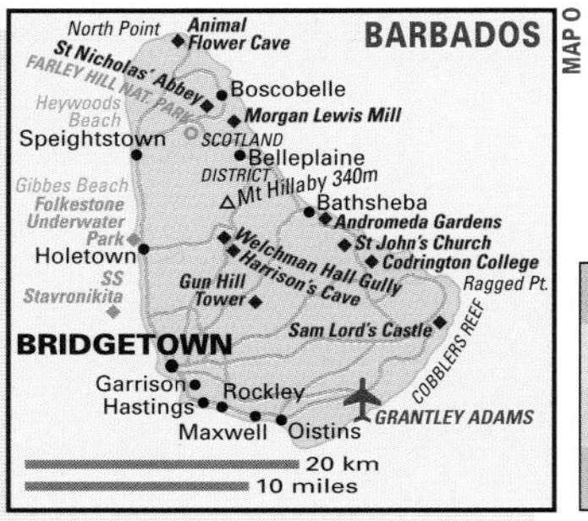
BARBADOS
MAP O
North Point
Animal Flower Cave
St Nicholas' Abbey
FARLEY HILL NAT. PARK
Boscobelle
Heywoods Beach
Morgan Lewis Mill
Speightstown
SCOTLAND DISTRICT
Belleplaine
Mt Hillaby 340m
Bathsheba
Gibbes Beach
Andromeda Gardens
Folkestone Underwater Park
St John's Church
Welchman Hall Gully
Codrington College
Holetown
Harrison's Cave
SS Stavronikita
Gun Hill Tower
Ragged Pt.
Sam Lord's Castle
COBBLERS REEF
BRIDGETOWN
Garrison
Rockley
Hastings
Maxwell
Oistins
GRANTLEY ADAMS
20 km
10 miles

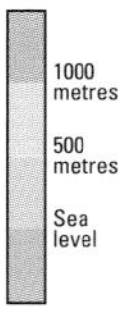
1000 metres
500 metres
Sea level

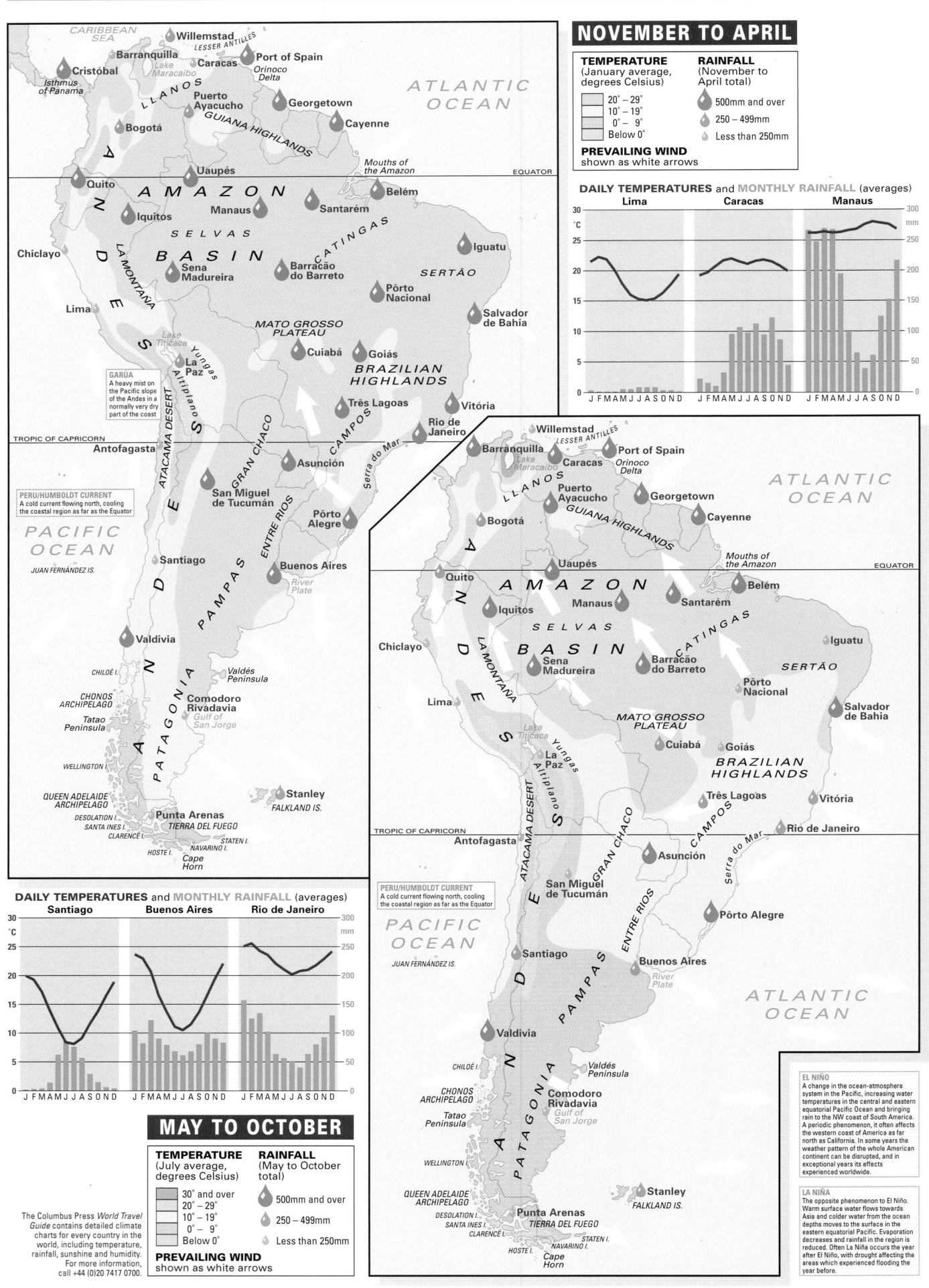

CLIMATE

TEMPERATURE CONVERSION

°Celsius	−10	0	10	20	30	40
°Fahrenheit	14	32	50	68	86	104

RAINFALL CONVERSION

Millimetres	102	203	305	406	508	610
Inches	4	8	12	16	20	24

NOVEMBER TO APRIL

TEMPERATURE
(January average, degrees Celsius)

- 20° – 29°
- 10° – 19°
- 0° – 9°
- Below 0°

RAINFALL
(November to April total)

- 500mm and over
- 250 – 499mm
- Less than 250mm

PREVAILING WIND
shown as white arrows

DAILY TEMPERATURES and **MONTHLY RAINFALL** (averages)

Lima   Caracas   Manaus

DAILY TEMPERATURES and **MONTHLY RAINFALL** (averages)

Santiago   Buenos Aires   Rio de Janeiro

MAY TO OCTOBER

TEMPERATURE
(July average, degrees Celsius)

- 30° and over
- 20° – 29°
- 10° – 19°
- 0° – 9°
- Below 0°

RAINFALL
(May to October total)

- 500mm and over
- 250 – 499mm
- Less than 250mm

PREVAILING WIND
shown as white arrows

The Columbus Press *World Travel Guide* contains detailed climate charts for every country in the world, including temperature, rainfall, sunshine and humidity. For more information, call +44 (0)20 7417 0700.

GARÚA
A heavy mist on the Pacific slope of the Andes in a normally very dry part of the coast

PERU/HUMBOLDT CURRENT
A cold current flowing north, cooling the coastal region as far as the Equator

PERU/HUMBOLDT CURRENT
A cold current flowing north, cooling the coastal region as far as the Equator

EL NIÑO
A change in the ocean-atmosphere system in the Pacific, increasing water temperatures in the central and eastern equatorial Pacific Ocean and bringing rain to the NW coast of South America. A periodic phenomenon, it often affects the western coast of America as far north as California. In some years the weather pattern of the whole American continent can be disrupted, and in exceptional years its effects experienced worldwide.

LA NIÑA
The opposite phenomenon to El Niño. Warm surface water flows towards Asia and colder water from the ocean depths moves to the surface in the eastern equatorial Pacific. Evaporation decreases and rainfall in the region is reduced. Often La Niña occurs the year after El Niño, with drought affecting the areas which experienced flooding the year before.

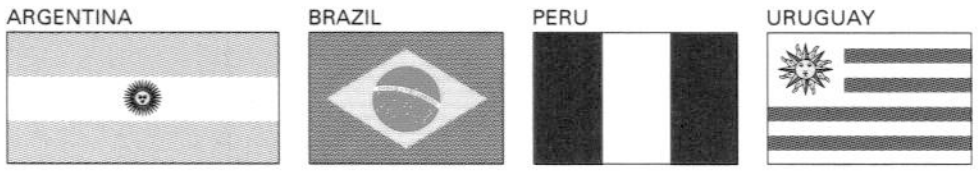

SOUTH AMERICA

See pages 50–53 for general maps

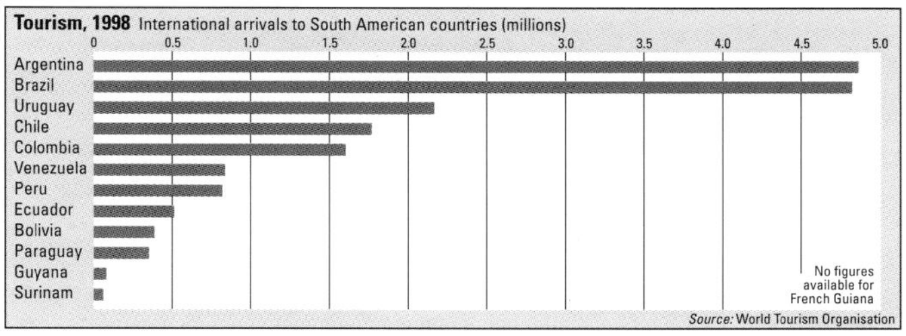

Tourism, 1998 International arrivals to South American countries (millions)

Argentina	
Brazil	
Uruguay	
Chile	
Colombia	
Venezuela	
Peru	
Ecuador	
Bolivia	
Paraguay	
Guyana	
Surinam	

0 0.5 1.0 1.5 2.0 2.5 3.0 3.5 4.0 4.5 5.0

No figures available for French Guiana

Source: World Tourism Organisation

OFFICIAL LANGUAGES
(Numbers refer to the notes on right)

- Spanish
- Portuguese
- English
- French
- Dutch

1 Spanish, English, Italian, French and German are widely spoken, especially in tourist areas.
2 Most of the population speak a Creole *patois*.
3 *Sranan Tongo*, originating in Creole, is the popular language. The other main languages are Hindi and Javanese. English, Chinese, French and Spanish are also spoken.
4 Creole, Hindi, Urdu and Amerindian are also spoken.
5 English, French, German and Portuguese are spoken by some sections of the community.
6 Local Indian dialects and some English, French, German and Italian are spoken.
7 Quechua, the Inca tongue, and other indigenous languages are common. Some English is spoken.
8 Quechua is the most important native language and is spoken in the majority of the Andean cities. Aymará is spoken in some areas of Puno Department. Many other dialects exist in the jungle regions. English is spoken in major tourist areas.
9 The Indians of the Altiplano speak Aymará and elsewhere Quechua is spoken. English is also spoken by a small number of officials and businessmen in commercial centres.
10 Guaraní is widely spoken. Most Paraguayans are bilingual, but prefer to speak Guaraní outside Asunción.
11 English is widely spoken.
12 English, German, French and Italian are sometimes spoken.
13 Some English is spoken in tourist resorts.

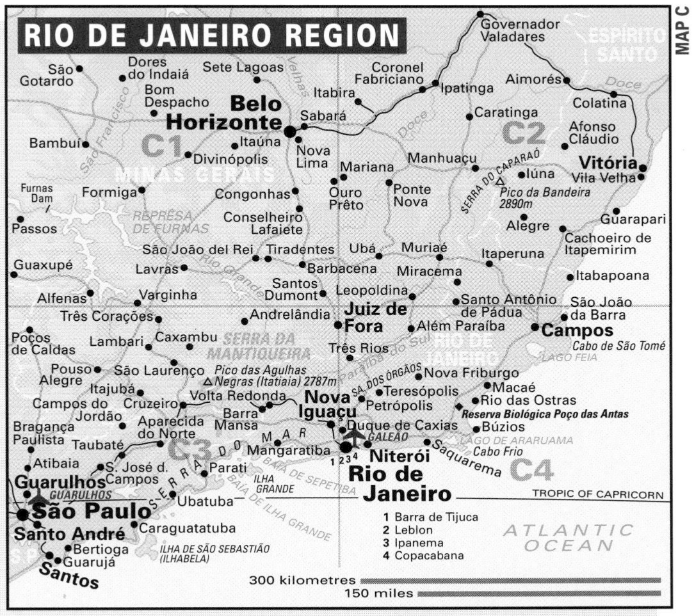

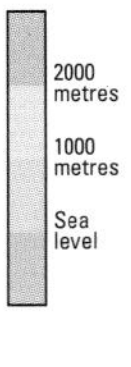

RIO DE JANEIRO REGION

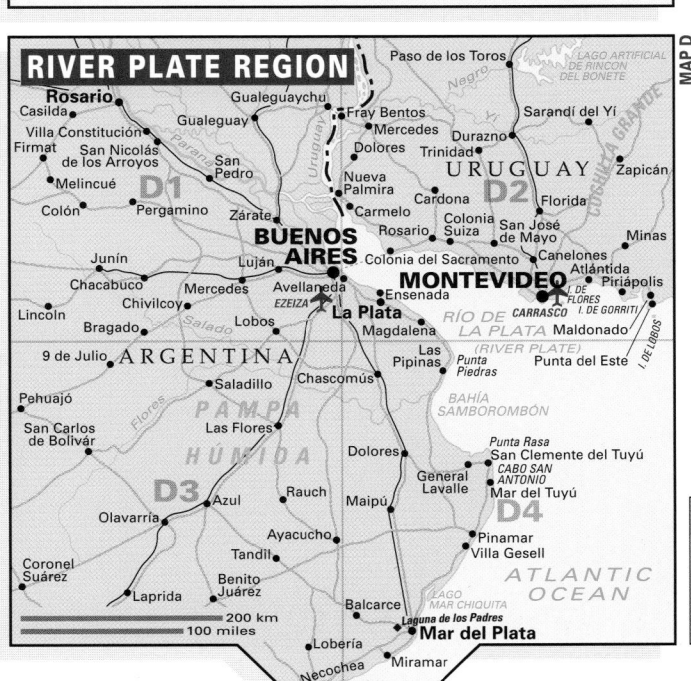

SOUTHERN PERU

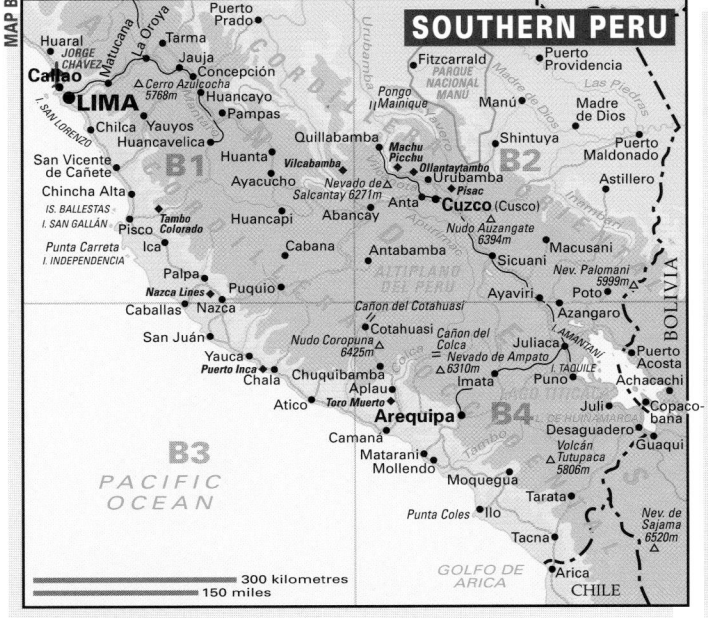

RIVER PLATE REGION

WORLD

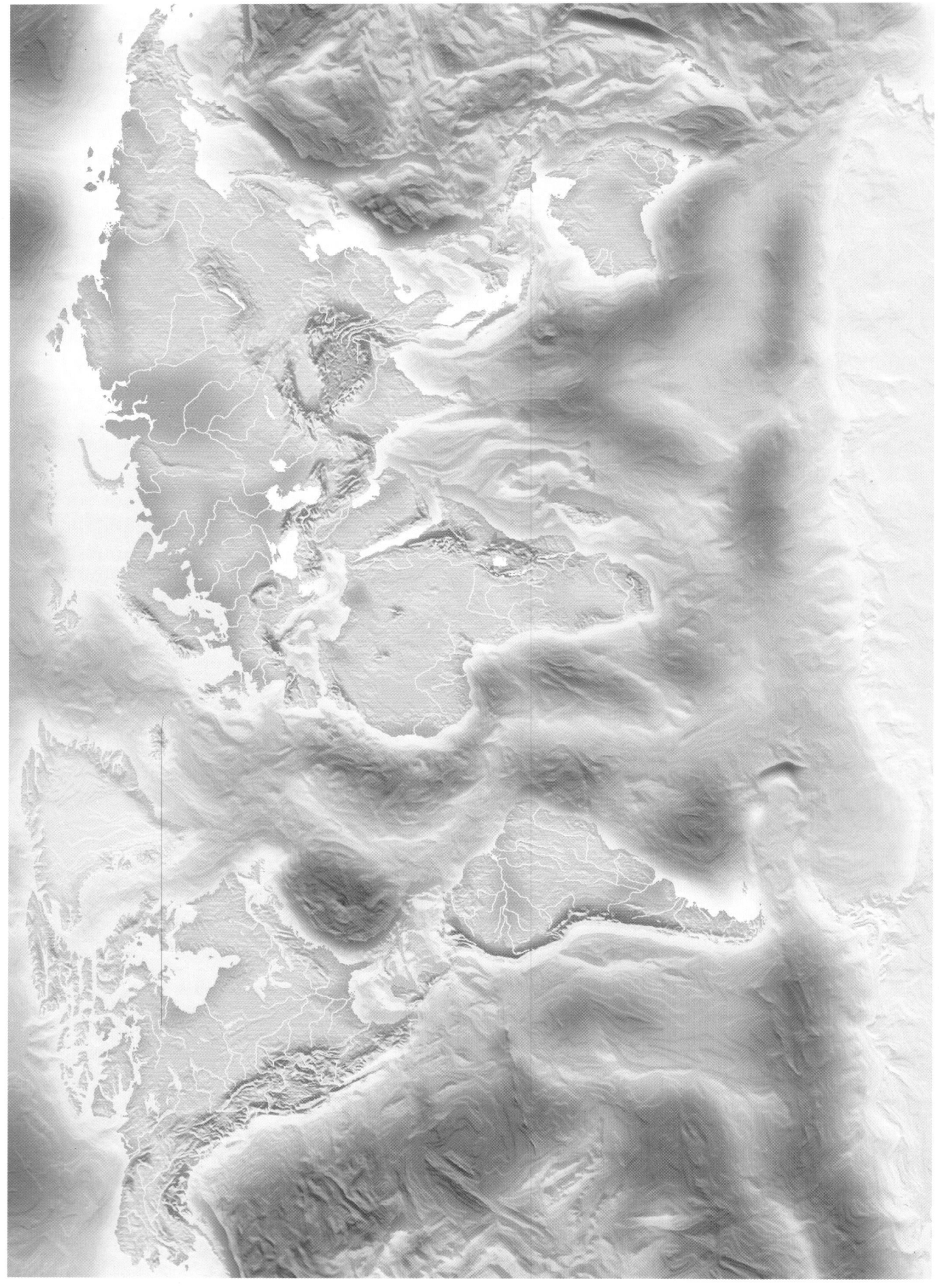

EUROPE

The British Isles

The Alps

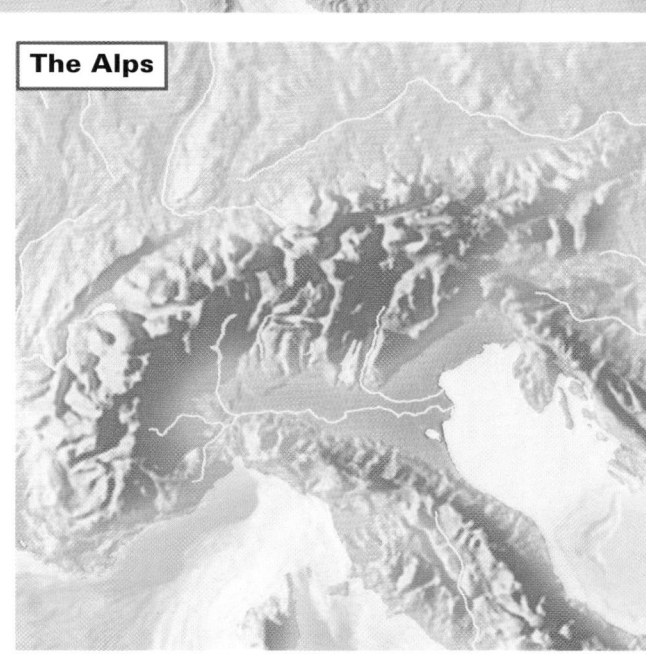

AFRICA

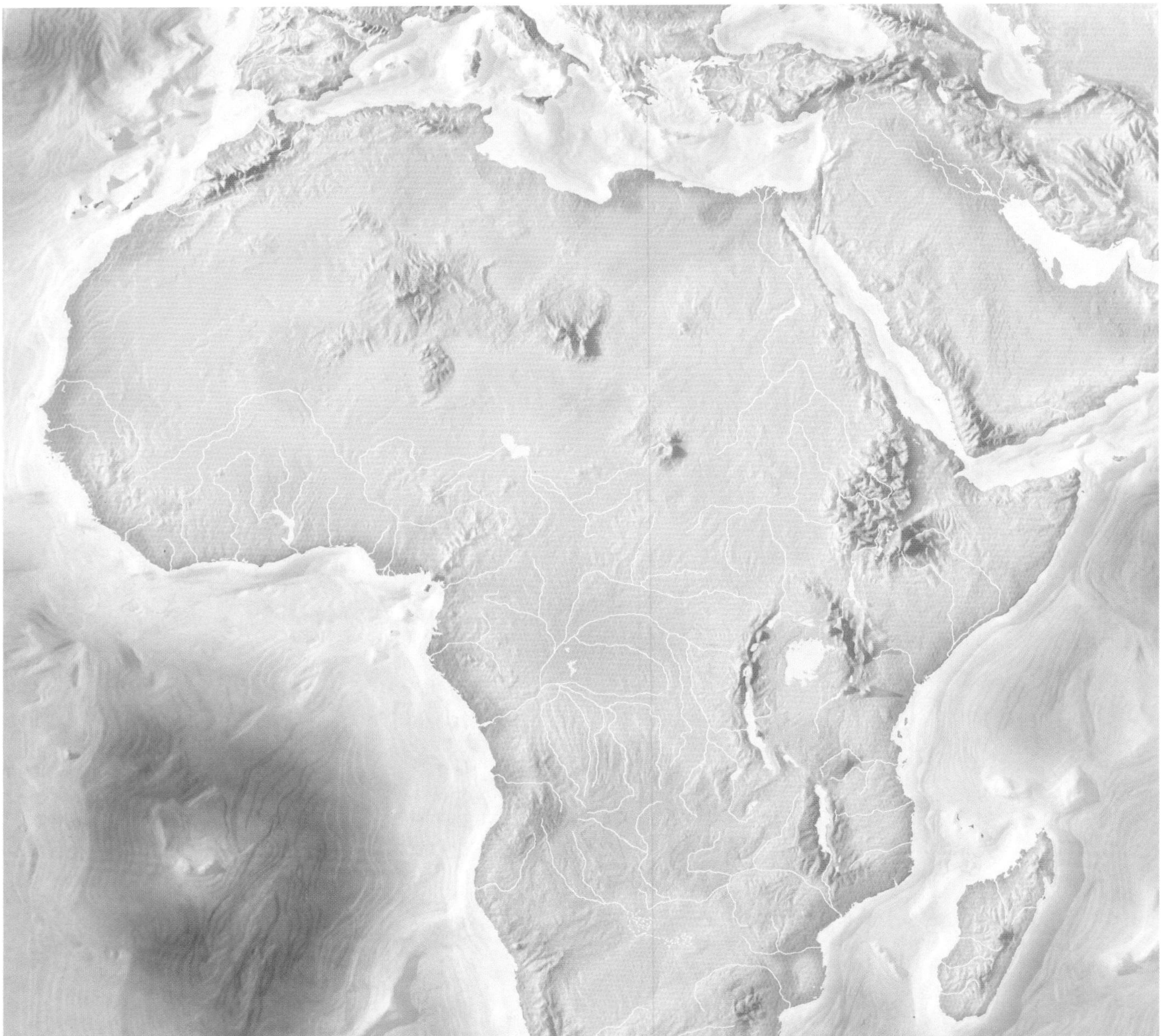

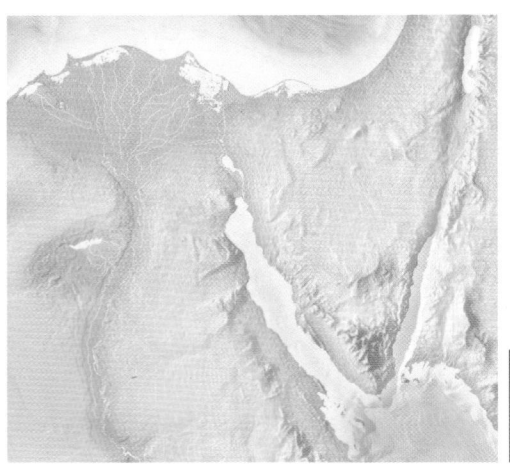

Nile Delta, Sinai and the Suez Canal

Lake Victoria region

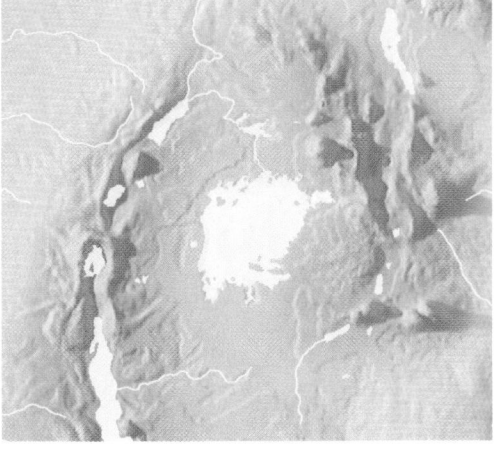

ASIA

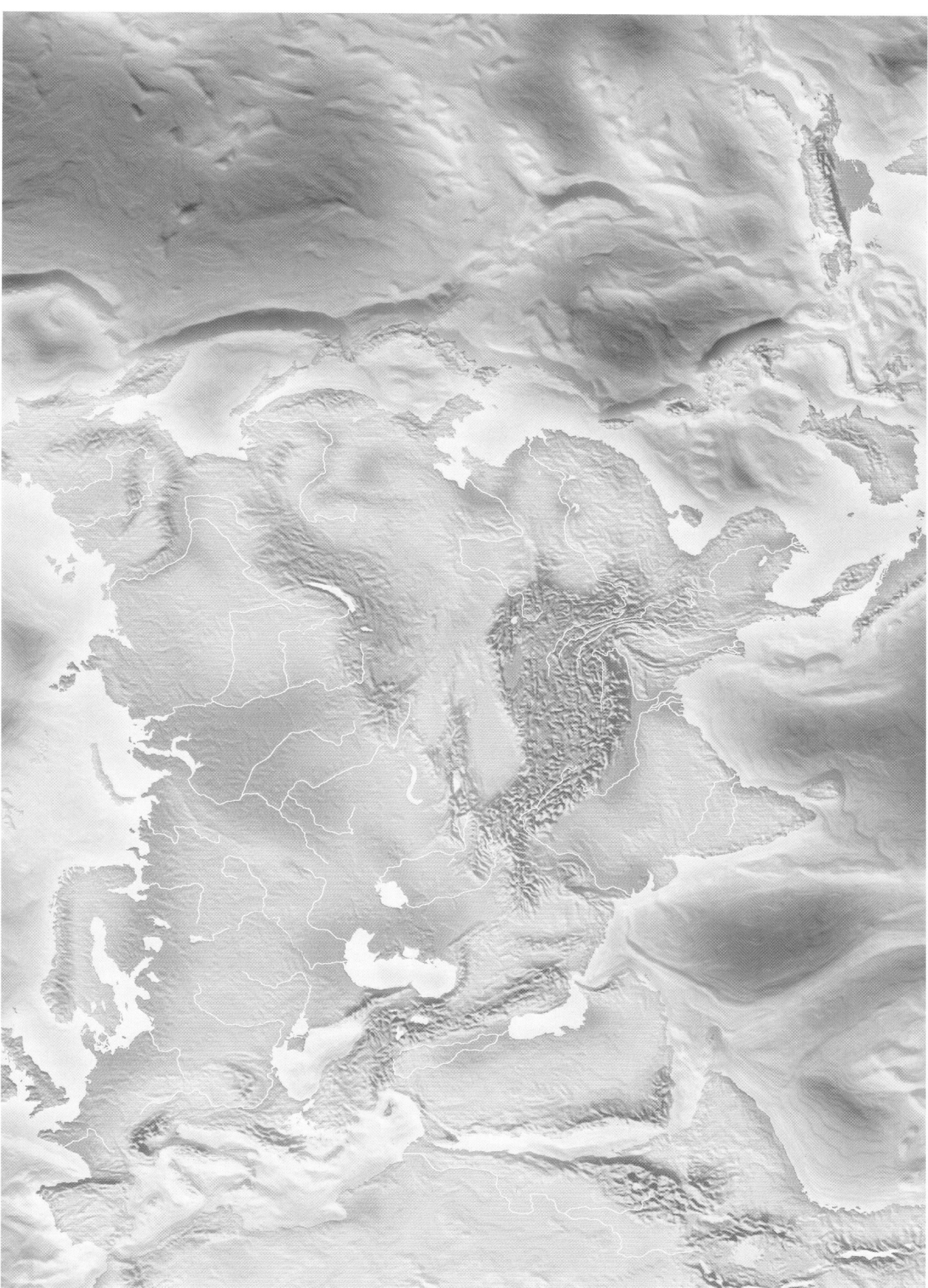

NORTH AMERICA

Hawaii

Panama

Northern Caribbean

SOUTH AMERICA

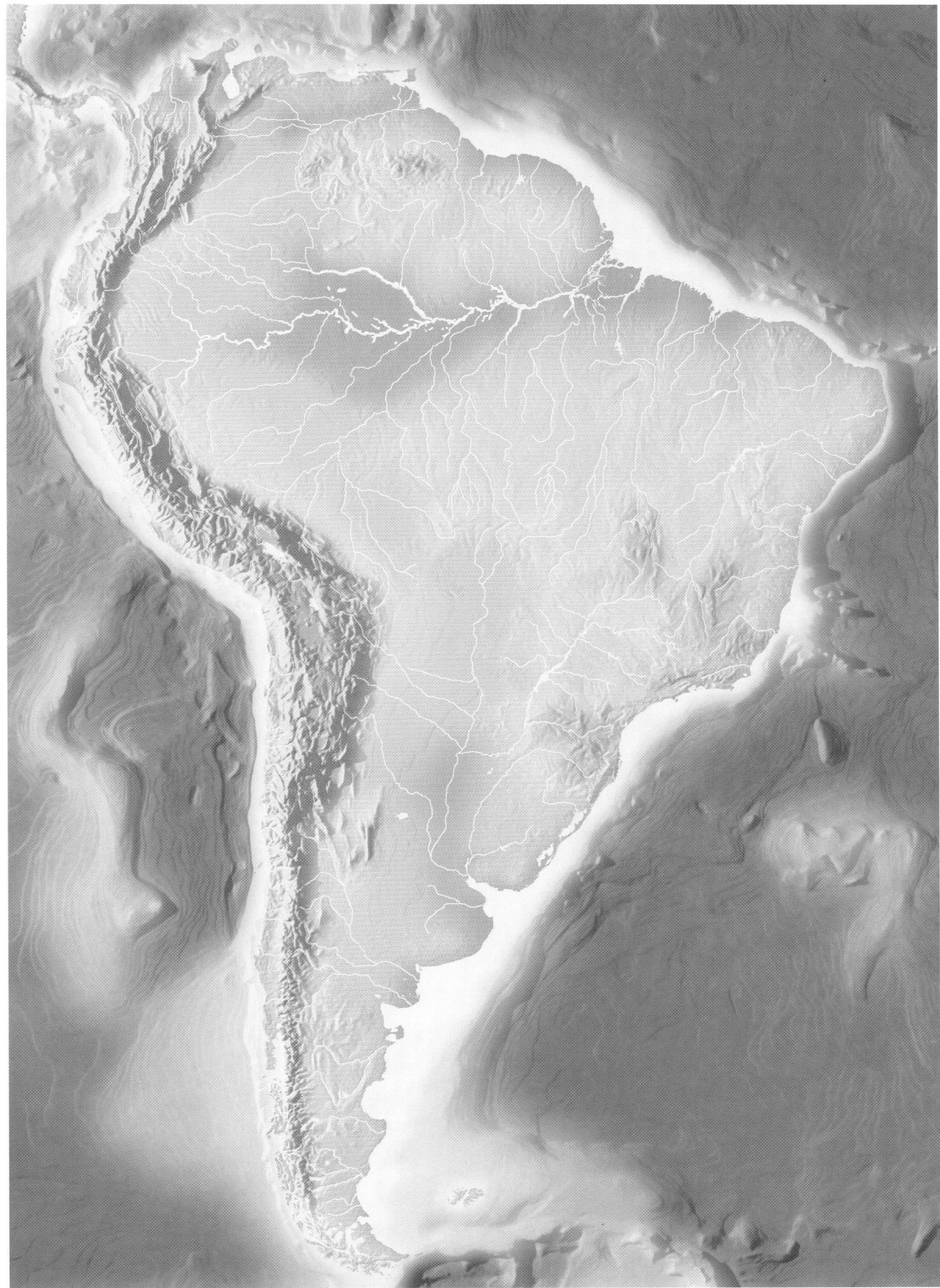

AUSTRALIA AND NEW ZEALAND

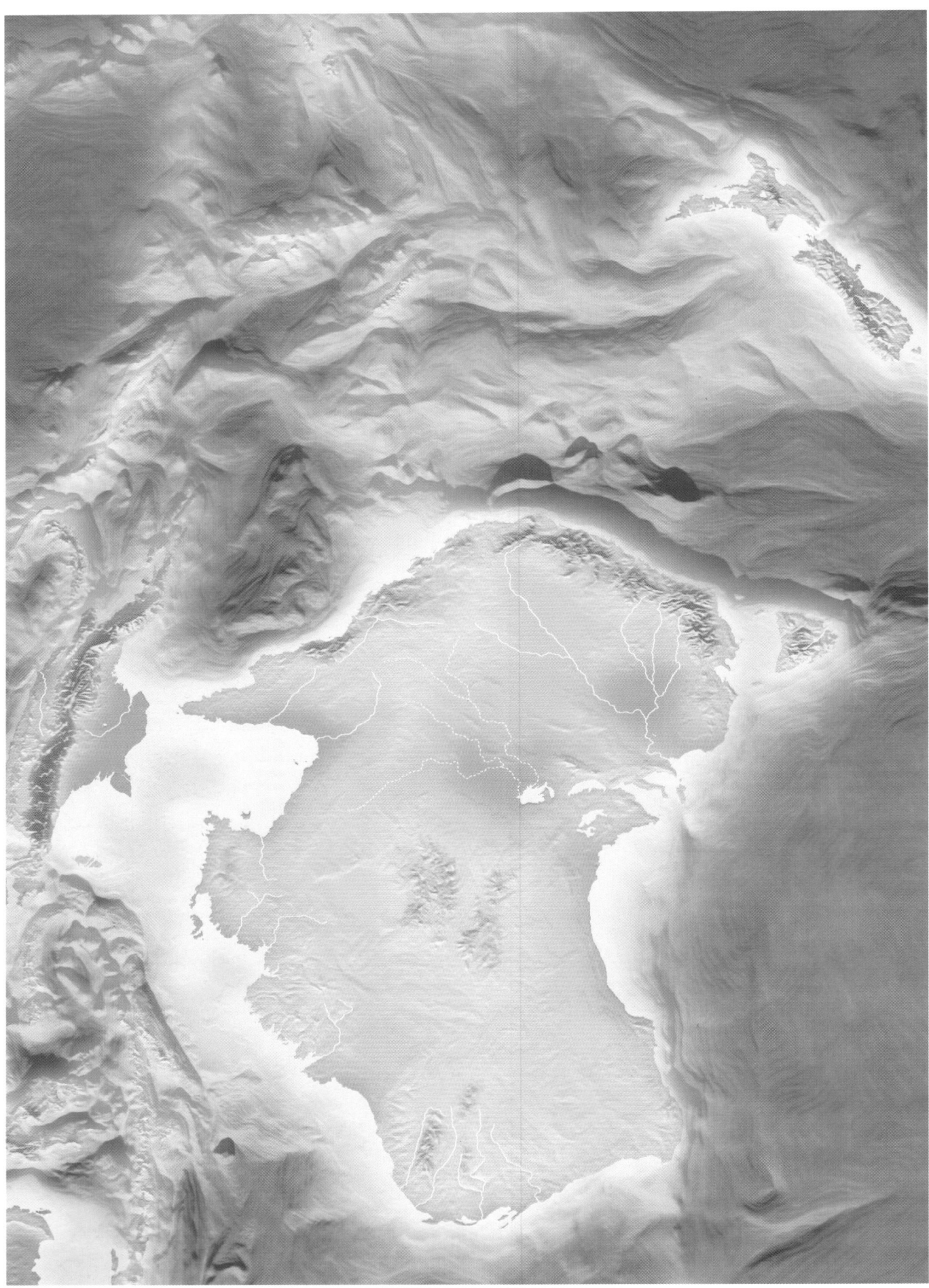

POLAR REGIONS

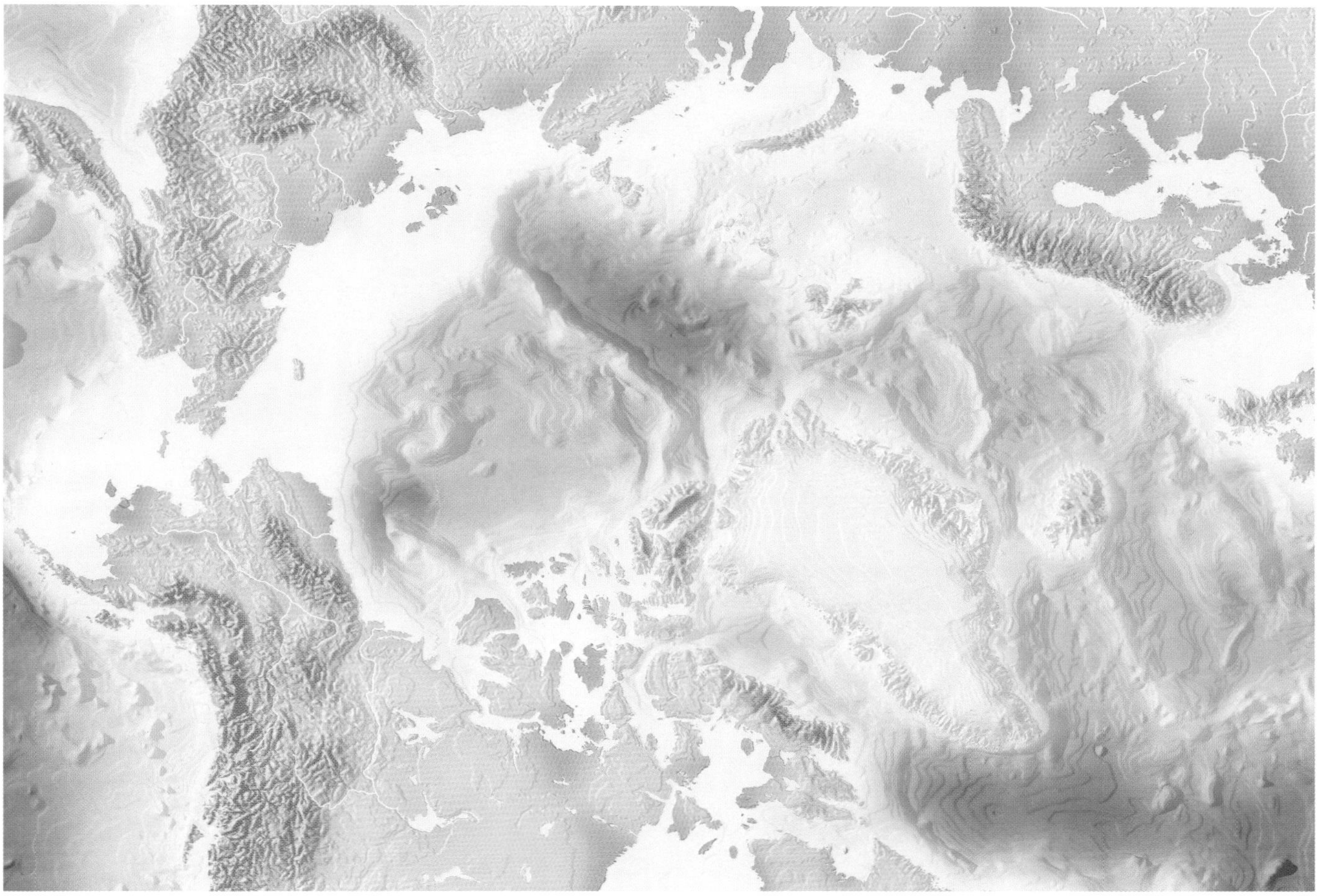

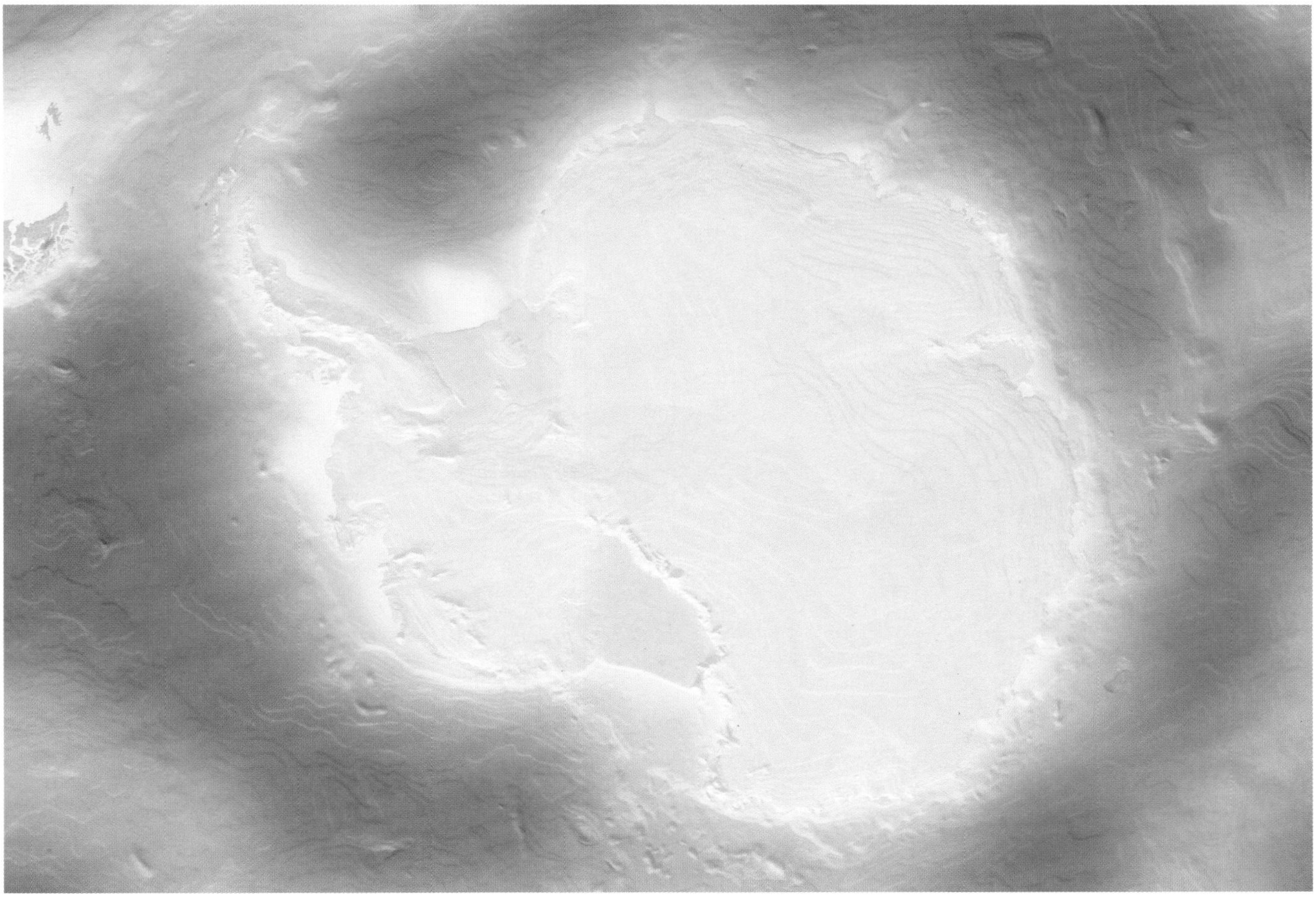

EARTH FROM SPACE

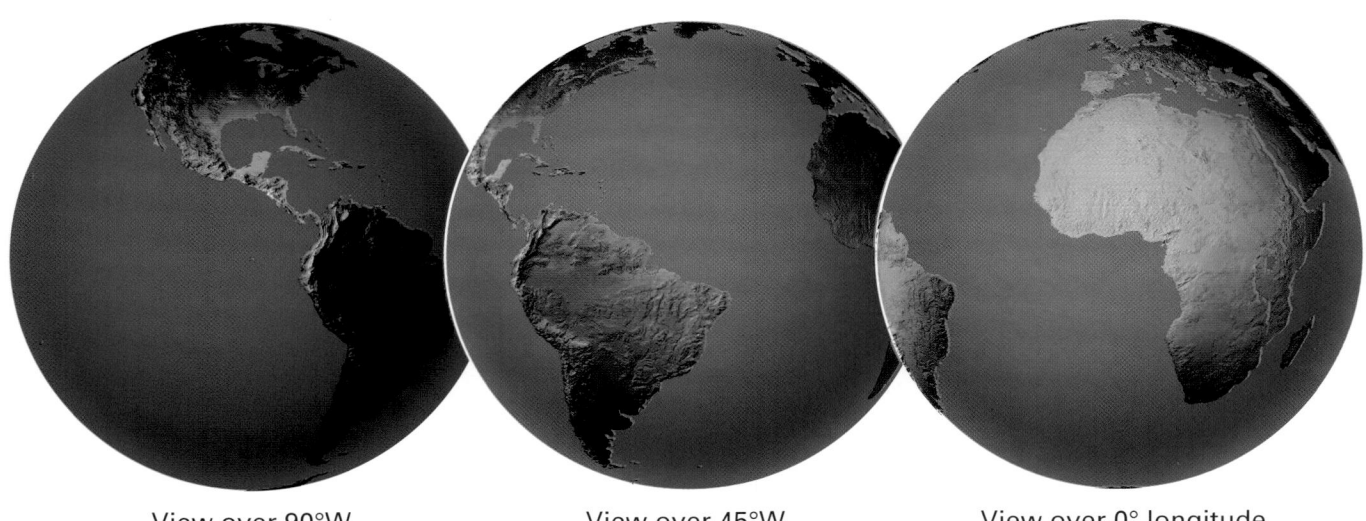

View over 90°W   View over 45°W   View over 0° longitude

PACIFIC OCEAN

ATLANTIC OCEAN

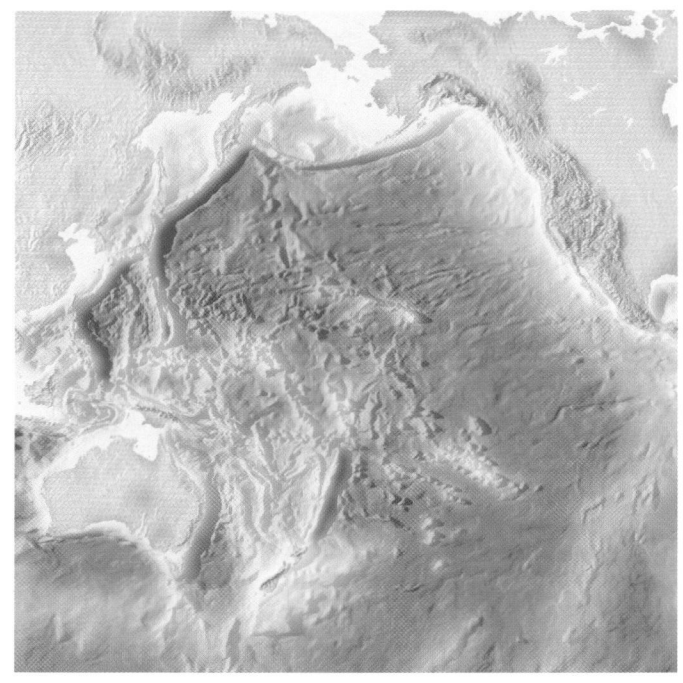

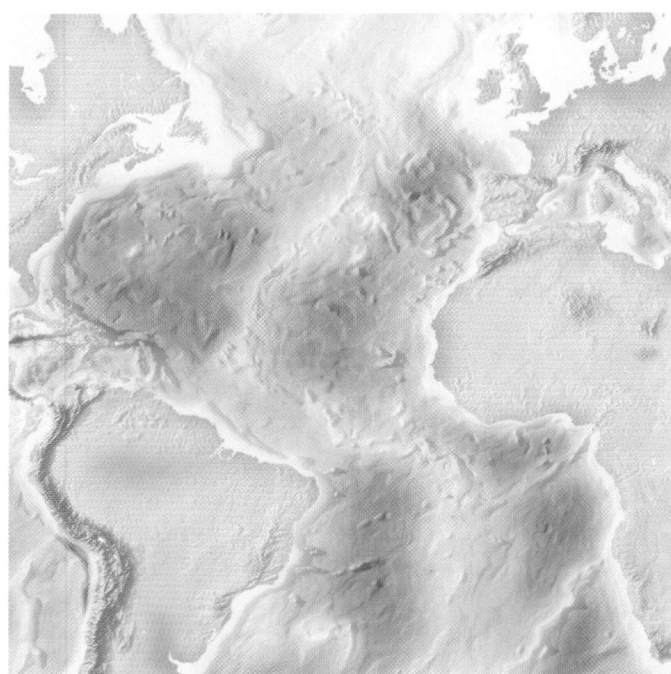

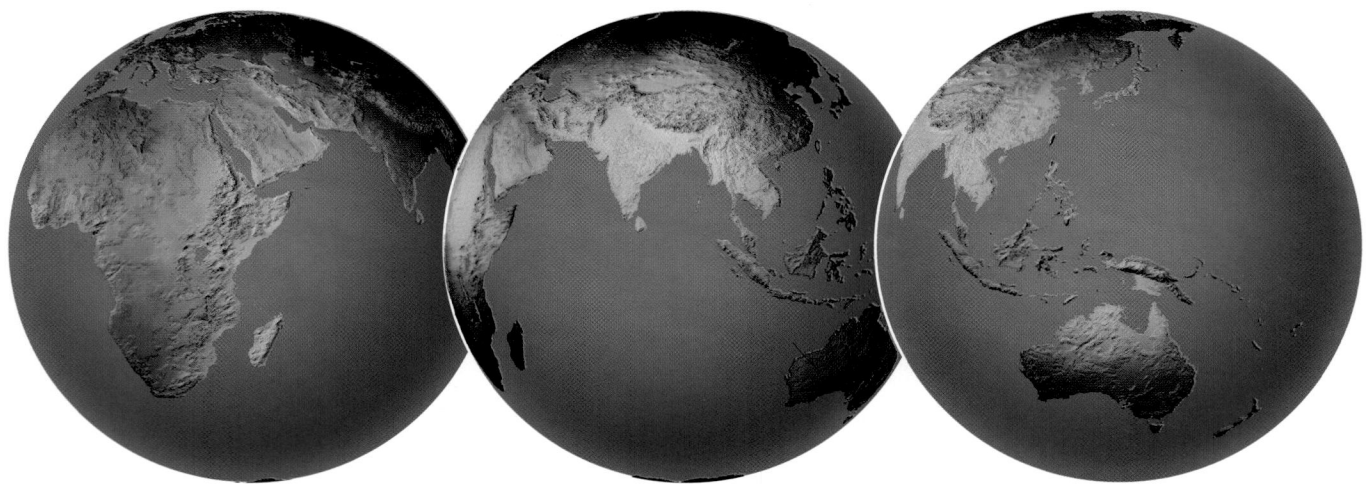

View over 45°E   View over 90°E   View over 135°E

APPENDICES

1: GEOGRAPHICAL DEFINITIONS

The following list includes names and abbreviations which appear in this atlas, together with other terms that are commonly used in the travel industry. Various authorities differ on the exact definitions of some of these entries; the definitions given here are those which are generally understood within the travel trade. For principal world and regional organisations, see pages 70-71.

Arabian Peninsula
Geographical region comprising: Bahrain, Kuwait, Oman, Qatar, Saudi Arabia, United Arab Emirates, Yemen.

Australasia
Geographical region comprising: Australia, New Caledonia, New Zealand, Solomon Islands, Vanuatu and the island of New Guinea including all of Papua New Guinea. Often described as equivalent to all of Oceania between the Equator and 47°S. The term is not commonly used, especially in Australia and New Zealand because of confusion with Australia.

Bahama Islands
Group of islands in the Atlantic Ocean comprising the Commonwealth of The Bahamas and the Turks and Caicos Islands.

Balkans, The
The Balkan Peninsula, which is bordered by the Adriatic and Ionian Seas to the west, the Aegean and Black Seas to the east and the Mediterranean Sea to the south. The countries occupying this peninsula are described as Balkan states: Albania, Bosnia-Herzegovina, Bulgaria, Croatia, Greece, Former Yugoslav Republic of Macedonia, Romania, Slovenia, Federal Republic of Yugoslavia and the European part of Turkey.

Borneo
Island in the Malay Archipelago (qv) divided between Brunei, Indonesia (the provinces of Central, East, South and West Kalimantan) and Malaysia (the states of Sabah and Sarawak).

British Isles
Geographical region comprising: United Kingdom (qv), Republic of Ireland, Isle of Man, Channel Islands.

Caribbean
General tourist destination term used to describe the West Indies (qv).

Caroline Islands
Archipelago in the west Pacific Ocean. Islands comprise the Federated States of Micronesia and Palau.

Celebes
Island in the Malay Archipelago (qv), Sulawesi in Indonesian.

Central America
Geographical region comprising: Belize, Costa Rica, El Salvador, Guatemala, Honduras, Nicaragua, Panama. Usually considered part of the North American (qv) continent.

Ceylon
Island off the southeast coast of India, officially Sri Lanka.

Channel Islands
Group of islands comprising Jersey, Guernsey, Alderney, Sark and Herm, situated off the northwest coast of France. They are possessions of the British Crown and not officially part of the United Kingdom (qv).

East Indies
General geographical term sometimes applied loosely to India, Indochina and the Malay Archipelago (qv). Often used as alternative to the Malay Archipelago or the Republic of Indonesia itself. The term is rarely used.

Europe
Continent. Northern boundary formed by Arctic Ocean. Eastern boundary formed by Ural Mountains, Ural River and Caspian Sea. Southern boundary formed by Caucasus Mountains, Black Sea, Bosporus, Aegean Sea and Mediterranean Sea. Western boundary formed by Atlantic Ocean. Includes Iceland, Svalbard and area of Turkey west of the Bosporus.

Far East
General geographical term describing east and South-East Asia: Brunei, Cambodia, China, Indonesia, Japan, Democratic People's Republic of Korea (North Korea), Republic of Korea (South Korea), Laos, Malaysia, Myanmar, the Philippines, Singapore, Taiwan, Thailand, Vietnam. Sometimes extended to include Mongolia and the eastern Siberian region of the Russian Federation.

Formosa
Island off the southeast coast of the People's Republic of China, known variously as the Republic of China or Taiwan.

Great Britain
Geographical region comprising: England, Scotland, Wales.

Greater Antilles
Group of Caribbean islands comprising: Cayman Islands, Cuba, Hispaniola, Jamaica, Puerto Rico.

Hispaniola
Island in the Greater Antilles (qv) divided between the Dominican Republic and Haiti.

IATA (International Air Transport Association)
An association which acts as a governing body of the major airlines, responsible for establishing fare levels and for rules and regulations concerning international passenger and cargo services. It has over 100 tariff members and a further 100 trade associate airlines.

Iberia
Peninsula in southwest Europe occupied by Spain, Portugal, Andorra and Gibraltar.

Indochina
Geographical region comprising: Cambodia, Laos, Malaysia (Peninsular), Myanmar, Singapore, Thailand, Vietnam.

Lesser Antilles
Group of Caribbean islands comprising: Leeward Islands (qv), Windward Islands (qv), Aruba, Barbados, Bonaire, Curaçao, Trinidad and Tobago. Also includes the chain of small Venezuelan islands east of Bonaire.

Leeward Islands
Group of Caribbean islands comprising: Anguilla, Antigua and Barbuda, Dominica, Guadeloupe, Montserrat, Saba, St Eustatius, St Kitts and Nevis, St Maarten/St Martin, Virgin Islands.

Low Countries
Geographical region comprising: Belgium, Luxembourg, The Netherlands.

Maghreb
Arabic name for northwest Africa and, during the Moorish period, Spain. Algeria, Morocco and Tunisia are described as Maghreb countries.

Malay Archipelago
The largest island group in the world, off the southeast coast of Asia and between the Indian and Pacific Oceans. Major islands include Borneo (qv), Sulawesi (Celebes, qv), Jawa (Java), New Guinea and Sumatera (Sumatra). Countries within this archipelago: Brunei, Indonesia, Malaysia (East), Papua New Guinea, the Philippines.

Mediterranean
General tourist destination term used to describe the islands of the Mediterranean Sea and the countries bordering it.

Melanesia
Collective name for the islands in the southwest Pacific Ocean, south of the Equator and northeast of Australia. Includes: Fiji, Nauru, New Caledonia, Papua New Guinea (excluding New Guinea mainland), Solomon Islands, Vanuatu.

Micronesia
Collective name for the islands in the west Pacific Ocean, north of the Equator and east of the Philippines. Includes: Guam, Kiribati (west), Marshall Islands, Federated States of Micronesia, Northern Mariana Islands, Palau.

Middle East
General geographical term describing a loosely defined area comprising: countries of the Arabian Peninsula, Egypt, Iran, Iraq, Israel, Jordan, Lebanon, Syria. Sometimes extended to include Algeria, Cyprus, Libya, Morocco, Sudan, Tunisia and Turkey.

Near East
Rarely used general geographical term describing an area of SW Asia: the Arabian Peninsula, Cyprus, Israel, Jordan, Lebanon, Syria, Turkey. Often extended to Egypt and Sudan.

Netherlands Antilles
Islands of the West Indies administered by The Netherlands, comprising: Bonaire, Curaçao, Saba, St Eustatius, St Maarten. Aruba, formerly part of the Netherlands Antilles is now administered from The Netherlands separately.

New Guinea
Island in the Malay Archipelago (qv) divided between Papua New Guinea and the Indonesian province of Irian Jaya.

North America
Continent comprising: Bermuda, Canada, Mexico, USA, West Indies (qv). Usually considered to also include Central America and Greenland.

Oceania
General geographical term describing the islands of the central and south Pacific Ocean, including Melanesia, Micronesia and Polynesia. Sometimes extended to include Australia, New Zealand and the Malay Archipelago (qv).

Polynesia
Collective name for the islands of the central and south Pacific Ocean. Includes: American Samoa, Cook Islands, Easter Island, French Polynesia, Hawaii, Kiribati (east), New Zealand, Niue, Pitcairn Islands, Tokelau, Tonga, Tuvalu, Wallis and Futuna, Western Samoa.

Scandinavia
Geographical region comprising: Denmark, Norway, Sweden. Often extended to include Finland and Iceland.

South America
Continent comprising: countries on mainland south of Panama, Falkland Islands, Galapagos Islands.

Ulster
Geographical region comprising Northern Ireland plus the counties of Cavan, Donegal and Monaghan in the Republic of Ireland. It is often used (incorrectly) as an unofficial term to describe Northern Ireland.

United Kingdom
Country comprising Great Britain (qv) and Northern Ireland. The Isle of Man and the Channel Islands are Crown dependencies and not officially part of the UK.

West Indies
Islands enclosing the Caribbean Sea, comprising: Bahama Islands (qv), Greater Antilles (qv), Lesser Antilles (qv).

Windward Islands
Group of Caribbean islands comprising: Grenada, Martinique, St Lucia, St Vincent and The Grenadines.

WWF (World-Wide Fund For Nature / World Wildlife Fund)
One of the world's largest private international nature conservation organisations. Its aim is to conserve nature by preserving genetic, species and ecosystem diversity.

2: HIGHEST AND LOWEST

Name	Metres	Feet	Country
AFRICA			
Kilimanjaro (Kibo)	5,895	19,340	Tanzania
Lake Assal	–155	–509	Djibouti
ANTARCTICA			
Vinson Massif	5,140	16,860	Antarctica
(ice covered)	–2,538	–8,327	Antarctica
ASIA			
Everest (Qomolangma Feng/ Sagarmatha)	8,848	29,028	China-Nepal
Dead Sea	–395	–1,296	Israel-Jordan
AUSTRALASIA			
Cook	3,764	12,349	New Zealand
Lake Eyre	–16	–52	Australia
EUROPE			
Elbrus	5,642	18,510	Russian Fed.
Caspian Sea	–28	–92	
NORTH AMERICA			
McKinley (Denali)	6,194	20,320	Alaska, USA
Death Valley	–86	–282	California, USA
SOUTH AMERICA			
Aconcagua	6,960	22,834	Argentina
Gran Bajo de San Julián	–105	–344	Argentina

Name	Metres	Feet	Country
SOME OTHER SIGNIFICANT MOUNTAINS			
K2 (Godwin Austin/ Qogir Feng)	8,611	28,250	China-Kashmir
Kangchenjunga	8,586	28,170	India-Nepal
Makalu	8,463	27,766	China-Nepal
Dhaulagiri	8,167	26,795	Nepal
Nanga Parbat	8,126	26,660	Kashmir
Annapurna	8,091	26,545	Nepal
Gosainthan (Xixabangma Feng)	8,012	26,286	China
Ismoili Somoni	7,495	24,590	Tajikistan
Ojos del Salado	6,863	22,516	Argentina-Chile
Huascarán	6,768	22,205	Peru
Logan	5,951	19,524	Yukon, Canada
Citlaltépetl (Orizaba)	5,700	18,701	Mexico
Damavand	5,670	18,602	Iran
Kenya (Kirinyaga)	5,199	17,057	Kenya
Ararat	5,165	16,946	Turkey
Mont Blanc	4,810	15,781	France-Italy
Ras Dashen	4,620	15,158	Ethiopia
Whitney	4,418	14,495	California, USA
Kinabalu	4,101	13,455	Malaysia
Fuji	3,776	12,388	Japan

3: THE WORLD'S LONGEST RIVERS

Lengths include the river plus the tributaries comprising the longest watercourse, shown to the nearest 10 km/miles. Local names are shown in square brackets: [ ].

River	Length: (km)	(miles)	Source(s) and outflow
Nile-Kagera-Ruvuvu-Luvironza	6,690	4,160	Lake Victoria region – Mediterranean Sea
Amazon-Ucayali-Tambo-Ene-Apurimac	6,570	4,080	Peruvian Andes – Atlantic Ocean
Mississippi-Missouri-Beaverhead-Red Rock	6,020	3,740	SW Montana – Gulf of Mexico
Chang Jiang (Yangtze)-[Jinsha-Tongtian-Tuotuo]	5,980	3,720	Tanggula Shan, China – East China Sea
Yenisey-Angara-Selenga-Ider	5,870	3,650	Western Mongolia – Kara Sea
Amur-Argun-Kerulen	5,780	3,590	Eastern Mongolia – Sea of Japan
Ob-Irtysh-[Ertix]	5,410	3,360	Altay Mountains, China – Kara Sea
Paraná-Rio Grande	4,880	3,030	Serra da Mantiquera, Brazil – Atlantic Ocean
Huang He (Yellow)	4,840	3,010	Bayan Har Shan, China – Yellow Sea
Congo-Lualaba	4,630	2,880	Katanga Plateau, Congo D.R. – Atlantic Ocean
Lena	4,400	2,730	Baikal Mtns, Russian Fed., – Laptev Sea
Mackenzie-Slave-Peace-Finlay	4,240	2,630	Omineca Mtns, BC, Canada– Beaufort Sea
Mekong-[Lancang-Za]	4,180	2,600	Tanggula Shan, China – South China Sea
Niger-[Joliba/Kworra]	4,100	2,550	Guinea/Sierra Leone border – Gulf of Guinea

4: CONVERSIONS

Kilometres	10	20	30	40	50	60	70	80	90	100
Miles	6.2	12.4	18.6	24.9	31.1	37.3	43.5	49.7	55.9	62.1
Metres	10	20	30	40	50	60	70	80	90	100
Feet	33	66	98	131	164	197	230	262	295	328

Centimetres	10	20	30	40	50	60	70	80	90	100	
Inches	3.9	7.9	11.8	15.7	19.7	23.6	27.6	31.5	35.4	39.4	
°Centigrade	-10	-5	0	5	10	15	20	25	30	35	40
°Fahrenheit	14	23	32	41	50	59	68	77	86	95	104

APPENDICES

5: FOREIGN GEOGRAPHICAL TERMS

The following list provides the English equivalents for some of the most common foreign geographical terms used in this atlas and other international atlases.

A

Å, -å	Danish, Norwegian	Stream
Abar, Abyar	Arabic	Wells
Açude	Portuguese	Reservoir
Adalar	Turkish	Islands
Adasi	Turkish	Island
Agia, Ágios	Greek	Saint
Aiguille(s)	French	Peak(s)
Ain, Aïn	Arabic	Spring, well
-air	Indonesian	Stream
Ákra, Akrotírion	Greek	Cape, point
Ala-	Finnish	Lower
A'lá	Arabic	Upper
Alt-	German	Old
Alta, Alto	Italian, Portug., Spanish	Upper
Altiplanicie	Spain	High plain, mesa
Älv, -älven	Swedish	River
am, an	German	On, upon
Áno	Greek	Upper
Anse	French	Bay
Ao	Chinese, Thai	Bay
'Aqabat	Arabic	Pass
Arrecife	Spanish	Reef
Arroio / Arroyo	Portuguese / Spanish	Watercourse
Archipiélago	Spanish	Archipelago
Aust-	Norwegian	East, eastern
Austral	Spanish	Southern
'Ayn	Arabic	Spring, well

B

Baai	Afrikaans	Bay
Bab	Arabic	Strait
Bach	German	Stream
Bad	German	Spa
Badiyat	Arabic	Desert
Bælt	Danish	Strait
Baharu	Malay	New
Bahía	Spanish	Bay
Bahiret	Arabic	Lagoon
Bahr	Arabic	Bay, canal, lake
Bahra / Bahrat	Arabic	Lagoon / Lake
Baía / Baie	Portuguese / French	Bay
Baixo	Portuguese	Lower
Baja, Bajo	Spanish	Lower
Bala	Persian	Upper
Ban	Cambodian, Laotian, Thai	Village
-bana	Japanese	Cape, point
Bañado	Spanish	Marshy land
Banc / Banco	French / Spanish	Sandbank
Bandao	Chinese	Peninsula
Bandar	Arabian, Malay, Persian	Inlet, port
-bando	Korean	Peninsula
Baraj, Baraji	Turkish	Dam
Barat	Indonesian, Malay	West, western
Barqa	Arabic	Hill
Barra	Portuguese	Sandbank
Barracão	Portuguese	Dam, weir
Barragem	Portuguese	Reservoir
Baruun	Mongolian	Western
Bas, Basse	French	Lower
Bassin	French	Basin
Batin, Batn	Arabic	Depression
Becken	German	Basin
Beek	Flemish	Stream
bei	German	At, near
Bei	Chinese	North, northern
Beinn, Ben	Gaelic	Mountain
Belogor'ye	Russian	Mountain
Bereg	Russian	Bank, shore
-berg	Norwegian, Swedish	Mountain
Berg(e)	German	Mountain(s)
Besar	Indonesian, Malay	Big, great
Bir, Bîr / Bi'ar	Arabic	Well / Wells
Birkat, Birket	Arabic	Pool, well
-bjerg	Danish	Hill
Boca	Portuguese, Spanish	Mouth
Bocche	Italian	Estuary, mouths
Bodden	German	Bay, gulf
Bogazi	Turkish	Strait
Bogen	Norwegian	Bay
Bois	French	Woods
Boloto	Russian	Bog, marsh
Bol'sh-aya, -iye, -oy, -oye	Russian	Big
-bong	Korean	Mountain
Boquerón	Spanish	Pass
Bor	Polish	Forest
-botn / -botten	Norwegian / Swedish	Valley floor
Bouche	French	Estuary, mouth
-bre, -breen	Norwegian	Glacier
Bredning	Danish	Bay
Bron	Afrikaans	Spring, well
-brønn	Norwegian	Spring, well
Bucht / Bugt	German / Danish	Bay
Buhayrat, Buheirat	Arabic	Lake
Bukhta	Russian	Bay
Bukit	Malay	Hill
Bukt, Bukten	Norwegian, Swedish	Bay
Bulag	Mongolian	Spring
Bulak	Russian, Uighur	Spring
Burg	German	Castle
Burun, Burnu	Turkish	Cape, point
Büyük	Turkish	Big

C

Cabeço	Portuguese	Summit
Cabeza	Spanish	Summit
Cabo	Portuguese, Spanish	Cape, headland
Cachoeira	Portuguese	Waterfall
Cala / Caleta	Catalan / Spanish	Inlet
Cañada	Spanish	Ravine
Cañadón	Spanish	Gorge
Canal	Portuguese, Spanish	Channel
Caño	Spanish	Stream
Cañon	Spanish	Canyon
Cap / Capo	Catalan, French / Italian	Cape, headland
Catarata	Spanish	Waterfall
Cayo(s)	Spanish	Islet(s), rock(s)
Cerro	Spanish	Hill, peak
Chaco	Spanish	Plain
Chaîne	French	Mountain chain
Chalb	Arabic	Watercourse
Chapada	Portuguese	Hills, uplands
Chebka	Arabic	Hill
-chedo	Korean	Archipelago
Chenal	French	Channel
Chiang	Thai	Town
-ch'on	Korean	River
Chong	Thai	Bay
Chott	Arabic	Marsh, salt lake
Chuluu	Mongolian	Mountain
Chute	French	Waterfall
Ci	Indonesian	Stream
Ciénaga	Spanish	Marshy lake
Cima / Cime	Italian / French	Summit
Città / Ciudad	Italian / Spanish	City, town
Co	Tibetan	Lake
Col	French	High pass
Collado	Spanish	Hill, saddle
Colle	Italian	Pass
Collina	Italian	Hill
Colline(s)	French	Hill(s)
Combe	French	Valley
Conca	Italian	Hollow
Cordillera	Spanish	Mountain chain
Corne / Corno	French / Italian	Peak
Costa	Italian, Portug., Spanish	Coast, shore
Côte	French	Coast, slope
Coteau(x)	French	Hill(s)
Cove	Catalan	Cave
Cuchilla	Spanish	Mountain chain
Cuenca	Spanish	River basin
Cueva	Spanish	Cave
Cun	Chinese	Village

D

Da	Chinese	Big
Dag / Dagh	Turkish / Persian	Mountain
Daglar	Turkish	Mountain
-dake	Japanese	Peak
-dal	Afrikaans, Danish, Norwegian, Swedish	Valley
Danau	Indonesian	Lake
Dao	Chinese	Island
Darreh	Persian	Valley
Daryacheh	Persian	Lake
Dasht	Persian, Urdu	Desert
Davaa	Mongolian	Pass
Denizi	Turkish	Sea
Dhar	Arabic	Hills, mountain
-diep	Flemish	Channel
Djebel / Djibâl	Arabic	Mountain / Mtns.
-do	Korean	Island
Dolina	Russian	Valley
Dolna / Dolní	Bulgarian / Czech	Lower
Dolny	Polish	Lower
Dong	Chinese	East, eastern
Dong	Thai	Mountain
-dong	Korean	Village
Donja, Donji	Serbo-Croat	Lower
Dorf	German	Village
-dorp	Afrikaans	Village
Dür	Arabic	Mountains
Dzüün	Mongolian	East, eastern

E

Eiland(en)	Afrikaans, Flemish	Island(s)
-elv, -elva	Norwegian	River
Embalse	Spanish	Reservoir
Embouchure	French	Estuary
Ensenada	Spanish	Bay
Erg	Arabian	Desert & dunes
Eski	Turkish	Old
Estero	Spanish	Inlet, estuary, swamp
Estrecho	Spanish	Strait
Estreito	Portuguese	Strait
Étang	French	Lake, lagoon

F

Fajj	Arabic	Watercourse
Fels	German	Rock
Feng	Chinese	Peak
Fiume	Italian	River
-fjäll, -fjället	Swedish	Mountain
-fjärden	Swedish	Fjord
-fjell, -fjellet	Norwegian	Mountain
-fjord, -fjorden	Danish, Norwegian	Fjord, lagoon
Fleuve	French	River
Foce	Italian	River-mouth
-fonn	Norwegian	Glacier
Förde	German	Inlet
Forêt / Forst	French / German	Forest
-foss	Norwegian	Waterfall
Fuente	Spanish	Source, well

G

-gan	Japanese	Rock
Gang	Chinese	Harbour
Garet	Arabic	Hill
Gardaneh	Persian	Pass
Gat	Flemish	Channel
-gata	Japanese	Inlet, lagoon
Gau	German	District
Gave	French	Torrent
-gawa	Japanese	River
Gebel	Arabic	Mountain
Gebergte	Afrikaans	Mountain range
Gebiet	German	District, region
Gebirge	German	Mountains
Gedigi	Turkish	Pass
Gezîret / Gezâir	Arabic	Island / Islands
Ghadfat	Arabic	Watercourse
Ghadir	Arabic	Well
Ghard	Arabic	Sand dunes
Ghubbat	Arabic	Bay
Gipfel	German	Peak
Gletscher	German	Glacier
Gobi	Mongolian	Desert
Gol	Mongolian	River
Göl, Gölü	Turkish	Lake
Golfe	French	Bay, gulf
Golfete	Spanish	Bay
Golfo	Italian, Spanish	Bay, gulf
Gora	Bulgarian	Forest
Gora / Góra	Russian, Serbo-Croat / Polish	Mountain
Górka	Polish	Hill
Gornja, Gornji	Serbo-Croat	Upper
Gory / Góry	Russian / Polish	Mountains
Goulet	French	Narrow entrance
Graben	German	Ditch, trench
-grad	Bulgarian, Russian, Serbo-Croat	Town, castle
Grand, Grands	French	Big
Grat	German	Crest, ridge
Greben'	Russian	Ridge
-gród	Polish	Town, castle
Groot	Afrikaans	Big
Gross, -e, -en, -er	German	Big
Grotta / Grotte	Italian / French	Cave, grotto
Grund	German	Ground, valley
Gryada	Russian	Ridge
Guan	Chinese	Pass
Guba	Russian	Bay
Guelta	Arabic	Well
-gunto	Japanese	Island group
Gunung	Indonesian, Malay	Mountain

H

Hadabat	Arabic	Plain
Hadh, Hadhat	Arabic	Sand dunes
-haehyop	Korean	Strait
Hafar	Arabic	Wells
Hafen	German	Harbour, port
Haff	German	Bay
Hai	Chinese	Sea
Halbinsel	German	Peninsula
-halvøya	Norwegian	Peninsula
Hamad-a, -et	Arabic	Plateau
Hammad-ah, -at	Arabic	Plain, rocky plateau
-hamn	Norwegian, Swedish	Harbour
Hamun	Persian	Marsh
-hanto	Japanese	Peninsula
Hardt	German	Wooded hills
Harrat	Arabic	Lava fields
Hassi, Hasy	Arabic	Well
-haug	Norwegian	Hill
Haut, -e	French	Upper
Hawr	Arabic	Lake
-havn	Danish, Norwegian	Harbour
Hazm	Arabic	Plateau
He	Chinese	River
-hede	Danish, Norwegian	Heath
-hegység	Hungarian	Mountains
-hei / Heide	Norwegian / German	Heath, moor
Hersónisos	Greek	Peninsula
Higashi-	Japanese	East, eastern
-hisar	Turkish	Castle
Hisn	Arabic	Fort
-hø	Norwegian	Peak
Hoch / Hoë	German / Afrikaans	High
Hoek	Flemish	Cape, point
Hög / -høg(d)	Swedish / Norwegian	High, height
Höhe, Hohen-	German	Height
Hoog	Flemish	High
-høoj	Danish	Hill
Hora / Hory	Czech	Mountain / Mtns
Horn	German	Peak, summit
Horní	Czech	Upper
Hot	Mongolian	Town
-høy	Norwegian	Height
-hrad	Czech	Castle
Hu	Chinese	Lake
Hügel	German	Hill

I

Idd	Arabic	Well
Idhan	Arabic	Sand dunes
'Idwet	Arabic	Mountain
Île(s) / Ilha(s)	French / Portuguese	Island(s)
Illa, Illes	Catalan	Island, islands
im, in	German	In
Inférieur, -e	French	Lower
Insel(n)	German	Island(s)
Irmak	Turkish	Large river
'Irq	Arabic	Sand dunes
Isla(s) / Isle	Spanish / French	Island(s)
Islote	Spanish	Small island
Iso	Finnish	Big
Ísola, Isole	Italian	Island, islands
Istmo	Spanish	Isthmus

J

Jabal	Arabic	Mountain
-järvi	Finnish	Lake
-jaure, -javrre	Lappish	Lake
Jazirat / Jaza'ir	Arabic	Island / Islands
Jbel, Jebel	Arabic	Mountain
Jezero / Jezioro	Serbo-Croat / Polish	Lake
Jiang	Chinese	River
Jiao	Chinese	Point, reef
Jibal	Arabic	Mountains
-jima	Japanese	Island
-joki / -jokka	Finnish / Lappish	River
-jøkulen	Norwegian	Glacier
-jökull	Icelandic	Glacier
Jun	Arabic	Bay

K

Kaap	Afrikaans	Cape
-kai	Japanese	Sea, bay, inlet
Kali	Indonesian	River
Kamm	German	Crest, ridge
Kampung	Indonesian, Malay	Village
Kanaal / Kanal	Flemish / German, Russian	Canal
-kapp	Norwegian	Cape
Karif	Arabic	Well
Kathib	Arabic	Sand dunes
Káto	Greek	Lower
-kawa	Japanese	River
Kecil	Indonesian, Malay	Small
Kepulauan	Indonesian	Archipelago
Kereb	Arabic	Hill, ridge
Keski-	Finnish	Central, middle
Khalig, Khalij	Arabic	Bay, gulf
Khao	Thai	Peak
Khashm	Arabic	Mountain
Khawr, Khor / Khowr	Arabic / Persian	Inlet
Khrebet	Russian	Mountain range
Kis-	Hungarian	Small
Kita-	Japanese	North, northern
Klamm	German	Ravine
Klein	Afrikaans, German	Small
Klint / Klit	Danish	Cliff / Dunes
Klong	Thai	Canal, creek
Kloof	Afrikaans	Gorge
Ko / Koh	Thai / Cambodian	Island
-ko	Japanese	Lake, inlet
Kólpos	Greek	Gulf
Koog	German	Polder
Kop / Kopf	Afrikaans / German	Hill
Körfezi	Turkish	Bay, gulf
Kotlina	Czech, Polish	Basin, depression
Kotlovina	Russian	Depression
-köy	Turkish	Village
Kraj	Czech, Polish, Serbo-Croat	Region
Kray	Russian	Region
Kreis	German	District
Kryazh	Russian	Ridge
Kuala	Malay	Estuary
Küçük	Turkish	Small
Kuduk	Russian	Spring, well
Kuh	Persian	Mountain
Kul'	Russian	Lake
Kület	Arabic	Hill
Kum	Russian	Sandy desert
-kundo	Korean	Island group
-kylä	Finnish	Village

L

Lac	French	Lake
Laem	Thai	Point
Lago	Italian, Portug., Spanish	Lake
Lagoa	Portuguese	Lagoon
Laguna	Spanish	Lagoon, lake
Lam	Thai	Stream
Län	Swedish	Province
Land	German	Province, area
Lande	French	Heath, sandy moor
Las / Les	Polish / Czech, Russian	Forest, wood
Laut	Indonesia	Sea
Lednik	Russian	Glacier
lès, lez	French	Beside, near
Liedao	Chinese	Island group
Lille	Danish, Norwegian	Small
Liman	Russian	Bay, gulf
Liman, Limani	Turkish	Harbour, port
Limni	Greek	Lake, lagoon
Ling	Chinese	Mountain range
Llano	Spanish	Plain, prairie
Loma	Spanish	Hill
-luoto	Finnish	Rocky island
-lyng	Danish	Heath

M

Macizo	Spanish	Massif
Madinat	Arabic	City, town
Mae Nam	Thai	River
Mala / Malé	Serbo-Croat / Czech	Small
Malaya, -oye, -yy	Russian	Small
-man	Korean	Bay
Manâqîr	Arabic	Hills
Mar	Portuguese, Spanish	Sea
Marais	French	Marsh, swamp
Mare	Italian / Romanian	Sea / Big
Marsá	Arabic	Anchorage, inlet
Marsch	German	Fen, marsh
Masabb	Arabic	Estuary
Mashâsh	Arabic	Well
Massif	French	Mountains, upland
Mayor	Spanish	Higher, larger
Meer	Afrikaans, Flemish, German	Lake, sea
Méga, Megál-a, -i, -o	Greek	Big
Menor	Portuguese, Spanish	Lesser, smaller
Mer	French	Sea
Mersa	Arabic	Anchorage, inlet
Mesa, Meseta	Spanish	Tableland
Mesto	Czech, Serbo-Croat	Town
Mezzo	Italian	Middle, mid-
Miasto	Polish	Town
Mic / Mikr-i, ón	Romanian / Greek	Small
Mina'	Arabic	Harbour, port
Minami-	Japanese	South, southern
Minqâr	Arabic	Hill
-misaki	Japanese	Cape, point
Mishâsh, Mushâsh	Arabic	Well
Miti	Greek	Cape
Mittel-, Mitten-	German	Central, middle
Mjesto	Serbo-Croat	Town
Monasterio / Moni	Spanish / Greek	Monastery
Mont / Monte	French / Italian, Portuguese, Spanish	Mountain
Montagne(s)	French	Mountain(s)
Monti	Italian	Mountains
Moor	German	Bog, moor, swamp
Moos	German	Bog, moss
More	Russian	Sea
Mörön	Mongolian	River
Morro	Portuguese	Hill, mountain
-mose	Danish	Bog, moor
Moyen, -ne	French	Middle, mid-
Muara	Indonesian	Estuary
Mudiriyat	Arabic	Province
Muntii	Romanian	Mountains
-myr	Norwegian, Swedish	Moor, swamp
Mys	Russian	Cape

N

na	Bulgarian, Russian, Serbo-Croat	On
nad	Czech, Polish, Russian	Above, over
-nada	Japanese	Gulf, sea
Nádrz	Czech	Reservoir
-naes	Danish	Cape, point
Nafud	Arabic	Desert, dune
Nagor'ye	Russian	Highland, uplands
Nagy-	Hungarian	Big, great
Nahr	Arabic	River
Nakhon	Thai	Town
Nam	Korean, Vietnamese	South, southern
Nam	Burmese, Thai, Vietnamese	River
Nan	Chinese	South, southern
Naqb	Arabic	Pass
Nasb	Arabic	Hill, mountain
Né-a, -on, -os	Greek	New
Neder-	Flemish	Lower
Nehri	Turkish	River
Nei	Chinese	Inner
-nes	Icelandic, Norwegian	Cape, point
Neu- / Neuf, Neuve	German / French	New
Nevado	Spanish	Peak
-ni	Korean	Village
Nieder-	German	Lower
Nieu	Afrikaans	New
Nieuw, -e, -en, -er	Flemish	New
Nishi	Japanese	West, western
-nisi	Greek	Island
Nizhn-eye, -iy, -iye, -yaya	Russian	Lower
Nízina / Nizini	Czech	Lowland / Lower
Nizmennost'	Russian	Lowland
Noord-	Flemish	North, northern
Nord	Danish, French, German	North, northern
Nordre, Nørre	Danish	Northern
Norra	Swedish	Northern
Norte	Portuguese, Spanish	North
Nos	Bulgarian, Russian	Point, spit
Nótios	Greek	Southern
Nou	Romanian	New
Nouv-eau, -elle	French	New
Nova	Italian	New
Nova, Novi	Bulgarian, Serbo-Croat	New
Nova, Novo	Portuguese	New
Nová, Nové, Novy	Czech	New
Nov-aya, -o, -oye, -yy, -yye	Russian	New
Nowa, Nowe, Nowy	Polish	New
Nudo	Spanish	Mountain
Nueva, Nuevo	Spanish	New
Nuruu	Mongolian	Mountains
Nusa	Indonesian	Island
Nuur	Mongolian	Lake
Ny-	Danish, Norweg., Swedish	New

O

-ö, -ön / -ø	Swedish / Danish	Island
-oaivi, -oaivve	Lappish	Hill, mountain
Ober-	German	Upper
Oblast'	Russian	Province
Occidental	Spanish	Western
-odde	Danish, Norwegian	Cape, point
Ogla, Oglet	Arabic	Well
Okrug	Russian	District
Ömnö-	Mongolian	South, southern
Onder	Flemish	Lower
Öndör-	Mongolian	Upper
-oog	German	Island
Oost, -er, -elijk	Flemish	East, eastern
Orasu	Romanian	Town
Oriental, -e	French, Romanian, Spanish	Eastern
Ormani	Turkish	Forest
Órmos	Greek	Bay
Óros / Óri	Greek	Mountain / Mtns.
Ost- / Øster-	German / Danish, Norweg.	East, eastern
Ostan	Persian	Province
Östra-	Swedish	East, eastern
Ostrov(a)	Russian	Island(s)
Otok / Otoci	Serbo-Croat	Island / Islands
Oud, -e, -en, -er	Flemish	Old
Oued	Arabic	Dry river-bed
Ovasi	Turkish	Plain
Over-	Danish, Flemish	Upper
Över-, Övre-	Norwegian, Swedish	Upper

APPENDICES

-øy, -a	Norwegian	Island
Ozero, Ozera	Russian	Lake, lakes
P		
-pää	Finnish	Hill
Palai-á, -ó, Palió	Greek	Old
Parbat	Urdu	Mountain
Parc	French	Park
Pas	French	Low pass, strait
Paso	Spanish	Pass, strait
Pass / Passo	Spanish / Italian	Pass
Pays	French	Region
Pegunungan	Indonesian	Mountain range
Peña(s)	Spanish	Cliff(s), rocks(s)
Pendi	Chinese	Basin
Penisola	Italian	Peninsula
Peñon	Spanish	Cliff
Pereval	Russian	Pass
Perv-o, -yy	Russian	First
Peski	Russian	Sands, desert
Petit, -e, -es	French	Little
Pic	French, Spanish	Peak, summit
Pico / Picacho	Portuguese, Spanish	Peak, summit
Pik	Russian	Peak, summit
Pingyuan	Chinese	Plain
Pizzo	Italian	Peak, summit
-plaat	Dutch	Sandbank, shoal
Plage	French	Beach
Plaine / Planicie	French / Spanish	Plain
Plaj(i)	Turkish	Beach(es)
Planalto	Portuguese	Plateau
Planina	Bulgarian, Serbo-Croat	Mountains
Platja / Playa	Catalan / Spanish	Beach
Plato	Afrikaans, Bulg., Russian	Plateau
Platte	German	Plateau, plain
Plosina	Czech	Tableland
Ploskogor'ye	Russian	Plateau
pod	Czech, Russian	Under
Pohor-i, -ie	Czech	Mountain range
Pointe	French	Cape, point
Poluostrov	Russian	Peninsula
Półwysep	Polish	Peninsula
Pongo	Spanish	Water gap
Ponta, Pontal	Portuguese	Point
Portile	Romanian	Gate
Portillo	Spanish	Gap, pass
Porto	Catalan, Italian, Portug.	Harbour, port
Pradesh	Hindi	State
Praia	Portuguese	Beach, shore
près	French	Near
Presqu'île	French	Peninsula
Pri-	Russian	Near
Proliv	Russian	Strait
Protoka	Russian	Channel
Prusmyk	Czech	Pass
Przelecz	Polish	Pass
Pubu	Chinese	Waterfall
Pueblo	Spanish	Village
Puente	Spanish	Bridge
Puerta	Spanish	Narrow pass
Puerto	Spanish	Harbour, port
Puk-	Korean	North, northern
Pulau	Indonesian, Malay	Island
Puna	Spanish	Desert plateau
Punta	Catalan, Italian, Spanish	Cape, point
Puntjak	Indonesian	Mountain
Puy	French	Peak
Q		
Qa	Arabic	Depression
Qalamat, Qalib	Arabic	Well
Qanat	Arabic, Persian	U'ground conduit
Qararat	Arabic	Depression
Qâret	Arabic	Hill
Qiao	Chinese	Bridge
Qiuling	Chinese	Hills
Qoz	Arabic	Hill
Qu	Tibetan	Stream
Quan	Chinese	Spring
Quedas	Portuguese	Rapids
Qulban	Arabic	Wells
Qum	Persian	Sand
Qundao	Chinese	Archipelago
Qûr, Qurayyat	Arabic	Hills
Qurnat	Arabic	Peak
Quwayrat / Qurûn	Arabic	Hill / Hills
R		
Ramlat	Arabic	Sands
Râs / Ra's	Arabic / Arabic, Persian	Cape, point
Raso	Portuguese	Upland
Ravnina / Razlivy	Russian	Plain
Região	Portuguese	Region
Reprêsa	Portuguese	Dam
Reshteh	Persian	Mountain range
-retto	Japanese	Island chain
-rev	Norwegian	Cliff, reef
Ri	Tibetan	Mountain
-ri	Korean	Village
Ria / Ria	Portuguese / Spanish	River-mouth
Ribeirão	Portuguese	River
Ribeiro	Portuguese	Stream
Rio / Río	Portuguese / Spanish	River
Rivier / Rivière	Afrikaans / French	River
Rocher	French	Cliff, rock
Rocque	French	Rock
Rt	Serbo-Croat	Cape, point
Rücken	German	Ridge
Rud, Rudkhaneh	Persian	River
Rudohorie	Czech	Mountains
S		
-saari	Finnish	Island
Sabkhat	Arabic	Salt-flat
Sagar, Sagara	Hindi	Lake
Sahl	Arabic	Plain
Sahra	Arabic	Desert
-saki	Japanese	Cape, point
Salada / Salar, Salina	Spanish	Salt lake / Salt pan
Salto	Portuguese, Spanish	Waterfall
-san	Japanese, Korean	Mountain
-sanchi	Japanese	Mountainous area
Saniyat	Arabic	Well
Sanmaek	Korean	Mountain range
-sanmyaku	Japanese	Mountain range
San	Italian, Portug., Spanish	Saint
Sankt / Sant	German / Catalan	Saint
Santa, Santo	Italian, Portug., Spanish	Saint
São	Portuguese	Saint
Satu	Romanian	Village
Schloss	German	Castle, mansion
Schutzgebeit	German	Reserve
Sebkra	Arabic	Salt-flat
See	German	Lake
-sehir	Turkish	Town
Selat	Indonesian	Channel, strait
Selatan	Indonesian, Malay	South, southern
-selkä	Finnish	Open water, ridge
Selo	Russian, Serbo-Croat	Village
Selva	Spanish	Forest, wood
-sen	Japanese	Mountain
Serra / Serrania	Catalan, Portug. / Span.	Mountain range
-seto	Japanese	Channel, strait
Sever-naya, -noye, -nyy, -o	Russian	North, northern
Sfîntu	Romanian	Saint
Shahr	Persian	Town
Sha'ib, -an	Arabic	Watercourse
Shamo	Chinese	Desert
Shan	Chinese	Mountain(s)
Shandi	Chinese	Mountainous area
Shang	Chinese	Upper
Shankou	Chinese	Pass
Shanmai	Chinese	Mountain range
Sharm	Arabic	Cove, inlet
Shatt	Arabic	River, river-mouth
-shima	Japanese	Island
-shoto	Japanese	Island group
Shuiku	Chinese	Reservoir
Sierra	Spanish	Mountain range
Silsilesi	Turkish	Mountain range
Sint	Afrikaans, Flemish	Saint
-sjø / sjön	Norwegian / Swedish	Lake
Skala, Skaly	Czech	Cliff, rock
-skog	Norwegian	Woods
-slette	Norwegian	Plain
Sliabh, Slieve	Gaelic	Mountain, upland
Sloboda	Russian	Suburb, large village
Sø	Danish, Norwegian	Lake
Söder-, Södra	Swedish	Southern
Solonchak	Russian	Salt lake
Sommet	French	Peak, summit
Sønder-	Danish	Southern
Søndre	Danish, Norwegian	Southern
Sopka	Russian	Hill
Sør	Norwegian	Southern
sous	French	Under
Spitze	German	Peak
Sredn-a, -i	Bulgarian	Central, middle
Sredn-e, -eye, -iy, -yaya	Russian	Central, middle
-stad	Afrikaans, Norwegian, Swedish	Town
-stadt	German	Town
Stara, Stari	Serbo-Croat	Old
Stará, Staré	Czech	Old
Star-aya, oye, -yy, -yye	Russian	Old
Stausee	German	Reservoir
Stenó	Greek	Pass, strait
Step'	Russian	Steppe
Stit	Czech	Peak
Stor-, Stora / Store	Swedish / Danish	Big
Strand	Gaelic, German	Beach
-strand	Danish, Norweg., Swedish	Beach
Strasse	German	Road
-strede	Norwegian	Passage, strait
Strelka	Russian	Spit
Stretto	Italian	Strait
Sud	French	South
Süd(er)	German	South (southern)
Suhul	Arabic	Plain
Suid	Afrikaans	South
-suido	Japanese	Channel, strait
Sul	Portuguese	South
sul, sull'	Italian	On
Sund	Swedish	Sound, strait
Sungai	Indonesian, Malay	River
-suo	Finnish	Marsh, swamp
Supérieur / Superior	French / Spanish	Upper
Sur	Spanish	South
sur	French	On
Sveti	Serbo-Croat	Saint
Szent-	Hungarian	Saint
T		
-take	Japanese	Peak
Tal	German	Valley
Tall(ät)	Arabic	Hill(s)
Tang	Persian	Pass, strait
Tanjung	Indonesian, Malay	Cape, point
Taraq	Arabic	Hills
Tasek	Malay	Lake
Tau	Russian	Mountain(s)
Tekojärvi	Finnish	Reservoir
Tell	Arabic	Hill
Teluk	Indonesian	Bay
Tengah	Indonesian	Middle
Teniet	Arabic	Pass
Tepe, Tepesi	Turkish	Hill, peak
Tepeler, Tepeleri	Turkish	Hills, peaks
Terre / Tierra	French / Spanish	Land
Thale	Thai	Lake
Tilat	Arabic	Hill
Timur	Indonesian	East, eastern
-tind, -tinderne	Norwegain	Peak, peaks
Tir'at	Arabic	Canal
-tji	Indonesian	Stream
-to	Japanese	Island
-toge	Japanese	Pass
-tong	Korean	Village
Tonle	Cambodian	Lake
-topp	Norwegian	Peak
Torrente	Spanish	Rapids
Travesia	Spanish	Desert
Tulul	Arabic	Hills
Túnel	Spanish	Tunnel
U		
über	German	Above
-udden	Swedish	Cape, point
Új-	Hungarian	New
Ujung	Indonesian	Cape, point
-umi	Japanese	Inlet
Unter-	German	Lower
'Uqlat	Arabic	Well
-ura	Japanese	Inlet
'Urayq	Arabic	Sand ridge
'Uruq	Arabic	Area of dunes
Ust'ye	Russian	Estuary
Utara	Indonesian	North, northern
Uttar	Hindi	Northern
Uul	Mongolian	Mountains
Uval	Russian	Hill
'Uyun	Arabic	Springs
V		
-vaara(t)	Finnish	Hill(s)
-vaart	Flemish	Canal
-våg	Norwegian	Bay
Val, Vall	Italian, Spanish	Valley
Vale	Portuguese, Romanian	Valley
Valle / Vallée	Italian, Spanish / French	Valley
Vallon	French	Small valley
-vann	Norwegian	Lake
-város	Hungarian	Town
-varre	Norwegian	Mountain
Väster, Västra	Swedish	Western
-vatn	Icelandic, Norwegian	Lake
-vatnet	Norwegian	Lake
-vatten, vattnet	Swedish	Lake
Vaux	French	Valleys
Vecchio	Italian	Old
Vechi	Romanian	Old
Velha, Velho	Portuguese	Old
Velik-a, -i	Serbo-Croat	Big
Velik-aya, -iy, -iye	Russian	Big
Vel'k-á, -é, -ý	Czech	Big
Verkhn-e, -eye, -iy, -yaya	Russian	Upper
-vesi	Finnish	Lake, water
Vester	Danish	Western
Vest, Vestre	Norwegian	West, western
-vidda	Norwegian	Plateau
Vieja, Viejo / Vieux	Spanish / French	Old
Vig / -vik	Danish / Norwegian	Bay
Vila	Portuguese	Small town
Ville	French	Town
Viztároló	Hungarian	Reservoir
Vodokhranilishche	Russian	Reservoir
Volcán	Spanish	Volcano
Vorota	Russian	Channel, strait
Vostochn-aya, -oye, -yy	Russian	Eastern
Vozvyshennost'	Russian	Uplands
Vpadina	Russian	Depression
Vrch(y)	Czech	Mountain(s)
Vrchovina	Czech	Mountainous area
Vysocina	Czech	Upland
Vysok-aya, -oye	Russian	Upper
W		
Wad	Flemish	Sand-flat
Wâdi, Wadi	Arabic	Watercourse
Wahat	Arabic	Oasis
Wai	Chinese	Outer
Wald	German	Forest
Wan / -wan	Chinese / Japanese	Bay
Wand	German	Cliff
Wasser	German	Lake, water
Wes-	Afrikaans	West
West, Wester	Flemish, German	West
Wielk-a, -i, -ie, -o	Polish	Big
Wysok-a, -i, -ie	Polish	Upper
X		
Xi	Chinese	Stream, west
Xia	Chinese	Gorge, lower
Xian	Chinese	County
Xiao	Chinese	Small
Xu	Chinese	Islet
Y		
-yama	Japanese	Mountain(s)
Yang	Chinese	Ocean
Yarimadasi	Turkish	Peninsula
Yeni	Turkish	New
Yli-	Finnish	Upper
Ytre-	Norwegian	Outer
Ytter-	Norwegian, Swedish	Outer
Yuan	Chinese	Spring
Yugo-	Russian	Southern
Yunhe	Chinese	Canal
Yuzhn-aya, -o, -oye, -yy	Russian	South, southern
Z		
-zaki	Japanese	Cape, point
Zalew	Polish	Bay, inlet, lagoon
Zaliv	Russian	Bay
-zan	Japanese	Mountain
Zapadn-aya, -o, -oye, -yy	Russian	West, western
Zatoka	Polish	Gulf
-zee	Flemish	Sea
Zemlya	Russian	Land
-zhen	Chinese	Town
Zhong	Chinese	Middle
Zhou	Chinese	Islet
Zui	Chinese	Point, spit
Zuid	Flemish	South
Zuid-elijk, er	Flemish	Southern

6: CLIMATE TERMS

An alphabetical list of all the terms featured on the regional climate maps.

Benguela Current *Africa maps*
A cold current flowing north along the west coast of South Africa, cooling the coastal region.

Berg Wind *Africa May–October map*
A hot dry wind which blows from the interior to the coastal regions of Namibia and South Africa.

Bora *Europe Winter map*
A cold dry wind which blows from the N and NE, affecting the Adriatic coastlines of Croatia, Italy and Slovenia.

California Current *North America Summer map*
A cold current which flows south along the west coast of California and Mexico, cooling the coastal region, and responsible for the frequent sea fogs particularly during the summer.

Canary Current *Africa maps*
An extension of the North Atlantic Drift (qv), flowing south along the NW Africa coast and moderating temperatures in the coastal region.

Chinook *North America Winter map*
A warm dry wind which blows down the eastern slopes of the Rockies, rapidly melting lying snow.

Crachin *Asia November–April map*
Light rain in the northern mountains and coastal regions of Vietnam.

El Niño *South America maps*
A change in the ocean-atmosphere system in the Pacific, increasing water temperatures in the central and eastern equatorial Pacific Ocean and bringing rain to the NW coast of South America. A periodic phenomenon, it often affects the western coast of America as far north as California. In some years the weather pattern of the whole American continent can be disrupted, and in exceptional years its effects experienced worldwide.

Etesian Wind / Meltemi *Europe Winter map*
A wind blowing from the N and NW in the eastern Mediterranean and the Aegean, often creating rough seas.

Föhn *Europe Winter map*
A wind which blows down Alpine valleys, warming as it descends, and melts snow rapidly.

Garúa *South America November–April map*
A heavy mist on the Pacific slope of the Andes in a normally very dry part of the coast.

Ghibli *Africa May–October map*
Local name for the Sirocco (qv) in Libya.

Guinea Monsoon *Africa May–October map*
Warm humid winds blowing from the SW in West Africa between April and September, associated with the rainy season.

Gulf Stream
North America Summer map (mentioned in 'Labrador current' box)
A warm current which flows NE from the Gulf of Mexico. After passing Newfoundland, it divides and follows three separate routes: 1. northwest towards Europe (the North Atlantic Drift (qv)); 2. southeast; 3. recirculating around an area north of Bermuda.

Harmattan *Africa November–April map*
A dry and dusty NE wind in West Africa blowing from the Sahara, associated with the dry season; cool at night and warm in the day. Opposite of the Guinea Monsoon (qv).

Kharif *Asia May–October map*
The rainy season in northern India and Arab countries.

Khamsin / Sharav *Africa May–October map*
A hot dry wind blowing from the S and SE in the eastern Mediterranean, warming the coastal region and helping to create dust storms and a hazy atmosphere.

Labrador Current *North America Summer map*
A cold current flowing south along the east coast of Canada, carrying icebergs and keeping the coastal region relatively cool druing the summer; fogs are caused off the Newfoundland coast where the current meets the warmer Gulf Stream flowing NE from the Gulf of Mexico.

La Niña *South America maps*
The opposite phenomenon to El Niño. Warm surface water flows towards Asia and colder water from the ocean depths moves to the surface in the eastern equatorial Pacific. Evaporation decreases and rainfall in the region is reduced. Often La Niña occurs the year after El Niño, with drought affecting the areas which experienced flooding the year before.

Leveche *Europe Winter map*
A hot, dry and dusty wind in southern Spain which blows from the Sahara.

Mistral *Europe Winter map*
A strong cold dry wind blowing from the north in southern France; known as Cers in Aude département.

Monsoon Winds *Asia maps*
Seasonal winds which change direction during the year; during the dry season in India the NE monsoon blows dry air from the land and during the wet season the SW monsoon blows wet air from the ocean. The term is also used in Africa and Australasia.

Mozambique Current / Agulhas Current *Africa May–October map*
A warm current flowing south and west along the coast of Mozambique and eastern South Africa, warming the coastal region.

North Atlantic Drift *Europe Winter map*
An extension of the Gulf Stream (qv) which helps to maintain relatively mild winters in the British Isles and along the Norwegian coast.

Peru Current / Humboldt Current *South America maps*
A cold current flowing north along the west coast of South America and cooling the coastal region as far as the Equator.

Shamal *Africa May–October map*
A hot dry wind which blows from the NW in Iraq and The Gulf.

Sirocco *Europe Summer map*
A hot dusty wind blowing towards Europe from north Africa. Known as the Ghibli (qv) in Libya and Leveche (qv) in Spain. Its origins are the same as the Khamsin (qv) or Sharav (qv). On the northern Mediterranean coast, particularly in southern Italy, the wind is moist after crossing the Mediterranean.

APPENDICES

7: US STATES

ISO abbrev.*	Name	Nickname	Date of admission to the Union	State capital
AL	Alabama	Heart of Dixie	14th Dec 1819	Montgomery
AK	Alaska	The Last Frontier	3rd Jan 1959	Juneau
AZ	Arizona	Grand Canyon State	14th Feb 1912	Phoenix
AR	Arkansas	Land of Opportunity	15th June 1836	Little Rock
CA	California	Golden State	9th Sept 1850	Sacramento
CO	Colorado	Centennial State	1st Aug 1876	Denver
CT	Connecticut	Constitution State / Nutmeg State	9th Jan 1788 †	Hartford
DE	Delaware	First State / Diamond State	7th Dec 1787 †	Dover
DC	District of Columbia *(Federal District, coextensive with the city of Washington)*			
FL	Florida	Sunshine State	3rd Mar 1845	Tallahassee
GA	Georgia	Empire State of the South / Peach State	2nd Jan 1788 †	Atlanta
HI	Hawaii	Aloha State	21st Aug 1959	Honolulu
ID	Idaho	Gem State	3rd July 1890	Boise
IL	Illinois	Prairie State	3rd Dec 1818	Springfield
IN	Indiana	Hoosier State	11th Dec 1816	Indianapolis
IA	Iowa	Hawkeye State	28th Dec 1846	Des Moines
KS	Kansas	Sunflower State	29th Jan 1861	Topeka
KY	Kentucky	Bluegrass State	1st June 1792	Frankfort
LA	Louisiana	Pelican State	30th Apr 1812	Baton Rouge
ME	Maine	Pine Tree State	15th Mar 1820	Augusta
MD	Maryland	Old Line State	28th Apr 1788 †	Annapolis
MA	Massachusetts	Bay State	6th Feb 1788 †	Boston
MI	Michigan	Great Lakes State / Wolverine State	26th Jan 1837	Lansing
MN	Minnesota	Gopher State / North Star State	11th May 1858	St Paul
MS	Mississippi	Magnolia State	10th Dec 1817	Jackson
MO	Missouri	Show Me State	10th Aug 1821	Jefferson City
MT	Montana	Treasure State	8th Nov 1889	Helena
NC	North Carolina	Old North State / Tar Heel State	21st Nov 1789 †	Raleigh
ND	North Dakota	Flickertale State	2nd Nov 1889	Bismarck
NE	Nebraska	Cornhusker State	1st Mar 1867	Lincoln
NV	Nevada	Silver State	31st Oct 1864	Carson City
NH	New Hampshire	Granite State	21st June 1788 †	Concord
NJ	New Jersey	Garden State	18th Dec 1787 †	Trenton
NM	New Mexico	Land of Enchantment	6th Jan 1912	Santa Fe
NY	New York	Empire State	26th July 1788 †	Albany
OH	Ohio	Buckeye State	1st Mar 1803	Columbus
OK	Oklahoma	Sooner State	16th Nov 1907	Oklahoma City
OR	Oregon	Beaver State	14th Feb 1859	Salem
PA	Pennsylvania	Keystone State	12th Dec 1787 †	Harrisburg
RI	Rhode Island	Ocean State / Little Rhody	29th May 1790 †	Providence
SC	South Carolina	Palmetto State	23rd May 1788 †	Columbia
SD	South Dakota	Mount Rushmore State	2nd Nov 1889	Pierre
TN	Tennessee	Volunteer State	1st June 1796	Nashville
TX	Texas	Lone Star State	29th Dec 1845	Austin
UT	Utah	Beehive State	4th Jan 1896	Salt Lake City
VT	Vermont	Green Mountain State	4th Mar 1791	Montpelier
VA	Virginia	Old Dominion	25th June 1788 †	Richmond
WA	Washington	Evergreen State	11th Nov 1889	Olympia
WV	West Virginia	Mountain State	20th June 1863	Charleston
WI	Wisconsin	Badger State	29th May 1848	Madison
WY	Wyoming	Cowboy State / Equality State	10th July 1890	Cheyenne

* International Standards Organisation. † Original thirteen states: date of ratification of the Constitution.

8: CANADIAN PROVINCES AND TERRITORIES

ISO abbrev.	Name	Language*	Date of entry to the Dominion	Province/ territory capital
AL	Alberta	English	1st Sept 1905	Edmonton
BC	British Columbia	English	20th July 1871	Victoria
MN	Manitoba	English	15th July 1870	Winnipeg
NB	New Brunswick	English †	1st July 1867	Fredericton
NF	Newfoundland and Labrador	English	31st March 1949	St John's
NT	Northwest Territories	English	1870	Yellowknife
NS	Nova Scotia	English	1st July 1867	Halifax
NU	Nunavut (territory)	Inuktitut **	1st April 1999	Iqaluit
OT	Ontario	English	1st July 1867	Toronto
PE	Prince Edward Island	English	1st July 1873	Charlottetown
QU	Québec	French	1st July 1867	Québec
SA	Saskatchewan	English	1st Sept 1905	Regina
YT	Yukon Territory	English	13th June 1898	Whitehorse

* Although Canada is officially bilingual (English & French), this column indicates the most commonly-spoken language in each region. † Approx. 35% of the population are French-speaking. ** The language of the Inuit.

9: AUSTRALIAN STATES AND TERRITORIES

ISO abbrev.	Name	Nickname	Date of granting of responsible gov't	State/territory capital
AC	Australian Capital Territory	Nation's Capital	1911 *	Canberra
CL	Coral Sea Territory *(External Territory bordering the Queensland coast and Gt. Barrier Reef)*			
NS	New South Wales	Premier State	1788 †	Sydney
NT	Northern Territory	Outback Australia	1911 **	Darwin
QL	Queensland	Sunshine State	1859	Brisbane
SA	South Australia	Festival State	1856	Adelaide
TS	Tasmania	Holiday Isle	1856	Hobart
VI	Victoria	Garden State	1855	Melbourne
WA	Western Australia	State of Excitement	1890	Perth

* Canberra became the seat of the Australian government on 9th May 1927. † Date of first settlement: New South Wales originally covered the whole island with the exception of Western Australia. ** Transferred to Commonwealth from South Australia in 1911, self-government within the Commonwealth granted 1978.

10: FRENCH DÉPARTEMENTS

Dept. no.	Name	Département capital	Region
01	Ain	Bourg-en-Bresse	Rhône-Alpes
02	Aisne	Laon	Picardie
03	Allier	Moulins	Auvergne
04	Alpes-de-Haute-Provence	Digne	Provence-Alpes-Côte d'Azur
05	Hautes-Alpes	Gap	Provence-Alpes-Côte d'Azur
06	Alpes-Maritimes	Nice	Provence-Alpes-Côte d'Azur
07	Ardèche	Privas	Rhône-Alpes
08	Ardennes	Charleville-Mézières	Champagne-Ardenne
09	Ariège	Foix	Midi-Pyrénées
10	Aube	Troyes	Champagne-Ardenne
11	Aude	Carcassonne	Languedoc-Roussillon
12	Aveyron	Rodez	Midi-Pyrénées
13	Bouches-du-Rhône	Marseille	Provence-Alpes-Côte d'Azur
14	Calvados	Caen	Basse-Normandie
15	Cantal	Aurillac	Auvergne
16	Charente	Angoulême	Poitou-Charentes
17	Charente-Maritime	La Rochelle	Poitou-Charentes
18	Cher	Bourges	Centre
19	Corrèze	Tulle	Limousin
20 [2A	Corse-du-Sud	Ajaccio	Corse
20 [2B	Haute-Corse	Bastia	Corse
21	Côte-d'Or	Dijon	Bourgogne
22	Côtes-d'Armor	St Brieuc	Bretagne
23	Creuse	Guéret	Limousin
24	Dordogne	Périgueux	Aquitaine
25	Doubs	Besançon	Franche-Comté
26	Drôme	Valence	Rhône-Alpes
27	Eure	Évreux	Haute-Normandie
28	Eure-et-Loir	Chartres	Centre
29	Finistère	Quimper	Bretagne
30	Gard	Nîmes	Languedoc-Roussillon
31	Haute-Garonne	Toulouse	Midi-Pyrénées
32	Gers	Auch	Midi-Pyrénées
33	Gironde	Bordeaux	Aquitaine
34	Hérault	Montpellier	Languedoc-Roussillon
35	Ille-et-Vilaine	Rennes	Bretagne
36	Indre	Châteauroux	Centre
37	Indre-et-Loire	Tours	Centre
38	Isère	Grenoble	Rhône-Alpes
39	Jura	Lons-le-Saunier	Franche-Comté
40	Landes	Mont-de-Marsan	Aquitaine
41	Loir-et-Cher	Blois	Centre
42	Loire	St Étienne	Rhône-Alpes
43	Haute-Loire	Le Puy	Auvergne
44	Loire-Atlantique	Nantes	Pays de la Loire
45	Loiret	Orléans	Centre
46	Lot	Cahors	Midi-Pyrénées
47	Lot-et-Garonne	Agen	Aquitaine
48	Lozère	Mende	Languedoc-Roussillon
49	Maine-et-Loire	Angers	Pays de la Loire
50	Manche	St Lô	Basse-Normandie
51	Marne	Châlons-sur-Marne	Champagne-Ardenne
52	Haute-Marne	Chaumont	Champagne-Ardenne
53	Mayenne	Laval	Pays de la Loire
54	Meurthe-et-Moselle	Nancy	Lorraine
55	Meuse	Bar-le-Duc	Lorraine
56	Morbihan	Vannes	Bretagne
57	Moselle	Metz	Lorraine
58	Nièvre	Nevers	Bourgogne
59	Nord	Lille	Nord-Pas-de-Calais
60	Oise	Beauvais	Picardie
61	Orne	Alençon	Basse-Normandie
62	Pas-de-Calais	Arras	Nord-Pas-de-Calais
63	Puy-de-Dôme	Clermont-Ferrand	Auvergne
64	Pyrénées-Atlantiques	Pau	Aquitaine
65	Hautes-Pyrénées	Tarbes	Midi-Pyrénées
66	Pyrénées-Orientales	Perpignan	Languedoc-Roussillon
67	Bas-Rhin	Strasbourg	Alsace
68	Haut-Rhin	Colmar	Alsace
69	Rhône	Lyon	Rhône-Alpes
70	Haute-Sâone	Vesoul	Franche-Comté
71	Saône-et-Loire	Mâcon	Bourgogne
72	Sarthe	Le Mans	Pays de la Loire
73	Savoie	Chambéry	Rhône-Alpes
74	Haute-Savoie	Annecy	Rhône-Alpes
75	Paris	Paris	Île-de-France
76	Seine-Maritime	Rouen	Haute-Normandie
77	Seine-et-Marne	Melun	Île-de-France
78	Yvelines *(canton)*	Versailles	Île-de-France
79	Deux-Sèvres	Niort	Poitou-Charentes
80	Somme	Amiens	Picardie
81	Tarn	Albi	Midi-Pyrénées
82	Tarn-et-Garonne	Montauban	Midi-Pyrénées
83	Var	Toulon	Provence-Alpes-Côte d'Azur
84	Vaucluse	Avignon	Provence-Alpes-Côte d'Azur
85	Vendée	La Roche-sur-Yon	Pays de la Loire
86	Vienne	Poitiers	Poitou-Charentes
87	Haute-Vienne	Limoges	Limousin
88	Vosges	Épinal	Lorraine
89	Yonne	Auxerre	Bourgogne
90	Territoire-de-Belfort	Belfort	Franche-Comté
91	Essonne *(canton)*	Évry	Île-de-France
92	Hauts-de-Seine *(canton)*	Nanterre	Île-de-France
93	Seine-St-Denis *(canton)*	Bobigny	Île-de-France
94	Val-de-Marne *(canton)*	Créteil	Île-de-France
95	Val-d'Oise *(canton)*	Cergy	Île-de-France

APPENDICES

11: WORLD FEDERATION OF GREAT TOWERS

The World Federation of Great Towers is an association of international monuments which join together to foster global awareness and develop international opportunities for promotion. The structure must fulfil four criteria: it must be in the form of a tower; have an observatory open to visitors or reception rooms/restaurants at the top accessible to the public; must be the most representative of the town or country concerned, due its history, height or other remarkable fact; and have been in operation for at least three years.

Name	Location	Total height (m)	Upper observation level (m)	Inauguration date	Name	Location	Total height (m)	Upper observation level (m)	Inauguration date
CN Tower	Toronto, Canada	553	447	26th June 1976	Sky Tower	Auckland, New Zealand	328	220	3rd Aug 1997
Ostankino Tower	Moscow, Russian Federation	540	337	5th Nov 1967	AMP Tower	Sydney, Australia	304	250	23rd Sept 1981
Oriental Pearl Tower	Shanghai, China	468	350	1st May 1995	Collserola Tower	Barcelona, Spain	288	135	27th June 1992
John Hancock Centre	Chicago, USA	444	314	3rd Mar 1970	Rialto Towers	Melbourne, Australia	253	236	19th July 1994
Empire State Building	New York, USA	443	381	1st May 1931	Donauturm	Vienna, Austria	252	170	16th April 1964
Menara Tower	Kuala Lumpur, Malaysia	421	276	23rd July 1996	Seoul Tower	Seoul, Republic of Korea	237	135	15th Oct 1980
Tian Tower	Tianjin, China	415	253	1st Oct 1991	Telstra Tower	Canberra, Australia	195	66	15th May 1980
Central Radio & TV Tower	Beijing, China	405	248	30th Sept 1992	Euromast	Rotterdam, The Netherlands	185	104	25th Mar 1960
Tashkent Tower	Tashkent, Uzbekistan	375	97	15th Jan 1985	Latinoamericana Tower	Mexico City, Mexico	181	139	30th Apr 1956
Fernsehturm (TV Tower)	Berlin, Germany	365	203	3rd Oct 1969	Harbour Centre Tower	Vancouver, Canada	177	129	13th Aug 1977
Tokyo Tower	Tokyo, Japan	333	250	23rd Dec 1958	Olympic Tower	Montreal, Canada	175	166	21st Nov 1987

12: WORLD MONUMENTS WATCH

The World Monuments Fund is a New York-based non-profit organisation dedicated to preserving and protecting endangered works of historic art and architecture around the world. The World Monuments Watch List of 100 Most Endangered Sites, a programme of the World Monuments Fund, is issued every other year. Below is the list for the year 2000.

CANADA & UNITED STATES
VDL Research House II, Los Angeles, California
Tree Studios and Medinah Temple, Chicago, Illinois
Lancaster County, Pennsylvania
Eastern State Penitentiary, Philadelphia, Pennsylvania
Seventh Regiment Armory, New York

MEXICO, CENTRAL AMERICA & CARIBBEAN
Madera cave dwellings, Mexico
San Juan de Ulúa Fort, Veracruz, Mexico
Teotihuacán archaeological site, Mexico
Santa Prisca Parish Church, Taxco, Mexico
Yaxchilán archaeological zone, Mexico
Suchitoto City, El Salvador
San Lorenzo and San Gerónimo Forts, Colón & Portobelo, Panama
National Schools of Art, Cubanacán, La Habana (Havana), Cuba
Santa Teresa de Jesús Cloisters, La Habana (Havana), Cuba
San Isidro de los Destiladeros, Trinidad, Cuba
Falmouth historic town, Jamaica
Puerto Plata Lighthouse, Dominican Republic

SOUTH AMERICA
Jodensavanne archaeological site, Redi Doti, Surinam
San Francisco Church, Coro, Venezuela
Los Pinchudos archaeological site, Río Abiseo, Peru
Machu Picchu, Peru
Cuzco historic centre, Peru
Santo Antonio do Paraguaçu, São Francisco do Paraguaçu, Brazil
Vila de Paranapiacaba, Santo André, Brazil
Orongo ceremonial site, Easter Island

EUROPE (including Turkey)
St Brendan's Cathedral, Clonfert, Ireland
St Francis Church and Monastery, Manchester, England
Abbey Farmstead, Faversham, England
Tour and Taxis transport hub, Brussels, Belgium
Gartenreich Dessau-Wörlitz, Dessau, Germany
Thomaskirche, Leipzig, Germany
Cathédrale St Pierre, Beauvais, France
Cinque Terre, Italy
Bridge of Chains, Bagni di Lucca, Italy
Santi Quattro Coronati Cloister, Roma (Rome), Italy
Pompei, Italy
Vistula Mouth Fortress, Gdansk, Poland
Kuks Forest sculptures, Czech Republic
Basil the Great Church, Krajné Cierno, Slovak Republic
Vukovar City, Croatia
Mostar historic centre, Bosnia-Herzegovina
Subotica Synagogue, Federal Republic of Yugoslavia
Butrunti (Buthrotum) archaeological site, Albania
Bánffy Castle, Bontida, Romania
Ivanovo rock chapels, Bulgaria
Kahal Shalom Synagogue, Rhodes, Greece
Zeyrek Mosque, Istanbul, Turkey
Catalhöyük, Cumra, Turkey
Nemrut Dagi archaelogical site, Turkey
Ani archaeological site, Ocarli Köyü, Turkey
Mnajdra prehistoric temples, Malta

FORMER SOVIET UNION
Zhovkva Synagogue, Zhovkva, Ukraine
Castle bridge, Kamyanets Podilskyy, Ukraine
Paanajärvi Village, Russian Federation
Viipuri Library, Vyborg, Russian Federation
Oranienbaum State Museum, Lomonosov, Russian Federation
Arkhangelskoye State Museum, Moskva (Moscow), Russian Federation
Russakov Club, Moskva (Moscow), Russian Federation
Rostov historic centre, Russian Federation
Irktusk historic centre, Russian Federation
Ikorta Church of the Archangel, Zemo Artsevi, Georgia
Tbilisi historic district, Georgia
Merv archaeological site, Mary, Turkmenistan
Abdulazizkhan complex, Bukhoro (Bukhara), Uzbekistan

AFRICA
Tipasa archaeological park, Algeria
Giraffe rock art site, Niger
Sultan Qa'itbay complex, Cairo, Egypt
Valley of the Kings, Egypt
Khasekhemwy at Hierakonpolis, Egypt
Gebel Barkal archaeological site, Kuraymah, Sudan
Mentewab-Qwesqwam Palace, Gonder, Ethiopia
Thimlich Ohinga cultural landscape, Migori, Kenya
Khami Ruins National Monument, Zimbabwe

MIDDLE EAST
Enfeh archaeological site, near Tripoli, Lebanon
Tel-Dan Canaanite Gate, Upper Galilee, Israel
White Mosque archaeological site, Ramla, Israel
Petra archaeological site, Jordan
Arbil Citadel, Iraq
Tarim historic city, Yemen

SOUTH, EAST & SE ASIA
Uch monument complex, near Bahawalpur, Pakistan
Basgo Gompa (Maitreya Temples), Ladakh, India
Jaisalmer Fort, India
Champaner archaeological site, India
St Anne Church, Talulaim, Goa, India
Metropolitan Building, Calcutta, India
Itum Monastery, Kathmandu, Nepal
Teku Thapatali monument zone, Kathmandu, Nepal
Bogd Khaan Palace Museum, Ulaanbaatar (Ulan Bator), Mongolia
Dulan County royal tomb group, China
Palpung Monastery, Babang Village, Sichuan, China
Xuanjian Tower, Yuci City, Shanxi, China
Temple of Agriculture, Beijing, China
Minh Mang Tomb, Hue, Vietnam
My Son temple complex, near Da Nang, Vietnam
Banteay Chhmar Temple of Jayavarman VII, Thmar Puok, Cambodia
George Town historic enclave, Malaysia
Kampung Cina river frontage, Kuala Terengganu, Malaysia
Rice terraces of the Cordilleras, the Philippines
Omo Hada (royal palace complex), Nias, Indonesia
Tanah Lot Temple, Bali, Indonesia

COUNTRIES A–Z

This chart provides exact data relevant to many of the thematic maps which appear elsewhere in this atlas: over 6,000 figures in all. Attention in drawn to the notes at the foot of page 182. Various sources have been used in the compilation of these statistics and these are specified on the maps themselves, as are the year/s to which the information relates.

The matter of deciding what is and what is not a country is by no means clear-cut, but no political or other subjective stance has been adopted in compiling this chart. Many countries have dependencies, overseas possessions, colonies and the like; for various reasons (mainly connected with the availability, reliability or relevance of statistical data) some have been listed separately, some have had their figures amalgamated with those for their mother country and some have been excluded. Again, the notes will give more information on this point. For more information on countries worldwide, consult the 19th edition of the Columbus *World Travel Guide*.

The data figures have been rounded up or down to either a whole number or two decimal places. The only exceptions are the Human Development Index, which is an exact figure to three decimal places; and Population Density, which has been rounded to the nearest whole number for figures above 9.5 (rounded to 10), and to the nearest single decimal place for those under 9.49 (rounded to 9.5).

The red numbers in the second row for each country give the country's ranking for that category, in descending order. The top 10 countries in each category have their ranking figure in bold. Countries whose figures are equal according to whatever rounding has been employed for that category have been ranked equally. Throughout the chart, n/a means that data was not available, not reliable or not relevant at the time of going to press. For details of other abbreviations used please see the notes on page 182.

Country	Capital / Map reference	Area '000 sq km	Population '000	Population Density People/sq km	International Arrivals '000	Visitor Receipts US$ million	Income per Person US$ million	External Debt US$ million	Energy Production Million tonnes oil equiv.	Energy Consumption Tonnes oil equiv./person	Fixed Tel. Lines Lines/100 people	Mobile Tel. Lines Lines/100 people	Internet Usage Subscribers/100 people	Human Dev't Index	Agricultural Land % of national area
Afghanistan	Kabul R4	652.10	24,965	38	4	1	400	1,499	0.29	0.03	0.10	nn	ns	n/a	58
		41	37	145	201	196	181	120	122	197	220	—	—	—	42
Albania	Tirana O4	28.70	3,324	116	20	27	700	781	1.93	0.64	3.70	0.09	0.03	0.656	41
		142	127	77	186	160	161	139	94	125	155	157	155	105	96
Algeria	Algiers N5	2,381.70	29,318	12	678	20	1,300	33,260	141.88	1.12	5.30	0.06	<0.01	0.746	16
		11	34	191	82	164	134	31	15	100	148	169	177	82	165
American Samoa	Pago Pago A7	0.20	62	310	21	10	6,000	60	0.00	3.39	22.30	4.46	n/a	n/a	15
		210	201	29	185	177	67	183	—	39	88	70	—	—	167
Andorra	Andorra la Vella M4	0.45	64	142	n/a	n/a	18,000	n/a	n/a	n/a	44.10	18.82	7.03	n/a	58
		195	199	64	—	—	25	—	—	—	43	23	28	—	42
Angola	Luanda O7	1,246.70	11,659	9.4	50	9	230	10,612	38.86	0.20	0.60	0.08	0.02	0.344	25
		23	63	197	174	179	207	57	38	160	194	161	160	156	141
Anguilla	The Valley H5	0.16	11	69	44	58	3,000	9	n/a	n/a	55.20	4.49	n/a	n/a	<1
		213	217	110	178	140	92	192	—	—	23	69	—	—	211
Antigua & Barbuda	St John's H5	0.44	66	150	230	275	7,100	466	0.00	2.42	40.80	1.86	4.55	0.895	27
		196	198	62	131	98	63	148	—	60	50	91	35	29	136
Argentina	Buenos Aires H9	2,780.40	35,677	13	4,860	5,363	8,900	93,841	83.07	1.77	20.30	7.81	0.84	0.888	62
		8	31	188	29	21	56	12	26	76	92	51	87	36	30
Armenia	Yerevan P4	29.80	3,787	127	32	14	440	552	0.82	0.69	15.00	0.16	0.11	0.674	44
		141	120	72	181	172	177	145	106	124	106	146	130	99	81
Aruba	Oranjestad H6	0.18	89	494	647	675	9,000	285	0.00	2.92	36.70	3.76	2.58	n/a	11
		211	194	16	84	69	54	154	—	50	56	74	58	—	180
Australia	Canberra V8	7,682.30	18,532	2.4	4,167	5,694	17,627	273,797	199.30	6.01	51.40	28.89	16.19	0.932	60
		6	51	216	33	19	26	**3**	12	17	30	**10**	**10**	15	35
Austria	Vienna N3	83.90	8,072	96	17,352	11,560	18,625	22,000	12.02	4.00	49.10	27.55	13.63	0.933	42
		115	86	92	**10**	**8**	24	42	63	33	34	12	15	13	92
Azerbaijan	Baku Q4	86.60	7,600	88	170	160	420	435	15.20	2.26	8.90	0.72	0.01	0.623	48
		113	89	94	139	114	179	150	57	65	124	113	165	110	71
Bahamas	Nassau H5	13.90	289	21	1,590	1,415	9,900	91	0.00	3.53	33.30	2.13	4.15	0.893	1
		158	173	171	59	53	51	176	—	37	65	88	40	32	208
Bahrain	Manama Q5	0.71	620	873	1,922	270	7,700	3,200	8.68	11.45	24.60	9.44	3.23	0.872	8
		186	161	**8**	53	100	61	98	69	**4**	81	46	51	43	186
Bangladesh	Dhaka S5	148.40	123,633	833	172	56	280	16,083	6.64	0.08	0.30	0.06	<0.01	0.371	80
		93	**9**	**10**	138	143	199	50	73	176	209	169	177	147	**6**
Barbados	Bridgetown J6	0.43	265	616	512	725	7,100	581	0.08	1.58	40.80	3.01	1.89	0.909	42
		197	175	11	94	64	64	144	136	82	51	82	65	24	92
Belarus	Minsk O3	207.60	10,267	49	355	26	1,800	1,071	2.14	2.62	24.10	0.12	0.07	0.783	45
		85	74	134	111	161	120	128	91	59	83	149	141	68	77
Belgium	Brussels N3	30.50	10,190	334	6,218	5,375	21,623	22,300	11.95	6.33	50.00	17.24	7.85	0.933	45
		139	75	24	22	20	14	41	64	14	32	27	24	12	77
Belize	Belmopan G5	23.00	230	10	161	86	2,300	288	0.00	0.43	13.80	1.49	4.35	0.807	5
		150	178	194	140	128	103	153	—	142	109	99	38	63	200
Benin	Porto Novo N6	112.60	5,796	51	152	33	330	1,594	0.17	0.05	0.70	0.11	0.04	0.378	21
		100	100	131	142	156	190	118	127	189	190	154	151	145	156
Bermuda	Hamilton H4	0.05	63	1,260	369	480	25,000	n/a	0.00	3.33	83.60	13.33	31.75	n/a	<1
		219	200	**6**	109	81	**9**	—	—	40	**2**	38	**3**	—	211
Bhutan	Thimphu S5	46.50	737	16	5	6	170	87	0.44	0.16	1.00	nn	ns	0.347	8
		131	157	180	199	183	217	177	117	166	182	—	—	155	186
Bolivia	note[1] H8	1,098.60	7,767	7.1	387	185	920	5,174	5.25	0.41	6.90	11.49	0.13	0.593	26
		28	88	205	104	110	153	79	77	144	137	41	126	116	139
Bosnia-Herzegovina	Sarajevo O4	51.10	2,346	46	100	15	700	4,076	0.71	0.85	9.00	0.69	0.02	n/a	39
		127	139	138	155	169	161	87	109	112	123	115	160	—	103
Botswana	Gaborone O8	581.70	1,533	2.6	740	185	2,900	613	0.52	0.72	5.60	new n.	0.65	0.678	47
		47	146	213	80	110	95	112	123	146	—	92	97	72
Brazil	Brasília J7	8,547.40	163,689	19	4,818	3,678	4,290	179,047	129.13	1.17	12.10	4.68	1.83	0.809	28
		5	**5**	177	30	30	76	**6**	19	99	111	68	66	62	133
British Virgin Is.	Road Town H5	0.13	19	146	250	215	12,000	61	0.00	1.05	50.60	6.32	n/a	n/a	60
		215	212	63	127	105	38	182	—	103	31	57	—	—	35
Brunei	Bandar Seri Begawan U6	5.80	308	53	800	37	20,000	0	19.35	5.29	24.70	15.60	3.25	0.889	3
		168	172	126	78	154	20	195	54	20	80	33	50	35	202
Bulgaria	Sofia O4	111.00	8,312	75	3,000	500	1,100	9,819	11.28	2.84	32.90	0.84	1.81	0.789	55
		102	84	108	41	79	140	60	66	52	66	111	67	67	50
Burkina Faso	Ouagadougou M6	274.00	10,474	38	140	39	180	1,294	0.02	0.03	0.40	0.02	0.01	0.219	35
		74	70	145	145	151	216	123	149	197	203	184	165	172	114
Burundi	Bujumbura O7	27.80	6,435	231	12	1	130	1,127	0.03	0.03	0.30	0.01	<0.01	0.241	89
		145	95	39	193	196	220	147	149	197	209	189	177	170	**2**
Cambodia	Phnom Penh T6	181.00	10,480	58	287	157	280	2,111	0.02	0.02	0.20	0.57	<0.01	0.422	24
		89	69	121	122	115	199	112	149	202	216	121	177	140	145
Cameroon	Yaoundé N6	475.40	13,936	29	135	40	590	9,515	1.19	0.14	0.50	0.03	0.03	0.481	19
		53	61	159	146	148	172	61	103	169	199	178	165	132	160
Canada	Ottawa E3	9,970.60	30,287	3.0	18,825	9,393	17,533	253,000	436.95	10.07	63.50	17.56	24.76	0.960	8
		2	33	211	**8**	**9**	27	**4**	**5**	**8**	11	26	**5**	**1**	186
Cape Verde	Praia L5	4.00	401	100	52	17	980	211	0.00	0.12	9.80	0.25	0.50	0.591	17
		171	169	87	172	167	147	162	—	172	119	138	97	117	161
Cayman Is.	George Town G5	0.26	36	138	404	510	20,000	82	n/a	3.33	62.60	8.17	n/a	n/a	8
		204	207	65	102	76	21	180	—	41	12	50	—	—	186
Central African Rep.	Bangui O6	622.40	3,418	5.5	20	6	290	928	0.02	0.37	0.30	0.02	<0.01	0.347	8
		43	126	208	187	183	197	134	149	146	209	184	177	154	186

Country	Capital / Map reference	Area '000 sq km	Population '000	Population Density People/sq km	International Arrivals '000	Visitor Receipts US$ million	Income per Person US$ million	External Debt US$ million	Energy Production Million tonnes oil equiv.	Energy Consumption Tonnes oil equiv./person	Fixed Tel. Lines Lines/100 people	Mobile Tel. Lines Lines/100 people	Internet Usage Subscribers/100 people	Human Dev't Index	Agricultural Land % of national area
Chad	Ndjaména	1,284.00	7,153	5.6	8	10	200	997	0.00	0.01	0.10	nn	<0.01	0.318	39
	O5	21	91	207	196	177	213	131		206	220		177	163	103
Chile	Santiago	736.90	14,622	20	1,767	991	4,300	27,411	8.09	1.52	18.00	2.80	2.05	0.893	23
	H9	39	58	173	56	58	75	37	70	84	100	83	63	31	151
China	Beijing	9,536.70	1,227,177	129	25,073	12,600	700	128,817	905.83	0.74	6.80	1.06	0.17	0.650	53
	T4	3	1	69	6	7	161	9	3	120	138	106	120	106	55
China: Hong Kong [2]	–	1.10	6,502	5,911	9,575	7,109	21,500	0	0.00	2.34	55.80	47.47	15.38	0.909	8
	U5	179	94	3	18	14	16	195	—	61	22	2	12	25	186
China: Macau [2]	–	0.02	448	22,400	3,590	3,300	12,000	0	0.00	1.18	40.90	15.37	6.70	n/a	<1
	U5	220	163	1	37	32	39	195	—	96	49	34	31	—	211
Colombia	Bogotá	1,141.70	40,042	35	1,600	955	2,100	28,859	68.20	0.74	17.60	4.91	0.43	0.850	44
	H6	26	28	151	57	59	110	36	29	120	101	65	101	53	81
Comoros	Moroni	1.90	518	273	27	28	360	206	0.01	0.06	0.80	nn	0.04	0.411	52
	Q7	176	162	36	183	158	187	163	154	184	187	—	151	141	58
Congo	Brazzaville	341.80	2,708	7.9	44	3	600	5,240	13.90	0.19	0.80	0.04	<0.01	0.519	29
	Q7	63	132	202	179	191	171	77	59	162	187	173	177	128	130
Congo, Dem. Rep. [3]	Kinshasa	2,344.90	46,709	20	32	2	100	12,826	3.22	0.07	< 0.1	0.02	<0.01	0.383	10
	Q7	12	24	173	182	193	222	55	85	178	221	184	177	143	181
Cook Is.	Avarua	0.23	19	83	49	45	2,200	141	0.00	1.05	26.70	0.55	n/a	n/a	22
	B7	209	213	99	177	144	106	171	—	103	73	123	—	—	153
Costa Rica	San José	51.10	3,464	68	943	829	2,672	3,454	1.20	0.83	16.20	1.78	2.89	0.889	57
	G6	127	125	111	70	62	101	94	102	115	104	95	54	34	46
Côte d'Ivoire [4]	note [4]	320.80	14,211	44	301	97	640	19,713	1.94	0.29	1.20	0.64	0.07	0.368	53
	M6	68	59	141	121	126	169	47	93	155	180	117	141	148	55
Croatia	Zagreb	56.50	4,768	84	4,112	2,740	3,700	4,634	5.28	2.10	34.80	4.07	4.20	0.759	43
	O4	126	108	96	34	34	84	81	76	69	62	73	39	76	87
Cuba	Havana	110.90	11,059	100	1,390	1,626	2,000	35,000 [5]	1.95	0.99	3.40	0.03	0.23	0.729	58
	G5	103	65	87	63	50	114	29	92	106	160	178	113	85	42
Cyprus [6]	Nicosia	9.30	747	80	2,223	1,671	9,800	2,423	0.00	3.24	58.50	16.83	4.02	0.913	17
	P4	165	156	101	48	49	52	103	—	46	18	31	43	23	161
Czech Rep.	Prague	78.90	10,304	131	16,325	3,719	4,100	20,094	41.87	4.53	36.40	9.39	3.88	0.884	54
	N3	117	71	67	12	29	77	46	37	25	58	47	44	39	53
Denmark	Copenhagen	43.10	5,284	123	2,072	3,036	26,642	40,279	20.04	4.59	65.40	27.37	18.93	0.928	65
	N3	133	103	74	51	35	8	26	53	23	8	13	9	18	24
Djibouti	Djibouti	23.20	636	27	20	4	900	241	n/a	0.96	1.30	0.04	0.08	0.324	9
	P6	149	160	167	188	189	154	158	—	107	177	173	139	162	184
Dominica	Roseau	0.75	74	99	66	42	3,100	111	< 0.01	0.54	25.20	0.63	2.70	0.879	25
	H5	183	197	89	168	147	91	174	158	128	77	118	56	41	141
Dominican Rep.	Santo Domingo	48.40	8,107	168	2,309	2,142	1,633	4,310	0.49	0.58	8.80	1.61	0.25	0.720	73
	H5	130	85	56	46	44	126	83	115	126	125	98	109	88	13
Ecuador	Quito	275.80	11,937	43	508	285	1,232	14,491	23.42	0.77	8.80	2.53	0.13	0.767	29
	G7	73	62	142	95	97	137	51	48	119	125	84	126	73	130
Egypt	Cairo	997.70	60,348	60	3,213	2,555	1,100	31,407	65.26	0.74	6.00	0.14	0.17	0.612	2
	O5	30	18	119	40	39	140	32	31	120	145	148	120	112	205
El Salvador	San Salvador	21.00	5,928	282	542	125	1,874	2,894	0.75	0.39	8.00	1.76	0.51	0.604	64
	F6	152	98	34	92	117	119	101	107	145	129	96	95	114	26
Equatorial Guinea	Malabo	28.10	420	15	n/a	2	950	282	2.62	0.13	1.30	0.12	0.12	0.465	13
	N6	144	166	181	—	193	148	155	87	171	177	149	129	135	173
Eritrea	Asmara	93.70	3,773	40	188	75	210	46	0.00	0.14	0.70	nn	<0.01	0.275	61
	P5	109	121	144	137	131	208	187	—	169	190	—	177	168	31
Estonia	Tallinn	45.20	1,458	32	825	499	2,900	405	< 0.01	1.80	34.30	16.99	10.29	0.758	34
	O3	132	147	155	75	80	96	151	158	75	63	28	19	77	117
Ethiopia	Addis Ababa	1,104.30	59,750	54	117	40	100	10,077	0.46	0.02	0.60	new n.	0.01	0.252	53
	P6	22	19	124	151	148	222	58	116	202	194	—	165	169	55
Falkland Is.	Stanley	12.20	3	0.2	n/a	n/a	12,000	n/a	0.00	3.33	76.50	nn	n/a	n/a	99
	J10	159	222	222	—	—	40	—	—	42	3	—	—	—	1
Faroe Is.	Tórshavn	1.40	44	31	n/a	n/a	15,000	699	0.02	n/a	53.80	10.74	4.55	n/a	6
	M2	178	205	156	—	—	31	141	149	—	27	44	35	—	197
Fiji Is. [7]	Suva	18.30	815	45	371	266	2,200	217	0.11	0.54	9.20	0.67	0.61	0.869	24
	Y8	155	155	139	108	101	107	160	133	128	121	116	93	44	145
Finland	Helsinki	338.10	5,140	15	1,858	1,972	19,223	82,065	7.95	5.77	55.10	57.28	28.66	0.942	8
	O2	64	105	182	54	46	22	15	71	19	24	1	4	6	186
France	Paris	549.10	58,607	107	70,000	29,700	20,802	117,600	122.04	4.15	57.00	18.78	3.41	0.946	55
	M3	49	21	83	1	3	18	11	21	31	19	24	47	2	50
French Guiana	Cayenne	85.50	157	1.8	n/a	n/a	10,000	1,200	0.00	2.10	27.70	2.40	0.96	n/a	<1
	J6	114	185	219	—	—	47	125	—	70	70	85	82	—	211
French Polynesia	Papeete	4.20	224	53	189	354	14,000	390	0.04	1.34	23.00	4.79	1.34	n/a	12
	C7	170	179	126	136	90	35	152	142	89	86	66	76	—	176
Gabon	Libreville	267.70	1,153	4.3	192	8	3,700	4,213	20.18	1.27	3.30	0.83	0.17	0.568	20
	N7	76	150	209	135	180	85	85	51	93	161	112	120	120	158
Gambia, The	Banjul	10.70	1,181	110	91	33	310	452	0.00	0.07	2.10	0.40	0.21	0.291	27
	L6	163	149	79	159	156	192	149	—	178	171	133	116	165	136
Georgia	Tbilisi	69.70	5,427	78	317	440	700	1,356	1.73	0.87	11.40	0.55	0.09	0.633	38
	P4	121	101	104	119	83	161	122	96	110	113	123	136	108	107
Germany	note [8]	357.00	82,071	230	16,511	15,859	21,983	n/a	136.80	4.32	56.60	16.95	7.31	0.925	49
	N3	62	12	49	11	6	13	—	16	27	20	29	27	19	69
Ghana	Accra	238.50	17,985	75	335	274	342	6,202	1.78	0.16	0.60	0.12	0.03	0.473	41
	M6	81	52	108	114	99	188	73	95	166	194	149	155	133	96
Gibraltar	Gibraltar	0.01	27	4,500	73	300	15,000	n/a	n/a	n/a	62.50	3.58	n/a	n/a	<1
	M4	223	210	5	165	93	32	—	—	—	13	77	—	—	211
Greece	Athens	132.00	10,522	80	11,077	4,050	10,361	34,174	8.75	2.80	52.20	19.41	3.33	0.924	68
	O4	96	67	101	16	27	46	30	68	54	29	22	48	20	20
Greenland	Nuuk	2,166.10	56	0.03	n/a	n/a	12,000	243	n/a	n/a	41.70	11.56	1.79	n/a	1
	K2	14	203	223	—	—	41	157	—	—	46	40	68	—	208
Grenada	St George's	0.34	96	282	116	61	2,900	120	0.00	0.50	26.30	1.35	2.08	0.851	36
	H6	201	193	35	152	138	97	173	—	133	74	102	62	51	112
Guadeloupe	note [9]	1.70	427	251	693	583	6,000	n/a	0.00	1.48	44.50	3.21	0.47	n/a	32
	H5	177	164	44	81	73	68	—	—	85	40	80	100	—	123
Guam	Agaña	0.54	146	270	1,137	1,378	12,000	n/a	0.00	7.47	45.30	3.61	1.37	n/a	37
	W6	190	186	38	67	54	42	—	—	12	37	74	—	—	111
Guatemala	Guatemala City	108.90	10,519	97	636	394	1,400	3,785	1.39	0.27	4.10	1.03	0.48	0.615	41
	F5	104	68	91	86	87	130	91	100	156	153	107	99	111	96
Guinea	Conakry	245.90	6,920	28	99	1	500	3,240	0.05	0.07	0.50	0.28	<0.01	0.277	24
	M6	78	93	165	156	183	173	97	139	178	199	137	177	167	145
Guinea-Bissau	Bissau	36.10	1,137	31	n/a	n/a	210	937	0.00	0.10	0.80	0.01	0.03	0.295	50
	L6	137	152	156	—	—	208	133	—	175	190	189	155	164	68
Guyana	Georgetown	215.00	848	3.9	80	60	791	1,631	< 0.01	0.06	7.10	0.17	0.24	0.670	8
	J6	84	154	210	162	139	159	117	158	184	134	141	111	100	186

Country	Capital / Map ref.	Area '000 sq km	Population '000	Population Density People/sq km	International Arrivals '000	Visitor Receipts US$ million	Income per Person US$	External Debt US$ million	Energy Production Million tonnes oil equiv.	Energy Consumption Tonnes oil equiv./person	Fixed Tel. Lines Lines/100 people	Mobile Tel. Lines Lines/100 people	Internet Usage Subscribers/100 people	Human Dev't Index	Agricultural Land % of national area
Haiti	Port-au-Prince	27.80	7,492	269	150	58	340	897	0.08	0.06	0.80	nn	<0.01	0.340	51
	H5	145	90	39	143	140	189	135	137	184	187		177	159	62
Honduras	Tegucigalpa	112.10	5,986	53	318	164	663	4,453	0.50	0.32	3.70	0.53	0.30	0.573	32
	G5	101	97	126	118	112	167	82	114	151	155	125	106	119	123
Hungary	Budapest	93.00	10,155	109	15,000	2,568	3,900	26,958	13.86	2.70	30.40	10.53	2.95	0.857	66
	O3	110	76	81	14	38	81	38	60	56	67	45	53	47	21
Iceland	Reykjavík	103.00	271	2.6	232	202	23,423	3,424	1.53	9.30	61.40	37.60	36.90	0.943	23
	L2	105	174	213	130	107	12	95	99	9	15	5	2	5	151
India	New Delhi	3,065.00	953,954	311	2,359	3,124	393	89,827	232.68	0.31	1.90	0.09	0.05	0.451	61
	S5	7	2	28	45	34	183	14	10	153	172	157	146	139	31
Indonesia	Jakarta	1,919.40	200,390	104	4,900	5,325	925	129,033	189.01	0.46	2.70	0.52	0.15	0.679	24
	U7	16	4	84	28	22	152	8	13	138	168	126	125	96	145
Iran	Tehran	1,648.00	60,929	37	900	400	2,100	21,183	244.76	1.72	10.10	0.37	0.16	0.758	38
	Q4	18	16	148	71	86	110	45	7	80	118	134	123	78	107
Iraq	Baghdad	438.30	21,847	50	340	13	800	200,000 [10]	65.64	1.35	3.20	nn	ns	0.538	21
	P4	58	45	132	113	173	158	5	30	88	162			127	156
Ireland	Dublin	70.30	3,661	52	6,073	3,159	15,261	45,406	2.29	3.31	43.50	25.70	8.19	0.930	81
	M3	120	124	130	24	33	30	23	88	44	44	14	23	17	4
Israel	Jerusalem	21.90	5,836	266	1,950	2,700	14,000	51,851	0.04	2.95	45.00	28.32	7.71	0.913	28
	P4	151	99	40	52	37	36	20	142	48	39	11	26	22	133
Italy	Rome	301.30	57,523	191	34,829	30,427	17,256	66,000	36.73	3.33	45.10	35.53	5.22	0.922	56
	N4	71	22	52	4	2	28	17	40	43	38	7	34	21	47
Jamaica	Kingston	11.40	2,554	224	1,225	1,162	1,400	4,041	0.04	1.38	16.60	2.15	1.96	0.735	44
	G5	161	135	50	65	57	130	88	142	87	103	87	64	84	81
Japan	Tokyo	377.80	126,091	334	4,106	4,154	28,543	0	107.77	4.22	47.90	37.46	13.28	0.940	14
	W4	61	8	25	35	25	6	195	22	30	36	6	17	8	170
Jordan	Amman	91.90	4,437	48	1,256	810	1,520	8,118	0.28	1.21	7.00	1.18	1.37	0.729	14
	P4	111	114	136	64	63	128	64	123	94	136	104	75	87	170
Kazakhstan	Astana [11]	2,717.30	15,801	5.8	n/a	289	1,300	2,920	60.22	3.15	10.80	0.07	0.13	0.695	80
	R3	9	55	206		96	134	100	32	47	115	165	126	93	6
Kenya	Nairobi	582.60	28,612	49	951	358	310	6,893	1.00	0.12	0.90	0.02	0.05	0.463	45
	P6	46	35	134	69	89	192	71	104	172	184	184	146	137	77
Kiribati	Bairiki	0.72	83	115	5	1	820	12	0.00	0.96	3.50	0.03	0.36	n/a	51
	Y7	185	195	78	200	196	157	190		108	159	178	102		62
Korea, DPR (North)	Pyongyang	122.80	22,893	186	130	n/a	1,000	11,900	43.51	2.02	4.80	nn	ns	0.766	16
	V4	98	41	53	149		145	56	36	73	151			75	165
Korea, Rep. (South)	Seoul	99.40	45,991	463	4,250	5,807	8,501	54,542	21.63	4.06	44.40	15.02	6.75	0.894	22
	V4	107	25	17	32	18	57	19	49	32	41	35	30	30	153
Kuwait	Kuwait City	17.80	1,809	102	79	188	18,981	7,300	125.58 [12]	9.01 [12]	23.10	11.79	3.32	0.848	8
	Q5	156	144	86	163	109	23	68	20	10	85	39	49	54	186
Kyrgyzstan	Bishkek	199.90	4,635	23	13	7	450	789	4.08	1.29	7.70	0.03	0.05	0.633	51
	R4	86	112	170	191	182	176	138	81	92	132	178	146	109	62
Laos	Vientiane	236.80	4,849	20	209	80	330	2,263	0.32	0.05	0.60	0.12	ns	0.465	6
	T5	82	107	173	132	130	190	109	121	189	194	149		136	197
Latvia	Riga	64.60	2,465	38	242	211	2,020	472	0.52	1.75	38.30	6.25	4.06	0.704	40
	O3	124	137	145	128	106	113	147	113	78	55	58	42	92	100
Lebanon	Beirut	10.50	4,146	395	631	1,285	3,000	3,996	0.22	1.18	19.40	15.67	2.41	0.796	31
	P4	164	118	21	87	55	93	90	125	96	96	32	60	66	126
Lesotho	Maseru	30.40	2,014	66	150	20	610	654	0.00	0.08	1.00	0.48	0.01	0.469	77
	O8	140	141	112	144	164	170	142		176	182	129	165	134	11
Liberia	Monrovia	99.10	2,886	29	n/a	n/a	300	2,107	0.05	0.07	0.20	new n.	<0.01	n/a	63
	M6	108	130	160			195	113	139	178	216		177		28
Libya	Tripoli	1,775.50	5,201	2.9	50	6	5,000	4,300	84.65	2.81	6.80	0.17	ns	0.806	9
	N5	17	104	212	175	183	74	84	25	53	138	141		64	184
Liechtenstein	Vaduz	0.16	31	194	59	n/a	45,000	0	note [13]	note [13]	64.30	note [13]	n/a	n/a	63
	N3	214	209	51	171		1	195			10				28
Lithuania	Vilnius	65.30	3,706	57	1,416	505	2,300	1,286	3.18	2.29	30.00	7.23	2.16	0.750	54
	O3	123	123	122	62	77	103	124	86	63	68	54	61	79	53
Luxembourg	Luxembourg	2.60	422	162	802	309	35,570	1,023	0.02	10.47	69.20	22.19	11.85	0.900	45
	N3	173	165	57	77	92	2	130	149	5	4	18	18	26	77
Macedonia, FYR	Skopje	25.70	1,997	78	157	15	900	1,659	1.65	1.69	19.90	0.60	1.00	0.749	51
	O4	148	142	104	141	169	154	116	98	81	94	120	81	80	62
Madagascar	Antananarivo	587.00	14,148	24	133	74	210	4,175	0.13	0.04	0.30	0.03	0.02	0.348	46
	Q8	45	60	169	148	134	208	86	128	192	209	178	160	153	76
Malawi	Lilongwe	118.50	10,276	87	205	8	210	2,312	0.27	0.05	0.40	0.10	0.02	0.334	38
	P7	99	73	95	133	180	208	108	124	189	203	156	160	161	107
Malaysia	Kuala Lumpur	329.80	21,667	66	5,551	2,061	3,900	39,777	77.40	0.19	19.80	7.52	3.69	0.834	15
	U6	66	46	112	27	45	82	27	27	162	95	52	45	60	167
Maldives	Malé	0.30	256	853	396	292	1,080	167	n/a	0.43	6.60	0.47	0.59	0.683	13
	R6	203	176	9	103	94	143	165		142	141	130	94	95	173
Mali	Bamako	1,248.60	10,290	8.2	85	28	190	3,020	0.05	0.03	0.30	0.04	0.01	0.236	27
	M5	22	72	201	160	158	214	99	139	197	209	173	165	171	136
Malta	Valletta	0.32	375	1,172	1,182	677	8,375	953	0.00	1.87	49.90	5.87	5.33	0.899	41
	N4	202	171	7	66	68	59	132		74	33	60	33	27	96
Marshall Is.	Majuro	0.18	60	333	6	3	1,550	125	note [14]	note [14]	6.20	0.57	0.00	n/a	60
	Y6	211	202	27	197	191	127	172			143	121	175		35
Martinique	Fort-de-France	1.10	393	357	549	415	6,000	180	0.00	1.76	44.30	14.14	0.51	n/a	33
	H5	179	170	23	91	85	69	164		77	42	37	95		120
Mauritania	Nouakchott	1,030.70	2,461	2.4	n/a	11	400	2,363	0.01	0.49	0.50	n/a	0.04	0.361	38
	M5	29	138	216		176	181	105	154	135	199		151	149	107
Mauritius	Port Louis	2.00	1,148	574	558	503	3,300	1,818	0.03	0.79	21.20	5.27	1.09	0.833	55
	R8	175	151	13	90	78	89	114	147	116	90	62	80	61	50
Mayotte	Dzaoudzi	0.37	108	292	n/a	n/a	4,000	87	n/a	n/a	11.40	n/a	n/a	n/a	n/a
	P7	199	191	31			78	177			113				n/a
Mexico	Mexico City	1,967.20	94,349	48	19,810	7,897	3,621	157,125	227.36	1.53	10.40	3.45	1.43	0.855	52
	F5	15	11	136	7	13	86	7	11	83	117	78	73	49	58
Micronesia, Fed. States	Palikir [15]	0.70	111	159	11	n/a	1,800	47	n/a	n/a	7.60	n/a	0.90	n/a	n/a
	X6	187	190	59	194		120	185			133		84		n/a
Moldova	Chisinău	33.70	4,312	128	20	4	420	834	0.12	0.79	15.00	0.21	0.08	0.610	80
	O3	138	117	70	189	189	179	136	131	116	106	140	139	113	6
Monaco	Monaco-Ville	0.00	32	16,000	278	n/a	32,000	n/a	n/a	n/a	99.00	16.88	n/a	n/a	<1
	N4	224	208	2	124		4				1	30			211
Mongolia	Ulan Bator	1,565.00	2,542	1.6	135	23	390	524	1.24	0.79	3.70	0.08	0.05	0.669	81
	T3	19	136	220	147	162	184	146	101	116	155	161	146	181	4
Montserrat	Plymouth [16]	0.10	n/a	n/a	6	5	2,000	10	0.00		39.40	0.70	0.16	n/a	n/a
	H5	217			198	188	114	191			53	114			n/a
Morocco	Rabat	458.70	24,731	54	3,243	1,705	1,200	21,767	0.57	0.37	5.40	0.42	0.16	0.557	69
	M4	55	38	124	39	48	138	43	111	146	147	132	123	125	19

Country	Capital / Map reference	Area '000 sq km	Population '000	Population Density People/sq km	International Arrivals '000	Visitor Receipts US$ million	Income per Person US$	External Debt US$ million	Energy Production Million tonnes oil equiv.	Energy Consumption Tonnes oil equiv./person	Fixed Tel. Lines Lines/100 people	Mobile Tel. Lines Lines/100 people	Internet Usage Subscribers/100 people	Human Dev't Index	Agricultural Land % of national area
Mozambique	Maputo	799.40	16,630	21	n/a	n/a	130	5,842	0.04	0.04	0.40	0.04	0.02	0.281	60
	P8	35	53	171	–	–	220	76	142	192	203	173	160	166	35
Myanmar	Yangon 17	676.60	43,893	65	196	35	700	5,184	2.28	0.06	0.50	0.02	ns	0.481	17
	T5	40	26	114	134	155	161	78	89	184	199	184		131	161
Namibia	Windhoek	824.30	1,623	2.0	560	339	1,900	43	0.00	0.47	6.10	1.17	0.31	0.644	47
	O8	34	145	218	89	91	118	188	–	137	144	105	105	107	72
Nauru	Yaren District	0.02	10	500	n/a	n/a	10,000	33	n/a	6.00	20.00	5.60	n/a	n/a	<1
	Y7	220	218	14	–	–	48	189	–	18	93	61	–	–	211
Nepal	Kathmandu	140.80	22,321	159	435	124	210	2,413	0.33	0.03	0.90	new n.	0.06	0.351	32
	S5	95	44	60	99	119	208	104	120	197	184	–	144	152	123
Netherlands	Amsterdam 18	41.50	15,607	376	9,102	6,806	20,913	0	71.46	6.22	59.30	21.29	10.25	0.941	59
	N3	134	56	22	19	16	17	195	28	15	17	20	20	7	40
Netherlands Antilles	Willemstad	0.80	210	263	751 19	638 19	9,000	1,780	0.00	18.33	36.60	6.36	0.24	n/a	10
	H5	182	180	41	79	71	55	115	–	2	57	55	111	–	181
New Caledonia	Nouméa	18.60	202	11	104	111	11,000	n/a	0.13	3.66	23.90	6.33	0.25	n/a	12
	X8	154	181	192	154	123	44	–	128	36	84	56	109	–	176
New Zealand	Wellington	270.50	3,761	14	1,485	1,883	14,344	50,021	17.19	5.24	48.00	14.91	15.95	0.939	64
	Y9	75	122	184	61	47	34	21	55	21	35	36	11	9	26
Nicaragua	Managua	130.70	4,677	36	411	90	430	5,929	0.42	0.32	3.10	0.45	0.32	0.547	56
	G6	97	110	149	101	127	178	74	118	151	163	131	104	126	47
Niger	Niamey	1,186.40	9,799	8.3	19	18	150	1,557	0.12	0.04	0.20	0.01	<0.01	0.207	10
	N5	25	78	200	190	166	218	119	131	192	216	189	177	173	181
Nigeria	Abuja 20	923.80	117,897	128	640	124	250	31,407	131.63	0.18	0.40	0.01	<0.01	0.391	80
	N6	32	10	71	85	119	205	33	17	165	203	189	177	142	6
Niue	Alofi	0.26	2	7.7	2	1	2,100	n/a	0.00	0.50	25.00	n/a	n/a	n/a	31
	A8	204	223	203	202	196	110	–	–	133	78	–	–	–	126
Northern Mariana Is.	Saipan	0.46	54	117	660	647	10,000	0	note 14	note 14	40.00	2.00	n/a	n/a	40
	W5	193	204	76	83	70	49	195			52	89	–	–	–
Norway	Oslo	323.80	4,404	14	2,829	2,212	29,161	60,515	238.78	10.09	62.10	47.39	22.71	0.943	3
	N2	67	115	184	43	43	5	18	9	7	14	3	7	3	202
Oman	Muscat	309.50	2,256	7.3	612	112	5,300	3,415	52.59	2.65	9.20	4.33	0.89	0.771	5
	Q5	70	140	204	88	122	73	96	35	57	121	72	85	71	200
Pakistan	Islamabad	796.10	128,457	161	381	104	384	29,901	27.40	0.34	1.90	0.08	0.05	0.453	34
	R5	36	7	58	105	125	186	34	46	148	172	161	146	138	117
Palau	Koror	0.51	17	33	64	–	4,000	100	0.01	0.84	n/a	n/a	n/a	n/a	n/a
	V6	191	214	152	169	–	79	175	154	114	–	–	–	–	–
Palestine NAR 21	Jerusalem 22	6.20	2,570	415	n/a	n/a	1,700	2	n/a	n/a	4.10	1.45	n/a	n/a	59
	P4	167	134	20	–	–	124	193	–	–	153	100	–	–	40
Panama	Panama City	75.50	2,719	36	439	376	2,855	6,990	0.94	1.31	13.40	0.62	1.10	0.868	29
	G6	118	131	149	98	88	98	70	105	91	110	119	79	45	130
Papua New Guinea	Port Moresby	462.80	4,501	9.7	67	75	950	2,359	4.33	0.24	1.10	0.07	<0.01	0.507	1
	W7	54	113	195	166	131	148	106	79	158	181	165	177	129	208
Paraguay	Asunción	406.80	5,085	13	350	710	1,752	2,141	13.18	0.48	4.30	1.66	0.20	0.707	61
	J8	59	106	188	112	66	122	111	62	136	152	97	117	91	31
Peru	Lima	1,285.20	24,371	19	815	878	2,300	29,176	10.57	0.52	6.80	1.79	0.82	0.729	24
	G7	20	39	177	76	61	103	35	67	131	138	94	88	86	145
Philippines	Manila	300.00	73,527	245	2,149	2,421	1,070	41,214	5.54	0.33	2.90	1.80	0.20	0.677	35
	V6	72	14	45	50	40	144	24	75	149	165	93	118	98	114
Poland	Warsaw	312.70	38,650	124	18,820	8,000	3,000	40,895	95.45	2.73	22.80	4.98	4.09	0.851	61
	O3	69	30	73	9	12	94	25	23	55	87	64	41	52	31
Portugal 23	Lisbon	91.90	9,945	108	11,200	4,665	9,703	14,067	3.42	2.28	41.40	30.88	6.03	0.892	44
	M4	111	77	82	15	24	53	52	84	64	47	9	32	33	81
Puerto Rico	San Juan	8.90	3,827	430	3,396	2,233	7,500	n/a	0.09	2.24	35.10	4.44	2.61	n/a	35
	H5	166	119	19	38	42	62	–	134	66	71	57	–	–	114
Qatar	Doha	11.40	721	63	451	n/a	12,500	0	53.18	22.01	26.00	10.87	2.77	0.840	6
	Q5	161	158	116	96	–	37	195	34	1	75	43	55	57	197
Réunion	Saint-Denis	2.50	678	271	377	250	8,000	n/a	0.13	1.18	35.60	7.38	1.33	n/a	24
	Q8	174	159	37	107	102	60	–	128	96	60	53	77	–	145
Romania	Bucharest	236.40	22,554	95	2,966	547	1,400	8,291	34.21	2.12	16.70	0.89	0.67	0.767	65
	O3	83	43	93	42	74	130	63	42	67	102	110	91	74	24
Russian Federation	Moscow	17,075.40	147,307	8.6	15,810	7,107	2,700	124,785	1,021.33	4.52	18.30	0.33	0.68	0.769	12
	S2	1	6	199	13	15	100	10	2	26	99	135	90	72	176
Rwanda	Kigali	26.30	7,895	300	2	17	190	1,034	0.04	0.04	0.30	new n.	0.01	n/a	66
	O7	147	87	30	203	167	214	129	142	192	209	–	165	–	21
St Helena	Jamestown	0.12	6	50	n/a	n/a	1,500	n/a	0.00	0.33	34.30	nn	n/a	n/a	12
	M8	216	221	132	–	–	129	–	–	149	64	–	–	–	176
St Kitts & Nevis	Basseterre	0.26	41	158	93	71	5,600	58	0.00	0.85	41.80	0.50	3.66	0.854	42
	H5	204	206	61	158	136	72	184	–	112	45	127	46	50	92
St Lucia	Castries	0.62	159	256	252	290	3,500	142	0.00	0.44	26.80	1.29	1.26	0.839	34
	H5	189	184	42	126	95	88	170	–	140	72	103	78	58	117
St Pierre et Miquelon	St Pierre	0.24	7	29	n/a	n/a	10,000	n/a	n/a	4.57	54.30	n/a	n/a	n/a	13
	J3	207	220	160	–	–	50	–	–	24	25	–	–	–	173
St Vincent & the Gren.	Kingstown	0.39	112	287	67	72	2,200	87	< 0.01	0.54	18.40	0.07	1.79	0.845	33
	H5	198	189	32	167	135	108	177	158	128	98	165	69	55	120
Samoa 24	Apia	2.80	174	62	78	39	1,100	167	0.01	0.44	5.00	0.91	0.23	0.694	43
	A7	172	183	118	164	151	140	165	154	140	149	109	113	94	87
San Marino	San Marino	0.06	26	433	532	n/a	24,000	n/a	n/a	n/a	68.30	10.88	n/a	n/a	17
	N4	218	211	18	93	–	11	–	–	–	5	42	–	–	161
São Tomé e Príncipe	São Tomé	1.00	138	138	2	2	260	261	< 0.01	2.03	2.20	nn	0.29	0.563	39
	N7	181	187	66	204	193	202	156	158	72	170	–	108	121	103
Saudi Arabia	Riyadh	2,200.00	20,266	9.2	3,700	1,462	6,900	n/a	529.58 12	5.16 12	14.30	3.11	0.10	0.778	58
	P5	13	49	198	36	52	65	–	4	22	108	81	134	70	42
Senegal	Dakar	196.20	8,790	45	332	161	480	3,663	0.06	0.16	1.50	0.25	0.09	0.342	28
	L5	87	82	139	115	113	175	93	138	166	176	138	136	158	133
Seychelles	Victoria	0.46	78	170	128	111	6,300	148	0.00	2.31	24.40	1.38	2.56	0.845	15
	Q7	193	196	55	150	123	66	168	–	62	82	101	59	56	167
Sierra Leone	Freetown	73.30	4,748	65	50	57	150	1,167	0.00	0.07	0.40	nn	0.11	0.185	39
	M6	119	109	114	176	142	218	126	–	178	203	–	130	174	103
Singapore	Singapore	0.65	3,104	4,775	5,630	4,984	24,500	0	0.00	10.23	56.20	34.60	24.16	0.896	8
	T6	188	129	4	26	23	10	195	–	6	21	8	6	28	186
Slovak Rep.	Bratislava	49.00	5,383	110	830	480	3,200	7,704	5.73	3.46	28.60	8.65	9.29	0.875	51
	O3	129	102	79	74	82	90	66	74	38	69	49	22	42	62
Slovenia	Ljubljana	20.30	1,986	98	977	931	8,400	4,031	3.61	3.72	36.40	4.70	10.07	0.887	43
	N3	153	143	90	60	58	58	89	83	35	58	67	21	37	87
Solomon Is.	Honiara	28.40	403	14	13	13	830	145	0.00	1.32	1.90	0.17	0.50	0.560	3
	X7	143	168	184	192	173	156	169	–	90	172	141	97	123	202
Somalia	Mogadishu	637.70	8,775	14	10	n/a	90	2,643	0.00	0.02	0.20	< 0.01	0.00	n/a	71
	Q6	42	83	184	195	–	224	102	–	202	216	190	175	–	17

Country	Capital / Map ref.	Area '000 sq km	Population '000	Population Density People/sq km	International Arrivals '000	Visitor Receipts US$ million	Income per Person US$ million	External Debt US$ million	Energy Production Million tonnes oil equiv.	Energy Consumption Tonnes oil equiv./person	Fixed Tel. Lines Lines/100 people	Mobile Tel. Lines Lines/100 people	Internet Usage Subscribers/100 people	Human Dev't Index	Agricultural Land % of national area
South Africa	note 25	1,224.70	40,604	33	5,981	2,389	2,506	23,590	129.60	2.65	10.70	3.69	3.12	0.717	78
	O9	24	27	152	41	102	40	18	58	116	75	52	89		10
Spain 26	Madrid	504.80	39,323	78	47,749	29,585	11,796	48,565	29.07	2.85	41.40	17.91	4.41	0.935	60
	M4	51	29	104	2	4	43	22	43	51	48	25	37	11	35
Sri Lanka	note 27	65.60	18,552	283	381	233	740	7,995	0.73	0.19	2.80	0.94	0.11	0.716	36
	S6	122	50	33	106	104	160	65	108	162	166	108	130	90	112
Sudan	Khartoum	2,505.80	27,737	11	34	6	260	16,972	4.78	0.06	0.60	0.03	<0.01	0.343	51
	O6	10	36	192	180	183	202	48	78	184	194	178	177	157	62
Surinam	Paramaribo	163.80	412	2.5	62	45	1,200	217	0.63	2.11	15.20	1.81	1.75	0.796	<1
	J6	91	167	215	170	144	138	161	110	68	105	92	70	65	211
Swaziland	Mbabane	17.40	958	55	325	40	1,370	220	0.09	0.46	3.10	0.49	0.10	0.597	73
	P8	157	153	123	116	148	133	159	134	138	164	128	134	115	13
Sweden	Stockholm	450.00	8,849	20	2,568	4,107	21,623	361,005	34.54	6.09	67.90	46.41	39.55	0.936	8
	N2	56	81	173	44	26	11	2	41	16	6	4	1	10	186
Switzerland	Bern	41.10	7,088	172	11,025	8,208	32,278	0	15.00	4.29	67.50	23.52	14.11	0.930	40
	N3	135	92	54	17	11	3	195	58	28	7	17	13	16	100
Syria	Damascus	185.20	14,895	80	890	712	4,000	21,240	37.23	1.19	8.80	new n.	0.01	0.749	75
	P4	88	57	101	72	65	80	44	39	95	125		165	81	12
Taiwan	Taipei	36.20	21,615	597	2,299	3,450	10,567	165	11.94	3.92	52.50	21.59	13.93	n/a	30
	V5	136	47	12	47	31	45	167	65	34	28	19	14		129
Tajikistan	Dushanbe	143.10	6,017	42	n/a	n/a	310	707	3.65	0.94	3.70	0.01	n/a	0.575	31
	R4	94	96	143	–	–	192	140	82	109	155	189	–	118	126
Tanzania	Dodoma	945.00	31,316	33	447	431	234	7,412	0.38	0.04	0.40	0.09	0.01	0.358	44
	P7	31	32	152	97	84	206	67	119	192	203	157	165	150	81
Thailand	Bangkok	513.10	60,602	118	7,720	6,392	2,148	90,824	27.83	1.04	8.00	3.33	0.33	0.838	42
	T5	50	17	75	21	17	109	13	45	105	129	79	103	59	92
Togo	Lomé	56.80	4,345	76	96	15	260	1,463	< 0.01	0.07	0.70	0.17	1.73	0.380	49
	N6	125	116	107	157	169	202	121	158	178	190	141	71	144	69
Tonga	Nuku'alofa	0.75	98	131	27	12	1,700	70	0.00	0.51	7.90	0.30	0.20	n/a	73
	A7	183	192	68	184	175	124	181		132	131	136	119		13
Trinidad & Tobago	Port of Spain	5.10	1,307	256	325	200	3,799	2,242	15.40	7.44	20.70	1.87	1.53	0.880	26
	H6	169	148	43	117	108	83	110	56	13	91	90	72	40	140
Tunisia	Tunis	154.50	9,215	60	4,718	1,550	1,750	9,887	7.75	0.87	7.10	0.08	0.11	0.744	52
	N4	92	80	119	31	51	123	59	72	110	135	161	130	83	58
Turkey	Ankara	779.50	63,745	82	8,960	8,300	2,848	73,592	26.10	1.08	25.40	5.25	0.71	0.782	52
	P4	37	15	100	20	10	99	16	47	101	76	63	89	69	58
Turkmenistan	Ashgabat	488.10	4,658	9.5	304	119	700	825	28.93	1.41	8.20	0.06	ns	0.660	66
	Q4	52	111	196	120	121	161	137	44	86	128	169	–	103	21
Turks & Caicos Is.	Cockburn Town	0.50	14	28	106	125	6,000	1	n/a	n/a	27.00	n/a	n/a	n/a	2
	H5	192	216	165	153	117	70	194	–	–	71	–	–		205
Tuvalu	Funafuti	0.02	10	500	1	n/a	1,000	n/a	0.00	n/a	5.00	n/a	n/a	n/a	<1
	Y7	220	219	15	205	–	145	–		–	149	–	–		211
Uganda	Kampala	241.00	20,317	84	238	142	300	3,674	0.20	0.02	0.30	0.15	0.07	0.340	43
	P6	80	48	96	129	116	195	92	126	202	209	147	141	160	87
Ukraine	Kyyiv (Kiev)	603.70	50,698	84	6,208	3,760	930	9,335	87.38	3.25	18.50	0.11	0.30	0.665	73
	P3	44	23	96	23	28	151	62	24	45	97	154	106	102	13
United Arab Emirates	Abu Dhabi	83.70	2,580	31	1,810	540	16,500	14,000	162.11	16.91	38.90	20.96	7.75	0.855	2
	Q5	116	133	156	55	75	29	53	14	3	54	21	25	48	205
United Kingdom 28	London	243.50	59,009	242	25,750	21,233	20,269	16,200	286.00	4.27	54.20	25.23	13.36	0.932	71
	M3	79	20	46	5	5	19	49	6	29	26	16	16	14	17
United States 29	Washington DC	9,372.60	267,636	29	46,395	71,116	26,992	1,292,400	1,807.90	8.80	64.40	25.60	22.42	0.943	44
	F4	4	3	160	3	1	7	1	1	11	9	15	8	4	81
US Virgin Is.	Charlotte Amalie	0.35	117	334	415	605	15,000	n/a	0.00	n/a	60.10	n/a	0.86	n/a	47
	H5	200	188	26	100	72	33	–		–	16	–	86		72
Uruguay	Montevideo	176.20	3,266	19	2,163	695	5,700	5,899	1.67	1.06	25.00	5.96	7.02	0.885	84
	J9	90	128	177	49	67	71	75	97	102	79	59	29	38	3
Uzbekistan	Tashkent	447.40	23,667	53	270	21	950	2,319	54.68	2.05	6.40	0.07	0.04	0.659	56
	R4	57	40	126	125	163	148	107	33	71	142	165	151	104	47
Vanuatu	Port Vila	12.20	177	15	52	45	1,250	47	0.00	0.11	2.80	0.12	0.06	0.559	14
	Y8	159	182	183	173	144	136	185		174	166	149	144	124	170
Venezuela	Caracas	916.50	22,777	25	837	1,229	3,538	35,344	239.94	2.95	11.70	8.67	0.22	0.860	25
	H6	33	42	168	73	56	87	28	8	49	112	48	115	46	141
Vietnam	Hanoi	331.70	76,711	231	1,520	86	290	26,764	20.72	0.20	2.60	0.17	0.01	0.560	22
	U5	65	13	48	60	128	197	39	50	160	169	141	165	122	153
Wallis & Futuna	Matu Utu	0.24	15	63	n/a	n/a	2,000	n/a	n/a	n/a	9.70	n/a	n/a	n/a	25
	A7	207	215	116	–	–	114	–		–	120	–	–		141
Western Sahara	al-Aioun	252.10	253	1.0	n/a	n/a	500	n/a	0.00	0.30	n/a	n/a	n/a	n/a	43
	M5	77	177	221	–	–	173	–		154	–	–	–		87
Yemen	San'a	555.00	16,072	29	81	69	280	6,356	20.11	0.22	1.30	0.05	0.03	0.356	33
	Q5	48	54	160	161	137	199	72	52	159	177	172	155	151	120
Yugoslavia, Fed. Rep.	Belgrade	102.20	10,614	104	283	39	2,000	13,439	13.42	1.73	21.80	2.26	0.94	n/a	n/a
	O4	106	66	84	123	151	114	54	61	79	89	86	83		–
Zambia	Lusaka	752.60	9,443	13	362	75	390	7,113	2.23	0.26	0.90	0.04	0.03	0.378	47
	O7	38	79	188	110	131	185	69	90	157	184	173	155	146	72
Zimbabwe	Harare	390.70	11,468	29	1,600	246	650	5,005	4.09	0.55	1.70	0.09	0.09	0.507	20
	O8	60	64	160	58	103	168	80	80	127	175	157	136	130	158

Country: some names have been abbreviated for reasons of space.
Capitals: some countries have more than one, or in the process of changing over from one to another. *See the notes below.*
Map Reference: this locates the country on the map on *pages 2 & 3*.
Area, Population & Population Density: *see page 59*. Most population figures are from 1997, but some are based on estimates from 1994, 1995, 1996 or 1998: these exceptions relate to very small countries and have not therefore been specified.
International Arrivals & Visitor Receipts: *see page 60*.
Income per Person & External Debt: *see page 61*.
Energy Production: *see page 64*.
Energy Consumption: *see page 65*.
Fixed Telephone Lines & Mobile Telephone Lines: *see page 66*.
Internet Subscribers: *see page 67*.
Human Development Index: *see page 68*.
Agricultural Land: *see page 72*.
nn: no network.
new n: new network: no figures yet available.
ns: no service.

1. La Paz (administrative); Sucre (Legislative)
2. Although Hong Kong and Macau are now part of China, figures have been included separately.
3. Formerly Zaire.
4. Yamoussoukro (administrative); Abidjan (commercial).
5. Estimate comprising US$11 billion to western institutions and US$24 billion to the former Soviet Union.
6. All figures relate to the Republic of Cyprus only.
7. Formerly Fiji.
8. Berlin is the capital and Bonn the administrative capital. Berlin will become the administrative capital by 2002.
9. Basse-Terre (administrative) & Pointe-à-Pitre (commercial).
10. Figures derived from UN estimates.
11. The former capital was Almaty (Alma-Ata).
12. Figures for Kuwait and Saudi Arabia include each country's share of the Neutral Zone production.
13. Figures included in those for Switzerland.
14. Figures included in those for Palau.
15. The former capital was Pohnpei.

16. Plymouth was destroyed during recent volcanic activity. Discussions are currently being held concerning the site and name of the new capital.
17. Formerly Burma.
18. Amsterdam (capital) & The Hague (seat of government).
19. Figures include all of St Maarten/St Martin.
20. The former capital was Lagos.
21. Palestine National Authority Region.
22. Jerusalem was declared the capital by the Palestine National Assembly in November 1988.
23. Figures include Madeira and the Azores.
24. Formerly Western Samoa.
25. Pretoria (administrative); Cape Town (legislative); & Bloemfontein (judicial). This arrangement is currently under review.
26. Figures include the Balearic and Canary Islands.
27. The new capital is Sri Jayewardenepura Kotte, a suburb of Colombo.
28. Figures do not include the Channel Islands or the Isle of Man.
29. Figures include Alaska and Hawaii.

COMPREHENSIVE INDEX TO THE COMPLETE ATLAS

This index lists all locations and features which appear throughout this atlas, with the exception of the following special-subject map pages:

- World climate
- World time
- Natural world
- World statistical maps
- World health
- World sport
- World driving
- World airports*
- World flight times
- Europe climate
- Europe empires
- European Union
- Europe rail and ferries
- Europe museums and art galleries*
- UK geographical and administrative divisions
- UK railways
- London airports and connections
- The Netherlands attractions
- Africa climate
- Asia climate
- North America climate
- US and Canada airports and railways
- US and Canada museums and art galleries*
- South America climate

Maps marked * include a list of locations on the page itself

GENERAL ABBREVIATIONS

(for Australian, Canadian and US state/province abbreviations, see appendices)

Arch.	Archaeological
Hist.	Historic/Historical
I.	Island, Ile and equivalents
Int.	International
Is.	Islands, Iles and equivalents
Mem.	Memorial
Mon.	Monument
Mt	Mount/Mont
Mtn	Mountain/Montagne
Mtns	Mountains/Monts
Nac.	Nacional
Nat.	National
Naz.	Nazionale
Prov.	Provincial
St	Saint/Sankt/Sint

(All 'St' entries are treated as if spelt 'Saint' and are located in the index accordingly)

Ste	Sainte
Vdkhr.	Vodokhranilishche

Countries and principal territories (listed on pages 178-182) are shown in CAPITALS

Hyphens and some accents have been removed in certain cases for consistency and ease of viewing. The correct form appears on the map pages.

The following names, which appear in bold, indicate the entry is featured on one of the special subject maps:

Beach	Beach map
Castle	German castle map
Dive	Diving site map
Hill Sta	Indian hill station map
Park L	Leisure park map
Park N	National Park map
Ski	Ski map
Spa	German spa map
Heritage C	UNESCO cultural heritage map
Heritage N	UNESCO natural heritage map

The following abbreviations appear occasionally, particularly to distinguish features with the same name:

[Adm]	Administrative region
[Apt]	Airport
[Riv]	River

A • Norway 16 G3
A Coruña • Spain 11 C1
A Coruña **Beach** • Spain 96 [92]
A la Ronde House • United Kingdom 104 F5
A Pobra do Caramiñal **Beach** • Spain 96 [92]
A'ali an Nil • Sudan 23 E2
A'nyêmaqên Shan • China 29 B4
Aachen **Heritage C** • Germany 86 [48]
Aachen • Germany 112 D1
Aaiún, El • Western Sahara 20 C3
Aalborg **Beach** • Denmark 96 [48]
Aalborg • Denmark 125 F5
Aalborg Bugt • Denmark 125 F6
Aalen • Germany 9 F8
Aalsmeer • Netherlands 109 F2
Aalst • Belgium 109 D14
Äänekoski • Finland 125 E2
Aarau • Switzerland 9 D9
Aare • Switzerland 119 G2
Aargub, El • Western Sahara 20 B4
Aarschot • Belgium 109 D15
Aazanèn • Morocco 11 H9
Aba • Nigeria 22 F3
Aba • Dem. Rep. of Congo 23 E3
Abadan • Iran 18 E3
Abadeh • Iran 18 F3
Abadia, El • Algeria 11 M8
Abaetetuba • Brazil 53 (1) B2
Abagnar Qi • China 29 F2
Abajo Peak • UT, United States 45 H3
Abakan • Russian Fed. 26 P7
Abakan [Riv] • Russian Fed. 26 P7
Abala • Niger 20 F6
Abalak • Niger 20 G5
Abancay • Peru 163 B2
Abano • Italy 121 E7
Abashiri • Japan 30 M2
Abasolo • Mexico 157 G1
Abau • Papua New Guinea 35 (1) D3
Abay • Ethiopia 21 G5
Abay • Kazakstan 26 L8
Abaya, Lake • Ethiopia 23 F2
Abbeville • France 10 G3
Abbeville • AL, United States 48 E5
Abbeville • SC, United States 48 F3
Abbeville • LA, United States 153 F3
Abbeyfeale • Ireland 108 C6
Abbot, Mt • QL, Australia 34 I4
Abbotsbury • United Kingdom 104 F6
Abbotsford • BC, Canada 42 D2
Abbotsinch [Apt] • United Kingdom 104 B3
Abd al Kuri • Yemen 18 F7
Abdul Ghadir • Somalia 23 G1
Abdulino • Russian Fed. 17 I4
Abe, Lake • Ethiopia 21 H5
Abéché • Chad 21 D5
Abengourou • Côte d'Ivoire 22 D3
Abenrå **Beach** • Denmark 96 [45]
Abenrå • Denmark 125 F13
Abensberg • Germany 9 G8
Abeokuta • Nigeria 22 E3
Aberaeron • United Kingdom 7 H9
Aberaeron **Beach** • United Kingdom 101 [197]
Aberdare Nat. Park • Kenya 131 G3
Aberdare Nat. Park **Park** • Kenya 133 [79]
Aberdare Range • Kenya 23 F4
Aberdaron **Beach** • United Kingdom 101 [206]
Aberdeen • United Kingdom 6 J4
Aberdeen • South Africa 134 C3
Aberdeen • Hong Kong, China 139 B5
Aberdeen • SD, United States 43 G4
Aberdeen • MD, United States 44 G6
Aberdeen • MS, United States 48 C4
Aberdeen • WA, United States 152 B1
Aberdeen Country Park • Hong Kong, China 139 B5
Aberdeen Lake • NU, Canada 38 L4
Aberdour **Beach** • United Kingdom 101 [13-14]
Aberdour • United Kingdom 104 B4
Abereiddy **Beach** • United Kingdom 101 [184]
Aberfeldy • United Kingdom 104 B1
Aberffraw **Beach** • United Kingdom 101 [216]
Aberfoyle • United Kingdom 104 B1
Abergavenny • United Kingdom 104 D3
Abergele **Beach** • United Kingdom 101 [211]
Abernathy • TX, United States 46 E6
Aberporth **Beach** • United Kingdom 101 [189]
Abers, Côte des • France 114 C1
Abert, Lake • OR, United States 152 B3
Aberystwyth • United Kingdom 7 H9
Aberystwyth **Beach** • United Kingdom 101 [199-200]
Abez • Russian Fed. 26 J4
Abha • Saudi Arabia 18 D6
Abidjan • Côte d'Ivoire 22 D3
Abilene • KS, United States 46 G3
Abilene • TX, United States 47 E1
Abingdon • United Kingdom 104 D4
Abingdon • VA, United States 48 F2
Abisko • Sweden 16 J2
Abisko Nat. Park **Park N** • Sweden 89 [17]
Abitibi • OT, Canada 39 O6
Abkhazia • Georgia 17 G6
Abo • Finland 125 E3
Abo, Massif d' • Chad 21 C3
Abomey • Benin 22 E3
Abomey **Heritage C** • Benin 85 [112]
Abondance **Ski** • France 100 [8]
Abong Mbang • Cameroon 22 G4
Abony • Hungary 13 I10
Aborigen, pik • Russian Fed. 27 O4
Abraham Lincoln Birthplace Nat. Hist. Site **Park N** • KY, United States 151 [231]
Abraham's Bay • Bahamas 158 B4
Abrántes • Portugal 11 C5
Abri • Sudan 21 F3
Abrolhos, Arquipelago dos • Brazil 53 (1) D5
Abruzzo • Italy 12 H6
Abruzzo, Parco Naz. d' **Park N** • Italy 89 [86]
Abruzzo, Parco Naz. d' • Italy 121 F4
Absaroka Range • MT/WY, United States 42 K4
Abu Dhabi • United Arab Emirates 18 F5
Abu Galawa (tugboat) **Dive** • Red Sea 135 B2
Abu Hamad • Sudan 21 F4
Abu Hills • India 137 C5
Abu Libdah, Khashm • Saudi Arabia 21 I3
Abu Madd, Ra's • Saudi Arabia 18 C5
Abu Matariq • Sudan 23 D1
Abu Mena **Heritage C** • Egypt 86 [273]
Abu Mena • Egypt 131 F1
Abu Road • India 137 C5
Abu Shagara, Ras • Sudan 21 G3
Abu Simbel • Egypt 131 F5
Abu Simbel to Philae **Heritage C** • Egypt 85 [97]
Abuja • Nigeria 22 F3
Abuko Nature Reserve **Park** • Gambia 133 [10]
Abut Head • New Zealand 35 C6
Abuyemeda • Ethiopia 23 F1
Aby • Ostergötland, Sweden 125 D3
Aby • Kalmar, Sweden 125 F8
Abyad, Ar Ra's al • Saudi Arabia 18 C5
Abyar ash Shuwayrif • Libya 21 B2
Abybro • Denmark 125 F5
Abydos • Egypt 131 F4
Açaba, El • Mauritania 20 C5
Acadia Nat. Park **Park N** • ME, United States 151 [342]
Acadia Nat. Park • ME, United States 44 K3
Acadia Valley • AL, Canada 42 J1
Acámbaro • Mexico 37 (1) B1
Acaponeta • Mexico 37 (1) A1
Acapulco • Mexico 157 G4
Acará • Brazil 51 H4
Acarai, Serra • Brazil 51 F3
Acaraú • Brazil 53 (1) C2
Acarigua • Venezuela 51 D2
Accra • Ghana 22 D3
Accra **Heritage C** • Ghana 85 [111]
Aceh • Indonesia 143 G1
Acerenza • Italy 90 A19
Achacachi • Bolivia 163 B4
Achaguas • Venezuela 51 D2
Achegour • Niger 20 H5
Achern • Germany 9 D8
Achill **Beach** • Ireland 96 [63]
Achill Head • Ireland 108 C1
Achill I. • Ireland 108 C1
Achim • Germany 8 E3
Achinsk • Russian Fed. 26 P6
Achonry • Ireland 108 C2
Aci Gölü • Turkey 123 F1
Aci Gölü • Turkey 123 G1
Aci Trezza • Sicily, Italy 120 D4
Acireale • Sicily, Italy 120 D4
Acklins I. • Bahamas 158 B4
Acoma Pueblo • NM, United States 153 E2
Aconcagua, Cerro • Argentina/Chile 52 C5
Açores • Atlantic Ocean 20 (1) B2
Acquasanta • Italy 121 E12
Acquasparta • Italy 121 F1
Acqui Terme • Italy 121 E6
Acraman, Lake • SA, Australia 34 G6
Acre • Brazil 51 C5
Acre • Israel 135 A1
Acre [Riv] • Bolivia/Brazil 51 D6
Acropolis • Rhodes, Greece 122 D12
Acroverde • Brazil 53 (1) D3
Actaeon Group • French Polynesia 33 N8
Action Planet **Park L** • Belgium 98 [47]
Ad Dawhah • Qatar 18 F4
Ada • OH, United States 44 D5
Ada • OK, United States 46 G5
Adair, Bahía del • Mexico 45 F6
Adair, Cape • NU, Canada 39 Q2
Adak I. • AK, United States 49 F5
Adale • Somalia 23 H3
Adam, Mt • Falkland Is. 53 D6
Adam's Bridge • India/Sri Lanka 138 D11
Adam's Peak • Sri Lanka 138 D15
Adamandás **Beach** • Greece 97 [207]
Adamaoua • Cameroon 22 G3
Adámas • Greece 122 D7
Adams • MA, United States 44 I4
Adams, Mt • WA, United States 42 E3
Adams Nat. Hist. Site **Park N** • MA, United States 151 [329]
Adamstown • Pitcairn Is. 33 O8
Adan • Yemen 18 E7
Adana • Turkey 123 G4
Adapazari • Turkey 15 L3
Adarama • Sudan 18 B6
Adare • Ireland 108 C6
Adare, Cape • Antarctica 81 A10
Adavale • QL, Australia 34 H5
Adda • Italy 121 E2
Addis Ababa • Ethiopia 23 F2
Addis Zemen • Ethiopia 23 F1
Addo Elephant Nat. Park **Park** • South Africa 133 [126]
Addo Elephant Nat. Park • South Africa 134 C8
Addu Atoll • Maldives 138 F3
Adeje **Beach** • Tenerife, Canary Is. 96 [109]
Adeje • Tenerife, Canary Is. 116 E1
Adel • GA, United States 48 F5
Adelaide • SA, Australia 34 G6
Adelaide • Bahamas 158 B3
Adelaide I. • Antarctica 81 A10
Adelaide Peninsula • NU, Canada 38 L3
Adelaide [Riv] • NT, Australia 34 F2
Adelaide River • NT, Australia 34 F2
Adelboden **Ski** • Switzerland 100 [89]
Adelboden • Switzerland 119 G6
Adéle **Beach** • Crete, Greece 97 [213]
Adéle • Crete, Greece 123 E2
Ademuz • Spain 11 J4
Aden • Yemen 18 E7
Aden, Gulf of • Africa/Asia 19 I4
Adenau • Germany 112 E1
Aderbissinat • Niger 20 G5
Adi • Indonesia 32 (1) D3
Adige • Italy 121 E7
Adigrat • Eritrea 21 G5
Adilabad • India 28 C5
Adiri • Libya 21 B2
Adirondack Mtns • NY, United States 44 H3
Adis Abeba • Ethiopia 23 F2
Adjuntas • Puerto Rico 159 H3
Adjuntas, Presa de las • Mexico 47 E5
Admiralty Inlet • NU, Canada 39 N2
Admiralty Is. • Papua New Guinea 35 (1) D1
Admiralty Is. • AK, United States 49 O4
Adok • Sudan 23 E2
Adoni • India 138 D2
Adour • France 115 J2
Adra **Beach** • Spain 96 [116]
Adra • Spain 116 B8
Adrano • Sicily, Italy 12 I11
Adrar • Algeria 20 E3
Adrar Bou Nasser • Morocco 131 D2
Adrar des Iforas • Mali 20 F5
Adrian • MI, United States 44 C5
Adrian • TX, United States 46 D5
Adriana, Villa • Italy 121 F1
Adrianople • Turkey 90 A15
Adriatic Coast • Croatia 128 A2
Adriatic Riviera • Italy 121 E12
Adriatic Sea • Europe 12 I5
Adula • Switzerland 12 D2
Adulis • Eritrea 21 G4
Adwa • Ethiopia 21 G5
Adygalakh • Russian Fed. 27 O4
Adygeya • Russian Fed. 17 G6
Adzopé • Côte d'Ivoire 22 D3
Aegean Coast • Turkey 122 A2
Aegean Sea • Greece/Turkey 122 D
Aegina • Greece 122 D7
Ærø • Denmark 125 F14
Æroskøbing • Denmark 125 F14
Afafi, Massif d' • Chad 21 C3
Afándou **Beach** • Rhodes, Greece 97 [211]
Afek • Israel 135 A5
Afétes **Beach** • Greece 97 [188]
Affollé • Mauritania 20 C5
Affroun • Algeria 11 N8
AFGHANISTAN • Asia 18 I3
Afif • Saudi Arabia 18 D5
Afikpo • Nigeria 22 F3
Afiq • Syria 135 A4
Afitos • Greece 122 D1
Aflou • Algeria 20 F2
Afmadow • Somalia 23 G3
Afonso Cláudio • Brazil 163 C2
Afore • Papua New Guinea 34 I1
Afragola • Italy 12 I8
Africa-India cruise area • Indian Ocean 81 A5/8
Africains, Bancs • Seychelles 133 K2
African Lion Safari • OT, Canada 155 B9
African Lion Safari **Park L** • OT, Canada 156 [J]
African Mzamba Village • South Africa 134 B5
Africana, Reserva • Majorca, Spain 117 H2
Afsluitdijk • Netherlands 109 D3
Afton • WY, United States 42 J5
Afton • OK, United States 46 H4
Afton Alps **Ski** • MN, United States 149 [121]
Afuá • Brazil 51 G4
Afyon • Turkey 15 L5
Afyonkarahisar • Turkey 18 B2
Agadem • Niger 20 H5
Agadez • Niger 20 G5
Agadir • Morocco 131 D5
Agadyr • Kazakstan 26 L8
Agalega • Mauritius 24 (2) C3
Agalta, Sierra de • Honduras 37 D4
Agana • Guam 33 F4
Agano • Japan 30 J6
Agartala • India 28 F4
Agate Fossil Beds Nat. Mon. **Park N** • NE, United States 150 [161]
Agathonissi • Greece 122 D8
Agats • Indonesia 32 (1) E4
Agatti I. • India 138 D9
Agattu I. • AK, United States 49 D5
Agawa • OT, Canada 44 C2
Agawam • MA, United States 44 I4
Agay • France 115 H4
Agboville • Côte d'Ivoire 22 D3
Agde • France 11 O1
Agdz • Morocco 20 D2
Agen • France 115 G4
Ageo • Japan 140 C2
Agger • Germany 111 B4
Agger Tange • Denmark 125 F5
Aggtelek Caves **Heritage N** • Hungary/Slovak Rep. 83 [58]
Aggtelek Nat. Park **Park N** • Hungary 89 [103]
Agía Fotiá • Crete, Greece 123 E7
Agía Galíni • Crete, Greece 123 E6
Agía Marína • Léros, Greece 15 H6
Agía Marína • Attica, Greece 122 D4
Agía Marína • Crete, Greece 123 E1
Agía Pelagía • Cerigo, Greece 122 D7
Agía Pelagía • Crete, Greece 123 E3
Agía Rouméli • Crete, Greece 123 E5
Agía Sofia • Crete, Greece 123 E1
Agía Triáda **Beach** • Greece 97 [191]
Agía Triáda • Crete, Greece 123 E6
Agiássos • Greece 15 H4
Agincourt • France 90 A7
Agio Oros • Greece 122 D1
Agios Apóstoli • Greece 122 D4
Agios Dimitrios **Beach** • Greece 97 [188]
Agios Dimitrios • Greece 122 D4
Agios Efstratios • Greece 122 D4
Agios Górdis • Corfu, Greece 122 B1
Agios Ioánnis **Beach** • Crete, Greece 97 [215]
Agios Ioánnis, Akra • Crete, Greece 123 E4
Agios Kirikos • Greece 122 D8
Agios Mironas • Crete, Greece 123 E7
Agios Nikitas • Levkas, Greece 122 C1
Agios Nikólaos **Beach** • Halkidikí, Greece 97 [192]
Agios Nikólaos **Beach** • Crete, Greece 97 [215]
Agios Nikólaos • Crete, Greece 123 E8
Agios Stefanos • Corfu, Greece 122 B1
Agiou Orous, Kólpos • Greece 15 E3
Aglona • Latvia 126 B4
Agnes Creek • SA, Australia 145 D4
Agnew • WA, Australia 34 D5
Agnita • Romania 14 L4
Agonda Beach • Goa, India 137 B2
Agordat • Eritrea 21 G4
Agordo • Italy 120 B4
Agostinho, I. de • Madeira 118 C2
Agra • India 137 C3
Agra Fort **Heritage C** • India 85 [136]
Agreda • Spain 11 J3
Agriá • Greece 122 D4
Agriates, Désert des • Corsica, France 115 L2
Agrigento **Heritage C** • Sicily, Italy 86 [158]
Agrigento • Sicily, Italy 120 D3
Agrínio • Greece 15 C5
Agro Romano • Italy 121 F1
Agrópoli **Beach** • Italy 97 [149]
Agrópoli • Italy 121 G4
Agua • Brazil 52 F2
Agua Caliente • Mexico 40 E6
Agua de Pena • Madeira 118 C2
Agua Prieta • Mexico 157 F2
Agua Vermelha, Represa • Brazil 52 F2
Aguada Bay • Goa, India 137 B1
Aguada de Pasajeros • Cuba 158 D2
Aguada Fort • Goa, India 137 B1
Aguada Grande • Mexico 157 H2
Aguada, I. • Mexico 157 H3
Aguadilla • Puerto Rico 159 H1
Aguadilla, Bahía de • Puerto Rico 159 H1
Aguadulce • Spain 116 B8
Aguas Buenas, Cuevas de • Puerto Rico 159 H4
Aguas de Moura • Portugal 118 D2
Aguascalientes • Mexico 157 G1
Aguascalientes [Adm] • Mexico 157 E4
Agudo • Spain 11 G6
Agueda • Spain 11 E4
Aguelhok • Mali 20 F5
Agüenit • Western Sahara 20 C4
Aguilar • CO, United States 46 C4
Aguilar de Campóo • Spain 11 G2
Aguilas • Spain 11 J7
Aguilas **Beach** • Spain 96 [117]
Agujereada, Punta • Puerto Rico 159 H1
Agulhas, Cape • South Africa 134 C6
Agulhas Negras, Pico das • Brazil 163 C3
Agung, Gunung • Bali, Indonesia 143 H2
Aguni-jima • Japan 140 A10
Agva • Turkey 15 K2
Ahaggar • Algeria 20 G4
Aharnés • Greece 15 E5
Ahaus • Germany 8 B4
Aheim • Norway 124 C1
Ahelóos • Greece 15 C4
Ahfir • Morocco 131 D2
Ahirli • Turkey 123 F2
Ahlada **Beach** • Crete, Greece 97 [214]
Ahlada • Crete, Greece 123 E3
Ahlbeck **Beach** • Germany 97 [30]
Ahlen • Germany 8 C5
Ahmadabad • India 28 B4
Ahmadnagar • India 28 B5
Ahmar • Ethiopia 23 G2
Ahmedpur-Mandvi **Beach** • India 138 E3
Ahon, Tarso • Chad 20 I4
Ahr • Germany 112 E1
Ahrensburg • Germany 8 F3
Ahrenshoop **Beach** • Germany 96 [32]
Ahrntal • Italy 120 B2
Ahrtal • Germany 112 E1
Ahtäri • Finland 125 E2
Ahungalla • Sri Lanka 138 D15
Ahus • Sweden 125 F11
Ahvaz • Iran 18 E3
Ahvenanmaa • Finland 125 E3
Ahwar • Yemen 18 E7
Aibonito • Puerto Rico 159 H4
Aichach • Germany 9 G8
Aichi • Japan 140 A4
Aiea • HI, United States 154 G5
Aierbach • Germany 9 H6
Aigle, l' • France 5 D6
Aigóual, Mt • France 10 I9
Aigrettes, I. aux • Mauritius 132 J4
Aigrettes, Pointe des • Réunion 132 H1
Aiguablava • Spain 117 D2
Aigues • France 10 K9
Aiguillon-sur-Mer, l' **Beach** • France 96 [83]
Aiguillon-sur-Mer, l' • France 114 D3
Aihole • India 138 D2
Aihui • China 27 K6
Aiken • SC, United States 48 G4
Ailao Shan • China 31 C2
Aileron • NT, Australia 145 D2
Aim • Russian Fed. 27 L5
Aimorés • Brazil 163 C2
Ain [Adm] • France 115 F1
Aïn Beïda • Algeria 20 G1
Aïn Defla • Algeria 11 M8
Aïn el Hadjel • Algeria 11 O9
Aïn Galakka • Chad 20 I5
Aïn Ouessera • Algeria 20 F1
Ain [Riv] • France 10 K7
Aïn Sefra • Algeria 20 E2
Aïn Taya • Algeria 11 O8
Ainazi • Latvia 16 M8
Aínos Nat. Park **Park N** • Greece 89 [137]
Aínsa • Spain 11 L2
Ainsdale-on-Sea **Beach** • United Kingdom 101 [240]
Aïr • Niger 20 G5
Air Force I. • NU, Canada 39 Q3
Air Hitam • Penang, Malaysia 141 F1
Air Hitam Dam • Penang, Malaysia 141 F1
Aïr Natural Reserve **Heritage N** • Niger 83 [87]
Aïr, Natural Reserve **Park** • Niger 133 [4]
Airão • Brazil 51 E4
Aire • France 5 I5
Aire • United Kingdom 7 K8
Aire, Canal d' • France 5 F4
Aire, I. de l' • Minorca, Spain 117 F4
Aire-sur-l'Adour • France 115 G3
Aire-sur-la-Lys • France 5 F4
Airolo • Switzerland 119 G7
Aisawan Tippaya Asna • Thailand 142 C1
Aisch • Germany 9 F7
Aisne • France 10 I4
Aïssa, Djebel • Algeria 20 E2
Aït Benhaddou **Heritage C** • Morocco 86 [255]
Aït Benhaddou • Morocco 131 D5
Aitape • Papua New Guinea 35 (1) C1
Aitken • MN, United States 43 J3
Aitutaki • Cook Is. 33 K7
Aiud • Romania 14 K3
Aiviekste • Latvia 126 B4
Aix-en-Provence • France 115 H3
Aix-la-Chapelle **Heritage C** • Germany 86 [48]
Aix-la-Chapelle • Germany 112 D1
Aix-les-Bains • France 115 F1
Aizawl • India 28 F4
Aizuwakamatsu • Japan 30 J6
Ajaccio • Corsica, France 115 L3
Ajaccio, Golfe d' • Corsica, France 115 L3
Ajanta Caves **Heritage C** • India 85 [141]
Ajax • OT, Canada 44 F4
Ajdabiya • Libya 21 D1
Ajigasawa • Japan 30 K4
Ajim • Tunisia 131 E6
Ajka • Hungary 13 G10
Ajlun • Jordan 135 A4
Ajmer • India 137 C6
Ajo • AZ, United States 153 E3
Ajo, Cabo de • Spain 11 H1
Aju, Kepulauan • Indonesia 32 (1) D2
Ak Dag • Turkey 15 K7
Akagera, Parc nat. de l' **Park** • Rwanda 133 [72]
Akaishi-sanmyaku • Japan 30 I7
Akaka Falls State Park • HI, United States 154 G8
Akaki • Ethiopia 23 F2
Akanthou • Cyprus 123 J2
Akaroa • New Zealand 35 D6
Akashi • Japan 140 B1
Akashi-kaikyo • Japan 140 B3
Akayzi • Turkey 15 L3
Akbaytal • Tajikistan 26 L10
Akçakoca • Turkey 15 M2
Akçakoca **Beach** • Turkey 97 [238]
Akçay • Turkey 123 F3
Akçay [Riv] • Turkey 15 J6
Akdag • Izmir, Turkey 15 H5
Akdag • Kütahya, Turkey 15 J4
Akdag • Denizli, Turkey 15 K5
Aké • Mexico 157 H1
Aker • Sweden 125 D3
Akersberga • Sweden 125 D4
Akershus • Norway 124 B2
Aketi • Dem. Rep. of Congo 23 C3
Akgöl • Turkey 123 G1
Akhdar, Al Jabal al • Oman 18 G5
Akhdar, Al Jabal al • Libya 21 D1
Akhisar • Turkey 122 D6
Akhtopol • Bulgaria 128 E4
Akhtubinsk • Russian Fed. 17 H5
Akimiski • NU, Canada 39 O6
Akinci Burun • Turkey 123 G4
Akirkeby • Denmark 125 F16
Akita • Japan 30 K5
Akita [Adm] • Japan 140 A4
Akjoujt • Mauritania 20 C5
Akka • Morocco 20 D3
Akkajaure • Sweden 16 J3
Akko • Israel 135 A1
Akköy • Turkey 15 I6
Aklavik • NT, Canada 49 N2
Akmeqit • China 26 M10
Akobo • Sudan 23 E2
Akobo [Riv] • Ethiopia/Sudan 23 E2
Akola • India 28 C4
Akören • Turkey 15 N6
Akosombo Dam • Ghana 22 E3
Akpatok I. • NU, Canada 39 R4
Akranes • Iceland 16 (1) B2
Akrehamn • Norway 124 C5
Akritas, Akra • Greece 15 C7
Akron • OH, United States 44 E5
Akrotíri • Greece 122 D8
Akrotiri • Cyprus 123 J3
Akrotiri Bay • Cyprus 123 J3
Akrotíri, Hersónisos • Crete, Greece 123 E1
Aksai Chin • China 28 C1
Aksakal • Turkey 15 J3
Aksaray • Cyprus 15 O8
Aksaray • Turkey 123 G1
Aksayqin Hu • China 28 C1
Aksehir • Turkey 15 M5
Aksehir Gölü • Turkey 15 M5
Akseki • Turkey 123 F2
Aksha • Russian Fed. 27 H6
Aksoran • Kazakstan 26 M8
Aksu • China 26 N9
Aksu • Turkey 123 F1
Aksu [Riv] • Turkey 123 F4
Aksum • Ethiopia 21 G5
Aksum **Heritage C** • Ethiopia 85 [98]
Aktau • Uzbekistan 26 J9
Aktion • Greece 122 C1
Aktogay • Kazakstan 26 M8
Akumal • Mexico 157 H2
Akune • Japan 30 F9
Akure • Nigeria 22 F3
Akureyri • Iceland 16 (1) D2
Akuseki-jima • Japan 140 A11
Akutan • AK, United States 49 H5
Al • Norway 124 C4
Al Hoceïma • Morocco 131 D2
Al Jaghbub • Libya 21 D2
Al Jahrah • Kuwait 21 I2
Al Khasab • Oman 81 E
Al Khums • Libya 21 B1
Al Kuwayt • Kuwait 18 E4
Al Mird • Palestine 135 A8
Al Qaryah ash Sharqiyah • Libya 21 B1
Al Qatrun • Libya 21 B3
Al Uwaynat • Libya 21 B2
Al-Ayn **Heritage C** • Oman 85 [124]
Al-Khutm **Heritage C** • Oman 85 [124]
Ala Dag • Turkey 15 N6
Alabama [Adm] • United States 48 D4
Alabama [Riv] • AL, United States 48 D5
Alaçam Daglari • Turkey 15 J4
Alaçati • Turkey 15 H5
Alacranes, Arrecife • Mexico 157 E6
Aladzha manastir • Bulgaria 128 E4
Alagna-Valsésia **Ski** • Italy 100 [207]
Alagnon • France 10 I8
Alagoas • Brazil 53 (1) D3
Alagoinhas • Brazil 52 I1
Alahan • Turkey 123 G3
Alaior **Beach** • Minorca, Spain 96 [127]
Alaior • Minorca, Spain 117 F4
Alajuela • Costa Rica 51 A1
Alakanuk • AK, United States 49 I3
Alaköl • Kazakstan 26 N8
Alakurtti • Russian Fed. 16 P3
Alam • QU, Canada 156 D1
Alamagan • Northern Mariana Is. 33 F4
Alameda • CA, United States 45 A3
Alamein, El • Egypt 131 F1
Alamo • Somalia 23 G3
Alamogordo • NM, United States 153 E4
Alamos • Mexico 157 F4
Alamosa • CO, United States 153 E2
Aland • Finland 125 E3
Aland [Adm] • Finland 125 E3
Alands Hav • Finland/Sweden 125 D2
Alantika, Mts • Cameroon 22 G3
Alanya • Turkey 123 F4
Alaotra, Lac • Madagascar 24 H3
Alapayevsk • Russian Fed. 26 J6
Alapli • Turkey 15 M2
Alara Han • Turkey 123 F4
Alarcon, Embalse de • Spain 11 I5
Alarcos • Spain 90 A16
Alas • Indonesia 143 G1
Alasasua • Spain 11 I2
Alasehir • Turkey 122 D6
Alaska • United States 49 K2
Alaska Highway • BC, Canada 155 C1
Alaska Peninsula • AK, United States 49 J4
Alaska Range • AK, United States 36 B3
Alaska/Canada cruise area • N. America 80 A2
Alássio • Italy 121 E9
Alatri • Italy 12 H7
Alatyr • Russian Fed. 17 H3
Alava, Cape • WA, United States 42 C2
Alavus • Finland 125 E2
Alayskiy • Kyrgyzstan 26 L10
Alazeya • Russian Fed. 27 P2
Alba • Italy 121 E5
Alba Iulia • Romania 14 K3
Albacete • Spain 11 J5
Albæk • Denmark 125 F6
Albæk Bugt • Denmark 125 F6
Albanel, Lac • QU, Canada 39 Q6
ALBANIA • Europe 15 A2
Albano, Lago • Italy 121 F3
Albano Laziale • Italy 121 F3
Albany • WA, Australia 34 C6
Albany • OT, Canada 39 O6
Albany • GA, United States 48 E5
Albany • OR, United States 152 B3
Albany • NY, United States 153 D3
Albardón • Argentina 52 C5
Albatross Bay • QL, Australia 34 H2
Albatross Point • New Zealand 145 F1
Albéces, Chaine des • France 11 N2
Albemarle • NC, United States 48 G3
Albemarle Sound • NC, United States 48 H3
Albena • Bulgaria 128 E4
Albenga • Italy 121 E9
Alberche • Spain 11 G4
Alberdi • Paraguay 52 E4
Alberga • SA, Australia 145 D4
Alberobello **Heritage C** • Italy 86 [156]
Albert • France 5 F4
Albert Edward • Papua New Guinea 35 (1) D2
Albert Falls Nature Reserve • South Africa 134 B3
Albert Kanaal • Belgium 5 H3
Albert, Lake • Uganda/Dem. Rep. of Congo 23 E3
Albert, Lake • OR, United States 42 E5
Albert Lea • MN, United States 43 J5
Albert Nile • Uganda 23 E3
Albert Town • Jamaica 159 F1
Alberta • Canada 38 H5
Albertville • France 115 F2
Albertville • AL, United States 48 D3
Albi • France 115 G4
Albina, Ponta • Angola 24 A3
Albion • MI, United States 44 C4
Albion • NY, United States 44 F4
Albion • NE, United States 46 F2
Albisola Marina **Beach** • Italy 96 [141]
Alblasserwaard • Netherlands 109 F4
Alborán, I. de • Spain 11 H9
Alborz, Reshteh-ye Kuhha-ye • Iran 18 F2
Alboux • Spain 11 I7
Albrechtsburg **Castle** • Germany 113 [197]
Albufeira **Beach** • Portugal 96 [100]
Albufeira • Portugal 118 E6
Albufeira, Lagoa de • Portugal 118 D1
Albuquerque • NM, United States 153 E2
Albuquerque, Cayos de • West Indies 160 A18
Albury • NS, Australia 144 C3
Alcácer do Sal • Portugal 11 C6
Alcalá de Chivert **Beach** • Spain 96 [120]
Alcalá de Guadaira • Spain 11 F7
Alcalá de Henares • Spain 11 H4
Alcalá de Henares **Heritage C** • Spain 86 [103]
Alcalá del Júcar • Spain 11 J5
Alcalá la Real • Spain 116 B3
Alcalar, Túmulos de • Portugal 118 E6
Alcamo • Sicily, Italy 12 G11
Alcanar **Beach** • Spain 96 [121]
Alcañiz • Spain 11 K3
Alcántara, Embalse de • Spain 11 E5
Alcantarilha • Portugal 118 E6
Alcantarilla • Spain 11 J6
Alcaraz • Spain 11 I6
Alcaraz, Sierra de • Spain 11 I6
Alcaria do Cume, Serra de • Portugal 118 E4
Alcaudete • Spain 11 G7
Alcázar de San Juan • Spain 11 H5
Alcira • Spain 11 K5
Alcobaça • Portugal 11 C5
Alcobaça **Heritage C** • Portugal 86 [116]
Alcobaça **Beach** • Portugal 96 [97]
Alcobendas • Spain 11 H4
Alcochete • Portugal 118 D2
Alcolea del Pinar • Spain 11 I3
Alcoutim • Portugal 118 E4
Alcoy • Spain 117 C1
Alcúdia **Beach** • Majorca, Spain 96 [126]
Alcúdia • Majorca, Spain 117 H2
Alcúdia, Badia d' • Majorca, Spain 117 H2
Aldabra, Groupe d' **Heritage N** • Seychelles 83 [109]
Aldabra, Groupe d' • Seychelles 133 K3
Aldama • Mexico 47 B3
Aldan • Russian Fed. 27 K5
Aldan [Riv] • Russian Fed. 27 L4
Aldanskoye Nagorye • Russian Fed. 27 K5
Aldeburgh • United Kingdom 5 E2
Aldeburgh **Beach** • United Kingdom 101 [59]
Alderney • Channel Is. 7 J12
Aldershot • United Kingdom 5 C3
Aleg • Mauritania 20 C5
Alegranza • Canary Is. 117 E6
Alegre • Brazil 163 C2
Alegrete • Brazil 52 E4
Aleksandrov • Russian Fed. 126 C4
Aleksandrovsk-Sakhalinskiy • Russian Fed. 27 N6
Aleksandrów Lodzki • Poland 13 I6
Alem • Sweden 125 F8
Além Paraíba • Brazil 163 C4
Alençon • France 10 F5
Alenhuihaha Channel • HI, United States 154 G8
Alenquer • Portugal 118 D2
Aleppo • Syria 18 C2
Aléria • Corsica, France 115 L4
Alert • NU, Canada 36 J1
Alès • France 10 J9
Ales stenar • Sweden 125 F15
Alessándra • Italy 121 E6
Alestrup • Denmark 125 F5

Alesund

Alesund • Norway 124 C1
Aleutian Is. •
　AK, United States 49 F5
Aleutian Trench •
　AK, United States 25 T5
Alexander Archipelago •
　AK, United States 38 D5
Alexander, Cape • Solomon Is. .. 35 (1) F2
Alexander City •
　AL, United States 48 E4
Alexanderbaai • South Africa 24 B5
Alexandra • New Zealand 145 G2
Alexandria • Turkey 123 G4
Alexandria • Romania 128 E1
Alexandria • Egypt 131 F1
Alexandria • South Africa 134 C8
Alexandria • MN, United States 43 I4
Alexandria • LA, United States 153 F1
Alexandria • VA, United States 153 D9
Alexandroúpoli Beach • Greece .. 97 [197]
Alexandroúpoli • Greece 122 D2
Aleysk • Russian Fed. 26 N7
Alf • Germany 5 K4
Alfambra • Spain 11 J4
Alfatar • Bulgaria 128 E1
Alfaz del Pi Beach • Spain .... 96 [118]
Alfaz del Pi • Spain 117 C2
Alfenas • Brazil 163 C1
Alfios • Greece 15 C6
Alföld • Hungary 13 J11
Alfred Faure [Base] •
　Pacific Ocean 54 (1) K5
Algajola • Corsica, France 115 L1
Algarás • Sweden 125 F7
Algarve • Portugal .... 118 E
Algeciras Beach • Spain .... 96 [113]
Algeciras • Spain 116 B6
Algeciras, Bahia de • Spain 11 F8
Alger • Algeria 20 F1
Alger Heritage C • Algeria .... 86 [257]
ALGERIA • Algeria 20 F3
Aghero • Sardinia, Italy 120 C1
Algiers • Algeria 20 F1
Algiers Heritage C • Algeria ...... 86 [257]
Algoa Bay • South Africa 134 C8
Algodonales • Spain 116 B6
Algona • IA, United States 43 I5
Algonquin Park • OT, Canada 44 F3
Algonquin Prov. Park •
　OT, Canada 155 B1
Algoz • Portugal 118 E6
Algutsrum • Sweden 125 F8
Alhambra • CA, United States 45 C4
Alholm • Denmark 125 F14
Aliabad • Iran 18 G4
Aliaga • Spain 11 K4
Aliaga • Turkey 122 D5
Alibates Flint Quarries Nat. Mon.
　Park N • TX, United States ...... 150 [132]
Alibey • Turkey 122 D5
Alicante Beach • Spain .... 96 [118]
Alicante • Spain 117 C1
Alice • TX, United States 154 J5
Alice, Punta • Italy 12 L9
Alice Springs • NT, Australia 145 D2
Alice Town • Bahamas 158 B1
Alicudi, I. • Italy 120 D2
Aligarh • India 137 C3
Alijos, Rocas • Mexico 157 E3
Alikampos • Crete, Greece 114 A5
Alikés • Zante, Greece 122 C3
Alikianós • Crete, Greece 123 E1
Alima • Congo 22 H5
Alimatha • Maldives 138 F1
Alimnía • Greece 15 G4
Alimos Beach • Greece .... 97 [185]
Alimos • Greece 122 D7
Alingsås • Sweden 125 F3
Aliquippa • PA, United States 45 E4
Alivéri • Greece 15 F5
Aliwal Shoal • South Africa 134 B5
Aljezur Beach • Portugal .... 96 [100]
Aljezur • Portugal 118 E1
Alkmaar • Netherlands 109 D7
All Saints • Antigua & Barbuda .... 161 K
Allahabad • India 137 C8
Allakh-Yun • Russian Fed. 27 M4
Allanmyo • Myanmar 28 G5
Allatoona Lake •
　GA, United States 48 E3
Alleghe Ski • Italy .... 100 [227]
Alleghe • Italy 120 B4
Allegheny • PA, United States 153 D5
Allegheny Forest •
　PA, United States 153 D5
Allegheny Mtns •
　VA/WV, United States 48 G2
Allegheny Portage Railroad Nat. Hist. Site
　Park N • PA, United States ...... 151 [294]
Allegheny Portage Railroad Nat. Hist. Site •
　PA, United States 153 D5
Allen • Philippines 31 G4
Allen, Bog of • Ireland 108 B1
Allen, Lough • Ireland 7 D7
Allendale • SC, United States 48 G4
Allende • Mexico 47 D3
Allentown • PA, United States 153 D6
Alleppey • India 138 D10
Aller • Germany 8 E4
Allerheiligen • Germany 112 D6
Allgäu • Germany 112 F6
Allgäuer Alpen • Germany 112 F6
Alliance • NE, United States 43 E5
Alliance • OH, United States 44 E5
Allier • France 10 I7
Allihies • Ireland 108 C7
Allingåbro • Denmark 125 F10
Alloa • United Kingdom 104 B3
Allonby Beach • United Kingdom .. 101 [245]
Allstedt Castle • Germany .... 113 [208]
Alma • MI, United States 44 C4
Alma • NE, United States 46 F5
Almada Beach • Portugal .... 96 [99]
Almada • Portugal 118 D1
Almadén • Spain 11 G6
Almalik • Kazakhstan 127 D2
Almansa • Spain 11 J6
Almansil • Portugal 118 E7
Almanzor, Pico de • Spain 11 F4
Almanzora • Spain 11 I7
Almas, Picos da • Brazil 52 H1
Almaty • Kazakhstan 26 M9
Almazán • Spain 11 I3
Almeirim • Brazil 51 G4
Almelo • Netherlands 109 D9
Almenar de Soria • Spain 11 I3
Almendra, Embalse de • Spain 11 E3
Almendralejo • Spain 116 A4
Almere-Haven • Netherlands 109 F2
Almere-Stad • Netherlands 109 F2
Almería Beach • Spain .... 96 [116]
Almería • Spain 116 B8
Almería, Costa de • Spain 116 B8
Almería, Golfo de • Spain 116 B8
Almhult • Sweden 125 F11
Almijara, Sierra de • Spain 116 B7
Almirante • Panama 51 A2
Almirante Brown [Base] •
　Antarctica 54 (1) II3
Almirós Beach • Greece .... 97 [188]
Almirós • Greece 123 E2
Almodôvar • Portugal 118 E3
Almodóvar del Pinar • Spain 11 J5
Almodóvar del Río • Spain 116 B2

Almonte Beach • Spain .... 96 [112]
Almonte • Spain 116 B1
Almora • India 137 C3
Almora Hill Sta • India 138 E1
Almsta • Sweden 125 D2
Almuñécar Beach • Spain .... 96 [115]
Almuñécar • Spain 116 B7
Alofi • Wallis & Futuna 35 (2) E1
Alofi • Niue 35 (2) G2
Aloha • OR, United States 42 D4
Aloka • OK, United States 46 G5
Alónissos • Greece 122 D4
Alor, Kepulauan • Indonesia 32 (1) B4
Alorna Fort • Goa, India 137 B1
Alotau • Papua New Guinea 35 (1) E3
Alpach • Austria 119 H3
Alpe d'Huez Ski • France .... 100 [58]
Alpe d'Huez • France 115 F3
Alpe di Pampeago Ski • Italy .... 100 [218]
Alpe di Suisi • Italy 120 B3
Alpe du Grand Serre Ski •
　France .... 100 [56]
Alpen • Germany 111 B1
Alpena • MI, United States 44 D3
Alpental Ski •
　WA, United States .... 149 [50]
Alpental • WA, United States 152 B1
Alpes Cottiennes •
　France/Italy 10 L8
Alpes de Haute-Provence •
　France 115 H1
Alpes Graies • France/Italy 10 M8
Alpes Maritimes • France/Italy 10 L9
Alpes Maritimes [Adm] • France .. 115 H2
Alpes Pennines •
　France/Switzerland 10 M7
Alpes Pennines •
　Italy/Switzerland 119 G6
Alphen aan den Rijn •
　Netherlands 109 F1
Alphonse • Seychelles 133 K2
Alpi Bernina • Italy 119 G8
Alpi Carniche • Italy 121 E4
Alpi Cozie • France/Italy 121 E5
Alpi di Pampeago • Italy 120 B3
Alpi Lepontine •
　Italy/Switzerland 119 G7
Alpi Marittime • France/Italy 12 B4
Alpi Orobie • Italy 119 G8
Alpi Retiche •
　Italy/Switzerland 119 G4
Alpi Sarentine • Italy 120 B3
Alpi Venoste • Italy 121 E3
Alpine • AZ, United States 45 H5
Alpine • TX, United States 47 C2
Alpine Meadows Ski •
　CA, United States .... 149 [61]
Alpine Valley Ski •
　WI, United States .... 149 [134]
Alpine Valley Ski •
　MI, United States .... 149 [147]
Alpine Valley Ski •
　OH, United States .... 149 [159]
Alpirsbach • Germany 112 D6
Alps • Europe 4 L7
Alqueria Blanca •
　Majorca, Spain 117 H4
Alquèva, Barragem de • Portugal .. 118 A3
Als • Denmark 125 F13
Alsace • France 10 M5
Alsandak • Cyprus 15 O8
Alsfeld • Germany 112 D2
Alslev • Denmark 8 G2
Alsten • Norway 124 A4
Alt St Johann • Switzerland 119 G3
Alta • Norway 16 L1
Alta Heritage C • Norway .... 85 [82]
Alta Ski • UT, United States .... 149 [94]
Alta Badia Ski • Italy .... 100 [231]
Alta Gracia • Argentina 52 D5
Altaelva • Norway 16 L2
Altafulla Beach • Spain .... 96 [121]
Altagracia • Margarita .... 160 V
Altamira • Brazil 51 G4
Altamira Cave Heritage C •
　Spain .... 86 [96]
Altamont • OR, United States 152 B3
Altamonte Springs •
　FL, United States 49 C3
Altamura • Italy 12 K8
Altar • Mexico 45 G6
Altar, Desierto de • Mexico 45 E5
Altas, Rías • Spain 11 C1
Altavilla Irpina • Italy 121 G2
Altay • Russian Fed. 26 O7
Altay • Mongolia 29 B1
Altay, Golden Mountains of Heritage N •
　Russian Fed. .... 83 [74]
Altayn Nuruu • Mongolia 29 A1
Altdorf bei Nürnberg • Germany 9 G7
Alte • Portugal 118 E7
Alte Bischöflicher Residenz, Passau
　Castle • Germany .... 113 [124]
Alte Hofhaltung, Bamberg Castle •
　Germany .... 113 [162]
Altea Beach • Spain .... 96 [118]
Altea • Spain 117 C2
Altena • Germany 111 C2
Altenahr • Germany 111 E1
Altenburg • Germany 9 H6
Altenkirchen • Germany 112 E2
Altenmarkt • Austria 119 H4
Altenmarkt-Zauchensee Ski •
　Austria .... 100 [178]
Alter do Chão • Brazil 80 A3
Alternative Reefs Dive •
　Red Sea 135 B1
Altet [Apt] • Spain 117 C1
Altevatnet • Norway 16 J2
Altinkum • Turkey 123 F3
Altinoluk • Turkey 15 H4
Altissima, I • Austria/Italy 120 B1
Altlandsberg • Germany 111 C2
Altmark • Germany 8 E4
Altmühl • Germany 9 G8
Alto Alentejo • Portugal 11 D6
Alto Cedro • Cuba 158 D8
Alto Douro • Portugal 11 D3
Alto Paraguai • Brazil 52 E1
Alto Parnaíba • Brazil 53 (1) B3
Alto, Pico • Brazil 53 (1) D2
Alto Velo, I. • Dominican Rep. 159 G6
Alto Vista Chapel • Aruba .... 160 Y
Altomünster • Germany 112 F3
Alton • MO, United States 46 J4
Alton • IL, United States 46 J3
Alton Towers Park L •
　United Kingdom .... 98 [25]
Altoona • PA, United States 153 D5
Altötting • Germany 112 F4
Altun-Shan • China 26 O10
Altura • Portugal 118 E8
Alturas • CA, United States 152 C1
Altus • OK, United States 46 F5
Altus Lake • OK, United States 48 B5
Altwood • TN, United States 48 C3
Aluksne • Latvia 126 B4
Alur Setar • Malaysia 32 C1
Alva • OK, United States 46 F4
Alvdalen • Sweden 125 F2
Alvesta • Sweden 125 F7
Alvik • Norway 124 C3
Alvin • TX, United States 154 I3
Alvkarleby • Sweden 16 I6
Alvor • Portugal 118 E6

Alvsborg • Sweden 125 F7
Alwar • India 137 C2
Alyangula • NT, Australia 34 G2
Alywarra Aboriginal Land •
　NT, Australia 145 D2
Alysbyn • Sweden 16 K4
Alytus • Lithuania 126 B5
Alz • Germany 112 F4
Alzada • MT, United States 43 D4
Alzamay • Russian Fed. 26 O6
Alzey • Germany 112 E4
Am Dam • Chad 21 C1
Am Gérédo • Chad 23 C1
Am Timan • Chad 21 D5
Amacon • France 10 J6
Amada • Egypt 131 F5
Amadeus, Lake • NT, Australia 145 D3
Amadjuak Lake • NU, Canada 39 G3
Amadora • Portugal 118 D1
Amadror • Algeria 20 G3
Amagasaki • Japan 140 B2
Amager • Denmark 125 F11
Amagi-san • Japan 140 C3
Amahai • Indonesia 32 (1) C4
Amakusa • Japan 30 E8
Amal • Sweden 125 F3
Amalfi • Italy 121 G4
Amaliáda Beach • Greece .... 97 [180]
Amami • Japan 29 H5
Amami-shoto • Japan 31 H1
Amana • IA, United States 46 J2
Amana, Punta • Greece 35 (1) C1
Amanab • Papua New Guinea 35 (1) C1
Amanda Park • WA, United States .. 152 B1
Amanningen • Sweden 125 D1
Amanzimtoti • South Africa 134 B5
Amapá • Brazil 51 G3
Amapá [Adm] • Brazil 51 G3
Amara • Ethiopia 21 G5
Amara, Al • Iraq 18 E3
Amaranth • MN, Canada 43 G1
Amaravati • India 138 D3
Amari • Crete, Greece 123 E6
Amarillo • TX, United States 46 E5
Amasra • Turkey 15 N2
Amata • SA, Australia 145 D3
Amathus • Cyprus 123 J3
Amazon • S. America 50 E5
Amazon Basin • S. America 163 A1
Amazon, Mouths of the • Brazil 163 A1
Amazonas • Brazil 51 F4
Amazonas [Adm] • Brazil 51 D4
Ambala • India 28 C2
Ambam • Cameroon 22 G4
Ambanja • Madagascar 24 H2
Ambarchik • Russian Fed. 27 R3
Ambato • Ecuador 51 B4
Amber • India 137 C2
Amber Coast • Dominican Rep. 159 G3
Amberg • Germany 9 G7
Amberieu-en-Bugey • France 115 F1
Amblehole • Madagascar 24 J2
Amble Links Beach •
　United Kingdom .... 101 [20]
Ambleside • United Kingdom 104 C4
Amblève • Belgium 109 D15
Ambo • Peru 51 B6
Amboise • France 114 D2
Amboise [Château] • France 114 D2
Ambon • Indonesia 32 (1) C3
Ambon [I.] • Indonesia 32 (1) C3
Ambongo • Madagascar 24 H3
Amboseli Nat. Park • Kenya 131 G3
Amboseli Nat. Park Park • Kenya .. 133 [83]
Ambositra • Madagascar 24 H4
Ambre, C. d' • Madagascar 24 H2
Ambre, I. d' • Mauritius 132 J2
Ambre, Mt d' • Madagascar 24 H2
Ambri • Angola 23 A5
Ambrym • Vanuatu 35 (2) B2
Ambunten • Indonesia 143 J4
Ambunti • Papua New Guinea 35 (1) C1
Amchitka Cove • Belize 49 E5
Amderma • Russian Fed. 26 J4
Ambo • China 28 F2
Ameixal • Portugal 118 E3
Ameland Beach • Netherlands .... 96 [66]
Ameland • Netherlands 109 B8
Amelia • AL, United States 48 C3
Amelia I. • FL, United States 49 C2
Amendolara • Italy 12 K9
America's Stonehenge •
　NH, United States 153 D4
American Adventure Park L •
　United Kingdom .... 98 [27]
American Falls •
　ID, United States 42 I5
American Fork •
　UT, United States 45 J1
American Highland • Antarctica .. 54 (1) M2
AMERICAN SAMOA • Pacific Ocean 35 (2) F1
Americus • GA, United States 48 F4
Amersfoort • Netherlands 109 F2
Amery Ice Shelf • Antarctica 54 (1) M3
Ames • IA, United States 43 J5
Ametlla de Mar, l' Beach •
　Spain .... 96 [121]
Amfilohía • Greece 15 C5
Amga • Russian Fed. 27 L4
Amga [Riv] • Russian Fed. 27 L4
Amgaena • Russian Fed. 27 L4
Amguid • Algeria 20 G3
Amgun [Adm] • Algeria 20 G3
Amgun • Russian Fed. 27 M6
Amherst • NY, United States 44 F4
Amherst • MA, United States 44 I4
Amherst • MA, United States 153 D3
Amherst • NS, Canada 156 D7
Amherst, Fort • PE, Canada 156 D7
Amherstburg • OT, Canada 44 D5
Amiens • France 10 H4
Amiens Heritage C • France ...... 86 [62]
Amik Gölü • Turkey 123 G4
Amini I. • India 138 C9
Amistad Nat. Recreation Area Park N •
　TX, United States .... 150 [137]
Amistad Reservoir •
　Mexico/United States 47 D3
Amitié Estate • Seychelles 133 K4
Amlapura • Bali, Indonesia 143 H2
Amli • Norway 125 I6
Amlwch • United Kingdom 7 H8
Amman • Jordan 18 D3
Ammarnäs • Sweden 16 I3
Ammassalik • Greenland 4 C3
Ammassalik • Greenland 39 X3
Ammersee • Germany 112 F2
Amnok • Greece 15 O3
Amnok-kang •
　China/D.P.R. Korea 29 H2
Amok • China/D.P.R. of Korea 30 D4
Amol • Iran 18 F2
Amoliani • Greece 122 D1
Amorbach • Germany 112 D4
Amorgós • Greece 122 D8
Amory • MS, United States 48 C4
Amorosa, Fontana • Cyprus 123 J3
Amot • Telemark, Norway 124 I1
Amot • Buskerud, Norway 124 I1
Ampato, Nevado de • Peru 163 B4
Amper • Germany 112 F3

Ampezzo, Valle d' • Italy 120 B4
Ampolla, l' Beach • Spain .... 96 [121]
Amposta • Spain 11 L4
Amravati • India 28 C4
Amritsar • India 28 B2
Amroth Beach • United Kingdom .. 101 [160]
Amrum • Germany 8 D2
Amsittene, Jebel • Morocco 20 D2
Amstelveen • Netherlands 109 F2
Amsterdam Heritage C •
　Netherlands .... 86 [31]
Amsterdam • Netherlands 109 F2
Amsterdam • NY, United States 153 D3
Amsterdam, Fort • St Maarten .... 160 D
Amsterdam-Rijnkanaal •
　Netherlands 109 F2
Amsterdamse Waterleiding Duinen •
　Netherlands 109 F1
Amstetten • Austria 13 D9
Amu Darya • Turkmenistan 18 H2
Amundsen Gulf • NT, Canada 38 G2
Amundsen Sea • Pacific Ocean 54 (1) EE4
Amundsen-Scott Station [Base] •
　Antarctica 54 (1) A1
Amuntai • Indonesia 32 F3
Amur • Russian Fed. 27 K6
Amurang • Indonesia 32 (1) B2
Amursk • Russian Fed. 27 M6
An Loc • Vietnam 141 E1
An Nabi Samu'il • Palestine 135 A5
An Tan • Vietnam 31 D3
An Uaimh • Ireland 108 B1
Ana Maria, Golfo de • Cuba 158 D7
Anabar • Russian Fed. 27 H2
Anabarskoye Ploskogorye •
　Russian Fed. 26 S3
Anacapri Beach • Italy .... 97 [148]
Anacapri • Italy 121 G3
Anaconda • MT, United States 42 I3
Anacortes • WA, United States 152 B1
Anadarko • OK, United States 46 F5
Anadyr • Russian Fed. 27 U4
Anadyrskiy Zaliv • Russian Fed. .. 27 V4
Anadyrskoye Ploskogorye •
　Russian Fed. 27 T3
Anáfi • Greece 122 D8
Anáfonitria • Zante, Greece 123 C7
Anagni • Italy 121 F4
Anaheim • CA, United States 45 D5
Anahuac • Mexico 47 D4
Anáhuac Beach • Italy 47 D4
Anai Mudi • India 138 D10
Analalava • Madagascar 24 H2
Anamur • Turkey 123 G3
Anambas, Kepulauan • Indonesia .. 32 D2
Anambra • Nigeria 22 F3
Anamosa • IA, United States 43 K5
Anamur Burun • Turkey 123 G3
Anan • Japan 30 H8
Anantapur • India 138 D2
Anantnag • Pakistan 18 K3
Anápa • Russian Fed. 17 F6
Anápolis • Brazil 52 G2
Anaraki • Iran 18 F3
Anascaul Beach • Ireland 108 B6
Anascaul • Ireland 108 C5
Anastásio • Greece 123 H1
Añasco • Puerto Rico 159 H1
Añasco, Río Grande de •
　Puerto Rico 159 H1
Anatolia • Turkey 15 L5
Anatolia, Central • Turkey 122 A3
Anatolia, Eastern • Turkey 122 A4
Anatoliki Rodópi • Greece 15 G2
Anatom • Vanuatu 35 (2) B3
Añatuya • Argentina 52 D4
Anávissos Beach • Greece .... 97 [185]
Anávissos • Greece 122 D7
Anazah, Jabal • Saudi Arabia 21 G1
Anbyon • D.P.R. of Korea 30 C3
Ancão, I. do • Portugal 118 E7
Ancaster • OT, Canada 44 F4
Ancenis • France 114 D1
Anchorage • AK, United States 49 J3
Anclote Keys •
　FL, United States 154 H5
Anchuma, Nevado • Bolivia 52 C2
Ancona • Italy 121 E12
Ancud • Chile 53 B4
Anda • China 27 K7
Andalgalá • Argentina 52 C4
Andalo • Italy .... 100 [214]
Andalsnes • Norway 124 C2
Andalucía • Spain 11 G7
Andalucía • AL, United States 48 D5
Andaman Is. • India 28 F6
Andaman Sea • India/Myanmar .. 31 B4
Andara • Namibia 24 C3
Andelys, les • France 115 E1
Andenes • Norway 16 I2
Andenne • Belgium 5 I4
Anderanboukane • Mali 20 F5
Anderdalen Nat. Park Park N •
　Norway .... 89 [8]
Andermatt Ski • Switzerland .... 100 [105]
Andernach • Germany 112 E1
Andernos-les-Bains Beach •
　France .... 96 [85]
Anderson • NT, Canada 38 F3
Anderson • IN, United States 44 C5
Anderson • MO, United States 46 H4
Anderson • SC, United States 48 F3
Andersonville Nat. Hist. Site Park N •
　GA, United States .... 151 [208]
Andes • S. America 50 D7
Anson Bay • NT, Australia 34 F2
Andhra Pradesh • India 138 D3
Andijon • Uzbekistan 18 J1
Andikithira • Greece 122 D10
Andípaxos • Greece 122 C2
Andirlangar • China 28 D1
Andkhvoy • Afghanistan 18 I2
Ando, Rep. of Korea 30 E6
Andorra Beach • Italy .... 96 [141]
ANDORRA • Europe 115 K1
Andorra la Vella • Andorra 115 K1
Andover • OH, United States 44 E5
Andøya • Norway 16 I2
Andradina • Brazil 52 F3
Andújar • Spain 11 G6
Andulo • Angola 23 B6
Andutan • South China Sea 31 E5
Aneby • Sweden 125 F7
Anéfis • Mali 20 F5
Anegada • British Virgin Is. ...... 160 B
Anegada Passage • West Indies .. 37 I4
Aneto, Pico de • Spain 115 K1

Aney • Niger 20 H5
Angaga • Maldives 138 F1
Angamos, Punta • Chile 52 B3
Angara • Russian Fed. 27 E5
Angarsk • Russian Fed. 27 F6
Ange • Sweden 16 H5
Ange Beach • Sweden .... 99 [24]
Angel de la Guarda, I. • Mexico .. 157 F1
Angel Falls • Venezuela 51 E2
Angeles • Philippines 31 G3
Angelholm Beach • Sweden .... 96 [9]
Angelholm • Sweden 125 F11
Angelina • TX, United States 47 G2
Angermanälven • Sweden 16 I5
Angermünde • Germany 8 J3
Angers • France 114 D1
Angers [Château] • France 114 D1
Angkor • Cambodia 31 C4
Angkor Heritage C • Cambodia .. 85 [198]
Anglem, Mt • New Zealand 35 A8
Anglesberg • Sweden 125 D1
Anglesey • United Kingdom 7 H8
Angoche • Mozambique 24 F3
Angol • Chile 53 B3
ANGOLA • Africa 24 B2
Angola • IN, United States 44 C5
Angoram • Papua New Guinea .. 35 (1) C1
Angoulême • France 115 G1
Angra do Heroísmo Heritage C •
　Terceira, Azores .... 84 [79]
Angra do Heroísmo Beach •
　Terceira, Azores .... 96 [104]
Angra do Heroísmo • Azores 118 J2
Anguilla • Bahamas 49 C6
ANGUILLA • West Indies .... 160 C
Anguilla Cays • Bahamas 158 B3
Anguilla Channel • West Indies .... 160 C
Anguillita I. • Anguilla .... 160 C
Anholt Castle • Germany .... 113 [15]
Anholt • Denmark 125 F9
Anholt I. • China 139 A8
Aniakchak Nat. Mon. •
　AK, United States .... 151 [50]
Aniakchak Nat. Mon. & Preserve Park N •
　AK, United States .... 150 [10]
Anie, Pic d' • France/Spain 11 K2
Animal Kingdom •
　FL, United States 151 C1
Animas Peak • NM, United States .. 45 H6
Aniva, mys • Russian Fed. 27 N7
Aniva, Zaliv • Russian Fed. 27 N7
Anjar Heritage C • Lebanon ...... 86 [280]
Anji • China 139 C3
Anjou • France 114 D1
Anjouan • Comoros 24 G2
Anjuna Beach • Goa, India 137 B1
Ankang • China 29 D4
Ankara • Turkey 15 N4
Ankara [Riv] • Turkey 15 N4
Ankara-Altindag • Turkey 15 N4
Ankara-Çankaya • Turkey 15 N4
Ankara-Yenimahalle • Turkey 15 O4
Ankaratra • Madagascar 24 H3
Ankarsrum • Sweden 125 F8
Ankeny • IA, United States 43 J6
Ankhor • Somalia 23 H1
Anklam • Germany 8 I3
Anlong • China 31 D2
Ann Arbor • MI, United States 44 D4
Ann, Cape • MA, United States 153 D4
Anna • IL, United States 46 K4
Anna Plains • WA, Australia 34 B2
Annaba • Algeria 131 E1
Annaberg Ski • Austria .... 100 [181]
Annaberg-Buchholz • Germany 9 I6
Annam • Vietnam 31 C3
Annandale • VA, United States 44 G6
Annandale Falls • Grenada .... 160 S
Annapolis • MD, United States 153 D10
Annapolis Royal • NS, Canada 156 D7
Annapurna • Nepal 28 D2
Anne, Fort • NS, Canada 156 D7
Annecy • France 115 F1
Anneville • Belgium 109 D15
Anniston • AL, United States 48 E4
Annobón • Gabon 22 F5
Annonay • France 115 F3
Annotto Bay • Jamaica 159 B2
Annweiler • Germany 112 D6
Ano Merá Beach • Greece .... 97 [204]
Ano Síros Beach • Greece .... 97 [203]
Ano Viános • Crete, Greece 123 E7
Anógia • Crete, Greece 123 E6
Anoka • MN, United States 43 J4
Anópolis Beach • Crete, Greece .. 97 [214]
Anqing • China 29 E4
Ansbach • Germany 112 E4
Ansbach Castle • Germany .... 113 [148]
Anse Boileau Bay • Seychelles .. 133 K1
Anse Courtois • Mauritius 132 J1
Anse d'Hainault • Haiti 159 G5
Anse La Raye • St Lucia .... 161 P
Anse Lavoute • St Lucia .... 161 P
Anse Royale • Seychelles 133 K1
Anse Royale Bay • Seychelles 133 K3
Anse Volbert Village •
　Seychelles 133 K4
Anse-Bertrand • Guadeloupe ...... 161 L
Anses-d'Arlets, les •
　Martinique .... 161 N
Anshan • China 29 G2
Anshun • China 29 D5
Anson • TX, United States 47 E1
Ansongo • Mali 20 F5
Ansruther Beach •
　United Kingdom .... 101 [9]
Anta • Peru 163 B2
Antabamba • Peru 163 B2
Antagnod Ski • Italy .... 100 [105]
Antakya • Turkey 123 G4
Antalaha • Madagascar 24 I2
Antalya • Turkey 123 F3
Antalya [Adm] • Turkey 123 F3
Antalya Beach • Turkey .... 96 [...]
Antananarivo • Madagascar 24 H3
Antarctic cruise area •
　Antarctica 81 A10
Antarctic Peninsula •
　Antarctica 54 (1) II2
Antenor • Italy 13 B11
Antequera • Spain 116 B3
Anthony • TX, United States 47 B1
Anthony I. Heritage C •
　BC, Canada .... 84 [1]
Anti Atlas • Morocco 131 D5
Antibes Beach • France .... 96 [134]
Antibes • France 115 H4
Antibes, Cap d' • France 115 H4
Antigo • WI, United States 156 D2
Antietam Nat. Battlefield Park N •
　MD, United States .... 151 [262]
Antietam Nat. Battlefield •
　MD, United States 153 D9
Antifer, Cap d' • France 5 D5
Antigo • NY, United States 43 L4
Antigua Heritage C • Honduras .. 84 [32]
Antigua •
　Fuerteventura, Canary Is. 117 E2
Antigua • Antigua & Barbuda .... 161 K
ANTIGUA & BARBUDA • West Indies 161 J/K
Antikira Beach • Greece .... 97 [177]
Antilla • Cuba 158 D8
Antilla • Aruba .... 160 Y
Antilles • St Vincent & Gren. ...... 161 R

Antioch • Turkey 123 G4
Antioch • CA, United States 45 B3
Antioche, Pertuis d' • France 10 D7
Antiphnitis Monastery • Cyprus .. 123 J2
Antivari •
　Fed. Rep. of Yugoslavia 90 A14
Antlers • OK, United States 46 H5
Antofagasta • Chile 52 B3
Antofalla, Volcán • Argentina 52 C4
Antongil, Baie d' • Madagascar 24 H3
Antonio • Spain 116 B3
Antonine Wall • United Kingdom .. 90 A2
Antonito • CO, United States 46 B4
Antrim • United Kingdom 7 F7
Antrim Mtns • United Kingdom 7 F6
Antriol • Bonaire .... 160 W
Antrodoco • Italy 12 H6
Antsalova • Madagascar 24 G3
Antsirabe • Madagascar 24 H4
Antsiranana • Madagascar 24 H2
Antu • China 30 E3
Antwerp • Belgium 109 D10
Antwerpen Beach • 109 D10
Antwerpen [Adm] • Belgium 109 D15
Anupgarh • India 137 C1
Anuradhapura Heritage C •
　Sri Lanka .... 85 [153]
Anuradhapura • Sri Lanka 138 D15
Anxi • China 29 B2
Anyang • China 29 E3
Anyer • Java, Indonesia 143 J1
Anza-Borrego Desert •
　United States 152 C6
Anzanigo • Spain 11 K2
Anzère • Switzerland 119 G6
Anzhero-Sudzhensk •
　Russian Fed. 26 O6
Anzhou, Ostrova • Russian Fed. .. 27 N1
Anzio • Italy 121 F3
Anzob • Tajikistan .... 18 ...
Ko Phuket, Thailand 142 E1
Aoba • Vanuatu 35 (2) B2
Aoga-shima • Japan 140 C3
Aogi-shima • Japan 140 C3
Aoki • China 28 F2
Aokigahara • Japan 140 C1
Aomori • Japan 30 K4
Aomori [Adm] • Japan 140 A1
Aoraki • New Zealand 35 C6
Aoste • Italy 121 E1
Aotea Harbour • New Zealand 145 F1
Aotou • China 139 B2
Aouk, Bahr •
　Central African Rep./Chad 21 C6
Aoukâle •
　Central African Rep./Chad 23 C1
Aoukâr • Mauritania 20 D5
Aoulef • Algeria 20 F3
Aozou • Chad 21 C3
Ap Lei Chau • Hong Kong, China .. 139 B5
Apacha • Russian Fed. 27 Q6
Apalachee Bay •
　FL, United States 49 A3
Apalachicola •
　FL, United States 154 H2
Apalachicola [Riv] •
　FL, United States 154 H2
Apaporis • Colombia 163 C3
Aparecida do Norte • Brazil 163 C1
Aparri • Philippines 31 G3
Apatity • Russian Fed. 17 E1
Apeldoorn • Netherlands 109 D8
Apennines • Italy 12 G5
Apere • Bolivia 52 C1
Apex Ski • BC, Canada .... 149 [3]
Api • Nepal 28 D2
Apia • Samoa 35 (2) F1
Apiacás, Serra dos • Brazil 51 F6
Apio • Solomon Is. 35 (1) G2
Aplau • Peru 163 B4
Apo, Mt • Philippines 31 H5
Apolda • Germany 9 G5
Apollo Bay • VI, Australia 146 G6
Apollo Beach • Greece 122 D7
Apollonia • Albania 15 A3
Apollonia • Libya 21 D1
Apopka, Lake •
　FL, United States 154 H5
Apostle Is. • WI, United States 43 K3
Apostle Is. Nat. Lakeshore Park N •
　WI, United States .... 151 [156]
Apóstoli • Crete, Greece 123 E6
Apoteri • Guyana 51 F3
Appalachian Mtns •
　United States 48 F3
Appennino • Italy 12 E4
Appennino Calabro • Italy 12 K10
Appennino Campano • Italy 12 J8
Appennino Ligure • Italy 12 D5
Appennino Lucano • Italy 12 K8
Appennino Tosco-Emiliano •
　Italy 12 E4
Appenweier • Germany 5 K6
Appenzell • Switzerland 112 D7
Apple Mtn Ski •
　MI, United States .... 149 [146]
Apple Valley •
　MN, United States 43 J4
Appleby • United Kingdom 7 J7
Appleton • WI, United States 43 L4
Appleton • Jamaica 159 F1
Appomattox • VA, United States .. 48 H2
Appomattox Court House Nat. Hist. Site
　Park N • VA, United States .... 151 [247]
Appomattox Court House Nat. Hist. Site •
　VA, United States 153 D11
Aprica • Italy 121 E2
Aprilia • Italy 121 F3
Apt • France 115 H1
Aptera • Crete, Greece 123 E1
Apucarana • Brazil 52 F3
Apurímac • Peru 163 B2
Aqaba, Gulf of •
　Egypt/Saudi Arabia 131 F2
Aqabah, Al • Jordan 18 D4
Aqmola • China 26 P9
Aqqikkol Hu • China 28 E1
Aqsay • Kazakhstan 17 I4
Aqsu • Kazakhstan 26 17
Aqtöbe • Kazakhstan 26 J7
Aquidauana • Brazil 52 E3
Aquileia Heritage C • Italy .... 86 [135]
Aquileia • Italy 121 E4
Aquiles Serdán • Mexico 47 C2
Aquin • Haiti 159 G5
Aquitaine • France 10 F9
Ar Horqin Qi • China 27 J8
Ar Raqqah • Syria 18 C2
Ar Riyad • Saudi Arabia 18 E5
Ar Ruways •
　United Arab Emirates 18 F5
Ara • India 137 C8
Ara-kawa • Japan 140 C2
Arab • AL, United States 48 D3
Arab, Bahr al • Sudan 23 D2
Arabba • Italy .... 100 [232]
Arabba • Italy 120 B4
Arabba • Italy 48 C6
Arabian Oryx Sanctuary Heritage N •
　Oman .... 83 [112]
Arabian Sea • Asia 18 G6
Araç • Turkey 15 G2
Aracaju • Brazil 53 (1) D2
Araçatuba • Brazil 52 F3
Aracena • Spain 116 B1
Aracena, Sierra de • Spain 11 E7
Araçuaí • Brazil 53 (1) C5
Arad • Romania 14 I3

Arafali • Eritrea 21 G4
Arafura Sea • Australia/Indonesia 33 E7
Aragão [Adm] • Spain 52 F2
Aragón • Brazil 11 K3
Aragón [Riv] • Spain 11 J2
Aragona • Sicily, Italy 12 H11
Araguacema • Brazil 53 (1) B3
Araguaia • Brazil 52 F1
Araguaína • Brazil 53 (1) B3
Araguari • Brazil 52 G2
Araguatins • Brazil 53 (1) B3
Arak • Iran 18 E3
Arak • Algeria 20 F3
Arakan Yoma • Myanmar 31 A2
Araks • Azerbaijan 18 E2
Aral • Kazakstan 26 J8
Aral Sea • Kazakstan/Uzbekistan 26 J8
Aramac • QL, Australia 144 B3
Arambol • Goa, India 137 B1
Arambol Beach • Goa, India 137 B1
Aran I. • Ireland 7 D7
Aran Is. • Ireland 108 C3
Aranda de Duero • Spain 11 H3
Aranjuez • Spain 11 H4
Aransas Pass • TX, United States 47 F4
Araouane • Mali 20 E5
Arapahoe • NE, United States 46 F2
Arapahoe Basin Ski • CO, United States 149 [101]
Arapiraca • Brazil 53 (1) D3
Arápis, Akra • Greece 15 F3
Arapongas • Brazil 52 F3
Arapuni Dam • New Zealand 145 G2
Araranguá • Brazil 52 G4
Araraquara • Brazil 52 G3
Ararat • Turkey 18 D2
Ararat • VI, Australia 144 C3
Araruama, Lago de • Brazil 163 C4
Aras • Asia 18 D2
Arashi Beach • Aruba 160 V
Arashiyama • Japan 140 B2
Arauca • Colombia 51 C2
Aravalli Range • India 137 C5
Arawale Game Reserve • Kenya 131 G4
Arawua Bay • New Zealand 145 G2
Araxá • Brazil 52 G2
Araxos, Akra • Greece 15 C5
Arba • Spain 10 D11
Arba Minch • Ethiopia 23 F2
Arbanasi • Bulgaria 128 E3
Arbaoua • Morocco 131 D1
Arbatax • Sardinia, Italy 120 C4
Arbil • Iraq 18 D2
Arboga • Sweden 125 D3
Arbon • Switzerland 9 E9
Arborg • MN, Canada 43 H1
Arbroath • United Kingdom 104 B2
Arc • France 115 F4
Arc-et-Senans Heritage C • France 86 [73]
Arcachon Beach • France 96 [85]
Arcachon • France 115 G3
Arcachon, Bassin de • France 115 G3
Arcadia • Greece 15 D6
Arcadia • FL, United States 49 C4
Arcadins, Côte des • Haiti 159 G2
Arcata • CA, United States 42 C6
Arches Nat. Park Park N • UT, United States 150 [85]
Arches Nat. Park • UT, United States 45 H2
Archidona • Spain 11 G7
Arcidosso • Italy 12 F6
Arco • ID, United States 42 I5
Arcos de Valdevez • Portugal 11 C3
Arcs, les Ski • France 100 [30]
Arcs, les • France 115 F2
Arctic Bay • NU, Canada 36 J2
Arctic Red River • NT, Canada 38 E3
Arctic Red River [Riv] • NT, Canada 38 E3
Arctic Village • AK, United States 38 B3
Arda • Bulgaria 14 E2
Ardabil • Iran 18 E2
Ardakan • Iran 18 F3
Ardalstangen • Norway 124 C4
Ardee • Ireland 7 F8
Arden • Denmark 125 F5
Arden Town • CA, United States 45 B2
Ardennes • Belgium 109 D19
Ardennes, col des • France 5 H5
Ardfert Beach • Ireland 96 [60]
Ardfert • Ireland 108 C5
Ardila • Portugal 11 D6
Ardmore • OK, United States 154 J1
Ardrossan • United Kingdom 6 H6
Are • Sweden 16 G5
Arecibo • Puerto Rico 159 H1
Arecibo, Observatorio de • Puerto Rico 159 H1
Arecibo, Rio Grande de • Puerto Rico 159 H1
Arée, Mcnts d' • France 10 B5
Areia, Ponta de • Portugal 118 E8
Areiro, Pico de • Madeira 118 C2
Arena d'en Castell • Minorca, Spain 117 F2
Arenas, Punta de • Argentina 53 C6
Arend • Sweden 125 F8
Arendal • Norway 124 C4
Arenys de Mar • Spain 117 D4
Aréopoli • Greece 15 D7
Arequipa • Peru 163 B4
Arès Beach • France 96 [85]
Arès • France 115 G3
Areuse, Gorges de l' • Switzerland 119 G1
Areyonga • NT, Australia 145 D3
Arezzo • Italy 121 E11
Arga • Spain 10 D11
Arganda • Spain 11 H4
Argássi • Zante, Greece 122 C3
Argelès-Gazost • France 115 J2
Argelès-sur-Mer Beach • France 96 [128]
Argen • Germany 112 F8
Argent, Côte d' • France 115 G3
Argentan • France 10 E5
Argentera, Punta • Italy 115 K5
Argenteuil • France 10 E5
Argentia • NF, Canada 156 D4
ARGENTINA • S. America 53 B5
Argentino, Lago • Argentina 53 B6
Argenton-sur-Creuse • France 14 K3
Arges • Romania 14 M5
Arghandab • Afghanistan 28 A2
Argonne • France 5 I5
Argopuro, Gunung • Java, Indonesia 143 J8
Árgos • Greece 15 D6
Argostóli Beach • Cephalonia, Greece 97 [171]
Argostóli • Cephalonia, Greece 122 C2
Arguello, Point • CA, United States 45 B4
Arguineguín • Gran Canaria, Canary Is. 116 E4
Argun • Russian Fed. 27 J6
Argyle Beach • St Vincent & Gren. 161 Q
Argyle, Lake • WA, Australia 34 E3
Arhánes • Crete, Greece 123 E7
Arhángelos • Rhodes, Greece 122 D12
Århus • Denmark 125 F10

Århus [Adm] • Denmark 125 F10
Århus Bugt • Denmark 125 F10
Ari Atoll • Maldives 138 F1
Ariano Irpino • Italy 121 G2
Aribinda • Burkina Faso 20 F5
Arica • Chile 52 B2
Arica, Golfo de • Chile/Peru 163 B4
Aricha, El • Algeria 20 E2
Arid • Japan 140 B3
Aride, I. • Seychelles 133 K4
Aridéa • Greece 14 J9
Arieja • Greece 10 G10
Ariège • Romania 14 K3
Arild • Sweden 125 F11
Arima • Trinidad & Tobago 160 U
Arima Spa • Japan 140 B1
Arinagour • United Kingdom 106 B2
Aripo Caves • Trinidad & Tobago 160 U
Aripuanã • Brazil 51 E5
Arís • Ethiopia 23 G1
Arísh, El • Egypt 131 F2
Ariza • Spain 11 I3
Arizona • United States 153 E
Arjang • Sweden 124 B4
Arjeplog • Sweden 16 I3
Arjuna, Gunung • Java, Indonesia 143 J8
Arkabutla Lake • MS, United States 48 B3
Arkadelphia • AR, United States 46 I5
Arkádi, Moní • Crete, Greece 123 E6
Arkansas [Adm] • United States 46 I5
Arkansas City • KS, United States 46 G4
Arkansas Post Nat. Mem. Park N • AR, United States 151 [189]
Arkansas [Riv] • United States 46 E4
Arkanu • Libya 21 D3
Arkatag • China 26 O10
Arkhangel'sk • Russian Fed. 17 G2
Arklow Beach • Ireland 96 [55]
Arklow • Ireland 108 B4
Arkona, Kap • Germany 8 I2
Arkösund • Sweden 125 D3
Arkoúdi • Greece 122 C1
Arktícheskogo Instituta, Ostrov • Russian Fed. 26 N2
Arla • Sweden 125 D3
Arlanda [Apt] • Sweden 125 D3
Arlanza • Spain 10 B11
Arlbergpass • Austria 119 H5
Arles Heritage C • France 86 [77]
Arles • France 10 J10
Arlington • OR, United States 42 E4
Arlington • NY, United States 44 I3
Arlington • VA, United States 153 D9
Arlington • TX, United States 154 J1
Arlington Heights • IL, United States 44 A4
Arlington House Park N • VA, United States 151 [259]
Arlit • Niger 20 G5
Arlon • Belgium 109 D20
Arltunga Hist. Reserve • NT, Australia 145 D2
Arly, Parc nat. d' Park • Burkina Faso 133 [27]
Armação de Pera • Portugal 118 E6
Armadale • WA, Australia 34 C6
Armageddon • Israel 135 A3
Armagh • United Kingdom 7 F7
Armagnac • France 114 B3
Armando Bermudez, Parque Nac. • Dominican Rep. 159 G3
Armant • Egypt 21 C2
Armavir • Russian Fed. 17 G5
Armenia • Crete, Greece 123 E2
ARMENIA • Asia 18 D1
Armenia • Colombia 51 B3
Armentières • France 10 H3
Armidale • NS, Australia 34 J6
Armier Bay • Malta 123 H1
Armijo • NM, United States 45 I4
Armona, I. de • Portugal 118 E8
Armstrong • OT, Canada 43 L1
Armutcuk Dag • Turkey 15 I3
Armutlu • Turkey 15 J3
Arnaud • QU, Canada 39 J4
Arnauti, Cape • Cyprus 123 J3
Árnes • Greece 15 E3
Arnel, Ponta de • Azores 118 B2
Arnes • Norway 124 B2
Arnhem • Netherlands 109 D8
Arnhem, Cape • NT, Australia 34 G2
Arnhem Land • NT, Australia 34 F2
Árni • Greece 121 E11
Arnold • MO, United States 46 J3
Arnøy • Norway 16 H3
Arnprior • OT, Canada 155 B6
Arnsberg • Germany 8 D5
Arnstadt • Germany 9 G6
Arnuero Beach • Spain 96 [89]
Aroab • Namibia 24 B5
Aroche, Pico de • Spain 11 D5
Arolsen • Germany 112 F3
Arolsen Castle • Germany 113 [35]
Aroma • Italy 121 E2
Aroostook • ME, United States 44 K2
Aroræ • Kiribati 33 I6
Arosa Ski • Switzerland 100 [113]
Arosa • Switzerland 119 G4
Arosa, Ria de • Spain 11 C2
Arpajon • France 114 C3
Arqalyq • Kazakstan 26 K7
Arraias • Brazil 53 (1) B4
Arrábida, Serra da • Portugal 118 D2
Arran • United Kingdom 6 G6
Arras • France 10 H3
Arras Castle • Germany 113 [60]
Arras, Burg • Germany 112 E3
Arrecife Beach • Lanzarote, Canary Is. 96 [111]
Arrecife • Lanzarote, Canary Is. 117 E3
Arrieta • Lanzarote, Canary Is. 117 E3
Arrochar • United Kingdom 104 B1
Arrosim Beach • Goa, India 137 B2
Arrow Lake • BC, Canada 38 H6
Arrow, Lough • Ireland 108 C2
Arrowhead, Lake • TX, United States 154 J1
Arrowtown • New Zealand 145 G2
Arroyo • Puerto Rico 159 H4
Arroyo de la Luz • Spain 11 E5
Arroyo Grande • CA, United States 45 B4
Arroyo • Argentina 52 D5
Arrufó • Argentina 52 D5
Ars • Denmark 125 F5
Arsenyev • Russian Fed. 30 G2
Árta • Greece 15 B4
Artá • Majorca, Spain 117 H2
Artá, Coves d' • Majorca, Spain 117 H2
Artem • Russian Fed. 30 G3
Artemovsk • Russian Fed. 26 P7
Artesia • NM, United States 45 I4
Arthur • United Kingdom 46 E2
Arthur's Town • Bahamas 158 B2
Artibonite • Haiti 159 G2
Artigas • Uruguay 52 E5
Artillery Lake • NT, Canada 38 J4
Artois • France 10 G3
Artrutx, Cap d' • Minorca, Spain 117 F3
Artyk • Russian Fed. 27 O4

Aru, Kepulauan • Indonesia 32 (1) D4
Arua • Uganda 23 E3
ARUBA • West Indies 160 Y
Arucas • Gran Canaria, Canary Is. 116 E4
Arunachal Pradesh • India 28 F3
Arundel • United Kingdom 104 E3
Arungu • Nigeria 22 E2
Arusha • Tanzania 130 B2
Arusha Nat. Park • Tanzania 130 B2
Arusha Nat. Park Park • Tanzania 133 [90]
Aruwimi • Dem. Rep. of Congo 23 D3
Arvada • CO, United States 46 C3
Arvalem Caves • Goa, India 137 B1
Arvayheer • Mongolia 29 C1
Arvi • Crete, Greece 123 E7
Arviat • NU, Canada 38 M4
Arvidsjaur • Sweden 16 J4
Arvika • Sweden 124 B4
Arvksand • Norway 16 K1
Arykanda • Turkey 123 F3
Arys • Kazakstan 26 K9
Arzamas • Russian Fed. 17 G3
Arzew • Algeria 20 E1
Arzew, Gulf of • Algeria 11 K9
Arzgir • Russian Fed. 17 E5
As • Norway 124 B2
As • Czech Rep. 128 B1
As Sidr • Libya 21 C1
As Sidrah • Libya 21 C1
As Smara • Western Sahara 131 D5
As • Denmark 125 F6
Asa Wright Nature Centre • Trinidad & Tobago 160 U
Asahan • Indonesia 143 G2
Asahi • Japan 140 D3
Asahikawa • Japan 30 L3
Asan-man • Rep. of Korea 30 D6
Asansol • India 28 E4
Asbestos • QU, Canada 44 J3
Ascari Park • NJ, United States 115 J1
Ascension • Atlantic Ocean 19 C6
Ascension • Mexico 45 H6
Ascensión, Bahía de la • Mexico 157 H2
Aschaffenburg • Germany 112 D4
Aschau in Tirol Ski • Austria 100 [157]
Aschersleben • Germany 8 G5
Áscos, Gorges de l' • Corsica, France 115 L2
Ascoli Piceno • Italy 121 E12
Ascona • Switzerland 119 G7
Ascot • United Kingdom 104 E1
Asdhu Sun I. • Maldives 138 F2
Aseda • Sweden 125 F8
Asela • Ethiopia 23 F2
Asele • Sweden 16 I4
Asenovgrad • Bulgaria 14 L7
Aseral • Norway 124 B4
Asfendioú Beach • Greece 97 [210]
Åsgårdstrand • Norway 124 B4
Ash Shariqah • United Arab Emirates 18 G4
Ashanti traditional buildings Heritage C • Ghana 85 [110]
Ashbourne • Ireland 108 B2
Ashburton • New Zealand 35 C6
Ashdod • Israel 135 A5
Ashdown • AR, United States 46 H6
Ashdown Forest • United Kingdom 104 E3
Asheboro • NC, United States 48 H3
Ashern • MN, Canada 43 G1
Asherton • TX, United States 47 E3
Asheville • NC, United States 48 F3
Ashford • United Kingdom 104 E4
Ashfork • AZ, United States 45 F4
Ashgabat • Turkmenistan 18 H2
Ashington • United Kingdom 7 K6
Ashino-ko • Japan 140 C3
Ashizuri-misaki • Japan 30 G8
Ashkharah, Al • Oman 18 G5
Ashland • OR, United States 42 D5
Ashland • WI, United States 43 K3
Ashland • KY, United States 48 G1
Ashland • OH, United States 44 D5
Ashland • NE, United States 46 G2
Ashley • ND, United States 43 G3
Ashmûnein, El • Egypt 131 F2
Ashmyany • Belarus 16 M9
Ashtabula • OH, United States 44 E5
Ashtabula, Lake • ND, United States 43 G3
Ashton • ID, United States 42 J4
Ashuanipi Lake • QU, Canada 39 R6
Asia • Syria/Turkey 18 C2
Asia, Kepulauan • Indonesia 32 (1) D2
Asiago Ski • Italy 100 [217]
Asikkala • Finland 125 E2
Asilah • Morocco 131 D1
Asinara, Golfo del • Sardinia, Italy 120 C1
Asinara, I. • Sardinia, Italy 120 C1
Asinou Church • Cyprus 123 J3
Asir • Saudi Arabia 18 D6
Askepieion • Turkey 122 D5
Asker • Norway 124 B2
Askersund • Sweden 125 F3
Askham • United Kingdom 104 C2
Askim • Norway 124 B4
Asklipió Beach • Rhodes, Greece 97 [211]
Askoy • Norway 124 C3
Askvoll • Norway 124 C3
Asmara • Eritrea 125 F11
Asni • Morocco 131 D5
Asola • Italy 121 E7
Aspen Ski • CO, United States 149 [108]
Aspen • CO, United States 45 I2
Aspendos • Turkey 123 F4
Aspermont • TX, United States 46 E6
Aspiring, Mt • New Zealand 145 G2
Asprókavos, Akra • Corfu, Greece 122 B1
Asprovalta Beach • Greece 97 [193]
Assab • Eritrea 21 H5
Assal, Lake • Ethiopia 21 H5
Assam • India 28 F3
Assamakka • Niger 20 G5
Assateague I. • MD/VA, United States 44 H7
Assateague I. Nat. Seashore Park N • MD, United States 151 [269]
Assateague I. Nat. Seashore • MD, United States 153 D11
Assen • Netherlands 109 D4
Assens • Denmark 125 F13
Assiniboine • MN, Canada 38 L7
Assiniboine, Mt • BC, Canada 38 I6
Assiniboine, Mt, Prov. Park • BC, Canada 155 C4
Assis • Brazil 52 F3
Assisi • Italy 121 E12
Assisibola • SA, Canada 43 C2
Assmannshausen • Germany 112 E4
Assomption • Seychelles 133 K3
Assomada • Cephalonia, Greece 122 C2
Astakós • Greece 15 C5
Astana • Kazakstan 26 L7
Astérix, Parc • France 115 E2
Asteroúsia • Crete, Greece 123 E7
Asti • Italy 121 E5
Astillero • Peru 163 B2
Astipálea • Greece 122 D8
Astorga • Spain 11 E2
Astoria • OR, United States 152 B1

Astove • Seychelles 133 K3
Astrakhan • Russian Fed. 17 H5
Astura, Torre • Italy 121 F3
Asturias, Principado de • Spain 11 E1
Asunción • Paraguay 52 E3
Aswa • Uganda 23 E3
Aswân • Egypt 131 F5
Aswân Dam • Egypt 131 F5
Aswân High Dam • Egypt 131 F5
Asyût • Egypt 131 F3
Ata • Tonga 33 J8
Atacama • Chile 52 C3
Atafu • Tokelau 33 J6
Atagawa Spa • Japan 140 D3
Atakpamé • Togo 22 E2
Atalaya de Femés • Lanzarote, Canary Is. 117 E3
Atalánti Beach • Greece 97 [187]
Atalaya • Peru 51 C6
Atami • Japan 140 C3
Atâr • Mauritania 20 C4
Atascadero • CA, United States 45 B4
Asa • Kazakstan 26 L8
Ataturk [Apt] • Turkey 122 D3
Atauri • Spain 11 I2
Atáviros • Rhodes, Greece 122 D12
Atbara • Sudan 21 F4
Atbara [Riv] • Sudan 21 G4
Atbasar • Kazakstan 26 K7
Atchafalaya • LA, United States 153 F3
Atchafalaya Bay • LA, United States 153 F3
Atchinson • KS, United States 46 H3
Ateno • Italy 121 F2
Ath • Belgium 109 D14
Athabasca • AL, Canada 38 H6
Athabasca Lake • AL/SA, Canada 38 J5
Athabasca • Ireland 108 B1
Atheny • Ireland 108 C4
Athens Heritage C • Greece 86 [216]
Athens • Greece 122 D4
Athens • TX, United States 47 G1
Athens • AL, United States 48 D3
Athens • GA, United States 48 F4
Athens • TN, United States 48 E3
Athens • OH, United States 44 E6
Athens • QL, Australia 34 I3
Atherton • QL, Australia 144 B1
Atherton Tableland • QL, Australia 144 B1
Athi • Kenya 131 G4
Athína Heritage C • Greece 86 [216]
Athína • Greece 122 D4
Athlone • Ireland 7 E8
Athol • MA, United States 44 I4
Athol I. • Bahamas 158 B3
Athos Heritage C • Greece 86 [206]
Athos • Greece 122 D1
Athos, Greece Heritage N • Greece 83 [69]
Athi • United Kingdom 108 B3
Ati • Chad 21 C5
Atibaia • Brazil 163 C3
Atico • Peru 163 B3
Atikokan • OT, Canada 43 K2
Atka • Russian Fed. 27 P4
Atka • AK, United States 49 G5
Atlanta • GA, United States 48 E4
Atlanta • TX, United States 154 J2
Atlanta • IA, United States 46 H2
Atlantic • NC, United States 48 I3
Atlantic City • NJ, United States 153 D10
Atlantic Islands cruise area • Atlantic Ocean 81 A5
Atlantic Ocean 2 K5
Atlántida • Uruguay 163 D2
Atlas Bogdo-Ula • Mongolia 29 B2
Atlas Mtns • Algeria/Morocco 19 D2
Atlas Saharien • Algeria 20 F3
Atlin • BC, Canada 38 E5
Atlin Lake • YT, Canada 38 E4
Atoka • OK, United States 46 H5
Atokos • Greece 122 C1
Atol das Rocas • Brazil 53 (1) E2
Atran • Iran 18 G2
Atran • Sweden 125 F7
Atran [Riv] • Sweden 125 F7
Ataro • Colombia 51 B2
Atrek • Turkmenistan 18 G2
Atri • Italy 12 H6
Atrun, Al • Sudan 21 E4
Atsugi • Japan 140 C1
Atsumi • Japan 30 J5
Attaf, El • Algeria 11 M8
Attapu • Laos 31 C3
Attawapiskat • OT, Canada 39 O6
Attawapiskat [Riv] • OT, Canada 39 O6
Attersee • Austria 119 H4
Attica • OH, United States 44 D5
Attila Line • Cyprus 123 J4
Attitash-Bear Peak Ski • NH, United States 149 [225]
Attleborough • United Kingdom 7 K6
Attopeu • Laos 31 C3
Attu • AK, United States 49 D5
Attu I. • AK, United States 49 D5
Atuel • Argentina 52 C5
Atvidaberg • Sweden 125 F4
Atwater • CA, United States 45 B3
Atyrau • Kazakstan 17 I5
Au • Austria 119 H1
Au Vent • Réunion 132 H2
Auas Mtns • Namibia 24 B4
Aubagne • France 115 H3
Aube • France 10 J5
Aubry Lake • NT, Canada 38 F3
Auburn • WA, United States 44 C5
Auburn • IN, United States 44 C5
Auburn • NE, United States 46 H2
Auburn • CA, United States 45 B2
Auburn • AL, United States 152 C3
Auburn • NY, United States 153 D2
Aubusson • France 114 C4
Aucanquilcha, Cerro • Chile 52 C3
Auch • France 115 G4
Auckland • New Zealand 35 E3
Auckland [Adm] • New Zealand 145 E1
Auckland I. • New Zealand 35 (4) J2
Aue • Germany 112 C3
Aue [Riv] • Germany 5 M2
Auerbacher Schloss • Germany 112 E4
Auerbacher Schloss Castle • Germany 113 [58]
Auffach Ski • Austria 100 [148]
Auffach • Austria 119 H3
Aufsess Castle • Germany 113 [160]
Aughleam • QL, Australia 144 B5
Aughrim • Ireland 108 C4
Aughty, Slieve • Ireland 108 C4
Augrabies Falls • South Africa 24 C5
Augsburg • Germany 112 G6
Augusta • WA, Australia 34 C6
Augusta • Sicily, Italy 120 D4

Augusta • ME, United States 44 K3
Augusta • GA, United States 48 F4
Augustenborg • Denmark 125 F13
Augustin Codazzi • Colombia 51 C2
Augustów • Poland 13 M4
Augustus, Mt • WA, Australia 34 C4
Augustusburg Castle • Germany 113 [187]
Augustusburg, Brühl Castle • Germany 113 [31]
Auki • Solomon Is. 35 (1) G2
Aukstaitija Nat. Park Park N • Lithuania 89 [146]
Aukstaitija Nat. Park • Lithuania 126 B6
Aulavik Nat. Park Park N • NT, Canada 156 [15]
Aulendorf • Germany 112 F1
Aulla • Italy 12 E4
Aulnay • France 114 C1
Aulne • France 96 [76]
Ault Beach • France 96 [76]
Aumale • France 5 E5
Auob • Africa 24 C5
Aurach Ski • Austria 100 [159]
Aurangabad • India 28 C5
Auray • France 114 C4
Aurdal • Norway 124 C4
Aure • France 114 C4
Aurilac • France 10 H9
Aurina, Val • Italy 120 B2
Aurina • Italy 120 B2
Aurin • France 115 F3
Auris-en-Oisans Ski • France 100 [58]
Aurlandsvangen • Norway 124 C4
Auron Ski • France 100 [72]
Auron • France 115 H2
Aurora • IL, United States 44 A5
Aurora • OT, Canada 44 F3
Aurora • NE, United States 46 F2
Aurora • MO, United States 46 I4
Auroville • India 138 D7
Aurukun Mission • QL, Australia 34 H2
Ausoni, Monti • Italy 121 F4
Aust Agder • Norway 16 E2
Austad • Norway 124 C6
Austin • MN, United States 43 J5
Austin • NV, United States 152 C4
Austin • TX, United States 154 J3
Austin, Lake • WA, Australia 34 C5
Austintown • OH, United States 44 E5
Austnes • Norway 124 C1
Australasia cruise area • Oceania 81 A9
AUSTRALIA • Australasia 34
Australia's Wonderland • NS, Australia 144 C2
Australian Alps • NS/VI, Australia 144 C3
Australian Capital Territory • Australia 144 C3
AUSTRIA • Europe 4 M7
Austvågøy • Norway 16 H2
Autazes • Brazil 51 F4
Authie • France 10 G3
Autieuil • France 115 H3
Autun • France 10 J7
Auvergne • Switzerland 119 G1
Aux Sources, Mont • South Africa 24 D5
Auxerre • France 10 I6
Auxi-le-Château • France 5 F4
Auyan Tepuy • Venezuela 51 E2
Auyuittuq Nat. Park Park N • NU, Canada 156 [7]
Auzangate, Nudo • Peru 163 B3
Avadh • India 137 C4
Avaldsnes • Norway 124 C5
Avalon Peninsula • NF, Canada 156 D4
Avarua • Cook Is. 33 L8
Avebury Heritage C • United Kingdom 86 [22]
Avebury • United Kingdom 104 F3
Aveiro • Portugal 11 C4
Aveiro [Adm] • Portugal 118 A1
Avellaneda • Argentina 163 D2
Avellino • Italy 121 G2
Avenal • CA, United States 45 B3
Averbode Beach • Belgium 96 [73]
Averoya • Norway 16 D5
Aversa • Italy 121 G2
Avesnes-sur-Helpe • France 5 G4
Avesta • Sweden 125 D1
Aveyron • France 115 G4
Aveyron, Gorges de l' • France 115 G4
Avezzano • Italy 121 F2
Avgó • Greece 123 E3
Aviano • Italy 120 B2
Aviés • Spain 11 F1
Avigliano • Italy 121 G2
Avignon Heritage C • France 86 [76]
Avignon • France 10 J10
Avila Heritage C • Spain 86 [100]
Avila • Spain 11 G4
Avilés • Spain 11 F1
Aviñones, les • Réunion 132 H3
Avisio • Italy 120 B3
Avliótes Beach • Corfu, Greece 97 [170]
Avoca • Ireland 108 B4
Avoca, Vale of • Ireland 108 B4
Avola • Sicily, Italy 120 D4
Avon • CA, United States 45 B3
Avon • United Kingdom 104 D2
Avon Downs • NT, Australia 34 G4
Avon • United Kingdom 104 F3
Avon Gorge • United Kingdom 104 F3
Avon Spring • FL, United States 49 C4
Avondale • AZ, United States 45 F5
Avondale • NE, United States 38 F3
Avonmore • United Kingdom 104 F3
Avranches • France 10 E5
Avre • France 10 H4
Awaji • Japan 30 H7
Awa-shima • Japan 140 B3
Awajiku • Japan 30 J5
Awaji-shima • Japan 140 B3
Awakino • New Zealand 145 G2
Awash • Ethiopia 23 G2
Awash Nat. Park Park • Ethiopia 133 [62]
Awash [Riv] • Ethiopia 23 G1
Awaso • Ghana 22 D3
Awbari • Libya 21 B2
Awbari Sand Sea • Libya 21 B2
Awe, Loch • United Kingdom 104 B1
Awjilah • Libya 21 D2
Ax-les-Thermes • France 115 K1
Axarfjörður • Iceland 16 (1) E1
Axiós • Greece 122 D1
Axminster • United Kingdom 104 F3
Axios • Crete, Greece 123 E7
Ayabe • Japan 30 H7
Ayacucho • Argentina 163 D3
Ayacucho • Peru 51 C6
Ayaguz • Kazakstan 26 N8

Ayakkum Hu • China 28 E1
Ayame • Russian Fed. 127 A14
Ayamonte • Spain 11 D7
Ayan • Russian Fed. 27 G5
Ayan • Russian Fed. 27 M5
Ayan, Russian Fed. 27 S4
Ayas • Turkey 15 N3
Ayaviri • Peru 163 B2
Aydar • Afghanistan 28 A1
Aydin • Turkey 122 D9
Aydin Daglari • Turkey 15 I5
Aydingkol Hu • China 26 O9
Ayer • Singapore 141 Q6
Ayer Chawan • Singapore 141 Q6
Ayer Hitam • Malaysia 141 M4
Ayer Merbau • Singapore 141 H3
Ayers Rock • NT, Australia 145 D3
Ayers Rock Resort • NT, Australia 145 D3
Ayia Napa Beach • Cyprus 97 [220]
Ayia Napa • Cyprus 123 J4
Ayios Tychon Beach • Cyprus 97 [218]
Aykhal • Russian Fed. 27 H3
Aylmer • QU, Canada 44 H3
Aylmer, Lake • QU, Canada 44 J3
Aynunah • Saudi Arabia 18 B4
Ayod • Sudan 23 E2
Ayodhya • India 137 C8
Ayon, Ostrov • Russian Fed. 27 R3
Ayora • Spain 11 I5
Ayr • United Kingdom 6 H6
Ayr • QL, Australia 144 B1
Ayr [Riv] • United Kingdom 6 H6
Ayre, Point of • United Kingdom 6 H7
Aytos • Bulgaria 23 G1
Ayutthaya Heritage C • Thailand 85 [201]
Ayutthaya • Thailand 142 C1
Ayvacik • Turkey 122 D5
Ayvalik • Turkey 97 [237]
Ayvalik • Turkey 122 D5
Az Zahran • Saudi Arabia 18 E4
Az Zawiyah • Libya 21 B1
Azahar, Costa del • Spain 11 K5
Azaila • Spain 11 J3
Azamgarh • India 137 C8
Azapa • Peru 163 B4
Azaouâd • Mali 20 E5
Azaouak, Vallée de l' • Mali/Niger 20 F5
Azare • Nigeria 22 G2
Azay-le-Ferron [Château] • France 114 D4
Azay-le-Rideau [Château] • France 114 D2
Azbine • Niger 20 G5
Azdavay • Turkey 15 N3
Azemmour • Morocco 131 D1
Azemmao do Mar • Portugal 118 D1
Azinhal • Portugal 118 E8
AZERBAIJAN • Asia 18 E1
Azinhal • Portugal 118 E8
Azogues • Ecuador 51 B4
Azores • Atlantic Ocean 118 B
Azov, Sea of • Russian Fed./Ukraine 17 F5
Azpeitia • Spain 11 I1
Azrou • Morocco 131 D2
Azrou • Russian Fed. 45 H3
Aztec Ruins Nat. Mon. Park N • NM, United States 150 [122]
Aztec Ruins Nat. Mon. • NM, United States 153 E2
Azua de Compostela • Dominican Rep. 159 G7
Azuaga • Spain 11 F6
Azuchi Castle • Japan 140 B2
Azuero, Peninsula de • Panama 37 E6
Azul • Argentina 53 (1) A2
Azul • Argentina 163 D3
Azulcoca, Cerro • Peru 163 B1
Azur, Côte d' • France 115 H
Azure Window • Malta 123 H1
Azzel Matti, Sebkha • Algeria 20 F3
Azzurra, Grotta • Italy 121 G3

Ba'qubah • Iraq 18 D3
Baa • Indonesia 32 (1) B5
Baâba • New Caledonia 35 (2) A3
Baalbek Heritage C • Lebanon 86 [281]
Baam • Netherlands 109 F2
Baba Burun • Çanakkale, Turkey 15 H4
Baba Burun • Zonguldak, Turkey 15 M2
Baba Dagi • Turkey 15 K7
Babadag • Romania 128 E2
Babaeski • Turkey 15 I2
Babanango • South Africa 134 B4
Babar • Indonesia 32 (1) C4
Babayevo • Russian Fed. 126 C2
Babbacombe Bay • United Kingdom 104 F5
Babenhausen • Germany 112 F2
Baberu • South Africa 24 E5
Babian Jiang • China 29 C6
Babine Lake • BC, Canada 38 F6
Babiogórski Nat. Park Park N • Poland 89 [96]
Babiogórski Nat. Park • Poland 128 (1) D3
Babo • Indonesia 32 (1) D3
Babol • Iran 18 F2
Baboquivari Peak • AZ, United States 45 G6
Babr • Poland 13 E6
Babruysk • Belarus 17 D4
Babuna • F.Y.R. of Macedonia 14 I8
Babuyan • Philippines 31 F4
Babuyan Is. • Philippines 31 G3
Babylon • Iraq 18 D3
Bac Lieu • Vietnam 141 E3
Bac Thai • Vietnam 31 D2
Bacabal • Brazil 53 (1) C2
Bacau • Romania 14 N3
Baccarat • France 112 E4
Bacharach • Germany 112 E4
Bacharach Castle • Germany 113 [70]
Back • NU, Canada 38 L3
Backa Topola • F.R. of Yugoslavia 14 G4
Backbone Mtn • WV, United States 44 F6
Bäckefors • Sweden 125 F2
Backnang • Germany 9 E8
Bacolod • Philippines 31 F4
Bad • Iran 18 F3
Bad Aibling • Germany 112 F3
Bad Aussee • Germany 119 H4
Bad Bayersoien • Germany 112 H4
Bad Bergzabern Spa • Germany 113 [h4]
Bad Bergzabern • Germany 112 D4
Bad Berka • Germany 5 L3
Bad Bevensen Spa • Germany 113 [k1]
Bad Birnbach • Germany 112 F4
Bad Breisig • Germany 112 D3
Bad Brückenau Spa • Germany 113 [s15]
Bad Buchau • Germany 112 F1
Bad Doberan • Germany 8 G2
Bad Düben Spa • Germany 113 [s18]
Bad Dürkheim • Germany 112 D4
Bad Ems • Germany 112 E2
Bad Ems Spa • Germany 113 [s6]

Bad Endorf • Germany ... 112 F4
Bad Feilnbach • Germany ... 112 F7
Bad Freienwalde • Germany ... 8 J4
Bad Godesberg • Germany ... 112 E1
Bad Goisem • Austria ... 119 H4
Bad Harzburg • Germany ... 8 F5
Bad Harzburn • Germany ... 112 F7
Bad Herrenalb Spa • Germany ... 113 [h5]
Bad Hersfeld • Germany ... 9 E6
Bad Hofgastein Ski • Austria ... 100 [171]
Bad Hofgastein • Austria ... 119 H8
Bad Homburg Spa • Germany ... 113 [s5]
Bad Homburg vor der Höhe • Germany ... 112 E2
Bad Honnef • Germany ... 112 E1
Bad Homningen • Germany ... 112 E1
Bad Ischl • Austria ... 119 H4
Bad Kissingen • Germany ... 9 F6
Bad Kissingen Spa • Germany ... 113 [s14]
Bad Kleinkirchheim Ski • Austria ... 100 [193]
Bad Kohlgrub • Germany ... 112 F6
Bad Kreuznach • Germany ... 112 E4
Bad Kreuznach Spa • Germany ... 113 [s7]
Bad Krozingen • Germany ... 9 C9
Bad Langensalza • Germany ... 9 F5
Bad Langensalza Spa • Germany ... 113 [s16]
Bad Lauterberg • Germany ... 8 F5
Bad Mergentheim • Germany ... 9 E7
Bad Mergentheim Castle • Germany ... 113 [90]
Bad Münstereifel • Germany ... 112 E1
Bad Nauheim • Germany ... 9 D6
Bad Neuenahr-Ahrweiler • Germany ... 112 E1
Bad Neustadt an der Saale • Germany ... 9 F6
Bad Oldesloe • Germany ... 16 F10
Bad Orb • Germany ... 5 M4
Bad Orb Spa • Germany ... 113 [s3]
Bad Pyrmont • Germany ... 8 E5
Bad Pyrmont Spa • Germany ... 113 [s1]
Bad Reichenhall • Germany ... 112 F8
Bad Reichenhall Spa • Germany ... 113 [s13]
Bad Salzuflen • Germany ... 8 D4
Bad Salzungen • Germany ... 9 F6
Bad Schussenried • Germany ... 112 F1
Bad Schwalbach • Germany ... 112 E4
Bad Schwartau • Germany ... 8 F3
Bad Segeberg • Germany ... 8 F3
Bad Suderode Spa • Germany ... 113 [h15]
Bad Tölz • Germany ... 112 F7
Bad Tölz Spa • Germany ... 113 [s11]
Bad Urach • Germany ... 112 D6
Bad Vilbel Spa • Germany ... 113 [s4]
Bad Waldsee • Germany ... 112 F1
Bad Wiessee • Germany ... 112 F7
Bad Wiessee Spa • Germany ... 113 [s12]
Bad Wildbad • Germany ... 112 D6
Bad Wildbad Spa • Germany ... 113 [s9]
Bad Wildungen • Germany ... 9 E5
Bad Wildungen Spa • Germany ... 113 [s2]
Bad Wimpfen • Germany ... 112 D4
Bad Windsheim • Germany ... 9 F7
Bad Wörishofen • Germany ... 112 F2
Bad Wurzach • Germany ... 112 F1
Bad Zwischenahn • Germany ... 8 D3
Badain Jaran Shamo • Mongolia ... 29 C2
Badajoz • Spain ... 11 E6
Badalona • Spain ... 117 D4
Badami • India ... 138 D2
Badanah • Saudi Arabia ... 18 D3
Badda • Ethiopia ... 23 I3
Bade • Indonesia ... 32 (1) E4
Baden • Switzerland ... 9 C9
Baden • Austria ... 13 F9
Baden-Baden • Germany ... 112 D6
Baden-Baden Spa • Germany ... 113 [s8]
Baden-Württemberg • Germany ... 9 E8
Badenweiler • Germany ... 112 D7
Badenweiler Spa • Germany ... 113 [s10]
Badgastein Ski • Austria ... 100 [170]
Badgastein • Austria ... 119 H8
Badia, Val • Italy ... 120 B2
Badiyat ash Sham • Iraq/Jordan ... 18 C3
Badlands • United States ... 152 A2
Badlands Nat. Park Park N • SD, United States ... 150 [152]
Badr Hunayn • Saudi Arabia ... 18 C5
Badu I. • QL, Australia ... 34 H2
Badulla • Sri Lanka ... 138 D15
Badung, Bukit • Bali, Indonesia ... 143 H4
Badung, Selat • Indonesia ... 143 H4
Badwater Basin • CA, United States ... 152 C4
Baena • Spain ... 116 B3
Bafang • Cameroon ... 22 G3
Bafatá • Guinea-Bissau ... 22 A3
Baffin Bay • Canada/Greenland ... 36 K2
Baffin Bay • TX, United States ... 154 J5
Baffin I. • NU, Canada ... 39 P2
Baffing • Guinea/Mali ... 22 B2
Bafia • Cameroon ... 22 G4
Bafoulabé • Mali ... 20 C6
Bafoussam • Cameroon ... 22 G3
Bafq • Iran ... 18 G3
Baga • Goa, India ... 137 B1
Baga Beach • Goa, India ... 137 B1
Bagamoyo • Tanzania ... 130 B2
Bagan Datuk • Malaysia ... 141 G1
Bagansiapiapi • Indonesia ... 143 G3
Bagata • Dem. Rep. of Congo ... 23 B4
Bagdad • AZ, United States ... 45 F4
Bagdad • Mexico ... 47 F5
Bagdarin • Russian Fed. ... 27 H6
Bagé • Brazil ... 52 F5
Bagenkop • Denmark ... 125 F14
Bagerhat Heritage C • Bangladesh ... 85 [152]
Baggs • WY, United States ... 46 B2
Baghdad • Iraq ... 18 D3
Baghelkhand Plateau • India ... 137 C8
Baghlan • Afghanistan ... 18 I2
Baghwan Mahaveer Wildlife Sanctuary • Goa, India ... 137 B2
Baginton [Apt] • United Kingdom ... 104 D2
Bagnères-de-Bigorre • France ... 11 L1
Bagnères-de-Luchon • France ... 11 L2
Bagno di Romagna • Italy ... 12 F5
Bagoe • Mali ... 22 C2
Bagua • Peru ... 51 B5
Baguio • Philippines ... 31 G3
Bagzane, Mts • Niger ... 20 G5
Bahamas Is. • West Indies ... 37 F2
Bahama Sea • West Indies ... 158 D3
BAHAMAS • West Indies ... 158 B
Bahamas Nat. Trust Park • Bahamas ... 158 B4
Bahariya Oasis • Egypt ... 131 F3
Bahau • Malaysia ... 141 G4
Bahawalnagar • Pakistan ... 28 B3
Bahawalpur • Pakistan ... 28 B3
Bahçe • Turkey ... 123 G2
Bahia • Brazil ... 52 H1
Bahia Blanca • Argentina ... 53 D3
Bahia de los Angeles • Mexico ... 157 F1
Bahia Grande • Majorca, Spain ... 117 H3
Bahia Honda • Cuba ... 157 I3
Bahia Honda State Recreation Area • FL, United States ... 154 H8
Bahia, Is. de la • Honduras ... 160 A11
Bahia Kino • Mexico ... 157 F2
Bahia Negra • Paraguay ... 52 E3
Bahia Tortugas • Mexico ... 157 F3

Bahias, Camarones Cabo dos • Argentina ... 53 C4
Bahla Heritage C • Oman ... 85 [123]
Bahoruco, Sierra de • Dominican Rep. ... 159 G6
Bahr Chad/Sudan ... 21 D5
Bahr al Abyad, Al • Sudan ... 21 F5
Bahr al Azraq, Al • Sudan ... 21 F5
Bahr al Ghazal • Sudan ... 23 D2
Bahr Dar • Ethiopia ... 21 G5
Bahr el Arab • Sudan ... 19 G4
Bahraich • India ... 137 C3
Bahrain • Asia ... 18 F4
Bai Bung, Mui • Vietnam ... 141 E3
Bàia Mare • Romania ... 14 K2
Baia Sardinia • Sardinia, Italy ... 120 C2
Baião • Brazil ... 53 (1) B2
Baibokoum • Chad ... 21 C6
Baicheng • China ... 29 G1
Baie Comeau • QU, Canada ... 156 D1
Baie Lazare Village • Seychelles ... 133 K3
Baie Verte • NF, Canada ... 156 D3
Baiersbronn • Germany ... 112 D6
Baiguan • China ... 139 C4
Baijiahohu • China ... 139 B3
Baikal, Lake • Russian Fed. ... 27 G6
Baikal, Lake Heritage N • Russian Fed. ... 83 [75]
Baikal-Amur Railway • Russian Fed. ... 126 A13
Baikonur Cosmodrome • Kazakhstan ... 126 A11
Baile Atha Cliath • Ireland ... 108 B2
Bailén • Spain ... 11 H6
Baildón • Angola ... 23 B6
Baina Beach • Goa, India ... 137 B1
Bainbridge • FL, United States ... 154 H2
Baing • Indonesia ... 32 (1) B5
Baingoin • China ... 28 E2
Baio Grande • Spain ... 11 C1
Baird Peninsula • NU, Canada ... 39 P3
Bairiki • Kiribati ... 33 I5
Bairnsdale • VI, Australia ... 144 C3
Baise • France ... 10 F10
Baitenghu Resort • Zhuhai, China ... 139 B3
Baitou • D.P.R. of Korea ... 30 E4
Baixo Alentejo • Portugal ... 11 C6
Baixo Longa • Angola ... 24 B3
Baiyun [Apt] • China ... 139 B1
Baja • Hungary ... 13 H11
Baja California • Mexico ... 157 F
Baja California [Adm] • Mexico ... 40 D6
Baja California Sur • Mexico ... 40 D6
Baja Nuevo • West Indies ... 158 A1
Bajas, Rías • Spain ... 11 C2
Bajos de Haina • Dominican Rep. ... 159 G7
Bajsa • Mexico ... 23 E3
Bakadzicite • Bulgaria ... 15 H1
Bakal • Russian Fed. ... 26 I7
Bakala • Central African Rep. ... 22 I3
Bakanas • Kazakhstan ... 26 M9
Bakauheni • Indonesia ... 143 J1
Bakchar • Russian Fed. ... 26 N6
Bake • Indonesia ... 32 C3
Bakel • Senegal ... 22 B2
Baker • Pacific Ocean ... 33 J5
Baker • MT, United States ... 43 D3
Baker • CA, United States ... 45 D4
Baker • LA, United States ... 47 I2
Baker • OR, United States ... 152 B4
Baker City • OR, United States ... 42 G4
Baker Lake • NU, Canada ... 38 L4
Baker Lake [Lake] • NU, Canada ... 38 L4
Bakersfield • CA, United States ... 152 C6
Bakhta • Russian Fed. ... 26 O5
Bakhtaran • Iran ... 18 E3
Bakhuhn, Kuh-e • Iran ... 18 G4
Bakir • Azerbaijan ... 18 E1
Bakir • Turkey ... 15 I4
Bakirköy • Turkey ... 122 D3
Bakken Park L • Denmark ... 98 [174]
Bakony • Hungary ... 13 G10
Bakoye • Mali ... 20 D6
Baku • Azerbaijan ... 18 E1
Bakungan • Indonesia ... 143 G1
Bala • Turkey ... 15 K5
Bala Morghab • Afghanistan ... 26 J10
Balabac • Philippines ... 31 F5
Balabac [I.] • Philippines ... 31 F5
Balabac, Selat • Malaysia/Philippines ... 31 F5
Balaban • Turkey ... 15 O4
Balaghat • India ... 28 C4
Balagne • Corsica, France ... 115 L1
Balaguer • Spain ... 11 L3
Balakovo • Russian Fed. ... 17 H4
Balan [Apt] • Turkey ... 15 J7
Balankanché • Mexico ... 157 H2
Balashov • Russian Fed. ... 17 G4
Balassagyarmat • Hungary ... 13 G11
Balaton • Hungary ... 13 G11
Balatonfüred • Hungary ... 13 G11
Balaurin • Indonesia ... 32 (1) B4
Balazote • Spain ... 11 I6
Balbi • Papua New Guinea ... 35 (1) E2
Balboa • Panama ... 80 B9
Balbriggan • Ireland ... 108 B2
Balcarce • Argentina ... 163 D4
Balchik Beach • Bulgaria ... 97 [243]
Balchik • Bulgaria ... 128 E4
Balclutha • New Zealand ... 145 G4
Balcones Escarpment • TX, United States ... 154 J3
Bald Knob • WV, United States ... 44 E6
Bald Mtn • NV, United States ... 45 E3
Baldenschwang • Germany ... 112 F5
Baldeneysee • Germany ... 111 B2
Baldwin Park • CA, United States ... 45 D4
Baldy Peak • AZ, United States ... 153 E4
Bale Gong Palace • Bali, Indonesia ... 143 H4
Bale Mtns Nat. Park Park • Ethiopia ... 133 [64]
Baleares, Is. • Spain ... 11 N5
Balearic Is. • Spain ... 11 N5
Baleia, Gunung • Indonesia ... 32 (1) B3
Baleia, Ponta de • Brazil ... 53 (1) D5
Baleine, Falls of • St Vincent & Gren. ... 161 Q
Baleine, Grande Rivière de la • QU, Canada ... 39 P5
Baleine, Rivière à la • QU, Canada ... 39 R5
Baler • Philippines ... 31 G3
Baleshwar • India ... 28 E4
Balestrand • Norway ... 124 C4
Baley • Russian Fed. ... 27 I6
Balfour Town • Turks & Caicos Is. ... 158 C2
Bali • Indonesia ... 143 H
Bali Aga • Bali, Indonesia ... 143 H4
Bali Handara • Bali, Indonesia ... 143 H2
Bali Sea • Indonesia ... 143 H2
Bali, Selat • Indonesia ... 143 H1
Balice John Paul II [Apt] • Poland ... 128 C2
Baliceaux • St Vincent & Gren. ... 161 R
Balik Pulau Forest Reserve • Penang, Malaysia ... 141 F3
Balikesir • Turkey ... 122 D3

Balikpapan • Indonesia ... 32 F3
Balimbing • Indonesia ... 32 C4
Balimo • Papua New Guinea ... 35 (1) C2
Balintang Channel • Philippines ... 112 D6
Ball Lake • OT, Canada ... 43 I1
Ball's Pyramid • NS, Australia ... 34 K6
Balladonia • WA, Australia ... 34 D6
Ballaghaderreen • Ireland ... 108 C2
Ballangen • Norway ... 16 I2
Ballantrae • United Kingdom ... 104 B3
Ballarat • VI, Australia ... 144 C3
Ballaró • Egypt ... 21 F3
Ballenita, Punta • Chile ... 52 B4
Ballina • India ... 137 C8
Ballina • NS, Australia ... 144 B6
Ballinasloe • Ireland ... 108 C4
Ballinger • TX, United States ... 47 E2
Ballinrobe • Ireland ... 108 C3
Ballinskelligs Beach • Ireland ... 96 [60]
Ballinskelligs • Ireland ... 108 C7
Ballintober Abbey • Ireland ... 108 C3
Ballivor • Ireland ... 108 B2
Ballranald • NS, Australia ... 144 C1
Ballwin • MO, United States ... 46 J3
Ballybunion Beach • Ireland ... 96 [60]
Ballycastle Beach • United Kingdom ... 101 [250]
Ballycastle • United Kingdom ... 106 A9
Ballydehob • Ireland ... 108 C7
Ballyhaunis • Ireland ... 108 C3
Ballyheige Beach • Ireland ... 96 [60]
Ballyheige • Ireland ... 108 C5
Ballylynan • Ireland ... 108 B3
Ballymena • United Kingdom ... 7 F7
Ballymore Eustace • Ireland ... 108 B3
Ballymote • Ireland ... 108 C3
Ballyshannon • Ireland ... 7 D7
Ballyvaughan Beach • Ireland ... 96 [61]
Ballyvaughan • Ireland ... 108 C4
Ballywaughan • Ireland ... 108 C4
Balmerrown • OT, Canada ... 43 J1
Balmoral • United Kingdom ... 6 I4
Balmorhea • TX, United States ... 47 C2
Balnibi • Ko Phuket, Thailand ... 142 E1
Balochistan • Pakistan ... 18 H4
Balonne • QL, Australia ... 144 B5
Balotra • India ... 137 C5
Balpyk • Kazakhstan ... 26 L8
Balqash Köli • Kazakhstan ... 26 M8
Balranald • NS, Australia ... 34 H6
Bals • Romania ... 14 L5
Balsa • Brazil ... 53 (1) B3
Balsas • Mexico ... 157 G4
Bålsta • Sweden ... 125 D2
Balt • Moldova ... 14 O2
Baltic Coast • Poland ... 128 A1
Baltic cruise area • Europe ... 81 A4
Baltic Sea • Europe ... 16 J8
Baltim • Egypt ... 131 F1
Baltimore • Ireland ... 108 C8
Baltimore • MD, United States ... 153 D10
Baltimore-Washington [Apt] • MD, United States ... 153 D10
Baltinglass • Ireland ... 108 B3
Baltiysk • Russian Fed. ... 13 I3
Baltrum • Germany ... 8 C3
Balve • Germany ... 9 C5
Balya • Turkey ... 15 I4
Bam • Iran ... 18 G4
Bam Co • China ... 28 E2
BAM Railway • Russian Fed. ... 127 A13
Bama • Nigeria ... 22 H2
Bamaga • QL, Australia ... 34 H2
Bamako • Mali ... 20 D6
Bambari • Central African Rep. ... 23 C2
Bamberg • Germany ... 9 F7
Bamberg Heritage C • Germany ... 86 [57]
Bambili • Dem. Rep. of Congo ... 23 D3
Bambio • Central African Rep. ... 22 H4
Bambolim Beach • Goa, India ... 137 B1
Bambous • Mauritius ... 132 J3
Bambouto, Mts • Cameroon ... 22 G3
Bambui • Brazil ... 163 C1
Bamburi Beach • Kenya ... 131 G5
Bamenda • Cameroon ... 22 G3
Bamian • Afghanistan ... 18 I3
Bamingui • Central African Rep. ... 23 C2
Bamingui-Bangoran, Parc nat. du Park • Central African Rep. ... 133 [44]
Bamovskoye • Russian Fed. ... 127 A14
Bampur [Riv] • Iran ... 18 H4
Bampur • Iran ... 18 G4
Ban Bang Po • Ko Samui, Thailand ... 142 D1
Ban Bophut • Ko Samui, Thailand ... 142 D1
Ban Chaweng • Ko Samui, Thailand ... 142 D1
Ban Chaweng Noi • Ko Samui, Thailand ... 142 D2
Ban Chiang Heritage C • Thailand ... 85 [199]
Ban Chiang • Thailand ... 142 A1
Ban Hong • Thailand ... 142 B3
Ban Houayxay • Laos ... 31 C2
Ban Hua Thanon • Ko Samui, Thailand ... 142 D2
Ban Klaeng • Thailand ... 142 C4
Ban Laem • Thailand ... 142 C3
Ban Lamai • Ko Samui, Thailand ... 142 D2
Ban Lipa Noi • Ko Samui, Thailand ... 142 D1
Ban Maenam • Ko Samui, Thailand ... 142 D1
Ban Me Thuot • Vietnam ... 141 E2
Ban Pae • Thailand ... 142 C4
Ban Phang Ka • Ko Samui, Thailand ... 142 D2
Ban Pong • Thailand ... 142 C1
Ban Sa Ket • Ko Samui, Thailand ... 142 D2
Ban Sa Kret • Ko Samui, Thailand ... 142 D1
Ban Tah • Thailand ... 142 D1
Ban Tai • Ko Samui, Thailand ... 142 D2
Ban Taling Ngam • Ko Samui, Thailand ... 142 D2
Ban Thale • Ko Samui, Thailand ... 142 D2
Ban Thong Krut • Ko Samui, Thailand ... 142 D2
Ban Thong Tanot • Ko Samui, Thailand ... 142 D2
Ban Thurian • Ko Samui, Thailand ... 142 D2
Ban Tong Yang • Ko Samui, Thailand ... 142 D2
Banaadir • Somalia ... 23 G3
Banaba • Kiribati ... 33 I6
Banados del Izozog • Bolivia ... 52 D2
Banamba • Mali ... 22 C2
Banana • Dem. Rep. of Congo ... 23 A4
Banana • Mali ... 28 F7
Banas, Rás • Egypt ... 131 F5
Banaz • Romania ... 14 I4
Banaz [Riv] • Turkey ... 15 K5
Banaz • Turkey ... 15 K5
Banbury • United Kingdom ... 104 D4
Banc d'Arguin Nat. Park Heritage N • Mauritania ... 83 [80]
Banc d'Arguin Nat. Park Park • Mauritania ... 133 [1]
Banca C • Grenada ... 160 S
Banca • OT, Canada ... 155 B6
Banda Aceh • Indonesia ... 143 G1
Banda, Kepulauan • Indonesia ... 32 (1) C3

Banda, Punta • Mexico ... 45 D6
Banda Sea • Indonesia ... 32 (1) G4
Bandak • Norway ... 124 C6
Bandama • Côte d'Ivoire ... 22 D3
Bandama • Gran Canaria, Canary Is. ... 116 E4
Bandar Seri Begawan • Brunei ... 32 E2
Bandar-e 'Abbas • Iran ... 18 G4
Bandar-e Anzali • Iran ... 18 E2
Bandar-e Khomeyni • Iran ... 18 E3
Bandar-e Langeh • Iran ... 18 F4
Bandar-e Maqam • Iran ... 18 F4
Bandar-e Torkeman • Iran ... 18 F2
Bandaranayake [Apt] • Sri Lanka ... 138 D15
Bandeira, Pico da • Brazil ... 163 C2
Bandelier Nat. Mon. Park N • NM, United States ... 150 [127]
Bandelier Nat. Mon. • NM, United States ... 153 E2
Bandera • TX, United States ... 47 E3
Banderas, Bahía de • Mexico ... 37 (1) A1
Bandiagara Cliffs Heritage N • Mali ... 83 [79]
Bandirma • Turkey ... 122 D3
Bandirma Körfezi • Turkey ... 15 J3
Bandol Beach • France ... 96 [133]
Bandol • France ... 115 H3
Bandon • OR, United States ... 152 B3
Bandon • Ireland ... 108 C7
Bandos • Maldives ... 138 F4
Bandundu • Dem. Rep. of Congo ... 23 B4
Bandundu [Adm] • Dem. Rep. of Congo ... 23 B4
Bandung • Java, Indonesia ... 143 J2
Bandungan • Java, Indonesia ... 143 J2
Baneasa [Apt] • Romania ... 128 E1
Baneasa • Cuba ... 158 D8
Banes • Cuba ... 158 D8
Banff • AL, Canada ... 155 C4
Banff Nat. Park • AL, Canada ... 155 C4
Banff Nat. Park Park N • AL, Canada ... 156 [17]
Bang Kaong Beach • Ko Phuket, Thailand ... 142 E1
Bang Pa-In • Thailand ... 142 C1
Bang Saen • Thailand ... 142 C4
Bang Thao • Ko Phuket, Thailand ... 142 E1
Bang Thao Beach • Ko Phuket, Thailand ... 142 E1
Bangalore • India ... 138 D6
Banganapalle • India ... 138 D3
Bangang Co • China ... 28 C2
Bangaram I. • India ... 138 D9
Bangassou • Central African Rep. ... 23 C3
Bangeta • Papua New Guinea ... 35 (1) D2
Banggai • Indonesia ... 32 (1) B3
Banggi • Malaysia ... 31 F5
Banghazi • Libya ... 21 C1
Bangil • Java, Indonesia ... 143 J8
Bangka • Indonesia ... 32 D3
Bangkalan • Indonesia ... 143 J4
Bangkao Bay • Ko Samui, Thailand ... 142 D2
Bangkok • Thailand ... 142 C1
Bangkok, Bight of • Thailand ... 142 C3
BANGLADESH • Asia ... 28 E4
Bangli • Bali, Indonesia ... 143 H4
Bangor • N. Ireland, UK ... 7 G7
Bangor • Wales, UK ... 7 H8
Bangor • ME, United States ... 44 K3
Bangui • Central African Rep. ... 23 B3
Bangweulu, Lake • Zambia ... 24 D2
Bangyai • Ko Phuket, Thailand ... 142 E2
Bani • Mali ... 22 C2
Bani • Dominican Rep. ... 159 G7
Bani Walid • Libya ... 21 I4
Baniyas • Syria ... 135 A2
Banja Luka • Bosnia-Herz. ... 14 E5
Banjar • Bali, Indonesia ... 143 H1
Banjar • Java, Indonesia ... 143 J6
Banjarmasin • Indonesia ... 32 E3
Banjul • Gambia ... 22 A2
Bank I. • BC, Canada ... 155 A2
Bankas • Mali ... 22 D2
Bankberg • South Africa ... 134 C4
Bankeryd • Sweden ... 125 F7
Bankhead Lake • AL, United States ... 48 D4
Banks I. • QL, Australia ... 34 H2
Banks I. • NT, Canada ... 38 G2
Banks Is. • Vanuatu ... 35 (2) B1
Banks Peninsula • New Zealand ... 35 D6
Banks Strait • TS, Australia ... 34 I8
Bann • United Kingdom ... 7 F7
Banning • CA, United States ... 45 D4
Bannockburn • United Kingdom ... 104 B3
Bannu • Pakistan ... 28 B2
Bansin Beach • Germany ... 97 [30]
Banská Bystrica • Slovak Rep. ... 13 I9
Banská Stiavnica • Slovak Rep. ... 13 H9
Banská Stiavnica Heritage C • Slovak Rep. ... 86 [177]
Banten • Java, Indonesia ... 143 J1
Bantry • Ireland ... 108 C7
Bantry Bay • Ireland ... 108 C7
Banyak, Kepulauan • Indonesia ... 143 G3
Banyalbufar • Majorca, Spain ... 117 H1
Banyo • Cameroon ... 22 G3
Banyoles • Spain ... 11 N2
Banyuls-sur-Mer Beach • France ... 96 [128]
Banyumas • Java, Indonesia ... 143 J6
Banyuwangi • Java, Indonesia ... 143 J8
Banyuwedang • Bali, Indonesia ... 143 H1
Bao Loc • Vietnam ... 141 E2
Bao'an • China ... 139 B3
Baoding • China ... 29 F3
Baoji • China ... 29 D4
Baoqing • China ... 27 L7
Baoshan • Yunnan, China ... 29 B5
Baoshan • Shanghai, China ... 139 D3
Baotou • China ... 29 E2
Baoulé • Côte d'Ivoire/Mali ... 22 C2
Bapaume • Mali ... 22 C2
Baquedano • Chile ... 52 C3
Bar • France ... 5 H5
Bar • F.R. of Yugoslavia ... 14 G7
Bar Am • Israel ... 135 A2
Bar Harbor • ME, United States ... 44 K3
Bar-le-Duc • France ... 10 K5
Barabinsk • Russian Fed. ... 26 M6
Barabinskaya Step • Russian Fed. ... 26 M6
Baraboo • WI, United States ... 43 L5
Baracaldo • Spain ... 11 H1
Baracoa • Cuba ... 158 D8
Barahona, Presqu'île des • Haiti ... 159 G5
Barafundle Bay Beach • United Kingdom ... 101 [170]
Barahona • Dominican Rep. ... 159 G7
Baraganul, Cimpia • Romania ... 14 L4
Baraki Barak • Afghanistan ... 18 I3
Baranja • Hungary ... 14 N10
Barano d'Ischia • Italy ... 121 G3
Baranof I. • AK, United States ... 49 N4
Barancheya Step • Russian Fed. ... 26 M6
Baranya • Hungary ... 14 F9
Barat Daya, Kepulauan • Indonesia ... 143 F7
Baratang • India ... 28 F6
Barataria Bay • LA, United States ... 48 C6
Barawe • Somalia ... 23 G3

Barbacena • Brazil ... 163 C1
BARBADOS • West Indies ... 161 O
Barbar • Sudan ... 21 F4
Barbastro • Spain ... 11 L2
Barbate de Franco • Spain ... 116 B5
Barberton • OH, United States ... 115 G1
Barbuda • Antigua & Barbuda ... 161 J
Barca de Alva • Portugal ... 11 E3
Barcaldine • QL, Australia ... 144 B3
Barcarès, la Beach • France ... 96 [128]
Barcarrota • Spain ... 11 E6
Barcellona Pozzo di Gotto • Sicily, Italy ... 12 J10
Barcelona • Venezuela ... 51 F5
Barcelona Heritage C • Spain ... 86 [85-86]
Barcelona Beach • Spain ... 96 [122]
Barcelona • Spain ... 117 D3
Barcelonette • France ... 115 H2
Barcelos • Brazil ... 51 E4
Barcoo • QL, Australia ... 144 A3
Barcs • Hungary ... 14 E4
Bardai • Chad ... 21 C3
Bardejov • Slovak Rep. ... 13 K8
Bardere • Somalia ... 23 G3
Bardeskan • Iran ... 26 I10
Bardo • Tunisia ... 12 E12
Bardolino • Italy ... 121 E7
Bardonecchia Ski • Italy ... 100 [200]
Bardonecchia • Italy ... 121 E5
Bareda • Somalia ... 23 I1
Barèges • France ... 115 J2
Bareilly • India ... 137 C3
Barentin • France ... 10 F4
Barents Sea • Arctic Ocean ... 4 S2
Barentsburg • Svalbard ... 54 N2
Barentu • Eritrea ... 21 G4
Barfleur, Pointe de • France ... 5 B5
Barga • China ... 28 D2
Bargal • Somalia ... 23 I1
Bargarh • India ... 28 D4
Barguzinskiy Khrebet • Russian Fed. ... 27 H6
Bari • Italy ... 12 K7
Bari • Venezuela ... 51 C2
Barinas • Venezuela ... 51 C2
Baringo, Lake • Kenya ... 131 G1
Baripada • India ... 28 E4
Barisal • Bangladesh ... 28 E4
Barito • Indonesia ... 32 E3
Barka • Oman ... 18 G5
Barkerville • BC, Canada ... 155 C1
Barkley, Lake • KY, United States ... 48 D2
Barkley Sound • BC, Canada ... 42 C2
Barkly Tableland • NT, Australia ... 34 G3
Barlee, Lake • WA, Australia ... 34 C5
Barletta • Italy ... 12 K7
Barlinek • Poland ... 13 E4
Barlovento de Jandia, Playa de • Fuerteventura, Canary Is. ... 117 C2
Barma • Indonesia ... 32 (1) D3
Barmer • India ... 137 C5
Barmera • SA, Australia ... 34 H6
Barmouth • United Kingdom ... 104 C4
Barnaul • Russian Fed. ... 26 N7
Barnes Bay • Anguilla ... 160 C
Barneville-Carteret • France ... 10 D3
Barneville-Carteret Beach • France ... 96 [78]
Barnsley • United Kingdom ... 7 K8
Barnstaple • United Kingdom ... 104 C5
Barmwell • SC, United States ... 48 G4
Barolo • Italy ... 121 E5
Baronia • Sardinia, Italy ... 120 C2
Baros • Maldives ... 138 F4
Barossa Valley • SA, Australia ... 144 A7
Bargah al Bahriyah • Egypt ... 21 E1
Barqu, Jabal • Tunisia ... 12 D12
Barquisimeto • Venezuela ... 51 D2
Barra • United Kingdom ... 6 E4
Barra • Brazil ... 53 (1) C4
Barra de Navidad • Mexico ... 157 G3
Barra de Tijuca • Brazil ... 163 C3
Barra do Cuanza • Angola ... 23 A5
Barra Falsa, Ponta da • Mozambique ... 24 E4
Barra Mansa • Brazil ... 163 C3
Barra, Ponta de • Mozambique ... 24 F4
Barração do Barra • Brazil ... 51 B4
Barranca • Peru ... 51 B4
Barrancabermeja • Colombia ... 157 F4
Barranca • Venezuela ... 51 E2
Barranco do Velho • Portugal ... 118 E3
Barranqueras • Argentina ... 52 E4
Barranquilla • Colombia ... 51 C1
Barre • VT, United States ... 44 J3
Barre de l'Isle • St Lucia ... 161 P
Barre des Écrins • France ... 115 F4
Barreiras • Brazil ... 53 (1) C4
Barreiro • Portugal ... 118 D2
Barreiros Beach • Brazil ... 96 [91]
Barren • Madagascar ... 24 G3
Barren Grounds • NU, Canada ... 155 A2
Barren River Lake • KY, United States ... 48 D2
Barretos • Mexico ... 47 B3
Bareta, I. da • Portugal ... 118 E7
Barretos • Brazil ... 52 G3
Barrie • OT, Canada ... 155 B5
Barrier Reef Reserve System Heritage N • Belize ... 82 [22]
Barrington, Fort • Montserrat ... 161 H
Barrington Tops • NS, Australia ... 34 J6
Barron • WI, United States ... 43 K4
Barroualie • St Vincent & Gren. ... 161 Q
Barrow • United Kingdom ... 7 F9
Barrow • AK, United States ... 49 J1
Barrow Creek • NT, Australia ... 145 D2
Barrow I. • WA, Australia ... 34 C4
Barrow, Point • AK, United States ... 49 J1
Barrow-in-Furness • United Kingdom ... 104 C3
Barry • United Kingdom ... 104 C5
Barry's Amusement Park Park L • United Kingdom ... 98 [211]
Barry's Bay • OT, Canada ... 155 B6
Barsac • France ... 114 B3
Barsinghausen • Germany ... 8 E4
Barstow • CA, United States ... 152 C6
Barth • Germany ... 8 H2
Bartica • Guyana ... 51 G2
Barth • Turkey ... 15 N2
Bartle Frere, Mt • QL, Australia ... 144 B1
Bartlesville • OK, United States ... 46 H4
Bartlet Town • Bahamas ... 158 B2
Bartlett • TN, United States ... 48 C3
Bartoszyce • Poland ... 13 J3

Bartow • FL, United States ... 49 C4
Baru, Volcán • Panama ... 37 E6
Barúmini • Sardinia, Italy ... 120 C4
Barun • Indonesia ... 143 G4
Barun Bagdo-Ula • Mongolia ... 29 C1
Barung • Indonesia ... 143 J8
Barysaw • NS/QL, Australia ... 144 A8
Barycz • Poland ... 13 F6
Barysaw • Belarus ... 17 D4
Bas Médoc • France ... 114 B3
Basak • Cambodia ... 141 E1
Basankusu • Dem. Rep. of Congo ... 23 B3
Basauri • Spain ... 11 I1
Bascuñan, Cabo • Chile ... 52 B4
Basdorf • Germany ... 111 C2
Basel • Switzerland ... 9 C9
Basey • Philippines ... 31 H4
Bashi Haixia • Taiwan ... 31 G2
Bashkortostan • Russian Fed. ... 31 G5
Basildon • United Kingdom ... 104 E2
Basilicata • Italy ... 12 K8
Basin • MA, United States ... 153 D3
Basingstoke • United Kingdom ... 7 K10
Baskatong, Réservoir • QU, Canada ... 155 B3
Basle • Switzerland ... 112 D7
Basoko • Dem. Rep. of Congo ... 23 C3
Basque Coast • Spain ... 116 A2
Basque, Côte • France ... 115 J1
Basque Country • Spain ... 116 A2
Basque, Pays • France ... 115 J1
Basra, Al • Iraq ... 18 E3
Basrah, Al • Iraq ... 18 E3
Bass Lake • CA, United States ... 152 C3
Bass Strait • TS/VI, Australia ... 34 I7
Bassae Heritage C • Greece ... 86 [212]
Bassano • AL, Canada ... 42 I1
Bassar • Togo ... 22 E3
Bassas da India • Reunion ... 24 F4
Basse Casamance, Parc nat. de Park • Senegal ... 133 [8]
Basse Normandie • France ... 114 A1
Basse-Pointe • Martinique ... 161 N
Basse-Terre • Guadeloupe ... 161 L
Bassein • Myanmar ... 31 A3
Bassein • India ... 28 D4
Bassenthwaite • United Kingdom ... 104 C1
Bassenthwaite Lake • United Kingdom ... 104 C1
Basseterre • St Kitts & Nevis ... 161 G
Bassett • NE, United States ... 43 G5
Bassila • Benin ... 22 E3
Bassins Bleus • Haiti ... 159 G6
Basso, Plateau de • Chad ... 21 D4
Bassum • Germany ... 5 L2
Båstad Beach • Sweden ... 96 [8]
Båstad • Sweden ... 125 F11
Bastelica • Corsica, France ... 115 L3
Basti • India ... 137 C4
Bastia • Italy ... 12 G5
Bastia • Corsica, France ... 115 L2
Bastogne • Belgium ... 109 D19
Bastrop • LA, United States ... 153 F1
Bastrop • TX, United States ... 154 J3
Basu Heritage C • Oman ... 85 [124]
Bat'umi • Georgia ... 17 G6
Bata • Equatorial Guinea ... 22 F4
Batabanó, Golfo de • Cuba ... 158 D1
Batagay • Russian Fed. ... 27 L3
Batagay-Alyta • Russian Fed. ... 27 L3
Batak • Bulgaria ... 14 L8
Bataklik Gölü • Turkey ... 15 O6
Bataklik Gölü • Turkey ... 123 G1
Batalha Heritage C • Portugal ... 86 [115]
Batan Is. • Philippines ... 31 G2
Batang • China ... 29 B5
Batangafo • Central African Rep. ... 23 B2
Batanghari • Indonesia ... 32 C3
Batangas • Philippines ... 31 G4
Batavia • NY, United States ... 153 D11
Batchelor • NT, Australia ... 34 F2
Batchelor, Mt • OR, United States ... 152 B3
Batéké, Plateaux • Congo ... 22 G5
Bateman's Bay • NS, Australia ... 144 C3
Batesburg • SC, United States ... 48 G4
Batesville • NF, Canada ... 46 J5
Bath Heritage C • United Kingdom ... 86 [21]
Bath • United Kingdom ... 104 F3
Bath • Jamaica ... 159 F4
Bath • NY, United States ... 44 G4
Bath • NC, United States ... 48 H3
Batha • Chad ... 21 C5
Bathaway Beach • Grenada ... 160 S
Bathgate • United Kingdom ... 104 B4
Baths, The • British Virgin Is. ... 160 B
Bathsheba • Barbados ... 161 O
Bathurst • NS, Australia ... 144 C2
Bathurst • NU, Canada ... 156 D2
Bathurst, Cape • NT, Canada ... 38 F2
Bathurst I. • NT, Australia ... 34 F2
Bathurst I. • NU, Canada ... 54 J3
Bathurst Inlet • NU, Canada ... 38 J3
Batna • Algeria ... 20 G1
Bato-Bato • Philippines ... 31 F5
Baton Rouge • LA, United States ... 153 F4
Batouri • Cameroon ... 22 H3
Bats Cave Beach • Cayman Is. ... 159 E3
Battambang • Cambodia ... 141 D1
Battenberg • Germany ... 9 D5
Batti Maly • India ... 28 F7
Batticaloa • Sri Lanka ... 138 D16
Battipaglia • Italy ... 121 G4
Battle • United Kingdom ... 104 E4
Battle • AL, Canada ... 38 I6
Battle Creek • MI, United States ... 44 C4
Battle Harbour • NF, Canada ... 39 T6
Battle Mtn • NV, United States ... 152 C2
Battowia • St Vincent & Gren. ... 161 R
Batu • Ethiopia ... 23 F2
Batu Berinchang, Gunung • Malaysia ... 141 G1
Batu Caves • Malaysia ... 141 G4
Batu Gajah • Malaysia ... 141 G1
Batu Pahat • Malaysia ... 141 G5
Batu, Kepulauan • Indonesia ... 143 G4
Batu Putih, Gunung • Malaysia ... 141 G1
Batuasa • Indonesia ... 32 (1) H2
Batuata • Indonesia ... 143 H2
Batubara, Gunung • Bali, Indonesia ... 143 H2
Batur, Danau • Bali, Indonesia ... 143 H2
Batur, Gunung • Bali, Indonesia ... 143 H2
Batur Temple • Bali, Indonesia ... 143 H2
Baturaja • Indonesia ... 32 C3
Baturino • Russian Fed. ... 26 O6
Batusangkar • Indonesia ... 32 (1) B4
Bauchi • Nigeria ... 22 F2
Bauchi [Adm] • Nigeria ... 22 F2
Baudette • MN, United States ... 43 I2
Baudry [Château] • France ... 114 D2
Bauld, Cape • NF, Canada ... 156 D2
Baule-Escoublac, la • France ... 114 A2
Bauru • Brazil ... 52 G3
Bauska • Latvia ... 13 N1
Bautzen • Germany ... 9 J5
Bavarian Alps • Germany ... 111 A8
Bávaro • Dominican Rep. ... 159 G8
Bavella, Col de • Corsica, France ... 115 L4

Båven • Sweden ... 125 D3
Baw Sang • Thailand ... 142 B1
Bawamataluo • Indonesia ... 143 G3
Bawe • Indonesia ... 32 (1) D3
Bawiti • Egypt ... 131 F3
Bawku • Ghana ... 22 D2
Baxoi • China ... 28 G2
Bay Area • CA, United States ... 152 C3
Bay City • MI, United States ... 44 D4
Bay City • TX, United States ... 154 J6
Bay Is. • Honduras ... 160 A11
Bay Minette • AL, United States ... 48 D5
Bay of Islands • New Zealand ... 35 E2
Bay of Isles • South Georgia ... 81 A10
Bay of Plenty [Adm] • New Zealand ... 145 L1
Bay Shore • NY, United States ... 44 I5
Bay St Louis • MS, United States ... 48 C5
Bay View • New Zealand ... 145 F4
Bayad, Al • Saudi Arabia ... 18 E5
Bayadh, El • Algeria ... 20 F2
Bayah Har Shan • China ... 28 G2
Bayahibe • Dominican Rep. ... 159 G8
Bayamo • Cuba ... 158 D8
Bayamón • Puerto Rico ... 159 H2
Bayan • Mongolia ... 26 Q9
Bayan Har Shan • China ... 29 B4
Bayan Lepas • Penang, Malaysia ... 141 F3
Bayan Lepas [Apt] • Penang, Malaysia ... 141 F3
Bayan Obo • China ... 29 D2
Bayan Uul • Mongolia ... 27 H7
Bayana • India ... 137 C6
Bayanga • Central African Rep. ... 23 B3
Bayard • NM, United States ... 45 H5
Bayda, Al • Libya ... 21 D1
Baydaratskaya Guba • Russian Fed. ... 26 K4
Bayerische Alpen • Germany ... 112 F7
Bayerischer Wald • Germany ... 9 I8
Bayern • Germany ... 9 G8
Bayeux • France ... 114 E4
Baykal, Ozero • Russian Fed. ... 25 L4
Baykalsky Khrebet • Russian Fed. ... 27 G6
Baykit • Russian Fed. ... 26 O5
Bayona • Spain ... 11 C2
Bayonne • France ... 115 J1
Bayou Bodcau Reservoir • LA, United States ... 47 H1
Bayou Cane • LA, United States ... 48 B6
Bayou D'Arbonne Lake • LA, United States ... 47 H1
Bayramaly • Turkmenistan ... 18 H2
Bayramiç • Turkey ... 15 H4
Bayreuth • Germany ... 9 G7
Bayrischer Wald, Nationalpark Park N • Germany ... 89 [64]
Bayrischzell Ski • Germany ... 100 [4]
Bayrischzell • Germany ... 112 F7
Bayrischzell Spa • Germany ... 113 [h14]
Bayrut • Lebanon ... 18 B3
Bays, Lake of • OT, Canada ... 44 F3
Baytik Shan • China ... 26 O8
Baytown • TX, United States ... 154 J5
Bayy al Kabir • Libya ... 21 B1
Baza • Spain ... 11 B4
Bazar Dyuzi • Azerbaijan ... 17 H6
Bazas • France ... 115 G3
Be'er Shiva • Israel ... 18 B3
Beach • ND, United States ... 43 E3
Beachy Head • United Kingdom ... 104 E3
Beacon • NY, United States ... 44 I5
Béalanana • Madagascar ... 24 H2
Bear, Cap • France ... 115 K2
Bear Cove • BC, Canada ... 155 C3
Bear I. • Ireland ... 108 C7
Bear Lake • ID, United States ... 42 J5
Bear Mtn Ski • CA, United States ... 149 [73]
Bear Valley Ski • CA, United States ... 149 [66]
Beara Peninsula • Ireland ... 108 C7
Beardmore • OT, Canada ... 43 M2
Beardstown • IL, United States ... 46 J2
Béarn • France ... 115 J2
Bearpaw Mtns • MT, United States ... 42 K2
Beata, Cabo • Dominican Rep. ... 159 G6
Beata, I. • Dominican Rep. ... 159 G6
Beatrice • NE, United States ... 46 G2
Beatty • OR, United States ... 42 E5
Beatty • NV, United States ... 152 C4
Beau Bassin • Mauritius ... 132 J3
Beau Vallon, Baie • Seychelles ... 133 K1
Beaufort • Malaysia ... 32 F1
Beaufort • Luxembourg ... 109 D20
Beaufort • SC, United States ... 48 G4
Beaufort I. • Hong Kong, China ... 139 B6
Beaufort Sea • Arctic Ocean ... 36 C2
Beaufort West • South Africa ... 134 C3
Beaugency • France ... 114 D2
Beaujolais • France ... 114 B4
Beaulieu-sur-Mer • France ... 115 H2
Beaumaris Beach • United Kingdom ... 101 [236]
Beaumont • France ... 5 B5
Beaumont • New Zealand ... 145 G4
Beaumont • TX, United States ... 154 J4
Beaune • France ... 114 B4
Beauport • QU, Canada ... 10 J6
Beaupré • QU, Canada ... 44 J2
Beauregard [Château] • France ... 114 D2
Beauséjour • Fort NB, Canada ... 156 D7
Beauté, I. de • France ... 114 B4
Beauvais • France ... 115 E1
Beauval • SA, Canada ... 38 J5
Beauvoir-sur-Mer • France ... 10 C7
Beaver • UT, United States ... 45 F2
Beaver • OK, United States ... 46 F4
Beaver Creek Ski • CO, United States ... 149 [104]
Beaver Creek • YT, Canada ... 49 M3
Beaver Dam • WI, United States ... 43 L5
Beaver Falls • PA, United States ... 44 E5
Beaver I • MI, United States ... 44 C3
Beaver Lake • AR, United States ... 46 I4
Beaver [Riv] • OK, United States ... 46 F4
Beaver Valley Ski • OT, Canada ... 149 [23]
Beavercreek • OH, United States ... 44 C6
Beaverton • OR, United States ... 42 E3
Beawar • India ... 137 C6
Bebedouro • Brazil ... 52 G3
Bebra • Germany ... 9 E6
Becal • Mexico ... 157 H3
Becan • Mexico ... 157 H3
Becej • F.R. of Yugoslavia ... 14 H4
Béchar • Algeria ... 20 E2
Bechet • Romania ... 14 K6
Bechyne • Czech Rep. ... 128 B4
Beckum • Germany ... 8 D5
Bective Abbey • Ireland ... 108 I1
Bedarra I. • QL, Australia ... 144 F3
Bedburg • Germany ... 111 B3
Bedford • United Kingdom ... 7 L9
Bedford • IN, United States ... 44 B6
Bedford • KY, United States ... 48 E1
Bedford • PA, United States ... 153 D5
Bedford Level • United Kingdom ... 5 C2

Bedulu • Bali, Indonesia ... 143 H4
Beech Grove • IN, United States ... 44 B6
Beechy • SA, Canada ... 42 L1
Beef I. [Apt] • British Virgin Is. ... 160 B
Beek [Apt] • Netherlands ... 109 D15
Beekse Bergen • Netherlands ... 109 D11
Beemster, Droogmakerij de Heritage C • Netherlands ... 86 [30]
Beemster Polder Heritage C • Netherlands ... 86 [30]
Beersheba • Israel ... 135 A7
Beesands Beach • United Kingdom ... 101 [125]
Beeston • United Kingdom ... 7 K9
Beeville • TX, United States ... 154 J5
Bega • NS, Australia ... 144 C4
Begejski Kanal • F.R. of Yugoslavia/Romania ... 14 H4
Begna • Norway ... 16 E6
Begur Beach • Spain ... 96 [123]
Begur • Spain ... 117 D2
Beherobie • France ... 115 J1
Behshahr • Iran ... 18 F2
Bei Jiang • China ... 31 E2
Bei'an • China ... 27 K7
Beida He • China ... 29 B3
Beihai • China ... 29 D6
Beijing • China ... 29 F3
Beijing Heritage C • China ... 85 [165-167]
Beijing [Adm] • China ... 139 A3
Beila • Mauritania ... 20 B5
Beilstein • Germany ... 112 E3
Beira • Mozambique ... 24 E3
Beira Alta • Portugal ... 11 D4
Beira Baixa • Portugal ... 11 D5
Beira Litoral • Portugal ... 11 C4
Beirut • Lebanon ... 18 B3
Beit el Wali • Egypt ... 131 F5
Beitbridge • Zimbabwe ... 134 D1
Beius • Romania ... 14 J3
Beja • Portugal ... 11 D6
Béja • Tunisia ... 131 E1
Beja [Adm] • Portugal ... 118 A3
Béjaïa • Algeria ... 20 G1
Béjar • Spain ... 11 F4
Beji Temple • Bali, Indonesia ... 143 H2
Bekal • India ... 138 D6
Bekasi • Java, Indonesia ... 143 J1
Bekdash • Turkmenistan ... 18 F1
Békés • Hungary ... 13 K11
Bekily • Madagascar ... 24 H4
Bel Air • Mauritius ... 132 J4
Bela • Pakistan ... 28 A3
Bela, Costa • Portugal ... 118 D2
Bela Crkva • F.R. of Yugoslavia ... 14 I5
Bela Pratapgarh • India ... 137 C8
Bela Vista • Mozambique ... 24 E5
Belaga • Malaysia ... 32 J2
Belang • Indonesia ... 32 (1) B2
BELARUS • Europe ... 17 D4
Belawan • Indonesia ... 143 G2
Belaya • Russian Fed. ... 4 V6
Belaya • Russian Fed. ... 27 T3
Belayan • Indonesia ... 32 F2
Belchatów • Poland ... 13 I6
Belchen • Germany ... 112 D8
Belcher Is. • NU, Canada ... 39 P5
Belchite • Spain ... 10 E12
Beldibi Beach • Turkey ... 97 [227]
Beldibi • Turkey ... 123 F3
Beled Weyne • Somalia ... 23 H3
Belek Beach • Turkey ... 97 [224]
Belek • Turkey ... 123 F4
Belém • Brazil ... 53 (1) B2
Belém • Portugal ... 118 D1
Belén • France ... 123 G4
Belen • NM, United States ... 153 E2
Belep, Is. • New Caledonia ... 35 (2) A2
Beleye • Ethiopia ... 23 F1
Belfast • United Kingdom ... 7 G7
Belfast • MI, United States ... 44 K3
Belfield • ND, United States ... 43 E3
Belfort • United Kingdom ... 6 I6
Belfort • France ... 10 L6
Belfort • Lebanon ... 135 A2
Belfry, The • United Kingdom ... 104 D2
Belgaum • India ... 138 D2
BELGIUM • Europe ... 109
Belgodere • Corsica, France ... 115 L1
Belgorod • Russian Fed. ... 17 F4
Belgrade • F.R. of Yugoslavia ... 14 H5
Belgrade • MT, United States ... 42 J4
Belhaven Bay Beach • United Kingdom ... 101 [17]
Bélice • Sicily, Italy ... 120 D1
Beliche • Portugal ... 118 E5
Bélinga • Gabon ... 22 G4
Belisirma • Turkey ... 123 G3
Beltung • Indonesia ... 32 D3
BELIZE • C. America ... 37 D4
Belize City • Belize ... 37 D4
Beljanica • F.R. of Yugoslavia ... 14 I5
Bell • QU, Canada ... 39 P7
Bell Peninsula • NU, Canada ... 39 O4
Bell Ville • Argentina ... 52 D5
Bella Coola • BC, Canada ... 38 H4
Bella Vista • AR, United States ... 46 H4
Bellac • France ... 114 D4
Belladère • Haiti ... 159 G6
Bellágio • Italy ... 121 E2
Bellaire • TX, United States ... 159 H6
Bellamonte Ski • Italy ... 100 [223]
Bellamonte • Italy ... 120 B3
Bellaria • Italy ... 12 G4
Bellavista • Italy ... 138 D2
Belle Fourche • SD, United States ... 43 E4
Belle Fourche [Riv] • SD/WY, United States ... 43 D5
Belle Glade • FL, United States ... 154 H6
Belle Ile • France ... 114 C4
Belle Isle • IL, United States ... 151 C2
Belle Isle • NF, Canada ... 156 D5
Belle Isle, Strait of • NF, Canada ... 156 D5
Belle Mare Beach • Mauritius ... 132 J2
Belle-Anse • Haiti ... 159 G6
Belleayre Ski • NY, United States ... 149 [192]
Belleayre • NY, United States ... 153 D3
Bellefontein • OH, United States ... 44 D5
Bellegarde-sur-Valserine • France ... 115 F1
Bellepais Abbey • Cyprus ... 123 J1
Belleterre • QU, Canada ... 44 F2
Belleville • KS, United States ... 46 G3
Belleville • IL, United States ... 46 K3
Belleville • OT, Canada ... 155 B6
Belleville • OH, United States ... 44 D5
Belleville • NT, United States ... 46 H2
Belleville • WA, United States ... 152 B1
Bellevue, Col • Réunion ... 132 H4
Bellevue, Grotte de • France ... 115 G4
Bellewaerde Park Park L • Belgium ... 98 [46]
Bellewaerde Park • Belgium ... 109 D13
Bellingham • WA, United States ... 152 B1
Bellingshausen [Base] • Antarctica ... 54 (1) JJ4
Bellingshausen Sea • Pacific Ocean ... 54 (1) GG4
Bellinzona • Switzerland ... 119 G7

Bello • Colombia ... 51 B2
Bellows Falls • VT, United States ... 44 I4
Belluno • Italy ... 120 B4
Bellville • South Africa ... 134 C5
Bellwald • Switzerland ... 119 G6
Belm • Germany ... 8 D4
Belmonte • Brazil ... 52 I2
Belmopan • Belize ... 37 D4
Belmullet Beach • Ireland ... 96 [63]
Belmullet • Ireland ... 108 C1
Belo Horizonte • Brazil ... 163 C1
Belo Tsiribihina • Madagascar ... 24 G3
Belogorsk • Russian Fed. ... 27 K6
Beloit • WI, United States ... 43 L5
Beloix • KS, United States ... 46 F3
Belomorsk • Russian Fed. ... 17 F2
Beloretsk • Russian Fed. ... 26 I7
Belot, Lac • NT, Canada ... 38 F3
Belovezhskaya Pushcha Heritage N • Belarus/Poland ... 83 [57]
Belovo • Russian Fed. ... 26 O7
Beloye More • Russian Fed. ... 17 F1
Beloye Ozero • Russian Fed. ... 17 F2
Belozersk • Russian Fed. ... 17 F3
Belp [Apt] • Switzerland ... 119 G2
Belton • MO, United States ... 46 H3
Belton • TX, United States ... 47 F2
Belton Reservoir • TX, United States ... 47 F2
Belukha, gora • Kazakstan/Russian Fed. ... 26 O8
Belur • India ... 138 D6
Belvidere • IL, United States ... 46 K1
Belvoir • Israel ... 135 A4
Belyando • QL, Australia ... 144 B3
Belyy, Ostrov • Russian Fed. ... 26 L3
Belz • Ukraine ... 13 N5
Bembé • D.R. of Congo ... 22 G6
Bembibre • Spain ... 11 D2
Bembridge • Cook Is. ... 33 K8
Bemidji • MN, United States ... 43 I3
Ben Gardane • Tunisia ... 131 E6
Ben Mehidi • Algeria ... 12 B12
Bena Dibele • Dem. Rep. of Congo ... 23 C4
Benagoil • Ireland ... 10 F11
Benago Beach • Grenada ... 160 S
Benalla • VI, Australia ... 144 C3
Benalmádena Beach • Spain ... 96 [114]
Benalmádena Costa • Spain ... 116 B7
Benares • India ... 137 C8
Benavente • Portugal ... 118 D2
Benavente • Spain ... 11 F3
Benbulbin • Ireland ... 108 C2
Bend • OR, United States ... 152 B3
Bendara, Bukit • Penang, Malaysia ... 141 F1
Bendel • Nigeria ... 22 F3
Bender • Moldova ... 14 O3
Bender Bayla • Somalia ... 23 I2
Bendigo • VI, Australia ... 144 C3
Bendinat, Castell de • Majorca, Spain ... 117 H3
Bénémérail [Apt] • France ... 112 E1
Bénéna • Mali ... 20 E6
Benenden Prinsen • St Maarten ... 128 B2
Benevento • Severocesky, Czech Rep. ... 128 B2
Benevento • Italy ... 121 G2
Bengal, Bay of • Indian Ocean ... 28 E5
Bengbu • China ... 29 F4
Benghazi • Libya ... 21 C1
Bengkalis • Indonesia ... 32 C2
Bengkulu • Indonesia ... 32 C3
Bengo, Baia do • Angola ... 22 G6
Bengough • SA, Canada ... 43 D2
Bengtsfors • Sweden ... 125 F2
Benguela • Angola ... 23 A6
Benguerir • Morocco ... 131 D3
Bengut, Cap • Algeria ... 20 F1
Beni • Dem. Rep. of Congo ... 23 D3
Beni • Bolivia ... 52 C1
Beni Abbès • Algeria ... 20 E2
Beni Bouffah • Morocco ... 11 G9
Beni Hammad Heritage C • Algeria ... 86 [258]
Beni Hasan • Egypt ... 131 F3
Beni Mellal • Morocco ... 20 D2
Beni Saf • Algeria ... 11 J9
Beni Suef • Egypt ... 131 F1
Benicarló • Spain ... 11 L4
Benicàssim Beach • Spain ... 96 [120]
Benicàssim Beach • Spain ... 96 [119]
Benidorm Beach • Spain ... 96 [118]
Benidorm • Spain ... 117 C2
BENIN • Africa ... 22 E3
Benin, Bight of • Nigeria ... 22 E3
Benin City • Nigeria ... 22 F3
Benin Forcados • Nigeria ... 22 E3
Benissa Beach • Spain ... 96 [118]
Benissa • Spain ... 117 C2
Bénitiers, I. aux • Mauritius ... 132 J3
Benito Juárez • Argentina ... 163 D3
Benito Juárez [Apt] • Mexico ... 157 G4
Benitses • Corfu, Greece ... 122 B1
Benjamin Constant • Brazil ... 51 D4
Benjamin Hill • Mexico ... 157 F2
Benkovac • Croatia ... 14 C5
Benllech Beach • United Kingdom ... 101 [232]
Bennettsville • SC, United States ... 48 H3
Bennington • VT, United States ... 153 D3
Benny • OT, Canada ... 44 E2
Benoa Port • Bali, Indonesia ... 143 H4
Benoni • Malaysia ... 141 G2
Benone Beach • United Kingdom ... 101 [247]
Benoni • South Africa ... 24 D5
Bénoué • Cameroon/Chad ... 22 G3
Bénoué, Parc nat. de la Park • Cameroon ... 133 [39]
Benrath Castle • Germany ... 113 [28]
Benrath, Schloss • Germany ... 111 B3
Bensafrim • Portugal ... 118 E5
Bensberg (Bergisch Gladbach) • Germany ... 111 B4
Bensheim • Germany ... 112 E4
Benson • AZ, United States ... 153 E4
Bent's Old Fort Nat. Hist. Site Park N • CO, United States ... 150 [96]
Benteng • Sebarang • Malaysia ... 141 G2
Benteng • Togian, Indonesia ... 32 (1) B3
Benteng • Selajar, Indonesia ... 32 (1) B4
Bentiu • Sudan ... 23 D2
Benton • AR, United States ... 46 I5
Benton Harbor • MI, United States ... 44 B4
Bentota • Sri Lanka ... 138 D15
Bentota Beach • Sri Lanka ... 138 D15
Benue • Nigeria ... 22 G3
Benue [Adm] • Nigeria ... 22 G3
Benwee Head • Ireland ... 108 C1
Benxi • China ... 29 G2
Beo • Indonesia ... 32 (1) C2
Beograd • F.R. of Yugoslavia ... 14 H5
Beppu • Japan ... 30 F8
Bequia • St Vincent & Gren. ... 161 E2

Ber-Chogur • Kazakstan ... 26 I8
Berach • India ... 137 C6
Berane • F.R. of Yugoslavia ... 15 A3
Berat • Albania ... 15 A3
Beratus, Gunung • Indonesia ... 32 F3
Berbérati • Central African Rep. ... 23 B3
Berchtesgaden • Germany ... 112 F8
Berchtesgaden, Nationalpark Park N • Germany ... 89 [65]
Berchtesgaden, Nationalpark • Germany ... 112 F8
Berck • France ... 10 G3
Berck-sur-Mer Beach • France ... 96 [75]
Berdichiv • Ukraine ... 17 D5
Berdyans'k • Ukraine ... 17 F5
Berea • KY, United States ... 48 E2
Berechid • Morocco ... 131 D1
Berettyóújfalu • Hungary ... 13 K10
Bereznik • Russian Fed. ... 17 G2
Bereznik • Russian Fed. ... 26 I6
Berezovo • Russian Fed. ... 26 J5
Berg • Germany ... 112 F3
Berga • Spain ... 117 D1
Berga • Sweden ... 125 F7
Bergama • Turkey ... 122 D5
Bérgamo • Italy ... 121 E6
Bergara • Spain ... 11 I1
Bergby • Sweden ... 16 I6
Bergeggi Beach • Italy ... 96 [141]
Bergen • Niedersachsen, Germany ... 8 E4
Bergen • Mecklenburg-Vorpommern, Germany ... 8 I2
Bergen Heritage C • Norway ... 86 [1]
Bergen • Norway ... 124 C3
Bergen op Zoom • Netherlands ... 109 D10
Bergerac • France ... 115 G2
Bergisch Gladbach • Germany ... 111 B4
Bergischer Dom • Germany ... 111 B4
Bergkamen • Germany ... 111 B2
Bergkvara • Sweden ... 125 F12
Bergnäsudd • Sweden ... 125 D2
Bergsjö • Sweden ... 16 G6
Bergville • South Africa ... 134 B3
Berhampur • India ... 28 E4
Bering Land Bridge Nat. Preserve Park N • AK, United States ... 150 [1]
Bering Sea • Russian Fed./US ... 49 F4
Bering Strait • Russian Fed./US ... 49 H2
Bering, Ostrov • Russian Fed. ... 27 S5
Beringen • Belgium ... 5 I3
Beringov Proliv • Russian Fed. ... 27 X3
Berja • Spain ... 11 I8
Berkåk • Norway ... 16 F5
Berkakit • Russian Fed. ... 27 J5
Berkel • Netherlands ... 109 F4
Berkner I. • Antarctica ... 54 (1) JJ2
Berkshire Downs • United Kingdom ... 7 K10
Berkshire East Ski • MA, United States ... 149 [203]
Berkshire East • MA, United States ... 153 D3
Berlengas, Is. • Portugal ... 11 B5
Berlevåg • Norway ... 16 O1
Berlin Heritage C • Germany ... 86 [39-40]
Berlin • Germany ... 111 C2
Berlin • NH, United States ... 44 J3
Berlin [Adm] • Germany ... 111 C2
Bermejo • Argentina ... 52 C5
Bermeo • Spain ... 10 C10
Bermeo Beach • Spain ... 96 [88]
Bermillo de Sayago • Spain ... 11 E3
BERMUDA • Atlantic Ocean ... 159 J
Bermuda Aquarium • Bermuda ... 159 J3
Bermuda Beach • Bermuda ... 159 J3
Bermuda I • Bermuda ... 159 J3
Bermuda Maritime Museum • Bermuda ... 159 J1
Bern Heritage C • Switzerland ... 86 [120]
Bern • Switzerland ... 119 G2
Bernalda • Italy ... 12 K8
Bernalillo • NM, United States ... 45 I4
Bernau • Germany ... 111 G1
Bernau bei Berlin • Germany ... 111 C2
Bernay • France ... 114 D1
Bernburg • Germany ... 8 G5
Berne Heritage C • Switzerland ... 86 [120]
Berne • Switzerland ... 119 G2
Berner Alpen • Switzerland ... 119 G2
Berner Oberland • Switzerland ... 119 G2
Bernina, Passo del • Switzerland ... 119 G8
Bernina, Piz • Italy/Switzerland ... 119 G8
Bernkastel-Kues • Germany ... 112 E3
Beroroha • Madagascar ... 24 H4
Beroun • Germany ... 13 D8
Berounka • Czech Rep. ... 128 B1
Berovo • F.Y.R. of Macedonia ... 15 D2
Berrow Beach • United Kingdom ... 101 [153]
Berry • France ... 10 H7
Berry Is. • Bahamas ... 158 B1
Bertioga • Brazil ... 163 C3
Bertoua • Cameroon ... 22 G4
Beruas • Malaysia ... 141 G1
Beruwala • Sri Lanka ... 138 D15
Berwick • PA, United States ... 44 G5
Berwick-upon-Tweed • United Kingdom ... 6 J6
Besakih Temple • Bali, Indonesia ... 143 H2
Besalampy • Madagascar ... 24 H4
Besançon • France ... 10 L6
Besar, Gunung • Indonesia ... 32 F3
Besikama • Indonesia ... 32 (1) B4
Beskid Niski • Poland ... 13 K8
Beskra • Turkey ... 14 P5
Besna Kobila • F.R. of Yugoslavia ... 14 J7
Besparmak Dagi • Turkey ... 123 F4
Bessarabia • Moldova ... 14 P2
Bessemer • AL, United States ... 48 D4
Bestensee • Germany ... 111 C4
Bestyakh • Russian Fed. ... 27 J3
Betafo • Madagascar ... 24 H3
Betancuria • Fuerteventura, Canary Is. ... 117 E2
Betanzos, Ria de • Spain ... 11 C1
Betatakin • AZ, United States ... 45 I4
Betence • France ... 115 J1
Beth Horon • Palestine ... 135 A5
Beth-zur • Palestine ... 135 A6
Bethany • OK, United States ... 46 I2
Bethany • MO, United States ... 46 I2
Bethany Beach • DE, United States ... 153 D10
Béthel • Palestine ... 135 A5
Bethel Park • PA, United States ... 44 E5
Bethesda • MD, United States ... 44 F6
Bethesdaweg • South Africa ... 134 C4
Bethlehem • South Africa ... 24 D5
Bethlehem • Palestine ... 135 A7

Bethlehem • PA, United States ... 153 D6
Béthune • France ... 10 H3
Béthune [Riv] • France ... 5 E5
Betioky • Madagascar ... 137 C8
Betong • Malaysia ... 141 F3
Bétou • Congo ... 23 G1
Betpaqdala • Kazakstan ... 26 K8
Betroka • Madagascar ... 24 H4
Bette • Libya ... 21 C3
Bettendorf • IA, United States ... 46 J2
Bettex, le Ski • France ... 100 [26]
Bettmeralp Ski • Switzerland ... 100 [94]
Bettmeralp • Switzerland ... 119 G6
Bettna • Sweden ... 125 D3
Betul • Madhya Pradesh, India ... 28 C4
Betul • Goa, India ... 137 B2
Betul Beach • Goa, India ... 137 B2
Betwa • India ... 137 C7
Betzdorf • Germany ... 9 C6
Beuil-les-Launes Ski • France ... 100 [74]
Beulah • ND, United States ... 43 E3
Beuren, Kloster • Germany ... 112 D8
Beveridge • Cook. Is. ... 33 K8
Beverley • United Kingdom ... 7 I8
Beverly Hills • ... 45 C4
Beverungen • Germany ... 8 E5
Beverwijk • Netherlands ... 109 F1
Bexhill-on-Sea Beach • United Kingdom ... 101 [81]
Bexhill-on-Sea • United Kingdom ... 104 E4
Bey Daglari • Turkey ... 123 F3
Beykoz • Turkey ... 123 E1
Beymelek • Kazakstan ... 26 I8
Beyneu • Kazakstan ... 18 G1
Beypazari • Turkey ... 15 M3
Beysehir • Turkey ... 123 F2
Beysehir Gölü • Turkey ... 126 C2
Bezhetsk • Russian Fed. ... 17 E3
Béziers • France ... 10 I10
Bhadravati • India ... 138 D6
Bhagalpur • India ... 28 E3
Bhaktapur • Nepal ... 137 C4
Bhamo • Myanmar ... 31 B2
Bharatpur • India ... 137 C2
Bharuch • India ... 28 B4
Bhatinda • India ... 28 B4
Bhatpara • India ... 28 E4
Bhavnagar • India ... 28 B4
Bhawanipatna • India ... 28 E4
Bheemunipatnam Beach • India ... 138 E4
Bhekuzulu • South Africa ... 134 B1
Bheri • Nepal ... 28 D3
Bhojpur • India ... 137 C6
Bhilwara • India ... 137 C6
Bhima • India ... 28 C4
Bhiwani • India ... 137 C2
Bhopal • India ... 28 C4
Bhubaneswar • India ... 28 E4
Bhuj • India ... 28 A4
Bhumiphol Reservoir • Thailand ... 142 B3
BHUTAN • Asia ... 28 E3
Bi'r al Hakim • Libya ... 21 D1
Bi'r al Wa'r • Libya ... 21 B3
Bi'r Allaq • Libya ... 21 A2
Bi'r Misalah • Egypt ... 21 E3
Bia Nat. Park • Ghana ... 133 [25]
Biabou • St Vincent & Gren. ... 161 Q
Biafra, Bight of • Africa ... 22 F4
Biak • Indonesia ... 32 (1) E3
Biak [I.] • Indonesia ... 32 (1) E3
Biala Podlaska • Poland ... 13 M5
Biala Slatina • Bulgaria ... 14 K6
Bialogard • Poland ... 13 G2
Bialowieski Nat. Park Park N • Poland ... 89 [94]
Bialowieza Forest Heritage N • Belarus/Poland ... 83 [57]
Bialystok • Poland ... 13 M4
Biarritz • France ... 115 J1
Biasca • Switzerland ... 119 G7
Bibai • Japan ... 30 K3
Bibione Beach • Italy ... 96 [164]
Bibione • Italy ... 121 B4
Bicaz • Romania ... 14 M3
Bicholim • Goa, India ... 137 B1
Bickerton I. • NT, Australia ... 34 G2
Bida • Nigeria ... 22 F3
Biddeford • ME, United States ... 44 J4
Bideford • United Kingdom ... 104 F2
Bideford Bay • United Kingdom ... 104 F2
Bidwell Mansion State Hist. Park • CA, United States ... 152 C1
Bie, Planalto do • Angola ... 23 B6
Biebrich Castle • Germany ... 113 [45]
Biebrza • Poland ... 13 L4
Biebrzanski Nat. Park Park N • Poland ... 89 [93]
Biedenkopf • Germany ... 9 D6
Bielefeld • Germany ... 119 G2
Bieler See • Switzerland ... 119 G2
Biella • Italy ... 12 B6
Bielsk Podlaski • Poland ... 13 M5
Bielsko-Biala • Poland ... 13 I8
Bien Hoa • Vietnam ... 141 E1
Bienville, Lac • QU, Canada ... 39 O5
Bierset [Apt] • Belgium ... 109 D19
Biertan Heritage C • Romania ... 86 [195]
Bierut • Netherlands ... 109 D10
Biesbosch • Netherlands ... 109 F4
Biesenthal • Germany ... 111 C2
Bieszczady • Poland ... 13 L8
Bieszczadzki Nat. Park Park N • Poland ... 89 [95]
Bifuka • Japan ... 30 L2
Big Ambergris Cay • Turks & Caicos Is. ... 158 C2
Big Bear Lake • CA, United States ... 152 C6
Big Bend Nat. Park Park N • TX, United States ... 150 [136]
Big Bend Nat. Park • TX, United States ... 47 C3
Big Boulder Ski • PA, United States ... 149 [176]
Big Boulder • PA, United States ... 153 D5
Big Cypress Nat. Preserve Park N • FL, United States ... 151 [220]
Big Cypress Nat. Preserve • FL, United States ... 154 H8
Big Cypress Swamp • FL, United States ... 154 H8
Big Fork • MT, United States ... 42 J3
Big Hole Nat. Battlefield Park N • MT, United States ... 150 [67]
Big Lake • TX, United States ... 47 D2
Big Mtn Ski • MT, United States ... 149 [82]
Big Muddy Lake • SA, Canada ... 43 D2
Big Pine Key • FL, United States ... 154 H8
Big Piney • WY, United States ... 42 J5
Big Powderhorn Mtn Ski • MI, United States ... 149 [136]
Big Rapids • MI, United States ... 44 C4

Big Sand Cay • Turks & Caicos Is. ... 158 C2
Big Sheep Range • MT, United States ... 43 C3
Big Sioux • IA/SD, United States ... 38 L8
Big Sky Ski • MT, United States ... 149 [83]
Big Smoky Valley • NV, United States ... 152 C4
Big Snowy Mtns • MT, United States ... 42 K3
Big Spring • TX, United States ... 47 D1
Big Sur • CA, United States ... 152 C3
Big Thicket Nat. Preserve Park N • TX, United States ... 151 [142]
Big Thicket Nat. Preserve • TX, United States ... 154 J4
Big Timber • MT, United States ... 42 K4
Big Trout Lake • OT, Canada ... 39 M6
Big Vanilla at Davos Ski • NY, United States ... 149 [190]
Big White Ski • BC, Canada ... 149 [6]
Bigadiç • Turkey ... 15 I3
Bigadic • Turkey ... 122 D6
Bigbury Bay • United Kingdom ... 104 F5
Bigbury-on-Sea Beach • United Kingdom ... 101 [129]
Biggar • United Kingdom ... 104 B4
Biggs • OR, United States ... 42 E4
Bighorn Canyon Nat. Recreation Area Park N • MT, United States ... 150 [68]
Bighorn Lake • MT/WY, United States ... 42 K4
Bighorn Mtns • WY, United States ... 42 L2
Bignona • France ... 115 J2
Biguglia, Etang de • Corsica, France ... 115 L2
Bihac • Bosnia-Herz. ... 14 C5
Bihar • India ... 28 E4
Bihar [Adm] • India ... 28 E4
Biharamulo • Tanzania ... 130 B1
Bihoro • Japan ... 30 M3
Bijapur • India ... 138 D2
Bijawar • India ... 137 C6
Bijeljina • Bosnia-Herz. ... 14 G5
Bijoutier • Seychelles ... 133 K4
Bikaner • India ... 137 C1
Bikin • Russian Fed. ... 29 I1
Bikin [Riv] • Russian Fed. ... 28 M7
Bikini • Marshall Is. ... 33 H4
Bikoro • Dem. Rep. of Congo ... 22 H5
Bila Tserkva • Ukraine ... 17 E5
Bilaspur • India ... 28 D4
Bilauktaung Range • Myanmar/Thailand ... 31 B4
Bilbao • Spain ... 11 I1
Bilecik • Turkey ... 15 K3
Bilesha Plain • Kenya ... 23 G3
Bilibino • Russian Fed. ... 27 S3
Bilin • Myanmar ... 142 B3
Bilina • Czech Rep. ... 30 B5
Bill Baggs Cape Florida State Recreation Area • FL, United States ... 154 H8
Billings • MT, United States ... 42 K4
Billund • Denmark ... 125 F9
Bilma • Niger ... 20 H5
Bilma, Grand Erg de • Niger ... 20 H5
Biloela • QL, Australia ... 144 B4
Bilogora • Croatia ... 14 D4
Bilohorsk • Poland ... 13 L7
Biloku • Guyana ... 51 F3
Biloxi • MS, United States ... 153 F4
Bilthoven • Netherlands ... 109 F2
Biltine • Chad ... 21 D5
Bimberi Peak • AC/NS, Australia ... 34 I7
Bimbo • Central African Rep. ... 23 B3
Bimini Is. • Bahamas ... 158 B1
Bin Qurdan, Jabal • Libya ... 21 C3
Bina • India ... 137 C7
Binbirkilise • Turkey ... 123 G1
Bindura • Zimbabwe ... 130 C2
Binga • Zimbabwe ... 130 C1
Bingemans Action Park Park L • OT, Canada ... 156 [G]
Bingen • Germany ... 112 E4
Bingham • ME, United States ... 44 K3
Binghamton • NY, United States ... 153 D2
Biniancolla • Minorca, Spain ... 117 F4
Binibequer Vell • Minorca, Spain ... 117 F4
Binissafúller • Minorca, Spain ... 117 F4
Binjai • Indonesia ... 143 G2
Bintan • Indonesia ... 32 C2
Bintulu • Malaysia ... 32 E2
Bintumani, Mt Park • Sierra Leone ... 133 [13]
Binz • Germany ... 8 I2
Binz • Germany ... 96 [31]
Binz Spa • Germany ... 113 [c24]
Biobio • Chile ... 53 B3
Biograd na Moru • Croatia ... 12 J5
Biograd na Moru • Croatia ... 128 D3
Biogradska Gora Nat. Park Park N • Fed. Rep. of Yugoslavia ... 89 [119]
Bioko • Equatorial Guinea ... 22 F4
Biokovo • Croatia ... 14 E6
Bir • India ... 28 C5
Bir Gandus • Western Sahara ... 20 B4
Bir Lehlu • Western Sahara ... 20 C3
Bir Mogrein • Mauritania ... 20 C3
Bir Shalatein • Egypt ... 21 G3
Bira Racing Circuit • Thailand ... 142 C4
Birak • Libya ... 21 B2
Biratnagar • India ... 137 C4
Birao • Central African Rep. ... 28 E3
Biratnagar • Nepal ... 28 E3
Birchington Beach • United Kingdom ... 101 [72]
Bird • MN, United States ... 38 M5
Bird I. • Seychelles ... 133 K2
Bird I. [Base] • South Georgia ... 54 (1) B4
Bird of Paradise I. • Trinidad & Tobago ... 160 T
Birdsville • QL, Australia ... 34 G5
Bireuen • Indonesia ... 143 G1
Birganj • Nepal ... 28 D3
Birhet el Bibane • Tunisia ... 131 E6
Birjand • Iran ... 18 G3
Birk, Al • Saudi Arabia ... 18 D6
Birka Heritage C • Sweden ... 125 F1
Birkeland • Norway ... 7 I8
Birkenhead • United Kingdom ... 7 I8
Birkenwerder bei Berlin • Germany ... 111 C1
Birlad • Romania ... 14 O3
Birled [Riv] • Romania ... 14 N3
Birling Gap Beach • United Kingdom ... 101 [84]
Birmingham • United Kingdom ... 104 D2
Birmingham • AL, United States ... 48 D4
Birni Nkonni • Niger ... 20 G6
Birnin • Kiribati ... 33 J6
Birnin Gwari • Nigeria ... 20 G6
Birnin Kebbi • Nigeria ... 22 E2
Birobidzhan • Russian Fed. ... 27 L7
Birr • Ireland ... 7 E8
Birsk • Russian Fed. ... 17 J3
Birstonas • Lithuania ... 126 B5
Birtle • MN, Canada ... 43 F1
Biru • China ... 28 F2
Biryusa • Russian Fed. ... 27 E5
Birzai • Lithuania ... 126 B4
Birżebbuga • Malta ... 123 H4
Bisanadi Game Reserve • Kenya ... 131 G2
Bisau • India ... 137 C2

Biscarosse • France 115 G3
Biscay, Bay of • France 4 J8
Biscayne Bay •
FL, United States 49 C5
Biscayne Nat. Park **Park N** •
FL, United States .... 151 [222]
Biscayne Nat. Park •
FL, United States 154 H8
Bisceglie • Italy 14 D8
Bischofshofen • Austria 9 I8
Bischofswerda • Germany 9 J5
Biscotasi Lake • OT, Canada 44 D2
Biscotasing • OT, Canada 44 D2
Biserta • Tunisia 90 A18
Bisevo • Croatia 128 D3
Bišev's kanal • Croatia 14 D6
Bishkek • Kyrgyzstan 26 I3
Bisho • South Africa 24 D6
Bishop • CA, United States 152 C4
Bishop Auckland •
United Kingdom 7 K7
Bishop's Stortford •
United Kingdom 104 E1
Biskra • Algeria 20 G2
Biskupiec • Poland 13 J4
Bislig • Philippines 31 H5
Bismarck • ND, United States 43 F3
Bismarck Archipelago •
Papua New Guinea 35 (1) D1
Bismarck Sea • Pacific Ocean 35 (1) D1
Bismo • Norway 124 C1
Bison • SD, United States 43 E4
Bissau • Guinea-Bissau 22 A2
Bistcho Lake • AL, Canada 38 H5
Bistrita • Romania 14 L2
Bistrita [Riv] • Romania 14 M2
Bitam • Gabon 22 G4
Bitburg • Germany 112 E3
Bitche • France 5 K5
Bitea • Chad 21 D5
Bithia • Sardinia, Italy 120 C4
Bitkine • Chad 20 I6
Bitola • F.Y.R. of Macedonia 14 I8
Bitonto • Italy 12 K7
Bitra • India 138 D9
Bitterfeld • Germany 8 H5
Bitterfontein • South Africa 24 B6
Bitterroot Range •
ID/MT, United States 152 B2
Bittersweet **Ski** •
MI, United States .... 149 [152]
Bitti • Sardinia, Italy 14 A6
Bitumount • AL, Canada 38 I5
Biu • Nigeria 22 G2
Bivolari • Romania 14 O2
Biwa-ko • Japan 140 B2
Biya • Russian Fed. 26 O7
Biyadoo • Maldives 138 F4
Biysk • Russian Fed. 26 O7
Bizana • South Africa 134 B5
Bizana • South Africa 134 B5
Bizerte • Tunisia 131 E2
Bjarrehalvön • Sweden 125 F11
Bjelolasica • Croatia 14 B4
Bjelovar • Croatia 128 D2
Bjergsted **Beach** • Denmark .... 96 [43]
Bjerringbro • Denmark 125 F9
Bøshkët e Nemuna •
Albania/F.R. of Yugoslavia 14 G7
Bjørkelangen • Norway 124 B2
Björklinge • Sweden 125 D2
Björkö • Sweden 125 D2
Björkvik • Sweden 125 D3
Björna • Sweden 125 E1
Bjørnafjorden • Norway 124 C3
Björneborg • Finland 125 E1
Björnlunda • Sweden 125 D3
Björnön • Arctic Ocean 4 O2
Bla • Mali 22 C2
Blåbjerg **Beach** • Denmark .... 96 [51]
Black Bay • OT, Canada 43 L2
Black Canyon •
AZ/NV, United States 153 E1
Black Canyon City •
United States 45 F4
Black Canyon of the Gunnison Nat. Mon.
Park N • CO, United States .... 150 [89]
Black Country • United Kingdom 104 D2
Black Forest • Germany 112 D8
Black Head • United Kingdom 104 F4
Black Hills •
SD/WY, United States 43 E5
Black Lady Mtn • Vietnam 141 E1
Black Mesa • AZ, United States 45 G3
Black Mesa • OK, United States 46 D4
Black Mountains •
United States 104 D3
Black Mtn • KY, United States 48 F2
Black Range • NM, United States ... 45 I5
Black [Riv] • China/Vietnam 141 D1
Black River • Jamaica 159 F3
Black River Falls •
WI, United States 43 K4
Black Rock Desert •
NV, United States 152 C2
Black Sea • Europe 17 E6
Black Sea Coast • Turkey 122 A3
Black Sea Coast •
Bulgaria/Romania .... 128 E
Black Sea cruise area •
Asia/Europe .... 81 C
Black Sugarloaf, The •
NS, Australia 34 J6
Black Umfolozi • South Africa 134 B2
Blackall • QL, Australia 144 B3
Blackbeard's Grave • Bahamas 158 B3
Blackburn • United Kingdom 7 J8
Blackburn, Mt •
AK, United States 38 C4
Blackdown Hills •
United Kingdom 104 F2
Blacksburg • VA, United States 48 G2
Blacksod Bay • Ireland 108 C1
Blackstone River Valley Nat. Heritage
Corridor • MA, United States 153 D4
Blackwater • Neath, Ireland 108 B1
Blackwater • Cork, Ireland 108 C8
Blackwell • OK, United States 46 C5
Blåfjellhatten • Norway 16 G4
Blagnac [Apt] • France 115 G4
Blagoevgrad • Bulgaria 14 K7
Blagoveshchensk • Russian Fed. 27 K6
Blaine • MN, United States 43 J4
Blaine • WA, United States 152 B1
Blair • NE, United States 46 G2
Blair Athol • QL, Australia 144 B3
Blair Drummond Safari Park •
United Kingdom 104 B3
Blairgowrie • United Kingdom 104 B2
Blaj • Romania 14 K3
Blakely • GA, United States 48 E5
Blambangan, Semenanjung •
Java, Indonesia 143 J10

Blanc, Cap • Majorca, Spain 11 N5
Blanc, Cap • Tunisia 131 E2
Blanc, Mont • France/Italy 115 F2
Blanc Sablon • QU, Canada 156 D5
Blanca, Bahia • Argentina 53 D3
Blanca, Costa • Spain .... 117 C
Blanca, I. • Mexico 157 H2
Blanca Peak • CO, United States ... 40 E4
Blanche, Lake • SA, Australia 34 G5
Blanco • Bolivia 52 D2
Blanco, Cape •
OR, United States 152 B3
Blandford Forum •
United Kingdom 104 F3
Blanding • UT, United States 45 H3
Blanes **Beach** • Spain .... 96 [133]
Blanes • Spain 117 D4
Blangkejeren • Indonesia 143 G1
Blangy-sur-Bresle • France 5 E5
Blankaholm • Sweden 125 F8
Blankenberge • Belgium 109 E2
Blankenfelde • Germany 111 C4
Blankenheim • Germany 112 E1
Blanquilla • Venezuela 51 E1
Blansko • Czech Rep. 13 F8
Blantyre • Malawi 24 F3
Blantyre-Limbe • Malawi 24 E3
Blarney • Ireland 108 C8
Blåsjøen • Norway 124 C6
Blatna • Czech Rep. 128 B3
Blaubeuren • Germany 112 F7
Blåvands Huk **Beach** • Denmark .... 96 [51]
Blåvands Huk • Denmark 125 F9
Blavet • France 114 C4
Blaye • France 115 G1
Błędna • Slovenia 128 D1
Bledos, Is. • Ibiza, Spain 117 G1
Blefjell • Norway 124 B1
Bleikenge • Sweden 125 F12
Blenheim • New Zealand 35 O5
Blenheim • OT, Canada 44 E4
Blenheim Palace **Heritage C** •
United Kingdom .... 86 [23]
Blenheim Palace •
United Kingdom 104 D4
Blessington • Ireland 108 B3
Bletchley • United Kingdom 7 L10
Blida • Algeria 11 N8
Blidö • Sweden 125 D4
Blies • Germany 5 K5
Blieskastel • Germany 112 D3
Bligh Sound • New Zealand 145 G1
Blind River • OT, Canada 39 O7
Blitar • Java, Indonesia 143 J7
Blitta • Togo 22 E3
Blizzard **Beach** •
FL, United States 151 C1
Block I. • RI, United States 153 D8
Block I. Sound •
RI, United States 44 J5
Bloemfontein • South Africa 24 D5
Blois • France 114 D2
Blois [Château] • France 114 D2
Blommesteinmeer, W.J. van, Meer •
Surinam 51 F3
Blood River • South Africa 134 B1
Bloody Bay • Cayman Is. 159 E1
Bloomfield • NM, United States 45 H3
Bloomfield • NM, United States 44 B6
Bloomington • MN, United States ... 43 J4
Bloomsburg • PA, United States 44 G5
Blowing Point • Anguilla .... 160 C
Blowing Point **Beach** • Anguilla .. 160 C
Bludenz • Austria 119 H5
Blue Bay • Mauritius 132 J4
Blue Bell **Dive** • Red Sea 135 B3
Blue Earth • MN, United States 43 I5
Blue Grotto • Malta 123 H4
Blue Hole • Jamaica 159 F2
Blue Lagoon • Malta 123 H1
Blue Mtn **Ski** • OT, Canada .... 149 [24]
Blue Mtn **Ski** •
PA, United States .... 149 [175]
Blue Mtn • CA, United States 42 E6
Blue Mtn • NJ, United States 153 D6
Blue Mtn Lake •
NY, United States 44 H4
Blue Mtn Peak • Jamaica 159 F4
Blue Mtns • NS, Australia 144 C2
Blue Mtns • Jamaica 159 F4
Blue Mtns • OR, United States 152 B4
Blue Nile • Sudan 21 F5
Blue Rapids • KS, United States 46 G3
Blue Ridge •
NC/VA, United States 48 G2
Blue Ridge • United States 152 A8
Blue Ridge Parkway **Park N** •
NC/VA, United States .... 151 [239]
Blue Springs •
MO, United States 46 H3
Blue Star • WA, United States 42 F2
Bluefield • WV, United States 48 G2
Bluefields • Jamaica 159 F1
Bluefields • Nicaragua 37 E5
Bluefields Bay • Jamaica 159 F3
Bluenose Lake • NU, Canada 38 H3
Bluff • New Zealand 145 G4
Bluff • UT, United States 45 H3
Bluff Point • WA, Australia 34 B5
Bluff Point **Dive** • Red Sea 135 B1
Bluff Point Wreck **Dive** •
Red Sea 135 B1
Bluffton • IN, United States 44 C5
Blumberg •
Baden-Württemberg, Germany ... 9 D9
Blumberg • Brandenburg, Germany .. 111 C2
Blumenau • Brazil 52 G4
Blyth • United Kingdom 7 K6
Blythe • CA, United States 45 E5
Blytheville • AR, United States 46 K5
Bo • Sierra Leone 22 B3
Bo • Norway 124 B3
Bo Hai • China 29 F3
Bo Sai • Ko Phuket, Thailand 142 E1
Boa Esperança, Represa • Brazil ... 53 (1) C3
Boa Vista • Cape Verde 22 (1) B1
Boa Vista • Brazil 51 E3
Boac • Philippines 31 G4
Boardman • OH, United States 44 E5
Boaventura • Madeira 118 C1
Boaz I. • Bermuda 158 J3
Bobadilla • Spain 116 B2
Bobbejaanland **Park L** • Belgium .. 98 [48]
Bóbbio • Italy 12 D4
Bobingen • Germany 112 F2
Böblingen • Germany 112 D6
Bobo Dioulasso • Burkina Faso 22 D2
Bóbr • Poland 111 D6
Bóbr • Russian Fed. 17 G4
Boby, Pic • Madagascar 24 H3
Boca Chica • Dominican Rep. 159 G8
Boca de Valeria • Brazil 80 A3
Boca do Acre • Brazil 51 D5
Boca Grande • Venezuela 51 E2
Boca Grande • FL, United States ... 154 H5
Boca Onima Caves • Bonaire .... 160 W
Boca Tabla • Curaçao .... 160 X
Bocaranga •
Central African Rep. 22 H3
Bocas del Amazonas • Brazil 51 H3
Bochnia • Poland 128 C4

Bocholt • Germany 8 B5
Bochsburg **Castle** • Germany ..... 113 [199]
Bochum • Germany 111 B2
Bocognano • Corsica, France 115 L4
Boda • Central African Rep. 22 H4
Bodafors • Sweden 125 F7
Bodaybo • Russian Fed. 27 H5
Boden Bay • Cayman Is. 159 E4
Bodden Town • Cayman Is. 159 E4
Bode • Germany 8 G5
Bodega Bay • CA, United States 45 A2
Bodegraven • Netherlands 109 F3
Bodelé • Chad 21 C4
Boden • Sweden 16 I4
Bodensee • Germany 112 F5
Bodhgaya • India 137 C8
Bodiam Castle • United Kingdom ... 104 E4
Bodmin • United Kingdom 104 E4
Bodmin Moor • United Kingdom 104 E4
Bodø • Norway 16 H3
Bodrum **Beach** • Turkey .... 97 [235]
Bodrum • Turkey 122 D9
Bodufinolhu • Maldives 138 F4
Boduhithi Coral Isle • Maldives 138 F2
Boende • Dem. Rep. of Congo 23 C4
Bœuf, Nez de • Réunion 132 H4
Bogalusa • LA, United States 153 F4
Bogarra • Spain 11 I6
Bogbonga • Dem. Rep. of Congo ... 22 H4
Bogcang Zangbo • China 28 E2
Bogda Feng • China 26 O9
Bogda Shan • China 28 O9
Bogen • Norway 16 I2
Bogenfels • Namibia 24 B5
Bogense • Denmark 125 F10
Boggeragh Mtns • Ireland 108 C8
Boggy Peak • Antigua & Barbuda ... 161 K
Bogia • Papua New Guinea 35 (1) C1
Bognegab **Beach** • Goa, India 137 B1
Bognor Regis **Beach** •
United Kingdom .... 101 [88]
Bognor Regis • United Kingdom 104 E3
Bogolyubovo • Russian Fed. 126 C4
Bogor • Java, Indonesia 143 J1
Bogotá • Colombia 51 C3
Bogotol • Russian Fed. 26 O6
Bogra • Bangladesh 137 D9
Boguchany • Russian Fed. 26 Q6
Bogué • Mauritania 20 C5
Bogue Banks • NC, United States ... 48 I3
Bogue Forts Museum • China 139 B2
Bogus Basin **Ski** •
ID, United States .... 149 [80]
Bohain • Belgium 109 D19
Bohemia • Czech Rep. .... 128 B
Bohemia, Garden of • Czech Rep. .. 128 B2
Bohemian Forest • Germany 111 A6
Bohemian Switzerland •
Czech Rep. 128 B1
Böhmen • Czech Rep. 13 D8
Böhmerwald • Germany 9 H7
Bohol • Philippines 31 G4
Bohol Sea • Philippines 31 G4
Boiaçu • Brazil 51 E4
Boiano • Italy 14 D3
Bois Blanc • Réunion 132 H4
Bois Blanc I. •
MI, United States 44 C3
Bois d'Attilly, Parc zoologique du •
France 115 E4
Bois, Lac des • NT, Canada 38 F3
Bois-Plage-en-Re, le **Beach** •
France .... 96 [84]
Boise • ID, United States 152 B4
Boise City • OK, United States 46 D4
Boissevain • MN, Canada 43 F2
Boizenburg • Germany 8 F3
Bojador, Cabo • Morocco 20 C3
Bojano • Italy 12 I7
Bojnurd • Iran 18 G2
Bojonegoro • Java, Indonesia 143 J3
Bok Tower Gardens •
FL, United States 154 H5
Boka Kotorska •
F.R. of Yugoslavia 14 F7
Bokaro • India 137 C8
Boknafjorden • Norway 124 C5
Boko • Congo 22 G5
Bokol Mayo • Ethiopia 23 G3
Bokoro • Chad 22 H2
Bokpyin • Myanmar 31 B4
Bol • Chad 21 B5
Bolama • Guinea-Bissau 20 B6
Bolans • Antigua & Barbuda .... 161 K
Bole • Ghana 22 D3
Bole • China 26 N9
Bolekhiv • Ukraine 13 M9
Boleslawiec • Poland 13 E6
Bolgatanga • Ghana 22 D2
Bolhrad • Ukraine 14 P4
Bolia • Dem. Rep. of Congo 23 B4
Boliden • Sweden 16 K4
Bolitush • Maldives 138 F4
Boliqueime • Portugal 118 E7
Bolivar • MO, United States 46 I4
Bolivar • TN, United States 46 K4
Bolivar, Cerro • Venezuela 51 C2
Bolivar, Cerro • Venezuela 37 I6
BOLIVIA • S. America 52 D2
Bolivia, Altiplano de • Bolivia 52 C2
Boljevac • Serbia 14 I6
Bolkhov • Russian Fed. 125 F7
Bollnäs • Sweden 16 I6
Bollon • QL, Australia 144 B5
Bolmen • Sweden 125 F7
Bolobo • Dem. Rep. of Congo 23 B4
Bologna • Italy 121 C2
Bolognesi • Peru 51 C6
Bologoye • Russian Fed. 126 C1
Bolomba • Dem. Rep. of Congo 23 B3
Bolomba • Dem. Rep. of Congo 23 C4
Bolovens Plateau • Laos 141 E1
Bolsena • Italy 121 F1
Bolsena, Lago di • Italy 12 G6
Bolshaya Murta • Russian Fed. 26 P6
Bolshevik, Ostrov •
Russian Fed. 4 M2
Bolshezemelskaya Tundra •
Russian Fed. 26 I4
Bolshoy Anyuy • Russian Fed. 27 R3
Bolshoy Begichev, Ostrov •
Russian Fed. 27 H2
Bolshoy Kamen • Russian Fed. 30 G3
Bolshoy Lyakhovskiy, Ostrov •
Russian Fed. 27 N2
Bolsón, Cerro del • Argentina 52 C3
Bolsón de Mapimi • Mexico 40 F6
Bolton • United Kingdom 7 J8
Bolton Valley **Ski** •
VT, United States .... 149 [213]
Bolu • Turkey 15 M3
Bolu Daglari • Turkey 15 N3
Boluntay • China 28 F1
Bolvadin • Turkey 15 N5
Bolzano • Italy 120 B3
Bom Despacho • Brazil 163 C1
Bom Jesus da Lapa • Brazil 52 H1
Boma • Dem. Rep. of Congo 23 A5
Boma • Dem. Rep. of Congo 23 A5
Bomassa • Congo 22 H4
Bombay • India 28 B5
Bomberai, Jazirah • Indonesia .. 32 (1) D3

Bomba • Dem. Rep. of Congo 22 H4
Bomi • China 28 F2
Bomi Hills • Liberia 22 B3
Bamlafjorden • Norway 124 C5
Bømlo • Norway 124 C5
Bommelerwaard • Netherlands 109 F4
Bomu • Central African Rep./Dem.
Rep. of Congo 23 C3
Bon Accueil • Mauritius 132 J2
Bon, Cap • Tunisia 131 E2
Bon Echo Prov. Park •
OT, Canada 155 B6
Bona • Algeria 90 A18
Bonaire • West Indies .... 160 W
Bonao • Dominican Rep. 159 G3
Bonaparte Archipelago •
WA, Australia 34 D3
Bonasse • Trinidad & Tobago ...... 160 U
Bonavista • NF, Canada 156 D4
Bonavista Bay • NF, Canada 156 D4
Bondeno • Italy 12 F4
Bonda Wildlife Sanctuary •
Goa, India 137 B1
Bondo • Dem. Rep. of Congo 23 C3
Bondoukou • Côte d'Ivoire 22 D3
Bondowoso • Java, Indonesia 143 J8
Bonerate, Kepulauan • Indonesia ... 143 F7
Bonete, Cerro • Argentina 52 C4
Bongabong • Philippines 31 G4
Bongandanga •
Dem. Rep. of Congo 23 C3
Bongo • Chad 21 C5
Bongor • Chad 21 C5
Bongolava • Madagascar 24 H3
Bonham **Game Reserve** • Kenya ... 131 G4
Bonifacio • Corsica, France 115 L4
Bonifacio, Strait of •
France/Italy 12 D7
Bonifica del Volturno • Italy 121 G1
Bonin Is. • Japan 140 A13
Bonita, Playa • Cuba 158 D7
Bonita Springs •
FL, United States 154 H7
Bonn • Germany 112 D1
Bonners Ferry •
ID, United States 152 B2
Bonneval • France 114 D2
Bonneville • France 119 G5
Bonneville Salt Flats •
UT, United States 152 C2
Bonny • Nigeria 22 F4
Bonorva • Sardinia, Italy 12 C8
Bontebok Nat. Park **Park** •
South Africa .... 133 [123]
Bontebok Nat. Park •
South Africa 134 C6
Booby Cay • Cayman Is. 159 E3
Booker T. Washington Nat. Mon.
Park N • VA, United States .... 151 [246]
Booligal • NS, Australia 144 C1
Bön Tsagaan Nuur • Mongolia 29 B1
Boone • IA, United States 43 J5
Boone • NC, United States 48 G2
Boonville • MO, United States 46 I3
Boot • United Kingdom 104 C3
Boothia, Gulf of • NU, Canada 38 M2
Boothia Peninsula • NU, Canada ... 38 M2
Booué • Gabon 22 G4
Bopfingen • Germany 9 F8
Bophut **Beach** •
Ko Samui, Thailand 142 D1
Boppard • Germany 112 E2
Boquerón • Puerto Rico 159 H3
Boquerón, Bahía de •
Puerto Rico 159 H3
Boquillas • TX, United States 47 C3
Boquillas del Carmen • Mexico 47 C3
Bor • Russian Fed. 17 G3
Bor • Sudan 23 E2
Bor • Turkey 123 G2
Bor • Czech Rep. 128 B3
Bora Bora • French Polynesia 80 A1
Borah Peak • ID, United States 42 I4
Borås • Sweden 16 G6
Boraema, Planalto da •
Brazil 53 (1) D3
Borca di Cadore • Italy 120 B4
Borchen • Germany 8 D5
Bordeaux • France 115 G3
Bordeaux Mtn • US Virgin Is. ..... 160 Z
Bordeira • Portugal 118 E5
Bordeira • Portugal 118 E7
Borden Peninsula • NU, Canada 38 O2
Bordertown • SA, Australia 34 H7
Bordeyri • Iceland 16 I1 (1/2)
Bordighera **Beach** • Italy .... 96 [104]
Bordighera • Italy 121 E9
Bordj Bou Arreridj • Algeria 20 F1
Bordj el Kiffan • Algeria 11 O8
Bordj Fly St Marie • Algeria 20 E2
Bordj Menaïel • Algeria 11 O8
Bordj Messouda • Algeria 20 G2
Bordj Moktar • Algeria 20 F4
Bordj Omar Driss • Algeria 20 G3
Boreal **Ski** • CA, United States ... 149 [60]
Borensberg • Sweden 125 F4
Boréon, le • France 115 H2
Borgå • Finland 125 E4
Borgafjäll • Sweden 16 H4
Borgarnes • Iceland 16 I1 (1/2)
Børgefjell • Norway 16 G4
Børgefjell Nat. Park **Park N** •
Norway .... 89 [10]
Borger • TX, United States 46 E5
Borgholm **Beach** • Sweden .... 97 [17]
Borgholm • Sweden 125 F8
Borglund stavkirke • Norway 124 B1
Borgo • Corsica, France 115 L2
Borisoglebsk • Russian Fed. 17 G4
Borj Bourguiba • Tunisia 131 E6
Borja • Peru 51 B4
Borken •
Nordrhein-Westfalen, Germany .. 8 B5
Borken • Hessen, Germany 8 E5
Børkop **Beach** • Denmark .... 96 [46]
Borkop • Denmark 125 F9
Borkou • Chad 21 C4
Borkum • Germany 8 B3
Borkum **Spa** • Germany .... 113 [c9]
Borlänge • Sweden 16 H6
Borlu • Turkey 15 J5
Bormes-les-Mimosas **Beach** •
France .... 96 [133]
Bormio **Ski** • Italy .... 100 [209]
Bormio • Italy 121 B3
Borna • Germany 9 H5
Borneo • East Indies .... 96 [35]
Bornholm [Adm] • Denmark 124 A9
Bornholm [I.] • Denmark 125 F15
Bornholmsgattet •
Denmark/Sweden 125 F15
Börnicke • Germany 111 C1
Borno • Nigeria 22 G2
Bornova • Turkey 15 I5
Borobudur **Heritage C** •
Java, Indonesia .... 85 [205]
Borobodur • Java, Indonesia 143 J7
Borodino • Russian Fed. 26 J5
Borohoro Shan • China 25 J5
Boron • East Indies 20 E6
Boron • CA, United States 45 D4
Borovets • Bulgaria 128 A2

Borovichi • Russian Fed. 126 C1
Borroloola • NT, Australia 34 G3
Borrowdale • United Kingdom 104 C2
Borsa • Romania 14 L2
Borth **Beach** • United Kingdom .. 101 [202]
Boryslav • Ukraine 13 M8
Borzya • Russian Fed. 27 I6
Bosa **Beach** • Sardinia, Italy ..... 96 [136]
Bosa • Sardinia, Italy 120 C1
Bosanska Dubica • Bosnia-Herz. ... 12 K3
Bosanska Gradiska •
Bosnia-Herz. 12 L3
Bosanski Petrovac •
Bosnia-Herz. 12 K4
Bosansko • Somalia 23 H1
Boscastle • United Kingdom 104 E4
Boscobel • NY, United States 153 D7
Boscobel House • United Kingdom .. 104 D1
Boscobelle • Barbados .... 161 O
Bosherston **Beach** •
United Kingdom .... 101 [171]
Boshnyakovo, gora •
Russian Fed. 27 N7
Boskoop • Netherlands 109 F3
Bosna • Bosnia-Herz. 14 F5
Bosnia • Bulgaria 15 I1
BOSNIA-HERZEGOVINA • Europe .. 14 F6
Bosnik • Indonesia 32 (1) D3
Boso-hanto • Japan 140 C4
Bosporus • Turkey 15 J3
Bosra **Heritage C** • Syria .... 86 [279]
Bossango •
Central African Rep. 23 B2
Bossangoa • Madagascar 24 H3
Bossembélé •
Central African Rep. 23 B2
Bosso • Niger 20 H6
Bosten Hu • China 26 O9
Boston • United Kingdom 7 L8
Boston • Indonesia 143 J5
Boston • MA, United States 153 D4
Boston African American Nat. Hist. Site
Park N • MA, United States .... 151 [330]
Boston Harbor Is. Nat. Recreation Area
Park N • MA, United States .... 151 [331]
Boston Mills **Ski** •
OH, United States .... 149 [158]
Boston Mtns • AR, United States ... 46 I5
Boston Nat. Hist. Park **Park N** •
MA, United States .... 151 [332]
Boswarsheng Wassenaar •
Netherlands 109 F1
Bosworth Field • United Kingdom .. 104 C1
Botany Bay • NS, Australia 144 C2
Botevgrad • Bulgaria 15 E1
Bothnia, Gulf of •
Finland/Sweden 16 J6
Bothwell Castle •
United Kingdom 104 B3
Botlek • Netherlands 109 F3
Botosani • Romania 14 N2
Botrange • Belgium 5 J4
Botswana • Africa 24 C4
Botte Donato • Italy 12 K9
Bottineau • ND, United States 43 F2
Bottle Creek •
Turks & Caicos Is. 158 C5
Bottrop • Germany 111 B1
Botucatu • Brazil 52 G3
Botwood • NF, Canada 156 D3
Bötzow • Germany 111 C1
Bou Djebéha • Mali 20 E5
Bou Grara, Golfe de • Tunisia 131 E6
Bou Saâda • Algeria 20 F1
Bou Izakarn • Morocco 20 D3
Bou Maad, Djebel • Algeria 11 N8
Bouaké • Côte d'Ivoire 22 C3
Bouar • Central African Rep. 23 A2
Bouârfa • Morocco 20 E2
Bouba Ndjida, Parc nat. de **Park** •
Cameroon .... 133 [40]
Bouca • Central African Rep. 22 H3
Bouchet, le [Château] • France 114 D4
Boudenib • Morocco 20 E2
Boudeuse • Seychelles 133 K2
Boudarik • Asia 11 N8
Bougainville • Papua New Guinea . 35 (1) F2
Bougouni • Mali 22 C2
Bouguenais • France 12 D6
Bouillon • Belgium 109 D19
Bouira • Algeria 11 O8
Boulder • France •
St Barthélemy .... 160 E
Boulder • CO, United States 46 C2
Boulder City •
NV, United States 45 E4
Boulder Peak •
CA, United States 42 E6
Boulogne-Billancourt • France 5 F6
Boulogne-sur-Mer • France 10 G3
Boultoum • Niger 20 H6
Boumois [Château] • France 114 D1
Bouna • Côte d'Ivoire 22 D3
Boundiali • UT, United States 42 J6
Bourail • New Caledonia 35 (2) B3
Bourbonnais • France 44 B5
Bourbonnais • IL, United States ... 44 B5
Bourdeilles • France 115 G2
Bourem • Mali 20 E5
Bourg • France 114 B3
Bourg-en-Bresse • France 115 F3
Bourg-St Maurice • France 115 F2
Bourges • France 10 H6
Bourges **Heritage C** • France ..... 86 [70]
Bourget, le [Apt] • France 115 E2
Bourgneuf, Baie de • France 10 G6
Bourgogne • France 10 J6
Bourgueil • France 114 B1
Bourke • NS, Australia 144 B1
Bournemouth **Beach** •
United Kingdom .... 101 [93-94]
Bournemouth • United Kingdom ... 104 F3
Bournscheid • Luxembourg 109 D20
Bourton-on-the-Water •
United Kingdom 104 D4
Boussay [Château] • France 114 D4
Boussens • France 11 L1
Bousso • Chad 23 B1
Boutilimit • Mauritania 20 C5
Bouvines • France 5 H4
Bouzina • Algeria 90 A7
Bova Marina • Italy 12 J11
Bovalstrand • Sweden 125 F2
Bovec • Slovenia 128 D1
Bovan • St Eustatius .... 161 F
Boven Bolivia • Bonaire .... 160 W
Boven Prinsen • St Maarten .... 160 D
Bovey Tracey • United Kingdom 104 F5
Bovigo • Italy 38 I6
Bow Island • AL, Canada 42 J2
Bowbells • ND, United States 43 E2
Bowdle • SD, United States 43 G4
Bowen • QL, Australia 144 B1
Bowen • TX, United States 154 J1
Bowie •
OH, United States 44 D5
Bowling Green •
MO, United States 46 I3
Bowling Green •
KY, United States 48 D2
Bowman • ND, United States 43 E3
Bowness-on-Windermere •
United Kingdom 104 C3
Bowo • China 28 F2
Bowral • NS, Australia 144 C2
Bowron Lake Prov. Park •
BC, Canada 155 C1

Boxholm • Sweden 125 F4
Boxmeer • Netherlands 5 I3
Boxtel • Netherlands 5 I3
Boyana **Heritage C** • Bulgaria .... 86 [199]
Boyle • Ireland 108 C2
Boyne • Ireland 108 B1
Boyne Highlands **Ski** •
MI, United States .... 149 [139]
Boyne Mtn **Ski** •
MI, United States .... 149 [138]
Boynton **Beach** •
FL, United States 154 H8
Bozcaada • Turkey 15 J3
Bozcaada [I.] • Turkey 122 D2
Bozel • Turkey 15 J6
Boz Dagi • Turkey 15 K6
Boz Daglari • Turkey 15 J5
Bozanski Novi • Bosnia-Herz. 12 K3
Bozashchy Tübegi • Kazakstan 17 J7
Bozburun • Turkey 15 J7
Bozdurun Dagi • Turkey 15 M6
Bozburun • Turkey 15 K4
Bozcaada [I.] • Turkey 122 D2
Bozdogan • Turkey 15 J6
Bozeman • MT, United States 42 J4
Bozen • Italy 120 B3
Bozene • Dem. Rep. of Congo 22 H4
Bozkir • Turkey 123 F2
Bozkir • Turkey 123 G1
Bozouls • France 10 H9
Bozoum • Central African Rep. 23 B2
Bozova • Turkey 123 F1
Bozovici • Romania 14 I5
Bözüyük • Turkey 15 L4
Bozyazi • Turkey 123 G3
Bra • Italy 12 B4
Brabant Wallon • Belgium 109 D15
Bracciano • Italy 128 D4
Bracciano • Italy 121 F1
Bracciano, Lago di • Italy 121 F1
Bracebridge • OT, Canada 44 F3
Bräcke • Sweden 16 H5
Brackenheim • Germany 112 D6
Brackettville •
TX, United States 47 D3
Brackla kanal • Croatia 14 D6
Bracknell • United Kingdom 7 L10
Brad • Romania 14 J3
Bradano • Italy 12 K8
Bradenton • FL, United States 154 H5
Bradford • United Kingdom 7 K8
Bradford • PA, United States 153 D1
Bradley • IL, United States 44 B5
Brady • TX, United States 47 E2
Braemar • United Kingdom 6 I4
Braga • Portugal 11 C3
Braga • Portugal 118 A1
Bragança • Argentina 163 D1
Bragança • Portugal 11 E3
Bragança • Brazil 53 (1) D2
Bragança [Adm] • Portugal 118 A1
Bragança Paulista • Brazil 163 C3
Brahami • Romania 28 E4
Brahestad • Finland 16 M4
Brahmapur • India 28 E3
Brahmaputra • Asia 28 E3
Braila • Romania 128 E2
Brainerd • MN, United States 43 I3
Braithwaite • United Kingdom 104 C1
Braj • India 137 C2
Brake • Germany 8 D3
Brålanda • Sweden 125 F2
Bramadero, Bahía • Puerto Rico ... 159 H3
Bramming • Denmark 125 F9
Brampton • OT, Canada 155 B9
Brampton I. • QL, Australia 144 B3
Bramsche • Germany 8 C4
Branco • Brazil 51 E3
Brand • Austria 119 H5
Brandaris • Bonaire .... 160 W
Brandberg • Namibia 24 A4
Brandbu • Norway 124 B2
Brande • Denmark 125 F9
Brandenburg • Germany 8 H4
Brandenburg [Adm] • Germany 8 I4
Brandenburger Tor • Germany 111 C2
Brandon • MN, Canada 38 I7
Brandon I. • United States 49 B4
Brandon Mtn • Ireland 108 C5
Brands Hatch • United Kingdom ... 104 E1
Brandval • Norway 124 B2
Brandywine **Ski** •
OH, United States .... 149 [158]
Brandywine Battlefield State Hist.
Park • PA, United States 153 D10
Branesti • Romania 128 E1
Branféré, Parc zoologique de •
France 114 C4
Brani • Singapore 141 H4
Braniewo • Poland 13 I3
Bransby Point • Montserrat .... 161 H
Brantas • Java, Indonesia 143 J8
Brantford • OT, Canada 155 B9
Brantley • AL, United States 48 D5
Brantôme • France 115 G2
Bras d'Or Lake • NS, Canada 156 D8
Bras-Panon • Réunion 132 H2
Brasil, Planalto do • Brazil 56 B2
Brasileia • Brazil 51 D6
Brasília • Brazil 52 G2
Brasília **Heritage C** • Brazil ...... 84 [66]
Braslaw • Belarus 16 N9
Brasov • Romania 14 M4
Brass • Nigeria 22 F4
Brasschaat • Belgium 5 H3
Brasstown Bald •
GA, United States 48 F3
Brastagi • Indonesia 143 G2
Brataj • Albania 15 A3
Bratan, Danau • Bali, Indonesia ... 143 H2
Bratislava • Slovak Rep. 13 G9
Bratsk • Russian Fed. 26 R6
Bratskoye Vdkhr. • Russian Fed. ... 27 F5
Brattleboro • VT, United States 153 D3
Brattvåg • Norway 124 C2
Braubach • Germany 112 E2
Braunfels • Germany 112 E2
Braunfels **Castle** • Germany ..... 113 [41]
Braunlage • Germany 50 E5
Braunschweig • Germany 119 G3
Brauweiler • Germany 111 B3
Brava • Cape Verde 22 (1) B2
Brava, Costa • Spain .... 117 D
Braway • CA, United States 45 E5
Bray • Ireland 108 B4
Bray • NU, Canada 39 P3
Bray Head • Ireland 108 B4
Brazey • S. America 44 B6
Brazil • S. America 51 E6
Brazilian Highlands • Brazil 163 A2
Brazo Casiquiare • Venezuela 51 D3
Brazos • TX, United States 154 J3
Brazzaville • Congo 22 H5
Brčko • Bosnia-Herz. 14 F5
Breadalbane • United Kingdom 104 B2
Breakers • Cayman Is. 159 E4
Bream Bay • New Zealand 145 G3
Bream **Beach** • United Kingdom .. 101 [154]
Brebes • Java, Indonesia 143 J2
Breckenridge **Ski** •
CO, United States .... 149 [106]
Breckenridge •
MN, United States 43 H3
Breckenridge •
TX, United States 47 E1
Breckerfeld • Germany 111 B4
Breckland • United Kingdom 5 D2

Breclav • Czech Rep. ... 13 F9
Brecon • United Kingdom ... 7 I10
Brecon Beacons • United Kingdom ... 7 I10
Brecon Beacons Nat. Park Park N • United Kingdom ... 89 [49]
Breda • Netherlands ... 109 D11
Bredasdorp • South Africa ... 134 C6
Bredebro • Denmark ... 125 F13
Bredene-aan-Zee • Belgium ... 109 E1
Bredstedt • Germany ... 8 D2
Bree • Belgium ... 109 D11
Breede • South Africa ... 134 C6
Breganica • F.Y.R. of Macedonia ... 14 J8
Bregenz • Austria ... 119 H1
Bréhat, I. • France ... 114 C2
Breheimen • Norway ... 124 C1
Breidafjördur • Iceland ... 16 [1] B2
Breimsvatnet • Norway ... 124 C1
Breisach • Germany ... 12 D7
Breitachklamm • Germany ... 112 F6
Breitenfeld • Germany ... 90 A8
Brejeira, Serra da • Portugal ... 118 E2
Brekke • Norway ... 124 C3
Brekstad • Norway ... 16 E5
Bremangerlandet • Norway ... 124 C1
Bremen • Germany ... 8 D3
Bremen [Adm] • Germany ... 111 A1
Bremerhaven • Germany ... 8 D3
Bremerton • WA, United States ... 152 B1
Bremervörde • Germany ... 8 E3
Bremnes • Norway ... 124 C3
Brendon Hills • United Kingdom ... 104 F2
Brenham • TX, United States ... 154 J3
Brenner Pass • Austria/Italy ... 119 H7
Brent • OT, Canada ... 44 F2
Brenta • Italy ... 121 E3
Brenta [Riv] • Italy ... 12 F3
Brentwood • United Kingdom ... 7 M10
Brenta • Italy ... 121 E6
Breskens • Netherlands ... 109 D10
Breslau • Poland ... 90 A9
Bressanone • Italy ... 100 [241]
Bressanone • Italy ... 120 B1
Bresse-Hohneck, la Ski • France ... 100 [6]
Bressuire • France ... 114 D3
Brest • Belarus ... 13 M5
Brest • France ... 114 C1
Bretagne • France ... 10 B5
Bretagne, Pont de • Réunion ... 132 H3
Brétignolles-sur-Mer Beach • France ... 96 [83]
Breton, Pertuis • France ... 10 D7
Breton Sound • LA, United States ... 153 F4
Bretonne Corniche • France ... 114 C1
Brett, Cape • New Zealand ... 35 E2
Bretten • Germany ... 9 D7
Bretton Woods Ski • NH, United States ... 149 [224]
Breuberg Castle • Germany ... 113 [57]
Breueh • Indonesia ... 143 G1
Breuil-Cervinia Ski • Italy ... 100 [203]
Breuil-Cervinia • Italy ... 121 E1
Breves • Brazil ... 52 H3
Brewarrina • NS, Australia ... 34 I5
Brewster • NE, United States ... 46 F2
Brewton • AL, United States ... 48 D5
Brezno • Slovak Rep. ... 13 I9
Bria • Central African Rep. ... 23 C2
Brian Head Ski • UT, United States ... 149 [95]
Briançon Ski • France ... 100 [62]
Briançon • France ... 115 F4
Bribie • QL, Australia ... 144 B6
Brices Cross Roads Nat. Battlefield Site Park N • MS, United States ... 151 [198]
Brides-les-Bains Ski • France ... 100 [40]
Bridge of Orchy • United Kingdom ... 104 B1
Bridgend • United Kingdom ... 7 I10
Bridgeport • CA, United States ... 45 C2
Bridgeport • NE, United States ... 46 E2
Bridgeport • CT, United States ... 153 D7
Bridger Peak • WY, United States ... 42 L6
Bridgeton • NJ, United States ... 153 D10
Bridgetown • WA, Australia ... 34 E6
Bridgetown • Barbados ... 161 O
Bridgewater • NS, Canada ... 156 D7
Bridgnorth • United Kingdom ... 104 D1
Bridgwater • United Kingdom ... 104 F3
Bridgwater • United Kingdom ... 7 I7
Bridlington Beach • United Kingdom ... 101 [35-36]
Bridport • United Kingdom ... 104 F3
Brie • France ... 115 E4
Brielle • Netherlands ... 109 F3
Brienzer See • Switzerland ... 119 G2
Brieselang • Germany ... 111 F2
Brievenapt • Curaçao ... 160 X
Briey • France ... 5 I5
Brig • Switzerland ... 119 G6
Briggsdale • CO, United States ... 46 C2
Brigham City • UT, United States ... 42 I6
Brightlingsea Beach • United Kingdom ... 101 [62]
Brighton • United Kingdom ... 104 E3
Brighton Ski • UT, United States ... 149 [92]
Brighton • CO, United States ... 46 C2
Brignoles • France ... 115 H3
Brimstone Hill Fortress • St Kitts & Nevis ... 161 G
Brimstone Hill Fortress Nat. Park Heritage C • St Kitts & Nevis ... 84 [45]
Brindisi • Italy ... 12 L8
Brindisi • AR, United States ... 46 J5
Brisbane • QL, Australia ... 144 B6
Brissac [Château] • France ... 114 D1
Brissago • Switzerland ... 119 G7
Bristol • United Kingdom ... 104 F3
Bristol • CT, United States ... 44 I5
Bristol • TN, United States ... 48 F2
Bristol • PA, United States ... 153 D6
Bristol • RI, United States ... 153 D8
Bristol Bay • AK, United States ... 49 I4
Bristol Channel • United Kingdom ... 7 H7
Bristol Mtn Ski • NY, United States ... 149 [187]
Bristol Mtn • NY, United States ... 153 D1
British Columbia • Canada ... 38 F5
British Indian Ocean Territory • Indian Ocean ... 3 R7
British Mtns • Canada/United States ... 38 C3
BRITISH VIRGIN IS. • West Indies ... 160 B
Britstown • South Africa ... 24 C6
Brittany • France ... 114 C
Brittas Bay • Ireland ... 108 C4
Briton • United States ... 43 H4
Brive-la-Gaillarde • France ... 115 G2
Brixen Ski • Italy ... 100 [241]
Brixen • Italy ... 120 B1
Brixen im Thale Ski • Austria ... 100 [149]
Brixham Beach • United Kingdom ... 101 [121]
Brixham • United Kingdom ... 104 F5
Brnik [Apt] • Slovenia ... 13 F10
Brno • Czech Rep. ... 13 F8
Broad Haven Beach • United Kingdom ... 101 [179]
Broad Sound • QL, Australia ... 144 B3
Broadback • QU, Canada ... 39 P6
Broadford • United Kingdom ... 104 B1
Broads, The • United Kingdom ... 5 E2
Broadsands Beach • United Kingdom ... 101 [120]

Broadstairs Beach • United Kingdom ... 101 [74-75]
Broadstairs • United Kingdom ... 104 E2
Broadus • MT, United States ... 43 D4
Broadway • United Kingdom ... 104 D4
Brocken • Germany ... 8 F5
Brockhole Visitor Centre • United Kingdom ... 104 C4
Brockton • MA, United States ... 153 D4
Brockville • OT, Canada ... 155 B7
Brodeur Peninsula • NU, Canada ... 39 N2
Brodick • United Kingdom ... 6 G6
Brodie Ski • MA, United States ... 149 [201]
Brodie • MA, United States ... 153 D3
Brodnica • Poland ... 13 I4
Broek in Waterland • Netherlands ... 109 F2
Broek op Langedijk • Netherlands ... 109 D7
Broich, Schloss • Germany ... 111 B1
Bromley Mtn Ski • VT, United States ... 149 [208]
Bromley Mtn • VT, United States ... 153 D3
Bromma [Apt] • Sweden ... 125 D4
Bromo, Gunung • Java, Indonesia ... 143 J8
Bromolla • Sweden ... 125 F11
Bromont Ski • QU, Canada ... 149 [39]
Brøndby Beach • Denmark ... 96 [39]
Brønderslev • Denmark ... 125 F6
Brønnøysund • Norway ... 16 G4
Bronte • Sicily, Italy ... 12 I11
Brønshøj • United States ... 153 D7
Brook's Point • Philippines ... 31 F5
Brookhaven • MS, United States ... 153 F2
Brookton • WA, Australia ... 34 C6
Brookings • OR, United States ... 42 C5
Brookings • SD, United States ... 43 H4
Brooklyn • MA, United States ... 44 J4
Brooklyn • NY, United States ... 153 D7
Brookneal • VA, United States ... 48 H2
Brooks • AL, United States ... 38 I6
Brooks Range • AK, United States ... 49 K2
Brooksville • FL, United States ... 49 B3
Broome • WA, Australia ... 34 C6
Broome • WA, Australia ... 34 D3
Brora • United Kingdom ... 6 I3
Brothers • OR, United States ... 42 E5
Brothers Is. Dive • Red Sea ... 135 B2
Brouage • France ... 115 G1
Brougham Castle • United Kingdom ... 104 C2
Broughton in Furness • United Kingdom ... 104 C3
Broughty Ferry • United Kingdom ... 104 B2
Brovst Beach • Denmark ... 96 [48]
Brovst • Denmark ... 125 F5
Brown Hills • NJ, United States ... 44 H6
Brown v. Board of Education Nat. Hist. Site Park N • KS, United States ... 151 [169]
Brownfield • TX, United States ... 46 D6
Brownhill • TX, United States ... 42 I2
Brownlee Dam • ID/OR, United States ... 42 G4
Brownsea I. • United Kingdom ... 104 F3
Brownsville • TX, United States ... 47 F4
Brownsville • TN, United States ... 48 C3
Brownwood • TX, United States ... 154 J3
Brú, Jökulsá á • Iceland ... 16 [1] F2
Brú na Bóinne Heritage C • Ireland ... 86 [13]
Brú na Bóinne • Ireland ... 108 B2
Bruay-en-Artois • France ... 10 H3
Bruce, Mt • WA, Australia ... 33 C8
Bruce Peninsula • OT, Canada ... 44 E3
Bruce Peninsula Nat. Park Park N • OT, Canada ... 156 [25]
Bruce Rock • WA, Australia ... 34 C6
Bruche • France ... 5 K6
Bruchsal • Germany ... 112 D6
Bruchsal Castle • Germany ... 113 [79]
Bruck an der Mur • Austria ... 13 E10
Bruckmühl • Germany ... 112 F3
Bruges • Belgium ... 109 E2
Brugge • Belgium ... 109 E2
Brühl Heritage C • Germany ... 86 [50]
Brühl • Germany ... 112 D1
Brûlé, le • Réunion ... 132 H1
Brumado • Brazil ... 52 H1
Brumunddal • Norway ... 16 F6
Brundidge • AL, United States ... 48 E5
Bruneck • Italy ... 31 E6
BRUNEI • Asia ... 31 E6
Brunico • Italy ... 120 B2
Brunnen • Switzerland ... 119 G3
Brunsbüttel • Germany ... 8 E3
Brunswick • Germany ... 90 A8
Brunswick • OH, United States ... 44 E5
Brunswick • ME, United States ... 44 K4
Brunswick • MO, United States ... 46 I3
Brunswick • MO, United States ... 48 G5
Brusa • Turkey ... 90 A20
Brush • CO, United States ... 46 D2
Bruson Ski • Switzerland ... 100 [79]
Bruson • Switzerland ... 119 G6
Brusque • Brazil ... 52 G4
Brussel Heritage C • Belgium ... 86 [35]
Brussel • Belgium ... 109 D14
Brussels Heritage C • Belgium ... 86 [35]
Brussels • Belgium ... 109 D14
Bruxelles Heritage C • Belgium ... 86 [35]
Bruxelles • Belgium ... 109 D14
Bryan • OH, United States ... 44 C5
Bryan • TX, United States ... 154 J3
Bryansk • Russian Fed. ... 17 E4
Bryce Canyon Nat. Park Park N • UT, United States ... 150 [80]
Bryce Canyon Nat. Park • UT, United States ... 45 F3
Bryrup • Denmark ... 125 F9
Brzeg • Poland ... 13 G7
Bu Craa • Western Sahara ... 20 C3
Bu'ayrat al Hasun • Libya ... 21 C1
Bua • Sweden ... 125 F6
Bua Yai • Thailand ... 31 C3
Buala • Solomon Is. ... 35 [1] F2
Buapinang • Indonesia ... 32 [1] B3
Buatan • Indonesia ... 32 C2
Buba • Guinea-Bissau ... 15 I5
Buca • Turkey ... 123 F1
Bucak • Turkey ... 123 G3
Bucaramanga • Colombia ... 51 C2
Buccoo • Trinidad & Tobago ... 160 T
Buccoo Reef • Trinidad & Tobago ... 160 T
Buch (Berlin) • Germany ... 111 C2
Buchan • Australia ... 144 A3
Buchanan • Liberia ... 22 D2
Buchanan, Lake • TX, United States ... 47 E2
Bucharest • Romania ... 128 E1
Buchen • Germany ... 9 E7
Buchholz in der Nordheide • Germany ... 8 E3
Buchloe • Germany ... 112 F2
Buchow (Berlin) • Germany ... 111 C4
Buck Hill Ski • MN, United States ... 149 [122]
Buck I. • US Virgin Is. ... 160 Z
Buck I. Reef Nat. Mon. • US Virgin Is. ... 160 Z
Bückeburg Castle • Germany ... 113 [11]
Buckeye • AZ, United States ... 45 E4
Buckfastleigh • United Kingdom ... 104 F5
Buckhannon • WV, United States ... 44 F6
Buckhorn Lake • OT, Canada ... 44 F3

Buckingham • QU, Canada ... 44 H3
Buckland Abbey • United Kingdom ... 104 F5
Buckland Tableland • QL, Australia ... 144 B3
Buco Zau • Angola ... 22 G5
Bucuresti • Romania ... 128 E1
Bucyrus • OH, United States ... 44 D5
Bud • Norway ... 16 D5
Budapest • Hungary ... 13 I10
Budapest Heritage C • Hungary ... 86 [182]
Budardalur • Iceland ... 16 [1] D2
Budaun • India ... 137 C3
Bude Beach • United Kingdom ... 101 [145-148]
Bude • United Kingdom ... 104 F4
Bude • MS, United States ... 48 B5
Bude Bay • United Kingdom ... 104 F1
Büdelsdorf • Germany ... 8 E2
Budennovsk • Russian Fed. ... 17 G6
Budennovsk • Russian Fed. ... 112 D2
Budleigh Salterton • United Kingdom ... 104 F5
Budva • Yugoslavia ... 14 P3
Budzjak • Moldova ... 45 B4
Buea • Cameroon ... 149 [117]
Buena Vista • CO, United States ... 45 I2
Buenaventura • Colombia ... 51 B3
Buenos Aires • Argentina ... 163 D1
Buenos Aires, Lago • Argentina/Chile ... 53 B5
Buer (Gelsenkirchen) • Germany ... 111 B2
Bueu Beach • Spain ... 96 [93]
Buff Bay • Jamaica ... 159 F2
Buffalo • WY, United States ... 42 L4
Buffalo • SD, United States ... 43 E4
Buffalo • OK, United States ... 46 F4
Buffalo • NY, United States ... 44 F4
Buffalo • TX, United States ... 154 J4
Buffalo Bill Dam • WY, United States ... 42 K4
Buffalo Lake • NT, Canada ... 38 H4
Buffalo Narrows • SA, Canada ... 38 K5
Buffalo Springs Game Reserve • Kenya ... 131 G2
Buffels • South Africa ... 134 B1
Buffels Bay • South Africa ... 134 C7
Buftea • Romania ... 128 E1
Buga • Colombia ... 51 B3
Bugala • Uganda ... 131 F2
Bugel • SA, Canada ... 123 H2
Buglie • Malta ... 123 H2
Bugojno • Bosnia-Herz. ... 12 L4
Bugulma • Russian Fed. ... 17 I4
Buhi • Philippines ... 28 C4
Bühl • Germany ... 9 D8
Bühl • ID, United States ... 42 H5
Bühlertal • Germany ... 112 E6
Bui Nat. Park Park • Ghana ... 133 [22]
Builth Wells • United Kingdom ... 7 I9
Buin • Indonesia ... 32 [1] C3
Buin • Papua New Guinea ... 35 [1] F2
Buinsk • Russian Fed. ... 17 H3
Buir Nur • Mongolia ... 29 F1
Bujanovac • F.R. of Yugoslavia ... 11 K3
Bujaraloz • Spain ... 8 D4
Bujumbura • Burundi ... 23 B3
Bük • Hungary ... 14 D2
Buka • Papua New Guinea ... 35 [1] E2
Bukama • Dem. Rep. of Congo ... 23 D5
Bukavu • Dem. Rep. of Congo ... 23 D4
Bukhara • Uzbekistan ... 18 I6
Bukhara Heritage C • Uzbekistan ... 85 [95]
Bukhoro • Uzbekistan ... 18 I6
Bukhoro Heritage C • Uzbekistan ... 85 [95]
Bukit Ferringhi • ... 141 F1
Bukit Gemuruh Forest Reserve • Penang, Malaysia ... 141 F3
Bukit Genting Forest Reserve • Penang, Malaysia ... 141 F3
Bukit Juru Forest Reserve • Penang, Malaysia ... 141 F3
Bukit Kerajaan Forest Reserve • Penang, Malaysia ... 141 F1
Bukit Mertajam • Malaysia ... 31 C5
Bukit Pulau • Penang, Malaysia ... 141 F3
Bukit Relau Forest Reserve • Penang, Malaysia ... 141 F4
Bukit Tengah • Penang, Malaysia ... 141 F4
Bukit Timah Nature Reserve • Singapore ... 141 H1
Bukittinggi • Indonesia ... 143 G4
Bukk Nat. Park Park N • Hungary ... 89 [104]
Bukoba • Tanzania ... 130 B1
Bukoba • Dem. Rep. of Congo ... 23 D4
Bukovina • Ukraine ... 14 M1
Bula • Indonesia ... 32 [1] D3
Bulan • Philippines ... 31 G4
Bulawayo • Zimbabwe ... 130 C3
Buldan • Turkey ... 122 D6
Bulgan • Mongolia ... 29 B2
BULGARIA • Europe ... 14 L7
Bull Point • Falkland Is. ... 163 C1
Bull Shoals Lake • AR/MO, United States ... 46 I4
Bulla Regia • Tunisia ... 123 E1
Bullaher • Somalia ... 21 H5
Bullenbaai • Curaçao ... 160 X
Bullfinch • WA, Australia ... 34 C6
Bullhead City • Rhodes, Greece ... 122 D12
Bullhead City • AZ, United States ... 45 E4
Bulloo • Australia ... 144 B5
Bulls • New Zealand ... 35 [1] C3
Bulo Berde • Somalia ... 23 H3
Bulolo • Papua New Guinea ... 35 [1] D2
Bulukumba • Indonesia ... 32 [1] B4
Bulungu • Dem. Rep. of Congo ... 23 C3
Bumba • Dem. Rep. of Congo ... 23 C3
Bumi Hills • Zimbabwe ... 130 C1
Bunbury • WA, Australia ... 8 D4
Bundaberg • QL, Australia ... 144 B4
Bünde • Germany ... 8 D4
Bundelkhand Riva • India ... 137 C7
Bundi • India ... 137 C6
Bundoran Beach • Ireland ... 96 [65]
Bundoran • Ireland ... 108 C2
Bungku • Indonesia ... 32 [1] B3
Bungle Bungle • WA, Australia ... 144 A2
Bungo • Angola ... 22 H6
Bungo [Riv] • Angola/Zambia ... 24 C2
Bünian. Nat. Park Park N • Uganda ... 83 [97]
Bunkie • LA, United States ... 47 H2
Bunmahon Beach • Ireland ... 96 [58]
Bunnaharty Castle • Ireland ... 108 C6
Bunratty • Ireland ... 108 C6
Bünyan • Turkey ... 123 F1
Buol • Indonesia ... 30 B4
Buon Ma Thuot • Vietnam ... 141 E4
Buong Long • Cambodia ... 141 E4
Buorkhaya, Guba • Russian Fed. ... 27 L2
Buqum • Saudi Arabia ... 134 G6
Bur Gabo • Somalia ... 23 G4
Bur Hakkaba • Somalia ... 23 G3
Bur Sa'id • Egypt ... 135 D1
Bur Sudan • Sudan ... 21 G4
Buraydah • Saudi Arabia ... 18 D4
Burbach • Germany ... 9 D6
Burbank • CA, United States ... 45 C4
Burdekin • Australia ... 144 A2
Burdur [Adm] • Turkey ... 123 B1
Burdur Gölü • Turkey ... 123 F1
Burdwan • India ... 28 E4
Bure • United Kingdom ... 23 F1
Bure • Ethiopia ... 21 F4
Bureinskiy Khrebet • Russian Fed. ... 27 L6
Bureia Beach • Spain ... 96 [91]
Büren • Germany ... 8 D5
Bürenhayrhan • Mongolia ... 26 P8

Burg • Germany ... 8 G2
Burg bei Magdeburg • Germany ... 8 G4
Burg, Schloss • Germany ... 111 B4
Burgas • Bulgaria ... 128 E3
Burgaski Zaliv • Bulgaria ... 14 O7
Burgau • Germany ... 112 F2
Burgau • Portugal ... 118 E5
Burgdorf • Germany ... 119 G2
Burgenland • Austria ... 13 E10
Burgeo • NF, Canada ... 156 D3
Burghausen • Germany ... 112 F4
Burghausen Castle • Germany ... 113 [122]
Burgkirchen • Germany ... 112 F4
Burglengenfeld • Germany ... 9 H7
Burgos • Spain ... 8 C3
Burgos Heritage C • Spain ... 86 [93]
Burgsteinfurt Castle • Germany ... 113 [12]
Burgsvik • Sweden ... 16 J8
Burgundy • France ... 114 A2
Burhaniye • Turkey ... 15 I4
Burhanpur • India ... 28 C4
Burias • Philippines ... 31 G4
Burica, Punta • Costa Rica ... 51 A2
Burin Peninsula • NF, Canada ... 156 D4
Burjasot • Spain ... 11 K5
Burketown • TX, United States ... 19 A4
Burley • ID, United States ... 42 I5
Burlington • VT, United States ... 44 I3
Burlington • IA, United States ... 46 J2
Burlington • CO, United States ... 46 D3
Burlington • NC, United States ... 48 G2
Burlington • WI, United States ... 153 D6
Burlington • NJ, United States ... 155 B9
Burma • Asia ... 31 B2
Burma Road • China/Myanmar ... 29 B5
Burmah, Al • Tunisia ... 21 A1
Burnaby • BC, Canada ... 42 C7
Buron, Serranias del • Mexico ... 47 C3
Burnazului, Cimpia • Romania ... 14 M6
Burney • CA, United States ... 42 E6
Burnham-on-Sea • United Kingdom ... 104 F3
Burnie • TS, Australia ... 34 I8
Burnley • United Kingdom ... 7 J8
Burns • OR, United States ... 152 B4
Burnside • NU, Canada ... 38 I3
Burqin • China ... 26 D8
Burra • SA, Australia ... 34 G6
Burrell • Albania ... 15 B2
Burren, The • Ireland ... 108 C4
Burriana • Spain ... 11 L5
Bursa • Turkey ... 122 D3
Burscheid • Germany ... 111 B4
Bürserberg • Austria ... 119 H5
Burt Lake • MI, United States ... 44 C3
Burton • MI, United States ... 44 D4
Burton-upon-Trent • United Kingdom ... 7 K9
Buru • Indonesia ... 32 [1] C3
Burun Shibertuy, gora • Russian Fed. ... 27 G7
BURUNDI • Africa ... 23 D4
Burwash Landing • YT, Canada ... 38 D4
Buruun Urt • Mongolia ... 27 H7
Burwell • NE, United States ... 46 F2
Burwick • United Kingdom ... 106 A6
Bury • United Kingdom ... 7 J8
Bury St Edmunds • United Kingdom ... 7 M9
Buryatia • Russian Fed. ... 27 H6
Busch Gardens Tampa Bay Park L • FL, United States ... 151 [DD]
Busch Gardens Tampa Bay • FL, United States ... 154 H5
Busch Gardens the Old Country Park L • VA, United States ... 151 [GG]
Busch Gardens the Old Country • VA, United States ... 153 D11
Bushehr • Iran ... 18 F4
Bushkill • PA, United States ... 153 C6
Busing • Singapore ... 141 H3
Businga • Dem. Rep. of Congo ... 23 C3
Buskerud • Norway ... 16 E6
Busko-Zdrój • Poland ... 128 C2
Bussana • Italy ... 121 E9
Busselton • WA, Australia ... 34 A6
Bussum • Netherlands ... 109 F2
Busto Arsizio • Italy ... 12 C3
Busuanga • Philippines ... 31 A4
Büsum • Germany ... 8 D2
Buta • Dem. Rep. of Congo ... 23 D3
Buta Ranquil • Argentina ... 52 D3
Butaleja • Uganda ... 18 B6
Butare • Rwanda ... 23 D4
Butaritari • Kiribati ... 33 I5
Bute • United Kingdom ... 6 G6
Butembo • Dem. Rep. of Congo ... 23 D3
Butha Qi • China ... 29 E1
Buthrotum Heritage C • Albania ... 86 [192]
Buthrotum • Albania ... 122 B1
Butiá • Brazil ... 52 F5
Butler • PA, United States ... 44 F5
Butler, Lake •
Butrint Heritage C • Albania ... 86 [192]
Butrinti • Albania ... 122 B1
Butt of Lewis • United Kingdom ... 6 F3
Butte • MT, United States ... 42 I4
Butterfly Valley • Rhodes, Greece ... 122 D12
Buttermere [Lake] • United Kingdom ... 104 C1
Butternut Beach • United States ... 108 C7
Butternut Basin Ski • MA, United States ... 149 [200]
Butterworth • Penang, Malaysia ... 141 F2
Buttevant • Ireland ... 108 C6
Butung • Indonesia ... 32 [1] B4
Butzbach • Germany ... 112 E2
Buxar • India ... 137 C8
Buxtehude • Germany ... 8 E3
Buxton • United Kingdom ... 7 K8
Buy • Russian Fed. ... 17 G3
Buyan, Danau • Bali, Indonesia ... 143 H2
Buyende • Uganda ... 32 [1] B3
Büyük Agri Dag • Turkey ... 18 D2
Büyük Kemiki Burnu • Turkey ... 15 H3
Büyük Menderes • Turkey ... 15 K5
Büyüm • China ... 30 B4
Buzau • Romania ... 128 E1
Buzau [Riv] • Romania ... 14 M6
Buzet • France ... 114 B3
Búzios • Brazil ... 163 C4
Buzuluk • Russian Fed. ... 17 I4
Bwindi • Rwanda • Zimbabwe ... 132 D6
Bwindi Nat. Park Heritage N • Uganda ... 83 [97]
Byala • Lovec, Bulgaria ... 14 M6
Byala • Ruse, Bulgaria ... 128 E4
Byam Martin I. • NU, Canada ... 39 P2
Byam Martin, Cape • NU, Canada ... 39 P2
Byblos Heritage C • Lebanon ... 86 [283]
Bydgoszcz • Poland ... 13 H5
Byers • CO, United States ... 46 C3
Bygdin • Norway ... 124 C3
Bygland • Norway ... 124 C6
Bygstad [Adm] • Norway ... 125 F1
Byhalia • MS, United States ... 48 C4
Bykle • Norway ... 124 C5
Bykovski • Russian Fed. ... 27 L2
Bylot I. • NU, Canada ... 39 N2
Byoido-in • Japan ... 140 B2
Byrranga, Gory • Russian Fed. ... 26 P3
Bystrzca Klodzka • Poland ... 13 F7

Bytca • Slovak Rep. ... 13 H8
Bytom • Poland ... 128 C1
Bytov • Poland ... 13 G3
Byxelkrok • Sweden ... 125 F8
Bzura • Poland ... 13 I5

C.J. Strike Dam • ID, United States ... 42 H5
C.W. McConaughy, Lake • NE, United States ... 46 E2
Ca Mau • Vietnam ... 141 E3
Caaguazú • Paraguay ... 52 E4
Caballas • Peru ... 163 B3
Caballo • Peru ... 51 C4
Caballo Reservoir • NM, United States ... 153 E4
Caballos Mesteños, Llano de los • Mexico ... 47 B3
Cabana • Peru ... 163 B1
Cabanas • Portugal ... 118 E8
Cabanatuan • Philippines ... 31 G3
Cabarete • Dominican Rep. ... 159 G3
Caberfae Peaks Ski • MI, United States ... 149 [143]
Cabimas • Venezuela ... 51 C1
Cabinda • Angola ... 22 G6
Cabinda [Adm] • Angola ... 22 G6
Cabinet Mtns • MT, United States ... 152 B2
Cable Beach • Bahamas ... 158 B3
Cabo Bojador • Western Sahara ... 20 C3
Cabo de Rama Fort • Goa, India ... 137 B2
Cabo Negro • Morocco ... 131 D2
Cabo San Lucas • Mexico ... 157 F4
Cabo San Lucas [Cape] • Mexico ... 157 F4
Cabonga, Reservoir • QU, Canada ... 39 P7
Cabool • MO, United States ... 46 I4
Caborca • Mexico ... 157 F2
Caboro Bassa Dam • Mozambique ... 24 E3
Caboro Bassa, Lago • Mozambique ... 24 E3
Cabot Strait • NF/NS, Canada ... 156 D3
Cabra • Spain ... 11 G7
Cabral • Dominican Rep. ... 159 G4
Cabrera, I. de • Spain ... 117 H4
Cabri • SA, Canada ... 42 K1
Cabriel • Spain ... 11 K5
Cabrillo Nat. Mon. Park N • CA, United States ... 150 [56]
Cabritos, I. • Dominican Rep. ... 159 G6
Cabrits Nat. Park • Dominica ... 161 M
Cabrón, Cabo • Dominican Rep. ... 159 G4
Caçador • Brazil ... 52 F4
Cacahuamilpa • Mexico ... 157 G4
Cacak • F.R. of Yugoslavia ... 14 H6
Caçapava do Sul • Brazil ... 52 F5
Cáceres • Spain ... 11 E5
Cáceres • Brazil ... 52 E2
Cáceres Heritage C • Spain ... 86 [106]
Cache Peak • ID, United States ... 42 I5
Cachimbo • Brazil ... 51 G5
Cachimbo, Serra do • Brazil ... 51 F5
Cachoeira • Brazil ... 52 J1
Cachoeira de Paulo Afonso • Brazil ... 53 [1] D3
Cachoeira do Sul • Brazil ... 52 F5
Cachoeiro de Itapemirim • Brazil ... 163 C4
Cacolo • Angola ... 22 H6
Cacocum • Cuba ... 158 D8
Caconda • Angola ... 24 B2
Caculé • Brazil ... 52 H1
Cadaqués • Spain ... 117 D2
Cadereyta • Mexico ... 47 D5
Cadca • Slovak Rep. ... 13 H8
Cadale Lake • TX, United States ... 154 J4
Cadena Costero Catalana • Spain ... 11 M3
Cadenàbbia • Italy ... 121 E2
Cades Reef • Antigua & Barbuda ... 161 K
Cadillac • MI, United States ... 44 C3
Cadiz • Philippines ... 31 G4
Cádiz Beach • Spain ... 96 [113]
Cádiz • Spain ... 116 B5
Cádiz, Bahía de • Spain ... 116 B5
Cádiz, Golfo de • Spain ... 11 E7
Cadolzburg Castle • Germany ... 113 [150]
Cadore • Italy ... 120 B2
Cadouin • France ... 114 D2
Caen • France ... 10 E4
Caernarfon • United Kingdom ... 7 H8
Caernarfon Bay • United Kingdom ... 7 H8
Caerphilly • United Kingdom ... 7 I10
Caesarea • Israel ... 135 A3
Caesarea Philippi • Syria ... 135 A2
Cafayate • Argentina ... 52 C4
Cafres, Plaine des • Réunion ... 132 H4
Cagayan • Philippines ... 31 G3
Cagayan de Oro • Philippines ... 31 G5
Cagayan Sulu • Philippines ... 31 F5
Çagis • Turkey ... 15 J4
Cagliari • Sardinia, Italy ... 120 C4
Cagliari, Golfo di • Sardinia, Italy ... 120 C4
Cagnes-sur-Mer • France ... 115 H4
Caguas • Puerto Rico ... 159 H4
Caherciveen Beach • Ireland ... 96 [60]
Caherciveen • Ireland ... 96 [60]
Caherdaniel Beach • Ireland ... 96 [61]
Caherdaniel • Ireland ... 108 C7
Cahir • Ireland ... 7 E9
Cahokia • IL, United States ... 46 J4
Cahokia Mounds State Hist. Site Heritage C • IL, United States ... 84 [9]
Cahul • Moldova ... 14 P4
Caiapó, Serrra do • Brazil ... 52 E2
Caibarién • Cuba ... 158 D3
Caicara • Venezuela ... 37 H6
Caicos Bank • Turks & Caicos Is. ... 158 C1
Caicos Passage • West Indies ... 158 C1
Caille I. • Grenada ... 161 R
Caimancita • Venezuela ... 160 V
Caimanera • Cuba ... 158 D2
Caimito, Playa del • Cuba ... 158 D2
Caine • Bolivia ... 51 C1
Cairngorm Mtns • United Kingdom ... 6 I4
Cairnryan • United Kingdom ... 106 A10
Cairns • QL, Australia ... 144 B1
Cairo Heritage C • Egypt ... 86 [275]
Cairo • Egypt ... 135 D1
Cairo • GA, United States ... 48 E5
Cairo • IL, United States ... 46 K4
Caiundo • Angola ... 24 B3
Cajabamba • Peru ... 51 B5
Cajamarca • Peru ... 51 B5
Cajapió • Brazil ... 52 H3
Cajàzeiras • Brazil ... 52 H3
Çakirlar • Turkey ... 123 F3
Çakmak • Turkey ... 15 H6
Cakovec • Croatia ... 13 F10
Cala Antena • Majorca, Spain ... 117 H4
Cala Bassa • Ibiza, Spain ... 117 H4
Cala Blanca • Minorca, Spain ... 117 F1
Cala Blanes • Minorca, Spain ... 117 F4
Cala Blava • Majorca, Spain ... 117 H3
Cala Bona • Majorca, Spain ... 117 H4
Cala Conta • Ibiza, Spain ... 117 H3
Cala d'Or • Majorca, Spain ... 117 H4
Cala de Sant Vicenç • Ibiza, Spain ... 117 G2
Cala de Sant Vicenç • Majorca, Spain ... 117 H2

Cala de Santandria • Minorca, Spain ... 117 F1
Cala Egos • Majorca, Spain ... 117 H3
Cala Egos • Majorca, Spain ... 117 H4
Cala En Bosc • Minorca, Spain ... 117 F4
Cala En Porter • Minorca, Spain ... 117 F4
Cala Estany • Majorca, Spain ... 117 H2
Cala Figuera • Majorca, Spain ... 117 H4
Cala Figuera, Cap de • Majorca, Spain ... 117 H3
Cala Forcat • Minorca, Spain ... 117 F4
Cala Fornells • Majorca, Spain ... 117 H3
Cala Gració • Ibiza, Spain ... 117 G1
Cala Liberotto • Sardinia, Italy ... 120 C2
Cala Llenya • Ibiza, Spain ... 117 G2
Cala Llombarts • Majorca, Spain ... 117 H4
Cala Llonga • Minorca, Spain ... 117 F4
Cala Llonga • Ibiza, Spain ... 117 G2
Cala Llonga • Majorca, Spain ... 117 H3
Cala Marçal • Majorca, Spain ... 117 H4
Cala Millor • Majorca, Spain ... 117 H4
Cala Mondragó • Majorca, Spain ... 117 H4
Cala Morell • Minorca, Spain ... 117 F1
Cala Murada • Majorca, Spain ... 117 H4
Cala d'Or • Majorca, Spain ... 117 H4
Cala Ratjada • Majorca, Spain ... 117 H3
Cala Tarida • Ibiza, Spain ... 117 F2
Cala Torret • Minorca, Spain ... 117 F1
Cala Vadella • Ibiza, Spain ... 117 G1
Cala Vinyes • Majorca, Spain ... 117 H3
Calabar • Nigeria ... 22 F3
Calabozo • Venezuela ... 51 D2
Calàbria • Italy ... 12 K9
Calàbria, Parco Naz. della Park N • Italy ... 89 [88]
Calacuccia • Corsica, France ... 115 L1
Calafat • Romania ... 14 J6
Calafate • Argentina ... 53 B6
Calafell Beach • Spain ... 96 [121]
Calahonda • Spain ... 116 B7
Calahorra • Spain ... 11 I2
Calais • France ... 10 G3
Calais • ME, United States ... 44 L3
Calakmul • Mexico ... 157 H3
Calalaste, Sierra de • Argentina ... 52 C4
Calama • Chile ... 52 C3
Calamian Group • Philippines ... 31 F4
Calamocha • Spain ... 11 J4
Calanche, les Heritage N • Corsica, France ... 83 [51]
Calanche, les • Corsica, France ... 115 L1
Calang • Indonesia ... 143 G1
Calangute • Goa, India ... 137 B1
Calangute Beach • Goa, India ... 137 B1
Calanques, Côte des • France ... 115 H4
Calapan • Philippines ... 31 G4
Calarasi • Moldova ... 14 P2
Calarasi • Romania ... 128 E1
Calatayud • Spain ... 11 J3
Calatrava Park L • AL, Canada ... 156 [B]
Calbayog • Philippines ... 31 G4
Calbogie Peaks Ski • OT, Canada ... 149 [17]
Calcare, Cava di • Italy ... 121 G1
Calcasieu Lake • LA, United States ... 153 F3
Calcatoggio • Corsica, France ... 115 L3
Calçoene • Brazil ... 51 G3
Calcutta • India ... 28 E4
Caldas da Rainha • Portugal ... 11 B5
Caldbeck • United Kingdom ... 104 C2
Calderào, Serra do • Portugal ... 118 E3
Calder Hall • United Kingdom ... 104 C3
Caldera • Chile ... 52 B4
Caldera de Taburiente, Parque Nac. de Park N • La Palma, Canary Is. ... 89 [76]
Caldera de Taburiente, Parque Nac. de • La Palma, Canary Is. ... 117 E5
Caldonazzo, Lago di • Italy ... 120 B3
Caldwell • ID, United States ... 152 B4
Caledon • South Africa ... 134 C5
Caledon Ski • OT, Canada ... 149 [26]
Caledon • OT, Canada ... 44 E4
Caledon [Riv] • South Africa ... 24 D6
Caledonian Canal • United Kingdom ... 6 H4
Calella Beach • Spain ... 96 [122]
Calella • Spain ... 117 D4
Calenzana • Corsica, France ... 115 L1
Cales Coves • Minorca, Spain ... 117 F4
Cales de Mallorca • Majorca, Spain ... 117 H4
Caleta de Fustes • Fuerteventura, Canary Is. ... 117 E2
Caleta Olivia • Argentina ... 53 C5
Caleton Blanc • Cuba ... 120 C2
Caletta, la • Sardinia, Italy ... 120 C2
Calexico • CA, United States ... 155 C4
Calgary • AL, Canada ... 155 C4
Calheta • Azores ... 118 C1
Calheta • Madeira ... 118 C1
Calhoun • GA, United States ... 48 E3
Cali • Colombia ... 51 B3
Calibishie • Dominica ... 161 M
Calico Ghost Town • CA, United States ... 152 C6
Calicut • India ... 138 D10
Cálida, Costa • Spain ... 117 C3
California • United States ... 152 C4
California, Golfo de • Mexico ... 157 F
California Lighthouse • Aruba ... 160 Y
Calilabad •
Calipatria • CA, United States ... 45 E5
Calistoga • CA, United States ... 45 A2
Calitzdorf • South Africa ... 134 C6
Calivigny I. • Grenada ... 160 S
Callabonna, Lake • Australia ... 34 G5
Callaghan, Mt • NV, United States ... 45 D2
Callao • Peru ... 163 B1
Caldas de Segura • Spain ... 11 K6
Calonge Beach • Spain ... 96 [123]
Caloosahatchee • FL, United States ... 49 C4
Caltagirone • Sicily, Italy ... 121 G2
Caltanissetta • Sicily, Italy ... 12 I11
Caluango • Angola ... 22 I6
Calulo • Angola ... 22 G6
Calvados, Côte du • France ...
Calvi • Corsica, France ... 115 L1
Calvià Beach • Majorca, Spain ... 96 [126]
Calvinia • South Africa ... 134 B5
Calw • Germany ... 112 D6
Cam • United Kingdom ... 7 M9
Cam Ranh • Vietnam ... 141 E4
Cam Ranh Bay • Vietnam ... 141 E4
Camabatela • Angola ... 23 B5
Camaçari • Brazil ... 52 J1
Camagüey • Cuba ... 158 D7
Camagüey, Archipiélago de • Cuba ... 158 D3
Camaioré Beach • Italy ... 96 [144]
Camamu • Brazil ... 52 I1

Camaná • Peru.... 163 B4
Camaquã • Brazil.... 52 F5
Câmara de Lobos • Madeira.... 118 C1
Çamardi • Turkey.... 123 G2
Camargo • Spain.... 11 H1
Camargo • Mexico.... 47 E4
Camargue • France.... 10 J10
Camariñas • Spain.... 11 B1
Camarón, Cabo • Honduras.... 37 D4
Camarones • Argentina.... 53 C4
Camas • Spain.... 11 F7
Camas • WA, United States.... 42 D4
Cambados • Spain.... 11 C2
Camber Beach • United Kingdom.... 101 [79]
Cambo-les-Bains • France.... 115 J1
CAMBODIA • Asia.... 31 C4
Camborne • United Kingdom.... 104 F4
Cambrai • France.... 10 I3
Cambria • CA, United States.... 45 B4
Cambrian Mtns • United Kingdom.... 7 M9
Cambridge • United Kingdom.... 7 P7
Cambridge • New Zealand.... 145 F1
Cambridge • MN, United States.... 43 J4
Cambridge • OH, United States.... 44 E5
Cambridge • OT, Canada.... 44 E4
Cambridge • NY, United States.... 153 C4
Cambridge • ME, United States.... 44 K3
Cambridge • MD, United States.... 153 D10
Cambridge Bay • NT, Canada.... 38 J3
Cambrils Beach • Spain.... 96 [121]
Cambrils de Mar • Spain.... 117 D3
Camden • NY, United States.... 44 H4
Camden • ME, United States.... 44 K3
Camden • AR, United States.... 46 I6
Camden • AL, United States.... 48 D5
Camden • SC, United States.... 48 G3
Camden • NJ, United States.... 153 D10
Camelback Ski •
  PA, United States.... 149 [177]
Camelback • PA, United States.... 153 D6
Camelford • United Kingdom.... 104 F4
Camelot Theme Park Park L •
  United Kingdom.... 98 [23]
Camenca • Moldova.... 14 P1
Cameron • AZ, United States.... 45 G4
Cameron • MO, United States.... 46 H3
Cameron • TX, United States.... 47 F2
Cameron Highlands • Malaysia.... 141 G1
Cameron Hills • NT, Canada.... 38 H4
Cameron Mtns • New Zealand.... 145 G3
CAMEROON • Africa.... 22 G3
Cameroon, Mt • Cameroon.... 22 F4
Cametá • Brazil.... 51 H4
Camilla • GA, United States.... 48 E5
Caminha Beach • Portugal.... 96 [94]
Camino de Santiago Heritage C •
  Spain.... 86 [95]
Çamlıköyü • Turkey.... 123 F2
Çamoçin • Brazil.... 53 I1 (1) C2
Camooweal • QL, Australia.... 34 G3
Camopi • French Guiana.... 51 G3
Camorta • India.... 28 F7
Camp David • MD, United States.... 153 D9
Camp de Mar • Majorca, Spain.... 117 H3
Camp Verde • AZ, United States.... 45 G4
Campagna • Italy.... 121 G4
Campal Beach • Goa, India.... 137 B1
Campana, I. • Chile.... 53 A5
Campanella, Punta • Italy.... 121 G3
Campania • Italy.... 12 J8
Campbell • OH, United States.... 44 E5
Campbell • MO, United States.... 46 J4
Campbell, Cape • New Zealand.... 35 E5
Campbell Town • TS, Australia.... 34 I8
Campbellsville •
  KY, United States.... 48 E2
Campbelltown • NS, Australia.... 144 C2
Campbellton • NB, Canada.... 156 D2
Campbeltown • United Kingdom.... 6 G6
Campeche Heritage C • Mexico.... 84 [29]
Campeche • Mexico.... 157 H1
Campeche [Adm] • Mexico.... 37 C4
Campeche, Bahía de • Mexico.... 37 C4
Campechuela • Cuba.... 158 D7
Campello Beach • Spain.... 96 [116]
Campello • Spain.... 117 C2
Campi Dano • Sardinia, Italy.... 12 C9
Campiglia Marittime • Italy.... 12 E5
Campina Grande • Brazil.... 53 I1 (1) D3
Campinas • Brazil.... 52 F3
Campitello di Fassa Ski • Italy.... 100 [235]
Campitello di Fassa • Italy.... 120 B3
Campo del Oro [Apt] •
  Corsica, France.... 115 L3
Campo Felice • Italy.... 121 F2
Campo Grande • Brazil.... 52 F3
Campo Maior • Brazil.... 53 I1 (1) C2
Campo Mourão • Brazil.... 52 F3
Campo Tures • Italy.... 120 B2
Campoamor • Spain.... 117 C3
Campobasso • Italy.... 12 I7
Campos • Brazil.... 53 I1 (1) C4
Campos • Majorca, Spain.... 117 H4
Campos • Brazil.... 163 C4
Campos do Jordão • Brazil.... 163 C3
Campotosto, Lago di • Italy.... 12 H7
Campsie Fells • United Kingdom.... 104 B3
Campton Ski • NH, United States.... 149 [221]
Camrose • AL, Canada.... 38 I6
Camsell Portage • SA, Canada.... 38 J5
Camyuva • Turkey.... 122 D2
Çan • Turkey.... 122 D2
Can Pastilla • Majorca, Spain.... 117 H3
Can Picafort • Majorca, Spain.... 117 H2
Can Tho • Vietnam.... 141 E3
Cana of Galilee • Israel.... 135 A4
Canaan • Trinidad & Tobago.... 160 T
Canaan Valley Ski •
  VA, United States.... 149 [167]
CANADA • N. America.... 36
Cañada de Gomez • Argentina.... 52 D5
Cañadas del Teide, Parque Nac. de las •
  Park N • Tenerife, Canary Is..... 89 [78]
Cañadas del Teide, Parque Nac. de las •
  Tenerife, Canary Is..... 116 E1
Canadian • TX, United States.... 46 G5
Canadian (Riv) • United States.... 46 G5
Canadian Rocky Mtns Parks Heritage N •
  AL/BC, Canada.... 82 [4]
Canadian Shield • Canada.... 38/39
Canaguinim Beach • Goa, India.... 137 B2
Canaima, Parque Nac. Heritage N •
  Venezuela.... 82 [30]
Çanakkale • Turkey.... 122 D1
Çanakkale Bogazi • Turkey.... 122 D2
Canal du Midi Heritage C •
  France.... 86 [80]
Canal Flats • BC, Canada.... 42 H1
Canandaigua Lake •
  NY, United States.... 153 D1
Cananea • Mexico.... 157 F2
Canaria, Costa •
  Gran Canaria, Canary Is..... 116 E4
Canarias, Islas •
  Atlantic Ocean.... 19 C3
Canaries • St Lucia.... 161 P
Canarreos, Archipiélago de los •
  Cuba.... 158 D2
Canary Is. • Atlantic Ocean.... 117 E
Canaveral Nat. Seashore Park N •
  FL, United States.... 151 [218]
Canaveral Nat. Seashore •
  FL, United States.... 154 H6
Canazei Ski • Italy.... 100 [236]
Canazei • Italy.... 120 B3
Canberra • ACT, Australia.... 144 C2
Canby • CA, United States.... 45 C2
Cancale Beach • France.... 96 [79]
Cancale • France.... 114 C2
Canche • France.... 5 E4
Cancún • Mexico.... 157 H2
Cancún, I. • Mexico.... 157 H2

Çandarli • Turkey.... 15 H5
Çandarli Körfezi • Turkey.... 15 H5
Candelaria •
  Tenerife, Canary Is..... 116 E1
Candelaria • Mexico.... 157 H3
Candi Kuning Temple •
  Bali, Indonesia.... 143 H2
Candi Sukuh Temple •
  Java, Indonesia.... 143 J7
Candidasa Beach •
  Bali, Indonesia.... 143 H4
Candolim Beach • Goa, India.... 137 B1
Cane River Creole Nat. Hist. Park Park N •
  LA, United States.... 151 [191]
Canea • Crete, Greece.... 123 E1
Canefield [Apt] • Dominica.... 161 M
Canelones • Uruguay.... 163 D2
Canet d'En Berenguer Beach •
  Spain.... 96 [119]
Canet Plage • France.... 115 K2
Cañete • Spain.... 11 J4
Canfranc • Spain.... 11 H2
Cangamba • Angola.... 24 B2
Cangas • Spain.... 11 C2
Cangas Beach • Spain.... 96 [93]
Canggu Beach • Bali, Indonesia.... 143 H4
Cango Caves • South Africa.... 134 C2
Cangzhou • China.... 39 F6
Caniapiscau, Lac • QU, Canada.... 156 C2
Caniçal • Madeira.... 118 C2
Canicattì • Sicily, Italy.... 12 H11
Caniço • Madeira.... 118 C2
Canindé • Brazil.... 53 (1) D2
Cankiri • Turkey.... 15 O3
Cannanore • India.... 138 D6
Cannanore Beach • India.... 138 E3
Cannes Beach • France.... 96 [134]
Cannes • France.... 115 H4
Cannock • United Kingdom.... 5 A2
Cannock Chase • United Kingdom.... 104 D2
Cannon Ski • NH, United States.... 149 [223]
Cannon [Apt] •
  NV, United States.... 152 C3
Cannon Ball • ND, United States.... 43 H3
Cannon Beach •
  OR, United States.... 152 B1
Cannonball • ND, United States.... 43 H3
Canonsburg Ski •
  MI, United States.... 149 [151]
Canoas • Brazil.... 52 F4
Cañon City • CO, United States.... 46 C3
Canonica, la • Corsica, France.... 115 L2
Canonniers Point • Mauritius.... 132 J1
Canora • SA, Canada.... 43 E1
Canosa di Puglia • Italy.... 14 D8
Canouan • St Vincent & Gren..... 161 R
Canove Ski • Italy.... 100 [217]
Cansaulim Beach • Goa, India.... 137 B2
Canso, Strait of • NS, Canada.... 156 D8
Cantabria • Spain.... 11 G1
Cantábrica, Cordillera • Spain.... 11 F2
Cantábrico, Mar • Spain.... 11 E1
Cantanhede Beach • Portugal.... 96 [96]
Cantera, I. de la • Spain.... 117 C1
Canterbury Heritage C •
  United Kingdom.... 86 [27]
Canterbury • United Kingdom.... 104 E4
Canterbury • New Zealand.... 145 E3
Canterbury Bight • New Zealand.... 35 C6
Canterbury Plains • New Zealand.... 145 E3
Canton • China.... 139 B1
Canton • SD, United States.... 43 H5
Canton • OH, United States.... 44 E5
Canton • PA, United States.... 153 C4
Canton • NY, United States.... 44 H3
Canton • IL, United States.... 46 J2
Canton • MS, United States.... 153 F2
Canton Lake • OK, United States.... 46 H4
Canumã • Brazil.... 51 F4
Canvey I. • United Kingdom.... 104 E3
Canyon • TX, United States.... 46 E5
Canyon de Chelly Nat. Mon. Park N •
  AZ, United States.... 150 [101]
Canyon de Chelly Nat. Mon. •
  AZ, United States.... 153 E2
Canyon Lake • TX, United States.... 47 E3
Canyonlands Nat. Park Park N •
  UT, United States.... 150 [84]
Canyonlands Nat. Park •
  UT, United States.... 45 H2
Caombo • Angola.... 22 H6
Caorle • Italy.... 121 E8
Cap aux Meules • QU, Canada.... 156 D2
Cap d'Ail Beach • France.... 96 [134]
Cap d'Ambre • Madagascar.... 24 H2
Cap de la Madeleine •
  QU, Canada.... 155 B4
Cap Malheureux • Mauritius.... 132 J2
Cap, Pointe du • St Lucia.... 161 P
Cap Rock Escarpment •
  TX, United States.... 47 D1
Cap-Haïtien • Haiti.... 159 G2
Cap-Pelé • Brazil.... 53 (1) B2
Caparaó, Serra do • Brazil.... 163 C2
Caparra • Puerto Rico.... 159 H2
Capbreton • France.... 115 G3
Capdepera Beach •
  Majorca, Spain.... 96 [126]
Capdepera • Majorca, Spain.... 117 H2
Cape Breton Highlands Nat. Park •
  NS, Canada.... 156 D8
Cape Breton Highlands Nat. Park •
  Park N • NS, Canada.... 156 [35]
Cape Breton I. • NS, Canada.... 156 D8
Cape Canaveral •
  MA, United States.... 154 H6
Cape Coast • Ghana.... 22 D3
Cape Cod Bay •
  MA, United States.... 153 D4
Cape Cod Nat. Seashore Park N •
  MA, United States.... 151 [328]
Cape Cod Nat. Seashore •
  MA, United States.... 153 D4
Cape Coral • FL, United States.... 154 H7
Cape Cross Reserve Park •
  Namibia.... 133 [120]
Cape Evans • Antarctica.... 81 A10
Cape Girardeau •
  MO, United States.... 46 K4
Cape Hatteras Nat. Seashore Park N •
  NC, United States.... 151 [243]
Cape Krusenstern Nat. Mon. Park N •
  AK, United States.... 150 [2]
Cape Krusenstern Nat. Mon. •
  AK, United States.... 49 I2
Cape Lookout Nat. Seashore Park N •
  NC, United States.... 151 [242]
Cape May • NJ, United States.... 153 D11
Cape of Good Hope Nature Reserve •
  South Africa.... 133 [122]
Cape of Good Hope Nature Reserve •
  Park • South Africa.... 134 C3
Cape Peninsula • South Africa.... 134 C5
Cape Region • Mexico.... 157 F4
Cape Sounio • Greece.... 122 D7
Cape Town • South Africa.... 134 C5
CAPE VERDE • Atlantic Ocean.... 22 I1
Capella I. • US Virgin Is..... 160 Z
Capella Telefomin • Indonesia.... 32 (1) F3
Capelle aan den IJssel •
  Netherlands.... 109 F3
Capelle, la • France.... 10 I4
Capernaum • Israel.... 135 A2
Capesterre-Belle-Eau •
  Guadeloupe.... 161 L
Capiera • Spain.... 116 B3
Capitán Arturo Prat [Base] •
  Antarctica.... 54 (1) JJ4

Capitan Peak •
  NM, United States.... 46 C6
Capitol Reef Nat. Park Park N •
  UT, United States.... 150 [81]
Capitol Reef Nat. Park •
  UT, United States.... 45 G2
Capo Bci • Sardinia, Italy.... 120 C4
Capodimonte • Italy.... 121 G1
Capodimonte • Italy.... 121 F1
Cappadocia • Italy.... 121 F2
Cappadocia rock sites Heritage N •
  Turkey.... 83 [71]
Cappadocia rock sites Heritage C •
  Turkey.... 86 [228]
Cappenberg, Schloss • Germany.... 111 B2
Caprája, I. di • Italy.... 121 E10
Caprera, I. • Sardinia, Italy.... 120 C2
Capri • Italy.... 121 G3
Capri • Italy.... 121 G3
Capriate San Gervasio • Italy.... 121 E6
Capricorn Channel •
  QL, Australia.... 144 B4
Capricorn Group • QL, Australia.... 144 B4
Caprivi Strip • Namibia.... 24 C3
Capt. Keith Roberts, MV •
  Cayman Is..... 159 E2
Captain Cook •
  HI, United States.... 154 G8
Captiva I. • FL, United States.... 154 H7
Câpua • Italy.... 121 G1
Capucin, Cape • Dominica.... 161 M
Capulin • NM, United States.... 46 C4
Caplin Volcano Nat. Mon. Park N •
  NM, United States.... 150 [130]
Caputh • Germany.... 111 C3
Caquetá • Colombia.... 51 C4
Car Nicobar • India.... 28 F7
Caracal • Romania.... 14 I5
Caracaraí • Brazil.... 51 E3
Caracas • Venezuela.... 51 D1
Caracollo • Bolivia.... 52 C2
Caraguatatuba • Brazil.... 163 C3
Carais, Serra dos • Brazil.... 51 G5
Carajás • Brazil.... 51 G5
Caransebes • Romania.... 14 J4
Caranzalem Beach • Goa, India.... 137 B1
Caraquet • NB, Canada.... 156 D2
Caratasca, Laguna de • Honduras.... 37 E4
Caratinga • Brazil.... 163 C2
Carauari • Brazil.... 51 D5
Caravaca de la Cruz • Spain.... 11 J6
Caravelas • Brazil.... 52 I2
Caravelle, Presqu'île la •
  Martinique.... 161 N
Carazinho • Brazil.... 52 F4
Carballo • Spain.... 11 C1
Carballo Beach • Spain.... 96 [92]
Carberry • MN, Canada.... 43 G2
Carbet, la • Martinique.... 161 N
Carbo • Mexico.... 157 F2
Carbon, Cap • Algeria.... 11 K9
Carbonara, Capo •
  Sardinia, Italy.... 120 D4
Carbondale • CO, United States.... 45 I2
Carbondale • IL, United States.... 46 K4
Carbondale • PA, United States.... 153 C4
Carboneras Beach • Spain.... 96 [116]
Carboneras • Spain.... 116 B4
Carbonia • Sardinia, Italy.... 120 C4
Carbury • Ireland.... 108 E3
Carcans Beach • France.... 96 [85]
Carcans • France.... 115 G1
Carcassonne Heritage C • France.... 86 [79]
Carcross • YT, Canada.... 49 O3
Cardak • Çanakkale, Turkey.... 15 H3
Cardak • Denizli, Turkey.... 15 K6
Cardamom Hills • India.... 138 D10
Cárdenas • Cuba.... 158 D2
Cardiff • United Kingdom.... 104 F2
Cardigan • United Kingdom.... 7 H9
Cardigan Bay • United Kingdom.... 7 H9
Cardona • Spain.... 163 D2
Cardrona • New Zealand.... 145 G2
Cardston • AL, Canada.... 42 I2
Carei • Romania.... 14 J2
Carentan • France.... 10 D4
Carey, Lake • WA, Australia.... 34 D5
Cerezza, Lago di • Italy.... 120 B3
Cargados Carajos • Indian Ocean.... 19 J7
Cargèse • Corsica, France.... 115 L3
Cargo boat Dive • Red Sea.... 135 B2
Carhaix-Plouguer • France.... 114 C1
Caria • Turkey.... 122 D9
Cariacica • Brazil.... 163 C2
Carib Reserve • Dominica.... 161 M
Caribbean Sea • America.... 37 G4
Caribbean/Florida cruise area •
  America.... 80 B
Cariboo Mtns • BC, Canada.... 38 G6
Caribou • MN, Canada.... 38 L5
Caribou • ME, United States.... 44 K2
Caribou I. • OT, Canada.... 43 L1
Caribou Mtns • AL, Canada.... 38 H5
Carignan • France.... 5 I5
Carinhanha • Brazil.... 52 H1
Carinthia • Austria.... 119 F3
Carinthia Ski •
  VT, United States.... 149 [206]
Caripito • Venezuela.... 51 E1
Carita • Java, Indonesia.... 143 J1
Carl Sandburg Home Nat. Hist. Site •
  Park N • NC, United States.... 151 [238]
Carleton Place • OT, Canada.... 155 B6
Carlin • NV, United States.... 42 G6
Carlinville • IL, United States.... 46 J3
Carlisle • PA, United States.... 153 D5
Carlow • Ireland.... 108 B3
Carlow [Adm] • Ireland.... 108 A2
Carlsbad • CA, United States.... 45 D5
Carlsbad • NM, United States.... 47 B1
Carlsbad Caverns Nat. Park Heritage N •
  NM, United States.... 82 [14]
Carlsbad Caverns Nat. Park Park N •
  NM, United States.... 150 [120]
Carlsbad Caverns Nat. Park •
  NM, United States.... 47 B1
Carlyle • SA, Canada.... 43 E2
Carmacks • YT, Canada.... 38 D4
Carmagnola • Italy.... 12 B4
Carmarthen • United Kingdom.... 7 H10
Carmarthen Bay • United Kingdom.... 7 H10
Carmaux • France.... 10 H9
Carmel • IN, United States.... 44 B6
Carmel • CA, United States.... 152 C4
Carmel, Mount • Israel.... 135 A3
Carmelo • Uruguay.... 163 D2
Carmen, I. • Mexico.... 157 H3
Carmen, I. • Mexico.... 157 H3
Carmen, Ponto do • Madeira.... 118 C2
Carmi • IL, United States.... 48 C1
Carmichael • CA, United States.... 152 C1
Carmona • Spain.... 116 B2
Carna • Ireland.... 108 C3
Carnac • France.... 114 C2
Carnamah • WA, Australia.... 34 B4
Carnarvon • WA, Australia.... 34 B4
Carnarvon • South Africa.... 134 C3
Carnati • India.... 138 D11
Carnatic Dive • Red Sea.... 135 B2
Carnegie, Lake • WA, Australia.... 34 D5
Carnot • Central African Rep..... 23 B3
Carnot • Central African Rep..... 104 B2
Carnsore Point • Ireland.... 7 F9
Carol City • FL, United States.... 154 M
Carolina • Brazil.... 53 (1) B3
Carolina • Puerto Rico.... 159 H2
Caroline • Kiribati.... 33 L7

Caroline I. •
  Fed. States of Micronesia.... 33 F5
Carondelet • Kiribati.... 33 J6
Caroni • Venezuela.... 37 I6
Caroni Bird Sanctuary •
  Trinidad & Tobago.... 160 U
Carora • Venezuela.... 51 C1
Carpathians • Europe.... 4 O7
Carpatii Meridionali • Romania.... 14 K4
Carpatii Occidentali • Romania.... 13 L11
Carpentaria, Gulf of •
  NT/QL, Australia.... 34 G3
Carpi • Italy.... 121 E8
Carpinteria • CA, United States.... 45 C4
Carr Pond Mtn •
  ME, United States.... 44 K2
Carra, Lough • Ireland.... 108 C4
Carrabelle • FL, United States.... 49 A3
Carrantuohill • Ireland.... 7 H11
Carrara • Italy.... 121 E10
Carraroe • Ireland.... 108 C5
Carraroe Beach • Ireland.... 96 [62]
Carrarroe • Ireland.... 108 C5
Carrasco • Uruguay.... 163 D2
Carreta, Punta • Peru.... 163 B1
Carriacou • Grenada.... 161 R
Carrick-on-Shannon • Ireland.... 7 D8
Carrick-on-Suir • Ireland.... 7 E9
Carrickfergus • United Kingdom.... 7 G8
Carrigadrohid Reservoir •
  Ireland.... 108 C7
Carrington • ND, United States.... 43 G3
Carrizo Springs •
  TX, United States.... 47 D3
Carrizozo • NM, United States.... 46 C6
Carroll • IA, United States.... 46 I3
Carrollton • OH, United States.... 44 E5
Carrollton • GA, United States.... 48 E4
Carrollton • TX, United States.... 47 F1
Carrollton • KY, United States.... 48 E4
Carroz d'Arâches, les • France.... 115 F2
Carroz, les Ski • France.... 100 [18]
Carruantoohil • Ireland.... 108 C7
Carson City • NV, United States.... 152 C3
Carson, Fort • United States.... 46 C3
Cartagena Heritage C • Colombia.... 84 [48]
Cartagena • Colombia.... 51 B1
Cartagena Beach • Spain.... 96 [117]
Cartagena • Spain.... 11 J7
Cartago • Costa Rica.... 37 E6
Cartago • Colombia.... 51 B3
Carter, Mt • OL, Australia.... 34 H2
Cartersville •
  GA, United States.... 48 E3
Carthage Heritage C • Tunisia.... 86 [264]
Carthage • Tunisia.... 131 E2
Carthage • IL, United States.... 46 H4
Carthage • TX, United States.... 47 G1
Carthage [Apt] • Tunisia.... 131 E2
Carúpano • Venezuela.... 51 E1
Caruthersville •
  MO, United States.... 48 C2
Carvoeiro • Portugal.... 118 E6
Carvoeiro, Cabo • Portugal.... 11 F5
Cary • NC, United States.... 48 H3
Cas Concos • Majorca, Spain.... 117 [149]
Casa de Campo, Parque de Atracciones •
  Park L • Spain.... 98 [77]
Casa Grande • AZ, United States.... 153 E3
Casa Grande Ruins Nat. Mon. Park N •
  AZ, United States.... 150 [111]
Casa Grande Ruins Nat. Mon. •
  AZ, United States.... 153 E3
Casablanca • Morocco.... 131 D1
Casale Monferrato • Italy.... 121 E6
Casalmaggiore • Italy.... 121 E7
Casamari, Abbazia di • Italy.... 121 F4
Casares • Spain.... 116 A4
Casasos • Mexico.... 47 E6
Cascade • ID, United States.... 42 G4
Cascade Dam • ID, United States.... 42 G4
Cascade Mtn Ski •
  WI, United States.... 149 [132]
Cascade Range •
  OR/WA, United States.... 152 B
Cascades, Pointe des • Réunion.... 132 H4
Cascais Beach • Portugal.... 96 [98]
Cascais • Portugal.... 118 D6
Cascavel • Brazil.... 52 F4
Cascina • Italy.... 12 E5
Caselle [Apt] • Italy.... 121 E5
Caserta Heritage C • Italy.... 86 [149]
Caserta • Italy.... 121 G1
Casey [Base] • Antarctica.... 54 (1) Q3
Casey Bay • Antarctica.... 54 (1) J3
Caseyr, Râs • Somalia.... 23 I1
Cashel • Ireland.... 163 D1
Casilda • Argentina.... 52 C5
Casino • NS, Australia.... 144 B6
Casino • Czech Rep..... 128 B2
Caspe • Spain.... 11 K3
Casper • WY, United States.... 42 E5
Caspian Depression •
  Kazakstan/Russian Fed..... 17 H5
Caspian Sea • Asia.... 4 T8
Cass Lake • MN, United States.... 43 I3
Cassano allo Ionio • Italy.... 12 K9
Casselberry • FL, United States.... 49 C3
Casselton • ND, United States.... 43 H3
Cassino • BC, Canada.... 38 F5
Cassino • Italy.... 12 I7
Cassino Beach • Brazil.... 52 F5
Cassville • MO, United States.... 46 I4
Castagneto Carducci Beach •
  Italy.... 96 [146]
Castagneto Carducci • Italy.... 121 E11
Castanhal • Brazil.... 52 G1
Castel del Monte Heritage C •
  Italy.... 86 [154]
Castel di Sangro • Italy.... 12 I7
Castelbuono • Italy.... 12 H11
Castelfranco Véneto • Italy.... 12 F3
Castellabate • Italy.... 12 I8
Castellammare di Stábia • Italy.... 121 G3
Castellammare, Golfo di •
  Sicily, Italy.... 120 D4
Castellana Grotte • Italy.... 12 L8
Castellane • France.... 115 H2
Castelldefels • Spain.... 117 D3
Castelli Romani • Italy.... 121 F3
Castelló d'Empúries Beach •
  Spain.... 96 [123]
Castellón de la Plana • Spain.... 11 K4
Castelltallat • Spain.... 11 K4
Castelsaudany • France.... 11 M1
Castelo Branco • Portugal.... 11 G5
Castelo Branco [Adm] • Portugal.... 118 C2
Castelo, Ponto do • Madeira.... 118 C2
Castelsardo Beach •
  Italy.... 96 [137]
Castelsardo • Sardinia, Italy.... 120 C1
Castelvetrano • Sicily, Italy.... 12 G11
Castera • Trinidad & Tobago.... 160 T
Castiglione del Lago • Italy.... 121 F2
Castiglione della Pescáia •
  Italy.... 121 E11

Castle Bruce • Dominica.... 161 M
Castle Clinton Nat. Mon. Park N •
  NY, United States.... 151 [312]
Castle Dale • UT, United States.... 45 G2
Castle Drogo • United Kingdom.... 104 F5
Castle Harbour • Bermuda.... 159 H2
Castle Hill • NF, Canada.... 108 C6
Castle Matrix • Ireland.... 108 C6
Castle Peak • Hong Kong, China.... 139 B5
Castle Rock • WA, United States.... 42 D3
Castle Rock • CO, United States.... 46 C3
Castle Rock Lake •
  WI, United States.... 43 L5
Castlebar • Ireland.... 108 B2
Castlebay • United Kingdom.... 106 B2
Castleconnell • Ireland.... 108 C6
Castledermot • Ireland.... 108 B1
Castledown House • Ireland.... 108 B1
Castlegar • BC, Canada.... 42 G2
Castlegregory Beach • Ireland.... 96 [60]
Castlegregory • Ireland.... 108 C5
Castleisland • Ireland.... 108 C6
Castlepoint • New Zealand.... 35 F5
Castlereagh • NT, Australia.... 34 G2
Castlerock • United Kingdom.... 108 D1
Castleton • Jamaica.... 159 F2
Castletownbere • Ireland.... 108 B1
Castres • France.... 10 H10
Castricum • Netherlands.... 109 D7
Castries • St Lucia.... 161 P
Castro • Brazil.... 52 F3
Castro • Chile.... 53 B4
Castro Marim Beach • Portugal.... 96 [100]
Castro Marim • Portugal.... 118 E4
Castro Urdiales Beach • Spain.... 96 [89]
Castrojeriz • Spain.... 11 H2
Castrop-Rauxel • Germany.... 111 B2
Castrovillari • Italy.... 12 K9
Caswell Bay Beach •
  United Kingdom.... 101 [157]
Caswell Sound • New Zealand.... 145 G1
Cat Cay • Bahamas.... 49 D5
Cat Lake (Lake) • OT, Canada.... 43 K1
Catahoula Lake •
  LA, United States.... 47 H2
Catak • Turkey.... 15 J4
Catalão • Brazil.... 52 G2
Çatalca • Turkey.... 15 J2
Catalina • AZ, United States.... 45 G5
Catalina, I. • Dominican Rep..... 159 D8
Catalina, Punta • Chile.... 53 C6
Catalonia • Spain.... 116 A2
Cataluña • Spain.... 11 M3
Catalunya • Spain.... 11 M3
Catamarca • Argentina.... 52 C4
Catanduanes • Philippines.... 31 G4
Catandvava • Brazil.... 52 F3
Catánia • Sicily, Italy.... 120 D4
Catánia, Golfo di •
  Sicily, Italy.... 120 D4
Catano • Puerto Rico.... 159 H2
Catanzaro • Italy.... 12 K10
Cataratas Ruancaná •
  Angola/Namibia.... 24 A3
Catbalogan • Philippines.... 31 G4
Catemu • Chile.... 53 A3
Catania Costiera • Italy.... 12 K9
Catena dei Lagorai • Italy.... 120 B3
Catholic I. •
  St Vincent & Gren..... 161 R
Catía • Colombia.... 51 B2
Catoca • Angola.... 22 H6
Catoosa • OK, United States.... 46 H4
Cato I. • CL, Australia.... 34 K4
Catoche, Cabo • Mexico.... 157 H2
Catoctin Mtn Park Park N •
  MD, United States.... 151 [273]
Catriló • Argentina.... 52 D6
Catskill Mtns •
  NY, United States.... 153 D3
Cattólica • Italy.... 121 E12
Catu • Brazil.... 53 (1) D3
Cauca • Colombia.... 51 B2
Caucasia • Colombia.... 51 B2
Caucasus • Asia/Europe.... 17 G6
Caucasus, Western Heritage N •
  Russian Fed..... 83 [72]
Caucete • Argentina.... 52 C5
Caudry • France.... 5 G4
Caulnes • France.... 114 C2
Caulonia • Italy.... 12 K10
Caungula • Angola.... 22 H6
Cauquenes • Chile.... 53 A4
Caura • Venezuela.... 51 E2
Causani • Moldova.... 14 Q3
Causeway Bay • Hong Kong, China.... 139 B6
Cautín • Chile.... 53 A4
Cauto • Cuba.... 158 D6
Cauvery • India.... 138 D6
Cauvery Delta • India.... 138 D11
Caux, Pays de • France.... 5 D5
Cava de' Tirreni • Italy.... 121 G4
Cavado • Portugal.... 11 F3
Cavalaire-sur-Mer • France.... 115 H4
Cavalese Ski • Italy.... 100 [219]
Cavalese • Italy.... 120 B3
Cavalier • ND, United States.... 43 H2
Cavalleria, Cap de •
  Minorca, Spain.... 117 F2
Cavalli Is. • Corsica, France.... 115 L4
Cavallo, I. • Corsica, France.... 115 L4
Cavan • Côte d'Ivoire/Liberia.... 7 E8
Cavan • Ireland.... 108 A1
Cavan [Adm] • Ireland.... 108 A1
Cavalcante • France.... 12 G3
Cavdir • Turkey.... 123 F1
Cave Creek • AZ, United States.... 45 G5
Cave Junctions •
  OR, United States.... 42 D5
Cavelossim Beach • Goa, India.... 137 B2
Cavernoso • Brazil.... 51 G3
Cavour • Italy.... 12 B4
Cavtat • Croatia.... 128 D4
Çavus Burun • Turkey.... 123 F3
Çavus • Turkey.... 123 E2
Cawnpore • India.... 28 C3
Cawood • Brazil.... 163 C3
Caxias • Brazil.... 53 (1) C2
Caxias do Sul • Brazil.... 52 F4
Caxito • Angola.... 23 A5
Cay Sal Bank • Bahamas.... 49 C6
Cayambe, Volcán • Ecuador.... 51 B3
Cayenne • French Guiana.... 51 G3
Cayey • Puerto Rico.... 159 H2
Cayman Brac • Cayman Is..... 159 E2
Cayman Is. • West Indies.... 159 C2
Cayman Trench • West Indies.... 160 A7
Cayman Turtle Farm • Cayman Is..... 159 E3
Cayo Coco • Cuba.... 158 D3
Cayo Guin • Cuba.... 159 G2
Cayton Bay Beach •
  United Kingdom.... 101 [32]
Cayuga Lake • NY, United States.... 153 D2
Cazombo • Angola.... 24 B2
Ceananmas Mór • Ireland.... 108 B1
Ceará • Brazil.... 53 (1) C2
Cebollera, Sierra • Spain.... 11 G2
Cebreros • Spain.... 11 G4
Cebu • Philippines.... 31 G4
Cebu [I.] • Philippines.... 31 G4

Ceccano • Italy.... 121 F4
Cece • Hungary.... 14 F3
Cecina • Italy.... 12 E5
Cecis • Latvia.... 126 B4
Cedar • ND, United States.... 43 E3
Cedar • IA, United States.... 43 K6
Cedar Breaks Nat. Mon. Park N •
  UT, United States.... 150 [79]
Cedar City • UT, United States.... 45 F3
Cedar Creek Dam •
  ID, United States.... 42 H5
Cedar Creek Lake •
  TX, United States.... 47 F1
Cedar Falls • IA, United States.... 43 J5
Cedar Grove • Antigua & Barbuda.... 161 K
Cedar Key • FL, United States.... 49 B3
Cedar Key Nat. Wildlife Refuge •
  FL, United States.... 154 H3
Cedar Lake • MN, Canada.... 38 K6
Cedar Lake • IN, United States.... 44 B5
Cedar Point Park L •
  OH, United States.... 151 [T]
Cedar Pride Dive • Red Sea.... 135 B1
Cedar Rapids •
  IA, United States.... 46 J2
Cedar Tree Point •
  Antigua & Barbuda.... 161 J
Cedartown • GA, United States.... 48 E4
Cederberg • South Africa.... 134 C1
Cedros • Mexico.... 36 F7
Cedros I. • Mexico.... 157 F1
Ceduna • SA, Australia.... 34 F6
Cefalú • Sicily, Italy.... 120 D2
Cegar Perah • Malaysia.... 141 G2
Cegléd • Hungary.... 13 I10
Cehegín • Spain.... 11 J6
Ceiba • Puerto Rico.... 159 H2
Ceiba Fields • Ireland.... 108 C2
Cekik • Bali, Indonesia.... 143 H1
Celano • Italy.... 121 F2
Celaya • Mexico.... 157 G1
Celebes • Indonesia.... 32 (1) A3
Celebes Sea • Indonesia.... 32 (1) B3
Celerina Ski • Switzerland.... 100 [116]
Celerina • Switzerland.... 100 [116]
Celestún • Mexico.... 157 H1
Celina • OH, United States.... 44 C5
Celje • Slovenia.... 13 I11
Celje • Slovenia.... 128 D1
Celldömölk • Hungary.... 13 G10
Celle • Germany.... 8 F4
Celle Castle • Germany.... 113 [5]
Celle Ligure Beach • Italy.... 96 [141]
Celoricó da Beira • Portugal.... 11 D4
Celtic Sea • Ireland/UK.... 7 E10
Celuk • Bali, Indonesia.... 143 H4
Cemaes Bay Beach •
  United Kingdom.... 101 [230-231]
Cemlyn Beach • United Kingdom.... 101 [229]
Cenajo, Embalse de • Spain.... 11 J6
Cenderawasih, Teluk • Indonesia.... 35 (1) A1
Cennet ve Cehennem • Turkey.... 123 G3
Cento • Italy.... 121 E7
Centola Beach • Italy.... 97 [149]
Central • Hong Kong, China.... 139 B5
CENTRAL AFRICAN REPUBLIC •
  Africa.... 23 C2
Central Australia Aboriginal Land •
  WA, Australia.... 145 D3
Central Butte • SA, Canada.... 42 L1
Central City •
  KY, United States.... 48 D2
Central City •
  NE, United States.... 46 G2
Central eastern rainforest reserves •
  Heritage N • Australia.... 83 [143]
Central Forest Reserve •
  AL, United States.... 48 D4
Central I. Nat. Park Heritage N •
  Kenya.... 83 [98]
Central I. Nat. Park • Kenya.... 131 G1
Central Lowland • United States.... 41 H3
Central Makran Range • Pakistan.... 18 H4
Central Plains • Thailand.... 142 A2
Central Plateau • Russian Fed..... 4 R6
Central Plateau • New Zealand.... 145 F4
Central Range •
  Papua New Guinea.... 35 (1) C2
Central Siberian Plateau •
  Russian Fed..... 25 L3
Central Siberian Uplands •
  Russian Fed..... 26 Q5
Central, Sistema • Spain.... 11 F4
Central-Leatherstocking •
  NY, United States.... 153 D2
Centralia • IL, United States.... 48 C1
Centralia • WA, United States.... 152 B1
Centre • France.... 114 A1
Centre • AL, United States.... 48 E3
Centre, Canal du Heritage C •
  Belgium.... 86 [36]
Centre du Flaq • Mauritius.... 132 J4
Centre Hills • Montserrat.... 161 H
Centreville Park L • OT, Canada.... 156 [L]
Centreville (Toronto) •
  Canada.... 155 B9
Cephalonia • Greece.... 122 C2
Cepu • Java, Indonesia.... 143 J3
Cerbère Beach • France.... 96 [128]
Cerbère • France.... 115 K2
Cerbicale, Is. •
  Corsica, France.... 115 L4
Ceres • Brazil.... 52 G2
Ceres • CA, United States.... 45 B3
Cerf, I. au • Seychelles.... 133 K3
Cerfs, I. aux • Mauritius.... 132 J4
Cergy-Pontoise • France.... 114 A1
Ceringola • Italy.... 12 J7
Cergy • Greece.... 122 D7
Çerkes • Turkey.... 15 I3
Çerkezköy • Turkey.... 15 I2
Cermei • Romania.... 13 K11
Cermenika • Albania.... 14 H8
Cerna Skala •
  Bulgaria/F.Y.R. of Macedonia.... 15 I1
Cernavodă • Romania.... 128 E2
Cerni vrah • Bulgaria.... 15 E1
Cernóbbio • Italy.... 121 E2
Ceralvo • Mexico.... 47 E4
Cerralvo I. • Mexico.... 157 F3
Cerritos • Mexico.... 157 H2
Cerro Azul • Brazil.... 52 G3
Cerro de las Mesas • Mexico.... 157 G3
Cerro de Pasco • Peru.... 51 B6
Cerro del Aripo •
  Trinidad & Tobago.... 160 U
Certosa di Padula Heritage C •
  Italy.... 86 [153]
Cervaro • Italy.... 12 J7
Cervená Lhota • Czech Rep..... 128 B4
Cervéteri • Italy.... 12 G6
CerviaAldo • Italy.... 121 E8
Cerviale, Monte • Italy.... 121 G4
Cervo Beach • Italy.... 96 [91]
Cervo Beach • Italy.... 96 [140]
Cesana Ski • Italy.... 100 [196]
Cesena • Italy.... 12 G4
Cesenático • Italy.... 121 E8
České Budejovice • Czech Rep..... 128 B4
České Švycarsko • Czech Rep..... 128 B1
Ceské Zeme • Czech Rep..... 13 D8
Ceskomoravská Vysocina •
  Czech Rep..... 13 E8

Cesky Krumlov **Heritage C** •
Czech Rep. .... 86 [172]
Cesky Krumlov • Czech Rep. ... 128 B4
Cesky Les • Czech Rep. 128 B3
Cesky Sternberk • Czech Rep. .. 128 B2
Çeşme • Turkey 122 D5
Cessnock • NS, Australia 144 C2
Cestos • Côte d'Ivoire/Liberia ... 22 C3
Cetarro • Italy 12 J9
Cetinje • F.R. of Yugoslavia 14 F7
Ceuta • Africa 131 D2
Ceva-i-Ra • Fiji Is. 35 (2) C3
Cévennes • France 10 I9
Cévennes, Parc nat. des **Park N** •
France .... 89 [70]
Cevizli • Turkey 123 F2
Ceyhan • Turkey 123 G4
Ceyhan [Riv] • Turkey 123 G2
Ceylon • Asia 28 D7
Ch'an • Rep. of Korea 30 D6
Ch'ongju • D.P.R. of Korea 30 C4
Ch'ongju • Rep. of Korea 30 D6
Ch'orwon • Rep. of Korea 30 C5
Ch'unch'on • Rep. of Korea 30 D6
Ch'ungju • Rep. of Korea 30 D6
Cha-Am • Thailand 142 C3
Chaâlis, Abbaye de • France 115 F2
Chablais • France 115 F2
Chablis • France 114 B2
Chacabuco • Argentina 163 D1
Chacachacare I. •
Trinidad & Tobago .... 160 U
Chachua, Laguna de • Mexico ... 157 G4
Chachapoyas • Peru 51 B5
Chachoengsao • Thailand 142 C2
Chacmultún • Mexico 157 H1
Chaco Austral • Argentina 52 D4
Chaco Boreal • Paraguay 52 D3
Chaco Central • Argentina 52 D3
Chaco Culture Nat. Hist. Park
Heritage C • NM, United States ... 84 [7]
Chaco Culture Nat. Hist. Park **Park N** •
NM, United States .... 150 [123]
Chaco Culture Nat. Hist. Park •
NM, United States 153 E2
CHAD • Africa 21 C4
Chad, Lake • Africa 21 B5
Chadan • Russian Fed. 26 P7
Chadileuvú • Argentina 52 C6
Chadron • NE, United States ... 43 E5
Chafarinas, Is. • Spain 11 I9
Chagai Hills • Pakistan 18 H4
Chagcharan • Afghanistan 18 I3
Chagda • Russian Fed. 27 L5
Chaguanas • Trinidad & Tobago .. 160 U
Chagyl • Turkmenistan 18 G1
Chah Bahar • Iran 18 H4
Chahar Borjak • Afghanistan ... 18 H3
Chaillu, Massif du • Gabon 22 G5
Chainat • Thailand 31 C3
Chaitén • Chile 53 B4
Chake Chake • Tanzania 130 B2
Chakwara • Afghanistan 18 H3
Chala • Peru 163 B3
Chalbi Desert • Kenya 131 G1
Chaleur Bay • NB/QU, Canada .. 156 D2
Chalky Inlet • New Zealand 145 G3
Challaborough **Beach** •
United Kingdom .... 101 [130]
Challapata • Bolivia 52 C2
Challenger Deep •
Fed. States of Micronesia 25 P8
Challis • ID, United States 42 H4
Chalmette • LA, United States .. 48 C6
Chalon-sur-Saône • France 10 J7
Chalong • Ko Phuket, Thailand .. 142 E2
Chalong Bay •
Ko Phuket, Thailand 142 E2
Chalong, Wat •
Ko Phuket, Thailand 142 E2
Châlons-sur-Marne • France ... 10 J5
Chalusset, Château de • France .. 115 G2
Cham • Germany 9 H7
Chám • Mauritania 20 B4
Chaman • Pakistan 28 A2
Chamarel • Mauritius 132 J3
Chamba • India 28 C2
Chamba • Tanzania 130 B4
Chamba **Hill Sta** • India 138 E1
Chambal • India 137 C6
Chamberlain • SD, United States .. 43 G5
Chamberlain Lake •
ME, United States 44 K2
Chambers Pillar • NT, Australia .. 145 D4
Chambéry • France 115 F1
Chambeshi • Zambia 24 E2
Chambi, Jebel • Tunisia 131 E3
Chambly • France 115 E1
Chambly, Fort • QU, Canada ... 155 B7
Chambord **Heritage C** • France .. 86 [71]
Chambord [Château] • France .. 114 D2
Chamizal Nat. Mem. **Park N** •
TX, United States .... 150 [133]
Chamois • Italy 121 E1
Chamonix • France 115 F2
Chamonix-Mont Blanc **Ski** •
France .... 100 [27]
Champ du Feu • France 10 M5
Champagne Castle • South Africa .. 134 B3
Champagne-Ardenne • France .. 114 A2
Champagnole • France 10 K7
Champagny-en-Vanoise **Ski** •
France .... 100 [35]
Champaign • IL, United States .. 44 A5
Champaner **Hill Sta** • India .. 138 E1
Champaqui, Cerro • Argentina .. 52 D5
Champasak • Laos 141 D2
Champawat • India 137 C3
Champéry • Switzerland 119 G5
Champéry-Planachaux **Ski** •
Switzerland .... 100 [78]
Champex • Switzerland 119 G6
Champigny-sur-Marne • France .. 115 E4
Champlain, Lake •
VT, United States 44 I3
Champoluc **Ski** • Italy ..... 100 [205]
Champotón • Mexico 157 H3
Champoussin **Ski** • Switzerland .. 100 [77]
Champoussin • Switzerland 119 G5
Champs, Château de • France .. 115 E4
Champsosse **Ski** • France ... 100 [53]
Chan Chan • Peru 51 B5
Chan Chan **Heritage C** • Peru .. 84 [55]
Chan Santa Cruz • Mexico 157 H4
Chances Peak • Montserrat .... 161 H
Chandalar • AK, United States .. 38 B3
Chandelaur Is. •
LA, United States 48 C6
Chandeleur Sound •
LA, United States 153 F4
Chanderi • India 137 C2
Chandigarh • India 28 C2
Chandigarh [Adm] • India 137 A1
Chandler • AZ, United States ... 45 G5
Chandler • QU, Canada 156 D2
Chandor • Goa, India 137 B2
Chandragiri • India 138 D3
Chandraprabha Wildlife Sanctuary •
India 137 C3
Chang • India 28 C2
Chang Jiang • China 29 F4
Chang, Ko • Thailand 31 C4
Chang Zhou • China 139 C1
Changjin Nuruu • Mongolia 25 K5
Changan • China 127 D6
Changane • Mozambique 24 E4
Changbai • China 30 E4
Changbai Shan • China 30 D4
Changcheng • China 29 D3
Changchun • China 29 H2
Changde • China 29 E5

Changhua • Taiwan 29 G6
Changi [Apt] • Singapore 141 H2
Changjiang Kou • China 29 G4
Changjin-Up • D.P.R. of Korea .. 30 D4
Changping • China 139 B2
Changsha • China 29 E5
Changshu • China 139 C2
Changxing • China 139 C2
Changyon • D.P.R. of Korea ... 30 C5
Channhasen • MN, United States .. 43 J4
Channel Country • QL, Australia .. 144 A7
Channel Is. • Europe 7 J12
Channel Is. • CA, United States .. 152 C5
Channel Is. Nat. Park **Park N** •
CA, United States .... 150 [54]
Channel Is. Nat. Park •
CA, United States 152 C5
Channel Port-aux-Basques •
NF, Canada 156 D3
Channel Tunnel • France/UK ... 104 E4
Chantada • Spain 11 D2
Chantada, Faro de • Spain 11 D2
Chanthaburi • Thailand 31 C4
Chantilly • France 115 E2
Chantilly, Forêt de • France ... 115 E2
Chanute • KS, United States ... 48 H4
Chao Phraya • Thailand 142 C1
Chaouèn • Morocco 131 D2
Chaozhou • China 29 F6
Chapada das Mangabeiras •
Brazil 53 (1) B3
Chapada Diamantina • Brazil ... 52 H1
Chapaev • Kazakhstan 17 I5
Chapala, Laguna de • Mexico .. 157 G1
Chapecó • Brazil 52 F4
Chapel Hill • NC, United States .. 48 B1
Chapelle d'Abondance, la **Ski** •
France .... 100 [8]
Chapleau • QU, Canada 39 O7
Chaplin • SA, Canada 42 L1
Chaplino, mys • Russian Fed. ... 27 W4
Chapmanville •
WV, United States 48 G2
Chapora • Goa, India 137 B1
Chapora Fort • Goa, India 137 B1
Chapra • India 20 C4
Char • Mauritania 20 C4
Chara • Russian Fed. 27 I5
Chard • United Kingdom 104 F3
Charentais • France 114 B3
Charente [Adm] • France 115 G1
Charente [Riv] • France 115 G1
Charente-Maritime • France ... 115 G1
Chari • Chad 21 C5
Charity • Guyana 51 F2
Chärjew • Turkmenistan 18 H2
Charleroi • Belgium 109 D14
Charles, Cape • NF, Canada ... 39 T6
Charles, Cape •
VA, United States 153 D11
Charles City •
IA, United States 43 J5
Charles I. • NU, Canada 39 Q4
Charles Mound •
IL, United States 43 K5
Charles, Peak • WA, Australia .. 34 D6
Charles Pinckney Nat. Hist. Site **Park N** •
SC, United States .... 151 [233]
Charles Sound • New Zealand .. 145 G1
Charlesbourg • QU, Canada 44 J2
Charleston • IL, United States .. 44 A6
Charleston • WV, United States .. 48 G2
Charleston • MO, United States .. 46 K4
Charleston • SC, United States .. 48 H4
Charleston • Ireland 108 C2
Charlestown •
St Vincent & Gren. .... 161 R
Charlestown • St Kitts & Nevis .. 161 G
Charleville • QL, Australia 144 B5
Charleville-Mézières • France .. 10 J4
Charlevoix • MI, United States .. 44 C3
Charlotte • MI, United States .. 44 C4
Charlotte • NC, United States .. 48 G3
Charlotte Amalie •
US Virgin Is. .... 160 Z
Charlotte, Fort •
St Vincent & Gren. .... 161 R
Charlotte, Fort •
Bahamas 158 B3
Charlotte, Fort •
St Vincent & Gren. .... 161 Q
Charlotte, Fort • St Lucia ..... 161 P
Charlotte Harbor •
FL, United States 154 H5
Charlottenburg **Castle** • Germany .. 113 [219]
Charlottenburg, Schloss •
Germany 111 C1
Charlottesville **Heritage C** •
VA, United States .... 84 [10]
Charlottesville •
VA, United States 153 D11
Charlottetown • PE, Canada ... 156 D7
Charlotteville •
Trinidad & Tobago .... 160 T
Charlton • VI, Australia 144 C3
Charlton • AL/MO, United States .. 46 I2
Charmouth **Beach** •
United Kingdom .... 101 [110]
Charnwood Forest •
United Kingdom 104 D2
Charters Towers • QL, Australia .. 144 B1
Chartres **Heritage C** • France .. 86 [64]
Chartres • France 115 E1
Chartwell • United Kingdom ... 104 E3
Chascomús • Argentina 163 D4
Chasong • D.P.R. of Korea 30 C4
Chassagne • Angola 23 G3
Château-Arnoux • France 10 L9
Château-d'Oex **Ski** • Switzerland .. 100 [86]
Château-d'Oex • Switzerland ... 119 G6
Château-du-Loir • France 10 F6
Château-Gontier • France 10 E6
Château-Salins • France 5 J6
Château-Thierry • France 115 E2
Chateaubelair •
St Vincent & Gren. .... 161 Q
Chateaubelair I. •
St Vincent & Gren. .... 161 Q
Châteaubriant • France 114 D2
Châteaudun • France 114 D2
Châteauguay • QU, Canada 44 I3
Châteaulin • France 10 A5
Châteauneuf-du-Pape • France .. 114 D4
Châteaux, Pointe des •
Guadeloupe .... 161 L
Châtel **Ski** • France .... 100 [9]
Châtel • France 115 F2
Châtelet • Belgium 5 H4
Châtellerault • France 114 D4
Chatham • United Kingdom 104 E2
Chatham • OT, Canada 44 D4
Chatham • NB, Canada 156 C3
Chatham I. • New Zealand 35 (3) B1
Chatham Is. • New Zealand 35 (3)
Châtillon-sur-Indre • France ... 114 D4
Châtillon-sur-Seine • France ... 114 D3
Chau Doc • Vietnam 141 E1
Chaudière [Riv] • France 114 D2
Chauk • India 137 B2
Chaumont • France 114 D2
Chaumont [Château] • France .. 114 D2

Chaunskaya Guba • Russian Fed. .. 27 S3
Chauny • France 5 G5
Chautauqua-Allegheny •
NY, United States 153 D1
Chautauqua • NY, United States .. 153 D1
Chauvigny • France 114 D4
Chavantina • Brazil 52 F1
Chaves • Portugal 11 D3
Chaves • Brazil 51 G4
Chávez, Jorge [Apt] • Peru ... 163 B1
Chavuma • Zambia 24 C2
Chaweng Beach •
Ko Samui, Thailand 142 D1
Chayamangkalaram, Wat •
Penang, Malaysia 141 F2
Chbika • Tunisia 131 E3
Cheaha Mtn • AL, United States .. 48 E4
Cheb • Czech Rep. 128 B1
Cheboksary • Russian Fed. 17 H3
Cheboygan • MI, United States .. 44 C3
Chech, Erg • Algeria 20 C2
Cheddar • United Kingdom 104 F3
Cheddar Gorge • United Kingdom .. 104 F3
Chedube • Myanmar 31 A3
Chedworth Roman Villa •
United Kingdom 104 D4
Cheektowaga • NY, United States .. 44 F4
Cheerala • India 138 D3
Chegga • Mauritania 20 D3
Chegutu • Zimbabwe 130 C2
Chehalis • WA, United States .. 42 D3
Cheju • Rep. of Korea 30 D8
Cheju I. • Rep. of Korea 30 D8
Cheju-Haehyop • Rep. of Korea .. 30 D8
Chek Lap Kok • Hong Kong, China .. 139 B5
Chela • Angola 23 G3
Chelan • WA, United States ... 42 F1
Cheliff, Plaine du • Algeria 11 L8
Cheliff [Riv] • Algeria 20 F1
Chelm • Poland 13 M6
Chelmno • Poland 13 H4
Chelmsford • United Kingdom .. 104 E4
Chelmsford Nature Reserve •
South Africa 134 B1
Chelmza • Poland 13 H4
Chelsea • United Kingdom 104 E1
Cheltenham • United Kingdom .. 104 D4
Chelva • Spain 11 J5
Chelyabinsk • Russian Fed. 26 J6
Chelyuskin, mys • Russian Fed. .. 26 S2
Chembe • Zambia 23 D6
Chembersburg •
PA, United States 153 D9
Chemdal'sk • Russian Fed. 26 R6
Chemery [Château] • France .. 114 D2
Chemillé • France 114 D3
Chemin Grenier • Mauritius ... 132 J3
Chemnitz • Germany 9 H6
Chemult • OR, United States .. 152 B3
Chenab • Pakistan 28 B2
Chenachane • Algeria 20 E3
Chenachane [Riv] • Algeria 20 E3
Cheney • WA, United States ... 42 G3
Cheney Reservoir •
KS, United States 46 G4
Chengde • China 29 F2
Chengde **Heritage C** • China .. 85 [164]
Chengdu • China 29 D5
Chengshan Jiao • China 29 G3
Chenini • Tunisia 131 E6
Chennai • India 138 D3
Chenonceaux [Château] • France .. 114 D2
Chentijn Nuruu •
Mongolia/Russian Fed. 27 H7
Chenxian • China 29 E5
Cheongmon Bay •
Ko Samui, Thailand 142 D1
Chepca • Russian Fed. 17 I3
Chepes • Argentina 52 C5
Chepstow • United Kingdom ... 104 D3
Cher • France 10 G6
Cherangany Hills • Kenya 23 F3
Cherating • Malaysia 141 D3
Cheraw • SC, United States ... 48 H3
Cherbaniani Reef • India 138 C3
Cherbourg • France 10 D4
Cherchell • Algeria 11 N8
Cheremkhovo • Russian Fed. ... 26 R4
Cherepovets • Russian Fed. ... 126 C2
Cheriton Terminal •
United Kingdom 106 A19
Cherkasy • Ukraine 13 D9
Cherkesk • Russian Fed. 17 G6
Cherlak • Russian Fed. 26 L7
Chernihiv • Ukraine 17 E4
Chernivtsi • Ukraine 14 M1
Chernomorets • Bulgaria 128 E3
Chernyakhovsk • Russian Fed. .. 13 K3
Chernysevsky • Russian Fed. ... 27 H4
Cherokee • IA, United States .. 43 I5
Cherokee • OK, United States .. 46 F4
Cherokee Lake •
TN, United States 48 F2
Cherokees, Lake of the •
OK, United States 46 H4
Cherrapunji • India 28 F3
Cherry Hills •
NJ, United States 44 H6
Cherskiy • Russian Fed. 27 R3
Chervonohrad • Ukraine 13 N7
Chesapeake • VA, United States .. 153 D11
Chesapeake Bay •
VA, United States 153 D11
Chesapeake & Ohio Canal Nat. Hist. Park
Park N • MD, United States ... 151 [264]
Cheshskaya Guba • Russian Fed. .. 17 H1
Chesil Beach • United Kingdom .. 104 F6
Chesne, le • France 5 H5
Chessington World of Adventures **Park L** •
United Kingdom .... 98 [35]
Chessington World of Adventures •
United Kingdom 104 E1
Chester • United Kingdom 7 J8
Chester • CA, United States ... 42 E6
Chester • MT, United States .. 42 J1
Chester • IL, United States ... 46 K4
Chester • PA, United States ... 48 G3
Chester • PA, United States ... 153 D10
Chesterfield • United Kingdom .. 7 K8
Chesterfield Inlet • NU, Canada .. 39 N4
Chesterton • IN, United States .. 44 B5
Chestnut Mtn **Ski** •
IL, United States .... 149 [127]
Chesuncook Lake •
ME, United States 44 K2
Chettlatt I. • India 138 D5
Cheung Chau • Hong Kong, China .. 139 B5
Chevanny • France 114 B1
Cheverny [Château] • France .. 114 D2
Cheviot Hills • United Kingdom .. 7 J6
Cheviot, The • United Kingdom .. 7 J6
Chevreau, I. • St Barthélemy .. 160 E
Chevron Bahir • Ethiopia/Kenya .. 23 F3
Chewore safari area **Heritage N** •
Zimbabwe .... 83 [105]
Cheyenne • WY, United States .. 46 C2
Cheyenne •
SD/WY, United States 43 F5
Cheyenne Wells •
CO, United States 46 D3
Cheyne Bay • WA, Australia ... 34 C6
Chi • Thailand 142 A2
Chia • Sardinia, Italy 120 C4
Chiang Dao • Thailand 142 B1

Chiang Kham • Thailand 142 B2
Chiang Khan • Thailand 142 B4
Chiang Khong • Thailand 142 B2
Chiang Mai • Thailand 142 B2
Chiang Rai • Thailand 142 B2
Chiang Saen • Thailand 142 B2
Chianje • Angola 24 A3
Chianti • Italy 121 E11
Chiapas • Mexico 37 C4
Chiari • Italy 24 C2
Chiavenna • Angola 24 C2
Chiayi • Taiwan 29 G6
Chiba • Japan 140 C2
Chiba [Adm] • Japan 140 C2
Chibougamou • QU, Canada ... 39 Q6
Chicago • IL, United States ... 44 B5
Chicago Heights •
IL, United States 163 D1
Chicagof I. • AK, United States .. 49 N4
Chicanná • Mexico 157 H3
Chichaoua • Morocco 20 D2
Chichén-Itzá **Heritage C** •
Guatemala .... 84 [31]
Chichén-Itzá • Mexico 157 H2
Chichester • United Kingdom .. 104 E3
Chichibu • Japan 140 C2
Chichibu-Tama Nat. Park • Japan .. 140 C1
Chichijima-retto • Japan 140 A13
Chickamauga & Chattanooga Nat. Military
Park **Park N** • GA, United States .. 151 [203]
Chickamauga Lake •
TN, United States 48 E3
Chickasaw Nat. Recreation Area **Park N** •
OK, United States .... 151 [161]
Chickasawhay •
MS, United States 153 F2
Chicksha • OK, United States .. 46 G5
Chiclana de la Frontera **Beach** •
Spain .... 96 [113]
Chiclana de la Frontera • Spain .. 11 B5
Chiclayo • Peru 163 B3
Chico • CA, United States 152 C1
Chicopee • MA, United States .. 44 I4
Chicoutimi • QU, Canada 156 C1
Chicualacuala • Mozambique .. 130 C4
Chidambaram • India 138 D11
Chidley, Cape • NU, Canada ... 39 S4
Chiefland • FL, United States .. 154 H2
Chiemsee • Germany 112 F4
Chiengi • Zambia 23 D5
Chiesa • Italy 121 E2
Chieti • Italy 12 I6
Chiêut **Beach** • Italy .... 97 [158]
Chifeng • China 29 F2
Chiginagak, Mt •
AK, United States 49 J4
Chignik • AK, United States ... 49 J4
Chiguo Co • China 28 F3
Chigubo • Mozambique 24 E3
Chihuahua • Mexico 47 A3
Chihuahua [Adm] • Mexico ... 40 E6
Chikitu, Playa • Bonaire ...... 160 W
Chikurachki, Vulkan •
Russian Fed. 27 Q6
Chilca • Peru 163 B1
Chilcott I. • QL, Australia 34 J3
Childers • QL, Australia 144 B6
Childress • TX, United States .. 46 E5
CHILE • S. America 50 C7
Chile-Chico • Chile 53 B5
Chilecito • Argentina 52 C5
Chilián • Chile 52 B6
Chillicothe • OH, United States .. 44 D6
Chillicothe • MO, United States .. 46 I3
Chilliwack • BC, Canada 42 E2
Chiloé, I. de • Chile 53 B4
Chiloquin • OR, United States .. 42 E5
Chilpancingo • Mexico 157 G4
Chiltern Hills • United Kingdom .. 104 E1
Chilumba • Malawi 24 E2
Chilung • Taiwan 29 G5
Chilwa, Lake • Malawi 24 F3
Chimanimani • Zimbabwe 130 C4
Chimanimani Nat. Park •
Zimbabwe 130 C4
Chimayo • NM, United States .. 46 B4
Chimbay • Uzbekistan 26 I9
Chimborazo, Volcán • Ecuador .. 51 B4
Chimbote • Peru 51 B5
Chin • Rep. of Korea 30 D7
Chin • Myanmar 31 A2
China • Mexico 47 E5
China Folk Culture Villages •
Shenzhen, China 139 B3
CHINA, PEOPLE'S REPUBLIC OF •
Asia 25 L6
Chinandega • Nicaragua 37 D5
Chinati Peak •
TX, United States 47 B3
Chincha Alta • Peru 163 B1
Chinchilla • QL, Australia 144 B6
Chinchorro, Banco • Mexico ... 157 H4
Chincoteague •
VA, United States 153 D11
Chindwin • Myanmar 31 A2
Chinese & Japanese Garden •
Singapore 141 H1
Chingola • Zambia 24 C2
Chinguetti • Mauritania 20 C4
Chinguetti **Heritage C** •
Mauritania .... 85 [106]
Chinhae • Rep. of Korea 30 E7
Chinhoyi • Zimbabwe 130 C2
Chinju • Rep. of Korea 30 D7
Chinko • Africa 23 C2
Chinle • AZ, United States 153 E2
Chino Valley •
AZ, United States 45 F4
Chinon • France 114 B1
Chinon [Château] • France ... 114 D4
Chinook • MT, United States .. 42 K1
Chinook, Lake •
OR, United States 42 E4
Chióggia • Italy 121 E10
Chios **Heritage C** • Greece ... 86 [218]
Chios • Greece 122 D5
Chipata • Zambia 24 E2
Chipione • Mozambique 24 E2
Chipinda Pools • Zimbabwe ... 130 C4
Chiping • Zimbabwe 130 C4
Chipiona **Beach** • Spain .... 96 [113]
Chipiona • Spain 11 B5
Chipman • NB, Canada 156 D7
Chippenham • United Kingdom .. 104 F3
Chippewa • United Kingdom ... 43 K4
Chippewa Falls •
WI, United States 43 K4
Chippewa, Lake •
WI, United States 43 K4
Chiquinquirá • Colombia 51 C2
Chiquito Jesuit mission **Heritage C** •
Bolivia .... 84 [64]
Chiquitos, Llanos de • Bolivia .. 52 D2
Chirchiq • Uzbekistan 26 K9
Chiredzi • Zimbabwe 130 C4
Chirfa • Niger 20 H4
Chiri • Rep. of Korea 30 D7
Chiricahua Nat. Mon. **Park N** •
AZ, United States .... 150 [117]
Chiricahua Nat. Mon. •
AZ, United States 153 E4
Chirikof I. • AK, United States .. 49 J4
Chirip, vulkan • Russian Fed. .. 27 D7
Chirpan • Bulgaria 128 E3
Chirripó • Costa Rica 37 E6
Chirundu • Zimbabwe 130 C1
Chisamba • QU, Canada 39 P6
Chisasibi • QU, Canada 39 P6
Chişinău • Moldova 14 P2
Chistopol • Russian Fed. 17 I3
Chita • Russian Fed. 27 H6
Chitina • AK, United States ... 38 C4

Chitradurga • India 138 D6
Chitrakut • India 137 C7
Chitral • Pakistan 28 B1
Chitré • Panama 37 E6
Chittagong • Bangladesh 28 F4
Chittaurgarh • India 137 C6
Chittoor • India 138 D7
Chitungwiza • Zimbabwe 130 C2
Chiumbe • Angola 24 C2
Chiume • Angola 24 C2
Chiunzi, Válico de • Italy 121 G4
Chiusa • Italy 120 B1
Chiusi • Italy 121 E11
Chivasso • Italy 121 E5
Chivhu • Zimbabwe 130 C4
Chivilcoy • Argentina 163 D1
Chiwan • Shenzhen, China 139 B5
Chizarira Nat. Park • Zimbabwe .. 130 C1
Chizha • Russian Fed. 17 G1
Chobe • Botswana/Namibia ... 24 C4
Chobe Nat. Park **Park N** • Botswana .. 133 [115]
Chodov • Czech Rep. 13 B7
Chodziez • Poland 13 F5
Choele-Choel • Argentina 53 C3
Choirokoitia **Heritage C** •
Cyprus .... 86 [236]
Choirokoitia • Cyprus 123 J3
Choiseul • Solomon Is. 35 (1) F2
Choiseul • St Lucia .... 161 P
Choisy Beach • Mauritius 132 J1
Choix • Mexico 157 F4
Chojnice • Poland 13 G4
Chojnów • Poland 13 E6
Chokai • Japan 30 K5
Choke • Ethiopia 23 F1
Cholet • France 114 D3
Cholula • Mexico 157 G4
Chom Thong • Thailand 142 B3
Choma • Zambia 24 D3
Chomutov • Czech Rep. 128 B1
Chon Buri • Thailand 142 C4
Chone • Ecuador 51 A4
Chongkrum, Laem •
Ko Samui, Thailand 142 D2
Chongming • China 139 C2
Chongming Dao • China 139 C2
Chongmyo Shrine **Heritage C** •
Rep. of Korea .... 85 [182]
Chongqing • China 29 D5
Chongqing [Adm] • China 139 A7
Chongup • Rep. of Korea 30 D7
Chonju • Rep. of Korea 30 D7
Chonos, Archipiélago de los •
Chile 53 A5
Choral I. • Goa, India 137 B1
Chornobyl • Ukraine 17 E4
Chorwad **Beach** • India 138 E3
Chorzow • Poland 128 C1
Choshi • Japan 140 D2
Choszczno • Poland 13 E4
Chota Nagpur • India 137 A3
Choteau • MT, United States .. 42 I3
Chott Ech Chergui • Algeria .. 20 F2
Choum • Mauritania 20 C4
Chowchilla • CA, United States .. 45 B3
Choybalsan • Mongolia 27 H7
Choyr • Mongolia 29 D1
Chrisosalitissas, Moni •
Crete, Greece 123 E5
Chrisoula **Dive** • Red Sea .. 135 B1
Christchurch • New Zealand ... 35 D6
Christian, Cape • NU, Canada .. 39 R2
Christian I. • OT, Canada 44 E3
Christian Sound •
AK, United States 38 D5
Christiania • Norway 90 A3
Christiana • Jamaica 159 F1
Christiansburg •
VA, United States 48 G2
Christiansfeld • Denmark 125 F13
Christianso • Denmark 125 F16
Christiansted • US Virgin Is. ... 160 Z
Christie Bay • NT, Canada 38 I4
Christmas • Kiribati 33 L5
Christmas Creek • WA, Australia .. 34 E3
Christmas I. • Indian Ocean ... 32 D5
Christtianshåb • Greenland ... 39 U3
Chrysorroyiatissa Monastery •
Cyprus 123 J3
Chrzanów • Poland 128 C1
Chu Xian • China 139 C1
Chu Yang Sin • Vietnam 141 E2
Chu Zhou • China 139 C1
Chuansha • China 139 C2
Chubokulaki, gora •
Russian Fed. 27 P3
Chudovo • Russian Fed. 126 C1
Chudskoye Ozero •
Estonia/Russia 16 N7
Chugach Mtns •
AK, United States 49 L3
Chugoku • Japan 140 A3
Chugoku-sanchi • Japan 30 G7
Chugwater • WY, United States .. 43 D6
Chukai • Malaysia 32 C2
Chukchi • AK, United States .. 38 B3
Chukchi Sea • Russian Fed./US .. 49 G2
Chukotskiy Poluostrov •
Russian Fed. 27 W3
Chukotskoye More • Russian Fed. .. 54 GG2
Chula Vista • CA, United States .. 45 D5
Chulman • Russian Fed. 27 J5
Chulucanas • Peru 51 A5
Chulym • Russian Fed. 26 N6
Chumikan • Russian Fed. 27 M6
Chumphon • Thailand 31 B4
Chun'an • China 139 C3
Chunar • India 137 C8
Chunskiy • Russian Fed. 26 Q6
Chuvayeche • Mexico 157 H2
Chur Phnum Krâvanh •
Cambodia/Thailand 31 C4
Chur • Switzerland 119 G4
Churapcha • Russian Fed. 27 L4
Church Bay **Beach** •
Bermuda 159 J3
Church Bay • Bermuda 159 J3
Churchill • SA, Canada 38 N5
Churchill • MN, Canada 39 S6
Churchill Falls • SA, Canada .. 155 A8
Churchill Falls [Falls] •
NF, Canada 39 S6
Churchill Lake • SA, Canada .. 38 J5
Churchill Peak • BC, Canada .. 38 F5
Churchs Ferry •
ND, United States 43 G2
Churu • India 137 C2
Churuguara • Venezuela 51 D1
Churún Merú • Venezuela 51 E2
Churwalden **Ski** • Switzerland .. 100 [110]
Chuse-Montmorency, Parc de la •
QU, Canada 156 D1

Ciechanowiec • Poland 13 L5
Ciego de Avila • Cuba 158 D3
Ciénaga • Colombia 51 C1
Ciénaga de Flores • Mexico ... 47 D5
Cienfuegos • Cuba 158 C2
Cieszyn • Poland 128 C3
Ciezar • Spain 117 C1
Çiftehan • Turkey 123 G2
Çifteler • Turkey 15 M4
Çiftlik • Turkey 123 G2
Cihanbeyli Platosu • Turkey ... 15 N5
Cijara, Embalse de • Spain 11 G5
Cijulang • Java, Indonesia 143 J6
Cilacap • Java, Indonesia 143 J6
Cilaos • Réunion 132 H3
Cilavrú • Argentina 163 D1
Cilaos, Bras de la • Réunion ... 132 H3
Cilaos, Cirque de • Réunion ... 132 H3
Ciledug • Java, Indonesia 143 J2
Cilento **Heritage C** • Italy ... 86 [153]
Cilento • Italy 121 G4
Cilicia • Turkey 123 G3
Cilician Gates • Turkey 123 G2
Cilo Dag • Turkey 18 D2
Cimahi • Java, Indonesia 143 J2
Cimarron • OK, United States .. 46 F4
Cimini, Monti • Italy 121 F1
Cimone • Italy 12 E4
Cina • Romania 14 M4
Cina, Tanjung • Indonesia 14 M4
Cinarcik • Turkey 15 K3
Cinca • Spain 10 F11
Cincar • Bosnia-Herz. 14 E6
Cincinnati • OH, United States .. 44 C6
Cindrelu, Vírful • Romania 14 K4
Cine • Turkey 122 D9
Ciney • Belgium 5 I4
Cinque Terre **Heritage C** • Italy .. 86 [139]
Cinque Terre • Italy 121 E10
Cinto, Monte • Corsica, France .. 115 L1
Cintra, Golfe de •
Western Sahara 20 B4
Ciotat **Beach** • France ...... 96 [132]
Ciotat, la • France 115 H3
Cipó • Brazil 52 I1
Circeo, Parco Naz. del **Park N** •
Italy .... 89 [87]
Circeo, Parco Naz. del • Italy .. 121 F4
Circle • MT, United States 43 D3
Circle • AK, United States 49 M2
Circleville • OH, United States .. 44 D6
Circus Circus **Park L** •
NV, United States .... 150 [K]
Cireben • Java, Indonesia 143 J2
Cirene, Gunung •
Java, Indonesia 143 J2
Cirencester • United Kingdom .. 104 D4
Cirò Marina • Italy 12 L9
Cisco • MT, N. Canada 39 S5
Cisco • AK, United States 45 H2
Cisco • TX, United States 154 J1
Cisnadie • Romania 14 L4
Citadelle, La **Heritage C** •
Haiti .... 84 [42]
Citadelle, La • Haiti 159 G2
Città di Castello • Italy 121 E2
Cittadella • Italy 121 E7
City of Rocks Nat. Reserve **Park N** •
ID, United States .... 150 [61]
City of Rocks Nat. Reserve •
ID, United States 152 B4
Ciucasu, Vírful • Romania 14 M4
Ciudad Acuña • Mexico 47 D3
Ciudad Altamirano • Mexico .. 157 G3
Ciudad Bolívar • Venezuela ... 51 E2
Ciudad Camargo • Mexico 47 B4
Ciudad Constitución • Mexico .. 157 F4
Ciudad de Guatemala • Guatemala .. 37 C5
Ciudad de México **Heritage C** •
Mexico .... 84 [22]
Ciudad de México • Mexico ... 157 G9
Ciudad del Carmen • Mexico .. 157 H3
Ciudad del Este • Paraguay ... 37 F6
Ciudad Guayana • Venezuela .. 51 E2
Ciudad Juárez • Mexico 47 A2
Ciudad Lerdo • Mexico 40 F6
Ciudad Madero • Mexico 157 G2
Ciudad Mante • Mexico 157 G2
Ciudad Mier • Mexico 47 D4
Ciudad Obregón • Mexico 157 F4
Ciudad Ojeda • Venezuela 51 C1
Ciudad Piar • Venezuela 51 E2
Ciudad Real • Spain 11 H6
Ciudad Rodrigo • Spain 11 E4
Ciudad Valles • Mexico 157 G2
Ciudad Victoria • Mexico 157 G2
Ciutadella • Minorca, Spain ... 117 F1
Cividale del Friuli • Italy 13 C11
Civita Castellana • Italy 121 F1
Civitanova Marche • Italy 121 E2
Civitavécchia • Italy 121 F1
Çivril • Turkey 15 K5
Çixi • China 139 C4
Cizre • Turkey 18 D2
Clackmannanshire •
United Kingdom 104 B2
Clara • Ireland 108 C5
Claraville • NF, Canada 156 D4
Clare • Ireland 108 D6
Clare • MI, United States 44 C4
Clare • SA, Australia 108 C6
Clare I. • Ireland 108 D5
Clare Island **Beach** • Ireland .. 96 [63]
Claregalway Abbey • Ireland ... 108 C4
Claremont • Jamaica 159 F2
Claremont • NH, United States .. 44 I4
Claremore • OK, United States .. 46 H4
Claremorris • Ireland 108 C2
Clarence • Chile 163 A4
Clarence Town • Bahamas 158 B4
Clarendon • TX, United States .. 46 E5
Claresholm • AL, Canada 42 H2
Clarinda • IA, United States ... 46 H2
Clarín • Spain 43 G5
Clarion • PA, United States ... 153 D5
Clark • SD, United States 43 H4
Clark Fork • ID, United States .. 38 H7
Clarks Hill Lake •
GA/SC, United States 48 F4
Clarksburg • WV, United States .. 44 E6
Clarksdale • MS, United States .. 48 B3
Clarkston • WA, United States .. 42 G3
Clarksville • AR, United States .. 46 I5
Clarksville • IN, United States .. 48 E1
Clarksville • VA, United States .. 48 F2
Clarksville • TN, United States .. 42 D3
Clatsop, Fort, Nat. Mem. •
OR, United States 152 B1
Clauholm • Denmark 125 F10
Claviere **Ski** • Italy .... 100 [197]
Claviere • Italy 121 E5
Clay Belt • OT/QU, Canada ... 39 O6

Claymont • DE, United States 44 H6
Clayton • NM, United States 46 G4
Clayton • MO, United States 46 J3
Clayton • GA, United States 48 F3
Cle Elum • WA, United States 42 E3
Clear • WY, United States 43 C4
Clear, Cape • Ireland 108 C7
Clear I. • Ireland 108 C7
Clear Lake • IA, United States 43 J5
Clear Lake • CA, United States 47 H2
Clear Lake Reservoir •
  CA, United States 42 E6
Clear Water Bay •
  Hong Kong, China 139 B6
Clearfield • PA, United States 153 D5
Clearfield • UT, United States 42 I6
Clearfield • PA, United States 44 F5
Clearlake Oaks •
  CA, United States 45 A2
Clearwater • AL/SA, Canada 38 I5
Clearwater • FL, United States 154 H5
Clearwater Lake •
  WI, United States 43 L4
Clearwater Lake •
  MO, United States 46 J4
Clearwater Mtns •
  ID, United States 42 H4
Cleator Moor • United Kingdom 104 C1
Cleburne • TX, United States 154 J1
Cleethorpes • United Kingdom 7 L8
Cleethorpes Beach •
  United Kingdom ..... 101 [37]
Clemenswerth Castle • Germany ..... 113 [4]
Clemson • SC, United States 48 F3
Clermont • France 115 E2
Clermont • QL, Australia 144 B3
Clermont • FL, United States 151 C1
Clermont-Ferrand • France 10 I8
Clervaux • Luxembourg 109 D20
Clevedon • United Kingdom 104 F3
Cleveland • OH, United States 44 E5
Cleveland • MS, United States 48 B4
Cleveland • TN, United States 48 E3
Cleveland • TX, United States 154 J4
Cleveland Heights •
  OH, United States 44 E5
Clew Bay • Ireland 108 C1
Clewiston • FL, United States 154 H6
Clifden • Ireland 108 C3
Clifden • New Zealand 145 G3
Clifton • St Vincent & Gren. ..... 161 R
Clifton • AZ, United States 153 E4
Clingmans Dome •
  NC/TN, United States 48 F3
Clinton • BC, Canada 38 G6
Clinton • IN, United States 44 B6
Clinton • OT, Canada 44 E4
Clinton • IA, United States 43 J5
Clinton • OK, United States 46 F5
Clinton • MO, United States 46 I3
Clinton • IL, United States 46 K2
Clinton • MS, United States 48 B4
Clinton • SC, United States 48 G3
Clinton • NC, United States 48 H3
Clinton-Colden Lake •
  NT, Canada 38 J4
Clodomira • Argentina 52 D4
Cloghane • Ireland 108 C5
Clogher Head • Ireland 108 B2
Clogherhead Beach • Ireland ..... 96 [53]
Clonakilty Beach • Ireland ..... 96 [59]
Clonakilty • Ireland 108 C8
Clonakilty Bay • Ireland 108 C8
Cloncurry • QL, Australia 144 B1
Clonea Beach • Ireland ..... 96 [58]
Clonmel • Ireland 7 E9
Clonmellon • Ireland 108 B1
Clontarf • Ireland 90 A6
Clorinda • Argentina 52 E4
Cloud Peak • WY, United States 42 L4
Clovelly • United Kingdom 104 F2
Cloverdale • CA, United States 45 A2
Clovis • CA, United States 45 C3
Clovis • NM, United States 46 G5
Cluane Lake • YT, Canada 38 D4
Cluj-Napoca • Romania 14 K3
Clun Forest • United Kingdom 104 D1
Clusaz, la Ski • France ..... 100 [21]
Clusaz, la • France 115 F2
Clutha • New Zealand 145 G4
Clutha District • New Zealand 145 G4
Clyde • NU, Canada 54 V2
Clyde • United Kingdom 104 B3
Clyde • OH, United States 44 D5
Clyde, Firth of •
  United Kingdom 6 G6
Clydebank • United Kingdom 104 B3
Coahuila • Mexico 40 F6
Coal I. • New Zealand 145 G3
Coal River • BC, Canada 49 P4
Coaldale • NV, United States 45 D2
Coalinga • CA, United States 45 C3
Coalville • United Kingdom 7 K9
Coalville • UT, United States 42 I6
Coamo • Puerto Rico 159 H4
Coari • Brazil 51 E4
Coast Mtns • BC, Canada 38 F6
Coast Ranges •
  CA/OR, United States 42 D7
Coastal Plain • United States ..... 154 J
Coatesville • PA, United States 44 H6
Coaticook • QU, Canada 44 J3
Coats I. • NU, Canada 39 O4
Coatzacoalcos • Mexico 37 C4
Cobá • Mexico 157 H2
Cobán • Guatemala 37 C4
Çobanisa • Turkey 123 F3
Cobar • NS, Australia 34 I6
Cobblers Reef • Barbados ..... 161 O
Cóbh • Ireland 108 C8
Cobija • Bolivia 51 D6
Cobleskill • NY, United States 44 I5
Cobo Bay Beach • United Kingdom ..... 101 [256]
Cobourg • OT, Canada 44 F3
Cobourg Peninsula •
  NT, Australia 34 F2
Côbue • Mozambique 23 E6
Coburg • Germany 9 D6
Cochabamba • Bolivia 52 C2
Coche, I. de • Venezuela ..... 160 V
Cochem • Germany 112 E1
Cochem Castle • Germany ..... 113 [61]
Coches, Iles Ski • France ..... 100 [34]
Cochin • India 138 D10
Cochin China • Vietnam 141 E3
Cochino, Bahia de • Cuba 158 D2
Cochran • GA, United States 48 F4
Cochrane • OT, Canada 39 O7
Cockburn Harbour •
  Turks & Caicos Is. 158 C2
Cockburn I. • OT, Canada 44 D3
Cockburn Town • Bahamas 158 C2
Cockburn Town •
  Turks & Caicos Is. 158 C2
Cockermouth • United Kingdom 104 C1
Cockpit Country • Jamaica 159 F1
Coco • Pacific Ocean 50 A4
Coco • Honduras/Nicaragua 37 E5
Coco, Cayo • Cuba 158 D3
Coco Channel • India 28 F6
Coco, I. • St Barthélemy ..... 160 E
Coco Is. • India 28 F6
Coco, Parque Nac. Isla del Heritage N •
  Costa Rica ..... 82 [25]
Cocoa • FL, United States 151 C2
Cocoa Beach • FL, United States 154 H6
Cocoa I. • Maldives 138 F4
Cocoa Point • Antigua & Barbuda ..... 161 J
Cocos Bay • Trinidad & Tobago ..... 160 U
Cod, Cape • MA, United States 153 D4

Coda Cavallo, Capo •
  Sardinia, Italy 12 D8
Codajás • Brazil 51 E4
Codigoro • Italy 12 G4
Codrington • Antigua & Barbuda ..... 161 J
Codrington College • Barbados ..... 161 O
Codrington Lagoon •
  Antigua & Barbuda ..... 161 J
Cody • WY, United States 42 K4
Coesfeld • Germany 8 C5
Coëtivy • Seychelles 133 K4
Coeur d'Alene •
  ID, United States 152 B2
Coevorden • Netherlands 109 D8
Coffeyville • KS, United States 46 H4
Coffs Harbour • NS, Australia 34 J6
Cofrentes • Spain 11 K5
Cogalnic • Moldova 14 P3
Cogama • OT, Canada 44 E2
Coglians, Monte • Austria/Italy 121 E4
Cognac • France 115 G1
Cogolin Beach • France ..... 96 [133]
Cogolin • France 115 H4
Cohoes • NY, United States 44 I4
Coiba • Panama 37 E6
Coihaique • Chile 53 B5
Coimar • Cuba 158 D2
Coimbatore • India 138 D10
Coimbra • Portugal 11 C4
Coimbra [Adm] • Portugal 118 A2
Coin • Spain 11 G8
Colac • VI, Australia 34 I8
Colares • Portugal 118 D1
Colatina • Brazil 163 C2
Colby • KS, United States 46 F3
Colca • Peru 163 B4
Colca, Cañon del • Peru 163 B4
Colchester • United Kingdom 104 E2
Cold Bay • AK, United States 49 I4
Cold Spring • MN, United States 43 I4
Cold Spring • NJ, United States 44 H6
Coldfoot • AK, United States 49 K2
Colditz Castle • Germany ..... 113 [201]
Coldwater • MI, United States 44 C5
Coldwater • KS, United States 46 F4
Colebrook • NH, United States 44 J3
Coleford Nature Reserve •
  United Kingdom 134 B5
Coleman • TX, United States 47 E2
Colenso • South Africa 134 B3
Coleraine • United Kingdom 7 F6
Coles, Punta • Peru 163 B4
Colfax • WA, United States 42 G3
Colfosco Ski • Italy ..... 100 [231]
Colfosco • Italy 120 B2
Colihaut • Dominica ..... 161 M
Colima • Mexico 40 G5
Colima [Adm] • Mexico 37 (1) B2
Coll • United Kingdom 6 F5
College • AK, United States 49 L3
College Station •
  TX, United States 154 J3
Collier Bay • WA, Australia 34 D3
Colliers • Cayman Is. 159 E4
Collingwood • New Zealand 35 D5
Collingwood • OT, Canada 155 B5
Collins • MS, United States 153 F2
Collinstown Beach • Ireland ..... 96 [57]
Collinsville • QL, Australia 144 B1
Collinsville •
  IL, United States 46 K3
Collioure Beach • France ..... 96 [128]
Collioure • France 115 K2
Collonges-la-Rouge • France 115 G2
Collooney • Ireland 108 C2
Colmar • France 10 M5
Colmenar Viejo • Spain 11 H4
Colôane • Macau, China 139 B3
Colôane Village • Macau, China 139 B3
Cologne Heritage C • Germany ..... 86 [49]
Cologne • Germany 111 B3
Coloma • CA, United States 152 C3
Colomb Beach • Goa, India 137 B2
COLOMBIA • S. America 51 C3
Colombier • Switzerland 119 C1
Colombier • St Martin ..... 160 D
Colombier • St Barthélemy ..... 160 E
Colombier, Pointe à •
  St Barthélemy ..... 160 E
Colombo • Sri Lanka 138 D15
Colombo, Cristofo [Apt] • Italy 120 (1) A1
Colón • Cuba 158 D2
Colón • Argentina 163 D1
Colón • Panama 37 F6
Colón, Archipiélago de •
  Pacific Ocean 51 (1) A1
Colona • SA, Australia 34 F6
Colonet, Cabo • Mexico 45 D6
Colònia de Sant Jordi •
  Majorca, Spain 117 H4
Colonia del Sacramento Heritage C •
  Uruguay ..... 84 [73]
Colonia del Sacramento •
  Uruguay 163 D2
Colonia Las Heras • Argentina 53 C5
Colonia Suiza • Uruguay 163 D2
Colonial Heights •
  VA, United States 48 I2
Colonial Nat. Hist. Park Park N •
  VA, United States ..... 151 [249]
Colonial Nat. Hist. Park •
  VA, United States 153 D11
Colonial Park •
  PA, United States 44 G5
Colonna, Capo • Italy 12 L9
Colonsay • United Kingdom 6 F5
Colorado • Argentina 53 D3
Colorado [Adm] • United States 40 E4
Colorado Aqueduct •
  CA, United States 45 E5
Colorado City •
  AZ, United States 45 F3
Colorado City •
  TX, United States 47 D1
Colorado Desert •
  CA, United States 152 C6
Colorado Nat. Mon. Park N •
  CO, United States ..... 150 [88]
Colorado Plateau •
  United States 153 E1
Colorado Point Lighthouse •
  Aruba ..... 160 Y
Colorado [Riv] •
  Mexico/United States 40 D5
Colorado [Riv] •
  TX, United States 47 E2
Colorado Springs •
  CO, United States 46 C3
Colton • UT, United States 45 G2
Columbia • PA, United States 44 G6
Columbia • MO, United States 46 I3
Columbia • SC, United States 48 G3
Columbia • TN, United States 48 D3
Columbia • LA, United States 153 F1
Columbia Basin •
  WA, United States 152 B2
Columbia City •
  IN, United States 44 C5
Columbia Falls •
  MT, United States 42 H2
Columbia Gorge •
  OR/WA, United States 152 B1
Columbia, Icefield • AL, Canada 155 C4
Columbia, Mt • AL/BC, Canada 155 C4
Columbia Mtns • BC, Canada 38 G6
Columbia Plateau •
  United States 152 B4

Columbia [Riv] •
  Canada/United States 38 H6
Columbia [Riv] •
  Canada/United States 40 B2
Columbia Road Reservoir •
  SD, United States 43 G4
Columbine, Cape • South Africa 134 C1
Columbus • MT, United States 42 K4
Columbus • IN, United States 44 C6
Columbus • OH, United States 44 D6
Columbus • NE, United States 46 G2
Columbus • MS, United States 48 C4
Columbus • GA, United States 48 E4
Columbus • TX, United States 154 J3
Columbus Mon. • Bahamas 158 B4
Columbus Park • Jamaica 159 F1
Colville • WA, United States 42 G2
Colva Beach • Goa, India 137 B2
Colva • WA, United States 49 K2
Colville • AK, United States 49 K2
Colville Channel • New Zealand 35 E3
Colville Lake • NT, Canada 38 F3
Colwell Bay Beach •
  United Kingdom ..... 101 [98]
Colwyn Bay • United Kingdom 7 I8
Comácchio • Italy 12 G4
Comácchio, Lido di • Italy 121 E8
Coman, Mt • Antarctica 54 (1) I2
Comanche • TX, United States 47 E2
Comaruga • Spain 117 D3
Comarelles, Groote des •
  France 115 G2
Combe Martin Beach •
  United Kingdom ..... 101 [152]
Combermere Bay • Myanmar 31 A3
Combloux Ski • France ..... 100 [25]
Comendador • Dominican Rep. 159 G2
Comerío • Puerto Rico 159 H4
Comillas Beach • Spain ..... 96 [89]
Comino • Malta 123 H1
Cominotto • Malta 123 H1
Commandersbaai • Aruba ..... 160 Y
Commerce • TX, United States 47 F1
Commerce City •
  CO, United States 46 C3
Commercy • France 5 I6
Comminges • France 115 K1
Commissioner's Point • Bermuda 159 J1
Como • Italy 12 G4
Como, Lago di • Italy 121 E2
Comodoro Rivadavia • Argentina 53 C5
Comores, Archipel des •
  Indian Ocean 24 G2
Comorin, Cape • India 138 D14
COMOROS • Indian Ocean 24 G2
Compiègne • France 115 E2
Compiègne, Forêt de • France 115 E2
Comrat • Moldova 14 P3
Con Dao • Vietnam 114 B3
Conakry • Guinea 22 B3
Carcarneau • France 114 C3
Conceição • Portugal 118 E8
Conceiçao do Araguaia • Brazil 51 H5
Concepción • Chile 52 B6
Concepción • Argentina 52 D4
Concepción • Bolivia 52 D2
Concepción • Paraguay 52 E3
Concepción • Peru 163 B1
Concepción del Uruguay •
  Argentina 52 E5
Conception • Seychelles 133 K1
Conception I. • Bahamas 158 B4
Conception, Point •
  CA, United States 152 C5
Conch Bar • Turks & Caicos Is. 158 C1
Conchas Lake •
  NM, United States 46 C5
Concord • CA, United States 45 A3
Concord • NC, United States 48 G3
Concord • MA, United States 153 D4
Concord • NH, United States 153 D4
Concordia • Argentina 52 E5
Concordia • KS, United States 46 G3
Concordia Baai • St Eustatius ..... 161 F
Condé • Brazil 52 I1
Condobolin • NS, Australia 144 C1
Condor, Cordillera del •
  Ecuador/Peru 51 B4
Condroz • Belgium 5 I4
Cone Mtn • AK, United States 49 J2
Conegliano • Italy 12 G3
Conero, Costa • Italy 121 E12
Coney Beach Park L •
  United Kingdom ..... 98 [32]
Coney I. • Bermuda 159 J2
Confolens • France 115 G2
Cong • Ireland 108 C4
Congaree Swamp Nat. Mon. Park N •
  SC, United States ..... 151 [234]
CONGO • Africa 23 C4
Congo [Riv] •
  Congo/Dem. Rep. of Congo 23 C4
Congonhas Heritage C • Brazil ..... 84 [73]
Congonhas • Brazil 163 C1
Conil de la Frontera Beach •
  Spain ..... 96 [113]
Conil de la Frontera • Spain 116 B5
Coniston • United Kingdom 7 H4
Coniston Water • United Kingdom 104 C4
Conn, Lough • Ireland 108 C2
Connacht • Ireland 7 D8
Connaught • Ireland 7 D8
Conneaut • OH, United States 44 E5
Connecticut [Adm] •
  United States 153 D7
Connecticut [Riv] •
  United States 153 D3
Connell • WA, United States 42 F3
Connellsville •
  PA, United States 44 F5
Connemara • Ireland 108 C3
Connemara Nat. Park Park N •
  Ireland ..... 89 [39]
Connemara Nat. Park • Ireland 108 C3
Connersville •
  IN, United States 44 C6
Conny-Land Park L • Switzerland ..... 98 [80]
Conrad • MT, United States 42 J2
Conroe • TX, United States 154 J4
Conroe, Lake •
  TX, United States 47 G2
Conselheiro Lafaiete • Brazil 163 C1
Consett • United Kingdom 7 K7
Constance • Germany 112 D8
Constance, Lake • Germany 112 F5
Constanta • Romania 128 E2
Constantina • Spain 116 B2
Constantine • Algeria 20 G1
Constantine Bay Beach •
  United Kingdom ..... 101 [142]
Constantinople • Turkey 90 A15
Constitución • Chile 52 B6
Constitution of 1857, Parque Nac. •
  Mexico 157 F1
Constitution Gardens Park N •
  United States ..... 151 [274]
Consuegra • Spain 11 H5
Consuelo Peak • QL, Australia 34 I4
Consul • SA, Canada 42 K2
Contamines-Montjoie, les Ski •
  France ..... 100 [29]
Contamines-Montjoie, les •
  France 115 F2

Contoy, I. • Mexico 157 H2
Contreras, • Spain 11 J5
Contwoyto Lake • NT/NU, Canada 35 (2) C3
Conway • Fiji Is. 35 (2) C3
Conway • FL, United States 151 C2
Conway • AR, United States 46 I5
Conway, Cape • QL, Australia 144 B1
Conway, Mt • NT, Australia 145 D2
Conway • United Kingdom 7 I8
Coober Pedy • SA, Australia 34 F5
Cook • SA, Australia 34 F6
Cook Inlet • AK, United States 49 K4
Cook Is. • Pacific Ocean 33 K7
Cook, Mt • New Zealand 35 E5
Cook Strait • New Zealand 35 E5
Cookes Peak • NM, United States 46 E6
Cookeville • TN, United States 48 E2
Cookhouse • South Africa 134 C4
Cooktown • QL, Australia 34 I3
Coolangatta • QL, Australia 144 B6
Coolgardie • WA, Australia 34 D6
Coolidge • AZ, United States 45 G5
Cooma • NS, Australia 144 C4
Coon Rapids • MN, United States 43 J4
Coonabarabran • NS, Australia 144 C2
Coonoor • India 138 D10
Conoor Hill Sta • India 138 E2
Cooper • AK, United States 38 C4
Cooper Creek • QL/SA, Australia 34 H5
Cooper I. • New Zealand 145 G3
Cooper I. • British Virgin Is. ..... 160 B
Coos Bay • OR, United States 152 B3
Cooperstown • ND, United States 43 G3
Cooperstown • NY, United States 153 D2
Coorg • India 138 D6
Coos Bay • OR, United States 152 B3
Cootamundra • NS, Australia 144 C1
Cootehill • Ireland 108 B2
Copacabana • Bolivia 163 B4
Copacabana • Brazil 163 C4
Copán Heritage C • Panama ..... 84 [34]
Copán • Honduras 37 D5
Copano Bay • TX, United States 154 J5
Copeland Forest •
  United Kingdom 104 C1
Copenhagen Beach • Denmark ..... 96 [40]
Copenhagen • Denmark 125 F11
Copiapó • Chile 52 B4
Copoco • Angola 24 A2
Copper Center •
  AK, United States 49 L3
Copper Harbor •
  MI, United States 43 M3
Copper Mtn Ski •
  CO, United States ..... 149 [105]
Copperas Cove •
  TX, United States 154 J3
Coppermine • NU, Canada 38 H3
Coppermine Point • OT, Canada 44 C2
Coppermine [Riv] •
  NT/NU, Canada 38 H3
Coqen • China 28 E2
Coquille • OR, United States 42 C5
Coquimbo • Chile 52 B5
Corabia • Romania 14 I6
Coral Bay • Cyprus 123 J3
Coral Bay • US Virgin Is. ..... 160 Z
Coral Gables •
  FL, United States 154 H8
Coral Harbour • NU, Canada 39 O4
Coral Heights • Bahamas 158 B3
Coral Sea • Australia 33 G7
Coral Sea Is. Territory •
  Australia 34 I3
Coral Springs •
  FL, United States 154 H8
Coralarium, Sentosa • Singapore 141 H4
Corallo, Riviera del •
  Sardinia, Italy 120 C1
Corantijn • Guyana/Surinam. 51 F3
Corato • Italy 14 D8
Corbeil-Essonnes • France 115 E2
Corbett Nat. Park • India 137 C3
Corbier, le Ski • France ..... 100 [47]
Corbie • United Kingdom 7 I9
Corbières • France 115 K2
Corby • United Kingdom 104 D2
Corcaigh • Ireland 108 C8
Córcega • Puerto Rico 159 H1
Corcoran • CA, United States 45 C3
Corcovado, Golfo • Chile 53 B4
Corcovado, Volcán • Chile 53 B4
Cordèle • GA, United States 48 F5
Cordevole • Italy 120 B4
Cordilheiras, Serra das •
  Brazil 53 (1) B3
Cordillera Central • Colombia 51 B3
Cordillera Central • Peru 51 B5
Cordillera Central • Bolivia 52 C2
Cordillera Central Heritage C •
  Philippines ..... 85 [203]
Cordillera Central •
  Puerto Rico 159 H3
Cordillera Central •
  Dominican Rep. 159 G3
Cordillera Real • Ecuador 51 B4
Cordillera Occidental •
  Bolivia/Chile 52 C2
Cordillera Oriental • Peru 51 B5
Cordillera Oriental • Colombia 51 C2
Cordillera Oriental •
  Bolivia/Peru 52 C2
Cordillera Oriental •
  Dominican Rep. 159 G3
Córdoba • Argentina 52 D5
Córdoba Heritage C • Spain ..... 86 [109]
Córdoba • Spain 116 B2
Córdoba • Mexico 157 G4
Córdoba, Sierras de • Argentina 52 D5
Corfe Castle • United Kingdom 104 F6
Corfu Beach • Corfu, Greece ..... 97 [170]
Corfu • Corfu, Greece 122 B1
Corfu [I.] • Greece 11 E5
Coria • Spain 11 E5
Coria del Río • Spain 11 E7
Coricudgy, Mt • NS, Australia 144 C3
Corigliano Calabro • Italy 12 K9
Corinaldo • Italy 121 E12
Coringa Is. • CL, Australia 34 J3
Corinth • Greece 15 C3
Corinth • MS, United States 48 C3
Corinth • TX, United States 154 J4
Corinto • Brazil 163 C1
Corjuem Fort • Goa, India 137 B1
Cork • Ireland 108 C8
Cork [Adm] • Ireland 108 C8
Çorlu • Turkey 15 I1
Çorlu [Riv] • Turkey 15 I2
Corn Is. • Nicaragua 160 A18
Cornas • France 114 B4
Cornélio • Brazil 52 F3
Corner Brook • NF, Canada 126 D3
Corner Point • Saba ..... 161 F
Corning • NY, United States 44 G5
Corno Grande • Italy 121 F2
Cornouaille • France 114 C2
Cornudas • TX, United States 47 B2
Cornwall • United Kingdom 104 F4
Cornwall • Jamaica 159 E4
Cornwall • OT, Canada 155 B7
Cornwall, Cape • United Kingdom 104 F4
Cornwallis I. • NU, Canada 38 L1
Coro • Venezuela 51 D1
Coro Heritage C • Venezuela ..... 84 [47]

Covelong Beach • India 138 E3
Coventry • United Kingdom 104 D2
Coverack • United Kingdom 104 F4
Covilhã • Portugal 11 D4
Covington • MI, United States 43 L3
Covington • KY, United States 44 C6
Covington • VA, United States 48 F3
Covington • TN, United States 48 C3
Covington • VA, United States 48 G2
Cow and Calves •
  St Vincent & Gren. ..... 161 Q
Cowansville • QU, Canada 44 I3
Cowboy Country •
  NV, United States 152 C2
Cowdenbeath • United Kingdom 104 B4
Cowes • United Kingdom 5 B4
Cowes Beach • United Kingdom ..... 101 [99-100]
Cowes • United Kingdom ..... 106 D
Cowpens Nat. Battlefield Park N •
  SC, United States ..... 151 [237]
Covra • NS, Australia 144 C2
Cox's Bazar • Bangladesh 28 F4
Coxsackie • NY, United States 153 D3
Coyame • Mexico 47 B3
Cozad • NE, United States 157 H2
Cozumel • Mexico 157 H2
Cozumel, I. • Mexico 157 H2
Cracow Heritage C • Poland ..... 86 [165]
Cracow • Poland 128 C2
Cradock • South Africa 134 C4
Craig • CO, United States 45 I1
Craig • AK, United States 42 G3
Craigmont • ID, United States 42 G3
Craignure • United Kingdom 106 B2
Crail Beach • United Kingdom ..... 101 [8]
Crailsheim • Germany 9 F7
Craiova • Romania 14 K5
Cranborne Chase •
  United Kingdom 104 F3
Cranbrook • WA, Australia 34 C6
Cranbrook • BC, Canada 155 C4
Crane • OR, United States 42 F5
Cranfield Beach •
  United Kingdom ..... 101 [253]
Cranmore Ski •
  United States ..... 149 [226]
Crans-Montana Ski • Switzerland ..... 100 [91]
Crans-Montana • Switzerland 119 G6
Cranston • RI, United States 44 J5
Crasna • Romania 14 J2
Crater Lake •
  St Vincent & Gren. ..... 161 Q
Crater Lake • OR, United States 42 D5
Crater Lake (Lake) •
  OR, United States 42 D5
Crater Lake Nat. Park Park N •
  OR, United States ..... 150 [35]
Crater Lake Nat. Park •
  OR, United States 152 B3
Crater Mtn • CA, United States 45 C3
Craters of the Moon Nat. Mon. Park N •
  United States ..... 150 [63]
Crateús • Brazil 53 (1) C3
Crati • Italy 12 K9
Crato • Brazil 53 (1) D3
Craufurd, Cape • NU, Canada 39 O2
Cravo Norte • Colombia 51 C2
Crawford • NE, United States 43 E5
Crawford Bay • BC, Canada 42 G2
Crawfordsville •
  IN, United States 44 B5
Crawley • United Kingdom 104 E3
Crécy • France 90 A7
Crediton • United Kingdom 104 F2
Cree Lake • SA, Canada 38 J5
Creede • CO, United States 45 I3
Creek • Cayman Is. 159 E2
Creel • Mexico 157 F2
Creerlea Abbey • Ireland 108 C2
Creeslough Beach • Ireland ..... 96 [65]
Creil • France 115 E2
Crema • Italy 121 E6
Cremona • Italy 121 E6
Crépy-en-Valois • France 115 E2
Cres • Croatia 128 D1
Cres [I.] • Croatia 128 D1
Crescent City •
  FL, United States 49 S3
Crescent City •
  CA, United States 152 C1
Crescent I. • Hong Kong, China 139 B4
Crescent Lake •
  FL, United States 49 S3
Crespi d'Adda Heritage C •
  Italy ..... 86 [130]
Crested Butte Ski •
  CO, United States ..... 149 [109]
Crested Butte •
  CO, United States 45 I2
Crestline • OH, United States 44 D5
Creston • IA, United States 46 H2
Crestone Peak •
  CO, United States 46 C4
Crestview • FL, United States 48 D5
Creswell Bay • NU, Canada 38 M2
Crete • Greece ..... 123 E
Crete • NE, United States 46 G2
Crete, Sea of • Greece 122 D11
Créteil • France 115 E4
Creus, Cap de • Spain 117 D2
Creuse • France 114 D4
Creusot, le • France 10 J7
Crevillente • Spain 117 C1
Crewe • United Kingdom 7 J8
Crianlarich • United Kingdom 104 B1
Crichton Castle •
  United Kingdom 104 B4
Criciuma • Brazil 52 G4
Crieff • United Kingdom 104 B1
Crikvenica • Croatia 128 D1
Crimea • Ukraine 17 E5
Crimmitschau • Germany 9 H6
Crinkley Bottom •
  United Kingdom 104 F3
Cripple Creek •
  CO, United States 46 C3
Crisan • Romania 128 E2
Crisfield • MD, United States 153 D11
Cristal, Sierra del • Cuba 158 D8
Cristal • Spain 51 H6
Cristóbal • Panama 80 B9
Cristóbal Colón • Colombia 51 C1
Crisul Negru • Romania 13 L11
Crisul Repede • Romania 13 L10
Crna • F.Y.R. of Macedonia 15 C2
Crna Gora • F.R. of Yugoslavia 14 H8
Crni Drim • Albania 15 C1
Crni vrh • Slovenia 13 E11
Croagh Patrick • Ireland 108 C1
CROATIA • Europe 14 D4
Crockett • TX, United States 154 J4
Crocodile Farm • Singapore 141 H2
Crocodile Farm •
  Bangkok, Thailand 142 C2
Crocodile Paradise • Singapore 141 H1
Crocus Bay • Anguilla ..... 160 C
Crocus Hill • Anguilla ..... 160 C
Crocworld • South Africa 134 C5
Croisic, le • France 114 C3
Croix-des-Bouquets • Haiti 43 K2
Croix-Valmer, la Beach • France ..... 96 [133]
Croix-Valmer, la • France 115 H4
Croker I. • NT, Australia 34 F2
Cromarty • United Kingdom 7 N9
Cromer Beach • United Kingdom ..... 101 [46]
Cromer • United Kingdom 155 G2
Crook • United Kingdom 104 C1
Crooked I. • Hong Kong, China 139 B4
Crooked I. • Bahamas 158 B4
Crooks • OT, Canada 43 L2
Crookston • MN, United States 43 H3

Crosby • ND, United States 43 E2
Cross Cays • Bahamas 158 B2
Cross River • Nigeria 22 F3
Cross River Nat. Park **Park •**
Nigeria .... 133 [36]
Cross Sound • AK, United States 49 N4
Crossett • AR, United States 46 J6
Crosshaven • Ireland 108 C8
Crossmolina • Ireland 108 C2
Crossville • TN, United States 48 E3
Croton • CT, United States 44 I5
Crotone • Italy 12 L9
Crow Agency • MT, United States 42 L4
Crow Indian Reservation •
MT, United States 42 K4
Crowell • TX, United States 46 F6
Crowley • LA, United States 47 H2
Crown Point [Apt] •
Trinidad & Tobago .... 160 T
Crown Prince Frederik •
NU, Canada 39 N2
Crownpoint • NM, United States 45 H4
Crowsnest Pass • AL, Canada 38 I7
Crowsnest Pass • AL, Canada 42 H2
Croyde Bay **Beach •**
United Kingdom .... 101 [149]
Croydon • QL, Australia 34 H3
Croydon • United Kingdom 104 E1
Crozes-Hermitage • France 114 B4
Crozet, Is. • Indian Ocean 19 J10
Crozon, Presqu'île de • France 114 C1
Cruces • Cuba 158 D2
Cruese • France 10 O7
Crummock Water • United Kingdom 104 C1
Cruz Alta • Brazil 52 F4
Cruz Bay • US Virgin Is. .... 160 Z
Cruz, Cabo • Cuba 158 D7
Cruz, Cayo • Cuba 158 F3
Cruz del Eje • Argentina 52 D5
Cruzeiro • Brazil 163 C3
Cruzeiro do Oeste • Brazil 52 F3
Cruzeiro do Sul • Brazil 51 C5
Crystal Caves • Bermuda 159 J2
Crystal City •
TX, United States 47 E3
Crystal Falls •
MI, United States 43 L3
Crystal Lake •
IL, United States 44 A4
Crystal Mtn **Ski •**
WA, United States .... 149 [51]
Crystal Mtn **Ski •**
MI, United States .... 149 [145]
Crystal River •
FL, United States 49 B3
Crystal Springs •
MS, United States 48 B5
Cserhát • Hungary 14 G2
Csurgó • Hungary 14 E3
Ctesiphon • Iraq 127 D4
Cu Chi Tunnels • Vietnam 141 I1
Cu Lao Hon • Vietnam 141 E4
Cuamba • Mozambique 24 F2
Cuangar • Angola 24 B3
Cuango • Angola 23 B5
Cuango [Riv] • Angola 23 B5
Cuanza • Angola 23 B6
Cuanza • Argentina 53 D2
CUBA • West Indies .... 158 D
Cuba • Portugal 11 B6
Cuba • NM, United States 45 I3
Cuba • MO, United States 46 J3
Cubagua, I. de • Venezuela .... 160 V
Cubelles **Beach** • Spain .... 96 [122]
Cubells • Ibiza, Spain 117 G3
Cubuk • Turkey 15 O3
Cuchilla Grande • Uruguay 53 F2
Cuchilla Grande • Uruguay 163 D2
Cuchillas de Toa • Cuba 158 D8
Cucc **Beach** • France .... 96 [75]
Cucuí • Brazil 51 D3
Cúcuta • Colombia 51 C2
Cuddalore • India 138 D7
Cuddapah • India 138 D7
Cue • WA, Australia 34 C5
Cuéllar • Spain 11 G3
Cuenca • Spain 11 I4
Cuenca • Ecuador 51 B4
Cuenca **Heritage C** • Ecuador .... 84 [53]
Cuenca **Heritage C** • Spain .... 86 [91]
Cuenca, Serranía de • Spain 11 J4
Cuernavaca • Mexico 157 G4
Cuero • TX, United States 47 F3
Cueto • Cuba 158 D8
Cueva de Bellamar • Cuba 158 D2
Cuevas de Almanzora **Beach** •
Spain .... 96 [116]
Cuevas de Camuy • Puerto Rico 159 H1
Cuevas del Indio • Cuba 158 D1
Cuí Hong • China 139 B2
Cuiabá • Brazil 52 E2
Cuilo • Angola 23 B5
Cuima • Angola 24 B2
Cuito • Angola 24 B3
Culapan • Mexico 157 G1
Cul-de-Sac • St Martin 160 D1
Culatra, I. da • Portugal 118 E7
Culbertson • MT, United States 43 D2
Culbone Church • United Kingdom 104 F2
Culcairn • NS, Australia 144 C1
Culdaff **Beach** • Ireland .... 96 [65]
Culebra Peak •
CO, United States 46 C4
Culemborg • Netherlands 109 F4
Culgoa • QL, Australia 144 A8
Culiacán • Mexico 157 F4
Culik • Bali, Indonesia 143 H2
Culion • Philippines 31 F4
Culion [I.] • Philippines 31 F4
Cullera • Spain 11 K5
Cullera **Beach** • Spain .... 96 [119]
Cullman • AL, United States 48 D3
Culpeper • VA, United States 153 D9
Culross • United Kingdom 104 B4
Culuene • Brazil 157 H2
Culver, Point • WA, Australia 34 D6
Cuma • Italy 121 G3
Cumana • Venezuela 51 E1
Cumbal, Volcán • Colombia 51 B3
Cumberland •
KY/TN, United States 48 E2
Cumberland • MD, United States 153 D9
Cumberland, Cape • Vanuatu 35 (2) B1
Cumberland Gap Nat. Hist. Park **Park N** •
KY, United States .... 151 [229]
Cumberland I. •
GA, United States 48 G5
Cumberland I. Nat. Seashore **Park N** •
GA, United States .... 151 [212]
Cumberland, Lake •
KY, United States 48 E2
Cumberland Peninsula •
NU, Canada 39 R3
Cumberland Plateau •
TN, United States 48 E2
Cumberland Sound • NU, Canada 39 R3
Cumbernauld • United Kingdom 104 B3
Cumbre del Libertador General San Martín •
Argentina 52 C3
Cumbre, Paso de la •
Argentina/Chile 52 B5
Cumbrian Mtns • United Kingdom 7 I1
Cumerna • Bulgaria 14 M7
Çumra • Turkey 123 G1
Cunene • Angola/Namibia 24 A3
Cuneo • Italy 121 E5
Cunit **Beach** • Spain .... 96 [121]
Cunnamulla • QL, Australia 144 B5
Cunningham • United States 44 B4
Cuokka rassa • Norway 16 M2

Cupar • United Kingdom 104 B2
Cupica, Golfo de • Colombia 51 B2
Cupids • NF, Canada 156 D4
Cupra Marittima **Beach** • Italy .... 97 [162]
Cupra Marittima • Italy 121 E12
Curaçao • West Indies .... 160 X
Curaçao Seaquarium • Curaçao .... 160 X
Curaçao Underwater Park •
Curaçao .... 160 X
Curacautín • Chile 53 B3
Curdimurka • SA, Australia 34 G5
Cure • France 10 I6
Curecanti Nat. Recreation Area **Park N** •
CO, United States .... 150 [90]
Curepipe • Mauritius 132 J3
Curiapo • Venezuela 51 E2
Curicó • Chile 52 B5
Curieuse • Seychelles 133 K4
Curitabanos • Brazil 52 F4
Curitiba • Brazil 52 G4
Curium • Cyprus 123 J3
Curoca • Angola 24 A3
Curonian Spit •
Lithuania/Russian Fed. 126 B5
Curracloe **Beach** • Ireland .... 96 [56]
Curragh, The • Ireland 108 B3
Currais Novos • Brazil 53 (1) D3
Curral das Freiras • Madeira 118 C1
Curral-Velho • Cape Verde 22 (1) B1
Currane, Lough • Ireland 108 C7
Current • MO, United States 46 J4
Currie • TS, Australia 34 H7
Currie • NV, United States 45 E1
Currituck Sound •
NC, United States 48 J2
Curtea de Argeş • Romania 14 L4
Curtis • New Zealand 33 J9
Curtis • NE, United States 46 E2
Curtis Channel • QL, Australia 144 B4
Curtis I. • QL, Australia 144 B4
Curuguaty • Paraguay 52 F3
Curupira, Sierra de •
Brazil/Venezuela 51 D3
Curuzú Cuatiá • Argentina 52 F4
Curvelo • Brazil 52 H2
Cusco • Peru 163 B2
Cushing • OK, United States 46 G5
Cut Back • MT, United States 42 I2
Cuthbert • GA, United States 23 B6
Cutervo • Peru 51 B5
Cuthbert • SA, United States 48 E5
Cutler Ridge •
FL, United States 49 C5
Cutro • Italy 12 L9
Cuttack • India 28 E4
Cuvo • Angola 23 A6
Cuxhaven • Germany 8 D3
Cuxhaven **Spa** • Germany .... 113 [c5]
Cuya • Chile 52 B2
Cuyahoga Falls •
OH, United States 44 E5
Cuyahoga Valley Nat. Recreation Area
Park N • OH, United States ..... 151 [185]
Cuyuni • Guyana/Venezuela 51 E2
Cuzco **Heritage C** • Peru .... 84 [59]
Cuzco • Peru 163 B2
Cwmtydu **Beach** • United Kingdom 101 [194]
Cyclades • Greece 122 D8
Cynthiana • KY, United States 48 E1
Cypress Hills • AL/SA, Canada 38 I7
CYPRUS • Europe .... 123 J
Cyrenaica • Libya 21 D1
Cyrene • Libya 21 D1
Cyrene **Heritage C** • Libya .... 86 [272]
Cyril E. King [Apt] •
US Virgin Is. .... 160 Z
CZECH REPUBLIC • Europe 13 D8
Czechowice-Dziedzice • Poland 128 C3
Czersk • Poland 13 G4
Czestochowa • Poland 128 C1

D.F. Wouda steam pumping station
Heritage C • Netherlands .... 86 [28]
D.F. Woudagemaal • Netherlands 109 D3
D'Arros • Seychelles 133 K2
D'Entrecasteaux Is. •
Papua New Guinea 35 (1) E2
D'Urville I. • New Zealand 35 D5
Da Hinggan Ling • China 27 I8
Da Lat • Vietnam 141 E2
Da Lat Plateau • Vietnam 141 E2
Da Nang • Vietnam 31 D3
Da Qaidam • China 29 B3
Da Yunhe • China 29 F4
Da Vinci, Leonardo [Apt] •
Italy 121 F3
Da Xi • China 31 F1
Da Yunhe • China 29 F3
Daba Shan • China 29 D3
Dabakala • Côte d'Ivoire 22 D3
Dabas • Hungary 13 I10
Dabeiba • Colombia 51 B2
Dabie Shan • China 29 F4
Dabola • Guinea 22 B3
Daboya • Ghana 141 D1
Dabolim [Apt] • Goa, India 137 B1
Dabsan Hu • China 28 F1
Dachau • Germany 112 F3
Dachstein • Austria 119 H4
Dacre Heights **Ski** • OT, Canada .. 149 [18]
Dadanawa • Guyana 51 F3
Dade City • FL, United States 49 B3
Dadès, Gorges du • Morocco 20 B2
Dâdejö • Sweden 125 F8
Dadra • India 28 B4
Dadu • Pakistan 28 A3
Dadu He • China 29 C4
Daeni • Romania 128 E2
Dafnoúdi, Akra •
Cephalonia, Greece 122 C2
Dafok, Am • Sudan 23 C1
Dagali • Norway 124 C4
Dagana • Senegal 20 B5
Dagestan • Russian Fed. 17 H6
Dagg Sound • New Zealand 145 G1
Dagomys • Russian Fed. 17 F6
Dagomys • Russian Fed. 126 A10
Daguapan • Philippines 31 G3
Dahab • Egypt 131 F4
Dahlem (Berlin) • Germany 111 C3
Dahme • Germany 8 E4
Dahna, Ad • Saudi Arabia 18 E4
Dahner 'Schlosser' **Castle** •
Germany .... 113 [74]
Dahongliutan • China 28 C1
Dahra • Algeria 118 L8
Dahra • Libya 21 C2
Dahra • Senegal 22 A1
Dahshur • Egypt 131 F1
Dai Shan • China 139 C4
Daiet el Kisria • Algeria 11 N9
Dailekh • Nepal 28 D3
Daimanji • India 11 H5
Daimiel, Parque Nac. de las Tablas de
Park N • Spain .... 89 [74]
Daio-zaki • Japan .... 89 [74]
Daishan • China 139 C4
Daito-shoto • Japan 29 I5
Dajabón • Dominican Rep. 159 G2
Dajarra • QL, Australia 34 G4
Dajtit Nat. Park **Park N** •
Albania .... 89 [125]
Dakar • Senegal 22 A2
Dakhla • Western Sahara 20 B4
Dakhla Oasis • Egypt 131 F3
Dakoro • Niger 20 G6

Dakovica • F.R. of Yugoslavia 14 H7
Dakovo • Croatia 14 F4
Dal • Norway 124 B2
Dala • Angola 24 C2
Dalaas • Austria 119 H5
Dalaba • Guinea 22 B2
Dalälven • Sweden 16 I6
Dalaman • Turkey 122 D9
Dalaman [Riv] • Turkey 15 J7
Dalandzadgad • Mongolia 29 C2
Dalarnas • Sweden 16 G6
Dalard • Sweden 125 D4
Dalbandin • Pakistan 18 H4
Dalbosjön • Sweden 125 F3
Dalby • Sweden 125 F11
Dalby • QL, Australia 144 B6
Dale **Beach** • United Kingdom ...... 101 [174]
Dale • Sogn og Fjordane, Norway 124 C3
Dale • Hordaland, Norway 124 C3
Dale City • VA, United States 44 G6
Dale Hollow Lake •
TN, United States 48 E2
Dalem Temple • Bali, Indonesia 143 H4
Dalen • Norway 124 C6
Daleville • AL, United States 48 E5
Dalhart • TX, United States 46 D4
Dalhousie **Hill Sta** • India 138 C1
Dalhousie Springs •
SA, Australia 145 D4
Dali • China 29 C5
Dalian • China 29 G3
Dalkey • Ireland 108 B2
Dalkey I. • Ireland 108 B2
Dall I. • AK, United States 38 E6
Dallas • OR, United States 42 D4
Dallas • TX, United States 154 J1
Dallgow • Germany 111 C1
Dallol Bosso • Niger 20 F6
Dalmacia • Croatia 12 F8
Dalmeny • United Kingdom 104 B4
Dalnegorsk • Russian Fed. 27 M8
Dalnyaya, gora • Russian Fed. 27 U3
Daloa • Côte d'Ivoire 22 C3
Dalou Shan • China 29 D5
Dalry • United Kingdom 21 F3
Dalrymple, Mt • QL, Australia 144 B3
Daslands kanal • Sweden 125 F2
Dalton • South Africa 134 B3
Dalton • GA, United States 48 E3
Dalton-in-Furness •
United Kingdom 104 C3
Daltonganj • India 137 C8
Dalus, Gorges de • France 115 H2
Dalwallinu • WA, Australia 34 C6
Daly • NT, Australia 34 F2
Daly City • CA, United States 45 A3
Daly Waters • NT, Australia 34 F1
Dalyan • Turkey 122 D9
Dam Qu • China 28 F2
Daman • India 28 B4
Daman **Beach** • India 138 E3
Daman [Adm] • India 28 B4
Damanhûr • Egypt 21 F1
Damar • Indonesia 32 (1) C4
Damascus • Syria 18 B2
Damascus **Heritage C** • Syria ...... 86 [278]
Damaturu • Nigeria 20 H6
Damazin, Ad • Sudan 23 E1
Damba • Angola 23 A5
Dambulla Golden Rock Temple
Heritage N • Sri Lanka .... 83 [119]
Dambulla Golden Rock Temple
Heritage C • Sri Lanka .... 85 [156]
Dambulla Golden Rock Temple •
Sri Lanka 138 D15
Dame-Marie, Cap • Haiti 159 G5
Dametta • Egypt 131 F2
Damietta Mouth • Egypt 131 F2
Damir, Ad • Sudan 21 F4
Dammam, Ad • Saudi Arabia 18 E4
Damme • Germany 8 D3
Damoh • India 137 C7
Damon **Spa** • Germany .... 113 [c13]
Dampier • WA, Australia 34 C4
Damqawt • Yemen 18 F6
Damqog Kanbab • China 28 D3
Damüls • Austria 119 H1
Damville • France 10 H5
Damxung • China 28 E3
Dandancheng • China 139 C4
Dandaneng • China 130 C1
Dandeldhura • Nepal 28 D3
Dandenong • VI, Australia 144 C3
Dangan Liedao • Zhuhai, China 139 B4
Dange, Point • South Africa 134 C5
Dangoura, Mt •
Central African Rep. 23 D2
Dangtu • China 139 C1
Dania • VI, United States 154 H8
Danilov • Russian Fed. 126 C2
Danish Riviera • Denmark 125 F11
Danjo-gunto • Japan 140 A6
Danmarks Havn • Greenland 36 O1
Dannemora • Sweden 125 D2
Dannenberg • Germany 8 G3
Dannevirke • New Zealand 35 F5
Danshui • China 139 B4
Dansville • NY, United States 153 D1
Danube • Europe 4 P8
Danube Delta **Heritage N** •
Romania .... 83 [64]
Danube Delta • Romania 128 E2
Danville • IL, United States 44 B5
Danville • PA, United States 44 H5
Danville • KY, United States 48 E2
Danville • VA, United States 48 H2
Danyang • China 139 C1
Danzig • Poland 13 H3
Dao Phu Quoc • Vietnam 31 C4
Dao Timni • Niger 20 H4
Dapaong • Togo 22 E3
Dapqing • China 29 G1
Dar Bouâzza • Morocco 131 D1
Dar es Salaam • Tanzania 130 B4
Dar Rounga •
Central African Rep./Sudan 23 C2
Dar Sila • Chad 23 C1
Dar'a • Syria 18 C3
Daraban • Romania 14 N1
Daracya Yarimadasi • Turkey 15 J7
Daravica • F.R. of Yugoslavia 14 H7
Darbhanga • India 28 E3
Dardanelle • AR, United States 46 I5
Dardanelle, Lake •
AR, United States 46 I5
Dardanelles • Turkey 122 D2
Darfo Boario Terme • Italy 121 E7
Darfur • Chad/Sudan 130 A2
Darfur al Janubiyah • Sudan 23 C1
Dargaville • New Zealand 35 E1
Dargasata • Turkmenistan 18 G1
Dargol • Niger 141 C1
Darhan • Mongolia 27 G7
Darién • Panama 51 B2
Darién, Golfo del •
Colombia/Panama 51 B2
Darién, Parque Nac. del **Heritage N** •
Panama .... 82 [27]
Darién, Serranía del •
Colombia/Panama 51 B2
Darjeeling • India 28 E3
Darjeeling **Hill Sta** • India 138 C3
Darjeeling Himalayan Railway
Heritage C • India .... 85 [150]
Darling • Australia 5 N9
Darling Downs • QL, Australia 144 B6
Darling Range • WA, Australia 33 C9
Darlington • United Kingdom 7 K7
Darlington • SC, United States 48 G3
Darlowo • Poland 13 F3
Darmstadt • Germany 112 E4
Darnah • Libya 21 D1
Daroca • Spain 11 J3

Darrah Wildlife Sanctuary •
India 137 C6
Darregueira • Argentina 52 D6
Darrington • WA, United States 42 E2
Darss • Germany 8 H2
Dart • United Kingdom 104 F5
Dartmoor **Hill Sta** • India 138 D7
Dartmoor Nat. Park **Park N** •
United Kingdom .... 89 [51]
Dartmoor Nat. Park •
United Kingdom 104 F5
Dartmouth • United Kingdom 104 F5
Dartmouth • NS, Canada 156 D3
Daru • Papua New Guinea 35 (1) C2
Daru Lake (Lake) • NF, Canada 156 D3
Daru Lake [Lake] • NF, Canada 156 D3
Deer Lodge • MT, United States 42 I3
Deer Park • WA, United States 42 G3
Darwin • NT, Australia 34 F2
Darwin • Galapagos Is. 51 (1) A1
Daryacheh-ye Hamun-e Hirmand •
Afghanistan/Iran 18 H3
Dashen, Ras • Ethiopia 21 G5
Dashhowuz • Turkmenistan 18 G1
Dassel • Germany 8 E4
Dasseri I. • South Africa 134 C5
Dassià • Corfu, Greece 122 B1
Datça **Beach** • Turkey .... 97 [234]
Datça • Turkey 122 D9
Date • Japan 30 K3
Datia • India 137 C7
Datong • China 29 E2
Daugava • Latvia 126 B4
Daugava • Latvia 126 B4
Daugavpils • Latvia 126 B4
Daun • Germany 112 E1
Daun **Spa** • Germany .... 113 [k5]
Daunia, Monti della • Italy 14 G8
Dauphin • MN, Canada 38 L6
Dauphin • MN, Canada 48 C5
Dauphin Lake • MN, Canada 43 G1
Dauphiné • France 10 K8
Davangere • India 138 D6
Davao • Philippines 31 H5
Davao Gulf • Philippines 31 H5
Davar Panah • Iran 18 H4
Davenport • IA, United States 42 F3
Davenport • IA, United States 46 J2
David • Panama 37 E6
David Point • Grenada .... 160 S
Davidson • SA, Canada 43 C1
Davis • FL, United States 49 C4
Davis • CA, United States 45 B2
Davis Bay • Antarctica 54 (1) N3
Davis Bay • US Virgin Is. .... 160 Z
Davis Dam •
AZ/NV, United States 153 E1
Davis Mtns • TX, United States 47 B2
Davis Strait • Canada/Greenland 39 T4
Davos **Ski** • Switzerland .... 100 [114]
Davos • Switzerland 119 G4
Davos • NY, United States 153 D6
Dawa • China 30 B4
Dawa • Ethiopia 131 G2
Dawlish **Beach** • United Kingdom .. 101 [111]
Dawlish Warren **Beach** •
United Kingdom .... 101 [111]
Dawson • QL, Australia 144 B5
Dawson • YT, Canada 38 D4
Dawson • ND, United States 43 F1
Dawson Creek • BC, Canada 155 C1
Dawu • China 29 C4
Dax • France 115 G3
Daxue Shan • China 29 C5
Daydream I. • QL, Australia 144 B1
Daylesford • VI, Australia 144 C3
Dayr • Sudan 21 F5
Dayr az Zawr • Syria 18 C2
Dayton • WA, United States 42 F3
Dayton • OH, United States 44 D6
Dayton • TN, United States 48 E3
Dayton Aviation Nat. Hist. Park **Park N** •
OH, United States .... 151 [181]
Daytona Beach •
FL, United States 154 H4
Dazu rock carvings **Heritage C** •
China .... 85 [178]
De Aar • South Africa 24 C6
De Bay, Laguna • Philippines 31 G4
De Efteling **Park L** •
Netherlands .... 98 [44]
De Efteling • Netherlands 109 D11
De Funiak Springs •
FL, United States 154 F4
De Grey • WA, Australia 34 D4
De Haan • Belgium 109 D2
De Haar • Netherlands 109 F2
De Hoge Veluwe, Nat. Park **Park N** •
Netherlands .... 89 [53]
De Hoop Nature Reserve •
South Africa 134 C6
De Kalb, Tanjung • Indonesia 32 (1) E4
De Kalb • IL, United States 46 K2
De Kalb • TX, United States 154 J2
De Land • FL, United States 154 H4
De Leon Springs •
FL, United States 49 C3
De Panne • Belgium 109 E1
De Pere • WI, United States 44 A3
De Quincy Village • Seychelles 133 K1
De Ridder • LA, United States 47 H2
De Rust • South Africa 134 C7
De Smet • SD, United States 43 H4
De Soto Nat. Mem. **Park N** •
FL, United States .... 151 [219]
De Soto Nat. Mem. •
FL, United States 154 H5
De Tour Village •
MI, United States 44 C3
De Witt • NY, United States 44 G4
De Witt • IA, United States 46 J2
De Zijpe • Netherlands 109 D3
Dead Sea • Asia 135 A4
Deal • United Kingdom 104 E4
Dean, Forest of •
United Kingdom 104 D3
Deán Funes • Argentina 52 D5
Dease • BC, Canada 38 E5
Dease Arm • NT/NU, Canada 38 F5
Dease Lake • BC, Canada 38 E5
Dease Strait • NU, Canada 38 H4
Death Valley •
CA, United States 45 D3
Death Valley Nat. Park **Park N** •
CA, United States .... 150 [53]
Death Valley Nat. Park •
CA, United States 45 D3
Deauville • France 5 D1
Debica • Poland 13 K7
Debin • Russian Fed. 27 P4
Deblin • Poland 13 K6
Dèbo, Lac • Mali 20 E5
DeBoulie Mtn •
ME, United States 44 K2
Debrecen • Hungary 14 K2
Debre Berhan • Ethiopia 21 G5
Debre Markos • Ethiopia 21 G5
Debrecen • United States 154 J1
Decatur • CO, United States 46 C3
Decatur • IN, United States 44 C5
Decatur • AL, United States 48 D3
Deccan • India 138 D2
Decele, Réservoir •
QU, Canada 44 F2

Deception Bay •
Papua New Guinea 35 (1) C2
Déroute, Passage de la • France 2 B5
Derry • NH, United States 44 J4
Derrynasaggart Mtns • Ireland 108 C8
Derventa • Bosnia-Herz. 14 E5
Derwent • Cumbria, UK 104 C1
Derwent • Derbyshire, UK 5 B1
Derwent • Italy 137 C2
Deep Bay • China 139 C2
Deep Cove • New Zealand 145 G1
Deep River • OT, Canada 44 G2
Deer I. • NB, Canada 156 D6
Derwent • Cumbria, UK 104 C1
Derwent Water • United Kingdom ... 104 C1
Des Moines • IA, United States 46 I2
Des Moines [Riv] •
IA, United States 46 I2
Des Plaines • IL, United States 44 A4
Desaguadero • Argentina 52 C5
Desaguadero • Peru 163 B4
Désappointement •
French Polynesia 33 M7
Desaru • Malaysia 141 D3
Descartes • France 114 D4
Deschutes • OR, United States 152 B3
Dese • Ethiopia 21 G5
Deseado • Argentina 53 C5
Desembogue • Mexico 45 F6
Desengaño, Punta • Argentina 53 C5
Desenzano • Italy 121 E7
Desert Center •
CA, United States 45 E5
Desert Springs • India 137 C1
Desierto Central de Baja California, Parque
Natural del • Mexico 157 F1
Désirade, la • Guadeloupe .... 161 L
Deskáti • Greece 15 C4
Desna • Ukraine 17 E4
Desnoeufs • Seychelles 133 K2
Desolation, Valley of •
South Africa 134 C3
Despotiko • Greece 122 D7
Desroches • Seychelles 133 K2
Dessau • Germany 8 H5
Dessau **Heritage C** • Germany ... 86 [71]
Dessel **Beach** • Belgium .... 96 [71]
Destin • FL, United States 154 F4
Destruction Bay • YT, Canada 49 N3
Dete • Romania 14 I4
Dete • Zimbabwe 130 C1
Detmold • Germany 8 D5
Detmold **Castle** • Germany ... 113 [24]
Detroit • MI, United States 44 D4
Detroit Lakes •
MN, United States 43 I3
Detva • Slovak Rep. 13 I9
Deurne [Apt] • Belgium 109 D10
Deutsche Bucht • North Sea 8 C2
Deux Alpes, les **Ski** • France ... 100 [59]
Deux Alpes, les • France 115 F2
Deux Sèvres • France 114 D3
Deva • Romania 14 J4
Deventer • Netherlands 109 D8
Devil River Peak • New Zealand 35 D5
Devil's Bridge •
Antigua & Barbuda .... 161 K
Devil's I. • French Guiana 80 A3
Devil's Woodyard •
Trinidad & Tobago .... 160 U
Devils Head **C** •
WI, United States .... 149 [133]
Devils Postpile Nat. Mon. **Park N** •
CA, United States .... 150 [50]
Devils Postpile Nat. Mon. •
CA, United States 152 C4
Devils Tower •
WY, United States 43 D4
Devils Tower Nat. Mon. **Park N** ... 150 [70]
WY, United States .... 150 [70]
Devin • Bulgaria 14 L8
Devizes • United Kingdom 104 F3
Devoloraine • TS, Australia 34 I8
Delphi • Greece 15 D5
Delphi **Heritage C** • Greece ..... 86 [210]
Delphi • IN, United States 44 C5
Delphos • OH, United States 44 C5
Delray Beach •
FL, United States 154 H4
Delta • UT, United States 45 F2
Delta • CA, United States 45 B1
Delta, Country of •
MS, United States 153 F2
Delta del Saloum, Parc nat. du **Park •**
Senegal .... 133 [7]
Delta Junction •
AK, United States 49 L3
Deltebre **Beach** • Spain .... 96 [121]
Delvin • Ireland 108 B1
Delvináki • Greece 15 B4
Demak • Java, Indonesia 143 J3
Demba • Dem. Rep. of Congo 23 C2
Dembi Dolo • Ethiopia 21 F5
Demidov • Russian Fed. 126 C3
Demici • Turkey 15 J4
Demirci • Turkey 15 J4
Demirkazik Tepe • Turkey 123 G2
Demirköy • Turkey 15 I2
Demirtas • Turkey 123 F4
Demmin • Germany 8 H3
Demone, Val • Sicily, Italy 120 D2
Demopolis • AL, United States 48 D4
Demta • Indonesia 32 (1) H3
Demyanskoye • Russian Fed. 26 I5
Den Chai • Thailand 142 E4
Den Haag • Netherlands 109 F1
Den Helder **Beach** • Netherlands . 96 [67]
Den Helder • Netherlands 109 D3
Denain • France 10 I3
Denali Nat. Park •
AK, United States 49 K3
Denali Nat. Park & Preserve **Park N** •
AK, United States .... 150 [7]
Denau • Uzbekistan 18 I2
Denbigh • OT, Canada 44 G2
Dendang • Indonesia 32 D3
Dendermonde • Belgium 109 D3
Deng Xian • China 29 E4
Dêngqên • China 28 F2
Denham • WA, Australia 34 B5
Denia **Beach** • Spain .... 96 [118]
Denia • Spain 117 C2
Deniliquin • NS, Australia 144 C1
Denis, I. • Seychelles 133 K1
Denison • IA, United States 43 I5
Denison • TX, United States 46 G6
Denison Dam •
OK/TX, United States 154 J1
Denizli • Turkey 122 D9
Denloo • NV, United States 45 E2
Denmark • WA, Australia 34 K6
Denmark • SC, United States 48 G4
DENMARK • Europe .... 125 F
Denmark Strait •
Greenland/Iceland 4 E3
Dennery • St Lucia .... 161 P
Denpasar • Bali, Indonesia 143 H4
Denton • MD, United States 44 G6
Denton • TX, United States 154 J1
Denver • CO, United States 46 C3
Deogarh • India 137 C7
Deol • India 137 C1
Deoli • India 137 C1
Deping • China 139 C2
Der, Lac du • France 5 H6
Derbent • Russian Fed. 17 H6
Derby • United Kingdom 104 D2
Derby • WA, Australia 34 D3
Derby • KS, United States 46 G4
Derbyshire Dales • United Kingdom . 7 J8
Dereköy • Turkey 15 I2
Derg, Lough • Ireland 108 C4

Derinkuyu • Turkey 123 G2
Decize • Czech Rep. 128 B2
Decize • France 10 I7
Decorah • IA, United States 43 K5
Dedegöl Dag • Turkey 123 F2
Dee • Scotland, UK 6 J4
Dee • England/Wales, UK 7 I9
Deeg • India 137 C2
Deep Bay • China 139 C2
Deer I. • NB, Canada 156 D6
Deer Lake • NF, Canada 156 D3
Deer Lake [Lake] • NF, Canada 156 D3
Deer Valley **Ski** •
UT, United States .... 149 [89]
Deerfield Beach •
FL, United States 49 C4
Defiance • OH, United States 44 C5
Degeberga • Sweden 125 F11
Degeh Bur • Ethiopia 23 G2
Degelis • QU, Canada 44 K2
Degerhamn • Sweden 125 F12
Deggendorf • Germany 9 H8
Degirmendere • Turkey 15 I5
Degirmenlik • Cyprus 123 J2
Dehibat • Tunisia 20 H2
Dehiwala • Sri Lanka 138 D15
Dehra Dun • India 28 C2
Dehra Dun **Hill Sta** • India 138 C2
Dehui • China 27 K8
Deinze • Belgium 5 G3
Deià • Majorca, Spain 117 H1
Deje • Sweden 124 C2
Déjeanne • Belgium 5 G3
Dekese • Dem. Rep. of Congo 23 C4
Dekoa • Central African Rep. 22 H3
Del City • OK, United States 46 G5
Del Rio • TX, United States 47 D3
Del Norte • CA, United States 152 C3
Delarem • Afghanistan 18 H3
Delaware • OH, United States 44 D5
Delaware [Adm] • United States 153 D10
Delaware Bay •
DE/NJ, United States 153 D10
Delaware • NF, United States 153 D6
Delaware Mtns •
TX, United States 47 B2
Delaware [Riv] • United States 153 D6
Delaware Water Gap Nat. Recreation Area
Park N • PA, United States ... 151 [302]
Delaware Water Gap Nat. Recreation
Area • PA, United States 153 D6
Delegate • NS, Australia 144 C4
Delémont • Switzerland 9 C9
Delfi • Greece 15 D5

Didiéni • Mali 20 D6
Didyma • Turkey 122 D8
Die • France 10 K9
Dieburg • Germany 9 D7
Diefenbaker, Lake • SA, Canada 42 L1
Diego Suarez • Madagascar 24 H2
Diekirch • Luxembourg 109 D20
Diélette • France .... 106 C
Diéma • Mali 22 C2
Diemel • Germany 8 D5
Diem Bien Phu • Vietnam 31 D2
Dieng Plateau • Java, Indonesia 143 J6
Dienten am Hochkönig Ski •
  Austria .... 100 [167]
Diepholz • Germany 8 D4
Dieppe • France 10 G4
Dieppe Beach • France .... 96 [77]
Dieppe Bay • St Kitts & Nevis .... 161 G
Dierhagen Beach • Germany .... 96 [32]
Dießen-Rieden • Germany 112 F2
Diest • Belgium 109 D15
Dieuze • France 5 J6
Diez • France 112 E2
Diffa • Niger 20 H6
Differdange • Luxembourg 5 I5
Difnein I. Dive • Red Sea 135 B4
Digby • NS, Canada 156 D7
Digha Beach • India 138 E4
Digne • France 115 H1
Digne • France 10 I7
Digoin • France 10 I7
Digue, la • Seychelles 133 K4
Digul • Indonesia 32 (1) E4
Dihang • India 28 F3
Dijlah • Iraq 18 D2
Dijon • France 10 K6
Dik • Chad 23 B2
Dikili • Turkey 15 H4
Diksmuide • Belgium 109 E1
Dikson • Russian Fed. 26 N3
Diktéon Antron • Crete, Greece 123 E7
Diktineon • Crete, Greece 123 E1
Dikwa • Nigeria 22 G2
Dili • East Indies 32 (1) B4
Dillenburg • Germany 112 D2
Dillia • Niger 21 B4
Dilling • Sudan 23 D1
Dillingen • Germany 90 A8
Dillingen Castle • Germany .... 113 [134]
Dillingham • AK, United States 49 J4
Dillon • MT, United States 42 I4
Dilly • Mali 20 D6
Diolo • Dem. Rep. of Congo 23 C6
Dilos Heritage C • Greece .... 86 [217]
Dilos • Greece 122 D8
Dimashq • Syria 18 C3
Dimashq Heritage C • Syria .... 86 [278]
Dimokrio • Côte d'Ivoire 22 D3
Dimboola • VI, Australia 34 H7
Dimbovita • Romania 128 E1
Dimitrovgrad • Russian Fed. 17 H4
Dimitrovgrad • Bulgaria 128 E3
Dinagat • Philippines 31 H4
Dinajpur • Bangladesh 28 E3
Dinan • France 114 C2
Dinant • Belgium 109 D19
Dinar • Turkey 15 L5
Dinara • Bosnia-Herz./Croatia 128 D4
Dinard • France 114 C2
Dinaric Alps •
  Bosnia-Herz./Croatia 128 A2
Dinas Cross Beach •
  United Kingdom .... 101 [186]
Dinder Nat. Park Park • Sudan .... 133 [60]
Dindigul • India 138 D11
Dinga • Dem. Rep. of Congo 22 H6
Dinga • China 139 C4
Dingle • Ireland 108 C5
Dingle Bay • Ireland 108 C5
Dingle Peninsula • Ireland 108 C5
Dingli Cliffs • Malta 123 H4
Dingolfing • Germany 9 H8
Dingwall • United Kingdom 6 H4
Dingxian • China 29 F3
Dinkelsbühl • Germany 9 F7
Dinkelsbühl Castle • Germany .... 113 [146]
Dinorwic • OT, Canada 43 J2
Dinorwic Lake • OT, Canada 43 J2
Dinosaur Nat. Mon. Park N •
  CO, United States .... 150 [86]
Dinosaur Prov. Park Heritage N •
  AL, Canada .... 82 [6]
Dinosaurier Park Münchehagen Park L •
  Germany .... 98 [55]
Dinotown • BC, Canada 155 C3
Dinslaken • Germany 111 B1
Dinuba • CA, United States 45 C3
Dioila • Mali 22 C2
Dionísiades • Greece 123 E4
Dioura • Mali 20 D6
Diourbel • Senegal 22 A2
Dipkarpaz • Cyprus 123 J2
Dipolog • Philippines 31 G5
Dire Dawa • Ethiopia 23 G1
Dirfis, Oros • Greece 15 E5
Dirj • Libya 21 A1
Dirk Hartog I. • WA, Australia 34 B5
Dirkou • Niger 20 H5
Dirranbandi • QL, Australia 34 I5
Disappointment, Lake •
  WA, Australia 34 D4
Discovery Bay • Jamaica 159 F1
Discovery Coast Atlantic forest reserves
  Heritage N • Brazil .... 82 [39]
Dishforth •
  FL, United States 151 C1
Disentis • Switzerland 119 G3
Disko • Greenland 39 U3
Disney-MGM Studios •
  FL, United States 151 C1
Disneyland Park L •
  CA, United States .... 150 [H]
Disneyland • CA, United States 152 C6
Disneyland Paris Park L •
  France .... 98 [72]
Disneyland Paris • France 115 E4
Dispur • India 28 F3
Disraeli • QU, Canada 44 J3
Distington • United Kingdom 104 C1
Distrito Federal • Brazil 53 (1) B5
Ditiki Rodópi • Greece 15 C3
Diu • India 28 B4
Diu Beach • India 138 E3
Diu [Adm] • India 28 B4
Diver I. • Goa, India 137 B1
Dives • France 5 C5
Divide • MT, United States 42 I4
Divinópolis • Brazil 163 C1
Divisões, Serra das • Brazil 52 F2
Divisor, Serra de • Brazil/Peru 51 C5
Divjaka Nat. Park Park N •
  Canada/United States 49 O5
Diyala • Iraq 18 D2
Diyarbakir • Turkey 18 D2
Dja • Cameroon/Congo 22 G4
Dja, Réserve du Heritage N •
  Cameroon .... 83 [90]
Dja, Réserve du Park • Cameroon .... 133 [38]
Djado • Niger 20 H4
Djado, Plateau de • Niger 20 H4
Djambala • Congo 22 G5
Djanet • Algeria 20 G4
Djaret • Algeria 20 F3

Djavat • F.Y.R. of Macedonia 15 C2
Djedi • Algeria 20 F2
Djelfa • Algeria 20 F2
Djemila • Algeria 20 G1
Djemila Heritage C • Algeria .... 86 [259]
Djenne • Mali 20 E6
Djenne Heritage C • Mali .... 85 [108]
Djerdap Nat. Park Park N •
  Fed. Rep. of Yugoslavia .... 89 [116]
Djerem • Cameroon 22 G3
Djibo • Burkina Faso 22 D2
DJIBOUTI • Africa 21 H5
Djibouti • Djibouti 21 H5
Djoua • Congo/Gabon 22 G4
Djougou Nat. Bird Sanctuary Heritage N •
  Senegal .... 83 [81]
Djoudj, Parc nat. des Oiseaux du Park •
  Senegal .... 133 [5]
Djouf, El • Mali/Mauritania 20 D4
Djoum • Cameroon 22 G4
Djourab, Erg du • Chad 22 H1
Djúpivogur • Iceland 16 (1) F2
Djurs Sommerland Park L •
  Denmark .... 98 [15]
Djurs Sommerland • Denmark 125 F10
Djursdala • Sweden 125 F8
Djursland • Denmark 125 F10
Dmitriya Lapteva, Proliv •
  Russian Fed. 27 N2
Dmitrov • Russian Fed. 126 C4
Dnipro • Ukraine 17 E5
Dniprodzerzhyns'k • Ukraine 17 E5
Dnipropetrovs'k • Ukraine 17 F5
Dnister • Ukraine 17 D5
Doaktown • NB, Canada 156 D7
Doba • Chad 23 B2
Dobbiaco • Italy 120 B2
Dobele • Latvia 126 B3
Döbeln • Germany 9 I5
Doberai, Jazirah • Indonesia 32 (1) D3
Dobiacco Ski • Italy .... 100 [245]
Dobo • Indonesia 32 (1) D3
Doboj • Bosnia-Herz. 14 F5
Dobreta-Turnu Severin • Romania 14 J5
Dobrich • Bulgaria 128 E4
Dobrodsja • Romania 128 E2
Doce • Brazil 163 C2
Docker River • NT, Australia 145 D3
Doctor González • Mexico 47 E5
Doctor Phillips •
  FL, United States 151 C2
Doda Betta • India 138 D10
Dodecanese • Greece 122 D8
Dodekánissa • Greece 15 I7
Dodge City • KS, United States 46 E3
Dodge Ridge Ski •
  CA, United States .... 149 [67]
Dodoma • Tanzania 130 B2
Dodóni • Greece 15 B4
Dodori Game Reserve • Kenya 131 G4
Doe Mtn Ski • PA, United States .... 149 [174]
Doe Mtn •• PA, United States 153 D6
Doetinchem • Netherlands 5 J3
Dofa • Indonesia 32 (1) C3
Dog I. • Anguilla .... 160 C
Dog I. • FL, United States 154 H2
Dog Lake • OT, Canada 43 L2
Dog Lake • OT, Canada 44 C1
Dogai Coring • China 28 E2
Doganbey • Turkey 123 F2
Dogashima • Japan 140 C3
Dogger Bank • North Sea 7 N7
Dogo • Japan 30 G6
Dogs, The • British Virgin Is. .... 160 B
Dogu Karadeniz Daglari • Turkey 18 D1
Dogubayazit • Turkey 122 A4
Dogwood Point •
  St Kitts & Nevis .... 161 G
Doha • Qatar 18 F4
Dohad • India 18 J5
Doi Inthanon • Thailand 142 B3
Doi Inthanon Nat. Park •
  Thailand 142 B3
Doi Khun Tan Nat. Park •
  Thailand 142 B3
Doi Suthep Nat. Park • Thailand 142 B3
Dokhara, Dunes de • Algeria 20 G2
Dokkum • Netherlands 109 D7
Dokós • Greece 122 D7
Dol-de-Bretagne • France 114 C2
Dole • France 32 (1) E4
Dôle • France 10 K6
Dolent, Mt •
  France/Italy/Switzerland 119 G5
Dolfinarium Harderwijk Park L •
  Netherlands .... 98 [41]
Dolfinarium Harderwijk •
  Netherlands 109 D7
Dolgellau • United Kingdom 7 I9
Dolina • Ukraine 14 K1
Dollard • Germany/Netherlands 8 C3
Dollywood Park L •
  TN, United States .... 151 [Y]
Dolny Kubín • Slovak Rep. 13 I8
Dolo • Ethiopia 23 G3
Dolomites • Italy .... 120 B
Dolomiti • Italy .... 120 B
Dolonnur • China 29 F2
Dovrefjell • Norway 16 E3
Dolores • Uruguay 163 D2
Dolores • Argentina 163 D4
Dolphin, Cape • Falkland Is. 53 E6
Dolphin Coast • South Africa 134 B4
Dolphin Reef (Berenice) Dive •
  Red Sea 135 B2
Dolphin Reef (Eilat) Dive •
  Red Sea 135 B1
Dolus-d'Oléron Beach • France .... 96 [84]
Dom Pedrito • Brazil 52 F5
Domazlice • Czech Rep. 124 C2
Dombás • Norway 16 E3
Dombóvár • Hungary 13 H11
Domburg • Belgium 5 G3
Domfront • France 114 D2
DOMINICA • West Indies .... 161 M
DOMINICAN REPUBLIC •
  West Indies .... 159 G
Domme • France 115 G4
Dommel • Netherlands 5 H4
Domo • Ethiopia 23 H2
Domodedovo [Apt] • Russian Fed. 126 D4
Domodóssola • Italy 121 E2
Domokós • Greece 15 D4
Domuyo, Volcán • Argentina 52 B6
Don • Russian Fed. 6 J4
Don • Mexico 157 F4
Don Benito • Spain 11 F4
Don Martin • Mexico 47 E4
Don Muang [Apt] • Thailand 142 C2
Don Sak • Thailand 142 C4
Dona Paula Beach • Goa, India 137 B1
Donabate Beach • Ireland .... 96 [54]
Donabate • Ireland 108 B2
Donaldsonville •
  LA, United States 47 I2
Donau • Austria/Germany 9 G8
Donaueschingen • Germany 112 D8
Donauwörth • Germany 9 F8
Doncaster • United Kingdom 7 K8
Dondo • Angola 23 A5
Dondo • Mozambique 109 D13
Dondra Head • Sri Lanka 24 G3
Dondra Head • Sri Lanka 138 D15
Donegal • Ireland 7 D7
Donegal [Adm] • Ireland 108 A1
Donegal Bay • Ireland 7 D7
Donegal Mtns • Ireland 7 D7

Donets Basin •
  Russian Fed./Ukraine 126 A10
Donets'k • Ukraine 17 F5
Dong Bai • China 29 G1
Dong Hai • Asia 29 H5
Dong Hoi • Vietnam 31 D3
Dong Jiang • China 31 F2
Dong Ujimqin Qi • China 27 I7
Dongara • WA, Australia 34 B5
Donggala • China 31 C1
Dongfang • China 31 D3
Donggou • China 30 C5
Dongkala • Indonesia 32 (1) B4
Dongnan Qiuling • China 31 E2
Dongping • China 29 E5
Donipah • MO, United States 46 J4
Danna • Norway 16 G3
Donnacona • QU, Canada 44 J2
Donner Pass • CA, United States 152 C3
Donner Ski Ranch Ski •
  CA, United States .... 149 [57]
Donnybrook • WA, Australia 34 C6
Donore • Ireland 108 B2
Donostia • Spain 11 J1
Donoússa • Greece 122 D8
Doolin • Ireland 108 C6
Doonass, Falls of • Ireland 108 C6
Doorn • Netherlands 109 F4
Dor • Israel 135 A3
Dora Baltea • Italy 121 E5
Dora Riparia • Italy 10 M8
Dorada, Costa • Spain 117 D3
Dorado • Puerto Rico 159 H2
Dorchester • United Kingdom 7 K10
Dordogne • France 115 G1
Dordogne [Adm] • France 115 G1
Dordogne, Gorges de la • France 115 G2
Dordrecht • Netherlands 109 F3
Dore • France 10 I8
Doré Lake • SA, Canada 42 L3
Dores do Indaiá • Brazil 163 C1
Dorfen • Germany 112 F3
Dorfgastein • Austria 119 H4
Dorgali • Sardinia, Italy 12 D8
Dori • Burkina Faso 22 D2
Doring • South Africa 134 I6
Dormagen • Germany 111 B3
Dormaa • Austria 119 H1
Dornoch • United Kingdom 6 I3
Dornoch Beach • United Kingdom .... 101 [3]
Dornoch Firth • United Kingdom 6 I4
Dorog • Hungary 13 H10
Dorohoi • Romania 14 N2
Dorotea • Sweden 16 G3
Dorset • United Kingdom 104 F3
Dorset • OT, Canada 44 F3
Dorsten • Germany 111 B1
Dortmund • Germany 111 B2
Dortmund: Florianturm • Germany 111 B2
Dortmund: Tierpark • Germany 111 B2
Dortmund-Ems-Kanal • Germany 111 B1
Dörtyol • Turkey 123 G4
Dorval [Apt] • QU, Canada 155 B7
Dos Hermanas • Spain 11 F7
Dösmealti • Turkey 123 F1
Dospat • Bulgaria 15 E2
Dosso • Niger 22 E2
Dothan • AL, United States 154 H2
Douai • France 10 I3
Douala • Cameroon 22 F4
Dournenez • France 114 C3
Double, Fôret de la • France 115 G1
Double I. • Hong Kong, China 139 B4
Doubs • France 10 L6
Doubtful Sound • New Zealand 146 A6
Douentza • Mali 21 N8
Douera • Algeria 116 C2
Dougga Heritage C • Tunisia .... 86 [262]
Dougga • Tunisia 131 E1
Douglas • Isle of Man 7 H7
Douglas • South Africa 134 C5
Douglas • WY, United States 43 D5
Douglas • GA, United States 48 F5
Douglas • AZ, United States 153 E4
Douglas Lake •
  TN, United States 48 F2
Douglas, Mt • QL, Australia 144 B3
Douglas • IA, Levkas, Greece 122 C7
Doullens • France 10 H3
Doumen • Zhuhai, China 139 B1
Dourada, Costa da • Portugal 118 A3
Dourados • Brazil 52 F3
Dourdan • France 115 E3
Douro • Portugal 11 D3
Dout • Tunisia 131 E5
Dove Cottage • United Kingdom 104 C2
Dove Creek • CO, United States 45 H3
Dover • United Kingdom 104 E4
Dover • OH, United States 44 E5
Dover • NH, United States 153 D4
Dover • DE, United States 153 D10
Dover, Strait of • France/UK 104 E4
Dover-Foxcroft •
  ME, United States 44 K3
Dovercourt Beach •
  United Kingdom .... 101 [60]
Dovrefjell • Norway 16 E3
Dovrefjell Nat. Park Park N •
  Norway .... 89 [12]
Dovrefjell Nat. Park • Norway 124 C2
Dowagiac • MI, United States 44 B5
Downey • CA, United States 152 C6
Downings Beach • Ireland .... 96 [65]
Downpatrick • United Kingdom 7 G7
Downpatrick • NS, Australia 34 H11
Dowth • Ireland 108 B2
Dozois, Réservoir • QU, Canada 44 G2
Draa • Algeria/Morocco 131 D5
Draa, Cap • Morocco 131 D5
Draa al Baguel • Algeria 20 G2
Dráa, Vallée du • Morocco 131 D6
Drac • France 115 F3
Drac, Coves de' •
  Majorca, Spain 117 H2
Drachenfels • Germany 112 E1
Drachten • Netherlands 5 J1
Dragan • Sweden 16 H4
Dragasani • Romania 14 L5
Dragonáda • Greece 123 E4
Dragonera I. • Majorca, Spain 117 H1
Dragsholm Beach • Denmark .... 96 [43]
Draguignan • France 115 H4
Drake • ND, United States 43 F2
Drake Passage • Antarctica 54 (1) HH4
Drakensberg • South Africa 24 D6
Dráma • Greece 128 B1
Drammen • Norway 124 B3
Drangajökull • Iceland 16 (1) B1
Drangedal • Norway 124 B3
Drápano, Akra • Crete, Greece 123 E2
Drassburg • Austria 13 D11
Drau • Austria 13 D11
Drava • Europe 14 E4
Drayton • ND, United States 43 H2
Drayton Manor Park Park L •
  United Kingdom .... 98 [29]
Drayton Manor Park •
  United Kingdom 104 D2
Dreamworld • QL, Australia 144 B6
Dreihennspitze • Austria/Italy 109 D13
Drenthe • Netherlands 109 D4
Drépano, Akra • Greece 15 E4
Dresden • Germany 9 I5
Dreux • France 115 E3
Drievliet, Familiepark Park L •
  Netherlands .... 98 [43]

Drina • F.R. of Yugoslavia 14 G5
Drinit, Gjiri • Albania 14 G8
Driochead Atha • Ireland 108 B2
Drøbak • Norway 124 B2
Drochia • Moldova 14 O1
Drogheda • Ireland 108 B2
Drohobych • Ukraine 13 M8
Droichead Nua • Ireland 108 B3
Drôme • France 10 I8
Dronfield • United Kingdom 104 E3
Dronninglund Beach • Denmark .... 96 [48]
Drosia • Greece 34 I4
Drottningholm • Sweden 125 D4
Drottningholm Palace Heritage C •
  Sweden .... 86 [6]
Drovyannaya • Russian Fed. 54 H2
Druif Beach • Aruba .... 160 Y
Drumcliff • Ireland 108 C2
Drumheller • AL, Canada 155 C4
Drummond • MT, United States 42 I3
Drummond I. • MI, United States 44 D3
Drummondville • QU, Canada 155 B4
Drusillas Park • United Kingdom 104 E3
Druzba • Kazakstan 26 N8
Druzhba • Bulgaria 128 E4
Drvar • Bosnia-Herz. 14 D5
Drvenik • Croatia 128 C4
Dry Falls • WA, United States 152 B2
Dry Harbour Mtns • Jamaica 159 F1
Dry Tortugas Nat. Park Park N •
  FL, United States .... 151 [223]
Dry Tortugas Nat. Park •
  FL, United States 154 H7
Dryden • OT, Canada 43 J2
Drygalski Ice Tongue •
  Antarctica 54 (1) W2
Drysdale • WA, Australia 34 E2
Drysdale River Nat. Park •
  WA, Australia 34 E3
Dschang • Cameroon 22 G3
Du Quoin • IL, United States 44 B6
Du'ayn, Ad • Sudan 23 D1
Duarte, Pico • Dominican Rep. 159 G3
Dubai • United Arab Emirates 18 G4
Dubasari • Moldova 14 O2
Dubawnt • NT, Canada 38 K4
Dubawnt Lake • NT/NU, Canada 38 K4
Dubbo • Australia 34 I6
Dublin • Ireland 108 B2
Dublin • GA, United States 48 F4
Dublin [Adm] • Ireland 108 B2
Dublin Bay • Ireland 108 B2
Dubna • Russian Fed. 126 C4
Dubois • WY, United States 42 K5
Dubois • CO, United States 153 D5
Dubovka • Russian Fed. 126 E6
Dubreka • Guinea 22 A3
Dubrovnik Heritage C • Croatia .... 86 [187]
Dubrovnik • Croatia 128 D4
Dubuc, Château • Martinique .... 161 N
Dubuque • IA, United States 43 K5
Duc de Gloucester •
  French Polynesia 33 M8
Duchcov • TN, United States 45 G1
Duchess • QL, Australia 34 G4
Ducie • Pitcairn Is. 33 O8
Duddon • United Kingdom 104 C3
Duden • Turkey 123 F1
Düdenbasi • Turkey 123 F1
Düdensuyu • Turkey 123 F1
Duderstadt • Germany 8 F5
Dudhsagar Falls • Goa, India 137 B2
Dudhwa Nat. Park • India 137 C3
Dudinka • Russian Fed. 26 O4
Duero • Spain 11 E3
Dugi Otok • Croatia 128 D3
Duino • Italy 121 E4
Duinrell Park L • Netherlands 98 C2
Duinrell • Netherlands 109 F1
Duisburg • Germany 111 B1
Duitama • Colombia 51 C2
Duiveland • Netherlands 109 D10
Dujuma • Somalia 23 G3
Dukagjini • Albania 14 G8
Dukhan • Qatar 18 F4
Dukku • China 29 C5
Dulan • China 29 B3
Dulce • Argentina 52 D4
Dulce • NM, United States 45 I3
Duleek • Ireland 108 B2
Dulles [Apt] •
  VA, United States 153 D9
Dülmen • Germany 8 C5
Dumaguete • Philippines 31 G5
Dumai • Indonesia 143 G4
Dumas Beach • India 138 E3
Dumas • AR, United States 46 E5
Dumas • TX, United States 46 E5
Dumbarton • United Kingdom 104 C4
Dumfries • United Kingdom 7 I6
Dumford, Punta • Western Sahara 20 B4
Dümmersee • Germany 5 L2
Dumon, QU, Canada 44 G2
Dumoine, Lac • QU, Canada 44 G2
Dumont d'Urville [Base] •
  Antarctica 54 (1) T3
Dumont d'Urville Sea •
  Antarctica 54 (1) S3
Dumpu • Papua New Guinea 35 (1) D2
Dún Aengus • Ireland 108 C3
Dún Dealgan • Ireland 7 F7
Dún Laoghaire • Ireland 108 B2
Duna • Hungary 13 H11
Duna-Tisza Köz • Hungary 13 H11
Dunaj • Slovak Rep. 13 G9
Dunajec • Poland 128 C4
Dunajská Sreda • Slovak Rep. 13 G9
Dunántúl • Hungary 13 G11
Dunarea • Romania 14 K6
Dunas Beach • Goa, India 137 B1
Dunaújváros • Hungary 13 H11
Dunav • Europe 14 L6
Dunay • Russian Fed. 30 D2
Dunbartonshire • United Kingdom 104 B3
Dunblane • United Kingdom 104 B1
Dunboyne • Ireland 108 B2
Duncan • OK, United States 46 G5
Duncan • BC, Canada 155 C3
Duncan Passage • India 28 F6
Duncannon Beach • Ireland .... 96 [56]
Dundalk • Ireland 7 F8
Dundalk • MD, United States 44 G6
Dundalk Bay • Ireland 7 F8
Dundas • OT, Canada 44 G4
Dundas Peninsula • NT, Canada 38 I2
Dundee • United Kingdom 104 C1
Dundee • South Africa 134 B4
Dunedin • New Zealand 35 C7
Dunedin • FL, United States 151 C1
Dunfanaghy • Ireland 7 E6
Dunfermline • United Kingdom 104 B1
Dungarvan • Ireland 7 E9
Dungeness • United Kingdom 104 E4
Dunguaire Castle • Ireland 108 C6
Dunhua • China 29 K2
Dunhuang • China 27 K8
Dunk I. • QL, Australia 144 B1
Dunkeld • United Kingdom 104 B2
Dunkery Beacon • United Kingdom 7 I10
Dunkirk • France 109 D13
Dunkirk • NY, United States 153 D1
Dunlavin • Ireland 108 B3
Dunloe, Gap of • Ireland 108 C5
Dunmanus Bay • Ireland 108 C5
Dunmanway • Ireland 108 C5

Dunmarra • NT, Australia 34 F3
Dunmore • Ireland 108 C4
Dunmore East Beach • Ireland .... 96 [58]
Dunmore Town • Bahamas 158 B1
Dunn's River Falls • Jamaica 159 F2
Dunnville • OT, Canada 155 B9
Dunnet Head • United Kingdom 6 I3
Dunquin • Ireland 108 C5
Dunmore Dive • Red Sea 135 B1
Dunshaughlin • Ireland 108 B1
Dunstan Mtns • New Zealand 145 G3
Dunster • United Kingdom 104 F2
Duntroon • New Zealand 35 C7
Duolun • China 29 F2
Dupnitsa • Bulgaria 15 E1
Duqm • Oman 18 I6
Duque de Caxias • Brazil 163 C4
Durack Ranges • WA, Australia 34 E3
Durance • France 10 L9
Durango • Spain 11 I1
Durango • Mexico 40 F7
Durango • CO, United States 153 E2
Durango [Adm] • Mexico 40 F7
Durankulak • Bulgaria 128 E2
Durant • OK, United States 46 G5
Durant • MS, United States 153 F2
Durant • OK, United States 154 J1
Durazno • Uruguay 163 D2
Durazzo • Albania 90 A19
Durban • South Africa 134 B5
Düren • Germany 112 D1
Durgapur • India 28 E4
Durham • United Kingdom 7 K7
Durham Heritage C •
  United Kingdom .... 86 [18]
Durmitor • F.R. of Yugoslavia 14 F6
Durmitor Nat. Park Heritage N •
  F.R. of Yugoslavia .... 83 [61]
Dürres • Albania 14 G8
Durrest, Gjiri i • Albania 14 G8
Dursey I. • Ireland 108 C7
Dursunbey • Turkey 122 D6
Durusu Gölü • Turkey 15 J2
Duruz • Syria 21 G1
Dusa Mareb • Somalia 23 G2
Dushan • China 31 D1
Dushanbe • Tajikistan 18 I2
Dusky Sound • New Zealand 145 G3
Düsseldorf • Germany 111 B3
Dutch Country •
  PA, United States 153 D6
Dutch Harbor •
  AK, United States 49 H5
Dutch John • UT, United States 45 H1
Duvenstette, Fort •
  St Vincent & Gren. .... 161 Q
Duvkh Tsirkov, gora •
  Russian Fed. 27 S3
Duwayhin • United Arab Emirates 18 G5
Duwaym, Ad • Sudan 21 F5
Duyfken Point • QL, Australia 34 H2
Duyun • China 31 D1
Düzce • Turkey 15 M3
Dvinskaya Guba • Russian Fed. 27 F4
Dwarka Beach • India 138 E1
Dwingelderveld, Nat. Park Park N •
  Netherlands .... 89 [52]
Dwingelderveld, Nat. Park •
  Netherlands 109 D4
Dworshak Reservoir •
  ID, United States 42 H3
Dyck Castle • Germany .... 113 [27]
Dyersburg • TN, United States 48 C2
Dyersville • IA, United States 43 K5
Dyje • Czech Rep. 13 F9
Dylewska Góra • Poland 13 I4
Dymchurch Beach •
  United Kingdom .... 101 [77]
Dymchurch • United Kingdom 104 E4
Dyrehavsbakken Park L • Denmark .... 98 [17]
Dzamin Üüd • Mongolia 29 E2
Dzanga-Sangha, Réserve du Park •
  Central African Rep. .... 133 [45]
Dzaoudzi • Comoros 24 H2
Dzerzhinsk • Belarus 16 N10
Dzerzhinsk • Russian Fed. 17 G3
Dzhankoy • Ukraine 17 E5
Dzhardzhan • Russian Fed. 27 I3
Dzhebel • Bulgaria 15 F2
Dzhugdzhur, Khrebet •
  Russian Fed. 27 M5
Dzialdowo • Poland 13 J4
Dzialoszyce • Poland 128 C2
Dzibilchaltún • Mexico 157 H1
Dzibilnocac • Mexico 157 H3
Dzierzoniów • Poland 13 F7
Dzier-Stausee • Germany 5 M3
Dzodze • Ghana 15 D3
Dziekanów • Germany 5 H2
Dzukija Nat. Park Park N •
  Lithuania .... 89 [148]
Dzukija Nat. Park • Lithuania 126 B6
Dzungaria •
  Kazakstan 26 N8
E.T. Joshua [Apt] •
  St Vincent & Gren. .... 161 Q
Eads • CO, United States 46 D3
Eagar • AZ, United States 45 H4
Eagle • AK, United States 49 M3
Eagle Beach • Aruba .... 160 Y
Eagle Butte • SD, United States 43 F4
Eagle Farm [Apt] •
  QL, Australia 144 B6
Eagle Lake • CA, United States 42 E6
Eagle Lake • OT, Canada 43 J2
Eagle Lake • ME, United States 44 K2
Eagle Pass • TX, United States 46 F7
Eagle Peak • CA, United States 42 E6
Eagle Peak • TX, United States 47 B2
Eagle River • WI, United States 43 L4
Ear Falls • OT, Canada 43 J1
Earlton • OT, Canada 44 F2
Earn • United Kingdom 104 B1
Earn, Loch • United Kingdom 104 B1
Earnslaw, Mt • New Zealand 145 G2
Earth • TX, United States 46 D5
Easley • SC, United States 48 F3
East Alligator • NT, Australia 34 F2
East Aurora • NY, United States 153 D1
East Branch Delaware •
  NY, United States 153 D2
East Caicos •
  Turks & Caicos Is. 158 C2
East Cape • New Zealand 35 G3
East Coast Park • Singapore 141 M4
East Cowes • United Kingdom .... 106 C
East Falkland • Falkland Is. 53 E6
East Grinstead • United Kingdom 104 E4
East Hampton •
  NY, United States 153 D7
East Hartford •
  CT, United States 44 I5
East Lansing •
  MI, United States 44 C4
East Las Vegas •
  NV, United States 45 E3
East Liverpool •
  OH, United States 153 D1
East London • South Africa 24 D6
East Los Angeles •
  CA, United States 45 C5

East Millinocket •
  ME, United States 44 K3
East Moline • IL, United States 43 K5
East Neuk • United Kingdom 104 B2
East Peoria • IL, United States 46 K2
East Point • Cayman Is. 159 E1
East Point • US Virgin Is. .... 160 Z
East Point • QA, United States 48 F4
East Prussia • Poland 13 J3
East Range • NV, United States 42 G6
East Retford • United Kingdom 5 C1
East Siberian Sea •
  Arctic Ocean 54 I12
East St Louis •
  IL, United States 46 J3
East Stroudsburg •
  PA, United States 44 H5
East Tawas • MI, United States 44 D3
East Windsor •
  NJ, United States 153 D5
East York • OT, Canada 44 F4
Eastbourne Beach •
  United Kingdom .... 101 [83]
Eastbourne • United Kingdom 104 E3
Eastend • SA, Canada 42 K2
Easter I. • Pacific Ocean 33 O8
Eastern Cape • South Africa 24 E6
Eastern Desert • Egypt 131 F4
Eastern Mediterranean Coast •
  Turkey .... 123 G
Eastern Valleys • Norway 124 A6
Eastfield • TX, United States 47 E1
Eastleigh • United Kingdom 7 K11
Eastmain • QU, Canada 39 P6
Eastmain (Riv] • QU, Canada 39 Q6
Eastman • GA, United States 48 F4
Eastnor Castle • United Kingdom 104 F3
Eastport • ME, United States 44 L3
Eatonton • GA, United States 48 F4
Eau Claire • WI, United States 43 K4
Ebbw Vale • United Kingdom 7 I10
Ebebiyin • Equatorial Guinea 22 G4
Ebeltoft Beach • Denmark .... 96 [47]
Ebeltoft • Denmark 125 F10
Ebensburg • PA, United States 153 D6
Eber Gölü • Turkey 15 M5
Eberbach • Germany 112 E4
Eberbach, Kloster • Germany 112 E4
Eberswalde-Finow • Germany 8 I4
Ebey's Landing Nat. Hist. Reserve Park N •
  WA, United States .... 150 [25]
Eboli • Italy 121 G4
Ebolowa • Cameroon 22 G4
Ebre, Delta de l' • Spain 11 L4
Ebro • Spain 11 K3
Ebro, Embalse del • Spain 11 H2
Ebschloh • Germany 5 L3
Ecab • Mexico 157 H2
Echdeina • Western Sahara 20 C3
Echo Bay • NT, Canada 38 H3
Echterdingen [Apt] • Germany 112 D6
Echternach • Luxembourg 109 D20
Echuca • VI, Australia 144 C3
Ecija • Spain 116 B2
Eckartal • Germany 9 G7
Eckental • Germany 9 G7
Eckernförde Spa • Germany .... 113 [c14]
Eckernförde • Germany 8 E2
Eckerö • Finland 125 E3
Eclipse Sound • NU, Canada 39 P2
Ecouen, Château d' • France 115 E1
Ecrins, Parc nat. des Park N •
  France .... 89 [67]
Ecrins, Parc nat. des • France 115 F4
ECUADOR • S. America 51 B4
Ed • Sweden 125 F2
Edam • Netherlands 109 F2
Edam • Netherlands 6 J2
Echtera • Western Sahara 20 C3
Eddystone Rocks •
  United Kingdom 104 F5
Ede • Nigeria 22 E3
Ede • Netherlands 109 D7
Ede • Cameroon 22 G4
Edelstmimme • Germany 112 E3
Edelweiss Valley Ski •
  QU, Canada .... 149 [30]
Edemissen • Germany 8 F4
Eden • NS, Australia 104 C2
Eden • NC, United States 144 C4
Eden • TX, United States 47 E2
Eden • NC, United States 48 G2
Edendale • South Africa 134 B3
Edendale • New Zealand 108 B1
Edenderry • Ireland 108 B1
Edenlandia Park L • Italy .... 98 [86]
Edenton • NC, United States 48 H3
Edenvale • South Africa 9 D5
Eder-Stausee • Germany 5 M3
Edessa • Greece 15 D3
Edewecht • Germany 8 C3
Edfu • Egypt 131 F5
Edgar Allen Poe Nat. Hist. Site Park N •
  PA, United States .... 151 [299]
Edgar Ranges • WA, Australia 34 D3
Edgeleh • Algeria 20 G3
Edgeley • ND, United States 43 G3
Edgell I. • NU, Canada 39 S4
Edinburg • TX, United States 47 E4
Edinburgh Heritage C •
  United Kingdom .... 86 [15]
Edinburgh • United Kingdom 104 B4
Edincik • Turkey 15 J2
Edirne • Turkey 15 H2
Edirne • Turkey 14 H5
Edison Nat. Hist. Site Park N •
  NJ, United States .... 151 [322]
Edland • Norway 124 C6
Edmond • OK, United States 46 G5
Edmonds • WA, United States 47 F3
Edmonton • AL, Canada 155 C2
Edmundston • NB, Canada 156 D1
Edna • TX, United States 47 F3
Edremit • Turkey 122 D5
Edremit Körfezi • Turkey 15 H4
Edsbro • Sweden 125 C2
Eduardo Castex • Argentina 52 C5
Eduni, Mt • NT, Canada 49 P3
Edward, Lake •
  Uganda/Dem. Rep. of Congo 23 D4
Edwards Creek • SA, Australia 34 G5
Edwards Plateau •
  TX, United States 47 D2
Edwardsville •
  IL, United States 46 K3
Edzna • Mexico 157 H3
Edzo • NT, Canada 38 H4
Eeklo • Belgium 5 G3
Eelde [Apt] • Netherlands 109 D4
Eemshaven • Netherlands 109 D4
Efaté • Vanuatu 35 (2) B2
Eferding • Austria 9 I8
Effigy Mounds Nat. Mon. Park N •
  IA, United States .... 151 [164]
Eflani • Turkey 15 N2
Eforie Nord • Romania 128 E2
Eforie Sud • Romania 128 E2
Efxinoúpolis Beach • Greece .... 97 [188]
Ega • Spain 11 C1
Ega, Val • Italy 120 B1
Ega • Italy 120 D1
Eger • Hungary 13 J10
Eger • Hungary 9 H6
Egersund • Norway 124 C6
Egeskov • Denmark 125 F14

Eggenfelden • Germany 112 F4
Eghezée • Belgium 5 H4
Egiana • Greece 127 D7
Egio • Greece 15 C5
Eğirdir Beach • Turkey . . . . 97 [240]
Eglab Dersa • Algeria 20 E3
Eglab, El • Algeria 20 E3
Egmont, Cape • New Zealand 145 F3
Egmont, Mt • New Zealand 145 F3
Egmont Nat. Park • New Zealand . 145 F3
Egnazia • Italy 14 E9
Egremont • United Kingdom 104 C1
Eğridir • Turkey 123 F2
Eğridir Gölü • Turkey 15 L5
Eğrigöz Dagi • Turkey 15 K4
Egvekinot • Russian Fed. 27 V3
EGYPT • Africa . . . . 131 F
Ehime • Japan 140 A7
Ehingen • Germany 112 F1
Ehrenberg • AZ, United States 45 E5
Ehrenbreitstein • Germany 112 E2
Ehrenbreitstein Castle •
   Germany . . . . 113 [64]
Ehrwald Ski • Austria . . . . 100 [137]
Ehrwald • Austria 119 H2
Eibar • Spain 11 I1
Eichenzell [Fasanerie] Castle •
   Germany . . . . 113 [52]
Eichstätt • Germany 9 G8
Eichwalde • Germany 111 C4
Eidanger • Norway 124 B3
Eider • Germany 8 E2
Eidfjord • Norway 124 C4
Eidfjorden • Norway 124 C4
Eidsdal • Norway 124 C2
Eidsfoss • Norway 124 B1
Eidskog • Norway 124 B2
Eidsvoll • Norway 124 B2
Eifel • Germany 112 D1
Eifelpark Park L • Germany . . . . . . 98 [61]
Eifelpark • Germany 112 E3
Eigat • Egypt 21 G3
Eiger • Switzerland 119 G2
Eight Degree Channel •
   Indian Ocean 138 D13
Eight Mile Rock • Bahamas 49 D4
Eikeren • Norway 124 B1
Eikesdalsvatnet • Norway 124 C2
Eilat • Israel 18 B4
Eilethyia • Crete, Greece 123 E3
Einasleigh • QL, Australia 143 H3
Einbeck • Germany 8 E5
Eindhoven • Netherlands 109 D11
Einsiedeln • Switzerland 119 G3
Einslow • KS, United States 153 E1
Eirunepé • Brazil 51 D5
Eisenach • Germany 9 F6
Eisenberg • Germany 9 G6
Eisenerz • Austria 13 D10
Eisenhower Birthplace State Hist. Site •
   TX, United States 154 J1
Eisenhower Nat. Hist. Site Park N •
   PA, United States . . . . 151 [295]
Eisenhüttenstadt • Germany 8 J4
Eisenstadt • Austria 13 F10
Eisenwurzen • Austria 14 B2
Eisleben • Germany 8 G5
Eisleben Heritage C • Germany . . . 86 [41]
Eitorf • Germany 5 K4
Eivissa • Ibiza, Spain 117 G2
Eivissa [I.] • . . . . 117 G
Eje, Sierra del • Spain 11 E2
Ejea de los Caballeros • Spain 11 J2
Ek Balam • Mexico 157 H2
Ekalaka • MT, United States 153 B7
Ekenäs • Finland 125 E4
Eketorpsborg • Sweden 125 F12
Ekibastuz • Kazakhstan 26 M7
Eklingji • India 137 C5
Ekoli • Dem. Rep. of Congo 23 C4
Ekoln • Sweden 125 D2
Ekonda • Russian Fed. 26 S3
Eksjö • Sweden 125 F8
Ekwan • OT, Canada 39 O6
El Abrigo •
   Tenerife, Canary Is. 116 E1
El Arahal • Spain 11 F7
El Arco • Mexico 157 F1
El Banco • Colombia 51 C2
El Baúl • Venezuela 51 D2
El Cabo de Gata • Spain 116 B8
El Cajon • CA, United States 45 D5
El Callao • Venezuela 51 E2
El Campo • TX, United States 154 J5
El Cañuelo • Puerto Rico 159 H2
El Carmen de Bolivar • Colombia . . 51 B2
El Centro • CA, United States 45 E5
El Cerro • Bolivia 52 D2
El Cuy • Argentina 53 C3
El Cuyo • Mexico 157 H2
El Descanso • Mexico 45 D5
El Dorado • Venezuela 37 I6
El Dorado • KS, United States 46 G4
El Dorado • AR, United States 46 I6
El Ejido Beach • Spain . . . . 96 [116]
El Ejido • Spain 116 B8
El Encanto • Colombia 51 C4
El Escorial • Spain 11 G4
El Escorial Heritage C • Spain . . . 86 [102]
El Ferrol • Spain 11 C1
El Fuerte de Samaipata Heritage C •
   Bolivia . . . . 84 [63]
El Gîza • Egypt 131 F1
El Jem Heritage C • Tunisia . . . . 86 [268]
El Macao • Dominican Rep. 159 G8
El Maestrazgo • Spain 11 K4
El Maitén • Argentina 53 B4
El Malpais Nat. Mon. Park N •
   NM, United States . . . . 150 [125]
El Malpais Nat. Mon. •
   NM, United States 153 E2
El Masnou Beach • Spain . . . . . . 96 [122]
El Masnou • Spain 117 D4
El Meco • Mexico 157 H2
El Medano •
   Tenerife, Canary Is. 116 E1
El Mirador • Guatemala 157 H3
El Molinar • Majorca, Spain 117 H1
El Monte • CA, United States 45 C4
El Morro • Cuba 158 D8
El Morro, Castillo •
   Puerto Rico 159 H2
El Morro Nat. Mon. Park N •
   NM, United States . . . . 150 [124]
El Morro Nat. Mon. •
   NM, United States 153 E2
El Nevado, Cerro • Argentina 52 C6
El Palo • Spain 116 B7
El Paso • TX, United States 153 E4
El Pico • Bolivia 52 D2
El Pilar • Formentera, Spain 117 G4
El Pital • Mexico 157 G2
El Port de la Selva Beach •
   Spain . . . . 96 [123]
El Portal • CA, United States 45 C3
El Porvenir • Mexico 47 B2
El Potosi • Mexico 37 A3
El Prat de Llobregat • Spain 11 N3
El Prat de Llobregat [Apt] •
   Spain 117 D3
El Puerto de Santa Maria •
   Spain 116 B5
El Qâhira Heritage C • Egypt . . . . 86 [275]
El Reno • OK, United States 46 G5
El Rey • Mexico 157 H2
El Rompido • Spain 116 B1
El Rosario • Mexico 157 F1
El Sahuaro, Estacion • Mexico . . . 45 F6

El Salto • Mexico 37 (1) A1
EL SALVADOR • C. America 37 D5
El Sauz • Mexico 47 A3
El Seibo • Dominican Rep. 159 G8
El Socorro • Mexico 157 F1
El Sueco • Mexico 47 A3
El Tajín Heritage C • Mexico . . . . 84 [20]
El Tajín • Mexico 157 G2
El Tigre • Venezuela 51 E2
El Torro • Minorca, Spain 117 F2
El Turbio • Argentina 53 B6
El Vendrell Beach • Spain . . . . . 96 [121]
El Vendrell • Spain 117 D3
El Vizcaino whale sanctuary Heritage N •
   Mexico . . . . 82 [19]
El Yunque • Puerto Rico 159 H2
Elaea Beach • Greece . . . . 97 [182]
Elafonisi • Crete, Greece 123 E5
Eland Sanctuary • Zimbabwe 130 C4
Elassóna • Greece 15 D4
Elat • Israel 18 B4
Eláti • Levkas, Greece 15 B5
Eláziğ • Turkey 18 C2
Elba, I. d' • Italy 121 E10
Elbasan • Albania 14 H8
Elbe • Germany 8 F3
Elbers • Georgia/Russian Fed. 17 G6
Elbeuf • France 10 F4
Elblag • Poland 13 I3
Elche Beach • Spain . . . . 96 [118]
Elche • Spain 117 C1
Elcho I. • NT, Australia 34 G2
Elcho I. • NT, Australia 117 C1
Elda • Spain 23 H2
Eldab • Somalia 23 H2
Eldikaturt • Russian Fed. 8 G3
Eldikaürı • Russian Fed. 27 M4
Eldora Mtn Ski •
   CO, United States . . . . 149 [98]
Eldorado • TX, United States 47 D2
Eldorado • IL, United States 48 C2
Eldorado • Kenya 50 B7
Eleanor Roosevelt Nat. Hist. Site Park N •
   NY, United States . . . . 151 [309]
Elephant Butte Reservoir •
   NM, United States 153 E4
Elephant Village •
   Pattaya, Thailand 142 C4
Elephanta Caves Heritage C •
   India . . . . 85 [143]
Elephantine I. • Egypt 131 F5
Eleuthera I. • Bahamas 158 B1
Elgin • United Kingdom 6 I4
Elgin • OR, United States 45 C1
Elgin • ND, United States 43 F3
Elgin • IL, United States 44 A4
Elginsky • Russian Fed. 27 N4
Elgon, Mt • Kenya/Uganda 131 G1
Elgoïbar • Ethiopia 23 G2
Elguar • Russian Fed. 27 I4
Elia Beach • Crete, Greece . . . . . 97 [214]
Elias Pita • Dominican Rep. 159 G2
Elie Beach • United Kingdom . . 101 [10-11]
Elie • MN, Canada 43 H2
Elila • Dem. Rep. of Congo 23 D4
Elkhay • France 14 K1
Eliot • NT, Australia 34 F3
Elista • Russian Fed. 17 G5
Elizabeth • SA, Australia 34 A3
Elizabeth • NJ, United States 153 D7
Elizabeth City •
   NC, United States 48 H3
Elizabeth Reef • Australia 33 H9
Elizabethtown •
   TN, United States 48 F2
Elizabethtown •
   PA, United States 44 G5
Elizabethtown •
   KY, United States 48 E2
Elk • Poland 13 L4
Elk City • ID, United States 46 G4
Elk City • OK, United States 46 F5
Elk I. Nat. Park • AL, Canada 155 C2
Elk I. Nat. Park Park N •
   AL, Canada . . . . 156 [15]
Elk Ridge • UT, United States 45 H3
Elkhart • IN, United States 44 C5
Elkhovo • Bulgaria 128 E3
Elkins • WV, United States 44 F6
Elko • NV, United States 152 C2
Elkwater • AL, Canada 42 J2
Ellendale • ND, United States 43 G3
Ellensburg • WA, United States . . . 152 B2
Elortin, Plains of • Ireland 108 C4
Ellesmere I. • NU, Canada 36 I2
Ellesmere I. Nat. Park Park N •
   NU, Canada . . . . 156 [6]
Ellice Is. • Tuvalu 33 I6
Ellingen Castle • Germany . . . . . 113 [145]
Elliot Lake • OT, Canada 39 O7
Elliot • ND • QL, Australia 143 H4
Elliston • SA, Australia 34 F6
Ellmau Ski • Austria . . . . 100 [154]
Ellmau • Austria 119 H3
Ellora Caves Heritage C • India . . 85 [142]
Ellsworth • WI, United States 43 J4
Ellsworth • ME, United States 44 K3
Ellsworth • KS, United States 46 F3
Ellsworth Land • Antarctica 54 (1) FF2
Ellwangen • Germany 9 F8
Elma • WA, United States 42 D3
Elma • MN, Canada 43 H2
Elmali • Turkey 123 F3
Elmas [Apt] • Sardinia, Italy 120 C4
Elmdon [Apt] • United Kingdom . . 104 D2
Elmira • NY, United States 153 D2
Elmshorn • Germany 8 E3
Elne • France 11 I2
Elorza • Venezuela 51 D2
Eloy • AZ, United States 45 E5
Elrose • SA, Canada 42 K1
Elsdorf • Germany 111 B3
Else • Germany 5 L2
Elsehul • South Georgia 81 A10
Elsen Nur • China 28 F1
Elstal • Germany 111 C1
Elsterwerda • Germany 8 I5
Eltanin Bay • Antarctica 54 (1) GG2
Eltham • New Zealand 145 F3
Eltville • Germany 112 E4
Elura • India 9 C8
Elura • India 138 D3
Elvas • Portugal 11 E6
Elverum • Norway 16 F6
Elwell, Lake •
   MT, United States 42 J2
Elwood • IN, United States 44 C5
Elx Beach • Spain . . . . 96 [118]
Elx • Spain 117 C1
Ely • United Kingdom 7 M9
Ely • NV, United States 152 C4
Ely • MN, United States 43 J2
Ely Harbour • Bermuda 159 J3
Elyria • OH, United States 44 D5
Elzas • France 9 C8
Emal • Vanuatu 35 (2) B2
Emamshahr • Iran 18 G2
Emån • Sweden 125 F8
Emangusi • South Africa 134 B2
Emao • Vanuatu 35 (2) B2
Embarcación • Argentina 52 D3
Embarras Portage • AL, Canada . . . 38 I5
Embi • Kazakhstan 26 I8
Embona • Rhodes, Greece 122 D12

Embrun • France 115 F4
Embudhu • Maldives 138 F4
Embudhu Finolhu • Maldives 138 F4
Emden • Germany 8 C3
Emei Shan Heritage N • China . . 83 [125]
Emei Shan • China . . . . 85 [179]
Emei Shan • China 139 A7
Emerald • QL, Australia 144 B3
Emerald Coast •
   FL, United States 154 H2
Emerald Pool • Dominica . . . . . . 161 M
Emeraude, Côte d' • France 114 C2
Emet • Turkey 15 K4
Emi Koussi • Chad 21 C4
Emilia-Romagna • Italy 121 E7
Emily Rock • Pacific Ocean 50 B7
Emine, Nos • Bulgaria 14 O7
Emirdaag • Turkey 15 M4
Emkendorf Castle • Germany . . . 113 [3]
Emlichheim • Germany 8 B4
Emmaboda • Sweden 126 B1
Emmaste • Estonia 126 B1
Emmaus • PA, United States 44 H5
Emmelord • Netherlands 109 D7
Emmen • Netherlands 9 C8
Emmendingen • Germany 9 C8
Emmerich • Germany 5 J3
Emmet • QL, Australia 34 H4
Emmet • ID, United States 42 G5
Emory Peak • TX, United States . . . 40 F6
Empalme • Mexico 157 F1
Empangeni • Italy 12 E5
Emporda • Spain 117 D2
Emporia • KS, United States 46 G3
Emporia • VA, United States 153 D11
Empúries • Spain 117 D2
Ems • Germany 8 C4
Ems-Jade-Kanal • Germany 8 C4
Emsdetten • Germany 5 K2
Emsland • Germany 8 C4
En Colom, I. d' •
   Minorca, Spain 117 F4
En Gedi • Israel 135 A8
Enarotali • Indonesia 32 (1) D3
Enare Träsk • Finland 16 N2
Encantada • Mexico 40 C5
Encarnación • Paraguay 52 E4
Enchi • Ghana 22 D3
Encinal • TX, United States 47 E3
Enclave • Indonesia 32 (1) B4
Endelave • Denmark 125 F10
Enderby Land • Antarctica 54 (1) K3
Enderlin • ND, United States 43 H3
Endicott • NY, United States 44 G4
Endwell • NY, United States 44 G4
Ené • Peru 52 B1
Enez • Turkey 15 H3
Enez Körfezi • Turkey 15 G3
Enfidaville • Tunisia 12 E12
Engaño, Cabo • Dominican Rep. . . 159 G8
Engelberg Ski • Switzerland . . . . 100 [104]
Engelberg • Switzerland 119 G2
Engels • Russian Fed. 17 H4
Engelsberg Heritage C • Sweden . 86 [4]
Engelskirchen • Germany 111 B4
Enggano • Indonesia 32 C4
England • United Kingdom 7
England, Southeast •
   United Kingdom . . . . 104 E
Englee • NF, Canada 156 D5
Englewood • OH, United States . . . 44 C6
English Channel • France/UK 10 D3
English Harbour •
   Antigua & Barbuda . . . . 161 K
English Harbour Town •
   Antigua & Barbuda . . . . 161 K
English River • OT, Canada 43 K2
Enh-Gaivan • Mongolia 26 Q8
Enið • OK, United States 46 G4
Enid Lake • MS, United States 48 C3
Eniwetok • Marshall Is. 33 H4
Enkhuizen • Netherlands 109 D7
Enkirch • Germany 112 E3
Enköping • Sweden 125 D2
Enna • Sicily, Italy 120 D4
Ennadai Lake • NU, Canada 38 K4
Ennedi • Chad 21 D4
Ennepetal • Germany 111 B4
Ennerdale Water •
   United Kingdom 104 C1
Ennis • Ireland 108 C6
Enniscorthy • Ireland 108 B4
Enniskean • Turkey 123 G3
Enniskillen • United Kingdom 7 E7
Ennistymon • Ireland 108 A4
Eno • Austria 13 D10
Enonekiö • Finland 16 L2
Enonkoski Beach • Finland . . . . 96 [127]
Es Mercadal Beach •
   Minorca, Spain 117 F3
Es Mercadal • Minorca, Spain . . . 117 F3
Es Migjorn Redones Gran Sant Cristóbal •
   Minorca, Spain 117 F3
Es Pla • Majorca, Spain 117 H2
Es Pujols • Formentera, Spain . . . 117 G4
Es Savina • Formentera, Spain . . . 117 G4
Es Tudóns, Naveta d' •
   Minorca, Spain 117 F1
Esashi • Japan 30 L2
Esbjerg • Denmark 125 E9
Esbo • Finland 125 D3
Escala, I. Beach • Spain . . . . . . 96 [123]
Escala • Spain 117 D2
Escalante • UT, United States 45 G3
Escalante Desert •
   NV/UT, United States 45 E3
Escalier, l' • Mauritius 132 J4
Escambia • AL/FL, United States . . 154 H1
Escanaba, Sierra del • Cuba 158 D2
Escanaba • MI, United States 43 K3
Escárcega • Mexico 157 G3
Escaut • France 109 D14
Esch-sur-Alzette • Luxembourg . . 109 D20
Esch-sur-Sûre • Luxembourg . . . 109 D20
Eschwege • Germany 9 F5
Eschweiler • Germany 9 B6
Escondido • Colombia 51 B2
Escondida, Bahia •
   Dominican Rep. 159 G3
Escondido • CA, United States . . . 152 C6
Escuintla • Guatemala 37 C5
Esfahan • Iran 18 F3
Esfahan Heritage C • Iran . . . . . 85 [126]
Eshowe • South Africa 134 B4
Eshtemoa • Palestine 135 A8
Esil • Kazakhstan 26 K7
Esil • Kazakhstan 26 K7
Esk • United Kingdom 104 C3
Eskilstuna • Sweden 125 D3
Eskimo Lake • NT, Canada 38 E3
Eskisehir • Turkey 125 F11
Eslöv • Sweden 15 J5
Esme • Turkey 123 F1
Esmeraldas • Ecuador 51 B3
Esna • Egypt 131 F4
Esnagi Lake • OT, Canada 43 K1
Española, I. • Ibiza, Spain 117 G4
Española • Galapagos Is. 51 (1) B2
Española • OT, Canada 39 O7
Española • NM, United States 46 B4
Espardell, I. • Ibiza, Spain 117 G4
Espelkamp • Germany 5 L2
Esperance • WA, Australia 34 D6
Espérance [Apt] • St Martin . . . . 160 D
Esperance Bay • WA, Australia . . . 34 D6

Equateur • Dem. Rep. of Congo . . . 23 C3
Equatorial Channel • Maldives . . . 138 F3
EQUATORIAL GUINEA • Africa 22 F4
Er Rachidia • Morocco 131 D4
Eraclea Minoa • Sicily, Italy 120 D3
Erbach • Germany 9 M5
Erbach • Germany 112 F1
Erbalunga • Corsica, France 115 L2
Erbeskopf • Germany 9 C7
Ercan [Apt] • Cyprus 123 J2
Erciyes Dag • Turkey 123 H2
Erculano • Italy 121 G3
Erd • Hungary 13 H10
Erdao • China 30 D3
Erdek • Turkey 122 D3
Erdek Körfezi • Turkey 15 I3
Erdeven Beach • France . . . . . . 96 [81]
Erdeven • France 114 C4
Erdi • Chad 21 D4
Erdi Ma • Chad. 21 D4
Erding • Germany 112 F3
Erdre • France 10 D6
Erebus, Mt • Antarctica 54 (1) W2
Erechim • Brazil 52 E4
Ereglı • Turkey 15 M2
Ereglı • Turkey 123 G1
Ereke • Indonesia 32 (1) B3
Eremitage, Bayreuth Castle •
   Germany . . . . 113 [155]
Erenhot • China 29 E2
Erenköy • Cyprus 123 J2
Eressós Beach • Greece . . . . . . 97 [199]
Eressós • Greece 122 D5
Erétria • Greece 15 E5
Erétria Beach • Greece . . . . . . 97 [186]
Erfoud • Morocco 131 D6
Erft • Germany 5 J4
Erft • Germany 111 B3
Erftstadt • Germany 112 D1
Erfurt • Germany 9 G6
Erg Abu Ramada Dive • Red Sea . 135 K3
Ergene • Turkey 15 H2
Ergıi, Bahr • Chad 22 C2
Ergun He • China 27 J6
Ergun Zuoqi • China 27 J6
Erice • Sicily, Italy 120 D1
Ericeira • Portugal 118 D1
Erie • PA, United States 44 E4
Erie Canal • NY, United States . . . 153 D1
Erie, Lake •
   Canada/United States 44 E4
Erigabo • Somalia 23 H1
Erimanthos • Greece 15 C6
Erimo-misaki • Japan 30 L4
Eringsbode • Sweden 125 F12
Eritrea • Africa 21 G4
Eriyadu • Maldives 138 F2
Erken • Sweden 125 D2
Erkner • Germany 111 C4
Erkrath • Germany 111 B3
Erl • Austria 119 H3
Erlangen • Germany 9 F7
Erlanger • KY, United States 44 C6
Erldunda • NT, Australia 145 E4
Erlebnispark Tripsdrill Park L •
   Germany . . . . 98 [63]
Erlebnispark Tripsdrill •
   Germany 112 D6
Erlong Shan • China 27 K8
Ermak • Russian Fed. 26 M7
Ermelo • South Africa 24 E5
Ermenek • Turkey 123 G3
Ermesinde • Portugal 11 C3
Ermones • Corfu, Greece 122 B1
Ernabella • SA, Australia 145 D3
Ernakulam • India 138 D10
Erne, Lough, Lower •
   United Kingdom 7 E7
Erne, Lough, Upper •
   United Kingdom 7 E7
Ernest Legouvé • Pacific Ocean . . 33 L9
Erode • India 138 D10
Erpeler Ley • Germany 112 E1
Erquy • France 114 C2
Erqy • Mozambique 24 F5
Erritso • Denmark 125 F9
Erromango • Vanuatu 35 (2) B2
Erstein • France 109 D8
Ertis • Kazakhstan 26 M7
Erzen • Albania 15 A2
Erzgebirge • Germany 9 I6
Erzin • Russian Fed. 26 Q7
Erzincan • Turkey 122 A4
Erzurum • Turkey 18 D2
Euboea • Greece 122 D4
Eucla • WA, Australia 34 E6
Euclid • OH, United States 44 D5
Eucumbene, Lake • NS, Australia . 144 D5
Eufaula • AL, United States 48 E5
Eufaula Lake •
   OK, United States 46 H5
Eugene • OR, United States 152 B2
Eugene O'Neill Nat. Hist. Site Park N •
   CA, United States . . . . 150 [47]
Eugenia, Punta • Mexico 157 F1
Eugmo • Finland 16 L5
Eunice • LA, United States 47 I1
Eunice • NM, United States 153 F3
Eupen • Belgium 5 K4
Euphrates • Asia 18 D3
Eupora • MS, United States 48 C4
Eura • Finland 125 E1
Eurajoki • Finland 125 E1
Eure • France 10 G5
Eureka • MT, United States 42 H2
Eureka • SD, United States 43 G3
Eureka • KS, United States 46 G4
Eureka • CA, United States 152 C1
Eureka • NV, United States 152 C2
Eureka Springs •
   AR, United States 46 I4
Euromart (Rotterdam) •
   Netherlands 109 F3
Euromos • Turkey 122 D9
Europa Park • Germany 112 D7
Europa, Picos de • Spain 11 G1
Europa, Punta de • Gibraltar 11 G8
Europa-Park Park L • Germany . . 98 [66]
Europoort • Netherlands 109 F3
Euskadi • Spain 116 A2
Euskirchen • Germany 112 E1
Eustis • FL, United States 49 C3
Eutaw • AL, United States 48 D4
Evale • Angola 24 B3
Evander • South Africa 124 C3
Evans • CO, United States 46 D2
Evans, Lac • QC, Canada 39 P6
Evans Strait • NU, Canada 39 O4
Evanston • WY, United States 45 H3
Evanston • IL, United States 44 B4
Evansville • IN, United States 48 D2
Evant • TX, United States 47 E2
Eveciler • Turkey 15 H4
Evdir Hani • Turkey 123 F1
Evelyn, Mt • NT, Australia 34 F2
Evensk • Russian Fed. 27 U4
Everest, Mt • China/Nepal 28 E3
Everett • WA, United States 154 H8
Everglades Nat. Park Heritage N •
   FL, United States . . . . 82 [18]
Everglades Nat. Park Park N •
   FL, United States . . . . 151 [221]
Everglades Nat. Park •
   FL, United States 154 H8

Evergreen • CO, United States 46 C3
Evergreen • AL, United States 48 D5
Evesham • United Kingdom 104 D4
Evesham, Vale of •
   United Kingdom 104 D4
Evia • Greece 122 D4
Evian-les-Bains • France 115 F2
Evinayong • Equatorial Guinea . . . 22 G4
Evje • Norway 125 F1
Evora • Portugal 11 D6
Évora Heritage C • Portugal . . . . 86 [119]
Évora [Adm] • Portugal 118 A3
Évora • Portugal 10 G5
Evros • Greece 15 G4
Evry • France 115 E4
Ewa Beach • HI, United States . . 154 G5
Ewaso Ngiro • Kenya 131 G2
Ewo • Congo 23 C3
Excelsior Springs •
   MO, United States 46 H3
Exe • United Kingdom 104 F2
Exeter • United Kingdom 104 F2
Exeter • NH, United States 153 D4
Exmoor • United Kingdom 104 F2
Exmoor Nat. Park Park N •
   United Kingdom . . . . 89 [50]
Exmoor Nat. Park •
   United Kingdom 104 F2
Exmouth • WA, Australia 34 B4
Exmouth • United Kingdom 104 F5
Exmouth Gulf • WA, Australia 33 C8
Expoland • Japan 140 B2
Exposition, Parc des (Paris) •
   France 115 E2
Externsteine • Germany 5 L3
Extremadura • Spain 11 F5
Exuma Cays • Bahamas 158 B3
Exuma Cays Land & Sea Park •
   Bahamas 158 B1
Eyasi, Lake • Tanzania 130 B2
Eyl • Somalia 23 H2
Eymouthers • France 115 G2
Eyre • WA, Australia 34 E6
Eyre, Lake, North •
   SA, Australia 34 G5
Eyre, Lake, South •
   SA, Australia 34 G5
Eyre Mtns • New Zealand 145 G2
Eyre Peninsula • SA, Australia . . . 34 G6
Ezakheni • South Africa 134 B3
Ezcaray • Spain 11 I2
Ezeiza [Apt] • Argentina 163 D1
Ezequiel Ramos Mexia, Embalse •
   Argentina 53 C3
Ezine • Turkey 122 D2

Faan, Ko • Thailand 142 D1
Fabens • TX, United States 47 A2
Faber Lake • NT, Canada 38 H4
Fåborg Beach • Denmark . . . . . . 96 [44]
Fåborg • Denmark 125 F14
Fabriano • Italy 12 G5
Fachi • Niger 20 H5
Fada • Chad 21 D4
Fada-Ngourma • Burkina Faso . . . 22 E2
Faddeya, Zaliv • Russian Fed. . . . 26 S2
Faddeyevskiy, Ostrov •
   Russian Fed. 27 N1
Fadiffolu Atoll • Maldives 138 F1
Faenza • Italy 121 E7
Fafan • Ethiopia 23 G2
Fagaras • Romania 14 L4
Fagerhult • Sweden 125 E8
Fagerberg • Norway 16 E6
Fagersta • Sweden 125 D1
Fagita • Indonesia 32 (1) D3
Faguibine, Lac • Mali. 20 E5
Faguibine, Lac Park • Mali. . . . . 133 [2]
Fahan Beach • Ireland . . . . 96 [65]
Fahrland • Germany 111 C3
Fahrländer See • Germany 111 C3
Fahs, El • Tunisia 12 D12
Fai di Paganella • Italy 120 B3
Faial Beach • Azores . . . . 96 [101]
Faial • Azores 118 B1
Faial • Madeira 118 C2
Fair Isle • United Kingdom 6 K2
Fair Park Park L •
   TX, United States . . . . 151 [M]
Fairbanks • AK, United States 49 L3
Fairborn • OH, United States 44 C6
Fairburn • NE, United States 46 F2
Fairburn • OH, United States 44 C6
Fairfield • AL, United States 44 I5
Fairfield • CA, United States 45 B3
Fairfield • IA, United States 46 J2
Fairfield • IL, United States 48 C1
Fairford Reserve • MN, Canada . . . 43 H3
Fairmont • WV, United States 44 E6
Fairmont • MN, United States 43 I5
Fairmont • WV, United States 44 E6
Fairmont • NE, United States 46 G2
Fairmount Hot Springs •
   BC, Canada 155 C4
Fairview Heights •
   IL, United States 46 K3
Fairview Park •
   Hong Kong, China 139 B3
Fairweather, Mt •
   Canada/United States 38 D5
Fairymbridge • Ireland 108 B2
Faisalabad • Pakistan 28 E2
Faith • SD, United States 43 E4
Faiyûm, El • Egypt 131 F1
Faizabad • India 137 C8
Fakfak • Indonesia 32 (1) D3
Fakse • Denmark 125 F14
Fakse Bugt • Denmark 125 F14
Ladse Ladeplads • Denmark . . . 125 F14
Falaise • France 10 E5
Falaise de Tiguidit • Niger 20 G5
Falaise, Gorges de la •
   Martinique . . . . 161 N
Falam • Myanmar 31 A2
Falásarna • Crete, Greece 123 E1
Falcade Ski • Italy . . . . 100 [126]
Falcade • Italy 120 B3
Falcon • Algeria 11 K9
Falcon, Cap • Algeria 11 K9
Falcon Reservoir •
   TX, United States 47 E4
Falconara • Italy 121 E12
Falconara Marittima • Italy 12 H5
Falémé • Mali/Senegal 22 B2
Falfurrias • TX, United States 154 J5
Faliráki • Rhodes, Greece 122 D12
Falkenberg Beach • Sweden . . . . 96 [4]
Falkenberg • Sweden 125 E8
Falkenstein • Germany 111 C1
Falkenstein Castle • Germany . . 113 [209]
Falkirk • United Kingdom 104 B3
FALKLAND IS. • Atlantic Ocean . . . 53 E6
Falköping • Sweden 125 D1
Fall River • MA, United States . . . 153 D8
Fall River Mills • CA, United States . 8 E4
Fallingbostel • Germany . . . . . . 113 [k2]
Fallon • NV, United States 152 C4
Falls City • NE, United States 46 H2
Falmouth • United Kingdom 104 F2
Falmouth • Jamaica 159 F1
Falmouth • Antigua & Barbuda . . 161 K

Falmouth • MA, United States ... 44 J5
False Bay • South Africa ... 134 C5
Falso, Cabo • Dominican Rep. ... 159 G6
Falster • Denmark ... 125 F14
Falsterbo • Sweden ... 125 F15
Falticeni • Romania ... 14 N2
Falun • Sweden ... 16 H6
Famagusta • Cyprus ... 123 J4
Famagusta Bay • Cyprus ... 123 J2
Familien-Freizeitpark Tolk-Schau Park L • Germany ... 98 [50]
Fan Si Pan • Vietnam ... 31 C2
Fana • Mali ... 20 D6
Fana • Norway ... 124 C3
Fanári Beach • Greece ... 97 [196]
Fanari • Greece ... 122 D2
Fanchang • China ... 139 C3
Fancy • St Vincent & Gren. ... 161 Q
Fang • Thailand ... 142 B1
Fanling • Hong Kong, China ... 139 B3
Fanø Beach • Denmark ... 96 [51]
Fano • Italy ... 121 E12
Fanø • Denmark ... 125 F13
Fanø Bugt • Denmark ... 125 F13
Fantasy Fair Park L • OT, Canada ... 156 [E]
Fantasylandia • Ibiza, Spain ... 117 G2
Far East cruise area • Asia ... 81 A8
Faraday [Base] • Antarctica ... 54 (1) I13
Farafangana • Madagascar ... 24 H4
Farafra Oasis • Egypt ... 131 F3
Faráh • Afghanistan ... 18 H3
Faráh [Riv] • Afghanistan ... 18 H3
Farallón • Margarita ... 160 V
Faranah • Guinea ... 22 B2
Farasan, Jaza'ir • Saudi Arabia ... 18 D6
Farbairn Reservoir • QL, Australia ... 144 B3
Fareham • United Kingdom ... 7 K11
Farewell • ME, United States ... 44 J3
Farewell, Cape • New Zealand ... 35 D5
Farewell, Cape • Greenland ... 39 W5
Farewell Spit • New Zealand ... 35 C5
Farghona • Uzbekistan ... 18 J1
Fargo • ND, United States ... 43 H3
Faribault • MN, United States ... 43 J4
Faridabad • India ... 137 C2
Farilhões, Is. • Portugal ... 11 B5
Farim • Guinea-Bissau ... 22 A2
Färjestaden • Sweden ... 125 F8
Farley Hill Nat. Park • Barbados ... 161 O
Farmakonissi • Greece ... 122 D8
Farmers Branch • TX, United States ... 47 F1
Farmington • ME, United States ... 44 J3
Farmington • MO, United States ... 46 J4
Farmington • NM, United States ... 153 E2
Farmington Hills • MI, United States ... 44 D4
Farmville • VA, United States ... 153 D11
Färnebofjärden • Sweden ... 125 D1
Farnham • United Kingdom ... 104 E3
Färö • Sweden ... 16 J8
Faro • Portugal ... 118 E7
Faro • YT, Canada ... 49 O3
Faro, Punta del • Sicily, Italy ... 12 J10
Faro [Adm] • Portugal ... 118 E7
FAROE IS. • Atlantic Ocean ... 4 I4
Färösund • Sweden ... 16 J8
Farquhar, Atoll de • Seychelles. ... 133 K3
Farrukhabad • India ... 137 C3
Fársala • Greece ... 15 D4
Faro Beach • Denmark ... 96 [48]
Farsø • Denmark ... 125 F5
Farson • WY, United States ... 42 K5
Farsund • Norway ... 16 D7
Farukolhufushi • Maldives ... 138 F4
Fárup • Denmark ... 125 F9
Fárup Aquapark & Sommerland Park L • Denmark ... 98 [14]
Fárup Sommerland • Denmark ... 125 F5
Fasano • Italy ... 12 L8
Fashir, Al • Sudan ... 21 E5
Fasil Ghebbi Heritage C • Ethiopia ... 85 [99]
Fasillar • Turkey ... 123 F2
Fatehpur • Rajasthan, India ... 137 C2
Fatehpur • Uttar Pradesh, India ... 137 C3
Fatehpur Sikri Heritage C • India ... 85 [138]
Fatehpur Sikri • India ... 137 C3
Fathom Five Nat. Marine Conservation Area Park N • OT, Canada ... 156 [23]
Fátima • Portugal ... 11 C5
Fatrade Beach • Goa, India ... 137 B2
Fatu Hiva • French Polynesia ... 33 N7
Faucigny • France ... 115 F2
Faugères • France ... 114 B4
Faulkton • SD, United States ... 43 G4
Faurei • Romania ... 128 E1
Fauske • Norway ... 16 H3
Faute-sur-Mer, la Beach • France ... 96 [83]
Favara • Sicily, Italy ... 12 H11
Favàritx, Cap de • Minorca, Spain ... 117 F2
Favignana, I. • Italy ... 120 D1
Favorite Castle • Germany ... 113 [101]
Fawn • OT, Canada ... 39 N6
Faxaälven • Sweden ... 16 H5
Faya-Largeau • Chad ... 21 C4
Faye, Pas de la • France ... 115 H2
Fayette • AL, United States ... 48 B4
Fayetteville • AR, United States ... 46 H4
Fayetteville • NC, United States ... 48 H3
Fayetteville • TN, United States ... 48 D3
Fazao-Malfakassa, Parc nat. de Park • Togo ... 22 C3
Fazilka • India ... 18 J3
Fazzan • Libya ... 21 B2
Fderick • Mauritania ... 20 C4
Feale • Ireland ... 108 C6
Fear, Cape • NC, United States. ... 48 I4
Fécamp • France ... 114 C1
Federación • Argentina ... 53 E2
Federal, Distrito [Adm] • Mexico ... 157 E9
Federal Hall Nat. Mem. Park N • NY, United States ... 151 [313]
Federal Way • WA, United States ... 42 D3
Fehmarn • Germany ... 8 G2
Fehmarnbelt • Germany ... 8 G2
Feia, Lago • Brazil ... 163 C4
Feijó • Brazil ... 51 C5
Feilding • New Zealand ... 35 E5
Feira de Santana • Brazil ... 52 I1
Feke • Turkey ... 123 G2
Felanitx Beach • Majorca, Spain ... 96 [126]
Felanitx • Majorca, Spain ... 117 H4
Feldafing • Germany ... 119 H4
Feldberg Ski • Germany ... 100 [1]
Feldberg • Germany ... 112 D8
Feldkirch • Austria ... 119 H5
Feletto Corsica • France ... 115 L4
Félicité • Seychelles ... 133 K4
Felidu Atoll • Maldives ... 138 F1
Felipe Carillo Puerto • Mexico ... 157 H4
Felixstowe • United Kingdom ... 104 E2
Fell Foot Park • United Kingdom ... 104 E1
Felsberg Castle • Germany ... 113 [37]
Feltre • Italy ... 120 B4

Fengcheng • China ... 30 C4
Fenghua • China ... 139 C4
Fengjie • China ... 29 D4
Fengshui Shan • China ... 27 J6
Fengxian • China ... 139 C4
Fenit Beach • Ireland ... 96 [60]
Fenit • Ireland ... 108 C5
Fennimore • WI, United States ... 43 K5
Fens, The • United Kingdom ... 115 K2
Fensfjorden • Norway ... 7 M9
Fenyang • China ... 124 C3
Feolin Ferry • United Kingdom ... 29 E3
Fer, Cap de • Algeria ... 106 B2
Feraklós • Rhodes, Greece ... 20 G1
Ferdows • Iran ... 122 D12
Fère-Champenoise • France ... 18 G3
Fères • Greece ... 5 H6
Ferfer • Ethiopia ... 15 H3
Fergana Basin • Uzbekistan ... 23 H2
Fergus Falls • MN, United States ... 126 A11
Ferguson Lake • NU, Canada ... 43 H3
Ferguson • Papua New Guinea ... 38 J3
Ferienzentrum Schloss Dankern Park L • Germany ... 35 (1) E2
Ferkéssédougou • Côte d'Ivoire ... 98 [52]
Ferlo • Senegal ... 22 C3
Ferlo [Riv] • Senegal ... 20 C6
Fermain Bay Beach • United Kingdom ... 20 B5
Fermo • Italy ... 101 [259]
Fermoy • Ireland ... 12 H5
Fern Gully • Jamaica ... 108 C8
Fernandina Beach • FL, United States ... 159 F2
Fernandina • Galapagos Is. ... 154 H3
Fernando de Noronha, Território de • Brazil ... 51 (1) A2
Fernando Póo • Equatorial Guinea ... 53 (1) E2
Fernándópolis • Brazil ... 22 F4
Fernie • BC, Canada ... 52 F3
Fernie Snow Valley Ski • BC, Canada ... 42 H2
Fernley • NV, United States ... 149 [10]
Fernmeldeturm Germany ... 45 C2
Fernwood • IL, United States ... 119 H4
Ferragudo • Portugal ... 42 G3
Ferrandina • Italy ... 118 E6
Ferté-Bernard, la • France ... 12 K8
Ferrara Heritage C • Italy ... 86 [136]
Ferrara • Italy ... 121 E7
Ferraria, Ponta da • Azores ... 118 B1
Ferreira do Alentejo • Portugal ... 11 C6
Ferreiras • Portugal ... 11 E6
Ferreries Beach • Minorca, Spain ... 96 [127]
Ferreries • Minorca, Spain ... 117 F1
Ferret, Cap • France ... 115 G3
Ferrey • LA, United States ... 47 I2
Ferriday • FL, United States ... 120 C1
Ferruz, Es Cap de • Majorca, Spain ... 11 O5
Ferté-Bernard, la • France ... 114 D2
Ferté-Macé, la • France ... 5 C6
Fès • Morocco ... 131 D2
Fès Heritage C • Morocco ... 86 [251]
Festós • Crete, Greece ... 123 E6
Fetesti • Romania ... 128 E1
Fethiye • Turkey ... 122 D9
Fethiye Körfezi • Turkey ... 5 I5
Fettar • United Kingdom ... 6 L1
Fetsund • Norway ... 124 B2
Feuchtwangen • Germany ... 9 F7
Feuilles, Rivière aux • QU, Canada ... 39 O5
Feurs • France ... 10 J8
Fevzipasa • Turkey ... 123 G2
Feyzabad • Afghanistan ... 18 J2
Fezzan • Libya ... 20 H3
Ffestiniog • United Kingdom ... 104 E1
Fiabilandia Park L • Italy ... 98 [84]
Fianarantsoa • Madagascar ... 24 H4
Fiche • Ethiopia ... 23 G1
Fichtelgebirge • Germany ... 9 H6
Fichtenwalde • Germany ... 111 C3
Fidenza • Italy ... 121 E6
Fideris Ski • Switzerland ... 100 [115]
Fieberbrunn Ski • Austria ... 100 [156]
Fieberbrunn • Austria ... 119 H3
Fiemme, Val di • Italy ... 120 B3
Fier • Albania ... 15 A3
Fiesch Ski • Switzerland ... 100 [96]
Fiesch • Switzerland ... 119 G6
Fiésole • Italy ... 121 E11
Figari • Corsica, France ... 115 L4
Figeac • France ... 114 B4
Figeholm • Sweden ... 125 F8
Figueira da Foz • Portugal ... 11 C5
Figueira de Foz Beach • Portugal ... 96 [96]
Figueres • Spain ... 117 D2
Figuig • Morocco ... 131 D4
Fihalhohi • Maldives ... 138 F4
FIJI IS. • Pacific Ocean ... 35 (2) D2
Filadélfia • Brazil ... 51 H5
Filchner Ice Shelf • Antarctica ... 54 M3
Filey Beach • United Kingdom ... 101 [33]
Filfla • Malta ... 123 H4
Filiasi • Romania ... 14 K5
Filiátes • Greece ... 15 B4
Filiatrá • Greece ... 15 C6
Filicudi, I • Italy ... 120 D2
Filingué • Niger ... 22 C2
Filipiáda • Greece ... 15 B4
Filipstad • Sweden ... 16 H7
Fillefjell • Norway ... 124 C4
Fillmore • UT, United States ... 45 F2
Filmpark Babelsberg • Germany ... 111 C3
Filosoma • Corsica, France ... 115 L1
Filzmoos Ski • Austria ... 100 [184]
Filzmoos • Austria ... 119 H4
Fimana • Greece ... 15 H6
Fimi • Dem. Rep. of Congo ... 23 B4
Finale Emilia • Italy ... 121 B4
Finale Ligure • Italy ... 120 C3
Finale Ligure Beach • Italy ... 96 [141]
Findel [Apt] • Luxembourg ... 109 D20
Findlater • SA, Canada ... 43 D1
Findlay • OH, United States ... 44 D5
Finestrat Beach • Spain ... 96 [118]
Finestrat • Spain ... 117 C2
Finger Lakes • NY, United States ... 153 D2
Fingly • BC, Canada ... 38 F5
Finhaut • Switzerland ... 119 G5
Finike • Turkey ... 123 F3
Finike Körfezi • Turkey ... 5 I5
Finikoúndas Beach • Greece ... 97 [181]
Finistère • France ... 114 C1
Finisterre, Cabo • Spain ... 11 B2
Finke • NT, Australia ... 145 D4
Finke Gorge Nat. Park • Australia ... 145 D4
Finke • NT, Australia ... 34 F6
Finke [Riv] • NT/SA, Australia ... 145 D4
Finkenberg Ski • Austria ... 100 [142]
Finkenberg • Austria ... 119 H7
FINLAND • Europe ... 16
Finland, Gulf of • Europe ... 16 M7
Finnemarka • Norway ... 124 B1
Finnigan, Mt • QL, Australia ... 34 I3
Finnish Archipelago • Finland ... 124 A8
Finnish Lakeland • Finland ... 124 A8
Finnis, Cape • SA, Australia ... 34 F6

Finnmark • Norway ... 16 L2
Finnmark • Sweden ... 125 F7
Finschhafen • Papua New Guinea ... 35 (1) D2
Finse • Norway ... 124 C4
Finsterwalde • Germany ... 8 I5
Finsteraarhorn • Switzerland ... 119 G6
Finnphort • United Kingdom ... 6 F5
Fiordland Nat. Park • New Zealand ... 145 G1
Firat • Turkey ... 18 C2
Firatkin • Turkey ... 123 G2
Fire I. Nat. Seashore Park N • NY, United States ... 151 [321]
Fire I. Nat. Seashore • NY, United States ... 153 D7
Firefly • Jamaica ... 159 F2
Firenze Heritage C • Italy ... 86 [140]
Firenze • Italy ... 121 E11
Firminy • France ... 10 J8
Firozabad • India ... 137 C3
Firozpur • India ... 28 B2
Fischen • Germany ... 112 F6
Fish • Namibia ... 24 B4
Fish River Canyon • Namibia ... 24 B5
Fishbourne • United Kingdom ... 106 D
Fisher River • NT, Canada ... 43 H1
Fisher Strait • NU, Canada ... 39 O4
Fishers I. • NY, United States ... 153 D8
Fishguard • United Kingdom ... 7 H10
Fishnish • United Kingdom ... 106 B2
Fiskárs • Cephalonia, Greece ... 122 C2
Fiskarhalvön • Russian Fed. ... 17 E1
Fiskebäckskil • Sweden ... 125 E2
Fisterra Beach • Spain ... 96 [92]
Fitchburg • MA, United States ... 44 I6
Fitou • France ... 114 B4
Fitri, Lac • Chad ... 21 H2
Fitzcarrald • Peru ... 163 B2
Fitzgerald • GA, United States ... 48 F5
Fitzroy • WA, Australia ... 34 D3
Fitzroy • QL, Australia ... 144 B4
Fitzroy Crossing • WA, Australia ... 34 E3
Fitzroy • QL, Australia ... 144 B1
Fitzwilliam I. • OT, Canada ... 44 E3
Fiumicino • Italy ... 121 F3
Fiumicino [Apt] • Italy ... 121 F3
Fiumorbo • Corsica, France ... 115 L4
Five Cays • Turks & Caicos Is. ... 158 C1
Five Is. Harbour • Antigua & Barbuda ... 161 K
Fjällbacka • Sweden ... 125 F2
Fjärásbräcka • Sweden ... 125 F6
Fjerritslev Beach • Denmark ... 96 [48]
Fjerritslev • Denmark ... 125 F5
Fjöllum, Jökulsá á • Iceland ... 16 (1) E2
Flå • Norway ... 124 B1
Flachau Ski • Austria ... 100 [175]
Flachau • Austria ... 119 H4
Flachauwinkel Ski • Austria ... 100 [173]
Flagler • CO, United States ... 46 D3
Flagstaff • South Africa ... 134 B5
Flagstaff, Mt • United States ... 153 E1
St Martin, West Indies ... 160 D
Flaine Ski • France ... 100 [19]
Flaine • France ... 115 F2
Flåm • Norway ... 124 C4
Flamants, I. • Mauritius ... 132 J4
Flambards Victorian Village • United Kingdom ... 104 F4
Flambeau, Lac de • WI, United States ... 43 K3
Flamborough Beach • United Kingdom ... 101 [34]
Fläming • Germany ... 119 G1
Flaming Gorge Reservoir • WY, United States ... 115 K2
Flamingo • FL, United States ... 42 K6
Flamingo [Apt] • Bonaire ... 49 C5
Flamingo Sanctuary • Bonaire ... 160 W
Flanders • Belgium/France/Neths. ... 109 D13
Flanders • BC, Canada ... 38 G5
Flanders: Beguinages Heritage C • Belgium ... 86 [33]
Flandre-Zuydcoote Beach • France ... 96 [74]
Flåsjon • Sweden ... 16 I4
Flat I. • South China Sea ... 31 F4
Flat I. • Mauritius ... 132 J2
Flatey • Norway ... 124 B2
Flathead Lake • MT, United States ... 152 B2
Flattery, Cape • WA, United States ... 152 B1
Flatts Village • Bermuda ... 159 J2
Flåvatn • Norway ... 124 B3
Flaxafloi • Iceland ... 16 (1) B2
Flèche, la • France ... 114 D1
Fleetwood • United Kingdom ... 7 I8
Flekkefjord • Norway ... 16 D7
Flemingsburg • KY, United States ... 48 F1
Flen • Sweden ... 125 D3
Flensburg • Germany ... 8 E2
Flers • France ... 5 C6
Flesberg • Norway ... 124 B1
Flesland [Apt] • Norway ... 124 C3
Fleuve Maroni • French Guiana/Surinam ... 51 G3
Flevoland • Netherlands ... 109 D7
Flevoland [Adm] • Netherlands ... 109 D7
Flims Ski • Switzerland ... 100 [107]
Flims • Switzerland ... 119 G3
Flin Flon • MN, Canada ... 38 K6
Flinders • QL, Australia ... 34 I3
Flinders I • TS, Australia ... 34 I8
Flinders Passage • QL, Australia ... 144 B1
Flinders Ranges • SA, Australia ... 34 G6
Flinders Reefs • CL, Australia ... 144 B1
Flint • United Kingdom ... 7 I8
Flint • MI, United States ... 33 L7
Flint • AL, United States ... 44 D4
Flint • GA, United States ... 48 E5
Flint • GA, United States ... 44 F6
Flint Hills • KS, United States ... 46 G4
Flisa • Norway ... 124 B1
Flix • Spain ... 10 F12
Flóa • Germany ... 9 I6
Flora • IL, United States ... 46 J4
Florence Heritage C • Italy ... 86 [140]
Florence • Italy ... 121 E11
Florence • KY, United States ... 44 C6
Florence • AZ, United States ... 45 E1
Florence • SC, United States ... 48 H3
Florence • OR, United States ... 152 B3
Florencia • Colombia ... 51 B3
Florenville • Belgium ... 109 D19
Flores • Indonesia ... 32 (1) B4
Flores • Azores ... 118 B1
Flores • Argentina ... 53 E2
Flores • Guatemala ... 37 C4
Flores, I. de • Uruguay ... 163 D2
Flores, Laut • Indonesia ... 25 N10
Flores Sea • Indonesia ... 32 (1) B4
Floresti • Moldova ... 14 P2
Florida • TX, United States ... 154 J5
Floriana • Malta ... 123 H4
Floriano • Brazil ... 53 (1) C3
Florianópolis • Brazil ... 52 G4
Florida • Cuba ... 158 D7
Florida • Uruguay ... 163 D2

Florida • United States ... 154 H
Florida Caverns State Park • FL, United States ... 154 H2
Florida Citrus Bowl • FL, United States ... 151 C2
Florida Citrus Tower • FL, United States ... 151 C2
Florida City • FL, United States ... 154 H8
Florida Keys • FL, United States ... 154 H8
Florida's Cypress Gardens • FL, United States ... 154 H5
Florida's Silver Springs Park L • FL, United States ... 151 [AA]
Florida's Silver Springs • FL, United States ... 154 H3
Floridablanca • Colombia ... 51 C2
Floridia • Sicily, Italy ... 15 C3
Florissant • MO, United States ... 46 J3
Florissant Fossil Beds Nat. Mon. Park N • CO, United States ... 150 [95]
Flora • Norway ... 124 C1
Flossenbürg Castle • Germany ... 113 [154]
Flowers Cove • NF, Canada ... 39 T6
Floyd, Mt • AZ, United States ... 45 F4
Floydada • TX, United States ... 46 E6
Flumendosa • Sardinia, Italy ... 120 C4
Flumserberg Ski • Switzerland ... 100 [108]
Flumserberg • Switzerland ... 119 G3
Flushing • United Kingdom ... 109 D10
Fluvià • Spain ... 10 H11
Flying Fish Cove • Indian Ocean ... 32 D5
Fly • Papua New Guinea ... 35 (1) C2
Flying Tigers Warbird Air Museum • FL, United States ... 151 C2
Fort Fun Abenteuerland Park L • Germany ... 98 [58]
Foca • Bosnia-Herz. ... 14 F6
Foça Beach • Turkey ... 97 [236]
Foça • Turkey ... 122 C9
Focsani • Romania ... 14 O4
Fogdön • Sweden ... 125 D3
Foggia • Italy ... 12 J7
Foggo • Nigeria ... 20 I6
Fogo • Cape Verde ... 22 (1) B2
Fogo • NF, Canada ... 156 D4
Fogo [I.] • NF, Canada ... 156 D4
Fohnsdorf • Austria ... 13 D10
Föhr • Germany ... 8 D2
Fóia • Portugal ... 118 E2
Foix • France ... 114 B5
Foix • France ... 115 K1
Foix [Region] • France ... 115 K1
Folda • Norway ... 16 G4
Foleland • Norway ... 16 G4
Folégandros • Greece ... 122 D7
Foleli • Corsica, France ... 115 L2
Foley I. • NU, Canada ... 39 O3
Foleyet • OT, Canada ... 44 D1
Folgaria Ski • Italy ... 100 [215]
Folgárida Ski • Italy ... 100 [210]
Folgefonna • Norway ... 124 C1
Folgoët, le • France ... 114 C1
Foligno • Italy ... 121 E12
Folkestone • United Kingdom ... 104 E4
Folkestone Underwater Park • Barbados ... 161 O
Follónica • Italy ... 121 E11
Folsom • CA, United States ... 45 B2
Fombuni • Comoros ... 24 G2
Fomento • Cuba ... 158 D2
Fond d'Or Bay • St Lucia ... 161 P
Fond du Lac • WI, United States ... 43 L5
Fond du Lac • SA, Canada ... 38 J5
Fondi • Italy ... 121 F4
Fonsagrada • Spain ... 11 D1
Fonseca, Golfo de • El Salvador/Nicaragua ... 37 D5
Font • United States ... 119 G1
Font-Romeu • France ... 115 K2
Fontainebleau Heritage C • France ... 86 [67]
Fontainebleau • France ... 115 E4
Fontainebleau, Forêt de • France ... 115 E4
Fontana • Sicily, Italy ... 120 B6
Fontas • BC, Canada ... 38 G5
Fonte alla Róccia • Italy ... 120 B2
Fonte Boa • Brazil ... 51 D4
Fontein Cave • Aruba ... 160 Y
Fontenay Heritage C • France ... 86 [68]
Fontenay-le-Comte • France ... 114 D3
Fontevraud • France ... 114 D2
Fontur • Iceland ... 16 (1) F1
Fonualei • Tonga ... 35 (2) F2
Fóppolo • Italy ... 121 E2
Föra • Sweden ... 125 F8
Fora, I. de Madeira • Madeira ... 118 C2
Forbach • France ... 10 L4
Forbach • Germany ... 112 F6
Forchheim • Germany ... 9 G7
Ford City • CA, United States ... 45 C4
Ford's Theatre Nat. Hist. Site Park N • DC, United States ... 151 [275]
Forde • Sogn og Fjordane, Norway ... 124 C1
Førde • Rogaland, Norway ... 124 C2
Fordefjorden • Norway ... 124 C1
Fordyce • AR, United States ... 46 I6
Fore Abbey • Ireland ... 108 B1
Forel, Mt • Greenland ... 39 X3
Foremost • AL, Canada ... 42 J2
Forest • MS, United States ... 48 C4
Forest City • NC, United States ... 48 F3
Forest Finland • Finland ... 124 A5
Forest Glen • CA, United States ... 42 D6
Forest Grove • OR, United States ... 42 D4
Forest of the Cedars of God Heritage C • Lebanon ... 86 [282]
Forest Park • GA, United States ... 48 E4
Forestville • QU, Canada ... 156 D1
Forez, Mts du • France ... 10 I8
Forfar • United Kingdom ... 104 B2
Forggensee • Germany ... 112 F6
Forillon Nat. Park Park N • QU, Canada ... 156 D2
Forillon Nat. Park Park N • QU, Canada ... 156 [31]
Forio • Italy ... 121 G3
Forks • WA, United States ... 42 C3
Forli • Italy ... 121 E7
Formby Beach • United Kingdom ... 96 [124]
Formentera • Spain ... 117 G4
Formentera Beach • Spain ... 96 [124]
Formentor • Majorca, Spain ... 117 H2
Formentor, Cap de • Majorca, Spain ... 117 H2
Formia • Italy ... 121 G3
Formiga • Brazil ... 163 C1
Formigas • Azores ... 118 B2
Formosa • Argentina ... 52 E2
Formosa • Brazil ... 52 G2
Formosa Strait • China ... 29 F6
Fornebu [Apt] • Norway ... 124 B2
Fornells • Minorca, Spain ... 104 B3
Forth, Firth of • United Kingdom ... 6 G5
Forth • Scotland ... 104 B2
Fortín Coronel Eugenio Garay • Paraguay ... 52 D3
Forssa • Sweden ... 125 D1
Forsyth • QL, Australia ... 34 H3
Forssa • Finland ... 125 E4
Forsyth • MT, United States ... 42 L3
Fort Albany • OT, Canada ... 39 O6
Fort Apache Indian Reservation • AZ, United States ... 153 E3
Foss Lake • OK, United States ... 46 G5
Fort Archambault • Chad ... 21 C6
Fort Augustus • United Kingdom ... 6 H4
Fort Bay • Saba ... 161 F
Fort Beaufort • South Africa ... 134 C4

Fort Belknap Indian Reservation • MT, United States ... 42 K2
Fort Benton • MT, United States ... 42 J3
Fort Bowie Nat. Hist. Site Park N • AZ, United States ... 150 [116]
Fort Bowie Nat. Hist. Site • AZ, United States ... 153 E4
Fort Bragg • CA, United States ... 152 C1
Fort Caroline Nat. Mem. Park N • FL, United States ... 151 [315]
Fort Caroline Nat. Mem. • FL, United States ... 154 H3
Fort Chipewyan • AL, Canada ... 38 I5
Fort Clatsop Nat. Mem. Park N • FL, United States ... 150 [33]
Fort Collins • CO, United States ... 46 C2
Fort Coulonge • QU, Canada ... 44 G3
Fort Davis • TX, United States ... 47 C2
Fort Davis Nat. Hist. Site Park N • TX, United States ... 150 [135]
Fort de France • Martinique ... 161 N
Fort de France, Baie de • Martinique ... 161 N
Fort Defiance • AZ, United States ... 45 H4
Fort Delaware State Park • DE, United States ... 153 D10
Fort Dodge • IA, United States ... 43 I5
Fort Donelson Nat. Battlefield Park N • TN, United States ... 151 [225]
Fort Erie • OT, Canada ... 155 B9
Fort Frances • OT, Canada ... 43 J2
Fort Frederica Nat. Mon. Park N • GA, United States ... 151 [211]
Fort Gadsden State Hist. Site • FL, United States ... 154 H2
Fort George • QU, Canada ... 39 P6
Fort Gibson Lake • OK, United States ... 46 H5
Fort Good Hope • NT, Canada ... 49 P2
Fort Hall Indian Reservation • ID, United States ... 42 J5
Fort Hope • OT, Canada ... 43 M1
Fort Kent • ME, United States ... 44 K2
Fort Laramie Nat. Hist. Site Park N • WY, United States ... 150 [71]
Fort Larned Nat. Hist. Site Park N • KS, United States ... 150 [167]
Fort Lauderdale • FL, United States ... 154 H8
Fort Liberté • Haiti ... 159 G2
Fort Lupton • CO, United States ... 46 C2
Fort Macleod • AL, Canada ... 155 C4
Fort Madison • IA, United States ... 46 J2
Fort Matanzas Nat. Mon. Park N • FL, United States ... 151 [217]
Fort McHenry Nat. Mon. & Hist. Shrine Park N • MD, United States ... 151 [270]
Fort McMurray • AL, Canada ... 38 I5
Fort McPherson • NT, Canada ... 38 E3
Fort Meade • FL, United States ... 49 C4
Fort Médoc • France ... 115 G1
Fort Miribel • Algeria ... 20 F3
Fort Morgan • CO, United States ... 46 D2
Fort Myers • FL, United States ... 154 H7
Fort Necessity Nat. Battlefield Park N • PA, United States ... 151 [292]
Fort Nelson • BC, Canada ... 9 G6
Fort Nelson [Riv] • BC, Canada ... 38 G5
Fort Norman • NT, Canada ... 48 E3
Fort Payne • AL, United States ... 48 E3
Fort Pearson • South Africa ... 134 B4
Fort Peck • ND, United States ... 42 L2
Fort Peck Dam • MT, United States ... 42 L2
Fort Peck Lake • MT, United States ... 42 L3
Fort Pierce • FL, United States ... 154 H6
Fort Pierre • SD, United States ... 43 F4
Fort Point Nat. Hist. Site Park N • CA, United States ... 150 [43]
Fort Providence • NT, Canada ... 48 I1
Fort Pulaski Nat. Mon. Park N • GA, United States ... 151 [210]
Fort Qu'Appelle • SA, Canada ... 43 E1
Fort Raleigh Nat. Hist. Site Park N • NC, United States ... 151 [244]
Fort Resolution • NT, Canada ... 38 I4
Fort Ross State Hist. Park • CA, United States ... 152 C3
Fort Scott • KS, United States ... 46 H4
Fort Scott Nat. Hist. Site Park N • KS, United States ... 151 [170]
Fort Severn • OT, Canada ... 39 N5
Fort Shevchenko • Kazakstan ... 17 I6
Fort Simpson • NT, Canada ... 38 I4
Fort Smith • AR, United States ... 46 H5
Fort Smith • NT, Canada ... 38 I4
Fort Smith Nat. Hist. Site Park N • AR, United States ... 151 [187]
Fort St James • BC, Canada ... 38 G6
Fort St John • BC, Canada ... 155 C1
Fort Stanwix Nat. Mon. Park N • NY, United States ... 151 [306]
Fort Stanwix Nat. Mon. • NY, United States ... 153 D2
Fort Steele • BC, Canada ... 155 C4
Fort Stockton • TX, United States ... 47 C2
Fort Sumner • NM, United States ... 153 F1
Fort Sumter Nat. Mon. Park N • SC, United States ... 151 [232]
Fort Totten • ND, United States ... 43 G3
Fort Union Nat. Mon. Park N • NM, United States ... 150 [129]
Fort Union Trading Post Nat. Hist. Site Park N • ND, United States ... 150 [146]
Fort Vancouver Nat. Hist. Site Park N • WA, United States ... 150 [32]
Fort Vermilion • AL, Canada ... 38 H5
Fort Walton Beach • FL, United States ... 154 H2
Fort Washington Park Park N • MD, United States ... 151 [266]
Fort Washington Park • MD, United States ... 153 D9
Fort Wayne • IN, United States ... 44 C5
Fort Wilderness • FL, United States ... 151 C1
Fort William • United Kingdom ... 6 G5
Fort Worth • TX, United States ... 154 J1
Fort Yates • ND, United States ... 43 F3
Fort Yukon • AK, United States ... 49 M2
Fortaleza • Brazil ... 53 (1) D2
Forte dei Marmi Beach • Italy ... 96 [144]
Forte dei Marmi • Italy ... 121 E10
Fortescue • WA, Australia ... 34 C4
Forth • United Kingdom ... 104 B3
Fortín Coronel Eugenio Garay • Paraguay ... 52 D3
Fortune • NF, Canada ... 156 D3
Fortune Bay • NF, Canada ... 156 D3
Fortuneswell • United Kingdom ... 104 F6
Fos-sur-Mer Beach • France ... 96 [132]
Fosforescente, Bahía • Puerto Rico ... 159 H3
Foshan • China ... 29 E5
Fosnvåg • Norway ... 124 C1
Fossano • Italy ... 12 B4
Fossanova, Abbazia di • Italy ... 121 F4
Fossil • OR, United States ... 42 E4

Fossil Butte Nat. Mon. Park N • WY, United States ... 150 [75]
Fossombrone • Italy ... 12 G5
Foster • VI, United States ... 144 C3
Fostoria • OH, United States ... 44 D5
Fougères • France ... 6 D1
Foula • United Kingdom ... 6 J1
Foulness • United Kingdom ... 104 E2
Foulness, Cape • New Zealand ... 35 G5
Foulwind, Cape • New Zealand ... 35 C4
Fouman • Cameroon ... 22 G3
Fountains Abbey Heritage C • United Kingdom ... 86 [19]
Four Mtns. Is. of • AK, United States ... 49 G5
Fouras Beach • France ... 96 [84]
Fouras • France ... 115 G1
Fourchue, I • St Barthélemy ... 160 E
Fourchue, I • St Barthélemy ... 123 E6
Fourmies • France ... 5 H4
Fournaise, Piton de la • Réunion ... 132 H4
Fourneau, I • Mauritius ... 132 J3
Foúrnoi • Greece ... 122 D8
Fouta • Senegal ... 22 A1
Fouta Djalon • Guinea ... 22 B2
Fouta-Cap-á • Haiti ... 159 G1
Foveaux Strait • New Zealand ... 145 G4
Fowey Beach • United Kingdom ... 101 [131]
Fowey • United Kingdom ... 104 F4
Fowlers Bay • SA, Australia ... 34 F5
Fox • MN, Canada ... 38 M5
Fox • WI, United States ... 43 L5
Fox's Bay • Montserrat ... 161 H
Fox Basin • NU, Canada ... 39 P3
Foxe Channel • NU, Canada ... 39 P4
Foxe Peninsula • NU, Canada ... 39 P4
Foxen • Sweden ... 124 B4
Foxford • Ireland ... 108 C2
Foyle, Lough • Ireland/UK ... 7 E6
Foynes • Ireland ... 108 C6
Foz de Cunene • Namibia ... 24 A3
Foz do Iguaçu • Brazil ... 52 F4
Frackville • PA, United States ... 44 G5
Fraga • Spain ... 11 L3
Frailes, Los • Venezuela ... 160 V
Framingham • MA, United States ... 44 J4
Francavilla al Mare Beach • Italy ... 96 [143]
Franca • Brazil ... 52 G3
FRANCE • Europe ... 10
Francés, Punta • Cuba ... 158 C1
Franceville • Gabon ... 22 A3
Franche Comte • France ... 10 K6
Francis Case, Lake • SD, United States ... 40 G3
Francisco Beltrão • Brazil ... 52 F4
Francisco I Madero • Mexico ... 24 A5
Francistown • Botswana ... 24 D4
Francs Peak • WY, United States ... 42 K5
Franeker • Netherlands ... 8 F3
Frankenberg • Germany ... 9 D5
Frankenberg • Germany ... 9 G6
Frankenstein, Burg • Germany ... 112 E4
Frankenthal • Germany ... 9 G6
Frankenwald • Germany ... 9 H6
Frankfort • MI, United States ... 44 B3
Frankfort • IN, United States ... 44 B5
Frankfort • KY, United States ... 48 F1
Frankfurt am Main • Germany ... 112 E4
Frankfurt an der Oder • Germany ... 8 J4
Fränkisch Alb • Germany ... 9 G7
Fränkische Saale • Germany ... 9 E6
Franklin • WI, United States ... 44 B6
Franklin • IN, United States ... 44 B6
Franklin • OH, United States ... 44 C6
Franklin • PA, United States ... 44 F5
Franklin • NH, United States ... 44 J4
Franklin • KY, United States ... 48 D2
Franklin • NC, United States ... 48 F3
Franklin • TX, United States ... 47 I3
Franklin • KY, United States ... 48 D2
Franklin • VA, United States ... 153 D11
Franklin Bay • NT, Canada ... 38 F3
Franklin D. Roosevelt [Apt] • St Eustatius ... 161 F
Franklin Delano Roosevelt Mem. Park N • DC, United States ... 151 [276]
Franklin Mtns • NT, Canada ... 38 G4
Franklin Strait • NU, Canada ... 38 J2
Frans, Playa • Bonaire ... 160 W
Frantiskovy Lazne • Czech Rep. ... 128 B1
Frantsa-Iosifa, Zemlya • Russian Fed. ... 126 A3
Franz • OT, Canada ... 43 K1
Franz Josef Land • Arctic Ocean ... 26 G1
Franz Joseph Strauss [Apt] • Germany ... 112 F5
Frasassi, Grotta di • Italy ... 121 E12
Frascati • Italy ... 121 F3
Fraser • BC, Canada ... 155 C3
Fraser I. Heritage N • Australia ... 83 [48]
Fraser • QL, Australia ... 144 B6
Fraser Range • WA, Australia ... 34 E5
Fraser's Hill • Malaysia ... 141 G2
Fraserburgh • United Kingdom ... 6 K4
Fraserburgh • South Africa ... 134 C2
Frauenfeld • Switzerland ... 9 D9
Fray Bentos • Uruguay ... 163 D2
Fredensborg Beach • Denmark ... 96 [46]
Fredericia • Denmark ... 125 F9
Frederick • OK, United States ... 46 F5
Frederick • MD, United States ... 153 D9
Frederick Douglass Nat. Hist. Site Park N • DC, United States ... 151 [277]
Fredericksburg • VA, United States ... 153 D10
Fredericksburg • TX, United States ... 154 J3
Fredericksburg & Spotsylvania County Battlefields Mem. Nat. Military Park Park N • VA, United States ... 151 [254]
Fredericksburg & Spotsylvania Nat. Military Park • VA, United States ... 153 D9
Frederiktown • MO, United States ... 46 J4
Frederikborg • Denmark ... 125 F10
Frederikshåb • Greenland ... 39 Y4
Frederikshavn Beach • Denmark ... 96 [48]
Frederikshavn • Denmark ... 125 F10
Frederiksted • US Virgin Is. ... 160 Z
Frederiksværk Beach • Denmark ... 96 [41]
Frederiksværk • Denmark ... 125 F10
Fredonia • AZ, United States ... 45 F3
Fredrikstad • Norway ... 124 B2
Free State • South Africa ... 24 D5
Freels, Cape • NF, Canada ... 156 D4
Freeport • IL, United States ... 46 K1
Freeport • Bahamas ... 158 E3
Freeport • TX, United States ... 154 J5
Freetown • Sierra Leone ... 22 B3
Freetown • Antigua & Barbuda ... 161 K
Frégate • Seychelles ... 133 K2
Fréhel, Cap • France ... 114 C2
Freiberg • Germany ... 9 I6
Freiberger Mulde • Germany ... 9 I6

Freiburg im Breisgau • Germany ...112 D8
Freilassing • Germany ...112 F8
Freising • Germany ...112 F3
Freistadt • Austria ...13 D9
Freital • Germany ...9 I6
Freizeit- und Miniaturpark Allgäu Park L • Germany ...98 [65]
Freizeit- und Miniaturpark Allgäu • Germany ...112 F5
Freizeit-Land Park L • Germany ...98 [64]
Freizeitpark Lochmuhle • Germany ...112 E2
Freizeitpark Schloss Beck • Germany ...111 B1
Fréjus Beach • France ...96 [133]
Fréjus • Var, France ...115 F4
Fréjus • Hautes-Alpes, France ...115 H4
Fréjus, Tunnel du • France/Italy ...115 F4
Fremantle • WA, Australia ...34 C6
Fremont • OH, United States ...44 D5
Fremont • NE, United States ...46 G2
Fremont • CA, United States ...152 C3
Fremont Mtns • OR, United States ...152 B3
French Cay • Turks & Caicos Is. ...158 C1
FRENCH GUIANA • S. America ...51 G3
French Pass • New Zealand ...144 C3
French Pass • New Zealand ...35 D5
FRENCH POLYNESIA • Pacific Ocean ...33 M8
Frenchglen • OR, United States ...42 F5
Frenchman • SA, Canada ...43 B2
Frenchville • ME, United States ...44 K2
Frere • South Africa ...134 B3
Freshwater Beach • United Kingdom ...101 [169]
Fresnillo • Mexico ...37 (1) B1
Fresno • CA, United States ...152 C3
Fresno Reservoir • MT, United States ...42 J2
Freu, Cap del • Majorca, Spain ...11 O5
Freudenberg • Germany ...9 C6
Freudenstadt • Germany ...112 D6
Freudenstadt Spa • Germany ...113 [h6]
Fri • Greece ...15 H8
Fria • Guinea ...22 B2
Frias • Argentina ...52 C4
Fribourg • Switzerland ...119 G2
Friday Harbor • WA, United States ...42 D2
Fridlevstad • Sweden ...125 F12
Fridtjof Nansen, Mt • Antarctica ...54 (1) Y1
Friedberg • Hesse, Germany ...112 D2
Friedberg • Bavaria, Germany ...112 F2
Friedberg Castle • Germany ...113 [49]
Friedenstein Castle • Germany ...113 [182]
Friedland Castle • Germany ...113 [226]
Friedrichshafen • Germany ...112 F5
Friendship Hill Nat. Hist. Site Park N • PA, United States ...151 [291]
Friendswood • TX, United States ...47 G3
Friesland • Germany/Neths. ...5 K1
Friesland [Adm] • Netherlands ...109 D3
Friesoythe • Germany ...8 C3
Frigate Bay • St Kitts & Nevis ...161 G
Frigate I. • Grenada ...161 R
Frio, Cabo • Brazil ...163 C4
Frisco Peak • UT, United States ...45 F2
Frisian Is. • Germany/Neths. ...8 B3
Frisian Is., East • Germany ...8 C3
Frisian Is., North • Germany ...8 D2
Frisian Is., West • Netherlands ...8 A3
Frisian Islands, West • Netherlands ...109 D3
Fristad • Sweden ...125 F7
Fritzlar • Germany ...9 E5
Friuli-Venezia Giulia • Italy ...121 E4
Frobisher Bay • NU, Canada ...39 R4
Frobisher Bay [Bay] • NU, Canada ...39 R4
Frobisher Lake • SA, Canada ...38 J5
Frohnau (Berlin) • Germany ...111 C1
Frohavet • Russian Fed. ...17 G5
Frome • United Kingdom ...104 F3
Frome, Lake • SA, Australia ...34 G6
Fronsac • France ...114 B3
Front Range • CO, United States ...46 B3
Front Royal • VA, United States ...153 D9
Frontenac Prov. Park • QU, Canada ...155 B4
Fronteras • Mexico ...159 D2
Frosinone • Italy ...121 F4
Froya • Norway ...16 E5
Frozen Strait • NU, Canada ...39 O3
Frunzivka • Ukraine ...14 O2
Fruska Gora • F.R. of Yugoslavia ...14 G4
Fruska Gora Nat. Park Park N • Fed. Rep. of Yugoslavia ...89 [115]
Frutal • Brazil ...52 G3
Frýdek Místek • Czech Rep. ...13 H8
Frýdlant • Czech Rep. ...128 B2
Fu Yang • China ...139 C3
Fuah Mulah Atoll • Maldives ...138 F3
Fuchskauten • Germany ...5 L4
Fuchu • Japan ...140 C2
Fuchun Jiang • China ...139 C3
Fucino, Piana del • Italy ...121 F2
Fuding • China ...29 G5
Fuengirola Beach • Spain ...96 [114]
Fuengirola • Spain ...116 B6
Fuente Alto • Chile ...52 B5
Fuentesaúco • Spain ...11 F3
Fuerte • Mexico ...157 F4
Fuerteventura • Canary Is. ...117 E2
Fügen • Austria ...119 H3
Fuggerschloss • Germany ...112 F2
Fuggerschloss Castle • Germany ...113 [103]
Fuhai • China ...26 O8
Fujairah • United Arab Emirates ...81 E
Fuji • Japan ...140 C3
Fuji Five Lakes • Japan ...140 C1
Fuji-Hakone-Izu Nat. Park • Japan ...140 C3
Fuji-san • Japan ...140 C3
Fujian • China ...139 A8
Fujin • China ...29 I1
Fujinomiya • Japan ...140 C3
Fujioka • Japan ...140 C1
Fujisawa • Japan ...140 C4
Fujiyoshida • Japan ...140 C1
Fukagawa • Japan ...30 K3
Fukaya • Japan ...140 C1
Fukuchiyama • Japan ...30 H7
Fukue • Japan ...30 E8
Fukue [I.] • Japan ...30 E8
Fukueichiao • Taiwan ...29 G5
Fukui • Japan ...30 I6
Fukui [Adm] • Japan ...140 A4
Fukuoka • Japan ...30 F8
Fukuoka [Adm] • Japan ...140 A1
Fukusaki • Japan ...30 K6
Fukushima • Japan ...140 A4
Fukushima [Adm] • Japan ...140 A4
Fukuyama • Japan ...30 G7
Fulda • Germany ...9 E5
Fulda Castle • Germany ...113 [51]
Fulda [Riv] • Germany ...9 E5
Fuling • China ...139 A6
Full Moon • Maldives ...138 F4
Fullerton • CA, United States ...45 D5
Fulpmes • Austria ...119 H6
Fulton • MO, United States ...46 I3
Fulton • KY, United States ...48 C2
Fulton • NY, United States ...153 D2
Fulton • AR, United States ...154 J2
Fumay • France ...5 H4

Fumimaggiore • Sardinia, Italy ...12 C9
Fun Acres Park L • United Kingdom ...98 [36]
Fun I. • Maldives ...138 F4
Funabashi • Japan ...140 C2
Funafuti • Kiribati ...33 I6
Funafuti [I.] • Kiribati ...33 I6
Funchal Beach • Madeira ...96 [108]
Funchal • Madeira ...118 C2
Fundão • Portugal ...11 D4
Fundy, Bay of • NB/NS, Canada ...156 D7
Fundy Nat. Park • NB, Canada ...156 D7
Fundy Nat. Park Park N • NB, Canada ...156 [33]
Fünen • Denmark ...125 F14
Fünfkirchen • Hungary ...90 A14
Fungus Rock • Malta ...123 H1
Fur • Denmark ...125 F5
Furana • Maldives ...138 F4
Furancungo • Mozambique ...24 E2
Furano • Japan ...30 L3
Furat, Al • Iraq/Syria ...18 D3
Furkapass • Switzerland ...119 G3
Furnas • Azores ...118 E1
Furnas Dam • Brazil ...163 C1
Furnas, Represa de • Brazil ...163 C1
Furneaux Group • TS, Australia ...34 I8
Furness Abbey • United Kingdom ...104 C3
Furness Fells • United Kingdom ...104 C3
Fürstenbischöflicher Residenz, Eichstätt Castle • Germany ...113 [141]
Fürstenfeld • Austria ...14 D2
Fürstenfeldbruck • Germany ...112 F3
Fürstenhof Castle • Germany ...113 [223]
Fürstenwalde • Germany ...8 J4
Fürth • Germany ...9 F6
Fürth im Wald • Germany ...9 H7
Furtwangen • Germany ...112 D8
Furukawa • Japan ...30 K5
Furuvik • Sweden ...98 [8]
Furuviksparken Park L • Sweden ...98 [8]
Fury & Hecla Strait • NU, Canada ...39 O3
Fury Shoal (Amphora wreck) Dive • Red Sea ...135 B2
Fusa • Norway ...124 C3
Fushë-Lura • Albania ...15 B2
Fushun • China ...29 G2
Fushun • China ...30 D3
Füssen • Germany ...112 F6
Futtsu • Japan ...140 C4
Futuna • Vanuatu ...35 (2) C2
Futuna • Wallis & Futuna ...35 (2) E1
Futuroscope Park L • France ...98 [73]
Futuroscope • France ...114 D4
Fuxian • China ...30 A5
Fuxin • China ...29 G2
Fuyang • China ...29 F4
Fuyu • China ...27 J8
Fuyu • China ...26 O8
Fuzhou • Fujian, China ...29 F5
Fuzhou • Jiangxi, China ...29 F5
Fyn [Adm] • Denmark ...125 F14
Fyn [I.] • Denmark ...125 F14
Fyne, Loch • United Kingdom ...6 G6
Fynshav • Denmark ...125 F13
Fyresdal • Norway ...124 C6
Fyresvatn • Norway ...124 C6

Gaafaru Atoll • Maldives ...138 F2
Gabbs • NV, United States ...152 C4
Gabela • Angola ...23 A6
Gabès • Tunisia ...131 E4
Gabès, Golfe de • Tunisia ...131 E4
Gabicce Mare • Italy ...121 E12
Gabon • Africa ...22 G5
GABON • Africa ...22 G5
Gaborone • Botswana ...24 D4
Gabriel I. • Mauritius ...132 J2
Gabriel Strait • NU, Canada ...39 R4
Gabrovo • Bulgaria ...128 E3
Gadag • India ...138 D2
Gadara • Jordan ...135 A4
Gäddede • Sweden ...16 H4
Gadsden • AL, United States ...48 E3
Gaeri • India ...128 E1
Gaeta • Italy ...121 F4
Gaeta, Golfo di • Italy ...12 H7
Gaferut • Fed. States of Micronesia ...33 F5
Gaffney • SC, United States ...48 G3
Gafsa • Tunisia ...131 E3
Gagarin • Russian Fed. ...126 C3
Gagnoa • Côte d'Ivoire ...22 C3
Gagnon • QU, Canada ...39 R6
Gai Xian • China ...30 B4
Gaillac • France ...115 G4
Gaillimh • Ireland ...108 C4
Gaitaler Alpen • Austria ...119 H4
Gainer Wildlife Sanctuary • India ...137 C1
Gainesville • MO, United States ...46 I4
Gainesville • GA, United States ...48 F3
Gainesville • FL, United States ...154 H3
Gainesville • TX, United States ...154 J1
Gainsborough • United Kingdom ...7 L8
Gairdner, Lake • SA, Australia ...34 G6
Gairloch • United Kingdom ...6 H4
Gal Oya Nat. Park • Sri Lanka ...138 D16
Gala • Turkey ...15 H3
Gala Güol • Turkey ...15 H3
Galán, Cerro • Argentina ...52 C4
Galana • Kenya ...131 G4
Galanta • Slovak Rep. ...13 G9
Galápagos Is. • Pacific Ocean ...51 (1) A1
Galápagos Is., Parque Nac. Heritage N • Pacific Ocean ...82 [33]
Galashiels • United Kingdom ...104 B4
Galata • Cyprus ...123 J3
Galata • Bulgaria ...128 E4
Galati • Romania ...128 E2
Galatina • Italy ...12 M8
Galdhøpiggen • Norway ...124 C2
Galè, Costa da • Portugal ...118 A3
Galeana • Mexico ...47 D5
Galeão • Brazil ...163 C4
Galena • AK, United States ...49 J3
Galeota Point • Trinidad & Tobago ...160 U
Galera Point • Trinidad & Tobago ...160 U
Galesburg • IL, United States ...46 J2
Galets, Pointe des • Réunion ...132 H1
Galets, Rivière des • Réunion ...132 H1
Galgibaga Beach • Goa, India ...137 B2
Galhak, El • Sudan ...21 F5
Galicia • Spain ...11 C2
Galicia • Poland ...13 L8
Galicica Nat. Park Park N • F.Y.R. of Macedonia ...89 [123]
Galilea • Israel ...135 A2
Galilee, Sea of • Israel ...135 A4
Galileo, Galileo [Apt] • Italy ...121 E11
Galina Point • Jamaica ...159 F2
Galion • OH, United States ...44 D5
Galite, Canal de la • Tunisia ...12 C11
Galite, La • Tunisia ...131 E1
Galka'yo • Somalia ...23 H2
Gallarus Oratory • Ireland ...108 C2
Gallatin • TN, United States ...48 E2
Gallatin Peak • NM, United States ...46 C5
Galliano • Italy ...12 M8
Gallipoli • Turkey ...122 D2
Gallipoli Peninsula • Turkey ...122 D2

Gallipolis • OH, United States ...44 D6
Gallivare • Sweden ...16 K3
Gällö • Sweden ...16 H5
Galloway, Mull of • United Kingdom ...7 H7
Gallup • NM, United States ...153 E2
Gallur • Spain ...11 J3
Galtür • Austria ...119 H5
Galty Mtns • Ireland ...108 C6
Galu Beach • Kenya ...131 G5
Galveston • TX, United States ...154 J6
Galveston Bay • TX, United States ...154 J6
Galveston I. • TX, United States ...154 J6
Gálvez • Argentina ...52 D5
Galway • Ireland ...108 C4
Galway [Adm] • Ireland ...108 C4
Galway Bay • Ireland ...108 C4
Galway City Beach • Ireland ...96 [62]
Galways Soufrière • Montserrat ...161 H
Gamarra • Colombia ...51 C2
Gamasa • Egypt ...131 F2
Gambell • AK, United States ...49 G3
Gambia [Riv] • Gambia/Senegal ...20 B6
Gambia • Senegal ...22 B2
Gambia • Senegal ...22 B2
GAMBIA, THE • Africa ...20 B6
Gambier • Senegal ...22 B2
Gambier • Bahamas ...158 B3
Gamboma • Congo ...22 H5
Gamkonora, Gunung • Indonesia ...32 (1) C2
Gamla Uppsala • Sweden ...125 D12
Gamleby • Sweden ...125 F14
Gammarth • Tunisia ...131 E2
Gammertingen • Germany ...112 F1
Gamph, Slieve • Ireland ...108 C4
Gamud • Ethiopia ...23 F3
Gamvik • Norway ...16 O1
Gan • Maldives ...138 F3
Gan Jiang • China ...29 F5
Ganado • AZ, United States ...45 H4
Gananoque • OT, Canada ...44 G3
Ganca • Azerbaijan ...18 E1
Gandadiwata, Bulu • Indonesia ...32 (1) A3
Gandajika • Dem. Rep. of Congo ...23 C5
Gandak • India ...137 C3
Gander • NF, Canada ...156 D4
Ganderkesee • Germany ...5 L1
Gandhi Dam • India ...137 C6
Gandhi, Indira [Apt] • India ...137 C2
Gandhi, Indira, Nahar • India ...137 C1
Gandhi, Indira, Wildlife Sanctuary • India ...138 D10
Gandhi Sagar • India ...137 C6
Gandhinagar • India ...28 B4
Gandia • Spain ...11 K6
Gandia Beach • Spain ...96 [119]
Gandria • Switzerland ...119 G7
Ganeb • Brazil ...52 I1
Ganetti • Sudan ...21 F4
Ganga • India ...28 D3
Gangaikondacholapuram • India ...138 D11
Gangaw • Myanmar ...28 C2
Gangca • China ...29 C3
Gangdhar • India ...137 C6
Gangdisê Shan • China ...28 D2
Ganges • India ...28 D3
Ganges Plain • India ...137 C7
Gangtok • India ...28 E3
Gangtok Hill Sta • India ...138 E2
Gani • Indonesia ...32 (1) C3
Gannett Peak • WY, United States ...42 K5
Gansbaai • South Africa ...134 C5
Gansu • China ...139 A3
Ganta • Liberia ...22 C3
Ganteng • China ...139 C3
Ganzhou • China ...121 F3
Ganzi • China ...29 E4
Gao • Mali ...20 E5
Gaochun • China ...139 C1
Gaolan • Zhuhai, China ...139 B3
Gaolan Dao • Zhuhai, China ...139 B3
Gaodong • China ...139 C4
Gaoyou Hu • China ...29 F4
Gap • France ...115 F3
Gara • Palestine ...18 G2
Gara, Lough • Ireland ...108 C2
Gara Muleta • Ethiopia ...23 G2
Gara'at • Somalia ...23 H2
Garabogazköl Aylagy • Turkmenistan ...26 H9
Garachico • Tenerife, Canary Is. ...116 E1
Garajonay, Parque Nac. de Heritage N • Gomera, Canary Is. ...83 [56]
Garajonay, Parque Nac. de Park N • Gomera, Canary Is. ...89 [77]
Garajonay, Parque Nac. de • Gomera, Canary Is. ...117 E5
Garama • Libya ...21 B2
Garamba, Parc nat. de la Heritage N • Dem. Rep. of Congo ...83 [92]
Garamba, Parc nat. de la Park • Dem. Rep. of Congo ...133 [53]
Garanhuns • Brazil ...53 (1) D3
Garar • Central African Rep. ...23 C2
Garberville • CA, United States ...42 D6
Garbsen • Germany ...8 E4
Garching bei München • Germany ...112 T3
Garda, Lago di • Italy ...121 E2
Gardaland Park L • Italy ...98 [82]
Gardaland • Italy ...121 E2
Garden City • NY, United States ...44 I5
Garden City • KS, United States ...46 E4
Garden City • TX, United States ...47 D2
Garden Grove • CA, United States ...45 C5
Garden I. • MI, United States ...44 C3
Garden Route • South Africa ...134 C7
Gardermoen [Apt] • Norway ...124 B3
Gardez • Afghanistan ...18 I3
Gardiki • Corfu, Greece ...122 B1
Gardiner • MT, United States ...42 J4
Gardner • MA, United States ...44 J4
Gardner I. • NV, United States ...45 C2
Gardone Riviera • Italy ...121 E7
Gärdsjö • Sweden ...125 F3
Gärdslösa • Sweden ...125 F8
Gargaliáni • Greece ...15 C6
Gargano • Italy ...12 J7
Gargellen • Austria ...119 H5
Gargždai • Lithuania ...125 H3
Garibaldi • OT, United States ...42 D4
Garibaldi Prov. Park • BC, Canada ...155 C3
Garicín Grad • F.R. of Yugoslavia ...14 I7
Garigliano • Italy ...121 F4
Gariwerd • VI, Australia ...144 A7
Garland • TX, United States ...47 F1
Garmisch-Partenkirchen Ski • Germany ...100 [3]
Garmisch-Partenkirchen • Germany ...112 F6
Garmisch-Partenkirchen Spa • Germany ...113 [h12]
Garner • IA, United States ...43 J5
Garnett • KS, United States ...46 H3
Garonne • France ...115 G4
Garonne, Canal latéral à la • France ...10 F9
Garoua • Cameroon ...22 G3
Garowe • Somalia ...23 H2
Garphyttan Nat. Park Park N • Sweden ...89 [25]
Garrett • IN, United States ...44 C5

Garrison • Barbados ...161 O
Garrison • ND, United States ...43 F3
Garrison • UT, United States ...45 F2
Garry Lake • NU, Canada ...38 K3
Garsa, Chott el • Tunisia ...131 E3
Garsen • Kenya ...23 F4
Gärtringen • Germany ...9 D8
Garut • Java, Indonesia ...143 J6
Garvie Mtns • New Zealand ...145 G2
Garwa • India ...137 C8
Garwolin • Poland ...13 K6
Gary • IN, United States ...44 B5
Garyarsa • China ...28 B2
Garzê • China ...29 C4
Garzón • Colombia ...51 B3
Gasan-Kuli • Turkmenistan ...18 F2
Gaschurn Ski • Austria ...100 [125]
Gaschurn • Austria ...119 H5
Gascogne • France ...10 F10
Gascony • France ...114 A3
Gascoyne • WA, Australia ...34 C5
Gasfinolhu • Maldives ...138 F2
Gashaka Game Reserve Park • Nigeria ...133 [34]
Gashua • Nigeria ...22 G2
Gaspar Hernández • Dominican Rep. ...159 G3
Gaspé • QU, Canada ...156 D2
Gaspé, Cap • QU, Canada ...156 D2
Gaspésie, Péninsule de • QU, Canada ...156 D2
Gassol • Nigeria ...22 G3
Gaston, Lake • VA, United States ...153 D11
Gastonia • NC, United States ...48 G3
Gastoúni • Greece ...15 C6
Gastouri • Corfu, Greece ...122 B1
Gata, Cabo de • Spain ...116 E8
Gata, Cape • Cyprus ...123 J3
Gata, Sierra de • Spain ...11 E4
Gatchina • Russian Fed. ...126 C1
Gates • NY, United States ...44 G4
Gates of the Arctic Nat. Park • AK, United States ...49 K2
Gates of the Arctic Nat. Park & Preserve Park N • AK, United States ...150 [5]
Gateshead • United Kingdom ...7 K7
Gatesville • TX, United States ...47 F2
Gateway • CO, United States ...45 H2
Gateway Nat. Recreation Area Park N • NJ/NY, United States ...151 [314]
Gatineau • QU, Canada ...44 H3
Gatineau Park • QU, Canada ...155 B2
Gatineau [Riv] • QU, Canada ...155 B2
Gatorland • FL, United States ...154 B4
Gatwick [Apt] • United Kingdom ...104 E3
Gauja • Latvia ...126 B4
Gauja Nat. Park Park N • Latvia ...89 [144]
Gauja Nat. Park • Latvia ...126 B4
Gauley River Nat. Recreation Area Park N • WV, United States ...151 [260]
Gaume, Fonte de • France ...115 G2
Gaupne • Norway ...124 C4
Gausta • Norway ...124 B1
Gaustablikk • Norway ...124 B1
Gauteng • South Africa ...24 D5
Gavarnie • France ...115 G2
Gavdopoúla • Greece ...123 E5
Gavdos • Greece ...122 D10
Gaviota • CA, United States ...45 B4
Gävle • Sweden ...16 I6
Gävleborg • Sweden ...16 I6
Gávrio • Greece ...122 D7
Gawler • SA, Australia ...34 G6
Gawler Ranges • SA, Australia ...34 G6
Gaya • Niger ...22 E2
Gaya • India ...137 C8
Gaylord • MI, United States ...44 C3
Gayndah • QL, Australia ...144 B6
Gayny • Russian Fed. ...17 I2
Gaza • Palestine ...18 G2
Gazanjyk • Turkmenistan ...18 G2
Gazi Beach • Kenya ...131 G5
Gaziantep • Turkey ...18 C2
Gazimagusa • Cyprus ...123 J4
Gazipasa • Turkey ...122 F4
Gazli • Uzbekistan ...18 H1
Gbadolite • Dem. Rep. of Congo ...22 I4
Gdańsk • Poland ...13 H3
Gdansk, Gulf of • Poland ...13 I3
Gdynia • Poland ...13 H3
Ge'gyai • China ...28 D2
Gebze • Turkey ...122 E2
Gecitkale [Apt] • Cyprus ...123 J3
Gedi Nat. Mon. • Kenya ...131 G5
Gediz • Turkey ...21 B2
Gediz [Riv] • Turkey ...122 D3
Gedser • Denmark ...125 F14
Gedung • Malaysia ...141 F4
Geel • Belgium ...5 H3
Geelong • VI, Australia ...144 C3
Geesthacht • Germany ...8 F3
Géfira • Greece ...15 D3
Geigar • Sudan ...23 E1
Geike • Norway ...124 C4
Geirangerfjorden • Norway ...124 C2
Geirangerfjord • Norway ...100 [146]
Geislingen an der Steige • Germany ...9 E8
Geita • Tanzania ...23 E4
Gela • Sicily, Italy ...12 M10
Gela • Sicily, Italy ...120 D4
Gela, Golfo di • Sicily, Italy ...120 D4
Geladi • Ethiopia ...23 H2
Gelderland • Netherlands ...109 D7
Geldermalsen • Netherlands ...109 F4
Geldern • Germany ...8 B5
Geleen • Netherlands ...109 D16
Gelendorf • Germany ...112 F2
Gelendzhik • Russian Fed. ...18 H3
Gelibolu • Turkey ...122 D3
Gelibolu Yarimadasi • Turkey ...122 D2
Gelinsor • Somalia ...23 H2
Gelliswick Beach • United Kingdom ...101 [173]
Gelnhausen • Germany ...9 E6
Gelsenkirchen • Germany ...111 B2
Gelugur • Penang, Malaysia ...141 F3
Gemas • Malaysia ...141 G4
Gembloux • Belgium ...90 A7
Gemena • Dem. Rep. of Congo ...23 B3
Gemerek • Turkey ...123 F2
Gemlik • Turkey ...123 D2
Gemlik Körfezi • Turkey ...122 D2
Gemmenich • Belgium ...9 E6
Gen. G. Luperón [Apt] • Dominican Rep. ...159 G3
Gen. Juan N. Alvarez [Apt] • Mexico ...157 G4
Gen. Santiago Mariño [Apt] • Margarita ...160 V
Genádio Beach • Rhodes, Greece ...97 [211]
Genádio • Rhodes, Greece ...122 D12
Gencale • Ethiopia ...23 G2
Gencek • Turkey ...123 F2
Genemuiden • Netherlands ...109 D16
Gênes • Italy ...121 E6

General Grant Nat. Mem. Park N • NY, United States ...151 [315]
General Lavalle • Argentina ...163 D4
General Manuel Belgrano, Cerro • Argentina ...52 C4
General Pico • Argentina ...52 D6
General Pinedo • Argentina ...52 D4
General Roca • Argentina ...53 C3
General Santos • Philippines ...31 H5
General Teran • Mexico ...47 E5
General Toševo • Bulgaria ...14 P6
General Trias • Mexico ...47 A3
General Villegas • Argentina ...52 D5
Genesco • NY, United States ...44 G4
Genesco • IL, United States ...46 J2
Genesee • NY, United States ...153 D1
Geneva • Switzerland ...119 G5
Geneva • IL, United States ...153 D2
Geneva, Lake of • Switzerland/France ...119 G5
Genève • Switzerland ...119 G5
Gengenbach • Germany ...112 D6
Genil • Spain ...11 G7
Genk • Belgium ...109 D15
Gennargentu, Monte del • Sardinia, Italy ...120 C2
Genoa • Italy ...121 E6
Génova • Italy ...121 E6
Génova, Golfo di • France/Italy ...121 E10
Genovesa • Galápagos Is. ...51 (1) B1
Gent • Belgium ...109 D14
Gent naar Oostende, Kanaal van • Belgium ...109 E2
Genteng • Indonesia ...143 J5
Genteng [I.] • Indonesia ...143 J8
Genthin • Germany ...8 H4
Genting Highlands • Malaysia ...141 G4
Genting Highlands Resort • Malaysia ...32 (1) 7
Geographe Bay • WA, Australia ...34 C6
Geok-Tepe • Turkmenistan ...18 G2
Georg von Neumayer [Base] • Antarctica ...54 (1) I3
George • South Africa ...134 C7
George, Fort • Grenada ...160 S
George, Fort • OT, Canada ...155 S
George, Lake • NS, Australia ...144 C2
George, Lake • NY, United States ...44 I4
George, Lake • FL, United States ...49 C3
George Rogers Clark Nat. Hist. Park Park N • IN, United States ...151 [178]
George Sound • New Zealand ...145 G1
George Town • TS, Australia ...34 I8
George Town • Penang, Malaysia ...141 F2
George Town • Cayman Is. ...159 E3
George VI Sound • Antarctica ...54 (1) I3
George Washington Birthplace Nat. Mon. Park N • VA, United States ...151 [252]
George Washington Birthplace Nat. Mon. • VA, United States ...153 D11
George Washington Carver Nat. Mon. Park N • MO, United States ...151 [274]
George Washington Mem. Parkway Park N • VA, United States ...151 [258]
Georgetown • Ascension ...19 C6
Georgetown • QL, Australia ...34 H3
Georgetown • Guyana ...51 F2
Georgetown • St Vincent & Gren. ...161 Q
Georgetown • CO, United States ...46 C3
Georgetown • SC, United States ...48 I4
Georgetown • KY, United States ...48 F1
Georgetown • TX, United States ...154 J3
GEORGIA • Asia ...17 G6
Georgia • United States ...48 F4
Georgia, Strait of • BC, Canada ...38 G7
Georgian Bay • OT, Canada ...44 E3
Georgian Bay Is. Nat. Park • OT, Canada ...155 B5
Georgian Bay Is. Nat. Park Park N • OT, Canada ...156 [24]
Georgina • NT/QL, Australia ...144 A3
Georgioúpoli • Crete, Greece ...123 E2
Georgsmarienhütte • Germany ...8 E4
Gera • Germany ...9 H6
Gera [Riv] • Germany ...9 G5
Gérardmer • France ...10 I5
Geráki • Greece ...15 D7
Gerakiní • Greece ...97 [192]
Gerakini • Greece ...122 D1
Geral do Goiás, Serra • Brazil ...53 (1) B4
Geral, Serra • Brazil ...52 F4
Gerald's • Montserrat ...161 H
Geraldine • New Zealand ...35 C7
Geraldton • WA, Australia ...34 B5
Geraldton • WA, Australia ...34 B5
Geranio Beach • Crete, Greece ...97 [212]
Gerasa • Jordan ...135 A4
Gerbichi gora • Russian Fed. ...26 S3
Gerede • Turkey ...123 F1
Gerede [Riv] • Turkey ...15 N3
Gerês, Serra de • Portugal ...11 D3
Gereshk • Afghanistan ...18 H3
Geretsried • Germany ...112 F3
Gérgeri • Crete, Greece ...123 E7
Gering • NE, United States ...46 D2
Gerizim, Mount • Palestine ...135 A6
Gerlach • Slovak Rep. ...13 J8
Gerlachovsky Stit • Slovak Rep. ...13 J8
Gerlos Ski • Austria ...100 [146]
Gerlos • Austria ...119 H7
Gerlovo • Bulgaria ...14 N6
German Town • WI, United States ...44 A4
Germantown • TN, United States ...48 C3
GERMANY • Europe ...8/9
Germi • Iran ...18 F3
Germencik • Turkey ...122 D4
Gernsheim • Germany ...112 E4
Gerolstein • Germany ...112 E1
Geroskipou Beach • Cyprus ...97 [217]
Gerrard Smith [Apt] • Cayman Is. ...159 E2
Gers • France ...115 G4
Gersau • Switzerland ...119 G3
Gersthofen • Germany ...112 F2
Gertak Sanggul • Penang, Malaysia ...141 F3
Gertak Sanggul, Tanjong • Penang, Malaysia ...141 F3
Gerze • China ...28 D2
Gesundaberget • Sweden ...16 H6
Geta • Finland ...125 E3
Getafe • Spain ...11 H4
Getaria Beach • Spain ...96 [87]
Gete • Belgium ...5 J4
Gets, les Ski • France ...100 [13]
Gets, les • France ...115 F2
Gettysburg • SD, United States ...43 G4
Gettysburg Nat. Military Park Park N • PA, United States ...151 [296]
Gettysburg Nat. Military Park • PA, United States ...153 D9
Geureudong, Gunung • Indonesia ...143 G1
Gevelsberg • Germany ...111 B2
Gevgelija • Macedonia ...15 D2
Gevne Çayi • Turkey ...123 G3
Gevrai • India ...137 C6
Geyik Dagi • Turkey ...15 N7
Geyikli • Turkey ...15 L4
Geyve • Turkey ...15 L3
Gezira • Sudan ...23 E1
Ghaghara • India ...137 C8
Ghain Tuffieha Bay • Malta ...123 H3
GHANA • Africa ...22 D3

Ghar Dalam • Malta ...123 H4
Gharb • Malta ...123 H1
Gharbi • Tunisia ...131 E4
Gharbiyah, Al Istiwa'iyah al • Sudan ...23 D2
Ghard Abu Muharik • Egypt ...21 E2
Ghardaïa • Algeria ...20 F2
Ghârib • Egypt ...21 F2
Gharyan • Libya ...21 B1
Ghat • Libya ...21 A2
Ghats, Eastern • India ...138 D3
Ghats, Western • India ...138 D6
Ghazal, Bahr al • Sudan ...23 E2
Ghazal, Bahr al • Chad ...21 C5
Ghazaouet • Algeria ...11 J9
Ghaziabad • India ...137 C2
Ghazipur • India ...137 C8
Ghazni • Afghanistan ...18 I3
Ghent • Belgium ...109 D14
Ghent • Romania ...14 K2
Ghisonaccia • Corsica, France ...115 L4
Ghisoni • Corsica, France ...115 L4
Ghoumrassen • Tunisia ...131 E6
Ghuzayyil, Sabkhat • Libya ...21 C2
Giáli • Greece ...122 D8
Gianades Beach • Corfu, Greece ...97 [170]
Gianades • Corfu, Greece ...122 B1
Gianisáda • Greece ...123 E4
Giannis D Dive • Red Sea ...135 B1
Giannutri, I. di • Italy ...120 A2
Giant's Castle • South Africa ...134 B3
Giant's Castle Game Reserve Park • South Africa ...133 [134]
Giant's Causeway • United Kingdom ...7 F6
Giant's Causeway and its coast Heritage N • United Kingdom ...83 [47]
Giants Ridge Ski • MN, United States ...149 [118]
Gianyar • Bali, Indonesia ...143 H4
Giao • Vietnam ...31 D4
Giardini-Naxos • Sicily, Italy ...120 D2
Giáros • Greece ...122 D7
Giarre • Sicily, Italy ...12 J11
Giba • Greece ...158 D8
Gibb River • WA, Australia ...34 E3
Gibb's Hill Lighthouse • Bermuda ...159 J3
Gibbes Beach • Barbados ...161 O
Gibeon • Namibia ...24 B5
Gibostad • Norway ...16 I2
Gibraltar • Europe ...116 B6
Gibraltar, Strait of • Morocco/Spain ...11 F9
Gibson Desert • WA, Australia ...34 D4
Gien • France ...10 H6
Giens • France ...115 H3
Giessen • Germany ...112 D2
Giethoorn • Netherlands ...109 D8
Gifford • NU, Canada ...39 O2
Gifhorn • Germany ...8 F4
Gifhorn Castle • Germany ...113 [6]
Giftün el-Saghir Dive • Red Sea ...135 B1
Gifu • Japan ...30 I7
Gifu [Adm] • Japan ...140 A4
Giglio • Italy ...12 E6
Gijón • Spain ...11 F1
Gila • NM, United States ...45 H5
Gila Bend • AZ, United States ...153 E3
Gila Cliff Dwellings Nat. Mon. Park N • NM, United States ...150 [118]
Gila Cliff Dwellings Nat. Mon. • NM, United States ...153 E4
Gila Desert • AZ, United States ...45 F5
Gila [Riv] • AZ/NM, United States ...153 E3
Gilbert • QL, Australia ...34 H3
Gilbert Is. • Kiribati ...33 I6
Gilbo'a, Mount • Israel/Palestine ...135 A4
Gildeskål • Brazil ...53 (1) B3
Giles Meteorological Station • WA, Australia ...34 E5
Gilgit • Jammu & Kashmir ...28 B1
Gilgit [Riv] • Jammu & Kashmir ...28 B1
Gilimanuk • Bali, Indonesia ...143 H4
Gill, Lough • Ireland ...108 C2
Gillam • MN, Canada ...38 M5
Gilleleje • Denmark ...125 F10
Gillette • WY, United States ...43 F4
Gillingham • United Kingdom ...104 F3
Gills Rock • WI, United States ...44 B3
Gilroy • CA, United States ...45 B3
Gimbi • Ethiopia ...23 F2
Gimie, Mt • St Lucia ...161 P
Gin Gin • QL, Australia ...144 B6
Ginger I. • British Virgin Is. ...160 B
Gingin • WA, Australia ...34 C6
Gingindlovu • South Africa ...134 B4
Gingoog • Philippines ...31 G5
Ginosa Beach • Italy ...97 [156]
Gioia del Colle • Italy ...12 K8
Gioúra • Greece ...122 D4
Gippsland • VI, Australia ...144 C3
Gippsland Lakes • VI, Australia ...144 C3
Giraglia, I. de la • Corsica, France ...115 L2
Girão, Cabo • Madeira ...118 C1
Girard • OH, United States ...44 E5
Girardot • Colombia ...51 C3
Giravara • Maldives ...138 F4
Giri • Dem. Rep. of Congo ...23 B3
Girne • Cyprus ...123 J1
Girolata, Golfe de Heritage N • Corsica, France ...83 [51]
Girolata, Golfe de • Corsica, France ...115 L1
Girona • Spain ...117 D2
Gironde • France ...115 G1
Gironde [Adm] • France ...115 G3
Gisborne • New Zealand ...35 G4
Gisborne [Adm] • New Zealand ...145 E1
Gislaved • Sweden ...125 F7
Gisors • France ...115 L1
Gistel • Belgium ...109 E1
Gitgit Waterfall • Bali, Indonesia ...143 H2
Githio • Greece ...15 D7
Githio Beach • Greece ...97 [182]
Giulianova • Italy ...121 E12
Giumalau, Virful • Romania ...14 M2
Giurgeni • Romania ...128 E2
Giurgiu • Romania ...128 E1
Give • Denmark ...125 F9
Giverny • France ...115 L1
Givet • France ...5 H4
Giza Pyramids • Egypt ...131 F1
Gizhiga • Russian Fed. ...27 R4
Gizhiginskaya Guba • Russian Fed. ...27 Q4
Gizo • Solomon Is. ...35 (1) Y2
Gizycko • Poland ...13 K3
Gjerstad • Norway ...124 B3
Gjirokastër • Albania ...15 B3
Gjoa Haven • NU, Canada ...38 L3
Gjøvik • Norway ...16 F6
Gjuhëzës, Kep i • Albania ...15 B3
Glace Bay • NS, Canada ...156 D8
Glacier • WA, United States ...42 E2
Glacier Bay Nat. Park • AK, United States ...49 N4
Glacier Bay Nat. Park & Preserve Park N • AK, United States ...150 [14]
Glacier Nat. Park Park N • MT, United States ...150 [65]
Glacier Nat. Park • MT, United States ...152 B2

Glacier Nat. Park • BC, Canada 155 C4
Glacier Nat. Park **Park N** • BC, Canada 156 [11]
Glacier Peak • WA, United States 42 E2
Gladbeck • Germany 111 B1
Gladenbach • Germany 9 D6
Gladmar • SA, Canada 43 D2
Gladstone • QL, Australia 144 B4
Gladstone • MI, United States 44 B3
Gladstone • MO, United States 46 H3
Glåma • Norway 16 F6
Glamis Castle • United Kingdom 104 B2
Glan • Germany 9 C7
Glan • Sweden 125 F4
Glarner Alpen • Switzerland 119 G3
Glasgow • United Kingdom 104 B3
Glasgow • MT, United States 42 L2
Glasgow • KY, United States 48 E2
Glashütte • Germany 9 I6
Glasriket • Sweden 125 F8
Glass Country • Sweden 125 F8
Glass Mtn • CA, United States 42 E6
Glass Mtns • TX, United States 47 C2
Glass Window Bridge • Bahamas 158 B1
Glassboro • NJ, United States 44 H6
Glasshouse Mtns Nat. Park • QL, Australia 144 B6
Glastonbury • United Kingdom 104 F3
Glastonbury Tor • United Kingdom 104 F3
Glauchau • Germany 9 H6
Glauchau • Germany 13 B7
Glazov • Russian Fed. 17 I3
Glen Canyon • UT, United States 45 G3
Glen Canyon Dam • AZ, United States 153 E1
Glen Canyon Nat. Recreation Area **Park N** • AZ/UT, United States 150 [99]
Glen Canyon Nat. Recreation Area • AZ/UT, United States 153 E1
Glen Eden **Ski** • OT, Canada 149 [27]
Glen Helen • NT, Australia 145 D1
Glen Innes • NS, Australia 34 J5
Glen Shee • United Kingdom 104 B2
Glen Ullin • ND, United States 43 F3
Glenbeigh **Beach** • Ireland 96 [60]
Glenbeigh • Ireland 108 C7
Glencoe • South Africa 134 B1
Glencoe • MN, United States 43 I4
Glencree • Ireland 108 B4
Glendale • WI, United States 44 A4
Glendale • CA, United States 45 C4
Glendale • AZ, United States 45 F5
Glendalough • Ireland 108 B4
Glendive • MT, United States 43 D3
Glendo Reservoir • WY, United States 43 D5
Gleneagles • United Kingdom 104 B1
Glengarriff • Ireland 108 C7
Glenmalure • Ireland 108 B4
Glennallen • AK, United States 49 L3
Glenns Ferry • ID, United States 42 H5
Glenorchy • New Zealand 145 G2
Glenridding • United Kingdom 104 C2
Glenrock • WY, United States 42 M5
Glenrothes • United Kingdom 104 B2
Glens Falls • NY, United States 44 I4
Glenshaw • PA, United States 44 E5
Glenveagh Nat. Park **Park N** • Ireland 89 [38]
Glenwood Springs • CO, United States 45 I2
Gletsch • Switzerland 119 G3
Glifáda • Corfu, Greece 122 B1
Glifáda • Greece 122 D7
Glinde • Germany 8 F3
Glindow • Germany 111 C3
Glittertind • Norway 124 C2
Gliwice • Poland 128 C1
Globe • AZ, United States 153 E3
Glogów • Poland 13 F6
Glomfjord • Norway 16 G3
Glommersträsk • Sweden 16 J4
Glorenza • Italy 121 E3
Glorieuses • Réunion 24 H2
Gloucester • United Kingdom 104 D3
Gloucester • MA, United States 153 D4
Gloucester • VA, United States 153 D11
Gloucester, Cape • Papua New Guinea 35 (1) D2
Gloucestershire • United Kingdom 104 D4
Gloversville • NY, United States 153 D3
Glowno • Poland 13 I6
Glucholazy • Poland 13 G7
Glücksburg **Castle** • Germany 113 [1]
Glückstadt • Germany 8 E3
Glurns • Italy 121 E3
Glyngøre • Denmark 125 F5
Gmund • Germany 112 F7
Gmünd • Austria 119 H8
Gmünd • Austria 128 B4
Gmunden • Austria 119 H4
Gnandstein **Castle** • Germany 113 [186]
Gnarp • Sweden 16 I5
Gnesen • Poland 90 A9
Gnesta • Sweden 125 D3
Gniezno • Poland 13 G5
Gnosjö • Sweden 125 F7
Gnowangerup • WA, Australia 34 C6
Goa **Heritage C** • India 85 [144]
Goa • India 137 B
Goa **Beach** • India 138 E3
Goa Lawah Cave • Bali, Indonesia 143 H4
Goat I. • Trinidad & Tobago 160 T
Goat I. • Antigua & Barbuda 161 J
Goat Point • Antigua & Barbuda 161 J
Goba • Ethiopia 23 G2
Gobabis • Namibia 24 B4
Gobernador Gregores • Argentina 53 B5
Gobi • China/Mongolia 29 D2
Gobo • Japan 30 H8
Goch • Germany 8 B5
Gochas • Namibia 24 B4
Göd • Hungary 13 I10
Godavari • India 28 D5
Godavari, Mouths of the • India 138 D4
Godbout • QU, Canada 156 D1
Gode • Ethiopia 23 G2
Godelbukta Breidvika • Antarctica 54 (1) H2
Gödene • Turkey 123 F3
Goderich • OT, Canada 44 E4
Godhavn • Greenland 39 U3
Godhra • India 28 B4
Godinne • Belgium 109 D15
Gödöllö • Hungary 13 I10
Godoy Cruz • Argentina 52 C5
Gods Lake • MN, Canada 38 M6
Godthåb • Greenland 39 U4
Goéland, Lac-au- • QU, Canada 39 P6
Goelo, Côte du • France 114 C2
Goeree **Beach** • Netherlands 96 [68]
Goeree • Netherlands 109 D10
Goes • Netherlands 5 G3
Gogrial • Sudan 23 D2
Goianésia • Brazil 52 G2
Goiânia • Brazil 52 G2
Goiás • Brazil 52 F2
Goiás [Adm] • Brazil 52 G1
Goiatuba • Brazil 52 G2
Goifulha Fehendhu Atoll • Maldives 138 F1
Going **Ski** • Austria 100 [154]
Göinge • Sweden 125 F11
Góis • Portugal 11 C4
Gojo • Japan 140 B4
Gök Tepe • Turkey 15 K7
Gokarn • India 138 D5
Gokayama **Heritage C** • Japan 85 [192]
Gökçe • Turkey 15 G3
Gökçeada • Turkey 122 D2
Gökova Körfezi • Turkey 15 I7
Göksu • Turkey 15 K3
Göksu • Turkey 123 G3
Göksun • Turkey 123 G2
Göktepe • Turkey 15 J6
Gokwe • Zimbabwe 130 C1
Gol • Norway 124 C4
Gola Forest Reserve **Park** • Sierra Leone 133 [15]
Golan Heights • Syria 135 A2
Golancz • Poland 13 G5
Golaninha • Brazil 53 (1) D3
Gölcük • Turkey 15 K3
Gold Beach • OR, United States 152 B3
Gold Coast • Ghana 22 D4
Gold Coast • QL, Australia 144 B6
Gold Coast • HI, United States 154 G8
Gold Coast • FL, United States 154 H8
Goldap • Poland 13 L3
Goldau • Switzerland 119 G3
Golden • CO, United States 46 C3
Golden Bay • New Zealand 35 D5
Golden Bay • Malta 123 H3
Golden Coast • Sweden 125 F6
Golden Gate • CA, United States 45 A3
Golden Gate Nat. Recreation Area **Park N** • CA, United States 150 [44]
Golden Horsehoe • OT, Canada 155 B9
Golden Mile • South Africa 134 B6
Golden Ring • Russian Fed. 126 C4
Golden Sands • Bulgaria 128 E4
Golden Spike Nat. Hist. Site **Park N** • UT, United States 150 [76]
Golden Triangle • India 137 C2
Golden Triangle • Laos/Myanmar/Thailand 141 D1
Golden Valley • United Kingdom 104 D3
Goldendale • WA, United States 42 E4
Goldsboro • NC, United States 48 H3
Goldsworthy • WA, Australia 34 C4
Goldthwaite • TX, United States 154 J3
Goléa, El • Algeria 20 F2
Goleniów • Poland 13 D4
Goleta • CA, United States 45 C4
Golfe-Juan • France 115 H4
Golfito • Costa Rica 37 E6
Golfo Aranci **Beach** • Sardinia, Italy 96 [137]
Golfo Aranci • Sardinia, Italy 120 C2
Golfo de Chiriqui • Panama 37 E6
Golfo de Santa Clara • Mexico 157 F1
Golija • F.R. of Yugoslavia 14 H6
Golm • Germany 111 C3
Gölmarmara • Turkey 15 I5
Golmud • China 28 F1
Golmud He • China 28 F1
Golo • Corsica, France 115 L2
Goma • Dem. Rep. of Congo 23 D4
Gombe • Nigeria 22 G2
Gombe Nat. Park • Tanzania 130 B1
Gombe Nat. Park **Park** • Tanzania 133 [92]
Gomera • Canary Is. 117 E5
Gómez Palacio • Mexico 40 F6
Gomi • Ethiopia/Sudan 21 F6
Gomo • China 28 E2
Gonabad • Iran 18 G3
Gonaïves • Haiti 159 G2
Gonarezhou Nat. Park • Zimbabwe 130 C4
Gonarezhou Nat. Park **Park** • Zimbabwe 133 [114]
Gonâve, Golfe de la • Haiti 159 G1
Gonâve, I. de • Haiti 158 A2
Gonâve, Ile de la • Haiti 159 G6
Gonbad-e Qabus • Iran 18 G2
Gonder • Ethiopia 21 G5
Gonder **Heritage C** • Ethiopia 85 [99]
Gondia • India 28 C4
Gondomar • Portugal 11 C3
Gönen • Turkey 122 D3
Gönen [Riv] • Turkey 15 I3
Gongbai • Zhuhai, China 139 B1
Gongbo'gyamda • China 28 F3
Gongga Shan • China 29 C5
Gonghe • China 29 C3
Gongola [Adm] • Nigeria 22 G3
Gongola [Riv] • Nigeria 22 G2
Gongshan • China 31 B1
Gonzales • TX, United States 47 F3
Good Hope, Cape of • South Africa 134 C5
Goodenough • Papua New Guinea 35 (1) E2
Goodhouse • South Africa 24 B5
Gooding • ID, United States 152 B4
Goodland • KS, United States 46 E3
Goodlands • Mauritius 132 J2
Goodrich • United Kingdom 104 D3
Goodwick Sands **Beach** • United Kingdom 101 [185]
Goodwood • United Kingdom 104 E3
Goole • United Kingdom 7 L8
Goomalling • WA, Australia 34 C6
Goondiwindi • QL, Australia 144 B6
Goonhilly Downs • United Kingdom 104 F4
Goor • Netherlands 5 J2
Goose Bay • NF, Canada 39 S6
Goose Creek • SC, United States 48 G4
Goose Lake • CA/OR, United States 152 B3
Gooty • India 138 D2
Gopalpur-on-Sea **Beach** • India 138 E4
Göppingen • Germany 9 E8
Gora • New Zealand 145 G4
Gorakhpur • India 137 C4
Gorczanski Nat. Park **Park N** • Poland 89 [96]
Gorczanski Nat. Park • Poland 128 C4
Gorda, Punta • CA, United States 152 C1
Gördes • Turkey 15 J5
Gordion • Turkey 15 N4
Gordon • NE, United States 43 E5
Gordon Reef **Dive** • Red Sea 135 B1
Gordonsville • VA, United States 44 F6
Gordonvale • QL, Australia 34 I3
Goré • Chad 22 H3
Gore • Ethiopia 23 F2
Gore Mtn **Ski** • NY, United States 149 [195]
Gorée, Ile de **Heritage C** • Senegal 85 [109]
Göreme • Turkey 123 G2
Göreme Nat. Park **Heritage N** • Turkey 83 [71]
Göreme Nat. Park **Heritage C** • Turkey 86 [228]
Göreme Nat. Park • Turkey 123 G2
Görenez Dagi • Turkey 15 J5
Gorey • Channel Is. 106 C
Gorgan • Iran 18 F2
Gorgona • Colombia 51 B3
Gorgona, I. di • Italy 121 E10
Gorinchem • Netherlands 109 F4
Gorízia • Italy 121 E4
Gorjanci • Croatia/Slovenia 14 C4
Gorkovskoye Vdkhr. • Russian Fed. 17 G3
Gørlev **Beach** • Denmark 96 [43]
Gørlev • Denmark 125 F10
Gorlice • Poland 128 C4
Gorling Bluff Lighthouse • Cayman Is. 159 E4
Görlitz • Germany 9 J5
Gorna Orjahovica • Bulgaria 128 E3
Gorno-Altaysk • Russian Fed. 26 O7
Gornozavodsk • Russian Fed. 29 K1
Gorochan • Ethiopia 23 F2
Gorodets • Russian Fed. 17 G3
Goroka • Papua New Guinea 35 (1) D2
Gorong, Kepulauan • Indonesia 32 (1) D3
Gorongosa, Parque Nac. da **Park** • Mozambique 133 [140]
Gorongoza, Serra da • Mozambique 24 E3
Gorontalo • Indonesia 32 (1) B2
Górowo Ilaweckie • Poland 13 J3
Gorriti, I. de • Uruguay 163 D2
Gorski Kotar • Croatia/Slovenia 14 B4
Gort • Ireland 108 C4
Gortipohl **Ski** • Austria 100 [126]
Górtis • Crete, Greece 123 E7
Gortyna • Crete, Greece 123 E7
Goru, Virful • Romania 14 N4
Gorumna I. • Ireland 108 C3
Gory Stolowe Nat. Park **Park N** • Poland 89 [98]
Gorzów Wielkopolski • Poland 13 E5
Gosau **Ski** • Austria 100 [182]
Gosau • Austria 119 H4
Gose • Japan 140 B4
Gosford • NS, Australia 144 C2
Goshen • Jamaica 159 F2
Goshen • NY, United States 153 D7
Gosier • Guadeloupe 161 L
Goslar • Germany 8 F5
Goslar **Heritage C** • Germany 86 [46]
Gospic • Croatia 128 D3
Gosport • United Kingdom 7 K11
Gossi • Mali 20 E5
Gossilies [Apt] • Belgium 109 D14
Gostivar • F.Y.R. of Macedonia 15 B2
Gostyn • Poland 13 G6
Gostynin • Poland 13 I5
Göta älv • Sweden 125 F2
Göta kanal • Sweden 125 F4
Göteborg **Beach** • Sweden 96 [1]
Göteborg • Sweden 125 F6
Göteborg och Bohus • Sweden 125 F2
Gotel Mtns • Cameroon/Nigeria 22 G3
Gotenba • Japan 140 C3
Götene • Sweden 125 F3
Gotha • Germany 9 F6
Gothenburg • Sweden 125 F6
Gothenburg • NE, United States 46 E2
Gothèye • Niger 20 F6
Gotland • Sweden 16 J8
Goto Meer • Bonaire 160 W
Goto-retto • Japan 30 E8
Gotowasi • Indonesia 32 (1) C2
Gotse Delchev • Bulgaria 14 K8
Gotska Sandön • Sweden 16 J7
Gotsu • Japan 30 G7
Göttingen • Germany 8 E5
Gottorf **Castle** • Germany 113 [2]
Gouda • Netherlands 109 F3
Goudiri • Senegal 20 C6
Goudoumaria • Niger 22 G2
Gough I. • Atlantic Ocean 19 C9
Gough I. Wildlife Reserve **Heritage N** • Atlantic Ocean 83 [111]
Gouin, Réservoir • QU, Canada 39 Q7
Goulburn • NS, Australia 144 C2
Goulburn [Riv] • VI, Australia 144 C3
Goulimine • Morocco 131 D5
Gouménissa • Greece 14 J9
Gouna • Cameroon 23 A2
Goundam • Mali 20 E5
Gourdon • France 10 G9
Gouré • Niger 20 H6
Gouritsmond • South Africa 134 C6
Gourma Rharous • Mali 20 E5
Gournay-en-Bray • France 115 E1
Gourniá • Crete, Greece 123 E8
Gourock • United Kingdom 106 B2
Gourock Range • NS, Australia 144 C2
Gourrama • Morocco 20 E2
Gouverneur • NY, United States 44 H3
Gouverneur, Anse du • St Barthélemy 160 E
Goúves **Beach** • Crete, Greece 97 [214]
Goúves • Crete, Greece 123 E3
Gouviá • Corfu, Greece 122 B1
Gouyave • Grenada 160 S
Gov'Altyan Nuruu • Mongolia 29 C2
Gove Peninsula • NT, Australia 34 G2
Govena, mys • Russian Fed. 27 S5
Governador Valadares • Brazil 163 C2
Govind Ballabh Pant Sagar • India 137 C8
Goya • Argentina 52 E4
Göynük • Turkey 15 L3
Göynük **Beach** • Turkey 97 [228]
Göynük • Turkey 123 F3
Goz Beida • Chad 23 C1
Gozha Co • China 28 D1
Gozo • Malta 123 H1
Graaff-Reinet • South Africa 134 C4
Graal-Müritz • Germany 8 H2
Graal-Müritz **Beach** • Germany 96 [33]
Graal-Müritz **Spa** • Germany 113 [c22]
Grabo • Côte d'Ivoire 22 C4
Grächen • Switzerland 119 G6
Gracias a Dios, Cabo • Nicaragua 37 E4
Graciosa **Beach** • Azores 96 [103]
Graciosa • Canary Is. 117 E3
Graciosa • Azores 118 B2
Gradaus, Serra dos • Brazil 51 G5
Grado • Spain 11 E1
Grado **Beach** • Italy 96 [166]
Grado • Italy 121 E8
Græsted-Gilleleje **Beach** • Denmark 96 [41]
Grafton • NS, Australia 34 J5
Grafton • ND, United States 43 H2
Grafton • WV, United States 44 E6
Grafton, Mt • NV, United States 45 E2
Graham • TX, United States 154 J1
Graham I. • BC, Canada 38 E6
Graham Land • Antarctica 54 (1) II3
Graham Moore, Cape • NU, Canada 39 P2
Graham, Mt • AZ, United States 45 H5
Grahamstown • South Africa 134 C4
Grain Coast • Liberia/Sierra Leone 22 B3
Grainau • Germany 112 F6
Grajau • Brazil 53 (1) B3
Grajewo • Poland 13 L4
Gram • Denmark 125 F13
Gramat, Causse de • France 115 G4
Grampian Mtns • United Kingdom 6 H5
Grampians, The • VI, Australia 144 A7
Gramvoúxa • Crete, Greece 123 E1
Gramvoúxa, Akria • Crete, Greece 123 E1
Gran • Hungary 90 A14
Gran • Norway 124 B2
Gran Cairo • Mexico 157 H2
Gran Canaria • Canary Is. 116 E4
Gran Chaco • Argentina/Paraguay 52 D3
Gran Desierto del Pinacate, Parque Natural del • Mexico 157 F1
Gran Paradiso • Italy 121 E5
Gran Paradiso, Parco Naz. del **Park N** • Italy 89 [85]
Gran Paradiso, Parco Naz. del • Italy 121 E5
Gran Piedra • Cuba 158 D8
Gran Pilastro • Austria/Italy 120 B1
Gran San Bernardo • Italy/Switzerland 12 B3
Gran Sasso d'Italia • Italy 121 F2
Gran Tarajal • Fuerteventura, Canary Is. 117 E2
Granada **Heritage C** • Spain 86 [110]
Granada • Spain 116 B3
Granada • Nicaragua 37 D5
Granbury, Lake • TX, United States 47 F1
Granby • CO, United States 45 I1
Granby • QU, Canada 155 B8
Grand • SD, United States 43 F4
Grand Anse • Grenada 160 S
Grand Anse Bay • Grenada 160 S
Grand Bahama I. • Bahamas 158 B2
Grand Baie • Mauritius 132 J2
Grand Ballon • France 9 C9
Grand Bank • NF, Canada 156 D3
Grand Bassam • Côte d'Ivoire 22 D3
Grand Bassin • Mauritius 132 J3
Grand Bay • Dominica 161 M
Grand Bernard • Réunion 132 H3
Grand Bourg • Guadeloupe 161 L
Grand Brière • France 114 C4
Grand Caicos • Turks & Caicos Is. 158 C1
Grand Canal • Ireland 7 E8
Grand Canal • China 29 F4
Grand Canyon • AZ, United States 153 E1
Grand Canyon Nat. Park **Heritage N** • AZ, United States 82 [13]
Grand Canyon Nat. Park **Park N** • AZ, United States 150 [98]
Grand Canyon Nat. Park • AZ, United States 153 E1
Grand Canyon of Pennsylvania • PA, United States 153 D5
Grand Canyon of the East • NY, United States 153 D1
Grand Canyon Village • AZ, United States 153 E1
Grand Case • St Martin 160 D
Grand Causses • France 10 I9
Grand Cayman • Cayman Is. 159 E
Grand Cess • Liberia 22 C4
Grand Coulee • WA, United States 42 F3
Grand Coulee Dam • WA, United States 152 B2
Grand Erg Occidental • Algeria 20 F2
Grand Erg Oriental • Algeria/Tunisia 20 G2
Grand Etang • Réunion 132 H2
Grand Etang • Grenada 160 S
Grand Etang Nat. Park • Grenada 160 S
Grand Falls • NB, Canada 156 D1
Grand Falls • NF, Canada 156 D3
Grand Fond • St Barthélemy 160 E
Grand Forks • BC, Canada 42 F2
Grand Forks • ND, United States 43 H3
Grand Gaube • Mauritius 132 J2
Grand Harbour • Malta 123 H4
Grand Haven • MI, United States 44 B4
Grand I. • MI, United States 44 B2
Grand I. • NE, United States 46 F2
Grand Isle • LA, United States 48 B6
Grand Junction **Ski** • CO, United States 149 A
Grand Junction • CO, United States 45 H2
Grand Lake • LA, United States 153 F3
Grand Lake • NF, Canada 156 D3
Grand Lake • NB, Canada 156 D7
Grand Manan I. • NB, Canada 156 D6
Grand Marais • MI, United States 44 C2
Grand Mère • QU, Canada 44 I2
Grand Mesa • CO, United States 45 I2
Grand Morin, Vallée du • France 115 E4
Grand Port • Mauritius 132 J4
Grand Portage • MN, United States 43 L3
Grand Portage Nat. Mon. **Park N** • MN, United States 151 [155]
Grand Prairie • TX, United States 154 J1
Grand Pré • NS, Canada 156 D7
Grand Pressigny, le [Château] • France 114 D4
Grand Rapids • MN, Canada 38 L6
Grand Rapids • MN, United States 43 J3
Grand Rapids • MI, United States 44 C4
Grand Récif de Cook • New Caledonia 35 (2) A2
Grand River • IA/MO, United States 46 H2
Grand' Rivière • Martinique 161 N
Grand Rivière Noire • Mauritius 132 J3
Grand Rivière SE • Mauritius 132 J4
Grand Roy • Grenada 160 S
Grand St-Bernard, Col du • Italy/Switzerland 119 G6
Grand Teton • WY, United States 42 J5
Grand Teton Nat. Park **Park N** • WY, United States 150 [74]
Grand Teton Nat. Park • WY, United States 42 J5
Grand Traverse Bay • MI, United States 44 C3
Grand Turk • Turks & Caicos Is. 158 C2
Grand Turk Wall • Turks & Caicos Is. 158 C2
Grand-Bornand, le **Ski** • France 100 [20]
Grand-Ilet • Réunion 132 H1
Grand-Motte, la **Beach** • France 96 [130]
Grand-Terre • Guadeloupe 161 L
Grand-Village-Plage, le **Beach** • France 96 [84]
Grandcamp-Maisy • France 10 D4
Grande • Brazil 52 G2
Grande, Bahía • Argentina 53 C6
Grande, Baía de I. • Brazil 163 C3
Grande Casse • France 10 L8
Grande Cayemite • Haiti 159 G5
Grande Comore • Comoros 24 G2
Grande, I. • Brazil 163 C3
Grande Lande, Ecomusée de la • France 115 G3
Grande Morin • France 5 G6
Grande Pointe • St Barthélemy 160 E
Grande Prairie • AL, Canada 155 C2
Grande, Rio • Bolivia 52 D2
Grande, Rio • Jamaica 159 F4
Grande, Serra • Brazil 53 (1) C3
Grande Vigie, Pointe de la • Guadeloupe 161 L
Grandfather Mtn • NC, United States 48 G2
Grandi, Playa • Curaçao 160 X
Grândola • Portugal 11 C6
Grândola **Beach** • Portugal 96 [99]
Grands-Jardins Prov. Park • QU, Canada 156 D1
Grandview • MN, Canada 43 F1
Grandview • MO, United States 46 H3
Grandville • MI, United States 44 C4
Grange-over-Sands • United Kingdom 104 C4
Grangemouth • United Kingdom 104 B4
Grangeville • ID, United States 42 G4
Granhult • Sweden 125 F8
Granit Rose, Côte de • France 114 C2
Granite City • IL, United States 46 J3
Granite Mtns • WY, United States 42 L5
Granite Peak • MT, United States 42 K4
Granite Peak • UT, United States 45 F1
Granite Peak • NV, United States 152 C2
Granites, The • NT, Australia 34 F4
Granitz **Castle** • Germany 113 [227]
Grankulla • Finland 125 E4
Granma, Parque Desembarco del • Cuba 158 D7
Granma, Parque Nac. Desembarco del **Heritage N** • Cuba 82 [28]
Gränna • Sweden 125 F3
Granollers • Spain 117 D4
Grant, Mt • NV, United States 45 C2
Grant-Kohrs Ranch Nat. Hist. Site **Park N** • MT, United States 150 [66]
Grantham • United Kingdom 7 L9
Grantley Adams [Apt] • Barbados 161 O
Grants • NM, United States 45 I4
Grants Pass • OR, United States 152 B3
Grantsville • UT, United States 45 F1
Granville • France 114 C2
Grapevine • TX, United States 47 F1
Grapevine Peak • NV, United States 45 D3
Graskop • South Africa 24 E4
Grasmere • United Kingdom 104 C2
Grasmere • BC, Canada 42 H2
Grasmoor • United Kingdom 104 C1
Gräsö • Sweden 16 J6
Grass I. • Hong Kong, China 139 B4
Grass Valley • CA, United States 152 C3
Grasse • France 115 H4
Grasslands Nat. Park • SA, Canada 42 L2
Grasslands Nat. Park **Park N** • SA, Canada 156 [20]
Grassy Butte • ND, United States 43 E3
Gråsten • Denmark 125 F13
Grau-du-Roi, le **Beach** • France 96 [131]
Graus • Spain 11 L2
Grave [Battlefield] • Netherlands 109 D11
Grave, la **Ski** • France 100 [60]
Grave, la • France 115 F4
Grave, Pointe de • France 115 G1
Gravelbourg • SA, Canada 42 L2
Gravelines • France 5 F3
Gravenhurst • OT, Canada 155 B5
Graves • France 114 B3
Gravesend • United Kingdom 104 E1
Gravina in Puglia • Italy 12 K8
Gravois, Pointe-à- • Haiti 159 G5
Gravonne • Corsica, France 115 L3
Grays Harbor • WA, United States 152 B1
Grays Lake • ID, United States 42 J5
Graz • Austria 13 E10
Graz **Heritage C** • Austria 86 [125]
Great Abaco • Bahamas 158 B1
Great Australian Bight • Australia 34 E6
Great Barrier I. • New Zealand 35 E3
Great Barrier Reef **Heritage N** • Australia 83 [144]
Great Barrier Reef • QL, Australia 144 B
Great Barrier Reef Marine Park • QL, Australia 34 J4
Great Barrington • MA, United States 44 I4
Great Basin • NV, United States 152 C2
Great Basin Nat. Park **Park N** • NV, United States 150 [60]
Great Basin Nat. Park • NV, United States 152 C4
Great Bear • NT, Canada 38 G4
Great Bear Lake • NT/NU, Canada 38 G3
Great Bend • KS, United States 46 F3
Great Bird I. • Antigua & Barbuda 161 K
Great Blasket I. • Ireland 108 C7
Great Camanoe • British Virgin Is. 160 B
Great Coxwell Barn • United Kingdom 104 D4
Great Cumbrae I. • United Kingdom 106 B2
Great Dismal Swamp • VA, United States 153 D11
Great Divide Basin • WY, United States 42 K6
Great Dividing Range • Australia 34 I4
Great Exhibition Bay • New Zealand 35 D2
Great Exuma • Bahamas 158 B3
Great Falls • MT, United States 42 J3
Great Falls of the Potomac • MD/VA, United States 153 D9
Great Fish • South Africa 134 C4
Great Gable • United Kingdom 104 C1
Great Gorge Resort Action Park **Park L** • NJ, United States 151 [MM]
Great Gorge Resort Action Park • NJ, United States 153 D7
Great Harbour Cay • Bahamas 158 B1
Great Harbour Deep • NF, Canada 156 D5
Great Inagua • Bahamas 158 B4
Great Karoo • South Africa 134 C3
Great Keppel I. • QL, Australia 144 B4
Great Lakes • Canada/United States 152 A4
Great Malvern • United Kingdom 104 D3
Great Nicobar • India 28 F7
Great Oasis, The • Egypt 131 F3
Great Palm I. • QL, Australia 144 B1
Great Pedro Bluff • Jamaica 159 F3
Great Plains • Canada/United States 40
Great [Riv] • Jamaica 159 F1
Great [Riv] • Grenada 160 S
Great Ruaha • Tanzania 130 B4
Great Sacandaga Lake • NY, United States 153 D3
Great Sale Cay • Bahamas 49 D4
Great Salt Lake • UT, United States 42 I6
Great Salt Lake Desert • UT, United States 45 F1
Great Salt Pond • St Maarten 160 D
Great Salt Pond • St Kitts & Nevis 161 G
Great Sand Dunes Nat. Mon. **Park N** • CO, United States 150 [94]
Great Sand Hills • SA, Canada 43 B1
Great Sandy Desert • WA, Australia 34 D4
Great Sandy Desert • OR, United States 152 B4
Great Skellig • Ireland 108 C7
Great Slave Lake • NT, Canada 38 H4
Great Smoky Mtns Nat. Park **Heritage N** • NC/TN, United States 82 [17]
Great Smoky Mtns Nat. Park **Park N** • NC/TN, United States 151 [227]
Great Smoky Mtns Nat. Park • NC/TN, United States 48 F3
Great Sound • Bermuda 159 J3
Great St James I. • US Virgin Is. 160 Z
Great Tobago • British Virgin Is. 160 B
Great Torrington • United Kingdom 104 F2
Great Valley • TN/VA, United States 41 J4
Great Victoria Desert • SA/WA, Australia 34 E5
Great Victoria Desert Nature Reserve • SA/WA, Australia 34 E5
Great Wall • China 29 D3
Great Wall **Heritage C** • China 85 [163]
Great White Heron Nat. Wildlife Refuge • FL, United States 154 H7
Great Yarmouth • United Kingdom 7 N9
Great Yarmouth **Beach** • United Kingdom 101 [49-50]
Great Zimbabwe Nat. Mon. **Heritage C** • Zimbabwe 85 [116]
Great Zimbabwe Nat. Mon. • Zimbabwe 130 C4
Greater Antilles • West Indies 37 G4
Greater St Lucia Wetland Park **Heritage N** • South Africa 83 [107]
Greater St Lucia Wetland Park **Park** • South Africa 133 [132]
Greater St Lucia Wetland Park • South Africa 134 B2
Greater Sunda Is. • Indonesia 32 E4
Greatstone-on-Sea **Beach** • United Kingdom 101 [78]
Grebbestad • Sweden 125 F2
Gréboun, Mt • Niger 20 G4
Greco, Cape • Cyprus 123 J4
Gredos, Sierra de • Spain 11 F4
GREECE • Europe 15
Greek Peak **Ski** • NY, United States 149 [188]
Greek Peak • NY, United States 153 D2
Greeley • CO, United States 46 C2
Greem Bell, Ostrov • Russian Fed. 126 A3
Green • KY, United States 48 D2
Green Bay • WI, United States 44 A3
Green Bay [Bay] • MI/WI, United States 44 B3
Green I. • QL, Australia 144 B1
Green I. • Grenada 160 S
Green I. • Antigua & Barbuda 161 K
Green Meadows Petting Farm • FL, United States 151 C2
Green [Riv] • UT/WY, United States 45 H2
Green River • WY, United States 42 K6
Green River • UT, United States 45 G2
Green River Reservoir • KY, United States 48 E2
Green Turtle Cay • Bahamas 158 B1
Green Valley • AZ, United States 153 E3
Greenbelt Park **Park N** • MD, United States 151 [271]
Greencastle • IN, United States 44 B6
Greeneville • TN, United States 48 F2
Greenfield • WI, United States 44 A4
Greenfield • IN, United States 44 C6
Greenfield • OH, United States 44 D6
Greenfield • MA, United States 44 I4
Greenfield • MO, United States 46 I4
GREENLAND • N. America 36 M2
Greenland Sea • Arctic Ocean 54 P2
Greenock • United Kingdom 104 B3
Greensboro • NC, United States 48 H2
Greensburg • IN, United States 44 C6
Greensburg • KS, United States 46 F4
Greenville • Liberia 22 C3
Greenville • MI, United States 44 C4
Greenville • OH, United States 44 C5
Greenville • PA, United States 44 E5
Greenville • AL, United States 48 D5
Greenville • SC, United States 48 F3
Greenville • NC, United States 48 I3
Greenville • MS, United States 153 F2
Greenville • TX, United States 154 J2
Greenwich • United Kingdom 7 M10
Greenwich • CT, United States 44 I5
Greenwood • IN, United States 44 B6
Greenwood • SC, United States 48 F3
Greenwood • MS, United States 153 F2
Greenwood Great House • Jamaica 159 F1
Greenwood, Lake • SC, United States 48 G3
Greer • SC, United States 48 F3
Greers Ferry Lake • AR, United States 46 I5
Greeson, Lake • AR, United States 46 I5
Gregorio • Brazil 51 C5
Gregory Lake • WA, Australia 34 E3
Gregory, Lake • SA, Australia 34 G5
Greifenstein **Castle** • Germany 113 [40]
Greifswald • Germany 8 I2
Greifswalder Bodden • Germany 8 I2
Greiggs • St Vincent & Gren. 161 Q
Grein • Austria 13 D9
Greiz • Germany 9 H6
Gremikha • Russian Fed. 17 F1
Grenå **Beach** • Denmark 96 [47]
Grenå • Denmark 125 F10
GRENADA • West Indies 160 S
Grenada • MS, United States 48 C4
Grenada Lake • MS, United States 48 C4
Grenen • Denmark 125 F6
Grenfell • SA, Canada 43 E1
Grenoble • France 115 F3
Grenville • Grenada 160 S
Grenville Bay • Grenada 160 S
Grenville, Cape • QL, Australia 34 H2
Gréolières-les-Neiges • France 115 H2
Gresham • OR, United States 42 D4
Gresik • Java, Indonesia 143 J4
Gressåmoen Nat. Park **Park N** • Norway 89 [11]
Gressoney-la-Trinité **Ski** • Italy 100 [206]
Gressoney-la-Trinité • Italy 121 E1
Gressoney-St Jean **Ski** • Italy 100 [206]
Gretna • LA, United States 48 B6
Greve **Beach** • Denmark 96 [38]
Greve Coeur • MO, United States 46 J3
Greven • Germany 8 C4
Grevená • Greece 15 C3
Grevenbroich • Germany 111 B3
Grevesmühlen • Germany 8 G3
Grey Is. • NF, Canada 156 D5
Grey Range • QL, Australia 34 H5
Greybull • WY, United States 42 K4
Greymouth • New Zealand 35 C6
Greystones **Beach** • Ireland 96 [55]
Greystones • Ireland 108 B4
Greytown • New Zealand 35 E5
Greytown • South Africa 134 B3
Gribës • Albania 15 A3
Gribingu • Central African Rep./Chad 22 H3
Griesheim • Germany 5 L5
Griesheim • Germany 112 E4
Griffin • GA, United States 48 E4
Griffith • NS, Australia 144 C1
Grimari • Central African Rep. 22 H3
Grimaud **Beach** • France 96 [133]
Grimentz • Switzerland 119 G6
Grimmen • Germany 8 I2
Grimsby • United Kingdom 7 L8
Grimsby • OT, Canada 44 F4
Grimselpass • Switzerland 119 G3
Grímsey • Iceland 16 (1) E1
Grímsstadir • Iceland 16 (1) E2
Grimstad • Norway 125 F1
Grindavik • Iceland 16 (1) B3
Grindelwald **Ski** • Switzerland 100 [103]
Grindelwald • Switzerland 119 G2
Grindsted • Denmark 125 F9
Grinnell • IA, United States 46 I2
Grintavec • Slovenia 13 D11
Gripsholm • Sweden 125 D3
Gris Gris, le • Mauritius 132 J3

Gris-Nez, Cap • France 10 G3
Grise Fjord • NU, Canada 36 I2
Grisons • Switzerland 119 G4
Grisslehamn • Sweden 125 D2
Grizedale Forest •
United Kingdom 104 C4
Grmec • Bosnia-Herz. 14 D5
Grodzisk Mazowiecki • Poland 13 J5
Groix, I. de • France 114 C3
Grójec • Poland 13 J6
Grömitz Spa • Germany .... 113 [c16]
Gröne Lunds Tivoli Park L •
Sweden .... 98 [7]
Gronant Beach • United Kingdom .. 101 [214]
Grönau • Germany 8 C4
Grönenbach • Germany 112 F2
Grong • Norway 16 G4
Groningen • Netherlands 109 D4
Groningen [Adm] • Netherlands .. 109 D4
Groot • South Africa 134 C3
Groot-Karasberge • Namibia 24 B5
Grootbaai • St Maarten .... 160 D
Groote Eylandt • NT, Australia 34 G2
Groote Peel, Nat. Park •
Netherlands 109 D11
Grootfontein • Namibia 24 B3
Gros Islet • St Lucia .... 161 P
Gros Morne • Haiti 159 G2
Gros Morne • NF, Canada 156 D3
Gros Morne Nat. Park Heritage N •
NF, Canada .... 82 [8]
Gros Morne Nat. Park •
NF, Canada 156 D3
Gros Morne Nat. Park Park N •
NF, Canada .... 156 [37]
Gros Piton • St Lucia .... 161 P
Gross-Gerau • Germany 112 E4
Grossari Ski • Austria .... 100 [172]
Grossbeeren • Germany 111 C4
Grosse Gay, Ile • Haiti 159 G6
Grosser Arber • Germany 9 I7
Großer Feldberg • Germany 112 E2
Grosser Inselsberg • Germany 9 F6
Grosser Müggelsee • Germany 8 F2
Grosser Plöner See • Germany 8 E1
Grosser Seddiner See • Germany 111 C3
Grosser Zernsee • Germany 111 C3
Grosserdhünne Stausee • Germany .. 111 B4
Grosseto • Italy 121 E11
Grosseto-Prugna Beach •
Corsica, France .... 96 [135]
Grosseto-Prugna •
Corsica, France 115 L3
Grossglockner • Austria 119 H8
Grossostheim • Germany 9 E7
Grossräschen • Germany 8 J5
Grossrotte • Austria 119 H7
Grossseditz Castle • Germany .... 113 [189]
Grossvenediger • Austria 13 B10
Grosswardein • Romania 90 A14
Grotli • Norway 124 C2
Grottaglie • Italy 12 L8
Grottammare • Italy 12 G5
Grou • Morocco 131 D1
Grouse Creek Mtns •
NV/UT, United States 42 H6
Grove City • OH, United States 44 D6
Grove City • PA, United States 44 E5
Grover Beach •
CA, United States 45 B4
Grozny • Russian Fed. 17 H6
Grudovo • Bulgaria 128 E3
Grudziadz • Poland 13 H4
Gruissan Beach • France .... 96 [129]
Grumeti • Tanzania 23 E4
Grünau • Namibia 24 B5
Grünberg • Germany 112 D2
Grundy • VA, United States 48 F2
Grundy Lake Prov. Park •
OT, Canada 155 B3
Grünes Schloss, Weimar Castle •
Germany .... 113 [184]
Grunewald • Germany 111 C3
Grünstadt • Germany 112 D4
Grünthal • Germany 111 C2
Grüsch • Switzerland 119 G4
Gruver • TX, United States 46 E4
Gruyères • Switzerland 119 F2
Gryazovets • Russian Fed. 126 C2
Gryfice • Poland 13 E4
Gryfino • Poland 13 D4
Gryon Ski • Switzerland .... 100 [84]
Gryon • Switzerland 119 G6
Gryt • Sweden 125 F4
Grytviken • South Georgia 54 (1) B4
Gstaad • Switzerland 119 G6
Gstaad-Saanenland Ski •
Switzerland .... 100 [87]
Guacanayabo, Golfo de • Cuba 158 D7
Guadalajara • Spain 117 C3
Guadalajara • Spain 11 H4
Guadalajara Heritage C • Mexico .... 84 [16]
Guadalcanal • Solomon Is. 35 (1) J2
Guadaleste • Spain 117 C2
Guadalimar • Spain 11 H6
Guadalope • Spain 11 K4
Guadalquivir • Spain 11 F7
Guadalupe • Spain 11 F7
Guadalupe Heritage C • Spain .... 86 [105]
Guadalupe • Chihuahua, Mexico 47 A2
Guadalupe • Nuevo León, Mexico .. 47 D5
Guadalupe • TX, United States 154 J5
Guadalupe [I.] • Mexico 36 F7
Guadalupe Mtns •
NM, United States 47 B1
Guadalupe Mtns Nat. Park Park N •
TX, United States .... 150 [134]
Guadalupe Mtns Nat. Park •
TX, United States 47 B2
Guadarrama, Sierra de • Spain 11 G4
GUADELOUPE • West Indies .... 161 L
Guadiana • Portugal/Spain 11 D7
Guadiana, Bahía de • Cuba 158 D1
Guadirikri Caves • Aruba .... 160 Y
Guadix • Spain 116 B4
Guaíba • Brazil 52 F5
Guáimaro • Cuba 158 D7
Guaiquinima • Venezuela 51 E2
Guaira • Brazil 52 F3
Guájaba, Cayo • Cuba 158 D7
Guajara Mirim • Brazil 51 D6
Guajataca • Puerto Rico 159 H1
Guaje, Llano el • Mexico 47 C4
Guajira, Península de •
Colombia 51 C1
Guakolak, Tanjung •
Java, Indonesia 143 J1
Gualdo Tadino • Italy 90 A13
Gualeguay • Argentina 163 D1
Gualeguaychú • Argentina 163 D1
GUAM • Pacific Ocean 33 F4
Guamá Indian Village • Cuba 158 D2
Guampi, Sierra de • Venezuela 37 H6
Guamúchil • Mexico 157 F4
Guana I. • British Virgin Is. .... 160 B
Guanacaste, Area de Conservación
Heritage N • Costa Rica .... 82 [24]
Guanaja • Honduras 160 A11
Guanajay • Cuba 158 D1
Guanajuato Heritage C • Mexico .... 84 [17]
Guanajuato • Mexico 157 F4
Guanajuato [Adm] • Mexico 37 (1) B1
Guanare • Venezuela 51 D2
Guane • Cuba 158 D1
Guangde • China 139 C3
Guangchang • China 139 A7
Guangmao Shan • China 31 C1
Guangming Ding • China 139 C3
Guangxi Zhuangzu Zizhiqu •
China 29 D6
Guangzhou • China 139 B1

Guangzhou East • China 139 B2
Guánica • Puerto Rico 159 H3
Guanimar, Playa • Cuba 158 D1
Guantánamo • Cuba 158 D8
Guantánamo Bay • Cuba 158 D8
Guapay • Bolivia 52 D2
Guapi • Colombia 51 B6
Guapí • Bolivia/Brazil 51 E6
Guaqui • Bolivia 52 C2
Guarabira • Brazil 53 (1) D3
Guarapari • Brazil 163 C2
Guarapuava • Brazil 52 F4
Guarda • Portugal 11 D4
Guarda [Adm] • Portugal 118 A1
Guardalatarca, Playa • Cuba 158 D8
Guardavacca • Cuba 158 D8
Guardamar del Segura Beach •
Spain .... 96 [118]
Guardamar del Segura • Spain 117 C3
Guàrdia Sanfranondi • Italy 121 G2
Guarujá • Brazil 163 C3
Guarulhos • Brazil 163 C3
Guarulhos [Apt] • Brazil 163 C3
Guasave • Mexico 157 F4
GUATEMALA • C. America 37 C4
Guatemala City • Guatemala 37 C5
Guaviare • Colombia 51 D3
Guaxupé • Brazil 163 C1
Guayama • Puerto Rico 159 H4
Guayanilla, Bahía de •
Puerto Rico 159 H3
Guayaquil • Ecuador 51 A4
Guayaquil, Golfo de • Ecuador 51 A4
Guaymas • Mexico 157 F2
Gubakha • Russian Fed. 26 I6
Guban • Somalia 23 H1
Gubbat Sawqirah • Oman 18 G6
Gúbbio • Italy 121 E12
Guben • Germany 8 J5
Gubin • Poland 8 J5
Gúdar, Sierra de • Spain 11 K4
Gudbrandsdalen • Norway 16 E6
Gudhjem • Denmark 125 F16
Gudur • Turkey 15 N3
Guéd, Mt • Chad 138 D7
Güeguen, Lac • QU, Canada 44 G1
Guellala • Tunisia 131 E6
Guelma • Algeria 20 G1
Guelph • OT, Canada 44 E4
Guelta Zemmur • Western Sahara .. 20 C3
Guène • Benin 20 F6
Guéra, Massif de • Chad 21 C5
Guérande • France 114 C4
Guéret • France 115 G2
Guernica • Spain 11 I1
Guernsey • Channel Is. 7 J12
Guernsey • WY, United States 43 D5
Guerrero • Mexico 47 D3
Guerrero [Adm] • Mexico 37 (1) B2
Guerrero Negro • Mexico 157 F1
Guge • Ethiopia 23 G2
Gugliones • Italy 12 I7
Guiana Highlands • S. America 51 E2
Guiana I. • Antigua & Barbuda .... 161 K
Guide • China 29 C3
Guidel Beach • France .... 96 [81]
Guidel • France 114 C3
Guider • Cameroon 23 A2
Guiglo • Côte d'Ivoire 22 C3
Guignes • France 115 E4
Guildford • United Kingdom 104 E3
Guilford Courthouse Nat. Military Park
Park N • NC, United States .... 151 [240]
Guilin • China 29 E5
Güímar • Tenerife, Canary Is. 116 E1
Guimarães • Portugal 11 D3
Guin • AL, United States 48 D4
Guincho Cay • Bahamas 158 D3
GUINEA • Africa 22 B2
Guinea, Gulf of • Africa 22 F4
GUINEA-BISSAU • Africa 20 B6
Güines • Cuba 158 D2
Guingamp • France 114 C2
Guiria • Venezuela 51 E1
Guiuan • Philippines 31 H4
Guixi • China 31 F1
Guiyang • China 29 D5
Guizhou • China 139 A7
Gujarat • India 28 B4
Gujranwala • Pakistan 28 B2
Gujrat • Pakistan 28 B2
Gulbarga • India 138 D2
Gulbene • Latvia 126 B4
Gulen • Norway 124 B2
Gulf Coast of FL, United States .. 154 H5
Gulf cruise area • Asia 81 A7
Gulf Is. Nat. Seashore Park N •
FL/MS, United States .... 151 [213]
Gulf Is. Nat. Seashore •
FL/MS, United States 154 H1
Gulf of Alaska •
AK, United States 49 M4
Gulf Shores • AL, United States 48 D5
Gulf, The • Asia 18 F4
Gulfport • FL, United States 49 B4
Gulfport • MS, United States 153 F4
Gulfstream Park •
FL, United States 154 H8
Gulhi • Maldives 138 F4
Guliston • Uzbekistan 26 K9
Gulkana • AK, United States 38 B4
Gull Harbor • MN, Canada 43 H1
Gull Lake • SA, Canada 42 K1
Gulane Bents Beach •
United Kingdom .... 101 [15]
Gullivers Kingdom Park L •
United Kingdom .... 98 [26]
Gullspång • Sweden 125 F3
Güllük • Turkey 122 D9
Güllük Körfezi • Turkey 15 I6
Gulmarg Hill Sta • India 138 E1
Gülnar • Turkey 123 G3
Gülpinar • Turkey 15 I4
Gulu • Uganda 23 E3
Gumbiri, Jabal • Sudan 18 F2
Gümdag • Turkmenistan 18 F2
Gumma • Japan 140 A4
Gummersbach • Germany 111 B4
Gummi • Nigeria 20 G6
Gümüssu • Turkey 15 K5
Gun Bay • Cayman Is. 159 L4
Gun Hill Tower • Barbados .... 161 O
Guna • Ethiopia 21 G5
Gundagai • Australia 123 C4
Güngör • Dem. Rep. of Congo 23 B5
Gunpar • SA, Canada 38 J5
Gunnbjørn Fjeld • Greenland 54 S2
Gunner's Quoin • Mauritius 34 J6
Gunnislake • United Kingdom 104 C7
Gunnison • CO, United States 45 J2
Gunstock Ski •
NH, United States .... 149 [219]
Guntakal • India 138 D2
Guntersville •
AL, United States 48 D3
Guntersville Lake •
AL, United States 48 D3
Guntur • India 138 D3
Gunung Kawi • Bali, Indonesia 143 H3
Gunungsitoli • Indonesia 143 G3

Günz • Germany 9 F8
Günzburg • Germany 112 F2
Gunzenhausen • Germany 9 F7
Gur, Lough • Ireland 108 C6
Guradu • Maldives 138 F4
Gurdon • AR, United States 46 I6
Güre • Turkey 15 K5
Gurgel • Sudan 137 D5
Gurha • India 137 D5
Gurktaler Alpen • Austria 14 A3
Gurskøy • Norway 124 C1
Gurupá • Brazil 51 G4
Gurupi • Brazil 53 (1) B4
Gurupi [Riv] • Brazil 53 (1) B2
Gurupi, Serra do • Brazil 53 (1) B2
Guruvayur • India 138 D10
Guruwe • Zimbabwe 130 C2
Gusau • Nigeria 22 F2
Gusev • Russian Fed. 13 L3
Gush Halav • Israel 135 A2
Gushan • China 30 B5
Gushgy • Turkmenistan 18 H2
Gusinaya, Guba • Russian Fed. 27 P2
Gusinoozersk • Russian Fed. 27 G6
Guspini • Sardinia, Italy 12 C9
Gustavia • St Barthélemy .... 160 E
Güstrow • Germany 8 H3
Güstrow (Renaissanceschloss) Castle •
Germany .... 113 [224]
Gusum • Sweden 125 F4
Gutach • Germany 112 D8
Güterfelde • Germany 111 C3
Güterslöh • Germany 8 D4
Guthega • NS, Australia 144 C4
Guthrie • OK, United States 46 G5
Guttenberg Castle • Germany .... 113 [82]
Guttenberg, Burg • Germany 112 E5
Guwahati • India 28 F3
GUYANA • S. America 51 F2
Guyang • China 29 E2
Guyenne • France 10 F9
Guymon • OK, United States 46 E4
Güzelsu • Turkey 123 F4
Güzelyurt • Cyprus 15 N8
Güzelyurt • Cyprus 123 J1
Güzelyurt Körfezi • Cyprus 15 N8
Gvardeysk • Russian Fed. 13 K3
Gvarv • Norway 124 B3
Gwadar • Pakistan 18 H4
Gwaii Haanas Nat. Park Park N •
BC, Canada .... 156 [8]
Gwalior • India 137 C7
Gwanda • Zimbabwe 130 C3
Gwda • Poland 13 F4
Gweebarra Bay • Ireland 7 D7
Gwei • Zimbabwe 130 C4
Gweru • Zimbabwe 130 C4
Gwinner • ND, United States 43 H3
Gyaca • China 28 F3
Gyangze • China 28 E3
Gyaring Co • China 28 F2
Gyaring Hu • China 28 G2
Gyda • Russian Fed. 26 M3
Gydan Peninsula • Russian Fed. .. 126 A3
Gydanskiy Poluostrov •
Russian Fed. 26 M3
Gympie • QL, Australia 144 B6
Gyóda • Japan 140 C2
Gyoma • Hungary 13 J11
Gyöngyös • Hungary 13 I10
Györ • Hungary 13 G10
Gypsumville • MN, Canada 43 G1
Gyula • Hungary 13 K11
Gyumri • Armenia 18 D1
Gyzylarbat • Turkmenistan 18 G2

H.P. Leu Botanical Gardens •
FL, United States 151 C2
Ha Giang • Vietnam 31 C2
Ha Long Bay Heritage N •
Vietnam .... 83 [132]
Ha Long Bay • Vietnam 141 D1
Ha Tien • Vietnam 141 E3
Ha Tinh • Vietnam 31 D3
Ha'apai Group • Tonga 35 (2) F7
Ha'il • Saudi Arabia 18 D4
Ha-ad Chao Samran • Thailand 142 C3
Haan • Germany 112 F4
Haan • Germany 111 B3
Haapsalu • Estonia 126 B1
Haar • Germany 112 F1
Haardt • Germany 9 C7
Haarlem • Netherlands 109 F1
Haarlemmermeer Polder •
Netherlands 109 F1
Haast • New Zealand 35 B6
Haast Bluff • NT, Australia 145 D1
Haast Pass • New Zealand 35 B7
Haasts Bluff Aboriginal Land •
NT, Australia 145 D1
Habarana • Sri Lanka 138 D15
Habaswein • Kenya 23 F3
Habomai-shoto • Russian Fed. 140 A2
Haboro • Japan 30 K2
Hachijo • Japan 30 J8
Hachinohe • Japan 30 K4
Hachioji • Japan 140 C1
Hacilar • Turkey 123 F1
Hackås • Sweden 16 H5
Hadamar • Germany 112 D3
Hadano • Japan 140 C3
Hadd, Al • Oman 18 G5
Hadd, Ra's al • Oman 18 G5
Hadded • Somalia 23 H1
Haddington • United Kingdom 104 B4
Haddumati Atoll • Maldives 138 F3
Hadejia • Nigeria 22 F2
Hadejia [Riv] • Nigeria 22 F2
Hadejia-Nguru Wetlands Park •
Nigeria .... 133 [32]
Hadeland • Norway 124 C2
Haderslev Beach • Denmark .... 96 [45]
Haderslev • Denmark 125 F13
Hadijah • Saudi Arabia 18 C4
Hadim • Turkey 123 G2
Hadithah, Al • Iraq 18 D3
Hadjout • Algeria 11 N8
Hadley Bay • NU, Canada 38 J2
Hadrian's Wall • United Kingdom .. 7 J6
Hadrian's Wall Heritage C •
United Kingdom .... 86 [17]
Hadsund Beach • Denmark .... 96 [48]
Hadsund • Denmark 125 F6
Haeinsa Temple Heritage C •
Rep. of Korea .... 85 [183]
Hafar al Batin • Saudi Arabia 18 E4
Hafirat al 'Ayda • Saudi Arabia 18 C4
Hafnarfjördur • Iceland 16 (1) B2
Hafun, Ras • Somalia 23 I1
Hagadera • Kenya 23 G3
Hagby • Sweden 125 F12
Hagen • Germany 111 B4
Hagenow • Germany 8 G3
Hagerman Fossil Beds Nat. Mon. Park N •
ID, United States .... 150 [62]
Hagerman Fossil Beds Nat. Mon. •
ID, United States 48 D3
Hagerstown • MD, United States .. 153 D9
Haghpat Heritage C • Armenia .... 85 [92]
Hagi • Japan 30 F7

Hagondange • France 10 L4
Hague, Cap de la • France 10 D4
Hague, The • Netherlands 109 F1
Haguenau • France 10 M5
Hagunia • Western Sahara 20 C3
Hahajima-retto • Japan 140 A13
Hahenklee Spa • Germany .... 113 [h1]
Hai'an • China 139 C2
Haifa • Israel 135 A2
Haiku • China 31 E2
Hailar • China 27 I7
Hailey • ID, United States 42 H5
Hailong • China 29 H1
Hailuoto • Finland 16 M4
Haimen • China 139 C2
Hainan • China 31 E3
Hainaut • Belgium 109 D14
Haines • AK, United States 49 N4
Haines City • FL, United States 49 N4
Haines Junction • YT, Canada 38 B4
Hainichen • Germany 9 I6
Haining • China 139 C4
Haiphong • Vietnam 31 D2
Haixan • China 139 C2
Haixin Shan • China 29 C3
Haiyan • China 139 C4
Hajar, Al • Iraq 18 D4
Hajdúböszörmény • Hungary 13 K10
Hajdúdorog • Hungary 13 K10
Hajdúhadhás • Hungary 13 K10
Hajdúnánás • Hungary 13 K10
Hajira Beach • India 138 E3
Hajla • F.R. of Yugoslavia 14 H7
Hajnówka • Poland 13 M5
Hakkari • Turkey 18 D3
Hakken-zan • Japan 140 B4
Hakodate • Japan 30 K4
Hakone • Japan 140 C3
Hakos • Namibia 24 C5
Haku, Mt • Japan 140 C2
Hakui • Japan 30 I6
Hal Saflieni Hypogeum Heritage C •
Malta .... 86 [232]
Hal Saflieni Hypogeum • Malta 123 H4
Hala Sultan Tekke • Cyprus 123 J4
Halab • Syria 18 C2
Halab Heritage C • Syria .... 86 [276]
Halabi • Egypt 21 G3
Häläveden • Sweden 125 F3
Halba • Lebanon 135 A1
Halcon, Mt • Philippines 31 G4
Haldemu Beach • India 138 F3
Halden • Norway 124 B4
Haldensleben • Germany 8 G4
Hale, Mt • WA, Australia 34 C5
Haleakala Crater •
HI, United States 154 G3
Haleakala Nat. Park Park N •
HI, United States .... 150 [18]
Haleakala Nat. Park •
HI, United States 154 G3
Halebid • India 138 D6
Haleiwa • HI, United States 154 C4
Halethorpe • MD, United States .. 123 E4
Half Moon I. • Antarctica 81 A10
Half Pass • New Zealand 35 B8
Halfa, Wadi • Egypt 21 F3
Halftmoon Bay • New Zealand 35 B8
Haliburton Highlands •
OT, Canada 155 B6
Halicarnassus • Turkey 122 D9
Halidon • India 138 D6
Halkida • Greece 122 D12
Halkidiki • Greece 122 D1
Hall Beach • NU, Canada 39 O3
Hall in Tirol • Austria 119 H2
Hall Peninsula • NU, Canada 39 R4
Halla • Rep. of Korea 125 D1
Halland • Sweden 125 F7
Hallandale • FL, United States 49 C5
Hallandsås • Sweden 125 F11
Hanshan • China 139 C1
Hansi • India 137 C2
Halle • Belgium 5 H4
Halle • Germany 8 G5
Halleberg • Sweden 125 D3
Hälleforsnäs • Sweden 125 D3
Hallein • Austria 13 C2
Hallett, Cape • Antarctica 81 A10
Hallettsville •
TX, United States 47 F3
Halley Bay • Antarctica 54 (1) J2
Hallingdalselva • Norway 16 E6
Hallingskarvet • Norway 124 C4
Hallock • MN, United States 43 H2
Halls Creek • WA, Australia 34 E3
Hallstahammar • Sweden 125 D1
Hallstatt-Dachstein-Salzkammergut
Heritage C • Austria .... 86 [124]
Hallstatt • Austria 13 C2
Hallstavik • Sweden 125 D2
Halmahera • Indonesia 32 (1) C2
Halmeu • Romania 14 K2
Halmstad Beach • Sweden .... 96 [51]
Halmstad • Sweden 125 F11
Haloze • Slovenia 14 C3
Hals Beach • Denmark .... 96 [48]
Hals • Denmark 125 F6
Halsskov • Denmark 125 F14
Halstad • Austria 119 H4
Haltern City •
TX, United States 47 F1
Halti • Finland 16 M1
Halver • Germany 111 B4
Hamad, A'l • Saudi Arabia 21 H1
Hamaca de Tinrhert • Algeria 20 G3
Hamaca del Haricha • Mali 20 E4
Hamadah al Hamrah, Al • Libya .. 21 B1
Hamacan • Iran 18 E3
Hamah • Syria 18 C2
Hamamatsu • Japan 30 I7
Hamar • Norway 16 F6
Hamat Gader • Israel 135 A4
Hamâta • Egypt 21 G3
Hamatonbetsu • Japan 30 L2
Hambantota • Sri Lanka 138 D15
Hamber Prov. Park • BC, Canada .. 156 A4
Hamborn (Duisburg) • Germany 111 B1
Hamburg • Germany 8 F3
Hamburg • NJ, United States 44 H5
Hamburg • AR, United States 153 F1
Hamburg • NY, United States 44 I6
Hamburg [Adm] • Germany 111 A1
Hamburgisches Wattenmeer, Nationalpark
Park N • Germany .... 89 [56]
Hamd, Wadi al • Saudi Arabia 21 G2
Hameln • Germany 8 E4
Hämelschenburg Castle • Germany 113 [10]
Hameenlinna • Finland 125 E4
Hämeenlinna • Finland 125 E4
Hameln • Germany 8 E4
Hamelsenburg Castle • Germany .. 113 [10]
Hamersley Ethiopia 140 B4
Hamersley Range • WA, Australia .. 34 C4
Hamgyong-Sanmaek •
D.P.R. of Korea 30 E4
Hamhung • D.P.R. of Korea 30 D5
Hamilton • VI, Australia 26 P9
Hamilton • Bermuda 80 A2
Hamilton • United Kingdom 104 B3
Hamilton • New Zealand 145 F1
Hamilton • KY, United States 44 C6
Harlan County Lake •
NE, United States 46 F2
Harlem • MT, United States 42 K2
Harlingen • Netherlands 109 D3
Harlingen • TX, United States 47 F5
Harlow • United Kingdom 104 E1

Hamilton • AL, United States 48 D3
Hamilton • OT, Canada 155 B9
Hamilton, Fort • Bermuda 159 J3
Hamilton Grange Nat. Mem. Park N •
NY, United States .... 151 [316]
Hamilton I. • QL, Australia 144 B1
Hamina • Finland 16 N6
Hamlet • NC, United States 48 E3
Hamm • Germany 8 D4
Hammam Lif • Tunisia 131 E2
Hammamet • Tunisia 131 E2
Hammamet, Golfe de • Tunisia 131 E2
Hammarsjön • Sweden 125 F11
Hammaslahti • Sweden 16 H5
Hammerdal • Sweden 16 H5
Hammerfest • Norway 16 L1
Hammondsport •
NY, United States 153 D1
Hammonton • NJ, United States 44 H6
Hamoyet, Jabal • Eritrea/Sudan .. 18 C6
Hampden • New Zealand 35 C7
Hampi Heritage C • India .... 85 [146]
Hampi • India 138 D2
Hampstead • United Kingdom 104 E1
Hampton • AR, United States 46 I6
Hampton • VA, United States 153 D11
Hampton Beach •
NH, United States 153 D4
Hampton Court • United Kingdom .. 104 E1
Hampton Nat. Hist. Site Park N •
MD, United States .... 151 [272]
Hampton Nat. Hist. Site •
MD, United States 153 D10
Hamra Nat. Park N • Sweden .... 89 [24]
Hamun-e Jaz Murian • Iran 18 G4
Han • Rep. of Korea 30 D6
Han Shui • China 29 E4
Han-sur-Lesse • Belgium 109 D19
Hana • HI, United States 154 G4
Hanahan • SC, United States 48 H4
Hanalei • HI, United States 47 K7
Hanamaki • Japan 30 K5
Hanang • Tanzania 130 B2
Hanau • Germany 112 D4
Hancedir • Moldova 14 P3
Hancock • MI, United States 43 L3
Hancock • MD, United States 44 F6
Hancock • NY, United States 44 H5
Hancock [Apt] •
NY, United States 153 D2
Handan • China 29 E3
Handen • Sweden 125 D4
Handlová • Slovak Rep. 13 H9
Haneda [Apt] • Japan 140 C2
Hanford • CA, United States 45 B4
Hangö • Finland 125 E4
Hangzhou • China 139 C3
Hangzhou Wan • China 139 C4
Hania • Crete, Greece 123 E1
Hania [Adm] • Crete, Greece 123 E1
Haniá • Crete, Greece 123 E1
Hanksville • UT, United States 45 J2
Hanmer Springs • New Zealand 35 D6
Hann, Mt • WA, Australia 34 E3
Hanna • AL, Canada 38 I6
Hannibal • MO, United States 46 J3
Hanno • Japan 140 C1
Hannover • Germany 13 D2
Hannoversch • Germany 125 F10
Hanoi • Vietnam 31 D2
Hanover • PA, United States 44 G6
Hanover • NH, United States 44 I4
Hanover, I. • Chile 52 B8
Hans Lollik I. • US Virgin Is. .... 160 Z
Hansapark Park L • Germany .... 98 [51]
Hanshan • China 139 C1
Hansi • India 137 C2
Hanstein Castle • Germany .... 113 [180]
Hantsholm • Denmark 125 F5
Hanumangarh • India 137 C2
Hanyu • Japan 140 C2
Hanzhong • China 29 D4
Hao • French Polynesia 33 M7
Haora • India 28 E4
Haouaria, El • Tunisia 131 E2
Haparanda • Sweden 16 M4
Hapcheon • D.P.R. of Korea 30 D6
Har Sai Shan • China 29 B3
Harad • Saudi Arabia 18 E5
Harahan • LA, United States 48 B6
Hárakas • Crete, Greece 15 G9
Haramachi • Japan 30 K6
Harare • Zimbabwe 130 C2
Harazah • Sudan 21 F4
Harazé Mangueigne • Chad 23 C2
Harbin • China 29 H1
Harbo • Sweden 125 D1
Harbour • Denmark 125 F9
Harbour Beach •
MI, United States 44 D4
Harbour Breton • NF, Canada 156 D3
Harbour Grace • NF, Canada 156 D4
Harbour, Lake • NU, Canada 39 R4
Harbour Park, Littlehampton Park L •
United Kingdom .... 98 [37]
Harburg Castle • Germany .... 113 [136]
Hardangerfjorden • Norway 124 C4
Hardangerjøkulen • Norway 124 C4
Hardangervidda • Norway 124 C3
Hardangervidda Nat. Park Park N •
Norway .... 89 [15]
Hardangervidda Nat. Park •
Norway 124 C4
Hardenberg • Netherlands 5 J2
Hardenberg Castle • Germany .... 113 [73]
Harderwijk • Netherlands 109 D7
Hardin • MT, United States 42 L4
Harding • South Africa 24 E6
Hardinsburg • KY, United States .. 48 D2
Hardisty Beach • United Kingdom .. 104 C3
Hardwick • GA, United States 48 E4
Hare Indian • NT, Canada 38 F7
Hareidlandet • Norway 124 C1
Haren • Germany 23 G2
Harer • Ethiopia 23 G2
Harestua • Norway 124 B2
Hargeysa • Somalia 23 G2
Hargrave Nat. Park Park N •
Somalia .... 133 [66]
Harghita, Muntii • Romania 14 M3
Haría Beach •
Lanzarote, Canary Is. .... 96 [111]
Haría • Lanzarote, Canary Is. 116 I6
Haridwar • India 137 C3
Haringvliet • Netherlands 109 F3
Haringvlietdam • Netherlands 109 F3
Harirud • Afghanistan 18 I3
Harjalvata • Finland 125 E4
Harlan • IA, United States 46 H2
Harlan • KY, United States 48 E2

Harlowtown • MT, United States .. 42 K3
Harmal • Goa, India 137 B1
Harmancik • Turkey 15 K4
Harmil • Eritrea 21 H4
Harney Basin •
OR, United States 152 B4
Harney Lake • OR, United States .. 152 B4
Harney Peak • SD, United States .. 40 F3
Hárnösand • Sweden 16 H5
Harold Johnson Nature Reserve •
South Africa 134 B4
Harpalpur • India 137 C7
Harper • Liberia 22 C4
Harpers Ferry Nat. Hist. Park Park N •
WV, United States .... 151 [261]
Harpers Ferry Nat. Hist. Park •
WV, United States 153 D9
Harrachov • Czech Rep. 128 B2
Harrat Al • Saudi Arabia 21 G1
Harrat al 'Uwayrid •
Saudi Arabia 21 G2
Harricana • QU, Canada 39 P6
Harrington Harbour • QU, Canada .. 39 T6
Harrington Sound • Bermuda 159 J2
Harrisburg • IL, United States 48 C2
Harrisburg • PA, United States 153 D6
Harrismith • South Africa 24 D5
Harrison • AR, United States 46 I4
Harrison Lake • BC, Canada 42 E2
Harrison's Cave • Barbados .... 161 O
Harrisonburg •
VA, United States 153 D9
Harrisonville •
MO, United States 46 H3
Harrodsburg • KY, United States .. 48 E2
Harrogate • United Kingdom 7 K8
Harry S. Truman Nat. Hist. Site Park N •
MO, United States .... 151 [151]
Harry S. Truman Reservoir •
MO, United States 46 I3
Harsho • Somalia 23 H1
Harstad • Norway 16 I2
Hart, Lake • FL, United States 151 C2
Hartegran • Norway 124 C4
Hartenfels Castle • Germany .... 113 [204]
Hartford • CT, United States 153 D7
Hartford City •
IN, United States 44 C5
Hartland • NB, Canada 44 L2
Hartland Covered Bridge •
NB, Canada 156 D6
Hartlepool • United Kingdom 104 F1
Hartlepool • United Kingdom 7 K7
Hartola • Finland 125 E2
Hartselle • AL, United States 48 D3
Hartsville • SC, United States 48 G3
Haruj al Aswad, Al • Libya 21 C2
Harvard • IL, United States 43 L5
Harvey • WA, Australia 34 B3
Harvey • ND, United States 43 F3
Harvey • IL, United States 44 B5
Harwich • United Kingdom 104 E2
Haryana • India 137 C2
Harz • Germany 8 F5
Hasa, Al • Saudi Arabia 18 E4
Hasakah, Al • Syria 18 D2
Hasbaya • Lebanon 135 A2
Hase • Germany 8 C4
Hashimoto • Japan 140 B4
Hasi Ausert • Western Sahara 20 C4
Haskell • TX, United States 46 F6
Haslemere • United Kingdom 7 I10
Hasleni • Denmark 125 F6
Hassan • India 138 D6
Hassel I. • US Virgin Is. .... 160 Z
Hasselt • Belgium 109 D15
Hassi Bel Guebbour • Algeria 20 G2
Hassi Messaoud • Algeria 20 G2
Hassi Serouenout • Algeria 20 G3
Hässleholm • Sweden 125 F11
Hastings • United Kingdom 104 E4
Hastings • New Zealand 145 F4
Hastings • Barbados .... 161 O
Hastings • MN, United States 43 J4
Hastings • NE, United States 46 F2
Hasvik • Norway 16 L1
Hat Yai • Thailand 31 C5
Hatay • Turkey 123 G4
Hatch • NM, United States 45 I5
Hatfield • United Kingdom 104 E1
Hatgal • Mongolia 27 F6
Hathras • India 137 C3
Hatibah, Ra's • Saudi Arabia 18 C5
Hatillo • Puerto Rico 159 H1
Hato [Apt] • Curaçao .... 160 X
Hato, Bocht van • Curaçao .... 160 X
Hato Cave • Curaçao .... 160 X
Hato Mayor • Dominican Rep. 159 G8
Hatra Heritage C • Iraq .... 86 [288]
Hatsu-shima • Japan 140 C3
Hatteras, Cape •
NC, United States 48 J3
Hattiesburg • MS, United States .. 153 F2
Hattingen • Germany 111 B1
Hattula • Finland 125 E2
Hattusha Heritage C • Turkey .... 86 [227]
Hatvan • Hungary 13 I10
Haugesund • Norway 124 E4
Hauhungaroa Range • New Zealand 145 F4
Haukeligrend • Norway 16 D7
Haukipudas • Finland 16 M4
Haukivesi • Finland 16 O5
Hauraki Gulf • New Zealand 35 E3
Hauroko, Lake • New Zealand 145 G3
Haus in Ennstal Ski • Austria .... 100 [186]
Hausa • Western Sahara 20 C3
Haut Atlas • Morocco 131 D4
Haut Médoc • France 114 B3
Haut Zaïre • Dem. Rep. of Congo .. 23 D3
Haute Corse • Corsica, France 115 L4
Haute Normandie • France 114 A1
Haute Savoie • France 115 F2
Haute-Touche, Parc de la •
France 114 D4
Hautefort • France 115 G2
Hautes Fagnes • Belgium 5 K4
Hautes Pyrénées • France 115 J2
Hautmont • France 5 G4
Hautot-sur-Mer Beach • France .... 96 [77]
Hauts Plateaux • Algeria 20 E2
Hauula • HI, United States 154 G1
Hauzenberg • Germany 9 I8
Havana • Cuba .... 84 [39]
Havana Heritage C • Cuba .... 84 [39]
Havana • Cuba 158 D1
Havant • United Kingdom 7 L11
Havasu, Lake •
AZ/NV, United States 153 C10
Havel • Germany 111 C1
Havelkanal • Germany 111 C3
Havelock • NC, United States 48 I3
Havelock North • New Zealand 145 F4
Havelte • Netherlands 109 D8
Haverfordwest •
Wales, United Kingdom 104 C2
Haverhill • MA, United States 44 J4
Haverthwaite • United Kingdom .. 104 E1
Havirov • Czech Rep. 13 H8
Havlíčkův Brod • Czech Rep. 128 C2
Havlíčkův Brod • Czech Rep. 128 C2
Havnsø • Denmark 125 F10
Havøysund • Norway 16 M1
Havre • MT, United States 42 K2
Havre-Aubert • QU, Canada 44 P4
Havre, le • France 10 F4
Havre-St Pierre • QU, Canada 156 D2

Havsa • Turkey ... 15 H2
Haw Par Dragon World • Singapore ... 141 H3
Hawaii • Pacific Ocean ... 154 G
Hawaii [I.] • HI, United States ... 154 G8
Hawaii Volcanoes Nat. Park Heritage N • HI, United States ... 82 [9]
Hawaii Volcanoes Nat. Park Park N • HI, United States ... 150 [22]
Hawaii Volcanoes Nat. Park • HI, United States ... 154 G8
Hawaiian Is. cruise area • Pacific Ocean ... 80 A1
Hawalli • Kuwait ... 18 E4
Hawd • Ethiopia/Somalia ... 23 H2
Hawea • New Zealand ... 145 G2
Hawea, Lake • New Zealand ... 145 G2
Hawera • New Zealand ... 145 F3
Haweswater Reservoir • United Kingdom ... 104 C2
Hawi • HI, United States ... 154 G8
Hawick • United Kingdom ... 6 J6
Hawke Bay • New Zealand ... 35 F4
Hawke's Bay [Adm] • New Zealand ... 145 F4
Hawkes, Mt • Antarctica ... 54 (1) JJ1
Hawkesbury • OT, Canada ... 44 H3
Hawkinsville • VA, United States ... 153 D9
Hawkshead • United Kingdom ... 104 C2
Hawksworth Pass • CA, United States ... 42 E7
Hawng Tuk • Myanmar ... 31 B2
Hawthorne • NV, United States ... 152 C4
Hawtho, Mt • Antarctica ... 54 (1) FF3
Hay • NT, Australia ... 144 C1
Hay • AL, Canada ... 38 H5
Hay River • NT, Canada ... 38 H5
Hay-on-Wye • United Kingdom ... 104 D3
Hayes • MN, Canada ... 38 M5
Hayes • SD, United States ... 43 F4
Hayes, Mt • AK, United States ... 49 L3
Hayle • United Kingdom ... 104 F4
Hayling I. Beach • United Kingdom ... 101 [90-91]
Hayman I. • QL, Australia ... 144 B1
Haymana • Turkey ... 15 N4
Haynesville • LA, United States ... 153 F1
Hayrabolu • Turkey ... 15 H2
Hays • KS, United States ... 46 F3
Haystack Ski • VT, United States ... 149 [206]
Haysville • KS, United States ... 46 G4
Hayward • CA, United States ... 45 A3
Haywards Heath • United Kingdom ... 104 E3
Hayya • Sudan ... 21 G4
Hazard • KY, United States ... 48 F2
Hazebrouck • France ... 10 H3
Hazen • ND, United States ... 43 F2
Hazleton • PA, United States ... 153 A2
Hazor • Israel ... 135 A2
He Xian • China ... 29 D4
Heacham Beach • United Kingdom 101 [42-43]
Head of Bight • SA, Australia ... 144 B1
Head-Smashed-In Buffalo Jump Heritage C • AL, Canada ... 84 [2]
Healdsburg • CA, United States ... 152 C3
Heard I. • Indian Ocean ... 19 (1) B2
Heard I. Heritage N • Southern Ocean ... 83 [151]
Hearne • TX, United States ... 154 J3
Hearst San Simeon State Hist. Mon. • CA, United States ... 152 C3
Heart of England • United Kingdom ... 104 D
Heathrow [Apt] • United Kingdom ... 104 E3
Heavenly Ski • NV, United States ... 149 [77]
Hebbronville • TX, United States ... 154 J5
Hebei • China ... 139 A3
Heber • AZ, United States ... 45 G4
Heber City • UT, United States ... 45 G1
Heber Springs • AR, United States ... 46 I5
Hebrides • China ... 29 E3
Hebrides, Inner • United Kingdom ... 6 F5
Hebrides, Outer • United Kingdom ... 6 E4
Hebrides, Sea of the • United Kingdom ... 6 E4
Hebron • Palestine ... 135 A7
Hebron • NF, Canada ... 39 S5
Hebron • NE, United States ... 46 G2
Hecate Strait • BC, Canada ... 38 E6
Hecate Strait • BC, Canada ... 38 E6
Hecelchakán • Mexico ... 157 H1
Hechingen • Germany ... 9 D8
Hechuan • China ... 29 D4
Hed • Sweden ... 125 D1
Heddal stavkirke • Norway ... 124 B1
Heddalsvatnet • Norway ... 124 B3
Hede • Sweden ... 16 G5
Hedemora • Sweden ... 16 I6
Hedesundafjärden • Sweden ... 125 F5
Hedmark • Norway ... 16 F5
Heemstede • Netherlands ... 109 F1
Heerenlogement Cave • South Africa ... 134 C1
Heerenveen • Netherlands ... 109 D3
Heerlen • Netherlands ... 109 D16
Hefa • Israel ... 135 A3
Hefei • China ... 29 E4
Hegang • China ... 29 I1
Hegura • Japan ... 30 I6
Hei Ling Chau • Hong Kong, China ... 139 B5
Heide • Germany ... 8 E2
Heide-Park Park L • Germany ... 98 [53]
Hedecksburg Castle • Germany ... 113 [185]
Heidelberg • Germany ... 112 D4
Heidelberg Castle • Germany ... 113 [77]
Heidenheim an der Brenz • Germany ... 112 D6
Heilbronn • Germany ... 112 D6
Heiligenberg Castle • Germany ... 113 [113]
Heiligenberg, Schloss • Germany ... 112 F5
Heiligenblut • Austria ... 119 H8
Heiligendamm Beach • Germany ... 96 [34]
Heiligendamm Spa • Germany ... 113 [c21]
Heiligenhafen • Germany ... 8 G2
Heiligenhafen Spa • Germany ... 113 [c15]
Heiligenhaus • Germany ... 111 B1
Heiligenstadt • Germany ... 9 F5
Heilong Jiang • China ... 27 K7
Heilongjiang • China ... 139 A4
Heimaey • Iceland ... 16 I5
Heimdal • Norway ... 16 F5
Heinola Beach • Finland ... 97 [28]
Heinola • Finland ... 125 E2
Heishan Xia • China ... 29 C3
Hekla • Iceland ... 16 I1
Hel • Poland ... 13 H3
Helagsfjället • Sweden ... 16 G5
Helen • GA, United States ... 153 D8
Helen Reef • Palau ... 32 (1) D2
Helena • MT, United States ... 42 J3
Helengeli • Maldives ... 138 F2
Helensburgh • United Kingdom ... 104 B3
Helgasjön • Sweden ... 125 G3
Helgeland • Norway ... 16 G3
Helgoland • Germany ... 8 E2
Helgoland Spa • Germany ... 113 [c1]
Helgolander Bucht • Germany ... 8 E2
Heliopolis • Egypt ... 21 I5
Hell • Cayman Is. ... 159 E3
Hell's Gate • Saba ... 161 F
Hell-Bourg • Réunion ... 132 H1
Hellesylt • Norway ... 124 C2
Hellevoetsluis • Netherlands ... 109 F3

Hellin • Spain ... 11 J6
Hellinikon [Apt] • Greece ... 122 D4
Hells Canyon • ID/OR, United States ... 40 C3
Hells Canyon Nat. Recreation Area • ID/OR, United States ... 152 B4
Hells Gate Nat. Park • Kenya ... 131 G3
Hellshire Hills • Jamaica ... 159 F4
Helmand • Afghanistan ... 18 H3
Helme • Germany ... 8 G5
Helmond • Netherlands ... 109 D11
Helmstedt • Germany ... 8 G4
Helong • China ... 30 E3
Helper • UT, United States ... 45 G2
Helsingborg Beach • Sweden ... 96 [10]
Helsingborg • Sweden ... 125 F11
Helsinge Beach • Denmark ... 96 [41]
Helsingfors • Finland ... 86 [9]
Helsingfors • Finland ... 125 E4
Helsinki Heritage C • Finland ... 86 [9]
Helsinki Beach • Finland ... 97 [27]
Helsinki • Finland ... 125 E4
Helston • United Kingdom ... 104 F4
Helvellyn • United Kingdom ... 104 C2
Helwân • Egypt ... 131 F2
Hemel Hempstead • United Kingdom ... 7 L10
Hemnes • Norway ... 124 B2
Hempstead • TX, United States ... 154 J4
Hemsedal • Norway ... 124 C4
Henan • China ... 139 A7
Henbury • NT, Australia ... 145 D4
Henbury meteorite craters • NT, Australia ... 145 D4
Hendala • Sri Lanka ... 138 D15
Hendaye • France ... 115 J1
Hende • Turkey ... 15 L3
Henderson • NC, United States ... 48 H2
Henderson • TN, United States ... 48 C3
Henderson • KY, United States ... 48 D2
Henderson • NV, United States ... 152 C4
Henderson • TX, United States ... 154 J3
Henderson I. Heritage N • Pitcairn Is. ... 82 [157]
Hendersonville • NC, United States ... 48 F3
Hendersonville • TN, United States ... 48 D2
Heng Shan • Shanxi, China ... 139 A3
Heng Shan • Hunan, China ... 139 A7
Hengduan Shan • China ... 31 B1
Hengelo • Netherlands ... 109 D8
Hengqin • China ... 139 B3
Hengshui • China ... 29 F3
Hengyang • China ... 29 E5
Hénin-Beaumont • France ... 5 F4
Hennebont • France ... 114 C4
Henneburg Castle • Germany ... 113 [170]
Hennigsdorf • Germany ... 111 C1
Henrietta Maria, Cape • OT, Canada ... 39 O5
Henry, Cape • VA, United States ... 153 D11
Henry E. Rohlsen [Apt] • US Virgin Is. ... 160 Z
Henryetta • OK, United States ... 46 H5
Henzada • Myanmar ... 31 B3
Heping • China ... 29 F6
Heppner • OR, United States ... 42 F4
Heptaepon • Israel ... 135 A4
Héradsvötn • Iceland ... 16 (1) D2
Herakleia • Turkey ... 122 D9
Herakleion • Crete, Greece ... 123 E3
Herald Cays • CL, Australia ... 144 B1
Herat • Afghanistan ... 18 H3
Herbert Hoover Nat. Hist. Site Park N • IA, United States ... 151 [165]
Herborn • Germany ... 112 D2
Herculaneum Heritage C • Italy ... 86 [151]
Herculaneum • Italy ... 121 G3
Herculaneum • Italy ... 111 B2
Heredia • Costa Rica ... 37 E5
Hereford • United Kingdom ... 104 D3
Hereford • TX, United States ... 46 D5
Herefordshire • United Kingdom ... 104 D1
Hereke • Turkey ... 15 K3
Herent • Belgium ... 109 D11
Hereford • Germany ... 8 D4
Hergiswil • Switzerland ... 119 G3
Hergla • Tunisia ... 131 E2
Heringsdorf • Germany ... 8 H2
Heringsdorf Beach • Germany ... 97 [30]
Heringsdorf Spa • Germany ... 113 [c25]
Herisau • Switzerland ... 119 F3
Herkimer • NY, United States ... 153 D2
Hermannsburg • NT, Australia ... 145 D2
Hermannsburg Aboriginal Land • NT, Australia ... 145 D2
Hermanus • Venezuela ... 51 E1
Hermansverk • Norway ... 124 C4
Hermanus • South Africa ... 134 C5
Hermiston • OR, United States ... 42 F4
Hermitage • France ... 114 B4
Hermitage • PA, United States ... 44 E5
Hermitage, The • Bahamas ... 158 B2
Hermon, Mount • Lebanon/Syria ... 135 A4
Hermosillo • Mexico ... 157 F2
Hernádsdorf • Germany ... 9 G6
Hernád • Slovak Rep. ... 13 K9
Hernando • FL, United States ... 49 B3
Herne • Germany ... 111 B2
Herne Bay Beach • United Kingdom ... 101 [70-71]
Herne Bay • United Kingdom ... 104 E2
Herning • Denmark ... 125 F9
Herodium • Palestine ... 135 A8
Heroine's monument • Ko Phuket, Thailand ... 142 E1
Herolds Bay • South Africa ... 134 C7
Heron I. • QL, Australia ... 144 B4
Hérouval, le Bois • France ... 115 E1
Herräng • Sweden ... 16 I6
Herrenchiemsee Castle • Germany ... 113 [120]
Herrenchiemsee, Schloss • Germany ... 112 F4
Herrenhausen, Hannover Castle • Germany ... 113 [8]
Herrera de Pisuerga • Spain ... 11 G2
Herrin • IL, United States ... 48 C2
Herrljunga • Sweden ... 125 E12
Hersbruck • Germany ... 112 E4
Herschung • Germany ... 112 F3
Hershey • PA, United States ... 153 D6
Hersheypark Park L • PA, United States ... 151 [JJ]
Herstal • Belgium ... 5 I4
Herten • Germany ... 111 B2
Hertford • United Kingdom ... 104 E1
Hertfordshire • United Kingdom ... 104 E1
Hervey Bay • QL, Australia ... 144 B4
Herzberg • Germany ... 8 F5
Herzogenaurach • Germany ... 9 F7
Herzogenrath • Germany ... 111 A1
Hesdin • France ... 5 F4
Hesbhon • Jordan ... 135 A6
Hesse • Germany ... 111 A5
Hessen • Germany ... 9 D6
Hessisch Lichtenau • Germany ... 9 E5
Hettingen • ND, United States ... 43 E3
Hettstedt • Germany ... 100 [128]
Hève Castle • United Kingdom ... 104 E3
Heves • Hungary ... 13 J10
Hewanorra [Apt] • St Lucia ... 161 P
Hexham • United Kingdom ... 7 J7
Hexrivierberge • South Africa ... 134 C6
Heysham • United Kingdom ... 106 A13

Heyuan • China ... 29 E6
Heywood • VI, Australia ... 34 H7
Heywoods Beach • Barbados ... 161 D
Heyworth • IL, United States ... 46 K2
Heze • China ... 29 F3
Hialeah • FL, United States ... 154 H8
Hiawatha • KS, United States ... 46 H3
Hibberdene • South Africa ... 134 B5
Hibbing • MN, United States ... 43 [70]
Hibiscus Coast • South Africa ... 134 B5
Hicacos, Peninsula • Cuba ... 158 D2
Hickory • NC, United States ... 48 G3
Hicksville • NY, United States ... 44 I5
Hida-sanmyaku • Japan ... 30 I6
Hidaka • Japan ... 140 C1
Hidaka-sanmyaku • Japan ... 30 L3
Hidalgo • Mexico ... 47 E5
Hidalgo [Adm] • Mexico ... 37 B3
Hidalgo del Parral • Mexico ... 40 E6
Hidcote Manor • United Kingdom ... 104 D4
Hidden Valley Ski • MO, United States ... 149 [126]
Hidden Valley Ski • PA, United States ... 149 [169]
Hidden Valley • PA, United States ... 153 D5
Hiddensee • Germany ... 8 G2
Hierakonpolis • Egypt ... 131 F5
Hierapolis • Turkey ... 122 D6
Hierapolis-Pamukkale Heritage N • Turkey ... 83 [70]
Hierapolis-Pamukkale Heritage C • Turkey ... 86 [223]
Hierro • Canary Is. ... 117 E5
Higashi-Matsuyama • Japan ... 140 C1
Higashiosaka • Japan ... 140 B2
High Butler Lake • NE, United States ... 46 E2
High Island • TX, United States ... 154 J4
High Island Reservoir • Hong Kong, China ... 139 B6
High Plains • United States ... 152 A2
High Point • NC, United States ... 48 H3
High River • AL, Canada ... 42 I1
High Rock • Bahamas ... 158 B2
High Rock Lake • NC, United States ... 48 G3
High Street • United Kingdom ... 104 C2
High Willhays • United Kingdom ... 104 F5
High Wycombe • United Kingdom ... 7 L10
Highgate • Jamaica ... 159 F2
Highland Park • Ko Samui, Thailand ... 142 D1
Highlands Forest Reserve • Penang, Malaysia ... 141 F1
Highlands Hammock State Recreation Area • FL, United States ... 154 H5
Highlands, North West • United Kingdom ... 6 G4
Highlands, The • Antigua & Barbuda ... 161 J
Highmore • SD, United States ... 43 G4
Highveld • Zimbabwe ... 133 E4
Higüero, Punta • Puerto Rico ... 159 H1
Higüey • Dominican Rep. ... 159 G8
Hiitola • Russian Fed. ... 16 I4
Hijar • Spain ... 11 K3
Hijaz, Al • Saudi Arabia ... 18 C5
Hikkaduwa • Sri Lanka ... 138 D15
Hikurangi • New Zealand ... 145 G2
Hikurangi [Mtn] • New Zealand ... 35 G3
Hila • Indonesia ... 32 (1) C4
Hiland • WY, United States ... 42 L5
Hildburghausen • Germany ... 9 F6
Hilden • Germany ... 111 B3
Hildesheim Heritage C • Germany ... 86 [47]
Hilisimaetano • Indonesia ... 143 G3
Hill End • NS, Australia ... 144 C2
Hillaby, Mt • Barbados ... 161 D
Hillah, Al • Iraq ... 18 D3
Hillah, Al • Saudi Arabia ... 18 E5
Hillcrest Center • CA, United States ... 45 C4
Hillegom • Netherlands ... 109 F1
Hillered • Denmark ... 125 F10
Hillsboro • OR, United States ... 42 D4
Hillsboro • ND, United States ... 43 H3
Hillsboro • OH, United States ... 44 D6
Hillsboro • TX, United States ... 154 J1
Hillsborough • Grenada ... 161 R
Hillsdale • MI, United States ... 44 C5
Hillswick • United Kingdom ... 6 K1
Hilo • HI, United States ... 154 G8
Hilpoltstein • Germany ... 9 G7
Hilton Head I. • SC, United States ... 48 G4
Hilvarenbeek • Netherlands ... 109 D11
Hilversum • Netherlands ... 109 F2
Himachal Pradesh • India ... 28 C2
Himalaya • Asia ... 28 E3
Himarë • Albania ... 15 A3
Himeji Heritage C • Japan ... 85 [188]
Himeji • Japan ... 140 B1
Himeville Nature Reserve • South Africa ... 134 B3
Himmafushi • Maldives ... 138 F2
Himmerland • Denmark ... 125 F5
Himos • Finland ... 125 E2
Hin Khom, Laem • Ko Samui, Thailand ... 142 D2
Hinamara • Norway ... 16 H2
Hinojosa del Duque • Spain ... 11 F6
Hins • Syria ... 18 C3
Hinterglemm • Austria ... 119 H3
Hintertux Ski • Austria ... 100 [141]
Hintertux • Austria ... 119 H7
Hinton • WV, United States ... 48 G2
Hios Heritage C • Greece ... 86 [218]
Hios • Greece ... 122 D5
Hios [I.] • Greece ... 122 D5
Hippos • Israel ... 135 A4
Hira-san • Japan ... 140 B2
Hirado • Japan ... 30 E8
Hirado-shima • Japan ... 140 A2
Hirakata • Japan ... 140 C3
Hirara • Japan ... 29 H6
Hiratsuka • Japan ... 140 D3
Hirebhasgar Reservoir • India ... 138 D6
Hirfanli Baraji Gölü • Turkey ... 15 G4
Hirhafok • Algeria ... 20 G4
Hiroo • Japan ... 30 L3
Hirosaki • Japan ... 30 K4
Hiroshima • Japan ... 30 G7
Hiroshima Heritage C • Japan ... 85 [186]
Hiroshima [Adm] • Japan ... 140 A7
Hirsau Castle • Germany ... 113 [99]
Hirschberg Castle • Germany ... 113 [140]
Hirschberg Ski • Austria ... 100 [128]
Hirshon • France ... 10 J4
Hirson • France ... 5 H4
Hirtshals Beach • Denmark ... 96 [48]
Hirtshals • Denmark ... 125 F4
Hisar • India ... 137 C2

Histria • Romania ... 128 E2
Hitachi • Japan ... 30 K6
Hitoyoshi • Japan ... 30 F8
Hitra • Norway ... 16 E5
Hiumaa • Estonia ... 126 B1
Hjallerup • Denmark ... 125 F6
Hjälmaren • Sweden ... 125 D3
Hjelm Bugt • Denmark ... 125 F6
Hjelmeland • Norway ... 124 C5
Hjø • Sweden ... 125 F3
Hjørring Beach • Denmark ... 96 [48]
Hjørring • Denmark ... 125 F6
Hlane Game Sanctuary Park • Swaziland ... 133 [136]
Hlohovec • Slovak Rep. ... 128 B4
Hluboká • Czech Rep. ... 128 B4
Hluhluwe-Umfolozi Game Reserve • South Africa ... 134 B4
Hluhluwe/Umfolozi Game Reserve Park • South Africa ... 133 [133]
Hlybokaye • Belarus ... 16 N9
Hö • Ghana ... 22 E3
Ho Chi Minh City • Vietnam ... 141 E1
Ho Da • Vietnam ... 141 E2
Hoanib • Namibia ... 24 A3
Hoani • Namibia ... 24 A3
Hoare Obbia • Somalia ... 23 H2
Hoch Harz, Nationalpark Park N • Germany ... 89 [63]
Hochdorf • Switzerland ... 119 G3
Hochburg Castle • Germany ... 113 [105]
Hochfeiler • Austria/Italy ... 120 B1
Hochgolling • Austria ... 9 I8
Hochgurgl Ski • Austria ... 100 [138]
Hochgurgl • Austria ... 119 H6
Höchneukirch • Germany ... 111 B3
Hochob • Mexico ... 157 H3
Hochschwab • Austria ... 13 E10
Hochstadt an der Aisch • Germany ... 9 F7
Hockenheim • Germany ... 5 L5
Hockenheim • Germany ... 112 D4
Hodeida • Yemen ... 18 D6
Hodgerville • KY, United States ... 48 E2
Hodh • Mauritania ... 20 D5
Hodmezővásárhely • Hungary ... 13 J11
Hodna, Chott el • Algeria ... 20 F1
Hodonin • Czech Rep. ... 13 G9
Hof • Iceland ... 16 (1) F2
Hofgeismar • Germany ... 8 E5
Hofors • Sweden ... 16 I6
Hofsjökull • Iceland ... 16 (1) D2
Hofu • Japan ... 30 F7
Hog I. • Grenada ... 160 S
Höganäs • Sweden ... 125 F11
Hogarth, Mt • NT, Australia ... 34 G4
Högby • Sweden ... 125 C7
Hoggar • Algeria ... 130 A1
Hogland • Russian Fed. ... 16 N6
Høgwörth • Germany ... 112 F8
Högsby • Sweden ... 125 F8
Høgsfjorden • Norway ... 124 C5
Hoh Xil Nur • China ... 28 F1
Hoh Zil Shan • China ... 28 F1
Hohe Acht • Germany ... 112 E1
Hohe Tauern, Nationalpark Park N • Austria ... 89 [82]
Hohe Tauern, Nationalpark • Austria ... 119 H8
Hohe Wilde • Austria/Italy ... 120 B1
Hohen Neuendorf • Germany ... 111 B2
Hohen-Limburg (Hagen) • Germany ... 111 B2
Hohenaschau Castle • Germany ... 113 [119]
Hohenbaden Castle • Germany ... 113 [102]
Hohenburg Castle • Germany ... 113 [109]
Hohenschwangau • Germany ... 112 F6
Hohenschwangau Castle • Germany ... 113 [116]
Hohenstein • Germany ... 113 [44]
Hohentübingen Castle • Germany ... 113 [107]
Hohenwald • Germany ... 112 D8
Hohenzollern Castle • Germany ... 113 [110]
Hohenzollern Castle • Germany ... 113 [106]
Hohenzollern, Schloss • Germany ... 112 D6
Hohes Schloss, Füssen Castle • Germany ... 113 [115]
Hohhot • China ... 29 E2
Hohneck • France ... 10 L5
Hohneck, Burg • Germany ... 112 E4
Hook of Holland • Netherlands ... 109 F3
Hooker • OK, United States ... 46 I6
Hoolehua • HI, United States ... 47 L8
Hoonah • AK, United States ... 49 N4
Hooper, Cape • NT, Canada ... 39 Q3
Hoopeston • IL, United States ... 44 B5
Höör • Sweden ... 125 F12
Hoorn • Netherlands ... 109 D7
Hoover I. • QL, Australia ... 144 B1
Hoover Dam • AZ/NV, United States ... 153 E1
Hopatkong • NJ, United States ... 44 I5
Hope • AR, United States ... 46 I6
Hope Bay • Antarctica ... 81 A10
Hope Bay • Jamaica ... 159 G2
Hope Town • Bahamas ... 158 B1
Hopes Advance, Cap • QU, Canada ... 39 R4
Hopetoun • WA, Australia ... 34 H7
Hopetoun House • United Kingdom ... 104 B4
Hopewell • VA, United States ... 48 I2
Hopewell Culture Nat. Hist. Park Park N • OH, United States ... 151 [182]
Hopewell Furnace Nat. Hist. Site Park N • PA, United States ... 151 [297]
Hopewell Furnace Nat. Hist. Site • PA, United States ... 153 D6
Hopfgarten im Brixental Ski • Austria ... 100 [150]
Hopi Indian Reservation • AZ, United States ... 153 E1
Hopkins, Lake • WA, Australia ... 145 D3
Hopkinsville • KY, United States ... 48 D2
Hopland • CA, United States ... 45 A2
Höör • Sweden ... 15 C6
Hora Stih • Ukraine ... 13 M9
Horain • Turkey ... 123 F3
Horasan • Turkey ... 15 G6
Horb • Germany ... 9 D8
Horbat Ashdod Yam • Israel ... 125 F11
Horby • Sweden ... 125 F11
Hordaland • Norway ... 124 B4
Horefto • Greece ... 122 D4
Horezu Heritage C • Romania ... 86 [193]
Horlivka • Ukraine ... 17 F5
Hormigueros • Puerto Rico ... 159 H3
Hormoz • Iran ... 18 G4
Hormuz, Strait of • Iran/Oman ... 18 G4
Horn • Iceland ... 16 (1) B1
Horn, Cape • Chile ... 53 C7
Horn I. • MS, United States ... 48 D4
Horn, Is. de • Wallis & Futuna ... 35 (2) E1
Horn Plateau • NT, Canada ... 38 H4
Hornavan • Sweden ... 16 H3
Hornberg Castle • Germany ... 113 [84]
Hornberg, Burg • Germany ... 112 D4
Horncastle • United Kingdom ... 5 C1

Holsnøy • Norway ... 124 C3
Holstebro • Denmark ... 125 F9
Holstein • IA, United States ... 43 I5
Holsworthy • United Kingdom ... 104 F2
Holton • KS, United States ... 46 H3
Holy Cross • AK, United States ... 49 K3
Holy I. • England, UK ... 6 K6
Holy I. • Wales, UK ... 7 H8
Holy Khoai • United Kingdom 101 [222-225]
Holy I. Beach • United Kingdom ... 135 A
Holy Land • Asia ... 86 [282]
Holy Valley Heritage C • Lebanon ... 86 [282]
Holyhead • United Kingdom ... 7 H8
Holyoke • MA, United States ... 44 I4
Holyoke • CO, United States ... 46 D2
Holzgau • Austria ... 119 H2
Holzkirchen • Germany ... 112 F3
Holzminden • Germany ... 8 E5
Holzwickede • Germany ... 111 B2
Homa Bay • Kenya ... 131 G3
Homalin • Myanmar ... 31 B2
Homberg • Germany ... 9 E5
Homberg (Duisburg) • Germany ... 111 B1
Hombori • Mali ... 20 E5
Homburg • Germany ... 9 C7
Homburg Castle • Germany ... 113 [175]
Home Bay • NU, Canada ... 39 R3
Home Hill • QL, Australia ... 144 B1
Home of Franklin Delano Roosevelt Nat. Hist. Site Park N • NY, United States ... 151 [311]
Homer • LA, United States ... 47 H1
Homer • AK, United States ... 49 K4
Homerville • GA, United States ... 48 F5
Homestead • FL, United States ... 154 H8
Homestead Nat. Mon. of America Park N • NE, United States ... 151 [163]
Homewood Ski • CA, United States ... 149 [62]
Homewood • AL, United States ... 48 B4
Homlijske Planina • F.R. of Yugoslavia ... 14 I5
Homosassa Springs State Wildlife Park • FL, United States ... 154 H5
Homyel • Belarus ... 16 N9
Homyel • Belarus ... 17 E4
Hon Chong • Vietnam ... 141 E3
Hon Khoai • Vietnam ... 141 E2
Hon Lon • Vietnam ... 141 E2
Hon Quan • Vietnam ... 141 E1
Hon Tre • Vietnam ... 141 E2
Honakaa • HI, United States ... 154 G8
Honaunau • HI, United States ... 47 M9
Honavar • India ... 138 D5
Honda Bay • Colombia ... 51 C2
Honda • Colombia ... 51 C2
Hondo • Japan ... 30 F8
Hondo • NM, United States ... 46 C6
Hondo • TX, United States ... 47 E3
Hondo • Belize/Mexico ... 47 H8
Honduras • C. America ... 37 D5
Honduras, Golfo de • C. America ... 37 D4
Honefoss • Norway ... 124 B1
Honesdale • PA, United States ... 44 H5
Honey Lake • CA, United States ... 42 E6
Honey Lake Resort • Shenzhen, China ... 139 B3
Honfleur • France ... 10 F4
Hong Kong Central • Hong Kong, China ... 139 B5
Hong Kong I. • Hong Kong, China ... 139 B6
HONG KONG SPECIAL ADMIN. REGION • China ... 139 B
Hong, Song • Vietnam ... 141 D1
Hongch'on • Rep. of Korea ... 30 D6
Hongor • Mongolia ... 29 E1
Hongqiao [Apt] • China ... 139 C2
Hongsong • Rep. of Korea ... 30 D6
Honiara • Solomon Is. ... 35 (1) F2
Honister Pass • United Kingdom ... 104 C1
Honiton • United Kingdom ... 104 F5
Honjo • Japan ... 30 K5
Honkajoki • Finland ... 125 E1
Hønne Strand • Denmark ... 125 F9
Hønningsvåg • Norway ... 16 M1
Honolulu • HI, United States ... 154 G6
Honolulu • Spain ... 11 I5
Honshu • Japan ... 30 J5
Hood, Fort • TX, United States ... 154 J3
Hood, Mt • OR, United States ... 152 B3
Hood River • OR, United States ... 42 E4
Hoofddorp • Netherlands ... 109 F1
Hoogeveen • Netherlands ... 109 D8
Hoogezand • Netherlands ... 109 D4
Hoogvliet • Netherlands ... 109 F3
Hook I. • QL, Australia ... 144 B1
Hook • United Kingdom ... 104 E3
Hooke • France ... 29 C7
Honeck, Burg • Germany ... 112 E4

Horneck Castle • Germany ... 113 [85]
Hörnefors • Sweden ... 16 J5
Hornell • NY, United States ... 153 C1
Hornindalsvatn • Norway ... 124 C1
Hornisgrinde • Germany ... 112 D6
Hornos, Cabo de • Chile ... 53 C7
Horodok • Ukraine ... 13 M8
Horovice • Czech Rep. ... 128 B3
Horqin • China ... 29 G1
Horqin Youyi Qianqqi • China ... 29 G1
Horqin Zuoyi Zhongqi • China ... 27 J8
Horred • Sweden ... 125 F7
Horse Is. • NF, Canada ... 156 D3
Horse Shoe Reef • Antigua & Barbuda ... 161 K
Horseley Hills • India ... 138 D7
Horsens Beach • Denmark ... 96 [46]
Horsens • Denmark ... 125 F9
Horseshoe Ski • OT, Canada ... 149 [22]
Horseshoe Bay • Bermuda ... 159 J3
Horseshoe Bend • ID, United States ... 42 G5
Horseshoe Bend Nat. Military Park Park N • AL, United States ... 151 [200]
Horseshoe Reef • British Virgin Is. ... 160 B
Horsh Arz el-Rab Heritage C • Lebanon ... 86 [282]
Horsham • VI, Australia ... 34 H7
Horsham • United Kingdom ... 104 E3
Horst, Schloss • Germany ... 111 B2
Horta • Azores ... 118 E1
Hortas do Tabual • Portugal ... 118 E5
Horten • Norway ... 124 B4
Hortobágyi Nat. Park Heritage C • Hungary ... 85 [190]
Hortobágyi Nat. Park Park N • Hungary ... 89 [105]
Horton • NT, Canada ... 38 F3
Horumersil Spa • Germany ... 113 [c7]
Horwood Lake • OT, Canada ... 44 D1
Horyu-ji Heritage C • Japan ... 85 [190]
Horyu-ji • Japan ... 140 B4
Hosaina • Ethiopia ... 23 F2
Hosbach • Germany ... 9 E6
Hosère Vokre • Cameroon ... 22 G3
Hoskins • Papua New Guinea ... 35 (1) E2
Hospet • India ... 138 D2
Hospitalet de Llobregat, l' • Spain ... 11 N3
Hossegor • France ... 115 C3
Hossmo • Sweden ... 125 F8
Hoste, I. • Chile ... 53 C7
Hot • Thailand ... 142 B3
Hot Springs • SD, United States ... 43 E5
Hot Springs • AR, United States ... 46 I5
Hot Springs Nat. Park Park N • AR, United States ... 151 [188]
Hotan • China ... 26 M10
Hotazel • South Africa ... 24 C5
Hoting • Sweden ... 16 H4
Hottah Lake • NT, Canada ... 38 H3
Hotte, Massif de la • Haiti ... 159 G5
Hottentots Holland Nature Reserve • South Africa ... 134 C6
Hotton • Belgium ... 109 D15
Houck • AZ, United States ... 45 H4
Houdan • France ... 115 E3
Houghton • MI, United States ... 43 L3
Houghton Lake • MI, United States ... 44 C3
Houlton • ME, United States ... 44 L2
Houma • LA, United States ... 153 F4
Houma • TX, United States ... 131 E4
Houmt-Souk • Tunisia ... 131 E4
Hounde • Burkina Faso ... 22 D2
Houphouët, Félix [Apt] • China ... 139 C2
Houssaye, Cap la • Réunion ... 132 H1
Houston • TX, United States ... 154 J4
Houston • BC, Canada ... 155 C1
Hov • Denmark ... 125 F10
Hovdehytta • Norway ... 124 C6
Hove • United Kingdom ... 7 L11
Hovenweep Nat. Mon. Park N • CO, United States ... 150 [91]
Hovgården Heritage C • Sweden ... 86 [5]
Howa • Chad/Sudan ... 21 D4
Howard City • MI, United States ... 44 C4
Howe, Cape • NS/VI, Australia ... 144 C4
Howes • SD, United States ... 43 E4
Howick • South Africa ... 134 B3
Howland • Pacific Ocean ... 33 J3
Howletts Park • United Kingdom ... 104 E3
Howser • BC, Canada ... 42 G1
Höxter • Germany ... 108 E2
Hoxie • AR, United States ... 46 I4
Höxvött • Germany ... 8 E5
Hoy • United Kingdom ... 6 I3
Høyanger • Norway ... 124 C3
Hoyerswerda • Germany ... 8 J5
Hoyle • OT, Canada ... 44 E1
Hozu-gawa • Japan ... 140 B2
Hpumhpu • Myanmar ... 31 B1
Hradec Králove • Czech Rep. ... 128 B3
Hrissi • Greece ... 123 E8
Hrissoúpoli • Greece ... 15 F3
Hristiani • Greece ... 123 E8
Hrodna • Belarus ... 13 M4
Hron • Slovak Rep. ... 13 H9
Hrubieszow • Poland ... 13 M7
Hruby Nisky Jesenik • Czech Rep. ... 13 G7
Hsinchu • Taiwan ... 29 G6
Hsophang • Myanmar ... 31 B2
Hu Men • China ... 139 B3
Hua Hin • Thailand ... 142 C3
Hua Shan • China ... 139 A3
Huacho • Peru ... 51 B6
Huacrachuco • Peru ... 51 B5
Huainan • China ... 29 F4
Huairen • China ... 29 F4
Huajuapan de León • Mexico ... 157 G4
Hualapai Indian Reservation • AZ, United States ... 153 E1
Hualapai Peak • AZ, United States ... 45 F4
Hualian • Taiwan ... 29 G6
Huambo • Angola ... 24 A2
Huancabamba • Peru ... 51 B6
Huancapi • Peru ... 163 B1
Huancavelica • Peru ... 163 B1
Huancayo • Peru ... 163 B1
Huang Hai • Asia ... 29 G3
Huang He • China ... 29 E3
Huang Shan Heritage N • China ... 83 [128]
Huang Shan Heritage C • China ... 85 [175]
Huang Shan • China ... 139 C3
Huanggang Liang • China ... 27 I8
Huanggang Heritage N • China ... 83 [124]
Huangmao Jian • China ... 31 F1
Huangpu • China ... 139 C3
Huangshi • China ... 139 A7
Huanren • China ... 30 C4
Huanta • Peru ... 163 B1
Huánuco • Peru ... 51 B6
Huaral • Peru ... 51 B5
Huaráz • Peru ... 51 B5
Huascarán, Parque Nac. Heritage N • Peru ... 82 [35]
Huatabampo • Mexico ... 157 G4
Hubbell Trading Post Nat. Hist. Site Park N • AZ, United States ... 150 [102]
Hubbell Trading Post Nat. Hist. Site • AZ, United States ... 153 E2
Hubei • China ... 139 A7

Hubertusburg **Castle** • Germany . . . . . 113 [203]
Hubli • India 138 D2
Hubsugul Nur • Mongolia 27 F6
Hückeswagen • Germany 111 B4
Hucknall • United Kingdom 7 K8
Huddersfield • United Kingdom 7 K8
Hudding • Sweden 125 D4
Hudhuveli • Maldives 138 F4
Hudhuveli • Maldives 138 F4
Hudiksvall • Sweden 16 I6
Hudson • NY, United States 153 D3
Hudson Bay • SA, Canada 38 K6
Hudson Bay [Bay] • Canada 39 N5
Hudson, Lake •
OK, United States 46 H4
Hudson [Riv] •
NY, United States 153 D3
Hudson Strait • NU/QU, Canada 39 O4
Hue • Vietnam 31 D2
Hue **Heritage C** • Vietnam . . . . 85 [194]
Huedin • Romania 14 K3
Huelgoat • France 114 C1
Huelva • Spain 116 E4
Huercal-Overa • Spain 116 B4
Huertas, Cabo de las • Spain 11 K6
Huesca • Spain 11 K2
Huéscar • Spain 116 B4
Huexotla • Mexico 157 G4
Hueytown • AL, United States 48 D4
Huftaray • Norway 124 C3
Hufuf, Al • Saudi Arabia 18 E4
Hügel, Villa • Germany 111 B1
Hugh Town • United Kingdom 7 F12
Hughenden • QL, Australia 34 H4
Hugo • OK, United States 154 J2
Hugo Lake • OK, United States 46 H5
Hugoton • KS, United States 46 E4
Hui • Brazil 51 C4
Hui Cheng • China 139 C3
Huiarau Range • New Zealand 145 F2
Huich'on • D.P.R. of Korea 29 H2
Huila • Colombia 51 B3
Huilai • China 31 F2
Huiñamarca, Lago de •
Bolivia/Peru 163 B4
Huisne • France 10 F5
Huiten Nur • China 28 F1
Huittinen • Finland 125 E2
Huiyang • China 139 B2
Huizen • Netherlands 109 F2
Huizhou • China 139 B2
Huka Falls • New Zealand 145 F2
Hvea • China 29 E3
Hukuntsi • Botswana 24 C4
Hula Valley • Israel 135 A2
Hulayfa' • Saudi Arabia 18 D4
Huliba Cave • Aruba . . . . 160 Y
Hulin • China 29 I1
Hull • IA, United States 43 H5
Hull • QU, Canada 155 B7
Hull City • SD, United States 155 B7
Hull City • KS, United States 46 F3
Hülshoff **Castle** • Germany . . . . 113 [13]
Hulst • Netherlands 5 H3
Hultsfred • Sweden 125 F8
Hulun Nur • China 27 I7
Humacao • Puerto Rico 159 H4
Humber • United Kingdom 51 D10
Humbert • New Caledonia 35 (2) B3
Humboldt • IA, United States 43 I5
Humboldt • TN, United States 48 C3
Humboldt • NV, United States 152 C2
Hume, Lake • NS, Australia 144 C3
Hume • China 139 B2
Humenné • Slovak Rep. 13 K9
Hümmling, Der • Germany 8 C4
Humphreys Peak •
AZ, United States 153 E1
Humppila • Finland 125 E4
Hun • Libya 21 C2
Hun • China 30 C4
Hunafljói • Iceland 16 (1) C2
Hunan • China 139 A7
Hunchun • China 30 F3
Hundested **Beach** • Denmark . . . . . 96 [41]
Hundested • Denmark 125 F10
Hunedoara • Romania 14 J4
Hünfeld • Germany 9 E6
Hungarian Plain • Hungary 128 A2
HUNGARY • Europe 13 I10
Hungnam • D.P.R. of Korea 30 D5
Hunjiang • China 30 D4
Hunneberg • Sweden 125 F3
Hunnebostrand • Sweden 125 F2
Hunsrück • Germany 112 E3
Hunstanton • United Kingdom 7 M9
Hunstanton **Beach** •
United Kingdom . . . . 101 [A4]
Hunte • Germany 8 D4
Hunter • New Caledonia 35 (2) C3
Hunter • NS, Australia 144 C2
Hunter Mtn **Ski** •
NY, United States . . . . 149 [193]
Hunter Mtn • NY, United States 153 D3
Hunter Mtns • New Zealand 145 G3
Hunter Valley • NS, Australia 144 A4
Hunting I. • SC, United States 48 G4
Huntingburg • IN, United States 48 D1
Huntingdon • WV, United States 41 J4
Huntingdon • IN, United States 44 C5
Huntingdon • QU, Canada 44 H3
Huntingdon • PA, United States 153 D5
Huntingdon • NY, United States 153 D7
Huntington Beach •
CA, United States 45 D5
Huntly • New Zealand 145 F1
Huntsville • AL, United States 48 D3
Huntsville • TX, United States 154 J4
Huntsville • OT, Canada 155 B5
Hünxe • Germany 111 B1
Hunza • Jammu & Kashmir 28 B1
Hunze • Netherlands 5 J2
Huocheng • China 26 N9
Huon Gulf • Papua New Guinea . . . 35 (1) D2
Huonville • TS, Australia 34 I8
Hura • Maldives 138 F2
Hurdalsjøen • Norway 124 E2
Hurdiyo • Somalia 23 I1
Hurghada • Egypt 131 F4
Huron • SD, United States 43 G4
Huron, Lake •
Canada/United States 44 D3
Hurricane • UT, United States 45 F3
Hurst • TX, United States 154 F1
Hürth • Germany 5 J4
Hurunui • New Zealand 35 D6
Húsavík • Iceland 16 (1) E1
Hushan • China 139 C4
Husi • Romania 14 P3
Huskvarna • Sweden 125 F7
Husum • Germany 18 I5
Husum • Sweden 16 J5
Hutag • Mongolia 27 F7
Hutanopan • Indonesia 143 G4
Hutch Mtn • AZ, United States 45 G4
Hutchinson • South Africa 134 C3
Hutchinson • MN, United States 43 I4
Hutchinson • KS, United States 46 G3
Huvhoyfun, gora • Russian Fed. 27 R5
Huwar • Al Yemen 18 E7
Huxley, Mt • New Zealand 35 B7
Huy • Belgium 109 D15
Huzhou • China 139 C3
Hvaler • Norway 124 B4

Hvannadalshnúkur • Iceland 16 (1) E2
Hvar • Croatia 128 D4
Hvar [Is] • Croatia 128 C4
Hvarski kanal • Croatia 14 D6
Hveragerdi • Iceland 16 (1) C3
Hvidbjerg • Denmark 125 F5
Hvítá • Iceland 16 (1) C2
Hvitsten • Norway 124 B2
Hvittingfoss • Norway 124 B3
Hwang-Hae • Asia 29 G3
Hwange • Zimbabwe 130 C1
Hwange Nat. Park • Zimbabwe 130 C3
Hwange Nat. Park **Park** •
Zimbabwe . . . . 133 [112]
Hyak **Ski** • WA, United States . . . . 149 [50]
Hyannis • NE, United States 43 F6
Hyannis • MA, United States 153 D8
Hycklinge • Sweden 125 F4
Hyde Park • NY, United States 153 D7
Hyderabad • Pakistan 28 A3
Hyderabad • India 138 D3
Hydra • Greece 122 D7
Hyères **Beach** • France . . . . 96 [133]
Hyères • France 115 H3
Hyères, Is. d' • France 115 H3
Hyères-Plage • France 115 H3
Hyesan • D.P.R. of Korea 30 E4
Hyland Post • BC, Canada 38 F5
Hylestad • Norway 124 C6
Hyltebruk **Beach** • Sweden . . . . . . 96 [7]
Hyltebruk • Sweden 125 F7
Hyndman Peak •
ID, United States 38 I8
Hyōgo • Japan 140 B1
Hythe • United Kingdom 104 E4
Hyuga • Japan 30 F8
Hyvinkää • Finland 125 E4

I-n-Abanrherit • Niger 20 G5
I-n-Afaleleh • Algeria 20 G4
I-n-Amenas • Algeria 20 G3
I-n-Azaoua • Niger 20 G4
I-n-Ezzane • Algeria 20 H4
I-n-Gall • Niger 20 G5
I-n-Guezzam • Algeria 20 G5
I-n-Saleh • Algeria 20 F3
I-n-Tabezas • Mali 20 F5
I-n-Tallak • Mali 20 F5
I-n-Techerène • Mali 20 E4
I-n-Tessoum • Niger 20 G5
Ialisos **Beach** • Rhodes, Greece . . 97 [211]
Ialisos • Rhodes, Greece 122 D12
Ialomita • Romania 14 O5
Iao Valley State Mon. •
HI, United States 154 G3
Iar-Chonnacht • Ireland 108 C4
Iasi • Romania 14 O2
Ibadan • Nigeria 22 E3
Ibague • Colombia 51 B3
Ibaraki • Japan 140 A4
Ibarra • Ecuador 51 B3
Ibarranguelua **Beach** • Spain . . . . 96 [88]
Ibarreta • Argentina 52 E4
Ibbenbüren • Germany 8 C4
Ibérico, Sistema • Spain 11 I3
Ibi • Spain 11 K6
Ibi • Nigeria 21 A6
Ibicaraí • Brazil 52 I1
Ibiza **Heritage N** • Spain . . . . 83 [53]
Ibiza **Heritage C** • Spain . . . . 86 [88]
Ibiza • Ibiza, Spain 117 G2
Ibiza [I.] • Spain . . . . 117 G
Ibri • Oman 18 G5
Ibri • Peru 163 B1
Icacos Point •
Trinidad & Tobago . . . . 160 U
Icama • Brazil 51 D3
Içel • Turkey 123 G4
Içel [Adm] • Turkey 123 G3
ICELAND • Atlantic Ocean 16 (1) D2
Içericümra • Turkey 123 G1
Ichihara • Japan 140 C2
Ichikawa • Japan 140 C2
Ichinskaya Sopka, Vulkan •
Russian Fed. 27 Q5
Ichkeul Nat. Park **Heritage N** •
Tunisia . . . . 83 [77]
Ichkeul Nat. Park • Tunisia 131 E2
Ichpaatun • Mexico 157 H4
Icmeler • Turkey 122 D9
Icod de los Vinos **Beach** •
Tenerife, Canary Is. . . . . 96 [109]
Icod de los Vinos •
Tenerife, Canary Is. 116 E1
Idabel • OK, United States 46 H6
Idah • Nigeria 22 F3
Idaho • United States 42 H5
Idaho City • ID, United States 152 B4
Idaho Falls • ID, United States 42 I5
Idan • Somalia 23 H2
Idar-Oberstein • Germany 112 E3
Ideles • Algeria 20 G4
Idéon Antron • Crete, Greece 123 E6
Idfu • Egypt 131 F5
Idhan Awbari • Libya 21 B3
Idhan Murzuq • Libya 21 B3
Idi Oros • Crete, Greece 123 E6
Idlib • Syria 123 G4
Idra • Greece 15 E6
Idra [I.] • Greece 122 D7
Idrettsm • Germany 9 D6
Ie-jima • Japan 140 A10
Ieper • Belgium 109 D13
Ierápetra **Beach** • Crete, Greece . . 97 [215]
Ierápetra • Crete, Greece 123 E8
Ierisoú, Kólpos • Greece 15 E3
Ierissós • Greece 15 E3
Ieshima-shoto • Japan 140 B1
Ifach, Peñon de • Spain 117 C2
Itakara • Tanzania 130 B4
Ife • Nigeria 22 E3
Iferouâne • Niger 20 G5
Ifetesene • Algeria 20 F3
Ifrane • Morocco 131 D2
Igarapé Miri • Brazil 53 (1) B2
Igarapé Tocantins • Brazil 26 O4
Iglesias • Sardinia, Italy 120 C3
Igloolik • NU, Canada 39 O3
Igls • Austria 119 H6
Ignace • OT, Canada 43 K2
Ignalina Nat. Park **Park N** •
Lithuania . . . . 89 [146]
Igneada Burun • Turkey 15 I2
Igneada • Turkey 15 I2
Igombe • Tanzania 23 B4
Igoumenítsa • Greece 15 B4
Igoumenítsa **Beach** • Greece . . . . 97 [173]
Igrim • Russian Fed. 26 J5
Iguaçu • Brazil 52 C4
Iguaçu, Parque Nac. do **Heritage N** •
Brazil . . . . 82 [41]
Iguaçu, Parque Nacional do •
Brazil 52 F4
Iguala • Mexico 157 G4
Igualada • Spain 117 D3
Iguatu • Brazil 53 (1) D3
Iguazú, Cataratas del •
Argentina/Brazil 52 F4
Iguazú, Parque Nac. de **Heritage N** •
Argentina . . . . 82 [42]
Iguéla • Gabon 22 D4
Iguéla, Réserve d' **Park** • Gabon . . 133 [48]

Iguidi, Erg •
Algeria/Mauritania 20 D3
Ih-Obo-Ula • Mongolia 26 O9
Iharana • Madagascar 24 H2
Iheya-jima • Japan 140 A10
Ihlara • Turkey 123 G1
Ihosy • Madagascar 24 H4
Ihuru • Maldives 138 F2
Iide • Japan 30 I7
IJ-Meer • Netherlands 109 F2
Ijebu Ode • Nigeria 22 E3
Ijmuiden • Netherlands 109 F1
IJssel • Netherlands 109 D8
IJsselmeer • Netherlands 109 D7
Ijuí • Brazil 52 F4
IJzendijke • Netherlands 109 D10
IJzer • Belgium 5 F4
Ikaalinen • Finland 125 E2
Ikali • Dem. Rep. of Congo 23 C4
Ikaria • Greece 122 D8
Ikast • Denmark 125 F9
Ikeda • Hokkaido, Japan 30 L3
Ikeda • Osaka, Japan 140 B2
Ikei • Ryusan Fed. 27 F6
Ikeja • Nigeria 22 E3
Iki • Japan 140 A7
Iki • Mexico 157 H2
Ikopa • Madagascar 24 H3
Ikungu • Philippines 31 G3
Ilawa • Poland 13 I4
Ilbenge • Russian Fed. 27 K4
Ile d'Anticosti Prov. Park •
QU, Canada 156 D2
Ile de France • France 10 H4
Ilebo • Dem. Rep. of Congo 23 C4
Ilek • Kazakstan/Russian Fed. 17 I6
Ilerh • Algeria 20 F4
Ilesha • Nigeria 22 E3
Ilfracombe • United Kingdom 104 F2
Ilgaz • Turkey 15 O3
Ilgaz Daglari • Turkey 15 O2
Ilgin • Turkey 15 M5
Ilha do Bananal • Brazil 53 (1) B3
Ilhabela • Brazil 163 C3
Ilhavo • Portugal 11 C4
Ilhavo **Beach** • Portugal . . . . 96 [95]
Ilhéus • Brazil 52 I1
Iliamna Lake •
AK, United States 49 J4
Iligan • Philippines 31 G5
Ilion • NY, United States 44 H4
Ilir • Russian Fed. 27 F6
Ilja • Romania 14 J4
Illapel • Chile 52 B5
Illertissen • Germany 112 F1
Illescas • Majorca, Spain 117 H3
Illiman, Nevado del • Bolivia 52 C2
Illinois [Adm] • United States 41 I4
Illinois [Riv] •
IL, United States 46 J3
Illizi • Algeria 20 G3
Ilm • Germany 9 G6
Ilmen, Ozero • Russian Fed. 26 H2
Ilmenau • Germany 9 G6
Ilo • Peru 163 B4
Iloilo • Philippines 31 G4
Ilomantsi • Finland 16 P5
Ilorin • Nigeria 22 E3
Ilulissat • Greenland 54 U3
Ilwaki • Indonesia 32 (1) C4
Imabari • Japan 30 E8
Imandra, Ozero • Russian Fed. 17 E1
Imari • Japan 30 E8
Imata • Peru 163 B4
Imatra • Finland 16 O6
Imbert • Dominican Rep. 159 G3
Imbituba • Brazil 52 G4
Imboden • AR, United States 46 J4
Imeni Gastello • Russian Fed. 27 O4
Imi • Ethiopia 23 G2
Imilili • Western Sahara 20 B4
Imin • D.P.R. of Korea 30 E4
Immakalee • FL, United States 49 C4
Immenstadt • Germany 112 F6
Imo • Nigeria 22 E3
Imogiri • Java, Indonesia 143 J7
Imola • Italy 121 E7
Imotski • Croatia 128 D4
Imperatorskaya Gavan •
Russian Fed. 27 M7
Imperia • Italy 53 (1) B3
Imperia • Italy 121 E9
Imperial • NE, United States 46 E2
Impfondo • Congo 28 F4
Imphal • India 119 H6
Imst • Austria 119 H6
Imuris • Mexico 45 G6
Imzouren • Morocco 11 H9
Inambari • Peru 163 B2
Inangahua Junction •
New Zealand 35 C5
Inanwatan • Indonesia 32 (1) D3
Iñapari • Peru 51 D6
Inari • Finland 16 N2
Inari [I.] • Finland 16 N2
Inatori Spa • Japan 140 C3
Inawashiro, Japan 117 H1
Inca • Majorca, Spain 117 H3
Inca de Oro • Chile 52 B4
Incaguasi • Chile 52 B4
Ince Burun • Turkey 15 I3
Incekum • Turkey 123 F4
Incekum Burun • Turkey 123 G3
Inch'on • Rep. of Korea 30 D6
Incir Han • Turkey 123 F2
Indalsälven • Sweden 16 I5
Indawgyi • Myanmar 28 E2
Independence •
IA, United States 43 K5
Independence •
KS, United States 46 H4
Independence •
MO, United States 46 H3
Independence Nat. Hist. Park **Park N** •
PA, United States . . . . 151 [300]
Independência • Brazil 53 (1) C3
Independencia, I. • Peru 163 B1
INDIA • Asia 28
Indian Ocean • 3 S8
Indian Peak • UT, United States 45 F2
Indian River •
MI, United States 44 C3
Indian Springs •
NV, United States 45 E3
Indian Town Point •
Antigua & Barbuda . . . . 161 K
Indiana • United States 41 I4
Indiana • PA, United States 153 D5
Indiana Dunes Nat. Lakeshore **Park N** •
IN, United States . . . . 151 [177]
Indianapolis •
IN, United States 44 B6
Indianhead Mtn & Bear Creek **Ski** •
MI, United States . . . . 149 [137]
Indianola • IA, United States 46 I2
Indianola • MS, United States 153 F2
Indiga • Russian Fed. 17 I1
Indija • Yugoslavia 14 H5
Indio • CA, United States 45 D5
INDONESIA • Asia 25 N10
Indore • India 28 C4
Indragiri • Indonesia 32 C3
Indramayu • Java, Indonesia 143 J2
Indravati • India 28 D5

Indre • France 114 D4
Indre [Adm] • France 114 D4
Indre • Norway 124 C3
Indre-et-Loire • France 114 D2
Induruwa • Sri Lanka 138 D15
Indus • Pakistan 28 A3
Inebolu • Turkey 15 O2
Inecik • Turkey 15 I3
Inegöl • Turkey 15 K3
Inezgane • Morocco 20 D2
Inezgane [Apt] • Morocco 131 D5
Infanta, Cape • South Africa 134 C6
Infantado • Portugal 118 D2
Ingalls, Mt • CA, United States 42 E6
Ingelstad • Sweden 125 F8
Ingeniero Jacobaci • Argentina 53 C4
Ingenio •
Gran Canaria, Canary Is. 116 E4
Ingenio Santa Ana • Argentina 52 C4
Ingham • QL, Australia 144 B1
Inglewood • QL, Australia 144 B6
Inglewood • New Zealand 145 F3
Ingolstadt • Germany 9 G8
Ingomar • MT, United States 42 L3
Ingushetia • Russian Fed. 17 H6
Inhambane • Mozambique 24 F4
Inhambane, Baía de • Mozambique . . 24 F4
Inhisar • Turkey 15 L3
Inhumas • Brazil 52 G2
Inirida • Colombia 51 D3
Inishark • Ireland 108 C3
Inishbofin • Ireland 108 C3
Inishcrone **Beach** • Ireland . . . . . 96 [64]
Inishcrone • Ireland 108 C3
Inisheer • Ireland 108 C3
Inishkea North • Ireland 108 C1
Inishkea South • Ireland 108 C1
Inishman • Ireland 108 C3
Inishmore • Ireland 108 C3
Inishmurray • Ireland 108 A1
Inishowan Peninsula • Ireland 108 A1
Inishturk • Ireland 108 C3
Injune • QL, Australia 144 B5
Inkisi • Dem. Rep. of Congo 23 B5
Inland Kaikoura Range •
New Zealand 35 D5
Inland Sea • Japan 30 G7
Inland Sea • Malta 123 H1
Inn • Austria/Germany 119 J3
Innamincka • SA, Australia 34 H5
Innbygda • Norway 16 G6
Inner Mongolia • China 29 E2
Inner Sound • United Kingdom 6 G4
Innfield • Ireland 108 B3
Innichen **Ski** • Italy . . . . 100 [247]
Innichen • Italy 120 B2
Innisfail • QL, Australia 144 B1
Innsbruck • Austria 119 H6
Innvikfjorden • Norway 124 C2
Inongo • Dem. Rep. of Congo 23 B4
Inönü • Turkey 15 L4
Intepe • Turkey 15 H4
Intercourse • PA, United States 153 D10
Interlaken **Ski** • Switzerland . . . . 100 [102]
Interlaken • Switzerland 119 G2
Internacional de las Americas [Apt] •
Dominican Rep. 159 G3
International Drive •
FL, United States 151 C2
International Falls •
MN, United States 43 J2
Intracoastal Waterway •
United States 153 F4
Inukjuak • QU, Canada 39 P5
Inuvik • NT, Canada 38 E3
Invercargill • New Zealand 145 G4
Inverell • New Zealand 145 F3
Inverness • United Kingdom 106 A5
Inverness • Ireland 6 H4
Inverness • FL, United States 49 B3
Inverness • NS, Canada 156 D7
Investigator Group •
SA, Australia 34 F6
Investigator Strait •
SA, Australia 34 G7
Inya • Russian Fed. 27 N5
Inya [Riv] • Russian Fed. 27 N5
Inyo, Mt • CA, United States 45 D3
Inyo Mtns • CA, United States 45 C3
Inzia • Dem. Rep. of Congo 22 H5
Ioánina • Greece 15 B4
Iola • KS, United States 46 H4
Ion Corvin • Romania 128 E2
Ionia • MI, United States 44 C4
Ionian Is. • Greece 122 B/C4
Ionian Sea • Europe 4 N9
Iónion Pélagos • Greece 15 B6
Ios **Beach** • Greece . . . . 97 [208]
Ios • Greece 122 D8
Ios [I.] • Greece 122 D8
Iowa • United States 41 H3
Iowa City • IA, United States 46 J2
Iowa Falls • IA, United States 43 J5
Iowa [Riv] • IA, United States 43 J6
Ipameri • Brazil 52 G2
Ipanema • Brazil 52 I2
Ipatinga • Brazil 52 H3
Ipek • Rep. of Yugoslavia 90 A14
Ipiales • Colombia 51 B3
Ipiaú • Brazil 52 I1
Ipirós • Greece 122 A1
Ipixuna • Brazil 51 C5
Ipoh • Malaysia 141 G1
Ipoly • Slovak Rep. 14 G1
Iporá • Brazil 52 C2
Iprona • Turkey 14 N9
Ipsala • Turkey 15 H3
Ipsos • Corfu, Greece 122 B1
Ipswich • United Kingdom 7 N9
Ipswich • QL, Australia 144 B6
Ipswich • SD, United States 43 G4
Ipú • Brazil 53 (1) C3
Iqaluit • NU, Canada 39 R4
Iquique • Chile 51 C4
Iquitos • Peru 51 C4
Iracoubo • French Guiana 51 G2
Iráklia • Greece 122 D8
Iráklio • Crete, Greece 123 E3
Iráklio [Adm] • Crete, Greece 123 E7
IRAN • Asia 18 F3
Iranshahr • Iran 18 I4
Iraník • Iran 18 H3
Irapuato • Mexico 157 F4
IRAQ • Asia 18 E3
Irati • Brazil 52 F4
Irazú, Volcán • Costa Rica 37 E5
Irbid • Jordan 18 E3
Irbil • Iraq 18 E3
Irebu • Dem. Rep. of Congo 26 J6
Irebu • Dem. Rep. of Congo 23 B4
IRELAND • Europe 6 F4
Ireland I. North • Bermuda 159 J1
Ireland I. South • Bermuda 159 J1
Irelands Eye • Ireland 108 B2
Iren • Rep. of Korea 30 D7
Irian [I.] • Indonesia 32 (1) I4
Irian Jaya • Indonesia 32 (1) I4
Iringa • Tanzania 130 B4
Iriomote • Japan 29 G6
Iriri • Brazil 51 G4
Irish Sea • Ireland/UK 7 H8
Irituia • Brazil 53 (1) B2

Itapebi • Brazil 52 I2
Itaperuna • Brazil 163 C2
Itapetinga • Brazil 52 H2
Itapetininga • Brazil 52 G3
Itapicuru • Brazil 53 (1) C2
Itapicuru-Mirim • Brazil 53 (1) C2
Itapipoca • Brazil 53 (1) D2
Itaqui • Brazil 52 E4
Itarsi • India 28 C4
Itatiaia • Brazil 163 C3
Itaúna • Brazil 163 C1
Itbay • Egypt 21 F2
Itchan Kala **Heritage C** •
Uzbekistan . . . . 85 [94]
Itéa **Beach** • Greece . . . . 97 [176]
Ithaca • Greece 122 C2
Ithaca • NY, United States 153 D2
Ithákï • Greece 122 C2
Ithákï [I.] • Greece 122 C2
Iti • Greece 15 D5
Iti Oros Nat. Park **Park N** •
Greece . . . . 89 [138]
Ito • Japan 140 C3
Iton • France 10 F5
Itremo, Massif de l' •
Madagascar 24 H4
Itsukushima Shrine **Heritage C** •
Japan . . . . 85 [187]
Itter • Austria 119 H3
Ittoqqortoormiit • Greenland 36 O2
Ituiutaba • Brazil 52 G2
Itumbiara • Brazil 52 G2
Iturup, Ostrov • Russian Fed. 27 O8
Itzehoe • Germany 8 E3
Iultin • Russian Fed. 27 V3
Iúna • Brazil 163 C2
Ivajlovgrad • Bulgaria 15 H2
Ivalo • Finland 16 N2
Ivalojoki • Finland 16 N2
Ivangorod • Russian Fed. 16 O7
Ivanhoe • NS, Australia 144 C1
Ivano-Frankivs'k • Ukraine 17 C5
Ivanovo **Heritage C** • Bulgaria . . . 86 [201]
Ivanovo • Russian Fed. 126 C4
Ivanovo • Bulgaria 128 C3
Ivdel • Russian Fed. 26 J5
Ivenack **Castle** • Germany . . . . . 113 [225]
Iveragh Peninsula • Ireland 108 C7
Ivindo • Congo/Gabon 22 G4
Ivittuut • Greenland 39 V4
Ivory Coast • Africa 22 C4
Ivõsjön • Sweden 125 F11
Ivrea • Italy 120 B2
Ivrindi • Turkey 15 I4
Ivujivik • QU, Canada 39 P4
Ivvavik Nat. Park • YT, Canada 49 N2
Ivvavik Nat. Park **Park N** •
YT, Canada . . . . 156 [1]
Iwaco • WA, United States 42 C3
Iwaizumi • Japan 30 K4
Iwaki [Mtn] • Japan 30 G4
Iwakuni • Japan 30 G7
Iwanai • Japan 30 K3
Iwate • Japan 140 A5
Iwate • Japan 30 K5
Iwatsuki • Japan 25 P7
Iwo • Japan 30 E4
Iwotori-shima • Japan 140 A10
Ixiamas • Bolivia 52 C1
Ixopo • South Africa 134 B5
Ixtapa • Mexico 157 G3
Ixtapan del Oro • Mexico 157 G4
Izabal, Lago de • Guatemala 37 D4
Izamal • Mexico 157 H2
Izhevsk • Russian Fed. 17 I3
Izmayil • Ukraine 14 P4
Izmir • Turkey 122 D5
Izmir Körfezi • Turkey 15 H5
Izmit • Turkey 15 K3
Izmit Körfezi • Turkey 15 K3
Iznajar, Embalse de • Spain 11 G7
Iznik • Turkey 122 D3
Iznik Gölü • Turkey 122 D3
Iztochni Rodopi • Bulgaria 14 M8
Izu-hanto • Japan 140 C3
Izu-shoto • Japan 140 J8
Izúcar de Matamoros • Mexico 157 G4
Izuhara • Japan 30 E7
Izumi-sanmakyu • Japan 140 B4
Izumiotsu • Japan 140 B3
Izumisano • Japan 140 B3
Izumo • Japan 30 G7
Izvestiy Tsik, Ostrova •
Russian Fed. 26 N2
Izyum • Ukraine 17 F5

Irkutsk • Russian Fed. 27 F6
Iro-zaki • Japan 140 C3
Iroise • France 114 C1
Iron Mtn • MI, United States 44 A3
Ironbridge • United Kingdom 104 D1
Ironbridge Gorge **Heritage C** •
United Kingdom . . . . 86 [20]
Irondequoit • NY, United States 44 G4
Ironside • OR, United States 42 G4
Ironton • OH, United States 44 D6
Ironton • MO, United States 46 J4
Ironwood • MI, United States 43 K3
Iroulëguy • France 114 B3
Irqah, Al • Yemen 18 E7
Irrawaddy • Myanmar 31 B3
Irrsdorf • Austria 119 H4
Irtysh • Asia 26 L6
Iruma • Japan 140 C1
Irum • Spain 11 J2
Irurzun • Spain 11 J2
Irvine • United Kingdom 6 H6
Irvine • CA, United States 45 D5
Irving • TX, United States 47 F1
Irwin • ID, United States 42 J5
Isa, Ra's • Yemen 21 H5
Isabel de Torres, Pico •
Dominican Rep. 159 G3
Isabela • Philippines 31 G5
Isabela • Galapagos Is. 51 (1) A2
Isabela • Puerto Rico 159 H1
Isabela, Cabo • Dominican Rep. 159 G3
Isabela de Sagua • Cuba 158 D2
Isabela, Cordillera •
Nicaragua 37 D5
Isabela • Philippines 31 G4
Isafjördur • Iceland 16 (1) D1
Isahaya • Japan 30 F8
Iseo, Lago di • Italy 115 F3
Isère • France 115 F3
Isère [Adm] • France 115 F3
Iserlohn • Germany 111 B2
Iset • Russian Fed. 26 K6
Iseyin • Nigeria 22 E3
Isfahan • Iran 18 F3
Isfahan **Heritage C** • Iran . . . . . . 85 [126]
Isfendiyar Daglari • Turkey 15 O2
Isfjorden • Norway 124 C2
Isha Baydabo • Somalia 23 G3
Isherton • Guyana 51 F3
Ishigaki • Japan 31 G2
Ishigaki-jima • Japan 140 A10
Ishikari-wan • Japan 30 K3
Ishim • Russian Fed. 26 L6
Ishim [Riv] • Russian Fed. 26 L6
Ishimskaya Step • Russian Fed. 26 K6
Ishinomaki • Japan 30 K5
Ishodnaya, gora • Russian Fed. 27 W4
Ishoej **Beach** • Denmark . . . . . . 96 [39]
Ishpeming • MI, United States 44 A3
Isigny-sur-Mer • France 5 B5
Isilkul • Russian Fed. 26 L7
Isiolo • Kenya 131 G2
Isipingo • South Africa 134 B5
Isiro • Dem. Rep. of Congo 23 D3
Iskandarîya, El • Egypt 131 F1
Iskele • Cyprus 123 G4
Iskenderun • Turkey 123 G4
Iskenderun Körfezi • Turkey 123 G4
Isla Cristina **Beach** • Spain . . . . . 96 [112]
Isla Cristina • Spain 116 B1
Isla Mujeres • Mexico 157 H2
Isla Vista • CA, United States 45 C4
Islahiye • Turkey 123 G4
Islamabad • Pakistan 28 B2
Islamorada • FL, United States 154 H8
Island Harbour • Anguilla . . . . 160 C
Island Park Reservoir •
ID, United States 42 J4
Islands, Bay of • NF, Canada 156 D3
Islantilla **Beach** • Spain . . . . 96 [112]
Islay • United Kingdom 6 F6
Isle • France 115 G1
Isle Royale Nat. Park **Park N** •
MI, United States . . . . 151 [157]
Isle Royale Nat. Park •
MI, United States 43 L3
Islote de Hilario •
Lanzarote, Canary Is. 117 E3
Ismâ'ïlîya • Egypt 131 F2
Ismoili Somoni • Tajikistan 26 L10
Isna • Egypt 131 F4
Isny • Germany 112 F5
Isny **Spa** • Germany . . . . 113 [h10]
Isoka • Zambia 24 E2
Isola 2000 • France 115 H2
Isonzo • Italy 121 E4
Isparta • Turkey 123 F1
Isparta [Adm] • Turkey 123 F1
Ispica • Sicily, Italy 12 I12
Ispica, Cava d' • Sicily, Italy 120 D4
ISRAEL • Asia 18 I8
Issoudun • France 10 H7
Issum • Germany 111 B1
Issyk-kul • Kyrgyzstan 159 F1
Ist • Croatia 128 B1
Istanbul **Heritage C** • Turkey . . . 86 [225]
Istanbul • Turkey 122 D3
Istanbul-Bakirköy • Turkey 15 J3
Istanbul-Kadiköy • Turkey 15 E5
Istappa, Lake •
FL, United States 49 C4
Istra • Croatia 128 D1
Istria • Croatia 128 A2
Itabaianinha • Brazil 52 I1
Itabapoana • Brazil 163 C2
Itaberaba • Brazil 52 H1
Itaberaí • Brazil 52 G2
Itabira • Brazil 163 C2
Itabuna • Brazil 52 H1
Itacoatiara • Brazil 51 F4
Itaguí • Colombia 51 B2
Itaipu, Represa de •
Brazil/Paraguay 52 F4
Itaituba • Brazil 51 F4
Itajaí • Brazil 52 G4
Itajubá • Brazil 163 C3
Itala Nature Reserve •
South Africa 134 B2
Italian Lake District • Italy 120 A1
ITALY • Europe 52 H2
Itambé, Pico da • Brazil 52 H2
Itambé • Brazil 52 I1
Itami [Apt] • Japan 140 B2
Itanagar • India 28 E3
Itanós • Crete, Greece 123 E8

J.A.D. Jensen Nunatakker •
Greenland 39 V4
J.B. Thomas, Lake •
TX, United States 47 D1
J.F. Mitchell [Apt] •
St Vincent & Gren. . . . . 161 R
J.N. 'Ding' Darling Nat. Wildlife Refuge •
FL, United States 154 H7
J. Percy Priest Lake •
TN, United States 48 D2
Ja'el • Somalia 23 I1
Jabal al Qarantal • Palestine 135 A6
Jabal, Bahr al • Sudan 23 E2
Jabalpur • India 28 C4
Jabbeke **Beach** • Belgium . . . . . 96 [70]
Jabbeke • Belgium 109 C2
Jabjabah, Wadi • Egypt 21 F3
Jablanica • Bosnia-Herz. 12 L5
Jablonec nad Nisou • Czech Rep. . . . 13 E7
Jablonné v Podjestedí •
Czech Rep. 128 B2
Jabridge Wilderness Area •
NV, United States 152 C2
Jabuticabal • Brazil 52 G3
Jaca • Spain 11 K2
Jacarezinho • Brazil 52 C4
Jáchal • Argentina 52 C4
Jáchymov • Czech Rep. 128 B1
Jack Frost **Ski** •
PA, United States . . . . 149 [178]
Jack Frost • PA, United States 153 D6
Jackman • ME, United States 44 J3
Jackpot • NV, United States 42 H6
Jacksboro • TX, United States 46 F6
Jackson • WY, United States 42 J5
Jackson • MN, United States 43 I5
Jackson • CA, United States 45 C4
Jackson • OH, United States 48 E1
Jackson • TN, United States 48 C3
Jackson • MS, United States 153 F2
Jackson Head • New Zealand 35 B7
Jackson Hole, Teton **Ski** •
WY, United States . . . . 149 [85]
Jackson Lake •
WY, United States 42 J5
Jackson, Mt • Antarctica 54 (1) II2
Jackson Prairie •
MS, United States 153 F2
Jackson Reef **Dive** • Red Sea . . . 135 B1
Jackson's Point • Cayman Is. 159 E1
Jacksonville •
OR, United States 42 D5
Jacksonville •
AR, United States 46 I5

Jacksonville •
    IL, United States 46 J3
Jacksonville •
    NC, United States 48 I3
Jacksonville •
    FL, United States 154 H3
Jacksonville •
    TX, United States 154 J2
Jacksonville Beach •
    FL, United States 48 C2
Jacmel • Haiti 159 G6
Jacob's Well • Palestine 135 A6
Jacobabad • Pakistan 28 A3
Jacobina • Brazil 53 (1) C4
Jacques-Cartier, Détroit de •
    QU, Canada 156 D2
Jacques-Cartier, Mt •
    QU, Canada 156 D2
Jacques-Cartier Prov. Park •
    QU, Canada 156 D1
Jacul, Rio • Brazil 52 F5
Jaddi, Ras • Pakistan 18 H4
Jadebusen • Germany 5 L1
Jadida, El • Morocco 131 D1
Jadu • Libya 21 B1
Jægerspris Beach • Denmark . . 96 [41]
Jaén • Spain 116 B3
Jaeren • Norway 16 C7
Jaffa • Israel 135 A5
Jaffa, Cape • SA, Australia 34 G7
Jaffar, Cirque de • Morocco 131 E2
Jaffna • Sri Lanka 138 D11
Jaffrey • NH, United States 44 I4
Jagaraga Temple •
    Bali, Indonesia 143 H2
Jagdalpur • India 28 D5
Jagodina • F.R. of Yugoslavia . . . 14 I6
Jagst • Germany 9 E7
Jaguaquara • Brazil 52 I1
Jaguarão • Brazil 52 F5
Jagüey Grande • Cuba 158 D2
Jahrom • Iran 18 F4
Jailolo • Indonesia 32 (1) C2
Jaina • Mexico 157 H1
Jaipur • India 137 C6
Jaisalmer • India 137 C1
Jajce • Bosnia-Herz. 12 D3
Jakarta • Java, Indonesia 143 J1
Jakobshavn • Greenland 54 U3
Jakobstad • Finland 16 L5
Jakupica • F.Y.R. of Macedonia . . 15 B2
Jalalabad • Afghanistan 28 B2
Jalapa • Mexico 157 G2
Jalasjärvi • Finland 16 L5
Jalgaon • India 28 C4
Jalisco • Mexico 37 (1) B1
Jalón • Spain 10 C12
Jalor • India 137 C5
Jamaare • Nigeria 20 G6
JAMAICA • West Indies . . . . 159 F
Jamalpur • Bangladesh 28 E4
Jamame • Somalia 23 G3
Jamanota • Aruba . . . . 160 Y
Jamantau, gora • Russian Fed. . . 26 I7
Jambi • Indonesia 32 C3
Jameos del Agua •
    Lanzarote, Canary Is. 117 E3
James • ND/SD, United States . . . 48 H4
James • SC, United States 48 H4
James • VA, United States 153 D11
James A. Garfield Nat. Hist. Site Park N •
    OH, United States . . . . 151 [184]
James Bay • NU, Canada 39 O6
James, Fort • Antigua & Barbuda . 161 K
James Ross Strait • NU, Canada . 38 L2
Jamestown • St Helena 19 D7
Jamestown • SA, Australia 34 L5
Jamestown • ND, United States . . 43 G3
Jamestown • NY, United States . . 153 D1
Jamestown • VA, United States . . 153 D11
Jammerbugten • Denmark 125 F5
Jammu • Jammu & Kashmir 28 B2
Jammu & Kashmir • Asia 28 C2
Jamnagar • India 28 B4
Jämsä • Finland 125 E2
Jämsänkoski • Finland 125 E2
Jamshedpur • India 28 E4
Jamtland • Sweden 16 F3
Jamti Historieland Park L •
    Sweden . . . . 98 [9]
Jan Mayen • Greenland Sea 4 I2
Janauca • Brazil 51 H3
Jandia •
    Fuerteventura, Canary Is. 117 E2
Jandía Playa •
    Fuerteventura, Canary Is. 117 E2
Jandía, Punta de •
    Fuerteventura, Canary Is. 117 E2
Jane Peak • New Zealand 145 G2
Janesville • WI, United States . . . 43 L5
Janos • Mexico 157 F2
Jánoshalma • Hungary 13 I11
Jánosháza • Hungary 12 L1
Janské Lázne • Czech Rep. 128 B2
Januária • Brazil 52 H2
JAPAN • Asia 30
Japan, Sea of • Asia 30 G4
Japan Trench • Pacific Ocean . . . 30 M6
Japanese Gardens Dive • Red Sea . 135 B1
Japim • Brazil 51 D4
Japura • Brazil 51 D4
Jarabacoa • Dominican Rep. . . . 159 G3
Jaragua, Parque Nac. •
    Dominican Rep. 159 G6
Jaramillo • Argentina 53 C5
Jarandilla • Spain 11 F4
Jard-sur-Mer Beach • France . . 96 [83]
Jard-sur-Mer • France 114 D3
Jardim • Brazil 52 E3
Jardin d'Acclimation Park L •
    France . . . . 98 [68]
Jardin de la France • France . . . 114 B1
Jardines de la Reina, Archipiélago
    de los • Cuba 158 D7
Jaren • Norway 124 B2
Jari • Brazil 51 G2
Järlåsa • Sweden 125 D1
Jarmah • Libya 21 B2
Järna • Sweden 125 D4
Järnlunden • Sweden 125 F4
Jarocin • Poland 13 G6
Jarorner • Czech Rep. 128 B2
Jaroslaw • Poland 13 L8
Järvenpää • Finland 125 E2
Jarvis • Pacific Ocean 33 K5
Jask • Iran 18 G4
Jaslo • Poland 13 K8
Jasmund, Nationalpark Park N •
    Germany . . . . 89 [59]
Jason Islands • Falkland Is. 53 D6
Jasper • AL, United States 48 D1
Jasper • IN, United States 48 D1
Jasper • TX, United States 154 J4
Jasper • AL, Canada 155 C2
Jasper Nat. Park • AL, Canada . 155 C2
Jasper Nat. Park Park N •
    AL, Canada . . . . 156 [16]
Jassy • Romania 90 A15
Jastrzebie Zdroj • Poland 128 C3
Jászárokszállás • Hungary 13 I10
Jászberény • Hungary 13 I10
Jatai • Brazil 52 F2
Jatibonico • Cuba 158 D3
Jatijajar Caves •
    Java, Indonesia 143 J6

Jatiwangi • Java, Indonesia 143 J2
Jaú • Brazil 52 G3
Jauja • Peru 163 B1
Jaunpur • India 137 C8
Java • Indonesia . . . . 143 J
Java Sea • Indonesia 32 D3
Java Trench • Indonesia 32 D3
Jávea Beach • Spain . . . . 96 [118]
Jávia • Spain 117 C2
Javier • Spain 11 J2
Javor Osa • Bosnia-Herz. 14 F5
Jawa • Indonesia 32 D4
Jawa Barat • Java, Indonesia . . . 143 J1
Jawa Tengah • Java, Indonesia . . 143 J3
Jawa Timur • Java, Indonesia . . . 143 J8
Jawf, Al • Saudi Arabia 18 C4
Jawf, Al • Libya 21 D3
Jawi • Penang, Malaysia 141 F4
Jawor • Poland 13 F6
Jaworzno • Poland 128 C1
Jaxartes • Asia 127 D2
Jay Peak Ski •
    VT, United States . . . . 149 [216]
Jaya Ancol Dreamland •
    Java, Indonesia 143 J1
Jaya, Puncak • Indonesia 32 (1) E3
Jayapura Grave •
    Bali, Indonesia 143 H1
Jayapura • Indonesia 32 (1) F3
Jayawijaya, Pegunungen •
    Indonesia 32 (1) E3
Jaziran, Al • Sudan 21 F5
Jazovir Iskar • Bulgaria 14 K7
Jean Lafitte Nat. Hist. Park •
    LA, United States 153 F4
Jean Lafitte Nat. Hist. Park & Preserve
    Park N • LA, United States . 151 [193]
Jeanerette • LA, United States . . 47 I3
Jebha • Morocco 11 G9
Jeddah • Saudi Arabia 18 C5
Jeddore Lake • NF, Canada 156 D3
Jedrzejów • Poland 128 C2
Jefferson • WI, United States . . . 43 L5
Jefferson • TX, United States . . 154 J2
Jefferson City •
    MO, United States 46 I3
Jefferson City •
    TN, United States 48 F2
Jefferson, Fort •
    FL, United States 154 H7
Jefferson, Mt •
    OR, United States 42 E4
Jefferson Nat. Expansion Mem. Park N •
    MO, United States . . . . . . 151 [175]
Jeffersontown •
    KY, United States 48 E1
Jeffersonville •
    KY, United States 48 E1
Jeffrey's Bay • South Africa . . . 134 C8
Jega • Nigeria 20 F6
Jekabpils • Latvia 126 B4
Jelai • Malaysia 141 G2
Jelena Gora • Poland 13 F7
Jelgava • Latvia 126 B3
Jelling Heritage C • Denmark . . . 86 [11]
Jelling • Denmark 125 F9
Jeløy • Norway 124 B4
Jels • Denmark 125 F13
Jelutong • Penang, Malaysia . . . 141 F2
Jem, El • Tunisia 131 E4
Jemaja • Indonesia 31 D6
Jember • Java, Indonesia 143 J8
Jemiste • Czech Rep. 128 B1
Jena • Germany 9 G6
Jendouba • Tunisia 12 C12
Jenner • Germany 112 F8
Jennings • LA, United States . . 153 F3
Jenolan Caves • NS, Australia . . 144 C2
Jensen Beach •
    FL, United States 49 C4
John F. Kennedy [Apt] •
    NY, United States 49 D3
John F. Kennedy Nat. Hist. Site Park N •
    MA, United States . . . . . . 151 [304]
John F. Kennedy Space Center •
    FL, United States 154 H6
John H. Kerr Reservoir •
    VA, United States 48 H7
John Muir Nat. Hist. Site Park N •
    CA, United States . . . . . . 150 [46]
John o'Groats • United Kingdom . . 6 I3
John Pennekamp Coral Reef State Park •
    FL, United States 154 H8
John Redmond Reservoir •
    KS, United States 46 H3
Johns Lake • FL, United States . . 151 C1
Johnson • KS, United States 46 E4
Johnson, Andrew, Nat. Hist. Site
    Park N • TN, United States . 151 [228]
Johnson City •
    NY, United States 44 H4
Johnson City •
    TN, United States 48 F2
Johnson Space Center •
    TX, United States 154 J4
Johnstown • PA, United States . . 153 D5
Johnstown Flood Nat. Mem. Park N •
    PA, United States . . . . 151 [293]
Johnstown Flood Nat. Mem. •
    PA, United States 153 D5
Johor • Malaysia 31 C6
Johor Baharu • Malaysia 141 H1
Johor Strait •
    Malaysia/Singapore 141 H2
Joigny • France 10 I6
Joinville • Brazil 52 G4
Joinville • France 10 K5
Jokkmokk • Sweden 16 J3
Jökulsárgljúfur Nat. Park Park N •
    Iceland . . . . 89 [1]
Joliet • IL, United States 44 A5
Joliette • QU, Canada 155 B3
Jolo • Philippines 31 J5
Jolo Group • Philippines 31 G5
Jolstravatnet • Norway 124 C1
Jombang • Java, Indonesia 143 J7
Jomfruland • Norway 124 B3
Jomsom • Nepal 137 C4
Jonava • Lithuania 126 B6
Jonesboro • AR, United States . . 46 J3
Jonesville • LA, United States . . 153 F1
Jonglei • Sudan 23 E2
Jonglei Canal • Sudan 23 E2
Jönköping • Sweden 125 F7
Jonquera, la • Spain 117 D2
Jonquière • QU, Canada 156 D1
Joplin • MO, United States 46 H4
Joppa • Israel 135 A5
JORDAN • Asia 18 B3
Jordan • MT, United States 42 L3
Jordan Lake • AL, United States . 48 D4
Jordan [Riv] • Israel 135 A6
Jordan Valley •
    OR, United States 42 G5
Jorhat • India 28 F3
Jörn • Sweden 16 K4
Jerpeland • Norway 124 C3
Jos • Nigeria 20 G6
Jos Plateau • Nigeria 20 G6
José de San Martin • Argentina . . 53 B4
José Miguel, Cuevas de • Cuba . 158 D1
Joseph Bonaparte Gulf •
    WA, Australia 34 G2
Joseph, Lac • NF, Canada 39 R6
Joshua Tree Nat. Park Park N •
    CA, United States . . . . 150 [57]
Joshua Tree Nat. Park •
    CA, United States 152 C6

Jilin [Adm] • China 139 A4
Jim Thorpe • PA, United States . . 44 H5
Jima • Ethiopia 23 F2
Jiman • Dominican Rep. 159 G6
Jimbaran Beach •
    Bali, Indonesia 143 H4
Jimbe • Angola 23 C6
Jimbolia • Romania 14 H4
Jimena de la Frontera • Spain . . . 11 F8
Jiménez • Mexico 47 B4
Jimani, Salto de •
    Dominican Rep. 159 G3
Jiminy Peak Ski •
    MA, United States . . . . 149 [202]
Jiminy Peak • MA, United States . 153 D3
Jimmy Carter Nat. Hist. Site Park N •
    GA, United States . . . . 151 [209]
Jin I • Hong Kong, China 139 B6
Jinan • China 29 F3
Jindrichuv Hradec • Czech Rep. . 128 B4
Jing Xian • China 139 C3
Jingde • China 139 C3
Jingdezhen • China 29 F5
Jinggang Shan • China 31 E1
Jinghe • China 26 N9
Jinghong • China 31 C2
Jingjiang • China 139 D4
Jingyu • China 30 D3
Jinhua • China 29 F5
Jining • Nei Monggol, China 29 E2
Jining • Shandong, China 29 F3
Jinja • Uganda 23 E3
Jinmen • Taiwan 31 F2
Jinsha • China 139 C2
Jinsha Jiang • China 31 C2
Jinshan • China 139 C4
Jintan • China 139 C1
Jinzhou • China 29 G2
Jiparaná • Brazil 51 E4
Jipijapa • Ecuador 51 A4
Jiuhua Shan • China 139 A8
Jiujiang • China 29 F5
Jiuquan • China 29 B3
Jiuzhaigou Valley Heritage N •
    China . . . . 83 [123]
Jiuzhou • China 139 B1
Jiwa, Al • United Arab Emirates . . 18 F5
Jiwani, Ras • Pakistan 18 H4
Jixi • Heilongjiang, China 29 I1
Jixi • Anhui, China 139 C3
Jizan • Saudi Arabia 18 D6
Jizo-zaki • Japan 30 G7
Jizzakh • Uzbekistan 26 K9
João Pessoa • Brazil 53 (1) E3
João Pinheiro • Brazil 52 G2
Jochberg Ski • Austria . . . . . . 100 [161]
Jochgrimm • Italy 120 B3
Jódar • Spain 11 H7
Jodhpur • India 137 C5
Joensuu • Finland 16 O5
Joetsu • Japan 30 J4
Jog Falls • India 138 D6
Joga-shima • Japan 140 C4
Jõgeva • Estonia 126 B2
Johannesburg • South Africa . . . 24 D5
Johannisburg Castle • Germany . 113 [173]
Johannterkastell Biebelried Castle •
    Germany . . . . 113 [165]
John D. Rockefeller Jr. Mem. Parkway
    Park N • WY, United States . 150 [73]
John Day • OR, United States . . . 42 F4
John Day Fossil Beds Nat. Mon. Park N •
    OR, United States . . . . 150 [34]
John Day Fossil Beds Nat. Mon. •
    OR, United States 152 B3

Josselin • France 114 C4
Jost van Dyke •
    British Virgin Is. . . . . 160 B
Jostedalsbreen • Norway 124 C2
Jostedalsbreen • Norway 124 C2
Jotunheimen • Norway 124 C2
Jotunheimen Nat. Park Park N •
    Norway . . . . 89 [14]
Jotunheimen Nat. Park • Norway . 124 C2
Joubertina • South Africa 134 C7
Joue du Loup, la Ski • France . . 100 [64]
Joumâa • Tunisia 131 E6
Joutsa • Finland 125 E2
Joutseno • Finland 16 O6
Jovellanos • Cuba 158 D2
Joya de Cerén Heritage C •
    Panama . . . . 84 [35]
Joyce's Country • Ireland. 108 C3
Juan de Fuca, Strait of •
    Canada/United States 155 C3
Juan de Nova • Réunion 24 G3
Juan Dolio • Dominican Rep. . . 159 G8
Juan Fernandez, Archipiélago •
    Pacific Ocean 50 B8
Juan Francisco, Playa • Cuba . . 158 D3
Juan les Pins • France 115 H4
Juancho Yrausquin [Apt] • Saba . 161 F
Juárez • Mexico 47 D4
Juázeiro • Brazil 53 (1) C3
Juázeiro do Norte • Brazil . . . 53 (1) D3
Juba • Sudan 23 E3
Jubaland • Somalia 23 G3
Jubba, Webi • Somalia 23 G3
Juby, Cap • Morocco 131 D2
Júcar • Spain 11 J5
Júcaro • Cuba 158 D3
Jüchen • Germany 111 B3
Judaberg • Norway 124 C5
Judaea • Israel/Palestine 135 A7
Judaea, Wilderness of •
    Israel/Palestine 135 A7
Judenburg • Austria 13 D10
Judith Basin •
    MT, United States 42 K3
Jueqiang • China 139 C2
Juelsminde Beach • Denmark . . . 96 [46]
Juelsminde • Denmark 125 F10
Juhu Beach Beach • India 138 E3
Jui • Romania 14 K5
Juist • Germany 8 B3
Juist Spa • Germany . . . . 113 [c10]
Juiz de Fora • Brazil 163 C4
Jukkeegga • Norway 124 C4
Juli • Peru 163 B4
Julia Creek • QL, Australia 34 H4
Juliaca • Peru 163 B4
Julian Alps • Slovenia 128 A2
Juliana Kanaal • Netherlands. . . . 5 I3
Juliana Top • Surinam 51 F3
Julianadorp • Curaçao . . . . 160 X
Jülich • Germany 9 B6
Julijske Alpe • Slovenia 12 H2
Julimes • Mexico 47 B3
Julita • Sweden 125 D3
Jullundur • India 28 C2
Jumba • Kenya 23 G5
Jumet • Belgium 111 C1
Junagadh • India 28 B4
Junaynah, Al • Sudan 21 D5
Junction • TX, United States 47 E2
Junction City •
    KS, United States 46 G3
June Lake • CA, United States . . 45 C3
June Mtn Ski •
    CA, United States . . . . 149 [68]
Juneau • AK, United States 49 O4
Junee • NS, Australia 144 C1
Jungfrau • Switzerland 119 G2
Junggar Basin • China 139 A1
Junggar Pendi • China 26 O8
Jungutbatu • Indonesia 143 H3
Juniata • PA, United States 153 D5
Junin • Argentina 163 D1
Junipero Serra Peak •
    CA, United States 45 B3
Junsele • Sweden 16 I5
Juntura • OR, United States 42 F5
Jupiá, Represa de • Brazil 52 F3
Jupiter • Romania 14 M6
Jura • United Kingdom 6 F6
Jura, Sound of • United Kingdom . 6 G6
Juradó • Colombia 51 B2
Jurançon • France 114 B3
Jurbarkas • Lithuania 126 B5
Jurilovca • Romania 14 L6
Jurmala • Latvia 126 B3
Jurong • China 139 C1
Jurong Bird Park • Singapore . . 141 H1
Jurong New Town • Singapore . . 141 H1
Juru • Penang, Malaysia 141 F4
Jurua • Brazil 51 C5
Juruena • Brazil 51 F6
Juruena [Riv] • Brazil 51 F5
Juruti • Brazil 51 F4
Justo Daract • Argentina 163 D1
Jutaí • Brazil 51 D5
Jutaí [Riv] • Brazil 131 G1
Jüterbog • Germany 8 I5
Jutland • Denmark 125 G1
Juuka • Finland 16 O5
Juva • Finland 16 N6
Juventud, I. de la • Cuba 158 D1
Jyderup • Denmark 125 F10
Jylland • Denmark 125 F9
Jyväskylä • Finland 125 E2

K'ut'aisi • Georgia 17 G6
K2 • China/Kashmir 28 C1
Ka • Nigeria 22 E2
Ka, Laem • Ko Phuket, Thailand . 142 E2
Kaabong • Uganda 23 F2
Kaakhka • Turkmenistan 18 G2
Kaala • MN, United States 154 G5
Kaamanen • Finland 16 N2
Kaarst • Germany 111 B3
Kaarta • Mali 22 C2
Kaatsheuvel • Netherlands 109 D11
Kaabonea • Indonesia 32 (1) B4
Kabah • Mexico 157 H1
Kabala • Sierra Leone 22 B3
Kabale • Uganda 130 B1
Kabalega Falls • Uganda 23 E3
Kabalo • Dem. Rep. of Congo . . 23 D5
Kabanjahe • Indonesia 143 G2
Kabardino-Balkaria •
    Russian Fed. 17 G6
Kabba • Nigeria 22 E3
Kábdalis • Sweden 16 K3
Kabinakagami Lake •
    ON, United States 43 J2
Kabin Buri • Thailand 142 C2
Kabinakagami Lake • OT, Canada . 155 A2
Kabinda • Dem. Rep. of Congo . 23 C5
Kableshkovo • Bulgaria 15 I1
Kablow-Ziegelei • Germany . . . 111 C4
Kabo • Central African Rep. 22 H3
Kabompo • Zambia 24 C6
Kabongo • Dem. Rep. of Congo . 23 C5
Kabul • Afghanistan 18 I3
Kabunda • Dem. Rep. of Congo . 24 D2

Kabwe • Zambia 24 D2
Kacanik • F.R. of Yugoslavia . . . 15 C1
Kachin • Myanmar 31 B1
Kachug • Russian Fed. 27 G6
Kacina • Czech Rep. 128 B2
Kackar Dagi • Turkey 18 D1
Kadad I. • India 138 D9
Kadan • Czech Rep. 128 B1
Kadan Kyun • Myanmar 31 B4
Kadei •
    Cameroon/Central African Rep. . 22 G4
Kadinhani • Turkey 15 N5
Kadiri • Turkey 123 G2
Kadoka • SD, United States 43 F5
Kadoma • Zimbabwe 130 C2
Kaduna • Nigeria 22 F2
Kaduna Plateau • Nigeria 22 F2
Kaduna [Riv] • Nigeria 22 F2
Kadugli • Sudan 21 E5
Kaduy • Russian Fed. 126 C2
Kadzherom • Russian Fed. 17 J2
Kaédi • Mauritania 20 C5
Kaena Point • HI, United States . 154 G5
Kaesong • D.P.R. of Korea 30 D6
Kaew Noi, Ko • Thailand 142 E1
Kaew Yai, Ko • Thailand 142 E1
Kafakumba • Dem. Rep. of Congo . 24 C1
Kaffrine • Senegal 20 B6
Kafiréa, Stenó • Greece 15 F6
Kafiréas, Akra • Greece 15 F6
Kafue • Zambia 24 D3
Kafue Dam • Zambia 24 D3
Kafue Flats • Zambia 24 D3
Kafue Nat. Park Park • Zambia . 133 [106]
Kaga • Japan 30 I6
Kaga Bandoro •
    Central African Rep. 23 B2
Kagan • Uzbekistan 18 H2
Kagawa • Japan 140 B2
Kagera • Africa 23 E4
Kagera • Rwanda/Tanzania 130 B1
Kagimba • Japan 30 F9
Kagoshima [Adm] • Japan 140 A11
Kagoshima • Japan 30 E9
Kahalu'u • HI, United States . . . 154 G5
Kahama • Tanzania 130 B1
Kahana Valley State Park •
    HI, United States 154 G5
Kahemba • Dem. Rep. of Congo . 23 B5
Kahla • Germany 9 D5
Kahler Asten • Germany 9 C5
Kahoolawe • HI, United States . 154 G7
Kahuku Point •
    HI, United States 154 G1
Kahului • HI, United States 154 G3
Kahuzi-Biega, Parc nat. du Heritage N •
    Dem. Rep. of Congo . . . . . . 83 [95]
Kahuzi-Biega, Parc nat. du Park •
    Dem. Rep. of Congo . . . . . 133 [57]
Kai Besar • Indonesia 35 (1) A2
Kai, Kepulauan • Indonesia . . 32 (1) D4
Kaiama • Nigeria 22 E3
Kaiapoi • New Zealand 35 D6
Kaibara • Japan 140 B1
Kaieteur Falls • Guyana 51 F2
Kaifeng • China 29 E4
Kaikohe • New Zealand 35 D2
Kaikoura • New Zealand 35 D5
Kailahun • Sierra Leone 22 J8
Kailua • HI, United States 154 G6
Kailua-Kona • HI, United States . 154 G8
Kaimana • Indonesia 32 (1) D3
Kaimanawa Mtns • New Zealand . 145 F4
Kainan • Japan 140 B3
Kainantu • Papua New Guinea . 35 (1) D2
Kainji Reservoir • Nigeria 22 E2
Kainuu • Finland 16 N4
Kaipara Flats • New Zealand . . . 145 F2
Kaiparowits Plateau •
    UT, United States 45 G3
Kairouan Heritage C • Tunisia . . 86 [267]
Kairouan • Tunisia 131 E4
Kaiserpfalz, Bad Wimpfen Castle •
    Germany . . . . 113 [86]
Kaiserpfalz, Gelnhausen Castle •
    Germany . . . . 113 [54]
Kaiserpfalz, Seligenstadt Castle •
    Germany . . . . 113 [56]
Kaiserslautern • Germany 112 D4
Kaiserstuhl • Germany 112 D7
Kaiserswerth (Düsseldorf) •
    Germany 111 B3
Kaitaia • New Zealand 35 D2
Kaiwi Channel •
    HI, United States 154 G3
Kaiyuan • China 140 B4
Kajaani • Finland 16 N4
Kajaapu • Indonesia 32 C4
Kajabbi • QL, Australia 34 H4
Kajang • Malaysia 141 G4
Kajmakcalan •
    Greece/F.Y.R. of Macedonia . . 15 C2
Kaka • Ethiopia 23 F2
Kakabeka Falls • OT, Canada . . . 43 L2
Kakadu Nat. Park •
    NT, Australia 34 F2
Kakadu Nat. Park Heritage N •
    Australia . . . . 83 [141]
Kakadu Nat. Park Heritage C •
    Australia . . . . 85 [208]
Kakamega • Kenya 130 B1
Kakamega Forest Game Reserve •
    Kenya 131 G1
Kakar Range • Pakistan 28 A2
Kakata • Liberia 22 B3
Kakeroma-jima • Japan 140 A11
Kakhovka • Ukraine 17 E5
Kakinada • India 138 D4
Kako-gawa • Japan 140 B1
Kakogawa • Japan 140 B1
Kakopetria • Cyprus 123 J3
Kaktovik • AK, United States . . . 49 M2
Kakum Nature Park Park • Ghana . 133 [26]
Kal-e Phuket, Thailand. 142 E3
Kala, El • Algeria 12 C12
Kalaâ Kabash • Tunisia 131 E3
Kalaallit Nunaat • Greenland . . . 39 V3
Kalabahi • Indonesia 32 (1) B4
Kalabsha • Egypt 131 F5
Kalacha Beach • Goa, India . . . 137 B1
Kaladan • India/Myanmar 28 F4
Kalahari • OT, Canada 155 B6
Kalahari Desert • Botswana 24 C4
Kalahari Gemsbok Nat. Park Park •
    South Africa . . . . 133 [118]
Kalaheo • HI, United States . 32 (1) B4
Kalai Mor • Turkmenistan 26 J10
Kalajoki Beach • Finland . . . . . . 97 [25]
Kalajoki • Finland 16 L4
Kalak Lookout •
    HI, United States 154 G5
Kalaka Beach • Zante, Greece . . 122 C3
Kálamaki • Zante, Greece 122 C3
Kalamata Beach • Greece . . . . . 97 [181]
Kalamazoo • MI, United States . . 44 A5
Kalambo Falls • Tanzania 130 B2
Kálamos • Crete, Greece 123 E1
Kálami • Crete, Greece 123 E1
Kalamunda • WA, Australia 34 C6
Kalándra Beach • Greece . . . . . 97 [192]
Kalándra • Greece 122 D1
Kalang • Indonesia 32 (1) B4
Kalaoa • HI, United States 154 G8
Kalasin • Indonesia 32 C4
Kalat • Pakistan 28 A3
Kálathos Beach • Rhodes, Greece . 97 [211]

Kalaupapa Nat. Hist. Park Park N •
    HI, United States . . . . 150 [17]
Kalaupapa Nat. Hist. Park •
    HI, United States 154 G3
Kalavárda • Rhodes, Greece . . 122 D12
Kale • Turkey 122 D9
Kale • Alanya, Turkey 123 F4
Kale • Antalya, Turkey 123 F4
Kalecik • Turkey 15 O3
Kalemie • Dem. Rep. of Congo . 23 D5
Kalesija • Bosnia-Herz. 14 F5
Kalewa • Myanmar 31 A2
Kaligoorlie • WA, Australia 34 D6
Kali Limènes • Crete, Greece . . 123 E6
Kaliakoúda • Greece 15 C5
Kaliakra, Nos • Bulgaria 14 M5
Kalima • Dem. Rep. of Congo . . 23 E3
Kalimantan • Indonesia 32 E3
Kálimnos • Greece 15 I7
Kálimnos [I.] • Greece 122 D8
Kalimpong Hill Sta • India 138 E2
Kaliningrad • Russian Fed. 13 J3
Kalinjar • India 137 C7
Kalispell • MT, United States . . 152 B2
Kalix • Sweden 128 B4
Kalix älv • Sweden 16 L3
Kalkan • Turkey 122 D9
Kalkim • Turkey 15 I4
Kalkrand • Namibia 24 B4
Kalkudah • Sri Lanka 138 D16
Kållandsö • Sweden 125 F3
Kallavesi • Finland 16 N5
Kallirhoe • Jordan 135 A8
Kalloni Beach • Greece . . . . . . 97 [199]
Kalloni • Greece 122 D5
Kallsjön • Sweden 16 G5
Kalmar • Sweden 125 F8
Kalmar [Adm] • Sweden 125 F8
Kalmarsund • Sweden 125 F8
Kalmykia • Russian Fed. 17 G5
Kaló Horió Beach •
    Crete, Greece . . . . 97 [215]
Kaló Horio • Crete, Greece . . . 123 E8
Kalocsa • Hungary 13 H11
Kalofer • Bulgaria 14 L7
Kaloko-Honokohau Nat. Park
    Park N • HI, United States . 150 [20]
Kaloko-Honokohau Nat. Hist. Park •
    HI, United States 154 G8
Kaloíimnos • Greece 122 D8
Kaloómo • Zambia 130 C1
Kalopanayotis • Cyprus 123 J3
Kalpáki • Greece 15 B4
Kalpeni I. • India 138 D9
Kalsubai • India 25 I8
Kaltenbach Ski • Austria . . . . 100 [145]
Kaltene • Latvia 126 B3
Kaluga • Russian Fed. 17 F4
Kalumburu Mission •
    WA, Australia 34 E2
Kalundborg Beach • Denmark . . 96 [43]
Kalundborg • Denmark 125 F10
Kalutara • Sri Lanka 138 D15
Kalvåg • Norway 124 C1
Kalwaria • Lithuania 13 M3
Kalwarja Zebrzydowska Heritage C •
    Poland . . . . 86 [166]
Kalwaria Zebrzydowska • Poland . 128 C3
Kalyazin • Russian Fed. 126 C4
Kam Shan Country Park •
    Hong Kong, China 139 B5
Kama • Russian Fed. 17 J4
Kaman • Chad 20 I4
Kamashi • Japan 30 K5
Kamakura • Japan 140 C4
Kaman • Turkey 15 O4
Kamanjab • Namibia 18 D6
Kamaran • Yemen 18 D6
Kamarang • Guyana 51 E2
Kamáres • Greece 15 F7
Kamári Beach • Greece . . . . . . 97 [209]
Kamas • UT, United States 45 G1
Kamativi • Zimbabwe 130 C1
Kambalda • WA, Australia 34 D6
Kambalnaya Sopka, Vulkan •
    Russian Fed. 27 R6
Kambanós, Akra • Greece 15 F6
Kamchatka Peninsula •
    Russian Fed. 127 A15
Kamchatka, Poluostrov •
    Russian Fed. 27 Q5
Kamchatka [Riv] • Russian Fed. . 27 Q6
Kamchatka volcanoes Heritage N •
    Russian Fed. . . . . 83 [76]
Kamchatskiy Zaliv •
    Russian Fed. 27 R5
Kamchiya • Bulgaria 14 M5
Kamchiya [Riv] • Bulgaria 14 06
Kamen • Russian Fed. 111 B2
Kamen • Germany 111 B2
Kamen-na-Obi • Russian Fed. . . 26 N9
Kámen • Czech Rep. 128 B4
Kámena Voúrla Beach • Greece . 97 [187]
Kámena Voúrla • Greece 122 D4
Kameniak, Rt • Croatia 128 D1
Kamenka • Russian Fed. 17 G4
Kamensk-Uralskiy • Russian Fed. . 26 J6
Kamenz • Germany 9 J5
Kameoka • Japan 140 B2
Kamet • India 28 C2
Kamien Pomorski • Poland 13 D4
Kamina • Dem. Rep. of Congo . 23 C5
Kámiros • Rhodes, Greece 122 D12
Kamloops • BC, Canada 155 C3
Kammarn • India 138 D4
Kamnarrok Game Reserve • Kenya . 131 G1
Kamp-Lintfort • Germany 111 B1
Kampala • Uganda 23 E3
Kampar • Malaysia 31 C6
Kampen • Indonesia 32 C2
Kampen • Netherlands 109 D7
Kampenwand • Germany 112 F8
Kampinoski Nat. Park Park N •
    Poland . . . . 89 [91]
Kamrau, Teluk • Indonesia . . . 35 (1) A1
Kamsack • SA, Canada 43 F1
Kamsar • Guinea 154 G8
Kamui-misaki • Japan 30 K3
Kamuku Wildlife Reserve Park •
    Nigeria . . . . 133 [31]
Kamvounía Ori • Greece 122 C3
Kamyshin • Russian Fed. 17 H4
Kanaaupscow • QU, Canada . . . 39 P6
Kanagawa • Japan 140 C1
Kanairiktok • NF, Canada 39 S6
Kanáli • Corfu, Greece 122 B1
Kananga • Dem. Rep. of Congo . 23 C5
Kanapolis Lake •
    KS, United States 46 G3
Kanab • UT, United States . . 32 (1) B4
Kanazawa • Japan 30 I6
Kanchanaburi • Thailand 142 C1
Kanchenjunga • India 28 E3
Kanchipuram • India 138 D7
Kandalaksha • Russian Fed. . . . 17 E1

Kandalakshskaya Guba •
  Russian Fed. 17 E1
Kandangan • Indonesia 32 F3
Kandanghaur • Java, Indonesia .. 143 J2
Kándanos • Crete, Greece 123 E1
Kandavu • Fiji Is. 35 (2) D2
Kandel • Germany 112 D8
Kandersteg • Switzerland 119 G6
Kandi • Benin 22 E2
Kandira • Turkey 15 L2
Kandla • India 28 B4
Kandooma • Maldives 138 F4
Kandrian • Papua New Guinea .. 35 (1) D2
Kandy Heritage C • Sri Lanka ... 85 [157]
Kandy • Sri Lanka 138 D15
Kane • PA, United States 153 D5
Kanem • Chad 21 B5
Kaneohe • HI, United States ... 154 G6
Kaneohe Bay • HI, United States 154 G6
Kánestron, Akra • Greece 15 E4
Kang • Botswana 24 C4
Kang Kra Chan • Thailand 142 C3
Kangaba • Mali 20 D6
Kangar • Malaysia 142 C5
Kangaroo I. • SA, Australia 34 G7
Kangasniemi • Finland 16 N6
Kangean, Kepulauan • Indonesia . 32 F4
Kangerlussuaq • Greenland 54 U3
Kangerlussuaq • Greenland 39 V3
Kanggye • D.P.R. of Korea 30 D4
Kangiqsualujjuaq • QU, Canada . 39 R5
Kangirsuk • QU, Canada 39 R4
Kangmar • India 28 E3
Kangnung • Rep. of Korea 30 E6
Kango • Gabon 22 G4
Kangra Hill Sta • India 138 E1
Kangrinboqê Feng • China 28 D2
Kanifinolhu • Maldives 138 F2
Kanin Nos • Russian Fed. 17 G1
Kanin Nos, mys • Russian Fed. .. 17 G1
Kanin, Poluostrov •
  Russian Fed. 17 I1
Kanjiza • F.R. of Yugoslavia 13 J11
Kankanpää • Finland 125 E1
Kankakee • IL, United States ... 44 B5
Kankan • Guinea 22 C2
Kankesanturai • Sri Lanka 138 D11
Kankroli • India 137 C6
Kankunskiy • Russian Fed. 27 K5
Kannapolis • NC, United States . 48 G3
Kannauj • India 137 C3
Kanniyakumari • India 138 D14
Kannonkoski Beach • India 138 E3
Kano • Nigeria 22 F2
Kano [Adm] • Nigeria 22 F2
Kanona • Zambia 23 E6
Kanoya • Japan 30 F9
Kanpur • India 137 C7
Kansai [Apt] • Japan 140 B3
Kansas [Adm] • United States .. 46 G3
Kansas City • KS, United States . 46 H3
Kansas City • MO, United States 46 H3
Kansas [Riv] •
  KS, United States 46 G3
Kansk • Russian Fed. 26 O6
Kansong • Rep. of Korea 30 E5
Kansyat • Indonesia 32 (1) E3
Kantara Castle • Cyprus 123 J2
Kantchari • Burkina Faso 20 F6
Kante • Togo 22 E3
Kanto • Japan 140 A4
Kanturk Castle • Ireland 108 C6
Kanye • Botswana 24 D4
Kanyemba • Zimbabwe 130 C2
Kanzak • Japan 140 B1
Kaohsiung • Taiwan 29 G6
Kaolack • Senegal 22 A2
Kaole • Tanzania 130 B4
Kapaa • HI, United States 154 G2
Kapanga • Dem. Rep. of Congo . 23 C5
Kapellskär • Sweden 125 G1
Kapenguria • Kenya 131 C3
Kapfenberg • Austria 13 E10
Kapidagi Yarimadasi • Turkey .. 15 I3
Kapit • Malaysia 32 E2
Kapka, Massif du • Chad/Sudan 21 D5
Kapos • Hungary 13 H11
Kappeln • Germany 8 F1
Kaprun Ski • Austria ...... 100 [164]
Kaprun • Austria 119 H4
Kapsan • D.P.R. of Korea 30 E4
Kapuas • Indonesia 32 E2
Kapuskasing • OT, Canada 39 O7
Kapuvár • Hungary 13 F10
Kara • Togo 22 E3
Kara Burun • Turkey 15 J7
Kara Dag • Turkey 15 O6
Kara Dong • China 26 N10
Kara Gölü • Turkey 15 K7
Kara Sea • Arctic Ocean 26 J3
Kara Strait • Russian Fed. 26 I4
Karabiga • Turkey 122 D2
Karabiga • Turkey 122 D3
Karaburun • Istanbul, Turkey ... 15 H5
Karaburun [Izmir], Turkey 15 J2
Karacabey • Turkey 122 D3
Karacaoglan • Turkey 15 I2
Karachay-Cherkessia •
  Russian Fed. 17 G6
Karachi • Pakistan 28 A3
Karadeniz Bogazi • Turkey 122 D3
Karaginskiy, Ostrov •
  Russian Fed. 27 R5
Karaginskiy Zaliv •
  Russian Fed. 27 R5
Karagos, gora • Russian Fed. .. 26 O7
Karaikal • India 138 D11
Karaikal Beach • India 138 E3
Karain • Turkey 123 F1
Karasaali • Turkey 123 G2
Karak • Kazakstan 26 J9
Karakax He • China 28 C2
Karakelong • Indonesia 32 (1) C2
Karakol • Kyrgyzstan 26 M9
Karakoram • Asia 28 C1
Karakorum • Mongolia 127 D3
Karakul, Ozero • China 18 J2
Karakum • Turkmenistan 18 H2
Karakumskiy Kanal •
  Turkmenistan 18 H2
Karam • Russian Fed. 27 G5
Karaman • Turkey 123 G1
Karaman [Adm] • Turkey 123 G3
Karamanli • Turkey 123 F1
Karamea • New Zealand 35 C5
Karamea • New Zealand 35 D5
Karamea Bight • New Zealand .. 35 C5
Karamiran He • China 28 E1
Karamiran Shankou • China ... 26 O10
Karamürsel • Turkey 15 K3
Karangasni Cave • Indonesia .. 143 H4
Karapinar • Turkey 123 G1
Karasburg • Namibia 24 B5
Karasjok • Norway 16 N2
Karasu • Turkey 15 L2
Karasu [Riv] • Turkey 18 C2
Karasuk • Russian Fed. 26 M7
Karatas • Turkey 15 J5
Karatepe • Turkey 123 G2
Karatas • Turkey 18 E3
Karatsu • Turkey 123 G4
Karatus Burun • Turkey 123 G4
Karaul • Russian Fed. 26 N3
Karauli • India 137 C6
Karavastase, Gjiri i • Albania .. 14 G9

Karawang • Java, Indonesia 143 J1
Karawanken • Austria/Slovenia . 13 D11
Karbala • Iraq 18 D3
Kårböle • Sweden 16 H6
Karcag • Hungary 13 K10
Kardam • Bulgaria 128 E2
Kardámena Beach • Greece .... 97 [210]
Kardámena • Greece 122 D8
Kardamila • Greece 15 H5
Kardamila Beach • Greece .... 97 [200]
Karditsa • Greece 15 C4
Kärdla • Estonia 126 B1
Kareedouw • South Africa 134 C7
Kareha, Jbel • Morocco 11 F9
Karelia • Russian Fed. 17 E2
Karelia [Adm] • Russian Fed. .. 17 E1
Karelia, Northern • Finland 124 A5
Kareliska Naset • Russian Fed. . 17 D2
Karen • India 28 F6
Karen • Myanmar 31 B3
Karesuando • Sweden 16 L2
Kargilik • China 28 C1
Kargopol • Russian Fed. 17 F2
Karhula • Finland 16 N6
Kari • Nigeria 20 H6
Kariai • Greece 15 F3
Kariani Beach • Greece .... 97 [194]
Karianous Nat. Park • Kenya ... 131 G3
Kariba • Zimbabwe 130 C1
Kariba Dam • Zambia/Zimbabwe 130 C1
Kariba, Lake • Zambia/Zimbabwe 130 C1
Karibib • Namibia 24 B4
Karidu Atoll • Maldives 138 F1
Kariega • South Africa 134 C3
Karigasniemi • Finland 17 D1
Karikari, Cape • New Zealand .. 35 D2
Karimata, Kepulauan • Indonesia 32 D3
Karimnagar • India 28 C5
Karimunjawa, Kepulauan •
  Indonesia 143 J3
Karin • Somalia 23 H1
Karin • Turkey 122 D8
Karis • Finland 125 E4
Karisimbi • Rwanda 23 D4
Káristos • Greece 122 D4
Karjaa • Finland 125 E4
Karkar • Papua New Guinea .. 35 (1) D1
Karkinits'ka Zatoka • Ukraine .. 17 E5
Karkonoski Nat. Park Park N •
  Poland .... 89 [98]
Karleby • Finland 16 L5
Karlik Shan • China 29 A2
Karlobag • Croatia 12 J4
Karlovac • Croatia 128 D1
Kárlovássi • Greece 122 D8
Karlovo • Bulgaria 14 L7
Karlovy Vary • Czech Rep. 128 B1
Karlsbad • Czech Rep. 128 B1
Karlsborg • Sweden 125 F3
Karlshamn • Sweden 125 F12
Karlskoga • Sweden 16 H7
Karlskrona Heritage C • Sweden 86 [3]
Karlskrona • Sweden 125 F12
Karlslunde • Denmark 125 F10
Karlsruhe • Germany 112 D6
Karlsruhe Castle • Germany ... 113 [80]
Karlstad • Sweden 16 G7
Karlstadt • Germany 9 G7
Kárlstein • Czech Rep. 128 B2
Karmah • Sudan 21 F4
Karmøy • Norway 124 C5
Karnak • Egypt 131 F4
Karnal • India 137 C2
Karnataka • India 138 D2
Karnataka Plateau • India 138 D2
Karnes City • TX, United States 47 F3
Karnische Alpen • Austria/Italy . 119 H7
Karnische Skiregion Ski •
  Austria .... 100 [194]
Karnobat • Bulgaria 128 E3
Kärnten • Austria 13 C11
Karo Batak Villages • Indonesia 143 G2
Karoi • Zimbabwe 130 C2
Karon • Ko Phuket, Thailand ... 142 E2
Karon Beach •
  Ko Phuket, Thailand 142 E2
Karonga • Malawi 24 E2
Karoo, Great • South Africa 134 C3
Karoo, Little • South Africa 134 C6
Karoo Nat. Park Park •
  South Africa .... 133 [124]
Karoo Nat. Park • South Africa . 134 C3
Karora • Sudan 21 G4
Karpackie, Pogórze • Poland ... 13 J8
Karpas Peninsula • Cyprus 122 D11
Kárpathos • Greece 122 D11
Kárpathos [I.] • Greece 122 D11
Karpathou, Stenó • Greece 15 I8
Karratha • WA, Australia 34 C4
Kars • Turkey 122 A4
Kärsämäki • Finland 16 M4
Karsiyaka • Turkey 122 D5
Karskoye Vorota, Proliv •
  Russian Fed. 26 I3
Karskoye More • Russian Fed. .. 54 H2
Kartal • Turkey 15 K3
Kartuzy • Poland 13 H3
Karumba • QL, Australia 34 H3
Karun • Iran 18 E3
Karungi • Sweden 16 L3
Karungu • Kenya 125 F9
Karur • India 138 D11
Karviná • Czech Rep. 13 H8
Karwendelgebirge • Austria 9 G9
Karwar • India 138 D1
Karymskoye • Russian Fed. 27 H6
Kas Beach • Turkey .... 97 [231]
Kas • Turkey 123 F1
Kasaali • Turkey 123 F2
Kasaba • Zambia 23 E6
Kasai • Dem. Rep. of Congo ... 23 C4
Kasai • Japan 140 B1
Kasai [Riv] •
  Dem. Rep. of Congo 23 C5
Kasama • Zambia 24 E2
Kasanga • Tanzania 130 B3
Kasanka Nat. Park Park • Zambia 133 [105]
Kasar, Ras • Sudan 21 G4
Kasaragod • India 138 D2
Kasempa • Zambia 24 D2
Kasenga • Dem. Rep. of Congo . 23 D5
Kasese • Uganda 23 E3
Kashan • Iran 18 F3
Kashi • China 26 M10
Kashihara • Japan 140 B4
Kashin • Russian Fed. 126 C4
Kashiwa • Japan 140 C2
Kashiwazaki • Japan 30 J6
Kashmar • Iran 18 H3
Kasimov • Russian Fed. 17 F3
Kaskinen • Finland 125 E1
Kaskö • Finland 125 E1
Kasongo • Dem. Rep. of Congo . 23 D4
Kasongo-Lunda •
  Dem. Rep. of Congo 23 B5
Kaspiyskiy • Russian Fed. 17 H5
Kassala • Sudan 21 G5
Kassándra • Greece 122 D1
Kassándras, Akra • Greece 15 E3
Kassándras, Kólpos • Greece .. 15 E3
Kassándria Beach • Greece .... 97 [192]
Kassel • Germany 9 E5

Kasselburg • Germany 112 E1
Kasselburg Castle • Germany .. 113 [59]
Kassiesbaai • Hungary 131 E3
Kassiópi Beach • Corfu, Greece 97 [170]
Kassiópi • Corfu, Greece 122 B1
Kássos • Greece 122 D11
Kastamonu • Turkey 15 O2
Kastaniés • Greece 15 H2
Kastélla • Greece 46 F2
Kastélli • Crete, Greece 123 E7
Kastelruth • Italy 120 B1
Kastelruth Ski • Italy .... 100 [239]
Kastélli • Italy 120 B1
Kasterlee Beach • Belgium .... 96 [71]
Kasterlee • Belgium 109 D11
Kastoriá • Greece 15 C3
Kastoriás, Limni • Greece 15 C3
Kastós • Greece 122 C1
Kástro Beach • Greece .... 97 [180]
Kástro • Greece 122 D4
Kasukabe • Japan 140 C2
Kasumiga-ura • Japan 140 C2
Kasungu • Malawi 24 E2
Kasungu Nat. Park Park • Malawi 133 [96]
Kasur • Pakistan 18 J3
Kata • Ko Phuket, Thailand 142 E2
Kata Noi Beach •
  Ko Phuket, Thailand 142 E2
Kata Yai Beach •
  Ko Phuket, Thailand 142 E2
Kataba • Zambia 24 D3
Katahdin, Mt •
  ME, United States 44 K3
Katanga • Dem. Rep. of Congo . 23 C5
Katanning • WA, Australia 34 C6
Katápola • Greece 122 D8
Katavi Nat. Park • Tanzania ... 130 B3
Katavia • Rhodes, Greece 122 D12
Katchall • India 28 F7
Katerini • Greece 15 D3
Katerini Beach • Greece ...... 97 [180]
Katha • Myanmar 31 B2
Katherina • Egypt 21 F2
Katherine • NT, Australia 34 F2
Katherine • NT, Australia 34 F2
Kathiawar • India 28 B3
Kathmandu • Nepal 28 E3
Kathmandu valley Heritage C •
  Nepal .... 85 [160]
Kathmandu • Nepal 156 D7
Kati • Mali 20 D6
Katikati • New Zealand 141 F1
Katiola • Côte d'Ivoire 22 C3
Katiti Aboriginal Land •
  NT, Australia 145 D3
Katiabuh, Ozero • Ukraine 14 P4
Katmai Nat. Park •
  AK, United States 49 J4
Katmai Nat. Park & Preserve Park N •
  AK, United States .... 150 [9]
Kató Ahaia • Greece 31 C5
Kató Korakiana Beach •
  Corfu, Greece .... 97 [170]
Kató Stavrós Beach • Greece .. 97 [193]
Kató Zákros • Crete, Greece ... 123 E8
Katoomba • NS, Australia 144 C2
Katowice • Poland 128 C1
Katrine, Loch • United Kingdom 104 B1
Katrineholm • Sweden 125 D3
Katsina • Nigeria 22 F2
Katsuura • Japan 140 C4
Kattakurgan • Uzbekistan 18 I2
Kattegat • Denmark/Sweden .. 125 F6
Katu • Ko Phuket, Thailand 142 E2
Katun • Russian Fed. 26 O7
Katwijk • Netherlands 109 F1
Katwijkse Duinen • Netherlands 109 F1
Katy Hill • Montserrat .... 161 H
Katz, Burg • Germany 112 E2
Kau • Indonesia 32 (1) C2
Kau Pualamada, Gunung •
  Indonesia 32 (1) C3
Kau Sai Chau • Hong Kong, China 139 B6
Kauai • HI, United States 154 G2
Kauai Channel •
  HI, United States 154 G2
Kaub • Germany 112 E4
Kaufbeuren • Germany 112 F2
Kaufungen • Germany 9 E5
Kauhajoki • Finland 16 L5
Kaukauna • WI, United States . 44 A3
Kaukauveld • Botswana/Namibia 24 C3
Kaukiainen • Finland 125 E3
Kaula I. • HI, United States ... 154 G1
Kaulakahi Channel •
  HI, United States 47 J8
Kaunakakai • HI, United States 154 G3
Kaunas • Lithuania 126 D9
Kaunos • Lithuania 126 B5
Kaupanger • Norway 124 C4
Kausambi • India 137 C7
Kautokeino • Norway 16 M2
Kavadarci • F.Y.R. of Macedonia 14 J8
Kavajë • Albania 14 G8
Kavak • Turkey 122 D1
Kavála Beach • Greece .... 97 [194]
Kavála • Greece 122 D1
Kaválas, Kólpos • Greece 15 F3
Kavalerovo • Russian Fed. 30 H2
Kavali • India 138 D3
Kavaratti • India 138 D9
Kavaratti I. • India 138 D9
Kavarna Beach • Bulgaria .... 97 [243]
Kavarna • Bulgaria 128 E4
Kavendou, Mt • Guinea 22 B2
Kavieng • Papua New Guinea .. 35 (1) E1
Kávos • Corfu, Greece 122 D7
Kavoúri • Greece 122 D7
Kavoússi • Crete, Greece 123 E8
Kaw Lake • OK, United States .. 46 G4
Kawa • Sudan 21 F4
Kawachi-Nagano • Japan 140 B4
Kawagoe • Japan 140 C2
Kawaguchi • Japan 140 C2
Kawaikini • HI, United States .. 154 G2
Kawambwa • Zambia 23 D5
Kawanee • IL, United States ... 46 K2
Kawartha Lakes • OT, Canada .. 44 F2
Kawasaki • Japan 140 C2
Kaweka Range • New Zealand . 145 F4
Kawerau • New Zealand 145 F2
Kawhia • New Zealand 145 F1
Kawhia Harbour • New Zealand 145 F1
Kawich Peak • NV, United States 45 D3
Kawich Range •
  NV, United States 45 D3
Kaxgar He • China 26 M10
Kaya • Burkina Faso 20 E6
Kayah • Myanmar 31 B3
Kayali Dagi • Turkey 15 H4
Kayan • Indonesia 32 E2
Kayenta • AZ, United States ... 45 G3
Kayes • Mali 22 B2
Kaymakli • Turkey 123 G2
Kayseri • Turkey 18 C2
Kayseri [Adm] • Turkey 123 G2
Kayuagung • Sumatra 32 (1) B3
Kazachye • Russian Fed. 27 M2
KAZAKSTAN • Asia 26 K8
Kazak Uplands • Kazakstan ... 26 K8
KAZAKSTAN • Asia 26 K8
Kazan • Russian Fed. 17 H3
Kazan • NU, Canada 38 L4
Kazan Retto • Japan 25 P7
Kazanluk Heritage C • Bulgaria 86 [204]
Kazanlik • Bulgaria 128 E3

Kazerun • Iran 18 F4
Käzim Karabekir • Turkey 123 G1
Kazincbarcika • Hungary 13 J9
Kaziranga Nat. Park Heritage N •
  India .... 83 [114]
Keoladeo Nat. Park • India 137 C2
Kepi • Indonesia 32 (1) E4
Kepice • Poland 13 F3
Kepno • Poland 13 G6
Kepsut • Turkey 15 J4
Kerala • NE, United States 46 F2
Kearns • UT, United States ... 42 I6
Kebili • Tunisia 131 E5
Kebnekaise • Sweden 16 J3
Kebumen • Java, Indonesia ... 143 J6
Kecel • Hungary 13 I11
Kechika • BC, Canada 38 F5
Kecskemét • Hungary 13 I11
Kedah • Malaysia 31 C5
Kedainiai • Lithuania 126 B5
Kédia d'Idjil • Mauritania 20 C4
Kediri • Java, Indonesia 143 J7
Kédougou • Senegal 22 B2
Kedzierzyn-Kozle • Poland 13 G7
Kedzierzyn-Kozle • Poland 128 C1
Keekorok Lodge • Kenya 131 G3
Keel • Ireland 108 C1
Keele Peak • YT, Canada 38 E4
Keene • NH, United States 153 D3
Keenmansthorp • Namibia ... 24 B5
Kef Lakhdar Chergui • Algeria . 11 O9
Kefalonía • Greece 122 C2
Kefalonía Nat. Park •
  Cephalonia, Greece 122 C2
Keflavík • Iceland 16 (1) B2
Kehl • Germany 9 C8
Kehlstein • Germany 112 F8
Keighley • United Kingdom ... 7 K8
Keihoku • Japan 140 B2
Keila • Estonia 126 B2
Keitele • Finland 16 M5
Keith • United Kingdom 104 C1
Keith Arm • NT, Canada 38 G3
Keizer • OR, United States ... 42 D4
Kejimkujik Nat. Park •
  NS, Canada 156 D7
Kejimkujik Nat. Park Park N •
  NS, Canada .... 156 [36]
Kek Lok Si Temple •
  Penang, Malaysia 141 F1
Kekaha • HI, United States ... 154 G2
Kekes • Hungary 13 I10
Kekova • Turkey 123 F3
Kel Tepe • Izmit, Turkey 15 K3
Kel Tepe • Zonguldak, Turkey .. 15 N2
Kelafo • Ethiopia 23 G2
Kelang • Malaysia 141 G3
Kelang [I.] • Malaysia 141 G3
Kelantan • Malaysia 31 C5
Kelbia • Tunisia 131 E2
Kelibia • Tunisia 22 G4
Kelkit • Turkey 122 A4
Kellerwand • Austria/Italy 119 H8
Kellet, Cape • NT, Canada 38 F2
Kellie Castle • Malaysia 104 B2
Ketchum • ID, United States . 42 H5
Ketou • Benin 22 E3
Ketrzyn • Poland 13 K3
Kettering • United Kingdom ... 7 L9
Kettering • OH, United States 44 C6
Kettleman City •
  CA, United States 45 C3
Ketzin • Germany 111 C3
Keuka Lake • NY, United States 153 D1
Keukenhof • Netherlands 109 F1
Keurusselka • Finland 125 E2
Keuruu • Finland 125 E2
Kew • Turks & Caicos Is. 158 C1
Kewaunee • WI, United States . 44 B3
Keweenaw Nat. Hist. Park Park N •
  MI, United States .... 151 [158]
Keweenaw Peninsula •
  MI, United States 43 L3
Keweenaw Point •
  MI, United States 44 B2
Key Biscayne •
  FL, United States 154 H8
Key Deer Nat. Wildlife Refuge •
  FL, United States 154 H8
Key Largo • FL, United States . 154 H8
Key Loup • Ireland 108 C2
Key West • FL, United States .. 154 H7
Keylong Hill Sta • India 138 E1
Keystone Ski •
  CO, United States .... 149 [102]
Keystone Reservoir •
  OK, United States 46 G4
Kezhma • Russian Fed. 26 R6
Kezmarok • Slovak Rep. 13 J8
Khabarovsk • Russian Fed. ... 27 M7
Khaburah, Al • Oman 18 G5
Khadra • Algeria 11 L8
Khairpur • Pakistan 28 A3
Khajuraho Heritage C • India . 85 [139]
Khajuraho • India 137 C7
Khakassia • Russian Fed. 26 O7
Khalesavey • Russian Fed. 26 M5
Khalij Sirt • Libya 21 C1
Khaluf • Oman 18 G5
Khambhat, Gulf of • India 28 B4
Khami Ruins Nat. Mon. Heritage C •
  Zimbabwe .... 85 [117]
Khami Ruins Nat. Mon. •
  Zimbabwe 130 C3
Khamir • Yemen 18 D6
Khamis, Ash Shallal al • Sudan 21 F4
Khamra • Russian Fed. 27 H4
Khan al Ahmar • Palestine 135 A6
Khandwa • India 28 C4
Khanka, Ozero • Russian Fed. . 27 L8
Khanpur • Pakistan 28 B3
Khanty-Mansiysk • Russian Fed. 26 K5
Khao Chamao • Thailand 142 C4
Khao Kheaw • Thailand 142 C3
Khao Kheaw Zoo • Thailand .. 142 C4
Khao Laem • Thailand 142 C4
Khao Mokochu • Thailand 31 B3
Khao Saming • Thailand 142 D4
Khao Yai • Thailand 142 C2
Kharabali • Russian Fed. 17 H5
Kharagpur • India 28 E4
Khareveddo Beach • Goa, India 137 D3
Khárga, El • Egypt 131 F3
Kharkiv • Ukraine 17 F4
Kharmanli • Bulgaria 128 D3
Kharovsk • Russian Fed. 17 F3
Khartoum • Sudan 21 F5
Khartoum • Sudan 23 F5
Khasab • Oman 18 F4
Khashm el Girba • Sudan 30 F3
Khash • Afghanistan 18 H3
Khaskovo • Bulgaria 26 R3
Khatanga • Russian Fed. 26 R3
Khatt Atoui • Mauritania 20 B4
Khawr Fakkan •
  United Arab Emirates ...... 81 E
Khayelitsha • South Africa ... 134 C7
Khemis Miliana • Algeria 11 N8
Khemisset • Morocco 20 D2
Khenchela • Algeria 20 G1
Khenifra • Morocco 131 D1
Kherson • Ukraine 17 E5
Kheta • Russian Fed. 26 R3
Kimball • NE, United States ... 46 E2
Kheta [Riv] • Russian Fed. 27 H4
Khilok • Russian Fed. 27 H6
Khilok [Riv] • Russian Fed. 27 H6
Khimki • Russian Fed. 126 C4
KENYA • Africa .... 131 G
Kenya, Mt • Kenya 131 G3
Khionótripa • Greece 15 D6
Kenyatta, Jomo [Apt] • Kenya . 131 G3
Khiva • Uzbekistan 18 H1

Khizi Pogost Heritage C •
  Russian Fed. .... 85 [90]
Khmel'nyts'kyy • Ukraine 17 D5
Kho Khot Kra • Myanmar 31 B4
Khodzheyli • Uzbekistan 18 G1
Khok Pip • Thailand 142 C2
Kholm • Afghanistan 28 A1
Kholmsk • Russian Fed. 27 N7
Khon Kaen • Thailand 31 C3
Khonuu • Russian Fed. 27 N3
Khoper • Russian Fed. 17 G4
Khorasan • Iran 18 G3
Khorat • Thailand 142 A2
Khorramabad • Iran 18 E3
Khorramshahr • Iran 18 E3
Khorugh • Tajikistan 18 J2
Khotan • China 127 D2
Khouribga • Morocco 131 D1
Khram, Ko • Thailand 142 C4
Khrysokhou Bay • Cyprus 123 J1
Khufayfiyah, Al • Saudi Arabia . 18 D5
Khujand • Tajikistan 18 I1
Khulna • Bangladesh 28 E4
Khun Yuam • Thailand 142 B1
Khuriya Muriya, Jaza'ir • Oman 18 G6
Khurtum, Al • Sudan 21 F4
Khurtum Bahri, Al • Sudan ... 21 F4
Khust • Ukraine 13 M9
Khwae Noi • Thailand 142 C1
Khyber Pass • Pakistan 28 B2
Kiamba • Philippines 31 G5
Kiang West Nat. Park Park •
  Gambia .... 133 [11]
Kiangarow, Mt • QL, Australia . 34 J5
Kiantajärvi • Finland 16 O4
Kiáton • Greece 15 D6
Kiboko • Kenya 23 F4
Kibombo • Dem. Rep. of Congo . 23 D4
Kibondo • Tanzania 130 B1
Kicevo • F.Y.R. of Macedonia .. 15 B2
Kicking Horse Pass •
  AL/BC, Canada 155 C4
Kidal • Antigua & Barbuda ... 161 J
Kidapawan • Philippines 20 F5
Kidderminster • United Kingdom 104 D1
Kidira • Senegal 22 B2
Kidnappers, Cape • New Zealand 145 F4
Kidricht • Germany 112 E4
Kiel • Germany 8 F2
Kielce • Poland 128 C2
Kieler Bucht • Germany 8 F2
Kierspe • Germany 111 B4
Kieta • Papua New Guinea .. 35 (1) F2
Kiev • Ukraine 17 E4
Kiev Heritage C • Ukraine .... 86 [241]
Kiffa • Mauritania 20 C5
Kifisós • Greece 15 D5
Kigoma • Tanzania 130 B2
Kihei • HI, United States 154 G3
Kihnu • Estonia 16 L7
Kii-sanchi • Japan 140 B4
Kii-suido • Japan 30 H8
Kiikoinen • Finland 125 E1
Kiiminki • Finland 16 N4
Kikambala • Kenya 131 G5
Kikinda • F.R. of Yugoslavia .. 14 H4
Kikládes • Greece 15 F6
Kikonai • Japan 30 K4
Kikori • Papua New Guinea .. 35 (1) C2
Kikori [Riv] • Papua New Guinea 35 (1) C2
Kikwit • Dem. Rep. of Congo .. 23 B5
Kilauea Caldera •
  HI, United States 154 G8
Kilbuck Mtns •
  AK, United States 49 I4
Kilchoan • United Kingdom ... 106 B2
Kilchu • D.P.R. of Korea 30 E4
Kilcock • Ireland 108 B1
Kilcolgan • Ireland 108 C4
Kilconnell Priory • Ireland 108 C4
Kilcrea Abbey • Ireland 108 C8
Kilcreggan • United Kingdom . 106 B2
Kilcullen • Ireland 108 B3
Kildare • Ireland 108 B3
Kildare [Adm] • Ireland 108 B3
Kildeer • ND, United States ... 43 E3
Kildonan • BC, Canada 42 C2
Kildrum • United Kingdom ... 108 C4
Kilgore • TX, United States ... 154 J2
Kilifi • Kenya 131 G5
Kilimanjaro, Mt • Tanzania ... 130 B2
Kilimanjaro Nat. Park Heritage N •
  Tanzania .... 83 [102]
Kilimanjaro Nat. Park •
  Tanzania 130 B2
Kilimanjaro Nat. Park Park •
  Tanzania .... 133 [89]
Kilindoni • Tanzania 130 B4
Kilini • Greece 15 D6
Kilitbahir • Turkey 122 D2
Kiliya • Ukraine 14 O4
Kilkee • Ireland 108 C5
Kilkenny • Ireland 7 E9
Kilkenny • Ireland 108 A2
Kilkenny [Adm] • Ireland 108 A2
Kilkis • Greece 15 D3
Killala Beach • Ireland ...... 96 [63]
Killala • Ireland 108 C2
Killala Bay • Ireland 108 C2
Killaloe • Ireland 108 C6
Killarney • Ireland 108 C7
Killarney • MN, Canada 43 G2
Killarney • OT, Canada 44 E2
Killarney, Lake • Bahamas 158 B3
Killarney Nat. Park • Ireland .. 108 C7
Killarney Nat. Park Park N •
  Ireland .... 89 [40]
Killarney Nat. Park • Ireland .. 108 C7
Killary Harbour • Ireland 108 C3
Killeen • TX, United States ... 47 F2
Killerton House •
  United Kingdom 104 F2
Killicrankie, Pass of •
  United Kingdom 104 B1
Killiney Beach • Ireland ..... 96 [54]
Killiney • Ireland 108 B4
Killini Ski •
  VT, United States .... 149 [210]
Killorglin • Ireland 108 C7
Killybegs Beach • Ireland .... 96 [65]
Kilmacduagh • Ireland 108 C4
Kilmallock • Ireland 108 C6
Kilmichael Point • Ireland 108 B4
Kilombero • Tanzania 23 F5
Kilosa • Tanzania 130 B4
Kilrane • Ireland 108 B4
Kilronan Beach • Ireland ..... 96 [62]
Kilronan • Ireland 108 C4
Kilrush Beach • Ireland ...... 96 [61]
Kilrush • Ireland 108 C6
Kiltan I. • India 138 D9
Kilwa • Dem. Rep. of Congo .. 23 D5
Kilwa Kisiwani Heritage C •
  Tanzania .... 85 [114]
Kilwa Kisiwani • Tanzania 130 B4
Kilwa Kivinje • Tanzania 130 B4
Kilwa Masoko • Tanzania 130 B4
Kilyos • Turkey 122 D2
Kim • CO, United States 46 E4
Kimball • NE, United States ... 46 D2
Kimbe • Papua New Guinea .. 35 (1) D2
Kimbe Bay • Papua New Guinea 35 (1) D2
Kimberley • South Africa 24 C5
Kimberley Ski • BC, Canada .. 149 [9]
Kimberley • OR, United States 42 F4

Kimberley Plateau

Kimberley Plateau •
  WA, Australia 34 E3
Kimch'aek • D.P.R. of Korea 30 E4
Kimch'on • Rep. of Korea 30 D6
Kimi • Greece 122 D4
Kimito • Finland 125 E3
Kimito [I.] • Finland 16 L6
Kimitsu • Japan 140 C4
Kimolos • Greece 122 D7
Kimon M Dive • Red Sea 135 B1
Kimry • Russian Fed. 126 C4
Kinabalu, Gunung • Malaysia 32 F1
Kinabatangan • Malaysia 32 F1
Kinaros • Greece 122 D8
Kinbasket Lake • BC, Canada 155 C4
Kincardine • United Kingdom 104 B4
Kincardine • OT, Canada 155 C6
Kind • Sweden 125 F7
Kinda • Sweden 125 F4
Kinder • LA, United States 153 F3
Kinder Scout • United Kingdom 5 B1
Kinderdijk • Netherlands 109 F3
Kinderdijk-Elshout Heritage C •
  Netherlands .... 86 [32]
Kindersley • SA, Canada 38 J6
Kindia • Guinea 22 B2
Kindu • Dem. Rep. of Congo 23 D4
Kineshma • Russian Fed. 17 G3
King City • CA, United States 45 B3
King Country, The • New Zealand .. 145 F1
King George I. • Antarctica 81 A10
King I. • TS, Australia 34 H7
King Leopold • WA, Australia 34 E3
King Peak • UT, United States 45 G1
King Salmon • AK, United States ... 49 J4
King Sound • WA, Australia 34 D3
King William I. • NU, Canada 38 L3
King William's Town •
  South Africa 24 D6
King's Bay Falls •
  Trinidad & Tobago .... 160 T
King's Lynn • United Kingdom 7 M9
Kingaroy • QL, Australia 144 B6
Kingfisher • OK, United States 51 H1
Kingisepp • Russian Fed. 16 O7
Kingman • Pacific Ocean 33 K5
Kingman • AZ, United States 153 E1
Kingoonya • SA, Australia 34 G6
Kings Beach • CA, United States ... 5 B1
Kings Canyon • NT, Australia 145 D3
Kings Canyon Nat. Park Park N •
  CA, United States .... 150 [51]
Kings Canyon Nat. Park •
  CA, United States 152 C4
Kings Landing • NB, Canada 156 D6
Kings Mtn Nat. Military Park Park N •
  SC, United States .... 151 [236]
Kings, Valley of the • Egypt 131 F4
Kingsbarns Beach •
  United Kingdom .... 101 [7]
Kingsbridge • United Kingdom 104 F5
Kingsburgh • South Africa 134 B5
Kingscote • SA, Australia 34 G7
Kingsford Smith [Apt] •
  NS, Australia 144 C2
Kingsport • TN, United States 48 F2
Kingston • New Zealand 145 G2
Kingston • Jamaica 159 F4
Kingston • ID, United States 42 G3
Kingston • PA, United States 44 H5
Kingston • NY, United States 153 D3
Kingston • OT, Canada 155 B6
Kingston South East •
  SA, Australia 34 G7
Kingston upon Hull •
  United Kingdom 7 L8
Kingston-upon-Thames •
  United Kingdom 104 E1
Kingstown • St Vincent & Gren. ... 161 Q
Kingstown Bay •
  St Vincent & Gren. .... 161 Q
Kingsville • TX, United States 154 J5
Kingussie • United Kingdom 6 H4
Kingwood • WV, United States 44 F6
Kinik • Turkey 15 I4
Kinki • Japan 140 A8
Kinna • Sweden 125 F7
Kinnairds Head • United Kingdom . 6 K4
Kinnegad • Ireland 108 B1
Kinnekulle • Sweden 125 F3
Kino-kawa • Japan 140 C8
Kinoosao • MN, Canada 38 K5
Kinpu-san • Japan 140 C4
Kinross • United Kingdom 104 B2
Kinross-shire • United Kingdom ... 104 B2
Kinsale • Ireland 108 C8
Kinsarvik • Norway 124 C4
Kinshasa • Dem. Rep. of Congo ... 23 B4
Kinsley • KS, United States 46 F4
Kinston • NC, United States 48 I3
Kintap • Indonesia 32 F3
Kintyre • United Kingdom 6 G6
Kintyre, Mull of •
  United Kingdom 7 G6
Kinvarra Beach • Ireland .... 96 [62]
Kinvarra • Ireland 108 C4
Kinyeti • Sudan 23 E3
Kinzig • Germany 9 D8
Kinzua Dam • PA, United States .. 153 D1
Kióni • Greece 122 C2
Kiparissiakós Kolpos • Greece 15 C6
Kipawa, Lac • QU, Canada 44 F5
Kipembawe • Tanzania 130 B3
Kipengere Range • Tanzania 130 B3
Kipili • Tanzania 130 B3
Kipushi • Dem. Rep. of Congo 24 D2
Kirakira • Solomon Is. 35 (1) G3
Kirazli • Turkey 15 H3
Kirby • AR, United States 46 I5
Kirbyville • TX, United States 154 J4
Kirchberg in Tirol Ski •
  Austria .... 100 [157]
Kirchdorf • Austria 119 H3
Kirchhain • Germany 112 D2
Kirchheim bei München • Germany . 112 F3
Kirchheim unter Teck • Germany .. 9 E8
Kirchheim-Bolanden • Germany ... 112 E4
Kireç • Turkey 15 J4
Kireli • Turkey 123 F2
Kirensk • Russian Fed. 29 H5
Kirgöz Hani • Turkey 123 F1
Kiri • Dem. Rep. of Congo 22 H5
KIRIBATI • Pacific Ocean 33 J6
Kirikhan • Turkey 123 G4
Kirikkale • Turkey 15 I4
Kirinyaga • Kenya 23 F3
Kirishi • Russian Fed. 16 O7
Kiritimati • Kiribati 33 L5
Kirkagaç • Turkey 15 I4
Kirkby Lonsdale •
  United Kingdom 7 J7
Kirkcaldy • United Kingdom 104 B4
Kirkenær • Norway 124 B2
Kirkenes • Norway 124 E1
Kirkintilloch • United Kingdom 104 B3
Kirkjubæjarklaustur • Iceland 16 (1) D3
Kirkkonummi • Finland 125 E4
Kirkland • WA, United States 5 B3
Kirkland Lake • OT, Canada 39 O7
Kirklareli • Turkey 15 I2
Kirkpatrick, Mt • Antarctica 154 (1) V1
Kirkstone Pass • United Kingdom . 104 C2
Kirksville • MO, United States 46 I2
Kirkuk • Iraq 18 D2
Kirkwall • United Kingdom 6 J3
Kirkwood • South Africa 134 C8

Kirkwood Ski •
  CA, United States .... 149 [65]
Kirn • Germany 5 K5
Kirov • Russian Fed. 17 E4
Kirovohrad • Ukraine 17 E5
Kirovsk • Russian Fed. 17 E1
Kirovskiy • Russian Fed. 27 K6
Kirriemuir • United Kingdom 104 B2
Kirs • Russian Fed. 17 I3
Kiruna • Sweden 16 K3
Kirsa • Sweden 125 F4
Kisalföld • Hungary 13 G10
Kisangani • Dem. Rep. of Congo .. 23 D3
Kisarazu • Japan 140 C4
Kishangarh • India 137 C6
Kishiwada • Japan 140 B4
Kisii • Kenya 131 G3
Kisite Nat. Park • Kenya 131 G5
Kiska • AK, United States 49 E5
Kiskörei Víztároló • Hungary 13 J10
Kiskőrös • Hungary 13 I11
Kiskunfélegyháza • Hungary 13 I11
Kiskunhalas • Hungary 13 I11
Kiskunmajsa • Hungary 13 I11
Kiskunság Nat. Park Park N •
  Hungary .... 89 [106]
Kislovodsk • Russian Fed. 17 G6
Kismanyo • Somalia 23 G4
Kismayo Nat. Park Park •
  Somalia .... 133 [67]
Kismayu • Somalia 23 G4
Kiso • Japan 30 I7
Kissámou Kastéli •
  Crete, Greece 123 E1
Kissámou, Kólpos •
  Crete, Greece 123 E1
Kissidougou • Guinea 22 B3
Kissimmee • FL, United States ... 151 C2
Kissimmee, Lake •
  FL, United States 49 C4
Kissing Bridge Ski •
  NY, United States .... 149 [185]
Kissing Bridge •
  NY, United States 153 D1
Kisújszállás • Hungary 13 J10
Kisumu • Kenya 131 G3
Kisvárda • Hungary 13 J9
Kita • Mali 22 C2
Kitadaito-jima • Japan 140 A11
Kitaiwo-jima • Japan 140 A13
Kitakyushu • Japan 30 F8
Kitale • Kenya 131 G3
Kitami • Japan 30 L3
Kitami-sanchi • Japan 30 L2
Kitayama-gawa • Japan 140 B4
Kitchener-Waterloo • OT, Canada . 155 B9
Kitee • Finland 16 P5
Kitessa • Central African Rep. 23 E3
Kitgum • Uganda 23 E3
Kithira • Greece 122 D10
Kíthira [I.] • Greece 122 D7
Kíthnos • Greece 122 D7
Kíthnou, Stenó • Greece 15 F6
Kiti • Cyprus 123 J4
Kiti, Cape • Cyprus 123 J4
Kitimat • BC, Canada 38 F6
Kitimat Ranges • BC, Canada 38 F6
Kitros • Greece 15 E5
Kittanning • PA, United States ... 44 F5
Kittery • ME, United States 44 J4
Kittilä • Finland 16 M3
Kitty Hawk • NC, United States ... 48 J2
Kitui • Kenya 23 F4
Kitunda • Tanzania 130 B3
Kitwe-Nkana • Zambia 24 C2
Kitzbühel Ski • Austria .... 100 [158]
Kitzbühel • Austria 119 H3
Kitzbüheler Alpen • Austria 119 H3
Kitzingen • Germany 9 F7
Kiu Tsui Chau •
  Hong Kong, China 139 B6
Kiunga • Kenya 23 G4
Kiunga • Papua New Guinea 35 (1) C2
Kiunga Marine Game Reserve •
  Kenya 131 G4
Kiuruvesi • Finland 16 N5
Kivéri Beach • Greece .... 97 [184]
Kivijärvi • Finland 16 M5
Kivik • Sweden 125 F11
Kivíóli • Estonia 126 B2
Kivu • Dem. Rep. of Congo 23 D4
Kivu, Lac •
  Rwanda/Dem. Rep. of Congo .. 23 D4
Kiwai • Papua New Guinea 35 (1) C2
Kizel • Russian Fed. 26 I6
Kizikkaya • Turkey 15 J3
Kizil Adalar • Turkey 122 D3
Kizil Dag • Turkey 15 N7
Kizil Irmak • Turkey 18 B1
Kizilcahaman • Turkey 15 N3
Kizilhisar • Turkey 122 D9
Kizilkadag • Turkey 123 F1
Kizimen Sopka, Vulkan •
  Russian Fed. 27 R5
Kizkalesi • Turkey 123 G3
Kjellerup • Denmark 125 F9
Kjevik [Apt] • Norway 125 F1
Kladanj • Bosnia-Herz. 14 F5
Kladno • Czech Rep. 128 B2
Kladruby • Czech Rep. 128 B3
Klaeng • Thailand 142 C4
Klagenfurt • Austria 13 D11
Klaipeda • Lithuania 126 B3
Klamath • CA/OR, United States . 152 C1
Klamath Falls •
  OR, United States 152 B3
Klamono • Indonesia 32 (1) D3
Klarälven • Sweden 16 G6
Klating Beach • Bali, Indonesia .. 143 H4
Klatovy • Czech Rep. 128 B3
Klausen • Italy 120 B1
Klawer • South Africa 134 C1
Klein Bonaire • Bonaire .... 160 W
Kleinarl Ski • Austria .... 100 [174]
Kleinburg • OT, Canada 155 B9
Kleinheubach Castle • Germany .. 113 [171]
Kleinmachnow • Germany 111 C3
Kleinwalsertal Ski • Austria .... 100 [128]
Klenci pod Cerchovem •
  Czech Rep. 128 B3
Klerksdorp • South Africa 24 D5
Kleve • Germany 8 B5
Klibreck, Ben • United Kingdom .. 6 H3
Klin • Russian Fed. 126 C4
Klingenbuerg • Germany 112 D4
Klingenthal • Germany 13 B7
Klinovec • Czech Rep. 128 B1
Klintehamn • Sweden 16 J8
Klintsy • Russian Fed. 16 O9
Klió Beach • Greece .... 97 [199]
Klippan • Sweden 125 F11
Klipplaat • South Africa 134 C3
Klitmøller • Denmark 125 F5
Klobuck • Poland 13 H7
Klodzko • Poland 13 F7
Klöfta • Norway 124 B2
Klondike • YT, Canada 38 D4
Klondike Gold Rush Nat. Hist. Park
  Park N • AK, United States ... 150 [13]
Klosterneuburg • Austria 13 F9
Klosters Ski • Switzerland ..... 100 [115]
Klosters • Switzerland 119 G4
Kloten • Switzerland 9 D9
Klotz, Mt • YT, Canada 49 M2

Kluane Nat. Park Heritage N •
  YT, Canada .... 82 [1]
Kluane Nat. Park • YT, Canada .. 49 N3
Kluane Nat. Park Park N •
  YT, Canada .... 156 [3]
Kluczbork • Poland 13 H7
Klungkung • Bali, Indonesia 143 H4
Klyuchevskaya Sopka, Vulkan •
  Russian Fed. 27 R5
Knäred • Sweden 125 F11
Knarvik • Norway 124 C3
Knebworth House •
  United Kingdom 104 E1
Knechtsteden • Germany 111 B3
Knídos • Turkey 122 D9
Knife River Indian Villages Nat. Hist. Site
  Park N • ND, United States ... 150 [148]
Knightshayes Court •
  United Kingdom 104 F2
Knin • Croatia 128 D4
Knislinge • Sweden 125 F11
Knittelfeld • Austria 13 D10
Knivskjellodden • Norway 16 M1
Knivsta • Sweden 125 D2
Knob Hill • Cayman Is. 159 E2
Knock • Ireland 108 C2
Knock [Apt] • Ireland 108 C1
Knockmealdown Mtns • Ireland .. 7 E9
Knoebels Grove •
  PA, United States 153 D6
Knokke-Heist • Belgium 109 C2
Knole • United Kingdom 104 E3
Knossós • Crete, Greece 123 E7
Knott's Berry Farm Park L •
  CA, United States .... 150 [G]
Knott's Camp Snoopy Park L •
  MN, United States .... 151 [R]
Knowth • Ireland 108 B2
Knox, Cape • BC, Canada 38 E6
Knoxville • IA, United States 46 I2
Knoxville • TN, United States 48 F3
Knutby • Sweden 125 D2
Knuthenborg Park • Denmark ... 125 F14
Knysna • South Africa 134 C7
Knysna Nat. Lake Area •
  South Africa 134 C7
Ko • Japan 30 J4
Kobayashi • Japan 30 F9
Kobe • Japan 140 B4
Kobe Portopia Land • Japan 140 B1
Kobenhavn Beach • Denmark ... 96 [40]
Kobenhavn • Denmark 125 F11
Kobern-Gondorf • Germany 112 E1
Kobeltag • Turkmenistan 18 G2
Koblenz • Germany 112 E2
Kobryn • Belarus 13 N5
Kobuk • AK, United States 49 J2
Kobuk Valley Nat. Park Park N •
  AK, United States .... 150 [3]
Kobuk Valley Nat. Park •
  AK, United States 49 J2
Kobyay • Russian Fed. 27 K4
Koca • Balıkesir, Turkey 15 I3
Koca • Zonguldak, Turkey 15 N2
Kocabas • Turkey 15 J3
Kocain • Turkey 123 F1
Kocevje • Slovenia 128 D1
Koch I. • NU, Canada 39 P3
Kochechum • Russian Fed. 26 Q4
Kochel • Germany 112 F7
Kochheisee • Germany 112 F8
Kocher • Germany 9 E7
Kochi • Japan 30 G8
Kochi [Adm] • Japan 140 A7
Kochisar Ovasi • Turkey 15 O5
Kochubey • Russian Fed. 17 H6
Kodagu • India 138 D10
Kodaikanal Hill Sta • India 138 E2
Kodiak • AK, United States 49 K4
Kodiak I. • AK, United States ... 49 K4
Kodikkarai Bird Sanctuary •
  India 138 D11
Kodok • Sudan 23 F2
Kodougadlur • India 138 D10
Kodyma • Ukraine 14 Q1
Kodyma [Riv] • Ukraine 14 Q1
Kodzha Balkan • Bulgaria 14 N7
Koës • Namibia 24 B5
Kofa Mtns • AZ, United States ... 45 F5
Köflach • Austria 13 E10
Kofu • Japan 140 C1
Koga • Japan 140 C2
Koganeiceanu, Mihail [Apt] •
  Romania 128 E2
Koge • Denmark 125 F14
Koge Bugt • Denmark 125 F15
Kohat • Pakistan 28 B2
Kohila • Estonia 126 B2
Kohtla-Järve • Estonia 126 B2
Kohu Dagi • Turkey 15 K7
Kohunlich • Mexico 157 H4
Koje • Rep. of Korea 30 E7
Kojo • D.P.R. of Korea 30 D5
Kok • Thailand 142 B2
Kök Shal Tau • Kyrgyzstan 26 M9
Kok Yangak • Kyrgyzstan 18 J1
Kokand • Uzbekistan 127 D2
Kokas • Indonesia 32 (1) D3
Kokemäenjoki • Finland 125 E2
Kokemäki • Finland 125 E1
Kokini Hani • Crete, Greece 123 E3
Kokkina • Cyprus 123 J1
Kokkola • Finland 16 L5
Kokkoni Beach • Greece .... 97 [178]
Koko • Nigeria 22 E2
Koko Head Natural Park •
  HI, United States 154 G6
Koko Nor • China 29 C3
Kokoda • Papua New Guinea 34 I1
Kokomo • IN, United States 46 J6
Kokonau • Indonesia 32 (1) E3
Kokorin • Czech Rep. 128 B2
Kökshetau • Kazakhstan 26 K7
Koksijde-Bad • Belgium 109 C1
Koksoak • QU, Canada 39 R5
Kokstad • South Africa 134 B5
Kol'skiy Poluostrov •
  Russian Fed. 17 F1
Kola • Russian Fed. 16 Q2
Kola Peninsula • Russian Fed. .. 17 F1
Kolaka • Indonesia 32 (1) B3
Kolar • India 138 D7
Kolar Gold Fields • India 138 D7
Kolari • Finland 16 L3
Kolárovo • Slovak Rep. 13 G10
Kolašin • Yugoslavia 14 G6
Kolbermoor • Germany 112 F7
Kolda • Senegal 22 A2
Koléa • Algeria 11 N8
Kolguyev, Ostrov • Russian Fed. . 17 I1
Kolhapur • India 138 C8
Kolin • Czech Rep. 123 D5
Kolka • Latvia 126 B3
Kolksnag • Italy 120 B2
Kolmarden Djurpark • Sweden ... 16 [49]
Köln Heritage C • Germany ..... 86 [165]
Köln • Germany 111 B3
Kolo • Poland 13 H5
Kolobrzeg • Poland 13 E3
Kolokani • Mali 22 C2

Kololo • Ethiopia 21 H6
Kolomna • Russian Fed. 126 C4
Kolono • Indonesia 32 (1) B3
Kolpashevo • Russian Fed. 26 N6
Kolpino • Russian Fed. 126 C1
Kolsva • Sweden 125 D1
Kolumadulu Atoll • Maldives ... 138 F3
Kolweni • Russian Fed. 23 D6
Kolyma • Russian Fed. 27 O4
Kolyma Lowlands • Russian Fed. . 127 A7
Kolymskaya Nizmennost •
  Russian Fed. 27 P3
Kolymskoye Nagorye •
  Russian Fed. 27 Q4
Kom • Bulgaria 14 K6
Kom • Africa 22 J6
Kom Ombo • Egypt 131 F5
Koma tou Gialou • Cyprus 123 J2
Komadugu Gana • Nigeria 20 H6
Komandorskiye Ostrova •
  Russian Fed. 27 S5
Komárno • Slovak Rep. 14 F2
Komárom • Hungary 14 F2
Komatsushima • Japan 140 B3
Komi • Russian Fed. 17 J2
Komi virgin forests Heritage N •
  Russian Fed. .... 83 [73]
Komló • Hungary 13 H11
Kommunizm, Qullai • Tajikistan .. 18 J2
Komodo • Indonesia 32 (1) A4
Komodo Nat. Park Heritage N •
  Indonesia .... 83 [138]
Komoé •
  Burkina Faso/Côte d'Ivoire ... 22 D3
Komoé, Parc nat. de la Heritage N •
  Côte d'Ivoire .... 83 [84]
Komoé, Parc nat. de la Park •
  Côte d'Ivoire .... 133 [20]
Komoran • Indonesia 32 (1) E4
Komotiní • Greece 122 D2
Kompas Berg • South Africa 134 C4
Kompong Cham • Cambodia 141 E1
Kompong Chhnang • Cambodia .. 141 E1
Kompong Som • Cambodia 141 E1
Komsa • Russian Fed. 26 O5
Komsomol'sk-na-Amure •
  Russian Fed. 27 M6
Komsomolets, Ostrov •
  Russian Fed. 26 N1
Komsomolskiy • Russian Fed. ... 27 T3
Kömür Burnu • Turkey 15 H4
Kona • Mali 20 E6
Kona [Apt] • HI, United States .. 154 G8
Kona Coast • HI, United States .. 154 G8
Konakovo • Russian Fed. 126 C4
Konar • Afghanistan 28 B1
Konarak • India 28 E5
Konawa • IN, Australia 34 C6
Kondagon • India 28 D5
Kondinin • WA, Australia 34 C6
Kondoa • Tanzania 130 B2
Kondopoga • Russian Fed. 16 O5
Kondrovo • Russian Fed. 17 E2
Koné • New Caledonia 35 (2) B3
Kong Christian IX Land •
  Greenland 39 W3
Kong Frederik VI Kyst •
  Greenland 39 W4
Kongolo • Dem. Rep. of Congo .. 23 D5
Kongsberg • Norway 124 B1
Kongsvinger • Norway 124 B1
Königs Wusterhausen • Germany . 111 C4
Königsbrunn • Germany 112 F2
Königsbrunn • Germany 112 F2
Königsleiten Ski • Austria ..... 100 [147]
Königsschlosser Castle •
  Germany .... 113 [116-117]
Königssee • Germany 112 F8
Königstein Castle • Germany ... 113 [190]
Königstein im Taunus • Germany . 112 E2
Königstein im Taunus Castle •
  Germany .... 113 [47]
Königstein im Taunus Spa •
  Germany .... 113 [h3]
Königswinter • Germany 112 E1
Konin • Poland 13 H5
Konispol • Albania 15 B4
Konjic • Bosnia-Herz. 14 F6
Konkan • India 137 A4
Konopiste • Czech Rep. 128 B2
Konosha • Russian Fed. 17 F2
Konradsheim Castle • Germany . 113 [30]
Konskie • Poland 13 J6
Konstanz • Germany 112 D8
Kontagora • Nigeria 22 F2
Kontcha • Cameroon 22 G3
Kontich • Belgium 5 H3
Kontiomäki • Finland 16 O4
Kontókali • Corfu, Greece 122 B1
Kontum Plateau • Vietnam 141 D2
Konya • Turkey 123 G1
Konya [Adm] • Turkey 123 G1
Konya Ovasi • Turkey 123 G1
Konyaalti Beach • Turkey ...... 97 [226]
Konyaalti • Turkey 123 F3
Konz • Germany 5 J5
Koolau Range •
  HI, United States 154 G5
Koorda • WA, Australia 34 C6
Kootenay • Canada/United States 155 C4
Kootenay Nat. Park • BC, Canada 155 C4
Kootenay Nat. Park Park N •
  BC, Canada .... 156 [13]
Kopaonik • F.R. of Yugoslavia ... 14 H6
Kopavogur • Iceland 16 (1) C2
Köpenick (Berlin) • Germany 111 C4
Koper • Slovenia 128 D1
Kopervik • Norway 124 C5
Kopeysk • Russian Fed. 26 J6
Köping • Sweden 125 D1
Koplik • Albania 15 A1
Kopparberg • Sweden 16 H7
Koppom • Norway 124 A2
Koprivnica • Croatia 128 D2
Köprülü • Turkey 123 F4
Kora Nat. Park • Kenya 131 G4
Korabük • Turkey 15 N2
Korable • Ethiopia 23 G2
Korana • Crete, Greece 123 E6
Korarou • Mali 22 D1
Korat Plateau • Thailand 142 A2
Korba • Tunisia 12 E12
Korba • India 28 D4
Korbach • Germany 9 D5
Korçë • Albania 15 B3
Korce • Albania 122 B1
Korcula • Croatia 14 F6
Korcula [I.] • Croatia 128 C4
Korcula • Croatia 14 D6

Korolei • Somalia 23 G3
Korithí • Zante, Greece 122 C3
Koritnik •
  Albania/F.R. of Yugoslavia 14 H7
Koriyama • Japan 30 K6
Koriyama [Apt] • Japan 123 F1
Korla • China 26 O9
Kormakiti, Cape • Cyprus 123 J1
Kormilovka • Russian Fed. 13 F10
Kormy, gora • Russian Fed. ... 26 J5
Kornat • Croatia 128 D3
Kornati Nat. Park • Croatia ... 89 [112]
Kornati Nat. Park Park N •
  Croatia 128 D3
Kornelimünster • Germany 111 B3
Kornos • Cyprus 123 J4
Kornye • Hungary 124 B4
Koro Sea • Fiji Is. 35 (2) D2
Koro Toro • Chad 20 I5
Koroba • Papua New Guinea ... 35 (1) C2
Korogu Tepe • Turkey 15 M3
Korogwe • Tanzania 130 B2
Koronia, Limni • Greece 15 E3
Koronida Beach • Greece ..... 97 [206]
Koronowo • Poland 13 G4
Koror • Palau 33 E5
Körös • Hungary 13 J11
Korosten • Ukraine 14 O3
Korovin Volcano •
  AK, United States 49 G5
Korpilahti • Finland 125 E2
Korpo • Finland 125 E3
Korpo • Finland 125 E3
Korsakov • Russian Fed. 27 N7
Korschenbroich • Germany 111 B3
Korsnäs • Finland 16 K5
Korsør Beach • Denmark ...... 96 [43]
Korsør • Denmark 125 F14
Koru Dagi • Turkey 15 H3
Korucu • Turkey 15 I4
Korup, Parc nat. du Park •
  Cameroon .... 133 [37]
Koryakskiy Nagorye •
  Russian Fed. 27 T4
Koryakskaya, Vulkan •
  Russian Fed. 27 Q6
Koryazhma • Russian Fed. 17 H2
Kos • Greece 122 D8
Kos [I.] • Greece 122 D8
Kosa • Russian Fed. 17 I3
Kosan • Poland 13 F5
Koscian • Poland 13 G3
Kościeliny drewniany • Poland .. 128 C4
Kosciusko, MS, United States ... 153 F2
Kosciusko, Mt • NS, Australia .. 145 F4
Koshikijima-retto • Japan 30 E9
Kosi Bay • South Africa 134 B2
Kosi Bay Nature Reserve •
  South Africa 134 B2
Kosice • Slovak Rep. 13 K9
Koski • Finland 125 E4
Koskinoú Beach • Rhodes, Greece 97 [211]
Koslan • Russian Fed. 17 H2
Kosovo • F.R. of Yugoslavia ... 14 I7
Kosovo, Autonomous Prov of •
  F.R. of Yugoslavia 14 H7
Kosovska Mitrovica •
  F.R. of Yugoslavia 14 H7
Kosrae •
  Fed. States of Micronesia ... 33 H5
Kossou, Barrage de •
  Côte d'Ivoire 22 C3
Kostajnica • Croatia 125 F8
Koster • Sweden 125 F3
Kostomuksha • Russian Fed. ... 16 P4
Kostroma • Russian Fed. 126 C2
Kostromskoye Vdkhr. •
  Russian Fed. 126 C2
Kostrzyn • Gorzowskie, Poland .. 13 D5
Kostrzyn • Poznanskie, Poland .. 13 G5
Koszalin • Poland 13 F3
Koszeg • Hungary 13 F10
Kota • India 137 C6
Kota Baharu • Malaysia 142 A4
Kota Kinabalu • Malaysia 32 F1
Kotabaru • Indonesia 32 F3
Kotabumi • Indonesia 32 C3
Kotadabok • Indonesia 32 C3
Kotagiri Hill Sta • India 138 E2
Kotare Gorge • New Zealand ... 145 F3
Kotel • Bulgaria 14 N7
Kotelnich • Russian Fed. 17 H3
Kotelnyy, Ostrov • Russian Fed. . 27 M1
Köthen • Germany 8 G5
Kotka • Finland 16 N6
Kotlas • Russian Fed. 17 H2
Kotlin, Ostrov • Russian Fed. .. 126 C1
Kotovk • Ukraine 14 Q2
Kotopasa, Gunung • Indonesia .. 32 (1) B3
Kotor Heritage N •
  F.R. of Yugoslavia .... 83 [62]
Kotor Heritage C •
  F.R. of Yugoslavia .... 86 [188]
Kotovo • Russian Fed. 17 G4
Kotovsk • Ukraine 14 Q2
Kotsifoú, Farági •
  Crete, Greece 123 E6
Kottagudem • India 138 D10
Kotturu • Russian Fed. 17 H3
Kottayam • India 138 C2
Kotto • Central African Rep. ... 23 C2
Kotuy • Russian Fed. 126 A4
Kotzebue • AK, United States .. 49 I2
Kouba Modounga • Chad 22 H1
Kouchibouguac Nat. Park •
  NB, Canada 156 D7
Kouchibouguac Nat. Park Park N •
  NB, Canada .... 156 [32]
Koudougou • Burkina Faso 22 D2
Köpenick (Berlin) • Germany ... 111 C4
Koufonisi • Aegean Sea, Greece . 122 D8
Koufonisi •
  Mediterranean Sea, Greece .. 123 E8
Kougaberge • South Africa 134 C7
Kouklux, Great Plain of the •
  NU, Canada 39 Q3
Koulamoutou • Gabon 22 G5
Koulikoro • Mali 20 D6
Koumbi-Saleh • Mauritania 20 C5
Koumpentoum • Senegal 20 C6
Koupéla • Burkina Faso 22 E2
Kourou • French Guiana 51 G2
Kourou • French Guiana 20 D6
Kourtaliótiko Farági •
  Crete, Greece 123 E6
Koutiala • Mali 22 C2
Koutsounari • Crete, Greece ... 123 E8
Kouvola • Finland 16 N6
Kovalam Beach • India 138 D4
Kovdor • Russian Fed. 16 P3
Kovdozero • Russian Fed. 16 P3
Kovriga, gora • Russian Fed. .. 26 P5
Kovrov • Russian Fed. 17 G3
Kowloon • Hong Kong, China .. 139 B6
Kowloon City • Hong Kong, China 139 B6
Kowon • D.P.R. of Korea 30 D5
Koya-san • Japan 140 B4
Köyceğiz • Turkey 15 J7
Kozağaci • Turkey 123 F3
Kozan • Turkey 123 G2
Kozani • Greece 14 I8
Kozara Nat. Park • Bosnia-Herz. . 14 D4
Kozhim • Russian Fed. 17 J1
Kozienice • Poland 13 K6
Kozludza • Turkey 15 M2

Kozu • Japan 30 J7
Kozuf • F.Y.R. of Macedonia ... 14 J8
Kpalimé • Togo 22 E3
Kra, Isthmus of • Thailand 142 A3
Kraaifontein • South Africa 134 C5
Krabbfjärden • Sweden 125 D4
Kragerø • Norway 124 B3
Kragujevac • F.R. of Yugoslavia . 14 H5
Krajiste •
  Bulgaria/F.R. of Yugoslavia .. 14 J7
Krakatau • Java, Indonesia 143 J1
Krakatau Nature Reserve Heritage N •
  Indonesia .... 83 [137]
Kraków Heritage C • Poland .... 86 [165]
Kraków • Poland 128 C2
Krakowska, Jura • Poland 128 C2
Krakowskie, Bonaire .... 160 W
Kraljevo • F.R. of Yugoslavia ... 14 H6
Kralupy nad Vltavou •
  Czech Rep. 13 D7
Kramsach • Austria 119 H3
Kramsfors • Sweden 16 I5
Kranebitten [Apt] • Austria 119 H2
Kranidi • Greece 15 E6
Kranj • Slovenia 13 D11
Kranj • Slovenia 128 D1
Kranjska Gora • Slovenia 128 D1
Kranskloof Nature Reserve •
  South Africa 134 B5
Kraskino • South Africa 134 B3
Krapina • Croatia 128 D1
Krapkowice • Poland 13 G7
Krasavino • Russian Fed. 17 H2
Kraskino • Russian Fed. 30 F3
Kraslava • Latvia 126 B4
Krasnik • Poland 13 L7
Krasnodar • Russian Fed. 17 F5
Krasnogorsk • Russian Fed. 27 N7
Krasnokamensk • Russian Fed. .. 17 J3
Krasnoselkup • Russian Fed. .. 26 N4
Krasnoufimsk • Russian Fed. ... 26 I6
Krasnoural'sk • Russian Fed. ... 26 I5
Krasnovishersk • Russian Fed. .. 26 I5
Krasnoyarsk • Russian Fed. 26 O6
Krasnozatonsiy • Russian Fed. .. 17 I2
Krasnystaw • Poland 13 M7
Krasny Chikoy • Russian Fed. .. 27 G6
Kratie • Cambodia 31 D4
Kratochvíle • Czech Rep. 128 B4
Kratovo • F.Y.R. of Macedonia .. 128 D4
Krautheim Castle • Germany ... 113 [92]
Krazh Khara-Tas • Russian Fed. . 26 Q6
Krefeld • Germany 111 B1
Kremastón, Tehniti Límni •
  Greece 15 C5
Kremenchuk • Ukraine 17 E5
Kremenchuts'ke Vdskh. • Ukraine 17 E5
Kremmling • CO, United States . 45 I1
Krems • Austria 123 F1
Krems • Austria 14 C1
Kresta, Zaliv • Russian Fed. ... 27 V3
Kretinga • Lithuania 126 B3
Kreuzberg (Berlin) • Germany .. 111 C4
Kreuzlingen • Switzerland 9 E9
Kreuztal • Germany 9 D6
Kribi • Cameroon 22 F4
Krichim • Bulgaria 14 L7
Kriebstein Castle • Germany ... 113 [198]
Krim • Ukraine 17 E5
Kriml • Austria 119 H7
Krimpenerwaard • Netherlands .. 109 F4
Krims'ke-Hory • Ukraine 17 E6
Kriopigi Beach • Greece ...... 97 [192]
Kriopigi • Greece 122 D1
Kríos, Ákra • Crete, Greece ... 123 E7
Krishna • India 138 D3
Krishna, Mouths of the • India .. 138 D3
Krishnagiri • India 138 D7
Kristdala • Sweden 125 F8
Kristianopel • Sweden 125 F12
Kristiansand • Norway 125 F1
Kristiansand Dyrepark Park L •
  Norway .... 98 [1]
Kristiansand Dyrepark • Norway . 125 F1
Kristianstad Beach • Sweden ... 97 [14]
Kristianstad • Sweden 125 F11
Kristiinankaupunki • Finland ... 16 I5
Kristinehamn • Finland 125 D1
Krivi • Greece 122 D12
Kritinía • Rhodes, Greece 123 E7
Kritsá • Crete, Greece 123 E7
Krivoklát • Czech Rep. 128 B1
Krivolátska Vrchovina •
  Czech Rep. 128 B1
Krk • Croatia 128 D1
Krk Nat. Park Park N •
  Slovenia .... 89 [108]
Krka Nat. Park • Slovenia 128 D1
Krknosoe Nat. Park Park N •
  Czech Rep. .... 89 [99]
Krnov • Czech Rep. 13 G7
Krøderen • Norway 124 B2
Krøderen [Lake] • Norway 125 D3
Krokek • Sweden 125 D3
Krokom • Sweden 16 H5
Krokodil Heritage C •
  South Africa .... 85 [118]
Kromeriz Heritage C •
  Czech Rep. .... 86 [176]
Kronach • Germany 9 G6
Kronberg • Germany 112 E2
Kronberg Castle • Germany .... 113 [48]
Kronoberg • Sweden 125 F11
Kronoki • Russian Fed. 27 R6
Kronotskaya Sopka, Vulkan •
  Russian Fed. 27 R5
Kronshagen • Germany 8 F2
Kronstadt • Russian Fed. 126 C1
Kroonstad • South Africa 24 D5
Kropotkin • Russian Fed. 17 G5
Kropp • Germany 8 E2
Kropstädt • Sweden 125 F12
Krosno • Poland 13 K8
Krotoszyn • Poland 13 G6
Kroussónas • Crete, Greece 123 E7
Krøv • Germany 112 E3
Kroya • Java, Indonesia 143 J4
Krško • Slovenia 128 D1
Kruger Nat. Park • South Africa . 24 E4
Kruger Nat. Park Park N •
  South Africa .... 133 [129]
Krugersdorp • South Africa 24 D5
Kruibeke • Bonaire .... 160 W
Krumbach • Germany 112 F2
Krummbbel • Germany 112 F2
Krumovgrad • Bulgaria 14 M8
Krung Thep • Thailand 142 C1
Krünpelsee • Germany 111 C4
Krusevac • F.R. of Yugoslavia .. 14 H6
Krusne Hory • Czech Rep. 128 B1
Krychaw • Belarus 17 E3
Krylbo • Sweden 125 D1
Krynica • Poland 13 K8
Kryvyy Rih • Ukraine 17 E5
Ksabi • Algeria 11 I6
Ksar el Boukhari • Algeria 11 N9
Ksar el Kebir • Morocco 131 D1
Ksar es Srhir • Morocco 11 F9
Ksar Hadada • Tunisia 131 E6

Ksar Hellal • Tunisia ... 131 E4
Ksar Ouled Soltane • Tunisia ... 131 E6
Ksour, Mts des • Algeria ... 20 E2
Ktikados **Beach** • Greece ... 97 [202]
Ku-Ring-Gai Chase Nat. Park •
NS, Australia ... 144 C2
Kuala Belait • Brunei ... 32 E2
Kuala Dungun • Malaysia ... 32 C2
Kuala Kelawang • Malaysia ... 141 G4
Kuala Kerai • Malaysia ... 32 C1
Kuala Kubu Baharu • Malaysia ... 141 G4
Kuala Lipis • Malaysia ... 141 G2
Kuala Lumpur • Malaysia ... 141 G4
Kuala Selangor • Malaysia ... 141 G3
Kuala Terengganu • Malaysia ... 32 C1
Kuandang • Indonesia ... 32 (1) B2
Kuandian • China ... 30 C4
Kuantan • Malaysia ... 32 C2
Kuban • Russian Fed. ... 17 G5
Kubenskoye, Ozero •
Russian Fed. ... 126 C2
Kubokawa • Japan ... 30 G8
Kubutambahan • Bali, Indonesia ... 143 H2
Kuching • Malaysia ... 32 E2
Kuchinoerabu-jima • Japan ... 140 A7
Kuchinoshima • Japan ... 140 A7
Kuchurhan • Ukraine ... 14 Q2
Kucova • Albania ... 15 A3
Küçük Menderes • Turkey ... 15 I5
Kudahithi • Maldives ... 138 F2
Kudarebe • Aruba ... 160 Y
Kudat • Malaysia ... 32 F1
Kudus • Java, Indonesia ... 143 J3
Kudymkar • Russian Fed. ... 17 I3
Kuenga • Russian Fed. ... 127 A13
Kufrah Oasis • Libya ... 21 D3
Kufri **Hill Sta** • India ... 138 E1
Kufstein • Austria ... 119 H3
Kugluktuk • NU, Canada ... 38 H3
Kühlungsborn • Germany ... 8 C2
Kühlungsborn **Beach** • Germany ... 96 [34]
Kühlungsborn **Spa** • Germany ... 113 [c20]
Kuhmo • Finland ... 16 O4
Kuito • Angola ... 23 B6
Kujani Game Reserve **Park** •
Ghana ... 133 [23]
Kujawy • Poland ... 13 I2
Kuju • Japan ... 30 K4
Kuju • Japan ... 30 F8
Kuki • Japan ... 140 C2
Kul • Iran ... 18 F4
Kul'sary • Kazakstan ... 26 H8
Kula • F.R. of Yugoslavia ... 14 G4
Kula • Bulgaria ... 14 J6
Kula • Turkey ... 15 J5
Kular • Russian Fed. ... 27 M2
Kulata • Bulgaria ... 14 K8
Kuldiga • Latvia ... 126 B3
Kulgera • NT, Australia ... 145 D4
Kulmbach • Germany ... 9 G6
Kulob • Tajikistan ... 18 I2
Kulpsville • PA, United States ... 44 H5
Kulu • Turkey ... 15 Q4
Kulu • Russian Fed. ... 27 Q4
Kulu **Hill Sta** • India ... 138 E1
Kulunda • Russian Fed. ... 26 M7
Kuma • Russian Fed. ... 4 T7
Kumagaya • Japan ... 140 C1
Kumai • Indonesia ... 32 E3
Kumamoto • Japan ... 30 F8
Kumamoto [Adm] • Japan ... 140 A7
Kumano • Japan ... 30 H8
Kumanovo • F.Y.R. of Macedonia ... 14 I7
Kumasi • Ghana ... 22 D3
Kumaun • India ... 137 C3
Kumba • Cameroon ... 22 F4
Kumbakonam • India ... 138 D11
Kumbe • Indonesia ... 32 (1) F4
Kumbhalgarh • India ... 137 C5
Kumdah • Saudi Arabia ... 21 I3
Kume • Japan ... 29 H5
Kumhwa • Rep. of Korea ... 30 D5
Kumköy • Turkey ... 15 K2
Kumkuduk • China ... 26 P9
Kumla • Örebro, Sweden ... 16 H7
Kumla • Västmanland, Sweden ... 125 D1
Kumluca • Turkey ... 123 F3
Kumo älv • Finland ... 125 E2
Kumul • China ... 29 A2
Kumyali • Cyprus ... 123 J2
Kunashir, Ostrov • Russian Fed. ... 27 O8
Kunashiri-To • Russian Fed. ... 27 O8
Kunashirskiy Proliv •
Russian Fed. ... 27 O8
Kundapura • India ... 138 D6
Kundelungu, Mtns •
Dem. Rep. of Congo ... 23 D6
Kundelungu, Parc nat. de **Park** •
Dem. Rep. of Congo ... 133 [59]
Kundiawa • Papua New Guinea ... 35 (1) C2
Kunduchi • Tanzania ... 130 B4
Künes He • China ... 26 N9
Kung Bay • Ko Phuket, Thailand ... 142 E1
Kungagraven • Sweden ... 125 F11
Kungälv • Sweden ... 125 F6
Kungey-Alatau • Kazakstan ... 26 M9
Kungsbacka • Sweden ... 125 F6
Kungshamn • Sweden ... 125 F2
Kungsör • Sweden ... 125 D3
Kungu • Dem. Rep. of Congo ... 23 B3
Kungur • Russian Fed. ... 17 J3
Kunhing • Myanmar ... 31 B2
Kunjamuk Mtn •
NY, United States ... 44 H4
Kunlun Shan • China ... 28 E1
Kunlun Shankou • China ... 28 F1
Kunming • China ... 29 C5
Kunsan • Rep. of Korea ... 30 D7
Kunshan • China ... 139 C2
Kununurra • WA, Australia ... 34 E3
Künzelsau • Germany ... 9 E7
Kuomi • Japan ... 140 C1
Kuopio • Finland ... 16 N5
Kuopio **Beach** • Finland ... 97 [29]
Kuopio [Adm] • Finland ... 16 N5
Kuopio [Adm] • Finland ... 124 A5
Kupa • Croatia/Slovenia ... 128 C1
Kupang • Indonesia ... 32 (1) B5
Kupiano • Papua New Guinea ... 35 (1) D3
Kupino • Russian Fed. ... 26 M7
Kupiskis • Lithuania ... 126 B4
Kupreanof Is. •
AK, United States ... 38 E5
Kuqa • China ... 26 N9
Kur • Azerbaijan ... 18 E1
Kuramathi • Maldives ... 138 F1
Kuranda • QL, Australia ... 34 F3
Kuremäe • Estonia ... 126 B2
Kuressaare • Estonia ... 126 B1
Kurgan • Russian Fed. ... 26 K6
Kuri Bay • WA, Australia ... 34 D3
Kurikka • Finland ... 16 L5
Kuril Is. • Russian Fed. ... 27 P7
Kuril'sk • Russian Fed. ... 27 O7
Kurilskiye Ostrova •
Russian Fed. ... 25 P5
Kurmuk • Sudan ... 23 E1
Kurnool • India ... 138 D3
Kurobe • Japan ... 30 I6

Kuroishi • Japan ... 30 K4
Kurort Schmalkalden • Germany ... 9 F6
Kurpfalzpark • Germany ... 112 D4
Kursenai • Lithuania ... 126 B3
Kursiu Nerija Nat. Park •
Lithuania ... 126 B5
Kursk • Russian Fed. ... 17 F4
Kürten • Germany ... 111 B4
Kuru • Finland ... 125 E2
Kurucasile • Turkey ... 15 N2
Kurukshetra • India ... 137 C2
Kuruman • South Africa ... 24 C5
Kurumbu • Maldives ... 138 F4
Kurume • Japan ... 30 F8
Kurunegala • Sri Lanka ... 138 D15
Kurutag • China ... 26 O9
Kurzeme • Latvia ... 126 B3
Kus Gölü • Turkey ... 122 D3
Kusadasi • Turkey ... 122 D8
Kusadasi Körfezi • Turkey ... 15 H6
Kusamala • Bali, Indonesia ... 143 H4
Kusatsu • Japan ... 140 B2
Kushikino • Japan ... 30 F9
Kushimoto • Japan ... 30 H8
Kushinagar • India ... 137 C4
Kushiro • Japan ... 30 M3
Kuskokwim • AK, United States ... 49 I3
Kuskokwim Mtns •
AK, United States ... 49 J3
Kussharo-ko • Japan ... 30 O5
Kussnacht • Switzerland ... 119 G3
Kusti • Sudan ... 21 F5
Kusva • Russian Fed. ... 26 I6
Kut, Al • Iraq ... 18 E3
Kut, Ko • Thailand ... 31 C4
Kuta • Bali, Indonesia ... 143 H4
Kutaisi **Heritage C** • Georgia ... 86 [249]
Kütahya • Turkey ... 15 K4
Kutch, Gulf of • India ... 28 A4
Kutch, Rann of • India ... 28 A4
Kutina • Croatia ... 128 D2
Kutná Hora **Heritage C** •
Czech Rep. ... 86 [169]
Kutná Hora • Czech Rep. ... 128 B2
Kutno • Poland ... 13 I5
Kuttanad • India ... 138 D10
Kutu • Dem. Rep. of Congo ... 23 B4
Kuty • Ukraine ... 14 M1
Kuujjuaq • QU, Canada ... 39 R5
Kuujjuarapik • QU, Canada ... 39 P5
Kuusamo • Finland ... 16 O3
Kuwait • Asia ... 18 E4
KUWAIT • Asia ... 18 E4
Kuwait City • Kuwait ... 18 E4
Kuygan • Kazakstan ... 26 L8
Kuytun • China ... 26 O9
Kuznetsk • Russian Fed. ... 17 H4
Kuznetskiy Alatau •
Russian Fed. ... 26 O7
Kuzomen • Russian Fed. ... 17 F1
Kvænangen • Norway ... 16 K1
Kvaløy • Norway ... 16 L1
Kvaløya • Norway ... 16 L1
Kvarner • Croatia ... 128 D1
Kvarneric • Croatia ... 128 D3
Kvicksund • Sweden ... 125 D3
Kvikkjokk • Sweden ... 16 I3
Kviteseid • Norway ... 124 C6
Kwa • Dem. Rep. of Congo ... 23 B4
Kwahu Plateau • Ghana ... 22 D3
Kwai Chung Port •
Hong Kong, China ... 139 B5
Kwajalein • Marshall Is. ... 33 H5
Kwakoegon • Surinam ... 51 G5
Kwale • Kenya ... 131 G5
Kwambonambi • South Africa ... 134 B4
KwaMashu • South Africa ... 134 B3
Kwando • Africa ... 24 C3
Kwangju • Rep. of Korea ... 30 D7
Kwango • Dem. Rep. of Congo ... 23 B4
Kwanmo • D.P.R. of Korea ... 30 E4
Kwara • Nigeria ... 22 F3
Kwazulu-Natal • South Africa ... 134 B3
Kwekwe • Zimbabwe ... 130 C2
Kwidzyn • Poland ... 13 H4
Kwikila • Papua New Guinea ... 34 I1
Kwilu • Dem. Rep. of Congo ... 23 B4
Kwoka, Gunung • Indonesia ... 32 (1) D3
Kyabé • Chad ... 23 B1
Kyakkam • Myanmar ... 31 B3
Kyakhta • Russian Fed. ... 27 G6
Kyancutta • SA, Australia ... 34 G6
Kyaukpyu • Myanmar ... 28 F5
Kyelang • India ... 28 C2
Kyjov • Czech Rep. ... 13 G9
Kyle, Lake • Zimbabwe ... 130 C4
Kyle of Lochalsh •
United Kingdom ... 6 G4
Kyll • Germany ... 112 E3
Kyllburg **Spa** • Germany ... 113 [k7]
Kymi • Finland ... 16 N6
Kymi • Finland ... 124 A8
Kymijoki • Finland ... 16 N6
Kymmene älv • Finland ... 16 N6
Kynnefjäll • Sweden ... 125 F2
Kyoga, Lake • Uganda ... 23 E3
Kyoga-misaki • Japan ... 30 H7
Kyonggi-man • Rep. of Korea ... 30 C6
Kyongju • Rep. of Korea ... 30 E7
Kyongju **Heritage C** •
Rep. of Korea ... 85 [184]
Kyongsong • D.P.R. of Korea ... 30 E4
Kyoto **Heritage C** • Japan ... 85 [189]
Kyoto • Japan ... 140 B2
Kyoto [Adm] • Japan ... 140 A4
Kyperounda • Cyprus ... 123 J3
Kyren • Russian Fed. ... 27 F6
Kyrenia • Cyprus ... 123 J1
Kyrenia Mtns • Cyprus ... 123 J2
KYRGYZSTAN • Asia ... 26 L9
Kyrkhult • Sweden ... 125 F11
Kytay, Ozero • Ukraine ... 14 Q4
Kythrea • Cyprus ... 123 J2
Kyushu • Japan ... 30 F8
Kyushu-sanchi • Japan ... 30 F8
Kyustendil • Bulgaria ... 14 J7
Kyusyur • Russian Fed. ... 27 K2
Kyyiv • Ukraine ... 11 H6
Kyyiv **Heritage C** • Ukraine ... 86 [241]
Kyzyl • Russian Fed. ... 26 P7
Kyzylart • China ... 26 M10
Kyzilca Dagi • Turkey ... 15 L6
Kyzl-Orda • Kazakstan ... 26 K9
Kyzltu • Kazakstan ... 26 L7

L'Ancresse Bay **Beach** •
United Kingdom ... 101 [258]
L'Annonciation • QU, Canada ... 44 H2
L'Anse au Loup • NF, Canada ... 156 D5
L'Anse aux Meadows Hist. Park
Heritage C • NF, Canada ... 84 [5]
L'Aquila • Italy ... 121 F7
L'Erée Bay **Beach** •
United Kingdom ... 101 [254]
L'Europa • Reunion ... 24 G4
L'Ile Rousse • Corsica, France ... 115 L1
L'viv • Ukraine ... 17 C5
L'viv **Heritage C** • Ukraine ... 86 [240]

L'vov • Ukraine ... 17 C5
L'vov **Heritage C** • Ukraine ... 86 [240]
La Almunia de Doña Godina •
Spain ... 11 J3
La Ametlla de Mar • Spain ... 11 L4
La Antilla • Spain ... 116 B1
La Asunción • Margarita ... 160 V
La Asunción • Mexico ... 47 C3
La Babia • Mexico ... 47 B4
La Banda • Argentina ... 52 D4
La Bañeza • Spain ... 11 F2
La Bomba • Mexico ... 45 E6
La Boquilla • Mexico ... 47 B4
La Boquilla, Presa de • Mexico ... 47 B4
La Cadena • Puerto Rico ... 159 H1
La Caleta •
Tenerife, Canary Is. ... 116 E1
La Canal • Ibiza, Spain ... 117 G3
La Ceiba • Honduras ... 37 D4
La Chaux-de-Fonds • Switzerland ... 119 G1
La Chorrera • Panama ... 51 B2
La Chorrera • Colombia ... 51 C4
La Crescent • MN, United States ... 43 K5
La Crosse • WI, United States ... 43 K5
La Crosse • VA, United States ... 153 D11
La Dorada • Colombia ... 51 C4
La Esmeralda • Venezuela ... 51 D3
La Española • West Indies ... 37 G3
La Esperanza • Cuba ... 158 D1
La Estrada • Spain ... 11 C2
La Fayette • LA, United States ... 48 E3
La Gi • Vietnam ... 31 C3
La Fortaleza **Heritage C** •
Puerto Rico ... 84 [44]
La Fortaleza • Puerto Rico ... 159 H2
La Gloria • Mexico ... 47 E4
La Goulette • Tunisia ... 131 E2
La Gran Sabana • Venezuela ... 51 D4
La Grande • OR, United States ... 152 B4
La Grande Rivière • QU, Canada ... 39 P6
La Grange • GA, United States ... 48 E4
La Grita • Venezuela ... 37 H5
La Guaira • Venezuela ... 51 D3
La Guardia • Portugal ... 11 C3
La Guardia, Ensenada •
Margarita ... 160 V
La Habana **Heritage C** • Cuba ... 84 [39]
La Habana • Cuba ... 158 D1
La Isabela • Dominican Rep. ... 159 G3
La Isleta •
Lanzarote, Canary Is. ... 117 E3
La Junta • CO, United States ... 46 D4
La Junta • Mexico ... 157 F2
La Línea • Spain ... 116 B6
La Línea de la Concepción **Beach** •
Spain ... 96 [113]
La Maddalena **Beach** •
Sardinia, Italy ... 96 [137]
La Mancha • Spain ... 11 H5
La Mancha • France/UK ... 117 H1
La Manga del Mar Menor • Spain ... 117 C3
La Mármora, Punta •
Sardinia, Italy ... 120 C4
La Marque • TX, United States ... 47 G3
La Marsa • Tunisia ... 131 E2
La Mauricie Nat. Park •
QU, Canada ... 155 B4
La Mauricie Nat. Park **Park N** •
QU, Canada ... 156 [28]
La Mesa • CA, United States ... 45 D6
La Montaña • Peru ... 51 C5
La Neuveville • Switzerland ... 119 G2
La Oliva •
Fuerteventura, Canary Is. ... 117 E2
La Orotava •
Tenerife, Canary Is. ... 116 E1
La Oroya • Peru ... 163 B1
La Palma • Canary Is. ... 117 E5
La Palma • Panama ... 37 F6
La Panchita • Cuba ... 158 D1
La Paragua • Venezuela ... 51 D4
La Pared, Istmo de •
Fuerteventura, Canary Is. ... 117 E2
La Paz • Bolivia ... 52 C2
La Paz • Mendoza, Argentina ... 52 C5
La Paz • Entre Ríos, Argentina ... 52 D5
La Paz • Mexico ... 157 F4
La Pedrera • Colombia ... 51 D4
La Peralejo • Spain ... 11 I4
La Perla • Mexico ... 47 B3
La Pérouse Strait •
Russian Fed. ... 27 N7
La Pesa • Mexico ... 47 F6
La Pine • OR, United States ... 42 E5
La Place • LA, United States ... 48 B5
La Plaine • Dominica ... 161 M
La Plata • Argentina ... 52 D5
La Plata, Río de •
Argentina/Uruguay ... 163 D2
La Playa de Mogán •
Gran Canaria, Canary Is. ... 116 E4
La Playa de Tauro •
Gran Canaria, Canary Is. ... 116 E4
La Pocatière • QU, Canada ... 44 J2
La Point Beach • WI, United States ... 161 P
La Porte • IN, United States ... 44 B5
La Porte • TX, United States ... 47 G3
La Puntilla • Ecuador ... 51 A4
La Purisma • Mexico ... 157 F4
La Purisma Mission State Hist. Park •
CA, United States ... 152 C5
La Quiaca • Argentina ... 52 C3
La Rapita • Majorca, Spain ... 117 H4
La Restinga, Laguna • Margarita ... 160 V
La Rioja • Spain ... 11 I2
La Rioja • Argentina ... 52 C4
La Robla • Spain ... 11 F2
La Roche-en-Ardenne • Belgium ... 109 D19
La Rochelle **Beach** • France ... 96 [84]
La Rochelle • France ... 114 D3
La Roda • Spain ... 11 I5
La Romana • Dominican Rep. ... 159 G8
La Ronde **Park L** • QU, Canada ... 156 [N]
La Ronge • SA, Canada ... 38 J5
La Rosita • Mexico ... 47 B3
La Sabana • Colombia ... 51 D3
La Salle • IL, United States ... 43 L4
La Serena • Spain ... 11 F6
La Serena • Chile ... 52 B4
La Solana • Spain ... 11 H6
La Spézia • Italy ... 121 E10
La Tagua • Colombia ... 51 C4
La Tuque • QU, Canada ... 44 I2
La Tzoumas **Ski** • Switzerland ... 100 [81]
La Unión • Chile ... 53 B4
La Unión • Spain ... 117 C3
La Vanille Crocodile Park •
Mauritius ... 132 J3
La Vega • Dominican Rep. ... 159 G3
La Veguita •
Lanzarote, Canary Is. ... 117 E3
La Vela • Venezuela ... 51 D1
La Vérendrye Prov. Reserve •
QU, Canada ... 155 B2
La Verna, Abbazia • Italy ... 121 E11
La Victoria • Venezuela ... 51 D1
La Vila Joiosa **Beach** • Spain ... 96 [118]
La Viña • Peru ... 51 B5
La Voz • China ... 28 D2
Laamene • Belgium ... 109 D14
Laas **Ski** • Switzerland ... 100 [106]
Laax • Switzerland ... 119 G3
Labe • Guinea ... 22 B2

Labe • Czech Rep. ... 128 B2
Labezanga • Niger ... 20 F6
Laborie • St Lucia ... 161 P
Labota • Indonesia ... 32 (1) B3
Labouheyre • France ... 115 G3
Laboulaye • Argentina ... 52 D5
Labrador • NF/QU, Canada ... 39 R6
Labrador City • NF, Canada ... 39 R6
Labrador, Coast of • NF, Canada ... 39 S5
Labrador Mtn **Ski** •
NY, United States ... 149 [189]
Labrador Mtn •
NY, United States ... 153 D2
Labrador Sea • Atlantic Ocean ... 36 M4
Lábrea • Brazil ... 51 E5
Labuha • Indonesia ... 32 (1) C3
Labuhan • Java, Indonesia ... 143 J1
Labuhanbajo • Indonesia ... 32 (1) A4
Labuhanbilik • Indonesia ... 143 G2
Labuk, Teluk • Malaysia ... 31 F5
Labutta • Myanmar ... 31 A3
Labytnangi • Russian Fed. ... 26 K4
Lac • Albania ... 15 A2
Lac • Bonaire ... 160 W
Lac du Bonnet • MN, Canada ... 43 H1
Lac la Biche • AL, Canada ... 38 I6
Lac la Martre • NT, Canada ... 38 H4
Lac Mégantic • QU, Canada ... 155 B4
Lacanau • France ... 115 G1
Laccadive Is. • India ... 25 H8
Lacepede Bay • SA, Australia ... 34 G7
Lacey • WA, United States ... 152 B1
Lachay, Punta • Peru ... 51 B6
Lachi • Cyprus ... 123 J3
Lachlan • NS, Australia ... 144 C1
Lachute • QU, Canada ... 155 B3
Lackawanna • NY, United States ... 44 F4
Lacken Reservoir • Ireland ... 108 B4
Lackland AFB •
AR, United States ... 46 J6
Laconia • NH, United States ... 44 J4
Lacq • France ... 115 G3
Lacre Punt • Bonaire ... 160 W
Ladakh • Jammu & Kashmir ... 137 C1
Ladhiqiyah, Al • Syria ... 18 C2
Ladispoli • Italy ... 121 F1
Ladner • WA, United States ... 42 D2
Ladoga, Lake • Russian Fed. ... 17 E2
Ladozhskoye, Ozero •
Russian Fed. ... 17 E2
Lady Ann Strait • NU, Canada ... 39 P1
Lady Elliot I. • QL, Australia ... 144 B4
Ladysmith • South Africa ... 134 B3
Ladysmith • WI, United States ... 43 J4
Lae • Papua New Guinea ... 35 (1) D2
Laem Chabang • Thailand ... 142 C4
Laem So Pagoda •
Ko Samui, Thailand ... 142 D2
Lærdalsøyri • Norway ... 124 C4
Læsø • Denmark ... 16 E6
Læsø **Beach** • Denmark ... 125 F6
Læsø Rende • Denmark ... 125 F6
Lafayette • IN, United States ... 44 B5
Lafayette • CO, United States ... 46 C2
Lafayette • LA, United States ... 153 F3
Lafia • Nigeria ... 22 F3
Lafiagi • Nigeria ... 22 F3
Lafite, Château • France ... 115 G1
Lafleche • SA, Canada ... 42 L2
Lågan • Sweden ... 125 F7
Laganás • Zante, Greece ... 122 C3
Lågen • Norway ... 16 F6
Laghouat • Algeria ... 20 F2
Lago de Moreno • Mexico ... 157 G1
Lago **Beach** • Portugal ... 96 [100]
Lagoa **Beach** •
São Miguel, Azores ... 96 [105]
Lagoa • Azores ... 118 B1
Lagoa • Portugal ... 118 B1
Lagoa Vermelha • Brazil ... 52 E4
Lagoníssi • Greece ... 122 D7
Lagos • Nigeria ... 22 E3
Lagos **Beach** • Portugal ... 96 [100]
Lagos • Portugal ... 118 B6
Lagos [Adm] • Nigeria ... 22 E3
Lagos, Baia de • Portugal ... 118 E6
Lagosa • Tanzania ... 130 B1
Lagrange • IN, United States ... 44 C5
Laguardia • Spain ... 11 I2
LaGuardia [Apt] •
NY, United States ... 153 D7
Lagun, Playa • Curaçao ... 160 X
Laguna • Brazil ... 52 E4
Laguna • NM, United States ... 153 E2
Laguna, Picacho de la • Mexico ... 157 F2
Lagunillas • Bolivia ... 52 D2
Lahad Datu • Malaysia ... 32 F1
Lahaina • HI, United States ... 154 G3
Lahat • Indonesia ... 32 C3
Lahemaa Nat. Park **Park N** •
Estonia ... 89 [143]
Lahemaa Nat. Park • Estonia ... 126 B1
Lahewa • Indonesia ... 143 G3
Lahn • Germany ... 112 D2
Lahnstein • Germany ... 112 E2
Lahore **Heritage C** • Pakistan ... 85 [133]
Lahore • Pakistan ... 28 B2
Lahr • Germany ... 112 F1
Lahti • Finland ... 125 E4
Lahti [Adm] • Finland ... 125 E4
Lai • Chad ... 23 B2
Lai Chau • Vietnam ... 31 C2
Lai'an • China ... 139 C1
Laiagam • Papua New Guinea ... 35 (1) C2
Laie • HI, United States ... 154 G1
Laigueglia **Beach** • Italy ... 96 [141]
Laigueglia • Italy ... 121 E9
Laikipia Game Reserve • Kenya ... 131 G1
Laingsburg • South Africa ... 16 K2
Lainio älv • Sweden ... 16 K2
Laitila • Finland ... 125 E4
Laiwui • Indonesia ... 32 (1) D3
Laja • Chile ... 52 B6
Lajes • Brazil ... 52 F4
Lajes do Pico • Azores ... 118 B1
Lajosmizse • Hungary ... 13 I10
Lake Bogoria Game Reserve •
Kenya ... 131 G1
Lake Bronson •
MN, United States ... 43 H2
Lake Buena Vista •
FL, United States ... 151 C2
Lake Charles •
LA, United States ... 153 F3
Lake Chelan Nat. Recreation Area
Park N • WA, United States ... 150 [28]
Lake Chelan Nat. Recreation Area •
WA, United States ... 152 B1
Lake City • MN, United States ... 43 J4
Lake City • CO, United States ... 46 C3
Lake City • FL, United States ... 48 H4
Lake City • SC, United States ... 154 H3
Lake Clark Nat. Park •
AK, United States ... 49 K3
Lake Clark Nat. Park & Preserve
Park N • AK, United States ... 150 [8]
Lake District Nat. Park **Park N** •
United Kingdom ... 89 [43]
Lake District Nat. Park •
United Kingdom ... 104 C

Lake Grace • WA, Australia ... 34 C6
Lake Havasu City •
AZ, United States ... 153 E1
Lake Isabella •
CA, United States ... 45 C4
Lake Jackson •
TX, United States ... 47 G3
Lake King • WA, Australia ... 34 C6
Lake Louise **Ski** • AL, Canada ... 149 [12]
Lake Louise • AL, Canada ... 155 C4
Lake Mackay Aboriginal Land •
NT, Australia ... 145 D1
Lake Malawi Nat. Park **Heritage N** •
Malawi ... 83 [104]
Lake Malawi Nat. Park **Park** •
Malawi ... 133 [97]
Lake Mead Nat. Recreation Area
Park N • NV, United States ... 150 [59]
Lake Mead Nat. Recreation Area •
AZ/NV, United States ... 153 E1
Lake Meredith Nat. Recreation Area
Park N • TX, United States ... 150 [131]
Lake Monroe • FL, United States ... 154 H6
Lake Murray • Papua New Guinea ... 35 (1) C2
Lake Nakuru Nat. Park • Kenya ... 131 G3
Lake Nakuru Nat. Park **Park** •
Kenya ... 133 [80]
Lake of the Woods •
Canada/United States ... 43 I3
Lake Oswego • OR, United States ... 42 D4
Lake Placid **Ski** •
NY, United States ... 149 C
Lake Placid • NY, United States ... 44 I3
Lake Providence •
LA, United States ... 47 I1
Lake River • OT, Canada ... 39 O6
Lake Roosevelt Nat. Recreation Area
Park N • WA, United States ... 150 [29]
Lake Roosevelt Nat. Recreation Area •
WA, United States ... 152 B2
Lake Tekapo • New Zealand ... 35 C7
Lake Town • UT, United States ... 42 J6
Lake Village •
AR, United States ... 48 A3
Lake Wales • FL, United States ... 154 H5
Lake Worth • FL, United States ... 49 C4
Lakefield Nat. Park •
QL, Australia ... 34 H3
Lakeland • FL, United States ... 154 H5
Lakemba • Fiji Is. ... 35 (2) E2
Lakes Entrance • VI, Australia ... 144 C3
Lakeview • OR, United States ... 152 B3
Lakeville • MN, United States ... 43 J4
Lakewood • OH, United States ... 44 E5
Lakewood • NJ, United States ... 44 H5
Lakewood • CO, United States ... 46 C3
Lakewood Center •
WA, United States ... 42 D3
Lákmos • Greece ... 15 C4
Lakonikós Kólpos • Greece ... 15 D7
Lakópetra **Beach** • Greece ... 97 [179]
Lakota • ND, United States ... 43 G2
Laksamana Forest Reserve •
Penang, Malaysia ... 141 F1
Laksefjorden • Norway ... 16 N1
Laksforsen • Norway ... 16 H3
Lakshadweep • India ... 138 D9
Lakshadweep Sea • India ... 138 D10
Lalapasa • Turkey ... 15 H2
Lalibela • Ethiopia ... 21 G5
Lalibela **Heritage C** • Ethiopia ... 85 [100]
Lalín • Spain ... 11 C2
Lalitpur • India ... 137 D4
Lalmanir Hat • Bangladesh ... 137 D4
Lalzit, Gjiri i • Albania ... 14 G8
Lam Po Reservoir • Thailand ... 142 A2
Lam Tseun Country Park •
Hong Kong, China ... 139 B3
Lamai Beach •
Ko Samui, Thailand ... 142 D2
Lamanai • Belize ... 157 H4
Lamar • CO, United States ... 46 D3
Lambaréné • Gabon ... 22 G5
Lambari • Brazil ... 163 C3
Lambasa • Fiji Is. ... 35 (2) D2
Lambay I. • Ireland ... 108 B2
Lambert's Bay • South Africa ... 134 C1
Lambton, Cape • NT, Canada ... 38 G2
Lame Deer • MT, United States ... 42 L4
Lamego • Portugal ... 11 D3
Lamèque, I. • NB, Canada ... 156 D2
Lamesa • TX, United States ... 47 D1
Lamézia Terme • Italy ... 12 K10
Lamía • Greece ... 15 D5
Lamington Nat. Park •
QL, Australia ... 144 B6
Lamma I. • Hong Kong, China ... 139 B5
Lammermuir Hills •
United Kingdom ... 104 B4
Lammhult • Sweden ... 125 F7
Lamon Bay • Philippines ... 31 G4
Lamongan • Java, Indonesia ... 143 J4
Lampang • Thailand ... 31 B2
Lampasas • TX, United States ... 154 J3
Lampedusa • Italy ... 12 G13
Lampertheim • Germany ... 9 D7
Lamphun • Thailand ... 142 B3
Lamu • Kenya ... 131 G4
Lamu I. • Kenya ... 131 G4
Lan Yu • Taiwan ... 29 G6
Lan, Ko • Thailand ... 142 C4
Lanao, Lake • Philippines ... 31 G5
Lanark • United Kingdom ... 104 B3
Lancang Jiang • China ... 29 B5
Lancashire • United Kingdom ... 7 J8
Lancaster • United Kingdom ... 7 J7
Lancaster • NH, United States ... 44 D6
Lancaster • NY, United States ... 44 F4
Lancaster • OH, United States ... 44 J3
Lancaster • CA, United States ... 45 C4
Lancaster • MO, United States ... 46 I2
Lancaster • SC, United States ... 48 E3
Lancaster • PA, United States ... 153 D6
Lancaster Sound • NU, Canada ... 39 O2
Lance aux Epines • Grenada ... 160 S
Lancelin • WA, Australia ... 34 C6
Lancha He • China ... 139 B5
Lanciano • Italy ... 12 I6
Lancut • Poland ... 13 L7
Land of the Midnight Sun cruise area •
Norway ... 81 A4
Land van Altena • Netherlands ... 109 F4
Landau an der Isar • Germany ... 13 B9
Landau in der Pfalz • Germany ... 112 D6
Landeck • Austria ... 119 H8
Landen • NT, Australia ... 34 F4
Lander • WY, United States ... 42 K5
Landes, Côte des • France ... 115 G1
Landes, les • France ... 115 G3
Landete • Spain ... 11 J5
Lands End • United Kingdom ... 104 C1
Landsberg am Lech • Germany ... 112 F2
Landshut • Germany ... 9 H8
Landskrona • Sweden ... 125 D4
Landsort • Sweden ... 125 D4
Landusky • MT, United States ... 42 K3
Landvetter [Apt] • Sweden ... 125 F6
Lanesborough • Ireland ... 119 H7
Lanett • AL, United States ... 48 E4

Langcang Jiang • China ... 28 G2
Langdale Fell • United Kingdom ... 104 C2
Langdon • ND, United States ... 43 G2
Langeac [Château] • France ... 114 C2
Langeberg • South Africa ... 134 C6
Langeland • Denmark ... 125 F14
Langelmävesi • Finland ... 125 E2
Langen • Germany ... 8 D3
Langenfeld • Germany ... 111 B3
Langenhagen • Germany ... 9 E6
Langenselbold • Germany ... 8 D3
Langeoog • Germany ... 9 E6
Langer See • Germany ... 111 C4
Langesund • Norway ... 124 B3
Langevåg •
More og Romsdal, Norway ... 124 C1
Langevåg • Rogaland, Norway ... 124 C5
Langevin, Pointe de • Réunion ... 132 H4
Langfjorden • Norway ... 124 C2
Langjökull • Iceland ... 16 (1) C2
Langkawi • Malaysia ... 32 B1
Langkloof • South Africa ... 134 C7
Langley • BC, Canada ... 42 D2
Langnau • Switzerland ... 119 G2
Langney • France ... 10 I9
Langø • France ... 115 G3
Langøy • Norway ... 16 H2
Langres • Spain ... 11 F1
Langres • France ... 10 K6
Langsele • Sweden ... 16 I5
Langue de Barbarie, Parc nat. de la **Park** •
Senegal ... 133 [6]
Languedoc • France ... 10 I10
Languedoc-Roussillon • France ... 114 A4
Langwedel • Germany ... 8 E4
Langxi • China ... 139 C2
Langzhong • China ... 29 D4
Lanhydrock House •
United Kingdom ... 104 F4
Lankaran • Azerbaijan ... 53 B3
Lankaranihu • Maldives ... 138 F4
Länkäran • Azerbaijan ... 18 E2
Lannemezan • France ... 115 J2
Lannion • France ... 114 C1
Lansdowne **Beach** • India ... 44 H5
Lansdowne **Hill Sta** • India ... 138 E1
Lansdowne • OT, Canada ... 44 G3
Lansing • MI, United States ... 44 C4
Lanta, Ko • Thailand ... 142 A4
Lantau Country Parks •
Hong Kong, China ... 139 B5
Lantau I. • Hong Kong, China ... 139 B5
Lantau Peak • Hong Kong, China ... 139 B5
Lante, Villa • Italy ... 121 F1
Lanton **Beach** • France ... 96 [85]
Lanzarote • Canary Is. ... 29 C3
Lanzhou • China ... 29 C3
Lao • Thailand ... 142 B2
Lao Cai • Vietnam ... 31 C2
Lao Ling • China ... 30 D4
Laoag • Philippines ... 31 G3
Laocheng • China ... 29 F3
Laodicea • Turkey ... 122 D9
Laois • Ireland ... 108 B3
Laon • France ... 10 I4
LAOS • Asia ... 31 C2
Laou • Morocco ... 11 F9
Lapa • Brazil ... 52 E4
Lapeer • MI, United States ... 44 D4
Lapithos • Cyprus ... 123 J1
Lapland • Finland/Sweden ... 124 A5
Lappeenranta • Finland ... 16 O6
Lappersdorf • Germany ... 9 H7
Lappi • Finland ... 16 N3
Lappijärvi • Finland ... 16 L5
Lapponian area **Heritage N** •
Sweden ... 83 [45]
Lapponian area **Heritage C** •
Sweden ... 85 [83]
Laprida • Argentina ... 163 D3
Lapseki • Turkey ... 15 H3
Lapta • Cyprus ... 123 J1
Laptev Sea • Arctic Ocean ... 54 C2
Laptevykh, More • Arctic Ocean ... 16 L5
Lapy • Poland ... 13 L4
Laquiat al Arba'in • Sudan ... 18 F4
Lar • Iran ... 21 H4
Lara, Playa • Turkey ... 123 F3
Larache • Morocco ... 131 D1
Laramie Mtns •
WY, United States ... 43 D6
Laramie [Riv] •
WY, United States ... 43 D5
Larantuka • Indonesia ... 32 (1) D4
Larba • Algeria ... 11 O8
Lárdos **Beach** • Rhodes, Greece ... 97 [211]
Lárdos, Akra • Rhodes, Greece ... 122 D12
Laredo • Spain ... 11 H1
Laredo **Beach** • Spain ... 96 [89]
Laredo • TX, United States ... 47 E4
Laren • Netherlands ... 109 F2
Larestan • Iran ... 18 E4
Largo I. • Grenada ... 161 R
Largo • FL, United States ... 49 B4
Largo, Cayo • Cuba ... 158 D1
Largo • United Kingdom ... 104 B3
Larino • Italy ... 12 I6
Lárissa • Greece ... 15 D4
Larkana • Pakistan ... 28 A3
Larnaca **Beach** • Cyprus ... 97 [219]
Larnaca • Cyprus ... 123 J4
Larnaca Bay • Cyprus ... 123 J4
Larne • United Kingdom ... 7 G7
Larned • KS, United States ... 46 E3
Larrau • France ... 115 G3
Larrimah • NT, Australia ... 34 F3
Larsen Ice Shelf • Antarctica ... 54 (1) II3
Larsen, Mt • Antarctica ... 54 (1) V2
Larvik • Norway ... 124 B3
Las Animas • CO, United States ... 46 D3
Las Casitas • Mexico ... 40 E7
Las Cruces • NM, United States ... 153 E4
Las Flores • Argentina ... 163 D3
Las Galletas •
Tenerife, Canary Is. ... 116 E1
Las Heras • Argentina ... 52 C5
Las Lajas • Argentina ... 53 B3
Las Marécottes • Switzerland ... 119 G3
Las Marismas • Spain ... 116 B1
Las Médulas **Heritage C** • Spain ... 86 [94]
Las Navas de la Concepción • Spain ... 90 A16
Las Palmas de Gran Canaria **Beach** •
Gran Canaria, Canary Is. ... 96 [110]
Las Palmas de Gran Canaria •
Gran Canaria, Canary Is. ... 116 E4
Las Piedras • Uruguay ... 52 E5
Las Piedras, Río de • Peru ... 52 C1
Las Pipinas • Argentina ... 163 D3
Las Plumas • Argentina ... 53 C4
Las Qoray • Somalia ... 23 H1
Las Salinas • Dominican Rep. ... 159 G3
Las Terrenas • Dominican Rep. ... 159 G4
Las Vegas • NM, United States ... 46 C5
Las Vegas • NV, United States ... 152 C4
Las'anod • Somalia ... 23 H2
Lascano • Uruguay ... 52 E5
Lascaux, Grotte de • France ... 115 G2
Lash-e Joveyn • Afghanistan ... 18 H3
Lashio • Myanmar ... 31 B2

Lashkar Gah

Lashkar Gah • Afghanistan 18 H3
Lask • Poland 13 I6
Lassen Peak • CA, United States 42 E6
Lassen Volcanic Nat. Park Park N • CA, United States ...... 150 [40]
Lassen Volcanic Nat. Park • CA, United States 152 C1
Lassi • Cephalonia, Greece 122 C2
Lassithi • Crete, Greece 123 E7
Lassithi [Adm] • Crete, Greece 123 E7
Last Chance • CO, United States 46 D3
Last Mountain Lake • SA, Canada 38 J6
Lastovo • Croatia 128 D4
Latakia • Syria 18 C2
Latchford • OT, Canada 44 F2
Late • Tonga 35 (2) F2
Làtemar • Italy 120 B3
Latgale • Latvia 126 B4
Latin • Spain 11 C2
Latina • Italy 121 F4
Latmos • Turkey 122 D9
Lató • Crete, Greece 123 E8
Latoritsya • Ukraine 13 L9
Latrobe • PA, United States 153 D5
Latrobe Valley • VI, Australia 144 C3
Lattari, Monti • Italy 121 G3
Latur • India 28 C5
LATVIA • Europe ...... 126 B
Lau Group • Fiji Is. 35 (2) E2
Lauchammer • Germany 8 I5
Lauenburg • Germany 8 F3
Lauf • Germany 9 G7
Laufen • Germany 112 F4
Laughlin • NV, United States 152 C6
Laughlin Peak • NM, United States 46 C4
Laukaa • Finland 125 E2
Launceston • TS, Australia 34 I8
Launceston • United Kingdom 104 F5
Lauphem • Germany 112 F3
Lauterbach • Germany 112 D2
Lauterbrunnen Ski • Switzerland ...... 100 [38]
Lauterbrunnen • Switzerland 119 G2
Lauttawar, Danau • Indonesia 143 G1
Lauzon • QU, Canada 44 J2
Lava Beds Nat. Mon. Park N • CA, United States ...... 150 [38]
Lava Beds Nat. Mon. • CA, United States 152 C1
Lavagna Beach • Italy. ...... 96 [142]
Lavagna • Italy 121 E6
Laval • France 114 D1
Laval • QU, Canada 44 I3
Lavandou, le Beach • France ...... 96 [133]
Lavandou, le • France 115 H3
Lavapié, Punta • Chile 52 B6
Lavarone Ski • Italy ...... 100 [216]
Lavayai, Ko • Thailand 142 E1
Laverne • OK, United States 46 F4
Laverton • WA, Australia 34 C5
Lavezzi, I. • Corsica, France 115 L4
Lavik • Norway 124 C3
Lavon Lake • TX, United States 154 J1
Lavras • Brazil 163 C1
Lávrio • Greece 122 D7
Lavumisa • Swaziland 24 E5
Lawang • Java, Indonesia 143 J8
Lawit, Gunung • Indonesia 32 E2
Lawra • Burkina Faso 20 E6
Lawrah • Afghanistan 28 A2
Lawrence • IN, United States 148 B6
Lawrence • MA, United States 44 J4
Lawrence • KS, United States 46 H3
Lawrenceburg • TN, United States 48 D3
Lawrenceville • KY, United States 48 E1
Lawson • Papua New Guinea 35 (1) D2
Lawton • OK, United States 46 F5
Lawu, Gunung • Java, Indonesia 143 J7
Lawz • Saudi Arabia 21 G2
Laxå • Sweden 125 F3
Laxe Beach • Spain ...... 96 [92]
Lay Lake • AL, United States 148 D6
Laycock Abbey • United Kingdom 104 F3
Layla • Saudi Arabia 18 E5
Layou • St Vincent & Gren. ...... 161 Q
Layton • UT, United States 46 B2
Lázaro Cárdenas • Mexico 157 G3
Lazdijai • Lithuania 13 M3
Lazio • Italy 121 F1
Lazo • Italy 121 F1
Le Borgne • Haiti 159 G2
Le Bourget [Apt] • France. 115 E2
Le Brassus • Switzerland 119 G1
Le Châble Ski • Switzerland ...... 100 [79]
Le Havre • France 10 F4
Le Kef • Tunisia 131 E1
Le Lamentin [Apt] • Martinique ...... 161 N
Le Locle • Switzerland 119 G1
Le Mans • France 114 D2
Le Mars • IA, United States 43 H5
Le Phang Bay • Ko Phuket, Thailand 142 E1
Le Raizet [Apt] • Guadeloupe ...... 161 L
Le Relais Ski • QU, Canada ...... 149 [44]
Le Rœulx • Belgium 109 D14
Le Vaud • Switzerland 119 G5
Lea • United Kingdom 5 C3
Lead • SD, United States 43 E4
Leader • SA, Canada 42 K1
Leadore • ID, United States 42 I4
Leadville • CO, United States 45 I2
Leaf • MS, United States 48 E5
League City • TX, United States 47 G3
Leamington • OT, Canada 44 D4
Leamington Caves • Bermuda 159 J2
Leap • Ireland 108 C8
Learmonth • WA, Australia 34 B4
Leavenworth • WA, United States 42 E3
Leavenworth • KS, United States 43 G3
Leba • Poland 13 H3
LEBANON • Asia 18 B3
Lebanon • OR, United States 42 D4
Lebanon • IN, United States 48 B5
Lebanon • NH, United States 44 I4
Lebanon • MO, United States 46 I4
Lebanon • TN, United States 48 D2
Lebanon • KY, United States 48 E2
Lebanon • PA, United States 153 D6
Leblon • Brazil 163 C4
Lebombo Mtns • South Africa 24 E4
Lebork • Poland 13 G3
Lebu • Chile 53 B9
Lecce • Italy 12 M8
Lecco • Italy 121 E2
Lech Ski • Austria ...... 100 [129]
Lech • Austria 119 H5
Lech [Riv] • Austria/Germany 112 F6

Lechi, Playa • Bonaire ...... 160 W
Lechtaler Alpen • Austria 119 H2
Leczna • Poland 13 L6
Leczyca • Poland 13 I5
Ledbury • United Kingdom 104 D3
Ledesma • Spain 11 F3
Lednice-Valtice Heritage C • Czech Rep. ...... 86 [174]
Lédo, Cabo • Angola 26 A1
Ledyanaya, gora • Russian Fed. 27 T4
Lee • Ireland 108 C8
Leech Lake • MN, United States 43 I3
Leeds • United Kingdom 7 K8
Leeds Castle • United Kingdom 104 E4
Leegebruch • Germany 111 C1
Leek • Netherlands 109 D4
Leer • Germany 111 C1
Leerdam • Netherlands 109 F4
Leesburg • FL, United States 49 C3
Leesville • LA, United States 47 H2
Leeuwarden • Netherlands 109 D3
Leeuwin, Cape • WA, Australia 34 C6
Lefka • Greece 123 J3
Lefká Óri • Crete, Greece 123 E1
Lefká Óri Nat. Park • Crete, Greece 123 E5
Lefkáda • Levkas, Greece 122 C1
Lefkáda [I.] • Greece 122 C1
Lefkara • Cyprus 123 J3
Lefke • Cyprus 123 J3
Lefkími Beach • Corfu, Greece ...... 97 [170]
Lefkími • Corfu, Greece 122 B1
Leganés • Spain 11 H4
Legazpi • Philippines 31 G4
Lège-Cap-Ferret Beach • France ...... 96 [85]
Legendes, Côte des • France 114 C1
Leggett • CA, United States 42 D7
Leghorn • Italy 121 E11
Legian Beach • Bali, Indonesia 143 H4
Legionowo • Poland 13 J5
Legnano • Lombardia, Italy 12 C3
Legnano • Veneto, Italy 121 E7
Legnica • Poland 13 F6
Legoland Park L • Denmark ...... 98 [16]
Legoland Park L • United Kingdom ...... 98 [33]
Legoland • United Kingdom 104 E1
Legoland • Denmark 125 F9
Legoland • CA, United States 152 C6
Legundi • Indonesia 143 J1
Leh • Jammu & Kashmir 28 C2
Leh Hill Sta • India 138 E1
Lehená • Greece 15 C6
Lehigh Acres • United States 49 C4
Lehigh Valley [Apt] • PA, United States 153 D6
Leighton • PA, United States 44 H5
Lehinch Beach • Ireland ...... 96 [61]
Lehinch • Ireland 108 C4
Lehrte • Germany 8 E4
Leicester • United Kingdom 7 K8
Leichlingen • Germany 111 B3
Leiden • Netherlands 109 F1
Leie • Belgium 5 G4
Leigh Creek • SA, Australia 34 G6
Leigh-on-Sea Beach • United Kingdom ...... 101 [66]
Leignitz • Poland 90 A9
Leikanger • Norway 124 C4
Leimen • Germany 112 E1
Leinefelde • Germany 9 F5
Leinster • Ireland 7 E8
Leipnitzsee • Germany 111 C2
Leipzig • Germany 9 H5
Leiria • Portugal 11 C5
Leiria Beach • Portugal ...... 96 [97]
Leiria [Adm] • Portugal 118 A2
Leirvik • Norway 124 C5
Leisure I. • Maldives 138 F2
Leith • United Kingdom 104 B4
Leitha • Austria 13 H11
Leitheim Castle • Germany ...... 113 [137]
Leitrim • Ireland 108 A1
Leitzkau Castle • Germany ...... 113 [215]
Leixa • Colombia 51 C3
Leixlip • Ireland 108 B2
Lejre Beach • Denmark ...... 96 [42]
Lek • Netherlands 109 D7
Leka • Norway 124 A4
Lekánis • Greece 15 F2
Leketi, Mts de la • Congo 22 G5
Lekitobi • Indonesia 32 (1) B3
Lek*nes • Norway 16 G2
Leksozero • Russian Fed. 16 P5
Leksula • Indonesia 32 (1) C3
Leland • MS, United States 48 B4
Lelång • Sweden 124 B4
Lelystad • Netherlands 109 F2
Léman, Lac • Switzerland 119 G5
Lemba Harau Reserve • Indonesia 143 G4
Lembeck Castle • Germany ...... 113 [117]
Lemesós • Cyprus 123 J3
Lemgo • Germany 8 D4
Lemieux Is. • NU, Canada 39 S4
Lemland • Finland 125 E3
Lemmenjoki Nat. Park Park N • Finland ...... 89 [29]
Lemmer • Netherlands 5 I2
Lemmon • SD, United States 43 E4
Lemnos • Greece 122 D2
Lemoore • CA, United States 45 C3
Lemsid • Western Sahara 20 C3
Lemvig Beach • Denmark ...... 96 [50]
Lemvig • Denmark 125 F9
Lena • Russian Fed. 17 K3
Lena Delta • Russian Fed. 127 A8
Léndas • Crete, Greece 123 E7
Lenexa • KS, United States 46 H3
Lengerich • Germany 8 C4
Lenggries • Germany 112 F7
Lengua de Vaca, Punta • Chile 52 B5
Lengwe Nat. Park Park • Malawi ...... 133 [100]
Lenina, pik • Kyrgyzstan 18 J2
Leningradskaya [Base] • Antarctica 54 (1) U3
Leningradsky • Russian Fed. 54 HH3
Leninsk-Kuznetskiy • Russian Fed. 26 O7
Lenk Ski • Switzerland ...... 100 [90]
Lenk • Switzerland 119 G6
Lenne • Germany 9 E5
Lennox, Fort • QU, Canada 155 B8
Leno-Angarskoye Plato • Russian Fed. 27 F6
Lenoir • NC, United States 48 E3
Lens • France 10 H3
Lensk • Russian Fed. 27 I4
Lenti • Hungary 14 D3
Lentini • Sicily, Italy 12 J11
Lenvik • Finland 16 H1
Lenzerheide • Switzerland 119 G4
Lenzerheide-Valbella Ski • Switzerland ...... 100 [111]
Léo • Burkina Faso 22 D2
Leoben • Austria 13 E10
Leofels Castle • Germany ...... 113 [94]
Leogane • Haiti 159 G6
Leogang Ski • Austria ...... 100 [163]
Leok • Indonesia 32 (1) B2
Leominster • United Kingdom 104 D1
Leominster • MA, United States 153 D4
Léon • France 10 I10
León • France 11 F2

León • Nicaragua 37 D5
León • IA, United States 46 I2
León • Mexico 157 G1
León, Montes de • Spain 11 E2
León, Pays de • France 114 C1
Leonardville • Namibia 24 B4
Leonberg • Germany 9 E8
Leone, Monte • Italy/Switzerland 119 G6
Leonídio Beach • Greece ...... 97 [183]
Leonora • WA, Australia 34 D5
Leones • Lebanon 135 A2
Leopardstown • Ireland 108 B2
Leopoldina • Brazil 163 C2
Leova • Moldova 14 F3
Lepanto • Greece 90 A20
Lepe • Spain 116 B1
Lepe Country Park Beach • United Kingdom ...... 101 [92]
Lephepe • Botswana 24 D4
Lepini, Monti • Italy 121 F4
Lepsi • Kazakstan 26 M8
Lepsóni • Greece 15 G4
Leptis Magna • Libya 21 B1
Lercara Friddi • Sicily, Italy 12 H11
Leptis Magna Heritage C • Libya ...... 86 [271]
Léré • Chad 22 G3
Lérici • Italy 121 E10
Lérida • Spain 11 I3
Lérida • Colombia 51 C4
Lérins, Is. de • France 115 H4
Lerma • Spain 10 B11
Lermoos Ski • Austria ...... 100 [136]
Lermoos • Austria 119 H5
Léros • Greece 122 D8
Leross • SA, Canada 43 E1
Lerum • Sweden 125 F6
Lerwick • United Kingdom 6 K1
Les Amirantes • Seychelles 133 K2
Les Bioux • Switzerland 119 G1
Les Cayes • Haiti 159 G5
Les Collons Ski • Switzerland ...... 100 [83]
Les Crosets Ski • Switzerland ...... 100 [78]
Les Diablerets Ski • Switzerland ...... 100 [85]
Les Diablerets • Switzerland 119 G6
Les Mosses • Switzerland 119 G6
Lesbos • Greece 122 D5
Leshan • China 29 C5
Leshan Giant Buddha Heritage N • China ...... 83 [125]
Leshan Giant Buddha Heritage C • China ...... 85 [179]
Lésina, Lago di • Italy 12 J7
Lesjaskog • Norway 124 C2
Lesjaskogsvatnet • Norway 124 C2
Leskovar • F.R. of Yugoslavia 14 H7
Leskovik • Albania 15 B3
Lesleen M • St Lucia ...... 161 P
Lesnoye • Russian Fed. 17 I3
Lesosibirsk • Russian Fed. 26 P6
LESOTHO • Africa 24 D5
Lesozavodsk • Russian Fed. 27 L7
Lesser Sunda Is. • Indonesia 32 (1) B4
Lester B. Pearson [Apt] • OT, Canada 155 B9
Lésvos • Greece 122 D5
Leszno • Poland 13 F6
Letchworth State Park • NY, United States 153 D1
Lethbridge • AL/Canada 38 I7
Lethem • Guyana 51 F3
Leti, Kepulauan • Indonesia 143 F7
Leticia • Colombia 51 D4
Letmathe • Germany 111 B2
Letpadan • Myanmar 31 B3
Letterfrack • Ireland 108 C3
Letterkenny • United Kingdom 7 E7
Lettermore I. • Ireland 108 C3
Leu • Romania 14 L5
Leucate Beach • France ...... 96 [129]
Leucate • France 115 K2
Leucate, Etang de • France 115 K2
Leuchtenburg Castle • Germany ...... 113 [153]
Leuk • Switzerland 119 G6
Leukerbad • Switzerland 119 G6
Leuna • Germany 9 H5
Leuser, Gunung • Indonesia 143 G1
Leutkirch • Germany 112 F5
Leuven • Belgium 109 D15
Levanger • Norway 16 F5
Levant • Asia 81 C8
Levant, I. du • France 115 H3
Levantado, Cayo • Dominican Rep. 159 G4
Lévanto • Italy 121 E6
Lévanzo, I. de • Italy 120 D1
Levelland • TX, United States 46 D6
Leven, Loch • United Kingdom 104 B2
Levens Hall • United Kingdom 104 C4
Lévèque, Cape • WA, Australia 34 D3
Levera Point Nat. Park • Grenada ...... 160 S
Leverkusen • Germany 111 B3
Levice • Slovak Rep. 13 H9
Lévico Terme • Italy 120 B3
Levin • New Zealand 35 E5
Levis • QU, Canada 155 B4
Levitha • Greece 122 D8
Levittown • PA, United States 44 H5
Levittown • NY, United States 44 I5
Levkas • Greece 122 C1
Levoca • Slovak Rep. 13 J8
Levski • Bulgaria 128 E3
Levski • United Kingdom 104 E3
Lewes • DE, United States 153 D10
Lewes • United Kingdom 6 F3
Lewis Hills • NF, Canada 156 D3
Lewis, Mt • NV, United States 42 G6
Lewis Pass • New Zealand 35 D6
Lewis Range • MT, United States 42 I2
Lewis Smith Lake • AL, United States 48 D3
Lewisburg • PA, United States 44 G5
Lewisburg • TN, United States 48 D3
Lewisburg • WV, United States 48 G2
Lewiston • NY, United States 44 F4
Lewiston • ID, United States 42 H3
Lewistown • MT, United States 42 K3
Lewistown • PA, United States 153 D5
Lewisville • TX, United States 154 J1
Lewisville, Lake • TX, United States 47 F1
Lexington • NE, United States 46 F2
Lexington • TN, United States 48 C3
Lexington • NC, United States 48 F3
Lexington • KY, United States 48 E2
Lexington • VA, United States 48 H2
Lexington • MD, United States 44 G6
Leyre • France 10 E9
Leyritz, Plantation • Martinique ...... 161 N
Leysdown-on-Sea Beach • United Kingdom ...... 101 [69]
Lezajsk • Poland 13 L7
Lézardrieux • France 114 C1
Lézignan • France 115 J3
Lezhe • Albania 15 A2
Lhasa • China 29 B4
Lhasa Heritage C • China ...... 85 [161]
Lhaze • China 28 E3
Lhazhong • China 28 E2

Lho-Nga Beach • Indonesia 143 G1
Lhohifushi • Maldives 138 F2
Lhokseumawe • Indonesia 143 G1
Lhozhag • China 28 F3
Liamuiga, Mt • St Kitts & Nevis ...... 161 G
Liangpran, Gunung • Indonesia 32 E2
Lianhuashan • China 139 B2
Lianxian • China 29 E5
Lianyungang • China 29 F4
Liao He • China 29 G2
Liaodong • China 29 G2
Liaodong Wan • China 29 G2
Liaoning • China 139 A4
Liaoyang • China 29 G2
Liaoyuan • China 29 G2
Liard • Canada 38 G4
Liard River • BC, Canada 38 F5
Libby • MT, United States 42 H2
Libčice • Czech Rep. 128 B2
Libenge • Dem. Rep. of Congo 23 B3
Liberal • KS, United States 46 E4
Liberec • Czech Rep. 128 B2
LIBERIA • Africa 22 B3
Liberia • Costa Rica 37 D5
Liberty • NY, United States 44 H5
Liberty • MO, United States 46 H3
Liberty • TX, United States 154 J4
Libiyah, As Sahra al • Africa 21 E2
Libobo, Tanjung • Indonesia 32 (1) C3
Liboi • Kenya 23 G3
Libournais • France 114 B3
Libourne • France 115 G1
Libreville • Gabon 22 F4
Libya • Africa 21 C2
LIBYA • Africa 21 C2
Libyan Desert • Egypt 21 D2
Licantén • Chile 53 B2
Licata • Sicily, Italy 12 H11
Lichfield • United Kingdom 104 D2
Lichinga • Mozambique 24 F2
Lichnice • Czech Rep. 128 B2
Lichtenberg Castle • Germany ...... 113 [149]
Lichtenberg Castle • Germany ...... 113 [72]
Lichtenberg Castle • Germany ...... 113 [96]
Lichtenberg (Berlin) • Germany 111 C2
Lichtenfels (Berlin) • Germany 111 C4
Licosa, Punta • Italy 12 I8
Lida • Belarus 16 M10
Lida • Czech Rep. 128 B2
Lidingö • Sweden 125 D4
Lidköping • Sweden 125 F3
Lido de Camaiore • Italy 121 E10
Lido de Jésolo • Italy 12 G7
Lido di Ostia • Italy 12 G7
Lido di Ostia • Italy 121 F1
Lidoríki • Greece 15 D5
Lidzbark Warminski • Poland 13 J3
Liebenbeck, Burg • Germany ...... 113 [72]
Liebenstein, Burg • Germany 112 E2
Liebig, Mt • N. Terr., Australia 145 D1
Liechtenstein • Europe 119 H5
LIECHTENSTEIN • Europe 119 H5
Liège • Belgium 109 D15
Liège [Adm] • Belgium 109 D16
Lielupe • Latvia 126 B3
Lienz • Austria 13 D10
Liepāja • Latvia 126 A3
Lierbyen • Norway 124 B1
Lierneux • Belgium 109 D11
Liestal • Switzerland 119 G3
Liévin • France 10 H3
Liezen • Austria 13 D10
Liffey • Ireland 108 B1
Lifford • Ireland 7 E7
Lifjell • Norway 124 B3
Lifou • New Caledonia 35 (2) B3
Ligen Shkodrës • Albania 14 G7
Ligenc • IN, United States 44 B6
Lignan de Bazas • France 114 B3
Lighthouse Point • FL, United States 49 C4
Lighthouse Reef • Belize 157 H4
Lightwater Valley Park L • United Kingdom ...... 98 [24]
Lignano • Italy 121 E8
Lignano Sabbiadoro Beach • Italy ...... 96 [165]
Ligny-en-Barrois • France 5 I6
Ligórtinos • Crete, Greece 123 E7
Liguria • Italy 121 E6
Ligurian Sea • Italy 12 C5
Lihir • Papua New Guinea 35 (1) E1
Lihou Reef & Cays • CL, Australia 144 B2
Lihue • HI, United States 154 G2
Lijiang • China 29 C5
Lijiang Heritage C • China ...... 85 [180]
Lijoki • Finland 16 M4
Likasi • Dem. Rep. of Congo 23 D6
Likoni • Kenya 131 G5
Likouala • Congo 22 G4
Lilla Edet • Sweden 125 F2
Lille • France 10 H3
Lille Beach • Belgium ...... 96 [71]
Lille • Belgium 109 D11
Lille Bælt • Denmark 125 F13
Lillebonne • France 7 K12
Lillers • France 5 H4
Lillehammer • Norway 16 F6
Lillers • France 5 H4
Lillesand • Norway 125 F1
Lillestrøm • Norway 124 B2
Lillhärdal • Sweden 16 H6
Lilloet • BC, Canada 155 C3
Lilongwe • Malawi 24 E2
Lim • F.R. of Yugoslavia 14 H7
Lima Heritage C • Peru ...... 84 [57]
Lima • Peru 163 B1
Lima • OH, United States 44 D5
Limassol • Cyprus 123 J3
Limay • Argentina 52 B6
Limbe • Cameroon 22 F4
Limbe • Malawi 24 E3
Limbazi • Latvia 159 G2
Limbourg • Belgium 109 D12
Limburg • Netherlands 109 D12
Limburg • Belgium 109 D15
Limburg an der Lahn • Germany 112 E2
Limeira • Brazil 52 G3
Limenária • Greece 15 F2
Limenas Hersonissou Beach • Crete, Greece ...... 97 [214]
Limenas Hersonissou • Crete, Greece 123 E3
Limerick • Ireland 108 C5
Limerick [Adm] • Ireland 108 C6
Limes • United Kingdom 104 F3
Limfjorden • Denmark 125 F5
Limingen • Norway 16 G4
Liminka • Finland 16 M4
Límni • Greece 122 D4
Limnos • Greece 122 D2
Limoges • Brazil 53 (1) D3
Limoges • France 10 G7
Limogne, Causse de • France 115 G4
Limón • Costa Rica 37 E5
Limone Piemonte Ski • Italy ...... 100 [195]
Limone Piemonte • Italy 121 E5
Limousin • France 10 G8
Limoux • France 115 J3
Limpopo • Africa 24 D4
Lin'an • China 139 C3
Linares • Spain 11 H6
Linares • Chile 52 B6
Linares • Mexico 157 B3

Linares • Mexico 47 E5
Linariá • Greece 122 D4
Linaro, Capo • Italy 12 F5
Lincang • China 29 C6
Lincoln • United Kingdom 7 L8
Lincoln • Argentina 163 D1
Lincoln • MT, United States 42 I3
Lincoln • CA, United States 45 B2
Lincoln • NE, United States 46 G3
Lincoln • KS, United States 46 G3
Lincoln • IL, United States 46 K2
Lincoln City • OR, United States 152 B3
Lincoln Home Nat. Hist. Site Park N • IL, United States ...... 151 [176]
Lincoln Mem. Park N • DC, United States ...... 151 [279]
Lincoln Park • CO, United States 46 C3
Lincoln Village • OH, United States 44 D6
Lincolnton • NC, United States 48 G3
Lindås • Norway 124 C3
Lindau • Germany 112 F5
Lindbergh Field [Apt] • CA, United States 152 C6
Lindeman I. • QL, Australia 144 B1
Linden • Guyana 51 F2
Linden • TN, United States 48 D3
Lindenberg • Germany 111 C2
Lindenberg • Germany 111 C1
Lindenfels • Germany 112 D4
Lindenwold • NJ, United States 153 D6
Lindenhof Castle • Germany ...... 113 [118]
Lindhof, Schloss • Germany 112 F6
Linderödsåsen • Sweden 125 F11
Lindesberg • Sweden 16 H7
Lindi • Dem. Rep. of Congo 23 D3
Lindi • Tanzania 130 B4
Lindis Pass • New Zealand 145 G2
Lindisfarne • United Kingdom 6 K6
Lindlar • Germany 111 C4
Lindos Beach • Rhodes, Greece ...... 97 [211]
Lindos • Rhodes, Greece 122 D12
Lindsay • OK, United States 155 B5
Lindsay • OT, Canada 155 B5
Lindsdal • Sweden 125 F8
Line Is. • Kiribati 33 L6
Linfen • China 29 E3
Lingayen • Philippines 31 G3
Lingayen Gulf • Philippines 31 G3
Lingding I. • Zhuhai, China 139 B4
Lingen • Germany 8 C4
Lingga • Indonesia 32 C3
Lingga, Kepulauan • Indonesia 32 D3
Lingling • China 29 E5
Lingua • India 138 D2
Linguère • Senegal 20 C5
Linhai • China 29 G5
Linhares • Brazil 52 D2
Linjiang • China 30 D4
Linköping • Sweden 16 H7
Linli • China 139 D11
Linlithgow Palace • United Kingdom 104 B4
Linn, Burg • Germany 111 B1
Linn, Mt • CA, United States 42 D7
Linnansaari Nat. Park Park N • Finland ...... 98 [12]
Linnansaari Nat. Park Park N • Finland ...... 89 [34]
Linnhe, Loch • United Kingdom 6 G5
Linping • China 139 B4
Lins • Brazil 52 G3
Linstead • Jamaica 159 F4
Linton • IN, United States 44 B6
Lintorf • Germany 111 B1
Linxi • China 29 F2
Linxia • China 29 D3
Linyi • China 29 F3
Linz • Austria 13 D9
Linz • Germany 112 E1
Lion, Golfe du • Mediterranean Sea 10 J11
Lion Rock Country Park • Hong Kong, China 139 B6
Lioppa • Indonesia 32 (1) C4
Liouesso • Congo 22 G4
Lipa • Philippines 31 G4
Lipari, I. • Italy 120 D2
Lipari, Is. • Italy 120 D2
Lipcani • Moldova 14 N1
Lipenská Prehradní Nádrz • Czech Rep. 128 B2
Liperi • Finland 16 N5
Lipetsk • Russian Fed. 17 F4
Lipez, Cordillera de • Bolivia 52 C3
Lipiany • Poland 13 I5
Lipova • Romania 14 I3
Lippe • Germany 8 D5
Lippstadt • Germany 8 D5
Liptovský Mikuláš • Slovak Rep. 13 I8
Lira • Uganda 23 E3
Lirang • Indonesia 32 (1) C3
Liri • Italy 12 H7
Lisala • Dem. Rep. of Congo 23 C3
Lisalmi • Finland 16 N5
Lisboa Heritage C • Portugal ...... 86 [118]
Lisboa • Portugal 118 D2
Lisboa [Adm] • Portugal 118 A2
Lisboa, Costa de • Portugal 118 D1
Lisbon Heritage C • Portugal ...... 86 [118]
Lisbon • Portugal 118 D2
Lisbon • United Kingdom 7 F7
Lisburn • United Kingdom 7 F7
Lisburne, Cape • AK, United States 49 H2
Liscannor Bay • Ireland 108 C4
Lisdoonvarna • Ireland 108 C4
Liseberg Park L • Sweden ...... 98 [5]
Lishui • Jiangsu, China 139 C1
Lishui • Zhejiang, China 139 F1
Liski • Russian Fed. 14 N3
Liskeard • United Kingdom 104 F5
Lismore • Australia 34 J6
Lismore • NS, Canada 156 D4
Lismore • Ireland 108 C6
Lista • Norway 16 F8
Lister, Mt • Antarctica 54 (1) V2
Lisle • IL, United States 44 B4
Lissadell House • Ireland 108 C2
Lisse • Netherlands 109 F1
Lista • Norway 16 F8
Listowel • OT, Canada 44 E4
Listowel • Ireland 108 C6
Litang • China 29 C4
Lit-et-Mixe, Fôret de • France 115 G3
Litani • Lebanon 135 A2
Litchfield • CT, United States 44 I5
Litchfield • IL, United States 46 K3
Litchfield • MN, United States 43 H4
Litchfield Nat. Park Park N • Australia ...... 146 [170]
Lith, Al • Saudi Arabia 18 D5
Lithgow • NS, Australia 34 I6
Lithino, Akra • Crete, Greece 123 E6
LITHUANIA • Europe ...... 126 B
Litle Abaco • Bahamas 158 B1
Litohóro Beach • Greece ...... 97 [106]
Litomerice • Czech Rep. 128 B2
Litomysl Castle Heritage C • Czech Rep. ...... 86 [170]
Little • TX, United States 154 J4
Little Ambergris Cay • Turks & Caicos Is. 158 C2

Little Andaman • India 28 F6
Little Belt Mtns • MT, United States 42 J3
Little Bighorn Battlefield Nat. Mon. Park N • MT, United States ...... 150 [69]
Little Cayman • Cayman Is. 159 E1
Little Current • OT, Canada 39 O7
Little Exuma • Bahamas 158 B4
Little Falls • MN, United States 43 I4
Little Falls • NY, United States 44 H4
Little Haven Beach • United Kingdom ...... 101 [178]
Little Hura • Maldives 138 F2
Little Inagua • Bahamas 158 B4
Little Karoo • South Africa 134 C6
Little Lake • CA, United States 45 D3
Little Missouri • MT/ND, United States 43 D4
Little Nicobar • India 28 F7
Little River Canyon Nat. Preserve Park N • AL, United States ...... 151 [201]
Little Rock • AR, United States 46 I5
Little Scrub I. • Anguilla ...... 160 C
Little Skellig • Ireland 108 C7
Little Sound • Cayman Is. 159 E3
Little Sound • Bermuda 159 J3
Little Tobago • Trinidad & Tobago ...... 160 T
Littlefield • TX, United States 46 D6
Littlehampton Beach • United Kingdom ...... 101 [87]
Littlehampton • United Kingdom 104 E4
Littleton • NH, United States 44 J3
Littleton • CO, United States 46 C3
Litvinov • Czech Rep. 128 B1
Liuhe • China 30 C3
Liuzhou • China 29 D6
Livádia • Greece 122 D4
Livanates Beach • Greece ...... 97 [187]
Live Oak • FL, United States 49 B2
Live Oak Springs • CA, United States 45 D5
Livengood • AK, United States 49 L2
Livermore • CA, United States 45 B3
Livermore, Mt • TX, United States 47 B2
Liverpool • United Kingdom 7 J8
Liverpool • NS, Canada 156 D7
Liverpool Bay • United Kingdom 7 I8
Liverpool Bay • NT, Canada 38 E3
Livigno Ski • Italy ...... 100 [218]
Livigno • Italy 121 E2
Livingston • United Kingdom 104 B4
Livingston • MT, United States 42 J4
Livingston • CA, United States 45 B3
Livingston • TX, United States 154 J4
Livingston, Lake • TX, United States 154 J4
Livingstone • Zambia 24 D3
Livingstone, Chutes de • Dem. Rep. of Congo 23 A5
Livingstone Falls • Dem. Rep. of Congo 23 A5
Livingstone Mtns • Tanzania 23 E5
Livingstone Mtns • New Zealand 145 G2
Livingstonia • Malawi 23 E5
Livno • Bosnia-Herz. 14 D6
Livny • Russian Fed. 14 N2
Livonia • Estonia/Latvia 126 B4
Livonia • MI, United States 44 D4
Livorno • Italy 121 E11
Liwale • Tanzania 130 B4
Liwonde Nat. Park Park • Malawi ...... 133 [98]
Lixoúri • Cephalonia, Greece 122 C1
Liyang • China 139 C1
Liyuan • China 139 C2
Lizard Point • United Kingdom 104 F4
Ljubinje • Bosnia-Herz. 14 F7
Ljubljana • Bosnia-Herz./F.R. of Yugoslavia 14 F6
Ljubljana • Slovenia 13 D11
Ljugarn • Sweden 16 I5
Ljungan • Sweden 16 I5
Ljungby • Sweden 125 F7
Ljungsbro • Sweden 125 F4
Ljusdal • Sweden 16 I6
Ljusnan • Sweden 16 H6
Ljusterö • Sweden 125 D2
Llafranc • Spain 117 D2
Llançà Beach • Spain ...... 96 [123]
Llançà • Spain 117 D2
Llandanwg Beach • United Kingdom ...... 101 [205]
Llanddona Beach • United Kingdom ...... 101 [234]
Llandrindod Wells • United Kingdom 7 I9
Llandudno Beach • United Kingdom ...... 101 [208]
Llanelli • United Kingdom 7 H10
Llanenddwyn Beach • United Kingdom ...... 101 [204]
Llanes • Spain 11 G1
Llanes Beach • Spain ...... 96 [90]
Llanfaelog Beach • United Kingdom ...... 101 [217-219]
Llanfaethlu Beach • United Kingdom ...... 101 [227]
Llanfwrog Beach • United Kingdom ...... 101 [226]
Llangrannog Beach • United Kingdom ...... 101 [192-193]
Llano • TX, United States 154 J3
Llano Estacado • NM/TX, United States 46 D6
Llano [Riv] • TX, United States 154 J3
Llanos • Colombia/Venezuela 51 D2
Llanos de Concepcion • Fuerteventura, Canary Is. 117 E2
Llanrhystud Beach • United Kingdom ...... 101 [198]
Llantwit Major • United Kingdom 104 F2
Llerena • Spain 11 F6
Llevant, Serra de • Majorca, Spain 117 H4
Llíria • Spain 11 K5
Llívia • Spain 117 D1
Llobregat, el • Spain 117 D1
Llogara Nat. Park Park N • Albania ...... 89 [128]
Lloret de Mar Beach • Spain ...... 96 [123]
Lloret de Mar • Spain 117 D4
Lloyd George, Mt • BC, Canada 38 F5
Lluc • Majorca, Spain 117 H1
Lluc Alcari • Majorca, Spain 117 H1
Lluc, Monestir de • Majorca, Spain 117 H1
Llucmajor • Majorca, Spain 117 H3
Lo Wu • Hong Kong, China 139 B6
Loa • Chile 52 C3
Loano • Italy 12 C4
Löbau • Germany 9 J5
Lobaye • Central African Rep. 22 H4
Lobería • Argentina 163 D3
Lobito • Angola 23 A6
Lobo • Indonesia 32 (1) D3

Lobos • Canary Is. ... 117 E2
Lobos • Argentina ... 163 D1
Lobos, I. de • Uruguay ... 163 D2
Locarno • Switzerland ... 119 G7
LOchaline • United Kingdom ... 106 B2
Loches [Château] • France ... 114 D4
Lochgilphead • United Kingdom ... 6 G5
Lochinvar Nat. Park Park • Zambia ... 133 [107]
Lochinver • United Kingdom ... 6 G3
Lochmaddy • United Kingdom ... 6 E4
Lochnagar • United Kingdom ... 6 I5
Lochranza • United Kingdom ... 106 B2
Lochy, Loch • United Kingdom ... 6 H5
Lock Haven • PA, United States ... 44 G5
Lockhart • TX, United States ... 154 J3
Lockport • NY, United States ... 153 D1
Locmariaquer Beach • France ... 96 [81]
Locmariaquer • France ... 114 C4
Locminé • France ... 10 C6
Locri • Italy ... 12 K10
Locronan • France ... 114 C3
Lod • Israel ... 135 A5
Lodève • France ... 10 I10
Lodeynoye Pole • Russian Fed. ... 17 E2
Lodi • Italy ... 121 E6
Lodi • CA, United States ... 45 B2
Lodingen • Norway ... 16 H2
Lodja • Dem. Rep. of Congo ... 23 C4
Lodore Falls • United Kingdom ... 104 D1
Lodwar • Kenya ... 131 G1
Lódz • Poland ... 13 I6
Loei • Thailand ... 142 B4
Loerie • South Africa ... 134 C8
Loffa • Liberia ... 22 B3
Lofoten • Norway ... 16 G2
Loftahammar • Sweden ... 125 F4
Lofthus • Norway ... 124 C4
Logan • UT, United States ... 42 J6
Logan • OH, United States ... 44 D6
Logan • NM, United States ... 46 D5
Logan • WV, United States ... 48 F2
Logan [Apt] • MA, United States ... 153 D4
Logan, Mt • YT, Canada ... 38 C4
Logansport • IN, United States ... 44 B5
Logansport • LA, United States ... 153 F1
Logone • Angola ... 23 A5
Logone • Chad ... 21 C5
Logroño • Spain ... 11 I2
Lagster Beach • Denmark ... 96 [48]
Løgstør • Denmark ... 125 F5
Logudoro • Sardinia, Italy ... 12 C8
Lagumkloster • Denmark ... 125 F13
Lágurinn • Iceland ... 16 [1] F2
Lohausen [Apt] • Germany ... 111 B3
Lohja • Finland ... 125 E4
Lohmar • Germany ... 112 D1
Löhne • Germany ... 8 D4
Lohne • Germany ... 8 D4
Lohne • Germany ... 9 E6
Lohria Crete, Greece ... 123 E6
Loi-kaw • Myanmar ... 31 B3
Lobl • Slovenia ... 13 D11
Loimaa • Finland ... 125 E4
Loir • France ... 114 D2
Loir-et-Cher • France ... 114 D2
Loire • France ... 10 G6
Loix Beach • France ... 96 [84]
Loiza Aldea • Puerto Rico ... 159 H2
Loiza, Rio Grande de • Puerto Rico ... 159 H4
Loja • Ecuador ... 51 B4
Loja • Spain ... 116 B3
Lokan tekojärvi • Finland ... 16 N3
Lokeren • Norway ... 124 B2
Lokeren • Belgium ... 5 G3
Loket • Czech Rep. ... 128 B1
Lokitaung • Kenya ... 23 F3
Løkken • Denmark ... 125 F5
Løkken-Vrå Beach • Denmark ... 96 [48]
Lokoja • Nigeria ... 22 F3
Lokolo • Cameroon ... 23 B3
Loks Land • NU, Canada ... 39 S4
Lokwe Kangole • Kenya ... 131 G1
Lolland • Denmark ... 125 F14
Lolo Hot Springs • MT, United States ... 42 H3
Lolo Pass • MT, United States ... 152 B2
Lom • Bulgaria ... 14 K6
Lom • Norway ... 124 C2
Lom Sak • Thailand ... 142 B4
Loma Mtns • Guinea/Sierra Leone ... 22 B3
Lomami • Dem. Rep. of Congo ... 23 C5
Lombarda, Serra • Brazil ... 51 G3
Lombardia • Italy ... 121 E6
Lombardsijde-Bad • Belgium ... 109 E1
Lombardy • Italy ... 120 A1
Lomela • Dem. Rep. of Congo ... 32 F4
Lome • Togo ... 22 E3
Lomela • Dem. Rep. of Congo ... 23 C4
Lomié • Cameroon ... 22 G4
Lommel • Belgium ... 5 I3
Lomond, Loch • United Kingdom ... 104 B3
Lomonosov • Russian Fed. ... 17 D3
Lompoc • CA, United States ... 45 B4
Lomza • Poland ... 13 L4
Lonavala Hill Sta • India ... 138 E2
Londe-les-Maures, la Beach • France ... 96 [133]
Londerzeel Beach • Belgium ... 96 [73]
Londerzeel • Belgium ... 109 D14
London Heritage C • United Kingdom ... 86 [24-26]
London • United Kingdom ... 104 E1
London • OT, Canada ... 39 O8
London • OH, United States ... 44 D6
London • KY, United States ... 48 E2
London City [Apt] • United Kingdom ... 104 E1
Londonderry • United Kingdom ... 7 E7
Londonderry, Cape • WA, Australia ... 34 E2
Lone Pine • CA, United States ... 45 C3
Long Akah • Malaysia ... 31 E6
Long Bay • Jamaica ... 159 F4
Long Bay • Anguilla ... 160 C
Long Bay • SC, United States ... 48 H4
Long Bay [Bay] • Jamaica ... 159 F3
Long Beach • NY, United States ... 44 I5
Long Beach • CA, United States ... 152 C6
Long Branch • NJ, United States ... 153 D7
Long Cay • Bahamas ... 158 B4
Long Cay • Turks & Caicos Is. ... 158 C2
Long Ground • Montserrat ... 160 H
Long Hai • Vietnam ... 142 E7
Long I. • Papua New Guinea ... 35 (1) D2
Long I. • Bahamas ... 144 B1
Long I. • New Zealand ... 145 G3
Long I. • Bahamas ... 158 B4
Long I. • Antigua & Barbuda ... 161 K
Long I. • United Kingdom ... 153 D7
Long I. Sound • NY, United States ... 153 D7
Long Lake ND, United States ... 43 F3
Long Mynd, The • United Kingdom ... 104 D1
Long Point • New Zealand ... 145 G3
Long Point • OT, Canada ... 155 B9
Long Range Mtns • NF, Canada ... 156 D3
Long Xuyen • Vietnam ... 141 E4
Long, Pointe • Russian Fed. ... 27 U3
Longarone • Italy ... 120 D4
Longboat Key • FL, United States ... 154 H5
Longchamp • France ... 115 E3

Longeville-sur-Mer Beach • France ... 96 [83]
Longfellow Mtns • ME/NH, United States ... 44 J3
Longfellow Nat. Hist. Site Park N • MA, United States ... 151 [335]
Longford • Ireland ... 7 E8
Longford [Adm] • Ireland ... 108 A1
Longgang • China ... 139 B2
Longlac • QT, Canada ... 39 N7
Longleat House & Safari Park • United Kingdom ... 104 F3
Longmalinau • Indonesia ... 32 F2
Longmont • CO, United States ... 46 C2
Longnan • China ... 139 B2
Longnoot Nat. Park • Kenya ... 131 G3
Longpuangam • Indonesia ... 32 F2
Longreach • QL, Australia ... 34 H4
Longs Peak • CO, United States ... 45 J1
Longue, I. • Seychelles ... 133 K1
Longueuil • QL, Canada ... 44 I3
Longuyon • France ... 10 K4
Longview • WA, United States ... 152 B1
Longview • TX, United States ... 154 J2
Longwood • FL, United States ... 49 C3
Longwood Gardens • PA, United States ... 153 D10
Longwy • France ... 5 I5
Longxi • China ... 29 C3
Longxi Shan • China ... 31 F1
Longyearbyen • Svalbard ... 54 N2
Löningen • Germany ... 8 C4
Lons-le-Saunier • France ... 10 K7
Looe • United Kingdom ... 104 F5
Looe Key Nat. Marine Sanctuary • FL, United States ... 154 H8
Lookout, Cape • NC, United States ... 48 I3
Lookout Mtn • NM, United States ... 45 H4
Lookout Pass • ID/MT, United States ... 40 C2
Loolmalassin • Tanzania ... 23 F4
Loon Ski • NH, United States ... 149 [222]
Loon • OT, Canada ... 43 L2
Loop Head • Ireland ... 108 C5
Loosdrechtse Plassen • Netherlands ... 109 F2
Lop Buri • Thailand ... 31 C4
Lop Nur • China ... 26 P9
Lopatina, gora • Russian Fed. ... 27 R6
Lopatka, mys • Russian Fed. ... 25 U4
Lopé, Réserve de Park • Gabon ... 133 [46]
Lopez, Cap • Gabon ... 22 F5
Lopez, Cap, Baie du • Gabon ... 22 F5
López Collada, Estacion • Mexico ... 45 F6
Loppikervaard • Netherlands ... 109 F4
Loppem • Belgium ... 109 E2
Lora del Rio • Spain ... 11 F7
Lorain • OH, United States ... 44 D5
Lorca • Spain ... 11 J7
Lorch • Germany ... 112 E4
Lorch • Germany ... 34 K6
Lord Howe island group Heritage N • Australia ... 83 [150]
Lordsburg • NM, United States ... 153 E4
Loreley • Germany ... 112 E4
Lorengau • Papua New Guinea ... 35 (1) D1
Lorentz Nat. Park Heritage N • Indonesia ... 83 [139]
Loreto • Bolivia ... 52 D2
Loreto • Italy ... 121 E12
Loreto • Mexico ... 157 F3
Loreto • Mexico ... 157 F4
Loreto Jesuit mission Heritage C • Argentina ... 84 [74]
Lorian Swamp • Kenya ... 131 G2
Lorient • France ... 114 C3
Lorient • St Barthélemy ... 160 E
Lörinci • Hungary ... 13 I10
Lorn, Firth of • United Kingdom ... 6 G5
Lörrach • Germany ... 112 D7
Lorraine • France ... 10 K4
Lörsch Heritage C • Germany ... 86 [53]
Lorsch • Germany ... 112 E4
Los Alamos • NM, United States ... 153 E2
Los Alcázares Beach • Spain ... 96 [117]
Los Alcázares • Spain ... 117 C3
Los Aldamas • Mexico ... 47 E4
Los Angeles • Chile ... 53 B3
Los Angeles • CA, United States ... 152 C6
Los Arenales del Sol • Spain ... 117 C1
Los Banos • CA, United States ... 45 B3
Los Blancos • Argentina ... 52 D3
Los Cristianos • Tenerife, Canary Is. ... 116 E1
Los Gatos • CA, United States ... 45 B3
Los Gigantes • Tenerife, Canary Is. ... 116 E1
Los Glaciares, Parque Nac. Heritage N • Argentina ... 82 [44]
Los Haïtises, Parque Nac. • Dominican Rep. ... 159 G4
Los Hernández • Margarita ... 160 V
Los, Is. de • Guinea ... 22 B3
Los Katios, Parque Nac. Heritage N • Colombia ... 82 [31]
Los Mochis • Mexico ... 157 F4
Los Monegros • Spain ... 11 K3
Los Monos • Mexico ... 157 G3
Los Padres, Laguna de • Argentina ... 163 D4
Los Palacios • Cuba ... 158 D1
Los Palacios y Villafranca • Spain ... 11 F7
Los Pinos, Costa de • Majorca, Spain ... 117 H2
Los Pocillos • Lanzarote, Canary Is. ... 117 C3
Los Rodeos [Apt] • Tenerife, Canary Is. ... 116 E1
Los Teques • Venezuela ... 51 D2
Los Vilos • Chile ... 52 B5
Losai Game Reserve • Kenya ... 131 G2
Losinj • Croatia ... 128 D3
Lost River Range • ID, United States ... 42 I4
Lost Trail Pass • MT, United States ... 152 B2
Lostwithiel • United Kingdom ... 104 F4
Lot • France ... 10 G9
Lot • Sudan ... 21 E4
Lot [Adm] • France ... 115 C4
Lot's Wife • Japan ... 140 A8
Lota • Chile ... 52 B6
Lotkipi Plain • Kenya ... 131 G1
Loto • Dem. Rep. of Congo ... 23 C4
Lotuka, Jabal • Sudan ... 23 E3
Lotus Mtn • China ... 139 B2
Louangphabang • Laos ... 31 C3
Louangphrabang Heritage C • Laos ... 85 [197]
Loubomo • Congo ... 22 G5
Loudéac • France ... 114 C2
Loudima • Congo ... 22 G5
Loudun • France ... 114 D3
Loue • France ... 10 E6
Louga • Senegal ... 22 I1
Loughborough • United Kingdom ... 104 D2
Loughrea Beach • Ireland ... 96 [62]
Loughrea • Ireland ... 108 C4
Loughwood Meeting House • United Kingdom ... 104 F3
Louhans • France ... 48 F1
Louisa, Lake • FL, United States ... 151 C1
Louisa, Lake, State Park • FL, United States ... 151 C1

Louisbourg, Fortress of • NS, Canada ... 156 D8
Louisburgh Beach • Ireland ... 96 [63]
Louisburgh • Ireland ... 108 C1
Louisiade Archipelago • Papua New Guinea ... 35 (1) E2
Louisiana • United States ... 153 F1
Louisville • GA, United States ... 48 F4
Louisville • MS, United States ... 153 F2
Loulan • China ... 123 D3
Loulan Yiji • China ... 26 O9
Loulé Beach • Portugal ... 96 [100]
Loulé • Portugal ... 118 E7
Loup • France ... 115 H2
Loup • NE, United States ... 46 G2
Loup City • NE, United States ... 46 F2
Loup, Gorges du • France ... 115 H2
Lourdes • France ... 115 J2
Louth • United Kingdom ... 7 M8
Louth • Ireland ... 108 A1
Loutrá • Greece ... 122 D7
Loutrá Edipsoú • Greece ... 122 D4
Loutráki Beach • Greece ... 97 [178]
Louvière • Belgium ... 5 H4
Louviers • France ... 10 G4
Lóvanger • Sweden ... 16 K4
Lövänger • Sweden ... 16 K4
Lovat • Russian Fed. ... 126 C3
Lovcan • F.R. of Yugoslavia ... 14 F7
Lovcen Nat. Park N • Fed. Rep. of Yugoslavia ... 89 [120]
Lovech • Bulgaria ... 14 L6
Loveland Ski • CO, United States ... 149 [100]
Loveland • CO, United States ... 46 C2
Lovell • WY, United States ... 42 K4
Lovelock • NV, United States ... 152 C2
Lover's Leap • Jamaica ... 159 F4
Loves Park • IL, United States ... 43 L5
Lovina Beach • Bali, Indonesia ... 143 H2
Lovington • NM, United States ... 47 C1
Lovoi • Dem. Rep. of Congo ... 23 D5
Lovosice • Czech Rep. ... 125 F4
Lövstad • Sweden ... 125 F4
Low, Cape • NU, Canada ... 39 N4
Low Newton Beach • United Kingdom ... 101 [18]
Lowa • Dem. Rep. of Congo ... 23 D4
Lowell • ID, United States ... 42 H3
Lowell • IN, United States ... 44 B5
Lowell • MA, United States ... 153 D4
Lowell Nat. Hist. Park Park N • MA, United States ... 151 [338]
Lower Austria • Austria ... 119 F4
Lower Burrell • PA, United States ... 44 F5
Lower Egypt • Egypt ... 131 F1
Lower Hutt • New Zealand ... 35 E5
Lower Post • YT, Canada ... 38 F4
Lower Red Lake • MN, United States ... 43 I3
Lower Saxony • Germany ... 111 A3
Loyalty Is. • New Caledonia ... 35 (2) B3
Loyangalani • Kenya ... 131 G1
Loyauté, Is. • New Caledonia ... 35 (2) B3
Lozenets • Bulgaria ... 128 E4
Lozère, Mt • France ... 10 I9
Loznica • F.R. of Yugoslavia ... 14 G5
Ltyentye Apurte Aboriginal Land • NT, Australia ... 145 D2
Lu Shan Heritage C • China ... 85 [176]
Lu'an • China ... 29 F4
Lua • Dem. Rep. of Congo ... 22 H4
Luacano • Angola ... 24 C2
Luachimo • Angola ... 23 C5
Luachimo [Riv] • Angola ... 23 C5
Luahasibuka • Indonesia ... 143 G4
Lualaba • Dem. Rep. of Congo ... 23 D5
Luama • Dem. Rep. of Congo ... 23 D4
Luana Point • Jamaica ... 159 F3
Luanda • Angola ... 23 A5
Luang Po Ban Laem • Thailand ... 142 C3
Luang Prabang Heritage C • Laos ... 85 [197]
Luang Prabang Range • Laos/Thailand ... 142 B4
Luapinga • Angola/Zambia ... 24 C2
Luangwa • Zambia ... 130 C2
Luangwa [Riv] • Zambia ... 24 D2
Luanshya • Zambia ... 24 D2
Luapula • Dem. Rep. of Congo/Zambia ... 23 D6
Luarca • Spain ... 11 E1
Luba • Equatorial Guinea ... 22 F4
Luban • Poland ... 22 B3
Lubanas Ezers • Latvia ... 126 B4
Lubang • Philippines ... 31 G4
Lubango • Angola ... 24 A2
Lubao • Dem. Rep. of Congo ... 23 D5
Lubartów • Poland ... 13 L6
Lübbecke • Germany ... 8 D4
Lübben • Germany ... 8 I5
Lübbenau • Germany ... 8 I5
Lubbock • TX, United States ... 46 E6
Lübeck • Germany ... 8 F3
Lübeck Heritage C • Germany ... 86 [38]
Lübecker Bucht • Germany ... 8 G2
Lubenec • Czech Rep. ... 9 I6
Lubilash • Dem. Rep. of Congo ... 13 F6
Lubin • Poland ... 13 F6
Lublin • Poland ... 128 C1
Lubliniec • Poland ... 13 I6
Lubnán, Jabal • Lebanon ... 13 E4
Lubny • Ukraine ... 17 E4
Lubon • Poland ... 13 F5
Lubsko • Poland ... 13 D6
Lubudi • Dem. Rep. of Congo ... 23 C6
Lubuklinggau • Indonesia ... 32 D3
Lubumbashi • Dem. Rep. of Congo ... 23 D6
Luc • France ... 115 H3
Luc-sur-Mer • France ... 115 H3
Luca • Italy ... 22 H6
Lucala • Angola ... 22 H6
Lucan • Ireland ... 108 B4
Lucapa • Angola ... 23 B5
Lucaya • Bahamas ... 158 B2
Lucaya Estates • Bahamas ... 158 B2
Lucca • Italy ... 121 E11
Luce Bay • United Kingdom ... 7 H7
Lucea • Jamaica ... 159 F3
Lucedale • MS, United States ... 48 C5
Lucena • Philippines ... 31 G4
Lucena del Cid • Spain ... 11 K4
Lucena • Italy ... 14 C8
Lucerne • Switzerland ... 119 G3
Lucerne, Lake of • Switzerland ... 119 G3
Lucheringo • Mozambique ... 23 F6
Lucira • Angola ... 24 A2
Luckau • Germany ... 8 I5
Luckenwalde • Germany ... 8 I5
Lucknow • India ... 137 D1

Luzhou • China ... 29 D5
Luziânia • Brazil ... 52 G2
Luznice • Czech Rep. ... 128 B4
Luzon • Philippines ... 31 G3
Luzon Strait • Philippines ... 31 G2
Lyakhovskiy Ostrova • Russian Fed. ... 127 A6
Lyall, Mt • New Zealand ... 145 G1
Lycaonia • Turkey ... 123 G1
Lycia • Turkey ... 123 F3
Lycksele • Sweden ... 16 J4
Lydd • United Kingdom ... 104 E4
Lydd [Apt] • United Kingdom ... 104 E4
Lydford Cay • Bahamas ... 158 B3
Lydia • Turkey ... 122 D6
Lydstep Beach • United Kingdom ... 101 [167]
Lyman • WY, United States ... 42 J6
Lyme Bay • United Kingdom ... 104 F6
Lyme Regis • United Kingdom ... 104 F3
Lymington • United Kingdom ... 7 K11
Lymira • Turkey ... 123 F3
Lyna Alie • Poland ... 13 J3
Lynchburg • VA, United States ... 153 D11
Lynden • WA, United States ... 34 H3
Lyndhurst • WA, Australia ... 152 B3
Lyndon B. Johnson Mem. Grove Park N • DC, United States ... 151 [280]
Lyndon B. Johnson Nat. Hist. Park N • TX, United States ... 150 [138]
Lyndon B. Johnson Nat. Hist. Park • TX, United States ... 154 J3
Lynn • IN, United States ... 44 C5
Lynn • MA, United States ... 44 J4
Lynn Lake • MN, Canada ... 38 K5
Lynnay, gora • Russian Fed. ... 27 R4
Lynton • United Kingdom ... 104 F2
Lynx Lake • NT, Canada ... 38 I4
Lyny Heritage C • France ... 86 [74]
Lyon • France ... 115 F1
Lyons • WA, Australia ... 34 C4
Lys • France ... 5 F4
Lysebotn • Norway ... 124 C6
Lysefjorden • Norway ... 124 C5
Lysekil • Sweden ... 125 F2
Lysva • Russian Fed. ... 26 I6
Lysychans'k • Ukraine ... 17 F5
Lytham St Anne's • United Kingdom ... 7 I8
Lyubertsy • Russian Fed. ... 126 C4
Lyubimets • Bulgaria ... 15 H2

M.R. Gomez, Presa • Mexico ... 47 E4
M'Sila • Algeria ... 20 F1
M'Zab valley Heritage C • Algeria ... 86 [261]
Ma On Shan Country Park • Hong Kong, China ... 139 B6
Ma, Oued el • Mauritania ... 20 D4
Ma Wan • Hong Kong, China ... 139 B5
Ma'an • Jordan ... 18 B3
Ma'anshan • China ... 139 C1
Ma'aza Plateau • Egypt ... 131 F4
Ma'tan as Sarra • Libya ... 21 D3
Maafushi • Maldives ... 138 F4
Maam Turk Mtns • Ireland ... 108 C3
Maarianhamina • Finland ... 125 E3
Maarssen • Netherlands ... 109 F2
Maas • Netherlands ... 109 D12
Maas en Waal, Land van • Netherlands ... 109 F4
Maaseik • Belgium ... 5 I3
Maassluis • Netherlands ... 109 F3
Maastricht • Netherlands ... 109 D15
Maasvlakte • Netherlands ... 109 F3
Mablethorpe Beach • United Kingdom ... 101 [38]
Mableton • GA, United States ... 48 E4
Mabote • Mozambique ... 24 E4
Macaé • Brazil ... 163 C4
Macanao, Peninsula de • Margarita ... 160 V
Macanet • Spain ... 117 D2
Macapá • Brazil ... 51 G3
Macará • Ecuador ... 51 B4
Macas • Ecuador ... 51 B4
Macau • Brazil ... 53 (1) D2
MACAU SPECIAL ADMIN. REGION • China ... 139 B1
Macaúbas • Brazil ... 52 H1
Macauley • New Zealand ... 33 J9
Macaya, Parque Nac. • Haiti ... 159 G5
Macclesfield • United Kingdom ... 7 J8
Macclesfield Bank • South China Sea ... 139 A8
Macdhui, Ben • United Kingdom ... 6 I4
Macdoel • CA, United States ... 42 D6
Macdonald, Lake • NT/WA, Australia ... 145 D1
Macdonnell Ranges • NT, Australia ... 145 D2
Maceda de Cavaleiros • Portugal ... 11 E3
Macedonia • Greece ... 122 A1
MACEDONIA, FORMER YUGOSLAV REPUBLIC OF • Europe ... 14 I8
Maceió • Brazil ... 53 (1) D3
Macenta • Guinea ... 22 C3
Macerata • Italy ... 12 H5
Macgillicuddy's Reeks • Ireland ... 108 C7
Machaerus • Jordan ... 135 A8
Machakos • Kenya ... 131 G3
Machala • Ecuador ... 51 B4
Machareti • Bolivia ... 52 D3
Machattie, Lake • QL, Australia ... 34 G4
Macheke • Zimbabwe ... 24 E3
Machgaon • India ... 137 E2
Machias • ME, United States ... 44 L3
Machico • Madeira ... 118 C2
Machida • Japan ... 140 C2
Machilipatnam India ... 138 E3
Machilipatnam Beach • India ... 138 E3
Machiques • Venezuela ... 51 C2
Machu Picchu • Peru ... 163 B2
Machu Picchu, Santuario histórico Heritage N • Peru ... 82 [36]
Machu Picchu, Santuario histórico Heritage C • Peru ... 84 [58]
Macia • Mozambique ... 24 E4
Macina Gourma • Mali ... 22 D1
Macinaggio • Corsica, France ... 115 L2
Macizo Galaico • Spain ... 11 D2
Mackay • QL, Australia ... 144 B3
Mackay • ID, United States ... 42 I5
Mackay, Lake • NT/WA, Australia ... 145 D1
Mackenzie • NT, Canada ... 38 G3
Mackenzie Bay • Kerguelen Is. ... 54 (1) L3
Mackenzie Bay • YT, Canada ... 38 D3
Mackenzie Delta • NT, Canada ... 155 A1
Mackenzie Mtns • NT/YT, Canada ... 38 F4
Mackerricher State Park • CA, United States ... 152 C1
Mackinac, Strait of • MI, United States ... 39 O7
Mackinaw City • MI, United States ... 44 C3
Mackinnon Road • Kenya ... 131 G5
Maclear • South Africa ... 24 D6
MacLeod, Lake • WA, Australia ... 144 B2
Macmillan • YT, Canada ... 38 E4
Macomb • IL, United States ... 46 J2
Macomer • Sardinia, Italy ... 120 C1
Mâcon • France ... 115 F1

Macon • MO, United States ... 46 I3
Macon • GA, United States ... 48 F4
Macondo • Angola ... 24 C2
Mâconnais • France ... 114 B2
Macquarie I. • Southern Ocean ... 3 X10
Macquarie I. Heritage N • Southern Ocean ... 83 [152]
Macroom • Ireland ... 108 C8
Macugnaga • Italy ... 121 E1
Macujer • Colombia ... 51 C3
Macusari • Peru ... 163 B2
Mad • Jordan ... 135 A8
Madadeni • South Africa ... 134 B1
MADAGASCAR • Indian Ocean ... 24 H3
Madama • Niger ... 20 H4
Madan • Bulgaria ... 14 M8
Madang • Papua New Guinea ... 35 (1) D2
Madaoua • Niger ... 20 G6
Madara Heritage C • Bulgaria ... 86 [202]
Madara • Bulgaria ... 128 E3
Maddalena, I. • Sardinia, Italy ... 120 C2
Madeira • Brazil ... 51 E5
Madeira • Atlantic Ocean ... 118 C
Madeira, Lauraísiva de Heritage N • Madeira ... 83 [55]
Mädelegabel • Austria/Germany ... 112 F6
Madeleine, Is. de la • QU, Canada ... 156 D2
Madelia • MN, United States ... 43 I4
Madera • WI, United States ... 43 K3
Madera • CA, United States ... 45 B3
Madera • Mexico ... 157 F2
Madera, Sierra • TX, United States ... 47 C2
Madésimo • Italy ... 121 E2
Madhar, Ra's • Saudi Arabia ... 21 G2
Madhya Pradesh • India ... 28 C4
Madikeri • India ... 138 D6
Madinah, Al • Saudi Arabia ... 18 C5
Madiran • France ... 114 B3
Madison • SD, United States ... 43 H4
Madison • WI, United States ... 43 L5
Madison • IN, United States ... 44 C6
Madison • ME, United States ... 44 K3
Madison • WV, United States ... 48 G1
Madisonville • KY, United States ... 48 D2
Madiun • Java, Indonesia ... 143 J7
Madoc • OT, Canada ... 44 G3
Madoi • China ... 28 G1
Madona • Latvia ... 126 B4
Madonie • Sicily, Italy ... 120 D2
Madonna di Campiglio Ski • Italy ... 100 [213]
Madonna di Campiglio • Italy ... 121 E3
Madra Dagi • Turkey ... 15 I4
Madrakah, Ra's al • Oman ... 18 G6
Madras • India ... 138 D7
Madras • OR, United States ... 42 E4
Madre de Dios • Peru ... 163 B2
Madre de Dios [Riv] • Bolivia/Peru ... 52 C1
Madre, Laguna • Mexico ... 47 F5
Madre, Laguna • TX, United States ... 47 F4
Madre, Sierra • Mexico ... 37 C4
Madrid • Spain ... 11 H4
Madrid, Comunidad de • Spain ... 11 H4
Madridejos • Spain ... 11 H5
Madura • Java, Indonesia ... 143 J8
Madura, Selat • Java, Indonesia ... 143 J8
Madurai • India ... 138 D11
Madurodam • Netherlands ... 109 F3
Madyan • Saudi Arabia ... 21 G3
Mae Hong Son • Thailand ... 142 B1
Mae La Noi • Thailand ... 142 B3
Mae Ping Nat. Park • Thailand ... 142 B2
Mae Rim • Thailand ... 142 B1
Mae Sai • Thailand ... 142 B1
Mae Sariang • Thailand ... 142 B3
Mae Suai • Thailand ... 142 B1
Mae Taeng • Thailand ... 142 B1
Maebashi • Japan ... 30 J6
Mael • Norway ... 124 B1
Maenam Beach • Ko Samui, Thailand ... 142 D1
Maestra, Sierra • Cuba ... 158 D8
Maevatanana • Madagascar ... 24 H3
Maéwo • Vanuatu ... 35 (2) B1
Mafeteng • Lesotho ... 24 D5
Mafia I. • Tanzania ... 130 B4
Mafikeng • South Africa ... 24 D5
Mafra • Brazil ... 52 G4
Mafra • Portugal ... 118 D1
Magadan • Russian Fed. ... 27 P5
Magadino • Switzerland ... 119 G7
Magalluf • Majorca, Spain ... 117 H3
Magangué • Colombia ... 51 C2
Magaria • Niger ... 22 F2
Magarida • Papua New Guinea ... 34 I2
Magda Plateau • NU, Canada ... 39 O2
Magdagachi • Russian Fed. ... 27 K6
Magdalena • Colombia ... 51 C3
Magdalena • Bolivia ... 52 D1
Magdalena • Argentina ... 163 D2
Magdalena • Mexico ... 45 G6
Magdalena • NM, United States ... 45 I4
Magdalena, I. • Mexico ... 157 F4
Magdalena [Riv] • Mexico ... 45 F6
Magdeburg • Germany ... 8 F8
Magdelaine Cays • CS, Australia ... 34 J3
Magelang • Java, Indonesia ... 143 J7
Magellan, Strait of • Chile ... 53 B6
Magens Bay • US Virgin Is. ... 160 Z
Mageroya • Norway ... 16 N1
Maggie L. Walker Nat. Site Park N • VA, United States ... 151 [250]
Maggiore, Lago • Italy ... 121 E2
Maghágha • Egypt ... 131 F3
Maghnia • Algeria ... 20 E2
Magic Hill Farm • OT, Canada ... 155 B5
Magic Kingdom • FL, United States ... 151 C1
Magic Valley • NS, Canada ... 156 [S]
Magic Valley Park L • NS, Canada ... 156 [S]
Magical World of Fantasy Island Park L • United Kingdom ... 98 [28]
Maglaj • Bosnia-Herz. ... 12 M4
Maglic • F.R. of Yugoslavia ... 14 F6
Maglie • Italy ... 12 M9
Magnetic I. • QL, Australia ... 144 B1
Magnitogorsk • Russian Fed. ... 26 I7
Magnolia • AR, United States ... 46 I6
Magnor • Norway ... 124 B1
Magny-en-Vexin • France ... 115 E1
Mago • Russian Fed. ... 27 N6
Mago Nat. Park • Ethiopia ... 133 [66]
Magoebaskloof • South Africa ... 24 D4
Magoé • QU, Canada ... 44 I3
Magwe • Myanmar ... 31 B3
Maha Sarakham • Thailand ... 31 C3
Mahabad • Iran ... 18 E2
Mahabaleshwar Hill Sta • India ... 138 E2
Mahabe • India ... 85 [148]
Mahabharat • India ... 138 D7
Mahabalipuram Heritage C • India ... 138 D8
Mahabalipuram Beach • India ... 138 D8
Mahafaly, Plateau • Madagascar ... 24 G4
Mahajan • India ... 137 C2

Mahajanga

Mahajanga • Madagascar 24 H3
Mahakam • Indonesia 32 F3
Mahalapye • Botswana 24 D4
Mahanadi • India 28 D4
Mahanoy City • PA, United States 44 G5
Maharashtra • India 28 C4
Mahaut • Dominica 161 M
Mahaweli Ganga • Sri Lanka 138 D15
Mahbubnagar • India 138 D3
Mahdia • Guyana 51 F2
Mahdia • Tunisia 131 E4
Mahé • Seychelles 133 K1
Mahe • India 138 D10
Mahe **Beach** • India 138 E3
Mahébourg • Mauritius 132 J4
Mahenge • Tanzania 130 B4
Mahesana • India 28 B4
Mahi • India 28 B4
Mahia Peninsula • New Zealand 35 F4
Mahilyow • Belarus 17 E4
Mahlow • Germany 111 C4
Mahón **Beach** • Minorca, Spain 96 [127]
Mahón • Minorca, Spain 117 F4
Mähren • Czech Rep. 13 F8
Mahrès • Tunisia 131 E4
Mai Khao Beach • Ko Phuket, Thailand 142 E1
Mai Ndombe, Lac • Dem. Rep. of Congo 23 B4
Mai Po Marsh • Hong Kong, China 139 B3
Mai-Ndombe, Lac • Dem. Rep. of Congo 22 H5
Maicao • Colombia 51 C1
Maiden Castle • United Kingdom 104 F3
Maidstone • United Kingdom 104 E4
Maiduguri • Nigeria 22 G2
Maihar • India 137 C7
Maiko, Parc nat. de la **Park** • Dem. Rep. of Congo 133 [56]
Maikona • Kenya 23 F3
Maili • HI, United States 154 G5
Main • Germany 9 E7
Main Barrier Range • NS, Australia 34 H6
Main Channel • OT, Canada 44 E3
Main-Donau-Kanal • Germany 9 G7
Mainalon • Greece 15 D6
Mainau • Germany 112 F5
Mainburg • Germany 9 G8
Maine • France 10 D5
Maine • United States 44 K2
Maine, Gulf of • Canada/United States 39 R8
Maine, Gulf of • United States 153 D4
Maine-et-Loire • France 114 D1
Mainique, Pongo • Peru 163 B2
Mainland • Orkney, UK 6 I2
Mainland • Shetland, UK 6 K1
Maintenon • France 115 E3
Mainz • Germany 112 E4
Maio • Cape Verde 22 (1) B1
Maipadu **Beach** • India 138 E3
Maipo, Volcá • Argentina 52 C5
Maipú • Argentina 163 D4
Maira • Italy 10 M9
Mais Gaté [Apt] • Haiti 159 G6
Maisi, Cabo • Cuba 158 D8
Maitland • NS, Australia 144 C2
Maíz, Is. del • Nicaragua 51 A1
Maíz, Is. del • Nicaragua 160 A18
Maizhokunggar • China 28 F3
Maizuru • Japan 30 H7
Majalengka • Java, Indonesia 143 J2
Majene • Indonesia 32 (1) A3
Majerten • Somalia 23 H2
Majete Game Reserve **Park** • Malawi 133 [99]
Majevica • Bosnia-Herz. 14 F5
Maji • Ethiopia 23 F2
Major General Rodgers • US Virgin Is. 160 Z
Major, Puig • Majorca, Spain 117 H1
Majorca • Spain 117 H
Majorda • Goa, India 137 B2
Majorda Beach • Goa, India 137 B2
Majuro • Marshall Is. 33 I5
Makaha • HI, United States 154 G5
Makakan • Indonesia 32 F3
Makakilo City • HI, United States 154 G5
Makale • Indonesia 32 (1) A3
Makallé • Argentina 52 E4
Makalondi • Niger 20 F6
Makambako • Tanzania 130 B3
Makanza • Dem. Rep. of Congo 23 B3
Makari Mtns • Tanzania 130 B1
Makarikari • Botswana 24 D4
Makarov • Russian Fed. 27 N7
Makarska • Croatia 128 D4
Makassar, Selat • Indonesia 25 M10
Makassar Strait • Indonesia 32 F3
Makat • Kazakstan 17 I5
Makatini Flats • South Africa 134 B2
Makaw • Myanmar 31 B1
Makaza • Bulgaria/Greece 14 M8
Makedonía • Greece 15 D3
Makeni • Sierra Leone 22 B3
Makgadikgadi Pans • Botswana 24 D3
Makgadikgadi Pans Game Reserve **Park** • Botswana 133 [117]
Makhachkala • Russian Fed. 17 H6
Makhan • Ko Phuket, Thailand 142 E2
Makhan Bay • Ko Phuket, Thailand 142 E2
Makhan Beach • Ko Phuket, Thailand 142 E2
Makheras Monastery • Cyprus 123 J3
Makinsk • Kazakstan 26 L7
Makkah • Saudi Arabia 18 C5
Makó • Hungary 13 J11
Makokou • Gabon 22 G4
Makongolosi • Tanzania 130 B3
Makorako, Mt • New Zealand 145 F4
Makoua • Congo 22 H4
Makran • Iran/Pakistan 18 H4
Makrigialós **Beach** • Greece 97 [190]
Makrigialós • Crete, Greece 123 E8
Makthar • Tunisia 131 E1
Makunudhoo • Maldives 138 F2
Makunudu Atoll • Maldives 138 F1
Makurazaki • Japan 30 F9
Makurdi • Nigeria 22 F3
Malå • Sweden 16 J4
Malá Fatra Nat. Park • Slovak Rep. 128 C3
Mala Kapela • Croatia 14 C5
Mala Panew • Poland 128 C1
Mala, Punta • Panama 37 E6
Malabang • Philippines 31 G5
Malabar Coast • India 138 D10
Malabo • Equatorial Guinea 22 F4
Malacca • Malaysia 141 D3
Malacca, Strait of • Indonesia/Malaysia 32 B2
Malacky • Slovak Rep. 13 G9
Malad City • ID, United States 42 I5
Maladzyechna • Belarus 16 N9
Málaga • Colombia 51 C2
Málaga **Beach** • Spain 96 [114]
Málaga • Spain 116 B7
Malagarasi • Tanzania 130 B1
Malahide • Ireland 108 B2
Malaimbandy • Madagascar 24 H4
Malaita • Solomon Is. 35 (1) G2
Malakal • Sudan 23 E2
Malakula • Vanuatu 35 (2) B2
Malan, D.F. [Apt] • South Africa 134 C5
Malang • Java, Indonesia 143 J8
Malanje • Angola 23 B5
Malanville • Benin 20 F6
Mälaren • Sweden 125 D3
Malartic • QU, Canada 44 F1
Malatya • Turkey 18 C2
MALAWI • Africa 24 E2
Malawi, Lake • Africa 24 E2
Malay Peninsula • Malaysia 31 C5
Malaya Vishera • Russian Fed. 126 C1
Malaybalay • Philippines 31 G5
MALAYSIA • Asia 31 C6
Malbork • Poland 13 I3
Malbork **Heritage C** • Poland 86 [160]
Malbun • Liechtenstein 119 H5
Malcésine • Italy 121 E3
Malchin • Germany 8 H3
Malchow • Germany 8 H3
Malden • Kiribati 33 L6
Malden • MA, United States 44 J4
Malden • MO, United States 46 K4
MALDIVES • Indian Ocean 138 F
Maldon • United Kingdom 7 M10
Maldonado • Uruguay 163 D2
Malé • Maldives 138 F4
Malé Atoll • Maldives 138 F2
Maléas, Akra • Greece 122 D7
Malegaon • India 28 B4
Máleme **Beach** • Crete, Greece 97 [212]
Máleme • Crete, Greece 123 E1
Målerås • Sweden 125 F8
Malgomaj • Sweden 16 H4
Malgrat de Mar **Beach** • Spain 96 [122]
Malgrat de Mar • Spain 117 D4
Malha Wells • Sudan 21 E4
Malhalla el Kubra, El • Egypt 131 F1
Malheur • OR, United States 42 G5
Malheur Lake • OR, United States 152 B4
MALI • Africa 20 E5
Mali i Krabit • Albania 14 G7
Mália **Beach** • Crete, Greece 97 [214]
Mália • Crete, Greece 123 E7
Mália [Hist.] • Crete, Greece 123 E7
Malibu • CA, United States 152 C6
Malik, Wadi al • Sudan 21 E4
Malimba, Mtns • Dem. Rep. of Congo 23 D5
Malin Head • Ireland 6 E6
Malindi • Kenya 131 G3
Malindi Marine Game Reserve • Kenya 131 G5
Malindi Marine Nat. Park • Kenya 131 G3
Malindidzimu • Zimbabwe 130 C3
Malino, Bukit • Indonesia 32 (1) B2
Malion, Kólpos • Crete, Greece 123 E3
Maljen • F.R. of Yugoslavia 14 G5
Malkara • Turkey 15 H3
Malko Turnovo • Bulgaria 15 I2
Mallacoota • VI, Australia 144 C4
Mallaig • United Kingdom 6 G4
Mallawi • Egypt 18 A4
Mallorca • Spain 11 O5
Mallow • Ireland 108 C8
Malmberget • Sweden 16 K3
Malmédy • Belgium 5 J4
Malmesbury • United Kingdom 104 D4
Malmesbury • South Africa 134 C5
Malmköping • Sweden 125 D3
Malmö **Beach** • Sweden 96 [11]
Malmö • Sweden 125 F11
Malmok • Bonaire 160 W
Malmok Beach • Aruba 160 Y
Malo • Vanuatu 35 (2) B2
Maloja **Ski** • Switzerland 100 [121]
Malolotja Nature Reserve **Park** • Swaziland 133 [137]
Malone • NY, United States 44 H3
Malonga • Dem. Rep. of Congo 24 C2
Malosmadulu Atoll North • Maldives 138 F1
Malosmadulu Atoll South • Maldives 138 F1
Måløy • Norway 124 C1
Malpelo • Colombia 51 A3
Malpensa [Apt] • Italy 121 E6
Malpica **Beach** • Spain 96 [92]
Malprabha • India 28 C5
Malsch • Germany 112 D6
MALTA • Europe 123 H
Malta • MT, United States 42 L2
Malta Channel • Italy/Malta 12 I12
Maltepe • Turkey 15 K3
Maluku, Kepulauan • Indonesia 32 (1) C2
Malunda • Indonesia 32 (1) A3
Malung • Sweden 16 G6
Malut • Sudan 23 E1
Maluu • Solomon Is. 35 (1) G2
Malvasia • Greece 90 A20
Malveira da Serra • Portugal 118 D1
Malvern • AR, United States 46 I5
Malvern Hills • United Kingdom 104 D3
Malvern Lake • KS, United States 46 H3
Malvinas, Is. • Atlantic Ocean 53 E6
Malwan • India 138 D1
Maly Karmakuly • Russian Fed. 26 H3
Malyy Lyakhovskiy, Ostrov • Russian Fed. 27 N2
Mama • Russian Fed. 27 H5
Mamaia-Bai • Romania 128 E2
Mamaia-Sat • Romania 128 E2
Mamallapuram **Heritage C** • India 85 [148]
Mamallapuram • India 138 D7
Mamallapuram **Beach** • India 138 E3
Mambéré • Africa 23 A2
Mambrui • Kenya 131 G3
Mammoth Cave Nat. Park **Heritage N** • KY, United States 82 [16]
Mammoth Cave Nat. Park **Park N** • KY, United States 151 [230]
Mammoth Hot Springs • WY, United States 42 J4
Mammoth Lakes • CA, United States 152 C4
Mammoth Mtn **Ski** • CA, United States 149 [69]
Mammoth Nat. Park • KY, United States 48 D2
Mamonovo • Russian Fed. 13 J3
Mamoré • Bolivia 52 C1
Mamou • Guinea 22 B2
Mamoutzou • Mayotte 23 H6
Mamuju • Indonesia 32 (1) A3
Mamuno • Botswana 24 C4
Mamunta-Mayoso Wildlife Sanctuary **Park** • Sierra Leone 133 [14]
Mamure Kalesi • Turkey 123 G3
Man • Côte d'Ivoire 22 C3
Man, Isle of • Europe 7 H7
Man'o War Bay • Trinidad & Tobago 160 T
Mana Pools Nat. Park **Heritage N** • Zimbabwe 83 [105]
Mana Pools Nat. Park • Zimbabwe 130 C2
Mana Pools Nat. Park **Park** • Zimbabwe 133 [109]
Manacapuru • Brazil 51 E4
Manacor **Beach** • Majorca, Spain 96 [126]
Manacor • Majorca, Spain 117 H2
Manado • Indonesia 32 (1) B2
Managua • Nicaragua 37 D5
Manakara • Madagascar 24 H4
Manali **Hill Sta** • India 138 E1
Manamah, Al • Bahrain 18 F4
Manambolo • Madagascar 24 H3
Manapouri • New Zealand 145 G3
Manapouri, Lake • New Zealand 145 G3
Manar • Yemen 21 H5
Manas • China 26 O9
Manas Wildlife Sanctuary **Heritage N** • India 83 [115]
Manassas • VA, United States 44 G6
Manassas Nat. Battlefield Park **Park N** • VA, United States 151 [256]
Manassas Nat. Battlefield Park • VA, United States 153 D9
Manatí • Puerto Rico 159 H1
Manati, Río Grande de • Puerto Rico 159 H2
Manaus • Brazil 51 E4
Manavgat **Beach** • Turkey 97 [222]
Manavgat • Turkey 123 F4
Manche, la • France/UK 10 D3
Manchester • United Kingdom 7 J8
Manchester • IA, United States 43 K5
Manchester • TN, United States 48 D3
Manchester • KY, United States 48 F2
Manchester • NH, United States 153 D4
Manchester Center • VT, United States 44 I4
Manchskaya Vpadina • Russian Fed. 17 G5
Manchuria • China 139 A4
Mand • Iran 18 F4
Manda • Sudan 21 D6
Manda • Tanzania 130 B3
Manda I. • Kenya 131 G4
Manda, Jabal • Sudan 23 C2
Mandab, Bab al • Africa/Asia 21 H5
Mandaguari • Brazil 52 F3
Mandal • Norway 125 F1
Mandala, Puncak • Indonesia 32 (1) F3
Mandalay • Myanmar 31 B2
Mandalgovi • Mongolia 29 D1
Mandalselva • Norway 125 F1
Mandan • ND, United States 43 F3
Mandara, Mts • Cameroon 21 B5
Mandas • Sardinia, Italy 12 D9
Mandawa • India 137 C2
Mandelieu **Beach** • France 96 [134]
Mandera • Kenya 131 G2
Mandera [Region] • Kenya 131 G2
Manderscheid • Germany 112 E3
Manderscheid **Spa** • Germany 113 [k6]
Mandeville • Jamaica 159 F3
Mandingues, Mts • Mali 22 B2
Mandla • India 28 C4
Mandore • India 137 C5
Mandoúdi • Greece 15 E5
Mandrem Beach • Goa, India 137 B1
Mandritsara • Madagascar 24 H3
Mandsaur • India 137 C6
Mandurah • WA, Australia 34 C6
Manduria • Italy 12 L8
Mandvi • India 18 I5
Mandzavinata **Beach** • Cephalonia, Greece 97 [171]
Mandzavinata • Cephalonia, Greece 122 C2
Manendragarh • India 28 D4
Manfalût • Egypt 18 A4
Manfredonia • Italy 12 J7
Manfredonia, Golfo di • Italy 12 K7
Manga • Niger 20 H6
Manga • Brazil 53 (1) C4
Mangalia • Romania 128 E2
Mangalore • India 138 D6
Mangalore **Beach** • India 138 E3
Mángana **Beach** • Greece 97 [195]
Mangaratiba • Brazil 163 C3
Mangareva • French Polynesia 33 N8
Manger • Norway 124 C3
Mangfall • Germany 112 F3
Manggar • Indonesia 32 D3
Mangin Yoma • Myanmar 31 B2
Manginipudi **Beach** • India 138 E3
Mangle, Punta • Margarita 160 V
Mangnai • China 28 F1
Mangoky • Madagascar 24 G4
Mangole • Indonesia 32 (1) C3
Mangrove Cay • Bahamas 49 D4
Mangueira, Lagoa • Brazil 52 F5
Mangueni, Plateau de • Niger 20 H4
Mangui • China 27 J6
Mangum • OK, United States 46 F5
Manhattan • KS, United States 46 G3
Manhattan • NY, United States 153 D7
Manheim • PA, United States 44 G5
Manhuaçu • Brazil 163 C2
Mani • Colombia 51 C3
Manía • Madagascar 24 H3
Manica • Mozambique 130 C2
Manicaland • Zimbabwe 130 C2
Manicouagan • QU, Canada 39 R6
Manicouagan, Réservoir • QU, Canada 39 R6
Manigotagan • MN, Canada 43 H1
Manihiki • Cook Is. 33 K7
Manila • Philippines 31 G4
Manila **Heritage C** • Java, Indonesia 85 [204]
Manila Bay • Philippines 31 G4
Manilva **Beach** • Spain 96 [114]
Manilva • Spain 116 B6
Maningrida Settlement • NT, Australia 34 F2
Maninjau, Danau • Indonesia 143 G4
Manipur • India 28 F4
Manises • Spain 11 K5
Manistee • MI, United States 44 B3
Manistique • MI, United States 44 B3
Manitoba • Canada 38 L5
Manitoba, Lake • MN, Canada 38 L6
Manitoulin I. • OT, Canada 39 O7
Manitowoc • WI, United States 44 B3
Maniwaki • QU, Canada 155 B2
Manizales • Colombia 51 B3
Manja • Madagascar 24 G4
Manjimup • WA, Australia 34 C6
Manjira • India 28 C5
Månkarbo • Sweden 125 D1
Mankato • MN, United States 43 J4
Mankono • Côte d'Ivoire 22 C3
Manley Hot Springs • AK, United States 49 K2
Manley, Norman [Apt] • Jamaica 159 F4
Manlleu • Spain 11 N3
Manly • Russian Fed. 27 S4
Manmanoc, Mt • Philippines 31 G3
Mann • NT, Australia 34 F2
Mann Ranges • NT/SA, Australia 145 D3
Manna • Indonesia 32 C3
Mannar • Sri Lanka 138 D11
Mannar, Gulf of • India/Sri Lanka 138 D15
Mannheim • Germany 112 D4
Mannheim **Castle** • Germany 113 [76]
Manning • AL, Canada 38 H5
Manning • SC, United States 48 G4
Mannu, Capu • Sardinia, Italy 12 C8
Mannu, Rio • Sardinia, Italy 12 C8
Manoa • Bolivia 51 D6
Manokwari • Indonesia 32 (1) D3
Manombo • Madagascar 24 G4
Mañón **Beach** • Spain 96 [92]
Manono • Dem. Rep. of Congo 23 D5
Manorbier **Beach** • United Kingdom 101 [168]
Manori **Beach** • India 138 E3
Manos, Cueva de las **Heritage C** • Argentina 84 [76]
Manosque • France 115 H1
Manouane • QU, Canada 44 H2
Manovo-Gounda-St Floris, Parc nat. **Park** • Central African Rep. 133 [43]
Manovo-Gounda-St Floris, Parc nat. de **Heritage N** • Central African Rep. 83 [89]
Manp'ojin • D.P.R. of Korea 30 D4
Manra • Kiribati 33 J6
Manresa • Spain 117 D3
Mans, le • France 114 D2
Mansa Konko • Gambia 22 A2
Mansel I. • NU, Canada 39 P4
Mansfield • United Kingdom 7 K8
Mansfield • OH, United States 44 D5
Mansfield • PA, United States 44 G5
Mansfield • MO, United States 48 A2
Mansfield • LA, United States 153 F1
Mansfield, Mt • VT, United States 44 I3
Mansura • LA, United States 153 F3
Mansûra, El • Egypt 131 F2
Manta • Ecuador 51 A4
Manta, Bahía de • Ecuador 51 A4
Manta Rota • Portugal 118 E8
Mantaro • Peru 163 B1
Manteca • CA, United States 45 B3
Manteo • NC, United States 48 J3
Mantes-la-Jolie • France 115 E1
Manti • UT, United States 45 G2
Mantiqueira, Serra da • Brazil 163 C3
Manton • MI, United States 44 C3
Mantova • Italy 121 E7
Mäntsälä • Finland 125 E4
Mänttä • Finland 125 E2
Mantua • Italy 121 E7
Manturovo • Russian Fed. 17 G3
Manú • Peru 163 B2
Manu Bay • New Zealand 145 F1
Manú, Parque Nac. **Heritage N** • Peru 82 [37]
Manú, Parque Nac. • Peru 163 B2
Manua • American Samoa 35 (2) G1
Manukau • New Zealand 35 E3
Manuoha, Mt • New Zealand 145 F2
Many • LA, United States 153 F1
Manyara Nat. Park • Tanzania 130 B2
Manyas • Turkey 122 D3
Manyas-Kuscenneti Nat. Park **Park N** • Turkey 89 [142]
Manyas-Kuscenneti Nat. Park • Turkey 122 D3
Manyoni • Tanzania 130 B1
Manzanar Nat. Hist. Site **Park N** • CA, United States 150 [52]
Manzanares • Spain 11 H5
Manzanillo • Cuba 158 D7
Manzanillo • Margarita 160 V
Manzanillo • Mexico 157 G3
Manzhouli • China 27 I7
Mao • Chad 21 B5
Maó **Beach** • Minorca, Spain 96 [127]
Maó • Minorca, Spain 117 F4
Mao • Dominican Rep. 159 G3
Mao Shan • China 139 C1
Maoke, Pegunungan • Indonesia 32 (1) E3
Maomao Shan • China 29 C3
Maoming • China 29 E6
Maotou Shan • China 31 C2
Mapelane Nat. Park • South Africa 134 B4
Mapi • Indonesia 32 (1) E4
Mapi [Riv] • Indonesia 32 (1) E4
Mapia, Kepulauan • Indonesia 32 (1) D2
Maple Creek • SA, Canada 38 J7
Maple Grove • MN, United States 43 J4
Mapou, Ko • Thailand 142 E2
Maprik • Papua New Guinea 35 (1) C1
Mapuera • Brazil 51 F4
Mapusa • Goa, India 137 B1
Maputaland • South Africa 134 B2
Maputo • Mozambique 24 E5
Maputo, Baia de • Mozambique 24 E5
Maputo Elephant Reserve **Park** • Mozambique 133 [139]
Maqaman Nabi Musá • Palestine 135 A8
Maquan He • China 28 D3
Maquinchao • Argentina 53 C4
Maquoketa • IA, United States 43 K5
Mar Chiquita, Lago • Argentina 163 D4
Mar Chiquita, Laguna • Argentina 52 D5
Mar del Plata • Argentina 163 D4
Mar del Tuyú • Argentina 163 D4
Mar, Serra do • Brazil 163 C3
Mara • Kenya/Tanzania 23 E4
Marabá • Brazil 51 H5
Maracá • Brazil 51 G3
Maracaibo • Venezuela 51 C1
Maracaibo, Lago de • Venezuela 51 C2
Maracaju • Brazil 52 E3
Maracaju, Serra de • Brazil 52 E3
Maracás • Brazil 52 H1
Maracas Bay • Trinidad & Tobago 160 U
Maracay • Venezuela 51 D1
Maradi • Niger 20 G6
Marahoué, Parc nat. de la **Park** • Côte d'Ivoire 133 [19]
Marahuaca • Venezuela 51 D3
Marais • MN, United States 43 K3
Marajó, Baía de • Brazil 53 (1) B2
Marajó, I. de • Brazil 51 G4
Maralal Game Reserve • Kenya 131 G1
Maralinga • SA, Australia 34 F6
Maramba • Zambia 24 D3
Maramures **Heritage C** • Romania 86 [197]
Marana • AZ, United States 45 G5
Marand • Iran 18 E2
Maranhão • Brazil 53 (1) B3
Marano, Laguna di • Italy 12 H3
Marañón • Peru 51 B4
Marão, Serra do • Portugal 11 D3
Maratea • Italy 12 J8
Maratea **Beach** • Italy 97 [150]
Maratea • Italy 120 A2
Marateca • Portugal 118 D2
Marathiá, Akra • Zante, Greece 122 C3
Marathón • Greece 122 D4
Marathon • OT, Canada 39 N7
Marathon • TX, United States 47 C2
Marathon • FL, United States 154 H8
Márathospilo • Crete, Greece 123 E2
Marawi • Sudan 21 F4
Marbella **Beach** • Spain 96 [114]
Marbella • Spain 116 B6
Marble Bar • WA, Australia 34 C4
Marble Canyon • AZ, United States 153 E1
Marble Falls • TX, United States 47 E2
Marble Mtn **Ski** • NF, Canada 149 [47]
Marburg • Germany 112 D2
Marburg **Castle** • Germany 113 [39]
Marcali • Hungary 12 L2
March • United Kingdom 7 M9
March • Austria 13 F9
Marche • France 10 G7
Marche • Italy 121 E12
Marche-en-Famenne • Belgium 109 D19
Marchena • Spain 11 F7
Marchena • Galapagos Is. 51 (1) A1
Märchenwald im Isartal • Germany 112 F3
Marches, The • United Kingdom 104 D1
Marcianise • Italy 121 G1
Marco I. • FL, United States 154 H7
Marconi, G [Apt] • Italy 121 E7
Marcos Juárez • Argentina 52 D5
Marcus • Pacific Ocean 33 G3
Mardan • Pakistan 28 B2
Mardin • Turkey 122 A4
Maré • New Caledonia 35 (2) B3
Mare aux Vacoas Reservoir • Mauritius 132 J3
Maree, Loch • United Kingdom 6 G4
Mareeba • QL, Australia 144 B1
Mareg • Somalia 23 H3
Maremma • Italy 121 E11
Marennes • France 115 G1
Maresme, Costa del • Spain 117 D4
Mareth • Tunisia 131 E6
Maréttimo, I. • Italy 120 D1
Marfa Point • Malta 123 H1
Margai Caka • China 28 E1
Margao • Goa, India 137 B2
Margaret • WA, Australia 34 C6
Margarita, I. de • Venezuela 160 V
Margaríti • Greece 15 B4
Margate **Beach** • United Kingdom 101 [73]
Margate • United Kingdom 104 E2
Margate • South Africa 134 B5
Margate • FL, United States 49 C4
Margaux • France 115 G1
Margeride, Mts de la • France 10 I8
Marguerite Bay • Antarctica 54 (1) HH3
Mari-El • Russian Fed. 17 H3
Maria • Tubuai Is., French Polynesia 33 L8
Maria • Gambier Is., French Polynesia 33 N8
Maria Alm **Ski** • Austria 100 [166]
María Elena • Chile 52 C3
Maria Is. • St Lucia 161 P
Maria Laach • Germany 112 E1
Mariana • Brazil 163 C2
Marianao • Cuba 158 D1
Marianas Trench • Pacific Ocean 25 Q8
Mariankani • Kenya 131 G5
Marianna • AR, United States 46 J5
Marianna • FL, United States 154 H2
Marianne • Seychelles 133 K4
Mariannelund • Sweden 125 F8
Mariánské Lázne • Czech Rep. 128 B1
Mariapfarr **Ski** • Austria 100 [190]
Marias, I. • Mexico 157 E4
Marias, Is • Mexico 37 (1) A1
Mariato, Punta • Panama 37 E6
Marib • Yemen 18 E6
Maribo • Denmark 125 F14
Maribor • Slovenia 13 E11
Maribor • Slovenia 128 D1
Marie Byrd Land • Antarctica 54 (1) BB2
Marie Louise • Seychelles 133 K2
Marie-Galante • Guadeloupe 161 L
Mariedamm • Sweden 125 F4
Mariefred • Sweden 125 D3
Mariehamn • Finland 125 E3
Mariel • Cuba 158 D1
Marienbad • Czech Rep. 128 B1
Marienberg, Würzburg **Castle** • Germany 113 [166]
Marienburg **Castle** • Germany 113 [9]
Marienheide • Germany 111 B4
Mariental • Namibia 24 B4
Mariestad • Sweden 125 F3
Marietta • OH, United States 44 E6
Marietta • OK, United States 46 G6
Marietta • GA, United States 48 E4
Marigot • St Martin 160 D
Marigot • Dominica 161 M
Marigot Bay • St Lucia 161 P
Mariinsk • Russian Fed. 26 O6
Marijampole • Lithuania 126 B5
Marília • Brazil 52 F3
Marilléva **Ski** • Italy 100 [211]
Marilléva • Italy 121 E3
Marimba • Angola 24 B1
Marín • Spain 11 C2
Marín **Beach** • Spain 96 [93]
Marin, Luis Muñoz [Apt] • Puerto Rico 159 H2
Marina • CA, United States 45 B3
Marina Bay • Singapore 141 H4
Marina del Rey • CA, United States 152 C6
Marina di Massa • Italy 121 E10
Marina di Pietrasanta • Italy 121 E10
Marina di Pisa • Italy 12 E5
Marina Real del Oeste • Bermuda 159 J1
Marinduque • Philippines 31 G4
Marine World Africa USA **Park L** • CA, United States 150 [A]
Marineland of Florida • FL, United States 154 H4
Marinella, Golfo di • Sardinia, Italy 120 C2
Marinette • WI, United States 44 B3
Maringa • Dem. Rep. of Congo 23 C3
Maringá • Brazil 52 F3
Marinha Grande • Portugal 11 C5
Marinha Grande **Beach** • Portugal 96 [97]
Marino • Italy 12 G7
Marion • IA, United States 43 K5
Marion • IN, United States 44 C5
Marion • OH, United States 44 D5
Marion • AL, United States 48 D4
Marion • SC, United States 48 H3
Marion • IL, United States 48 C2
Marion • KY, United States 48 C2
Marion • VA, United States 48 G2
Marion, Lake • SC, United States 48 G4
Marion Reef • CL, Australia 144 B2
Maripa • Venezuela 51 D2
Mariposa • CA, United States 152 C3
Marisa • Indonesia 32 (1) B2
Mariscal Estigarribia • Paraguay 52 D3
Marismas, Las • Spain 116 B1
Maritime Museum • Singapore 141 H4
Maritsa • Europe 14 M7
Mariupol • Ukraine 17 F5
Marj, Al • Libya 21 D1
Marka • Somalia 23 G3
Markaryd • Sweden 125 F11
Marken • Netherlands 109 F2
Markermeer • Netherlands 109 F2
Markerwaarddijk • Netherlands 109 D7
Market Harborough • United Kingdom 7 L9
Markha • Russian Fed. 27 J4
Markha [Riv] • Russian Fed. 27 I3
Markham • OT, Canada 44 F4
Markham, Mt • Antarctica 54 (1) V1
Marki • Poland 13 K5
Märkisch Wilmersdorf • Germany 111 C3
Markópoulo **Beach** • Greece 97 [185]
Markounda • Central African Rep. 22 H3
Markovo • Russian Fed. 27 T4
Marksburg **Castle** • Germany 113 [65]
Marksville • LA, United States 47 H2
Marktheidenfeld • Germany 9 E7
Marktoberdorf • Germany 112 F6
Marktredwitz • Germany 9 H6
Marl • Germany 5 K3
Marl • Germany 111 B2
Marlboro • VT, United States 153 D3
Marlborough • QL, Australia 144 B4
Marlborough • New Zealand 145 E2
Marle • France 5 G5
Marley Beach • Bermuda 159 J3
Marlin • TX, United States 154 J3
Marlin Coast • QL, Australia 144 B1
Marloes **Beach** • United Kingdom 101 [175]
Marlow • United Kingdom 104 E1
Marmalete • Portugal 118 E1
Marmande • France 115 G3
Marmara • Turkey 15 I3
Marmara Adasi • Turkey 122 D3
Marmara Ereglisi • Turkey 15 I3
Marmara Gölü • Turkey 15 I5
Marmara, Sea of • Turkey 122 D3
Marmári • Greece 122 D4
Marmaris **Beach** • Turkey 97 [232]
Marmaris • Turkey 122 D9
Mármaro • Greece 122 D5
Marmarole, Gruppo delle • Italy 120 B4
Marmion Lake • OT, Canada 43 K2
Marmolada • Italy 120 B4
Marmot Basin **Ski** • AL, Canada 149 [11]
Marne • France 10 I4
Marne au Rhin, Canal de la • France 10 J5
Maro • Chad 21 C6
Maro [Riv] • Chad 20 I5
Maroantsetra • Madagascar 24 H3
Maromokotro • Madagascar 24 H2
Marondera • Zimbabwe 130 C2
Marónia • Greece 122 D2
Maroochydore • QL, Australia 144 B6
Maróstica • Italy 121 E3
Maroua • Cameroon 22 G2
Márpissa **Beach** • Greece 97 [205]
Marquesas • French Polynesia 33 N6
Marquette • MI, United States 44 B2
Marquis I. • Grenada 160 S
Marrah • Sudan 21 D5
Marrah, Jabal • Sudan 21 D5
Marrakech **Heritage C** • Morocco 86 [254]
Marrakech • Morocco 131 D3
Marree • SA, Australia 34 G5
Marromeu • Mozambique 24 F3
Marromeu, Reserve de **Park** • Mozambique 133 [141]
Marsá al Burayquah • Libya 21 C1
Marsa Alam • Egypt 131 F5
Marsa, El • France 11 L8
Marsabit • Kenya 131 G2
Marsabit Game Reserve • Kenya 131 G2
Marsabit Nat. Park • Kenya 131 G2
Marsabit Nat. Park **Park** • Kenya 133 [74]
Marsala • Sicily, Italy 120 D1
Marsalforn • Malta 123 H1
Marsalforn Bay • Malta 123 H1
Marsaskala • Malta 123 H4
Marsaxlokk • Malta 123 H4
Marsaxlokk Bay • Malta 123 H4
Marsberg • Germany 8 D5
Marseille • France 115 H3
Marsh Harbour • Bahamas 158 B1
Marsh I. • LA, United States 153 F3
Marsh-Billings Nat. Hist. Park **Park N** • VT, United States 151 [340]
Marshall • MN, United States 43 I4
Marshall • MO, United States 46 I3
Marshall • TX, United States 154 J2
MARSHALL IS. • Pacific Ocean 33 H4
Marshalltown • IA, United States 43 J5
Marshfield • WI, United States 43 K4
Marssum • Netherlands 109 D3
Märsta • Sweden 125 D2
Marstal **Beach** • Denmark 96 [44]
Marstal • Denmark 125 F14
Marston Moor • United Kingdom 90 A7
Marstrand • Sweden 125 F6
Marta • TX, United States 47 B2
Martaban, Gulf of • Myanmar 31 B3
Marten River • OT, Canada 44 F2
Martha Brae • Jamaica 159 F1
Martha's Vineyard • MA, United States 153 D8
Marthaville • LA, United States 153 F1
Martí • Cuba 158 D7
Martí,José [Apt] • Cuba 158 D2
Martigny • Switzerland 119 G6
Martigues • France 10 K10
Martigues **Beach** • France 96 [132]
Martil • Morocco 131 D2
Martim Longo • Portugal 118 E4
Martin • Slovak Rep. 13 H8
Martin • SD, United States 43 F5
Martin • TN, United States 48 C2
Martin Lake • AL, United States 48 E4
Martin Luther King Jr. Nat. Historic Site **Park N** • GA, United States 151 [206]
Martin Van Buren Nat. Hist. Site **Park N** • NY, United States 151 [308]
Martin Van Buren Nat. Hist. Site • NY, United States 153 D3
Martin Vaz, Is. • Atlantic Ocean 19 B7
Martin's Haven **Beach** • United Kingdom 101 [176]
MARTINIQUE • West Indies 161 N
Martins Bay • New Zealand 145 G2
Martinsburg • WV, United States 153 D9
Martinsville • IN, United States 44 B6
Martinsville • VA, United States 48 H2
Marton • New Zealand 35 E5
Martorell • Spain 117 D3
Martos • Spain 11 H7
Martre, Lac la • NT, Canada 38 H4
Martti • Finland 16 O3
Marungu, Mtns • Dem. Rep. of Congo 23 D5
Marv-Dasht • Iran 18 F4
Marvão • Portugal 11 D5
Marve **Beach** • India 138 E3
Marvine, Mt • UT, United States 45 G2
Marwar • India 137 C5
Mary • Turkmenistan 18 H2
Mary **Heritage C** • Turkmenistan 85 [93]
Mary Jane **Ski** • CO, United States 149 [99]
Mary McLeod Bethune Council House Nat. Hist. Site **Park N** • DC, United States 151 [281]
Maryborough • QL, Australia 144 B6
Maryborough • VI, Australia 144 C3
Maryland • United States 153 D10
Maryport • United Kingdom 104 C1
Marysville • OH, United States 44 D5
Marysville • CA, United States 45 B2
Marysville • KS, United States 46 G3
Maryville • MO, United States 46 H2
Maryville • TN, United States 48 F3
Marzahn (Berlin) • Germany 111 C2
Masada • Israel 135 A8
Masai • Malaysia 141 H2
Masai Mara Game Reserve • Kenya 131 G3
Masai Mara Nat. Reserve **Park** • Kenya 133 [81]
Masai Steppe • Tanzania 130 B2
Masaka • Uganda 23 E4
Masalembo, Kepulauan • Indonesia 143 J4
Masan • Rep. of Korea 30 E7
Masasi • Tanzania 130 B4
Masbate • Philippines 31 G4
Masbate [I.] • Philippines 31 G4
Mascara • Algeria 20 F1
Mascouche • QU, Canada 44 I3
Maseru • Lesotho 24 D5
Mashabih • Saudi Arabia 21 G2
Mashhad • Iran 18 G2
Mashonaland • Zimbabwe 130 C2
Masindi • Uganda 23 E3
Masirah, Jazirat • Oman 18 G5
Masirah, Khalij • Oman 18 G6
Mask, Lough • Ireland 108 C4
Maskad, Al • Somalia 23 H1
Mason • TX, United States 47 E2
Mason City • IA, United States 43 J5

Mason's Limestone Valley • New Zealand ... 145 F1
Maspalomas • Gran Canaria, Canary Is. ... 116 K4
Masqat • Oman ... 18 G5
Massa • Italy ... 12 E4
Massa Lubrense • Italy ... 121 G3
Massa Marittima • Italy ... 121 E11
Massachusetts • United States ... 153 D3
Massachusetts Bay • United States ... 153 D4
Massafra • Italy ... 12 L8
Massaguet • Chad ... 23 B1
Massangena • Mozambique ... 24 E4
Massanutten Ski • WV, United States ... 149 [164]
Massanutten • VA, United States ... 153 D9
Massawa • Eritrea ... 21 G4
Massena • NY, United States ... 44 H3
Massénya • Chad ... 20 I6
Masset • BC, Canada ... 38 E6
Massif Central • France ... 10 H8
Massillon • OH, United States ... 44 C6
Massinga • Mozambique ... 24 F4
Massy • France ... 115 G3
Masterton • New Zealand ... 35 E5
Mastigouche Prov. Park • QU, Canada ... 155 B3
Masuda • Japan ... 30 F7
Masuguru • Tanzania ... 130 B4
Masuho • Japan ... 140 C1
Masurai, Gunung • Indonesia ... 32 C3
Masuria • Poland ... 128 A1
Masuriska Sjöarna • Poland ... 13 K4
Masvingo • Zimbabwe ... 130 C4
Mat Lang, Ko • Thailand ... 132 H2
Mât, Rivière du • Réunion ... 131 H4
Mata-Utu • Wallis & Futuna ... 35 (2) E1
Matabeleland • Zimbabwe ... 130 C3
Matachewan • OT, Canada ... 44 E2
Matadi • Dem. Rep. of Congo ... 23 A5
Matagalpa • Nicaragua ... 37 D5
Matagami • QU, Canada ... 39 P7
Matagorda Bay • TX, United States ... 154 J6
Matagorda I. • TX, United States ... 154 J5
Matagorda Peninsula • TX, United States ... 154 J6
Matakana I. • New Zealand ... 145 F2
Matala • Angola ... 24 B2
Matala • Crete, Greece ... 123 E6
Matalascañas, Playa de • Spain ... 116 B5
Matale • Sri Lanka ... 138 D15
Matam • Senegal ... 20 C5
Matamata • New Zealand ... 145 F2
Matamoros • Mexico ... 47 F5
Matamwe • QU, Canada ... 156 D1
Matanzas • Cuba ... 158 D2
Matanzas, Fort, Nat. Mon. • FL, United States ... 154 H4
Matapédia • QU, Canada ... 156 D2
Matara • Eritrea ... 21 G5
Matara • Sri Lanka ... 138 D15
Matarani • Indonesia ... 32 F4
Matarani • Peru ... 163 B4
Mataranka • NT, Australia ... 34 F2
Mataró • Spain ... 117 D4
Mataura • France ... 145 G4
Mataura [Riv] • New Zealand ... 145 G4
Matehuala • Mexico ... 47 E5
Matelica • Italy ... 121 E12
Matelot • Trinidad & Tobago ... 160 I
Matera • Italy ... 12 L8
Matera Heritage C • Italy ... 86 [155]
Matese, Monti del • Italy ... 121 G1
Mátészalka • Hungary ... 13 L10
Mateur • Tunisia ... 131 E2
Matheran Hill Sta • India ... 138 E2
Matheson • OT, Canada ... 44 E1
Mathis • TX, United States ... 47 F3
Mathura • India ... 137 C2
Mati • Albania ... 14 H8
Mati • Philippines ... 31 H5
Matlock • United Kingdom ... 7 K8
Matmata • Tunisia ... 131 E6
Mato Grosso • Brazil ... 52 E2
Mato Grosso • Brazil ... 52 E1
Mato Grosso do Sul • Brazil ... 52 E2
Mato Grosso, Planalto do • Brazil ... 50 E6
Matobo Nat. Park • Zimbabwe ... 130 C3
Matobo Nat. Park Park • Zimbabwe ... 133 [113]
Matochkin Shar • Russian Fed. ... 26 I3
Matosinhos • Portugal ... 11 C3
Matra • Hungary ... 13 I10
Matrah • Oman ... 18 G5
Matre • Norway ... 124 C3
Matrei • Austria ... 119 H7
Matrûh • Egypt ... 131 F1
Matsu Liehtao • Taiwan ... 29 G5
Matsubara-ko • Japan ... 140 C1
Matsudo • Japan ... 140 C2
Matsudona Nat. Park • Zimbabwe ... 130 C1
Matsudona Nat. Park Park • Zimbabwe ... 133 [110]
Matsue • Japan ... 30 G7
Matsumoto • Japan ... 30 I6
Matsuyama • Japan ... 30 G8
Mattagami • OT, Canada ... 39 O7
Mattagami Lake • OT, Canada ... 44 E2
Mattancheri • India ... 138 D10
Mattawa • OT, Canada ... 155 B1
Mattersey • United Kingdom ... 104 C2
Matterhorn • Italy/Switzerland ... 119 G6
Matterhorn • NV, United States ... 42 H6
Matthew Town • Bahamas ... 158 B4
Matthews Ridge • Guyana ... 51 E2
Mattoon • IL, United States ... 44 A6
Matucana • Peru ... 163 B1
Matuku • Fiji Is. ... 35 (2) D2
Maturín • Venezuela ... 51 F1
Mau • India ... 137 C8
Mau Escarpment • Kenya ... 23 F4
Mau Kyun • Myanmar ... 31 B4
Maubeuge • France ... 10 I3
Maubuisson • France ... 115 G1
Mauganj • India ... 137 C8
Mauguio Beach • France ... 96 [130]
Maui • HI, United States ... 154 G3
Maulbronn Heritage C • Germany ... 86 [55]
Mauléon • France ... 115 J1
Maullín • Chile ... 53 B4
Maumee • OH, United States ... 44 D5
Maumere • Indonesia ... 32 (1) B4
Maun • Botswana ... 24 C3
Mauna Kea • HI, United States ... 154 G8
Mauna Loa • HI, United States ... 154 G8
Maunoir, Lac • NT, Canada ... 38 F3
Maupin • OR, United States ... 42 E4
Maurepas, Lake • LA, United States ... 153 F4
Maures, Massif des • France ... 115 H3
Maurice, Lake • SA, Australia ... 34 F5
Mauriene • France ... 115 F4
MAURITANIA • Africa ... 20 C5
MAURITIUS • Indian Ocean ... 132 H
Maus, Burg • Germany ... 112 E2
Mäuseturm • Germany ... 112 E2
Mauterndorf Ski • Austria ... 100 [190]
Mavinga • Angola ... 24 C3
Mavrovo Nat. Park Park N • F.Y.R. of Macedonia ... 89 [122]
Mavrovoúni • Greece ... 14 K8
Mawan • Shenzhen, China ... 139 B3

Mawgan Porth Beach • United Kingdom ... 101 [140]
Mawkmai • Myanmar ... 142 B1
Mawlaik • Myanmar ... 28 F4
Mawson [Base] • Antarctica ... 54 (1) L3
Maxglan [Apt] • Austria ... 119 H4
Máximo Gómez • Cuba ... 158 D3
Maxwell • Barbados ... 161 O
May Day Mtns • Jamaica ... 159 F4
May Pen • Jamaica ... 159 F4
May Point, Cape • NJ, United States ... 153 D10
Maya • Russian Fed. ... 27 M5
Maya • Indonesia ... 32 D3
Mayaguana • Bahamas ... 158 B4
Mayagüez • Puerto Rico ... 159 H3
Mayagüez, Bahía de • Puerto Rico ... 159 H3
Mayapán • Mexico ... 157 H1
Mayari • Cuba ... 158 D8
Maybell • CO, United States ... 45 H1
Maychew • Ethiopia ... 20 B5
Mayen • Germany ... 112 E1
Mayenne • France ... 10 E5
Mayenne [Riv] • France ... 10 E6
Mayens-de-l'Ours Ski • Switzerland ... 100 [83]
Mayens-de-Riddes Ski • Switzerland ... 100 [81]
Mayfield • KY, United States ... 48 C2
Maykain • Kazakhstan ... 26 M7
Maykop • Russian Fed. ... 17 G6
Maynard Lake • OT, Canada ... 43 I1
Maynas • Peru ... 51 B4
Maynooth • Ireland ... 108 B1
Mayo • Ireland ... 108 C2
Mayo • YT, Canada ... 49 N3
Mayo, Plains of • Ireland ... 108 C2
Mayon, Mt • Philippines ... 25 N8
Mayor I. • New Zealand ... 145 F2
MAYOTTE • Indian Ocean ... 24 G2
Mayreau • St Vincent & Gren. ... 161 R
Mayrhofen Ski • Austria ... 100 [143]
Mayrhofen • Austria ... 119 H7
Mayshoß • Germany ... 112 E1
Maysville • KY, United States ... 44 D6
Mayville • ND, United States ... 43 H3
Mazabuka • Zambia ... 24 D3
Mazagão • Brazil ... 51 G4
Mazagón • Spain ... 116 B1
Mazamet • France ... 10 H10
Mazar • China ... 26 M10
Mazar-e Sharif • Afghanistan ... 18 I2
Mazara del Vallo • Sicily, Italy ... 12 G11
Mazara, Val di • Sicily, Italy ... 120 D1
Mazarrón Beach • Spain ... 96 [117]
Mazarrón • Spain ... 117 C3
Mazarrón, Golfo de • Spain ... 11 J7
Mazartag • China ... 26 N10
Mazatenango • Guatemala ... 37 C5
Mazatlán • Mexico ... 37 (1) A1
Mazeikiai • Lithuania ... 126 B3
Mazeppa • Lithuania ... 16 I5
Mazinga Shan • China ... 29 B2
Mazowe • Zimbabwe ... 130 C2
Mazowe [Riv] • Mozambique/Zimbabwe ... 130 C2
Mazurski Nat. Park Park N • Poland ... 89 [92]
Mazyr • Belarus ... 17 D4
Mazzarò • Sicily, Italy ... 120 D2
Mbabane • Swaziland ... 24 E5
Mbaiki • Central African Rep. ... 23 B3
Mbala • Zambia ... 23 E5
Mbalabala • Zimbabwe ... 24 D4
Mbale • Uganda ... 23 E3
Mbalmayo • Cameroon ... 23 G4
Mbamba Bay • Tanzania ... 130 B3
Mbandaka • Dem. Rep. of Congo ... 23 B3
Mbanga • Cameroon ... 22 F4
Mbanza Congo • Angola ... 23 A5
Mbanza-Ngungu • Dem. Rep. of Congo ... 23 A5
Mbarara • Uganda ... 23 D4
Mbé • Cameroon ... 23 G4
Mbéré • Cameroon/Central African Rep. ... 22 H3
Mbeya • Tanzania ... 130 B3
Mbinda • Congo ... 22 G5
Mbomou • Central African Rep./Dem. Rep. of Congo ... 23 D2
Mbour • Senegal ... 20 A2
Mbout • Mauritania ... 20 C5
Mbua • Fiji Is. ... 35 (2) D2
Mbuji-Mayi • Dem. Rep. of Congo ... 23 C5
Mbulu • Tanzania ... 130 B2
Mbwemburu • Tanzania ... 130 B4
McAdam • NB, Canada ... 44 I3
McAfee Peak • NV, United States ... 42 H6
McAlester • OK, United States ... 46 H5
McAllen • TX, United States ... 47 E4
McCall • ID, United States ... 152 B4
McCamey • TX, United States ... 47 C2
McCarran [Apt] • NV, United States ... 152 C4
McCarthy • AK, United States ... 49 M3
McClintock Channel • NU, Canada ... 38 K2
McClintock, Mt • Antarctica ... 54 (1) V1
McClure, Lake • CA, United States ... 45 B3
McClure Strait • NT, Canada ... 36 I2
McClusky • ND, United States ... 43 F3
McComb • MS, United States ... 153 F2
McCook • NE, United States ... 46 E2
McCreary • MN, Canada ... 43 G1
McDonald I. • Southern Ocean ... 3 R10
McDonald I. Heritage N • Southern Ocean ... 83 [151]
McDonald Peak • CA, United States ... 42 E6
McGrath • AK, United States ... 49 J3
McGregor Lake • AL, Canada ... 42 I1
McHenry • IL, United States ... 44 A4
Mchinga • Tanzania ... 130 B4
McIlwraith Range • QL, Australia ... 34 H2
McIntosh • SD, United States ... 43 F4
McKeesport • PA, United States ... 44 F5
McKenzie • TN, United States ... 48 C2
McKenzie Bridge • OR, United States ... 42 D4
McKerrow, Lake • New Zealand ... 145 G2
McKinley, Mt • AK, United States ... 49 K3
McKinney • TX, United States ... 154 J1
McLean Mtn • WA, United States ... 44 K2
McLean's Town • Bahamas ... 158 B2
McMillan, Lake • NM, United States ... 47 B1
McMinnville • TN, United States ... 48 E3
McMinnville • OR, United States ... 54 (1) V2
McMurdo [Base] • Antarctica ... 54 (1) V2
McPherson • KS, United States ... 46 G3
McRae • GA, United States ... 48 F4
Mdennah • Algeria/Mali ... 20 D4
Mdina • Malta ... 123 H4
Mdo • Morocco ... 131 D1
Me'arot Hever • Israel ... 135 A8
Mead, Lake • AZ/NV, United States ... 153 E1
Mead's Bay • Anguilla ... 160 C
Meade • KS, United States ... 46 E4
Meadow Lake • SA, Canada ... 38 J6
Meadview • AZ, United States ... 45 E4
Meadville • PA, United States ... 44 E5
Mealhada • Portugal ... 11 C4

Mealy Mtns • NF, Canada ... 39 T6
Meander • AL, Canada ... 38 H5
Meath • Ireland ... 108 B1
Meaux • France ... 115 E2
Mebridege • Angola ... 23 A5
Mecca • Saudi Arabia ... 18 C5
Mechelen • Belgium ... 109 D14
Mecheria • Algeria ... 20 E2
Mecidiye • Turkey ... 15 H3
Mecklenburg • Germany ... 112 E1
Mecklenburg-Vorpommern • Germany ... 8 H3
Mecklenburger Bucht • Germany ... 8 G2
Mecklenburgische Seenplatte • Germany ... 8 H3
Mecsek • Hungary ... 13 H11
Mecula • Mozambique ... 24 F2
Medan • Indonesia ... 143 G2
Medea • Algeria ... 11 N8
Mededsiz Tepe • Turkey ... 123 N2
Medellín • Colombia ... 51 B2
Medenine • Tunisia ... 131 E6
Mederdra • Mauritania ... 20 B5
Medewi Beach • Bali, Indonesia ... 143 H1
Medford • OK, United States ... 46 G4
Medford • OR, United States ... 152 B3
Medgidia • Romania ... 128 E2
Media Luna • Cuba ... 158 D7
Media Luna, Arrecife de la • Honduras/Nicaragua ... 160 A12
Medias • Romania ... 14 L3
Medical Springs • OR, United States ... 42 G4
Medicine Bow Mtns • CO/WY, United States ... 46 B2
Medicine Hat • AL, Canada ... 38 I6
Medicine Lodge • KS, United States ... 46 F4
Medina • Saudi Arabia ... 18 C5
Medina • OH, United States ... 44 D5
Medina • NY, United States ... 44 F4
Medina de Rioseco • Spain ... 11 E3
Medina del Campo • Spain ... 11 G3
Medina-Sidonia • Spain ... 11 F8
Medinaceli • Spain ... 11 I3
Mediterranean cruise area • Africa/Europe ... 81 C
Mediterranean Sea • Europe ... 4 N11
Mediterranean seaboard prehistoric rock-art sites Heritage C • Spain ... 86 [111]
Medjerda, Mts de la • Algeria/Tunisia ... 12 C12
Mednogorsk • Russian Fed. ... 26 I7
Mednyy, Ostrov • Russian Fed. ... 27 S6
Médoc • France ... 115 G1
Medora • ND, United States ... 43 E3
Medouneu • Gabon ... 22 G4
Medvednica • Russian Fed. ... 17 G4
Medvedica • Croatia ... 14 C4
Medvezh'yegorsk • Russian Fed. ... 17 E2
Medvezhi, Ostrovo • Russian Fed. ... 27 R2
Meekatharra • WA, Australia ... 34 C5
Meeker • CO, United States ... 45 I1
Meerkerk Nat. Park • NF, Canada ... 156 D3
Meenambakkam • India ... 138 D7
Meerane • Germany ... 9 H6
Meerbusch • Germany ... 111 B3
Meersburg • Germany ... 112 F5
Meersburg Castle • Germany ... 113 [114]
Meerut • India ... 137 C3
Meeteetse • WY, United States ... 42 K4
Mega • Ethiopia ... 23 F3
Mega • Indonesia ... 32 (1) D3
Megálo Khorion • Greece ... 15 I7
Megalópolis • Greece ... 15 D6
Meganisi • Greece ... 123 C4
Mégantic, Mont • QU, Canada ... 44 J3
Mégara • Greece ... 15 E6
Mégève Ski • France ... 100 [24]
Mégève • France ... 115 F2
Meghalaya • India ... 28 F3
Mégrit • Greece ... 123 F3
Meharry, Mt • WA, Australia ... 34 C4
Mehdiya-Plage • Morocco ... 131 D1
Mehran • Iran ... 18 F4
Mei Yuan • China ... 139 C1
Meiganga • Cameroon ... 22 G3
Meijinomori-Mino Quasi Nat. Park • Japan ... 140 B2
Meikтila • Myanmar ... 31 B2
Meinershagen • Germany ... 111 B4
Meiningen • Germany ... 9 F6
Meiringen • Switzerland ... 119 G2
Meiringspoort • South Africa ... 134 C7
Meisenheim • Germany ... 112 E4
Meissen • Germany ... 9 I5
Meizhou • China ... 29 F6
Mejez el Bab • Tunisia ... 131 E2
Mékambo • Gabon ... 22 G4
Meke Gölü • Turkey ... 123 G1
Mekele • Ethiopia ... 21 G5
Mekerrhane, Sebkha • Algeria ... 20 F3
Mékhé • Senegal ... 20 F3
Mekong • Asia ... 31 B4
Mekong, Mouths of the • Vietnam ... 141 E3
Mekongga, Gunung • Indonesia ... 32 (1) B3
Mekoryuk • AK, United States ... 49 H3
Mékrou • Africa ... 22 C2
Melaka • Malaysia ... 32 C2
Melanesia • Pacific Ocean ... 33 C3
Melaque • Mexico ... 157 G2
Melaselkä • Russian Fed. ... 16 N3
Melawi • Indonesia ... 32 E3
Melbourne • VI, Australia ... 144 C3
Melbourne • FL, United States ... 154 H6
Melbie • Norway ... 16 H2
Melbourne-Frith • Switzerland ... 119 G3
Meldorf • Germany ... 8 E2
Melfort • AL, Canada ... 42 I1
Melenki • Russian Fed. ... 125 E1
Melendugno • Italy ... 12 J8
Melfi • Italy ... 12 J8
Melfi • Chad ... 23 B1
Meli Park Park L • Belgium ... 109 [45]
Meli Park Beach • Belgium ... 109 E1
Melidoni • Crete, Greece ... 123 E2
Melilla • Africa ... 131 D2
Melilla • Argentina ... 163 D1
Melipilla • Chile ... 52 B5
Melissáni • Cephalonia, Greece ... 122 C2
Melita • MN, United States ... 43 F2
Melitopol' • Ukraine ... 17 F5
Mélivia • Greece ... 122 D1
Mellégue • Algeria/Tunisia ... 131 E1
Mellerud • Sweden ... 125 F3
Mellieha • Malta ... 123 H1
Mellient Abbey • Ireland ... 108 B2
Melmoth • South Africa ... 134 B4
Melnik • Czech Rep. ... 128 B2
Melo • Uruguay ... 52 F5
Melolo • Indonesia ... 32 (1) A4
Melrose • MN, United States ... 43 H4
Melsungen • Germany ... 9 E5
Meltaus • Finland ... 16 M3
Melton Mowbray • United Kingdom ... 104 C2
Melún • France ... 115 E4
Melville • SA, Canada ... 38 K6
Melville Bay • NT, Australia ... 34 G2

Melville, Cape • QL, Australia ... 34 H2
Melville Hall [Apt] • Dominica ... 161 M
Melville Hills • NT/NU, Canada ... 38 G3
Melville I. • NT, Australia ... 34 F1
Melville I. • NT/NU, Canada ... 36 F2
Melville Is. • Trinidad & Tobago ... 160 T
Melville, Lake • NF, Canada ... 39 T6
Melville Peninsula • NU, Canada ... 39 O3
Memba, Baía de • Mozambique ... 24 G2
Membaramo • Indonesia ... 32 (1) E3
Memboro • Indonesia ... 32 (1) A4
Memel • South Africa ... 134 B1
Memmert • Germany ... 9 B7
Memmingen • Germany ... 112 F2
Mempawah Heritage C • Egypt ... 86 [274]
Memphis • Egypt ... 131 F1
Memphis • TN, United States ... 48 B3
Mena • Ukraine ... 17 E4
Mena • AR, United States ... 46 H4
Menabe • Madagascar ... 24 G4
Menaggio • Italy ... 12 L8
Ménaka • Mali ... 20 F5
Menangkabu • Indonesia ... 32 (1) A4
Menara [Apt] • Morocco ... 131 D3
Menard • TX, United States ... 47 E2
Menasha • WI, United States ... 43 L4
Mendaya • Bali, Indonesia ... 143 H1
Mende • France ... 115 H2
Mendebo • Ethiopia ... 23 F2
Menden • Germany ... 9 B8
Mendenhall • MS, United States ... 48 C5
Menderes, Adnan [Apt] • Turkey ... 122 D5
Mendi • Papua New Guinea ... 35 (1) C2
Mendip Hills • United Kingdom ... 104 F3
Mendocino • CA, United States ... 152 C3
Mendocino, Cape • CA, United States ... 42 C6
Mendota • CA, United States ... 45 B3
Mendota I. • United States ... 46 K2
Mendoza • Argentina ... 52 C5
Menemen • Turkey ... 122 D5
Menen • Belgium ... 5 G4
Menfi • Sicily, Italy ... 12 G11
Menfi Beach • Sicily, Italy ... 97 [152]
Menfi • Sicily, Italy ... 120 D3
Mengen • Germany ... 112 F1
Menggala • Indonesia ... 32 D3
Mengkalihat, Tanjung • Indonesia ... 32 (1) E2
Menídio • Greece ... 15 E2
Menik, NS, Australia ... 34 G7
Meningie • SA, Australia ... 34 G7
Menjangan • Bali, Indonesia ... 143 H1
Menjapa, Gunung • Indonesia ... 143 H1
Menno • SD, United States ... 43 H5
Menomonee Falls • WI, United States ... 44 A4
Menongue • Angola ... 24 B2
Menor, Mar • Spain ... 117 C3
Menorca • Spain ... 11 P5
Mentakab • Malaysia ... 141 G4
Mentawai, Kepulauan • Indonesia ... 32 B3
Mentawai, Selat • Indonesia ... 32 B3
Mentok • Indonesia ... 32 C3
Mentor • OH, United States ... 44 E5
Menton Beach • France ... 96 [134]
Menton • France ... 115 H2
Menuires, les Ski • France ... 100 [42]
Menzies • WA, Australia ... 34 D5
Menzies, Mt • Antarctica ... 54 (1) L2
Meoqui • Mexico ... 47 B3
Meppel • Netherlands ... 109 D8
Meppen • Germany ... 8 C4
Meravia • Ethiopia ... 23 F3
Merak • Java, Indonesia ... 143 J1
Meran • Italy ... 120 B1
Merano • Italy ... 120 B1
Merapi, Gunung • Indonesia ... 143 G4
Merauke • Indonesia ... 32 (1) F4
Merbau, Gunung • Java, Indonesia ... 143 J7
Mercantour, Parc nat. du Park N • France ... 89 [68]
Mercantour, Parc nat. du • France ... 115 H2
Mercara • Italy ... 121 G4
Merced • CA, United States ... 45 B3
Mercedario • Argentina ... 52 C5
Mercedes • San Luis, Argentina ... 52 C5
Mercedes • Corrientes, Argentina ... 52 E4
Mercedes • Uruguay ... 163 D2
Mercedes • TX, United States ... 47 F4
Mercedes • Argentina ... 52 C5
Mercer Dam • QU, Canada ... 155 B2
Mercury I. • New Zealand ... 35 E3
Mercury, Cape • NU, Canada ... 39 S4
Meredoua • Algeria ... 35 (2) B1
Meredoua • Algeria ... 20 F3
Merefa • Ukraine ... 17 F5
Merenga • Russian Fed. ... 27 Q4
Mergenevo • Kazakhstan ... 17 I5

Merti • Kenya ... 23 F3
Mértola • Portugal ... 11 D7
Méru • France ... 115 E1
Meru • France ... 115 E1
Meru, Mt • Tanzania ... 130 B2
Meru Nat. Park • Kenya ... 131 G2
Meru Nat. Park Park • Kenya ... 131 G2
Merv Heritage C • Turkmenistan ... 85 [93]
Merv • Turkmenistan ... 127 D2
Meryemana • Turkey ... 122 D9
Merzig • Germany ... 9 B7
Mesa • AZ, United States ... 153 E3
Mesa Verde Nat. Park Heritage C • CO, United States ... 84 [6]
Mesa Verde Nat. Park Park N • CO, United States ... 150 [93]
Mesa Verde Nat. Park • CO, United States ... 153 E2
Mesabi Range • MN, United States ... 43 J3
Mesagne • Italy ... 12 L8
Mescalero • NM, United States ... 46 C6
Meschede • Germany ... 9 E5
Meschers-sur-Gironde Beach • France ... 96 [84]
Meseberg • Germany ... 9 B7
Meset • Turkey ... 15 G2
Meski • Morocco ... 131 D4
Meskiá • Crete, Greece ... 123 E5
Meso Gerakari Beach • Greece ... 97 [172]
Mesola • Italy ... 120 B2
Mesolóngi • Greece ... 15 C5
Mesolóngi Beach • Greece ... 97 [175]
Mesolóngi • Corfu, Greece ... 122 B1
Messotópos Beach • Greece ... 97 [199]
Mestá • Bulgaria ... 15 E2
Mestá • Greece ... 122 D5
Mesuji • Indonesia ... 32 D3
Meta • Colombia ... 51 C2
Meta • Italy ... 121 G3
Meta Incognita Peninsula • NU, Canada ... 39 R4
Métabief Ski • France ... 100 [7]
Metairie • LA, United States ... 48 B6
Metaline Falls • WA, United States ... 42 G2
Metamórfossi Beach • Greece ... 97 [192]
Metán • Argentina ... 52 D4
Metaponto • Italy ... 12 K8
Metéora Heritage N • Greece ... 83 [67]
Metéora Heritage C • Greece ... 86 [209]
Méthana • Greece ... 15 E6
Méthana [Peninsula] • Greece ... 122 D7
Methil • United Kingdom ... 104 D5
Methóni Beach • Greece ... 97 [181]
Methven • New Zealand ... 145 G3
Metionga Lake • OT, Canada ... 43 K2
Metković • Croatia ... 128 C4
Metlakatla • AK, United States ... 49 O4
Metmárfag • Western Sahara ... 20 C3
Metóhi Beach • Greece ... 97 [179]
Metohija • F.R. of Yugoslavia ... 14 H7
Metropolis • IL, United States ... 48 C2
Metsch • Germany ... 112 D3
Mettler • CA, United States ... 45 C4
Mettmann • Germany ... 111 B3
Metz • France ... 10 L4
Metzingen • Germany ... 112 F1
Meulaboh • Indonesia ... 143 G1
Meurthe • France ... 10 L5
Meurval • Indonesia ... 143 G1
Meuse • Belgium/France ... 109 D15
Meuse Valley • Belgium ... 109 D15
Meuselwitz • Germany ... 9 H5
Mevagissey • United Kingdom ... 104 F4
Mexia • TX, United States ... 47 F2
Mexiana • Brazil ... 51 H4
Mexicali • Mexico ... 157 F1
Mexican Riviera cruise area • Mexico/United States ... 80 A3
Mexicana, Altiplanicie • Mexico ... 40 F6
MEXICO • N. America ... 36 G8
Mexico • MO, United States ... 46 H3
México [Adm] • Mexico ... 157 E9
México City Heritage C • Mexico ... 86 [22]
Mexico City • Mexico ... 157 G4
Mexico, Gulf of • N. America ... 37 C2
Meymaneh • Afghanistan ... 18 H2
Mezen • Russian Fed. ... 17 G1
Mezen [Riv] • Russian Fed. ... 17 H2
Mezenskaya Guba • Russian Fed. ... 17 G1
Mezenskaya Guba • Russian Fed. ... 17 G1
Mezőkövesd • Hungary ... 13 J10
Mezőtúr • Hungary ... 128 C1
Mfanganu I • Uganda ... 131 G3
Mgarr • Malta ... 123 H1
Mgungundlovu • South Africa ... 134 B4
Mhamid • Morocco ... 131 D6
Mi • Japan ... 30 F7
Miami • FL, United States ... 154 H8
Miami • MO, United States ... 46 H4
Miami Beach • FL, United States ... 154 H8
Miami Seaquarium Park L • United States ... 151 [FF]
Miami Seaquarium • United States ... 154 H8
Miami Springs • United States ...
Miandrivazo • Madagascar ... 24 H3
Miangas • Indonesia ... 32 (1) C2
Mianduhe • China ... 29 C4
Mianwali • Pakistan ... 18 J3
Miaoli • Taiwan ... 29 G6
Mica Dam • BC, Canada ... 38 I6
Michelson, Mt • AK, United States ... 49 M2
Michendorf • Germany ... 111 C3
Michés • Dominican Rep. ... 159 G4
Michigan • United States ... 44 C4
Michigan [Adm] • United States ... 41 I2
Michigan City • IN, United States ... 44 B5
Michigan, Lake • United States ... 44 A4
Michipicoten Bay • OT, Canada ... 44 C2
Michipicoten I. • OT, Canada ... 39 N7
Michoacán • Mexico ... 37 (1) B2
Michurin • Bulgaria ... 128 E2
Michurinsk • Russian Fed. ... 17 G4
Micoud • St Lucia ... 161 P
Micronesia • Pacific Ocean ... 33 H5
MICRONESIA, FEDERATED STATES OF • Pacific Ocean ... 33 F5
Middelburg • South Africa ... 24 D5
Middelburg • Netherlands ... 109 D10
Middelburg • South Africa ... 134 C4
Middelfart Beach • Denmark ... 96 [44]
Middelfart • Denmark ... 125 F9
Middelharnis • Netherlands ... 109 E10
Middelkerke-Bad • Belgium ... 109 E1
Middle Andaman • India ... 28 F6

Middle Caoicos • Turks & Caicos Is. ... 158 C1
Middlebury • VT, United States ... 44 I3
Middlefield • CT, United States ... 48 F2
Middlesborough • United Kingdom ... 7 K7
Middlesex • United Kingdom ... 104 E1
Middlesex • Jamaica ... 159 F2
Middleton • WI, United States ... 43 L5
Middleton • NS, Canada ... 156 D7
Middleton Reef • Australia ... 33 H8
Middletown • OH, United States ... 44 C6
Middletown • PA, United States ... 44 G5
Middletown • NY, United States ... 44 H5
Middletown • CT, United States ... 44 I5
Middletown • RI, United States ... 44 J5
Midelt • Morocco ... 20 E2
Midès • Tunisia ... 131 E3
Midou • France ... 114 B4
Midi, Canal du • France ... 10 G10
Midi-Pyrénées • France ... 114 A3
Midland • MI, United States ... 44 C4
Midland • TX, United States ... 47 C2
Midland • OT, Canada ... 155 B5
Midleton • Ireland ... 108 C8
Midlothian • United Kingdom ... 104 B4
Midmar Nature Reserve • South Africa ... 134 B3
Midnight Sun Coast • Sweden ... 124 A4
Midongy Atsimo • Madagascar ... 24 H4
Midwest • WY, United States ... 42 L5
Midwest City • OK, United States ... 46 G5
Midzor • F.R. of Yugoslavia ... 14 J6
Mie • Japan ... 140 A8
Miechów • Poland ... 128 C2
Miedzyrzecz • Poland ... 13 E5
Mielan • France ... 115 J2
Mielec • Poland ... 128 C2
Miena • Australia ... 144 M3
Mier • India ... 137 C2
Miercurea Ciuc • Romania ... 14 M3
Mieres • Spain ... 11 F1
Miesbach • Germany ... 112 F7
Migiorn, Platja de • Formentera, Spain ... 117 G4
Migori • Kenya ... 131 G3
Miguel Hidalgo [Apt] • Mexico ... 157 G1
Mihaliçcik • Turkey ... 140 C4
Mihara-yama • Japan ... 140 C3
Miho • Japan ... 140 C3
Mijares • Spain ... 11 K4
Mijas Beach • Spain ... 96 [114]
Mijas Costa • Spain ... 116 B6
Mijdrecht • Netherlands ... 109 F2
Mikhaylovka • Russian Fed. ... 17 G4
Miki • Japan ... 140 B1
Mikines • Greece ... 15 D6
Mikkeli • Finland ... 16 N6
Mikkeli [Adm] • Finland ... 16 N6
Mikonos Beach • Greece ... 97 [204]
Mikonos • Greece ... 122 D8
Mikonou, Stenó • Greece ... 15 G6
Mikra Préspa, Limni • Greece ... 15 C3
Mikumi • Tanzania ... 130 B4
Mikumi Nat. Park • Tanzania ... 130 B4
Mikun • Russian Fed. ... 17 I2
Mikun-sanmyaku • Japan ... 30 J8
Mikura • Japan ... 30 J8
Milan Heritage C • Italy ... 86 [129]
Milan • Italy ... 121 E6
Milan • TN, United States ... 48 C3
Milan • Italy ... 121 E6
Milange • Mozambique ... 24 F3
Milano Heritage C • Italy ... 86 [129]
Milano • Italy ... 121 E6
Milano Maritima • Italy ... 121 E8
Milas • Turkey ... 122 D9
Milatos • Crete, Greece ... 123 E2
Milazzo • Sicily, Italy ... 120 D2
Mildenstein Castle • Germany ... 113 [202]
Mildura • NS, Australia ... 144 B3
Miles • QL, Australia ... 144 B6
Miles City • MT, United States ... 43 D3
Milestone • SA, Canada ... 43 D1
Miletus • Turkey ... 122 D8
Milevsko • Czech Rep. ... 128 B4
Milford • PA, United States ... 44 H5
Milford • NS, Australia ... 44 H6
Milford • VT, United States ... 45 F2
Milford Haven • United Kingdom ... 7 G10
Milford Lake • KS, United States ... 46 G3
Milford Sound • New Zealand ... 145 G2
Milford Track • New Zealand ... 145 G2
Milh, Ra's al • Libya ... 21 D1
Miliana • Algeria ... 11 N8
Miliés • Greece ... 15 E4
Milikapiti • NT, Australia ... 34 F2
Milk [Riv] • Canada/United States ... 42 J2
Milk River • AL, Canada ... 42 I2
Milk River Sap • Jamaica ... 159 F3
Milkovo • Russian Fed. ... 27 Q6
Mill I. • NU, Canada ... 39 P4
Millau • France ... 10 I9
Millbank • SD, United States ... 43 H4
Mille Lacs Lake • MN, United States ... 43 I3
Mille Lacs, Lac des • OT, Canada ... 43 K2
Milledgeville • GA, United States ... 48 F4
Millerovo • Russian Fed. ... 17 G5
Millersburg • PA, United States ... 44 G5
Millevaches, Plateau de • France ... 115 G2
Millicent • SA, Australia ... 34 H7
Millinocket • ME, United States ... 44 K3
Millwood Lake • AR, United States ... 46 I6
Milnthorpe • United Kingdom ... 104 C4
Milos Beach • Greece ... 97 [207]
Milos • Greece ... 122 D7
Milparinka • NS, Australia ... 34 H5
Miltenberg • Germany ... 112 D4
Milton • New Zealand ... 145 G5
Milton • PA, United States ... 44 G5
Milton • FL, United States ... 154 H1
Milton Freewater • OR, United States ... 42 F4
Milton Keynes • United Kingdom ... 7 L9
Milton-Malbay • Ireland ... 108 C6
Milville • NJ, United States ... 44 H6
Milwaukee • WI, United States ... 44 B4
Milyas • Turkey ... 123 F1
Mimaland • Malaysia ... 141 G4
Mimizan • France ... 115 G3
Mimizan, Fôret de • France ... 115 G3
Min • China ... 31 F1
Min • China ... 29 C4
Mina • Algeria ... 11 L9
Mina Sa'ud • Kuwait ... 18 E4
Minami Iwo-jima • Japan ... 140 A13
Minamata • Japan ... 30 J8
Minamiashigara • Japan ... 140 C3
Minamidaito-jima • Japan ... 140 A11
Minas • Uruguay ... 163 D2
Minas Gerais • Brazil ... 52 G2
Minbu • Myanmar ... 31 A2
Minch • United Kingdom ... 6 F4
Minch, North • United Kingdom ... 6 G3

Minchinmávida, Volcán • Chile 53 B4
Mincio • Italy 121 E7
Mindanao • Philippines 31 H5
Mindel • Germany 9 F8
Mindelheim • Germany 112 F2
Mindelo • Cape Verde 22 (1) B1
Minden • Germany 8 D4
Minden • QT, Canada 44 F3
Minden • NE, United States 46 F2
Minden • LA, United States 153 F1
Mindoro • Philippines 31 G4
Mindoro Strait • Philippines 31 G4
Mine Centre • OT, Canada 43 J2
Minehead • United Kingdom 104 F2
Mineiros • Brazil 52 F2
Mineola • TX, United States 154 J2
Mineral Mtns •
  UT, United States 45 F2
Mineral Wells •
  TX, United States 154 J1
Minerva Reefs • Pacific Ocean . . . 33 J3
Minervois • France 114 B3
Minfeng • China 28 D1
Ming Village • Singapore 141 H3
Mingan • QL, Canada 156 D2
Mingan Archipelago • QL, Canada 156 D2
Mingan Archipelago Nat. Park Park N •
  QL, Canada . . . . 156 [30]
Mingenew • WA, Australia 34 C5
Minglanilla • Spain 11 J5
Minhang Hi-Tech Zone • China . . 139 C4
Minho • Portugal 11 H2
Minho, Rio • Jamaica 159 F4
Minicoy I. • India 118 D13
Minilya • WA, Australia 34 B4
Minna • Nigeria 22 F3
Minneapolis • MN, United States . 43 J4
Minneburg Castle • Germany . . . 113 [81]
Minnedosa • MN, Canada 43 G1
Minnehaha, Lake •
  FL, United States 151 C1
Minnesota [Adm] • United States . 43 I3
Minnesota [Riv] •
  MN, United States 43 I4
Miño • Spain 11 D2
Miño Beach • Spain . . . . 96 [92]
Minorca • Spain . . . . 117 F
Minot • ND, United States 43 F2
Minsk • Belarus 17 D4
Minsk Mazowiecki • Poland 13 K5
Minto, Lac • QU, Canada 39 P5
Minto, Mt • Antarctica 54 (1) I2
Minturn • CO, United States 45 I2
Minusinsk • Russian Fed. 26 P7
Minute Man Nat. Hist. Park Park N •
  MA, United States . . . . 151 [339]
Minya, El • Egypt 131 F3
Miquasha Park Heritage N •
  QU, Canada . . . . 82 [7]
Mira • Italy 12 G3
Mira Beach • Portugal . . . . 96 [96]
Mira • Portugal 118 E2
Mirabad • Afghanistan 18 H3
Mirabel [Apt] • QU, Canada 155 B3
Mirabilandia Park L • Italy . . . . . 98 [83]
Mirabilandia • Italy 12 I4
Miracema • Brazil 163 C2
Miraflores • Boyacá, Colombia . . 51 C2
Miraflores • Guaviare, Colombia . 51 C3
Miragoâne • Haiti 159 G6
Miraj • India 138 D2
Miramar • Argentina 163 D4
Miramar • FL, United States 49 C4
Miramar [Apt] • Italy 121 E12
Miramar Beach • Goa, India 137 B1
Mirambeau • France 10 E3
Mirambelou, Kólpos •
  Crete, Greece 123 E8
Miranda de Ebro • Spain 11 H2
Mirándola • Portugal 11 D3
Mirándola • Italy 121 E7
Mirapolis Park L • France . . . . . 98 [67]
Mirapolis • France 115 E1
Mirbat • Oman 18 F6
Mirdita • Albania 14 H8
Mirebalais • Haiti 159 G6
Mirepoix • France 11 M1
Miri • Malaysia 32 E2
Miria • Niger 20 G6
Mirik Hill Sta • India 138 G4
Mirim, Lagoa • Brazil/Uruguay . . 52 F5
Mirina Beach • Greece . . . . 97 [198]
Mirina • Greece 122 D2
Mirny [Base] • Antarctica 54 (1) O3
Mirnyy • Russian Fed. 27 H4
Mirpur Khas • Pakistan 28 A3
Mirs Bay • China 139 B4
Mirtoan Sea • Greece 15 F7
Mirtós Pélagos • Greece 15 F7
Mirtos • Crete, Greece 123 E7
Mirzapur • India 137 C8
Misaki • Japan 140 B3
Misano Adriático • Italy 121 E12
Miscou I. • NB, Canada 156 D2
Miseno, Capo • Italy 121 G3
Mish, Slieve • Ireland 108 C5
Mishan • China 27 L7
Mishima • Japan 140 C3
Mishima [I.] • Japan 140 E4
Misima • Papua New Guinea . . . 35 (1) B4
Miskitos, Cayos • Nicaragua . . . 160 A12
Miskitos, Costa de • Nicaragua . . 37 E5
Miskolc • Hungary 13 J9
Misoöl • Indonesia 32 (1) D3
Misouah Hills •
  MN, United States 43 K3
Misratah • Libya 21 B1
Misrikh • India 137 C3
Missinaibi Lake • OT, Canada . . . 44 D1
Mission • SD, United States 43 F5
Mission • TX, United States 47 E4
Mission Beach • QL, Australia . . 144 B1
Mission San Javier • Mexico . . . 157 F4
Mississagi • OT, Canada 44 D2
Mississauga • OT, Canada 155 B9
Mississippi [Adm] •
  United States 48 C4
Mississippi [Riv] •
  United States 41 H3
Mississippi River Delta •
  LA, United States 153 F4
Mississippi Sound •
  LA/MS, United States 48 C6
Missoula • MT, United States . . 152 B2
Missouri [Adm] • United States . . 46 I3
Missouri Breaks •
  MT, United States 152 A2
Missouri [Riv] • United States . . . 41 H4
Missouri Valley •
  IA, United States 46 H2
Mistassibi • QU, Canada 39 Q6
Mistassini • QU, Canada 39 Q6
Mistassini, Lac • QU, Canada . . . 39 Q6
Mistassini [Riv] • QU, Canada . . . 39 Q7
Misterhult • Sweden 125 E4
Mistrás • Greece 15 D6
Mistrás Heritage C • Greece . . . 86 [213]
Misty Fjords •
  AK, United States 49 O4
Mitchell • QL, Australia 144 B5
Mitchell • OR, United States . . . 152 B4
Mitchell • SD, United States 43 G5
Mitchell Lake •
  AL, United States 48 D4
Mitchell, Mt •
  NC, United States 48 F3
Mitchell [Riv] • QL, Australia . . . 34 H3

Mitchell River Mission •
  QL, Australia 34 H3
Mitchelstown • Ireland 108 C6
Mithimna Beach • Greece . . . . . 97 [199]
Mithimna • Greece 122 D5
Mitikas Beach • Epirus, Greece . 97 [174]
Mitikas Beach •
  Greece (Western) . . . . 97 [175]
Mitikas • Epirus, Greece 122 C1
Mitikas • Greece (Western) 122 C1
Mitilini Beach • Greece . . . . 97 [199]
Mitilini • Greece 122 D5
Mitla • Mexico 157 G4
Mito • Japan 30 K6
Mitohama • Japan 140 C3
Mitte (Berlin) • Germany 111 C2
Mittelberg • Austria . . . . 100 [128]
Mittelfranken • Germany 9 G7
Mittelland • Switzerland 119 G2
Mittellandkanal • Germany 8 D4
Mittenwald • Germany 112 F7
Mittenwalde • Germany 111 C4
Mittersill Ski • Austria . . . . 100 [160]
Mittweida • Germany 9 H6
Mitú • Colombia 51 C3
Mitumba, Mtns •
  Dem. Rep. of Congo 23 D5
Mitwaba • Dem. Rep. of Congo . . 23 D5
Mitzic • Gabon 22 G4
Miura • Japan 140 C4
Miura-hanto • Japan 140 C4
Miyagi • Japan 140 A4
Miyake • Japan 30 J7
Miyako • Japan 30 K5
Miyako-shoto • Japan 29 H6
Miyakonojo • Japan 30 F9
Miyanoura • Japan 30 F9
Miyazaki • Japan 140 A7
Miyazaki [Adm] • Japan 140 A7
Miyoshi • Japan 30 G7
Mizdah • Libya 21 B1
Mizen Head • Wicklow, Ireland . . 108 B4
Mizen Head • Cork, Ireland 108 C7
Mizil • Romania 14 N5
Mizoram • India 28 F4
Mizuho [Base] • Antarctica 54 (1) J2
Mjölby • Sweden 125 F4
Mjendalen • Norway 124 B1
Mjörn • Sweden 125 F3
Mjøsa • Norway 16 F6
Mkhaya Nature Reserve Park •
  Swaziland . . . . 133 [138]
Mkhondvo • Swaziland 134 B2
Mkushi • Zambia 24 D2
Mkuze • South Africa 134 B2
Mkuzi Game Reserve Park •
  South Africa . . . . 133 [131]
Mkuzi Game Reserve •
  South Africa 134 B2
Mladá Boleslav • Czech Rep. . . 128 B2
Mlawa • Poland 13 I4
Mlibizi • Zimbabwe 130 C1
Mljet • Croatia 14 N5
Mljet Nat. Park Park N •
  Croatia . . . . 89 [113]
Mljet Nat. Park • Croatia 128 D4
Mmabatho • South Africa 24 D5
Mnajdra • Malta 123 H4
Mnarani • Kenya 131 G5
Mnichovo Hradiste • Czech Rep. 128 B2
Mo i Rana • Norway 16 H3
Moa • Sierra Leone 22 B3
Moa • QL, Australia 34 H2
Moa • Cuba 158 D8
Moab • Jordan 135 A8
Moab • UT, United States 45 H2
Moala • Fiji Is. 35 (2) D2
Moanda • Dem. Rep. of Congo . . 23 A5
Moa • Dem. Rep. of Congo . . . 23 A5
Mobara • Japan 140 C2
Mobaye • Central African Rep. . . 23 C3
Mobayi-Mbongo •
  Dem. Rep. of Congo 23 C3
Moberly • MO, United States . . . 46 I3
Mobile • AL, United States 154 H1
Mobile Bay • AL, United States . . 154 H1
Mobor Beach • Goa, India 137 B2
Mobridge • SD, United States . . . 43 F4
Moca • Dominican Rep. 159 G3
Moçambique • Mozambique . . . 24 F3
Moçambique, Canal de •
  Madagascar/Mozambique 24 G3
Moçambique, Ilha de Heritage C •
  Mozambique . . . . 85 [115]
Mocha • Yemen 18 D7
Mochudi • Botswana 24 D4
Mocimboa da Praia • Mozambique 23 G6
Möckeln • Sweden 125 F11
Môco, Serra • Angola 23 B5
Mocoa • Colombia 51 B3
Moctezuma • Mexico 47 A2
Moctezuma • Mexico 157 F2
Mocuba • Mozambique 24 F3
Modane • France 115 F4
Modave • Belgium 109 D15
Modena Heritage C • Italy . . . . 86 [138]
Modena • Italy 121 E7
Mödling • Austria 13 F9
Modica • Sicily, Italy 12 I12
Modesto • CA, United States . . . 45 B3
Modica • Sicily, Italy 12 I12
Mödling • Austria 13 F9
Moe • VI, Australia 144 C3
Moelv • Norway 16 F6
Moena • Italy 120 B3
Moena di Fassa Ski • Italy . . . . 100 [222]
Moengo • Surinam 51 G2
Moenkopi • AZ, United States . . 45 G3
Moers • Germany 109 D12
Moers • Germany 111 B1
Mogadishu • Somalia 23 F3
Mogadouro • Portugal 11 E3
Mogadouro, Serra do • Portugal . 11 E3
Mogami • Japan 30 K5
Mogán Beach •
  Gran Canaria, Canary Is. . . . . 96 [110]
Mogán •
  Gran Canaria, Canary Is. 116 E4
Mogao Caves Heritage C • China 85 [162]
Mogho • Ethiopia 23 G3
Mogoca • Russian Fed. 27 I6
Mogollon Mtns •
  NM, United States 45 H5
Mogollon Rim •
  AZ, United States 45 G4
Moguer Beach • Spain . . . . . . 96 [112]
Moguer • Spain 116 B1
Mohács • Hungary 13 H12
Mohall • ND, United States 43 F2
Mohammadia • Algeria 11 L9
Mohammed V [Apt] • Morocco . 131 D1
Mohammedia • Morocco 131 D1
Moharraq, El • Egypt 131 F5
Mohave, Lake •
  AZ/NV, United States 153 L1
Mohawk Mtn Ski •
  CT, United States . . . . 149 [198]
Mohawk Mtn • CT, United States 153 D3
Mohéli • Comoros 24 G2
Mohenjodaro • Pakistan 28 A3
Mohenjodaro Heritage C •
  Pakistan . . . . 85 [129]
Moher, Cliffs of • Ireland 108 C4
Mohinora • Mexico 40 B6
Möhne • Germany 8 D5
Moi • Myanmar/Thailand 142 B3
Moi [Apt] • Kenya 131 G5
Moineşti • Romania 14 N3

Moisie • QU, Canada 39 R6
Moissac • France 115 G4
Moïta • Corsica, France 115 L2
Mója • Sweden 125 D4
Mojácar Beach • Spain . . . . . . 96 [116]
Mojácar • Spain 116 B4
Mojave • CA, United States . . . 45 C4
Mojave Desert •
  CA, United States 152 C6
Mojave Nat. Preserve Park N •
  CA, United States . . . . 150 [58]
Mojave Nat. Preserve •
  CA, United States 152 C6
Mojokerto • Java, Indonesia . . . 143 J8
Mojos, Llanos de • Bolivia 52 C1
Mokapu Peninsula •
  HI, United States 154 G6
Mokau • New Zealand 145 F3
Mokau [Riv] • New Zealand . . . 145 F1
Mokine • Tunisia 131 E4
Mokp'o • Rep. of Korea 30 D7
Mokuleia Beech •
  HI, United States 154 G1
Mol • Belgium 5 I3
Mola di Bari • Italy 12 L7
Mólai • Greece 15 D7
Mólai Beach • Greece . . . . . . 97 [182]
Molalla • OR, United States . . . 42 D4
Molara • I., Sardinia, Italy 120 C2
Molat • Croatia 128 D3
Molatón • Spain 11 J5
Mold • United Kingdom 7 I8
Moldau • Czech Rep. 13 D8
Moldava • Romania 14 M4
Moldavian churches Heritage C •
  Romania . . . . 86 [198]
Molde • Norway 124 C2
MOLDOVA • Europe 14 P2
Moldova Noua • Romania 14 I5
Moldova [Riv] • Romania 14 M2
Moldoveanu, Virful • Romania . 14 L4
Môle, Cap du • Haiti 159 G1
Môle St Nicholas • Haiti 159 G1
Môle St Nicolas • Haiti 159 G1
Molepolole • Botswana 24 D4
Molfetta • Italy 12 K7
Molina de Aragón • Spain 11 J4
Molina de Segura • Spain 11 J6
Moline • IL, United States 46 J2
Molise • Italy 12 I7
Mollendo • Peru 163 B4
Mölln • Germany 8 F3
Mollösund • Sweden 125 F2
Mölndal • Sweden 125 F6
Molodezhnaya [Base] •
  Antarctica 54 (1) J3
Molokai • HI, United States . . . 154 G3
Molong • NS, Australia 144 C2
Molopo • Botswana/South Africa 24 C5
Moloundou • Cameroon 22 H4
Moloțdorf Castle • Germany . . 113 [182]
Molteno • South Africa 134 C4
Moluccas • Indonesia 32 (1) C3
Molucca Sea • Indonesia 32 (1) C2
Molygino • Russian Fed. 27 D5
Moma • Mozambique 24 F3
Moma • Russian Fed. 131 G5
Mombasa • Kenya 131 G5
Mombasa Marine Game Reserve •
  Kenya 131 G5
Mombasa Marine Nat. Park •
  Kenya 131 G5
Mombetsu • Japan 30 L2
Mompós • Colombia 51 C2
Mompós Heritage C • Colombia 84 [49]
Momski Khrebet • Russian Fed. 27 D3
Møn • Denmark 125 F15
Mona, I. • West Indies 161 A13
MONACO • Europe 115 H2
Monadhliath Mtns •
  United Kingdom 6 H4
Monaghan • Ireland 7 F7
Monaghan [Adm] • Ireland . . . 108 A1
Monahans • TX, United States . 47 C2
Monastir • Tunisia 131 E4
Monbetsu • Japan 30 L3
Moncalieri • Italy 12 B4
Monção • Portugal 11 C2
Moncarapacho • Portugal 118 E8
Monchegorsk • Russian Fed. . . 17 E1
Mönchengladbach • Germany . 111 B3
Monchique • Portugal 118 E2
Monchique, Serra de • Portugal 118 E2
Monchs Corner •
  SC, United States 48 H4
Monclova • Mexico 37 A2
Moncófar Beach • Spain . . . . . 96 [120]
Moncton • NB, Canada 156 D7
Mondego • Portugal 11 D4
Mondello • Sicily, Italy 120 D1
Mondlo • South Africa 134 B3
Mondo • Chad 22 H2
Mondorf-les-Bains • Luxembourg 109 D20
Mondovi • Italy 121 E5
Mondragone • Italy 121 G1
Mondsee • Austria 119 H4
Mondsee, Lake • Austria 119 H4
Mondy • Russian Fed. 27 F6
Moneague • Italy 121 E6
Monemvassia • Greece 122 C7
Monessen • PA, United States . 44 F5
Monett • MO, United States . . 46 I4
Monfalcone • Italy 12 H3
Monforte de Lemos • Spain . . . 11 D2
Mong Hang • Myanmar 142 B1
Mong Kok • Hong Kong, China . 139 B5
Monga • Dem. Rep. of Congo . . 23 C3
Mongalla • Sudan 23 E2
Monghyr • India 28 E3
Mongie, la • France 115 J2
Mongolia • Russian Fed. 27 H6
Mongoli Altayn Nuruu •
  China/Mongolia 26 O8
MONGOLIA • Asia 25 L5
Mongonu • Nigeria 22 G2
Mongororo • Chad 23 C1
Mongu • Zambia 24 C3
Monheim • Germany 111 B3
Monitor Range •
  NV, United States 45 D2
Monjes • West Indies 51 C1
Monmouth • United Kingdom . 104 D3
Monmouth • IL, United States . 46 J2
Monmouthshire • United Kingdom 109 F2
Monnickendam • Netherlands . 109 F2
Mono Lake • CA, United States 152 C4
Monocacy Nat. Battlefield Park N •
  MD, United States . . . . 151 [263]
Monocacy Nat. Battlefield •
  MD, United States 153 D9
Monolithos • Rhodes, Greece . 122 C14
Monopoli • Italy 12 L8
Monor • Hungary 13 I10
Monos • I., Trinidad & Tobago . 160 U
Monóvar • Spain 11 K6
Monowai, Lake • New Zealand . 145 A3
Monpazier • France 115 G4
Monreal del Campo • Spain . . . 11 J4
Monreale • Sicily, Italy 120 D1
Monroe • NC, United States . . 48 F3
Monroe • WI, United States . . . 48 D5
Monroe • MI, United States . . . 44 D3

Monroe • NC, United States . . 48 G3
Monroe • LA, United States . . 153 F1
Monroeville • AL, United States 48 D5
Monrovia • Liberia 22 B3
Mons • Belgium 109 D14
Mons Klint • Denmark 125 F15
Monschau • Germany 112 D1
Montoro • Spain 11 G6
Montpelier • ID, United States . 42 J5
Montpelier • VT, United States 161 H4
Montpellier • France 114 D2
Montpoupon [Château] • France 114 D2
Montréal • QU, Canada 155 B7
Montréal Nord • QU, Canada . . 44 I3
Montreal River Harbour •
  OT, Canada 44 C2
Montreuil • France 5 E4
Montreux • Switzerland 119 G5
Montrose • United Kingdom . . 6 J5
Montrose • CO, United States . 45 I2
Montrose • AR, United States . 48 J6
Monts Chic-Chocs prov. parks •
  QU, Canada 156 D2
Montsen • Spain 11 L2
MONTSERRAT • West Indies . 161 H
Monywa • Myanmar . . . . 161 H
Monza • Italy 121 E6
Monzón • Spain 11 L3
Mooi • South Africa 134 B3
Mooi River • South Africa . . . 134 B3
Mooirivier • South Africa 134 B3
Moonie • Ireland 108 C6
Moonie • QL, Australia 144 B6
Moonstone Ski • OT, Canada . 149 [20]
Moor Abbey • Ireland 108 C6
Moora • WA, Australia 34 C5
Moore • OK, United States . . . 46 G5
Moore, Lake • WA, Australia . 34 C5
Moorea • French Polynesia . . 80 A1
Moores Creek Nat. Battlefield Park N •
  NC, United States . . . . 151 [241]
Moorfoot Hills • United Kingdom 104 B4
Moorhead • MN, United States . 43 H3
Moorreesburg • South Africa . 134 B5
Moorslede • Belgium 109 D12
Moose • OK, United States . . . 46 G5
Moose, Lake • WA, Australia . 34 C5
Moose Jaw • SA, Canada 38 J6
Moosehead Lake •
  ME, United States 44 K3
Moosomin • SA, Canada 43 F1
Moosonee • OT, Canada 39 O6
Mopti • Mali 20 D6
Moquegua • Peru 163 B4
Mór • Hungary 13 H10
Mora • Portugal 11 C6
Mora • Spain 11 H5
Mora • Sweden 16 H6
Mora • Cameroon 22 H2
Mora • NM, United States . . . 46 C4
Mòra d'Ebre • Spain 11 L3
Moradabad • India 137 C3
Morag • Poland 13 I4
Moraira • Spain 117 C2
Morale • Poland 13 I4
Moraïtika • Corfu, Greece . . 122 R1
Moran • KS, United States . . 46 H4
Morane • French Polynesia . . 33 N8
Morant Bay • Jamaica 159 F4
Morant Pt • Jamaica 159 F4
Morar, Loch • United Kingdom 6 G5
Moratalla • Spain 11 J6
Moratuwa • Sri Lanka 138 D15
Morava • Czech Rep. 13 G9
Moravia • Czech Rep. 128 A1
Morawa • WA, Australia 34 C5
Morawhanna • Guyana 51 F2
Moray Firth • United Kingdom 6 I4
Morbach • Germany 112 E3
Morbihan, Golfe du • France . 114 C4
Mörbisch • Austria 128 A2
Mörbylånga • Sweden 125 F12
Morcenx • France 115 G2
Morcote • Switzerland 119 G7
Morden • MN, United States . 43 G2
Mordovia • Russian Fed. 17 G4
More • Sweden 125 E4
Mere, Glen • United Kingdom . 6 H4
Mere og Romsdal • Norway . 16 D5
Moreau [Riv] • United States . 43 F4
Morecambe • United Kingdom . 7 J7
Morecambe Bay • United Kingdom 7 J7
Moreau • France 114 B4
Morehead • Papua New Guinea 35 (1) C2
Morehead • NC, United States . 48 I3
Morehead • KY, United States . 48 F1
Moreiz, gora • Russian Fed. . 26 A4
Mörel-Breiten Ski • Switzerland 100 [95]
Morelia Heritage C • Mexico . 84 [21]
Morelia • Mexico 157 G1
Morella Beach • Spain 11 K4
Morella • Spain 11 K4
Morelos • Mexico 47 D3
Morelos • Mexico 157 E9
Morena, Sierra • Spain 11 G6
Morena • Romania 128 E1
Moresby I. • BC, Canada . . . 38 E6
Moreton Bay • QL, Australia . 34 J5
Moreton I. • QL, Australia . . 144 B6
Moreton-in-Marsh •
  United Kingdom 104 D4
Moreuil • France 5 F5
Morey's Pier Wildwood Park L •
  NJ, United States . . . . . . 151 [KK]
Mörfelden • Germany 112 E3
Morgan • SA, Australia . . . . 149 B
Morgan City • LA, United States 153 F4
Morgan Hill • CA, United States 45 B3
Morgan Lewis Mill • Barbados 161 Q
Morgan, Mt • QL, Australia . . 34 J4
Morganton • NC, United States 48 G3
Morgantown • WV, United States 44 E6
Morges • Switzerland 119 G5
Morghab • Afghanistan 18 I2
Morgins Ski • Switzerland . . 100 [76]
Morgins • Switzerland 119 G5
Mori • China 26 P9
Mori • Japan 30 K3
Moriarty • NM, United States . 45 I4
Morib • Malaysia 141 G3
Moriki • Nigeria 20 F6
Morioka • Japan 30 K5
Moritzburg Castle • Germany . 113 [196]
Moriyama • Japan 140 B2
Morjärv • Sweden 16 L3
Morjim Beach • Goa, India . . 137 B1
Mörkö • Sweden 125 D4
Morlaix • France 114 C1
Mörlunda • Sweden 125 F8
Mormagao • Goa, India 137 B1
Morne des Sauteurs • Grenada 160 S
Morne Diablotins • Dominica . 161 M
Morne Garu Mtns •
  St Vincent & Gren. . . . . . . 161 Q
Morne Seychellois • Seychelles 133 K1
Morne Seychellois Nat. Park •
  Seychelles 133 K1
Morne Trois Pitons • Dominica 161 M
Morne Trois Pitons Nat. Park
  Heritage N • Dominica . . . . 82 [29]
Morne Trois Pitons Nat. Park •
  Dominica . . . . 161 M
Mornington I. • QL, Australia . 34 G3
Moro • Pakistan 28 A3
Moro • Papua New Guinea . . 35 (1) D2
MOROCCO • Africa . . . . 131 D
Morogoro • Tanzania 130 B4
Morombe • Madagascar 24 G4

Mörön • Mongolia 27 F7
Morón • Cuba 158 D3
Morón de la Frontera • Spain . 11 F7
Moron Us He • China 28 F2
Moroni • Comoros 24 G2
Morotai • Indonesia 32 (1) C2
Moroto • Uganda 23 F3
Morotu • Japan 30 H8
Morphou • United Kingdom . . 7 K6
Morphou • Cyprus 123 J1
Morphou Bay • Cyprus 123 J1
Morrilton • AR, United States 46 I5
Morrinhos • Brazil 52 G2
Morrinsville • New Zealand . 145 F2
Morris • Montserrat . . . . . . 161 H
Morris • MN, United States . 43 H2
Morris • NB, Australia 43 I4
Morris • IL, United States . . 44 A5
Morris Jessup, Kap • Greenland 36 N1
Morrisburg • QU, Canada . . 155 B7
Morristown • NJ, United States 44 H5
Morristown • TN, United States 48 F2
Morro Bay • CA, United States 45 B4
Morro Bay [Bay] •
  CA, United States 45 B4
Morro Bay State Park •
  CA, United States 152 C5
Morro de Chapéu • Brazil . . 52 H1
Mörrum • Sweden 125 F12
Mors Beach • Denmark . . . . 96 [49]
Mors • Denmark 125 F5
Morsv-hansk • Russian Fed. . 17 G4
Morson • OT, Canada 43 I2
Mort, Costa de la • Spain . . 117 D2
Mortagne • France 10 L5
Mortain • France 5 C6
Morton • WA, United States . 42 D3
Morton • IL, United States . . 46 K2
Morton • MS, United States . 48 C4
Morundah • NS, Australia . . 144 B3
Morven • QL, Australia 144 B5
Morwell • VI, Australia 144 C3
Morzine Ski • France . . . . . 100 [12]
Morzine • France 115 F2
Mosbach • Germany 112 D4
Mosby • MT, United States . 42 L3
Moscow Heritage C •
  Russian Fed. . . . . 86 [244-245]
Moscow • Russian Fed. . . . 126 C4
Moscow • ID, United States . 152 B2
Mosel • Germany 112 E3
Mosel Valley • Germany . . . 112 E3
Moselle • France 10 L5
Moses Lake • WA, United States 42 F3
Moses Rock Dive • Red Sea . 135 B1
Mosgiel • New Zealand . . . 35 C7
Moshi • Tanzania 130 B2
Mosi-oa-Tunya Heritage N •
  Zambia/Zimbabwe . . . . . 83 [106]
Mosigkau Castle • Germany . 113 [213]
Mosinee • WI, United States . 43 L4
Mosjøen • Norway 16 G3
Moskenesøya • Norway . . . 16 G3
Moskva Heritage C •
  Russian Fed. . . . . 86 [244-245]
Moskva • Russian Fed. . . . 126 C4
Moskva [Riv] • Russian Fed. 126 C4
Moskvy, Kanal im • Russian Fed. 126 C4
Moslavacka Gora • Croatia . 14 D4
Mosonmagyaróvár • Hungary 13 G10
Mosquero • NM, United States 46 C5
Mosquitos, Costa de • Nicaragua 80 B9
Mosquitos, Golfo de •
  Costa Rica/Panama 37 E6
Moss • Norway 124 B4
Moss Park • FL, United States 151 C2
Moss Point • MS, United States 48 C5
Moss Town • Bahamas . . . 158 B3
Mossaka • Congo 23 B4
Mossel Bay • South Africa . 134 C7
Mossendjo • Congo 22 G5
Mossman • QL, Australia . . 34 I3
Mossoró • Brazil 53 (1) D3
Most • Czech Rep. 128 B1
Mosta • Malta 123 H4
Mostar • Bosnia-Herz. 20 F1
Mosul • Iraq 18 D2
Møsvatn • Norway 124 C6
Mota Lava • Vanuatu 35 (2) B1
Motaba • Congo 22 H4
Motagua • Guatemala 37 D4
Motala • Sweden . . . . 97 [19]
Motala Beach • Sweden . . . 125 F4
Motala • Sweden 16 H6
Motherwell • United Kingdom 104 B3
Motihari • India 137 C8
Motilla del Palancar • Spain . 11 J5
Motiti I. • New Zealand . . . 145 F2
Motril • Spain 116 B7
Motru • Romania 14 K4
Mott • ND, United States . . 43 E3
Motu One • French Polynesia 33 L7
Motueka • New Zealand . . 35 D5
Motuhora I. • New Zealand . 145 F2
Mouchard • France 10 K7
Mouche, Anse a la • Seychelles 133 K1
Moudjéra • Mauritania 20 C5
Moudon • France 122 C2
Mouila • Gabon 22 G5
Moukalaba, Réserve de la Park •
  Gabon . . . . 133 [50]
Moul • Niger 20 H5
Moulay Bousselham • Morocco 131 D1
Moulay Idriss • Morocco . . 131 D1
Moule à Chique, Cap • St Lucia 161 P
Moule • Guadeloupe . . . . 161 D
Moulin [Château] • France . 114 D2
Moulins • France 10 I7
Moulmein • Myanmar 31 B3
Moulouya • Morocco 131 D2
Moultrie • GA, United States 48 F5
Moultrie, Lake •
  SC, United States 48 G4
Mounda, Akra •
  Cephalonia, Greece 122 C2
Moundou • Chad 21 C6
Moundsville • WV, United States 44 E6
Mount Abu • India 137 C5
Mount Abu Hill Sta • India 138 I1
Mount Airy • NC, United States 48 G2
Mount Aspiring Nat. Park •
  New Zealand 145 G4
Mount Ayliff • South Africa 134 B5
Mount Ayr • IA, United States 46 H2
Mount Baker Ski •
  WA, United States . . . . 149 [48]
Mount Barker • WA, Australia 34 C6
Mount Brighton Ski •
  MI, United States . . . . . 149 [148]
Mount Buffalo • VI, Australia 144 C3
Mount Buller • VI, Australia 144 C3
Mount Carleton Prov. Park •
  NB, Canada 156 D2
Mount Carmel •
  PA, United States 44 G5
Mount Carmel •
  IL, United States 48 E1
Mount Carmel Junction •
  UT, United States 45 F3
Mount Currie Nature Reserve •
  South Africa 134 B5
Mount Darwin • Zimbabwe 130 C2
Mount Douglas • QL, Australia 34 I4

Mount Elgon Nat. Park • Kenya **131** G1
Mount Elgon Nat. Park **Park** •
Kenya .... **133** [75]
Mount Forest • OT, Canada **44** E4
Mount Gambier • SA, Australia **34** H7
Mount Hagen • Papua New Guinea . **35** (1) C2
Mount Holly **Ski** •
MI, United States .... **149** [149]
Mount Hood Meadows **Ski** •
OR, United States .... **149** [53]
Mount Horeb • WI, United States **43** L5
Mount Isa • QL, Australia **34** G4
Mount Kato **Ski** •
MN, United States .... **149** [124]
Mount Kenya Nat. Park • Kenya **131** G3
Mount Kenya Nat. Park **Park** •
Kenya .... **133** [78]
Mount Kenya Nat. Park and forest
Heritage N • Kenya .... **83** [99]
Mount Lavinia • Sri Lanka **138** D15
Mount Magnet • WA, Australia **34** C5
Mount Mansfield **Ski** •
VT, United States .... **149** [214]
Mount Manganui • New Zealand **145** F2
Mount Nimba Nature Reserve
Heritage N • Côte d'Ivoire/Guinea **83** [83]
Mount Pleasant • Cayman Is. **159** E3
Mount Pleasant •
MI, United States **44** C4
Mount Pleasant •
UT, United States **45** G2
Mount Pleasant •
IA, United States **46** J2
Mount Pleasant •
SC, United States **48** H4
Mount Prospect •
IL, United States **44** A4
Mount Rainier Nat. Park **Park N** •
WA, United States .... **150** [31]
Mount Rainier Nat. Park •
WA, United States **152** B1
Mount Revelstoke Nat. Park •
BC, Canada **155** C4
Mount Revelstoke Nat. Park **Park N** •
BC, Canada .... **156** [10]
Mount Robson Prov. Park •
AL, Canada **155** C2
Mount Rose **Ski** •
NV, United States .... **149** [76]
Mount Rushmore Nat. Mem. **Park N** •
SD, United States .... **150** [150]
Mount Shasta •
CA, United States **42** D6
Mount Snow **Ski** •
VT, United States .... **149** [206]
Mount Snow • VT, United States ... **153** D3
Mount St George •
Trinidad & Tobago .... **160** T
Mount St Helens Nat. Volcanic Mon. •
WA, United States **152** B1
Mount St Louis **Ski** • OT, Canada **149** [20]
Mount Sterling •
KY, United States **48** F1
Mount Sunapee **Ski** •
NH, United States .... **149** [218]
Mount Tom • NM, United States **153** D3
Mount Vernon • WA, Australia **34** C4
Mount Vernon •
WA, United States **42** D2
Mount Vernon •
OR, United States **42** F4
Mount Vernon •
OH, United States **44** D5
Mount Vernon •
^NY, United States **44** I5
Mount Vernon •
IL, United States **48** C1
Mount Vernon •
IN, United States **48** D2
Mount Vernon •
VA, United States **153** D9
Mount Washington **Ski** •
NH, United States .... **149** [1]
Mount's Bay • United Kingdom **104** F4
Mountain Brook •
AL, United States **48** D4
Mountain City •
TN, United States **48** G2
Mountain Creek **Ski** •
NJ, United States .... **149** [181]
Mountain High **Ski** •
CA, United States .... **149** [71]
Mountain Home •
ID, United States **42** H5
Mountain Home •
AR, United States **46** I4
Mountain View •
CA, United States **45** A3
Mountain Zebra Nat. Park **Park** •
South Africa .... **133** [125]
Mountain Zebra Nat. Park •
South Africa **134** C4
Mountainair • NM, United States **45** I4
Mountlake Terrace •
WA, United States **42** D3
Mountshannon • Ireland **108** C4
Mourão • Portugal **11** D6
Moura • QL, Australia **34** F3
Mourão • Portugal **11** D6
Mourdi, Dépression du • Chad **21** D4
Mourdiah • Mali **20** D6
Mourési **Beach** • Greece .... **97** [188]
Mourne Mtns • United Kingdom **7** G7
Mouscron • Belgium **5** G4
Moussoro • Chad **22** H2
Moutiers • France **115** F2
Mouton, Château • France **115** G1
Moutong • Indonesia **32** (1) B2
Mouydir • Algeria **20** F3
Moxey Town • Bahamas **158** B1
Moy • Ireland **108** C2
Moyale • Kenya **131** G2
Moyen Atlas • Morocco **131** D2
Moyne Abbey • Ireland **108** C2
Moyobamba • Peru **51** B5
Moyto • Chad **20** I6
Moyynty • Kazakhstan **26** L8
MOZAMBIQUE • Africa **24** F3
Mozambique, Canal de •
Madagascar/Mozambique **24** G3
Mozambique Channel •
Madagascar/Mozambique **24** G3
Mpanda • Tanzania **130** B1
Mpika • Zambia **24** E2
Mpouya • Congo **23** B4
Mpulungu • Zambia **24** E1
Mpumalanga • South Africa **134** C3
Mpumalanga [Adm] • South Africa . **24** D5
Mpungu Marine Nat. Park • Kenya . **131** G5
Mragowo • Poland **13** K4
Mráyer, El • Mauritania **130** C2
Mreiti, El • Mauritania **130** C2
Mrewa • Zimbabwe **130** C2
Mreyyé, El • Mali/Mauritania **130** C2
Msasam • Tanzania **130** B4
Msta • Russian Fed. **126** C1
Mt Bachelor **Ski** •
OR, United States .... **149** [55]
Mtarazi Falls Nat. Park •
Zimbabwe **130** C2
Mtelo • Kenya **131** G1
Mtensak • Russian Fed. **17** F4
Mtunzini • South Africa **134** D4
Mtwara • Tanzania **130** B4
Muang Khammouan • Laos **31** C3
Muang Khong • Laos **31** D4
Muang Mai • Ko Phuket, Thailand . **142** E1
Muang Pakxan • Laos **31** C3
Muang Sing • Laos **31** C2

Muang Xaignabouri • Laos **31** C3
Muar • Malaysia **32** C2
Muarasiberut • Indonesia **32** B3
Muaratebo • Indonesia **32** C3
Muarawenei • Indonesia **32** C3
Muaro Takus • Indonesia **143** G4
Mubarraz, Al • Saudi Arabia **18** E4
Mubi • Nigeria **22** G2
Muchinga Mtns • Zambia **24** E2
Muckross Abbey • Ireland **108** C7
Muconda • Angola **23** C6
Mud Butte • SD, United States **43** E4
Mud Lake • ID, United States **42** I5
Mud Lake • MN, United States **43** I2
Mudan Jiang • China **29** H2
Mudanjiang • China **29** H2
Mudanya • Turkey **122** D3
Muddus Nat. Park **Park N** •
Sweden .... **89** [18]
Muddy Gap • WY, United States **42** L5
Mudgee • NS, Australia **144** C2
Mudug • Somalia **23** H7
Mudumalai Wildlife Sanctuary •
India **138** D10
Mudurnu • Turkey **15** L3
Mueda • Mozambique **24** F2
Muela de San Juan • Spain **11** J4
Muertos, I. Caja de •
Puerto Rico **159** H3
Muezenti • Chad **20** I5
Mufulira • Zambia **24** D2
Mughalzhar Tauy • Kazakstan **26** I8
Mugla, Mtns •
Dem. Rep. of Congo **23** D5
Mugla • Turkey **122** D9
Muhammad Qol • Sudan **21** G3
Muhammad, Râs • Egypt. **131** F4
Mühlacker • Germany **9** D8
Mühlbach am Hochkönig **Ski** •
Austria .... **100** [168]
Mühlberg • Germany **90** A8
Mühldorf am Inn • Germany **112** F4
Mühlenbeck • Germany **111** C2
Mühlhausen • Germany **9** F5
Mühltal **Ski** • Austria .... **100** [148]
Muhos • Finland **16** N4
Muhu • Estonia **126** B1
Mui Wo • Hong Kong, China **139** B5
Muiden • Netherlands **109** F2
Muiderslot • Netherlands **109** F2
Muir Woods Nat. Mon. **Park N** •
CA, United States .... **150** [42]
Muirfield • United Kingdom **104** B4
Muite • Mozambique **24** F2
Mujeres, I. • Mexico **157** E6
Muji • China **28** C1
Muka Head • Penang, Malaysia ... **141** F1
Mukacheve • Ukraine **13** L9
Mukah • Malaysia **32** E2
Mukalla, Al • Yemen **18** E7
Mukawwar • Sudan **21** G3
Mukdahan • Thailand **31** C3
Mukha, Al • Yemen **18** D7
Mukinbudin • WA, Australia **34** C6
Mukogaoka Yuen • Japan **140** C2
Mukojima-retto • Japan **140** A13
Mula • Spain **11** J6
Mulaku Atoll • Maldives **138** F3
Mulan • China **27** K7
Mulanje Mtns • Malawi **24** F3
Mulde • Germany **8** H5
Mule Peak • NM, United States **46** C6
Muleshoe • TX, United States **46** D5
Mulgrave I. • Australia **32** (1) F4
Mulhacén • Spain **116** B3
Mülheim an der Ruhr • Germany . **111** B1
Mulhouse • France **10** M6
Mull • United Kingdom **6** G5
Mullaghareik Mtns • Ireland **108** C6
Mullaghmore **Beach** • Ireland ... **96** [164]
Mullaitivu • Sri Lanka **138** D11
Mullan • ID, United States **42** H3
Mullens • WV, United States **48** G2
Mullet Lake • MI, United States **44** C3
Mullet Peninsula • Ireland **108** C1
Mullewa • WA, Australia **34** C5
Mülheim • Germany **9** G6
Mullingar • Ireland **7** E8
Mullingar **Beach** • Ireland ...... **96** [57]
Mullsjö • Sweden **125** F3
Mulobezi • Zambia **130** C1
Mulranny **Beach** • Ireland .... **96** [163]
Mulranny • Ireland **108** C1
Multan • Pakistan **28** B2
Mumbai • Angola **23** B6
Mumford • NY, United States **153** D1
Mummelsee • Germany **112** D6
Münden • Germany **142** A2
Mun, Ko • Thailand **142** E2
Muna • Russian Fed. **27** J3
Muna • Indonesia **32** (1) B3
Muna • Mexico **157** H1
Munabao • India **18** I2
Münchberg • Germany **9** G6
München • Germany **112** F3
Muncie • IN, United States **44** C2
Munda • Solomon Is. **35** (1) F2
Mundaring • WA, Australia **34** C6
Münden • Germany **8** E5
Mundesley **Beach** •
United Kingdom .... **101** [47]
Mundiwindi • WA, Australia **34** D4
Mundo Nôvo • Brazil **52** H1
Munellës • Albania **15** B2
Mungbere • Dem. Rep. of Congo . **23** D3
Müngstener Brücke • Germany .. **111** B4
Munh-Hairhan-Ula • Mongolia **26** P8
Munhango • Angola **24** B2
Munich • Germany **112** F3
Muniesa • Spain **11** K3
Munifah • Saudi Arabia **18** E4
Munkedal • Sweden **125** F2
Munku Sardyk, gora •
Mongolia/Russian Fed. **27** F6
Munnar **Hill Sta** • India **138** D10
Munnar **Hill Sta** • India **138** E2
Münster • Ireland **7** C9
Münster • Germany **8** C5
Münsterland • Germany **8** C5
Münsterland, Water Castles of **Castle** •
Germany .... **113** [12-22]
Münsterländer Wasserburgen **Castle** •
Germany .... **113** [12-22]
Muntenia • Romania **128** C1
Muntii Apuseni • Romania **14** J3
Muntok • Indonesia **32** D3
Munyati • Zimbabwe **130** C1
Münzenberg • Germany .... **113** [50]
Münzenberg **Castle** • Germany . **113** [50]
Muojärvi • Finland **16** O3
Muong Sen • Vietnam **31** C3
Muonio • Finland **16** L3
Muonio älv • Finland **16** L2
Muonionjoki • Finland **16** L2
Muqdisho • Somalia **23** H3
Mur • Austria **13** D10
Mur • France **10** I3
Mura • Croatia **13** F9
Murad, Gunung • Malaysia **32** F2
Muranga • Kenya **131** G3
Murashi • Russian Fed. **17** H3
Murat • Turkey **18** D2
Murat Dagi • Turkey **15** K5
Muratli • Turkey **15** I2
Muratpasa **Beach** • Turkey ..... **97** [225]
Murau • Austria **14** B2

Murchison Falls • Uganda **23** E3
Murchison • WA, Australia **34** C5
Murchison, Mt • New Zealand **35** C6
Murcia • Spain **117** C3
Murcia [Adm] • Spain **11** J7
Murcia • SD, United States **43** F5
Mure, la • France **10** K9
Murère • Romania **14** K4
Muret • France **10** G10
Murfreesboro •
NC, United States **48** H3
Murfreesboro •
TN, United States **48** D3
Murg • Germany **9** D8
Murghob • Tajikistan **18** J2
Murgon • QL, Australia **144** B6
Müritz • Germany **8** H3
Müritz, Nationalpark **Park N** •
Germany .... **89** [60]
Murlaé • Brazil **163** C2
Murmansk • Russian Fed. **17** E1
Murmashi • Russian Fed. **17** E1
Muro • Spain **117** F7
Muro **Beach** • Majorca, Spain .. **96** [126]
Muro • Majorca, Spain **117** H2
Muron • Russian Fed. **17** G3
Muroran • Japan **30** K3
Muros • Spain **11** B2
Muros y Noya, Ria de • Spain **11** B2
Muroto-zaki • Japan **30** H8
Murphy • ID, United States **42** G5
Murray • Australia **34** H6
Murray • UT, United States **45** G1
Murray • KY, United States **48** D2
Murray Bridge • SA, Australia **34** G7
Murray R. • Papua New Guinea . **32** (1) F4
Murray •
SC, United States **48** G3
Murray's Anchorage • Bermuda .. **159** J2
Murraysburg • South Africa **134** C3
Murrhen **Ski** • Switzerland .... **100** [100]
Mürren • Switzerland **119** G2
Murrisk **Beach** • Ireland .... **96** [63]
Murrisk • Ireland **108** C1
Murrumbidgee • NS, Australia ... **144** C1
Murtensee • Switzerland **119** G2
Murter • Switzerland **119** G2
Murter • Croatia **128** D3
Murtosa **Beach** • Portugal ...... **96** [95]
Murud **Beach** • India **138** E3
Murupara • New Zealand **145** F2
Murura • French Polynesia **33** N8
Murwara • India **28** E4
Murwillumbah • NS, Australia ... **144** B6
Murzuq • Libya **21** B2
Mürzzuschlag • Austria **13** E10
Musa • Turkey **18** D2
Mus-Haya • Russian Fed. **27** N4
Musa • Lithuania **13** N1
Musala • Bulgaria **14** K7
Musala • Indonesia **143** G4
Musandam • Oman **30** E3
Musashi Hills Forest Park •
Japan **140** C1
Musashino • Japan **140** C2
Muscadet • France **114** B1
Muscat • Oman **30** J6
Muscatine • IA, United States **46** J2
Muscle Shoals •
AL, United States **48** D3
Musgrave • QL, Australia **34** H2
Musgrave Ranges • SA, Australia . **145** D3
Mushie • Dem. Rep. of Congo **23** B4
Muskego • WI, United States **44** A4
Muskegon • MI, United States **44** B4
Muskegon Heights •
MI, United States **44** B4
Muskö • Sweden **125** D4
Muskö [I.] • Sweden **125** D4
Muskogee • OK, United States **46** H5
Muskoka, Lake • OT, Canada **44** F3
Musoma • Tanzania **130** B1
Musselshell • MT, United States ... **42** K3
Mussende • Angola **23** B6
Mussoorie **Hill Sta** • India **138** E1
Mustafa Kemalpasa • Turkey **15** J3
Müstair **Heritage C** •
Switzerland .... **86** [122]
Müstair • Switzerland **119** G3
Müster • Switzerland **119** G3
Mustique • St Vincent & Gren. .... **161** R
Mustvee • Estonia **126** B2
Musu-dan • D.P.R. of Korea **30** E4
Mut • Turkey **123** G3
Mut • Egypt. **131** F3
Mutaf, Ra's al • Iran **18** F4
Mutare • Zimbabwe **130** C4
Mutis, Gunung • Indonesia ... **32** (1) F4
Mutoko • Zimbabwe **24** E3
Mutoray • Russian Fed. **26** R5
Mutsamudu • Comoros **24** G2
Mutshatsha • Dem. Rep. of Congo **23** D5
Mutsu • Japan **30** K4
Mutsu-wan • Japan **30** K4
Mutters • Austria **119** H6
Muwayh, Al • Saudi Arabia **21** H3
Muynľ • Mexico **157** H2
Muyinga • Burundi **23** E4
Muynoq • Uzbekistan **26** I9
Muyun Kum • Kazakhstan **123** T2
Muzaffarnagar • India **137** C8
Muzaffarpur • India **137** C8
Muzhi • Russian Fed. **26** J4
Múzquiz • Mexico **47** D4
Muztag • China **28** G1
Muztagata • China **26** N10
Muztau • China **26** O10
Mvomero • Tanzania **130** C4
Mwabwi Game Reserve **Park** •
Malawi .... **133** [101]
Mwanza • Tanzania **130** B1
Mwaya • Tanzania **130** B3
Mwea Game Reserve • Kenya ... **131** G4
Mweelrea • Ireland **108** C3
Mweka • Dem. Rep. of Congo **23** C4
Mwene-Ditu • Dem. Rep. of Congo **23** D6
Mwenso • Zambia **23** D6
Mweru, Lake •
Dem. Rep. of Congo/Zambia .. **23** D5
Mwinilunga • Zambia **24** C2
Mwnt **Beach** • United Kingdom . **101** [188]
My Son Sanctuary **Heritage C** •
Vietnam .... **85** [196]
My Tho • Vietnam **141** E3
Myakit • Russian Fed. **27** P4
Myakka River State Park •
FL, United States **154** H5
Myanaung • Myanmar **31** A3
MYANMAR • Asia **31** A2
Mycenae **Heritage C** • Greece . **86** [214]
Mycene • Greece **125** D6
Myingyan • Myanmar **31** B2
Myinmoletkat Taung • Myanmar .. **31** B3
Myitkyina • Myanmar **31** B1
Mykolayiv • Ukraine **17** E5
Mymensingh • Bangladesh **28** E4
Myra • Turkey **123** F3
Myrdal • Norway **124** B5
Myrdalsjökull • Iceland **16** (1) D3
Myre • Norway **16** H2
Myrtle **Beach** •
SC, United States **48** H4
Myrtle Creek •
OR, United States **42** D5

Myrtle Grove •
FL, United States **48** D5
Myrtle Point •
OR, United States **42** C5
Mys Shmidta • Russian Fed. **27** V3
Mysen • Norway **124** B4
Mysia • Turkey **122** C4
Myslenice • Poland **128** C4
Mysore • India **138** D6
Mystic • CT, United States **153** D8
Myszków • Poland **128** C4
Myszyniec • Poland **13** K4
Mytishchi • Russian Fed. **126** C4
Myvatn • Iceland **16** (1) E2
Mze • Czech Rep. **128** B1

N'Djamena • Chad **21** B5
Na Cailighe, Sliabh • Ireland **108** B1
Na Pali Coast State Park •
HI, United States **154** G2
Na Phra Lan, Laem •
Ko Samui, Thailand **142** D1
Naab • Germany **9** H7
Naalehu • HI, United States **154** G8
Naantali • Finland **125** E3
Naarden • Netherlands **109** F2
Naas • Ireland **108** B3
Nabadid • Somalia **21** H6
Nabari • Japan **140** B4
Naberezhnyye Chelny •
Russian Fed. **17** I3
Nabeul • Tunisia **131** E2
Nabi Shu'ayb • Yemen. **25** F8
Nabi Shu'ayb, Jabal an • Yemen .. **21** H4
Nabire • Indonesia **32** (1) E3
Nablus • Palestine **135** A6
Nacala • Mozambique **24** G2
Nachingwea • Tanzania **130** B4
Nachod • Czech Rep. **13** F7
Nachuge • India **28** F6
Nacimiento • Mexico **47** D3
Nacka • Sweden **125** D4
Naco • Mexico **45** H6
Nacogdoches • TX, United States . **46** H6
Nädendal • Finland **125** E3
Nadiad • India **28** B4
Nador • Morocco **131** D2
Nadur • Malta **123** H1
Nadvoitsy • Russian Fed. **17** E2
Nadym • Russian Fed. **26** L4
Nadym [Riv] • Russian Fed. **26** L5
Næstved **Beach** • Denmark .... **96** [37]
Nærøyfjorden • Norway **124** C4
Næstved • Denmark **125** F14
Náfpaktos • Greece **15** C5
Náfpaktos **Beach** • Greece .... **97** [175]
Náfplio • Greece **15** D6
Náfplio **Beach** • Greece .... **97** [184]
Nafud, an • Saudi Arabia **18** D4
Nafusah, Jabal • Libya **21** B1
Nag's Head • St Kitts & Nevis .... **161** G
Naga • Philippines **31** G4
Naga Hills • India **137** A3
Nagaland • India **28** F3
Nagaoka • Japan **30** J6
Nagaoka [Adm] • Japan **140** A4
Nagaoka • Japan **30** J6
Nagappattinam • India **138** D11
Nagar Haveli • India **28** B4
Nagarhole Nat. Park • India **138** D6
Nagarjuna Sagar • India **138** D3
Nagarjunakonda • India **138** D3
Nagasaki • Japan **30** E8
Nagasaki [Adm] • Japan **140** A7
Nagato • Japan **30** F7
Nagatoro • Japan **140** C1
Nagaur • India **137** C5
Nagda • India **137** C5
Nagercoil • India **138** D14
Nagina • India **137** C5
Nagledam Nature Reserve •
South Africa **134** B3
Nagno • Japan **30** G8
Nago • Japan **29** H5
Nagorny • Russian Fed. **27** J5
Nagoya • Japan **30** I7
Naggu • China **28** F2
Naggu • China **28** F2
Nagruawahia • New Zealand **145** F1
Nagua • Dominican Rep. **159** G3
Nagy-Milic • Slovak Rep. **14** I1
Nagyatád • Hungary **13** G11
Nagykálló • Hungary **13** K10
Nagykanizsa • Hungary **13** G11
Nagykáta • Hungary **13** I10
Nagykőrös • Hungary **13** I10
Naha • Japan **29** H5
Nahan **Hill Sta** • India **138** E1
Nahanni Butte • NT, Canada **38** G4
Nahanni Nat. Park **Heritage N** •
NT, Canada .... **82** [2]
Nahanni Nat. Park **Park N** •
NT, Canada .... **156** [4]
Nahariyya • Israel **135** A1
Nanuque • Brazil **52** H2
Nanus Fort • Goa, India **137** B1
Nahr Ouassei • Algeria **11** N9
Nai, Dong • Vietnam **141** E2
Nai Ham **Beach** •
Ko Phuket, Thailand **142** E2
Nai Yang **Beach** •
Ko Phuket, Thailand **142** E1
Nailsworth • United Kingdom **104** D3
Naimisharanya • India **137** C3
Nain • NF, Canada **39** S5
Nainital **Hill Sta** • India **138** E1
Naintal • India **137** C5
Nairn **Beach** • United Kingdom . **101** [4]
Nairobi • Kenya **131** G3
Nairobi Nat. Park • Kenya **131** G3
Nairobi Nat. Park **Park** • Kenya **133** [82]
Najaf, An • Iraq **18** D3
Najd • Saudi Arabia **21** H2
Najin • D.P.R. of Korea **30** E4
Najran • Saudi Arabia **18** D6
Naka Nci, Ko • Thailand **142** E1
Naka Yai, Ko • Thailand **142** E1
Naka-no • Japan **140** A7
Nakadori-jima • Japan **140** A7
Nakajō • Japan **30** J5
Nakamura • Japan **30** G8
Nakano-shima • Japan **140** A7
Nakasongola • Uganda **23** E3
Nakatchafushi • Maldives **138** F2
Nakatsu • Japan **30** F8
Nakfa • Eritrea **21** G4
Nakhodka • Russian Fed. **27** L8
Nakhon Nayok • Thailand **142** C2
Nakhon Pathom • Thailand **31** B4
Nakhon Phanom • Thailand **31** C3
Nakhon Ratchasima • Thailand ... **31** C3
Nakhon Sawan • Thailand **31** C3
Nakhon Si Thammarat • Thailand . **31** B5
Nakina • OT, Canada **43** N1
Nakło • Poland **128** C2
Naknek • AK, United States **36** E3
Nakodorada • Russian Fed. **26** K2
Nakskov • Denmark **125** F14
Nakskov **Beach** • Denmark .... **96** [37]
Nakten • Rep. of Korea **30** E7
Nakuru • Kenya **131** G3
Nakup • BC, Canada **42** G1

Nal • Pakistan **18** I4
Nalayha • Mongolia **27** G7
Nalchik • Russian Fed. **17** G6
Nalgonda • India **138** D3
Nallamalla Range • India **138** D3
Nallihan • Turkey **15** M3
Nalón • Spain **11** F1
Nalut • Libya **21** B1
Nam Cat Tien Nat. Park •
Vietnam **141** E2
Nam Co • China **28** F2
Nam Dinh • Vietnam **31** D2
Nam Tok Surin Nat. Park •
Thailand **142** B1
Namakan Lake •
Canada/United States **43** J2
Namakwaland • South Africa **134** B3
Namangan • Uzbekistan **18** J1
Namatanai • Papua New Guinea **35** (1) K1
Namatjira Mem. • NT, Australia . **145** D2
Namber • Indonesia **32** (1) D3
Nambour • QL, Australia **144** B6
Namchbarwa • China **28** G2
Namcha Barwa • China **28** G2
Namdalen • Norway **16** G4
Nämdo • Sweden **125** D4
Namialé • Mozambique **24** F3
Namib Desert • Namibia **24** A3
Namib-Naukluft Nat. Park **Park** •
Namibia .... **133** [121]
Namibe • Angola **24** A3
NAMIBIA • Africa **24** B4
Namja Namse La Shankou •
China/Nepal **28** D2
Namkham • Myanmar **31** B2
Namlea • Indonesia **32** (1) C3
Namous • Algeria **20** E2
Namp'o • D.P.R. of Korea **30** C5
Nampa • ID, United States **152** B4
Nampula • Mozambique **24** F3
Namrud • Syria **135** A2
Namsen • Norway **16** F4
Namsos • Norway **16** F4
Namuang Falls •
Ko Samui, Thailand **142** D2
Namuli, Serra • Mozambique **24** F3
Namur • Belgium **109** D15
Namur [Adm] • Belgium **109** D15
Namwon • Rep. of Korea **30** D7
Namyslow • Poland **13** G6
Nan • Thailand **142** B2
Nan Hai • China **29** F6
Nan Hulsan Hu • China **28** E1
Nan Jiang • China **139** C1
Nan Ling • China **29** E5
Nan [Riv] • Thailand **142** B2
Nanaimo • BC, Canada **155** C3
Nanam • D.P.R. of Korea **30** E4
Nanango • QL, Australia **144** B6
Nanchang • China **29** F5
Nanchong • China **29** D4
Nancowry • India **28** F7
Nancy • France **10** L5
Nancy **Heritage C** • France .... **86** [60]
Nancy Sound • New Zealand **145** G1
Nanda Devi • India **25** I7
Nanda Devi Nat. Park **Heritage N** •
India .... **83** [113]
Nandan • Japan **140** B3
Nanded • India **138** D3
Nandi • Fiji Is. **35** (2) D2
Nandikanima Pass • India **138** D3
Nandyal • India **138** D3
Nanfen • China **30** B4
Nanga Parbat • Jammu & Kashmir . **28** B1
Nangapinoh • Indonesia **32** E3
Nangatayap • Indonesia **32** E3
Nangnim • D.P.R. of Korea **30** D4
Nangnim-Sanmaek •
D.P.R. of Korea **30** D4
Nanhui • China **139** C4
Naning • China **29** D6
Nanling • China **139** C3
Nannup • WA, Australia **34** C6
Nanpan Jiang • China **29** C6
Nanping • China **29** F5
Nanpo-shoto • Japan **140** A8
Nanqiao • China **139** C4
Nansei-shoto • Japan **29** H5
Nansha • China **139** B2
Nansha Qundao • South China Sea . **31** E5
Nanshan • Shenzhen, China **139** B3
Nantais, Lac • QU, Canada **39** Q4
Nantes • France **114** D1
Nanticoke • PA, United States **44** G5
Nanton • AL, Canada **42** I1
Nantong • China **139** C2
Nantucket • MA, United States ... **80** A2
Nantucket • MA, United States ... **44** J5
Nantucket I. •
MA, United States **153** D8
Nantucket Sound •
MA, United States **153** D8
Nanumea • Tuvalu **33** I6
Nanuque • Brazil **52** H2
Nanwei Dao • South China Sea ... **31** E5
Nanyang • China **29** E4
Nanyuki • Kenya **131** G1
Nao, Cabo de la • Spain **117** C2
Naococcane, Lac • QU, Canada ... **39** Q6
Naoussa • Greece **15** D3
Napa • CA, United States **45** A2
Napa Valley • CA, United States . **152** C3
Napata • Sudan **21** F4
Naperville • IL, United States **44** A4
Napier • New Zealand **145** F4
Naples **Heritage C** • Italy .... **86** [150]
Naples • Italy **121** G3
Naples • FL, United States **154** H5
Napo • Peru **51** C4
Napoleon • OH, United States **44** C1
Napoléon, Route • France **115** F2
Nápoli **Heritage C** • Italy ..... **86** [150]
Nápoli, Golfo di • Italy **121** G3
Napoule, la • France **115** H4
Nappannee • IN, United States ... **44** C5
Nar • United Kingdom **5** D2
Nar yan Mar • Russian Fed. **26** I3
Nara • Mali **22** C1
Nara **Heritage C** • Japan ..... **85** [191]
Nara [Adm] • Japan **140** A3
Nara • Japan **140** B3
Nara Dreamland • Japan **140** B3
Naracoorte **Heritage N** •
Australia .... **83** [146]
Narayanganj • Bangladesh **28** E4
Narbonne • France **10** I10
Narbonne **Heritage C** • France . **86** [129]
Narbonne, Punta de • Angola **22** G4
Narcondam • India **28** F6
Nares Strait • Canada/Greenland . **54** V1
Narin Gol • China **28** E1
Narita • Japan **140** C2
Narita [Apt] • Japan **140** C2
Narita **Heritage C** • Japan ... **85** [191]
Nariva Swamp •
Trinidad & Tobago .... **160** U

Narmada • India **28** C4
Narnaul • India **137** C2
Narni • Italy **12** G6
Naro • Sicily, Italy **120** D3
Narodnaya, gora • Russian Fed. ... **17** J1
Narrabri • NS, Australia **34** I6
Narraberri • NS, Australia **144** C1
Narragansett •
RI, United States **153** D8
Narrogin • WA, Australia **34** I6
Narromine • NS, Australia **34** I6
Narsarsuaq • Greenland **39** V4
Narsimhapur • India **28** C4
Narta • Japan **140** B3
Naruto • Japan **140** B3
Naruto-kaikyo • Japan **140** B3
Narva • Estonia **126** B2
Narva • Russian Fed. **16** I2
Narym • Russian Fed. **26** N6
Naryn • Kazakstan **26** M9
Naryn [Riv] •
Kazakhstan/Uzbekistan **26** M9
Narynkol • Kazakstan **26** M9
Näsåker • Sweden **16** I5
Nasalot Game Reserve • Kenya . **131** G1
Naseby • United Kingdom **90** A7
Nash Point • United Kingdom **104** F2
Nashoba Valley **Ski** •
MA, United States .... **149** [205]
Nashoba Valley •
MA, United States **153** D4
Nashua • NH, United States **153** D4
Nashville • TN, United States **48** D2
Nashwaak Bridge • NB, Canada .. **44** L2
Nasice • Croatia **12** M3
Nasice • Croatia **128** D2
Näsijärvi • Finland **125** E2
Nasik • India **28** B4
Nasir • Sudan **23** E2
Nasiriyah, An • Iraq **18** E3
Nass • BC, Canada **38** F5
Nassau • Cook Is. **33** K7
Nassau • Bahamas **158** B2
Nasser, Lake • Egypt **131** F5
Nässjö • Sweden **125** F7
Nata • Botswana **24** D4
Nata [Riv] • Botswana/Zimbabwe . **24** D4
Natal • Brazil **53** (1) D3
Natal • Indonesia **143** G4
Natal Drakensberg Nat. Park •
South Africa **134** B3
Natal Mehlos • South Africa **134** B3
Natashquan • QU, Canada **156** D2
Natashquan [Riv] • QU, Canada .. **39** S6
Natchez • MS, United States **153** F1
Natchez Nat. Hist. Park **Park N** •
MS, United States .... **151** [194]
Natchez Trace Parkway **Park N** •
United States .... **151** [196]
Natchez Trace Parkway •
United States **153** F2
Natchitoches •
LA, United States **153** F1
Nathdwara • India **137** C5
Nathon • Ko Samui, Thailand **142** D1
National Agricultural Centre •
United Kingdom **104** D2
National Birds of Prey Centre •
United Kingdom **104** D3
National Capital parks **Park N** •
DC, United States .... **151** [282]
National City •
CA, United States **45** D5
National Exhibition Centre •
United Kingdom **104** D2
National Mall **Park N** •
DC, United States .... **151** [283]
National Park • New Zealand **145** F3
National Stadium • Singapore ... **141** H4
Natitingou • Benin **22** E2
Natividade • Brazil **51** H6
Natori • Japan **30** K5
Natron, Lake • Tanzania **130** B2
Natrona Heights •
PA, United States **44** F5
Nattawasaga Bay • OT, Canada . **155** B5
Natuna Besar • Indonesia **32** D3
Natuna Is. • Indonesia **31** D6
Natuna, Kepulauan • Indonesia . **143** F2
Natural Bridges Nat. Mon. **Park N** •
UT, United States .... **150** [83]
Naturaliste, Cape •
WA, Australia **34** C6
Nature's Valley • South Africa ... **134** C7
Naturita • CO, United States **45** H2
Nauders • Austria **119** H6
Nauen • Germany **111** C1
Nauujoli-Akmene • Lithuania **13** L1
Naukluft Mtns • Namibia **24** B4
Naul • Ireland **9** G5
Naumburg • Germany **9** G5
Nauplia • Greece **90** A20
NAURU • Pacific Ocean **33** H6
Nauta • Peru **51** C4
Nauvoo • IL, United States **46** J2
Nava • Mexico **47** D3
Navahermosa • Spain **11** G5
Navajo Dam • NM, United States . **45** I3
Navajo Indian Reservation •
AZ/NM, United States **153** E2
Navajo Nat. Mon. **Park N** •
AZ, United States .... **150** [100]
Navajo Nat. Mon. •
AZ, United States **153** E1
Navajo Reservoir •
CO/NM, United States **153** E2
Navalmoral de la Mata • Spain .. **11** F5
Navan • Ireland **108** B3
Navarin, mys • Russian Fed. **27** U4
Navarino • Greece **90** A20
Navarino, I. • Chile **53** C7
Navarra • Spain **11** J2
Navarre Beach •
FL, United States **154** H1
Navarro Mill Lake •
TX, United States **47** F2
Navasota • TX, United States **47** F2
Navasota • TX, United States **154** J4
Navasota R. • TX, United States . **154** J4
Navax Point, Pointe New Caledonia **35** (1) A3
Navojoa • Mexico **157** F4
Navrongo • Ghana **22** D2
Nawabshah • Pakistan **28** A3
Nawalgarh • India **137** C2
Nawiliwili • HI, United States ... **154** G2
Naxçivan • Azerbaijan **18** E2
Naxçivan [Adm] • Azerbaijan **18** E2
Náxos • Greece **122** D8
Náxos [I.] • Greece **122** D8
Nayarit • Mexico **45** D3
Nayarit [Adm] • Mexico **37** (1) A1
Nayoro • Japan **30** L2
Nazaré • Portugal **11** J5
Nazaré **Beach** • Portugal ...... **96** [197]
Nazareth • Israel **135** A4
Nazario Sauro **Dive** • Red Sea . **135** B4
Nazca • Peru **51** C6
Nazca **Heritage C** • Peru ..... **84** [60]
Nazca • Peru **163** B1
Nazca Lines • Peru **51** C6
Nazca Ridge • Pacific Ocean **51** C6
Naze • Japan **29** H5
Nazilli • Turkey **122** D7
Nazimovo • Russian Fed. **26** Q6
Nazran • Russian Fed. **17** G6
Nazwa • Oman **18** G5
Nchelnge • Zambia **23** D5
Ndalatando • Angola **23** B5

Ndali

Ndali • Benin 22 E3
Ndélé • Central African Rep. 23 C2
Ndendé, Réserve de Park • Gabon . . 133 [51]
Ndere I. Nat. Park • Kenya 131 G3
Ndola • Zambia 24 D2
Ndrhamcha, Sebkha du •
   Mauritania 20 B5
Nduindui • Solomon Is. 35 (1) F2
Ndumo Game Reserve Park •
   South Africa . . . . 133 [130]
Ndumo Game Reserve •
   South Africa 134 B2
Nea • Norway 16 F5
Néa Artáki • Greece 15 H8
Néa Fókea Beach • Greece . . . . . . 97 [192]
Néa Ionia • Greece 122 D4
Néa Kidonia Beach •
   Crete, Greece . . . . 97 [212]
Néa Moní • Greece 122 D5
Néa Póri Beach • Greece . . . . 97 [190]
Néa Róda Beach • Greece . . . . 97 [192]
Néa Skióni Beach • Greece . . . . . . 97 [192]
Néa Stíra • Greece 122 D4
Néa Zíhni • Greece 15 E2
Neagh, Lough • United Kingdom 7 F7
Neale, Lake • NT, Australia 145 D3
Neanderthal • Germany 111 B3
Neápoli • W. Macedonia, Greece 15 C3
Neápoli • Peloponnese, Greece 15 E7
Neápoli Beach • Greece . . . . 97 [182]
Neápoli • Crete, Greece 123 E7
Neapolitan Riviera • Italy 121 G4
Neath • United Kingdom 7 I10
Neath Bay • WA, United States 42 C2
Nebbio • Corsica, France 115 L2
Nebbou • Burkina Faso 20 E6
Nebesna • AK, United States 49 M3
Nebitdag • Turkmenistan 18 F2
Neblina • Brazil/Venezuela 51 D3
Nebo • QL, Australia 144 B3
Nebo, Mount • Jordan 135 A4
Nebraska • United States 40 F3
Nebraska City •
   NE, United States 46 H2
Nebrodi • Sicily, Italy 12 I11
Nechako • BC, Canada 155 C1
Neches • TX, United States 154 J4
Neckar • Germany 112 D6
Neckargemünd • Germany 5 L5
Neckarsulm • Germany 9 E7
Necochea • Argentina 163 D3
Neder-Rijn • Netherlands 5 I3
Nederland • TX, United States 47 G3
Nedong • China 27 K6
Nedstrand • Norway 124 C5
Needle • BC, Canada 42 F2
Needles • CA, United States 152 C6
Needles, The • United Kingdom 5 B4
Neenah • WI, United States 43 L4
Neepawa • MN, Canada 43 G1
Nefedova • Russian Fed. 26 L6
Nefta • Tunisia 131 E3
Neftekamsk • Russian Fed. 17 I3
Nefteyugansk • Russian Fed. 26 L5
Nefza • Tunisia 12 D12
Negage • Angola 22 H6
Negara • Bali, Indonesia 143 H1
Negaunee • MI, United States 23 F2
Negēlē • Ethiopia 23 F2
Negeri Sembilan • Malaysia 141 G4
Negev • Israel 21 F1
Negomano • Mozambique 24 F2
Negombo • Sri Lanka 138 D15
Negra • Peru 51 A5
Negra, Punta • Peru 51 A5
Negrais, Cape • Myanmar 31 A3
Negreira • Spain 11 C2
Negril • Jamaica 159 F1
Negro • Brazil 51 E4
Negro • Uruguay 52 E5
Negro • Argentina 53 D4
Negro, Cabo • Margarita . . . . 160 V
Negroponte • Greece 90 A20
Negros • Philippines 31 G4
Negru Vodă • Romania 128 E2
Nehe • China 27 J7
Neheim-Hüsten • Germany 8 C5
Nei Mongol Zizhiqu • China 29 E2
Neiba • Dominican Rep. 159 G6
Neiba, Sierra de •
   Dominican Rep. 159 G6
Neiderau Ski • Austria . . . . 100 [148]
Neidpath Castle •
   United Kingdom 104 B4
Neijiang • China 29 D5
Neipperg Castle • Germany . . . . . . 113 [87]
Neiva • Colombia 51 B3
Nekemt • Ethiopia 23 F2
Nekhen • Egypt 131 F5
Neksø • Denmark 125 F16
Nelichu • Sudan 23 E2
Neligh • NE, United States 126 C3
Neligh • NE, United States 43 G5
Nellore • India 138 D7
Nelma • Russian Fed. 27 M7
Nelsom • BC, Canada 42 G2
Nelson • New Zealand 35 D5
Nelson • BC, Canada 38 H7
Nelson • SA, United States 38 L5
Nelson, Cape • VIC, Australia 34 H7
Nelson Museum •
   St Kitts & Nevis . . . . 161 G
Nelson's Dockyard •
   Antigua & Barbuda . . . . 161 K
Nelspoort • South Africa 134 C3
Nelspruit • South Africa 24 E5
Nelyaty • Russian Fed. 27 I5
Néma • Mauritania 20 D5
Neman • Russian Fed. 13 K2
Nembrala • Indonesia 32 (1) H5
Neméa • Greece 15 D6
Neméa [Adm] • Greece 15 D6
Nēmērçkë • Albania 15 B3
Nemi, Lagi di • Italy 121 F3
Nemours • France 115 E4
Nemrut Daği Heritage C • Turkey . . . 86 [230]
Nemunas • Lithuania 126 B5
Nemuro • Japan 30 M3
Nen Jiang • China 27 K6
Nenagh • Ireland 108 C6
Nenana • AK, United States 49 L3
Nendal Ski • Switzerland . . . . 100 [82]
Nene • United Kingdom 7 M5
Nenjiang • China 27 K7
Néo Itilo Beach • Greece . . . . 97 [182]
Neohóri Beach • Greece . . . . 97 [200]
Néos Marmarás Beach • Greece . . 97 [192]
Néos Marmarás • Greece 122 D1
Neosho • MO, United States 46 H4
NEPAL • Asia 28 D3
Nepalganj • Nepal 28 D3
Nephi • UT, United States 45 G2
Nephin Beg Range • Ireland 108 C1
Neptun-Olimp • Romania 128 E2
Nera • Italy 121 F1
Neratovice • Czech Rep. 13 D7
Nererva • Bosnia-Herz. 12 L5
Neris • Lithuania 126 B6
Nerja Beach • Spain . . . . 96 [114]
Nerja • Spain 116 B7
Nerpio • Spain 11 I6
Nerva • Spain 11 E7
Nesbyen • Norway 124 C4
Nesebur Heritage C • Bulgaria . . . . 86 [203]
Nesebur Beach • Bulgaria . . . . 97 [242]
Nesebur • Bulgaria 128 E2
Neskaupstaður • Iceland 16 (1) F2

Neslandsvatn • Norway 124 B3
Nesna • Norway 16 G3
Ness • KS, United States 46 F3
Ness, Loch • United Kingdom 6 H4
Nessebar Heritage C • Bulgaria . . . . 86 [203]
Nessebar Beach • Bulgaria . . . . 97 [242]
Nessebar • Bulgaria 128 E3
Nesselwang • Germany 112 F6
Nesterov • Russian Fed. 13 L3
Nesterov • Ukraine 13 N8
Néstos • Greece 15 F2
Nesttun • Norway 124 B4
Netanya • Israel 135 A3
Netarhat Hill Sta • India 138 E2
NETHERLANDS • Europe 109
NETHERLANDS ANTILLES •
   West Indies 160/161
Neto • Italy 12 K9
Nette • Germany 112 E1
Nettilling Lake • NU, Canada 39 O3
Nettlé, Baie • St Martin . . . . 160 D
Nettuno • Italy 121 F3
Nettuno, Grotta di •
   Sardinia, Italy 120 C1
Neu-Anspach • Germany 112 E2
Neu-Ulm • Germany 112 F1
Neubrandenburg • Germany 8 I3
Neuburg • Germany 9 G8
Neuburg Castle • Germany . . . . . . 113 [123]
Neuchâtel • Switzerland 119 G1
Neuchâtel, Lac de • Switzerland . . 119 G1
Neue Bischöflicher Residenz, Passau
   Castle • Germany . . . . 113 [125]
Neue Residenz, Bamberg Castle •
   Germany . . . . 113 [163]
Neuenburg Castle • Germany . . . . 113 [206]
Neuenhagen bei Berlin • Germany . . 111 C2
Neuenstein Castle • Germany . . . . 113 [95]
Neues Palais (Potsdam) •
   Germany 111 C3
Neues Palais, Potsdam Castle •
   Germany . . . . 113 [216]
Neues Schloss, Bayreuth Castle •
   Germany . . . . 113 [156]
Neues Schloss, Ingolstadt Castle •
   Germany . . . . 113 [138]
Neues Schloss, Oberschleissheim
   Castle • Germany . . . . 113 [129]
Neufchâteau • France 10 K5
Neufchâteau • Belgium 109 D19
Neufchâtel-en-Bray • France 10 G4
Neuhof • Germany 9 E6
Neukirchen • Germany 111 C4
Neukölln (Berlin) • Germany 111 C4
Neuleiningen • Germany 112 D4
Neumagen-Dhron • Germany 112 E3
Neumarkt in der Oberpfalz •
   Germany 9 G7
Neumarkt-St Veit • Germany 112 F4
Neumarkter Sattel • Austria 14 B2
Neumünster • Germany 8 E2
Neunburg • Germany 9 O6
Neunkirchen • Austria 13 F10
Neunkirchen • Germany 112 D3
Neuquén • Argentina 53 C3
Neuruppin • Germany 8 H4
Neuschwanstein • Germany 112 E6
Neuschwanstein Castle • Germany 113 [117]
Neuse • NC, United States 48 I3
Neusiedler See • Austria 13 F10
Neuss • Germany 111 B3
Neustadt am Rübenberge •
   Germany 8 E4
Neustadt an der Aisch • Germany . . . 9 F7
Neustadt an der Weinstrasse •
   Germany 112 D4
Neustadt bei Coburg • Germany . . . 112 F2
Neustadt in Holstein • Germany 8 F2
Neustadt in Holstein Spa •
   Germany . . . . 113 [c17]
Neustift • Austria 119 H6
Neustift im Stubaital Ski •
   Austria . . . . 100 [140]
Neustrelitz • Germany 8 I3
Neuwied • Germany 112 E1
Nevada • MO, United States 46 H4
Nevada • United States . . . . 152 C
Nevada City • CA, United States . . . 152 C3
Nevada, Peña • Mexico 24 B3
Nevada, Sierra • Colombia 51 C1
Nevada, Sierra • Spain 116 B3
Nevada, Sierra •
   CA, United States 152 C3
Nevado • Colombia 51 C3
Neve, Serra da • Angola 24 A2
Nevel • Russian Fed. 17 I3
Nevers • France 10 I7
Nevesinje • Bosnia-Herz. 14 F6
Neviges • Germany 111 B2
Nevinnomyssk • Russian Fed. 17 G6
Nevis • St Kitts & Nevis . . . . 161 G
Nevis Peak • St Kitts & Nevis . . . . . 161 G
Nevşehir • Turkey 123 G2
Nevyansk • Russian Fed. 26 J6
New Albany • MS, United States . . . 48 C3
New Albany • IN, United States 48 E1
New Amsterdam • Surinam 51 F2
New Bedford • MA, United States . . 153 D8
New Bedford Whaling Nat. Hist. Park Park N •
   MA, United States . . . . 151 [327]
New Bern • NC, United States 48 I3
New Boston • TX, United States 46 H6
New Braunfels •
   TX, United States 154 J3
New Brighton • New Zealand 35 D6
New Britain • Papua New Guinea . . 35 (1) E2
New Castle • CT, United States 44 I5
New Brunswick •
   NJ, United States 153 D7
New Brunswick • Canada 156 D2
NEW CALEDONIA • Pacific Ocean . 35 (2) B3
New Castle • IN, United States 44 C6
New Castle • PA, United States 44 G3
New Castle • DE, United States . . . 153 D10
New Cuyama • CA, United States . . . 45 C4
New Delhi • India 137 C2
New England • ND, United States . . 43 E3
New England • United States 152 A4
New Exchequer Dam •
   CA, United States 45 B3
New Forest • United Kingdom 5 B4
New Georgia • Solomon Is. 35 (1) F2
New Georgia Sound • Solomon Is. . 35 (1) F2
New Glarus • WI, United States 23 K2
New Glasgow • NS, Canada 156 D7
New Guinea • Oceania 35 (1) C2
New Hampshire • United States 44 J4
New Hanover • Papua New Guinea . 35 (1) E1
New Haven • IN, United States 44 C5
New Haven • CT, United States . . . 153 D7
New Hazleton • BC, Canada 155 C1
New Hebrides • Vanuatu 35 (2) B2
New Iberia • LA, United States 47 I2
New Iberia • LA, United States 153 F3
New Ireland • Papua New Guinea . . 35 (1) E1
New Jersey • United States 153 D10
New Kensington •
   PA, United States 44 F5
New Lexington •
   OH, United States 44 D6
New Liskeard • OT, Canada 43 N3
New London • WI, United States . . . 43 L4
New London • CT, United States . . . 153 D8
New Market • VA, United States . . . 153 D9

New Martinsville •
   WV, United States 44 E6
New Meadows • ID, United States . . . 42 G4
New Mexico • United States 40 E5
New Milford • PA, United States 44 H5
New Norfolk • TS, Australia 34 I8
New Orleans • LA, United States . . . 153 F4
New Orleans Jazz Nat. Hist. Park Park N •
   LA, United States . . . . 151 [192]
New Paltz • NY, United States 153 D7
New Philadelphia •
   OH, United States 44 E5
New Pine Creek •
   OR, United States 42 E5
New Plymouth • New Zealand 145 F3
New Providence • Bahamas 158 B3
New Quay Beach •
   United Kingdom . . . . 101 [195-196]
New Roads • LA, United States 47 I2
New Rochelle •
   NY, United States 44 I5
New Ross • Ireland 7 F9
New Siberian Is. • Russian Fed. 27 N1
New Smyrna Beach •
   FL, United States 154 H4
New South Wales • NS, Australia . . . 34 I6
New Territories •
   Hong Kong, China 139 B5
New Town • ND, United States 43 E2
New Ulm • MN, United States 43 I4
New Valley, The • Egypt 131 F3
New Westminster • BC, Canada . . . 38 G7
New Winterplace Ski •
   VA, United States . . . . 149 [165]
New York • NY, United States 153 D7
New York [Adm] • United States . . . 44 H4
New York Mtn •
   CA, United States 45 E4
NEW ZEALAND • Australasia 35
New Zealand Sub-Antarctic islands
   Heritage N • Southern Ocean . . . 83 [153]
Newark • OH, United States 44 D5
Newark • NJ, United States 44 G4
Newark • NY, United States 153 D7
Newark-on-Trent •
   United Kingdom 7 L8
Newberg • OR, United States 42 D4
Newberry • SC, United States 48 G3
Newborough Beach •
   United Kingdom . . . . 101 [215]
Newburgh • NY, United States 153 D7
Newbury • United Kingdom 7 K10
Newcastle • NSW, Australia 1 G7
Newcastle • South Africa 134 B1
Newcastle • NS, Australia 144 C2
Newcastle • Jamaica 159 F4
Newcastle • St Kitts & Nevis . . . . . 161 G
Newcastle • United States 43 D5
Newcastle • OT, Canada 44 F4
Newcastle • NB, Canada 156 D2
Newcastle Creek • NT, Australia . . . 34 F3
Newcastle under Lyme •
   United Kingdom 7 J8
Newcastle upon Tyne •
   United Kingdom 7 K7
Newcastle West • Ireland 108 C6
Newcomb • NM, United States 45 H3
Newenham, Cape •
   AK, United States 49 I4
Newfoundland • NF, Canada 156 D3
Newfoundland & Labrador •
   Canada 39 T6
Newgale Beach • United Kingdom . . 101 [181]
Newgrange • Ireland 108 B2
Newhaven • United Kingdom 104 E3
Newman • WA, Australia 34 C4
Newman • GA, United States 48 E4
Newmarket • United Kingdom 7 M9
Newmarket • Ireland 108 C6
Newmarket • OT, Canada 44 F3
Newmarket • OT, Canada 155 B5
Newmarket on Fergus • Ireland . . . 108 C6
Newnan • GA, United States 48 D7
Newport •
   VA, United States 153 D11
Newport News •
   VA, United States 153 D11
Newport Sands Beach •
   United Kingdom . . . . 101 [187]
Newquay Beach •
   United Kingdom . . . . 101 [138-139]
Newquay • United Kingdom 104 F4
Newry • United Kingdom 7 F7
Newton • MA, United States 41 G4
Newton • MA, United States 44 J4
Newton • IA, United States 46 I3
Newton Abbot • United Kingdom . . 104 F5
Newtontoppen • Svalbard 54 N2
Newtown • United Kingdom 7 I9
Newtownabbey • United Kingdom . . . 7 G7
Newtownards • United Kingdom 7 G7
Newville • CA, United States 42 D7
Neya • Russian Fed. 17 I2
Neyagawa • Japan 140 B2
Neyshabur • Iran 18 E2
Neyveli • India 138 D11
Nez Perce Nat. Hist. Park Park N •
   ID, United States . . . . 150 [64]
Nez Perce Nat. Hist. Park •
   ID, United States 152 B2
Nga, Laem • Ko Phuket, Thailand . . 142 E2
Ngabé • Congo 23 C3
Ngami, Lake • Botswana 24 C4
Ngamiland • Botswana 24 C4
Ngangerdabi Plain • Kenya 23 G4
Ngangla Ringco • China 28 D2
Nganglong Kangri • China 28 D2
Nganze Co • China 28 E2
Ngao • Thailand 142 B2
Ngaoundéré • Cameroon 22 G3
Ngarurruro, Mt • New Zealand 145 F4
Ngo • Congo 22 H5
Ngoan Muc Pass • Vietnam 142 E3
Ngoc Linh • Vietnam 25 L8
Ngoko • Cameroon/Congo 23 B3
Ngola Shankou • China 29 B3
Ngoma • Zambia 28 G2
Ngoring Hu • China 28 G2
Ngorongoro Conservation Area
   Heritage N • Tanzania . . . . 83 [101]
Ngorongoro Conservation Area •
   Tanzania . . . . 133 [88]
Ngorongoro Conservation Area Park •
   Tanzania . . . . 133 [88]
Ngorongoro Crater • Tanzania 130 B2
Ngounié • Gabon 22 G5
Ngoura • Chad 23 B2
Ngudu • Tanzania 23 A3
Nguigmi • Niger 20 H6
Ngum, Ko • Thailand 142 E1
Nguni • Kenya 23 F4
Ngurah Rai [Apt] •
   Bali, Indonesia 143 H4
Nguru • Nigeria 22 H2
Nha Trang • Vietnam 141 E2
Nhlangano • Swaziland 134 B2

Nhulunbuy • NT, Australia 34 G2
Nia-Nia • Dem. Rep. of Congo 23 D3
Niafounké • Mali 20 E5
Niagara Falls •
   NY, United States 153 D1
Niagara Falls • OT, Canada 155 B9
Niagara Falls [Waterfall] •
   Canada/United States 155 B9
Niagara on the Lake •
   NY, United States 44 F4
Niah • Malaysia 32 E2
Niamey • Niger 20 F6
Niangara • Dem. Rep. of Congo 23 D3
Niangay, Lac • Mali 20 E5
Niangoloko • Burkina Faso 22 D2
Niantic • CT, United States 44 J5
Nianzishan • China 27 J7
Niao Dao • China 29 B3
Nias • Indonesia 143 G3
Nias • Indonesia 125 F5
NICARAGUA • C. America 37 D5
Nicaragua, Lago de • Nicaragua . . . 37 D5
Nice • France 115 H2
Nice-Côte d'Azur [Apt] • France . . . 115 H2
Nicholls Town • Bahamas 158 B1
Nicholson • WA, Australia 34 E4
Nicobar Is. • India 28 F7
Nicodemus Nat. Hist. Site Park N •
   KS, United States . . . . 150 [166]
Nicosia • Cyprus 123 J2
Nida • Lithuania 126 A5
Nida • Poland 128 C2
Nidda • Germany 9 E6
Nidda [Riv] • Germany 9 E6
Nideggen • Germany 112 D1
Nidgegen Castle • Germany . . . . . 113 [29]
Nidri • Levkas, Greece 122 C1
Nidzica • Poland 13 J4
Niebüll • Germany 8 D2
Niebla • Spain 11 E7
Niederau • Austria 119 H3
Niederbayern • Germany 9 H8
Niederdorf Ski • Italy . . . . 100 [246]
Niederlausitz • Germany 111 A4
Niederösterreich • Austria 13 E10
Niedersachsen • Germany 8 E4
Nienburg • Germany 8 E4
Niers • Germany 5 J3
Nieuw Amsterdam • Surinam 51 F2
Nieuwegein • Netherlands 109 F1
Nieuwpoort • Belgium 109 E1
Nieuwpoort • Curaçao . . . . 160 X
Nieuwpoort-aan-Zee • Belgium . . . 109 E1
Nieves, Pico de las •
   Gran Canaria, Canary Is. 117 B3
Niğde • Turkey 123 G2
Niğde [Adm] • Turkey 123 G2
NIGER • Africa 20 G5
Niger • Africa 22 F3
Niger Delta • Nigeria 22 F3
Niger [Riv] • Africa 22 D1
NIGERIA • Africa 22 F2
Night Hawk Lake • OT, Canada 44 E1
Nigrán Beach • Spain . . . . 96 [93]
Nigrita • Greece 14 K9
Nii • Japan 30 J7
Niigata • Japan 30 J6
Niigata [Adm] • Japan 140 A4
Niihama • Japan 30 G7
Niihau • HI, United States 154 G2
Niimi • Japan 140 B1
Nijar Beach • Spain . . . . 96 [116]
Nijar • Spain 116 B4
Nijmegen • Netherlands 109 D11
Nika • Maldives 138 F1
Nikel' • Russian Fed. 17 E1
Nikikas Beach • Greece . . . . 97 [192]
Niki • Benin 22 E3
Nikkō Heritage C • Japan . . . . 85 [193]
Nikolayevsk-na-Amure •
   Russian Fed. 27 N6
Nikol'sk • F.R. of Yugoslavia 14 F7
Nikolski • AK, United States 49 H5
Nikópol • Greece 17 E5
Nikopol • Greece 15 B4
Niksic • F.R. of Yugoslavia 14 F7
Nîl, Bahr el • Africa 21 F2
Nilandu Atoll North • Maldives 138 F1
Nilandu Atoll South • Maldives 138 F1
Nilaveli • Sri Lanka 138 D11
Nile • Africa 21 F2
Nile Delta • Egypt 131 F1
Nilgiri Hills • India 138 D10
Nilometer • Egypt 131 F5
Nilüfer • Turkey 15 J3
Nimba, Mts • Africa 22 C3
Nîmes • France 10 J10
Nin • Croatia 14 E5
Nine Degree Channel •
   Indian Ocean 138 D9
Ninety Mile Beach • New Zealand . . 35 D2
Ninety Mile Beach •
   New Zealand 144 C3
Ninety Six Nat. Hist. Site Park N •
   SC, United States . . . . 151 [235]
Ninevah • Iraq 18 D2
Ning Zhen Shan • China 139 C1
Ningbo • China 139 C4
Ningbo • China 139 C3
Ningde • China 139 C3
Ninghai • China 139 C4
Ningjing Shan • China 28 G2
Ningwu • China 29 E3
Ningxia Huizu Zizhiqu • China 29 D3
Ninh Hoa • Vietnam 141 E2
Niobrara • NE, United States 43 G5
Niobrara [Riv] •
   NE, United States 43 G5
Niokolo Koba, Parc nat. de Park •
   Senegal . . . . 133 [9]
Niokolo Koba, Parc nat. du Heritage N •
   Senegal . . . . 83 [82]
Niolo • Corsica, France 115 L1
Nioro du Sahel • Mali 20 D5
Niort • France 114 D3
Nipigon • OT, Canada 43 L2
Nipigon Bay • OT, Canada 43 L2
Nipigon, Lake • OT, Canada 23 N7
Nipissing, Lake • OT, Canada 155 B1
Niquelândia • Brazil 52 G1
Niquero • Cuba 158 D7
Nirasaki • Japan 140 C1
Nirmal • India 28 C5
Nis • F.R. of Yugoslavia 14 I6
Nisab • Yemen 18 D5
Niskayuna • NY, United States 44 I4
Nisko • Poland 13 L7
Nissáki • Corfu, Greece 122 B1
Nissedal • Norway 124 C6

Nisser • Norway 124 C6
Nissiros • Greece 122 C6
Nissum Bredning • Denmark 125 F5
Nissum Fjord • Denmark 125 F9
Nisswa • MN, United States 43 I3
Nistru • Moldova 14 G3
Niterói • Brazil 163 C4
Niton • United Kingdom 7 I6
Nithavris • Crete, Greece 123 E6
Nitra • Slovak Rep. 13 H9
Nitra • Slovak Rep. 13 H9
Nitra [Riv] • Slovak Rep. 14 D2
Nitray [Château] • France 114 D2
Nittedal • Norway 124 B2
Niuafo'ou • Tonga 35 (2) G2
Niuatoi Putapu • Tonga 35 (2) F2
NIUE • Pacific Ocean 35 (2) G2
Niut, Gunung • Indonesia 32 D2
Nivala • Finland 16 M5
Nivelles • Belgium 109 D14
Nivernais • France 10 I6
Niya • China 28 D1
Nizamabad • India 28 C5
Nizhnegansk • Russian Fed. 27 G5
Nizhnekamsk • Russian Fed. 17 I3
Nizhnevartovsk • Russian Fed. 26 D7
Nizhnevartovsk • Russian Fed. 26 M5
Nizhneyansk • Russian Fed. 27 M2
Nizhniy Novgorod • Russian Fed. . . 17 G3
Nizhniy Tagil • Russian Fed. 26 I6
Nizhnyaya Pesha • Russian Fed. . . 17 H1
Nizhnyaya Tunguska •
   Russian Fed. 26 P5
Nizina • Slovak Rep. 14 E2
Nizina Podlaska • Poland 13 L4
Nizke Tatry • Slovak Rep. 13 I9
Nízke Tatry Nat. Park Park N •
   Slovak Rep. . . . . 89 [101]
Njandoma • Russian Fed. 17 G2
Njave • Tanzania 24 F1
Njombe • Tanzania 130 B3
Njudung • Sweden 125 F8
Njvala • Finland 16 M5
Njunes • Norway 16 J2
Nkayi • Congo 23 A4
Nkongsamba • Cameroon 22 F4
Nkululu • Tanzania 23 E5
No Name City • Germany 112 E5
Noatak Nat. Preserve Park N •
   AK, United States . . . . 150 [4]
Nobeoka • Japan 30 F8
Noblesville • IN, United States 44 B6
Noce • Italy 120 B3
Nockberge, Nationalpark Park N •
   Austria . . . . 89 [83]
Noda • Japan 140 C2
Nodin • Mongolia 29 C2
Nogales • AZ, United States 153 E3
Nogales • Mexico 157 F2
Nogent-le-Rotrou • France 114 D2
Noginsk • Siberia, Russian Fed. . . . 26 P5
Noginsk • Moscow, Russian Fed. . . 126 C4
Nogliki • Russian Fed. 27 N6
Nogoa • QL, Australia 144 B3
Nogoyá • Argentina 52 E5
Nogueira, Serra da • Portugal 11 E3
Nohcacab • Mexico 157 H1
Nohfelden • Germany 5 K5
Noia • Spain 11 C2
Noirmoutier, I. de • France 10 C7
Noirmoutier-en-l'Ile Beach •
   France . . . . 96 [83]
Noja Beach • Spain . . . . 96 [89]
Noja • Spain 120 B2
Nok Kundi • Pakistan 18 H4
Nokaneng • Botswana 24 C3
Nokhra • India 137 C1
Nokia • Finland 125 E2
Nokomis • SA, Canada 43 D1
Nola • Central African Rep. 23 B3
Nola • Italy 121 E5
Noli Beach • Italy . . . . 96 [141]
Noli • Italy 121 E5
Nolinsk • Russian Fed. 17 H3
Nomad • Papua New Guinea 35 (1) C2
Nome • AK, United States 49 I3
Nomuka Group • Tonga 35 (2) F3
Nong Khai • Thailand 31 C3
Nong Nooch Garden • Thailand . . . 142 C4
Nongoma • South Africa 134 B2
Nonsuch I. • Bermuda 159 J2
Nonthaburi • Thailand 142 C3
Noord • Aruba . . . . 160 Y
Noord-Beveland • Netherlands 109 D10
Noord-Brabant • Netherlands 109 D11
Noord-Holland • Netherlands 109 D7
Noordoostpolder • Netherlands . . . 109 D7
Noordpunt • Curaçao . . . . 160 X
Noordwijk Beach • Netherlands . . . 96 [68]
Noordwijk • Netherlands 109 F1
Noordzee Kanaal • Netherlands . . . 109 F2
Noormarkku • Finland 125 E1
Noosa Heads • QL, Australia 144 B6
Nora • Sardinia, Italy 120 C4
Noranda • QU, Canada 39 P7
Norberg • Sweden 125 D1
Nord, I. du • Seychelles 133 K2
Nord-Ostsee-Kanal • Germany 8 E2
Nord-Ouest, Presqu'île de •
   Haiti 159 G2
Nord-Pas de Calais • France 114 A2
Nord-Trøndelag • Norway 16 G4
Nordagutu • Norway 124 B3
Nordborg Beach • Denmark . . . . . . 96 [45]
Nordborg • Denmark 125 F13
Nordby • Denmark 125 F9
Norddeich • Germany 8 C3
Norden • Germany 8 C3
Norden Spa • Germany . . . . 113 [c8]
Nordenham • Germany 8 D3
Nordenskjöld [Base] •
   Antarctica 54 (1) D2
Norderney Spa • Germany . . . . . . 113 [c11]
Norderstedt • Germany 8 E3
Nordeste Beach •
   São Miguel, Azores . . . . 96 [105]
Nordeste • Azores 118 B2
Nordfjord • Norway 124 C1
Nordfjorneset • Norway 124 C1
Nordfriesische Inseln • Germany . . . 8 D2
Nordfriesland • Germany 8 D2
Nordfrisiska Oarna •
   Denmark/Germany 16 E9
Nordhausen • Germany 8 F4
Nordhorn • Germany 8 C4
Nordic Mtn Ski •
   WI, United States . . . . 149 [131]
Nordjylland • Denmark 125 F5
Nordkapp • Norway 16 M1
Nordkinn • Norway 16 N1
Nordkinn-halvøya • Norway 16 N1
Nordland • Norway 16 G3
Nördlingen • Germany 9 F8
Nördlingen Castle • Germany . . . . 113 [135]
Nordrhein-Westfalen • Germany . . . 8 C4
Nordstrand • Germany 8 D2
Nore • Norway 124 B3
Norej • Moldova 14 P2
Norefjell • Norway 124 B1
Noresund • Norway 124 B1
Norfolk • United Kingdom 7 M9
Norfolk • VA, United States 43 H8

Norfolk • NE, United States 43 H5
Norfolk • VA, United States 153 D11
Norfolk I. •
   AR, United States 46 I4
Norheimsund • Norway 124 C3
Noril'sk • Russian Fed. 26 O4
Normal • IL, United States 46 K2
Norman • OK, United States 46 G5
Norman I. • British Virgin Is. . . . . . 160 B
Norman, Lake •
   NC, United States 48 G3
Norman Wells • NT, Canada 38 F3
Normanby • Papua New Guinea . . . 35 (1) E2
Normandie • France 10 E5
Normandie, Collines de • France . . . 10 E5
Normanton • QL, Australia 34 H3
Norra Kvarken • Finland/Sweden . . 16 K5
Norra Storfjället • Sweden 16 H4
Norrbotten • Sweden 16 K3
Norre Åby Beach • Denmark . . . . . 96 [44]
Norre Djurs Beach • Denmark . . . . 96 [47]
Norre Nebel • Denmark 125 F5
Norre Snede • Denmark 125 F5
Norre Vorupør • Denmark 125 F5
Norresundby • Denmark 125 F8
Norrhult • Sweden 125 E8
Norris Lake • TN, United States 48 F2
Norristown • PA, United States . . . 153 D6
Norrköping • Sweden 125 F4
Norrland Riviera • Sweden 124 A4
Norrtälje Beach • Sweden . . . . 97 [23]
Norrtälje • Sweden 125 E3
Norseman • WA, Australia 34 D6
Norsjö • Sweden 16 J4
Norsjö • Norway 124 B3
Norsk • Russian Fed. 27 L6
Norsoup • Vanuatu 35 (2) B2
Norte, Cabo • Brazil 51 G3
Norte, Punta • Argentina 53 D4
North Adams • MA, United States . . 44 I4
North Andaman • India 28 F6
North Arm • NT, Canada 38 I4
North Augusta •
   SC, United States 48 G4
North Battleford • SA, Canada 38 J6
North Bay • OT, Canada 155 B1
North Belcher Is. • NU, Canada . . . 39 P5
North Bend • OR, United States 42 C5
North Berwick Beach •
   United Kingdom . . . . 101 [16]
North Berwick • United Kingdom . . 104 B4
North Bimini I. • Bahamas 49 D5
North Branch Potomac •
   MD/WV, United States 153 D9
North Caicos •
   Turks & Caicos Is. 158 C1
North Cape • Norway 16 M1
North Cape • New Zealand 35 D2
North Cape • NS, Canada 156 D3
North Cape cruise area • Norway . . 81 A4
North Caribou Lake • OT, Canada . . 39 M6
North Carolina • United States 48 H3
North Cascades Nat. Park Park N •
   WA, United States . . . . 150 [26]
North Cascades Nat. Park •
   WA, United States 152 B1
North Channel • United Kingdom . . . 7 G7
North Channel • OT, Canada 44 D2
North Charleston •
   SC, United States 48 H4
North Cheyenne Indian Reservation •
   MT, United States 42 L4
North College Hill •
   OH, United States 44 C6
North Conway •
   NH, United States 44 J3
North Dakota • United States 43 F3
North Downs • United Kingdom . . . 104 E3
North East Point • Cayman Is. 159 E2
North Foreland • United Kingdom . . 7 N10
North Fork Pass • YT, Canada 38 D4
North Frigate Bay •
   St Kitts & Nevis . . . . 161 G
North Geomagnetic Pole •
   Greenland 54 V2
North Highlands •
   CA, United States 45 B2
North I. • New Zealand 35 E4
North Kitui Game Reserve •
   Kenya 131 G4
North Land • Russian Fed. 127 A5
North Las Vegas •
   NV, United States 45 E3
North Little Rock •
   AR, United States 46 I5
North Loup • NE, United States 43 F5
North Luangwa Nat. Park Park •
   Zambia . . . . 133 [103]
North Magnetic Pole • Canada 54 Z2
North Manitou I. •
   MI, United States 44 B3
North Mann Peak •
   CO, United States 45 I2
North Miami Beach •
   FL, United States 49 C6
North Negril Point • Jamaica 159 F1
North Olmsted •
   OH, United States 44 D5
North Ossetia • Russian Fed. 17 G6
North Palm Beach •
   FL, United States 49 C4
North Platte •
   NE, United States 43 E6
North Platte [Riv] •
   NE/WY, United States 46 C1
North Point • Seychelles 133 K1
North Point • Barbados . . . . 161 O
North Point • MI, United States 44 D3
North Rhine-Westphalia •
   Germany 111 A3
North Rim • AZ, United States 45 F3
North Rona • Ireland 6 G2
North Saskatchewan • AL, Canada . . 38 I6
North Sea • Europe 4 K6
North Sentinel • India 28 F6
North Shields • United Kingdom . . 106 A14
North Siberian Lowlands •
   Russian Fed. 127 A5
North Side • Cayman Is. 159 E4
North Slope • AK, United States . . . 49 J2
North Sound • Cayman Is. 159 E3
North Stradbroke I. •
   QL, Australia 144 B6
North Sydney • NS, Canada 156 D8
North Tonawanda •
   NY, United States 44 F4
North Uist • United Kingdom 6 E4
North Vancouver • BC, Canada 42 D2
North Vernon •
   IN, United States 44 C6
North West • South Africa 24 D5
North West Bluff • Montserrat . . . . 161 H
North West Cape • WA, Australia . . 34 B4
North York Moors Nat. Park Park N •
   United Kingdom . . . . 89 [45]
Northam • WA, Australia 34 C6
Northampton • United Kingdom 7 L9
Northampton • United States 44 I4
Northampton • MA, United States . . 153 D7
Northeast Aegean Is. • Greece 122 C4
Northeast Passage cruise area •
   N. America 80 A2
Northeim • Germany 8 F5
Northern Cape • South Africa 24 C6
Northern Capitals cruise area •
   Europe 81 A4
Northern Forest Reserve •
   Dominica . . . . 161 M

Northern Hills • Thailand 142 A1
Northern Indian Lake •
   MN, Canada 38 L5
Northern Ireland •
   United Kingdom 7 F7
NORTHERN MARIANA IS. •
   Pacific Ocean 33 F4
Northern Province •
   South Africa 24 D4
Northern Territory • Australia 34 F3
Northfield • MN, United States 43 J4
Northland • New Zealand 145 E1
Northport • MI, United States 44 C3
Northport • AL, United States 48 D4
Northstar-at-Tahoe Ski •
   CA, United States .... 149 [58]
Northumberland Is. •
   QL, Australia 144 B4
Northumberland Nat. Park Park N •
   United Kingdom .... 89 [42]
Northville • NY, United States 44 H4
Northway • AK, United States 38 C4
Northwest Providence Channel •
   Bahamas 49 D4
Northwest Territories • Canada 38 F4
Northwood • ND, United States 43 H3
Norton • KS, United States 46 F3
Norton Shores •
   MI, United States 44 B4
Norton Sound •
   AK, United States 49 I3
Norwalk • OH, United States 44 D5
Norwalk • CT, United States 44 I5
NORWAY • Europe 16
Norway • ME, United States 44 J3
Norwegian Fjords cruise area •
   Norway 81 A4
Norwegian Sea • Europe 4 K3
Norwich • United Kingdom 7 N9
Norwich • NY, United States 44 H4
Norwich • CT, United States 153 D8
Norwood • OH, United States 44 C6
Norwood • OT, Canada 44 F3
Noshiro • Japan 30 J4
Nosratabad • Iran 18 G4
Nossa Senhora das Candeias •
   Brazil 52 I1
Nossebro • Sweden 125 F3
Nossob • Africa 24 B4
Nostalgia Town • QL, Australia 144 B6
Nostra Señora de Guadelupe •
   Portugal 118 E5
Nostra Senyora de Cura, Santuari de •
   Majorca, Spain 117 H4
Nosy Bé • Madagascar 24 H2
Nosy Ste Marie • Madagascar 24 H3
Notch Peak • UT, United States 45 F2
Notec • Poland 13 F5
Noto • Sicily, Italy 12 J12
Noto • Japan 30 I6
Noto, Golfo di • Sicily, Italy 120 D4
Noto (Peninsula) • Japan 30 I6
Noto, Val di • Sicily, Italy 120 D4
Nototden • Norway 124 B3
Notre-Dame Bay • NF, Canada 156 D3
Notre-Dame de Lourdes •
   MN, Canada 43 G2
Notre-Dame, Mts • QU, Canada 156 D1
Notre-Dame-de-Bellecombe Ski •
   France .... 100 [22]
Notre-Dame-du-Nord • QU, Canada 44 F2
Nottaway • QU, Canada 39 P6
Nottekanal • Germany 111 C4
Nottingham • United Kingdom 7 K9
Nottingham I • NU, Canada 39 M5
Nottingham Road • South Africa 134 B3
Nouadhibou • Mauritania 20 B4
Nouadhibou, Dakhet • Mauritania 20 A4
Nouadhibou, Ras • Mauritania 20 A4
Nouakchott • Mauritania 20 B5
Nouamrhar • Mauritania 20 B5
Nouméa • New Caledonia 35 (2) B3
Noumbi • Burkina Faso 22 D2
Nouvelle Caledonie •
   Pacific Ocean 35 (3) A3
Nouvelle Decouverte • Mauritius 132 J2
Nouvelle France, Cap de •
   QU, Canada 39 Q4
Nouvelles Hébrides • Vanuatu 35 (2) B2
Nouzha, El [Apt] • Egypt 131 F1
Nova Friburgo • Brazil 163 C4
Nova Gaia • Angola 23 B6
Nova Gradiska • Croatia 128 C2
Nova Iguaçu • Brazil 163 C4
Nova Lamego • Guinea-Bissau 22 B2
Nova Levante • Italy 120 B3
Nova Lima • Brazil 163 C1
Nova Lisboa • Angola 24 B2
Nova Mambone • Mozambique 24 E4
Nova Scotia • Canada 156 D7
Nova Zagora • Bulgaria 128 E3
Novara • Italy 121 E6
Novato • CA, United States 45 A2
Novaya Sibir, Ostrov •
   Russian Fed. 27 O1
Novaya Zemlya • Russian Fed. 26 H3
Nové Zámky • Slovak Rep. 13 J8
Novelda • Spain 117 C1
Novgorod Heritage C •
   Russian Fed. .... 86 [243]
Novgorod • Russian Fed. 126 C1
Novi Ligure • Italy 12 C4
Novi Pazar • F.R. of Yugoslavia 14 H6
Novi Pazar • Bulgaria 128 E3
Novi Sad • F.R. of Yugoslavia 14 G4
Nôvo Hamburgo • Brazil 52 F4
Novo Mesto • Brazil 13 G9
Novo Mesto • Slovenia 128 D1
Novo Orjahovo • Bulgaria 128 E4
Novodvinsk • Russian Fed. 17 G5
Novohalinsk • Russian Fed. 17 I2
Novokhalinsk • Russian Fed. 17 H4
Novokuybyshev • Russian Fed. 17 H4
Novokuznetsk • Russian Fed. 26 O7
Novolazarevskaya [Base] •
   Antarctica 54 (1) G2
Novomoskovs'k • Ukraine 17 F5
Novomoskovsk • Russian Fed. 17 H4
Novorossiysk • Russian Fed. 17 I6
Novorybnoye • Russian Fed. 26 S3
Novosaya • Russian Fed. 17 I1
Novoshakhtinsk • Russian Fed. 17 F5
Novosibirskiye Ostrova •
   Russian Fed. 27 N1
Novozensk • Russian Fed. 17 H2
Novovolynsk • Ukraine 13 N7
Novoyeniseysk • Russian Fed. 26 P6
Novoyerudinskiy • Russian Fed. 26 P6
Novvy Port • Russian Fed. 26 L4
Novvy Vasyugan • Russian Fed. 26 M6
Nowa Ruda • Poland 13 F7
Nowa Sól • Poland 13 E6
Nowata • OK, United States 46 H4
Nowgong • India 137 C7
Nowogard • Poland 13 E4
Nowra • NS, Australia 144 C2
Nowy Dwór Mazowiecki • Poland 13 J5
Nowy Sacz • Poland 128 C4
Nowy Targ • Poland 128 C4
Nowy Wisnicz • Poland 128 C4
Noyon • France 10 H4
Nsukka • Nigeria 22 F3
Ntem •
   Cameroon/Equatorial Guinea 22 G4
Nu Jiang • China 28 F2
Nub's Nob Ski •
   MI, United States .... 149 [140]
Nubah, Jibal an • Sudan 21 F5
Nubian Desert • Sudan 21 F3

Nubiyah, As Sahra an • Sudan 21 F3
Nudow • Germany 111 C3
Nueces • TX, United States 154 J5
Nueltin Lake • NU, Canada 38 L4
Nueva Cádiz • Venezuela .... 160 V
Nueva Gerona • Cuba 158 D1
Nueva Palmira • Uruguay 163 D1
Nueva Rosita • Mexico 47 D4
Nueva San Salvador •
   El Salvador 37 D5
Nueve (9) de Julio • Argentina 163 D3
Nuevitas • Cuba 158 D3
Nuevo Casas Grandes • Mexico 157 F2
Nuevo, Golfo • Argentina 53 D4
Nuevo Guerrero • Mexico 47 E4
Nuevo Laredo • Mexico 47 E4
Nuevo Leon • Mexico 37 A2
Nuevo Mundo, Cerro • Bolivia 52 C3
Nuevo Rocafuerte • Ecuador 51 B4
Nugal • Somalia 23 H2
Nugget Point • New Zealand 35 B8
Nuhud, An • Sudan 21 E5
Nui Ba Den • Vietnam 141 E1
Nui Sam • Vietnam 141 E3
Nuiu'Erhu Shan • China 29 F2
Nukhaylak • Sudan 21 E4
Nuku Hiva • French Polynesia 33 M6
Nuku'alofa • Tonga 35 (2) E3
Nukunonu • Tokelau 35 J5
Nukus • Uzbekistan 18 G1
Nullagine • WA, Australia 34 D4
Nullarbor • SA, Australia 34 F6
Nullarbor Plain •
   SA/WA, Australia 34 E6
Numan • Nigeria 22 G3
Numancia • Philippines 31 H4
Numazu • Japan 140 C3
Numedalslågen • Norway 124 B1
Numfoor • Indonesia 35 (1) A1
Nummela • Finland 125 E4
Nunap Isua • Greenland 39 V5
Nunavut • Canada 38 L3
Nuneaton • United Kingdom 104 D2
Nungarin • WA, Australia 34 C6
Nungnain Sum • China 27 I7
Nungo • Mozambique 24 F2
Nunivak I • AK, United States 49 H3
Nuoro • Sardinia, Italy 120 C2
Nuqui • Colombia 51 B2
Nura • Kazakstan 26 L7
Nurage Santu Antine •
   Sardinia, Italy 12 C8
Nürburg • Germany 112 E1
Nürburgring • Germany 112 E1
Nuremberg • Germany 9 G7
Nuremberg Castle • Germany .... 113 [151]
Nuri • Sudan 21 F4
Nurki • Russian Fed. 27 M5
Nurmes • Finland 16 O5
Nürnberg • Germany 9 G7
Nürnberg Castle • Germany .... 113 [151]
Nurra, Ia • Sardinia, Italy 120 C1
Nusa Dua • Bali, Indonesia 143 H4
Nusa Dua Beach •
   Bali, Indonesia 143 H4
Nusa Penida • Indonesia 143 H4
Nusa Tenggara • Indonesia 25 N10
Nusa Tenggara Barat • Indonesia 143 F6
Nusa Tenggara Timur • Indonesia 143 F7
Nushima • Japan 140 B3
Nutak • NF, Canada 39 S5
Nuthe • Germany 111 C3
Nuuk • Greenland 39 U4
Nuussuaq • Greenland 39 U2
Nuwara Eliya • Sri Lanka 138 D15
Nuweiba • Egypt 131 F2
Nuweveldberge • South Africa 134 C2
Nyainqentanglha Feng • China 28 F2
Nyainqentanglha Shan • China 28 F2
Nyaka • Zimbabwe 130 C1
Nyala • Sudan 21 D5
Nyala • Kenya 131 G5
Nyali Beach • Kenya 131 G5
Nyamlett • Sudan 23 D2
Nyampanda • Zimbabwe 130 C1
Nyanga • Congo/Gabon 22 G5
Nyanga Nat. Park • Zimbabwe 130 C2
Nyangani • Zimbabwe 130 C2
Nyanza-Lac • Burundi 23 D4
Nyasvizh • Belarus 16 N10
Nyborg • Sweden 125 F14
Nybro • Sweden 125 F8
Nyda • Russian Fed. 26 L4
Nydala • Sweden 125 F7
Nyeri • Kenya 131 G3
Nyika Nat. Park Park • Malawi .... 133 [95]
Nyíregyháza • Hungary 13 K10
Nyírség • Hungary 14 J2
Nyíri • Kenya 131 G3
Nykarleby • Finland 16 L5
Nykøbing • Sjælland, Denmark 125 F10
Nykøbing • Falster, Denmark 125 F14
Nykøbing • Mors, Denmark 125 F5
Nykøbing Rørvig Beach • Denmark .... 96 [43]
Nykøping • Sweden 125 D3
Nymphenburg Castle • Germany ...... 113 [132]
Nynäshamn • Sweden 125 D4
Nyngan • NS, Australia 34 I6
Nyoman • Belarus 16 M10
Nyon • Switzerland 119 G5
Nyong • Cameroon 22 G4
Nyrud • Norway 16 O2
Nysa • Poland 13 G7
Nysh • Russian Fed. 27 N6
Nyslott • Finland 16 O6
Nyssa • OR, United States 42 G5
Nystad • Finland 125 E3
Nysted • Denmark 125 F14
Nyudo-zaki • Japan 30 J5
Nyurba • Russian Fed. 27 I4
Nyuya • Russian Fed. 27 I4
Nzega • Tanzania 130 B1
Nzérékoré • Côte d'Ivoire 22 C3
Nzeto • Angola 23 A5
Nzi • Côte d'Ivoire 22 D3
Nzilo, Barrage de •
   Dem. Rep. of Congo 24 D2

O • Japan 30 J4
O.C. Fisher Lake •
   TX, United States 47 D2
O Grove Beach • Spain .... 96 [93]
O'Fallon • MO, United States 46 K3
O'Neill • NE, United States 43 G5
O'Sullivan Dam •
   WA, United States 42 F3
Oahe Dam • SD, United States 43 F4
Oahe, Lake • SD, United States 43 F4
Oahu • HI, United States 154 G5
Oak Bay • Jamaica 159 G2
Oak Creek • WI, United States 44 B4
Oak Harbor • WA, United States 42 D2
Oak Hill • WV, United States 48 G2
Oak Lawn • IL, United States 44 B5
Oak Park • IL, United States 44 B5
Oak Ridge • OR, United States 44 D5
Oak Ridge • TN, United States 48 H5
Oakdale • CA, United States 45 B3
Oakdale • LA, United States 47 H2
Oakland • CA, United States 152 C3
Oakland Park •
   FL, United States 49 C4
Oakley • KS, United States 46 E3

Oakura • New Zealand 145 F3
Oakville • OT, Canada 44 F4
Oakwood Adventure Park L •
   United Kingdom .... 98 [31]
Oamaru • New Zealand 35 C7
Oaro • New Zealand 35 D6
Oasis de Nazaret •
   Lanzarote, Canary Is. 117 E3
Oaxaca Heritage C • Mexico .... 84 [27]
Oaxaca • Mexico 157 G4
Oaxaca [Adm] • Mexico 37 B4
Ob • Russian Fed. 26 K4
Ob Estuary • Russian Fed. 126 A3
Oban • Cameroon 22 G4
Oban • Japan 30 H7
Oban • United Kingdom 6 G5
Oban • Russian Fed. 35 B8
Oban Hills • Nigeria 22 F3
Obando • Colombia 51 D3
Obara • Bulgaria 128 E3
Ober Gatlinburg Ski •
   TN, United States .... 149 [160]
Oberá • Argentina 52 E4
Oberammergau • Germany 112 F6
Oberasbach • Germany 9 F7
Oberau Ski • Austria .... 100 [148]
Oberau • Austria 119 H3
Oberaudorf • Germany 112 F8
Oberbayern • Germany 112 F3
Oberburg, Kobern-Gondorf Castle •
   Germany .... 113 [63]
Obereggen Ski • Italy .... 100 [221]
Obereggen • Italy 120 B3
Oberfranken • Germany 9 G6
Obergurgl Ski • Austria .... 100 [138]
Obergurgl • Austria 119 H6
Oberharz Spa • Germany .... 113 [k3]
Oberhausen, Passau Castle •
   Germany .... 113 [126]
Oberhof • Germany 111 B1
Oberinntal • Austria 9 F6
Oberkirch • Germany 119 H6
Oberkirch • Germany 112 F6
Oberlausitz • Germany 111 A4
Oberlech Ski • Austria .... 100 [129]
Oberln • KS, United States 46 E3
Oberndorf • Germany 9 D8
Oberndorf • Austria 119 H4
Oberösterreich • Austria 13 D10
Oberpfalz • Germany 9 H7
Oberpfalzerwald • Germany 9 H7
Obersaxen • Switzerland 119 G3
Oberschleissheim • Germany 112 F3
Oberstaufen • Germany 112 F5
Oberstdorf Ski • Germany .... 100 [2]
Oberstdorf • Germany 112 F6
Oberstdorf Spa • Germany .... 113 [h11]
Obersdorf Ski • Austria .... 113 [k12]
Obertauern Ski • Austria .... 100 [177]
Obertauern • Austria 119 H4
Oberrtilliach • Austria 119 H4
Obervellach • Austria 119 H8
Oberwesel • Germany 112 E4
Obi • Indonesia 32 (1) C3
Obi Beach • Brazil 51 F4
Óbidos • Brazil 30 L3
Obihiro • Japan 140 C4
Obninsk • Russian Fed. 126 C4
Obo • Central African Rep. 23 D2
Obock • Djibouti 23 G1
Obonga Lake • OT, Canada 43 L2
Oborniki • Poland 13 F5
Obozerskiy • Russian Fed. 17 G2
Obrenovac • F.R. of Yugoslavia 14 H5
Obruk • Turkey 123 D1
Obskaya Guba • Russian Fed. 26 L4
Obuasi • Ghana 22 D3
Obzor • Bulgaria 128 E4
Oc, d' • France 114 B4
Ocajon, Pico • Spain 10 B12
Ocala • FL, United States 154 H3
Ocaña • Spain 11 H5
Ocaña • Colombia 51 C2
Ocean City • MD, United States 153 D10
Ocean City • NJ, United States 153 D10
Ocean Falls • BC, Canada 38 F6
Ocean Hole • Bahamas 158 B1
Ocean I • Kiribati 33 I6
Ocean Park • Hong Kong, China 139 B6
Ocean Park • WA, United States 42 E2
Ocean Springs •
   MS, United States 48 C5
Ocean World Water Park •
   Thailand 142 C4
Oceanside • CA, United States 45 D5
Ochagavia • Spain 11 J2
Ochils, The • United Kingdom 104 B2
Ocho Rios • Jamaica 159 F2
Ochrid • F.Y.R. of Macedonia 90 A19
Ochsenfurt • Germany 9 F7
Ochsenhausen • Germany 112 F1
Ocilla • Italy 140 A11
Ocmulgee • GA, United States 48 F5
Ocmulgee Nat. Mon. Park N •
   GA, United States .... 151 [207]
Ocoña • Moldova 14 O1
Ocoee • FL, United States 151 C1
Oconee • GA, United States 48 F4
Ocracoke I • NC, United States 48 J3
Oda • Sudan 21 G3
Oda • Ghana 22 D3
Oda • Japan 30 G7
Odadahraun • Iceland 16 (1) E2
Odate • Japan 30 K4
Odawara • Japan 140 C3
Odda • Norway 124 C4
Odder Beach • Denmark .... 96 [47]
Odder • Denmark 125 F10
Odeborg • Sweden 125 F2
Odeceixe • Portugal 118 E1
Odelette • Portugal 118 E4
Odelouca • Portugal 118 E2
Odemira • Turkey 122 D6
Odense • Denmark 125 F14
Odenthal • Germany 111 B4
Odenwald • Germany 112 D4
Oderbaff • Germany/Poland 111 B4
Oderzo • Italy 13 B12
Odesa • Ukraine 17 E5
Odeshög • Sweden 125 F3
Odessa • Ukraine 17 E5
Odessa • WA, United States 42 F3
Odessa • TX, United States 47 C2
Odessa • DE, United States 153 D10
Odiáxere • Portugal 118 E6
Odienné • Côte d'Ivoire 22 C3
Odle • It, Italy 120 B1
Odorheiu Secuiesc • Romania 14 M3
Odra • Poland 13 G6
Odžaci • Serbia 111 A1
Odzani Falls • Zimbabwe 130 C2
Oeiras • Portugal 118 E1
Oeiras • Brazil 53 (1) C3
Oeiras • Portugal 118 D1
Oelsnitz • Germany 9 H6
Old Crow • YT, Canada 49 N2
Old Devonshire Church • Bermuda 159 J4
Old Faithful •
   WY, United States 42 J4
Old Forge • NY, United States 44 H3
Old Fort Point • Montserrat .... 161 H
Old Goa • Goa, India 137 B1
Old Harbour • Jamaica 159 F4
Old Head of Kinsale Beach •
   Ireland .... 96 [59]
Old Head of Kinsale • Ireland 108 C8
Old Hickory Lake •
   TN, United States 48 D3
Old Kilcullen • Ireland 108 B3
Old Man Bay • Cayman Is. 159 F4

Ogallala • NE, United States 46 E2
Ogano • Japan 140 C1
Ogasawara-shoto • Japan 140 A13
Ogbomosho • Nigeria 22 E3
Ogden • UT, United States 42 J6
Ogden, Mt Ski •
   UT, United States .... 149 B
Ogdensburg • NY, United States 44 H3
Ogilvie Mtns • YT, Canada 38 C3
Ogliv • Italy 121 E6
Ognon • France 10 L6
Ob • Russian Fed. 23 H1
Ogoki • OT, Canada 39 N6
Ogoki Reservoir • OT, Canada 43 L1
Ogonék • Russian Fed. 27 M5
Ogooué • Gabon 22 G5
Ogosta • Bulgaria 14 L7
Ogote Spa • Japan 140 B2
Ograzden Belasica • Europe 15 D2
Ogre • Latvia 126 B4
Ogur • Nigeria 22 E3
Ohai • New Zealand 145 G4
Ohakune • New Zealand 145 F3
Ohanet • Algeria 20 G3
Ohata • Japan 30 K4
Ohio [Adm] • United States 44 D5
Ohio Peak • CO, United States 45 I2
Ohio [Riv] • United States 44 C5
Ohlstadt • Germany 112 F7
Ohope • New Zealand 145 F2
Ohopoho • Namibia 24 A3
Ohre • Czech Rep. 128 B1
Ohrid • Lake •
   Albania/F.Y.R. of Macedonia 15 B2
Ohrid Lake Heritage N •
   F.Y.R. of Macedonia .... 83 [63]
Ohrid Lake Heritage C •
   F.Y.R. of Macedonia .... 86 [191]
Ohridsko jezero •
   Albania/F.Y.R. of Macedonia 15 B2
Öhringen • Germany 9 E7
Oi City • PA, United States 44 F5
Oil City • OT, Canada 44 D5
Oildale • CA, United States 45 C4
Oinoanda • Turkey 123 C7
Oise • France 10 H4
Oiseaux, Parc des • France 115 E2
Oistins • Barbados .... 161 U
Oituz • Romania 14 L5
Oita • Japan 30 F8
Oita [Adm] • Japan 140 A7
Oituz • Romania 14 N3
Ojców Nat. Park Park N •
   Poland .... 89 [97]
Ojcówski Nat. Park • Poland 128 C2
Ojimaga • Mexico 47 B3
Ojo de Liebre, Parque Natural •
   Mexico 157 F3
Ojos del Salado, Nevada •
   Argentina/Chile 52 C4
Ojos Negros • Mexico 45 D6
Oka • Russian Fed. 17 G3
Okaba • Indonesia 32 (1) H4
Okahandja • Namibia 24 B4
Okanagan • Canada/United States 155 C4
Okanda, Parc nat. de l' Park •
   Gabon .... 133 [47]
Okapa • Papua New Guinea 35 (1) D2
Okapi, Réserve de Heritage N •
   Dem. Rep. of Congo .... 83 [93]
Okapi, Réserve du Park •
   Dem. Rep. of Congo .... 133 [54]
Okara • Pakistan 28 C3
Okarem • Turkmenistan 18 F2
Okaukuejo • Namibia 24 B3
Okavango • Africa 24 C3
Okavango Swamp • Botswana 24 C3
Okayama • Japan 30 G7
Okayama [Adm] • Japan 140 A7
Okazaki • Japan 30 I7
Okeechobee • FL, United States 49 C4
Okeechobee, Lake •
   FL, United States 154 H6
Okefenokee Swamp •
   GA, United States 154 H3
Okehampton • United Kingdom 104 F2
Okemo Mtn Ski •
   VT, United States .... 149 [209]
Okemos • MI, United States 44 C4
Okhota • Russian Fed. 27 N4
Okhotsk • Russian Fed. 27 N5
Okhotsk, Sea of • Russian Fed. 27 P5
Oki-shoto • Japan 30 G6
Okidaito-jima • Japan 140 A11
Okinawa [Adm] • Japan 140 A10
Okinawa-shoto • Japan 29 H5
Okinoerabu • Japan 29 H5
Oklahoma • United States 46 G4
Oklahoma [Adm] •
   OK, United States 46 G5
Oklahoma City Nat. Mem. Park N •
   OK, United States .... 151 [144]
Okmulgee • OK, United States 46 H5
Okoboji • IA, United States 43 H5
Okolona • KY, United States 48 E1
Okomo Sanctuary Park • Nigeria .... 133 [35]
Okondja • Gabon 22 G5
Oksbøl • Denmark 125 F9
Oktya'birskiy •
   Bashkortostan, Russian Fed. 17 I4
Oktyabr' • Kazakstan 26 I8
Oktyabr'sky •
   Kamchatka, Russian Fed. 27 Q6
Oktyabr'skoye • Russian Fed. 26 K5
Oktyabr'skoye Revolyutsii, Ostrov •
   Russian Fed. 126 A4
Okulovka • Russian Fed. 126 C1
Okushiri • Japan 30 J3
Okwa • Botswana/Namibia 24 C4
Ol-Doinyo Sapuk Nat. Park •
   Kenya 131 G3
Ola • Russian Fed. 27 P5
Ola • AR, United States 48 K5
Olaine • Latvia 126 B3
Oland • Sweden 125 F8
Olanesti • Moldova 14 O3
Olang Ski • Italy .... 100 [244]
Olang • Italy 120 B2
Olanta • KS, United States 46 H3
Olathe • KS, United States 46 H3
Olathe • CO, United States 45 I2
Olavarria • Argentina 163 D3
Olbia • Sardinia, Italy 120 C2
Old Bedford Village •
   PA, United States 153 D5
Old Colwyn Beach •
   United Kingdom .... 101 [202]

Old Man of Coniston •
   United Kingdom 104 C4
Old Road Bay • Montserrat .... 161 H
Old Road Town •
   St Kitts & Nevis .... 161 G
Old Sarai • Russian Fed. 127 D1
Old Sarum • United Kingdom 104 F3
Old Speck Mtn •
   ME, United States 44 J3
Old Station • CA, United States 42 E6
Old Town • ME, United States 44 K3
Old Wives Lake • SA, Canada 43 C1
Olden • Norway 124 C2
Oldenburg • Germany 8 D3
Oldenburg in Holstein • Germany 8 F2
Oldenburg • Netherlands 5 J2
Oldham • United Kingdom 7 J8
Olduvai Gorge • Tanzania 130 B2
Olean • NY, United States 153 D1
Olecko • Poland 13 L3
Oleiros Beach • Spain .... 96 [92]
Oleiros • Portugal 11 F5
Olekma • Russian Fed. 27 J5
Olema • CA, United States 45 A2
Olen • Norway 124 C5
Olenegorsk • Russian Fed. 17 E1
Olenek • Russian Fed. 27 J2
Olenëkskiy Zaliv • Russian Fed. 27 J2
Oleniy, Ostrov • Russian Fed. 26 M3
Oléron, I de • France 10 F5
Olesnica • Poland 13 G6
Oletta • Corsica, France 115 L2
Olga • Russian Fed. 27 M8
Olga, Mt • NT, Australia 145 D3
Olgod • Denmark 125 F9
Olhão • Portugal 118 E7
Olhuvalli • Maldives 138 F4
Oliana • Spain 11 M2
Olib • Croatia 128 D3
Oliena • Sardinia, Italy 120 C2
Olifants • Namibia 24 B4
Olifants • South Africa 134 C1
Olifants • South Africa 134 C7
Olimbía • Greece 15 C6
Olimbía Heritage N • Greece .... 83 [68]
Olimbía Heritage C • Greece .... 86 [211]
Olimbiáda Beach • Greece .... 97 [192]
Ólimbos •
   C. Macedonia/Thessaly, Greece 15 D3
Olimbos • Lesbos, Greece 15 H4
Olimbos • Scarpanto, Greece 122 D11
Olimbos Nat. Park Park N •
   Greece .... 89 [134]
Olinda Heritage C • Brazil .... 84 [69]
Olinda • Brazil 53 (1) E3
Olite • Spain 11 J2
Oliva • Spain 11 K8
Oliva • Argentina 52 D5
Oliva Beach • Spain .... 96 [119]
Oliva de la Frontera • Spain 11 E6
Oliveira do Brejinhos • Brazil 128 C2
Oljimaga • Mexico 47 B3
Olkhon, Ostrov • Russian Fed. 127 A13
Olkusz • Poland 128 C1
Ollantaytambo • Peru 163 B2
Olmedo • Spain 11 G3
Olmeto • Corsica, France 115 L3
Olmos • Peru 51 B5
Olmütz • Czech Rep. 90 A9
Olney • TX, United States 47 D1
Olofstrom • Sweden 125 F11
Olombo • Congo 23 B4
Olomouc • Czech Rep. 13 G8
Olonets • Russian Fed. 17 F2
Olonne-sur-Mer Beach • France ...... 96 [83]
Olopangon • Philippines 31 G3
Oloron, Gave d' • France 10 E10
Oloron-Ste Marie • France 115 J1
Olot • Spain 117 D2
Olovis • Crete, Greece 122 E8
Olsberg • Germany 9 D5
Olsztyn • Poland 13 J4
Olsztyn • Poland 128 C1
Olsztynek • Poland 13 J4
Olt • Romania 14 M4
Olten • Switzerland 119 G3
Oltenia • Romania 14 J5
Oltenita • Romania 128 E1
Oltet • Romania 14 L5
Oltina • Romania 16 D2
Oluanpi • Taiwan 29 G6
Olüdeniz • Turkey 122 D9
Olvesston • Montserrat .... 161 H
Olympia • Greece 15 C6
Olympia Heritage N • Greece .... 83 [68]
Olympia Heritage C • Greece .... 86 [211]
Olympia • WA, United States 152 B1
Olympiastadion (Berlin) •
   Germany 111 C1
Olympic Nat. Park Heritage N •
   WA, United States .... 82 [10]
Olympic Nat. Park Park N •
   WA, United States .... 150 [24]
Olympic Nat. Park •
   WA, United States 152 B1
Olympus • Cyprus 123 J3
Olympus, Mt • WA, United States 152 B1
Olympus Nat. Park Park N •
   Greece .... 89 [134]
Olyutorskiy, mys • Russian Fed. 27 T5
Om • Russian Fed. 26 L6
Omagh • United Kingdom 7 E7
Omaha • NE, United States 46 H2
Omak • WA, United States 42 F2
OMAN • Asia 19
Oman, Gulf of • Iran/Oman 18 G5
Omarama • New Zealand 35 B7
Omatako • Namibia 24 B4
Ombo • Norway 124 C5
Ombrone • Italy 12 F6
Ombu • China 28 E2
Omchak • Russian Fed. 27 O4
Omdurman • Sudan 21 F4
Omeo • VI, Australia 144 C3
Omerköy • Turkey 122 C5
Ometepec • Mexico 37 B4
Omihachiman • Japan 140 B2
Omihi • New Zealand 145 G4
Ominec Mtns • BC, Canada 38 F5
Omirpoli Beach • Greece .... 97 [200]
Omis • Croatia 128 D4
Omiya • Japan 140 C3
Ommanney Bay • NU, Canada 38 K2
Ommen • Netherlands 109 D8
Omo • Ethiopia 23 F2
Omo Lower Valley Heritage C •
   Ethiopia .... 101 [200]
Omo Nat. Park Park • Ethiopia ...... 133 [65]
Omokoroa • New Zealand 145 F2
Omolon • Russian Fed. 27 R3
Omsk • Russian Fed. 26 L7
Omsukchan • Russian Fed. 27 Q4
Omulew • Poland 13 K4
Omura • Japan 30 E8
Omuramba Omatako • Namibia 24 B3
Omuta • Japan 30 F8
Omutinsk • Russian Fed. 17 I3
Onalaska • WA, United States 42 E2
Onancock • VA, United States 153 D11
Onaping Lake • OT, Canada 44 E2
Onawa • IA, United States 46 G2

Onaway • MI, United States 44 C3
Onda • Spain 11 K5
Ondangua • Namibia 24 B3
Ondava • Slovak Rep. 13 K8
Öndör-Hayrhan • Mongolia 29 E1
Öndöl Öndörhaan • Mongolia 29 E1
Onega • Russian Fed. 17 F2
Onega, Lake • Russian Fed. 126 C1
Oneida • NY, United States 44 H4
Oneida Indian Reservation •
   NY, United States 153 D2
Oost-Vlaanderen • Belgium 109 D14
Oostduinkerke-Bad • Belgium 109 E1
Oostende • Belgium 109 E1
Oosterbeek (Battlefield) •
   Netherlands 109 D7
Oosterhout • Netherlands 5 H3
Oosterschelde • Netherlands 5 G3
Oostpunt • Curaçao .... 160 X
Oostvaardersplassen •
   Netherlands 109 F2
Ootacamund • India 138 D10
Ootacamund Hill Sta • India 138 E2
Ooty Hill Sta • India 138 E2
Opatija • Croatia 128 D1
Opava • Czech Rep. 13 G8
Opelika • AL, United States 48 E4
Opelousas • LA, United States 153 C4
Opeongo Lake • OT, Canada 44 F3
Opheim • MT, United States 42 L2
Opinaca • QU, Canada 39 N6
Opochka • Russian Fed. 17 D3
Opoczno • Poland 13 J6
Opole • Poland 13 G7
Oporto • Portugal 11 C3
Oporto Heritage C • Portugal .... 86 [112]
Optiki • New Zealand 145 F2
Oppdal • Norway 124 B2
Oppeln • Germany 13 G7
Oppenheim • Germany 112 E4
Oppland • Norway 16 E6
Opportunity • WA, United States 42 G3
Opryland USA Park L •
   TN, United States .... 151 [X]
Opunake • New Zealand 145 F3
Ora • Italy 120 B3
Oracabessa • Jamaica 159 F2
Oracle • AZ, United States 45 G5
Oradea • Romania 14 I2
Oradour-sur-Glane • France 115 G2
Oran • Algeria 20 E1
Orange • France 10 J9
Orange • Namibia/South Africa 24 B5
Orange Heritage C • France .... 86 [75]
Orange • NS, Australia 144 C2
Orange • TX, United States 154 C4
Orange, Cabo • Brazil 51 G3
Orange City • FL, United States 49 C3
Orange County •
   FL, United States 151 C1
Orangeburg • SC, United States 48 G4
Orangeville • OT, Canada 155 B9
Orango • Guinea-Bissau 22 A2
Oranienburg • Germany 111 C1
Oranje • Namibia/South Africa 24 A4
Oranje Baai • St Eustatius .... 161 F
Oranjestad • Aruba .... 160 Y
Oranjestad • St Eustatius .... 161 F
Orapa • Botswana 24 D4
Orastie Mountains Heritage C •
   Romania .... 86 [194]
Orava • Slovak Rep. 128 C3
Oravita • Romania 14 I4
Orayska priehradni nádrz •
   Slovak Rep. 13 I8
Orbe • Switzerland 119 G1
Orbetello • Italy 12 F6
Orbost • VI, Australia 144 C4
Orcadas [Base] • Antarctica 54 (1) A3
Orchila • India 137 C7
Orchila • Venezuela 51 D1
Orcières-Merlette Ski • France .... 100 [66]
Ord, Mt • WA, Australia 34 E3
Ordenes • Spain 11 C1
Ordesa, Parque Nac. de Park N •
   Spain .... 89 [72]
Ordos • China 139 A3
Orebro • Sweden 16 H7
Orebro [Adm] • Sweden 16 H7
Oregon • OH, United States 44 D5
Oregon • OR, United States 152 B3
Oregon Caves Nat. Mon. Park N •
   OR, United States .... 150 [36]
Oregon Caves Nat. Mon. •
   OR, United States 152 B3
Oregon City • OR, United States 152 B3
Oregon Dunes Nat. Recreation Area •
   OR, United States 152 B3
Oregon Inlet •
   NC, United States 48 J3
Oregrund • Sweden 125 D2
Orekhovo-Zuyevo • Russian Fed. 126 C4
Orel • Russian Fed. 17 F4
Orel, gora • Russian Fed. 27 M6
Orellana • Amazonas, Peru 51 B4
Orellana • Loreto, Peru 51 B4
Ören • Turkey 15 J6
Oren • Turkey 122 D5
Orenburg • Russian Fed. 17 J4
Orenburg • Russian Fed. 18 G1
Orepuki • New Zealand 145 G3
Öresund • Denmark/Sweden 125 F11
Orestiada • Greece 15 H2
Oreti • New Zealand 145 G4
Orford Ness • United Kingdom 5 E2
Organ Pipe Cactus Nat. Mon. Park N •
   AZ, United States .... 150 [112]
Organ Pipe Cactus Nat. Mon. •
   AZ, United States 153 E3
Orgãos, Sierra de los • Cuba 158 D1
Orgãos, Serra dos • Brazil 163 C4

Orhaneli • Turkey 15 K4
Orhangazi • Turkey 122 D3
Orhei • Moldova 14 P2
Orhon • Mongolia 27 F7
Oribi Gorge Nature Reserve • South Africa 134 B5
Orient • Majorca, Spain 117 H1
Orientale, Plaine • Corsica, France 115 L4
Orihuela **Beach** • Spain 96 [118]
Orihuela • Spain 117 C3
Oriku • Albania 15 A3
Orillia • OT, Canada 44 F3
Orimattila • Finland 125 E4
Orinoco • Colombia/Venezuela 51 D2
Orinoco, Delta del • Venezuela 51 E2
Orissa • India 28 D4
Orissaare • Estonia 126 B1
Oristano • Sardinia, Italy 120 C3
Oristano, Golfo di • Sardinia, Italy 120 C3
Orives • Finland 16 O5
Orivesi • Finland 125 E2
Orizaba • Mexico 37 B4
Orizaba, Pico de • Mexico 157 G4
Orje • Norway 124 B4
Orjiva • Spain 11 H8
Orkanger • Norway 16 E5
Orkelljunga • Sweden 125 F11
Orkney • South Africa 24 D5
Orkney Is. • United Kingdom 6 J3
Orkney, Neolithic **Heritage C** • United Kingdom 86 [14]
Orland • CA, United States 42 D7
Orlando • FL, United States 151 C2
Orlando Arena • FL, United States 151 C2
Orlando Museum of Art • FL, United States 151 C2
Orlando Science Center • FL, United States 151 C2
Orleanais • France 10 G6
Orléans • France 114 D2
Orleans • St Martin 160 D
Orléans, I. d' • QU, Canada 155 B4
Orlicke Hory • Czech Rep. 13 F7
Orlik • Russian Fed. 27 F6
Orlik • Czech Rep. 128 B4
Orlovista • FL, United States 151 C2
Orly [Apt] • France 115 E3
Ormara • Pakistan 18 H4
Ormea • Italy 121 E5
Ormília **Beach** • Greece 97 [192]
Ormiston Gorge Nat. Park • NT, Australia 145 D1
Ormoc • Philippines 31 G4
Ormond Beach • FL, United States 154 H4
Ormuz • Iran 127 D4
Orne • Lorraine, France 5 J5
Orne • Normandie, France 10 E4
Orneta • Poland 13 J3
Ornö • Sweden 125 D4
Ornö [I.] • Sweden 125 D4
Ornsköldsvik • Sweden 16 J5
Oro Verde • Cayman Is. 159 E3
Orocué • Colombia 51 C3
Orodara • Burkina Faso 22 D2
Orona • Kiribati 33 J6
Orono • ME, United States 44 K3
Orontes • Syria/Turkey 123 G4
Oropesa **Beach** • Spain 96 [120]
Oroqen Zizhiqi • China 27 J6
Oroquita • Philippines 31 G5
Oros Falakró • Greece 14 K8
Orosei • Sardinia, Italy 120 C2
Orosei, Golfo di • Sardinia, Italy 120 C2
Orosháza • Hungary 13 J11
Oroszlány • Hungary 13 H10
Orotukan • Russian Fed. 27 P4
Orovada • NV, United States 42 G6
Oroville • WA, United States 42 F2
Oroville • CA, United States 42 E7
Oroville, Lake • CA, United States 42 E7
Orpheus I. • QL, Australia 144 B1
Orrefors • Sweden 125 F8
Orres, les **Ski** • France 100 [69]
Orres, les • France 115 F4
Orrville • OH, United States 44 E5
Orsha • Belarus 17 E4
Orsk • Russian Fed. 26 I7
Orsoy • Germany 111 B1
Orsta • Norway 124 C1
Orsundsbro • Sweden 125 D1
Orta • Italy 121 E2
Ortaca • Turkey 122 D9
Ortakent • Turkey 122 D9
Ortaköy • Turkey 123 G1
Orte • Italy 121 F1
Ortegal, Cabo • Spain 11 D1
Ortenburg **Castle** • Germany 113 [191]
Orthez • France 115 J1
Ortigueira • Spain 11 D1
Ortisei **Ski** • Italy 100 [240]
Ortisei • Italy 120 B1
Ortles • Italy 12 E2
Ortona • Italy 12 I6
Ortonville • MN, United States 43 H4
Orumiyeh • Iran 18 D2
Orumiyeh, Daryacheh-ye • Iran 18 E2
Oruro • Bolivia 52 C2
Orust • Sweden 125 F2
Orval, Abbaye-d' • Belgium 109 D19
Orvieto • Italy 121 F1
Orzola • Lanzarote, Canary Is. 117 E3
Osaka • Japan 140 B2
Osaka [Adm] • Japan 140 B4
Osaka-wan • Japan 140 B3
Osan • Sweden 125 F3
Osborne • KS, United States 46 F3
Osby • Sweden 125 F11
Osceola • IA, United States 46 I2
Osceola • AR, United States 46 K5
Osceola County • FL, United States 151 C1
Oschiri • Sardinia, Italy 12 D8
Oscura Peak • NM, United States 45 I5
Ose-zaki • Japan 30 E8
Oserøya • Norway 124 C3
Osh • Kyrgyzstan 18 J1
Oshawa • OT, Canada 155 B9
Oshika • Japan 30 K5
Oshima • Japan 140 C3
Oshima [I.] • Japan 140 C4
Oshkosh • WI, United States 43 L4
Oshkosh • NE, United States 46 D2
Oshogbo • Nigeria 22 E3
Oshwe • Dem. Rep. of Congo 22 H5
Osian • India 137 C5
Osijek • Croatia 128 D2
Osimo • Italy 12 H5
Osizweni • South Africa 134 B1
Oskaloosa • IA, United States 46 I2
Oskarshamn • Sweden 125 F8
Oskemen • Kazakstan 26 N7
Oskerström • Sweden 125 F7
Oslo • Norway 124 B2
Oslofjorden • Norway 124 B4
Osmaneli • Turkey 15 L3
Osmaniye • Turkey 123 G4
Osmo • Sweden 125 D4
Osnabrück • Germany 8 D4
Osogovske Planine • F.Y.R. of Macedonia 15 D1
Osorno • Chile 53 B4
Osøyro • Norway 124 C3
Ospedaletti • Italy 121 E9
Oss • Netherlands 5 I3
Ossa • Greece 15 D4
Ossa, Mt • TS, Australia 34 I8
Ossabaw I. • GA, United States 48 G5
Osseo • WI, United States 43 K4
Ossora • Russian Fed. 27 R5
Ossun [Apt] • France 115 J2
Ostashkov • Russian Fed. 126 C3
Oste • Germany 8 E3
Ostend • Belgium 109 E1
Oster Hurup • Denmark 125 F6
Osterbymo • Sweden 125 F8
Osterdalälven • Sweden 16 G6
Osterdalen • Norway 16 F6
Ostergötland • Sweden 125 F4
Osterholz-Scharmbeck • Germany 8 D3
Osterode • Germany 8 F5
Ostersjön • Sweden 16 J7
Ostersund • Sweden 16 H5
Ostervåla • Sweden 125 D1
Ostfold • Norway 124 B4
Ostfriesische Inseln • Germany 8 C3
Ostfriesland • Germany 8 C3
Osthammar • Sweden 125 D2
Ostheim **Castle** • Germany 113 [179]
Ostia Antica • Italy 121 F3
Ostpreussen • Poland/Russian Fed. 16 K9
Ostrach • Germany 112 F1
Ostrava • Czech Rep. 13 H8
Ostrobothnia • Finland 124 A5
Ostróda • Poland 13 I4
Ostrogozhsk • Russian Fed. 17 F4
Ostroleka • Poland 13 K4
Ostrov • Russian Fed. 16 O8
Ostrov • Czech Rep. 128 B1
Ostrovul Delta Dunarii • Romania 14 Q4
Ostrów Mazowiecka • Poland 13 K5
Ostrów Wielkopolski • Poland 13 G6
Ostrowiec Swietokrzyski • Poland 13 K7
Ostrzeszów • Poland 13 G6
Osttirol • Austria 119 H7
Ostuni • Italy 12 L8
Ostuni **Beach** • Italy 97 [157]
Osumi-shoto • Japan 30 E9
Osuna • Spain 11 F7
Oswego • NY, United States 153 D2
Oswego [Riv] • NY, United States 155 B10
Oswestry • United Kingdom 7 I9
Oswiecim **Heritage C** • Poland 86 [167]
Oswiecim • Poland 128 C1
Otago • New Zealand 145 E3
Otago Peninsula • New Zealand 35 C7
Otaki • New Zealand 35 E5
Otaru • Japan 30 K3
Otautau • New Zealand 145 G4
Otava • Czech Rep. 9 I7
Otavi • Namibia 24 B3
Otawara • Japan 30 J6
Othello • WA, United States 42 F3
Othris • Greece 15 D4
Otira • New Zealand 35 C6
Otisco Lake • NY, United States 153 D2
Otish, Mtns • QU, Canada 39 Q6
Otjiwarongo • Namibia 24 B4
Otopeni [Apt] • Romania 128 E1
Otorohanga • New Zealand 145 F1
Otra • Norway 16 D7
Otranto • Italy 12 M8
Otranto, Canal d' • Italy 12 M8
Otrøy • Norway 124 C2
Otsu • Japan 140 B2
Otsuki • Japan 140 C1
Otta • Norway 16 E6
Ottadalen • Norway 124 C2
Ottaviano • Italy 121 G3
Ottawa • KS, United States 46 H3
Ottawa • IL, United States 46 K2
Ottawa • OT, Canada 155 B7
Ottawa [Riv] • OT/QU, Canada 155 B3
Otterøya • Norway 16 F4
Otterup • Denmark 125 F10
Ottobeuren • Germany 112 F2
Ottumwa • IA, United States 46 I2
Otway, Cape • VI, Australia 144 C3
Otwock • Poland 13 K5
Otztal • Austria 119 H6
Otztaler Alpen • Austria/Italy 119 H6
Ou-sanmyaku • Japan 30 K5
Ouachita • AR/LA, United States 153 F1
Ouachita, Lake • AR, United States 46 I5
Ouachita Mtns • AR/OK, United States 46 H5
Ouadane **Heritage C** • Mauritania 85 [106]
Ouadda • Central African Rep. 23 C2
Ouaddai • Chad 21 C5
Ouadi Qadisha **Heritage C** • Lebanon 86 [282]
Ouagadougou • Burkina Faso 22 D2
Ouahigouya • Burkina Faso 22 D2
Ouaka • Central African Rep. 23 C2
Oualata • Mauritania 20 D5
Oualata **Heritage C** • Mauritania 85 [106]
Oualidia • Morocco 20 D2
Ouanne, l' • France 10 I6
Ouargla • Algeria 20 G2
Ouarkziz, Jebel • Algeria/Morocco 20 D3
Ouarsenis, Massif de l' • Spain 11 M9
Ouarzazate • Morocco 131 D6
Ouatagouna • Mali 20 F5
Oubangi Chari • Central African Rep. 23 B2
Oubangui • Central African Rep./Congo 22 H4
Oud-Beijerland • Netherlands 109 F3
Oude Rijn • Netherlands 109 F4
Oudenaarde • Belgium 109 D14
Oudewater • Netherlands 109 F4
Oudna • Tunisia 131 E2
Oudon • France 10 E6
Oudong • Cambodia 141 E1
Oudref • Tunisia 131 E4
Oudtshoorn • South Africa 134 C7
Oued, El • Algeria 20 G2
Oued Rhiou • Algeria 11 L9
Oued Zem • Morocco 131 D1
Ouémé • Benin 22 E3
Ouerrha • Morocco 131 D2
Ouessant, I. d' • France 114 C1
Ouesso • Congo 23 B3
Oughterard • Ireland 108 C4
Ouham • Central African Rep./Chad 23 B2
Ouieft • Mauritania 20 C4
Ouistreham • France 10 E4
Oujda • Morocco 131 D2
Oukaïmeden • Morocco 131 D5
Oulanka Nat. Park **Park N** • Finland 89 [32]
Oulmès • Morocco 131 D1
Oulu • Finland 16 M4
Oulu [Adm] • Finland 16 N4
Oulu [Adm] • Finland 124 A5
Oulujärvi • Finland 16 N4
Oulujoki • Finland 16 N4
Oum Hadjer • Chad 22 H2
Oumm ed Droûs Guebli, Sebkhet • Mauritania 20 C4
Oumm ed Droûs Telli, Sebkhet • Mauritania 20 C4
Ounasjoki • Finland 16 M3
Oupeye • Belgium 5 I4
Our • Europe 5 J4
Our • Germany/Luxembourg 10 K3
Ouranópoli **Beach** • Greece 97 [192]
Ouranópoli • Greece 122 D1
Ourense • Spain 11 D2
Oureq • France 5 G5
Ourinhos • Brazil 52 G3
Ouro, Costa de • Portugal 118 A3
Ouro Prêto **Heritage C** • Brazil 84 [72]
Ouro Prêto • Brazil 163 C1
Ourthe • Belgium 109 D15
Ouse • United Kingdom 7 M9
Oust • France 10 C5
Outamba-Kilimi Nat. Park **Park** • Sierra Leone 133 [12]
Outão • Portugal 118 D2
Outeniqua Mtns • South Africa 134 C7
Outeniqua Pass • South Africa 134 C7
Outjo • Namibia 24 B4
Outlook • SA, Canada 42 L1
Outokumpu • Finland 16 O5
Ouvéa • New Caledonia 35 (2) B3
Ouyen • VI, Australia 34 H7
Ova • Turkey 15 N3
Ovalle • Chile 52 B5
Ovamboland • Namibia 24 B3
Ovar • Portugal 11 C4
Ovar **Beach** • Portugal 96 [95]
Overbecks • United Kingdom 104 F5
Overberg • South Africa 134 C6
Overflakkee • Netherlands 109 F3
OverIJssel • Netherlands 109 D8
Overkalix • Sweden 16 L3
Overland Park • KS, United States 46 H3
Overlida • Sweden 125 F7
Overloon • Netherlands 109 D11
Overton • NV, United States 152 C4
Overtorneå • Sweden 16 L3
Overum • Sweden 125 F4
Overuman • Sweden 16 H3
Oviedo • Spain 11 F1
Oviedo **Heritage C** • Spain 86 [97]
Ovre Anarjokka Nat. Park **Park N** • Norway 89 [5]
Ovre Ardal • Norway 124 C4
Ovre Dividal Nat. Park **Park N** • Norway 89 [7]
Ovre Pasvik Nat. Park **Park N** • Norway 89 [3]
Ovre Sirdal • Norway 124 C6
Ovre Soppero • Sweden 16 K2
Owabi Wildlife Sanctuary **Park** • Ghana 133 [24]
Owaka • New Zealand 145 G4
Owando • Congo 22 H5
Owasco Lake • NY, United States 153 D2
Owase • Japan 30 I7
Owatonna • MN, United States 43 J4
Owego • NY, United States 44 G4
Owen I. • Cayman Is. 159 E1
Owen, Mt • New Zealand 35 D5
Owen Roberts [Apt] • Cayman Is. 159 E3
Owen Sound • OT, Canada 39 O8
Owen Stanley Range • Papua New Guinea 35 (1) D2
Owens Lake • CA, United States 45 D3
Owensboro • KY, United States 48 D2
Owerri • Nigeria 22 F3
Owl Creek Mtns • WY, United States 42 K5
Owl's Head **Ski** • QU, Canada 149 [41]
Owo • Nigeria 22 F3
Owosso • MI, United States 44 C4
Owyhee • NV, United States 42 G6
Owyhee, Lake • OR, United States 42 G5
Owyhee Mtns • ID, United States 42 G5
Owyhee [Riv] • United States 152 B4
Ox Mtns • Ireland 108 C2
Oxcutzcab • Mexico 157 H1
Oxelösund • Sweden 125 D3
Oxford • United Kingdom 104 D4
Oxford • OH, United States 44 C6
Oxford • MS, United States 48 C3
Oxford • NC, United States 48 H2
Oxfordshire • United Kingdom 104 D4
Oxkintok • Mexico 157 H1
Oxnard • CA, United States 152 C5
Oxus • Asia 127 D2
Oy Mittelberg • Germany 112 F6
Oy Peter I. • Antarctica 54 (1) FF3
Oyahue • Chile 52 C3
Oyem • Gabon 22 G4
Oyeren • Norway 124 B2
Oykel • United Kingdom 6 H4
Oymyakon • Russian Fed. 27 N4
Oyo • Nigeria 22 E3
Oyster Bay • South Africa 134 C8
Oyten • Germany 8 E3
Oz-en-Oisans **Ski** • France 100 [57]
Ozamis • Philippines 31 G5
Ozark • AL, United States 48 E5
Ozark Plateau • MO, United States 46 I4
Ozd • Hungary 13 J9
Ozeblin • Croatia 14 C5
Ozernovskiy • Russian Fed. 27 Q6
Ozernoye, Zaliv • Russian Fed. 27 R5
Ozieri • Sardinia, Italy 12 D8
Ozinki • Russian Fed. 17 H4
Ozona • TX, United States 47 D2
Ozorków • Poland 13 I6
Ozouri • Gabon 22 F5

P

P'ohang • Rep. of Korea 30 E7
P'ot'i • Georgia 17 G6
P'ungsan • D.P.R. of Korea 30 E4
P'yongyang • D.P.R. of Korea 30 C5
Pa Sang • Thailand 142 B3
Pa-an • Myanmar 31 B3
Paar • Germany 9 G8
Paarl • South Africa 134 C5
Pabianice • Poland 13 I6
Pacaraima Mtns • Brazil/Guyana 51 E2
Pacaraima, Serra • Brazil/Venezuela 51 E3
Pachala • Sudan 23 E2
Pachino • Sicily, Italy 12 J12
Pachmarhi **Hill Sta** • India 138 E1
Pachuca • Mexico 157 G2
Pacific Grove • CA, United States 45 B3
Pacific Ocean • 2 C6
Pacific Palisades • HI, United States 154 G5
Pacific Ranges • BC, Canada 38 G6
Pacific Rim Nat. Park **Park N** • BC, Canada 156 [9]
Pacific Rim Nat. Park Reserve • BC, Canada 155 C3
Pacitan • Java, Indonesia 143 J7
Packwood • WA, United States 42 E3
Padang • Indonesia 143 G4
Padangbai • Bali, Indonesia 143 H4
Padanglawas • Indonesia 143 G4
Padangpanjang • Indonesia 143 G4
Padangsidempuan • Indonesia 143 G4
Padangtikar • Indonesia 32 D3
Padasjoki • Finland 125 E2
Paddock • South Africa 134 B5
Paderborn • Germany 8 D5
Paderne • Portugal 118 E7
Pades, Virful • Romania 14 J4
Padilla • Mexico 47 E5
Padirac, Gouffre de • France 115 G4
Padjelanta Nat. Park **Park N** • Sweden 89 [19]
Padmanabhapuram • India 138 D14
Pádova **Heritage C** • Italy 86 [133]
Pádova • Italy 121 E7
Padre I. • TX, United States 154 J5
Padre I. Nat. Seashore **Park N** • TX, United States 150 [141]
Padre I. Nat. Seashore • TX, United States 154 J5
Padstow • United Kingdom 104 F4
Padstow Bay • United Kingdom 104 F4
Padua **Heritage C** • Italy 86 [133]
Padua • Italy 121 E7
Paducah • TX, United States 46 E5
Paducah • KY, United States 48 C2
Paegam • D.P.R. of Korea 30 D4
Paengnyong • Rep. of Korea 30 C6
Paeroa • New Zealand 35 E3
Paestum **Heritage C** • Italy 86 [153]
Paestum • Italy 121 G4
Pafos **Heritage C** • Cyprus 86 [234]
Pafos • Cyprus 123 J3
Pafuri • Mozambique 24 E4
Pag • Croatia 128 D3
Pag [I.] • Croatia 128 D3
Pagadian • Philippines 31 G5
Pagai, Kepulauan • Indonesia 32 B3
Pagai Selatan • Indonesia 32 C3
Pagai Utara • Indonesia 32 C3
Pagalu • Equatorial Guinea 22 F5
Pagan • Northern Mariana Is. 33 F4
Pagassitikós Kólpos • Greece 15 D4
Pagatan • Indonesia 32 F3
Page • ND, United States 43 H3
Page • AZ, United States 153 E1
Pageland • SC, United States 48 G3
Paget • OT, Canada 44 E2
Paget I. • Bermuda 159 J2
Paget, Mt • South Georgia 54 (1) B4
Pági **Beach** • Corfu, Greece 97 [170]
Pago Pago • American Samoa 35 (2) F1
Pagosa Springs • CO, United States 45 I3
Pahala • HI, United States 47 M9
Pahalgam **Hill Sta** • India 138 E1
Pahang [Adm] • Malaysia 31 C6
Pahang [Riv] • Malaysia 32 C2
Paharpur **Heritage C** • Bangladesh 85 [151]
Pahiatua • New Zealand 35 E5
Páhnes • Crete, Greece 123 E5
Pahoa • HI, United States 47 M9
Pahokee • FL, United States 49 C4
Pahrump • NV, United States 45 E3
Pai • Thailand 142 B1
Paia • Vanuatu 35 (2) B2
Paide • Estonia 126 B2
Paignton **Beach** • United Kingdom 101 [118-119]
Paignton • United Kingdom 104 F5
Päijänne • Finland 125 E2
Paimpol • France 114 C2
Paine, Cerro • Chile 53 B6
Paine, Mt • Antarctica 54 (1) AA1
Painesville • OH, United States 44 E5
Painted Desert • AZ, United States 153 E1
País-Vasco • Spain 11 I1
Paisley • United Kingdom 104 B3
Paita • Peru 51 A5
Pajala • Sweden 16 L3
Pájara • Fuerteventura, Canary Is. 117 E2
Pajarito Mtn **Ski** • NM, United States 149 [112]
Pajaten • Peru 51 B5
Pakch'on • D.P.R. of Korea 30 C4
Pakhachi • Russian Fed. 54 II3
Paki • Nigeria 20 G6
PAKISTAN • Asia 18 I4
Paklenica Nat. Park **Park N** • Croatia 89 [111]
Paklenica Nat. Park • Croatia 128 D3
Pakokku • Myanmar 31 B2
Pakrac • Croatia 128 D2
Paks • Hungary 13 H11
Pakse • Laos 31 D3
Pakse • Laos 141 D2
Pakwach • Uganda 23 E3
Pakxe • Laos 31 D3
Pala • Chad 23 A2
Palacios • TX, United States 47 F3
Palafrugell **Beach** • Spain 96 [123]
Palafrugell • Spain 117 D2
Palagruza • Croatia 14 D7
Palamau Nat. Park • India 137 C8
Palamós **Beach** • Spain 96 [123]
Palamós • Spain 117 D2
Palana • Russian Fed. 27 Q5
Palanga • Lithuania 126 B3
Palangkaraya • Indonesia 32 E3
Palani • India 138 D10
Palanpur • India 137 C5
Palapye • Botswana 24 D4
Palatka • FL, United States 154 H3
PALAU • Pacific Ocean 33 E5
Palau • Sardinia, Italy 120 C2
Palauli • Samoa 35 (2) F1
Palawan • Philippines 31 F4
Paldiski • Estonia 126 B2
Palea Paphos • Cyprus 123 J3
Palékastro **Beach** • Crete, Greece 97 [215]
Palékastro • Crete, Greece 123 E8
Palembang • Indonesia 32 C3
Palencia • Spain 11 G3
Palendria • Cyprus 123 J3
Palenque **Heritage C** • Mexico 84 [28]
Palenque • Mexico 157 H3
Paleo Falíro • Greece 122 D7
Paleohóra **Beach** • Crete, Greece 97 [212]
Paleohóra • Crete, Greece 123 E5
Paleokastrítsa • Corfu, Greece 122 B1
Paleókipos **Beach** • Greece 97 [199]
Palermo • Sicily, Italy 120 D1
Páleros • Greece 122 C1
Palestine • TX, United States 154 J4
PALESTINE NATIONAL AUTHORITY REGION • Asia 18 B3
Palestrina • Italy 121 F4
Palghat • India 138 D10
Pali • India 137 C5
Palioúri • Greece 122 D1
Palisades • NJ/NY, United States 153 D7
Palisadoes • Jamaica 159 F4
Palk Bay • Sri Lanka 138 D11
Palk Strait • India/Sri Lanka 138 D11
Palkane • Finland 125 E2
Pallas-Ounastunturi Nat. Park **Park N** • Finland 89 [28]
Pallasovka • Russian Fed. 17 H4
Palliser, Cape • New Zealand 35 E5
Palliser, Is. • French Polynesia 33 M7
Palm Bay • FL, United States 154 H6
Palm Beach • Aruba 160 Y
Palm Beach • FL, United States 154 H6
Palm Desert • CA, United States 45 D5
Palm I. • St Vincent & Gren. 161 R
Palm Springs • CA, United States 152 C6
Palm Valley • NT, Australia 145 D4
Palma • Mozambique 24 G2
Palma, Badia de • Majorca, Spain 117 H3
Palma de Mallorca **Beach** • Majorca, Spain 96 [126]
Palma de Mallorca • Majorca, Spain 117 H1
Palma del Rio • Spain 116 B2
Palma Nova • Majorca, Spain 117 H3
Palma, Playa de • Majorca, Spain 117 H3
Palma Soriana • Cuba 158 D8
Palma Sur • Costa Rica 51 A2
Palmanova • Italy 121 E4
Palmar Beach • Mauritius 132 J4
Palmares • Brazil 53 (1) D3
Palmária, Isola **Heritage C** • Italy 86 [139]
Palmarito • Venezuela 51 C2
Palmas, Cape • Liberia 22 C4
Pálmas, Golfo di • Sardinia, Italy 120 C3
Palmdale • CA, United States 45 C4
Palmeira das Missões • Brazil 52 F4
Palmela • Portugal 118 D2
Palmer • AK, United States 49 L3
Palmer Station [Base] • Antarctica 54 (1) II3
Palmerston • Cook Is. 33 K7
Palmerston • New Zealand 35 C7
Palmerston North • New Zealand 35 E5
Palmetto Point • Cayman Is. 159 E3
Palmetto Point • Antigua & Barbuda 161 J
Palmi • Italy 12 J10
Palmira • Colombia 51 B3
Palmyra • Syria 18 C3
Palmyra **Heritage C** • Syria 86 [277]
Palmyra • NY, United States 153 D1
Palmyra Atoll • Pacific Ocean 33 K5
Palo Alto • CA, United States 45 A3
Palo Alto Battlefield Nat. Hist. Site **Park N** • TX, United States 150 [140]
Paloh • Indonesia 32 D2
Palolem Beach • Goa, India 137 B2
Palomani, Nevado • Bolivia/Peru 163 B2
Palomas • Mexico 45 I6
Palopo • Indonesia 32 (1) B3
Palos, Cabo de • Spain 117 C3
Palpa • Peru 163 B1
Palpala • Argentina 52 C3
Palu • Indonesia 32 (1) A3
Palyavaam • Russian Fed. 27 T3
Pama • Burkina Faso 22 E2
Pamekasan • Indonesia 143 J4
Pameungpeuk • Java, Indonesia 143 J6
Pamiers • France 10 G10
Pamir • Tajikistan 18 J2
Pâmiut • Greenland 39 V4
Pamlico • NC, United States 48 I3
Pamlico Sound • NC, United States 48 I3
Pampa • TX, United States 46 E5
Pampa Húmida • Argentina 163 D3
Pampas • Argentina 53 D3
Pampas • Peru 163 B1
Pampas • Mexico 47 B4
Pampatar • Margarita 160 V
Pamphylia • Turkey 123 F2
Pamplemousses • Mauritius 132 J2
Pamplona • Spain 11 J2
Pamplona • Colombia 51 C2
Pamporovo • Bulgaria 128 A2
Pampus • Netherlands 109 F2
Pamukkale • Turkey 122 D6
Pamukova • Turkey 15 L3
Pana • IL, United States 46 K3
Panache, Lake • OT, Canada 44 E2
Panagiá **Beach** • Greece 97 [194]
Panagyurishte • Bulgaria 15 F1
Panaitan • Indonesia 143 J1
Panaji • Goa, India 137 B1
Panajia Kerá • Crete, Greece 123 E8
Panalanes, Canal des • Madagascar 24 H4
PANAMA • C. America 37 E6
Panama Canal • Panama 37 F6
Panama City **Heritage C** • Panama 84 [37]
Panama City • Panama 37 F6
Panama City • FL, United States 154 H2
Panamá, Golfo de • Panama 51 B2
Panamá, Istmo de • Panama 51 B2
Panamint Range • CA, United States 45 D3
Panamint Springs • CA, United States 45 D3
Panao • Peru 51 B6
Panarea • Italy 12 J10
Panarea, I. • Italy 120 D2
Panáro • Italy 121 E7
Panay • Philippines 31 G4
Pancevo • F.R. of Yugoslavia 14 H5
Panchgani **Hill Sta** • India 138 E2
Pancicav vrh • F.R. of Yugoslavia 14 H6
Pandan • Philippines 31 G4
Pandava Caves • Goa, India 137 B2
Pandean • Indonesia 143 H1
Pandeleimónas **Beach** • Greece 97 [190]
Pandharpur • India 28 C5
Pándheon • Greece 15 D4
Pando • Uruguay 52 E5
Pandrup **Beach** • Denmark 96 [48]
Panevezys • Lithuania 126 B4
Panfilov • Kazakstan 26 M9
Pangan • Tanzania 23 F4
Pangandaran • Java, Indonesia 143 J6
Pangéo • Greece 15 F3
Panggoe • Solomon Is. 35 (1) F2
Pangkalanbrandan • Indonesia 143 G1
Pangkalaseang, Tanjung • Indonesia 32 (1) B3
Pangkalpinang • Indonesia 32 D3
Pangkor • Malaysia 141 G1
Pangnirtung • NU, Canada 39 R3
Pangrago, Gunung • Java, Indonesia 143 J1
Panguitch • UT, United States 45 F3
Pangutaran Group • Philippines 32 (1) B1
Panhala • India 138 D1
Panhala **Hill Sta** • India 138 E2
Panhandle • TX, United States 46 E5
Panié • New Caledonia 35 (2) A3
Panipat • India 137 C2
Panja • Afghanistan/Tajikistan 28 A1
Panjang • Indonesia 143 J1
Pankow (Berlin) • Germany 111 C2
Panmunjom • D.P.R. of Korea 30 D6
Panna • India 137 C7
Pannonhalma **Heritage C** • Hungary 86 [183]
Panorama • Brazil 52 F3
Panorama **Ski** • BC, Canada 149 [8]
Panoramapark Sauerland **Park L** • Germany 98 [59]
Pánormos • Crete, Greece 123 E2
Panshan • China 30 B4
Pantai Aceh Forest Reserve • Penang, Malaysia 141 F1
Pantai Suluban • Bali, Indonesia 143 H4
Pantanal • Brazil 52 E2
Pantar • Indonesia 143 F7
Pante Makassar • Indonesia 32 (1) B4
Pantelleria • Italy 12 G12
Pantoja • Peru 51 B4
Panuco • Mexico 37 B3
Pánuco • Mexico 157 G2
Panug, Ko • Thailand 142 E1
Panyu • China 139 B1
Panzi • Dem. Rep. of Congo 22 H6
Paola • Italy 12 K9
Paola • Malta 123 H4
Paola • KS, United States 46 H3
Paoli • IN, United States 48 D1
Paoli Peaks **Ski** • IN, United States 149 [155]
Paonta Sahib **Hill Sta** • India 138 E1
Pápa • Hungary 13 G10
Papago Indian Reservation • AZ, United States 153 E3
Papatowai • New Zealand 145 G4
Papeete • French Polynesia 33 M7
Papenburg • Germany 8 C3
Papendorp • South Africa 134 C1
Papendrecht • Netherlands 109 F3
Papey • Iceland 16 (1) F2
Paphos **Beach** • Cyprus 97 [217]
Papija • Bulgaria 15 I1
Papillon • NE, United States 46 G2
Papineau-Labelle Prov. Reserve • QU, Canada 155 B3
Papua, Gulf of • Papua New Guinea 35 (1) C2
PAPUA NEW GUINEA • Australasia 35 (1) D2
Papuk • Croatia 128 D2
Papun • Myanmar 142 B3
Papunya • NT, Australia 145 D1
Paquimé Casas Grandes **Heritage C** • Mexico 84 [14]
Paquimé Casas Grandes • Mexico 157 F2
Par **Beach** • United Kingdom 101 [132]
Pará • Brazil 51 G4
Paraburdoo • WA, Australia 34 C4
Paracatu • Brazil 52 G2
Paracel Is. • South China Sea 139 A7
Paradise • CA, United States 42 E7
Paradise • MI, United States 44 C2
Paradise Bay • Antarctica 81 A10
Paradise Bay • Malta 123 H1
Paradise I. • Bahamas 158 B3
Paradise Sea-Side Resort • BC, Canada 155 C3
Paradisi [Apt] • Rhodes, Greece 122 D12
Paragould • AR, United States 46 J4
Paragua • Venezuela 51 E2
Paragua • Bolivia 52 D1
Paraguarí • Paraguay 52 E4
PARAGUAY • S. America 52 E3
Paraguay [Riv] • S. America 52 E3
Paraíba • Brazil 53 (1) D3
Paraíba do Sul • Brazil 163 C4
Parainen • Finland 125 E3
Parakou • Benin 22 E3
Paralímni **Beach** • Cyprus 97 [220]
Paralimni • Cyprus 123 J4
Parálio Astros **Beach** • Greece 97 [183]
Paramaribo • Surinam 51 F2
Paramo Frontino • Colombia 51 B2
Paramount Canada's Wonderland • OT, Canada 155 B9
Paramount Canada's Wonderland **Park L** • OT, Canada 156 [F]
Paramount's Great America **Park L** • CA, United States 150 [B]
Paramount's Great America • CA, United States 152 C3
Paramount's Kings Dominion **Park L** • VA, United States 151 [HH]
Paramount's Kings Dominion • VA, United States 153 D11
Paramount's Kings I. **Park L** • OH, United States 151 [V]
Paramushir, Ostrov • Russian Fed. 27 Q6
Paraná • Argentina 52 D5
Paraná [Adm] • Brazil 52 F3
Paraná [Riv] • S. America 52 E4
Paraná [Riv] • Brazil 53 (1) B4
Paranaguá • Brazil 52 G4
Paranaíba • Brazil 52 G2
Paranapanema • Brazil 52 F3
Paranavaí • Brazil 52 F3
Parangtritis • Java, Indonesia 143 J7
Parás • Mexico 47 E4
Parati • Brazil 163 C3
Parbati • India 28 C4
Parbhani • India 28 C5
Parc Astérix **Park L** • France 98 [71]
Parc Astérix • France 115 E2
Parc des Princes (Paris) • France 115 E3
Parc Floral **Park L** • France 98 [69]
Parc Safari **Park L** • QU, Canada 156 [O]
Parchim • Germany 8 G3
Pardo • Brazil 53 (1) C5
Pardubice • Czech Rep. 128 B2
Parecis, Chapada dos • Brazil 51 E6
Paren • Russian Fed. 27 R4
Parepare • Indonesia 32 (1) A3
Párga • Greece 15 B4
Pargas • Finland 125 E3
Pargo, Ponta do • Madeira 118 C1
Parguera • Puerto Rico 159 H3
Parham • Antigua & Barbuda 161 K
Parham Harbour • Antigua & Barbuda 161 K
Paria, Gulf of • Trin. & Tob./Venezuela 160 U
Pariaguán • Venezuela 51 E2
Pariaman • Indonesia 143 G4
Parika • Guyana 51 F2
Parima, Serra • Brazil/Venezuela 51 E3
Pariñas, Punta • Peru 51 A4
Parintins • Brazil 51 F4
Paris **Heritage N** • France 83 [49]
Paris **Heritage C** • France 86 [66]
Paris • France 115 E3
Paris • IL, United States 44 B6
Paris • TN, United States 48 C2
Paris • KY, United States 48 E1
Paris • TX, United States 154 J2
Paris Expo • France 115 E3
Parish Closes • France 114 C1
Park City **Ski** • UT, United States 149 B
Park City **Ski** • UT, United States 149 [90]
Park City • UT, United States 45 G1
Park Forest • IL, United States 44 B5
Park Hills • MO, United States 46 J4
Park Rapids • MN, United States 43 I3
Parkano • Finland 125 E2
Parken Zoo i Eskilstuna **Park L** • Sweden 98 [6]
Parker • CO, United States 46 C3
Parker • AZ, United States 153 E3
Parker Dam • AZ/NV, United States 153 E3
Parkersburg • WV, United States 44 E6
Parkes • NS, Australia 144 C2
Parkland • WA, United States 42 D3
Parma • Italy 121 E7
Parma Heights • OH, United States 44 E5
Parnaiba • Brazil 53 (1) C2
Parnaiba [Riv] • Brazil 53 (1) C3
Parnassós • Greece 15 D5
Parnassós Nat. Park **Park N** • Greece 89 [139]
Parnassus • New Zealand 35 D6
Párnitha Nat. Park **Park N** • Greece 89 [140]
Párnitha, Oros • Greece 15 E5
Párnonas, Oros • Greece 15 D6
Pärnu • Estonia 126 B2
Páros • Greece 122 D8
Páros [I.] • Greece 122 D8
Parpaillon • France 12 A4
Parpan **Ski** • Switzerland 100 [112]
Parral • Chile 52 B6
Parramatta • NS, Australia 144 C2
Parrett • United Kingdom 104 F3

Parry I. • OT, Canada ... 44 E3
Parry Is. • NT/NU, Canada ... 38 L2
Parry Peninsula • NT, Canada ... 38 F2
Parry Sound • OT, Canada ... 155 B5
Parsons • KS, United States ... 46 H4
Partenen Ski • Austria ... 100 [124]
Partenen • Austria ... 119 H5
Parthenay • France ... 114 D3
Partinico • Sicily, Italy ... 12 H10
Partnachklamm • Germany ... 112 F6
Paru • Brazil ... 51 G4
Pas de la Casa • Andorra ... 115 K1
Pasadena • CA, United States ... 152 C6
Pasadena • TX, United States ... 154 J4
Pascagoula • MS, United States ... 154 H1
Pascagoula [Riv] •
   MS, United States ... 48 C5
Pascani • Romania ... 14 N2
Pasco • WA, United States ... 152 B2
Pascoal, Mt • Brazil ... 52 I2
Pascua, I. de • Pacific Ocean ... 33 Q8
Pasewalk • Germany ... 8 I3
Pasir Panjang •
   Penang, Malaysia ... 141 F3
Pasir Ras New Town • Singapore ... 141 H2
Pasirputih • Java, Indonesia ... 143 J8
Påskallavik • Sweden ... 125 F8
Pasman • Croatia ... 128 D3
Pasni • Pakistan ... 18 H4
Paso de Indios • Argentina ... 53 C4
Paso los Libres • Argentina ... 53 E8
Paso de los Toros • Uruguay ... 163 D2
Paso Real • Costa Rica ... 37 E6
Paso Robles • CA, United States ... 45 B4
Pass Thurn Ski • Austria ... 100 [160-161]
Passage to India cruise area •
   Indian Ocean ... 81 A5/8
Pássaro, Capo • Sicily, Italy ... 120 C4
Passau • Germany ... 9 I8
Passendale [Battlefield] •
   Belgium ... 109 D13
Passer • Italy ... 120 B1
Passo Fundo • Brazil ... 52 F4
Passo Rolle Ski • Italy ... 100 [225]
Passo Tonale Ski • Italy ... 100 [212]
Passos • Brazil ... 163 C1
Pastavy • Belarus ... 16 N9
Pasto • Colombia ... 51 B3
Pastos Bons • Brazil ... 53 (1) C3
Pasuruan • Java, Indonesia ... 143 H4
Pasut Beach • Bali, Indonesia ... 143 H4
Pasvikelva • Norway ... 16 O2
Pat Sin Leng Country Park •
   Hong Kong, China ... 139 B4
Patagonia • Argentina ... 53 B5
Patagonica, Cordillera •
   Argentina/Chile ... 53 B5
Patan • Nepal ... 28 C3
Patani • Indonesia ... 32 (1) C2
Patara • Turkey ... 122 D9
Patchogue • NY, United States ... 44 I5
Pate I. • Kenya ... 131 G4
Pate Manda • Kenya ... 23 G4
Patea • New Zealand ... 145 F3
Paternò • Sicily, Italy ... 12 I11
Paterson • South Africa ... 134 C8
Paterson • WA, United States ... 42 F4
Paterson • NJ, United States ... 153 D7
Paterson Range • WA, Australia ... 34 D4
Pathfinder Dam •
   WY, United States ... 42 L5
Pathfinder Reservoir •
   WY, United States ... 42 L5
Patia • Colombia ... 51 B3
Patillas, Puerto • Puerto Rico ... 159 H4
Pativilca • Peru ... 51 B6
Pátmos Heritage C • Greece ... 86 [220]
Pátmos • Greece ... 122 D8
Patna • India ... 137 C8
Patnem Beach • Goa, India ... 137 B2
Pato Branco • Brazil ... 52 F4
Patomskoye Nagorye •
   Russian Fed. ... 27 I5
Patong • Ko Phuket, Thailand ... 142 E2
Patong Bay •
   Ko Phuket, Thailand ... 142 E2
Patos • Brazil ... 53 (1) D3
Patos de Minas • Brazil ... 52 H2
Patos, Lagoa dos • Brazil ... 52 F5
Patquía • Argentina ... 52 C4
Pátra • Greece ... 15 C5
Patras • Greece ... 15 C5
Patrocínio • Brazil ... 52 G2
Pats Peak Ski •
   NH, United States ... 149 [217]
Pattadakal Heritage C • India ... 85 [145]
Pattadakal • India ... 138 D2
Pattaya • Thailand ... 142 C4
Patten • ME, United States ... 44 K2
Pattern of United Kingdom ... 104 C2
Patterson • CA, United States ... 45 B3
Patti • Sicily, Italy ... 12 I10
Patuca • Honduras ... 37 E4
Pátzcuaro • Mexico ... 157 G3
Pau • France ... 115 J2
Pauillac • France ... 115 G1
Pauini • Brazil ... 51 D5
Pauini [Riv] • Brazil ... 51 D5
Paul de Serra • Madeira ... 118 C1
Paul Sauer Bridge •
   South Africa ... 134 C7
Paulet I. • Antarctica ... 81 A10
Paulina Peak •
   OR, United States ... 42 E5
Paulo Afonso • Brazil ... 53 (1) D3
Paulpietersburg • South Africa ... 134 B1
Pauls Valley •
   OK, United States ... 46 G5
Pavia • Italy ... 121 E6
Pavia, Certosa di • Italy ... 121 E6
Pavlodar • Kazakhstan ... 26 M7
Pavlovsk • Russian Fed. ... 126 C1
Pawai • Singapore ... 141 H3
Paxi • Greece ... 15 B4
Paximada • Greece ... 123 E4
Paximádia • Greece ... 123 E6
Payakumbuh • Indonesia ... 143 G4
Payangan • Bali, Indonesia ... 143 H2
Payerne • Switzerland ... 119 G1
Payette • ID, United States ... 42 G4
Paynesville • VI, Australia ... 144 C3
Pays de la Loire • France ... 114 A1
Paysandú • Uruguay ... 52 E5
Payson • AZ, United States ... 45 G4
Payyer, gora • Russian Fed. ... 26 J4
Pazarbasi Burun • Turkey ... 15 L2
Pazardzik • Bulgaria ... 14 L7
Pazaryeri • Turkey ... 15 K4
Pazin • Croatia ... 128 D1
Pea I. • NC, United States ... 48 J3
Pea Ridge Nat. Military Park Park N •
   AR, United States ... 151 [186]
Peace • FL, United States ... 49 C4
Peace [Riv] • AL/BC, Canada ... 38 G5
Peace River • AL, Canada ... 155 C2
Peach Orchard •
   GA, United States ... 48 F4
Peach Springs •
   AZ, United States ... 45 F4
Peak District Nat. Park Park N •
   United Kingdom ... 89 [46]
Peale, Mt • UT, United States ... 45 H2
Pear • MS, United States ... 48 B4
Pearl • FL, United States ... 153 F2
Pearl City • HI, United States ... 154 G5

Pearl Harbor •
   HI, United States ... 154 G5
Pearl Land • Zhuhai, China ... 139 B2
Pearland • TX, United States ... 47 G3
Pearsall • TX, United States ... 47 E3
Pearson • GA, United States ... 48 F5
Pearson • South Africa ... 134 C4
Peary Land • Greenland ... 36 O1
Peatland World • Ireland ... 108 B1
Peaugres, Safari de • France ... 115 F3
Pebane • Mozambique ... 24 F3
Pebas • Peru ... 51 C4
Pec • F.R. of Yugoslavia ... 14 H7
Peche-Merle, Grotte du • France ... 115 G4
Pechenga • Russian Fed. ... 17 E1
Pechora • Russian Fed. ... 17 J1
Pechora [Riv] • Russian Fed. ... 17 I1
Pechorskaya Guba • Russian Fed. ... 17 I1
Pechorskoye More • Russian Fed. ... 26 H4
Pecos • TX, United States ... 47 C2
Pecos Nat. Hist. Park Park N •
   NM, United States ... 150 [128]
Pecos Nat. Hist. Park •
   NM, United States ... 153 E2
Pecos [Riv] •
   NM/TX, United States ... 47 C2
Pécs • Hungary ... 13 H11
Pedde Beach • Goa, India ... 137 B2
Pedernales • Dominican Rep. ... 159 G6
Pedra Azul • Brazil ... 52 H2
Pedráces Ski • Italy ... 100 [231]
Pedráces • Italy ... 120 B2
Pedraísches • Italy ... 120 B2
Pedreiras • Brazil ... 53 (1) C2
Pedro Afonso • Brazil ... 53 (1) B3
Pedro Castle • Cayman Is. ... 159 E3
Pedro Juan Caballero • Paraguay ... 52 E3
Pedro Luro • Argentina ... 53 D3
Pedro Osorio • Brazil ... 52 F5
Peebles • United Kingdom ... 104 B4
Peeblesshire • United Kingdom ... 104 B4
Peek'n Peak Ski •
   NY, United States ... 149 [182]
Peekskill • NY, United States ... 44 I5
Peel • YT, Canada ... 38 D3
Peel Sound • NU, Canada ... 38 L2
Peel's Grave, John •
   United Kingdom ... 104 C2
Peene • Germany ... 8 I3
Peene Peera Poolanna Lake •
   SA, Australia ... 34 G5
Péfki Beach • Crete, Greece ... 97 [215]
Péfki • Crete, Greece ... 123 E8
Pefkohóri Beach • Greece ... 97 [192]
Pefkohóri • Greece ... 122 D1
Péfkos • Crete, Greece ... 123 E7
Peg Barisan • Indonesia ... 25 L10
Pegasus Bay • New Zealand ... 35 D6
Peggys Cove • NS, Canada ... 156 D7
Pegnitz • Germany ... 9 G7
Pegnitz [Riv] • Germany ... 9 G7
Pegu • Myanmar ... 31 B3
Pegu Yoma • Myanmar ... 31 B2
Peguera • Majorca, Spain ... 117 H3
Pegunungan Iran •
   Indonesia/Malaysia ... 31 F6
Pehlivanköy • Turkey ... 15 H2
Pehuajó • Argentina ... 163 D3
Peillon • France ... 115 H2
Peine • Germany ... 8 F4
Peipsi järv •
   Estonia/Russian Fed. ... 126 B2
Peipus, Lake •
   Estonia/Russian Fed. ... 126 B2
Peisey-Nancroix-Vallandry Ski •
   France ... 100 [31]
Peissenberg • Germany ... 112 F6
Peixe • Brazil ... 53 (1) B4
Peixoto, Represa de • Brazil ... 52 G3
Pekalongan • Java, Indonesia ... 143 J2
Pekan • Malaysia ... 32 C2
Pekanbaru • Indonesia ... 143 G4
Pekelmeer • Bonaire ... 160 W
Peking • China ... 29 F3
Peking Heritage C • China ... 85 [165-167]
Pekulney, Khrebet •
   Russian Fed. ... 27 U3
Péla • Greece ... 15 D3
Pelabuhan Kelang • Malaysia ... 141 G3
Pelabuhanratu • Java, Indonesia ... 143 J1
Pelagonia •
   F.Y.R. of Macedonia ... 14 I8
Pélagos • Greece ... 122 D4
Pelat, Mont • France ... 115 H2
Pelawanbesar • Indonesia ... 32 F2
Peledaga, Virful • Romania ... 14 J4
Pelee • Malaysia ... 32 E3
Pekanbaru • Indonesia ... 143 G4
Pelekmeer • Bonaire ... 160 W
Pelée, Montagne • Martinique ... 161 N
Pelee I. • OT, Canada ... 44 D5
Pelée, Montagne • Martinique ... 161 N
Pelee Point • OT, Canada ... 44 D5
Pélekas Beach • Corfu, Greece ... 97 [170]
Pélekas • Corfu, Greece ... 122 B1
Peleng • Indonesia ... 32 (1) B3
Pelhrimov • Czech Rep. ... 128 B4
Pelican Cay Nat. Park Bahamas ... 158 B1
Pelinaíon • Greece ... 15 H5
Pella • Jordan ... 135 A4
Pella • IA, United States ... 46 I2
Pello • Finland ... 16 M3
Pellworm • Germany ... 8 D2
Pelly • YT, Canada ... 38 E4
Pelly Mtns • YT, Canada ... 38 E4
Peloponnisos • Greece ... 15 D6
Pelotas • Brazil ... 52 F5
Pelusium • Egypt ... 131 F2
Pemadumcook Lake •
   ME, United States ... 44 K3
Pemalang • Java, Indonesia ... 143 J2
Pematangsiantar • Indonesia ... 143 G2
Pemba • Mozambique ... 24 F2
Pemba I. • Tanzania ... 130 B2
Pemberton • WA, Australia ... 34 C6
Pembina • Canada/United States ... 38 L7
Pembrey Country Park Beach •
   United Kingdom ... 101 [159]
Pembroke Beach • United Kingdom 101 [268]
Pembroke • OT, Canada ... 155 B2
Pembrokeshire Nat. Park Park N •
   United Kingdom ... 89 [48]
Pembuang • Indonesia ... 32 E3
Pen Hills • PA, United States ... 44 F5
Peña Nevada • Mexico ... 40 F7
Peña, Sierra de la • Spain ... 11 K2
Penang • Malaysia ... 141 F
Penang Bird Park •
   Penang, Malaysia ... 141 F2
Penang Botanic Gardens •
   Penang, Malaysia ... 141 F1
Penang Hill • Penang, Malaysia ... 141 F1
Penang I. Bridge •
   Penang, Malaysia ... 141 F4
Penara Bukit Forest Reserve •
   Malaysia ... 141 F3
Peñarroya-Pueblonuevo • Spain ... 11 F6
Peñas, Cabo de • Spain ... 11 H1
Penbryn Beach • United Kingdom ... 101 [191]
Pend Oreille •
   United States ... 38 H7
Pend Oreille Lake •
   ID, United States ... 152 B2
Pendennis Castle •
   United Kingdom ... 104 C4
Pendik • Turkey ... 15 K3

Pendjari, Parc nat. de la Park •
   Benin ... 133 [30]
Pendleton • OR, United States ... 152 B4
Penebel • Bali, Indonesia ... 143 H2
Peneda, Serra de • Portugal ... 11 G1
Peneda-Gerês, Parque Nac. da Park N •
   Portugal ... 89 [80]
Penedo • Brazil ... 53 (1) D4
Penelokan • Bali, Indonesia ... 143 H2
Penetanguishene • OT, Canada ... 155 B5
Peng Chau • Hong Kong, China ... 139 B5
Pengambengan • Bali, Indonesia ... 143 H1
Penganga • India ... 28 C5
Pengastulan • Bali, Indonesia ... 143 H1
Penghu • Taiwan ... 139 A8
Penghu Liehtao • Taiwan ... 31 F2
Penibético, Sistema • Spain ... 11 G8
Penicé • Portugal ... 11 B5
Peniche Beach • Portugal ... 96 [97]
Penicuik • United Kingdom ... 6 I6
Peninsula [Apt] •
   CA, United States ... 152 C3
Peñíscola • Spain ... 11 L4
Peñíscola Beach • Spain ... 96 [120]
Penjat, I. des •
   Formentera, Spain ... 117 G4
Penmaenmawr Beach •
   United Kingdom ... 101 [207]
Penmarc'h, Pointe de • France ... 114 C3
Penmon Beach • United Kingdom ... 101 [235]
Penn Yan • NY, United States ... 44 G4
Penn's Cave • PA, United States ... 153 D5
Penne • Italy ... 138 D3
Penne, Punta • Italy ... 12 L8
Pennines • United Kingdom ... 7 J7
Pennsville • NJ, United States ... 44 H6
Pennsylvania • United States ... 44 F5
Pennsylvania Avenue Nat. Hist. Site
   Park N • DC, United States ... 151 [284]
Penny Highland • NU, Canada ... 39 R3
Penobscot Bay •
   ME, United States ... 44 K4
Penola • SA, Australia ... 34 H7
Penong • SA, Australia ... 34 F6
Penrhyn • Cook Is. ... 33 L6
Penrith • NS, Australia ... 34 J6
Penrith • United Kingdom ... 104 C2
Penryn • United Kingdom ... 154 H1
Penshurst Place •
   United Kingdom ... 104 E3
Pensiangan • Malaysia ... 32 F2
Pentecôte • Vanuatu ... 35 (2) B2
Penticton • BC, Canada ... 155 C4
Pentland Firth • United Kingdom ... 6 I3
Pentland Hills • United Kingdom ... 104 B4
Penukonda • India ... 138 D6
Penza • Russian Fed. ... 17 G4
Penzance • United Kingdom ... 104 F4
Penzberg • Germany ... 112 F7
Penzhinskaya Guba •
   Russian Fed. ... 27 R4
Peoria • AZ, United States ... 45 F5
Peoria • IL, United States ... 46 K2
Pequeno I. • Goa, India ... 137 B1
Perabumulih • Indonesia ... 32 C3
Peraea • Jordan ... 135 A6
Perai • Penang, Malaysia ... 141 F2
Perak [Adm] • Malaysia ... 31 C5
Perak [Riv] • Malaysia ... 141 G1
Pérama • Corfu, Greece ... 122 B1
Pérama • Crete, Greece ... 123 E2
Percé • QU, Canada ... 156 D2
Perche, Collines du • France ... 5 D6
Perdido, Monte Heritage N •
   France/Spain ... 83 [52]
Perdido, Monte Heritage C •
   France/Spain ... 86 [84]
Perdido, Mt • France/Spain ... 11 L2
Perdu, Mont Heritage N •
   France/Spain ... 83 [52]
Perdu, Mont Heritage C •
   France/Spain ... 86 [84]
Peréa Beach • Greece ... 97 [191]
Pereira • Colombia ... 51 B3
Pereira • Portugal ... 118 E4
Perentj • WA, Australia ... 34 C5
Perétola [Apt] • Italy ... 121 E11
Pereyaslav • Ukraine ... 90 A10
Pereybere Beach • Mauritius ... 132 J2
Perfect North Slopes Ski •
   IN, United States ... 149 [156]
Pergamino • Argentina ... 163 D3
Pergamon • Turkey ... 122 D5
Pergine • Turkey ... 123 F1
Périborca • QU, Canada ... 39 Q7
Perico • Argentina ... 52 C3
Périgord Blanc • France ... 115 G2
Périgord Noir • France ... 115 G2
Périgord Vert • France ... 115 G2
Périgueux • France ... 115 G2
Perija, Sierra de •
   Colombia/Venezuela ... 51 C2
Perim • Djibouti ... 21 H5
Perinet, Réserve de Park •
   Madagascar ... 133 [142]
Perisher Blue • NS, Australia ... 144 C4
Peristási Beach • Greece ... 97 [190]
Peristéra • Greece ... 122 D4
Periyar Wildlife Sanctuary •
   India ... 138 D10
Perkam, Tanjung • Indonesia ... 32 (1) E3
Perks Pleasure Park Park L •
   Ireland ... 98 [19]
Perl • Germany ... 112 D3
Perlak, Kuala • Malaysia ... 141 G1
Perlatuvier • Trinidad & Tobago ... 160 T
Perleberg •
   Brandenburg, Germany ... 8 G3
Perleberg •
   Niedersachsen, Germany ... 8 G3
Perlis • Malaysia ... 31 C5
Pernambuco • Brazil ... 53 (1) C3
Pernem • Goa, India ... 137 B1
Pernik • Bulgaria ... 14 K7
Perniö • Finland ... 125 E4
Pernis • Netherlands ... 109 F3
Péronne • France ... 5 F5
Peroulades Beach •
   Corfu, Greece ... 97 [170]
Perpignan • France ... 115 K2
Perros-Guirec • France ... 114 C1
Perry • IA, United States ... 46 H2
Perry • GA, United States ... 48 F4
Perry • FL, United States ... 48 E5
Perry's Victory & Int. Peace Mem.
   Park N • OH, United States ... 151 [183]
Perrysburg • OH, United States ... 44 D5
Perryton • TX, United States ... 46 E4
Perryville • MO, United States ... 46 J3
Persenk • Bulgaria ... 85 [127]
Persepolis Heritage C • Iran ... 85 [127]
Perseverancia • Bolivia ... 52 D1
Perstorp • Sweden ... 125 F11
Perth • WA, Australia ... 34 C6
Perth • United Kingdom ... 104 B2
Perth • OT, Canada ... 155 B6
Perth-Andover • NB, Canada ... 44 L2
Perthshire • United Kingdom ... 104 B1
Pertília • Italy ... 12 K8
Pertui • Ko Phuket, Thailand ... 142 E4
Pertusato, Capo •
   Corsica, France ... 115 L4
PERU • S. America ... 51 C5
Peru • IN, United States ... 44 B5
Peru • IL, United States ... 46 K2
Peru, Altiplano del • Peru ... 163 B2
Peru-Chile Trench •
   Pacific Ocean ... 52 B3

Perúgia • Italy ... 121 E12
Perumal Par I. • India ... 138 D9
Pervomay • Bulgaria ... 15 G1
Pésaro • Italy ... 121 E12
Pescadores • Taiwan ... 139 A8
Pescara • Italy ... 12 I6
Pescara [Riv] • Italy ... 12 I6
Peschanny, Ostrov •
   Russian Fed. ... 27 I2
Pesek • Singapore ... 141 H3
Peshawar • Pakistan ... 28 B2
Peshkoni • Albania ... 14 H8
Pessac • France ... 10 E9
Pescac-Léognan • France ... 114 B3
Pessáda • Cephalonia, Greece ... 122 C2
Pest • Hungary ... 90 A14
Pestel • Haiti ... 159 G5
Pestovo • Russian Fed. ... 126 C2
Petäjävesi Heritage C • Finland ... 85 [87]
Petäjävesi • Finland ... 125 E2
Petenwell Lake •
   WI, United States ... 46 J1
Petaling Jaya • Malaysia ... 141 G4
Petalion, Kólpos • Greece ... 15 F5
Petaloudes • Rhodes, Greece ... 122 D12
Petaluma • CA, United States ... 152 C3
Petare • Venezuela ... 51 D1
Petauke • Zambia ... 24 E2
Petchaburi • Thailand ... 142 C3
Petenwell Lake •
   WI, United States ... 43 L4
Peter I. • British Virgin Is. ... 160 B
Peterbell • OT, Canada ... 44 D1
Peterborough • United Kingdom ... 7 L9
Peterborough • SA, Australia ... 34 G6
Peterborough •
   NH, United States ... 153 D4
Peterborough • OT, Canada ... 155 B5
Peterhead • United Kingdom ... 6 K4
Peterlee • United Kingdom ... 7 K7
Petermann Aboriginal Land •
   NT, Australia ... 145 D3
Petermann Bjerg • Greenland ... 36 O2
Petermann Ranges •
   NT/WA, Australia ... 145 D3
Petersburg • AK, United States ... 38 D4
Petersburg • VA, United States ... 153 D11
Petersburg Nat. Battlefield Park N •
   VA, United States ... 151 [248]
Petersburg Nat. Battlefield •
   VA, United States ... 153 D11
Petionville • Haiti ... 159 G6
Petiot • BC, Canada ... 38 G5
Petit Bot Bay Beach •
   United Kingdom ... 101 [260]
Petit Canouan •
   St Vincent & Gren. ... 161 R
Petit Goâve • Haiti ... 159 G6
Petit Jean, I. • St Barthélemy ... 160 E
Petit Mécatina, Rivière du •
   France/Italy ... 10 I4
Petit Nevis •
   St Vincent & Gren. ... 161 R
Petit Piton • St Lucia ... 161 P
Petit St Bernard, Col du •
   France/Italy ... 115 F2
Petit St Vincent •
   St Vincent & Gren. ... 161 R
Petit-Loango, Réserve de Park •
   Gabon ... 133 [49]
Petite Martinique • Grenada ... 161 R
Petite Rivière de l'Artibonite •
   Haiti ... 159 G2
Petite Rivière Noire, Piton de la •
   Mauritius ... 132 J3
Petite Terre, Is. de la •
   Guadeloupe ... 161 L
Petite-Ile • Réunion ... 132 H4
Petites Pyrénées • France ... 11 M1
Petitsikapau Lake • NF, Canada ... 39 R6
Petkeljärvi Nat. Park Park N •
   Finland ... 89 [33]
Petoskey • MI, United States ... 44 C3
Petra Heritage C • Jordan ... 86 [287]
Pétra Beach • Greece ... 97 [199]
Petra Velikogo, Zaliv •
   Russian Fed. ... 30 F3
Petralona • Greece ... 122 D1
Petre, Point • OT, Canada ... 155 B10
Petreto-Bicchisano •
   Corsica, France ... 115 L3
Petrich • Bulgaria ... 14 K8
Pétrie, Récifs • New Caledonia ... 35 (2) A2
Petrified Forest Nat. Park Park N •
   AZ, United States ... 150 [103]
Petrified Forest Nat. Park •
   AZ, United States ... 153 E2
Petrila • Romania ... 14 K4
Petroglyph Nat. Mon. Park N •
   NM, United States ... 150 [126]
Petropavl • Kazakhstan ... 26 K7
Petropavlovsk-Kamchatskiy •
   Russian Fed. ... 27 Q6
Petropavlovsk-Kamchatskiy •
   Russian Fed. ... 27 Q6
Petrópolis • Brazil ... 163 C4
Petrovac • Russian Fed. ... 14 K4
Petrovsk • Russian Fed. ... 17 E1
Petrovsk-Zabaykalskiy •
   Russian Fed. ... 27 G6
Petrozavodsk • Russian Fed. ... 17 E2
Petsamo • Russian Fed. ... 17 E1
Petworth House • United Kingdom ... 104 E3
Peuetsagoe, Gunung • Indonesia ... 143 G1
Pevek • Russian Fed. ... 27 T3
Pevensey Bay Beach •
   United Kingdom ... 101 [82]
Pévia Beach • Cyprus ... 97 [217]
Peyia Basilica • Cyprus ... 123 J3
Peyriac-de-Mer Beach • France ... 96 [179]
Pezinok • Slovak Rep. ... 13 G9
Pfaffenhofen • Germany ... 112 D4
Pfalzgrafenstein • Germany ... 112 E4
Pfalzgrafenstein Castle •
   Germany ... 113 [69]
Pfarrkirchen • Germany ... 112 F4
Pfeiffer Big Sur State Park •
   CA, United States ... 152 C3
Pforzheim • Germany ... 112 F6
Pfronten • Germany ... 112 F6
Pfullendorf • Germany ... 112 F1
Pfullingen • Germany ... 9 E8
PGA National •
   FL, United States ... 154 H6
Pha Tai Caves • Thailand ... 142 B4
Phaestos • Crete, Greece ... 123 E6
Phai Rong Wua, Wat • Thailand ... 142 C1
Phalodi • India ... 137 C1
Phan • Thailand ... 142 B2
Phan Rang • Vietnam ... 31 D3
Phan Thiet • Vietnam ... 31 D3
Phanat Nikhom • Thailand ... 142 C4
Phangan, Ko • Thailand ... 31 B5
Phangnga • Thailand ... 31 B5
Phanom Dong Rak •
   Cambodia/Thailand ... 31 C4
Phanom Rung • Thailand ... 142 A2
Phantasialand Park • Germany ... 98 [60]
Pilaya • WA, Australia ... 144 A1
Pha, Ko Phuket, Thailand ... 142 E4
Pharr • TX, United States ... 47 E4
Phaselis • Turkey ... 123 I7
Phayao • Thailand ... 142 B2
Phet Buri • Thailand ... 142 B2
Phetchabun • Thailand ... 142 B2
Phi Phi, Ko • Thailand ... 142 E2
Philadelphia Heritage C •
   PA, United States ... 84 [11]
Philadelphia • Jordan ... 135 A6
Philadelphia •
   MS, United States ... 153 F2

Philadelphia •
   PA, United States ... 153 D10
Philae • Egypt ... 131 F5
Philippeville • Belgium ... 5 H4
Philippi • Greece ... 122 D1
Philippi • WV, United States ... 44 E6
Philippine Trench • Philippines ... 31 H4
PHILIPPINES • Asia ... 31 G4
Philippopolis • Bulgaria ... 90 A15
Philippsruhe Castle • Germany ... 113 [55]
Philipsburg • St Maarten ... 160 D
Philipsburg • NJ, United States ... 44 H5
Philistia • Israel ... 135 A7
Phillip • VI, Australia ... 144 C3
Phillipsburg • Germany ... 9 L5
Phimai • Thailand ... 142 A2
Phitsanulok • Thailand ... 142 B4
Phlu, Khao • Ko Samui, Thailand ... 142 B4
Phnom Penh • Cambodia ... 141 E1
Phoenicia • Israel/Lebanon ... 135 A1
Phoenix • Mauritius ... 132 J3
Phoenix • AZ, United States ... 153 E3
Phoenix Is. • Kiribati ... 33 K6
Phoenix Park • Ireland ... 108 B2
Phoi, Ko • Thailand ... 142 C4
Phôngsali • Laos ... 31 C2
Phou Bia • Laos ... 31 C3
Phra Buddha Sothorp • Thailand ... 142 C2
Phra Pathom Chedi • Thailand ... 142 C2
Phra Phutthabat • Thailand ... 142 C2
Phra Sriratana Mahathat, Wat •
   Thailand ... 142 C3
Phra Thong, Ko • Thailand ... 142 A4
Phra Thong, Wat •
   Ko Phuket, Thailand ... 142 E1
Phrae • Thailand ... 142 B2
Phu Hin Rongkla Nat. Park •
   Thailand ... 142 B4
Phu Luang Nat. Park • Thailand ... 142 B4
Phu Rua Nat. Park • Thailand ... 142 B4
Phuket, Ko • Thailand ... 142 E
Phumi Mlu Prey • Cambodia ... 31 D4
Piacenza • Italy ... 121 E6
Piana • Corsica, France ... 115 L1
Piancavallo • Italy ... 120 B4
Pianosa • Tyrrhenian Sea, Italy ... 12 E6
Pianosa • Adriatic Sea, Italy ... 12 J6
Piarco [Apt] •
   Trinidad & Tobago ... 160 U
Piaseczno • Poland ... 13 K5
Piatra Neamt • Romania ... 14 N3
Piatra-Olt • Romania ... 115 J2
Piau-Engaly • France ... 53 (1) C3
Piave • Italy ... 121 E3
Piazza Armerina • Sicily, Italy ... 120 C4
Pibor • Sudan ... 23 E2
Pibor Post • Sudan ... 23 E2
Pic Touside • Chad ... 21 C3
Picardie • France ... 10 H4
Picardy • France ... 114 A2
Picayune • MS, United States ... 48 C5
Piceno • Italy ... 12 H6
Picentini, Monti • Italy ... 121 G4
Pichilemu • Chile ... 52 B5
Pichl-Mandling Ski • Austria ... 100 [185]
Pickens, Fort •
   FL, United States ... 154 H1
Pickering • OT, Canada ... 44 F4
Pickle Lake • OT, Canada ... 39 M6
Pickwick Lake •
   MS/TN, United States ... 48 C3
Pico Ski • VT, United States ... 149 [211]
Pico • Azores ... 118 B1
Pico de Tre Signori •
   Austria/Italy ... 120 B2
Pico Truncado • Argentina ... 53 C5
Picos • Brazil ... 53 (1) C3
Picton • New Zealand ... 35 E5
Picton • OT, Canada ... 155 B10
Pictured Rocks Nat. Lakeshore Park N •
   MI, United States ... 151 [159]
Pidurutalagala • Sri Lanka ... 138 D10
Pie de la Cuesta • Mexico ... 157 H3
Piedade, Ponta da • Portugal ... 118 E6
Piedmont • Italy ... 120 A1
Piedmont • AL, United States ... 48 E4
Piedmont Matese • Italy ... 121 G1
Piedra, I. • Mexico ... 157 H1
Piedras • Peru ... 51 C6
Piedras Negras • Mexico ... 157 F1
Piedras, Punta • Argentina ... 163 D4
Piekary Slaskie • Poland ... 128 C1
Pieksämäki • Finland ... 16 N5
Pielavesi • Finland ... 16 N5
Pielavesi [Lake] • Finland ... 124 A5
Pielinen • Finland ... 16 P5
Pielekaise Nat. Park Park N •
   Sweden ... 89 [20]
Piemonte • Italy ... 121 E5
Pieninski Nat. Park Park N •
   Poland ... 89 [96]
Pieninski Nat. Park Park N •
   Slovak Rep. ... 89 [102]
Pienza Heritage C • Italy ... 86 [144]
Pienza • Italy ... 121 E11
Pierce Reservoirs • Singapore ... 141 H1
Piéria • Greece ... 15 D3
Pierre • SD, United States ... 43 F4
Pierrefonds • France ... 115 E2
Pierreville • Trinidad & Tobago ... 160 U
Pieskowa Skala • Poland ... 128 C2
Piest'any • Slovak Rep. ... 13 G9
Piet Retief • South Africa ... 134 B1
Pietarsaari • Finland ... 16 L5
Pieter Both • Mauritius ... 132 J1
Pietermaritzburg • South Africa ... 24 D4
Pietersburg • South Africa ... 134 A2
Pietra Ligure • Italy ... 121 E9
Pietrasanta • Italy ... 12 E5
Pietrosu, Virful • Romania ... 14 M2
Pieve di Cadore • Italy ... 120 B4
Pigeon I. Nat. Park • St Lucia ... 161 P
Pigeon Point Beach •
   Trinidad & Tobago ... 160 T
Piggott • AR, United States ... 46 J3
Pigi Beach • Crete, Greece ... 97 [213]
Pigi • Crete, Greece ... 123 E2
Pigs, Bay of • Cuba ... 158 D2
Pihlajavesi • Finland ... 16 O6
Pihlajaveri Heiau Temple •
   HI, United States ... 154 G4
Pikangikum • OT, Canada ... 43 J1
Pikes Peak • CO, United States ... 46 C3
Piketberg • South Africa ... 134 C1
Pikeville • KY, United States ... 48 F2
Pila • Poland ... 13 G7
Pilansberg Nat. Park Park N •
   South Africa ... 133 [128]
Pilar • Paraguay ... 52 E5
Pilar de la Horadada Beach •
   Spain ... 96 [118]
Pilar de la Horadada • Spain ... 117 C3
Pilão Arcado • Brazil ... 53 (1) C3
Pilbara • WA, Australia ... 144 A1
Pilcomayo • S. America ... 52 D3
Pilibhit • India ... 137 C3
Pilica • Poland ... 13 K4
Pílos • Greece ... 15 C7
Pílio • Greece ... 122 D4
Pilitz Castle • Germany ... 113 [194]
Pilot Mound • MN, Canada ... 43 G2
Pilsen • Czech Rep. ... 9 I6

Pilsrundale • Latvia ... 126 B3
Pinamar • Argentina ... 163 D4
Pinang • Spain ... 11 F8
Pinar, Cap d'es •
   Majorca, Spain ... 117 H2
Pinar del Rio • Cuba ... 158 D1
Pinarbasi • Turkey ... 123 G2
Pinarello • Corsica, France ... 115 L4
Pinarhisar • Turkey ... 15 I2
Pinatubo, Mt • Philippines ... 31 G3
Pinawa • MN, Canada ... 43 H1
Pincher Creek • AL, Canada ... 42 H2
Pinçon, Mt • France ... 5 C6
Pindos Nat. Park Park N •
   Greece ... 89 [135]
Pindos Oros • Greece ... 15 C4
Pine • MN, Canada ... 43 H2
Pine Bluff • AR, United States ... 46 I5
Pine Bluffs • WY, United States ... 46 C2
Pine Castle • FL, United States ... 151 C2
Pine Creek • NT, Australia ... 34 F2
Pine Creek Lake •
   OK, United States ... 46 H5
Pine Hills • FL, United States ... 151 C2
Pine I. • FL, United States ... 154 H7
Pine I. Bay • Antarctica ... 54 (1) EE2
Pine Keys • FL, United States ... 154 H7
Pine Knob Ski •
   MI, United States ... 149 [150]
Pine Pass • BC, Canada ... 38 G5
Pine Ridge • SD, United States ... 43 E5
Pine Springs •
   TX, United States ... 47 B2
Pineda de Mar Beach • Spain ... 96 [122]
Pineda de Mar • Spain ... 117 D4
Pineda, I. • Spain ... 117 D3
Pinedale • WY, United States ... 42 K5
Pinega • Russian Fed. ... 17 G2
Pinega [Riv] • Russian Fed. ... 17 H2
Pinehouse Lake • SA, Canada ... 38 H5
Pinehurst • NC, United States ... 48 H3
Pinel, Ilet • St Martin ... 160 D
Pinellas Park •
   FL, United States ... 49 B4
Pinerolo • Italy ... 121 E5
Pineview, Lake O' the •
   TX, United States ... 46 H6
Pineta • Sardinia, Italy ... 120 C4
Pineville • LA, United States ... 47 H2
Pineville • KY, United States ... 48 F2
Ping • Thailand ... 142 B3
Ping Chau • Hong Kong, China ... 139 B4
Pingdingshan • China ... 29 F4
Pinghu • China ... 139 C4
Pingliang • China ... 29 C4
Pingtung • Taiwan ... 29 G6
Pingwu • China ... 29 C4
Pingxiang • Guangxi, China ... 29 D6
Pingxiang • Jiangxi, China ... 29 E5
Pingyao Heritage C • China ... 85 [169]
Pinhel • Portugal ... 11 D4
Pini • Indonesia ... 143 G4
Piniós • Greece ... 15 C6
Pink Beach • Bonaire ... 160 W
Pinnacle, The •
   United States ... 44 F6
Pinnacles Nat. Mon. Park N •
   CA, United States ... 150 [148]
Pinnacles, The • WA, Australia ... 144 A5
Pinneberg • Germany ... 8 E3
Pinnes, Akra • Greece ... 15 F3
Pinny's Beach •
   St Kitts & Nevis ... 161 G
Pino • Corsica, France ... 115 L2
Pinolosean • Indonesia ... 32 (1) B2
Pinos, I. de • Cuba ... 158 D1
Pinos Altos • United States ... 45 C5
Pins, Anse aux • Seychelles ... 133 K1
Pins, Ile des • New Caledonia ... 35 (2) B3
Pinsk • Belarus ... 17 D4
Pinta • Galapagos Is. ... 51 (1) A1
Pinto • Argentina ... 52 D4
Pintu Gedong • Malaysia ... 141 G3
Pioche • NV, United States ... 45 E3
Piombino • Italy ... 121 E11
Pioneer Mtns •
   MT, United States ... 42 I4
Pioneer Territory •
   NV, United States ... 152 C4
Pioner, Ostrov • Russian Fed. ... 126 A4
Pionersky • Russian Fed. ... 13 J3
Pionki • Poland ... 13 K6
Piopio • New Zealand ... 145 F1
Piotrków Trybunalski • Poland ... 13 I6
Pipa Dingzi • China ... 29 H2
Pipalyatjara • SA, Australia ... 145 D3
Pipanunan, Réservoir •
   QU, Canada ... 156 D1
Pipe Spring Nat. Mon. Park N •
   AZ, United States ... 150 [97]
Pipe Spring Nat. Mon. •
   AZ, United States ... 153 E1
Pipestone • MN, United States ... 151 [153]
Pipestone Nat. Mon. Park N •
   MN, United States ... 151 [153]
Pipiriki • New Zealand ... 145 F3
Pipri Dam • India ... 137 C8
Piqua • OH, United States ... 44 C5
Piquiri • Brazil ... 52 F3
Piracicaba • Brazil ... 52 G3
Piraeus • Greece ... 122 D4
Piran Beach • Slovenia ... 97 [168]
Piran • Slovenia ... 128 D1
Pirapora • Brazil ... 52 H2
Pireás • Greece ... 122 D4
Pireás • Peloponnese, Greece ... 15 C6
Pirgos • Crete, Greece ... 123 E7
Pirgos • Crete, Greece ... 123 E7
Pirac-sur-Mer Beach • France ... 96 [82]
Piriac-sur-Mer • France ... 114 C4
Piriápolis • Uruguay ... 163 D2
Pirin • Bulgaria ... 14 K8
Pirin Nat. Park Heritage N •
   Bulgaria ... 83 [66]
Pirin Nat. Park Park N •
   Bulgaria ... 89 [132]
Pirineos • Spain ... 11 L2
Piripiri • Brazil ... 53 (1) C2
Pirmasens • Germany ... 112 D5
Pirna • Germany ... 9 J6
Pirongia, Mt • New Zealand ... 145 F1
Pirot • F.R. of Yugoslavia ... 14 K6
Piru • Indonesia ... 32 (1) C3
Pisa Heritage C • Italy ... 86 [141]
Pisa • Italy ... 121 E11
Pisa Range • New Zealand ... 145 G2
Pisac • Peru ... 163 B2
Piscataway Park Park N •
   MD, United States ... 151 [267]
Piscataway Park •
   MD, United States ... 153 D9
Pisco • Peru ... 163 B1
Pisek • Czech Rep. ... 128 B4
Pisidia • Turkey ... 123 F2
Pissouri Beach • Cyprus ... 97 [218]
Pissouri • Cyprus ... 123 J3
Pisticci • Italy ... 12 K8
Pistóia • Italy ... 121 E11
Pisz • Poland ... 13 K4
Pit • CA, United States ... 152 C1
Pitalito • Colombia ... 51 B3
Pitanga • Brazil ... 52 F3
Pitcairn I. • Pacific Ocean ... 33 O8
Pitcairn Is. • Pacific Ocean ... 33 O8
Pitch Lake • Trinidad & Tobago ... 160 U
Pite älv • Sweden ... 16 K4
Piteå • Sweden ... 16 K4
Pitesti • Romania ... 14 L5
Pithagório Beach • Greece ... 97 [201]

Pitjantjatjara Aboriginal Land •
SA, Australia..........145 D3
Pitkyaranta • Russian Fed..........17 E2
Pitlochry • United Kingdom..........104 B1
Pitsidia Beach • Cyprus..........97 [216]
Pitt I. • New Zealand..........35 (3) A2
Pitt I. • BC, Canada..........38 E6
Pitti I. • India..........138 D9
Pittsburg • KS, United States..........46 H4
Pittsburgh • PA, United States..........44 E5
Pittsfield • ME, United States..........44 K3
Pittsfield • MA, United States..........153 D3
Pitu • Indonesia..........32 (1) C2
Piura • Peru..........51 A5
Pivd. Bug • Ukraine..........17 D5
Placentia Bay • NF, Canada..........156 D4
Placetas • Cuba..........158 D2
Placeville • CA, United States..........45 B2
Plackovica •
F.Y.R. of Macedonia..........15 D2
Plage de la Corniche • Tunisia..........131 E2
Plage des Nations • Morocco..........131 D1
Plagne, la Ski • France..........100 [34]
Plagne, la • France..........115 F2
Plagne Montalbert Ski • France..........100 [34]
Plaine, Bras de la • Réunion..........132 H3
Plaine Champagne • Mauritius..........132 J3
Plaine des Palmistes, la •
Réunion..........132 H4
Plaine du Nord • Haiti..........159 G2
Plains • TX, United States..........46 D6
Plains • GA, United States..........48 E4
Plainview • NE, United States..........43 H5
Plainview • TX, United States..........46 E5
Plaisance • Haiti..........159 G2
Pláka Beach • Crete, Greece..........97 [212]
Pláka, Akra • Greece..........15 G4
Plake • F.Y.R. of Macedonia..........15 C2
Plakiás • Crete, Greece..........123 E6
Plana Cays • Bahamas..........158 B4
Planachaux • Switzerland..........119 G5
Planícies • Portugal..........118 A3
Plankinton • SD, United States..........43 G5
Plano • TX, United States..........154 J1
Plános Beach • Zante, Greece..........97 [172]
Plános • Zante, Greece..........122 C3
Plant City • FL, United States..........49 B3
Plasencia • Spain..........11 E4
Plassenburg Castle • Germany..........113 [157]
Plaster Rock • NB, Canada..........44 L2
Plastun • Russian Fed..........30 I2
Plasy • Czech Rep..........128 B1
Platamónas Beach • Greece..........97 [190]
Platanés • Crete, Greece..........97 [212]
Plátani • Sicily, Italy..........120 D3
Plataniás Beach • Crete, Greece..........97 [212]
Plataniás • Crete, Greece..........123 E1
Platanés • Crete, Greece..........123 E1
Plate, I. • Seychelles..........133 K2
Plate, River •
Argentina/Uruguay..........163 D2
Plati • Greece..........15 D3
Platja d'Aro • Spain..........117 G3
Platja de l'En Bossa •
Ibiza, Spain..........117 G3
Platja de Muro • Majorca, Spain..........117 H3
Platja dels Dols •
Majorca, Spain..........117 H4
Platja Talamanca • Ibiza, Spain..........117 G2
Plato • Colombia..........51 C2
Platres • Cyprus..........123 J3
Platte • SD, United States..........43 G5
Platte [Riv] •
NE, United States..........46 D2
Platteville • WI, United States..........43 K5
Plattsburgh • NY, United States..........44 I3
Plattsmouth • NE, United States..........46 H2
Plau • Germany..........8 H3
Plauen • Germany..........9 H6
Plauer See • Germany..........8 H3
Playa Azul • Mexico..........157 G3
Playa Blanca •
Lanzarote, Canary Is..........117 E3
Playa de Fajardo • Puerto Rico..........159 H2
Playa de Guayanés • Puerto Rico..........159 H4
Playa de Guayanilla •
Puerto Rico..........159 H3
Playa de la Arena •
Tenerife, Canary Is..........116 E1
Playa de la Balita •
Gran Canaria, Canary Is..........116 E4
Playa de las Américas •
Tenerife, Canary Is..........116 E1
Playa del Carmen • Mexico..........157 H2
Playa del Inglés •
Gran Canaria, Canary Is..........116 E4
Playa Dorada • Dominican Rep..........159 G3
Playa Girón • Cuba..........158 C2
Playa Grande • Dominican Rep..........159 G3
Playa Guacuco • Margarita..........160 V
Playa Larga • Cuba..........158 C2
Playa Paraíso •
Tenerife, Canary Is..........116 E1
Playland Park L • BC, Canada..........156 [A]
Pleasant Grove •
UT, United States..........45 G1
Pleasant, Mt •
VA, United States..........48 H2
Pleasanton • TX, United States..........47 G3
Pleasantville •
NJ, United States..........44 H6
Pleasure I • FL, United States..........151 C2
Pleasure Ridge Park •
KY, United States..........48 E1
Pleasurewood Hills Park L •
United Kingdom..........98 [30]
Plechy • Czech Rep..........128 B3
Pleiku • Vietnam..........31 D4
Pleiney, le Ski • France..........100 [52]
Plenty • NT, Australia..........145 D2
Plenty, Bay of • New Zealand..........35 F3
Plentywood • MT, United States..........43 D2
Plérin • France..........114 C2
Plesetsk • Russian Fed..........17 G2
Pless [Apt] • Croatia..........128 D1
Plessis-Bourré, le [Château] •
France..........114 D1
Plessisville • QU, Canada..........44 J2
Pleszew • Poland..........13 G6
Plettenberg • Germany..........9 C5
Plettenberg Bay • South Africa..........134 C7
Pleven • Bulgaria..........14 L6
Plevna • OT, Canada..........44 G3
Pliska • Bulgaria..........128 E3
Plitvica • Croatia..........128 D1
Plitvice Lakes Nat. Park Heritage N •
Croatia..........83 [60]
Plitvice Lakes Nat. Park Park N •
Croatia..........89 [110]
Plitvice Lakes Nat. Park •
Croatia..........128 D1
Pljesevica •
Bosnia-Herz./Croatia..........14 C5
Pljevlja • F.R. of Yugoslavia..........14 G6
Ploca, Rt • Croatia..........14 C6
Ploce • Bosnia-Herz..........12 L5
Ploce • Croatia..........128 D4
Plock • Poland..........13 I5
Plöckenstein •
Austria/Czech Rep..........9 I8
Ploërmel • France..........114 C4
Ploiesti • Romania..........14 L4
Plomári Beach • Greece..........97 [199]
Plomb du Cantal • France..........10 H8
Plön • Germany..........8 F2
Plonsk • Poland..........13 J5
Plotzin • Germany..........111 C2
Plougermeau • France..........10 A5
Plouha • France..........114 C2
Ploumanac'h • France..........114 C1

Plovdiv • Bulgaria..........14 L7
Plover • WI, United States..........43 L4
Plover Cove Country Park •
Hong Kong, China..........139 B4
Plover Cove Reservoir •
Hong Kong, China..........139 B4
Plummer, Mt • AK, United States..........49 J3
Plumtree • Zimbabwe..........130 C3
Plunge • Lithuania..........126 B3
Plymouth • United Kingdom..........104 F5
Plymouth • Trinidad & Tobago..........160 T
Plymouth • Montserrat..........161 H
Plymouth • IN, United States..........44 B5
Plymouth • NH, United States..........44 J4
Plymouth • MA, United States..........153 D4
Plzen • Czech Rep..........128 B1
Po • Italy..........121 E7
Po Basin • Italy..........120 A1
Po, Colline del • Italy..........121 E5
Po, Foci del • Italy..........121 E8
Po Lin Monastery •
Hong Kong, China..........139 B5
Po Toi • Hong Kong, China..........139 B6
Poarta Orientala • Romania..........14 J4
Pobeda, gora • Russian Fed..........25 P3
Pobedy, Pik • Kyrgyzstan..........26 N9
Pobla de Segur, la • Spain..........11 M2
Poblet Heritage C • Spain..........86 [87]
Poblet, Reial Monestir de •
Spain..........117 D3
Pobrezie • Bulgaria..........14 N6
Pocahontas • AR, United States..........46 J4
Pocatello • ID, United States..........42 I5
Pochentong [Apt] • Cambodia..........141 E1
Poço das Antas, Reserva Biológica •
Brazil..........163 C4
Poções • Brazil..........52 H1
Pocomoke City •
MD, United States..........44 G6
Pocono Mtns • PA, United States..........153 D6
Poços de Caldas • Brazil..........163 C3
Podebrady • Czech Rep..........128 B2
Podgorica • F.R. of Yugoslavia..........14 G7
Podhale • Poland..........128 C4
Podkammennaya Tunguska •
Russian Fed..........26 P5
Podol'sk • Russian Fed..........126 C4
Podor • Senegal..........20 C5
Podporozh'ye • Russian Fed..........17 E2
Podravina • Croatia..........128 D2
Podrima • F.R. of Yugoslavia..........14 I7
Podunajska • Slovak Rep..........14 E1
Poel • Germany..........8 G2
Pogradec • Albania..........15 B3
Pohjois-Karjala • Finland..........16 O5
Pohjois-Karjala • Finland..........124 A5
Pohnpei •
Fed. States of Micronesia..........33 G5
Pohorje • Slovenia..........13 E1
Point Arena • CA, United States..........42 D7
Point au Fer I. •
LA, United States..........153 F4
Point Fortin •
Trinidad & Tobago..........160 U
Point Hope • AK, United States..........49 H2
Point Lake • NT, Canada..........38 I3
Point Lisas • Trinidad & Tobago..........160 U
Point Pelee Nat. Park Park N •
OT, Canada..........156 [26]
Point Pleasant •
WV, United States..........44 D6
Point Pleasant •
NJ, United States..........153 D7
Point Reyes Nat. Seashore Park N •
CA, United States..........150 [41]
Point Salines [Apt] • Grenada..........160 S
Pointe au Sel • Seychelles..........133 K1
Pointe aux Piments Beach •
Mauritius..........132 J1
Pointe d'Esny Beach • Mauritius..........132 J4
Pointe du Bout • Martinique..........161 N
Pointe Noire • Congo..........22 G5
Pointe-à-Pitre • Guadeloupe..........161 L
Pointe-Noire • Guadeloupe..........161 L
Poissy • France..........5 F6
Poitevin, Marais • France..........114 D3
Poitiers • France..........114 D4
Poitou • France..........114 D3
Poitou-Charentes • France..........114 A3
Poivre • Seychelles..........133 K2
Poix-de-Picardie • France..........10 G4
Pojezierze Chelminskie • Poland..........13 I4
Pojezierze Dobrzynskie • Poland..........13 I5
Pojezierze Mazurskie • Poland..........13 J3
Pojezierze Pomorskie • Poland..........13 F4
Pojezierze Wielkopolsko-Kujawskie •
Poland..........13 F5
Pok Fu Lam Country Park •
Hong Kong, China..........139 B5
Pokaran • India..........137 C1
Pokhara • Nepal..........28 D3
Poko • Dem. Rep. of Congo..........23 D3
Pol-e Khomri • Afghanistan..........26 K10
Pola de Laviana • Spain..........11 F1
Pola de Lena • Spain..........11 F1
Pola de Siero • Spain..........11 F1
Polacca • AZ, United States..........45 G4
POLAND • Europe..........13
Polatli • Turkey..........15 N4
Polatsk • Belarus..........17 D4
Pole • Mexico..........157 H2
Polem Beach • Goa, India..........137 B2
Polesine • Italy..........121 E7
Polessje • Ukraine..........13 N6
Polessk • Russian Fed..........13 K3
Poli • Cameroon..........22 G3
Poliçan • Albania..........15 B3
Policastro, Golfo di • Italy..........12 J9
Police • Poland..........13 D4
Police, Pointe • Seychelles..........133 K3
Policoro • Italy..........12 K8
Policoro Beach • Italy..........97 [155]
Poliegos • Greece..........122 D7
Poligny • France..........10 K7
Poligus • Russian Fed..........26 P5
Polikastro • Greece..........15 H4
Polihnitos Beach • Greece..........97 [199]
Polihrono Beach • Greece..........97 [192]
Polikastro • Greece..........15 D2
Polilimnio • Greece..........31 G4
Polillo • Philippines..........31 G4
Polirinia • Crete, Greece..........123 E1
Pólis Beach • Cyprus..........97 [217]
Pólis • Cyprus..........123 J3
Politeni • Italy..........12 K10
Polk, Fort • LA, United States..........153 F3
Polkowice • Poland..........13 F6
Pollachi • India..........138 D10
Pollença • Majorca, Spain..........117 H2
Póllica • Italy..........12 J8
Polo, Marco [Apt] • Italy..........121 E8
Polonia [Apt] • Indonesia..........143 G2
Polonnaruwa Heritage C •
Sri Lanka..........85 [155]
Polonnaruwa • Sri Lanka..........138 D15
Polousnyy Kryazh • Russian Fed..........27 N3
Poltava • Ukraine..........17 E5
Põlva • Estonia..........126 B2
Polyarnyy • Russian Fed..........17 E1
Polynesia • Pacific Ocean..........33 K6
Polzeath Beach • United Kingdom..........101 [144]
Pomarkku • Finland..........125 E1
Pomerania • Poland..........128 A1
Pomerol • France..........114 B3
Pomio • Papua New Guinea..........35 (1) E2
Pomme de Terre Lake •
MO, United States..........46 I4

Pommersche Bucht •
Germany/Poland..........8 J2
Pomona • CA, United States..........45 D4
Pomona Lake • KS, United States..........46 H3
Pomongwe Cave • Zimbabwe..........130 C3
Pomorie • Bulgaria..........128 E3
Pomorska, Zatoka •
Germany/Poland..........8 J2
Pomorskiy Proliv • Russian Fed..........17 I1
Pompadour, Château de • France..........115 G2
Pompano Beach •
FL, United States..........154 H8
Pompei Heritage C • Italy..........86 [151]
Pompei • Italy..........121 G3
Pomposa Abbazia • Italy..........121 E8
Ponape •
Fed. States of Micronesia..........33 G5
Ponca City • OK, United States..........46 G4
Ponce • Puerto Rico..........159 H3
Ponchatula • LA, United States..........48 B5
Pond Inlet • NU, Canada..........39 P2
Ponda • Goa, India..........137 B1
Pondicherry • India..........138 D7
Pondland • India..........138 E3
Ponferrada • Spain..........11 E2
Pong Gu • China/Nepal..........28 E3
Ponagle •
Fed. States of Micronesia..........33 G5
Pongola •
Mozambique/South Africa..........24 E5
Pongola • South Africa..........134 B2
Pongola Bush Nature Reserve •
South Africa..........134 B1
Pongola [Riv] • South Africa..........134 B2
Pongolapoort Dam • South Africa..........134 B2
Pongolapoort Nature Reserve •
South Africa..........134 B2
Ponmudi • India..........138 D10
Ponmudi Hill Sta • India..........138 E2
Ponoy • Russian Fed..........17 G1
Pons • Spain..........10 G12
Pont-à-Mousson • France..........5 J6
Pont-Audemer • France..........10 F4
Pont-Aven • France..........114 C3
Pont-l'Abbé • France..........114 C2
Ponta Delgada Beach •
São Miguel, Azores..........96 [105]
Ponta Delgada • Azores..........118 B1
Ponta do Sol • Madeira..........118 C1
Ponta Grossa • Brazil..........52 F4
Ponta Porã • Brazil..........52 E3
Pontal • Portugal..........118 E5
Pontarlier • France..........119 G1
Pontchartrain, Lake •
LA, United States..........153 F4
Ponte de Lima Beach • Portugal..........96 [94]
Ponte di Legno • Italy..........121 E3
Ponte Leccia • Corsica, France..........115 L2
Ponte Nova • Brazil..........163 C2
Pontecagnano • Italy..........121 G4
Ponteix • SA, Canada..........42 L2
Pontevedra • Spain..........11 C2
Pontevedra, Ria de • Spain..........11 C2
Pontiac • SA, Australia..........144 D4
Pontiac • IL, United States..........46 K2
Pontianak • Indonesia..........32 D3
Pontivy • France..........114 C4
Pontoise • France..........5 B6
Pontrémoli • France..........121 E6
Pontresina Ski • Switzerland..........100 [122]
Pontresina • Switzerland..........119 G8
Pontypool • United Kingdom..........7 I10
Pony Express Territory •
NV, United States..........152 C2
Ponza • Italy..........12 G8
Ponziane, Is. • Italy..........12 G8
Pool Plateau • Antarctica..........54 (1) A1
Poole Beach • United Kingdom..........101 [95]
Poole • United Kingdom..........104 F3
Poona • India..........28 B5
Poopó • Bolivia..........52 C2
Poopó, Lago de • Bolivia..........52 C2
Poorman • AK, United States..........49 J3
Popayán • Colombia..........51 B3
Poperinge • Belgium..........109 D13
Popeye Village • Malta..........123 H1
Popigay • Russian Fed..........27 H2
Poplar Bluff •
MO, United States..........46 J4
Popocatépetl Heritage C •
Mexico..........84 [24]
Popocatépetl • Mexico..........157 G4
Popondetta • Papua New Guinea..........35 (1) D2
Popovo • Bulgaria..........128 E3
Poprad • Slovak Rep..........13 J8
Porbandar • India..........28 A4
Porbandar Beach • India..........138 E3
Porcupine •
Canada/United States..........38 C3
Porcupine Plain • YT, Canada..........38 D3
Pordenone • Italy..........120 B4
Porec Heritage C • Croatia..........86 [184]
Porec • Croatia..........128 D1
Poretta [Apt] • Corsica, France..........115 L2
Pori • New Zealand..........35 E5
Porkkala • Finland..........125 E4
Porlamar • Margarita..........160 V
Porlock • United Kingdom..........104 F2
Pornic Beach • France..........96 [82]
Pornichet • France..........114 C4
Poronaysk • Russian Fed..........27 N7
Póros • Greece..........15 E6
Póros Beach •
Cephalonia, Greece..........97 [171]
Póros • Cephalonia, Greece..........122 C2
Póros [I.] • Greece..........122 D6
Porpoise Bay • Antarctica..........54 (1) I3
Porpoise Bay • New Zealand..........145 G4
Porquerolles, I. de • France..........115 H3
Porsangen • Norway..........16 M1
Porsanger-Halvaya • Norway..........16 M1
Porsgrunn • Norway..........124 B3
Porsuk • Turkey..........15 M4
Porsuk Baraji • Turkey..........15 L4
Port a Piment • Haiti..........159 G5
Port Alberni • BC, Canada..........155 C3
Port Alfred • South Africa..........24 D6
Port Alice • BC, Canada..........38 F6
Port Angeles •
WA, United States..........152 B1
Port Antonio • Jamaica..........159 F2
Port Aransas •
TX, United States..........154 J5
Port Arthur • China..........29 G3
Port Arthur • TS, Australia..........34 I8
Port Arthur • TX, United States..........154 J4
Port Askaig • United Kingdom..........6 F6
Port au Choix • NF, Canada..........156 D5
Port au Prince • Haiti..........159 G6
Port Augusta • SA, Australia..........34 G6
Port Austin • MI, United States..........44 D3
Port aux Français •
Kerguelen Is..........19 (1) B1
Port Aventura Park L • Spain..........98 [75]
Port Aventura • Spain..........117 D3
Port Barcarès • France..........115 K2
Port Blair • India..........28 F6
Port Burwell • NU, Canada..........39 S4
Port Campbell Nat. Park •
Australia..........144 C3
Port Canaveral •
FL, United States..........154 H6
Port Cartier • QU, Canada..........39 R6
Port Chalmers • New Zealand..........35 C7
Port Clinton •
OH, United States..........44 D5
Port Colbourne • OT, Canada..........44 F4

Port Coquitlam • BC, Canada..........42 D2
Port Cros, I. de • France..........115 H3
Port Cros, Parc nat. de Park N •
France..........89 [69]
Port Cros, Parc nat. de •
France..........115 H3
Port d'Addaia • Minorca, Spain..........117 F2
Port d'es Torrent •
Ibiza, Spain..........117 G1
Port de Alcúdia •
Majorca, Spain..........117 H2
Port de Andratx •
Majorca, Spain..........117 H3
Port de Bouc • France..........10 K10
Port de Paix • Haiti..........159 G2
Port de Pollença •
Majorca, Spain..........117 H2
Port de Prince, Baie de • Haiti..........159 G6
Port de Sóller • Majorca, Spain..........117 H1
Port de Sóller •
Ibiza, Spain..........117 G2
Port des Barques Beach • France..........96 [84]
Port Dickson • Malaysia..........141 G4
Port Edward • South Africa..........134 B3
Port el Kantaoui • Tunisia..........131 E2
Port Elgin • OT, Canada..........44 E3
Port Elizabeth •
St Vincent & Gren..........161 R
Port Elizabeth •
South Africa..........134 C8
Port Ellen • United Kingdom..........6 F6
Port Erin • Isle of Man..........7 H7
Port Fitzroy • New Zealand..........35 E3
Port Gentil • Gabon..........22 F5
Port Gibson • MS, United States..........153 F2
Port Grimaud • France..........115 H4
Port Harcourt • Nigeria..........22 F4
Port Hardy • BC, Canada..........38 F6
Port Hawkesbury • NS, Canada..........156 D7
Port Hedland • WA, Australia..........34 C4
Port Hope • OT, Canada..........155 B9
Port Hope Simpson • NF, Canada..........39 T6
Port Hueneme •
CA, United States..........45 C4
Port Huron • MI, United States..........44 D4
Port Isabel • TX, United States..........154 J6
Port I. • Hong Kong, China..........139 B4
Port Jackson • NS, Australia..........144 E2
Port Jervis • NY, United States..........153 D6
Port Kelang • Malaysia..........141 G3
Port Kembla • NS, Australia..........144 D2
Port la Nouvelle • France..........115 K2
Port la Nouvelle Beach • France..........96 [129]
Port Lairge • Ireland..........7 E9
Port Lavaca • TX, United States..........154 J5
Port, le • Réunion..........132 H1
Port Leucate • France..........115 K2
Port Lincoln • SA, Australia..........34 G6
Port Lockroy • Antarctica..........81 A10
Port Louis • Mauritius..........132 J1
Port Louis • Guadeloupe..........161 L
Port Lympne Wildlife Park •
United Kingdom..........104 E3
Port Macquarie • NS, Australia..........34 J6
Port Maria • Jamaica..........159 F2
Port Menier • QU, Canada..........156 D2
Port Moody • BC, Canada..........42 D2
Port Morant • Jamaica..........159 F2
Port Moresby • Papua New Guinea..........35 (1) D2
Port Nocnes • TX, United States..........47 G3
Port O'Connor •
TX, United States..........154 J5
Port of Spain •
Trinidad & Tobago..........160 U
Port Orford • OR, United States..........42 C5
Port Phillip Bay •
Australia..........144 C3
Port Pirie • SA, Australia..........34 G6
Port Renfrew • BC, Canada..........42 C2
Port Royal • Jamaica..........159 F4
Port Royal des Champs, Abbaye de •
France..........115 E3
Port Royal Sound •
SC, United States..........48 G4
Port Salut • Haiti..........159 G5
Port Sanilac •
MI, United States..........44 D4
Port Saunders • NF, Canada..........156 D5
Port Shelter • Hong Kong, China..........139 B6
Port Shepstone • South Africa..........134 B5
Port Simpson • BC, Canada..........49 O5
Port Soif Bay Beach •
United Kingdom..........101 [257]
Port St Lucie •
FL, United States..........49 C4
Port Stanley • Falkland Is..........81 A10
Port Stephens • NS, Australia..........144 A4
Port Sudan • Sudan..........21 G4
Port Sulphur •
LA, United States..........48 C6
Port Talbot • United Kingdom..........7 I10
Port Townsend •
WA, United States..........42 D2
Port Vendres • France..........10 I11
Port Vendres Beach • France..........96 [128]
Port Vila • Vanuatu..........35 (2) B2
Port Wakefield • SA, Australia..........34 G6
Port-Cartier • QU, Canada..........39 R6
Port-en-Bessin •
United Kingdom..........101 [158]
Porta • Corsica, France..........115 L2
Portadown • United Kingdom..........7 F7
Portage • WI, United States..........44 C4
Portage • MI, United States..........44 B5
Portage la Prairie • MN, Canada..........38 L6
Portalegre • Portugal..........11 D5
Portalegre [Adm] • Portugal..........118 A2
Portales • NM, United States..........46 D5
Portalban • Switzerland..........119 H3
Portals Vells • Majorca, Spain..........117 H3
Portarlington • Ireland..........108 B3
Portavadie • United Kingdom..........106 D2
Portbou • Spain..........11 G2
Portbou Beach • Spain..........96 [123]
Porté Puymorens • France..........115 K1
Porte I • Brazil..........51 G4
Portel, le Beach • France..........96 [75]
Portel • Portugal..........118 C2
Portela [Apt] •
United Kingdom..........101 [261]
Porterville • CA, United States..........152 C3
Portes du Soleil • France..........119 G6
Portes, Punta de ses •
Ibiza, Spain..........117 G3
Porthcawl Beach •
United Kingdom..........101 [156]
Porthcawl • United Kingdom..........104 F2
Porthmadog • United Kingdom..........7 H9
Porthmeor Beach •
United Kingdom..........101 [133]
Porticcio • Corsica, France..........115 L3
Portici • Italy..........121 G3
Portiglione • Corsica, France..........115 L3
Portimão Beach • Portugal..........96 [100]
Portimão • Portugal..........118 E6
Portinho da Arrábida • Portugal..........118 D2
Portinatx • Ibiza, Spain..........117 G2
Portland • VI, Australia..........34 H7
Portland • IN, United States..........44 B6
Portland • ME, United States..........44 J4
Portland • OR, United States..........42 D3
Portland • TN, United States..........48 D2
Portland Bight • Jamaica..........159 F4
Portland Bill • United Kingdom..........104 F6
Portland, Isle of •
United Kingdom..........104 F6

Portland Point • Jamaica..........159 F4
Portlaoise • Ireland..........7 E8
Portmarnock • Ireland..........108 B2
Portmore • Jamaica..........159 F4
Portneuf • QU, Canada..........44 J2
Portnoo Beach • Ireland..........96 [65]
Porto • Portugal..........11 C3
Porto Heritage C • Portugal..........86 [112]
Porto Acre • Brazil..........51 C5
Porto Alegre • Brazil..........52 F5
Porto Amboim • Angola..........23 A6
Porto Azzurro • Italy..........121 E11
Porto Cervo • Sardinia, Italy..........120 C2
Porto Colom • Majorca, Spain..........117 H4
Porto Conte • Sardinia, Italy..........120 C1
Porto Cristo • Majorca, Spain..........117 H2
Porto da Cruz • Madeira..........51 G4
Porto de Moz • Brazil..........51 G4
Porto Empédocle • Sicily, Italy..........120 D3
Porto Franco • Brazil..........53 (1) B3
Porto Garibaldi • Italy..........121 E8
Porto, Golfe de Heritage N •
Corsica, France..........83 [51]
Porto, Golfe de •
Corsica, France..........115 L1
Porto Moniz Beach • Madeira..........96 [108]
Porto Moniz • Madeira..........118 C1
Porto Novo • Cape Verde..........22 (1) A1
Porto Rafael • Sardinia, Italy..........120 C2
Porto Recanati • Italy..........121 E12
Porto Rotondo • Sardinia, Italy..........120 C2
Porto San Giórgio • Italy..........12 H5
Pôrto Santana • Brazil..........51 G4
Porto Santo • Madeira..........20 B2
Porto Santo Beach • Madeira..........12 F6
Porto Santo Stefano • Italy..........52 I2
Porto Seguro • Brazil..........52 H2
Porto Tolle • Italy..........12 G4
Pôrto Tôrres • Sardinia, Italy..........120 C1
Porto Válter • Brazil..........51 E5
Portobelo Heritage C • Panama..........87 [36]
Portoferráio • Italy..........121 E10
Portofino Beach • Italy..........96 [122]
Portofino • Italy..........121 E6
Portogruaro • Italy..........12 G3
Portohéli Beach • Greece..........97 [184]
Portohéli • Greece..........122 D7
Portolà • CA, United States..........42 E3
Portonovo • Benin..........22 E3
Portoroz Beach • Slovenia..........97 [169]
Portoroz • Slovenia..........128 D2
Portoscuso • Sardinia, Italy..........120 C3
Portovénere Heritage C • Italy..........86 [139]
Portoviejo • Ecuador..........121 E10
Portpatrick • United Kingdom..........6 F7
Portree • United Kingdom..........6 E4
Portrush Beach • United Kingdom..........101 [249]
Portsea • United Kingdom..........106 D
Portsmouth • United Kingdom..........7 K11
Portsmouth • OH, United States..........44 D6
Portsmouth • NH, United States..........153 D4
Portsmouth • VA, United States..........153 D11
Portstewart Beach •
United Kingdom..........101 [248]
Portugal • Europe..........11
Portugalete • Spain..........11 H1
Portumna • Ireland..........108 C4
Porvenir • Bolivia..........51 D6
Porvenir • Chile..........53 B6
Porvoo • Finland..........125 E4
Posada • Sardinia, Italy..........120 C2
Posadas • Argentina..........52 E4
Posavina • Bosnia-Herz./Croatia..........14 F5
Posavina • Croatia..........128 D2
Poschiavo • Switzerland..........119 G8
Poseidon, Temple of • Greece..........122 D7
Posillipo • Italy..........121 G3
Posio • Finland..........16 O3
Positano Beach • Italy..........97 [149]
Positano • Italy..........121 G3
Poso • Indonesia..........32 G3
Poso, Danau • Indonesia..........32 (1) B3
Posse • Brazil..........53 (1) B4
Possession, I. • Réunion..........132 H1
Possum Kingdom Lake •
TX, United States..........47 E1
Post • TX, United States..........46 E6
Post Falls • ID, United States..........42 G3
Poste Lafayette • Mauritius..........132 J1
Postojna • Slovenia..........128 D1
Potamiés • Crete, Greece..........123 E2
Poteau • OK, United States..........46 H5
Potenza • Italy..........12 H5
Potenza [Riv] • Italy..........12 H5
Poteriteri, Lake • New Zealand..........145 G2
Potgietersrus • South Africa..........24 D4
Potiskum • Nigeria..........22 G3
Potnarvin • Vanuatu..........35 (2) B2
Poto • Peru..........163 B2
Potomac • United States..........153 D9
Potosi • Bolivia..........52 C3
Potosi Heritage C • Bolivia..........84 [61]
Potosí • MO, United States..........46 J4
Potsdam Heritage C • Germany..........111 C3
Potsdam • Germany..........111 C3
Pottsdown • PA, United States..........44 H5
Pottsville • PA, United States..........44 H5
Pottuvil • Sri Lanka..........138 D16
Potwoks Dam •
Antigua & Barbuda..........161 K
Poughkeepsie •
NY, United States..........153 D7
Pouilly-Fumé • France..........114 A2
Poule et les Poussins, la •
St Barthélemy..........160 E
Pouso Alegre • Brazil..........163 C3
Povazská Bystrica • Slovak Rep..........13 H8
Poverty Bay • New Zealand..........35 S
Poverty Point Nat. Mon. Park N •
LA, United States..........151 [190]
Poverty Point Nat. Mon. •
LA, United States..........153 F1
Pôvoa de Varzim • Portugal..........11 C3
Povoação • Azores..........118 B1
Powder • MT/WY, United States..........43 C5
Powder Mtn Ski •
UT, United States..........149 [86]
Powell • WY, United States..........42 K4
Powell, Lake •
United States..........45 G3
Powell River • BC, Canada..........38 G7
Powerscourt House • Ireland..........108 B4
Poyang Hu • China..........29 F5
Pöytyä • Finland..........125 E2
Poza Rica • Mexico..........157 G2
Pozantı • Turkey..........123 G2
Pozazal • Spain..........11 H1
Pozo Alegre • Brazil..........163 C3
Pozoblanco • Spain..........11 F5
Pozos, Punta • Argentina..........53 B5
Pozuelos • Venezuela..........51 E2
Pozza di Fassa Ski • Italy..........100 [33]
Pozza di Fassa • Italy..........120 D3
Pozzallo • Sicily, Italy..........121 G3
Pozzuoli • Italy..........121 G3
Pra • Ghana..........22 D3
Pra-Loup Ski • France..........100 [70]
Pra-Loup • France..........115 H2

Prachatice • Czech Rep..........128 B3
Prachin Buri • Thailand..........142 C2
Prachuap Kiri Khan • Thailand..........31 B4
Praded • Czech Rep..........13 G7
Prades • France..........115 K2
Præstø • Denmark..........125 F14
Prague Heritage C • Czech Rep..........86 [168]
Prague • Czech Rep..........128 B2
Praha Heritage C • Czech Rep..........86 [168]
Praha • Czech Rep..........128 B2
Praia • Cape Verde..........22 (1) B2
Praia da Benagil • Portugal..........118 E6
Praia da Falésia • Portugal..........118 E7
Praia da Luz • Portugal..........118 E7
Praia da Rocha • Portugal..........118 E6
Praia das Maças • Portugal..........118 D1
Praia de Balaia • Portugal..........118 E6
Praia de Castelo • Portugal..........118 E6
Praia de Galé • Portugal..........118 E6
Praia de Vale do Lobo •
Portugal..........118 E7
Praia do Guincho • Portugal..........118 D1
Praia Grande • Portugal..........118 D1
Praia Parede • Portugal..........118 D1
Praia Verde • Portugal..........118 E7
Prainha • Brazil..........51 G4
Prainha • Madeira..........118 C1
Prairie du Chien •
WI, United States..........43 K5
Prairie Village •
KS, United States..........46 H3
Prambanan Heritage C •
Java, Indonesia..........85 [206]
Prambanan • Java, Indonesia..........143 J7
Pranaburi Ski • Italy..........100 [237]
Pranita • India..........28 C5
Prapat • Indonesia..........143 G2
Prapoutel Ski • France..........100 [52]
Praslin Beach • Seychelles..........133 K4
Praslin Bay • St Lucia..........161 P
Prasonisi, Akra •
Rhodes, Greece..........122 D12
Prat Matalou • France..........115 K1
Prata • Brazil..........52 G2
Prata, Costa de • Portugal..........118 A2
Prata I. • China..........139 A8
Pratu • Italy..........121 E11
Prats-de-Mollo • France..........115 K2
Pratt • KS, United States..........46 F4
Prattville • AL, United States..........48 D4
Pravdinsk • Russian Fed..........13 K3
Pravia • Spain..........11 E1
Prawil Point • United Kingdom..........104 F5
Praz-de-Lys Ski • France..........100 [14]
Praz-sur-Arly Ski • France..........100 [23]
Prazeres • Madeira..........118 C1
Prêcheur, le • Martinique..........161 N
Predazzo Ski • Italy..........100 [220]
Predazzo • Italy..........120 B3
Preeté • Germany..........8 F2
Pregolya • Russian Fed..........13 J3
Preissac, Lac • QU, Canada..........44 F1
Prekmurje • Slovenia..........14 D3
Premnitz • Germany..........8 H4
Premuda • Croatia..........128 D3
Prenj • Bosnia-Herz..........14 E6
Prenn Falls • Vietnam..........141 E2
Prenzlau • Germany..........8 I3
Prenzlauer Berg (Berlin) •
Germany..........111 C2
Preobrazhenka • Russian Fed..........27 G5
Preparis North Channel •
Myanmar..........31 A3
Prerov • Czech Rep..........13 G8
Prerov nad Labem • Czech Rep..........128 B2
Prerow Beach • Germany..........96 [32]
Prescott • OT, Canada..........44 H3
Prescott • AZ, United States..........153 E1
Prescott Valley •
AZ, United States..........45 F4
Preservation Inlet •
New Zealand..........145 G3
Presho • SD, United States..........43 F5
Presidencia Roque Sáenz Peña •
Argentina..........52 D4
Presidente Epitácio • Brazil..........52 F3
Presidente Frei [Base] •
Antarctica..........54 (1) JJ4
Presidente Prudente • Brazil..........52 F3
Presidente R. Sáenz Peña • Brazil..........47 B3
Presidente • Bulgaria..........128 E3
Presidente • Slovak Rep..........13 K8
Prêspa Nat. Park Park N •
Greece..........89 [133]
Presque Isle •
ME, United States..........44 K2
Pressburg • Slovak Rep..........90 A14
Prestatyn Beach •
United Kingdom..........101 [213]
Prestice • Czech Rep..........9 I7
Preston • United Kingdom..........7 J8
Preston • United States..........42 J5
Preston • MN, United States..........43 J5
Preston • MN, United States..........46 I4
Preston Peak •
CA, United States..........42 D6
Prestwich [Apt] •
United Kingdom..........6 H6
Pretoria • South Africa..........24 D5
Pretorius, Willem Game Reserve Park •
South Africa..........133 [127]
Prevel, Fort • QU, Canada..........156 D2
Préveza • Greece..........122 C1
Pribilof Is. •
United States..........49 H4
Priboj • F.R. of Yugoslavia..........14 G6
Pribram • Czech Rep..........128 B3
Pribyslav • Czech Rep..........128 B4
Price • UT, United States..........45 G2
Prichard • AL, United States..........48 C5
Prickly Pear Cays • Anguilla..........160 C
Prickly Point • Grenada..........160 S
Pridz Bay • Antarctica..........54 (1) M3
Priego • Spain..........11 I4
Priego de Córdoba • Spain..........11 G7
Prien • Germany..........112 D4
Prievidza • Slovak Rep..........13 H9
Prijedor • Bosnia-Herz..........111 A2
Prijepolje • Bosnia-Herz..........12 K4
Prilep • F.Y.R. of Macedonia..........14 I8
Primaria [Base] • Antarctica..........53 (1) C2
Primeira Cruz • Brazil..........53 (1) C2
Primorsk • Russian Fed..........126 D6
Primorsk Beach • Bulgaria..........97 [242]
Primorsko • Bulgaria..........128 E3
Primorsko-Akhtarsk •
Russian Fed..........17 F5
Primosten • Croatia..........128 D3
Primosten • Croatia..........128 D3
Prince Albert • South Africa..........134 C4
Prince Albert • SA, Canada..........38 J5
Prince Albert Nat. Park Park N •
SA, Canada..........156 [19]
Prince Albert Peninsula •
NT, Canada..........38 H2
Prince Albert Road •
South Africa..........134 C2
Prince Albert Sound •
NT, Canada..........38 H2
Prince Alfreds Pass •
South Africa..........134 C7

Prince Charles I. • NU, Canada 39 P3
Prince Charles Mtns •
  Antarctica 54 (1) L2
Prince de Galles, Cap du •
  QU, Canada 39 Q4
Prince Edward I. • Canada 156 D7
Prince Edward I. Nat. Park •
  PE, Canada 156 D7
Prince Edward I. Nat. Park Park N •
  PE, Canada . . . . 156 [34]
Prince Edward Is. •
  Indian Ocean 19 H10
Prince George • BC, Canada 155 C1
Prince of Wales, Cape •
  AK, United States 36 A3
Prince of Wales I. •
  QL, Australia 34 H2
Prince of Wales I. • NU, Canada . . . 38 L2
Prince of Wales I. •
  AK, United States 49 O4
Prince of Wales Strait •
  NT, Canada 38 H2
Prince Regent Inlet •
  NU, Canada 39 N2
Prince Rupert • BC, Canada 38 F6
Prince Rupert Bay • Dominica 80 B11
Prince Rupert Bay • Dominica . . . . 161 M
Prince William Forest Park Park N •
  VA, United States . . . . 151 [255]
Prince William Forest Park •
  VA, United States 153 D9
Prince William Sound •
  AK, United States 49 L4
Princes Is. • Turkey 122 D3
Princess Charlotte Bay •
  QL, Australia 34 H2
Princess Juliana [Apt] •
  St Maarten . . . . 160 D
Princess Royal I. • BC, Canada 38 F6
Princeton • BC, Canada 42 E2
Princeton • IL, United States 46 I2
Princeton • IL, United States 46 K2
Princeton • IN, United States 48 D1
Princeton • WV, United States 48 G2
Princeton • NJ, United States 153 D6
Principe • Sao Tomé e Príncipe . . . 22 F4
Prineville • OR, United States 42 E4
Prineville Reservoir •
  OR, United States 42 E4
Prinos Beach •
  E. Macedonia, Greece . . . . 97 [194]
Prinos Beach • Crete, Greece . . . . 97 [213]
Prinos • Crete, Greece 123 E2
Prinzapolka • Nicaragua 51 A1
Pripyat • Belarus 17 D4
Priskaspiyskaya Nizmennost •
  Kazakstan 17 I5
Pristina • F.R. of Yugoslavia 14 I7
Pritzwalk • Germany 8 H3
Privas • France 10 J9
Priverno • Italy 121 F4
Prizren • F.R. of Yugoslavia 14 H7
Probolinggo • Java, Indonesia 143 J8
Prócida, II. • Italy 121 G3
Procópio • Brazil 52 F3
Prodhromos • Cyprus 123 J3
Profitis Ilías • Greece 115 J5
Profondeville • Belgium 109 D15
Progonati • Albania 15 A3
Progreso • Mexico 157 H1
Progress [Base] • Antarctica 54 (1) N3
Prokop'yevsk • Russian Fed. 26 O7
Prokuplje • F.R. of Yugoslavia 14 I6
Prome • Myanmar 31 B2
Promthep, Laem •
  Ko Phuket, Thailand 142 E2
Propriá • Brazil 53 (1) D4
Propriano • Corsica, France 115 L3
Proserpine • QL, Australia 144 B1
Prosna • Poland 13 G5
Prospect Beach • Cayman Is. 159 J4
Prospect, Fort • Bermuda 159 J4
Prospect Park • Cayman Is. 159 E2
Prosperidad • Philippines 31 H5
Prostejov • Czech Rep. 13 G8
Protaras • Cyprus 123 J4
Protea Banks • South Africa 134 B5
Provadiya • Bulgaria 14 L4
Provence • France 115 H1
Provence-Alpes-Côte d'Azur •
  France 114 A4
Providence • Seychelles 133 K4
Providence • RI, United States . . . 153 D4
Providence, Bancs • Seychelles . . 133 K3
Providencia, Cayo de •
  West Indies 160 A18
Providencia, I. de •
  West Indies 160 A18
Providenciales •
  Turks & Caicos Is. 158 C1
Providniya • Russian Fed. 54 GG3
Provincetown •
  MA, United States 44 J4
Provins • France 115 E4
Provo • UT, United States 45 G1
Provost • AL, Canada 38 I6
Prozor • Bosnia-Herz. 14 G6
Prudhoe Bay • AK, United States . . 49 L1
Prudnik • Poland 13 G7
Prüm • Germany 112 D1
Prune I. • St Vincent & Gren. . . . . 161 R
Prunn Castle • Germany . . . . . 113 [139]
Pruszcz Gdanski • Poland 13 H3
Pruszkow • Poland 13 J5
Prut • Ukraine 14 L1
Pruzhany • Belarus 13 N5
Pryluky • Ukraine 17 E4
Pryor • OK, United States 46 H4
Przasnysz • Poland 13 J4
Przemysl • Poland 13 L8
Psará • Greece 122 D5
Psérimos • Greece 122 D8
Psiloritis • Crete, Greece 123 E6
Pskov • Russian Fed. 17 D3
Pskovskoye Ozero • Russian Fed. . 126 B2
Ptolemaís • Libya 21 D1
Ptolemais • Israel 135 A1
Ptuj • Slovenia 121 H1
Pu'er • China 29 C6
Pu'uhonua o Honaunau Nat. Hist. Park
  Park N • HI, United States . . . . 150 [21]
Pu'uhonua o Honaunau Nat. Hist. Park •
  HI, United States 154 G8
Pucallpa • Peru 51 C5
Puck • Poland 13 H3
Puckasaw • OT, Canada 44 C1
Pudasjärvi • Finland 16 N4
Pudent, Estany •
  Formentera, Spain 117 G4
Pudong Special Development Area •
  China 139 C2
Pudsey • Russian Fed. 17 F2
Pudukkottai • India 138 D11
Puebla Heritage C • Mexico . . . . 84 [25]
Puebla • Mexico 157 E4
Puebla [Adm] • Mexico 37 B4
Pueblo • CO, United States 45 H3
Pueblo de Taos Heritage C •
  NM, United States . . . . 84 [8]
Pueblo Viejo • Dominican Rep. . . . 159 G7
Puelches • Argentina 55 C3
Puente Genil • Spain 11 C2
Puentearéas • Spain 11 C2
Puerto Acosta • Bolivia 52 C2
Puerto Aisén • Chile 53 B5
Puerto Alegre • Bolivia 52 D1
Puerto Angel • Mexico 157 B4
Puerto Armuelles • Panama 37 E6
Puerto Asís • Colombia 51 B3
Puerto Ayacucho • Venezuela 51 D2

Puerto Ayora • Galapagos Is. . . . 51 (1) A2
Puerto Banús • Spain 116 B6
Puerto Baquerizo Morena •
  Galapagos Is. 51 (1) B2
Puerto Barrios • Guatemala 37 D4
Puerto Berrio • Colombia 51 C2
Puerto Cabello • Venezuela 37 H5
Puerto Cabezas • Nicaragua 37 E5
Puerto Caldera • Costa Rica 80 B9
Puerto Carreño • Colombia 51 D2
Puerto Camarebo • Venezuela 51 D1
Puerto de la Cruz Beach •
  Tenerife, Canary Is. . . . . 96 [109]
Puerto de la Cruz •
  Tenerife, Canary Is. 116 E1
Puerto de la Peña •
  Fuerteventura, Canary Is. 117 E2
Puerto de Lajas • Mexico 40 E6
Puerto de Mazarrón • Spain 117 C3
Puerto de Santiago •
  Tenerife, Canary Is. 116 E1
Puerto del Carmen •
  Lanzarote, Canary Is. 117 E3
Puerto del Rosario •
  Fuerteventura, Canary Is. 117 E2
Puerto del Santiago Beach •
  Tenerife, Canary Is. . . . . 96 [109]
Puerto Deseado • Argentina 53 C5
Puerto Escondido •
  Oaxaca, Mexico 157 G4
Puerto Escondido •
  Baja Calif S., Mexico 157 F4
Puerto Francisco de Orellana •
  Ecuador 51 B4
Puerto Heath • Bolivia 51 C5
Puerto Huasco • Chile 52 B4
Puerto Huitoto • Colombia 51 C3
Puerto Inca • Peru 163 B3
Puerto Juárez • Mexico 157 H2
Puerto la Concordia • Colombia . . . 51 C3
Puerto la Cruz • Venezuela 51 E1
Puerto Leguizamo • Colombia 51 C4
Puerto Libertad • Mexico 157 F1
Puerto Limón • Colombia 51 B3
Puerto Limón • Costa Rica 51 A2
Puerto Lopez • Colombia 51 C3
Puerto Madryn • Argentina 80 A3
Puerto Maldonado • Peru 163 B2
Puerto Maunabo • Puerto Rico . . . 159 H4
Puerto Montt • Chile 53 B4
Puerto Morelos • Mexico 157 H2
Puerto Natilho • Venezuela 51 D3
Puerto Natales • Chile 53 B6
Puerto Ordaz • Venezuela 51 E2
Puerto Padre • Cuba 158 D8
Puerto Paez • Venezuela 51 D2
Puerto Peñasco • Mexico 157 F1
Puerto Plata • Dominican Rep. . . . 159 G3
Puerto Portalo • Majorca, Spain . . 117 H3
Puerto Portalo • Peru 163 B1
Puerto Princesa • Philippines 31 F5
Puerto Providencio • Peru 163 B2
Puerto Real • Spain 11 B8
PUERTO RICO • West Indies . . . . 159 H
Puerto Rico • Colombia 51 B3
Puerto Rico • Bolivia 51 D6
Puerto Rico •
  Gran Canaria, Canary Is. 116 E4
Puerto Rico Trench •
  West Indies 37 H4
Puerto San José • Guatemala 37 D4
Puerto Santa Cruz • Argentina . . . 53 C6
Puerto Siles • Bolivia 52 C1
Puerto Suárez • Bolivia 52 E2
Puerto Vallarta • Mexico 157 G1
Puerto Varas • Chile 53 B4
Puerto-Princesa Subterranean River
  Nat. Park Heritage N • Philippines . 83 [135]
Puertollano • Spain 11 G6
Puesti • Romania 14 O3
Puglia • Italy 12 K8
Puigcerdá • Spain 117 D1
Puigmal • France/Spain 11 N2
Puk'chong • D.P.R. of Korea 30 A1
Puka • Albania 15 A1
Pukapuka • French Polynesia 33 N7
Pukaskwa Nat. Park • OT, Canada . 44 B1
Pukaskwa Nat. Park Park N •
  OT, Canada . . . . 156 [22]
Puksoozero • Russian Fed. 17 G2
Puksubaek • D.P.R. of Korea 30 D4
Pula • Croatia 128 D1
Pulaski • NY, United States 44 G4
Pulaski • TN, United States 48 D3
Pulaski • VA, United States 48 G2
Pulau Pinang [Adm] • Malaysia . . . 141 F
Pulau Tikus • Penang, Malaysia . . 141 F2
Pulawy • Poland 13 K6
Pulguksa Temple Heritage C •
  Rep. of Korea . . . . 85 [185]
Pulheim • Germany 111 B3
Pulicat Lake • India 138 D7
Pulkkila • Finland 16 N4
Pulkovo [Apt] • Russian Fed. . . . 126 C1
Pullman • WA, United States . . . 152 B2
Pulog, Mt • Philippines 31 G3
Pulpi Beach • Spain . . . . 96 [116]
Pultusk • Poland 13 K5
Puma Yumco • China 28 E5
Pump Bay • St Kitts & Nevis . . . . 161 G
Punak • Ecuador 51 A4
Punchestown • Ireland 108 B3
Pune • India 28 B5
Punggol • Mozambique 24 E3
Púngoe • Mozambique 24 E3
Punia • Dem. Rep. of Congo 23 D4
Punjab [Adm] • Pakistan 28 B2
Punjab [Adm] • India 28 C2
Puno • Peru 163 B4
Punta Almina • Spain 11 F9
Punta Alta • Argentina 53 D3
Punta Arenas • Chile 53 B6
Punta Arenas • Margarita . . . . . 160 V
Punta Cana • Dominican Rep. . . . 159 G8
Punta, Cerro de • Puerto Rico . . . 159 H3
Punta del Este • Uruguay 163 D2
Punta Gorda • Belize 37 D4
Punta Gorda • FL, United States . . . 49 C4
Punta Prima • Margarita 157 F1
Punta Prima • Majorca, Spain . . . 117 J2
Punta Räisi [Apt] •
  Sicily, Italy 120 D1
Punta Umbría Beach • Spain . . . 96 [112]
Punta Umbría • Spain 11 B2
Puntarenas • Costa Rica 37 E6
Punto de Venezuela 51 C1
Punxsutawney •
  PA, United States 153 D5
Puolanka • Finland 16 N4
Pupapuka • Cook Is. 33 K7
Puquio • Peru 163 B1
Pur • Russian Fed. 26 M4
Puracé, Volcán • Colombia 51 B3
Purbeck, Isle of •
  United Kingdom 104 F6
Purbolinggo • Java, Indonesia . . . 143 J6
Purcell Mtns • AL/BC, Canada . . . 42 D4
Pureora Forest Park •
  New Zealand 145 F2
Purgatoire • CO, United States . . . 46 D4
Purgatory Ski •
  CO, United States . . . . 149 [111]
Puri Beach • India 138 E4
Purmerend • Netherlands 109 F2
Purnia • India 28 E4
Pursat • Cambodia 31 C4
Purulya • India 28 E4
Purus • Brazil 51 E5

Purwakarta • Java, Indonesia . . . 143 J1
Purwodadi • Java, Indonesia 143 J3
Purwokerto • Java, Indonesia . . . 143 J6
Pusan • Rep. of Korea 30 E7
Pushkar • India 137 C6
Pushkin • Russian Fed. 17 E3
Puspökladany • Hungary 13 K10
Pusteria, Val • Italy 120 B2
Pustertal • Austria/Italy 120 B2
Pusula Dagi • Turkey 15 N6
Puszcza Notecka • Poland 13 F5
Putao • Myanmar 31 B1
Putaruru • New Zealand 145 F2
Puteran • Indonesia 143 J4
Putian • China 29 F5
Putila • Ukraine 14 M2
Putnam • CT, United States 44 J5
Putorana, Plato • Russian Fed. . . . 26 P4
Putrajaya • Malaysia 141 G4
Putsborough Sands Beach •
  United Kingdom . . . . 101 [150]
Puttalam • Sri Lanka 138 D15
Puttaparthy • India 138 D6
Putten • Netherlands 109 F3
Puttgarden • Germany 8 G2
Putumayo • S. America. 51 C4
Putuo Shan • China 139 C4
Putussibau • Indonesia 32 E2
Puuc • Mexico 157 H1
Puukohola Heiau Nat. Hist. Site Park N •
  HI, United States . . . . 150 [19]
Puukohola Heiau Nat. Hist. Site •
  HI, United States 154 G8
Puulavesi • Finland 16 N6
Puuwai • HI, United States 154 G2
Puy, le • France 10 I8
Puy-l'Evêque • France 115 G4
Puyallup • WA, United States 42 D3
Puysegur Point • New Zealand . . . 145 G3
Pyalma • Russian Fed. 17 F2
Pyanskiy Zaliv • Russian Fed. 26 N3
Pyaozero • Russian Fed. 16 P3
Pyapon • Myanmar 31 B3
Pyasina • Russian Fed. 26 P3
Pyhä-Häkki Nat. Park Park N •
  Finland . . . . 89 [35]
Pyhäjärvi • Finland 125 E3
Pyhäjoki • Finland 16 L4
Pyhätunturi • Finland 16 N3
Pyhätunturi Nat. Park Park N •
  Finland . . . . 89 [31]
Pyhrnpaß • Austria 14 B2
Pyhäjoki • Finland 16 M4
Pyramid Canyon •
  AZ/NV, United States 153 E1
Pyramid Lake •
  NV, United States 152 C1
Pyrénées Occidentales, Parc nat. des
  Park N • France . . . . 89 [71]
Pyrénées-Occidentales, Parc nat. des •
  France . . . . 115 J
Pyrénées-Orientales • France . . . 115 K
Pyrénées-Orientales [Adm] •
  France 115 K2
Pyrgos Beach • Cyprus . . . . . . 97 [218]
Pyrzice • Poland 13 D4
Pyu • Myanmar 31 B3

Qaanaaq • Greenland 36 K2
Qadarif, Al • Sudan 21 G5
Qadimah, Al • Saudi Arabia 21 G3
Qadub • Yemen 18 F7
Qaidam Basin • China 139 A2
Qaidam He • China 28 G1
Qaidam Pendi • China 28 G1
Qairouan Heritage C • Tunisia . . . 86 [267]
Qairouan • Tunisia 131 E4
Qal'at al Jundi • Egypt 131 F2
Qal'at al Bishah • Saudi Arabia . . . 18 D6
Qal'eh-ye Now • Afghanistan 18 H3
Qala • Malta 123 H1
Qalat • Afghanistan 18 I3
Qalibah, Al • Saudi Arabia 18 C4
Qamdo • China 29 B4
Qandahar • Afghanistan 18 I3
Qang Ngai • Vietnam 31 D3
Qang Tri • Vietnam 31 D3
Qapshaghay • Kazakstan 26 M9
Qaqortoq • Greenland 39 V4
Qar Wager • Somalia 23 H1
Qarar • Afghanistan 18 I2
Qaraútaq • Kazakstan 26 J8
Qaraghandy • Kazakstan 26 L8
Qarasu as Sab'ah • Libya 21 C2
Qaratau • Kazakstan 26 L9
Qardo • Somalia 23 H2
Qarqan • China 28 E1
Qarqan He • China 26 O10
Qarsaqbay • Kazakstan 26 K8
Qarshi • Uzbekistan 18 I2
Qasigianguit • Greenland 39 U3
Qasimili • Azerbaijan 52 A4
Qasr Amra Heritage C • Jordan . . 86 [286]
Qasr, El • Egypt 131 F3
Qasr Faráfra • Egypt 21 E2
Qasr Haman • Saudi Arabia 18 E5
Qasr Ibrîm • Egypt 21 F4
Qasserine • Tunisia 131 E5
QATAR • Asia 18 E4
Qatif, Al • Saudi Arabia 18 E4
Qáttara • Egypt 21 E2
Qáttara Depression • Egypt 131 F1
Qáttara, Munkhaffad al • Egypt . . . 21 E2
Qawra • Malta 123 H2
Qayihab, Al • Saudi Arabia 18 D5
Qazrin • Syria 135 A2
Qazvin • Iran 18 E2
Qena • Egypt 131 F4
Qeqertarsuaq • Greenland 39 U3
Qeqertarsuaq [I.] • Greenland . . . 39 U3
Qerqenah Is. • Tunisia 131 E4
Qeshm • Iran 18 F4
Qezel Owzan • Iran 18 E2
Qian He • China 139 B1
Qian Gorlos • China 29 G1
Qian Shan • China 29 G2
Qianshan • Zhuhai, China 139 B1
Qiao Dao • Zhuhai, China 139 B2
Qiaowan • China 29 B2
Qiemo • China 28 E1
Qijiang • China 29 D3
Qikiqtaluk • NU, Canada 155 A4
Qilian Shan • China 29 B3
Qin Ling • China 29 D3
Qingdao • China 29 G3
Qinghai [Adm] • China 139 A2
Qinghai Hu • China 29 C3
Qinghe • China 29 F2
Qinghuangdao • China 139 F3
Qionghai • China 31 D2
Qiqihar • China 29 G1
Qira • China 28 D2
Qishn • Yemen 18 F6
Qitai • China 26 O9
Qitaihe • China 27 L7
Qixianshan • China 139 C1
Qizhou Yang • China 26 J9
Qoqir Feng • China/Kashmir 28 C1
Qojlleh-ye Damavand • Iran 18 F2

Qomolangma Feng • China/Nepal. . 28 E3
Qomsheh • Iran 18 F3
Qonduz • Afghanistan 18 I2
Qoraqalpoghiston • Uzbekistan . . . 26 J8
Qostanay • Russian Fed. 26 J7
Qu'Appelle • MN/SA, Canada 38 K6
Quabbin Reservoir •
  MA, United States 44 I4
Quadane • Mauritania 20 C4
Quakenbrück • Germany 8 C4
Quan Long • Vietnam 141 E3
Quanah • TX, United States 139 C1
Quantico • VA, United States . . . 153 D9
Quantock Hills • United Kingdom . 104 D9
Quanzhou • Guangxi, China 29 E5
Quanzhou • Fujian, China 29 F6
Quartier Militaire • Mauritius . . . 132 J4
Quartu San'Elena Beach •
  Sardinia, Italy . . . . 96 [139]
Quartu Sant'Elena •
  Sardinia, Italy 12 D9
Quartz Peak • CA, United States . . . 45 E5
Quatre Bornes • Mauritius 132 J3
Quatre Bornes • Seychelles 133 K3
Quatre, I. • St Vincent & Gren. . . . 161 R
Quba • Azerbaijan 17 H6
Quba • Iran 18 G2
Queanbeyan • NS, Australia . . . 144 C2
Quebec Heritage C • QU, Canada . 84 [3]
Québec • QU, Canada 155 B4
Québec [Adm] • Canada 39 P6
Qued el Kehir • Algeria 12 C12
Quedlinburg • Germany 8 G5
Quedlinburg Heritage C •
  Germany . . . . 86 [45]
Queen Alexandra Range •
  Antarctica 54 (1) U1
Queen, Cape • NU, Canada 39 P4
Queen Charlotte Is. •
  BC, Canada 38 E6
Queen Charlotte Sound •
  BC, Canada 38 E6
Queen Charlotte Strait •
  BC, Canada 38 F6
Queen Elizabeth Is. •
  NU, Canada 38 K2
Queen Elizabeth Nat. Park Park N •
  Uganda . . . . 133 [69]
Queen Maud Gulf • NU, Canada . . 38 K3
Queen Maud Land • Antarctica . . 54 (1) G2
Queen Maud Mtns • Antarctica . . 54 (1) CC1
Queen of Spains Valley •
  Jamaica 159 F1
Queens • NY, United States 153 D7
Queensborough • South Africa . . 24 D6
Queenstown • TS, Australia 34 I8
Queenstown • South Africa 134 C4
Queenstown • New Zealand 145 G2
Queenstown • New Town Singapore 141 H2
Quela • Angola 22 H6
Quelimane • Mozambique 24 F3
Quelpart • Rep. of Korea 30 D7
Queluz • Portugal 118 D1
Quemado • NM, United States . . . 45 H4
Quemoy • Taiwan 31 F2
Quenza • Corsica, France 115 L4
Quepem • Goa, India 137 B2
Quequén • Argentina 163 D3
Quérandi • Greenland 121 I11
Querétaro Heritage C • Mexico . . 84 [18]
Querétaro • Mexico 157 G2
Querfurt Castle • Germany . . . . 113 [207]
Querim Beach • Goa, India 137 B1
Queseda • Spain 11 H7
Quesnel • BC, Canada 155 C1
Quesnel Lake • BC, Canada 38 G6
Questa • NM, United States 46 C4
Questa • Pakistan 28 A2
Quevedo • Ecuador 51 B4
Queyras • France 115 H2
Quezaltenango • Guatemala 37 C5
Quezon • Palawan, Philippines . . . 31 F5
Quezon City •
  Luzon, Philippines 31 G3
Qufu Heritage C • China . . . . . . 85 [173]
Qui Nhon • Vietnam 31 D4
Quibdó • Colombia 51 B2
Quiberon • France 114 C4
Quickborn • Germany 8 E3
Quilbamba • Peru 163 B2
Quillacollo • Bolivia 52 C2
Quillan • France 115 K2
Quillota • Chile 52 B5
Quilmes • Argentina 52 E5
Quilon • India 138 D10
Quilon Beach • India 138 E3
Quilpie • QL, Australia 34 H5
Quimili • Argentina 52 D4
Quimper • France 114 C3
Quimperlé • France 114 C3
Quincy • France 114 B1
Quincy • IL, United States 46 J3
Quincy • MA, United States 152 C1
Quincy • WA, United States 153 D4
Quivican Marsh Is. 46 E6
Qulik Chain • Marshall Is. 33 N6
Quilota • Chile 52 B5
Quma • Nicaragua 51 A1
Qumdod, Al • Iraq 18 D4
Qumran • Palestine 135 A8
Qunfudhah, Al • Saudi Arabia . . . 18 D6
Quoin I. • QL, Australia 144 B4
Quoon • Uzbekistan 18 J1
Qurdud • Sudan 23 E1
Qurghonteppa • Tajikistan 18 J2
Quseir • Egypt 131 F4
Qusmuryn • Kazakstan 26 J7
Quthing • Lesotho 24 D5
Qüxü • China 28 F3

R'as al Khaymah •
  United Arab Emirates 18 G4
Ra's al Unif • Libya 21 C1
Ra's as Saffaniyah •
  Saudi Arabia 18 E4
Rãã • Sweden 125 F11
Raab • Austria 128 B3
Raahe • Sweden 13 F11
Raalte • Netherlands 5 J2
Raas • Indonesia 143 J4
Raasay, Sound of •
  United Kingdom 6 F4

Rab • Croatia 128 D3
Rab [I.] • Croatia 128 D3
Rába • Hungary 13 G10
Raba • Indonesia 32 (1) A4
Rabat • Poland 128 C4
Rabat • Malta 123 H4
Rabat • Morocco 131 D1
Rabaul • Papua New Guinea . . . 35 (1) E1
Rabbah • Jordan 135 A4
Rabbit I. • Antigua & Barbuda . . . 161 J
Rabi, Ash Shallal ar • Sudan 21 F4
Rabigh • Saudi Arabia 18 C5
Rabka • Poland 128 C4
Raccoon Point •
  LA, United States 47 I3
Race, Cape • NF, Canada 156 D4
Raceland • LA, United States 48 B6
Rach Gia • Vietnam 141 E3
Raciborz • Poland 128 C1
Rad, Ko • Thailand 142 E1
Radan • F.R. of Yugoslavia 14 I7
Radbuza • Czech Rep. 128 B3
Radcliff • KY, United States 48 E2
Råde • Norway 124 B4
Radeberg • Germany 13 C6
Radebeul • Germany 9 I5
Radevormwald • Germany 111 B4
Radford • VA, United States 48 G2
Radium Hot Springs • BC, Canada . 42 [3]
Radnor Forest • United Kingdom . 104 D1
Radolfzell • Germany 9 E9
Radom • Poland 13 K6
Radomir • Bulgaria 15 D1
Radomsko • Poland 13 I6
Radovis • F.R. of Macedonia 15 D3
Radøy • Norway 124 C3
Radstadt Ski • Austria . . . . . . 100 [179]
Radviliskis • Lithuania 126 B3
Radyn Castle • Czech Rep. 128 A3
Radzyn Podlaski • Poland 13 L6
Rae • NT, Canada 38 H4
Raesfeld Castle • Germany . . . . 113 [16]
Raetea • New Zealand 35 D2
Raetihi • New Zealand 145 F3
Raevavae • French Polynesia . . . 33 M8
Raf-Raf • Tunisia 131 E2
Rafaela • Argentina 52 D5
Rafaï • Central African Rep. 23 C2
Raffles Lighthouse • Singapore . . 141 H3
Rafha • Saudi Arabia 18 D4
Rafina • Greece 122 D4
Rafsanjan • Iran 18 G3
Ragged I. • Bahamas 159 F1
Ragged I. Range • Bahamas . . . 158 B3
Ragged, Mt • WA, Australia 34 D6
Ragged Point • Barbados . . . . . 161 O
Raging Waters Park L •
  CA, United States . . . . 150 [F]
Raglan • New Zealand 145 F1
Raglan Castle • United Kingdom . 104 D3
Raglan Harbour • New Zealand . . 145 F1
Ragley Hall • United Kingdom . . 104 D2
Ragusa • Croatia 90 A14
Ragusa • Sicily, Italy 120 D4
Raha • Indonesia 32 (1) B3
Rahad, Ar • Sudan 21 F5
Råhnes Beach • Greece . . . . . 97 [187]
Rahimyar Khan • Pakistan 28 B3
Rahole Game Reserve • Kenya . . 131 G2
Raichur • India 138 D2
Raiganj • India 28 D4
Rainbow Beach • US Virgin Is. . . 160 Z
Rainbow Bridge Nat. Mon. •
  UT, United States . . . . 150 [82]
Rainbow Bridge Nat. Mon. •
  UT, United States 153 E1
Rainbow Springs • New Zealand . 145 F2
Rainbow Valley Park L •
  PE, Canada . . . . 156 [Q]
Rainier, Mt • WA, United States . 152 B2
Rainy Lake •
  Canada/United States 43 J2
Rainy River • OT, Canada 43 I2
Raippaluoto • Finland 16 K5
Raipur • India 28 D4
Raisio • Finland 125 E3
Raja • Indonesia 143 J8
Raja No, Ko • Thailand 142 E2
Rajahmundry • India 138 D4
Rajang • Malaysia 32 E2
Rajapalaiyam • India 138 D10
Rajasthan • India 137 C2
Rajasthan Canal • India 137 B2
Rajbag Beach • Goa, India 137 B2
Rajkot • India 28 B4
Rajmahal • India 28 E4
Rajnandgaon • India 28 D4
Rajpur • India 28 C4
Rajshahi • Bangladesh 28 E4
Raka Zangbo • China 28 E3
Rakaia • New Zealand 145 G2
Rakhine • Myanmar 31 A2
Rakhiv • Ukraine 14 L1
Rakhmanovskiy Klyuchi •
  Russian Fed. 26 O8
Rakit • Indonesia 143 J2
Rakitovo • Bulgaria 14 L8
Rakkestad • Norway 124 B4
Rakoniewice • Poland 13 F5
Rakops • Botswana 24 C4
Rakovnik • Czech Rep. 9 I6
Rakvere • Estonia 126 B2
Raleigh • ND, United States 43 F3
Raleigh • NC, United States 48 H3
Raleigh Bay • NC, United States . . 48 I3
Ralik Chain • Marshall Is. 33 N6
Rama • Nicaragua 51 A1
Ramadi, Ar • Iraq 18 D3
Ramatuelle • France 115 H4
Rambervillers • France 9 B8
Rambouillet • France 115 E3
Rambouillet, Forêt de • France . . 115 F3
Rambat Siwi Temple •
  Bali, Indonesia 143 H1
Rameilerajo • Madagascar 138 D11
Rameswaram Beach • India . . . 138 E3
Ramgarh • India 28 E4
Ramgoolam, Sir S. [Apt] •
  Mauritius 132 J4
Ramiers Hist. Park Heritage C •
  Haiti . . . . 84 [42]
Ramla • Kenya 131 G3
Ramla • Israel 135 A5
Ramla Bay • Malta 123 H1
Ramlat Dahm • Saudi Arabia . . . 21 I4
Ramm • Ethiopia 131 H5
Rammenau Castle • Germany . . 113 [192]
Ramnagar • India 137 C8
Ramnäs • Sweden 125 E10
Ramonal • Mexico 157 H3
Rampur • India 137 D7
Ramree • Myanmar 31 A3
Ramsau am Dachstein Ski •
  Austria . . . . 100 [187]
Ramsau am Dachstein •
  Austria 112 F8
Ramsey • MN, United States 43 J4
Ramsey Lake • OT, Canada 44 C2
Ramsgate Beach • United Kingdom . 101 [76]
Ramsgate • United Kingdom . . . 105 J5
Ramsjö • Sweden 16 I5
Ramu • Laos 31 C2
Rana • Norway 124 D2
Ranai • Indonesia 32 D2
Rånåsfoss • Norway 124 B3
Ranaghat • India 28 E4
Rancagua • Chile 52 B5
Rance • France 114 C2

Ranchi • India 28 D4
Rancho California •
  CA, United States 45 D5
Rancho Cordova •
  CA, United States 45 B2
Rancho Luna, Playa • Cuba . . . 158 D2
Randaberg • Norway 124 C5
Randallstown •
  MD, United States 44 G6
Randers • Denmark 125 F10
Randolph • NE, United States . . . 43 H5
Randolph • VT, United States . . . 44 I4
Random I. • NF, Canada 156 D4
Ranfurly • New Zealand 35 C7
Rangeley • ME, United States . . . 44 J3
Rangely • CO, United States 45 H1
Ranger Lake • OT, Canada 44 D2
Rangiroa • French Polynesia 35 O6
Rangitaiki • New Zealand 145 F2
Rangitikei • New Zealand 145 F4
Rangkasbitung • Java, Indonesia . 143 J1
Rangoon • Myanmar 31 B3
Rangpur • Bangladesh 28 E3
Rangsdorf • Germany 111 C4
Rangsdorfer See • Germany . . . 111 C4
Ranielle • WV, United States . . . 48 G2
Raniket • India 137 C3
Raniket Hill Sta • India 138 E1
Rannalhi • Maldives 138 F4
Rannoch, Loch • United Kingdom . 104 B1
Ranomafana, Parc nat. de Park •
  Madagascar . . . . 133 [143]
Ranong • Thailand 31 B5
Ransdfjorden • Norway 124 B2
Ranskil • Indonesia 32 (1) D3
Rantaupanjang • Indonesia 32 E3
Rantauprapat • Indonesia 143 G4
Ranthambor Nat. Park • India . . 137 C6
Rantoul • IL, United States 46 K4
Ranua • Finland 16 N4
Ranyah, Wadi • Saudi Arabia . . . 21 H3
Raoul • New Zealand 33 J8
Rapa • French Polynesia 33 M8
Rapel • Mai • Mali 20 E5
Rapid el Ma Niafounke • Mali . . . 22 D1
Rapid City • SD, United States . . . 43 E4
Rapid Jumbo • Canada 23 G4
Rapid City • SD, United States . . . 43 E4
Rapa Nui, Parque Nac. Heritage C •
  Pacific Ocean . . . . 84 [77]
Rapallo • Italy 121 E6
Raper, Cape • NU, Canada 39 R3
Rapid City • SD, United States . . . 43 E4
Rapla • Estonia 126 B2
Raposeira • Portugal 118 E5
Rapperswil • Switzerland 119 G3
Rápulo • Bolivia 52 C1
Raroia • French Polynesia 33 M7
Rarotonga • Cook Is. 33 L8
Ras Beddouza • Morocco 20 D2
Ras el Ma • Egypt 131 F4
Ras el Má • Mali 20 E5
Ras el Ma Niafounke • Mali 22 D1
Rás Ghárib • Egypt 131 F4
Rás Jumbo • Somalia 23 G4
Râs Muhammad Dive • Red Sea . 135 B1
Râs Sidi Ali el Mekki • Tunisia . . 12 C11
Râs Umm Sid Dive • Red Sea . . 135 B1
Rasa • French Polynesia 33 M8
Rasa, Punta • Argentina 163 D4
Rascani • Moldova 14 O2
Rasdhu Atoll • Maldives 138 F1
Raseiniai • Lithuania 13 M2
Rashid • Egypt 21 E1
Rasht • Iran 18 E2
Raso, Cabo • Portugal 118 D1
Rason Lake • WA, Australia 34 D5
Rastatt • Germany 112 D6
Rastatt Castle • Germany . . . . 113 [100]
Rastede • Germany 8 D3
Rat Is. • AK, United States 49 E5
Ratak Chain • Marshall Is. 33 I5
Ratangarh • India 142 C1
Ratchaburi • Thailand 142 C1
Rath Luirc • Ireland 108 C6
Rathangan • Ireland 108 B3
Rathcoole • Ireland 108 B3
Rathdrum • Ireland 108 B4
Rathenow • Germany 8 H4
Rathkeale • Ireland 108 C6
Rathlin I. • United Kingdom 7 F6
Rathvilly • Ireland 108 B3
Ratibórice • Czech Rep. 128 B2
Ratingen • Germany 111 B3
Ratne • Ukraine 28 C4
Ratnagiri • India 138 D1
Ratne • Ukraine 13 N6
Raton • NM, United States 46 C4
Ratta • Russian Fed. 26 N5
Rattenberg • Austria 119 H3
Rattlesnake Hills •
  WY, United States 42 L5
Rattlesnake Nat. Recreation Area •
  MT, United States 152 B2
Ratz, Mt • BC, Canada 8 F3
Ratzeburg • Germany 8 F3
Raub • Malaysia 141 G2
Rauch • Argentina 163 D3
Rauland • Norway 124 C6
Rauma Heritage C • Finland . . . 85 [85]
Rauma • Norway 124 D3
Raurkela • India 28 D4
Raung, Gunung • Java, Indonesia . 143 J8
Raurkela • India 28 D4
Ravascletto • Italy 121 E4
Ravello • Italy 121 G4
Ravenglass • United Kingdom . . 104 C3
Ravenglass & Esdkale Railway •
  United Kingdom 104 C3
Ravenna Estuary •
  United Kingdom 104 C3
Ravenna Heritage C • Italy . . . . 86 [137]
Ravenna • Italy 121 E6
Ravenna • OH, United States . . . 44 E5
Ravensburg • Germany 112 F5
Ravenshoe • QL, Australia 144 B1
Ravensthorpe • WA, Australia . . 34 D6
Ravenswood • WV, United States . 48 F2
Ravi • Pakistan 28 B2
Ravinia • Turkmenistan 18 H2
Rawa Mazowiecka • Poland . . . 13 J6
Rawai • Ko Phuket, Thailand . . 142 E2
Rawai Beach •
  Ko Phuket, Thailand 142 E2
Rawaki • Kiribati 33 J6
Rawalpindi • Pakistan 28 B2
Rawicz • Poland 13 F6
Rawlins • WY, United States 45 H2
Rawlinna • WA, Australia 34 E6
Rawlinson Ranges •
  NT/WA, Australia 34 E5
Rawson • Argentina 53 C4
Raya • India 137 C4
Raya, Bukit • Indonesia 32 E3
Raychikhinsk • Russian Fed. . . . 27 K7
Raymondville •
  TX, United States 47 H4
Raymore • SA, Canada 43 D1
Rayong • Thailand 142 C4
Rayside-Balfour • OT, Canada . . 44 D2
Raytown • MO, United States . . . 46 H3
Razan • Iran 18 F3
Raz, Pointe de • France 114 C2
Razdel • Lac • Romania 128 E4
Razgrad • Bulgaria 126 B2
Razlog • Bulgaria 14 K8
Ré, Ile de • France 114 B1
Reach Falls • Jamaica 159 F4
Reading • PA, United States . . . 153 D6
Readstown • WI, United States . . 43 K5
Reboly • Russian Fed. 16 P5
Rebord Manambien • Madagascar . 24 H4

Rebun

Rebun • Japan 30 K2
Recherche, Archipelago of the • WA, Australia 34 D6
Recife • Brazil 53 (1) E3
Recife, Cape • South Africa 134 C8
Recklinghausen • Germany 111 B2
Recknitz • Germany 8 H2
Reconquista • Argentina 52 E4
Recreo • Argentina 52 C4
Red • China/Vietnam 29 C6
Red • United States 46 F5
Red Basin • China 139 A7
Red Bluff • CA, United States 152 C1
Red Bluff Lake • TX, United States 47 C2
Red Centre, The • NT, Australia 145 D
Red Cloud • NE, United States 46 F2
Red Deer • AL, Canada 155 C4
Red Deer [Riv] • AL, Canada 38 I6
Red Hill Patrick Henry Nat. Mem. • VA, United States 153 D11
Red Hills • KS, United States 46 F4
Red Lake • OT, Canada 43 J1
Red Lake [Lake] • OT, Canada 43 I1
Red Lodge • MT, United States 42 K4
Red Lodge Mtn **Ski** • MT, United States 149 [84]
Red Mtn **Ski** • BC, Canada 149 [7]
Red Oak • IA, United States 46 H2
Red River **Ski** • NM, United States 149 [113]
Red River of the North • Canada/United States 43 H2
Red Rock • MT, United States 42 I4
Red Rock • OT, Canada 43 L2
Red Rock, Lake • IA, United States 46 I2
Red Sea • Africa/Asia 21 G3
Red Sea cruise area • Africa/Asia 81 A5/7
Red Wharf Bay **Beach** • United Kingdom 101 [233]
Red Wing • MN, United States 43 J4
Redcar • United Kingdom 7 K7
Redcar **Beach** • United Kingdom 101 [26]
Redcliff • AL, Canada 42 J1
Redding • CA, United States 152 C1
Redditch • United Kingdom 7 J9
Redditt • OT, Canada 43 I2
Redeyef • Tunisia 131 E3
Redfield • SD, United States 43 G4
Redmond • WA, United States 42 D3
Redmond • OR, United States 42 E4
Redon • France 114 C4
Redondo • Portugal 11 D6
Redondo, Monte • Corsica, France 115 L2
Redruth • United Kingdom 104 F4
Redvers • SA, Canada 43 F2
Redwood City • CA, United States 45 A3
Redwood Falls • MN, United States 43 I4
Redwood Nat. Park **Heritage N** • CA, United States 82 [11]
Redwood Nat. Park **Park N** • CA, United States 150 [37]
Redwood Nat. Park • CA, United States 152 C1
Ree, Lough • Ireland 7 D8
Reed City • MI, United States 44 C4
Reedley • CA, United States 45 C3
Reedsburg • WI, United States 43 L5
Reedsport • OR, United States 42 C5
Reedville • VA, United States 44 G7
Reethi Rah • Maldives 138 F2
Reform • AL, United States 48 C4
Refugio • TX, United States 154 J5
Regen • Germany 9 I8
Regen [Riv] • Germany 9 H7
Regensburg • Germany 9 H7
Regenstauf • Germany 9 H7
Regenstein **Castle** • Germany 113 [210]
Reggane • Algeria 20 F3
Regge • Netherlands 5 J2
Reggio • LA, United States 48 C6
Réggio di Calabria • Italy 120 D2
Réggio nell' Emília • Italy 121 E7
Reghin • Romania 14 L3
Regina • French Guiana 51 G3
Regina • SA, Canada 38 K6
Regnitz • Germany 9 G7
Reguengos de Monsaraz • Portugal 11 D6
Rehoboth • Namibia 24 B4
Rehoboth Beach • DE, United States 153 D10
Rei, Costa • Sardinia, Italy 120 C4
Reichenbach • Germany 9 H6
Reichstag • Germany 111 C2
Reidsville • NC, United States 48 H2
Reigate • United Kingdom 104 E3
Reims • France 10 J4
Reims **Heritage C** • France 86 [61]
Reina Adelaida, Archipiélago • Chile 53 A6
Reina Beatrix [Apt] • Aruba 160 Y
Reina Sofia [Apt] • Tenerife, Canary Is. 116 E1
Reindeer • SA, Canada 38 K5
Reindeer Lake • MN/SA, Canada 38 K5
Reiner's Beach • Goa, India 137 B2
Reinga, Cape • New Zealand 35 D2
Reinhardstein, Château de • Belgium 109 D16
Reinickendorf (Berlin) • Germany 111 C2
Reis Magos Fort • Goa, India 137 B1
Reisa Nat. Park **Park N** • Norway 89 [6]
Reisaelva • Norway 16 K2
Reischach **Ski** • Italy 100 [243]
Reischach • Italy 120 B2
Reit im Winkl **Ski** • Germany 100 [5]
Reit im Winkl • Germany 112 F8
Rejmyre • Sweden 125 D3
Rekarne • Sweden 125 D3
Reliance • NT, Canada 38 J4
Relizane • Algeria 20 F1
Remada • Tunisia 131 E6
Remagen • Germany 112 E1
Remarkables, The • New Zealand 145 G2
Rembang • Java, Indonesia 143 J3
Rembau • Malaysia 141 G4
Remich • Luxembourg 109 D20
Remington • IN, United States 44 B5
Rémire • Seychelles 133 K2
Remiremont • France 10 L5
Remoulins **Heritage C** • France 86 [78]
Rempart, Rivière du • Mauritius 132 J2
Remparts, Rivière des • Réunion 132 H4
Remscheid • Germany 111 B4
Rémuzat • France 10 K9
Rend Lake • IL, United States 48 C1
Rendezvous Bay • Montserrat 161 H
Rendsburg • Germany 8 E2
Renfrew • OT, Canada 39 P7
Renfrewshire • United Kingdom 104 B3
Rengat • Indonesia 32 C3
Rengo • Chile 52 B5
Reni • Ukraine 14 P4
Renmark • SA, Australia 34 H6
Rennell • Solomon Is. 33 H7
Rennes • France 114 C4
Rennesøy • Norway 124 C5
Reno • Italy 12 F4
Reno • NV, United States 152 C1
Renon • Italy 120 B1
Renqiu • China 29 F3
Rensselaer • IN, United States 44 B5
Renton • WA, United States 42 D3
Reo • Indonesia 32 (1) B4
Réole, la • France 115 G3
Repentigny • QU, Canada 44 I3
Reposaari • Finland 125 E1
Republic • WA, United States 42 F2
Republican • KS/NE, United States 46 G3
Repulse Bay • NU, Canada 54 X3
Repulse Bay • Hong Kong, China 139 B6
Repulse Bay • QL, Australia 144 B3
Repvåg • Norway 16 M1
Requena • Spain 11 J5
Requena • Peru 51 C5
Réquista • France 10 H9
Reserve • NM, United States 45 H5
Rësheni • Albania 14 G8
Residenz, München **Castle** • Germany 113 [131]
Residenz, Würzburg **Castle** • Germany 113 [167]
Resistencia • Argentina 52 E4
Resita • Romania 14 I4
Resolute • NU, Canada 38 M2
Resolution I. • New Zealand 145 G3
Resolution I. • NU, Canada 39 S4
Reston • MN, Canada 43 F2
Restonica, Gorges de la • Corsica, France 115 L2
Retezat Nat. Park **Park N** • Romania 89 [129]
Rethel • France 10 J4
Réthimno **Beach** • Crete, Greece 97 [213]
Réthimno • Crete, Greece 123 E2
Réthimno [Adm] • Crete, Greece 123 E6
Rettenberg • Germany 112 F6
Retz • Austria 128 B4
Reuilly • France 114 B1
RÉUNION • Indian Ocean 132 H
Réunion, la • Seychelles 133 K4
Reus • Spain 117 D3
Reuss • Switzerland 119 G3
Reutlingen • Germany 112 D6
Reval • Estonia 90 A4
Revelstoke • BC, Canada 155 C4
Revillagigedo, Is. • Mexico 36 F8
Revin • France 10 J4
Rewa • India 137 C7
Rewari • India 137 C2
Rex, Mt • Antarctica 54 (1) HH2
Rexburg • ID, United States 42 J5
Rey • Iran 18 F2
Rey • Panama 51 B2
Reyes, Point • CA, United States 152 C3
Reykjahlid • Iceland 16 (1) E2
Reykjanes • Iceland 16 (1) B3
Reykjavík • Iceland 16 (1) B2
Reynolds Range • NT, Australia 145 D2
Reynoldsburg • OH, United States 44 D6
Reynosa • Mexico 47 E4
Rezé • France 10 D6
Rezekne • Latvia 126 B4
Reznas Ezers • Latvia 126 B4
Rezovo • Bulgaria 128 E4
Rezveya • Bulgaria/Turkey 15 I2
Rheda **Castle** • Germany 113 [22]
Rheda-Wiedenbrück • Germany 8 D5
Rhedyt **Castle** • Germany 113 [26]
Rhein • Germany/Switzerland 9 C6
Rheinbach • Germany 112 E1
Rheinberg • Germany 111 B1
Rheine • Germany 8 C4
Rheineck, Burg • Germany 112 E1
Rheinfelden • Germany 112 D8
Rheinfels **Castle** • Germany 113 [67]
Rheinfels, Burg • Germany 112 E2
Rheingau • Germany 112 E4
Rheinhausen (Duisburg) • Germany 111 B1
Rheinhessen • Germany 112 E4
Rheinisches Schiefergebirge • Germany 5 K4
Rheinland-Pfalz • Germany 9 C6
Rheinsberg • Germany 8 H3
Rheinsberg **Castle** • Germany 113 [218]
Rheinsberg **Spa** • Germany 113 [h16]
Rheinstein **Castle** • Germany 113 [71]
Rheinstein, Burg • Germany 112 E4
Rheinturm • Germany 111 B3
Rhenen • Netherlands 109 D11
Rhens • Germany 112 E2
Rheris • Morocco 20 E2
Rheurdt • Germany 111 B1
Rheydt, Schloss • Germany 111 B3
Rhin • France 10 M5
Rhine • Europe 112 D6
Rhine Gorge • Germany 112 E2
Rhineland-Palatinate • Germany 111 A5
Rhinelander • WI, United States 43 L4
Rhir, Cap • Morocco 131 D5
Rhode I. • RI, United States 153 D8
Rhode I. [Adm] • United States 153 D8
Rhodes **Heritage C** • Rhodes, Greece 86 [221]
Rhodes **Beach** • Rhodes, Greece 97 [211]
Rhodes • Greece 122 D12
Rhodes' Grave • Zimbabwe 130 C3
Rhodopi • Bulgaria/Greece 14 L8
Rhön • Germany 111 A5
Rhön, Hohe • Germany 9 F6
Rhondda • United Kingdom 7 I10
Rhône • France/Switzerland 10 J9
Rhône au Rhin, Canal du • France 9 C8
Rhone, RMS • British Virgin Is. 160 B
Rhône-Alpes • France 114 A4
Rhos-on-Sea **Beach** • United Kingdom 101 [209]
Rhosneigr **Beach** • United Kingdom 101 [220-221]
Rhyl • United Kingdom 7 I8
Rhyl **Beach** • United Kingdom 101 [212]
Riaño • Spain 11 F2
Riau • Indonesia 143 G4
Riau, Kepulauan • Indonesia 32 C2
Riaza • Spain 10 B12
Rib Mtn **Ski** • WI, United States 149 [130]
Rib Mtn • WI, United States 43 L4
Ribadeo • Spain 11 D1
Ribadeo **Beach** • Spain 96 [91]
Ribatejo • Portugal 11 C5
Ribble • United Kingdom 7 J8
Ribe • Denmark 125 F13
Ribe [Adm] • Denmark 125 F9
Ribeira • Spain 11 C2
Ribeira Grande • Azores 118 B1
Ribeirão Prêto • Brazil 52 G3
Ribnica • Slovenia 14 B4
Ribnitz-Damgarten • Germany 8 H2
Ricabayo, Embalse de • Spain 11 F3
Ricard, Circuit Paul • France 115 H3
Riccione • Italy 121 E12
Rice Lake • OT, Canada 44 F3
Rich • Morocco 20 E2
Richan • OT, Canada 43 J2
Richard Collinson Inlet • NT, Canada 38 I2
Richard Toll • Senegal 20 B5
Richards Bay • South Africa 134 B4
Richards Bay Nature Reserve • South Africa 134 B4
Richardson • TX, United States 47 F1
Richardson Mtns • New Zealand 145 G2
Richardson Mtns • NT/YT, Canada 38 D3
Richat, Guelb er • Mauritania 20 C4
Richborough Castle • United Kingdom 104 E2
Richelieu • France 10 F7
Richelieu • QU, Canada 155 B8
Richfield • UT, United States 45 F2
Richfield Springs • NY, United States 44 H4
Richland • OR, United States 42 G4
Richland • GA, United States 48 E4
Richland • WA, United States 152 B2
Richland Center • WI, United States 43 K5
Richmond • New Zealand 35 D5
Richmond • South Africa 134 C3
Richmond • South Africa 134 B5
Richmond • BC, Canada 42 D2
Richmond • IN, United States 44 C6
Richmond • CA, United States 45 A3
Richmond • MO, United States 46 H3
Richmond • KY, United States 48 E2
Richmond • VA, United States 153 D11
Richmond Beach • St Vincent & Gren. 161 Q
Richmond Hill • OT, Canada 44 F3
Richmond, Mt • New Zealand 35 D5
Richmond Nat. Battlefield Park **Park N** • VA, United States 151 [251]
Ridderkerk • Netherlands 109 F3
Riddle • ID, United States 42 G5
Rideau Lakes • OT, Canada 44 G3
Ridgecrest • CA, United States 45 D4
Riding Mtn Nat. Park **Park N** • MN, Canada 156 [21]
Ried • Austria 13 C9
Riederalp **Ski** • Switzerland 100 [101]
Riederalp • Switzerland 119 G6
Riedlingen • Germany 112 F1
Rienz • Italy 120 B1
Riesa • Germany 9 I5
Riesco, I. • Chile 53 B6
Rieti • Italy 121 F2
Rietini, Monti • Italy 121 F2
Riezlern **Ski** • Austria 100 [128]
Riezlern • Austria 119 H1
Rif • Morocco 131 D2
Rifle • CO, United States 45 I2
Rifstangi • Iceland 16 (1) E1
Rift Valley • Africa 130 A3
Riga **Heritage C** • Latvia 86 [238]
Riga • Latvia 126 B4
Riga, Gulf of • Estonia/Latvia 126 B1
Rigaud • QU, Canada 44 H3
Rigby • ID, United States 42 J5
Rigestan • Afghanistan 18 I3
Riggins • ID, United States 42 G4
Rihiveli Beach • Maldives 138 F4
Riihimäki • Finland 125 E4
Rijeka • Croatia 128 D1
Rijnsburg • Netherlands 109 F1
Rijswijk • Netherlands 109 F3
Rika • Ukraine 14 K1
Rila • Bulgaria 14 K7
Rila **Heritage C** • Bulgaria 86 [205]
Riley • OR, United States 42 F5
Riley • KS, United States 46 G3
Rima • Nigeria 20 G6
Rimau • Malaysia 141 F3
Rimavská Sobota • Slovak Rep. 13 J9
Rimbo • Sweden 125 D2
Rimbo Panti Reserve • Indonesia 143 G4
Rimforsa • Sweden 125 F4
Rímini • Italy 121 E12
Rîmnicu Sarat • Romania 14 O4
Rîmnicu Vîlcea • Romania 14 L4
Rimouski • QU, Canada 156 D1
Rimouski Prov. Reserve • QU, Canada 156 D1
Rincon • Bonaire 160 W
Rincón, Bahía de • Puerto Rico 159 H4
Rincon del Bonete, Lago Artificial de • Uruguay 163 D2
Ringe • Denmark 125 F14
Ringerike • Norway 124 B1
Ringkøbing **Beach** • Denmark 96 [50]
Ringkøbing • Denmark 125 F9
Ringkøbing [Adm] • Denmark 125 F9
Ringkøbing Fjord • Denmark 125 F9
Ringlades • Corfu, Greece 15 A4
Ringling • OK, United States 46 G5
Ringsjön • Sweden 125 F11
Ringsted **Beach** • Denmark 96 [43]
Ringsted • Denmark 125 F14
Ringvassøy • Norway 16 J1
Ringwood • NJ, United States 44 H5
Rínia • Greece 122 D8
Rinjani, Gunung • Indonesia 32 F4
Rinteln • Germany 8 E4
Río Abiseo, Parque Nac. **Heritage N** • Peru 82 [34]
Río Abiseo, Parque Nac. **Heritage C** • Peru 84 [54]
Río Azul • Guatemala 157 H3
Río Bec • Mexico 157 H3
Rio Branco • Brazil 51 D6
Río Bravo • Mexico 47 E5
Río Bravo del Norte • Mexico/United States 40 E5
Rio Bueno • Jamaica 159 F1
Rio Caribe • Venezuela 51 E1
Rio Claro • Trinidad & Tobago 160 U
Rio Colorado • Argentina 53 D3
Rio Cuarto • Argentina 52 D5
Rio das Ostras • Brazil 163 C4
Rio de Janeiro • Brazil 163 C4
Rio de Janeiro [Adm] • Brazil 163 C4
Río de la Plata • Puerto Rico 159 H2
Rio de Oro, Bahia de • Western Sahara 20 B4
Rio Dell • CA, United States 42 C6
Rio do Sul • Brazil 52 G4
Rio Formosa • Portugal 118 E7
Rio Gallegos • Argentina 53 C6
Rio Grande • Brazil 52 F5
Rio Grande • Argentina 53 C6
Rio Grande • Mexico/United States 40 F6
Rio Grande City • TX, United States 47 E4
Rio Grande do Norte • Brazil 53 (1) D3
Rio Grande do Sul • Brazil 52 F4
Río Lagartos • Mexico 157 H2
Rio Marina • Italy 121 E11
Rio Mayo • Argentina 53 B5
Rio Negro • Brazil 52 G4
Rio Pardo • Brazil 52 F4
Río Plátano, Reserva Biósfera **Heritage N** • Honduras 82 [23]
Rio Rancho • NM, United States 153 E2
Río San Juan • Dominican Rep. 159 G3
Rio Tercero • Argentina 52 D5
Rio Verde • Brazil 52 F2
Río Verde • Mexico 157 G2
Riobamba • Ecuador 51 B4
Riohacha • Colombia 51 C1
Riom • France 10 I8
Rionere in Vulture • Italy 12 J8
Ripley • WV, United States 44 E6
Ripley • MS, United States 48 C3
Ripoli • Spain 117 D1
Ripoll • Spain 11 N2
Ripon • United Kingdom 7 K7
Riposto • Sicily, Italy 12 J11
Riscone **Ski** • Italy 100 [243]
Riscone • Italy 120 B2
Rishiri • Japan 30 K2
Risle • France 5 D6
Risnjak • Croatia 14 B4
Risnjak Nat. Park **Park N** • Croatia 89 [109]
Risnjak Nat. Park • Croatia 128 D1
Risør • Norway 125 F1
Risoul **Ski** • France 100 [67]
Risoul • France 115 F4
Riss • Germany 9 E8
Ritchie's Archipelago • India 28 F6
Rittman • OH, United States 44 E5
Ritzville • WA, United States 42 F3
Riva del Garda • Italy 121 E3
Rivadavia • Argentina 52 C5
River Cess • Liberia 22 C3
River Kwai Bridge • Thailand 142 C1
Rivera • Argentina 52 D6
Rivera • Uruguay 52 E5
Riverina • NS, Australia 144 C1
Rivers • Nigeria 22 F3
Riversdale • South Africa 134 C6
Riverside • CA, United States 152 C6
Riverside [Apt] • United Kingdom 104 B2
Riversleigh **Heritage N** • Australia 83 [146]
Riverton • New Zealand 145 G4
Riverton • WY, United States 42 K5
Riverview • South Africa 134 B4
Rivesultes [Apt] • France 115 K2
Riviera • France/Italy 121 E10
Riviera Beach • FL, United States 49 C4
Riviera di Levante • Italy 121 E10
Riviera di Ponente • Italy 121 E9
Rivière des Outaouais • OT/QU, Canada 44 F2
Rivière du Loup • QU, Canada 156 D1
Rivière-Bleue • QU, Canada 44 K2
Rivière-Pilote • Martinique 161 N
Rivne • Ukraine 17 D4
Rivoli • Italy 12 B3
Rixensart • Belgium 109 D14
Riyadh • Saudi Arabia 18 E5
Rizhao • China 29 F3
Rizokarpaso • Cyprus 123 J2
Rjukan • Norway 124 B1
Roa • Spain 11 H3
Roa • Norway 124 B2
Road Bay • Anguilla 80 B7
Road Bay • Anguilla 160 C
Road Town • British Virgin Is. 160 B
Roan Cliffs • UT, United States 45 G2
Roan Plateau • CO, United States 45 H2
Roanne • France 10 J7
Roanoke • AL, United States 48 E4
Roanoke • VA, United States 48 H2
Roanoke Rapids • NC, United States 48 H3
Roanoke [Riv] • NC/VA, United States 48 H3
Roatán • Honduras 160 A11
Rob Roy's Grave • United Kingdom 104 B1
Robben I. **Heritage C** • South Africa 85 [119]
Robben I. • South Africa 134 C5
Robe • Ireland 108 C4
Robe, Mt • NS, Australia 34 H6
Röbel • Germany 8 H3
Robert L. Bradshaw [Apt] • St Kitts & Nevis 161 G
Robert Lee • TX, United States 47 D2
Robert S. Kerr Lake • OK, United States 46 H5
Roberts, Mt • QL, Australia 144 B6
Robertsfors • Sweden 16 K4
Robertsganj • India 137 C8
Robertson • South Africa 134 C6
Robertstown • Ireland 108 B3
Roberval • QU, Canada 156 D1
Robin • MN, Canada 43 F1
Robin Hood's Bay **Beach** • United Kingdom 101 [29]
Robinson • IL, United States 44 B6
Robinson Range • WA, Australia 34 C5
Robledal • Margarita 160 V
Robson, Mt • AL, Canada 155 C2
Robstown • TX, United States 47 F4
Roca, Cabo da • Portugal 118 D1
Rocamadour, Château de • France 115 G4
Rocas, Atol das • Brazil 163 A1
Rocca di Papa • Italy 121 F3
Rocha • Uruguay 52 F5
Rochdale • United Kingdom 7 J8
Roche-Ecrite, la • Réunion 132 H1
Roche-Guyon, la • France 115 E1
Roche-Racan [Château] • France 114 D2
Roche-sur-Yon, la • France 114 D3
Rochefort • Belgium 109 D19
Rochefort • France 115 G1
Rochefoucauld, la • France 115 G2
Rochegda • Russian Fed. 17 G2
Rochehaut • Belgium 109 D19
Rochelle • IL, United States 46 K2
Rochelle, la **Beach** • France 96 [84]
Rochelle, la • France 114 D3
Rocher River • NT, Canada 38 I4
Roches Noire • Mauritius 132 J2
Roches, Plaine des • Mauritius 132 J2
Rochester • United Kingdom 104 E2
Rochester • MN, United States 43 J4
Rochester • IN, United States 44 B5
Rochester • NH, United States 44 J4
Rochester • NY, United States 153 D1
Rochester Falls • Mauritius 132 J3
Rochford [Apt] • United Kingdom 104 E2
Rochlitz **Castle** • Germany 113 [200]
Rock Creek Park **Park N** • DC, United States 151 [285]
Rock Falls • IL, United States 46 K2
Rock Glen • SA, Canada 43 C2
Rock Hill • SC, United States 48 G3
Rock I. • IL, United States 46 J2
Rock Port • MO, United States 46 H2
Rock Rapids • IA, United States 43 H5
Rock River • WY, United States 42 M6
Rock Sound • Bahamas 158 B1
Rock Springs • WY, United States 42 K6
Rockall • Atlantic Ocean 4 H5
Rockdale • TX, United States 47 F2
Rockefeller Plateau • Antarctica 54 (1) BB1
Rockey I. Lake • OT, Canada 44 D2
Rockford • IL, United States 46 K1
Rockhampton • QL, Australia 144 B4
Rockingham • WA, Australia 34 C6
Rockingham • NC, United States 48 H3
Rocklake • ND, United States 43 G2
Rockland • ME, United States 44 K3
Rockledge • FL, United States 49 C3
Rockley • Barbados 161 O
Rockport • TX, United States 154 J5
Rocksprings • TX, United States 47 D2
Rockwood • TN, United States 48 E3
Rocky Boys Indian Reservation • MT, United States 42 K2
Rocky Ford • CO, United States 46 D3
Rocky I. **Dive** • Red Sea 135 B2
Rocky Mount • NC, United States 48 I3
Rocky Mtn Nat. Park **Park N** • CO, United States 150 [87]
Rocky Mtn Nat. Park • CO, United States 46 C2
Rocky Mtns • Canada/United States 36 F5
Rocky Mtns • Canada/United States 40
Rocky Point • Jamaica 159 F4
Rocky Reach Dam • WA, United States 42 E3
Rocque-Gageac, la • France 115 G4
Rocquefort • France 115 G3
Rocroi • France 5 H5
Rod Hill, Fort • BC, Canada 155 C3
Róda • Corfu, Greece 122 B1
Rødby • Denmark 16 F9
Rødby **Beach** • Denmark 96 [37]
Rødbyhavn • Denmark 125 F14
Rødeberg • Norway 124 B1
Rødenes • Norway 124 B2
Rødenessjøen • Norway 124 B4
Rödental • Germany 9 G6
Rodez • France 10 H9
Rodgau • Germany 5 L5
Rodgers Beach • Aruba 160 Y
Rodi Gargánico • Italy 12 J7
Rodi Gargánico **Beach** • Italy 97 [158]
Rodiá **Beach** • Crete, Greece 97 [214]
Rodiá • Crete, Greece 123 E3
Roding • United Kingdom 5 D3
Roding • Germany 9 H7
Rodnei, Muntii • Romania 14 L2
Rodney Bay • St Lucia 161 P
Rodolívos • Greece 15 E3
Rodonit, Kep i • Albania 14 G8
Rodopi • Greece 14 L8
Rodopi Planina • Bulgaria/Greece 14 L8
Rodópoi, Hersónisos • Crete, Greece 123 E1
Ródos **Heritage C** • Rhodes, Greece 86 [221]
Ródos **Beach** • Rhodes, Greece 97 [211]
Ródos • Greece 122 D12
Ródos [I.] • Greece 122 D12
Rodrigues • Indian Ocean 19 K8
Roebourne • WA, Australia 34 C4
Roermond • Netherlands 109 D12
Roes Welcome Sound • NU, Canada 39 N4
Roeselare • Belgium 5 G4
Rogaguado, Laguna • Bolivia 52 C1
Rogaland • Norway 16 D7
Roger Williams Nat. Mem. **Park N** • RI, United States 151 [325]
Rogers • AR, United States 46 H4
Rogers City • MI, United States 44 D3
Rogers, Mt • VA, United States 48 G2
Rogerson • ID, United States 42 H5
Rogliano • Corsica, France 115 L2
Rogue • OR, United States 42 C5
Rohnert Park • CA, United States 45 A2
Rohtak • India 137 C2
Rohtas **Heritage C** • Pakistan 85 [132]
Rohtas • India 137 C8
Roissy [Apt] • France 115 E2
Rojo, Cabo • Puerto Rico 159 H3
Rokan • Indonesia 143 G4
Rokiskis • Lithuania 126 B4
Rokitnokärren • Belarus 13 N5
Rokko-san • Japan 140 B1
Rokycany • Czech Rep. 128 B1
Rola Co • China 28 E1
Roland-Garros [Apt] • Réunion 132 H1
Rolandsbogen • Germany 112 E1
Røldal • Norway 124 C6
Rolla • MO, United States 46 J4
Rollag • Norway 124 B1
Rolle, Passo di • Italy 120 B3
Rolling Fork • MS, United States 48 B4
Rolvsøya • Norway 124 A2
Roma **Heritage C** • Italy 86 [148]
Roma • Italy 121 F3
Roma • QL, Australia 144 B5
Romainmôtier • Switzerland 119 G1
Roman • Romania 14 N3
Romang • Indonesia 32 (1) C4
ROMANIA • Europe 14 M4
Romans-sur-Isère • France 10 J8
Romanshorn • Switzerland 119 H1
Romantische Strasse • Germany 112 F2
Rombo Pass • Austria/Italy 120 B1
Rome **Heritage C** • Italy 86 [148]
Rome • Italy 121 F3
Rome • GA, United States 48 E3
Rome • NY, United States 153 D2
Romeleåsen • Sweden 125 F11
Romeoville • IL, United States 44 A5
Romerike • Norway 124 B2
Romilly-sur-Seine • France 10 I5
Romkamhaeng Nat. Park • Thailand 142 B4
Romney • United Kingdom 90 A7
Romney, Hythe & Dymchurch Light Railway • United Kingdom 104 E3
Romny • Ukraine 17 E4
Rømø • Denmark 125 F13
Romoranthin-Lanthenay • France 114 D2
Romsdalfjorden • Norway 124 C2
Roncador, Cayo de • West Indies 160 A18
Roncador, Serra do • Brazil 52 F1
Roncesvalles • Spain 11 J1
Ronda • Spain 116 B6
Ronda, Serranía de • Spain 116 B6
Rondane • Norway 16 E6
Rondane Nat. Park **Park N** • Norway 89 [13]
Rønde • Denmark 125 F10
Ronde, I. • Seychelles 133 K4
Ronde I. • Grenada 161 R
Rondón • Brazil 51 E3
Rondônia • Brazil 51 E6
Rondonópolis • Brazil 52 F2
Ronge, Lac la • SA, Canada 38 K5
Rønne • Denmark 125 F16
Ronne Bay • Antarctica 54 (1) HH2
Ronne Ice Shelf • Antarctica 54 (1) JJ2
Ronneby • Sweden 125 F12
Ronse • Belgium 5 G4
Roosboom • South Africa 134 B3
Roosendaal • Netherlands 109 D10
Roosevelt • Brazil 51 E6
Roosevelt • UT, United States 45 H1
Roosevelt Campobello Int. Park • NB, Canada 156 D6
Roosevelt, Franklin D., Lake • WA, United States 152 B2
Roosevelt, Mt • BC, Canada 38 F5
Roper • NT, Australia 34 F2
Roques • Venezuela 51 D1
Roquetas de Mar **Beach** • Spain 96 [116]
Roquetas de Mar • Spain 116 B8
Roraima [Adm] • Brazil 51 E3
Roraima [Mtn] • S. America 51 E2
Rorke's Drift • South Africa 134 B3
Røros • Norway 16 F5
Røros **Heritage C** • Norway 85 [81]
Rørvig • Denmark 125 F10
Rørvik • Norway 16 F4
Rosa, Lake • Bahamas 158 B4
Rosa, Monte • Italy/Switzerland 119 G6
Rosalie Moller **Dive** • Red Sea 135 B1
Rosario • Paraguay 52 E3
Rosário • Brazil 53 (1) C2
Rosario • Argentina 163 D1
Rosario • Uruguay 163 D2
Rosario de Lerma • Argentina 52 C3
Rosário do Sul • Brazil 52 F5
Rosário Oeste • Brazil 52 E1
Rosario, Sierra del • Cuba 158 D1
Rosarito • Mexico 157 F1
Rosarito • Mexico 157 F4
Rosarno • Italy 12 K10
Roscoff • France 114 C1
Roscommon • Ireland 108 C4
Roscommon [Adm] • Ireland 108 C2
Roscrea • Ireland 7 E9
Rose Belle • Mauritius 132 J4
Rose Hall • Jamaica 159 F1
Rose Hill • Mauritius 132 J3
Rose Peak • AZ, United States 45 H5
Roseau • Dominica 161 M
Rosebery • TS, Australia 34 I8
Roseburg • OR, United States 42 D5
Rosenberg **Castle** • Germany 113 [158]
Rosenberg • TX, United States 154 J6
Rosendal • Norway 124 C5
Rosenheim • Germany 112 F3
Rosenholm • Denmark 125 F10
Roses **Beach** • Spain 96 [123]
Roses • Spain 117 D2
Roses, Golf de • Spain 11 O2
Roses, Golf de • Spain 117 D2
Roses, Valley of • Bulgaria 128 E3
Rosethern • SA, Canada 38 J6
Roseto Capo **Beach** • Italy 97 [154]
Rosetown • SA, Canada 38 J6
Rosetta • Egypt 131 F1
Rosetta Mouth • Egypt 131 F1
Rosette • UT, United States 42 I6
Rosetto degli Abruzzi • Italy 12 I6
Roseville • MI, United States 44 D4
Roseville • CA, United States 45 B2
Rosière, la **Ski** • France 100 [38]
Rosière, la • France 115 F4
Rosignano Marittimo **Beach** • Italy 96 [146]
Rosignano Marittimo • Italy 121 E11
Rosiori de Vede • Romania 128 E1
Roskilde **Heritage C** • Finland 86 [10]
Roskilde **Beach** • Denmark 96 [42]
Roskilde • Denmark 125 F10
Roskilde [Adm] • Denmark 125 F10
Roslagen • Sweden 125 D2
Roslavl • Russian Fed. 17 E4
Rosmead • South Africa 134 C4
Ross • TS, Australia 34 I8
Ross • New Zealand 35 C6
Ross Abbey • Ireland 108 C4
Ross Barnett Reservoir • MS, United States 48 C4
Ross Carbery **Beach** • Ireland 96 [59]
Ross Carbery • Ireland 108 C8
Ross Ice Shelf • Antarctica 54 (1) Z1
Ross Lake Nat. Recreation Area **Park N** • WA, United States 150 [27]
Ross Lake Nat. Recreation Area • WA, United States 152 B1
Ross, Mt • Kerguelen Is. 54 (1) L5
Ross River • NT, Australia 145 D2
Ross River • YT, Canada 49 O3
Ross Sea • Antarctica 54 (1) Y2
Ross-on-Wye • United Kingdom 104 D3
Rossan Point • Ireland 7 D7
Rossano • Italy 12 K9
Rosseau Lake • OT, Canada 44 F3
Rosses Point **Beach** • Ireland 96 [64]
Rosses Point • Ireland 108 C2
Rossignol, Lake • NS, Canada 156 D7
Rosslare **Beach** • Ireland 96 [56]
Rosslare Harbour • Ireland 7 F9
Rosslau • Germany 8 H5
Rosslyn Chapel • United Kingdom 104 B4
Rosslyn Chapel • United Kingdom 104 B4
Rossnowlagh **Beach** • Ireland 96 [65]
Rosso • Mauritania 20 B5
Rossosh • Russian Fed. 17 F4
Røssvatnet • Norway 16 G4
Røst • Norway 16 G3
Rostock • Germany 8 H2
Rostocze • Poland 13 M7
Rostov • Russian Fed. 126 C4
Rostov-na-Donu • Russian Fed. 17 F5
Rostrenen • France 114 C1
Roswell • NM, United States 46 C6
Roswell • GA, United States 48 E3
Rot • Germany 112 F1
Rota • Northern Mariana Is. 33 F4
Rota **Beach** • Spain 96 [113]
Rota • Spain 116 B5
Rote • Indonesia 143 F7
Rotenburg • Germany 8 E3
Rotenburg an der Fulda • Germany 9 E5
Roth • Germany 9 G7
Rothaargebirge • Germany 9 D5
Rothenberg **Castle** • Germany 113 [152]
Rothenburg ob der Tauber • Germany 9 F7
Rothenburg on der Tauber **Castle** • Germany 113 [147]
Rothenfels **Castle** • Germany 113 [169]
Rothera [Base] • Antarctica 54 (1) II3
Rotherham • United Kingdom 7 K8
Rothesay • United Kingdom 106 B2
Roti • Indonesia 34 D2
Rotoehu, Lake • New Zealand 145 F2
Rotoiti, Lake • New Zealand 145 F2
Rotoma, Lake • New Zealand 145 F2
Rotorua • New Zealand 145 F2
Rotorua, Lake • New Zealand 145 F2
Rott • Germany 9 I8
Rottach-Egern • Germany 112 F7
Rottach-Egern **Spa** • Germany 113 [h13]
Rottal • Germany 112 F4
Rottenbuch • Germany 112 F6
Rottenburg am Neckar • Germany 112 D6
Rotterdam • Netherlands 109 F3
Rotterdam • NY, United States 44 H4
Rottnen • Sweden 125 F8
Rottumerplaat • Netherlands 8 B3
Rottweil • Germany 112 D8
Rotuma • Fiji Is. 35 (2) D1
Roubaix • France 10 I3
Roudnice nad Labem • Czech Rep. 13 D7
Rouen • France 10 G4
Rouergue • France 115 G4
Rouge-Matawan Prov. Reserve • QU, Canada 155 B3
Rougemont • Switzerland 119 G6
Rough River Lake • KY, United States 48 D2
Rougsø **Beach** • Denmark 96 [47]
Round I. • Mauritius 132 J2
Round Mountain, The • NS, Australia 34 J6
Round Rock • TX, United States 47 F2
Roundstone • Ireland 108 C3
Roundup • MT, United States 42 K3
Rousay • United Kingdom 6 I2
Roussillon • France 115 K2
Rouyn • QU, Canada 39 P7
Rovaniemi • Finland 16 M3
Rovereto • Italy 121 E3
Roviés • Greece 122 D4
Rovigo • Italy 121 E7
Rovinj • Italy 12 H3
Rovinj • Croatia 128 D1
Rovuma • Mozambique 23 G6
Rowley I. • NU, Canada 39 P3
Rowley Shoals • QL, Australia 33 C7
Roxas • Palawan, Philippines 31 F4
Roxas • Panay, Philippines 31 G4
Roxboro • NC, United States 48 H2
Roxborough • Trinidad & Tobago 160 T
Roxburgh • New Zealand 145 G4
Roxburgh, Lake • New Zealand 145 G2
Roxen • Sweden 125 F4
Roxo, Cap • Senegal 20 B6
Roy • UT, United States 42 I6
Roy Hill • WA, Australia 34 C4
Roya • France 115 H2
Royal & Ancient, The • United Kingdom 104 B2
Royal Canal • Ireland 7 E8
Royal Chitwan Nat. Park **Heritage N** • Nepal 83 [121]
Royal Dockyard • Bermuda 80 A2
Royal Leamington Spa • United Kingdom 104 D2
Royal Oak • MI, United States 44 D4

Royal St George's • United Kingdom 104 E4
Royal Tunbridge Wells • United Kingdom 104 E3
Royale, I. • MI, United States 43 L2
Royan • France 115 G1
Royaumont, Abbaye de • France 115 E1
Roye • France 5 F5
Røyrvik • Norway 16 G4
Røysheim • Norway 124 C2
Rózan • Poland 13 K5
Rozmberk • Czech Rep. 128 B4
Roznava • Slovak Rep. 13 J9
Rtishchevo • Russian Fed. 17 G4
Ruaha Nat. Park • Tanzania 130 B3
Ruaha Nat. Park **Park** • Tanzania 133 [93]
Ruahine Range • New Zealand 145 F4
Ruapehu, Mt • New Zealand 145 F4
Ruapuke I. • New Zealand 35 B8
Rub 'al Khali, Ar • Saudi Arabia 18 E6
Rubiku • Albania 15 A2
Rubio • Venezuela 51 C2
Rubondo I. Nat. Park • Tanzania 130 B1
Rubondo I. Nat. Park **Park** • Tanzania 133 [86]
Rubtsovsk • Russian Fed. 26 N7
Ruby • AK, United States 49 J3
Ruby Dome • NV, United States 42 H6
Ruby Mtns • NV, United States 152 C2
Ruda Slaska • Poland 128 C1
Rudall River Nat. Park • WA, Australia 34 D4
Rudbar • Afghanistan 18 H3
Rudbjerg **Beach** • Denmark 96 [37]
Rudelsburg **Castle** • Germany 113 [205]
Rüdersdorf • Germany 8 I4
Rüdersdorf • Germany 111 C4
Rüdesheim • Germany 112 E4
Rudkøbing **Beach** • Denmark 96 [44]
Rudkøbing • Denmark 125 F14
Rudnaya Pristan • Russian Fed. 27 M8
Rudnik • F.R. of Yugoslavia 14 H5
Rudnik • Bulgaria 15 I1
Rüdnitz • Germany 111 C2
Rudnyy • Kazakstan 26 J7
Rudolf, Lake • Kenya 23 F3
Rudolstadt • Germany 9 G6
Rudong • China 139 C2
Rudozem • Bulgaria 15 F2
Rue • France 5 E4
Rueil-Malmaison • France 115 E3
Ruffec • France 115 G1
Rufiji • Tanzania 130 B4
Rufino • Argentina 52 D5
Rufisque • Senegal 22 A2
Rufunsa • Zambia 24 D3
Rugao • China 139 C2
Rugby • United Kingdom 104 D2
Rugby • ND, United States 43 F2
Rügen • Germany 8 I2
Ruhnu Saar • Estonia 126 B1
Ruhpolding • Germany 112 F8
Ruhr • Germany 9 D5
Ruhrgebiet • Germany 111 B
Ruidosa • TX, United States 47 B3
Ruien • Bulgaria/F.Y.R. of Macedonia 15 D1
Ruijin • China 31 F1
Ruivo, Pico • Madeira 118 C1
Ruki • Dem. Rep. of Congo 23 B4
Rukwa, Lake • Tanzania 130 B3
Rum • United Kingdom 6 F4
Rum Cay • Bahamas 158 B4
Rum Jungle • NT, Australia 34 F2
Rum Point • Cayman Is. 159 E3
Ruma • F.R. of Yugoslavia 14 G4
Ruma Nat. Park • Kenya 131 G3
Rumbek • Sudan 23 D2
Rumburk • Czech Rep. 128 B2
Rumford • ME, United States 44 J3
Rumia • Poland 13 H3
Rumija • F.R. of Yugoslavia 15 A1
Rummah, Wadi ar • Saudi Arabia 21 H2
Rumoi • Japan 30 K3
Runanga • New Zealand 35 C6
Runaway Bay • Jamaica 159 F1
Runaway, Cape • New Zealand 35 F3
Runde • Zimbabwe 130 C4
Rundu • Namibia 24 B3
Rung, Ko • Thailand 142 E2
Rungwa • Tanzania 130 B3
Rungwa [Riv] • Tanzania 23 E5
Runhällen • Sweden 125 D1
Runkel • Germany 112 E2
Runkel **Castle** • Germany 113 [43]
Runmarö • Sweden 125 D4
Runnymede • United Kingdom 104 E1
Ruo Shui • China 29 C2
Ruokolahti • Finland 16 O6
Ruoqiang • China 26 O10
Ruovesi • Finland 125 E2
Rupat • Indonesia 143 G4
Rupert • QU, Canada 39 P6
Rupert • ID, United States 42 I5
Ruppiner Kanal • Germany 111 C1
Rur • Germany 9 B5
Rurutu • French Polynesia 33 L8
Rusalka • Bulgaria 128 E4
Rusape • Zimbabwe 130 C2
Rusayris, Ar • Sudan 21 F5
Rusayris, Khazzan ar • Sudan 21 F5
Rusayris, Lake • Sudan 23 E1
Ruse • Bulgaria 128 E1
Rusenski Lom Nat. Park **Park N** • Bulgaria 89 [130]
Rusenski Lom Nat. Park • Romania 128 E1
Rush • Ireland 108 B2
Rush • CO, United States 46 C3
Rush City • MN, United States 43 J4
Rushville • IN, United States 44 C6
Rushville • IL, United States 46 J2
Rusk • TX, United States 154 J4
Rusk Mtn • NY, United States 44 H4
Russbach **Ski** • Austria 100 [183]
Russborough House • Ireland 108 B3
Russel I. • NU, Canada 38 L2
Russell • New Zealand 35 E2
Russell • KS, United States 46 F3
Russell Cave Nat. Mon. **Park N** • AL, United States 151 [202]
Russell Springs • KY, United States 48 E2
Russellville • AR, United States 46 I5
Russellville • AL, United States 48 D3
Russellville • KY, United States 48 D2
Rüsselsheim • Germany 9 D6
Russian Black Sea Coast • Russian Fed. 126 A10
RUSSIAN FEDERATION • Asia/Europe 25 I3
Russkaya [Base] • Antarctica 54 (1) BB2
Rust'avi • Georgia 17 H6
Ruston • LA, United States 153 F1
Rutanzige, Lac • Uganda/Dem. Rep. of Congo 23 D4
Rutbah, Ar • Iraq 18 C3
Ruteng • Indonesia 32 (1) B4
Rutenga • Zimbabwe 130 C4
Rutland • India 28 F6
Rutland • VT, United States 44 I4
Rutog • China 28 C2
Ruvu • Tanzania 130 B2
Ruvuma • Mozambique/Tanzania 130 B4
Ruwenzori Mtns Nat. Park **Heritage N** • Uganda 83 [96]
Ruwenzori Nat. Park **Park** • Uganda 133 [68]
Ruya • Mozambique/Zimbabwe 24 E3
Ruzomberok • Slovak Rep. 13 I8
Ruzyne [Apt] • Czech Rep. 128 B2
RWANDA • Africa 23 E4
Ry **Beach** • Denmark 96 [47]
Ry • Denmark 125 F9
Ryazan • Russian Fed. 17 F4
Rybachiy, Poluostrov • Russian Fed. 16 Q2
Rybinsk • Russian Fed. 126 C2
Rybinskoye Vdkhr. • Russian Fed. 126 C2
Rybnik • Poland 128 C1
Rydaholm • Sweden 125 F7
Rydal Mt • United Kingdom 104 C2
Ryde **Beach** • United Kingdom 101 [101]
Ryde • United Kingdom 106 D
Rye • United Kingdom 104 E4
Ryfylke • Norway 124 C6
Rygge • Norway 124 B4
Ryotsu • Japan 30 J5
Rypin • Poland 13 I4
Rysy • Poland/Slovak Rep. 128 C4
Ryugasaki • Japan 140 C2
Ryujin Spa • Japan 140 B4
Ryukyu Is. • Japan 29 H5
Ryukyu-shoto • Japan 29 H5
Rzepin • Poland 13 D5
Rzeszów • Poland 13 L8
Rzhev • Russian Fed. 126 C3

S

S'Albufeira • Minorca, Spain 117 F2
S'Albufeira • Majorca, Spain 117 H2
S'Algar • Minorca, Spain 117 F4
S'Arenal • Majorca, Spain 117 H3
S'Argamassa • Ibiza, Spain 117 G2
S'Horta • Majorca, Spain 117 H2
S'Illot • Majorca, Spain 117 H2
s-Gravenhage • Netherlands 109 F1
s-Hertogenbosch • Netherlands 109 D11
Sa Calobra • Majorca, Spain 117 H1
Sa Coma • Majorca, Spain 117 H2
Sa Conillera • Ibiza, Spain 117 G1
Sa Keo • Thailand 142 C2
Sa Talaiassa de Sant Josep • Ibiza, Spain 117 G1
Sa'dah • Yemen 18 D6
Sa'idabad • Iran 18 G4
Saalach • Austria/Germany 112 F8
Saalbach • Austria 119 H3
Saalbach Hinterglemm **Ski** • Austria 100 [162]
Saale • Germany 8 G5
Saalfeld • Germany 9 G6
Saalfelden • Austria 119 H4
Saane • Switzerland 10 M7
Saanen • Switzerland 119 G6
Saanenmöser • Switzerland 119 G6
Saar • Germany 112 D3
Saarbrücken • Germany 112 D3
Saarburg • Germany 112 D3
Saaremaa • Estonia 126 B1
Saarijärvi • Finland 16 M5
Saaristomeri Nat. Park **Park N** • Finland 89 [37]
Saaristomeri Nat. Park • Finland 125 E3
Saarland • Germany 112 D3
Saarlouis • Germany 112 D3
Saas Fee **Ski** • Switzerland 100 [93]
Saas Fee • Switzerland 119 G6
Saba • West Indies 161 F
Sabac • F.R. of Yugoslavia 14 G5
Sabadell • Spain 117 D3
Sabah • Malaysia 32 F2
Sabaki • Kenya 131 G5
Saban, Archipiélago de • Cuba 158 D2
Sabana de la Mar • Dominican Rep. 159 G4
Sabang • Sulawesi, Indonesia 32 (1) A2
Sabang • Indonesia 143 G1
Sabanözü • Turkey 15 O3
Sabará • Brazil 163 C1
Sabarei • Kenya 23 F3
Sabáudia • Italy 121 F4
Sabáudia, Lago di • Italy 121 F4
Sabha • Libya 21 B2
Sabi • Mozambique/Zimbabwe 130 C4
Sabina • Italy 121 F1
Sabinal, Cayo • Cuba 158 D3
Sabiñánigo • Spain 11 K2
Sabinas • Mexico 47 D4
Sabinas Hidalgo • Mexico 47 D4
Sabine • LA/TX, United States 154 J2
Sabine Lake • LA/TX, United States 153 F3
Sabkhat Tawurgha • Libya 21 B1
Sable, Cape • FL, United States 154 H8
Sable, Cape • NS, Canada 156 D7
Sable I. • NS, Canada 156 D8
Sablé-sur-Sarthe • France 114 D1
Sables d'Olonne, les • France 10 D7
Sablukah, Ash Shallal as • Sudan 21 F4
Sabrata • Libya 21 B1
Sabratha **Heritage C** • Libya 86 [270]
Sabya • Saudi Arabia 18 D6
Sabzevar • Iran 18 G2
Saché [Château] • France 114 D2
Sachigo • OT, Canada 39 M6
Sachs Harbour • NT, Canada 38 G2
Sachsen • Germany 9 I5
Sachsen-Anhalt • Germany 8 G4
Sachsische Schweiz • Germany 9 J5
Sächsische Schweiz, Nationalpark **Park N** • Germany 89 [62]
Saco • MT, United States 42 L2
Saco • ME, United States 44 J4
Sacramento • Brazil 52 G2
Sacramento • CA, United States 152 C3
Sacramento Mtns • NM, United States 46 C6
Sacramento, Pampa del • Peru 51 B5
Sacramento [Riv] • CA, United States 152 C1
Sacramento Valley • CA, United States 40 B4
Sacred Falls State Park • HI, United States 154 G5
Sada Temple • Bali, Indonesia 143 H4
Sádaba • Spain 11 J2
Sadani • Tanzania 130 B2
Sadao • Thailand 142 A4
Saddle Mtn • ID, United States 42 I5
Sadiklar • Turkey 123 F4
Sadiya • India 28 G3
Sado • Portugal 11 C6
Sado • Japan 30 J5
Sado • Portugal 118 D2
Sadr, As • United Arab Emirates 18 F5
Saduak • Thailand 142 C1
Sæby **Beach** • Denmark 96 [48]
Sæby • Denmark 125 F6
Safad • Israel 135 A2
Safari- und Abenteuerpark **Park L** • Austria 98 [81]
Säffle • Sweden 16 G7
Safford • AZ, United States 45 H5
Saffron Walden • United Kingdom 7 M9
Safi • Morocco 131 D3
Safid • Iran 18 E2
Safonovo • Russian Fed. 17 E3
Safranbolu • Turkey 15 N2
Safranbolu **Heritage C** • Turkey 86 [226]
Sag Harbor • NY, United States 153 D7
Saga • Japan 30 F8
Sagaing • Myanmar 31 B2
Sagalassos • Turkey 123 F1
Sagami-nada • Japan 140 C4
Sagami-wan • Japan 140 C3
Sagamore Hill Nat. Hist. Site **Park N** • NY, United States 151 [320]
Sagar • India 137 C7
Sagarmatha • China/Nepal 28 E3
Sagarmatha Nat. Park **Heritage N** • Nepal 83 [122]
Sage, Mt • British Virgin Is. 160 B
Saggat • Sweden 16 I3
Saginaw • MI, United States 44 D4
Saginaw Bay • MI, United States 44 D4
Sagiz • Kazakstan 26 H8
Saglouc • QU, Canada 36 J3
Sagone • Corsica, France 115 L3
Sagone, Golfe de • Corsica, France 115 L3
Sagres • Portugal 118 E5
Sagres, Ponta de • Portugal 118 E5
Sagua de Tánamo • Cuba 158 D8
Sagua Grande • Cuba 158 D2
Saguache • CO, United States 45 I2
Saguaro Nat. Park **Park N** • AZ, United States 150 [115]
Saguaro Nat. Park • AZ, United States 153 E3
Saguenay • QU, Canada 39 Q7
Saguenay Prov. Park • QU, Canada 156 D1
Saguenay-St Lawrence Marine Park **Park N** • QU, Canada 156 [29]
Saguia el-Hamra • Western Sahara 20 C3
Sagunto • Spain 11 K5
Sagunto **Beach** • Spain 96 [119]
Sagwan • AK, United States 49 L1
Sahagún • Spain 11 F2
Saharanpur • India 28 C2
Sahel • Tunisia 131 E4
Sahiwal • Pakistan 28 B2
Sahlabad • Iran 18 G3
Sahr-i-Bahlol **Heritage C** • Pakistan 85 [130]
Sahra Bayyudah • Sudan 21 F4
Sahra Murzuq • Libya 21 B3
Sahra Rabyanah • Libya 21 C3
Sahuayo • Mexico 157 G1
Sahyadri • India 28 B5
Sai Gon [Riv] • Vietnam 141 E1
Sai Kung • Hong Kong, China 139 B6
Sai Kung Country Park • Hong Kong, China 139 B6
Sai, Laem • Ko Samui, Thailand 142 D1
Saïda • Algeria 20 F2
Saïdia • Morocco 131 D2
Saidor • Papua New Guinea 35 (1) D2
Saigon • Vietnam 141 E1
Saiki • Japan 30 F8
Saima Kanal • Finland/Russian Fed. 16 O6
Saimaa • Finland 16 N6
Saimaan Kanava • Finland/Russian Fed. 16 O6
St Agnes • United Kingdom 104 F4
St Alban's Head • United Kingdom 104 F6
St Albans • United Kingdom 104 E1
St Albans • VT, United States 44 I3
St Aldhelm's Head • United Kingdom 104 F6
St André • Réunion 132 H2
St André, Cap • Madagascar 24 G3
St Andrews **Beach** • United Kingdom 101 [5-6]
St Andrews • United Kingdom 104 B2
St Andrews • NB, Canada 156 D6
St Ann's Bay • Jamaica 159 F2
St Anne • Channel Is. 7 J12
St Anne-de-Beaupré • QU, Canada 156 D1
St Anthony • ID, United States 42 J5
St Anthony • NF, Canada 156 D5
St' Antíoco • Sardinia, Italy 120 C3
St' Antíoco, I. di • Sardinia, Italy 120 C3
St Anton am Arlberg **Ski** • Austria 100 [132]
St Anton am Arlberg • Austria 119 H6
St Arnaud • VI, Australia 144 C3
St Augustin • Germany 9 C6
St Augustin-Saguenay • QU, Canada 39 T6
St Augustine • FL, United States 154 H4
St Augustine, Baie de • Madagascar 24 G4
St Austell • United Kingdom 104 F4
St Avold • France 5 J5
St Barbe • NF, Canada 156 D5
St Barthélemy • West Indies 160 E
St Barts • West Indies 160 E
St Bee's Head • United Kingdom 104 C1
St Bees **Beach** • United Kingdom 101 [244]
St Benoît • Réunion 132 H2
St Blais, Cape • South Africa 134 C6
St Blaise • Switzerland 119 G1
St Blasien • Germany 112 D8
St Blasien **Spa** • Germany 113 [h9]
St Blasien **Spa** • Germany 113 [k10]
St Boniface • MN, Canada 38 L7
St Brevin • France 114 C4
St Brévin-les-Pins **Beach** • France 96 [82]
St Brides Haven **Beach** • United Kingdom 101 [177]
St Brieuc • France 114 C2
St Brieuc, Baie de • France 10 C5
St Calais • France 114 D2
St Cast • France 114 C2
St Catharines • OT, Canada 155 B9
St Catherine, Fort • Bermuda 159 J2
St Catherine, Monastery of • Egypt 131 F4
St Catherine, Mt • Grenada 160 S
St Catherine Point • Bermuda 159 J2
St Catherine's Point • United Kingdom 5 B4
St Catherines I. • GA, United States 48 G5
St Chamond • France 10 J8
St Charles • MO, United States 46 J3
St Chinian • France 114 B4
St Christina in Gröden • Italy 120 B1
St Christoffelberg • Curaçao 160 X
St Christoph am Arlberg **Ski** • Austria 100 [133]
St Christoph am Arlberg • Austria 119 H5
St Christopher • St Kitts & Nevis 161 G
St Christopher, Rocque • France 115 G2
St Cirq-Lapopie • France 115 G4
St Clair, Lake • Canada/United States 44 D4
St Clair Shores • MI, United States 44 D4
St Claude • Guadeloupe 161 L
St Cloud • MN, United States 43 I4
St Croix • US Virgin Is. 160 Z
St Croix I. Int. Hist. Site **Park N** • ME, United States 151 [343]
St Croix I. Int. Hist. Site • Canada/United States 156 D6
St Cyprien **Beach** • France 96 [128]
St Cyr-sur-Mer **Beach** • France 96 [133]
St Cyr-sur-Mer • France 115 H3
St David's **Beach** • United Kingdom 101 [182-183]
St David's Head • United Kingdom 7 G10
St David's Head • Bermuda 159 J2
St David's I. • Bermuda 159 J2
St Denis • France 115 E1
St Denis • Réunion 132 H1
St Denis d'Oléron **Beach** • France 96 [84]
St Dié • France 10 L5
St Dizier • France 10 J5
St Donat • QU, Canada 44 H2
St Elias, Mt • YT, Canada 38 C4
St Elias Mtns • Canada/United States 49 N3
St Elie • French Guiana 51 G3
St Emilion **Heritage C** • France 86 [82]
St Emilion • France 115 G1
St Estephe • France 114 B3
St Etienne • France 10 J8
St Étienne-de-Tinée **Ski** • France 100 [72]
St Etienne-du-Rouvray • France 5 E5
St Eustatius • West Indies 161 F
St Florent • Corsica, France 115 L2
St Florent, Golfe de • Corsica, France 115 L2
St Florentin • France 10 I6
St Flour • France 10 I8
St Francis • KS, United States 46 E3
St Francis Bay • South Africa 134 C8
St Francis, Cape • South Africa 134 C8
St Francisville • LA, United States 153 F4
St François • Seychelles 133 K4
St François • Guadeloupe 161 L
St Francois • QU, Canada 155 B4
St Francois, Lac • QU, Canada 44 J3
St François-Longchamp **Ski** • France 100 [45]
St Gallen • Switzerland 9 E9
St Gallen **Heritage C** • Switzerland 86 [121]
St Gallenkirch **Ski** • Austria 100 [127]
St Gaudens • France 115 J2
St Gaudens Nat. Hist. Site **Park N** • NH, United States 151 [341]
St George • QL, Australia 144 B5
St George • Bermuda 159 J2
St George • UT, United States 45 F3
St George, Cape • Papua New Guinea 35 (1) E1
St George I. • FL, United States 154 H2
St George, Monastery of • Palestine 135 A6
St George's • Bermuda 80 A2
St George's • Grenada 160 S
St George's Bay • NF, Canada 156 D3
St George's Channel • Ireland/UK 7 F10
St George's Harbour • Bermuda 159 J2
St George's I. • Bermuda 159 J2
St Georges • QU, Canada 44 J2
St Georges-de-la-Rivière **Beach** • France 96 [78]
St Germain, Forêt de • France 115 E1
St Germain-en-Laye • France 115 E1
St Gervais **Ski** • France 100 [26]
St Gervais-les-Bains • France 115 F2
St Giles Is. • Trinidad & Tobago 160 T
St Gilgen • Austria 119 H4
St Gilles-Croix-de-Vie **Beach** • France 96 [83]
St Gilles-les-Bains • Réunion 132 H1
St Girons • France 115 K1
St Goar • Germany 112 E2
St Gotthard Pass • Switzerland 119 G3
ST HELENA • Atlantic Ocean 19 D7
St Helena Bay • South Africa 134 C1
St Helena Sound • SC, United States 48 G4
St Helens • United Kingdom 7 J8
St Helens • TS, Australia 34 I8
St Helens **Beach** • United Kingdom 101 [104]
St Helens, Mt • WA, United States 152 B1
St Helier • Channel Is. 7 J12
St Hilaire-de-Riez **Beach** • France 96 [83]
St Hilarion Castle • Cyprus 123 J1
St Hubert • Belgium 5 I4
St Hyacinthe • QU, Canada 155 B4
St Idesbald • Belgium 109 E1
St Ignace • MI, United States 44 C3
St Ignace I. • OT, Canada 43 M2
St Ignatius • MT, United States 42 H3
St Ingbert • Germany 5 K5
St Ives **Beach** • United Kingdom 101 [136-137]
St Ives • United Kingdom 104 F4
St Ives Bay • United Kingdom 104 F4
St Jacques • QU, Canada 44 I3
St Jacut • France 114 C2
St Jakob am Arlberg **Ski** • Austria 100 [132]
St James, Cape • BC, Canada 38 E6
St Jean • QU, Canada 155 B8
St Jean [Apt] • St Barthélemy 160 E
St Jean, Baie de • St Barthélemy 160 E
St Jean d'Arves **Ski** • France 100 [48]
St Jean, Lac • QU, Canada 156 D1
St Jean-Cap-Ferrat • France 115 H2
St Jean-d'Angély • France 115 G1
St Jean-d'Aulps **Ski** • France 100 [11]
St Jean-de-Luz • France 115 J1
St Jean-Pied-de-Port • France 115 J1
St Jean-Port-Joli • QU, Canada 44 J2
St Jérôme • QU, Canada 39 P7
St Jérome • QU, Canada 44 H3
St Johann im Pongau **Ski** • Austria 100 [169]
St Johann im Pongau • Austria 119 H4
St Johann in Tirol **Ski** • Austria 100 [155]
St Johann in Tirol • Austria 119 H3
St John • US Virgin Is. 160 Z
St John • NB, Canada 156 D7
St John [Riv] • Canada/United States 156 D6
St John's • Montserrat 161 H
St John's • Antigua & Barbuda 161 K
St John's • NF, Canada 156 D4
St John's Church • Barbados 161 O
St Johns • MI, United States 44 C4
St Johns • AZ, United States 153 E2
St Johnsbury • VT, United States 44 I3
St Jorisbaai • Curaçao 160 X
St Joseph • France 114 B4
St Joseph • Réunion 132 H4
St Joseph • Seychelles 133 K2
St Joseph • Dominica 161 M
St Joseph • MI, United States 44 B5
St Joseph • MO, United States 46 H3
St Joseph I. • OT, Canada 44 D2
St Joseph, Lake • OT, Canada 39 M6
St Jovite • QU, Canada 44 H2
St Julian's • Malta 123 H4
St Julien • France 114 B3
St Just • United Kingdom 104 F4
St Kassian **Ski** • Italy 100 [231]
St Kassien • Italy 120 B2
St Kilda • United Kingdom 6 D4
St Kilda • New Zealand 35 C7
St Kilda **Heritage N** • United Kingdom 83 [46]
St Kitts • St Kitts & Nevis 161 G
ST KITTS & NEVIS • West Indies 161 G
St Lary Soulan • France 115 J2
St Laurent • French Guiana 51 G2
St Laurent • QU, Canada 39 R7
St Laurent • QU, Canada 44 I3
St Lawrence • QL, Australia 144 B3
St Lawrence • QU, Canada 39 R7
St Lawrence, Gulf of • QU, Canada 156 D2
St Lawrence I. • AK, United States 49 G3
St Lawrence Is. Nat. Park • OT, Canada 155 B6
St Lawrence Is. Nat. Park **Park N** • OT, Canada 156 [27]
St Lazaire • France 10 I11
St Léonard • QU, Canada 44 I3
St Léonard-de-Noblat • France 115 G2
St Leonhard **Ski** • Italy 100 [231]
St Leonhard in Passeier • Italy 120 B1
St Leu • Réunion 132 H3
St Lizier • France 115 K1
St Lô • France 10 D4
St Louis • France 9 C9
St Louis • Senegal 22 A1
St Louis • Réunion 132 H3
St Louis • MO, United States 46 J3
St Louis du Nord • Haiti 159 G2
ST LUCIA • West Indies 161 P
St Lucia • South Africa 134 B4
St Lucia, Cape • South Africa 24 E5
St Lucia, Lake • South Africa 134 B2
St Maarten • West Indies 160 D
St Malo • France 114 C2
St Malo, Golfe de • France 114 C2
St Marc • Haiti 159 G2
St Marc, Canal de • Haiti 159 G2
St Margarethen im Lungau **Ski** • Austria 100 [191]
St Märgen • Germany 112 D8
St Marie, Cap • Madagascar 24 H5
St Maries • ID, United States 42 G3
St Martin • West Indies 160 D
St Martin, Lake • MN, Canada 43 G1
St Martin-de-Belleville **Ski** • France 100 [41]
St Martinville • LA, United States 153 F3
St Mary • MT, United States 42 I2
St Mary Peak • SA, Australia 34 G6
St Mary's, Cape • NF, Canada 156 D4
St Marys • TS, Australia 34 I8
St Marys • OH, United States 44 C5
St Marys • AK, United States 49 I3
St Marys • PA, United States 153 D5
St Marys City • MD, United States 153 D11
St Mathieu, Point de • France 114 C1
St Matthew I. • AK, United States 49 G3
St Matthews • KY, United States 48 E1
St Maur-des-Fossés • France 5 F6
St Maurice • QU, Canada 39 Q7
St Maurice Prov. Reserve • QU, Canada 155 B4
St Mawes • United Kingdom 104 F4
St Maximin la Ste Baume • France 115 H3
St Memmie • France 5 H6
St Michael im Lungau **Ski** • Austria 100 [192]
St Michael's Mount • United Kingdom 104 F4
St Michel • Finland 16 N6
St Michel de l'Atalaye • Haiti 159 G2
St Michel-Chef-Chef **Beach** • France 96 [82]
St Michel-des-Saints • QU, Canada 44 H2
St Mihiel • France 5 I6
St Moritz **Ski** • Switzerland 100 [118]
St Moritz • Switzerland 119 G8
St Nazaire • France 114 C4
St Nicholas' Abbey • Barbados 161 O
St Nicolas-de-Port • France 5 J6
St Nicolas-de-Véroce **Ski** • France 100 [28]
St Niklaas • Belgium 109 D10
St Omer • France 10 H3
St Pamphile • QU, Canada 44 K2
St Paul • France 115 H2
St Paul • Réunion 132 H1
St Paul • AL, Canada 38 I6
St Paul • MN, United States 43 J4
St Paul, Baie de • Réunion 132 H1
St Paul I. • NS, Canada 156 D3
St Paul, Monastery of • Egypt 131 F4
St Paul's • St Kitts & Nevis 161 G
St Paul's Bay • Malta 123 H2
St Paul's Church Nat. Hist. Site **Park N** • NY, United States 151 [317]
St Paul's Is. • Malta 123 H2
St Paul-de-Montminy • QU, Canada 44 J2
St Pé, Parc zoologique • France 115 J2
St Peter • Germany 112 D8
St Peter • MN, United States 43 J4
St Peter Ording • Germany 8 D2
St Peter Ording **Spa** • Germany 113 [c4]
St Peter Port • Channel Is. 7 J12
St Peterburg **Heritage C** • Russian Fed. 86 [242]
St Peterburg • Russian Fed. 126 C1
St Peters • MO, United States 46 J3
St Petersburg **Heritage C** • Russian Fed. 86 [242]
St Petersburg • Russian Fed. 126 C1
St Petersburg • FL, United States 154 H5
St Philippe • Réunion 132 H4
St Pierre • Réunion 132 H3
St Pierre • Seychelles 133 K3
St Pierre • Martinique 161 N
St Pierre • St Pierre et Miquelon 156 D3
ST PIERRE ET MIQUELON • N. America 156 D3
St Pierre, Lac • QU, Canada 155 B4
St Pieters-Leeuw • Belgium 5 H4
St Pölten • Austria 13 E9
St Quay-Portrieux **Beach** • France 96 [80]
St Quay-Portrieux • France 114 C2
St Quentin • France 10 I4
St Raphaël • France 115 H4
St Regis • MT, United States 42 H3
St Sauveur-des-Monts • QU, Canada 155 B3
St Savin • France 114 D4
St Savin-sur-Gartempe **Heritage C** • France 86 [72]
St Sebastien, Cap • Réunion 24 H2
St Siméon • QU, Canada 156 D1
St Simons I. • GA, United States 48 G5
St Stephen • NB, Canada 156 D6
St Thégonnec • France 114 C1
St Thomas • US Virgin Is. 160 Z
St Thomas • OT, Canada 44 E4
St Thomas Bay • Malta 123 H4
St Tite • QU, Canada 44 I2
St Trojan-les-Bains **Beach** • France 96 [84]
St Tropez • France 115 H4
St Truiden • Belgium 5 I4
St Ulrich **Ski** • Italy 100 [240]
St Ulrich • Italy 120 B1
St Vaast-la-Hougue **Beach** • France 96 [78]
St Valéry-en-Caux • France 5 D5
St Veit an der Glan • Austria 13 D11
St Vigil in Enneberg • Italy 120 B2
St Vincent, Gulf • SA, Australia 34 G6
St Vincent I. • FL, United States 154 H2
ST VINCENT & THE GRENADINES • West Indies 161 Q
St Vincent-sur-Jard **Beach** • France 96 [83]
St Vith • Belgium 109 D16
St Wendel • Germany 9 C7
St Willibrordus • Curaçao 160 X
St Wolfgang • Austria 119 H4
Ste Agathe-des-Monts • QU, Canada 155 B3
Ste Anne • Réunion 132 H2
Ste Anne • Seychelles 133 K1
Ste Anne • Guadeloupe 161 L
Ste Anne • Martinique 161 N
Ste Anne Marine Nat. Park • Seychelles 133 K1
Ste Anne-des-Monts • QU, Canada 156 D2
Ste Anne-du-Lac • QU, Canada 44 H2
Ste Croix • Switzerland 119 G1
Ste Engrâce • France 115 J1
Ste Foy • QU, Canada 155 B4
Ste Foy-la-Grande • France 115 G3
Ste Marie • Réunion 132 H2
Ste Marie • Martinique 161 N
Ste Maxime • France 115 H4
Ste Menehould • France 5 H5
Ste Rose • Réunion 132 H4
Ste Rose • Guadeloupe 161 L
Ste Suzanne • Réunion 132 H2
Saintes • France 115 G1
Saintes, les • Guadeloupe 161 L
Saintonge • France 10 E8
Saipan • Northern Mariana Is. 33 F4
Sairecabur, Cerro • Bolivia 52 C3
Sais [Apt] • Morocco 131 D2
Saitama • Japan 140 C1
Saiwa Swamp Nat. Park • Kenya 131 G1
Sajak • Kazakstan 26 M8
Sajama • Bolivia 52 C2
Sajama, Nevado de • Bolivia 52 C2
Sajó • Hungary 13 J9
Sajószentpéter • Hungary 13 J9
Sakai • Japan 140 B4
Sakakah • Saudi Arabia 18 C4
Sakakawea, Lake • ND, United States 43 E3
Sakar • Bulgaria 15 H2
Sakaraha • Madagascar 24 G4
Sakarya • Turkey 15 L3
Sakata • Japan 30 J5
Sakenan Temple • Bali, Indonesia 143 H4
Sakha • Russian Fed. 27 H3
Sakhalin, Ostrov • Russian Fed. 27 N6
Sakhalinskiye Zaliv • Russian Fed. 27 N6
Sakhira • Tunisia 131 E4
Säki • Azerbaijan 17 H6
Sakishima-shoto • Japan 31 G2
Sakjiang • Singapore 141 H4
Sakra • Singapore 141 H3
Sakskøbing • Denmark 125 F14
Saku • Japan 140 C1
Sakura • Japan 140 C2
Sakurai • Japan 140 B4
Sal • Cape Verde 22 (1) B1
Sal'a • Slovak Rep. 13 G9
Sala • Chad 21 D4
Sala • Sweden 125 D1
Sala Consilina • Italy 12 J8
Sala y Gómez • Pacific Ocean 33 Q8
Salabangka, Kepulauan • Indonesia 32 (1) B3
Salacgriva • Latvia 126 B4
Saladillo • Argentina 163 D3
Salado • Argentina 52 C5
Salado • Argentina 52 D4
Salado • Cuba 158 D1
Salado • Argentina 163 D1
Salagle • Somalia 23 G3
Salal • Chad 22 H2
Salalah • Oman 18 F6
Salamanca • Spain 11 F4
Salamanca **Heritage C** • Spain 86 [99]
Salamanca • NY, United States 153 D1
Salamanca • Mexico 157 G1
Salamat, Bahr • Chad 21 C5
Salamína • Greece 15 E6
Salamína [I.] • Greece 122 D4
Salamis • Cyprus 123 J2
Salamiyah, As • Saudi Arabia 18 E5
Salas • Spain 11 E1
Salas de los Infantes • Spain 11 H2
Salatiga • Java, Indonesia 143 J7
Salavat • Russian Fed. 4 V6
Salawati • Indonesia 32 (1) D3
Salazie • Réunion 132 H2
Salazie, Cirque de • Réunion 132 H1
Salbris • France 10 H6
Salcantay, Nevado de • Peru 163 B2
Salcombe **Beach** • United Kingdom 101 [126-127]
Salcombe • United Kingdom 104 F5
Salda Gölü • Turkey 123 F1
Saldaña • Spain 11 G2
Saldanha • South Africa 134 C1
Saldanha Bay • South Africa 134 C1
Saldus • Latvia 126 B3
Salé • Morocco 131 D1
Sale • VI, Australia 144 C3
Salé [Apt] • Morocco 131 D1
Salekhard • Russian Fed. 26 K4
Salem • India 138 D11
Salem • Montserrat 161 H
Salem • SD, United States 43 H5
Salem • OH, United States 44 E5
Salem • NH, United States 44 J4
Salem • MO, United States 46 J4
Salem • IL, United States 48 C1
Salem • IN, United States 48 D1
Salem • VA, United States 48 G2
Salem • OR, United States 152 B3
Salem • MA, United States 153 D4
Salem Express **Dive** • Red Sea 135 B2
Salem Maritime Nat. Hist. Site **Park N** • MA, United States 151 [337]
Salema • Portugal 118 E5
Salemi • Sicily, Italy 12 G11
Salerno • Italy 121 G4
Salerno, Golfo di • Italy 121 G4
Salgotarján • Hungary 13 I9
Salgueiro • Brazil 53 (1) D3
Salida • CO, United States 45 I2
Salîm • Egypt 21 E1
Salina • UT, United States 45 G2
Salina • KS, United States 46 G3
Salina Bay • Malta 123 H2
Salina Cruz • Mexico 157 G4
Salina, I. • Italy 120 D2
Salinas • Ecuador 51 A4
Salinas • Puerto Rico 159 H4
Salinas • CA, United States 45 B3
Salinas, Bahia • Puerto Rico 159 H3
Salinas Cliff Dwellings Nat. Mon. • NM, United States 153 E4
Salinas Grandes • Argentina 52 D4
Salinas Pueblo Missions Nat. Mon. **Park N** • NM, United States 150 [121]
Saline • KS, United States 46 E3
Saline • AR, United States 46 I5
Saline I. • Grenada 161 R
Salines, Cap de ses • Majorca, Spain 11 O5
Salir • Portugal 118 E3
Salisbury • United Kingdom 104 F3
Salisbury • NC, United States 48 G3
Salisbury • MD, United States 153 D10
Salisbury I. • NU, Canada 39 P4
Salisbury Plain • United Kingdom 104 F3
Salla • Finland 16 O3
Sallingsund **Beach** • Denmark 96 [49]
Sallins • Ireland 108 B3
Sallisaw • OK, United States 46 H5
Salluit • QU, Canada 39 P4
Sallyana • Nepal 137 C4
Salmon • ID, United States 42 I4

Salmon Arm

Saratoga • CA, United States ... 45 A3
Saratoga Nat. Hist. Park Park N • NY, United States ... 151 [307]
Saratoga Nat. Hist. Park • NY, United States ... 153 D3
Saratoga Springs • NY, United States ... 153 D3
Saratov • Russian Fed. ... 17 H4
Saravan • Laos. ... 31 D3
Sarawak • Malaysia ... 32 E2
Saray • Turkey ... 15 I2
Sarayköy • Turkey ... 15 J6
Sárbogárd • Hungary ... 13 H11
Sardarshahar • India ... 137 C2
Sardegna • Italy ... 120 C
Sardindida Plain • Kenya ... 131 G2
Sardinia • Italy ... 120 C
Sardis • Turkey ... 122 D6
Sardis Lake • MS, United States. ... 48 C3
Sarek Nat. Park Park N • Sweden ... 89 (1) [93]
Sarektjåkkå • Sweden ... 16 I3
Sargasso Sea • Atlantic Ocean ... 50 E2
Sarh • Chad. ... 21 C6
Sarho, Jebel • Morocco ... 20 D2
Sari • Iran ... 18 F2
Sari d'Orcino • Corsica, France. ... 115 L3
Sária • Greece ... 122 D11
Sarigan • Northern Mariana Is. ... 33 F4
Sarigerne • Turkey ... 122 D9
Sarigöl • Turkey ... 15 J5
Sarina • Qld, Australia ... 144 B3
Sariñena • Spain ... 11 K3
Sariqamish Kuli • Turkmenistan ... 26 I9
Sarir Kalanshiyu • Libya ... 21 D2
Sarir Tibasti • Libya ... 21 C3
Sariska Nat. Park • India ... 137 C2
Sariwon • D.P.R. of Korea ... 30 C5
Sarıyer • Turkey ... 15 J2
Sark • Channel Is. ... 7 J12
Sarkad • Hungary ... 13 K11
Sarkikaraağaç • Turkey. ... 15 M5
Sarlat-la-Canéda • France ... 115 G2
Sarmi • Indonesia ... 32 (1) E3
Sarmiento • Argentina ... 53 C5
Särna • Sweden ... 16 G6
Sarnath • India ... 137 C8
Sarnen • Switzerland ... 119 G3
Sarnia • OT, Canada ... 39 O8
Sarny • Ukraine ... 17 D4
Saroma-ko • Japan ... 30 L2
Saronic Gulf • Greece ... 122 D7
Saronikós Kólpos • Greece ... 122 D7
Saronno • Italy ... 12 D3
Saros Körfezi • Turkey ... 15 H3
Sárospatak • Hungary ... 13 K9
Sarpsborg • Norway ... 124 B4
Sarqant • Kazakhstan ... 26 M8
Sarralbe • France ... 5 J5
Sarre • France ... 10 M5
Sarrebourg • France ... 10 L5
Sarreguemines • France ... 10 M4
Sarria • Spain ... 11 K4
Sarrión • Spain ... 11 K4
Sarstedt • Germany ... 8 E4
Sartène • Corsica, France ... 115 L3
Sarthe [Adm] • France ... 114 D2
Sarthe [Riv] • France ... 5 H2
Sarthe • Greece ... 97 [192]
Sárti • Greece ... 122 D1
Sárvár • Hungary ... 13 F10
Sárviz • Hungary ... 14 F3
Sarych, mys • Ukraine. ... 17 E6
Sarysu • Kazakhstan ... 26 K8
Sarzana • Italy ... 121 E10
Sasaram • India ... 137 C8
Sasayama • Japan ... 140 B1
Sasebo • Japan ... 30 E8
Saskatchewan [Adm] • Canada ... 38 J5
Saskatchewan [Riv] • MN/SA, Canada ... 38 K6
Saskatoon • SA, Canada. ... 38 J6
Saskylakh • Russian Fed. ... 27 H2
Sasovo • Russian Fed. ... 17 G4
Sassandra • Côte d'Ivoire ... 22 C3
Sassandra [Riv] • Côte d'Ivoire ... 22 C4
Sassari • Sardinia, Italy ... 120 C1
Sassenberg • Germany ... 8 D5
Sassnitz • Germany ... 8 I2
Sasso Marconi • Italy ... 12 F4
Sassuolo • Italy ... 12 E4
Sassuolo • Italy ... 121 E7
Sata-misaki • Japan ... 30 F9
Satan, Pointe de • Vanuatu ... 35 (2) B2
Satara • India ... 28 B5
Säter • Sweden ... 16 H6
Satipo • Peru ... 51 C6
Satna • India ... 28 D4
Satna • India ... 137 C7
Satoíás [Apt] • France ... 115 F1
Sátoraljaújhely • Hungary ... 13 K9
Satpayev • Kazakhstan ... 26 K8
Satsunan-shoto • Japan ... 31 H1
Sattahip • Thailand ... 142 C4
Satu Mare • Romania ... 14 J2
Satun • Thailand ... 128 E2
Saualpa • Austria ... 14 E3
Sauce • Argentina ... 52 E5
Saucillo • Mexico ... 47 B3
Sauda • Norway ... 16 E1
Saudárkrókur • Iceland ... 16 (1) D2
SAUDI ARABIA • Asia ... 18 E5
Sauerland • Germany ... 9 B7
Sauerland • Germany ... 9 C5
Saugus Iron Works Nat. Hist. Park Park N • MA, United States ... 151 [336]
Saugus Iron Works Nat. Hist. Site • MA, United States ... 153 D3
Sauk Centre • MN, United States. ... 43 I4
Saül • French Guiana ... 51 G3
Sauland • Norway ... 124 B1
Saulgau • Germany ... 112 F1
Sault Ste Marie • OT, Canada ... 39 O7
Sault Ste Marie • MI, United States ... 44 C2
Saum, Laem • Ko Phuket, Thailand. ... 142 E1
Saumarez Reef • Qld, Australia ... 144 B4
Saumâtre, Étang • Haiti ... 159 G6
Saumlaki • Indonesia ... 32 (1) D4
Saumur • France ... 114 D1
Saumur [Château] • France ... 114 D1
Saunderfoot Beach • United Kingdom ... 101 [162-163]
Saurimo • Angola ... 23 C5
Sausalito • CA, United States ... 152 C3
Saut d'Eau • Haiti ... 159 G6
Saut des Guit • France ... 114 B3
Sauteurs • Grenada ... 160 S
Sauteurs Bay • Grenada ... 160 S
Sauvage, Côte • France ... 114 C4
Sauve, la • France ... 115 G3
Sauveterre • France ... 115 J1
Sauze d'Oulx Ski • Italy ... 100 [199]
Sâuze d'Oulx • Italy ... 121 E5
Sava • Europe ... 14 E4
Savai'i • Samoa ... 35 (2) F1
Savalou • Benin ... 22 E3
Savan I. • St Vincent & Gren. ... 161 R
Savaneta • Aruba ... 160 Y
Savanna-la-Mar • Jamaica ... 159 F1
Savannah • GA, United States ... 48 C4
Savannah • TN, United States ... 48 C3
Savannah [Riv] • GA/SC, United States ... 49 C1
Savannakhet • Laos ... 31 D3
Savant Lake • OT, Canada ... 39 M6
Savant Lake • OT, Canada ... 43 K1
Savanur • India ... 138 D2
Savarsin • Romania ... 13 L11
Savastepe • Turkey ... 15 I4

Save • Benin ... 22 E3
Save • Mozambique ... 24 E4
Save • Sweden ... 125 F6
Saverdun • France ... 11 M1
Saverne • France ... 10 M5
Savinjske Alpe • Austria/Slovenia ... 14 B3
Savinski • Russian Fed. ... 17 G2
Savognin • Switzerland ... 119 G4
Savoie • France ... 121 E6
Savona • Italy ... 121 E6
Savonlinna • Finland ... 16 O6
Savoy • France ... 114 A4
Sävsjö • Sweden ... 125 F7
Sawai Madhopur • India ... 137 C6
Sawahlunhok • Thailand ... 142 B4
Sawantwadi • India ... 138 D1
Sawara • Japan ... 140 C2
Sawda, Jabal as • Libya ... 21 B2
Sawkanah • Libya ... 21 B2
Sawqirah • Oman ... 18 G6
Sawtooth Nat. Recreation Area • ID, United States ... 152 B4
Sawu • Indonesia ... 34 O2
Sawu Sea • Indonesia ... 32 (1) B4
Saxony • Germany ... 111 A4
Say • Niger ... 20 F6
Sayama • Japan ... 140 C2
Sayan • Russian Fed. ... 25 K4
Sayda • Lebanon ... 18 B3
Sayhut • Yemen ... 18 F5
Sayil • Mexico ... 157 H1
Saynshand • Mongolia ... 29 E2
Sayre • PA, United States ... 44 G5
Sayre • OK, United States ... 46 F5
Sázava • Czech Rep. ... 128 B2
Sázava [Riv] • Czech Rep. ... 128 B2
Sbaa • Algeria ... 20 E3
Sbeitla • Tunisia ... 131 E3
Scafell Pike • United Kingdom ... 104 C1
Scandinavia • Europe ... 16
Scandola, Réserve naturelle Heritage N • Corsica, France ... 83 [51]
Scandola, Réserve naturelle • Corsica, France ... 115 L1
Scanzano Iónico • Italy ... 120 A2
Scapa Flow • United Kingdom ... 6 I3
Scarborough • United Kingdom ... 7 L7
Scarborough Beach • United Kingdom ... 101 [30-31]
Scarborough • Trinidad & Tobago ... 160 T
Scarborough • OT, Canada. ... 44 F4
Scariff I. • Ireland ... 108 C7
Scarinish • United Kingdom ... 106 B2
Scarpanto • Greece ... 122 D11
Scaur, Fort • Bermuda ... 159 J3
Scenery, Mt • Saba ... 161 F
Schaalsee • Germany ... 8 F3
Schaffhausen • Switzerland ... 9 D9
Schafter • CA, United States ... 45 C4
Schäftlarn • Germany ... 112 F3
Schalksmühle • Germany ... 111 B4
Scharbeutz • Germany ... 8 F2
Scharbeutz-Haffkrug Spa • Germany ... 113 [c18]
Schärding • Austria ... 9 I8
Schärdhorn • Germany ... 8 D3
Scharmützelsee • Germany ... 8 J4
Schauinsland • Germany ... 112 D8
Schaumburg • IL, United States ... 44 A4
Scheffau Ski • Austria ... 100 [153]
Scheidegg • Switzerland ... 119 G2
Scheidegg • Germany ... 112 F5
Schelde • Belgium ... 109 D14
Schenectady • NY, United States ... 153 D3
Schermbeck • Germany ... 111 A3
Scherpenheuvel-Zichem • Belgium ... 109 D15
Scheveningen • Netherlands ... 109 F3
Schiedam • Netherlands ... 109 F3
Schieland • Netherlands ... 109 F3
Schiermonnikoog • Netherlands ... 109 F1
Schilde • Belgium ... 112 D8
Schildmeer • Germany ... 5 K6
Schiltach • France ... 5 K6
Schiphol [Apt] • Netherlands ... 109 F2
Schladming • Austria ... 100 [188]
Schladming • Austria ... 119 H4
Schlarigna • Switzerland ... 119 G4
Schleiden • Germany ... 9 B6
Schleswig • Germany ... 8 E2
Schleswig-Holstein • Germany ... 8 E2
Schleswig-Holsteinisches Wattenmeer, Nationalpark Park N • Germany ... 89 [57]
Schliersee • Germany ... 112 F7
Schluchsee • Germany ... 112 D8
Schlüchtern • Germany ... 9 E6
Schmallenberg • Germany ... 9 D5
Schneeberg • Germany ... 9 H6
Schneverdingen • Germany ... 5 M1
Schobüll • Austria ... 14 B2
Schölcher • Martinique ... 161 N
Schokland Heritage C • Netherlands ... 86 [29]
Schokland • Netherlands ... 109 D7
Schömberg Spa • Germany ... 113 [k8]
Schönau am Königssee • Germany ... 112 F7
Schönberg • Germany ... 112 E4
Schönburg Castle • Germany ... 113 [68]
Schönebeck • Germany ... 8 G4
Schöneberg (Berlin) • Germany ... 111 C4
Schönefeld [Apt] • Germany ... 111 C4
Schönebeck bei Berlin • Germany ... 111 C4
Schongau • Germany ... 112 F5
Schöningen • Germany ... 8 F4
Schönmünd Spa • Germany ... 113 [h7]
Schönwalde • Germany ... 111 C2
Schönwalde • Germany ... 111 C2
Schoonhoven • Netherlands ... 109 F3
Schopfheim • Germany ... 112 D8
Schorndorf • Germany ... 112 E2
Schortens • Germany ... 112 D2
Schottegat • Curaçao ... 160 X
Schotten • Germany ... 112 D2
Schouwen • Netherlands ... 109 D10
Schouwen-Duiveland Beach • Netherlands ... 96 [69]
Schramberg • Germany ... 9 D8
Schreiber • OT, Canada ... 39 N7
Schrems • Austria ... 119 H5
Schroon Lake • NY, United States ... 44 I4
Schruns • Austria ... 119 H5
Schulenburg • TX, United States ... 47 F3
Schull • Ireland ... 108 C7
Schultz Lake • NU, Canada ... 38 L3
Schulzendorf • Germany ... 111 C4
Schuss Mtn Ski • MI, United States ... 149 [142]
Schuyler • NE, United States ... 46 G2
Schwabach • Germany ... 9 F8
Schwaben • Germany ... 9 F8
Schwäbisch Gmünd • Germany ... 9 E8
Schwäbisch Hall • Germany ... 9 E8
Schwäbische Alb • Germany ... 9 E8
Schwäbisch-Bayerisches Alpenvorland • Germany ... 112 F2
Schwalmstadt • Germany ... 5 M4
Schwandorf • Germany ... 9 H7
Schwangau • Germany ... 112 F5
Schwanewede • Germany ... 111 C1
Schwarzach • Germany ... 9 H7
Schwarze Elster • Germany ... 9 H5
Schwarzenberg • Austria ... 119 H1
Schwarzenraben Castle • Germany ... 113 [23]
Schwarzwald • Germany ... 112 D8
Schwarzwald [Forest] • Germany ... 112 D8
Schwaz • Austria ... 9 G9
Schwedt an der Oder • Germany ... 8 J3
Schweich • Germany ... 112 A5
Schweinfurt • Germany ... 9 F6
Schweizer Mtn Ski • ID, United States ... 149 [78]
Schwelm • Germany ... 111 B4

Schwerin • Germany ... 8 G3
Schwerin Castle • Germany ... 113 [222]
Schweriner See • Germany ... 8 G3
Schwerte • Germany ... 5 K3
Schwerte • Germany ... 111 B2
Schwetzingen • Germany ... 112 D4
Schwetzingen Castle • Germany ... 113 [78]
Schwieberdingen • Germany ... 8 J4
Schwielochsee • Germany ... 8 I4
Schwyz • Switzerland ... 119 G3
Sciacca • Sicily, Italy ... 12 H11
Sciacca • Sicily, Italy ... 120 D3
Scicli • Sicily, Italy ... 12 I12
Scilly, Isles of • United Kingdom ... 7 F12
Scobey • MT, United States ... 43 D2
Scone Palace • United Kingdom ... 106 B1
Sconser • United Kingdom ... 106 B1
Scoresbysund • Greenland ... 36 O2
Scotland • United Kingdom ... 6
Scotland District • Barbados ... 161 O
Scotlandville • LA, United States ... 153 F4
Scott [Base] • Antarctica ... 54 (1) V2
Scott, Cape • NT, Australia ... 34 E2
Scott, Cape • BC, Canada ... 38 F6
Scott City • KS, United States ... 46 E3
Scott I. • Antarctica ... 54 (1) X3
Scottburgh • South Africa ... 134 B5
Scottish Lowlands • United Kingdom ... 104 B
Scotts Bluff Nat. Mon. Park N • NE, United States ... 150 [162]
Scotts Head • Dominica ... 161 M
Scottsbluff • NE, United States ... 46 D2
Scottsboro • AL, United States ... 48 D3
Scottsdale • TS, Australia ... 34 I8
Scottsdale • AZ, United States ... 45 D4
Scottsville • KY, United States ... 48 D2
Scrabster • United Kingdom ... 106 A5
Scranton • PA, United States ... 153 D6
Scrub I. • Anguilla ... 160 C
Scunthorpe • United Kingdom ... 7 L8
Scuol • Switzerland ... 119 G4
Scutari • Turkey ... 122 D3
Scutari, Lake • Albania/F.R. of Yugoslavia ... 14 G7
Scythopolis • Israel ... 135 A4
Se Mesquida de Baix • Majorca, Spain ... 117 H2
Sea Is. • GA, United States ... 41 J5
Sea Life Park • HI, United States ... 154 G6
Sea Palling Beach • United Kingdom ... 101 [48]
Sea World • Qld, Australia ... 144 B6
Sea World of California Park L • CA, United States ... 150 [J]
Sea World of California • CA, United States ... 152 C6
Sea World of Florida • FL, United States ... 151 C2
Sea World of Ohio Park L • OH, United States ... 151 [U]
Sea World of Texas Park L • TX, United States ... 151 [O]
Sea World of Texas • TX, United States ... 154 J5
Seaford Beach • United Kingdom ... 101 [85]
Seaford • United Kingdom ... 104 E3
Seaford • DE, United States ... 44 H6
Seaford Town • Jamaica ... 159 F1
Seagrove Bay Beach • United Kingdom ... 101 [103]
Seal, Cape • South Africa ... 134 C7
Seal River • MN, Canada ... 38 L5
Seapoint Beach • Ireland ... 96 [54]
Seapoint • Ireland ... 108 B2
Searchlight • NV, United States ... 45 C3
Searcy • AR, United States ... 46 J5
Seascale • United Kingdom ... 104 C1
Seaside • CA, United States ... 45 B3
Seaside • OR, United States ... 152 B1
Seaside • FL, United States ... 154 H2
Seaside Heights • NJ, United States ... 153 D10
Seaton • United Kingdom ... 104 F3
Seaton Carew Beach • United Kingdom ... 101 [25]
Seattle • WA, United States ... 152 B1
Seaward Kaikoura Range • New Zealand ... 35 D6
Seaward • Shenzhen, China ... 139 B3
Seba • Indonesia ... 32 (1) B5
Sebago Lake • ME, United States ... 44 J4
Sebarok • Singapore ... 141 H3
Sebastian • FL, United States ... 49 C4
Sebastián Vizcaino, Bahía • Mexico ... 157 F1
Sebes • Romania ... 14 K4
Sebes • Indonesia ... 143 J1
Sebis • Romania ... 14 J3
Sebkha de Tindouf • Algeria ... 131 D2
Sebou • Morocco ... 131 D2
Sebuca, El • Egypt ... 131 F5
Sebuku • Indonesia ... 143 J1
Séchelia • Italy ... 121 E7
Sechura, Bahía de • Peru ... 51 A5
Sechura, Desierto de • Peru ... 51 A5
Secretary I. • New Zealand ... 145 G1
Secunderabad • India ... 138 D3
Sécure • Bolivia ... 52 C2
Sedalia • MO, United States ... 46 I3
Sedan • France ... 10 J4
Sedan • KS, United States ... 46 G4
Sedeño • Spain ... 10 B11
Seddenga • Sudan ... 21 F3
Seddülbahir • Turkey ... 15 H3
Sedona • AZ, United States ... 153 E1
Sedro Wooley • WA, United States ... 42 D2
Sedrun • Switzerland ... 119 G3
Sée • France ... 5 B6
Seefeld • Austria ... 119 H2
Seeheim • Namibia ... 24 B5
Seehof Castle • Germany ... 113 [161]
Seeley Lake • MT, United States ... 42 I3
Seelig, Mt • Antarctica ... 54 (1) EE1
Seeon • Germany ... 112 F4
Sées • France ... 10 F5
Séesen • Germany ... 8 F5
Sefrou • Morocco ... 131 D2
Segesta • Sicily, Italy ... 120 D1
Segezha • Russian Fed. ... 17 F1
Ségou • Mali ... 22 C3
Segovia • Spain ... 11 G4
Segovia Heritage C • Spain ... 86 [101]
Segovia • Honduras/Nicaragua ... 37 E5
Segre, el • Spain ... 11 L3
Séguédine • Niger ... 20 H4
Séguéla • Côte d'Ivoire ... 22 C3
Segura • Spain ... 11 J6
Sehlabathebe Nat. Park Park • Lesotho ... 133 [135]
Seignosse Beach • France ... 96 [86]
Seiland • Norway ... 16 L1
Seili I. Dive • Red Sea ... 135 B4
Seiling • OK, United States ... 46 F4
Seille • France ... 5 J6
Seinäjoki • Finland ... 16 L5
Seine • France ... 10 G4
Seine, Baie de la • France ... 114 C1
Seine, Val de • France ... 115 F5
Seixal • Portugal ... 118 C1
Séjero Bugt • Denmark ... 125 F10
Sejlflod Beach • Denmark ... 96 [48]
Sekincau, Gunung • Indonesia ... 32 C3

Sekinchan • Malaysia ... 141 G3
Sekondi-Takoradi • Ghana. ... 22 D4
Selajar • Indonesia ... 32 (1) B4
Selangor • Malaysia ... 141 G3
Selaön • Sweden ... 125 F6
Selaru • Indonesia ... 32 (1) D4
Selatan, Selat • Penang, Malaysia ... 141 F4
Selatan, Tanjung • Indonesia ... 32 E3
Selb • Germany ... 9 H6
Selb • Germany ... 13 B7
Selby • United Kingdom ... 7 K8
Selby • SD, United States ... 43 F2
Selçuk • Turkey ... 122 D6
Selçuk Ski • Austria ... 119 H6
Sele • Italy ... 121 G4
Sele, Piana del • Italy ... 121 G4
Selebi-Phikwe • Botswana ... 24 D4
Selecka Planina • F.Y.R. of Macedonia ... 15 C2
Selendi • Turkey ... 15 J5
Selendi [Riv] • Turkey ... 15 J5
Selenga • Mongolia/Russian Fed. ... 27 G7
Selennyakh • Russian Fed. ... 27 N3
Serik • Turkey ... 123 F4
Sélestat • France ... 9 C8
Seletar Reservoir • Singapore ... 141 H1
Seletar Pierie • Turkey ... 123 G4
Seleucia • Iraq ... 127 D4
Seleucia Trachéotis • Turkey ... 123 G3
Selfoss • Iceland ... 16 (1) C3
Selga • Turkey ... 123 F2
Selibabi • Mauritania ... 20 C5
Seliger, Ozero • Russian Fed. ... 126 C3
Selimiye • Mugla, Turkey ... 15 I6
Selimiye • Antalya, Turkey ... 123 F4
Selinsgrove • PA, United States ... 120 D1
Selinunte • Sicily, Italy ... 120 D1
Selje • Norway ... 124 C1
Seljord • Norway ... 124 B3
Seljord stavkirke • Norway ... 124 B3
Seljordsvatnet • Norway ... 124 B3
Selkirk • United Kingdom ... 104 D4
Selkirk • MN, Canada ... 38 L6
Selkirk Mtns • BC, Canada ... 38 H7
Sella Nevea • Italy ... 121 E4
Sella, Passo di • Italy ... 120 B3
Sellafield • United Kingdom ... 104 C1
Selle • France ... 5 F5
Selle, La • Haiti ... 159 G6
Selle, Massif de la • Haiti ... 159 G6
Sells • AZ, United States ... 45 C4
Selma • CA, United States ... 45 C3
Selmer • TN, United States ... 48 C3
Selous Game Reserve Heritage N • Tanzania ... 83 [103]
Selous Game Reserve • Tanzania ... 130 B4
Selous Game Reserve Park • Tanzania ... 133 [94]
Selsey Bill • United Kingdom ... 5 C4
Sélune • France ... 5 C4
Selva de Cadore Ski • Italy ... 100 [229]
Selva di Cadore • Italy ... 120 B4
Selva di Val Gardena • Italy ... 120 B1
Selva Gardena Ski • Italy ... 100 [238]
Selvagens, Is • Madeira ... 20 A2
Selvas • Brazil ... 50 D5
Selworthy • United Kingdom ... 104 F2
Selwyn Lake • NT/SA, Canada ... 38 K5
Selwyn Mtns • NT/YT, Canada ... 38 E4
Selwyn Range • Ql, Australia ... 34 G4
Semakau • Singapore ... 141 H3
Semani • Albania ... 15 A3
Semarang • Java, Indonesia ... 143 J3
Sembé • Congo ... 22 G4
Semeru, Gunung • Java, Indonesia ... 143 J8
Semey • Kazakhstan ... 26 N7
Seminoe Dam • WY, United States ... 42 L5
Seminoe Reservoir • WY, United States ... 42 L5
Seminole • OK, United States ... 46 G5
Seminole • TX, United States ... 47 C1
Seminole, Lake • FL/GA, United States ... 48 E5
Semitau • Indonesia ... 32 E2
Semmering • Austria ... 14 D3
Semmering Railway Heritage C • Austria ... 86 [126]
Semnan • Iran ... 18 F2
Semnon • France ... 10 D6
Semois • Belgium/France ... 109 D19
Semporna • Malaysia ... 32 F2
Sempu • Indonesia ... 143 J8
Sena Madureira • Brazil ... 51 D5
Senaja • Malaysia ... 32 F1
Senang • Singapore ... 141 H3
Senanga • Zambia ... 24 C3
Sénart, Forêt de • France ... 115 E4
Senatobia • MS, United States ... 48 C3
Sendai • Kyushu, Japan ... 30 F9
Sendai • Honshu, Japan ... 30 K5
Sendai-wan • Japan ... 30 K5
Senden • Germany ... 112 F1
Seneca • SC, United States ... 48 F3
Seneca Falls • NY, United States ... 44 G4
Seneca Lake • NY, United States ... 153 D2
Seneffe, Château de • Belgium ... 109 D14
Senftenberg • Germany ... 8 I5
SENEGAL • Africa ... 20 C5
Senegal [Riv] • Mauritania/Senegal ... 20 C5
Senhor do Bonfim • Brazil ... 53 (1) C4
Senica • Slovak Rep. ... 13 G9
Senigallia Beach • Italy ... 97 [163]
Senigallia • Italy ... 121 E12
Senj • Croatia ... 128 D1
Senja • Norway ... 16 I2
Senkaku-shoto • Japan ... 29 G5
Senlin • China ... 30 F3
Senlis • France ... 115 E2
Sennen Cove Beach • United Kingdom ... 101 [135]
Senneterre • QU, Canada ... 39 P7
Sens • France ... 10 I5
Senta • F.R. of Yugoslavia ... 14 H4
Sentosa • Singapore ... 141 H4
Seoni • India ... 28 C4
Seoul • Rep. of Korea ... 30 D6
Seoul Heritage C • Rep. of Korea ... 85 [181]
Sepang • Malaysia ... 141 G4
Sepetiba, Baía de • Brazil ... 53 D5
Sepik • Papua New Guinea ... 35 (1) C1
Sepphoris • Israel ... 135 A3
Sept Laux, les Ski • France ... 100 [52]
Sept-Iles • QU, Canada ... 156 D2
Septemvri • Bulgaria ... 15 F1
Sept-Saar • Tunisia ... 131 E4
Sepúlveda • Spain ... 11 H3
Sequim • WA, United States ... 42 D2
Sequoia Nat. Park Park N • CA, United States ... 150 [51]
Sequoia Nat. Park • CA, United States ... 45 C3
Seraing • Belgium ... 5 I4
Seram • Indonesia ... 32 (1) B3
Seram, Laut • Indonesia ... 35 (1) A1
Seram • Indonesia ... 143 J1
Serang • Bali, Indonesia ... 143 H4
Serangan New Town • Singapore ... 141 H3
Seraya • Singapore ... 141 H3
Serbia • F.R. of Yugoslavia ... 14 H6
Serdo • Ethiopia ... 23 G5
Sered • Slovak Rep. ... 13 G9

Serefikoçhisar • Turkey ... 15 O5
Serein • France ... 10 I6
Seremban • Malaysia ... 141 G4
Serengeti Nat. Park Heritage N • Tanzania ... 83 [100]
Serengeti Nat. Park • Tanzania ... 130 B2
Serengeti Nat. Park Park • Tanzania ... 133 [87]
Serengeti Plain • Tanzania ... 130 B1
Serengeti Safaripark Park L • Germany ... 98 [54]
Séres • Greece ... 122 D1
Serfaus Ski • Austria ... 100 [135]
Serfaus • Austria ... 119 H6
Sergeya Kirova, Ostrova • Russian Fed. ... 26 P2
Sergino • Russian Fed. ... 54 I3
Sergipe • Brazil ... 52 I1
Sergiyev Posad Heritage C • Russian Fed. ... 86 [246]
Sergiyev Posad • Russian Fed. ... 126 C4
Serian • Malaysia ... 31 E6
Serifos • Greece ... 122 D7
Serifou, Stenó • Greece ... 15 F6
Serik • Turkey ... 123 F4
Sermata, Kepulauan • Indonesia ... 32 (1) C4
Seroe Colorado • Aruba ... 160 Y
Serón • Spain ... 11 I7
Serov • Russian Fed. ... 26 J6
Serowe • Botswana ... 24 D4
Serpent I. • Mauritius ... 132 J1
Serpukhov • Russian Fed. ... 126 C4
Serra da Capivara, Parque Nac. Heritage N • Brazil ... 82 [38]
Serra da Capivara, Parque Nac. Heritage C • Brazil ... 84 [67]
Serra dos Divisões • Brazil ... 52 F2
Serra do Caiapó • Brazil ... 52 F2
Serra do Navio • Brazil ... 51 G3
Serra Orrios, Villaggio nuragico di • Sardinia, Italy ... 160 A18
Serra Bank • West Indies ... 160 A18
Serrant [Château] • France ... 114 D1
Serrat, Cap • Tunisia ... 12 D11
Serre • France ... 5 G5
Serre-Chevalier Ski • France ... 100 [61]
Serre-Chevalier • France ... 115 F4
Serres • France ... 10 K9
Serrinha • Brazil ... 52 I1
Serrinha • Brazil ... 52 I2
Sertão • Brazil ... 163 A2
Serui • Indonesia ... 32 (1) E3
Servion • Switzerland ... 119 G1
Ses Ánimas, Mirador de • Majorca, Spain ... 117 H1
Ses Figueretes • Ibiza, Spain ... 117 G2
Ses Salines Beach • Majorca, Spain ... 96 [126]
Ses Salines • Majorca, Spain ... 117 H4
Sesa • Indonesia ... 32 F2
Seseganaga Lake • OT, Canada ... 43 K1
Seseh Beach • Bali, Indonesia ... 143 H4
Sesheke • Zambia ... 24 C3
Sesibi • Sudan ... 21 F3
Sesimbra Beach • Portugal ... 96 [99]
Sesimbra • Portugal ... 118 D2
Sessa Aurunca • Italy ... 121 G1
Sestao • Spain ... 11 I1
Sesto • Italy ... 120 [82]
Sesto Fiorentino • Italy ... 12 F5
Sesti Levante Beach • Italy ... 96 [112]
Sestri Levante • Italy ... 121 E6
Sestriere Ski • Italy ... 100 [198]
Sestriere • Italy ... 121 E5
Set, Laem • Ko Samui, Thailand ... 142 D2
Setal-gawa • Japan ... 140 B2
Setana • Japan ... 30 J3
Sète • France ... 10 I10
Sète Beach • France ... 96 [130]
Sete Cidades, Caldeiras das • Azores ... 118 B1
Sete Lagoas • Brazil ... 163 C1
Sete Quedas, Saltos das • Brazil/Paraguay ... 52 F3
Setesdal • Norway ... 124 C6
Sétif • Algeria ... 20 G1
Seto • Japan ... 30 I7
Setomaikai Nat. Park • Japan ... 131 D1
Settat • Morocco ... 131 D1
Setúbal • Portugal ... 118 D2
Setúbal, Baía de • Portugal ... 11 B6
Seu d'Urgell, la • Spain ... 117 D1
Seul, Lac • OT, Canada ... 39 M6
Sévaré • Mali ... 20 E6
Sevastopol • Ukraine ... 17 E6
Sevelen • Germany ... 111 B1
Seven Mile Beach • Cayman Is. ... 159 E3
Seven Springs Ski • PA, United States ... 149 [170]
Seven Springs • PA, United States ... 153 D5
Sévérac-le-Château • France ... 10 I9
Severn • United Kingdom ... 104 D3
Severn • OT, Canada ... 39 N5
Severnaya Dvina • Russian Fed. ... 104 D1
Severnaya Zemlya • Russian Fed. ... 26 Q2
Severnoye • Russian Fed. ... 26 M6
Severnyy Ural • Russian Fed. ... 26 I5
Severnyy Uvaly • Russian Fed. ... 17 G3
Severo Donets • Ukraine ... 4 R7
Severo-Sibirskaya Nizmennost • Russian Fed. ... 26 R3
Severobaikalsk • Russian Fed. ... 127 A13
Severodvinsk • Russian Fed. ... 17 F2
Severomorsk • Russian Fed. ... 17 E1
Sever Desert • UT, United States ... 45 F2
Sevier Lake • UT, United States ... 45 F2
Sevierville • TN, United States ... 48 F3
Sevilla • Colombia ... 51 B3
Sevilla Heritage C • Spain ... 86 [108]
Sevilla • Spain ... 116 B1
Seville Heritage C • Spain ... 86 [108]
Seville • Spain ... 116 B1
Seville Nueva • Jamaica ... 159 F2
Sevlievo • Bulgaria ... 128 C3
Sèvre Nantaise • France ... 114 D3
Sèvre Niortaise • France ... 114 D3
Sevre • Sierra Leone ... 22 B3
Seward • NE, United States ... 46 G2
Seward • AK, United States ... 49 I3
Seward Peninsula • AK, United States ... 49 I2
Sexten Ski • Italy ... 100 [248]
Sexten • Italy ... 120 B4
Seyakha • Russian Fed. ... 26 I3
Seychelles • Indian Ocean ... 133 K
Seydisehir • Turkey ... 123 F2
Seydisfjördur • Iceland ... 16 (1) F2
Seyhan • Turkey ... 123 G2
Seyitgazi • Turkey ... 15 L4
Seyla' • Somalia ... 23 G1
Seymour • VI, Australia ... 144 C3
Seymour • IN, United States ... 48 E2
Seymour • TX, United States ... 46 F6
Seyne-sur-Mer, la • France ... 10 K10
Seyssel • France ... 10 L5
Sézanne • France ... 10 I5
Sfakiá • Crete, Greece ... 123 E5
Sfântu Gheorghe • Covasna, Romania ... 14 M4
Sfântu Gheorghe • Tulcea, Romania ... 128 C2

Sha Tin • Hong Kong, China ... 139 B6
Sha'ab Abu Diab • Red Sea. ... 135 B3
Sha'ab Rumi: Precontinent II Dive • Red Sea ... 135 B3
Sha'ab Rumi: South Point Dive • Red Sea ... 135 B3
Shaanxi • China ... 139 A3
Shaba • Dem. Rep. of Congo ... 23 C5
Shaba Game Reserve • Kenya ... 131 G2
Shabelle, Webi • Somalia ... 23 G3
Shabla • Bulgaria ... 128 E4
Shache • China ... 26 M10
Shackleton Ice Shelf • Antarctica ... 54 (1) I3
Shadehill Reservoir • SD, United States ... 43 E4
Shadrinsk • Russian Fed. ... 26 J6
Shaftesbury • United Kingdom ... 104 F3
Shah Alam • Malaysia ... 141 G4
Shahad • India ... 137 C8
Shahganj • India ... 137 C8
Shahjahanpur • India ... 137 C6
Shahpura • India ... 137 C6
Shahrud • Iran ... 18 E2
Shakaland • South Africa ... 134 B4
Shaker Heights • OH, United States ... 44 E5
Shakhrisabz • Uzbekistan ... 18 I2
Shaki • Nigeria ... 22 E3
Shala, Lake • Ethiopia ... 23 F2
Shaldon Beach • United Kingdom ... 101 [114]
Shaler Mtn • NT, Canada ... 38 I2
Shalimar • United States ... 21 F3
Shalqar • Kazakstan ... 26 I8
Sham, Jabal ash • Oman. ... 18 F6
Shama, El • Somalia ... 23 G3
Shama, Irad/Syria ... 18 C4
Shammar, Jabal • Saudi Arabia ... 18 C4
Shamo, Lake • Ethiopia ... 23 F2
Shamokin • PA, United States ... 44 G5
Shamrock • TX, United States ... 46 E5
Shamva • Zimbabwe ... 130 C2
Shamwari Game Reserve • South Africa ... 134 C8
Shamwari Game Reserve • South Africa ... 134 C8
Shan • Myanmar ... 28 I2
Shanagarry Beach • Ireland ... 96 [59]
Shandi • Sudan ... 21 F4
Shandong • China ... 139 A4
Shandong Bandao • China ... 139 A4
Shandong Peninsula • China ... 139 A4
Shangani • Zimbabwe ... 130 C2
Shanghai • China ... 139 C4
Shanghai [Adm] • China ... 139 C4
Shangqiu • China ... 29 F4
Shangrao • China ... 29 F5
Shangri-La • Minorca, Spain ... 117 F4
Shangyu • China ... 29 G3
Shanhaiguan • China ... 27 K8
Shanjuan Cave • China ... 139 C1
Shanklin • United Kingdom ... 5 B4
Shanklin Beach • United Kingdom ... 101 [107]
Shannon [Apt] • Ireland ... 7 D9
Shannon [Riv] • Ireland ... 108 C4
Shannon, Mouth of the • Ireland ... 108 C5
Shantarskiye Ostrova • Russian Fed. ... 27 M5
Shantou • China ... 29 F6
Shanty Creek Ski • MI, United States ... 149 [142]
Shanxi • China ... 139 A3
Shanzu Becah • Kenya ... 131 G5
Shaoguan • China ... 29 F6
Shaowu • China ... 139 C1
Shaoxing • China ... 29 G3
Shaoyang • China ... 29 E5
Shap • United Kingdom ... 104 C2
Shap Abbey • United Kingdom ... 104 C2
Shap Fells • United Kingdom ... 104 C2
Shaqra • Yemen ... 18 E7
Shaqra, Ash • Saudi Arabia ... 18 E4
Sharafah • Sudan ... 23 I1
Shari • Japan ... 30 M3
Sharjah • United Arab Emirates ... 81 E
Shark Bay • WA, Australia ... 34 B5
Shark Bay Heritage N • Australia ... 83 [140]
Sharkiyah, Al Istiwa'iyah al • Sudan ... 23 E2
Sharm el Sheikh • Egypt ... 131 F4
Sharon • Israel ... 135 A3
Sharon Springs • KS, United States ... 46 E3
Sharp I. • Hong Kong, China ... 139 B6
Sharqiyah, Ash • Oman ... 18 G5
Shary • Saudi Arabia ... 18 C4
Shashe • Russian Fed. ... 17 H3
Shashe • Botswana/Zimbabwe ... 24 D4
Shashi • Botswana/Zimbabwe ... 24 D4
Shashi • China ... 29 E4
Shasta Lake • CA, United States ... 42 E6
Shasta, Mt • CA, United States ... 152 C1
Shati, Wadi ash • Libya ... 21 B2
Shattuqiao • Shenzhen, China ... 139 B4
Shattuck • OK, United States ... 46 F4
Shau Tau Kok • Hong Kong, China ... 139 B6
Shaunavon • SA, Canada ... 42 K2
Shawano • WI, United States ... 43 L4
Shawinigan-Sud • QU, Canada ... 44 I2
Shawnee Mtn Ski • PA, United States ... 149 [180]
Shawney • KS, United States ... 46 H3
Shawinigan • QU, Canada ... 155 B4
Shàyib el Banât • Egypt ... 21 F2
Shaykh 'Uthman • Yemen ... 18 E7
Shchel'yayur • Russian Fed. ... 17 I1
Shchuchinsk • Kazakhstan ... 26 L7
Shchuchyn • Belarus ... 13 N4
She Xian • China ... 139 C3
Shebele, Wabe • Ethiopia ... 23 G2
Sheberghan • Afghanistan ... 26 K10
Sheboygan • WI, United States ... 43 C3
Sheenjek • AK, United States ... 38 C3
Sheep Mtn • CO, United States ... 45 E3
Sheep Range • NV, United States ... 45 E3
Sheep's Head • Ireland ... 108 C7
Sheerness Beach • United Kingdom ... 101 [67-68]
Sheerness • United Kingdom ... 104 E2
Sheet Harbour • NS, Canada ... 156 D7
Sheffield • United Kingdom ... 7 K8
Sheffield • AL, United States ... 48 D3
Shek Kwu Chau • Hong Kong, China ... 139 B5
Shek O • Hong Kong, China ... 139 B6
Shek O Country Park • Hong Kong, China ... 139 B6
Shekerley Mtns • Antigua & Barbuda ... 161 K
Shelagskiy, mys • Russian Fed. ... 27 T2
Shelburne • NS, Canada ... 156 D7
Shelby • MS, United States ... 48 C3
Shelby • MT, United States ... 42 I2
Shelby • NC, United States ... 48 E3
Shelbyville • TN, United States ... 48 D3
Shelbyville • KY, United States ... 48 E2
Shelbyville, Lake • IL, United States ... 44 A6
Shelikhova, Zaliv • Russian Fed. ... 27 Q5
Shelikof Strait • AK, United States ... 49 K4

Shell Bay

Shell Bay **Beach** •
  United Kingdom .... 101 [12]
Shelley Beach • Kenya 131 G5
Shellharbour • NS, Australia 144 C2
Shelling Hill **Beach** • Ireland .. 96 [53]
Shelly • ID, United States 42 I5
Shelter Point • New Zealand 35 B8
Shelton • WA, United States 42 D3
Shenandoah • PA, United States .. 44 G5
Shenandoah • VA, United States .. 46 H2
Shenandoah • VA, United States .. 153 D9
Shenandoah Mtns •
  VA/WV, United States 153 D9
Shenandoah Nat. Park **Park N** •
  VA, United States .... 151 [253]
Shenandoah Nat. Park •
  VA, United States 153 D9
Shengsi Liedao • China 139 C4
Shengxian • China 139 C4
Shenkursk • Russian Fed. 17 G2
Shenmu • China 29 E3
Shenton, Mt • WA, Australia 34 D5
Shenyang • China 29 G2
Shenzhen • China 139 B3
Shenzhen Special Economic Zone •
  China 139 B3
Shepparton • VI, Australia 144 C3
Sheppey, Isle of •
  United Kingdom 104 E2
Sherard, Cape • NU, Canada 39 P2
Sherborne • United Kingdom 104 D3
Sherbro I. • Sierra Leone 22 B3
Sherbrooke • QL, Canada 155 B6
Sherbrooke Village • NS, Canada . 156 D7
Sherda • Chad 20 I4
Sherding Shan • China 29 I1
Shere Hill • Nigeria 22 F3
Sheremetyevo [Apt] •
  Russian Fed. 126 C4
Shergui • Tunisia 131 E4
Sheridan • WY, United States 42 L4
Sheringham • United Kingdom 5 E2
Sheringham **Beach** •
  United Kingdom .... 101 [45]
Sherkin I. • Ireland 108 C8
Sherman • TX, United States 154 J1
Sherwood Forest •
  United Kingdom 5 B1
Shetland Is. • United Kingdom 6 K1
Sheung Shui • Hong Kong, China .. 139 B3
Sheung Wan • Hong Kong, China .. 139 B5
Sheyenne • ND, United States 38 L7
Sheyenne • ND, United States 43 H3
Shibam • Yemen 18 E6
Shibam **Heritage C** • Yemen ... 85 [122]
Shibetsu • Japan 30 L2
Shibetsu • Japan 30 M3
Shibukawa • Japan 30 J6
Shibushi-Wan • Japan 30 F9
Shiel, Loch • United Kingdom 6 G5
Shift Run Gap •
  VA, United States 44 F6
Shiga • Japan 140 A4
Shiga [Adm] • Japan 140 B2
Shigaraki • Japan 140 B2
Shihezi • China 26 O9
Shihr, Ash • Yemen 18 F7
Shijiazhuang • China 29 E3
Shikarpur • Pakistan 28 A3
Shikoku • Japan 30 G8
Shikoku-sanchi • Japan 30 G8
Shikotan, Ostrov • Russian Fed. .. 27 O8
Shikotan-To • Russian Fed. 27 O8
Shikotsu-ko • Japan 30 K3
Shilega • Russian Fed. 17 G2
Shilka • Russian Fed. 27 J6
Shilka [Riv] • Russian Fed. 27 J6
Shillا • India 28 C2
Shillong • India 28 E2
Shillong **Hill Sta** • India 138 E2
Shiloh • Palestine 135 A6
Shiloh Nat. Military Park **Park N** •
  TN, United States .... 151 [224]
Shilong • China 139 B2
Shimabara • Japan 30 F8
Shimane • Japan 30 K5
Shimanovsk • Russian Fed. 27 K6
Shimba Hills Game Reserve •
  Kenya 131 G5
Shimizu • Wakayama, Japan 140 B4
Shimizu • Shizuoka, Japan 140 C3
Shimla • India 28 C2
Shimla **Hill Sta** • India 138 C2
Shimoda • Japan 140 C3
Shimoga • India 138 D6
Shimokama Spa • Japan 140 C2
Shimokita-hanto • Japan 140 A1
Shimoni • Kenya 131 G5
Shimonita • Japan 140 C1
Shimonoseki • Japan 30 F8
Shimotsuma • Japan 140 C2
Shin, Loch • United Kingdom 6 H3
Shindand • Afghanistan 18 H3
Shing Mun Country Park •
  Hong Kong, China 139 B5
Shingu • Japan 30 H8
Shingu • Japan 30 K5
Shinosaka • Japan 30 A5
Shinoussa • Greece 122 D8
Shintuya • Peru 163 B2
Shinyanga • Tanzania 130 B1
Shiono-misaki • Japan 30 H8
Ship Bottom • NJ, United States .. 44 H6
Ship I. • MS, United States 48 C5
Shipka Pass • Bulgaria 128 C2
Shipki La • China/India 28 C2
Shiprock • NM, United States 45 H3
Shiqi • China 139 B2
Shiquan He • China 28 D2
Shiquanhe • China 28 C2
Shiraito Falls • Japan 140 C3
Shirakami-Sanchi **Heritage N** •
  Japan .... 83 [131]
Shirakawa • Japan 30 I6
Shirakawa-Go **Heritage C** • Japan 85 [192]
Shirane • Gumma/Tochigi, Japan .. 30 J6
Shirane • Yamanashi, Japan 30 J7
Shiraz • Iran 18 F4
Shiren • China 30 K4
Shiriya-zaki • Japan 30 M2
Shirley, Cape •
  Antigua & Barbuda .... 161 K
Shirley, Fort • Dominica .... 161 N
Shirley Heights •
  Antigua & Barbuda .... 161 K
Shishaldin Volcano •
  AK, United States 54 FF4
Shitou Shan • China 27 K6
Shiucheng • China 31 C1
Shiveluch Sopka, Vulkan •
  Russian Fed. 27 R5
Shively • KY, United States 48 E1
Shivpuri • India 137 C6
Shivpuri Nat. Park • India 137 C6
Shiwa Ngandu • Zambia 24 E2
Shiyan Lake Hot Springs Resort •
  China 139 B2
Shize • Greece 122 D7
Shizuoka • Japan 140 C3
Shizuoka [Adm] • Japan 140 I4
Shkodër • Albania 14 G7
Shoal Lake • MN, Canada 43 C6
Shoalhaven • NS, Australia 144 C2
Shobara • Japan 30 G8
Shoeburyness **Beach** •
  United Kingdom .... 101 [64]
Shoeburyness **Beach** •
  United Kingdom .... 101 [63]

Shoreham-by-Sea •
  United Kingdom 7 L11
Shoreham • WI, United States 28 G7
Shorewood • WI, United States 44 B4
Shortland • Solomon Is. 35 (1) F2
Shosenkyo Gorge • Japan 140 C1
Shoshone • ID, United States 42 H5
Shoshone • CA, United States 45 D4
Shoshone Falls •
  ID, United States 152 B4
Shoshone Mtns •
  NV, United States 152 C4
Shoshone Range •
  NV, United States 42 G6
Shoshoni • WY, United States 42 K5
Show Low • AZ, United States 45 H4
Shreveport • LA, United States ... 153 F1
Shrewsbury • United Kingdom 104 D1
Shri Mahalsa Temple •
  Goa, India 137 B1
Shri Mallikarjun Temple •
  Goa, India 137 B2
Shri Mangesh Temple •
  Goa, India 137 B1
Shropshire • United Kingdom 104 D1
Shropshire Hills •
  United Kingdom 104 D1
Shu • Kazakhstan 26 L9
Shu [Riv] • Kazakhstan 26 K9
Shuangyashan • China 29 I1
Shuguri Falls • Tanzania 24 F1
Shule • China 18 K2
Shule • China 29 B2
Shumagin Is. •
  AK, United States 49 J4
Shumen • Bulgaria 128 E3
Shumerlya • Russian Fed. 17 H3
Shumshu, Ostrov • Russian Fed. .. 27 O6
Shunayn, Sabkhat • Libya 127 D6
Shunde • China 139 B1
Shurayk, Ash • Sudan 18 B6
Shusf • Iran 18 G3
Shute Harbour • QL, Australia 144 B1
Shuwak • Sudan 21 G5
Shuya • Russian Fed. 17 F4
Shwebo • Myanmar 31 B2
Shymkent • Kazakhstan 26 K9
Si Racha • Thailand 142 C4
Si Satchanalai • Thailand 142 B4
Si Satchanalai Nat. Park •
  Thailand 142 B4
Sia • Indonesia 32 (1) D4
Siak Kecil Reserve • Indonesia ... 143 G4
Sialkot • Pakistan 28 B2
Sian Ka'an, Reserva Biósfera
  Heritage N • Mexico .... 82 [20]
Sian Ka'an, Reserva Biósfera •
  Mexico 157 H4
Siargao • Philippines 31 H5
Siauliai • Lithuania 126 B3
Sibay • Russian Fed. 26 I7
Sibaya, Lake • South Africa 134 B2
Sibenik • Croatia 128 D3
Siberia • Russian Fed. 25 K3
Siberimanua • Indonesia 32 B3
Siberut, Pulau • Indonesia 32 B3
Sibi • Pakistan 28 A3
Sibigo • Indonesia 143 G1
Sibiloi Nat. Park **Heritage N** •
  Kenya .... 83 [98]
Sibiloi Nat. Park • Kenya 131 G1
Sibiloi Nat. Park **Park** • Kenya . 133 [73]
Sibiryakovo, Ostrov •
  Russian Fed. 26 M3
Sibiti • Congo 22 G5
Sibiu • Romania 14 L4
Sibolga • Indonesia 143 G4
Siboney, Playa • Cuba 158 D8
Sibu • Malaysia 32 E2
Sibut • Central African Rep. 23 B2
Sibuyan • Philippines 31 G4
Sibuyan I. • Philippines 31 G4
Sibuyan Sea • Philippines 31 G4
Sichang, Ko • Thailand 142 C4
Sichuan • China 139 A7
Sichuan Pendi • China 139 A7
Sicié, Cap • France 115 H3
Sicilia • Italy .... 120 D
Sicilia, Canale di •
  Mediterranean Sea 12 F1
Sicily • Italy 12 F1
Sicuani • Peru 163 B2
Sidári **Beach** • Corfu, Greece .. 97 [170]
Sidari • Corfu, Greece 122 B1
Side • Turkey 123 F4
Sideby • Finland 125 E1
Siderno • Italy 12 K10
Sideros, Akra • Crete, Greece 123 E4
Sidi Aïssa • Algeria 11 L8
Sidi Ali • Algeria 11 L8
Sidi Barrani • Egypt 21 E1
Sidi Bel Abbès • Algeria 20 E1
Sidi Bennour • Morocco 20 D2
Sidi Bou Saïd • Tunisia 131 E2
Sidi Daoud • Tunisia 131 E1
Sidi Ifni • Morocco 131 D5
Sidi Kacem • Morocco 131 D1
Sidi Moussa • Morocco 131 D1
Sidlaw Hills • United Kingdom 104 B2
Sidmouth • United Kingdom 104 F5
Sidney • OH, United States 44 C5
Sidney • NE, United States 46 D2
Sidney Lanier, Lake •
  GA, United States 48 F3
Sidorovsk • Russian Fed. 27 B3
Sidra, Gulf of • Libya 21 C1
Siebengebirge • Germany 112 D1
Siedlce • Poland 13 C5
Siegburg • Germany 9 C6
Siegburg • Germany 112 D1
Siegen • Germany 112 D2
Siegerwald • Germany 9 F7
Siem Reap • Cambodia 31 C4
Siemiatycze • Poland 13 L5
Siena **Heritage C** • Italy ...... 86 [143]
Siena • Italy 121 E11
Sienne • France 5 B6
Sieradz • Poland 13 H6
Sierpc • Poland 13 I5
Sierra Blanca Peak •
  NM, Australia 45 H5
Sierra Colorada • Argentina 53 C4
Sierra Madre •
  WY, United States 43 C6
Sierra Madre del Sur • Mexico 157 G4
Sierra Madre Occidental •
  Mexico 40 E6
Sierra Madre Oriental • Mexico ... 40 F7
Sierra Mojada • Mexico 47 C4
Sierra Nevada • Colombia 51 B3
Sierra Nevada • Spain 116 B3
Sierra San Pedro Mártir, Parque Nac. •
  Mexico 157 F1
Sierra Summit **Ski** •
  CA, United States .... 149 [70]
Sierra Vista •
  AZ, United States 45 G6
Sierra-at-Tahoe **Ski** •
  CA, United States .... 149 [64]
Sierre • Switzerland 119 G6
Siesta Key • FL, United States 154 H5
Siete Hermanos, Cayos •
  Dominican Rep. 159 G2
Sifnos • Greece 122 D7
Sig • Algeria 20 E1
Sigdal • Norway 124 B1
Sigean, Réserve africaine de •
  France 115 K2
Sigguup Nunaa • Greenland 39 U2
Sighetu Marmatiei • Romania 14 K2
Sighisoara • Romania 14 L3
Sighisoara **Heritage C** • Romania 86 [196]
Sigiriya **Heritage C** • Sri Lanka . 85 [154]

Sigiriya • Sri Lanka 138 D15
Sigli • Indonesia 28 G7
Sigmaringen • Germany 9 B9
Sigmaringen **Castle** • Germany . 113 [112]
Signy I. [Base] • Antarctica 54 (1) A3
Sígri • Greece 122 D6
Sigtuna • Sweden 125 D2
Siguanea • Cuba 158 D1
Siguenza • Spain 90 A17
Siguiri • Guinea 22 C2
Sigulda • Latvia 126 B4
Sihuas • Peru 51 B5
Siilinjärvi • Finland 16 N5
Siippy • Finland 125 E1
Sijunjung • Indonesia 143 G4
Sikakap • Indonesia 32 C3
Sikanni Chief • BC, Canada 38 G5
Sikar • India 137 C2
Sikasso • Mali 22 C2
Sikeston • MO, United States 46 K4
Sikhote-Alin • Russian Fed. 29 J1
Sikia • Peloponnese, Greece 15 D7
Sikia • Halkidiki, Greece 15 E3
Sikia **Beach** • Greece .... 97 [192]
Sikinos • Greece 122 D8
Siktyakh • Russian Fed. 27 K3
Sila, Jebel • United Arab Emirates . 18 F5
Silale • Lithuania 126 B5
Silba • Croatia 128 D3
Silchar • India 28 F4
Sile • Turkey 15 K2
Silecroft **Beach** •
  United Kingdom .... 101 [243]
Sileiro, Cabo • Spain 11 C2
Silencio, Costa del •
  Tenerife, Canary Is. 116 K1
Silesia • Poland 13 G7
Silet • Algeria 20 F4
Silhouette • Seychelles 133 K2
Silhana • Tunisia 12 D12
Silicon Valley •
  CA, United States 152 C3
Silifke • Turkey 123 G3
Siliguri • India 28 E2
Silipur • China 28 E2
Silistra • Bulgaria 128 E1
Silivri • Turkey 15 J2
Siljan • Sweden 16 H6
Siljan • Norway 124 B3
Silk Road • Asia 26 N9
Silkeborg • Denmark 125 F9
Silamäe • Estonia 16 N7
Sillé-le-Guillaume [Château] •
  France 114 D1
Sillil • Somalia 23 G1
Silloth **Beach** • United Kingdom 101 [246]
Sillyon • Turkey 123 F2
Siloam Springs •
  AR, United States 46 H4
Siloana Plains • Zambia 24 C3
Siloso, Fort • Singapore 141 H3
Sils • Switzerland 119 G6
Sils-Maria **Ski** • Switzerland ... 100 [119]
Sitou • Chad 21 C4
Silsatan, Gunung • Indonesia 143 G2
Silute • Lithuania 126 B5
Silvaplana • Switzerland 119 G6
Silvaplana-Surlej **Ski** •
  Switzerland .... 100 [120]
Silver Bay • MN, United States ... 43 K3
Silver City • NM, United States ... 153 E4
Silver Islet • OT, Canada 43 L2
Silver Lake Resort •
  Shenzhen, China 139 B3
Silver Mtn **Ski** •
  ID, United States .... 149 [79]
Silver Spring •
  MD, United States 44 G6
Silver Springs •
  NV, United States 45 C2
Silver Star **Ski** • BC, Canada .. 149 [5]
Silverton • OR, United States 42 D4
Silverton • CO, United States 45 I3
Silverwood • ID, United States ... 149 [163]
Silves **Beach** • Portugal .... 96 [100]
Silves • Portugal 118 E6
Silvretta **Ski** • Austria .... 100 [134]
Silvretta • Austria 119 H5
Sim, Cap • Morocco 20 D2
Simanggang • Malaysia 32 E2
Simard, Lac • QU, Canada 44 F2
Simareh • Iran 18 E3
Simav • Turkey 15 J4
Simav Gölü • Turkey 15 J4
Simav [Riv] • Turkey 15 J4
Simbach • Germany 112 F4
Simbirsk • Russian Fed. 17 H4
Simbruini, Monti • Italy 121 F2
Simcoe • OT, Canada 44 E4
Simcoe, Lake • OT, Canada 155 B5
Simei New Town • Singapore 141 H2
Simen • Ethiopia 21 G5
Siméto • Sicily, Italy 120 D4
Simeulue • Indonesia 143 G1
Simferopol • Ukraine 126 C5
Simi • Greece 15 I7
Simi [I.] • Greece 122 D9
Simi Valley • CA, United States ... 45 C4
Sidney • NE, United States 46 D2
Simien Nat. Park **Heritage N** •
  Ethiopia .... 83 [88]
Simien Nat. Park **Park** •
  Ethiopia .... 133 [61]
Simlångsdalen • Sweden 125 F7
Simleu Silvaniei • Romania 14 J2
Simmer • Germany 112 D2
Simmerath • Germany 5 J4
Simmern • Germany 112 E3
Simon's Town • South Africa 134 C5
Simonstorp • Sweden 125 D3
Simplonpass • Switzerland 119 G6
Simpson Bay Lagoon •
  St Martin, West Indies .... 160 D
Simpson Desert • Australia 34 G3
Simpson Desert Nat. Park •
  Australia 34 G5
Simpson Gap Nat. Park •
  NT, Australia 145 D2
Simpson Hill • WA, Australia 34 E5
Simpson I. • OT, Canada 43 L2
Simpson Peninsula • NU, Canada . 39 N3
Simrishamn • Sweden 125 F11
Simson Baai • St Maarten .... 160 D
Simsee • Germany 112 F4
Sin Cow • South China Sea 31 E5
Sinabang • Indonesia 143 G3
Sinai • Egypt 18 E2
Sinai, Mt • Egypt 131 F4
Sinaia • Romania 128 A2
Sinaloa • Mexico 40 E7
Sincelejo • Colombia 51 B2

Singapore Zoological Gardens •
  Singapore 141 H1
Singaraja • Bali, Indonesia 143 H2
Singen • Germany 9 D9
Singh Beach •
  Ko Phuket, Thailand 142 E2
Singida • Tanzania 130 B1
Singkaling Hkamti • Myanmar 28 G3
Singkarak, Danau • Indonesia 143 G4
Singkawang • Indonesia 32 D2
Singkep • Indonesia 32 C3
Singkil • Indonesia 143 G3
Singleton • NS, Australia 34 C5
Singleton • WI, Australia 144 C1
Singö • Sweden 125 D2
Singö [I.] • Sweden 125 D2
Sinharaja Forest Reserve **Heritage N** •
  Sri Lanka .... 83 [120]
Sinharaja Forest Reserve •
  Sri Lanka 138 D15
Sini • Sardinia, Italy 120 C3
Siniscola • Sardinia, Italy 12 D8
Siniscola **Beach** •
  Sardinia, Italy .... 96 [138]
Sinj • Croatia 128 D4
Sinjah • Sudan 21 F5
Sinjajevina •
  F.R. of Yugoslavia 14 G6
Sinnicolau Mare • Romania 14 H3
Sinoe, Lacul • Romania 128 E2
Sinop • Turkey 15 F3
Sinop **Beach** • Turkey .... 97 [239]
Sinquerim Beach • Goa, India 137 B1
Sinsheim • Germany 9 D7
Sintana • Romania 32 E2
Sintang • Indonesia 32 E2
Sinton • TX, United States 47 F3
Sintra **Heritage C** • Portugal .. 86 [117]
Sintra **Beach** • Portugal ...... 96 [98]
Sintra • Portugal 118 D1
Sintra, Serra de • Portugal 118 D1
Sinuiju • D.P.R. of Korea 30 C4
Sinzig • Germany 112 E1
Sinŭiju • D.P.R. of Korea 30 C4
Sion • Switzerland 119 G6
Siouville-Hague **Beach** • France 96 [78]
Sioux Center •
  IA, United States 43 H5
Sioux City **Park L** •
  Gran Canaria, Canary Is. ..... 98 [78]
Sioux City •
  Gran Canaria, Canary Is. 116 E4
Sioux City • IA, United States 43 H5
Sioux Falls • SD, United States .. 43 H5
Sioux Lookout • OT, Canada 39 M6
Sioux Narrows • OT, Canada 43 I2
Sipalay • Philippines 31 G5
Sipan • Croatia 128 D4
Sipcenski prohod • Bulgaria 128 C2
Sipiwesk • MN, Canada 38 L5
Siple **Ski** • PA, United States . 153 D9
Siple • Antarctica 54 (1) CC2
Siple Station [Base] •
  Antarctica 54 (1) GG2
Siponto • Italy 90 A19
Siquijor • Philippines 31 G5
Sir Bani Yas • United Arab Emirates 18 F5
Sir Edward Pellew Group •
  NT, Australia 34 G3
Sir Francis Drake Channel •
  British Virgin Is. .... 160 B
Sir Sam's **Ski** • OT, Canada ... 149 [19]
Sira • Norway 16 D7
Siracusa • Sicily, Italy 120 D4
Siraf • Iran 127 D4
Sirba • Burkina Faso/Niger 20 E6
Sire • Thailand 142 E2
Siret • Romania 14 N3
Siridao Beach • Goa, India 137 B1
Sirik • Iran 18 G4
Sirik, Tanjong • Malaysia 32 E2
Sirikit Reservoir • Thailand 142 B4
Sirino • Italy 121 F2
Sirmione • Italy 121 E7
Sirma • Greece 122 D8
Sirohi • India 137 C5
Sirolo **Beach** • Italy .... 97 [163]
Sirolo • Italy 121 E12
Sironj • India 28 C4
Sirsa • India 137 C2
Sirsa • India 137 C2
Sisak • Croatia 128 D3
Sisimiut • Greenland 39 U3
Sissano • Papua New Guinea 35 (1) C1
Sisseton • SD, United States 43 J8
Sisteron • France 115 H1
Sisters • OR, United States 42 E4
Sisters, The •
  Trinidad & Tobago .... 160 T
Sistiana • Italy 121 E6
Sitamala • Norway 16 E5
Sitapur • India 137 C3
Sitges **Beach** • Spain .... 96 [122]
Sitges • Spain 117 D3
Sithonía • Greece 122 D1
Sitia **Beach** • Crete, Greece .. 97 [215]
Sitía • Crete, Greece 123 E8
Sitka • AK, United States 49 N4
Sitka Nat. Hist. Park **Park N** •
  AK, United States .... 150 [15]
Sittard • Netherlands 109 D16
Sittoubondo • Java, Indonesia ... 143 J8
Sittwe • Turkey 15 K5
Sivasli • Turkey 15 K5
Sivrice **Beach** • Turkey .... 97 [241]
Sivrihisar • Turkey 15 M4
Sivry-sur-Meuse • France 5 I5
Siwa • Egypt 21 E2
Siwalik Range • India/Nepal 28 C3
Six Flags **Park N** • Netherlands . 98 [40]
Six Flags AstroWorld **Park L** •
  TX, United States .... 151 [P]
Six Flags AstroWorld •
  TX, United States 154 J4
Six Flags Fiesta **Park L** •
  TX, United States .... 151 [N]
Six Flags Fiesta •
  TX, United States 154 J3
Six Flags Great Adventure **Park L** •
  NJ, United States .... 151 [LL]
Six Flags Great Adventure •
  NJ, United States 153 D7
Six Flags Great America **Park L** •
  IL, United States .... 151 [S]
Six Flags Magic Mtn **Park L** •
  CA, United States .... 150 [D]
Six Flags Magic Mtn •
  CA, United States 152 D4
Six Flags over Georgia **Park L** •
  GA, United States .... 151 [2]
Six Flags over Mid-America **Park L** •
  MO, United States .... 151 [Q]
Six Flags over Texas **Park L** •
  TX, United States .... 151 [L]
Six Flags over Texas •
  TX, United States 154 J1
Six Flags WaterWorld **Park L** •
  TX, United States .... 151 [R]
Six Flags WaterWorld •
  TX, United States 154 J4
Sixt • France 119 G6
Sizergh Castle • United Kingdom . 104 C4
Sizewell **Beach** • United Kingdom 101 [57]
Sjælland • Denmark 125 F14
SINGAPORE • Asia .... 141 H
Singapore City • Singapore 141 H4
Singapore Crocadilarium •
  Singapore 141 H4
Singapore Science Centre •
  Singapore 141 H1
Singapore, Straits of • Asia 141 H4

Skælskør **Beach** • Denmark .... 96 [43]
Skælsør • Denmark 125 F14
Skærbæk **Beach** • Denmark ... 96 [52]
Skærbæk • Denmark 125 F9
Skaftafell Nat. Park **Park N** •
  Iceland .... 89 [2]
Skärthammar • Sweden 125 D2
Skagen **Beach** • Denmark .... 96 [48]
Skagen • Denmark 125 F6
Skagern • Sweden 125 F5
Skagerrak • Europe 125 F5
Skagway • AK, United States 49 N4
Skála **Beach** •
  Cephalonia, Greece .... 97 [171]
Skála • Cephalonia, Greece 122 C2
Skälderviken • Sweden 125 F11
Skalistyy Golets, gora •
  Russian Fed. 27 I5
Skalitsty Golec • Russian Fed. ... 54 B4
Skanderborg • Denmark 125 F8
Skanderborg **Beach** • Denmark 122 D4
Skåne • Sweden 125 F11
Skanés [Apt] • Tunisia 131 E4
Skanevik • Norway 16 C6
Skänninge • Sweden 125 F15
Skanör • Sweden 125 F11
Skara • Sweden 125 F3
Skaraborg • Sweden 125 F3
Skaralid • Sweden 125 F11
Skardu • Jammu & Kashmir ..... 97 [21]
Skarnes • Norway 124 B2
Skarzysko-Kamienna • Poland ... 13 J6
Skavsta [Apt] • Sweden 128 C4
Skawina • Poland 13 J7
Skeena • BC, Canada 38 F6
Skeena Mtns • BC, Canada 38 F5
Skegness • United Kingdom 7 M8
Skegness **Beach** • United Kingdom 101 [40]
Skei • Norway 124 C2
Skeleton Coast • Namibia 24 A3
Skellefteå • Sweden 16 K4
Skellefteälven • Sweden 16 J4
Skellig Michael **Heritage C** •
  Ireland .... 86 [12]
Skellig Michael • Ireland 108 C7
Skënderbut • Albania 15 A2
Skerries • Ireland 108 B2
Skhirat-Plage • Morocco 131 D1
Ski • Norway 124 B2
Ski Acres **Ski** •
  WA, United States .... 149 [50]
Ski Beech Mtn **Ski** •
  NC, United States .... 149 [161]
Ski Chantecler **Ski** • QU, Canada 149 [34]
Ski Dagmar **Ski** • OT, Canada . 149 [28]
Ski Liberty **Ski** •
  PA, United States .... 149 [171]
Ski Liberty • PA, United States .. 153 D9
Ski Morin Heights **Ski** •
  QU, Canada .... 149 [35]
Ski Roundtop **Ski** •
  PA, United States .... 149 [171]
Ski Roundtop •
  PA, United States 153 D6
Ski Snow Valley **Ski** •
  OT, Canada .... 149 [21]
Ski & Snowboard Ranch **Ski** •
  OT, Canada .... 149 [29]
Ski Sundown **Ski** •
  CT, United States .... 149 [199]
Ski Sundown • CT, United States . 153 D3
Ski Windham **Ski** •
  NY, United States .... 149 [194]
Ski Windham • NY, United States . 153 D3
Skiathos **Beach** • Greece .... 97 [186]
Skiathos • Greece 122 D4
Skibbereen **Beach** • Ireland .. 96 [59]
Skibbereen • Ireland 108 C8
Skibotn • Norway 16 I2
Skidda • Algeria 20 G1
Skidaw • United Kingdom 104 C2
Skiddaw Forest • United Kingdom 104 C2
Skien • Norway 124 B3
Skierniewice • Poland 13 I6
Skiftet Kihti • Finland 125 E3
Skilingaryd • Sweden 125 F4
Skinara • Zante, Greece 122 C2
Skinnskatteberg • Sweden 125 D1
Skipton • United Kingdom 7 J8
Skiros • Greece 15 F5
Skiros [I.] • Greece 122 D4
Skiti **Beach** • Greece .... 97 [189]
Skive • Denmark 125 F8
Skjærhalden • Norway 16 E5
Skjálfandafljót • Iceland 16 (1) E2
Skjálfandi • Iceland 16 (1) E1
Skjeberg • Norway 124 B4
Skjern • Denmark 125 F9
Skjolden • Norway 124 C2
Skład • Russian Fed. 27 K2
Sklavopoula • Crete, Greece 123 E5
Skocjan Caves **Heritage N** •
  Slovenia .... 83 [59]
Skocjan Caves • Slovenia 128 C3
Skopelos **Beach** • Greece ... 97 [188]
Skópelos • Lesbos, Greece ..... 97 [199]
Skópelos • Greece 122 D4
Skopje • F.Y.R. of Macedonia ... 14 I8
Skorba • Malta 123 H3
Skotfoss • Norway 124 B3
Skoura • Morocco 131 D2
Skövde • Sweden 125 F3
Skovorodino • Russian Fed. 27 J6
Skowhegan • ME, United States . 44 K3
Skrimfjella • Norway 124 B3
Skuleskogen Nat. Park **Park N** •
  Sweden .... 89 [21]
Sky Harbor [Apt] •
  United States 153 E3
Sky Lake • FL, United States 151 C2
Skye • United Kingdom 6 F4
Skylands • NJ, United States ... 153 D7
Slagbaai, Boca • Bonaire ...... 160 W
Slagelse **Beach** • Denmark ... 96 [43]
Slagelse • Denmark 125 F14
Slagharen, Attractiepark **Park L** •
  Netherlands .... 98 [38]
Slamet, Gunung •
  Java, Indonesia 143 J6
Slane • Ireland 108 B1
Slaney • Ireland 108 B1
Slantsy • Russian Fed. 16 O7
Slany • Czech Rep. 13 G7
Slask • Poland 13 G7
Slate Is. • OT, Canada 44 B1
Slatina • Romania 14 L5
Slave • SA, United States 43 J8
Slave Coast • Africa 22 E3
Slave Lake • AL, Canada 155 C2
Slave Lake, Lesser • AL, Canada . 38 H5
Slavgorod • Russian Fed. 26 M7
Slavonia • Croatia 15 E2
Slavonski Brod • Croatia 128 D6
Slavskovsky Les • Czech Rep. ... 128 B1
Slawno • Poland 13 F3
Slayton • MN, United States ... 43 I5

Sleat, Sound of •
  United Kingdom 6 G4
Sleeper Is. • NU, Canada 39 P5
Sleeping Bear Dunes Nat. Lakeshore
  Park N • MI, United States . 151 [160]
Slemmestad • Norway 124 B2
Slide Mtn • NY, United States ... 44 H4
Slidell • LA, United States 48 C5
Slidell • LA, United States 153 F4
Slidre • Norway 124 C1
Sliedrecht • Netherlands 109 F4
Sliema • Malta 123 H4
Slieve Aughty Mtns • Ireland ... 108 C4
Slieve Mish Mtns • Ireland 108 C5
Slievefelim Mtns • Ireland 7 D9
Sligo • Ireland 108 C2
Sligo [Adm] • Ireland 108 C2
Sligo Bay • Ireland 108 C2
Slioch • United Kingdom 104 B1
Sliven • Bulgaria 128 E3
Slobozia • Moldova 14 O3
Slobozia • Ialomita, Romania ... 128 E1
Slobozia • Pitesti, Romania 128 E1
Slough • United Kingdom 7 L10
Slovak karst **Heritage N** •
  Hungary/Slovak Rep. .... 83 [58]
SLOVAK REPUBLIC • Europe 13 H9
SLOVENIA • Europe 128 C3
Slovensko • Slovak Rep. 13 J9
Slovyans'k • Ukraine 17 F5
Slowinski Nat. Park **Park N** •
  Poland .... 89 [90]
Slunchev Bryag • Bulgaria 128 D1
Slunj • Croatia 128 D1
Slupsk • Poland 13 F3
Slutsk • Belarus 17 D5
Sluys • North Sea 90 A7
Snow Head • Ireland 108 C3
Smáland • Sweden 125 F4
Smålandsfarvandet • Denmark .. 125 F14
Smålandsstenar • Sweden 125 F7
Smallwood Reservoir •
  NF, Canada 39 S6
Smarhon • Belarus 16 N9
Smederevo • F.R. of Yugoslavia . 14 H5
Smedjebacken • Sweden 16 H6
Smeralda, Costa •
  Sardinia, Italy 120 C2
Smeraldo, Grotta di • Italy 121 E4
Smethport • PA, United States .. 44 F5
Smir-Restinga • Morocco 131 D2
Smith Arm • NT, Canada 38 G3
Smith, Cape • QU, Canada 39 P4
Smith Center •
  KS, United States 46 F3
Smith I. • NC, United States ... 159 J2
Smithfield • NC, United States .. 48 H3
Smiths Falls • OT, Canada 39 P7
Smiths Falls • OT, Canada 44 G3
Smithton • TS, Australia 34 I8
Smithville • TN, United States .. 48 E3
Smögen • Sweden 125 F2
Smoky • AL, Canada 38 H6
Smoky Hills • KS, United States . 46 F3
Smøla • Norway 16 D5
Smolensk • Russian Fed. 17 E4
Smólikas • Greece 15 B3
Smolyan • Bulgaria 14 L8
Smugglers' Notch **Ski** •
  VT, United States .... 149 [215]
Smyadovo • Bulgaria 128 E3
Smyrna • Turkey 122 C5
Smyrna • GA, United States 48 E4
Smyrna • DE, United States 153 D10
Snake • VT, Canada 38 E4
Snake I. • United States 42 F3
Snake River Plain •
  ID, United States 152 B4
Snake Temple, Penang •
  Penang, Malaysia 141 F3
Snasavatnet • Norway 16 G4
Sneem • Netherlands 109 D3
Sneem • Ireland 108 C7
Sneeuberg • South Africa 134 C4
Snettisham **Beach** •
  United Kingdom .... 101 [41]
Snina • Slovak Rep. 13 L9
Snøhetta • Norway 124 C2
Snoqualmie **Ski** •
  WA, United States .... 149 [50]
Snow Lake • MN, Canada 38 K6
Snow Mtn • ME, United States . 44 J3
Snow Summit **Ski** •
  CA, United States .... 149 [74]
Snow Trails **Ski** •
  OH, United States .... 149 [157]
Snow Valley **Ski** •
  CA, United States .... 149 [72]
Snowbason **Ski** •
  UT, United States .... 149 [87]
Snowbird **Ski** •
  UT, United States .... 149 [93]
Snowdon • United Kingdom 7 H8
Snowdonia • United Kingdom ... 7 H8
Snowdonia Nat. Park **Park N** •
  United Kingdom .... 89 [47]
Snowflake • AZ, United States .. 45 G4
Snowmass **Ski** •
  CO, United States .... 149 [107]
Snowshill Manor •
  United Kingdom 104 D2
Snowshoe **Ski** •
  VA, United States .... 149 [166]
Snowy Mtns • NS/VI, Australia .. 144 C4
Snowy Mtns • NS/VI, Australia .. 144 C4
Snowy Corner • Bahamas 158 B4
Snuol • Cambodia 141 E1
Snyder • OK, United States 46 F5
Snyder • TX, United States 47 D1
So, Laem • Ko Samui, Thailand . 142 D2
Soar • United Kingdom 5 E7
Soay • United Kingdom 104 B1
Soba • Nigeria 20 G6
Sobaek-Sanmaek • Rep. of Korea 30 D7
Sobat • Ethiopia/Sudan 23 B2
Sobotka • Czech Rep. 128 B1
Sobradinho, Reprêsa • Brazil ... 53 (1) C2
Sobral • Brazil 53 (1) C2
Soc Trang • Vietnam 141 E3
Sochaczew • Poland 13 J5
Sochi • Russian Fed. 17 F6
Society Is. • French Polynesia ... 33 L7
Socompa, Paso • Argentina/Chile 52 C3
Socorro • NM, United States ... 153 E4
Socorro • NM, United States ... 157 E7
Socorro, I. • Mexico 157 E7
Socotra • Yemen 18 F7
Soda Springs •
  ID, United States 42 J5
Sodankylä • Finland 16 M3
Sodegaura • Japan 140 C2
Söderåsen • Sweden 125 F11
Söderfors • Sweden 16 I6
Söderhamn • Sweden 125 F4
Södermanland • Sweden 125 D2
Södertälje **Beach** • Sweden .. 97 [20]
Södertälje • Sweden 125 D4
Södertörn • Sweden 125 D2
Sodo • Ethiopia 23 F2
Södra Kvarken • Finland/Sweden 16 J6
Sodus • NY, United States 44 G4
Sodwana Bay Nat. Park •
  South Africa 134 B2
Soekarno-Hatta [Apt] •
  Java, Indonesia 143 J1
Soest • Germany 8 D5

Soest • Germany 90 A8
Soest • Netherlands 109 F2
Soeste • Germany 8 C3
Sœurs, les • Seychelles 133 K4
Sofala • NS, Australia 144 C2
Sofala, Baia de • Mozambique 24 E4
Sofia • Bulgaria 14 K7
Sofia • Madagascar 24 H3
Sofiya • Bulgaria 14 K7
Sofiysk • Russian Fed. 27 L6
Sofporog • Russian Fed. 17 E1
Sofrino • Russian Fed. 126 C4
Sofu-iwa • Japan 140 A8
Sogamosa • Colombia 51 C2
Soganli • Turkey 15 N2
Sogda • Russian Fed. 27 L6
Sogeri • Papua New Guinea 35 (1) D2
Sogn og Fjordane • Norway 124 C1
Sogndal • Norway 124 C4
Sognefjorden • Norway 124 C3
Sogod • Philippines 31 G4
Sögüt Gölü • Turkey 15 K6
Sohâg • Egypt 131 F4
Sohano • Papua New Guinea 35 (1) E2
Sohna • India 137 C2
Sohuksan • Rep. of Korea 30 C7
Soignies • Belgium 5 H4
Soissons • France 115 E2
Sojoson-man • D.P.R. of Korea 30 C5
Soka Beach • Bali, Indonesia 143 H3
Sokal • Ukraine 13 N7
Söke • Turkey 122 D9
Sokele • Dem. Rep. of Congo 23 C5
Sokhumi • Georgia 17 G6
Sokkuram Grotto **Heritage C** • Rep. of Korea 85 [185]
Sokna • Norway 124 B1
Soko Is. • Hong Kong, China 139 B5
Sokodé • Togo 22 E3
Sokol • Russian Fed. 126 C2
Sokólka • Poland 13 M4
Sokolo • Mali 22 C2
Sokolov • Czech Rep. 128 B1
Sokolów Podlaski • Poland 13 L5
Sokosti • Finland 17 D1
Sokoto • Nigeria 22 F2
Sokoto [Adm] • Nigeria 22 F2
Sokoto [Riv] • Nigeria 22 F2
Sol, Costa del • Spain 116 B
Sol, Costa do • Portugal 118 D1
Sol y Nieve • Spain 116 B3
Sol-Iletsk • Russian Fed. 26 I7
Sola • Vanuatu 35 (2) B1
Sola • Venezuela 51 E1
Sola [Apt] • Norway 124 C5
Solapur • India 28 C5
Solda • Italy 121 E3
Sölden **Ski** • Austria 100 [139]
Sölden • Austria 119 H6
Soldotna • AK, United States 49 K3
Soledade • Brazil 52 F4
Solent, The • United Kingdom 7 K11
Solenzara • Corsica, France 115 L4
Solignac • France 115 G2
Solihull • United Kingdom 7 K9
Solikamsk • Russian Fed. 26 I6
Solimões • Brazil 51 E4
Solingen • Germany 111 B4
Solitude **Castle** • Germany 113 [98]
Solitude **Ski** • UT, United States 149 [91]
Solivella • Spain 11 M3
Söll **Ski** • Austria 100 [152]
Söll • Austria 119 H3
Sollefteå • Sweden 16 I5
Sollentuna • Sweden 125 D4
Sóller • Majorca, Spain 117 H1
Solna • Sweden 125 D4
Solo • Java, Indonesia 143 J7
Solo [Riv] • Java, Indonesia 143 J7
Solok • Indonesia 143 G4
Sololá • Guatemala 37 C5
Solomon • KS, United States 46 G3
SOLOMON IS. • Pacific Ocean 33 H6
Solomon Sea • Papua New Guinea/Solomon Is. 35 (1) E2
Solor, Kepulauan • Indonesia 32 (1) B4
Solothurn • Switzerland 119 G2
Solotvyn • Ukraine 14 L1
Solovetskiye Ostrova **Heritage C** • Russian Fed. 85 [89]
Solovyevsk • Russian Fed. 27 I7
Solsvik • Norway 124 C3
Solta • Croatia 128 D4
Soltau • Germany 8 E4
Solund • Norway 124 C3
Solvang • CA, United States 152 C5
Sølvegruvene • Norway 124 B1
Sölvesborg **Beach** • Sweden 97 [15]
Sölvesborg • Sweden 125 F11
Solway Firth • United Kingdom 7 I7
Solwezi • Zambia 24 D2
Som, Ko • Thailand 142 D1
Soma • Japan 30 K6
Soma • Turkey 122 D6
Somabhula • Zimbabwe 130 C4
Somali Peninsula • Somalia 130 A2
SOMALIA • Africa 23 H2
Sombo • Angola 24 C1
Sombor • F.R. of Yugoslavia 14 G4
Sombrerete • Mexico 37 (1) B1
Sombrero • Anguilla 160 C
Somerset • Australia 32 (1) F4
Somerset • United Kingdom 104 F3
Somerset • PA, United States 44 F5
Somerset • KY, United States 48 E2
Somerset Bridge • Bermuda 159 J3
Somerset East • South Africa 134 C4
Somerset I. • Bermuda 159 J3
Somerset I. • NU, Canada 38 M2
Somerset Village • Bermuda 159 J3
Somerset West • South Africa 134 C5
Somersworth • NH, United States 44 J4
Somerton • United Kingdom 104 F3
Somerton • AZ, United States 45 E5
Somerville • MA, United States 44 J4
Somerville Reservoir • TX, United States 47 F2
Somes • Romania 14 K2
Somme • France 10 H4
Sommen • Sweden 125 F4
Sömmerda • Germany 9 G5
Sommerresidenz, Eichstätt **Castle** • Germany 113 [142]
Somnath **Beach** • India 138 E3
Somnathpur • India 138 D6
Son • Norway 124 B4
Son • India 137 C8
Son Bou de Baix • Minorca, Spain 117 F4
Son Bou, Platja de • Minorca, Spain 117 F3
Son Moll • Majorca, Spain 117 H2
Son Parc • Minorca, Spain 117 F2
Son Sant Joan [Apt] • Majorca, Spain 117 H1
Son Servera **Beach** • Majorca, Spain 96 [126]
Sonagiri • India 137 C7
Sonamarg **Hill Sta** • India 138 E1
Sonch'on • D.P.R. of Korea 30 C5
Sønderborg **Beach** • Denmark 96 [45]
Sønderborg • Denmark 125 F13
Sønderjylland • Denmark 125 F13
Sondershausen • Germany 9 F5
Søndervig • Denmark 125 F9
Søndre Strømfjord • Greenland 39 V3
Sondrio • Italy 121 E2
Song Hong • Vietnam 31 C2
Song Shan • China 139 A3
Songea • Tanzania 130 B4
Songhua Hu • China 29 H2
Songhua Jiang • China 29 G1
Songjiang • China 139 C4
Songkhla • Thailand 31 C5
Songnim • D.P.R. of Korea 30 C5
Songo • Mozambique 24 E3
Songo Mnara **Heritage C** • Tanzania 85 [114]
Songo Mnara • Tanzania 130 B4
Sonid Youqi • China 29 E2
Sonipat • India 137 C2
Sonneberg • Germany 9 G6
Sonobe • Japan 140 B2
Sonoma • CA, United States 152 C3
Sonora • CA, United States 45 B3
Sonora • TX, United States 47 D2
Sonora • CA, United States 152 C3
Sonora • Mexico 157 F2
Sonora [Adm] • Mexico 40 D5
Sonoran Desert • AZ, United States 153 E3
Sonoyta • Mexico 157 F1
Sonsbeck • Germany 111 B1
Sonsorol Is. • Palau 32 (1) D2
Sonthofen • Germany 112 F6
Sooneck, Burg • Germany 112 E4
Soontornpoo Mon. • Thailand 142 C4
Sopelana **Beach** • Spain 96 [88]
Sopi, Tanjung • Indonesia 32 (1) C2
Sopocani Monastery **Heritage C** • F.R. of Yugoslavia 86 [190]
Sopot • Poland 13 H3
Sopot • Bulgaria 15 F1
Sopron • Hungary 13 F10
Sopur • Jammu & Kashmir 28 B2
Sør-Trøndelag • Norway 16 F5
Sora • Italy 121 F4
Sorak • Rep. of Korea 30 E5
Sorbas • Spain 11 I7
Sorel • QU, Canada 39 Q7
Sorel • QU, Canada 44 I2
Sörenberg **Ski** • Switzerland 100 [97]
Sörenberg • Switzerland 119 G2
Sorfjorden • Norway 124 C4
Soria • Spain 11 I3
Sorø **Beach** • Denmark 96 [43]
Sorø • Denmark 125 F14
Soroa • Cuba 158 D1
Soroca • Moldova 14 P1
Sorocaba • Brazil 52 G3
Sorong • Indonesia 32 (1) D3
Soroti • Uganda 23 E3
Sørøya • Norway 16 L1
Sorraia • Portugal 11 C6
Sørreisa • Norway 16 J2
Sorrento • Italy 121 G3
Sorsele • Sweden 16 I4
Sorsogon • Philippines 31 G4
Sortland • Norway 16 H2
Sosan • Rep. of Korea 30 D6
Sösdala • Sweden 125 F11
Sosnogorsk • Russian Fed. 17 I2
Sosnovka • Ukraine 13 N7
Sosnowiec • Poland 128 C1
Sosúa • Dominican Rep. 159 G3
Sosva • Khanty-Mansi, Russian Fed. 26 J5
Sosva • Yekaterinburg, Russian Fed. 26 J6
Sotavento de Jandía, Playa de • Fuerteventura, Canary Is. 117 E2
Sotavento, Is. de • West Indies 51 D1
Sotkamo • Finland 16 O4
Soto • Curaçao 160 X
Soto la Marina • Mexico 47 E6
Sotra • Norway 124 C3
Sottern • Sweden 125 F4
Sotteville-les-Rouen • France 5 E5
Souahel, Boukhalef [Apt] • Morocco 131 D1
Souanké • Congo 22 G4
Soúda • Crete, Greece 123 E1
Soúda, Ormos • Crete, Greece 123 E2
Souflí • Greece 122 D2
Soufrière • St Lucia 161 P
Soufrière • Guadeloupe 161 L
Soufrière • Dominica 161 M
Soufrière Bay • St Lucia 161 P
Soufrière Bay • Dominica 161 M
Soufrière Hills • Montserrat 161 H
Soufrière, La • St Vincent & Gren. 161 Q
Soúgia • Crete, Greece 123 E5
Souillac • France 115 G2
Souillac • Mauritius 132 J3
Souilly • France 5 I5
Souk Ahras • Algeria 20 G1
Souk el Arba du Rharb • Morocco 131 D1
Soul • Rep. of Korea 30 D6
Soul **Heritage C** • Rep. of Korea 85 [181]
Soulac-sur-Mer **Beach** • France 96 [85]
Soulac-sur-Mer • France 115 G1
Soúnio, Akra • Greece 122 D7
Soúnion Nat. Park **Park N** • Greece 89 [141]
Soûr **Heritage C** • Lebanon 86 [284]
Sour el Ghozlane • Algeria 20 F1
Soure • Brazil 51 H4
Souris • Canada/United States 38 K7
Souris • MN, Canada 43 F2
Souris • PE, Canada 156 D7
Souris [Riv] • Canada/United States 43 F2
Sous • Morocco 20 D2
Sous le Vent • Réunion 132 H3
Sous le Vent, Is. • French Polynesia 33 L7
Sousa • Brazil 53 (1) D3
Sousse **Heritage C** • Tunisia 86 [266]
Sousse • Tunisia 131 E2
Souterraine, la • France 114 D4
SOUTH AFRICA • Africa 24 D5
South America cruise area • S. America 80 A3
South Andaman • India 28 F6
South Aulatsivik I. • NU, Canada 39 S5
South Australia • Australia 34 F5
South Baymouth • OT, Canada 44 D3
South Beach • Bahamas 158 B3
South Bend • WA, United States 42 D3
South Bend • IN, United States 44 B5
South Bimini I. • Bahamas 49 D5
South Boston • VA, United States 153 D11
South Branch Potomac • WV, United States 153 D9
South Burlington • VT, United States 44 I3
South Caicos • Turks & Caicos Is. 158 C2
South Carolina • United States 48 G4
South China Sea • Asia 31 E3
South Dakota • United States 43 F4
South Downs • United Kingdom 104 E3
South East Cape • TS, Australia 34 I8
South East Point • VI, Australia 144 C3
South Euclid • OH, United States 44 E5
South Fork • CO, United States 45 I3
South Frigate Bay • St Kitts & Nevis 161 G
South Geomagnetic Pole • Antarctica 54 (1) Q2
South Georgia • Atlantic Ocean 50 G10
South Haven • MI, United States 44 B4
South Hole Sound • Cayman Is. 159 E1
South I. • New Zealand 35 B6
South I. Nat. Park • Kenya 131 G1
South Kitui Game Reserve • Kenya 131 G4
South Lake Tahoe • CA, United States 45 B2
South Luangwa Nat. Park **Park** • Zambia 133 [104]
South Magnetic Pole • Antarctica 54 (1) T3
South Milwaukee • WI, United States 44 B4
South Moll I. • QL, Australia 144 B1
South Nahanni • NT, Canada 38 F4
South Negril Point • Jamaica 159 F1
South Ogden • UT, United States 42 J6
South Orkney Is. • Antarctica 54 (1) A3
South Pacific cruise area • Pacific Ocean 80 A1
South Pacific cruise area • Pacific Ocean 81 A9
South Padre I. • TX, United States 47 F4
South Paris • ME, United States 44 J3
South Pass • WY, United States 42 K5
South Platte • CO/NE, United States 46 D2
South Pole • Antarctica 81 A10
South Portland • ME, United States 44 J4
South Rock • Turks & Caicos Is. 158 C2
South Ronaldsay • United Kingdom 6 J3
South Sandwich Is. • Antarctica 54 (1) C4
South Saskatchewan • SA, Canada 38 J6
South Shields • United Kingdom 7 K7
South Sioux City • NE, United States 43 H5
South Sound • Cayman Is. 159 E3
South Town • Cayman Is. 159 E1
South Turkana Game Reserve • Kenya 131 G1
South Twin Mtn • NH, United States 44 J3
South Uist • United Kingdom 6 E4
South Yarmouth • MA, United States 44 J5
Southampton • United Kingdom 7 K11
Southampton • NY, United States 44 I5
Southampton, Cape • NU, Canada 39 O4
Southampton I. • NU, Canada 39 O4
Southbridge • MA, United States 44 I4
Southbroom • South Africa 134 B5
Southeast Atlantic forest reserves **Heritage N** • Brazil 82 [40]
Southend • SA, Canada 38 K5
Southend-on-Sea **Beach** • United Kingdom 101 [65]
Southend-on-Sea • United Kingdom 104 E2
Southern Alps • New Zealand 35 C6
Southern Cross • WA, Australia 34 C6
Southern Indian Lake • MN, Canada 38 L5
Southern Is. • Japan 140 A8
Southern Uplands • United Kingdom 6 I6
Southey • SA, Canada 43 D1
Southey • MN, Canada 43 F1
Southfield • MI, United States 44 D4
Southland • New Zealand 145 G
Southport **Beach** • United Kingdom 101 [241]
Southport • QL, Australia 144 B6
Southsea • United Kingdom 106 D
Southwest Cape • New Zealand 35 A8
Southwest Florida [Apt] • FL, United States 154 H7
Southwest Is. • Japan 140 A10
Southwold • United Kingdom 5 E2
Southwold **Beach** • United Kingdom 101 [55-56]
Soutpansberg • South Africa 24 D4
Sovetsk • Russian Fed. 13 K2
Sovetskiy • Russian Fed. 26 J5
Soya-misaki • Japan 30 K2
Soyo • Angola 23 A5
Sozopol **Beach** • Bulgaria 97 [242]
Sozopol • Bulgaria 128 E3
Spa • Belgium 109 D16
Spa-Francorchamps • Belgium 109 D16
Spaandem • Netherlands 109 F1
Spaans Lagoen • Aruba 160 Y
Spaanswater • Curaçao 160 X
Space Coast • FL, United States 154 H6
SPAIN • Europe 11
Spalato • Croatia 90 A14
Spalding • United Kingdom 7 L9
Spánda, Akra • Crete, Greece 123 E1
Spandau **Castle** • Germany 113 [220]
Spandau (Berlin) • Germany 111 C1
Spangenberg **Castle** • Germany 113 [38]
Spanish • OT, Canada 44 E2
Spanish Peak • OR, United States 42 F4
Spanish Point • Bermuda 159 J3
Spanish Point • Antigua & Barbuda 161 J
Spanish Town • Jamaica 159 F4
Spanish Town • British Virgin Is. 160 B
Spanish Wells • Bahamas 158 B1
Spargi • Sardinia, Italy 12 D7
Sparks • NV, United States 152 C1
Sparreholm • Sweden 125 D3
Sparta • Greece 15 D6
Sparta • WI, United States 43 K5
Spartanburg • SC, United States 48 G3
Spartel, Cap • Morocco 131 D1
Spárti • Greece 15 D6
Spartilas **Beach** • Corfu, Greece 97 [170]
Spartivento, Capo • Calábria, Italy 12 K11
Spartivento, Capo • Sardinia, Italy 120 C4
Sparwood • BC, Canada 42 H2
Spassk-Dalniy • Russian Fed. 27 L8
Spearfish • SD, United States 43 E4
Speedway • IN, United States 44 B6
Speichersee • Germany 112 F3
Speightstown • Barbados 161 O
Spello • Italy 121 E12
Spence Bay • NU, Canada 36 H3
Spencer • ID, United States 42 I4
Spencer • IA, United States 43 I5
Spencer • WV, United States 44 E6
Spencer, Cape • SA, Australia 34 G7
Spencer Gulf • SA, Australia 34 G6
Spenser Mtns • New Zealand 35 D6
Sperillen • Norway 124 B1
Sperlonga **Beach** • Italy 96 [147]
Sperlonga • Italy 121 F4
Sperone, Capo • Sardinia 12 C10
Sperrin Mtns • United Kingdom 7 F7
Spessart • Germany 9 E7
Spetsai • Greece 122 D7
Spétses • Greece 122 D7
Spétses [I.] • Greece 15 E6
Spey • United Kingdom 6 I4
Speyer **Heritage C** • Germany 86 [54]
Speyer • Germany 112 D4
Speyside • Trinidad & Tobago 160 T
Sphinx • Egypt 131 F1
Spice Is. • Indonesia 143 F
Spiddal **Beach** • Ireland 96 [62]
Spiddal • Ireland 108 C4
Spiekeroog • Germany 8 C3
Spiez • Switzerland 119 G2
Spijkenisse • Netherlands 109 F3
Spíli • Crete, Greece 123 E6
Spílion Kamarón • Crete, Greece 123 E6
Spilva [Apt] • Latvia 126 B3
Spinalónga, Herson • Crete, Greece 123 E8
Spingdale • NF, Canada 156 D3
Spion Kop Nature Reserve • South Africa 134 B3
Spirit Lake • IA, United States 43 I5
Spirit Mtn **Ski** • MN, United States 149 [119]
Spisská-Nová Ves • Slovak Rep. 13 J9
Spisské Pohradie **Heritage C** • Slovak Rep. 86 [179]
Spithead • United Kingdom 5 B4
Spitsbergen • Arctic Ocean 4 M1
Spitsbergen • Arctic Ocean 54 N2
Spittal • Austria 119 H8
Spitzingsee • Germany 112 F7
Spjelkavik • Norway 124 C2
Splendid China • Shenzhen, China 139 B3
Splendid China • FL, United States 151 C1
Split **Heritage C** • Croatia 86 [186]
Split • Croatia 128 D4
Split Lake • MN, Canada 38 L5
Splügen • Switzerland 119 G3
Spodsbjerg • Denmark 125 F14
Spokane • WA, United States 152 B2
Spoleto • Italy 121 F1
Spongeorama • FL, United States 154 H5
Spontin • Belgium 109 D15
Spooner • WI, United States 43 K4
Sporades, N • Greece 122 D4
Sportgastein • Austria 119 H8
Sportsworld **Park L** • OT, Canada 156 [H]
Spot Bay • Cayman Is. 159 E2
Spotorno • Italy 121 E6
Spøttrup **Beach** • Denmark 96 [49]
Spratly Is. • South China Sea 31 E5
Spree • Germany 8 I4
Spreepark (Berlin) • Germany 111 C4
Spremberg • Germany 8 J5
Sprengisandur • Iceland 16 (1) D2
Spring Bay • Saba 161 F
Spring Hill • FL, United States 154 H5
Spring Valley • CA, United States 45 D5
Spring Valley • IL, United States 46 K2
Springbok • South Africa 24 B5
Springdale • AR, United States 46 H4
Springe • Germany 8 E4
Springer • NM, United States 46 C4
Springerville • AZ, United States 45 H4
Springfield • New Zealand 35 C6
Springfield • MN, United States 43 I4
Springfield • OH, United States 44 D6
Springfield • VT, United States 44 I4
Springfield • CO, United States 46 D4
Springfield • MO, United States 46 I4
Springfield • IL, United States 46 K3
Springfield • TN, United States 48 D2
Springfield • OR, United States 152 B3
Springfield • MA, United States 153 D3
Springfield Armory Nat. Hist. Site **Park N** • MA, United States 151 [326]
Springhill • NS, Canada 156 D7
Springs • South Africa 24 D5
Springvale **Beach** • United Kingdom 101 [102]
Springville • UT, United States 45 G1
Sprockhövel • Germany 111 B2
Spruce Knob • WV, United States 44 F6
Spui • Netherlands 109 F3
Spur • TX, United States 46 E6
Spurn Head • United Kingdom 7 M8
Squamish • BC, Canada 38 G7
Squaw Valley **Ski** • CA, United States 149 [63]
Squillace • Italy 12 K10
Squillace, Golfo di • Italy 12 K10
Sravanabelgola • India 138 D6
Sravasti • India 137 C4
Srbija • F.R. of Yugoslavia 14 H6
Srebarna • Bulgaria 128 E1
Srebarna Nature Reserve **Heritage N** • Bulgaria 83 [65]
Srebrenica • Bosnia-Herz. 14 G5
Sredinny Khrebet • Russian Fed. 27 Q5
Sredna Gora • Bulgaria 15 F1
Srednesibirskoye Ploskogorye • Russian Fed. 26 Q4
Sredni Verecki • Ukraine 14 K1
Sredniy Ural • Russian Fed. 26 I6
Srednrusskaya Vozvyshennost • Russian Fed. 17 E4
Srednyaya Olëkma • Russian Fed. 27 J5
Srem • Poland 13 G5
Sremska Mitrovica • F.R. of Yugoslavia 14 G5
Sretensk • Russian Fed. 27 I6
Sri Jayewardenepura Kotte • Sri Lanka 138 D15
SRI LANKA • Asia 138 D15
Srikakulam • India 28 D5
Srikalahasti • India 138 D7
Srinagar • Jammu & Kashmir 28 B2
Srinagar **Hill Sta** • India 138 E1
Srirangam • India 138 D11
Srirangapatnam • India 138 D6
Srisailam • India 138 D3
Sroda Wielkopolska • Poland 13 G5
Staaten River Nat. Park • QL, Australia 34 H3
Stabbursdalen Nat. Park **Park N** • Norway 89 [4]
Stade • Germany 8 E3
Stade de France (Paris) • France 115 E1
Stadskanaal • Netherlands 5 J1
Stadtallendorf • Germany 9 E6
Stadthagen • Germany 8 E4
Stadtresidenz, Landshut **Castle** • Germany 113 [128]
Staffelsee • Germany 112 F7
Staffelstein • Germany 9 F6
Stafford • United Kingdom 7 J9
Stafford • KS, United States 46 F4
Stagnone, I. della • Italy 120 D1
Stahnsdorf • Germany 111 C3
Staigue Fort • Ireland 108 C7
Stake Bay • Cayman Is. 159 E2
Stalheim • Norway 124 C4
Stalin, Mt • BC, Canada 38 G5
Stalingrad • Russian Fed. 4 T7
Stalís • Crete, Greece 123 E7
Stalowa Wola • Poland 13 L7
Stamford • United Kingdom 7 L9
Stamford • NY, United States 44 H4
Stamford • CT, United States 153 D7
Stamford Bridge • United Kingdom 90 A7
Stamnes • Norway 124 C3
Stampalia • Greece 122 D8
Stamsund • Norway 16 G2
Standerton • South Africa 24 D5
Standish • MI, United States 44 D3
Standley Chasm • NT, Australia 145 D2
Stanford • MT, United States 42 J3
Stanford • KY, United States 48 E2
Stanger • South Africa 134 B4
Stanley • TS, Australia 34 I8
Stanley • Falkland Is. 53 E6
Stanley • Hong Kong, China 139 B6
Stanley • ID, United States 42 H4
Stanley • ND, United States 43 E2
Stanley Falls • Dem. Rep. of Congo 23 D3
Stanley, Mt • Uganda 23 E3
Stanorvoye Nagorye • Russian Fed. 27 H5
Stanovoy Khrebet • Russian Fed. 27 J6
Stansted [Apt] • United Kingdom 104 E1
Stanthorpe • QL, Australia 34 J5
Stanton • ND, United States 43 F3
Staples • MN, United States 43 I3
Stapleton • NE, United States 46 E2
Stara Zagora • Bulgaria 128 E3
Staraplanina • Bulgaria 14 K7
Staraya Russa • Russian Fed. 126 C1
Starbuck • Kiribati 33 L6
Stargard Szczecinski • Poland 13 E4
Stari Ras **Heritage C** • F.R. of Yugoslavia 86 [190]
Starke • FL, United States 49 B3
Starkenburg • Germany 112 E3
Starkville • MS, United States 153 F2
Starnberg • Germany 112 F3
Starnberger See • Germany 112 F3
Starogard Gdanski • Poland 13 H4
Start Bay • United Kingdom 104 F5
Start Point • United Kingdom 104 F5
Staryy Oskol • Russian Fed. 17 F4
Staszów • Poland 128 C2
State College • PA, United States 153 D5
Staten I. • NY, United States 153 D7
Statesboro • GA, United States 48 G4
Statesville • NC, United States 48 G3
Stathelle • Norway 124 B3
Statue of Liberty **Heritage C** • NJ, United States 84 [12]
Statue of Liberty Nat. Mon. **Park N** • NY, United States 151 [318]
Statue of Liberty Nat. Mon. • NY, United States 153 D7
Staunton • VA, United States 153 D11
Stavanger • Norway 124 C5
Stavern • Norway 124 B3
Staverton [Apt] • United Kingdom 104 D4
Stavoren • Netherlands 109 D3
Stavronikita, SS • Barbados 161 O
Stavropol • Russian Fed. 17 G5
Stavropolskaya Vozvyshennost • Russian Fed. 17 G5
Stavrós • Thessaly, Greece 15 D4
Stavrós • Halkidiki, Greece 122 D1
Stavrós • Crete, Greece 123 E1
Stavrós, Akra • Crete, Greece 123 E3
Stavrovouni Monastery • Cyprus 123 J4
Stayton • OR, United States 42 D4
Steamboat **Ski** • CO, United States 149 [97]
Steamboat Springs **Ski** • CO, United States 149 A
Steamboat Springs • CO, United States 45 I1
Steamtown Nat. Hist. Site **Park N** • PA, United States 151 [303]
Stebnik • Ukraine 13 M8
Stechelberg **Ski** • Switzerland 100 [100]
Steele • ND, United States 43 G3
Steelville • MO, United States 46 J4
Steens Mtn • OR, United States 42 F5
Steenwijk • Netherlands 5 J2
Stefansson I. • NU, Canada 38 J2
Stege • Denmark 125 F14
Steglitz (Berlin) • Germany 111 C4
Steiermark • Austria 13 D10
Stein **Castle** • Germany 113 [121]
Steinach • Austria 119 H6
Steinau **Castle** • Germany 113 [53]
Steinau an der Strasse • Germany 112 D2
Steinbach • MN, Canada 43 H2
Steinfurt • Germany 8 C4
Steingaden • Germany 112 F6
Steinhuder Meer • Germany 5 M2
Steinkjer • Norway 16 F4
Steinsberg **Castle** • Germany 113 [88]
Steinsel • Luxembourg 109 D20
Stella Maris • Bahamas 158 B4
Stellenbosch • South Africa 134 C5
Stèlvio • Italy 121 E3
Stelvio, Parco Naz. dello **Park N** • Italy 89 [84]
Stelvio, Parco Naz. dello • Italy 121 E3
Stenay • France 10 K4
Stenbrohult • Sweden 125 F11
Stendal • Germany 8 G4
Stenhouse Bay • SA, Australia 34 G7
Stenó Andikíthiron • Greece 15 E8
Stenó Elafónissou • Greece 15 D7
Stenungsund • Sweden 125 F2
Stephens, Mt • Antarctica 54 (1) A1
Stephenville • TX, United States 154 J1
Stephenville • NF, Canada 156 D3
Sterkfontein **Heritage C** • South Africa 85 [118]
Sterkrade (Oberhausen) • Germany 111 B1
Sterkstroom • South Africa 134 C4
Sterling • VA, United States 44 G6
Sterling • CO, United States 46 D2
Sterling • IL, United States 46 K2
Sterling Heights • MI, United States 44 D4
Stern **Ski** • Italy 100 [231]
Stern • Italy 120 B2
Sternberk • Czech Rep. 13 G8
Stérnes **Beach** • Crete, Greece 97 [212]
Sterrenberg, Burg • Germany 112 E2
Sterzing • Italy 120 B1
Stes Maries-de-la-Mer • France 10 J10
Stessor Peak • Antarctica 54 (1) II3
Stetten **Castle** • Germany 113 [93]
Stettin • Poland 13 D4
Stettiner Haff • Germany/Poland 8 J3
Steubenville • OH, United States 44 E5
Stevenage • United Kingdom 7 L10
Stevens Pass **Ski** • WA, United States 149 [49]
Stevens Pass • WA, United States 42 E3
Stevens Point • WI, United States 43 L4
Stewart • BC, Canada 49 P4
Stewart I. • New Zealand 35 A8
Stewart Valley • SA, Canada 42 L1
Steynsburg • South Africa 134 C4
Steyr • Austria 13 D9
Steyr [Riv] • Austria 9 J9
Steytlerville • South Africa 134 C7
Stikine • BC, Canada 38 E5
Stilfs • Italy 121 E3
Stilída • Greece 15 D5
Still Bay • South Africa 134 C6
Still River • OT, Canada 44 E3
Stillwater • MN, United States 43 J4
Stillwater • OK, United States 46 G4
Stillwater Range • NV, United States 42 F6
Stip • F.Y.R. of Macedonia 14 J8
Stirling • United Kingdom 104 B3
Stirlingshire • United Kingdom 104 B3
Stjernøya • Norway 16 L1
Stjørdal • Norway 16 F5
Stobi • F.Y.R. of Macedonia 15 C2
Stockerau • Austria 13 F9
Stockholm **Heritage C** • Sweden 86 [7]
Stockholm **Beach** • Sweden 97 [22]
Stockholm • Sweden 125 D4
Stockholm [Adm] • Sweden 125 D4
Stockport • United Kingdom 7 J8
Stockton • KS, United States 46 F3
Stockton • CA, United States 152 C3
Stockton Lake • MO, United States 46 I4
Stockton-on-Tees • United Kingdom 7 K7
Stogovo • F.Y.R. of Macedonia 14 H8
Stoke-on-Trent • United Kingdom 7 J8
Stoke-sub-Hamdon Priory • United Kingdom 104 F3
Stokksund • Norway 16 F4
Stolberg • Germany 9 B6
Stolbovoy, Ostrov • Russian Fed. 27 M2
Stolpen **Castle** • Germany 113 [193]
Stolzenfels **Castle** • Germany 113 [66]
Stolzenfels, Schloss • Germany 112 E1
Stoneham **Ski** • QU, Canada 149 [45]
Stonehaven • United Kingdom 6 J5
Stonehenge **Heritage C** • United Kingdom 86 [22]
Stonehenge • United Kingdom 104 F3
Stones River Nat. Battlefield & Cemetery **Park N** • TN, United States 151 [226]
Stoney Creek • OT, Canada 44 F4
Stonington I. • Antarctica 81 A10
Stony Mtn • MN, Canada 43 H1
Stony Point • NY, United States 44 G4
Stony Rapids • SA, Canada 38 J5
Stora Le • Norway/Sweden 124 B4
Stora Lulevatten • Sweden 16 J3
Stora Sjöfallet Nat. Park **Park N** • Sweden 89 [19]
Storavan • Sweden 16 J4
Stord • Norway 124 C5
Stordal • Norway 124 C2
Store • Norway 124 C3
Store Bælt • Denmark 125 F14
Store Heddinge • Denmark 125 F15
Store Mosse Nat. Park **Park N** • Sweden 89 [27]
Store Mosse Nat. Park • Sweden 125 F7
Støren • Norway 16 F5
Størfjorden • Norway 124 C2
Storis Passage • NU, Canada 38 K3
Storkerson Bay • NT, Canada 38 F2
Storlien • Sweden 16 G5
Storm Lake • IA, United States 43 I5
Stornoway • United Kingdom 6 F3
Storsjøen • Norway 124 B2
Storsjön • Sweden 16 H5
Storsteinfjellet • Norway 16 I2
Storstrøm • Denmark 125 F14
Storuman • Sweden 16 I4
Storuman [Lake] • Sweden 16 I4
Storvreta • Sweden 125 D2
Storybook Land • NJ, United States 153 D10
Stöttingfjället • Sweden 16 I4
Stoughton • SA, Canada 43 E2
Stour • United Kingdom 5 D2
Stour • United Kingdom 5 E3
Stour • United Kingdom 104 F3
Stourbridge • United Kingdom 7 J9
Stourhead • United Kingdom 104 F3
Stourport • United Kingdom 104 D1
Stow-on-the-Wold • United Kingdom 104 D4
Stowbtsy • Belarus 16 N10
Stowe **Ski** • VT, United States 149 [214]
Strà • Italy 121 E7
Stradbally • Ireland 108 B3
Straits of Florida • N. America 49 C5
Strakonice • Czech Rep. 128 B3
Straldzha • Bulgaria 15 H1
Stralsund • Germany 8 I2
Stranda • Norway 124 C2
Strangford Lough • United Kingdom 7 G7
Strängnas • Sweden 125 D3
Strångsjö • Sweden 125 D3
Stranraer • United Kingdom 7 H7
Strasbourg • France 10 M5
Strasbourg **Heritage C** • France 86 [59]
Strasburg • ND, United States 43 F3
Strasburg • PA, United States 153 D10
Strassburg • France 90 A8
Stratford • New Zealand 145 F3
Stratford • CT, United States 44 I5
Stratford • OT, Canada 44 E4
Stratford • TX, United States 46 D4
Stratford-upon-Avon • United Kingdom 104 D2
Strath Earn • United Kingdom 104 B1
Strathcona Prov. Park • BC, Canada 155 C3
Strathgordon • TS, Australia 34 I8
Strathmore • United Kingdom 104 B2
Strathroy • OT, Canada 44 E4
Stratton **Ski** • VT, United States 149 [207]
Stratton • VT, United States 153 D3
Straubing • Germany 9 H8
Straumsjøen • Norway 16 H2
Strausberg • Germany 8 I4
Streaky Bay • SA, Australia 34 F6
Streaky Bay [Gulf] • SA, Australia 34 F6
Streator • IL, United States 46 K2
Streeter • ND, United States 43 G3
Strehaia • Romania 14 K5
Strelitza Coast • South Africa 134 B5
Strelka • Russian Fed. 26 P6
Stresa • Italy 121 E2
Strete Gate **Beach** • United Kingdom 101 [123]
Strezhevoy • Russian Fed. 26 M5
Strib • Denmark 125 F9
Strickland • Papua New Guinea 32 (1) F4
Strigno • Italy 120 B3
Strimónas • Greece 15 E3
Strimonikós Kolpos • Greece 15 E3
Strjama • Bulgaria 15 F1
Strómboli, I. • Italy 120 D2
Stromness • United Kingdom 6 I3
Strömsnäsbruk • Sweden 125 F11
Strömstad • Sweden 125 F2
Strömsund • Sweden 16 H5
Strongsville • OH, United States 44 E5
Stronsay • United Kingdom 6 J2
Stroud • United Kingdom 104 D3
Stroud • OK, United States 46 G5
Stroudsburg • PA, United States 153 D6
Struer **Beach** • Denmark 96 [50]
Struer • Denmark 125 F9
Struga • F.Y.R. of Macedonia 15 B2
Struisbaai • South Africa 134 C6
Struma • Bulgaria 14 K8
Strumica • F.Y.R. of Macedonia 14 J8
Struthers • OH, United States 44 E5
Stryn • Norway 124 C2
Strynsvatn • Norway 124 C2
Stryy • Ukraine 13 M8
Stryy [Riv] • Ukraine 13 M8
Strzelin • Poland 13 G7
Stuart Mem. • NT, Australia 145 D2
Stuart Mtns • New Zealand 145 G1
Stubbekøbing • Denmark 125 F14
Stubbenkammer • Germany 8 I2
Stubbs • St Vincent & Gren. 161 Q
Stuben • Austria 119 H5
Stubice • Poland 13 D5
Studen • Switzerland 119 G2
Studenica **Heritage C** • F.R. of Yugoslavia 86 [189]
Studley Royal Park **Heritage C** • United Kingdom 86 [19]
Study Butte • TX, United States 47 C3
Stung Treng • Cambodia 31 D4
Sturgeon Bay • WI, United States 44 B3
Sturgeon Falls • OT, Canada 155 B1
Sturgeon Lake • OT, Canada 43 K2
Sturgis • SD, United States 43 E4
Sturgis • MI, United States 44 C5
Sturt Creek • NT/WA, Australia 34 E3
Sturt Desert • QL/SA, Australia 34 H5
Sturt Nat. Park • NS, Australia 34 H5
Sturup [Apt] • Sweden 125 F11
Stuttgart • Germany 112 D6
Stuttgart • AR, United States 46 J5
Stykkishólmur • Iceland 16 (1) B2

Styr

Styr • Ukraine..................................17 D4
Styria • Austria...............................119 F4
Su Nuraxi • Sardinia, Italy..................120 C4
Su Nuraxi di Barúmini **Heritage C** •
Sardinia, Italy........................86 [159]
Suakin • Sudan................................21 G4
Suakin Archipelago • Sudan..............21 G4
Suavanao • Solomon Is............35 (1) F2
Subang • Java, Indonesia..................143 J2
Subbético • Spain.............................11 I6
Sublette • KS, United States..............46 E4
Submeseta •
Castilla i León, Spain..................11 F2
Submeseta •
Castilla-La Mancha, Spain...........11 H5
Subotica • F.R. of Yugoslavia..............14 G3
Suceava • Romania...........................14 N2
Sucia, Bahía • Puerto Rico..............159 H3
Suck • Ireland..................................108 C4
Suckling • Papua New Guinea...35 (1) D2
Sucre • Bolivia..................................52 C2
Sucre **Heritage C** • Bolivia.............84 [62]
Sud, Canal du • Haiti.......................159 G5
Sud, Costa del •
Sardinia, Italy...............................120 C3
Sud Ouest, Point • Mauritius.............132 J3
Sudama • Japan...............................140 C1
SUDAN • Africa.................................19 H4
Sudan [Region] • Africa....................22 F2
Sudbury • OT, Canada......................39 O7
Sudd, As • Sudan..............................23 E2
Sude • Germany.................................8 G3
Sudeten • Poland/Czech Rep.............13 F7
Sudety • Poland/Czech Rep...............13 F7
Sudirman, Pegunungan •
Indonesia................................32 (1) E3
Sudo • Singapore............................141 H3
Sue • Sudan.....................................23 D2
Sueca • Spain...................................11 K5
Sueca **Beach** • Spain....................96 [119]
Suez • Egypt....................................131 F2
Suez Canal • Egypt...........................131 F2
Suez, Gulf of • Egypt.......................131 F4
Suffolk • United Kingdom...................7 N9
Suffolk • VA, United States..............153 D11
Sugar Bowl **Ski** •
CA, United States....................149 [59]
Sugar Loaf **Ski** •
MI, United States....................149 [144]
Sugar Mtn **Ski** •
NC, United States....................149 [162]
Sugarbush **Ski** •
VT, United States....................149 [212]
Sugarbush Hill •
WI, United States...........................43 L4
Sugarloaf Mtn •
ME, United States...........................44 J3
Sugarloaf USA **Ski** •
ME, United States....................149 [230]
Sugla Gölü • Turkey........................123 F2
Sugoy • Russian Fed..........................27 O4
Suhar • Oman...................................18 G5
Suheli I. • India...............................138 D9
Suhl • Germany...................................9 F6
Suide • China....................................29 D3
Suihua • China..................................29 H1
Suippe • France..................................5 H5
Suippes • France.................................5 H5
Suir • Ireland......................................7 E9
Suitland • MD, United States..............44 G6
Suizhong • China................................29 G2
Sukabumi • Java, Indonesia.............143 J1
Sukadana • Indonesia........................32 D3
Sukaraja • Indonesia.........................32 E3
Sukhona • Russian Fed.......................18 E5
Sukhothai **Heritage N** • Thailand...83 [133]
Sukhothai **Heritage C** • Thailand...85 [200]
Sukhothai • Thailand........................142 B4
Suki • Sudan......................................21 F5
Sukkur • Pakistan...............................28 A3
Sukon • Indonesia.........................32 (1) B3
Sukses • Namibia...............................24 B4
Sukumo • Japan................................30 G8
Sukur **Heritage C** • Nigeria.........85 [113]
Sula • Norway..................................124 C3
Sula, Kepulauan • Indonesia...........143 F3
Sulaiman Range • Pakistan...........32 (1) A3
Sulawesi • Indonesia....................32 (1) A3
Sulayyil, As • Saudi Arabia................18 E5
Sule • Egypt.....................................21 F3
Suldalsvatn • Norway......................124 C6
Sulina • Italy...................................121 E3
Sulechów • Poland...........................13 E5
Suleskar • Norway...........................124 C6
Sulima • Sierra Leone........................22 B3
Sulina • Romania.............................128 E2
Sulingen • Germany............................5 L2
Sulitjelma • Norway...........................16 H3
Sulitjelma [Mtn] • Norway.................16 I3
Sullana • Peru...................................51 A4
Sullivan • MO, United States..............46 J3
Sulmona • Italy................................121 F2
Sulphur • OK, United States..............46 G5
Sulphur • LA, United States..............47 H2
Sulphur • AR/TX, United States........154 J2
Sulphur Springs •
TX, United States.........................154 J2
Sultan Dağları • Turkey...................15 M5
Sultanhanı • Turkey........................123 G1
Sultanpur • India.............................137 C8
Sulu Archipelago • Philippines...........31 G5
Sulu Sea • Philippines.......................31 F5
Sülüklü • Turkey...............................15 N5
Sulz am Neckar • Germany..............112 D6
Sulzbach-Rosenberg • Germany..........9 G7
Sulzberger Bay • Antarctica.........54 (1) AA2
Sumadija • F.R. of Yugoslavia............14 H5
Sumalata • Indonesia........................32 C3
Sumatera • Indonesia.......................143 G4
Sumatera Barat • Indonesia............143 G4
Sumatera Utara • Indonesia............143 G4
Sumatra • Indonesia.........................32 C3
Sumava • Czech Rep........................128 B3
Sumayh, As • Sudan..........................23 D2
Sumba • Indonesia......................32 (1) A4
Sumbawa • Indonesia...................32 (1) A4
Sumbawa Besar • Indonesia.........32 (1) A4
Sumbawanga • Tanzania.................130 B3
Sumbe • Angola................................23 A6
Sumbing, Gunung •
Java, Indonesia.............................143 J7
Sumbu • Zambia...............................23 E5
Sumbu Nat. Park **Park** • Zambia...133 [102]
Sumburgh • United Kingdom......106 A3
Sumburgh Head • United Kingdom.......6 K2
Sumenep • Indonesia......................143 J4
Summer Lake • OR, United States......42 E5
Summer Lake • OR, United States......42 E5
Summerland • BC, Canada................42 F2
Summerside • PE, Canada..............156 D7
Suzhou • China................................139 C2
Summersville •
WV, United States...........................44 E6
Summerville • GA, United States.......48 E3
Summerville • SC, United States........48 G4
Summit Lake • BC, Canada................38 G5
Summer Lake • NM, United States......46 C5
Sumperk • Czech Rep.......................13 F8
Sumqayıt • Azerbaijan.......................18 E1
Sumter • SC, United States................48 G4
Sumy • Ukraine.................................17 E4
Sun City • South Africa....................134 A1
Sun City • BC, United States..............45 D5
Sun City • UT, United States..............45 D5
Sun Kosi • Nepal...............................28 E3
Sun Peaks **Ski** • BC, Canada.......149 [4]
Sun Prairie • WI, United States..........43 L5
Sun Valley **Ski** •
ID, United States.......................149 [81]
Sun Valley • ID, United States..........152 B4
Sun Yat-sen's residence • China......139 B2

Sunak, gora • Kazakstan....................26 L8
Sunan • D.P.R. of Korea......................30 C5
Sunbury • VI, Australia......................34 H7
Sunbury • PA, United States..............44 G5
Sunch'on • Rep. of Korea...................30 D7
Sunchales • Argentina.......................52 D5
Sunda, Selat • Java, Indonesia.........143 J1
Sunda Strait • Indonesia....................32 D4
Sundance • WY, United States............43 D4
Sundarbans • Bangladesh/India.........28 E4
Sundarbans **Heritage N** •
Bangladesh.............................83 [118]
Sundarbans Nat. Park **Heritage N** •
India.......................................83 [117]
Sunday River **Ski** •
ME, United States....................149 [229]
Sunde • Norway..............................124 C5
Sunderland • United Kingdom.............7 K7
Sunderland Sound • New Zealand....145 G1
Sundern • Germany............................5 K3
Sundern • Germany.............................9 D5
Sündiken Dağları • Turkey................15 L4
Sundown **Mtn Ski** •
IA, United States.....................149 [125]
Sundsli • Norway.............................124 C6
Sundsvall • Sweden..........................16 I5
Sundybyberg • Sweden.....................125 D4
Sunflower, Mt •
KS, United States............................46 E3
Sungai Petani • Malaysia...................31 C5
Sungaigunting • Indonesia................32 C2
Sunndalsøra • Norway.....................124 C2
Sunne • Sweden................................16 G7
Sunnerbo • Sweden........................125 F7
Sunny Beach • Bulgaria...................128 E3
Sunnyside • WA, United States..........42 E3
Sunnyvale • CA, United States..........45 A3
Sunrise **Ski** •
AZ, United States....................149 [96]
Sunset Beach •
HI, United States.....................154 G1
Sunset Crater Volcano Nat. Mon.
Park N • AZ, United States.....150 [105]
Sunset Crater Volcano Nat. Mon. •
AZ, United States.....................153 E1
Sunshine Coast • QL, Australia........144 B6
Sunshine Village **Ski** •
AL, United States....................149 [13]
Suntar • Russian Fed..........................27 I4
Suntar Khayata, Khrebet •
Russian Fed..................................27 M4
Sunyani • Ghana...............................22 D3
Suolahti • Finland............................125 E2
Suomenlinna • Finland....................125 E4
Suomi • OT, Canada..........................43 L2
Suomussalmi • Finland......................16 O4
Suonenjoki • Finland........................16 N5
Suoyarvi • Russian Fed......................17 E2
Sup'ung-Chosuji • China...................30 C4
Super-Sauze • France.......................115 H2
Super-St-Bernard • Switzerland........119 G6
Superbagnères • France...................115 K1
Superdévoluy **Ski** • France.......100 [65]
Superior • WI, United States..............43 J3
Superior • AZ, United States..............45 G5
Superior • NE, United States..............46 F2
Superior, Lake •
Canada/United States....................41 I2
Suphan Buri • Thailand....................142 C4
Supiori • Indonesia......................32 (1) E3
Sur • Oman......................................18 G5
Sur • Lebanon................................135 A1
Sur, Point • CA, United States............45 B3
Surabaya • Java, Indonesia..............143 J8
Surahammar • Sweden....................125 D1
Surak • Iran......................................18 G4
Surakarta • Java, Indonesia.............143 J7
Surat • India.....................................28 C4
Surat • QL, Australia........................144 B5
Surat Thani • Thailand.....................142 B5
Suratgarh • India.............................137 C2
Surduc • Romania...........................13 M10
Süre • Luxembourg........................109 D20
Surfers Paradise •
QL, Australia................................144 B6
Surgidero de Batabano • Cuba.......158 D2
Surgut • Russian Fed..........................26 L5
Surgutikha • Russian Fed...................26 O5
Surhob • Asia...................................18 J2
Surigao • Philippines.........................31 H5
Surin **Beach** •
Ko Phuket, Thailand...................142 E1
Surin, Ko • Thailand........................142 A3
SURINAME • S. America.....................51 F3
Surinam • Mauritius........................132 A3
Surinam Quarters • Jamaica...........159 F3
Surrey • United Kingdom....................7 J9
Surrey • Jamaica.............................159 F4
Surt • Libya......................................21 C1
Surtsey • Iceland.........................16 (1) C1
Surud Ad • Somalia...........................25 F9
Suruga-wan • Japan........................140 C3
Susa • Italy......................................128 D3
Susac • Croatia................................128 D3
Susaki • Japan.................................30 G8
Susanville • CA, United States..........152 C1
Susice • Czech Rep..........................128 B3
Suso **Heritage C** • Spain.............86 [92]
Susoh • Indonesia............................143 G1
Susquehanna • United States..........153 D6
Sussex • United Kingdom................106 E3
Susuman • Russian Fed......................27 O4
Susurluk • Turkey............................122 D3
Sü
ltçüler • Turkey...........................123 F2
Sutherland • South Africa................134 C2
Sutherlin • OR, United States............42 D5
Sutjeska Nat. Park **Park N** •
Bosnia-Herz...............................89 [114]
Sutlej • India/Pakistan.......................28 B2
Sutter Creek •
CA, United States............................45 B2
Sutton on Sea **Beach** •
United Kingdom.......................101 [39]
Suursaari • Russian Fed...................16 N6
Suva • Fiji Is.................................35 (2) D2
Suva Planina •
F.R. of Yugoslavia.........................17 F4
Suvadiva Atoll • Maldives...............138 F3
Suwa • Japan...................................30 J6
Suwałki • Poland..............................13 I3
Suwannee • FL, United States............49 B3
Suwannee [Riv] •
FL/GA, United States.................154 H3
Suwarow-jima • Japan.................140 A11
Suweis, El • Egypt...........................131 F2
Suwon • Rep. of Korea......................30 D6
Suzdal **Heritage C** •
Russian Fed..............................86 [247]
Suzdal' • Russian Fed......................125 [174]
Suzhou **Heritage C** • China........85 [174]
Suzhou • China...............................139 C2
Suzu • Japan....................................30 J3
Suzu-misaki • Japan.........................30 I6
Suzu Han • Turkey..........................123 F1
Svalbard • Arctic Ocean....................54 N2
Svalyava • Ukraine.........................13 M9
Svaneti, Upper **Heritage C** •
Georgia.......................................86 [243]
Svarstad • Norway..........................124 B3
Svärtinge • Sweden........................125 D3
Svartisen • Norway............................16 H3
Svatovy Nos, mys • Russian Fed......13 O2
Svedala • Sweden............................16 H5
Sveg • Sweden..................................16 H5
Svelvik • Norway............................124 B2
Svendborg **Beach** • Denmark.....96 [44]
Svendborg • Denmark....................125 F14
Svene • Norway..............................124 B3
Svenljunga • Sweden......................125 E6
Sverdrup Is. • NU, Canada................36 H2

Sveshtari **Heritage C** • Bulgaria...86 [200]
Svetac • Croatia..............................128 D3
Svetla • Russian Fed..........................27 M7
Svetlograd • Russian Fed...................13 J3
Svetly • Russian Fed..........................27 K6
Svetlyy • Russian Fed........................18 G3
Sviahnúkar • Iceland....................16 (1) E2
Sviatoy Nos, mys • Russian Fed........17 F1
Svihov • Czech Rep.........................128 B3
Svilaja • Croatia..............................128 D3
Svilengrad • Bulgaria........................14 N8
Svinecea Mare, Virful • Romania.......14 J5
Svir • Russian Fed............................17 E2
Svishtov • Bulgaria.........................128 E1
Svitava • Czech Rep........................13 F8
Svitavy • Czech Rep........................13 F8
Svobodnyy • Russian Fed..................27 K6
Svolvær • Norway............................16 H2
Svrljig • F.R. of Yugoslavia................14 J6
Swain **Ski** • NY, United States....149 [186]
Swain • NY, United States...............153 D11
Swain Reefs • QL, Australia............144 B4
Swainsboro • GA, United States.........48 F4
Swakopmund • Namibia...................24 A4
Swan Hill • VI, Australia.................144 C11
Swan Is • Honduras.......................160 A11
Swanage **Beach** • United Kingdom.101 [96]
Swanage • United Kingdom.............104 F6
Swansea • United Kingdom...............7 I10
Swanson Reservoir •
NE, United States...........................46 E2
Swanton • VT, United States..............44 I3
Swartberg Pass • South Africa.........134 C7
Swartkrans **Heritage C** •
South Africa............................85 [118]
SWAZILAND • Africa..........................24 E5
SWEDEN • Europe.............................16
Swedish Lakeland • Sweden............125 F3
Sweet Home • OR, United States........42 D4
Sweetwater • WY, United States........38 J8
Sweetwater • TX, United States........47 D1
Sweetwater • TN, United States........48 E2
Swellendam • South Africa..............134 C6
Swidnica • Poland............................13 F7
Swidnik • Poland..............................13 E4
Swidwin • Poland.............................13 E4
Swiebodzin • Poland........................13 E5
Swiecie • Poland...............................13 I4
Swietokrzyski Nat. Park •
Poland...128 C2
Swietokrzyskie, Gory • Poland.........13 K7
Swift Current • SA, Canada................38 J6
Swilly, Lough • Ireland.......................7 E6
Swinburne, Cape • NU, Canada.........38 L2
Swindon • United Kingdom...............7 K10
Swinemünde • Poland....................13 D4
Swinoujscie • Poland......................13 D4
Swiss Nat. Park **Park N** •
Switzerland..............................89 [81]
Swiss Nat. Park • Switzerland.........119 G4
Swiss Valley **Ski** •
MI, United States....................149 [154]
SWITZERLAND • Europe......................4 L7
Swords • Ireland.............................108 B2
Sybaris • Italy...................................12 K9
Syburg (Dortmund) • Germany.......111 B2
Sydalsö **Beach** • Denmark..........96 [37]
Sydfalster **Beach** • Denmark.......96 [37]
Sydlangeland **Beach** • Denmark..96 [44]
Sydney • NS, Australia....................144 C2
Sydney • MT, United States...............43 D3
Sydney • NS, Canada......................156 D8
Sydney Mines • NS, Canada.............156 D8
Sydthy **Beach** • Denmark...........96 [49]
Sykkylven • Norway........................124 C2
Syktyvkar • Russian Fed...................17 I2
Sylacauga • AL, United States...........48 D4
Sylhet • Bangladesh.........................28 F4
Sylling • Norway.............................124 B1
Sylt • Germany...................................8 D2
Sylva • NC, United States..................48 F3
Sylvan **Ski** • MI, United States...149 [141]
Sylvania • OH, United States.............44 D5
Sylvania • GA, United States.............48 G4
Sylvensteinsee • Germany...............112 F7
Sylvester • GA, United States............48 F5
Symonds Yat • United Kingdom........104 D3
Syowa [Base] • Antarctica............54 (1) J3
Syr Darya • Kazakstan.......................26 K9
Syracuse • Sicily, Italy....................120 D4
Syracuse • KS, United States............46 E4
Syracuse • NY, United States..........153 D5
SYRIA • Asia.....................................18 D3
Syrian Desert • Asia..........................18 D3
Sytkya • Bulgaria.............................14 K8
Syvde • Norway..............................124 C1
Syzran • Russian Fed.........................17 H4
Szamotuły • Poland...........................13 F5
Szarvas • Hungary...........................13 J11
Szczawnica • Poland.......................128 C4
Szczecin • Poland..............................13 D4
Szczecinek • Poland..........................13 E4
Szczytno • Poland.............................13 J4
Székesfehérvár • Hungary..............13 H11
Szeksztard • Hungary......................13 H11
Szentendre • Hungary.....................13 J10
Szentes • Hungary...........................13 J11
Szeskie Wzgórza • Poland................13 L3
Szigetvár • Hungary........................13 G11
Szolnok • Hungary..........................13 J10
Szombathely • Hungary...................13 F10
Szprotawa • Poland.........................13 E6
Szubin • Poland..................................13 G4

T'aech'on • D.P.R. of Korea................30 C5
T'elavi • Georgia..............................17 H6
Ta'if, At • Saudi Arabia......................18 D5
Ta'izz • Yemen.................................18 D7
Tab • Hungary.................................13 G11
Tabar • Papua New Guinea..........35 (1) E1
Tabarka • Tunisia...........................131 E1
Tabasco • Mexico.............................37 C4
Tabasco y Campeche, Llanos de •
Mexico...37 C4
Tabasqueño • Mexico.....................157 H3
Tabatama • Mexico...........................45 G6
Tabelbala • Algeria...........................20 E3
Taber • AL, Canada..........................42 I2
Tabērg • Sweden.............................16 G5
Tablas • Niger..................................20 F6
Tablas • Philippines..........................31 G4
Table Bay • South Africa.................134 C5
Table Cape • New Zealand...............35 G4
Table Mtn • WA, United States..........34 E5
Tabletop, Mt • South Africa............132 H4
Talca • Chile...................................52 B6
Talcahuano • Chile...........................52 B6
Table, Pointe de la • Réunion.........132 H4
Table Rock Lake •
MO, United States...........................46 A2
Tábor • Czech Rep..........................128 B4
Tábor, Mount • Israel.....................135 A2
Tabou • Côte d'Ivoire.......................22 C4
Tabqa • Syria...................................18 D3
Tabriz • Iran...................................130 B1
Tabuaeran • Kiribati..........................33 L5
Tabuk • Saudi Arabia........................18 C4
Tabwemasana • Vanuatu...........35 (2) B2
Täby • Sweden................................125 D3
Tacheng • China..............................28 G1
Tachikawa • Japan..........................140 C1
Tachov • Czech Rep........................128 B3
Tacloban • Philippines.......................31 G4
Tacna • Peru...................................163 B4
Tacna • AZ, United States..................45 F6
Tacoma • WA, United States............152 B1

Tacoronte **Beach** •
Tenerife, Canary Is....................96 [109]
Tacoronte •
Tenerife, Canary Is....................116 E1
Tacuarembó • Uruguay.....................52 E5
Tademaït, Plateau du • Algeria.........20 F3
Tadjourah • Djibouti........................21 H5
Tadmur • Syria................................18 C3
Tadmur **Heritage C** • Syria.........86 [277]
Tadrart Acacus **Heritage C** •
Libya..85 [104]
Taebaek-Sanmaek •
D.P.R. of Korea/Rep. of Korea......30 E6
Taegu • Rep. of Korea......................30 E7
Taehan-Haehyop • Rep. of Korea.....29 H4
Taehuksan • Rep. of Korea...............30 C7
Taejon • Rep. of Korea......................30 D6
Tafahi • Tonga.............................35 (2) F2
Tafassasset • Algeria........................20 G4
Tafers • Switzerland........................119 G2
Taff • United Kingdom....................104 B2
Tafi Viejo • Argentina.......................52 C4
Tafilalt • Morocco...........................131 D6
Tafiré • Côte d'Ivoire.......................22 C3
Tafraoute • Morocco.......................131 D5
Taftan, Kuh-e • Iran........................18 H4
Taftan • Iran....................................18 H4
Taga Dzong • Bhutan.......................28 E3
Taganrog • Russian Fed....................17 F5
Tagant • Mauritania.........................20 D5
Tagbilaran • Philippines....................31 G5
Taggia **Beach** • Italy..................96 [140]
Tággia • Italy..................................121 F2
Tagliacozzo • Italy..........................121 F2
Tagliamento • Italy.........................128 C2
Tagomago, I. de • Ibiza, Spain.......117 G2
Tagouné • Morocco........................20 D3
Taguersimet • Western Sahara.........20 B4
Taguish Lake • YT, Canada...............38 D4
Tagus • Portugal/Spain...................116 A3
Tahan, Gunong • Malaysia...............20 A2
Tahat • Algeria................................20 G4
Tahcob • Mexico............................157 H1
Tahcok • Mexico.............................157 H1
Tahiti • French Polynesia.................33 M7
Tahlequah • OK, United States..........46 H5
Tahoe City • CA, United States..........45 B2
Tahoe, Lake •
CA/NV, United States..................152 C3
Tahoka • TX, United States...............46 E6
Taholah • WA, United States............42 C3
Tahoua • Niger...............................20 G6
Tahuna • Indonesia....................32 (1) C2
Tahu • China...................................139 C1
Tai Lam Country Park •
Hong Kong, China....................139 B5
Tai Mo Shan • Hong Kong, China......139 B5
Tai Mo Shan Country Park •
Hong Kong, China....................139 B5
Tai O • Hong Kong, China................139 B5
Taï, Parc nat. de **Heritage N** •
Côte d'Ivoire.............................83 [85]
Taï, Parc nat. de **Park N** •
Côte d'Ivoire.............................133 [18]
Tai Pang • Hong Kong, China..........139 B6
Tai Po Kau Country Park •
Hong Kong, China....................139 B6
Tai Shan **Heritage N** • China....83 [129]
Tai Shan **Heritage C** • China.....85 [172]
Tai Shan • China............................139 A4
Tai Tam Country Park •
Hong Kong, China....................139 B6
Taibai Shan • China.........................11 I6
Taicang • China..............................139 C2
Taibilla, Sierra de • Spain................11 I6
Taichung • Taiwan.........................139 D2
Taigetos, Oros • Greece.................15 D6
Taihape • New Zealand...................145 G4
Taimba • Russian Fed......................26 O5
Tainan • Taiwan.............................139 D2
Taipa • Macau, China......................139 B1
Taipa Village • Macau, China...........139 B1
Taiping • Malaysia...........................29 G6
Taiping • China...............................32 G2
Taiping Ling • China.........................29 G1
Taisetsu • Japan..............................30 L3
Taitao, Península de • Chile..............53 B5
Taitung • Taiwan...........................139 D2
Taivalkoski • Finland........................16 O4
Taiwan [Riv] • China.........................29 G6
TAIWAN • Asia................................139
Taiyuan • China..............................29 E3
Taizhou • China..............................139 C1
Taj Mahal **Heritage C** • India....85 [137]
TAJIKISTAN • Asia............................26 L10
Tajima • Japan..................................30 L10
Tajo • Spain....................................11 D5
Tajrish • Iran...................................18 F2
Tajumulco, Volcán • Guatemala........37 C4
Tajura • Libya..................................21 B1
Tak • Thailand...............................142 B4
Takahe, Mt • Antarctica.............54 (1) DD2
Takamatsu • Japan..........................30 H7
Takaoka • Japan..............................30 I6
Takapuna • New Zealand.................35 E3
Takara-jima • Japan..........................30 A9
Takarazuka Family Land • Japan.....140 B1
Takasago • Japan..............................30 J6
Takasaki • Japan..............................30 J6
Take Lake • BC, Canada....................38 F5
Take-shima • Japan..........................30 D6
Takeo • Cambodia..........................141 E4
Takern • Sweden.............................125 F3
Takhti-i-Bakhi **Heritage C** •
Pakistan.....................................85 [130]
Takijuq Lake • NU, Canada.............143 G1
Takingue • Indonesia......................143 G1
Takitimu Mtns • New Zealand.........145 G4
Takla Makan Shamo • China............26 N10
Takotna • AK, United States............139 A1
Takum • Nigeria...............................22 G3
Talaisigan • Indonesia......................32 F2
Talak • Niger...................................20 G6
Talara **Beach** • United Kingdom..101 [214]
Talaion • Crete, Greece...................123 E2
Talalero • Nigeria.............................22 F2
Talamanca, Cordillera de **Heritage N** •
Costa Rica/Panama......................82 [26]
Talara • Peru...................................51 A4
Talasea • Papua New Guinea.......35 (1) D2
Talata Mafara • Nigeria.....................20 F6
Talaud, Kepulauan • Indonesia...32 (1) C2
Talavera de la Reina • Spain............11 G5
Talbot • WA, United States...............34 E5
Talbotton • GA, United States...........48 E4
Talca • Chile...................................52 B6
Talcy [Château] • France.................114 D2
Taldygorghan • Kazakstan...............26 M9
Talence • France..............................10 E9
Talgar • Kazakstan.........................26 M9
Talguppa • Indonesia..................32 (1) B3
Talihina • OK, United States.............46 H5
Taljim Beach •
Ko Samui, Thailand...................142 D2
Talisakan • Indonesia.......................32 F2
Talish Mtns • Azerbaijan..................18 E2
Taliskan **Ski** • OT, Canada.........149 [25]
Talladega • AL, United States............48 D4
Talladega Nat. Preserve **Park N** •
KS, United States.....................151 [168]
Tallahassee • FL, United States........154 H2
Tallinn **Heritage C** • Estonia.......86 [207]
Tallinn • Estonia...............................16 M7
Tallulah • LA, United States..............47 I1

Tacoronte **Beach** •
Talmest • Morocco..........................20 D2
Talo • Ethiopia.................................23 H7
Talogan • Afghanistan.......................28 A1
Taloyoak • NU, Canada.....................38 M3
Taloyoak **Beach** • Goa, India......137 B2
Taltal • Chile...................................51 B4
Tam • France...................................10 G10
Tama • Japan..................................28 D3
Tama-gawa • Japan.......................140 C1
Tamale • Ghana................................22 D3
Taman Ayun Temple •
Bali, Indonesia...........................143 H4
Taman Negara Nat. Park •
Malaysia....................................141 D3
Tamanrasset • Algeria......................20 G4
Tamanrasset [Riv] • Algeria..............20 F4
Tamaqua • PA, United States...........44 G5
Tamar • United Kingdom................104 F5
Tamarac • FL, United States..............49 C4
Tamarin • Mauritius.........................132 J3
Tamarin **Beach** • Mauritius........132 J3
Tamarin Falls • Mauritius................132 J3
Tamarinda • Minorca, Spain...........117 F3
Tamarugal, Pampa del • Chile..........52 C2
Tamasag-Bulak • Mongolia.............29 F1
Tamási • Hungary...........................14 F3
Tamatave • Madagascar..................24 H3
Tamaulipas • Mexico........................37 B3
Tamaulipas, Sierra de • Mexico......157 G2
Tamazunchale • Mexico...................37 C2
Tambacounda • Senegal..................22 B2
Tambelan, Kepulauan • Indonesia..143 F2
Tambo • QL, Australia....................144 B5
Tambo • Peru.................................163 B4
Tambo Colorado • Peru..................163 B1
Tambora, Gunung • Indonesia....32 (1) A4
Tambov • Russian Fed......................17 G4
Tambre • Spain...............................11 C3
Tambunan • Malaysia.......................31 F5
Tambura • Sudan.............................23 D2
Tamchaket • Mauritania..................20 C5
Tame • Colombia.............................51 C2
Tâmega • Portugal..........................11 C3
Tamegroute • Morocco..................131 D6
Tamel Aike • Argentina....................53 B5
Tamenghest • Algeria.......................20 G4
Tamerza • Tunisia...........................131 E3
Tamga, Mts • Niger.........................20 G5
Tamgue, Massif du • Guinea............22 B2
Tamiahua, Laguna de • Mexico.......157 G2
Tamil Nadu • India.......................138 D11
Tamilngan, Danau •
Bali, Indonesia...........................143 H2
Tammerfors • Finland....................125 E2
Tammisaari • Finland.....................125 E4
Tämnaren • Sweden........................125 C3
Tampa • FL, United States...............154 H5
Tampa Bay • FL, United States.......154 H5
Tampere • Finland...........................125 E2
Tamper Sarkanniemi Oy **Park L** •
Finland..98 [11]
Tampico • Mexico...........................157 G2
Tampin • Malaysia..........................141 D3
Tampines • Singapore.....................141 H2
Tampon, le • Réunion......................132 H4
Tamsweg • Austria..........................13 C10
Tamuda • Morocco..........................20 D2
Tamuin • Mexico.............................37 B3
Tamworth • NS, Australia...............144 C2
Tamworth • United Kingdom...........104 D2
Tan An • Vietnam...........................141 E4
Tan Son Nhat [Apt] • Vietnam........141 E4
Tan-Tan • Morocco........................131 D5
Tana • Kenya..................................131 G4
Tana • Norway...............................124 E2
Tana [Riv] • Norway.......................16 N1
Tana, Lake • Ethiopia......................21 G5
Tana Lake Primate River Reserve •
Kenya...131 G4
Tanabe • Japan...............................30 H8
Tanacross • AK, United States..........38 C4
Tanafjorden • Norway....................16 O1
Tanah Merah • Malaysia.................141 G1
Tanahbala • Indonesia...................143 G1
Tanahgrogot • Indonesia.................32 F2
Tanahmasa • Indonesia..................143 G4
Tanami Desert • NT, Australia...........34 F3
Tanami Desert Wildlife Sanctuary •
NT, Australia............................145 D1
Tanana • AK, United States...............38 B4
Tanana [Riv] •
AK, United States..........................38 A4
Tanargue, le • France.......................10 J9
Tanaro • Italy.................................121 E5
Tanch'on • D.P.R. of Korea................30 E4
Tando Adam • Pakistan....................28 A3
Tando Adam **Beach** • Pakistan....28 A3
Tanega-shima • Japan.....................30 F9
Tanezrouft • Algeria.........................20 E4
Tanezrouft-n-Ahenet • Algeria.........20 F4
Tanezror Springs •
FL, United States........................154 H5
Tanguinia • Italy.............................12 I9
Tarragona **Beach** • Spain...........96 [121]
Tarragona • Spain..........................117 D3
Tàrrega • Spain...............................11 M3
Tarrytown • NY, United States.........153 D7
Tarso Emisou • Chad........................21 C4
Tarsus • Turkey..............................123 G4
Tart • China....................................28 F1
Tartagal • Argentina.........................52 D3
Tartu • Estonia...............................126 B2
Tarutao, Ko • Thailand.....................32 B1
Tarutung • Indonesia.....................143 G4
Tarxien Temples • Malta.................123 H4
Tasagaz • Turkey.............................123 F4
Tasejera, Sierra de la • Mexico.........47 B3
Tasawah • Libya..............................21 B2
Tash Kurgan • China.........................28 B2
Tash-Kömür • Kyrgyzstan.................18 I1
Tashk, Daryacheh-ye • Iran..............18 E3
Tashkent • Uzbekistan.....................26 K9
Tashkepri • Turkmenistan................18 H2
Tashtagol • Russian Fed...................26 O7
Tasikmalaya • Java, Indonesia........143 G4
Tåsinge • Denmark..........................8 F2
Tasman Bay • New Zealand.............35 D5
Tasman Sea • Australasia..................34 I8
Tasmania • TS, Australia...................34 I8
Tasmanian wilderness **Heritage N** •
Australia.................................83 [149]
Tasmanian wilderness **Heritage C** •
Australia.................................85 [211]
Tassa Takorat • Niger......................20 G5
Tassara • Niger................................20 G5
Tassili-n'Ajjer **Heritage N** •
Algeria.......................................83 [78]
Tassili-Oua-n-Ahaggar • Algeria.......20 G4
Tassili-n'Ajjer **Heritage C** •
Algeria.....................................85 [105]
Tata • Hungary..................................13 H10
Tata • Morocco................................20 D3
Tata Mailau • East Indies...........32 (1) C4
Tatabánya • Hungary......................13 H10
Tataouine • Tunisia.........................20 H3
Tatarbunary • Ukraine.....................14 O4
Tatarsk • Russian Fed.......................26 N6
Tatarskiy Proliv • Russian Fed..........27 N7
Tatarstan • Russian Fed....................18 F3
Tatebayashi • Japan........................140 C2

Taoyuan • Taiwan...........................31 G1
Tap Mun Chau • Hong Kong, China..139 B4
Tapa • Estonia................................126 B2
Tapachula • Mexico.........................37 C5
Tapah • Malaysia...........................141 G1
Tapajós • Brazil..............................51 F4
Tapaktuan • Indonesia...................143 G1
Tapan • Indonesia..........................32 C3
Tapanui • New Zealand...................51 E6
Taphao Noi, Ko • Thailand..............142 E2
Taphao Yai, Ko • Thailand..............142 E2
Tapini • Papua New Guinea........35 (1) D2
Tapolca • Hungary..........................13 G11
Tappan •
VA, United States..........................44 D7
Tappen • ND, United States..............43 G3
Tappi-zaki • Japan..........................30 K4
Tapti • India....................................28 B4
Tapul Group • Philippines...........32 (1) B1
Taquara • Brazil...............................52 F4
Taquile, I. • Peru............................163 B4
Tara • F.R. of Yugoslavia..................14 G6
Tara • Russian Fed...........................26 L6
Tara • Ireland.................................108 B1
Tara Nat. Park **Park N** •
F.R. of Yugoslavia.....................89 [117]
Tara [Riv] • F.R. of Yugoslavia........14 G6
Taraba • Nigeria..............................22 G3
Tarabuco • Bolivia...........................52 D2
Tarabulus • Libya.............................21 B1
Taraclia • Moldova..........................14 P4
Taradale • New Zealand..................145 F4
Taraghin • Libya..............................21 B2
Tarakan • Indonesia.........................32 F2
Tarakan [I.] • Indonesia..................32 F2
Taranaki [Adm] • New Zealand........145 F3
Taranaki, Mt • New Zealand............145 F3
Taranaki Bight, North •
New Zealand..............................145 F3
Taranaki Bight, South •
New Zealand..............................145 F3
Tarangire Nat. Park • Tanzania.......130 B2
Tarangire Nat. Park **Park** •
Tanzania.................................133 [91]
Tarantaise • France.........................90 A13
Táranto • Italy................................12 L8
Táranto, Golfo di • Italy.................12 L8
Tarapoto • Peru...............................51 B5
Taraqua • Brazil..............................51 D3
Tararua Range • New Zealand..........35 F5
Tarascon-sur-Ariège • France..........115 K1
Tarasp-Vulpera • Switzerland.........119 G4
Tarat • Algeria.................................20 G3
Tarata • Peru.................................163 B4
Tarauacá • Brazil.............................51 C5
Taravilla • Spain.............................11 I4
Taravo • Corsica, France................115 L3
Tarawa • Kiribati.............................33 I5
Tarawera, Lake • New Zealand........145 F2
Tarazona • Spain.............................11 J3
Tarazona de la Mancha • Spain.......11 J5
Tarbagatay • Kazakstan..................26 N8
Tarbert • United Kingdom.................6 F4
Tarbert • United Kingdom...............106 B2
Tarbes • France...............................115 J2
Tarboro • NC, United States............48 I3
Tarcoola • SA, Australia....................34 F6
Tardienta • Spain.............................11 K3
Tardoki Yani, gora •
Russian Fed..................................27 M7
Taree • NS, Australia........................34 J6
Tarentais • France...........................115 F2
Tarfaya • Morocco..........................131 D5
Tarifa • Spain.................................116 B6
Tarifa o Marroqui, Punta de •
Spain..116 B6
Tariku • Indonesia.......................32 (1) E3
Tariku-Taritatu • Indonesia........32 (1) E3
Tarim • Yemen................................18 E6
Tarim He • China............................139 A1
Tarim Basin • China.........................12 J8
Tarim Pendi • China.......................26 N10
Tarin Kowt • Afghanistan................18 I3
Taritatu • Indonesia....................32 (1) E3
Tarkhankut, mys • Ukraine..............17 E5
Tarkio • MO, United States...............46 H2
Tarko-Sale • Russian Fed................26 M5
Tarlac • Philippines..........................31 G3
Tarm • Denmark............................125 F9
Tarna • Peru..................................163 B1
Tarnaberg • Sweden.......................125 F5
Tarne • France................................10 H9
Tarn Hows • United Kingdom..........104 C4
Tärnaby • Sweden...........................16 H4
Tarnobrzeg • Poland........................13 K7
Tarnów • Poland.............................128 C4
Tärnsjö • Sweden...........................125 D1
Taro • Italy......................................12 E4
Taroom • QL, Australia...................144 B5
Taroudannt • Morocco...................131 D5
Tarp • Denmark..............................13 C11
Tarragona **Beach** • Spain...........96 [121]
Tarragona • Spain..........................117 D3

Tateyama • Japan 140 C4
Tathlina Lake • NT, Canada 38 H4
Tathlith • Saudi Arabia 18 D6
Tatilya Turizm Park L • Turkey .. 98 [87]
Tatilya Turizm • Turkey 122 D3
Tatlisu • Cyprus 123 J2
Tatnam, Cape • MN, Canada 39 M5
Tatra • Poland/Slovak Rep. 128 C4
Tatra • Poland/Slovak Rep. 128 C4
Tatry • Poland/Slovak Rep. 128 C4
Tatsenshenini-Alsek Prov. Wilderness Park
  Heritage N • BC, Canada .... 82 [1]
Tatsuno • Japan 140 B1
Tatum • NM, United States 47 C1
Tau • Norway 124 C5
Taubaté • Brazil 163 C3
Tauberbischofsheim • Germany 9 E7
Tauchik • Kazakstan 26 H9
Tauern, Hohe • Austria 119 H7
Tauern, Niedere • Austria 119 H8
Taufkirchen • Germany 112 F3
Taufstein • Germany 9 E6
Taum Sauk Mtn •
  MO, United States 46 J4
Taumarunui • New Zealand 145 F3
Taungdwingyi • Myanmar 28 G4
Taunggyi • Myanmar 31 B2
Taungup • Myanmar 31 A3
Taunton • MA, United States 44 J5
Taunus • Germany 112 E2
Taunus-Wunderland • Germany ... 112 E4
Taupitz! Ski • Austria .... 100 [189]
Taupo • New Zealand 145 F3
Taupo, Lake • New Zealand 145 F4
Taurage • Lithuania 126 B5
Tauranga • New Zealand 145 F2
Tauroa Point • New Zealand 35 D2
Taurus Mtns • Turkey 123 G3
Tavda • Russian Fed. 27 O5
Tavuskaya Guba • Russian Fed. 27 O5
Tavas • Turkey 15 K6
Tavas Ovasi • Turkey 15 K6
Tavda • Russian Fed. 26 K6
Tavda [Riv] • Russian Fed. 26 K6
Tavernes de la Valldigna Beach •
  Spain .... 96 [119]
Tavestehus • Finland 125 E4
Taveuni • Fiji Is. 35 (2) E2
Taviano • Italy 12 M9
Tavignano • Corsica, France 115 L2
Tavira Beach • Portugal .... 96 [100]
Tavira • Portugal 118 E8
Tavistock • United Kingdom 104 F5
Tavolara, I. • Sardinia, Italy 120 C2
Tavoy • Myanmar 31 B4
Tavropoú, Tehníti Límni •
  Greece 15 C4
Tavsanli • Turkey 15 K4
Taw • United Kingdom 104 F2
Tawakoni, Lake •
  TX, United States 154 J2
Tawangmangu • Java, Indonesia ... 143 J7
Tawau • Malaysia 32 F2
Tawitawi • Philippines 31 F5
Tawkar • Sudan 21 G4
Taxco • Mexico 157 G4
Taxila Heritage C • Pakistan .... 85 [131]
Taxila • Pakistan 127 D5
Taxkorgan • China 127 D2
Tay • United Kingdom 104 B1
Tay, Firth of • United Kingdom ... 104 B2
Tay, Loch • United Kingdom 104 B1
Tay Ninh • Vietnam 141 E1
Tayga • Russian Fed. 26 O6
Taygonos, mys • Russian Fed. 27 R4
Taygonos, Poluostrov •
  Russian Fed. 27 R4
Taylor • MI, United States 48 D3
Taylor • AK, United States 49 I2
Taylor • TX, United States 154 J3
Taylorville • IL, United States 46 K3
Tayma • Saudi Arabia 18 C4
Taymyr, Ozero • Russian Fed. 26 R3
Taymyr Peninsula • Russian Fed. . 127 A5
Taymyr, Poluostrov •
  Russian Fed. 26 S2
Taymyra • Russian Fed. 26 Q2
Taymyrlyr • Russian Fed. 26 R4
Tayshet • Russian Fed. 26 O6
Taytay • Philippines 31 F4
Tayu • Java, Indonesia 143 J3
Taza • Morocco 131 D2
Tazovsky • Russian Fed. 4 Z3
Tbilisi • Georgia 17 G6
Tchad, Lac • Africa 21 B5
Tchien • Liberia 22 C3
Tchin Tabardem • Niger 20 G5
Tchogha Zanbil Heritage C •
  Iran .... 85 [125]
Tczew • Poland 13 H3
Te Ana-Au Caves • New Zealand .. 145 G1
Te Anau • New Zealand 145 G1
Te Anau, Lake • New Zealand 145 G1
Te Araroa • New Zealand 35 G3
Te Aroha • New Zealand 145 F2
Te Awamutu • New Zealand 145 F1
Te Hapua • New Zealand 35 D2
Te Kaha • New Zealand 35 F3
Te Kao • New Zealand 35 D2
Te Kuiti • New Zealand 145 F1
Te Puke • New Zealand 145 F2
Te Urewera Nat. Park •
  New Zealand 145 F2
Te Waewae Bay • New Zealand ... 145 G3
Te Wahipounamu-Southwest New Zealand
  Heritage N • New Zealand .... 83 [154]
Teano • Italy 121 G1
Tebay • United Kingdom 104 C4
Tébessa • Algeria 131 E3
Tebingtinggi • Indonesia 143 G2
Téboursouk, Mts de • Tunisia 12 C12
Techirghiol • Romania 128 E2
Tecka • Argentina 53 B4
Tecomán • Mexico 157 G3
Tecuci • Romania 14 O4
Tecumseh • MI, United States 44 D5
Tecumseh • OK, United States 46 G5
Tees • United Kingdom 7 J7
Tees Bay • United Kingdom 7 K7
Tefé • Brazil 51 E4
Tefenni • Turkey 123 F1
Tegal • Java, Indonesia 143 J2
Tegéa • Greece 15 C6
Tegea Koripan Temple •
  Bali, Indonesia 143 H2
Tegel [Apt] • Germany 111 C1
Tegel (Berlin) • Germany 111 C1
Tegeler See • Germany 111 C1
Tegernsee • Germany 112 F7
Tegernsee [Lake] • Germany 112 F7
Teguidda • Niger 20 G5
Teguise Beach •
  Lanzarote, Canary Is. .... 96 [111]
Teguise • Lanzarote, Canary Is. .. 117 E3
Tehek Lake • NU, Canada 38 M4
Tehi-n-Isser • Algeria 20 D6
Tehran • Iran 18 E2
Tehuantepec • Mexico 37 B4
Tehuantepec, Golfo de • Mexico .. 37 B4
Tehuantepec, Istmo de • Mexico .. 37 C4
Teiche, la • France 115 G3

Teide, Pico de •
  Tenerife, Canary Is. 116 E1
Teifi, Afon • United Kingdom 7 H9
Teignmouth Beach •
  United Kingdom .... 101 [113]
Teignmouth • United Kingdom 104 F5
Teisendorf • Germany 112 F4
Teith • United Kingdom 104 B1
Tejakula • Bali, Indonesia 143 H2
Tejeda •
  Gran Canaria, Canary Is. 116 E4
Tejen • Turkmenistan 18 H2
Tejen [Riv] • Iran/Turkmenistan ... 18 H2
Tejo • Portugal 11 C5
Tejupan, Punta • Mexico 157 G3
Teke Burun • Turkey 15 H5
Tekeli • Kazakstan 26 M9
Tekeze • Africa 21 G5
Tekirdag • Turkey 15 I3
Tekirova Beach • Turkey .... 97 [230]
Tekirova • Turkey 123 F3
Tekke Burun • Turkey 15 H3
Tekulthili Lake • NT, Canada 38 I4
Tel 'Arad • Israel 135 A7
Tel Ashqelon • Israel 135 A7
Tel Aviv • Israel 135 A5
Tel Bet Shemesh • Israel 135 A6
Tel Dan • Israel 135 A2
Tel Lakhish • Israel 135 A7
Tel Meggido • Israel 135 A4
Tela • Honduras 37 D4
Teladgama Plateau • India 138 H2
Telc Heritage C • Czech Rep. .... 86 [173]
Telc • Czech Rep. 128 B4
Telciu • Romania 14 L2
Telde •
  Gran Canaria, Canary Is. 116 E4
Telegraph Creek • BC, Canada 38 E5
Telemark • Norway 16 F7
Telemark Sommerland Park L •
  Norway .... 98 [2]
Telemark Sommerland • Norway .. 124 B3
Telén • Indonesia 32 F2
Telén • Argentina 52 C6
Telenesti • Moldova 14 P2
Telescope Peak •
  CA, United States 45 D3
Telese • Italy 12 I7
Telford • United Kingdom 104 D1
Teli • Russian Fed. 26 P7
Tell Atlas • Algeria 4 K10
Tell City • IN, United States 48 D2
Tell Deir 'Alla • Jordan 135 A6
Tell el Amarna • Egypt 131 F3
Teller • AK, United States 49 H2
Telluride Ski •
  CO, United States .... 149 [110]
Telluride • CO, United States 45 I3
Telmessos • Turkey 122 D9
Telpoziz, gora • Russian Fed. 17 J2
Telsen • Argentina 53 C4
Telsiai • Lithuania 126 B3
Teltow • Germany 111 C3
Teltowkanal • Germany 111 C4
Teluk Anson • Malaysia 141 F1
Teluk Bahang • Penang, Malaysia . 141 F1
Teluk Bahang Forest Reserve •
  Penang, Malaysia 141 F1
Teluk Duyung • Penang, Malaysia . 141 F1
Teluk Intan • Malaysia 141 G1
Teluk Kumbar • Penang, Malaysia . 141 F1
Telukbetung • Indonesia 143 J1
Telukbutun • Indonesia 32 D2
Telukdalam • Indonesia 143 G3
Temagami, Lake • ON, Canada 44 E2
Temanggung • Java, Indonesia ... 143 J7
Témara Plage • Morocco 131 D1
Tembe Elephant Park •
  South Africa 134 B2
Tembeling • Malaysia 141 G2
Tembeling [Riv] • Malaysia 141 G2
Tembilahan • Indonesia 32 C3
Tembo • Angola 23 B5
Teme Valley • United Kingdom 104 D1
Temecula • CA, United States 45 D4
Temerloh • Malaysia 141 G4
Temesvár • Romania 14 I4
Teminabuan • Indonesia 32 (1) D3
Temirtau • Kazakstan 26 L7
Témiscaming • QU, Canada 155 F3
Témiscouata • NS, Australia 144 C1
Tempe • AZ, United States 45 G5
Tempelhof [Apt] • Germany 111 C4
Tempio Pausania •
  Sardinia, Italy 12 D8
Templar Park • Malaysia 141 G4
Temple • TX, United States 154 J3
Temple Terrace •
  FL, United States 49 B3
Templemore • Ireland 7 E9
Templetown Beach • Ireland .... 96 [53]
Templi, Valle dei •
  Sicily, Italy 120 D3
Templin • Germany 128 C1
Templiner See • Germany 111 C3
Temuco • Chile 53 B3
Temuka • New Zealand 35 C7
Ten Degree Channel • India 138 E4
Ten Thousand Is. •
  FL, United States 154 H8
Tenabo • Mexico 157 H1
Tenali • India 138 D3
Ténaro, Akra • Greece 15 C7
Tenasserim • Myanmar 31 B4
Tenby • United Kingdom 7 H10
Tenby Beach • United Kingdom 101 [164-166]
Tendaho • Ethiopia 23 G1
Tende • France 10 M9
Tendrara • Morocco 131 D2
Tenerife • Canary Is. 117 E3
Ténès • Algeria 20 F1
Tenga • Algeria 20 F1
Tengah, Kepulauan • Indonesia 143 (1) A4
Tengréla • Côte d'Ivoire 22 C3
Tenke • Dem. Rep. of Congo 23 D6
Tenkeli • Russian Fed. 27 N3
Tenkiller Lake •
  OK, United States 46 H5
Tenkodogo • Burkina Faso 20 E6
Tennant Creek • NT, Australia 34 F3
Tennessee [Adm] • United States .. 48 D3
Tennessee [Riv] • United States ... 48 D3
Tenojoki • Finland 124 A2
Tenosique • Mexico 157 H3
Tenri • Japan 140 B4
Tenryu • Japan 30 I7
Tenterfield • NS, Australia 145 F5
Teófilo Otoni • Brazil 52 H2
Teos • Turkey 122 D7
Teotepec, Cerro • Mexico 37 A4
Teotihuacán Heritage C • Mexico 84 [19]
Teotihuacán • Mexico 157 G2
Tepa • Indonesia 32 (1) C4
Tepa • Mexico 157 H3
Tepelena • Albania 14 F5
Tepic • Mexico 157 G3
Teplice • Czech Rep. 128 B1
Teplice • Czech Rep. 128 B1
Teposcolula • Mexico 157 G4
Tequila • Mexico 157 F2
Ter • Spain 117 D2

Ter Heijde • Netherlands 109 F3
Téra • Niger 20 F6
Teramo • Italy 121 F2
Terceira • Azores 118 B2
Tercero, Rio • Argentina 53 D2
Terengganu • Malaysia 31 C6
Teresina • Brazil 53 (1) C2
Teresina • Brazil 51 G3
Teresópolis • Brazil 163 C4
Teressa • India 28 F7
Terezin • Czech Rep. 128 B2
Tergnier • France 10 I4
Terhazza • Mali 20 D4
Termas de Río Hondo • Argentina . 52 D4
Terme • Turkey 12 E5
Termessos • Turkey 123 G2
Termez • Uzbekistan 18 I2
Términi Imerese • Sicily, Italy 12 H11
Términi Imerese, Golfo di •
  Sicily, Italy 120 D1
Terminillo • Italy 12 G6
Términos, Laguna de • Mexico ... 157 H3
Termit, Massif de • Niger 20 H5
Térmoli • Italy 12 I7
Térmoli Beach • Italy .... 97 [159]
Ternate • Indonesia 32 (1) C2
Terneuzen • Netherlands 109 D10
Terney • Russian Fed. 27 M7
Terni • Italy 121 F1
Ternopil • Ukraine 17 D5
Terpeniya, mys • Russian Fed. 27 N7
Terpeniya, Zaliv • Russian Fed. ... 27 N7
Terra Firma • South Africa 24 C5
Terra Nova Nat. Park •
  NF, Canada 156 D4
Terra Nova Nat. Park Park N •
  NF, Canada .... 156 [38]
Terrace Bay • OT, Canada 44 B1
Terracina • Italy 121 F4
Terralba • Sardinia, Italy 12 C9
Terrassa • Spain 117 D3
Terre Adelie • Antarctica 54 (1) S3
Terre Haute • IN, United States ... 44 B6
Terre Rouge, la • Mauritius 132 J4
Terre-de-Haut • Guadeloupe ..... 161 L
Terre-Neuve, Bancs de •
  NF, Canada 39 T7
Terreiro da Luta • Madeira 118 C2
Terrell • TX, United States 154 J1
Terry • MT, United States 43 D3
Terskan Gölü • Turkey 15 N5
Terschelling Beach •
  Netherlands .... 96 [66]
Terschelling • Netherlands 109 D3
Tersef • Chad 22 H2
Teruel • Spain 11 J4
Teruel Heritage C • Spain ...... 86 [90]
Tervel • Bulgaria 128 E1
Tervola • Finland 16 M3
Teseney • Eritrea 21 G4
Tésero Ski • Italy .... 100 [218]
Tésero • Italy 120 B3
Teshio • Japan 30 J1
Teshio [Mtn] • Japan 30 L2
Teshio [Riv] • Japan 30 L2
Teskraia • Tunisia 131 E1
Teslin • YT, Canada 38 E4
Teslin [Riv] • YT, Canada 38 E4
Tesovo-Netyl'skiy •
  Russian Fed. 126 C1
Tessalit • Mali 20 F4
Tessaoua • Niger 20 G6
Test • United Kingdom 5 B3
Test, Tizi n • Morocco 20 D2
Testa, Capo • Sardinia, Italy 120 C2
Teste-del Gargano • Italy 14 D8
Teste-de-Buch, la • France ...... 96 [85]
Teste-de-Buch, la • France 115 G3
Testigos • Venezuela 51 E1
Tét • France 115 K2
Tetas, Punta • Chile 52 B3
Tete • Mozambique 24 E3
Teterow • Germany 8 H3
Teteven • Bulgaria 14 L7
Tetouan Heritage C • Morocco .. 86 [250]
Tétouan • Morocco 131 D2
Tetovo • F.Y.R. of Macedonia 14 H7
Tettnang • Germany 112 F5
Teulada • Spain 117 C2
Teulada, Capo • Sardinia 12 C10
Teutoburger Wald • Germany 8 D5
Tévere • Italy 12 G6
Tewkesbury • United Kingdom 104 D4
Texarkana •
  AR/TX, United States 154 J2
Texas • United States 40 F5
Texas City • TX, United States ... 154 J6
Texas Safari Wildlife Park •
  TX, United States 154 J3
Texel • Netherlands 109 D3
Texoma, Lake •
  OK/TX, United States 154 J1
Teya • Russian Fed. 26 P5
Teykovo • Russian Fed. 126 C4
The Chin • Thailand 142 C1

The Valley • Anguilla .... 160 C
Thebes Heritage C • Egypt ..... 85 [96]
Thebes • Egypt 131 F4
Thedford • NE, United States 43 F6
Theile • France 115 E1
Theodore • QL, Australia 34 E3
Theodore Roosevelt Birthplace Nat. Hist. Site
  Park N • NY, United States ... 151 [319]
Theodore Roosevelt Dam •
  AZ, United States 153 E3
Theodore Roosevelt Inaugural Nat. Hist. Site
  Park N • NY, United States ... 151 [304]
Theodore Roosevelt Island Park N •
  DC, United States .... 151 [286]
Theodore Roosevelt Lake •
  AZ, United States 153 E3
Theodore Roosevelt Nat. Park Park N •
  ND, United States .... 150 [147]
Theódori, Agii • Crete, Greece ... 123 E1
Theológos Beach •
  Rhodes, Greece .... 97 [211]
Théoule-sur-Mer • France 5 F5
Théra • Greece 15 G3
Thermaikós Kólpos • Greece 122 D5
Thérmi • Greece 122 D7
Thérmo • Greece 122 C5
Thermia Beach • Greece .... 97 [184]
Thermopolis • WY, United States .. 42 K5
Thessalia • Greece 15 D4
Thessalon • OT, Canada 44 D2
Thessaloníki Heritage C •
  Greece .... 86 [207]
Thessaloníki • Greece 122 D5
Thessaly • Greece 122 A1
Thetford • United Kingdom 7 M9
Thetford Mines • QU, Canada 156 D6
Thethi Nat. Park Park N •
  Albania .... 89 [130]
Thibodaux • LA, United States ... 153 F4
Thief River Falls •
  MN, United States 43 H2
Thierbach Ski • Austria ...... 100 [148]
Thiers • France 112 D6
Thika • Kenya 131 G3
Thillot, le • France 9 B9
Thimphu • Bhutan 28 E3
Thinalio Beach • Corfu, Greece .. 97 [170]
Thingvallavatn • Iceland 16 (1) C2
Thingvellir • Iceland 16 (1) C2
Thira • New Caledonia 35 (2) B3
Thíonville • France 112 D1
Thíra • Greece 122 D8
Thíra [I.] • Greece 122 D8
Thirlmere • United Kingdom 104 C2
Thiruvarur • India 138 D11
Thisted Beach • Denmark ...... 96 [49]
Thisted • Denmark 125 F5
Thistilfjördur • Iceland 16 (1) F1
Thistlegorm Dive • Red Sea 135 B1
Thitu • South China Sea 31 E4
Thíva • Greece 15 E5
Thiviers • France 10 H8
Thjórsá • Iceland 16 (1) D2
Thoaims Stone Nat. Hist. Site Park N •
  MD, United States .... 151 [268]
Thoen • Thailand 31 B3
Thoiry, Parc zoologique de •
  France 115 C2
Tholen • Netherlands 109 D10
Thomas Jefferson Mem. Park N •
  DC, United States .... 151 [307]
Thomas Reef Dive • Red Sea 135 B1
Thomaston • NB, Canada 44 L3
Thomaston • GA, United States .. 48 F5
Thomasville • AL, United States .. 48 F5
Thomasville • GA, United States .. 48 F5
Thomasville • NC, United States .. 48 G3
Thompson • MN, Canada 39 H7
Thompson • BC, Canada 155 C3
Thompson Falls •
  MT, United States 42 H3
Thompson Sound • New Zealand 145 G1
Thomson • QL, Australia 34 H4
Thomson • GA, United States 48 F4
Thon Buri • Thailand 142 C1
Thon Buri floating market •
  Thailand 142 C1
Thong Krok, Laem •
  Ko Samui, Thailand 142 D2
Thonon-les-Bains • France 115 F2
Thoreau • NM, United States 45 I3
Thórisvatn • Iceland 16 (1) D2
Thorn • Poland 90 A9
Thornton • CO, United States 46 C3
Thoronet, Abbaye du • France ... 115 H3
Thorpe Park Park L •
  United Kingdom .... 98 [34]
Thorpe Park • United Kingdom .. 104 E1
Thorpeness Beach •
  United Kingdom .... 101 [58]
Thórshöfn • Iceland 16 (1) F1
Thouars • France 115 D2
Thousand Oaks •
  CA, United States 45 C4
Thrace • Greece/Turkey 14 N8
Thráki • Greece 15 H2
Thrakió Pélagos • Greece 15 G3
Thredbo • NS, Australia 144 C4
Three Forks • MT, United States .. 42 J4
Three Kings Is. • New Zealand ... 35 D2
Three Pagodas Pass •
  Myanmar/Thailand 31 B3
Three Points, Cape • Ghana 22 D4
Three Rivers •
  MI, United States 44 C5
Three Rivers •
  TX, United States 47 E3
Three Sisters •
  OR, United States 42 E4
Threlkeld • United Kingdom 104 C2
Throckmorton •
  TX, United States 46 F6
Thuburbo Majus • Tunisia 131 E2
Thuile, la Ski • Italy .... 100 [201]
Thuile, la • Italy 121 E1
Thule • Belgium 5 H4
Thule • Greenland 36 K2
Thulaghiri • Maldives 138 F2
Thulusdhu • Maldives 138 F2
Thun • Switzerland 119 G2
Thunder Bay • OT, Canada 39 N7
Thunder Bay [Bay] • OT, Canada . 43 L2
Thuner See • Switzerland 119 G2
Thung Salang Nat. Park •
  Thailand 142 B4
Thung Song • Thailand 31 B5
Thung Yai-Huai Kha Khaeng Wildlife Sanctuaries
  Heritage N • Thailand ...... 83 [134]
Thur • Switzerland 9 D9
Thüringen • Germany 9 F6
Thüringer Wald • Germany 9 F6
Thüringia • Germany 111 A6
Thurlestone Beach •
  United Kingdom .... 101 [214]
Thursday Island • QL, Australia .. 34 H1
Thurso • United Kingdom 104 A1
Thuy Duong • Vietnam 141 E4
Thy • Denmark 125 F5
Thyatira • Turkey 122 D6
Thyborøn • Denmark 125 F5
Thyborøn-Harbour Beach •
  Denmark .... 96 [50]

Thyon 2000 • Switzerland 119 G6
Ti Tree • NT, Australia 145 D2
Ti-n-Alkoum • Algeria 20 H4
Ti-n-Arkachie • Algeria 20 F4
Ti-n-Toumma • Niger 21 B4
Ti-n-Zaoâtene • Algeria 20 F4
Tianbaoshan • China 30 E3
Tianjin • China 29 F3
Tianjin [Adm] • China 139 A4
Tianjin • China 139 D3
Tianshui • China 29 D4
Tiaret • Algeria 20 F1
Tias Beach •
  Lanzarote, Canary Is. .... 96 [111]
Tías • Lanzarote, Canary Is. 117 E2
Tía, Ras el • Tunisia 131 E2
Tibati • Cameroon 22 G3
Tibbetts Turn • Cayman Is. 159 E2
Tiber • Italy 121 F1
Tiberias • Israel 135 A4
Tiberias, Lake • Israel 135 A4
Tiberio, Villa di • Italy 121 C3
Tibesti • Chad 21 C3
Tibet • China 28 E2
Tibet, Lake • FL, United States .. 151 C1
Tibet, Plateau of • China 139 A1
Tibidabo, Parque d'Atraccíons Park L •
  Spain .... 98 [74]
Tibro • Sweden 125 F3
Tiburón, I. • Mexico 157 F1
Tichít Heritage C • Mauritania .. 85 [106]
Tichla, Tizi n • Morocco 20 D2
Tichla • Western Sahara 20 C4
Ticino • Switzerland 119 G7
Ticino [Riv] •
  Italy/Switzerland 121 E2
Ticul • Mexico 157 H1
Tidaholm • Sweden 125 F3
Tidjikja • Mauritania 20 C5
Tidra, I. • Mauritania 20 B5
Tiefenbron • Germany 112 D6
Tiel • Netherlands 109 F4
Tielerwaard • Netherlands 109 F4
Tielongtan • China 28 C1
Tielt • Belgium 109 E2
Tien Shan • Asia 26 N9
Tienba • Côte d'Ivoire 22 C3
Tiemen • Belgium 109 D15
Tiergarten (Berlin) • Germany ... 111 C2
Tieroko, Tarso • Chad 20 I4
Tierpark Friedrichsfelde (Berlin) •
  Germany 111 C2
Tierra Amarilla • Chile 52 B4
Tierra del Fuego, I. Grande de •
  Argentina/Chile 53 C6
Tierradentro, Parque Arqueológico Nac.
  Heritage C • Colombia ..... 84 [50]
Tieté • Brazil 52 F3
Tiffin • OH, United States 44 D5
Tiflet • Morocco 131 D1
Tifton • GA, United States 154 H3
Tiga • New Caledonia 35 (2) B3
Tigani, Hersónisos •
  Crete, Greece 123 E1
Tigard • OR, United States 42 D4
Tigil • Russian Fed. 27 Q5
Tignes Ski • France .... 100 [32]
Tignes • France 115 F2
Tigra, Punta de • Margarita ..... 160 V
Tigre • Ecuador 51 B4
Tigre [Riv] • Peru 51 B4
Tihámat • Saudi Arabia 18 D6
Tijuana • Mexico 157 F1
Tikal • Guatemala 37 D5
Tikal, Parque Nac. Heritage N •
  Guatemala .... 82 [21]
Tikhoretsk • Russian Fed. 17 G5
Tikhvin • Russian Fed. 126 C1
Tiksi • Russian Fed. 27 K2
Tílea • Malaysia 141 F2
Tila Yak • Afghanistan 18 I2
Til-Châtel • France 112 E2
Tiladamati-Miladummadulu Atoll •
  Maldives 138 F1
Tilbury • Netherlands 109 D11
Tilbury • United Kingdom 104 E1
Tileagd • Romania 14 J2
Tilemsi, Vallée du • Mali 20 F5
Tilichiki • Russian Fed. 27 S4
Tilisos • Crete, Greece 123 E7
Tillabéry • Niger 20 F6
Tillamook • OR, United States ... 42 D4
Tillanchong • India 138 E4
Tillberga • Sweden 125 D1
Tilleul, le Beach • France ...... 96 [77]
Tillia • Niger 20 G5
Tillsonburg • OT, Canada 44 E4
Tiloa • Niger 20 F6
Tilos • Greece 122 D9
Tilos [I.] • Greece 122 D8
Tima • Egypt 21 F2
Timagami, Lake • OT, Canada ... 39 O7
Timanfaya, Parque Nac. de Park N •
  Lanzarote, Canary Is. ...... 89 [79]
Timanfaya, Parque Nac. de •
  Lanzarote, Canary Is. 117 E3
Timanskiy Kryazh • Russian Fed. .. 17 I2
Timashevsk • Russian Fed. 17 F5
Timassah • Libya 21 C2
Timbáki • Crete, Greece 15 F8
Timber Bay •
  LA, United States 47 I3
Timbedra • Mauritania 20 D5
Timber Ridge Ski •
  MI, United States .... 149 [153]
Timberlane •
  OR, United States .... 149 [54]
Timbuktu • Mali 20 E5
Timbuktu Heritage C • Mali ... 85 [107]
TimELEla Heritage C • Algeria .. 86 [260]
Timimoun • Algeria 20 F3
Timiris, Cap • Mauritania 20 B5
Timisoara • Romania 14 I4
Timmendorfer Strand Spa •
  Germany .... 113 [c19]
Timmernabben • Sweden 125 F8
Timmins • OT, Canada 39 O7
Timmins • OT, Canada .... 100 [245]
Timor • East Indies 32 (1) B4
Timor, Laut •
  Australia/Indonesia 25 N11
Timor Sea • Australia/Indonesia . 144 A1
Timote • Argentina 52 D6
Timpanogos Cave Nat. Mon. Park N •
  UT, United States .... 150 [77]
Timrå • Sweden 125 C1
Tims Ford Lake •
  TN, United States 48 D3
Tims Hill • WI, United States 43 K4
Timucuan Ecological & Hist. Preserve
  Park N • FL, United States ... 151 [214]
Timucuan Ecological & Hist. Preserve •
  FL, United States 154 H3
Tin Can Bay • QL, Australia 144 B6
Tin Fouye • Algeria 20 G3
Tin Shui Wai • Hong Kong, China 139 B5
Tinaca, Kaap • Philippines 31 H5
Tinajas • Mexico 157 H1
Tinazepte • Turkey 123 F2
Tíndari • Sicily, Italy 120 D3
Tindouf • Algeria 20 D3

Tineo • Spain 11 E1
Tinerhir • Morocco 131 D4
Tinetto, Isola del del Heritage C •
  Italy .... 86 [139]
Tinghert, Hamadat • Libya 21 B2
Tinglev • Denmark 125 F13
Tingo María • Peru 51 B5
Tingsryd • Sweden 125 F12
Tintern Abbey • United Kingdom . 104 D3
Tinker Field •
  FL, United States 151 C2
Tinn • Norway 124 B1
Tino, Isola del Heritage C •
  Italy .... 86 [139]
Tinogasta • Argentina 52 C4
Tinos • Greece 122 D8
Tinos [I.] • Greece 122 D8
Tínou, Stenó • Greece 15 G6
Tíntagel • United Kingdom 104 F4
Tinténiac • France 10 J4
Tío Beach • Malaysia 141 G3
Tipasa Heritage C • Algeria ... 86 [256]
Tipitapa • Nicaragua 37 D5
Tipperary • Ireland 7 D9
Tipperary • Ireland 7 E9
Tipperary • Ireland 108 C6
Tipuani, Serra do • Brazil 53 (1) B2
Tiracol Fort • Goa, India 137 B1
Tiradentes • Brazil 163 C1
Tiranë • Albania 14 G8
Tiranë • Albania 14 G8
Tíranë • Albania 14 G8
Tiraspol • Moldova 14 Q3
Tire • Turkey 122 D6
Tiree • United Kingdom 6 F5
Tirgovíste • Romania 128 E1
Tirgu Jiu • Romania 14 L3
Tirgu Mures • Romania 14 L3
Tirgu Neamt • Romania 14 N2
Tirintha • Greece 15 D6
Tirnava Mare • Romania 14 M3
Tirnava Mica • Romania 14 L3
Tirnaveni • Romania 14 L3
Tirnavos • Greece 15 D4
Tirnovo • Bulgaria 90 A15
Tirol • Austria 119 H3
Tirreno Beach • Italy .... 96 [145]
Tirrenia • Italy 121 E11
Tirso • Sardinia, Italy 120 C2
Tirstrup [Apt] • Denmark 125 F10
Tirtha Empul Temple •
  Bali, Indonesia 143 H2
Tiruchirappalli • India 138 D11
Tirukalikundram • India 138 D7
Tirumala • India 138 D7
Tirunchendur Beach • India ... 138 E3
Tirunelveli • India 138 D10
Tirupati • India 138 D10
Tiruppur • India 138 D10
Tiruvannamalai • India 138 D7
Tíryns • Greece 15 D6
Tiryns Heritage C • Greece ... 86 [214]
Tisararen • Sweden 125 E1
Tissemsilt • Algeria 11 M9
Tissville • Denmark 125 F6
Tisza • Hungary 13 J11
Tiszaföred • Hungary 13 J11
Tiszakecske • Hungary 13 J11
Tiszántúl • Hungary 13 J11
Tit-Ary • Russian Fed. 127 K2
Títhal Beach • India 138 E3
Titicaca, Lago • Bolivia/Peru .. 163 B4
Titisee • Germany 112 D8
Titlagarh • India 28 D4
Titov Veles •
  F.Y.R. of Macedonia 14 I8
Titov vrh • F.Y.R. of Macedonia . 14 H8
Tittmoning • Germany 112 F4
Titu • Romania 128 E1
Titus Mtn Ski •
  NY, United States .... 149 [197]
Titusville • PA, United States ... 44 F5
Titusville • FL, United States ... 154 H6
Titz • Germany 111 B3
Tiu • Malaysia 141 F2
Tivaouane • Mauritania 20 C5
Tiveden • Sweden 125 F3
Tiveden Nat. Park Park N •
  Sweden .... 89 [26]
Tiveden Nat. Park • Sweden 125 F3
Tivoli • Italy 121 C3
Tívoli Park L • Denmark .... 98 [18]
Tívoli • Italy 12 G6
Tivoli • Grenada .... 160 S
Tiwai I. Wildlife Sanctuary Park •
  Sierra Leone .... 133 [16]
Tiwi Beach • Kenya 131 G5
Tiya Heritage C • Ethiopia .... 85 [102]
Tizi Ouzou • Algeria 20 F1
Tizimin • Mexico 157 H2
Tiznit • Morocco 131 D5
Tjällmo • Sweden 125 E8
Tjeggelvas • Sweden 16 I3
Tjeukemeer • Netherlands 5 I2
Tjölöholm • Sweden 125 F1
Tjøme • Norway 124 B4
Tjørn • Sweden 125 F1
Tjust • Sweden 125 F8
Tlacotalpan Heritage C • Mexico 84 [26]
Tlacotalpan • Mexico 157 G4
Tlaxcala • Mexico 37 B4
Tlaxcala [Adm] • Mexico 37 B4
Tlaxco • Mexico 157 G2
Tlimsen • Algeria 20 F2
Tmarah • Indonesia 32 (1) F4
Toamasina • Madagascar 24 H3
Toapoon, Ko • Thailand 142 D2
Toay • Argentina 52 D6
Toba • China 28 F2
Toba • Java, Indonesia 143 G2
Toba, Lake • Indonesia 143 G2
Toba Range • Pakistan 28 A2
Tobago • Trinidad & Tobago .... 160 T
Tobago Cays •
  St Vincent & Gren. .... 161 R
Tobago Forest Reserve •
  Trinidad & Tobago .... 160 T
Tobelo • Indonesia 32 (1) C2
Tobercurry • Ireland 108 C2
Tobi • Palau 32 (1) D2
Tobin, Mt • NV, United States ... 42 G6
Toblach • Italy 120 B2
Toboali • Indonesia 143 G2
Tobol • Kazakstan 26 J7
Tobol [Riv] •
  Kazakstan/Russian Fed. 26 K6
Tobolsk • Russian Fed. 26 K6
Tobseda • Russian Fed. 17 I1
Toc Vers, Cap St-Barthélemy .. 160 E1
Tocantins [Adm] • Brazil 53 (1) B4
Tocantins [Riv] • Brazil 53 (1) B4
Tocoa • GA, United States 48 A4
Tochigi • Japan 140 A4
Tocoa • Trinidad & Tobago .... 160 U
Tocopilla • Chile 52 B3
Todi • Italy 121 E12
Todi • NT, Australia 145 B4
Todos-qa-saki • Japan 30 L5
Todos os Santos, Baía de •
  Brazil 52 I1
Todos Santos • Mexico 157 F4
Todra, Gorges du • Morocco ... 131 D4
Todtnau • Germany 112 D8
Tödy • Switzerland 12 C2

Toekomstig

Toekomstig Reservoir • Surinam **51** F3
Toetoes Bay • New Zealand **145** G4
Töfsingdalen Nat. Park **Park N** •
Sweden ...... **89** [22]
Tofte • Norway **124** B4
Toftlund • Denmark **125** F13
Tofua • Tonga **35** (2) E2
Togane • Japan **140** C2
Toggenburg • Switzerland **119** G3
Togiak • AK, United States **49** I4
Togian, Kepulauan • Indonesia **32** (1) B2
TOGO • Africa **22** E3
Togwotee Pass •
WY, United States **38** I3
Tohoku • Japan **140** A4
Toi-misaki • Japan **30** F9
Toijala • Finland **125** E2
Toisvesi • Finland **125** E2
Toiyabe Range •
NV, United States **45** D2
Tok • AK, United States **49** M3
Tokara-retto • Japan **140** A11
Tokelau • Pacific Ocean **33** J6
Tokkevatn • Norway **124** B4
Tokoroa • New Zealand **145** F2
Toknak • Kyrgyzstan **26** M9
Tokuno-shima • Japan **140** A11
Tokur • Russian Fed. **27** L6
Tokushima • Japan **140** B3
Tokushima [Adm] • Japan **140** A7
Tokyo • Japan **140** C2
Tokyo [Adm] • Japan **140** A8
Tokyo Disneyland • Japan **140** C2
Tokyo-wan • Japan **140** C2
Tol'yatti • Russian Fed. **17** H4
Tolaga Bay • New Zealand **35** G4
Tolañaro • Madagascar **24** H5
Toleant • Mexico **157** G2
Toledo • Spain **11** G5
Toledo • Brazil **52** F3
Toledo **Heritage C** • Spain ...... **86** [104]
Toledo • OR, United States **42** D4
Toledo • OH, United States **44** D5
Toledo • IA, United States **46** I2
Toledo Bend Reservoir •
LA/TX, United States **153** F1
Toledo, Montes de • Spain **11** G5
Tolentino • Italy **121** E12
Tolfa • Italy **121** F1
Tolfa, Monti della • Italy **121** F1
Toliara • Madagascar **24** G4
Tolima • Colombia **51** B3
Tolitoli • Indonesia **32** (1) B2
Tollarp • Sweden **125** F11
Tolmezzo • Italy **12** H2
Tolmin • Slovenia **14** A3
Tolmin • Slovenia **128** D1
Tolo • Dem. Rep. of Congo **22** H5
Tolo **Beach** • Greece ...... **97** [184]
Tolo Harbour • Hong Kong, China **139** B6
Tolosa • Spain **11** H2
Tolstoy, mys • Russian Fed. **27** Q5
Toluca • Mexico **157** G4
Toluca, Nevado de • Mexico **157** G4
Tom Price • WA, Australia **43** K3
Tomah • WI, United States **46** J2
Tomakomai • Japan **30** K3
Tomar • Portugal **11** G5
Tomar **Heritage C** • Portugal ...... **86** [114]
Tomaszow Lubelski • Poland **13** M7
Tomaszów Mazowiecki • Poland **13** J6
Tombigbee • AL, United States **48** C4
Tombôco • Angola **22** G6
Tomboctou • Mali **20** E5
Tombstone • AZ, United States **153** E4
Tomé • Chile **52** B6
Tomé-Açu • Brazil **53** (1) B2
Tomelilla • Sweden **125** F11
Tomini, Teluk • Indonesia **32** (1) B2
Tomi-saki • Japan **140** C4
Tomislavgrad • Bosnia-Herz. **14** E6
Tomkinson Ranges •
SA/WA, Australia **145** D3
Tommot • Russian Fed. **27** K5
Tomo • Colombia **51** C3
Tomogashima-suido • Japan **140** B3
Tomorit • Albania **15** B3
Tomorri Nat. Park **Park N** •
Albania ...... **89** [127]
Tompe • Indonesia **32** (1) A3
Tompo • Russian Fed. **27** M4
Tompo • Russian Fed. **26** O6
Tonaki-jima • Japan **140** A10
Tonala • Mexico **37** C4
Tonale, Passo del • Italy **121** E3
Tonbridge • United Kingdom **104** E3
Tondano • Indonesia **32** (1) B2
Tondbayashi • Japan **140** B4
Tønder • Denmark **8** E3
Tønder • Denmark **125** F13
Tone-gawa • Japan **140** C2
Tonesai Falls •
Ko Phuket, Thailand **142** E1
Toney • Antarctica **54** (1) DD2
Tong Phu Phum • Thailand **31** B4
TONGA • Pacific Ocean **35** (2) F2
Tonga Trench • Tonga **35** (2) F2
Tongaat • South Africa **134** B4
Tongariro Nat. Park **Heritage N** •
New Zealand ...... **83** [155]
Tongariro Nat. Park •
New Zealand **145** F4
Tongatapu • Tonga **81** A9
Tongatapu Group • Tonga **35** (2) E3
Tongchuan • China **29** D3
Tongeren • Belgium **5** I4
Tonghe • China **29** H1
Tonghua • China **29** D2
Tongjosŏn-man • D.P.R. of Korea **30** D5
Tongking • Vietnam **141** D1
Tongliao • China **29** G2
Tongling • China **29** F3
Tonglu • China **139** C3
Tongoa • Vanuatu **35** (2) B2
Tongtian Hel • China **28** G2
Tongue • United Kingdom **6** H3
Tongue • MT/WY, United States **38** J7
Tönisvorst • Germany **111** B1
Tonk • India **137** C6
Tonkawa • OK, United States **46** G4
Tonkin, Gulf of • China/Vietnam **31** D2
Tonle Sap • Cambodia **31** C4
Tönning • Germany **7** D2
Tönochi • Mexico **157** F2
Tonopah • NV, United States **152** C4
Tønsberg • Norway **124** B4
Tonto Nat. Mon. **Park N** •
AZ, United States ...... **150** [107]
Tonto Nat. Mon. •
AZ, United States **153** E3
Toowotee Pass •
WY, United States **42** J5
Tooele • UT, United States **45** F1
Toowoomba • QL, Australia **144** B6
Top End, The • NT, Australia **144** A2
Topçam Plaji • Turkey **123** F4
Topeka • KS, United States **46** H3
Topki • Russian Fed. **26** N4
Topko, gora • Russian Fed. **27** M5
Toplita • Romania **14** M3
Töplitz • Germany **111** C3
Topock • AZ, United States **153** H1
Topol'cany • Slovak Rep. **13** H1
Topolnica • Bulgaria **15** F1
Topolobampo • Mexico **157** F4
Topolovgrad • Bulgaria **128** E3
Toppenish • WA, United States **42** G3
Tor Bay • United Kingdom **104** F5

Torbali • Turkey **122** D6
Torbat-e Heydariyeh • Iran **18** G2
Torbat-e Jam • Iran **18** H2
Torch Lake • MI, United States **44** H1
Torcross **Beach** • United Kingdom ...... **101** [124]
Tordesillas • Spain **11** G3
Töreboda • Sweden **125** D3
Toresund • Sweden **125** D3
Torgelow • Germany **8** J3
Torghay • Kazakhstan **26** J8
Torgon Ski • Switzerland ...... **100** [75]
Torhamn • Sweden **125** F12
Torhout • Belgium **109** E2
Tori • India **137** C8
Toride • Japan **140** C2
Torino **Heritage C** • Italy ...... **86** [128]
Torino • Italy **121** E5
Torkovichi • Russian Fed. **126** C1
Tormes • Spain **11** F3
Torne älv • Sweden **16** K3
Torne-träsk • Sweden **16** J2
Torneå • Finland **16** M4
Tornesch • Germany **8** E3
Torngat Mtns • NF/QU, Canada **39** S5
Tornio • Finland **16** M4
Tornionjoki • Finland **16** M3
Toro • Japan **140** C3
Toro, Cerro del •
Argentina/Chile **52** C4
Toro Muerto • Peru **163** B4
Törökszentmiklós • Hungary **13** J10
Toronto • OT, Canada **155** B9
Toropets • Russian Fed. **126** C3
Tororo • Uganda **131** G1
Toros Daglari • Turkey **123** G3
Torö • Sweden **124** C4
Torquay **Beach** •
United Kingdom ...... **101** [115–117]
Torquay • United Kingdom **104** F5
Torralba • Portugal **118** E6
Torre Annunziata **Heritage C** •
Italy ...... **86** [151]
Torre Annunziata • Italy **121** G3
Torre de Areas • Portugal **118** E8
Torre de Carredo • Spain **11** G2
Torre de la Higuera • Spain **116** B1
Torre de Moncorvo • Portugal **11** E2
Torre del Greco • Italy **121** G3
Torre del Mar • Spain **116** D2
Torre-Pacheco • Spain **11** K7
Torreblanca • Spain **11** L4
Torreblanca **Beach** • Spain ...... **96** [120]
Torredembarra **Beach** • Spain ...... **96** [121]
Torredembarra • Spain **117** D3
Torredonjimeno • Spain **116** B3
Torreilles **Beach** • France ...... **96** [128]
Torrelavega • Spain **11** G2
Torremolinos **Beach** • Spain ...... **96** [114]
Torremolinos • Spain **116** B7
Torrens Creek • QL, Australia **144** B3
Torrens Lake • SA, Australia **34** G6
Torrens Point • Saba ...... **161** F
Torreón • Mexico **40** F6
Torres de Alcala • Morocco **131** D2
Torres Is • Vanuatu **35** (2) B1
Torres Strait • Australia **34** H1
Torres Vedras **Beach** • Portugal ...... **96** [98]
Torrevieja **Beach** • Spain ...... **96** [118]
Torrevieja • Spain **117** C3
Torridge • United Kingdom **104** C4
Torrington • WY, United States **43** D5
Torrington • CT, United States **44** I5
Torrox • Spain **116** D2
Torsås **Beach** • Sweden ...... **97** [16]
Torsby • Sweden **16** G6
Torshälla • Sweden **125** G5
Tórshavn • Faroe Is. **4** I4
Torö • Sweden **125** F3
Tortona • Italy **121** E6
Tortoreto **Beach** • Italy ...... **97** [161]
Tortosa • Spain **11** L4
Tortosa, Cabo de • Spain **11** L4
Tortue, Ile, de la • Haiti **159** G2
Tortue, la • St Barthélemy ...... **160** E
Tortuga • Venezuela **51** D2
Tortuga • Mexico **157** H3
Tortuga I. • Haiti **159** G2
Toruguari • China **26** M9
Torun • Poland **13** H4
Torun **Heritage C** • Poland ...... **86** [161]
Torup • Sweden **125** E1
Torver • United Kingdom **104** C4
Tory I. • Ireland **108** A1
Torzhok • Russian Fed. **126** C3
Toscana • Italy **121** E11
Toshiamaen • Japan **140** C2
Toshka Depression • Egypt **131** F5
Toson Hu • China **28** G2
Töss • Switzerland **9** D9
Tossa de Mar **Beach** • Spain ...... **96** [123]
Tossa de Mar • Spain **117** D4
Tostado • Argentina **52** D4
Tostedt • Germany **8** E3
Tostón •
Fuerteventura, Canary Is. **117** E2
Totak • Norway **124** B4
Totana • Spain **11** J7
Têtes • France **5** E5
Totland Bay **Beach** •
United Kingdom ...... **101** [97]
Totma • Russian Fed. **17** G2
Totnes • United Kingdom **104** F5
Totness • Surinam **51** F2
Totora • Bolivia **52** C2
Totora • Bolivia **53** (1) B2
Totoya • Fiji Is. **35** (2) E2
Totsu-gawa • Japan **140** B4
Tottori • Japan **30** H7
Tottori [Adm] • Japan **140** A3
Tottori **[Adm]** • Japan **140** A3
Touba • Côte d'Ivoire **22** C3
Toubkal, Jebel • Morocco **131** D5
Tougan • Burkina Faso **22** D2
Touggourt • Algeria **20** G2
Tougué • Guinea **20** C6
Tòúil • Algeria **22** C2
Toukoto • Mali **22** C2
Toul • France **10** K5
Toulon • France **115** H3
Toulouse • France **115** G4
Toummo • Niger **21** B3
Toungoo • Myanmar **31** B3
Touques • France **5** E5
Touquet-Paris-Plage, le •
France **5** E4
Touraine • France **114** D4
Tourcoing • France **10** H3
Tourinan, Cabo • Spain **11** B1
Tourine • Mauritania **20** C4
Tourmalet, Col du • France **115** F4
Tournai • France **109** D14
Tournan-en-Brie • France **115** F1
Touroparc • France **114** F1
Tours • France **114** D2
Toury • France **10** G5
Toussoro • Central African Rep. **23** C2
Toussuire, la **Ski** • France ...... **100** [46]
Toussuire, la • France **115** F4
Touws River • South Africa **134** C6
Tovdal • Norway **124** B5
Towanda • PA, United States **153** D6
Townsend • MT, United States **42** J3
Townsend, Cape • QL, Australia **144** B4
Townshend I. • QL, Australia **144** B4

Townsville • QL, Australia **144** B1
Towson • MD, United States **44** E6
Towton • United Kingdom **90** A7
Towuti, Danau • Indonesia **32** (1) B3
Toyama • Japan **30** I6
Toyama [Adm] • Japan **140** A4
Toyama-wan • Japan **30** I6
Toyapakeh • Indonesia **143** H4
Toyo'oka • Japan **30** H7
Toyohashi • Japan **30** I7
Toyota • Japan **140** C2
Tozeur • Tunisia **131** E3
Traben-Trarbach • Germany **112** E3
Tráblous • Lebanon **18** C3
Trabzon • Turkey **18** D1
Tracy • QU, Canada **44** I2
Trafalgar, Cabo • Spain **116** B5
Trafalgar Falls • Dominica ...... **161** M
Tragaki **Beach** • Zante, Greece ...... **97** [172]
Tragaki • Zante, Greece **122** C3
Traighli • Ireland **108** C5
Trail • OR, United States **42** D5
Trail • BC, Canada **155** C4
Trakai Nat. Park **Park N** •
Lithuania ...... **89** [147]
Trakai Nat. Park • Lithuania **126** B6
Tralee • Ireland **108** C5
Tralee Bay • Ireland **108** C5
Tramore • Ireland **108** E5
Tramuntana, Serra de •
Majorca, Spain **117** H1
Tranås • Sweden **125** F4
Tranebjerg • Denmark **125** F10
Tranemo • Sweden **125** F7
Trang • Thailand **31** B5
Trangan • Indonesia **32** (1) D4
Trani • Italy **12** K7
Trans World Radio • Bonaire ...... **160** W
Trans-Siberian Railway •
Russian Fed. **126** A11
Transylvania • Romania **14** L3
Transylvanian Alps • Romania **128** A2
Tranum Strand • Denmark **125** F5
Trápani • Sicily, Italy **120** D1
Trapper Peak •
ID/MT, United States **42** H4
Traralgon • VI, Australia **144** C3
Trarza • Mauritania **20** B5
Trás os Montes • Portugal **11** D3
Trasimeno, Lago • Italy **121** E11
Träslövsläge **Beach** • Sweden ...... **96** [3]
Trasvase, Canal de • Spain **11** I5
Traumland • Germany **112** D6
Traun • Austria **13** C9
Traun [Riv] • Austria **13** D9
Traunreut • Germany **112** F4
Traunsee • Austria **119** H4
Traunstein • Germany **112** F4
Travaux • Slovak Rep. **12** I6
Travemünde • Germany **8** F3
Travers, Mt • New Zealand **35** D5
Traverse City •
MI, United States **44** C3
Travis, Lake •
TX, United States **47** E2
Travnik • Bosnia-Herz. **14** E5
Travo • Corsica, France **115** L4
Trbovlje • Slovenia **13** E11
Treasure Beach • Jamaica **159** F3
Treasure Cay • Bahamas **158** B1
Trebaluger • Minorca, Spain **117** F4
Trebbin • Germany **111** C3
Treburden **Beach** • France ...... **96** [80]
Trébeurden • France **114** C1
Trebic • Czech Rep. **128** B4
Trebinje • Bosnia-Herz. **128** D4
Trebisov • Slovak Rep. **13** K9
Trebizond • Turkey **127** D1
Trebnje • Slovenia **13** D11
Trebon • Czech Rep. **128** B4
Trédrez **Beach** • France ...... **96** [80]
Trédrez • France **114** C1
Treetops **Ski** •
MI, United States ...... **149** [141]
Trégastel **Beach** • France ...... **96** [80]
Trégastel • France **114** C1
Tregosse Is. • QL, Australia **144** B2
Tréguier • France **114** C2
Treinta y Tres • Uruguay **52** F5
Treis-Karden • Germany **112** E1
Trelew • Argentina **53** C4
Trelleborg • Sweden **125** F15
Tremadoc **Beach** • France ...... **96** [190]
Tremblade, la **Beach** • France ...... **96** [84]
Tremblade, la • France **115** G1
Tremblant **Ski** • QU, Canada ...... **149** [37]
Tremblant, Mt • QU, Canada **44** H2
Tremblet, Pointe du • Réunion **132** H4
Tremezzo • Italy **121** E3
Tremiti, Is. • Italy **12** J6
Tremmen • Germany **111** C1
Tremonton • UT, United States **42** I6
Tremp • Spain **11** L2
Trencin • Slovak Rep. **13** H9
Trenque Lauguen • Argentina **52** D6
Trentino-Südtirol • Italy **121** E3
Trento • Italy **13** B10
Trenton • NJ, United States **153** D6
Trenton • OT, Canada **155** B6
Trepassey • NF, Canada **156** D4
Tréport, le • France **10** G3
Treptow (Berlin) • Germany **111** C4
Tres Arboles • Uruguay **52** E5
Tres Arroyos • Argentina **52** D6
Três Corações • Brazil **163** C3
Três Esquinas • Colombia **51** B3
Três Lagoas • Brazil **52** F3
Três Marias, Reprêsa • Brazil **52** G2
Tres Palos • Mexico **157** G4
Três Picos • Argentina **53** D3
Tres Puntas, Cabo • Argentina **53** C5
Três Rios • Brazil **163** C4
Tres Zapotes • Mexico **157** G4
Tresaith **Beach** • United Kingdom ...... **101** [190]
Treska • F.Y.R. of Macedonia **15** C2
Treskavica • Bosnia-Herz. **14** F6
Treuchtlingen • Germany **9** F8
Treuer Range • NT, Australia **145** D1
Treviglio • Italy **121** E6
Trevínca, Peña • Spain **11** E2
Treviño • Spain **11** I2
Treviso • Italy **121** E8
Trevone **Beach** • United Kingdom ...... **101** [143]
Trevose Head • United Kingdom **104** F4
Trévou-Treguignec **Beach** •
France ...... **96** [80]
Treyarnon Bay **Beach** •
United Kingdom ...... **101** [141]
Triánda • Rhodes, Greece **122** D12
Triberg • Germany **112** D8
Tribune • KS, United States **46** E3
Tricase • Italy **12** M9
Triconderoga •
NY, United States **44** I4
Trident Peak •
NV, United States **42** F6
Trier **Heritage C** • Germany ...... **86** [51]
Trier • Germany **112** E3
Trieste **Beach** • Italy ...... **97** [167]
Trieste • Italy **121** E8
Trieste, Golfo di •
Italy/Slovenia **121** E8
Trieux • France **114** C2
Trifels • Germany **112** D4
Triglav • Slovenia **13** B5
Triglav • Slovenia **128** D1
Triglav Nat. Park **Park N** •
Slovenia ...... **89** [107]

Triglav Nat. Park • Slovenia **128** D1
Trigno • Italy **121** F1
Trihonída, Límni • Greece **15** C5
Trikala • Greece **15** C4
Trikomo • Cyprus **123** J2
Trikora, Puncak • Indonesia **32** (1) E3
Trim • Ireland **108** C4
Trimburg **Castle** • Germany ...... **113** [177]
Trincomalee • Sri Lanka **138** D15
Trindade, I. d. •
Atlantic Ocean **19** B7
Trinec • Czech Rep. **13** H8
Trinidad • Bolivia **52** D1
Trinidad **Heritage C** • Cuba ...... **84** [40]
Trinidad • Cuba **158** D2
Trinidad • Uruguay **163** D2
Trinidad • CA, United States **42** D5
Trinidad • CO, United States **46** C4
Trinidad Jesuit mission **Heritage C** •
Paraguay ...... **84** [65]
TRINIDAD & TOBAGO • West Indies ...... **160** T/U
Trinidade, I. da • Brazil **163** B3
Trinitapoli • Italy **12** K7
Trinité, la • Martinique ...... **161** N
Trinity • TX, United States **154** J4
Trinity Bay • NF, Canada **156** D4
Trinity Center •
CA, United States **42** D6
Trinkstein • Italy **132** J1
Triolet • Mauritius **132** J1
Trípoli • Greece **15** D6
Tripoli • Lebanon **18** C3
Tripoli • Libya **21** B1
Tripolitania • Libya **21** B2
Tripura • India **28** F4
Tristan da Cunha •
Atlantic Ocean **19** C9
Trivandrum • India **138** D14
Trnava • Slovak Rep. **13** G9
Trobriand • Papua New Guinea **35** (1) G2
Trofors • Norway **16** G4
Trogir **Heritage C** • Croatia ...... **86** [185]
Trogir • Croatia **128** D4
Troglav • Bosnia-Herz./Croatia **128** D4
Tróia • Portugal **118** D2
Trois Fourches, Cap de •
Morocco **131** D2
Trois-Bassins • Réunion **132** H3
Trois-Ilets, les • Martinique ...... **161** N
Trois-Rivières • Guadeloupe ...... **161** L
Trois-Rivières • QU, Canada **155** B4
Troisdorf • Germany **5** K4
Troitsk •
Chelyabinsk, Russian Fed. **26** J7
Troitsk •
Krasnoyarsk, Russian Fed. **26** P6
Troitsko-Pechorsk •
Russian Fed. **17** J2
Trollhättan • Sweden **125** F2
Trollhaugen **Ski** •
WI, United States ...... **149** [129]
Troms • Norway **16** J2
Tromsø • Norway **16** J2
Trona • CA, United States **45** D4
Trondheim • Norway **16** F5
Trondheimsfjorden • Norway **16** F5
Troodos **Heritage C** • Cyprus ...... **86** [235]
Troodos • Cyprus **123** J3
Troodos Mtns • Cyprus **123** J3
Troon **Beach** • United Kingdom ...... **101** [70]
Tropea • Italy **12** J10
Tropical, Costa • Spain **116** B7
Trosa • Sweden **125** D4
Trossachs, The • United Kingdom **104** B1
Trostberg • Germany **112** F4
Trotus • Romania **14** N3
Trou aux Biches **Beach** •
Mauritius **132** J1
Trou d'Eau **Beach** • Mauritius **132** A4
Troussay (Château) • France **114** D2
Trout • LA, United States **47** H2
Trout Creek • OT, Canada **44** F2
Trout Lake • NT, Canada **38** G4
Trout Peak • WY, United States **42** K4
Troutbeck • United Kingdom **104** C4
Troutbeck • Zimbabwe **130** C2
Trouville-sur-Mer • France **10** G4
Trowbridge • United Kingdom **104** F3
Trowulan • Java, Indonesia **143** J8
Troy **Heritage C** • Turkey ...... **86** [224]
Troy • Turkey **122** D2
Troy • ID, United States **42** G3
Troy • MI, United States **44** D4
Troy • PA, United States **44** E5
Troy • AL, United States **48** E5
Troy • NY, United States **153** D6
Troy Peak • NV, United States **45** E2
Troyan • Bulgaria **14** L7
Troyes • France **10** J5
Truite, Lac à la • QU, Canada **44** F2
Trujillo • Spain **11** B5
Trujillo • Peru **51** B5
Trujillo • Venezuela **51** C2
Trumann • AR, United States **46** J5
Trumbull, Mt •
AZ, United States **45** F3
Trundholm **Beach** • Denmark ...... **96** [43]
Trung Phan • Vietnam **31** D3
Truro • NS, Canada **155** C7
Truro • United Kingdom **104** F4
Truth or Consequences •
NM, United States **153** E4
Trutnov • Czech Rep. **128** B2
Tryavna • Bulgaria **128** E3
Trysilelva • Norway **124** B3
Trzcianka • Poland **13** F4
Tsabong • Botswana **23** B4
Tsangarada **Beach** • Greece ...... **97** [188]
Tsarkoyo Selo • Russian Fed. **126** C1
Tsau • Botswana **24** C4
Tsavo • Kenya **23** F4
Tsavo East Nat. Park • Kenya **131** G4
Tsavo Nat. Park **Park N** • Kenya ...... **133** [84]
Tsavo West Nat. Park • Kenya **131** G4
Tseung Kwan O •
Hong Kong, China **139** B6
Tshane • Botswana **24** C4
Tshikapa • Dem. Rep. of Congo **23** C5
Tshuapa • Dem. Rep. of Congo **23** C4
Tshwaane • Botswana **24** H2
Tsiafajavona • Madagascar **24** H3
Tsim Sha Tsui •
Hong Kong, China **139** B6
Tsimlyanskoye Vdkhr. •
Russian Fed. **17** G5
Tsing Yi • Hong Kong, China **139** B5
Tsingy Benaraha, Réserve du
Heritage N • Madagascar ...... **83** [108]
Tsiroanomandidy • Madagascar **24** H3
Tsitsikamma Mtns • South Africa **134** C7
Tsitsikamma Nat. Park •
South Africa **134** C7
Tsodilo Hills • Botswana **29** C1
Tsqaltubo • Mongolia **23** H7
Tsu • Japan **140** C2
Tsuchiura • Japan **140** C2
Tsuen Wan • Hong Kong, China **139** B5
Tsugaru-kaikyo • Japan **30** K4
Tsukigase Garden • Japan **140** B2
Tsukuba • Japan **140** B3
Tsumeb • Namibia **24** B3
Tsuna • Japan **140** B3
Tsuru • Japan **140** C1
Tsurugi-saki • Japan **140** C1

Tsuruoka • Japan **30** J5
Tsushima • Japan **140** A2
Tsushima-kaikyo • Japan **30** E8
Tsuyama • Japan **30** G7
Tua • Portugal **11** D3
Tual • Indonesia **32** (1) D4
Tuam • Ireland **108** C4
Tuamotu • French Polynesia **33** M7
Tuapse • Russian Fed. **17** E6
Tuas • Singapore **141** H1
Tuatapere • New Zealand **145** G3
Tuba City • AZ, United States **153** E1
Tubai Is. • French Polynesia **33** L8
Tuban • Java, Indonesia **143** J3
Tubarão • Brazil **52** G4
Tubayq, Jabal at • Saudi Arabia **21** G2
Tubbataha Reef Marine Park **Heritage N** •
Philippines ...... **83** [136]
Tübingen • Germany **112** D6
Tubruq • Libya **21** D1
Tubuai • French Polynesia **33** M8
Tuchitua • YT, Canada **40** P3
Tuchola • Poland **13** G4
Tucker • GA, United States **48** E4
Tucker's Town • Bermuda **159** J2
Tucson • AZ, United States **153** E3
Tucumcari • NM, United States **46** D5
Tucupita • Venezuela **51** E2
Tucurui, Reprêsa de • Brazil **53** (1) B2
Tudela • Spain **11** J2
Tuen Mun • Hong Kong, China **139** B5
Tufi • Papua New Guinea **35** (1) D2
Tugela • South Africa **134** B4
Tugela Ferry • South Africa **134** B4
Tuguegarao • Philippines **31** G3
Tugur • Russian Fed. **27** M6
Tuineje •
Fuerteventura, Canary Is. **117** E2
Tuk Tuk • Indonesia **143** G2
Tukangbesi, Kepulauan •
Indonesia **32** (1) B4
Tuktoyaktuk • NT, Canada **38** E3
Tukums • Latvia **126** B3
Tula • Russian Fed. **126** B3
Tula • Mexico **157** G2
Tulamben • Bali, Indonesia **143** H2
Tulancingo • Mexico **157** G2
Tulare • CA, United States **45** C3
Tularosa • NM, United States **46** C6
Tularosa Valley •
NM, United States **45** I5
Tulayat al Ghassul • Jordan **135** A6
Tulbagh • South Africa **134** B6
Tulcan • Colombia **51** B3
Tulcea • Romania **128** E2
Tulelake • CA, United States **42** E6
Tuli, Fort • Zimbabwe **130** C1
Tulia • TX, United States **46** E5
Tulla • Ireland **108** C6
Tullahoma • TN, United States **48** D3
Tullamarine [Apt] •
VI, Australia **144** C3
Tullamore • Ireland **7** E8
Tulle • France **115** G2
Tulliow • Ireland **108** B3
Tullow • Ireland **144** B1
Tuloma • Russian Fed. **16** Q2
Tulsa • OK, United States **46** H4
Tulua • Colombia **51** B3
Tulum • Mexico **157** H2
Tulum • Russian Fed. **26** R7
Tulungagung • Java, Indonesia **143** J7
Tumacacori Nat. Hist. Park **Park N** •
AZ, United States ...... **150** [113]
Tumacacori Nat. Hist. Park •
AZ, United States **153** E3
Tumaco • Colombia **51** B3
Tumba • Sweden **125** D4
Tumbes • Peru **51** A4
Tumen [Riv] •
China/D.P.R. of Korea **30** E3
Tumkur • India **138** D6
Tummel • United Kingdom **104** B1
Tum • Sweden **125** F3
Tun Chung • Hong Kong, China **139** B5
Tunapuna • Trinidad & Tobago ...... **160** U
Tunas de Zaza • Cuba **158** D2
Tunduma • Tanzania **130** B3
Tunduru • Tanzania **130** B4
Tundzha • Bulgaria **14** N7
Tung Ling Chau •
Hong Kong, China **139** B6
Tungabhadra • India **138** D6
Tungelsta • Sweden **125** D4
Tungsten • NT, Canada **49** P3
Tunis **Heritage C** • Tunisia ...... **86** [263]
Tunis • Tunisia **131** E2
Tunis, Golfe de • Tunisia **131** E2
TUNISIA • Africa ...... **131** E
Tunja • Colombia **51** C2
Tunnsjøen • Norway **16** G4
Tunxi • China **139** C3
Tupá • Brazil **52** F3
Tupanciretã • Brazil **52** F4
Tupelo • MS, United States **48** C3
Tupelo Nat. Battlefield **Park N** •
MS, United States ...... **151** [197]
Tupiza • Bolivia **52** C3
Tupper Lake • NY, United States **44** H3
Tupungato, Cerro • Argentina **52** C5
Tuquan • China **27** J7
Tuquerre • Colombia **51** B3
Tur'ah Jonglei • Sudan **21** F6
Tûr, El • Egypt **131** F4
Turabah • Saudi Arabia **26** R5
Turabah • Saudi Arabia **18** D4
Turan • Russian Fed. **26** P7
Turana, Khrebet • Russian Fed. **27** L6
Turangi • New Zealand **145** F4
Turayf • Saudi Arabia **18** D3
Turbah, At • Yemen **21** H5
Turballe, la **Beach** • France ...... **96** [82]
Turballe, la • France **114** C4
Turbat • Pakistan **18** H4
Turbo • Colombia **51** B2
Turda • Romania **14** K3
Turek • Poland **13** H5
Turenne • France **115** G2
Turfan • China **26** M9
Turgay Basin • Kazakhstan **128** E3
Turgoviste • Bulgaria **128** E3
Turgutlu • Turkey **122** D6
Turgutlu, Al • Sudan **11** K5
Turiaçu, Baia de • Brazil **53** (1) B2
Turimiquire • Venezuela **51** H6
Turin **Heritage C** • Italy ...... **86** [128]
Turin • Italy **121** E5
Turinsk • Russian Fed. **26** J6
Turka • Kenya **23** F3
Turkana, Lake • Kenya **131** G3
TURKEY • Asia/Europe **4** R8
Turkestan • Kazakhstan **26** J9
Turkestan Range •
Tajikistan/Uzbekistan **31** C4
Turkey Creek • WA, Australia **26** K9
Turkmenabat • Turkmenistan **26** I10
TURKMENISTAN • Asia **26** I10
TURKS & CAICOS IS. •
West Indies ...... **158** C

Turks Island Passage •
Turks & Caicos Is. **158** C2
Turku • Finland **125** E3
Turku Archipelago • Finland **125** E3
Turkwel • Kenya **131** G1
Turlock • CA, United States **45** B3
Turnagain, Cape • New Zealand **35** F5
Turneffe Is. • Belize. **158** B2
Turnhout • Belgium **109** D11
Turnov • Czech Rep. **128** B2
Turnu Magurele • Romania **14** L6
Turoa • New Zealand **145** F4
Turpan • China **26** O9
Turpan Depression • China **26** P9
Turquino, Pico • Cuba **158** D8
Turrialba • Costa Rica ...... **123** F
Turtkul' • Uzbekistan **18** H1
Turtle I. • Bali, Indonesia **143** H4
Turtle I. • CA, United States **144** B2
Turtle Mtn • MN, Canada **43** F2
Turtmann • Russian Fed. **26** O4
Turtola • Finland **125** E3
Turtúla • Brazil **53** (1) C2
TusenFryd **Park L** • Norway ...... **98** [4]
Tuscaloosa • AL, United States **48** D4
Tuscania • Italy **121** F1
Tuscany • Italy **120** A1
Tuscola • TX, United States **47** E1
Tusenfryd • Norway **124** B4
Tuskegee Institute Nat. Hist. Site **Park N** •
AL, United States ...... **151** [199]
Tuticorin • India **138** D11
Tutóia • Brazil **53** (1) C2
Tuttle Creek Lake •
KS, United States **46** G3
Tuttlingen • Germany **112** D8
Tutuala • East Indies **32** (1) C4
Tutuila • American Samoa **35** (2) F1
Tutupaca, Volcán • Peru **163** B4
Tutwiler • MS, United States **48** C3
Tuul • Mongolia **27** G7
Tuvalu • Russian Fed. **26** O7
TUVALU • Pacific Ocean **33** I6
Tuvana-i-Ra • Fiji Is. **35** (2) E3
Tuvana-i-Tholo • Fiji Is. **35** (2) D3
Tuwayq, Jabal • Saudi Arabia **18** E5
Tuxpan • Mexico **157** G2
Tuxtla Gutiérrez • Mexico **157** G4
Tuy Hoa • Vietnam **31** D4
Tuz Gölü • Turkey **26** P9
Tuz, Lake • Turkey **122** A3
Tuzigoot Nat. Mon. **Park N** •
AZ, United States ...... **150** [107]
Tuzigoot Nat. Mon. •
AZ, United States **153** E1
Tuzla • Bosnia-Herz. **14** F5
Tuzlata • Bulgaria **128** E3
Tvedestrand • Norway **125** F1
Tveitsund • Norway **124** C6
Tver' • Russian Fed. **126** C4
Tverfjellet • Norway **124** C2
Tvøroyri • Faroe Is. **4** I4
Tvurditsa • Bulgaria **15** G1
Tweed • United Kingdom **6** J6
Tweedsmuir Prov. Park •
BC, Canada **155** C1
Twelve Apostles, The •
VI, Australia **144** C3
Twelve Bens • Ireland **108** C3
Twelve Mile Lake • SA, Canada **43** C2
Twentynine Palms •
CA, United States **45** D4
Twilight Cove • WA, Australia **34** E6
Twin Buttes Reservoir •
TX, United States **47** D2
Twin Falls • ID, United States **152** B4
Twin Is. • Canada **39** O6
Twin Mtns • NH, United States **44** J3
Twin Peaks **Ski** •
WI, United States ...... **149** B
Twisp • WA, United States **42** E2
Twistringen • Germany **8** E3
Two Harbors • MN, United States **43** K3
Two Rivers • WI, United States **44** C3
Two Thumb Range • New Zealand **35** C6
Twycross • United Kingdom **104** D2
Twyfelfontein **Heritage C** • Spain ...... **98** [76]
Tyana • Turkey **123** G2
Tybee I. • GA, United States **48** G5
Tychy • Poland **128** C1
Tyin • Norway **124** C4
Tyler • TX, United States **154** J2
Tyldosand • Sweden **125** F4
Tylösänd • Sweden **125** F4
Tymovskoye • Russian Fed. **54** A4
Tynda • Russian Fed. **27** K5
Tyndall • SD, United States **43** H5
Tyne • United Kingdom **7** K7
Tynemouth **Beach** •
United Kingdom ...... **101** [21–22]
Tynemouth **Beach** •
United Kingdom ...... **101** [203]
Tyre **Heritage C** • Lebanon ...... **86** [284]
Tyre • Lebanon **135** A1
Tyrella **Beach** • United Kingdom ...... **101** [252]
Tyrifjorden • Norway **124** B1
Tyrrhenian Sea •
Mediterranean Sea **12** G9
Tysa • Europe **12** K1
Tysnesøy • Norway **124** C4
Tysstranda • Norway **125** D3
Tyukalinsk • Russian Fed. **26** L6
Tyulenov • Bulgaria **14** P6
Tyumen • Russian Fed. **26** K6
Tywi, Afon • United Kingdom **7** H9
Tywyn • United Kingdom **7** H9
Tzaneen **Beach** • United Kingdom ...... **101** [203]
Tzermiádo • Crete, Greece **123** E7

Uaroo • WA, Australia **34** C4
Uaupés • Brazil **51** D4
Ubá • Brazil **163** C4
Ubaitaba • Brazil **52** I1
Ubangi • Dem. Rep. of Congo **23** B3
Ubatuba **Beach** • India **163** C4
Ubatuba • Brazil **163** C3
Ube • Japan **140** A3
Ubeda • Spain **11** H6
Uberaba • Brazil **52** G2
Überlandia • Brazil **52** G2
Überlingen • Germany **112** D7
Ubin • Singapore **141** H2
Ubina, Nevado • Peru **163** B4
Ubon Rat Reservoir • Thailand **142** A2
Ubon Ratchathani • Thailand **31** C3
Ubstadt-Weiher • Germany **112** D4
Ubsu-Nur • Mongolia **26** P8
Ubud • Bali, Indonesia **143** H3
Ubundu • Dem. Rep. of Congo **23** D4
Ucayali • Peru **51** C5
Uchami • Russian Fed. **26** Q5

U

Uchi Lake • OT, Canada 43 J1
Uchiura-wan • Japan 30 K3
Uchte • Germany 5 L2
Uckermark • Germany 8 I3
Uçpınar • Turkey 123 F2
Udachnyy • Russian Fed. 26 T4
Udaipur • India 137 C5
Udayapur • India 137 C7
Uddevalla • Sweden 125 F2
Uddjaure • Sweden 16 I4
Udgir • India 28 C5
Udhagamandalam • India 138 D10
Udine • Italy 121 E4
Udmurtia • Russian Fed. 17 I3
Udon Thani • Thailand 31 C3
Udskaya Guba • Russian Fed. 27 M5
Udupi • India 138 D6
Udupi Beach • India 138 E3
Uebonti • Indonesia 32 (1) B3
Uecker • Germany 8 J3
Ueckermünde • Germany 8 J3
Ueda • Japan 30 J6
Uele • Dem. Rep. of Congo. 23 C3
Uelen • Russian Fed. 27 X3
Uelzen • Germany 8 F3
Ueno • Japan 140 B2
Uetze • Germany 8 F4
Ufa • Russian Fed. 17 J4
Ufa [Riv] • Russian Fed. 26 I6
Ugab • Namibia 24 A4
Ugadamandalam Hill Sta • India 138 E2
UGANDA • Africa 23 E3
Ugine • France 115 F2
Uglekamensk • Russian Fed. 30 G3
Uglich • Russian Fed. 126 C4
Ugljan • Croatia 128 D3
Uherské Hradiste • Czech Rep. 13 G8
Uhersky • Czech Rep. 128 B3
Uhrichsville •
    OH, United States 44 E5
Uig • United Kingdom 6 F4
Uíge • Angola 23 B5
Uitenhage • South Africa 134 C8
Uithoorn • Netherlands 109 F2
Uithuizen • Netherlands 109 D4
Ufehertó • Hungary 13 K10
Uji • Japan 140 B2
Uji-gunto • Japan 30 E9
Ujjain • India 28 C4
Ujung • Bali, Indonesia 143 H4
Ujung Kulon Nat. Park Heritage N •
    Indonesia .... 83 [137]
Ujung Pandang • Indonesia 32 (1) A4
Ukhta • Russian Fed. 17 I2
Ukiah • OR, United States 42 F4
Ukiah • CA, United States 42 D7
Ukimi-do • Japan 140 B2
Ukmerge • Lithuania 126 B6
UKRAINE • Europe 17 E5
Uku-jima • Japan 30 E9
Ula • Turkey 122 D9
Ulá, Al • Saudi Arabia 18 C4
Ulaanbaatar • Mongolia 27 I7
Ulaangom • Mongolia 26 P8
Ulan Bator • Mongolia 27 I7
Ulan Tajga • Mongolia 26 P8
Ulan Ude • Russian Fed. 27 G6
Ulan Ul Hu • China 28 F2
Ulanhad • China 29 F2
Ular • Singapore 141 H3
Ulawa • Rep. of Korea 30 E6
Ulcinj • F.R. of Yugoslavia 15 A2
Ule älv • Finland 16 M4
Uleåborg • Finland 16 M4
Ulefoss • Norway 124 B3
Ulfborg • Denmark 125 F9
Ulfborg-Vemb Beach • Denmark ...... 96 [50]
Ulgiy • Mongolia 26 P8
Ulhasnagar • India 28 B5
Uliastay • Mongolia 26 Q8
Uliga • Marshall Is. 33 I5
Ullal Beach • India 138 E3
Ullapool • United Kingdom 6 G4
Ullared • Sweden 125 F7
Ulldecona • Spain 11 L4
Ullswater • United Kingdom 104 C2
Ulm • Germany 112 E1
Ulmen • Germany 112 E1
Ulricehamn • Sweden 125 F7
Ulsan • Rep. of Korea 30 E7
Ulsteinvik • Norway 124 C1
Ulster • Ireland/UK. 7 E7
Ulu Watu Temple •
    Bali, Indonesia 143 H4
Uluabat Gölü • Turkey 122 D3
Ulubey • Turkey 122 F8
Uludag • Turkey 122 D3
Uluguru Mtns • Tanzania 23 F5
Ulukisla • Turkey 123 G1
Ulundi • South Africa 134 B4
Ulupalakua • HI, United States 47 L8
Uluru • NT, Australia 145 D3
Uluru Nat. Park Heritage N •
    Australia .... 83 [145]
Uluru Nat. Park Heritage C •
    Australia .... 85 [209]
Uluru Nat. Park • NT, Australia 145 D3
Ulus Dag • Turkey 15 J4
Ulutau • Kazakstan 26 K8
Ulverston • United Kingdom 104 C4
Ulverstone • TS, Australia 34 I8
Ulvik • Norway 124 C4
Ulya • Russian Fed. 27 N5
Ulysses Dive • Red Sea 135 B1
Ulysses • KS, United States 46 E4
Ulysses S. Grant Nat. Hist. Site Park N •
    MO, United States .... 151 [174]
Uman • Ukraine 17 E5
Umán • Mexico 157 H1
Umba • Russian Fed. 17 E1
Umbargaon Beach • India 138 E3
Umboi I. • Papua New Guinea 35 (1) D2
Umbria • Italy 12 G6
Umbria Dive • Red Sea 135 B3
Ume älv • Sweden 16 J4
Umeå • Sweden 16 K5
Umhlanga Rocks • South Africa 134 B4
Umlalazi Nature Reserve •
    South Africa 134 B4
Umlazi • South Africa 134 B4
Umm ar Rizam • Libya 21 D1
Umm as Samim • Oman 18 G5
Umm Durman • Sudan 21 F4
Umm Lajj • Saudi Arabia 18 C4
Umnak I. • AK, United States 18 D4
Umpolo • Angola 24 B2
Umsini, Gunung • Indonesia 32 (1) D3
Umtamvuna Nature Reserve •
    South Africa 134 C7
Umtata • South Africa 52 F3
Umuarama • Brazil 52 F3
Umurbaba Dagi • Turkey 15 J4
Umurbey • Turkey 15 H3
Umzimkulu • South Africa 134 B5
Umzinto • South Africa 134 B5
Una • Bosnia-Herz. 14 D5
Unalakleet • AK, United States 49 H4
Unalaska • AK, United States 49 H5
Unalaska I. • AK, United States 49 H5
Unayzah • Saudi Arabia 18 D4
Uncompahgre Peak Ski •
    CO, United States .... 149 A
Uncompahgre Plateau •
    CO, United States 149 L2
Undandita • NT, Australia 145 D1

Unden • Sweden 125 F3
Underberg • South Africa 134 B5
Underdal • Norway 124 C4
Undu Point • Fiji Is. 35 (2) D2
Ungava, Baie d' • QU, Canada 39 R5
Ungava Peninsula • QU, Canada 36 J3
Ungava, Péninsule d' •
    QU, Canada 39 Q4
Unggi • D.P.R. of Korea 30 F3
Ungheni • Moldova 14 D2
Ungwana Bay • Kenya 131 G4
União da Vitória • Brazil 52 F4
Unicov • Czech Rep. 13 G8
Unije • Croatia 128 D3
Unimak I. • AK, United States 49 I5
Union • MO, United States 46 J3
Union • SC, United States 48 G3
Union City • TN, United States 48 C2
Union I. • St Vincent & Gren. .... 161 R
Union Springs •
    AL, United States 48 E4
Uniondale • South Africa 134 C7
Uniontown • PA, United States 44 F6
Uniontown • AL, United States 48 D4
UNITED ARAB EMIRATES • Asia 18 F5
UNITED KINGDOM • Europe 6/7
UNITED STATES • N. America 36
UNITED STATES VIRGIN IS. •
    West Indies .... 160 Z
Unity • SA, Canada 38 J6
Universal City •
    TX, United States 47 E3
Universal Studios Florida •
    FL, United States 151 C2
Universal Studios Hollywood Park L •
    CA, United States .... 150 [E]
Universales, Montes • Spain 11 J4
University Park •
    NM, United States 45 I5
Unna • Germany 5 K3
Unna • Germany 111 B2
Unst • United Kingdom 6 L1
Unstrut • Germany 9 F5
Unter Engadin • Switzerland 119 G4
Unteres Odertal, Nationalpark Park N •
    Germany/Poland .... 89 [61]
Unterfranken • Germany 9 E7
Unterinntal • Austria 119 H3
Unterwasser • Switzerland 119 G3
Unzha • Russian Fed. 17 G3
Upata • Venezuela 51 E2
Upemba, Parc nat. de l' Park •
    Dem. Rep. of Congo .... 133 [58]
Upernavik • Greenland 39 T2
Upin • Indonesia 32 (1) C3
Upington • South Africa 24 C5
Uplands [Apt] • OT, Canada 155 B7
Upolu • Samoa 35 (2) F1
Upper Arlington •
    OH, United States 44 D5
Upper Austria • Austria 119 G3
Upper Canada Village •
    OT, Canada 155 B7
Upper Darby • PA, United States 44 H6
Upper Egypt • Egypt 131 F4
Upper Hutt • New Zealand 35 B5
Upper Klamath Lake •
    OR, United States 152 B3
Upper Lake • CA, United States 42 E6
Upper Liard • YT, Canada 49 P3
Upper Red Lake •
    MN, United States 43 I2
Upper Sandusky •
    OH, United States 44 D5
Uppsala • Sweden 125 H2
Uppsala [Adm] • Sweden 125 D2
Upsala • OT, Canada 43 K2
Upshi • Jammu & Kashmir 28 C2
Uqlat as Sugur • Saudi Arabia 21 H2
Ur • Iraq 18 E3
Urakawa • Japan 30 L3
Ural • Russian Fed. 26 H7
Urals • Russian Fed. 26 J6
Urama Dive • Red Sea 135 B4
Uranium City • SA, Canada 38 J5
Uraricoera • Brazil 51 E3
Urawa • Japan 140 C2
Urbana • IL, United States 44 A5
Urbana • OH, United States 44 D5
Urbano Santos • Brazil 53 (1) C2
Urbino Heritage C • Italy .... 86 [145]
Urbino • Italy 121 E12
Uren • Russian Fed. 17 H3
Urengoy • Russian Fed. 26 M4
Urenui • New Zealand 145 F3
Ureparapara • Vanuatu 35 (2) B1
Urgal • Russian Fed. 27 L6
Urganch • Uzbekistan 18 H1
Ürgüp • Turkey 123 G2
Urho Kekkonen Nat. Park Park N •
    Finland .... 89 [30]
Urk • Netherlands 109 D7
Urla • Turkey 122 D5
Urnes Heritage C • Norway .... 85 [80]
Urnes stavkirke • Norway 124 C4
Urosevac • F.R. of Yugoslavia 14 F5
Urshult • Sweden 125 F12
Ursus • Poland 13 J5
Uruapan • Mexico 157 G3
Urubamba • Peru 163 B2
Urubamba • Peru 163 B2
Urucui • Brazil 53 (1) C3
Urucurituba • Brazil 51 F4
Uruguaiana • Brazil 52 E4
URUGUAY • S. America 52 E5
Uruguay [Riv] • S. America 52 E5
Ürümqi • China 26 O9
Urup, Ostrov • Russian Fed. 27 P7
Uryupinsk • Russian Fed. 17 F5
Urzhum • Russian Fed. 17 H3
Urziceni • Romania 128 E1
Urzig • Germany 112 E3
US East Coast cruise area •
    N. America 80 A2
Usa • Russian Fed. 4 W3
Usa • Russian Fed. 17 J2
Usak • Turkey 122 F8
Usak • Turkey 122 D6
Usambara Mtns • Tanzania 130 B2
Usborne, Mt • Falkland Is. 53 E6
Usedom • Germany 8 J3
Ushakova, Ostrov • Russian Fed. 126 A4
Ushakovskoye • Russian Fed. 27 V2
Ushant • France 114 C1
Ushkany, Ostrov • Russian Fed. 127 A13
Ushuaia • Argentina 17 J1
Usinsk • Russian Fed. 17 J1
Usk • United Kingdom 124 C5
Uskedal • Norway 124 C5
Üsküb • F.Y.R. of Macedonia 90 A14
Üsküdar • Turkey 122 D3
Üsküp • Turkey 15 I2
Uslar • Germany 5 M2
Usogorsk • Russian Fed. 17 H2
Usolye-Sibirskoye •
    Russian Fed. 27 F6

Ust-Kara • Russian Fed. 26 J4
Ust-Khayryuzovo • Russian Fed. 54 JJ4
Ust-Kut • Russian Fed. 27 G5
Ust-Kuyga • Russian Fed. 27 M3
Ust-Lyzha • Russian Fed. 17 J1
Ust-Maya • Russian Fed. 27 L4
Ust-Muya • Russian Fed. 27 I5
Ust-Nem • Russian Fed. 17 I2
Ust-Nera • Russian Fed. 27 N4
Ust-Nyukzha • Russian Fed. 27 J5
Ust-Olenëk • Russian Fed. 27 I3
Ust-Omchug • Russian Fed. 27 O4
Ust-Ordynskiy • Russian Fed. 27 F6
Ust-Pit • Russian Fed. 26 P6
Ust-Tsilma • Russian Fed. 17 I1
Ustaoset • Norway 124 C4
Ustek • Czech Rep. 128 B2
Usti nad Labem • Czech Rep. 128 B1
Usti nad Orlici • Czech Rep. 13 F8
Ustica Beach • Italy .... 97 [151]
Ustica, I. di • Italy 120 D1
Ustka • Poland 13 F3
Ustyurt Plateau •
    Kazakstan/Uzbekistan 26 I9
Ustyurt Plateau •
    Kazakstan/Uzbekistan 126 A10
Usu • China 26 N9
Usuki • Japan 30 F8
Usumacinta • Guatemala/Mexico. 37 C4
Utah • United States 40 D4
Utara, Selat • Penang, Malaysia 141 F2
Utena • Lithuania 126 B6
Utete • Tanzania 130 B4
Utica • Tunisia 131 E2
Utica • NY, United States 153 D2
Utiel • Spain 11 K5
Utila • Honduras 158 A11
Utlängen • Sweden 125 F12
Utne • Norway 124 C4
Utö • Sweden 125 D4
Utö [I.] • Sweden 125 D4
Utopia Aboriginal Land •
    NT, Australia 145 D2
Utorda Beach • Goa, India 137 B2
Utrecht • Netherlands 109 F4
Utrecht • South Africa 134 B1
Utrecht [Adm] • Netherlands 109 D7
Utrera • Spain 11 F7
Utsjoki • Finland 16 N2
Utsukushino-mori • Japan 140 C1
Utsunomiya • Japan 30 J6
Uttar Pradesh • India 137 C7
Uttaradit • Thailand 142 B4
Uttuado • Puerto Rico 159 H1
Utvær • Norway 124 C3
Uudenmaa • Finland 125 E4
Uusikaupunki • Finland 125 E3
Uvalde • TX, United States 47 E3
Uvdal • Norway 124 C6
Uvea • Wallis & Futuna 35 (2) G4
Uvinza • Tanzania 130 B1
Uvira • Dem. Rep. of Congo 23 D4
Uvongo • South Africa 134 B5
Uwajima • Japan 30 G8
Uwayl • Sudan 21 E3
Uwaynat Wannin • Libya 21 B2
Uxmal Heritage C • Guatemala .... 84 [30]
Uxmal • Mexico 157 H1
Uyar • Russian Fed. 26 P6
Uyedineniya, Ostrov •
    Russian Fed. 26 N2
Uygur Zizhiqu • China 29 A2
Uyuni, Salar de • Bolivia 52 C2
Uz • Slovak Rep. 13 L9
Uzbekistan •
    Kazakstan/Uzbekistan 26 J9
UZBEKISTAN • Asia 26 H9
Uzen • Kazakstan 115 G2
Uzerche • France 115 G2
Uzhhorod • Ukraine 13 L9
Uzhur • Russian Fed. 26 P6
Uzice • F.R. of Yugoslavia 14 G6
Uzum • Turkey 122 D5
Uzümlü • Turkey 123 F2
Uzuncaburç • Turkey 123 G3
Uzungwa Range • Tanzania 23 F5
Uzunköprü • Turkey 15 H2

V.C. Bird [Apt] •
    Antigua & Barbuda .... 161 K
Vaadhu Diving Paradise •
    Maldives 138 F4
Vaal • South Africa 24 D5
Vaala • Finland 16 N4
Vaaldam • South Africa 24 D5
Vaasa • Finland 16 K5
Vaasa Beach • Finland .... 97 [26]
Vaasa [Adm] • Finland 124 A8
Vabbinfaru • Maldives 138 F2
Vác • Hungary 13 I10
Vacaos • Mauritius 132 J3
Vacaria • Brazil 52 F4
Vacaville • CA, United States 159 B5
Vache, Ile-à- • Haiti 159 G5
Vaches, l. aux • Seychelles 133 K2
Vadeheuet • Denmark 96 J4
Vadheim • Norway 124 C3
Vadili • Cyprus 123 J4
Vadodara • India 28 B4
Vadsø • Norway 16 O1
Vadstena • Sweden 125 F4
Vaduz • Liechtenstein 119 G3
Vadvetjåkka Nat. Park Park N •
    Sweden .... 89 [16]
Værløse Beach • Denmark .... 96 [39]
Værøy • Norway 16 G3
Vågåmo • Norway 124 C2
Vaganski vrh • Croatia 14 C5
Vagator Beach • Goa, India 137 B1
Vågåvatn • Norway 124 C2
Vaggeryd • Sweden 125 F7
Vagharshad • Sweden 125 C2
Vagos Beach • Portugal .... 96 [95]
Vågsfjorden • Norway 16 I2
Vågslid • Norway 124 C6
Vågsøy • Norway 124 C1
Vah • Slovak Rep. 13 I8
Vaila • Crete, Greece 123 E8
Vail Ski • CO, United States ...... 149 [103]
Vail • CO, United States 45 I2
Vainguinim Beach • Goa, India 137 B1
Vaishali • India 137 C8
Vaksdal • Norway 124 C4
Val André, le • France 114 C2
Val Camónica Heritage C • Italy .... 86 [131]
Val Camónica • Italy 121 E3
Val Cenis Ski • France .... 100 [49]
Val d'Allos-La Foux Ski •
    France .... 100 [71]
Val d'Isère Ski • France .... 100 [33]
Val d'Isère • France 115 F2
Val d'Or Ski • France .... 100 [64]
Val d'Or • QU, Canada 39 P7
Val Marie • SA, Canada 42 L2
Val St Come Ski • QU, Canada .... 149 [38]
Val Thorens Ski • France .... 100 [43]
Val Thorens • France 115 F2
Val-d'Illiez Ski • Switzerland ..... 100 [78]
Valahima • Romania 14 K5
Valais • Switzerland 119 G6
Valandovo • F.Y.R. of Macedonia 119 G6
Valašské Mezirici • Czech Rep. 13 G8
Valbella • Switzerland 119 G4

Valberg Ski • France .... 100 [73]
Valcabrère • France 115 J2
Valchéta • Argentina 53 C4
Valdagno • Italy 121 E3
Valdáora Ski • Italy .... 100 [244]
Valcáora • Italy 120 B2
Valcay • Russian Fed. 4 Q5
Valcay • Russian Fed. 126 C1
Valcayskaya Vozvyshennost •
    Russian Fed. 126 C3
Valdecañas, Embalse de • Spain 11 F5
Valdegenga • Spain 11 J5
Valdemarsslot • Denmark 125 F14
Valdemarsvik • Sweden 125 F4
Valdepeñas • Spain 11 H6
Valdepeñas • Spain 11 H6
Valdes, Península Heritage N •
    Argentina .... 82 [43]
Valdés, Península • Argentina 53 D4
Valdez • AK, United States 49 L3
Valdivia • Chile 53 B3
Valdosta • GA, United States 154 H3
Valdoviño Beach • Spain .... 96 [92]
Vale de Parra • Portugal 118 E6
Vale do Côa Heritage C •
    Portugal .... 86 [113]
Vale Navio • Portugal 118 E7
Vale of Trent • United Kingdom 104 D2
Valea lui Mihai • Romania 14 J2
Valea Viseului • Romania 52 I1
Valença • France 114 B1
Valençay [Château] • France 114 D4
Valence • France 115 F3
Valencia • Spain 11 K5
Valencia • Venezuela 51 D2
Valencia Heritage C • Spain .... 86 [89]
Valencia Beach • Spain .... 96 [119]
Valencia, Costa de • Spain 116 A4
Valencia de Don Juan • Spain 11 F2
Valencia, Golfo de • Spain 11 L5
Valenciana, Comunidad de •
    Spain 11 K5
Valenciennes • France 10 I3
Valentia I. • Ireland 108 C7
Valentin • Russian Fed. 30 H3
Valentine • NE, United States 43 F5
Valera • Venezuela 51 C2
Valga • Estonia 126 B2
Valinco, Golfe de •
    Corsica, France 115 L3
Valjevo • F.R. of Yugoslavia 14 G5
Valkeakoski • Finland 125 E2
Valkenburg • Netherlands 109 D16
Valkenswaard • Netherlands 5 I3
Vall de Uxó • Spain 11 K5
Valladolid • Spain 11 G3
Valladolid • Mexico 157 H1
Valldal • Norway 124 C2
Valldemossa • Majorca, Spain 117 H1
Valle • Norway 124 C6
Valle d'Aosta • Italy 121 E1
Valle de Bravo • Mexico 157 G4
Valledupar • Colombia 51 C1
Vallée de Mai Nature Reserve •
    Seychelles 133 K4
Vallée de Mai Nature Reserve, Seychelles
    Heritage N • Seychelles .... 83 [110]
Vallée Jonction • QU, Canada 44 J2
Vallejo • CA, United States 45 A2
Vallejo • CA, United States 152 C3
Vallenar • Chile 52 B4
Vallendar • Germany 112 E2
Vallensbæk Beach • Denmark .... 96 [39]
Vallentuna • Sweden 125 H2
Valletta Heritage C • Malta .... 86 [233]
Valletta • Malta 123 H4
Valley City • ND, United States 43 G3
Valley de los Ingenios Heritage C •
    Cuba .... 84 [40]
Valley East • OT, Canada 44 E2
Valley Falls •
    OR, United States 42 E5
Valley Forge Nat. Hist. Park Park N •
    PA, United States .... 151 [298]
Valley Forge Nat. Hist. Park •
    PA, United States 153 D6
Valley of 1000 Hills •
    South Africa 134 B3
Valley of Fire State Park •
    NV, United States 152 C4
Valley Station •
    KY, United States 48 E1
Valleyfield • QU, Canada 155 B7
Vallo della Luciania • Italy 12 J8
Vallorcine • France 115 F4
Vallorbe • Switzerland 119 G1
Vallø • Denmark 117 D3
Valmeinier Ski • France .... 100 [50]
Valmiera • Latvia 126 B4
Valmorel Ski • France .... 100 [44]
Valognes • France 115 F2
Valparaíso • Chile 52 B5
Valparaiso • IN, United States 44 B5
Valparaiso • FL, United States 48 D5
Valpoi • Goa, India 137 B1
Valpolicella • Italy 121 E7
Vals • Switzerland 119 G3
Vals, Tanjung • Indonesia 32 (1) E4
Valsamonero, Moni •
    Crete, Greece 123 E6
Válthou, Ori • Greece 15 C4
Valtournenche Ski • Italy .... 100 [304]
Valtournenche • Italy 121 E1
Valtourenche • Italy 121 E1
Valverde del Camino • Spain 11 E6
Valzoldana Ski • Italy .... 100 [228]
Vammala • Finland 125 E2
Vámos • Crete, Greece 123 E2
Van • Turkey 18 D2
Van Buren • ME, United States 44 K2
Van Buren • AR, United States 46 H5
Van Diemen Gulf • NT, Australia 145 C1
Van Gölü • Turkey 18 D2
Van Horn • TX, United States 47 B2
Van Lake • Turkey 15 K2
Van Rees, Pegunungan •
    Indonesia 32 (1) E3
Vanavara • Russian Fed. 26 R5
Vanceburg • KY, United States 44 D6
Vancouver • WA, United States 152 B2
Vancouver • BC, Canada 155 C3
Vancouver I. • BC, Canada 155 C3
Vandalia • Ohio, United States 125 E4
Vandalia • IL, United States 46 K3
Vandellòs i l'Hospitalet de l'Infant
    Beach • Spain .... 96 [121]
Vanderbilt Mansion Nat. Hist. Site
    Park N • NY, United States ..... 151 [310]
Vanderhoof • BC, Canada 155 C1
Vänern • Sweden 16 G7
Vänersborg • Sweden 125 F3
Vang • Norway 124 C4
Vanga • Kenya 130 B3
Vangaindrano • Madagascar 23 H6
Vangunu • Solomon Is. 35 (1) F2
Vanimo • Papua New Guinea 35 (1) C1
Vanna • Norway 16 J1
Vännäs • Sweden 16 K5
Vannes Beach • France .... 96 [81]

Vannes • France 114 C4
Vannsjø • Norway 124 B4
Vanoise, Massif de la • France 12 A3
Vanoise, Parc nat. de la Park N •
    France .... 89 [66]
Vanoise, Parc nat. de la •
    France 115 F4
Vansbro • Sweden 16 H6
Vansittart Is. • NU, Canada 39 O3
Vanta • Finland 125 E4
Vantage • WA, United States 42 E3
Vanua Balavu • Vanuatu 35 (2) B1
Vanua Levu • Fiji Is. 35 (2) D2
VANUATU • Pacific Ocean 35 (2) B2
Vao, Ko • Thailand 142 E2
Var • France 115 H2
Var [Adm] • France 115 H3
Vara • Sweden 125 F3
Vara, Pico da • Azores 118 B1
Varadero • Cuba 158 D2
Varanasi • India 137 C8
Varanger-Halvøya • Norway 16 O1
Varangerfjorden • Norway 16 O1
Varano, Lago di • Italy 12 J7
Varano, Lago di • Italy 14 C8
Varazdin • Croatia 128 D2
Varberg Beach • Sweden .... 96 [2]
Varberg • Sweden 125 F6
Varca • Goa, India 137 B2
Varca Beach • Goa, India 137 B2
Varde • F.Y.R. of Macedonia 15 C2
Varde • Denmark 125 E4
Varde • Norway 16 P1
Varel • Germany 5 L1
Varel • Germany 8 D3
Varennes • France 115 H1
Vares • Italy 12 C3
Vårgårda • Sweden 125 F3
Varginha • Brazil 163 C1
Varkala • India 138 D14
Varkala Beach • India 138 E3
Varkaus • Finland 16 N5
Varkiza • Greece 122 D7
Värmdölandet • Sweden 125 D4
Värmland • Sweden 16 G6
Värmlandsnäs • Sweden 125 F3
Varna Beach • Bulgaria .... 97 [243]
Varna • Bulgaria 128 E2
Värnamo • Sweden 125 F7
Varneski Zaliv • Bulgaria 14 P6
Várpalota • Hungary 13 H10
Vars Ski • France .... 100 [63]
Vars • France 115 F4
Varzea Grande • Brazil 52 E2
Vasa • Finland 16 K5
Vasca, Costa • Spain 116 A2
Vascao • Portugal 118 E4
Vasco da Gama • Goa, India 137 B1
Vashka • Russian Fed. 17 H2
Vasiliki • Crete, Greece 123 E8
Vaslui • Romania 14 E2
Vassdalseggja • Norway 124 C3
Vassiliká • Greece 15 C3
Vassiliki • Levkas, Greece 122 C1
Vassilikós • Zante, Greece 122 C3
Västerås • Sweden 125 D3
Västerbotten • Sweden 16 K4
Västerdalälven • Sweden 16 H5
Västerhaninge • Sweden 125 D4
Västervik • Sweden 125 F11
Västernorrland • Sweden 16 J5
Västervik Beach • Sweden .... 97 [18]
Västervik • Sweden 125 F8
Västmanland • Sweden 16 H6
Vasto • Italy 12 I6
Vasto Beach • Italy .... 97 [160]
Váthi • Crete, Greece 123 E1
Vathípetro • Crete, Greece 123 E7
Vathy • Greece 122 C2
Vatican City Heritage C • Italy .... 86 [147]
Vatne • Norway 124 C1
Vatoa • Fiji Is. 35 (2) E2
Vatra Dornei • Romania 14 M2
Vättern • Sweden 125 F3
Vatthoima • Sweden 125 D3
Vauclin, le • Martinique .... 161 N
Vaucouleurs • France 5 I6
Vaujany • NM, United States 46 C5
Vaujany Ski • France .... 100 [57]
Vaux-le-Vicomte, Château de •
    France 115 F4
Vava'u Group • Tonga 35 (2) F2
Vaxholm • Sweden 125 D4
Vavuniya • Sri Lanka 138 D11
Vawkavysk • Belarus 13 N4
Vaxholm • Sweden 125 D4
Växjö • Sweden 125 F11
Vaygach, Ostrov • Russian Fed. 26 I3
Vaygach, Ostrov • Russian Fed. 126 A3
Vazon Bay Beach •
    United Kingdom .... 101 [255]
Vechelde • Germany 8 F4
Vechta • Germany 8 D4
Vechte • Germany 8 C4
Veckholm • Sweden 125 D1
Vecsés • Hungary 13 I10
Vedbaek • Denmark 125 E4
Veddige • Sweden 125 F6
Vedra, I. es • Ibiza, Spain 117 G3
Veendam • Netherlands 5 J1
Veendam • Netherlands 5 I2
Veere • Netherlands 109 D10
Veere Beach • Netherlands .... 96 [69]
Vega • Norway 124 B2
Vega Baja • Puerto Rico 159 H2
Vegår • Norway 124 B1
Veggli • Norway 124 B1
Vegorítida, Límni • Greece 15 B3
Veinge • Sweden 125 F11
Veitshöchheim Castle • Germany ... 113 [168]
Vejbystrand • Sweden 125 F11
Vejby Strand • Sweden 125 F11
Vejer de la Frontera • Spain 11 E7
Vejle Beach • Denmark .... 96 [46]
Vejle • Denmark 125 F9
Vejle [Adm] • Denmark 125 F9
Vel Veddo Beach • Goa, India 137 B2
Velas • Azores 118 A6
Velasany • Maldives 138 F4
Velay, Mts du • France 115 J1
Velbăzhd •
    Bulgaria/F.Y.R. of Macedonia 15 D1
Velddrif • South Africa 134 C1
Veldenz, Schloss • Germany 112 E3
Veldhoven • Netherlands 5 I3
Velebit • Croatia 128 D3
Velenje • Slovenia 128 C2
Veleta, Pico de • Spain 116 B3
Velez • Bosnia-Herz. 14 F6
Vélez-Málaga Beach • Spain .... 96 [121]
Vélez-Málaga • Spain 116 B7
Vélez-Rubio • Spain 116 B4
Velika • Croatia 163 C1
Vélia Heritage C • Italy .... 86 [138]
Veliginju Huraa • Maldives 138 F2
Velika Kapela • Croatia 14 B4
Velika • Greece 122 C3
Velikaya •
    Magadan, Russian Fed. 27 T4
Velikaya Ustyug • Russian Fed. 17 H2
Velikiye-Luki • Russian Fed. 17 E2
Veliko Turnovo • Bulgaria 128 E3
Velikovisechnoye • Russian Fed. 17 I1

Velingara • Senegal 22 B2
Velingrad • Bulgaria 15 F1
Velino [Mtn] • Italy 12 H6
Velino [Riv] • Italy 121 F2
Vella Lavella • Solomon Is. 35 (1) F2
Velletri • Italy 121 F3
Vellinge Beach • Sweden .... 96 [12]
Vellinge • Sweden 125 F15
Vellore • India 138 D7
Velmerstot • Germany 5 L3
Velsen Beach • Goa, India 137 B2
Velsk • Russian Fed. 17 G2
Velten • Germany 8 I3
Veluwezoom, Nat. Park Park N •
    Netherlands .... 89 [54]
Veluwezoom, Nat. Park •
    Netherlands 109 D8
Velvendos • Greece 125 F11
Venaco • Corsica, France 115 L2
Venado Tuerto • Argentina 52 D5
Vence • France 115 H2
Venda • South Africa 24 E4
Vendays-Montalivet Beach •
    France .... 96 [85]
Vendays-Montalivet • France 115 G1
Vendee • France 114 D3
Vendeval • Brazil 80 A3
Vendôme • France 114 D2
Véneta, Laguna • Italy 121 E8
Venetian Riviera • Italy 121 E8
Veneto • Italy 121 E7
Venézia Heritage C • Italy .... 86 [134]
Venézia • Italy 121 E8
Venézia, Golfo di •
    Croatia/Italy 121 E8
Venézia-Lido • Italy 12 G3
VENEZUELA • S. America 51 D2
Venezuela, Golfo de • Venezuela 51 C1
Venice Heritage C • Italy .... 86 [134]
Venice • Italy 121 E8
Venice • LA, United States 48 C6
Venice • FL, United States 49 B4
Venlo • Netherlands 109 D12
Vennesla • Norway 124 B1
Vénissieux • France 19 J8
Venlo • Netherlands 125 F5
Ventadour, Château de • France 115 G2
Ventimiglia • Italy 121 E4
Ventnor Beach • United Kingdom .... 101 [108]
Ventnor City •
    NJ, United States 44 H6
Ventry Beach • Ireland .... 96 [60]
Ventspils • Latvia 126 B3
Ventura • CA, United States 152 C5
Venus Baai • St Eustatius .... 161 F
Venus Bay • VI, Australia 34 O3
Venus-Aurora • Romania 128 E2
Venzone • Italy 121 E4
Vera • Argentina 52 D4
Vera Beach • Spain .... 96 [116]
Vera • Spain 116 B5
Veracruz • Mexico 157 G4
Veracruz [Adm] • Mexico 37 B3
Veraval • India 28 B4
Veraval Beach • India 138 E3
Verbánia • Italy 121 E5
Verbier Ski • Switzerland .... 100 [80]
Verbier • Switzerland 119 G6
Vercelli • Italy 121 E6
Vercors • France 115 G2
Verdala Palace • Malta 123 H4
Verdalsøra • Norway 16 F5
Verde • Paraguay 52 D3
Verde, Costa • Spain 11 E1
Verde, Costa • Portugal 118 A1
Verde • Sardinia, Italy 120 C3
Verden • Germany 8 E4
Vergennes • VT, United States 44 I3
Vergína Heritage C • Greece .... 86 [208]
Vergia • Greece 15 D3
Verín • Spain 11 D3
Veríngenstadt • Germany 112 F1
Verkhneimbatsk • Russian Fed. 27 C4
Verkhnetulomskiy • Russian Fed. 16 P2
Verkhnetulomskoye Vdkhr. •
    Russian Fed. 16 P2
Verkhni Kursy, Ozero •
    Russian Fed. 16 P4
Verkhoyansk • Russian Fed. 27 L3
Verkhoyanskiy Khrebet •
    Russian Fed. 27 K3
Verla Heritage C • Finland .... 85 [88]
Vermelho, Côte • France 115 K2
Vermilion Lake •
    MN, United States 43 J3
Vermillion • SD, United States 43 G4
Vermillion • OH, United States 44 D5
Vermillion Bay •
    LA, United States 47 I3
Vermont • United States 44 I4
Vermadsky [Base] • Antarctica 54 H1
Vernal • UT, United States 45 I1
Verneuil-sur-Avre • France 19 F5
Vérno • Greece 15 C3
Vernon • BC, Canada 38 H6
Vernon • France 115 E1
Vernon Crookes Nature Reserve •
    South Africa 134 B5
Vernon Valley •
    NJ, United States 153 D7
Verona • OR, United States 42 D4
Vero Beach • FL, United States 49 C4
Verona • Italy 121 E7
Verrettes • Haiti 159 G2
Versailles Heritage C • France .... 86 [65]
Versailles • France 114 D3
Versailles • IN, United States 44 C6
Versciaco Ski • Italy .... 100 [249]
Vert, Cap • Senegal 22 A2
Verte, Caye • St Martin .... 161 A
Vertientes • Cuba 158 D7
Vertiskos • Greece 15 E3
Verulam • South Africa 134 B4
Verviers • Belgium 109 D16
Veshenskaya • Russian Fed. 17 G5
Vesijärvi • Finland 16 N6
Vesoul • France 10 I6
Vest Agder • Norway 16 F7
Vest Sjælland • Denmark 125 F10
Vestavia Hills •
    AL, United States 48 D4
Veste Coburg Castle • Germany ... 113 [159]
Vestenia • Norway 124 B2
Vesterø Havn • Denmark 125 F6
Vestra Hani • Denmark 125 F9
Vestfjorden • Norway 16 H3
Vestfold • Norway 124 B3
Vestmannaeyjar • Iceland 16 (1) D3
Vestnes • Norway 124 C2
Vesuvio • Italy 121 G3
Vesuvius • Italy 121 G3
Veszeprém • Hungary 13 G10

Vetlanda

Vetlanda • Sweden ... 125 F8
Vetralla • Italy ... 121 F1
Vette, le • Italy ... 120 B4
Veurne • Belgium ... 109 E1
Vevey • Switzerland ... 119 G5
Vexin • France ... 115 E1
Veysonnaz Ski • Switzerland ... 100 [83]
Vézelay Heritage C • France ... 86 [69]
Vezen • Bulgaria ... 15 F1
Vézère • France ... 115 G2
Vézère, Gorges de la • France ... 115 G2
Vézère, Vallée du Heritage C • France ... 86 [81]
Vezzani • Corsica, France ... 115 L2
Viana del Bollo • Spain ... 11 D2
Viana do Castelo • Portugal ... 11 C3
Viana do Castelo Beach • Portugal ... 96 [94]
Viana do Castelo [Adm] • Portugal ... 118 A1
Vianden • Luxembourg ... 109 D20
Viangchan • Laos ... 31 C3
Viaréggio Beach • Italy ... 96 [144]
Viaréggio • Italy ... 121 E10
Vibo Valentia • Italy ... 12 K10
Viborg • Russian Fed. ... 17 D2
Viborg • Denmark ... 125 F9
Viborg [Adm] • Denmark ... 125 F9
Vic • Spain ... 117 D2
Vicarstown • Ireland ... 108 B3
Vicdessos • France ... 115 K1
Vicecomodoro Marambio [Base] • Antarctica ... 54 (1) JJ3
Vicedo Beach • Spain ... 96 [91]
Vicenza Heritage C • Italy ... 86 [132]
Vicenza • Italy ... 121 E7
Vichuga • Russian Fed. ... 17 G3
Vichy • France ... 10 I7
Vicksburg • MS, United States ... 153 F2
Vicksburg Nat. Military Park N • MS, United States ... 151 [195]
Vico • Corsica, France ... 115 L1
Vico Equense • Italy ... 121 G3
Vico, Lago di • Italy ... 121 F1
Victor Harbour • SA, Australia ... 34 G7
Victoria • NT, Australia ... 34 F3
Victoria • VI, Australia ... 34 H7
Victoria • Papua New Guinea ... 35 (1) D2
Victoria • Chile ... 53 B3
Victoria • Malta ... 123 H1
Victoria • Seychelles ... 133 K1
Victoria • Grenada ... 160 S
Victoria • TX, United States ... 154 J5
Victoria • BC, Canada ... 155 C3
Victoria Beach • MN, Canada ... 43 H1
Victoria de las Tunas • Cuba ... 158 D7
Victoria Falls Heritage N • Zambia/Zimbabwe ... 83 [106]
Victoria Falls • Zimbabwe ... 130 C1
Victoria Falls [Waterfall] • Zambia/Zimbabwe ... 130 C1
Victoria, Grand Lac • QU, Canada ... 44 G2
Victoria Harbour • Hong Kong, China ... 139 B5
Victoria I. • NT/NU, Canada ... 38 J2
Victoria, Lake • Africa ... 23 E4
Victoria Lake • NF, Canada ... 156 D3
Victoria Land • Antarctica ... 54 (1) V2
Victoria Lines • Malta ... 123 H4
Victoria, Mt • Myanmar ... 28 F4
Victoria, Mt • Myanmar ... 31 A2
Victoria Nile • Uganda ... 23 E4
Victoria Peak • Hong Kong, China ... 139 B5
Victoria Peak • TX, United States ... 47 B2
Victoria River Downs • NT, Australia ... 34 F3
Victoria Strait • NU, Canada ... 38 K3
Victoria West • South Africa ... 134 C3
Victorville • QU, Canada ... 44 J3
Victorville • CA, United States ... 45 D4
Victory • Papua New Guinea ... 35 (1) D2
Vicuña Mackenna • Argentina ... 52 D5
Vidal Junction • United States ... 45 E4
Vidalia • GA, United States ... 153 H1
Videira • Brazil ... 52 F4
Videle • Romania ... 14 J6
Vidin • Bulgaria ... 14 J6
Vidisha • India ... 28 C4
Vidor • TX, United States ... 47 G2
Vidöstern • Sweden ... 125 F7
Vidsel • Sweden ... 16 K4
Vidzeme • Latvia ... 126 B4
Viechtach • Germany ... 9 H7
Viedma • Argentina ... 53 D4
Viejo • Mexico ... 40 D5
Viella • Spain ... 11 D2
Viella, Túnel de • Spain ... 115 K1
Vienna • Austria ... 13 F9
Vienna Heritage C • Austria ... 86 [127]
Vienna • WV, United States ... 44 E6
Vienne • France ... 115 F1
Vienne [Adm] • France ... 114 D4
Vienne [Riv] • France ... 114 D4
Vientiane • Laos ... 31 C3
Vieques • Puerto Rico ... 159 H4
Viernheim • Germany ... 5 L5
Vierschach Ski • Italy ... 100 [249]
Viersen • Germany ... 111 B3
Vierwald Stätter See • Switzerland ... 119 G3
Vierzon • France ... 10 H6
Vieste • Italy ... 12 K7
Vieste Beach • Italy ... 97 [158]
Viet Tri • Vietnam ... 31 D2
VIETNAM • Asia ... 31 D3
Vietnam Veterans Mem. Park N • DC, United States ... 151 [288]
Vieux Fort • St Lucia ... 161 P
Vieux-Boucau-les-Bains • France ... 115 G3
Vigan • Philippines ... 31 G3
Vigan Heritage C • Philippines ... 85 [202]
Vigévano • Italy ... 121 E6
Vigia • Brazil ... 53 (1) B2
Vigie Beach • St Lucia ... 161 P
Vigo • Spain ... 11 C2
Vigo di Fassa Ski • Italy ... 100 [234]
Vigo di Fassa • Italy ... 120 B3
Vigo, Ria de • Spain ... 11 C2
Vigso Bugt • Denmark ... 125 F5
Vihorlat • Slovak Rep. ... 14 J1
Viiala • Finland ... 128 D1
Vijayadurg • India ... 138 D1
Vijayanagar • India ... 138 D2
Vijayapuri • India ... 138 D2
Vijayawada • India ... 138 D3
Vijfherenlanden • Netherlands ... 109 F4
Vijosë • Albania ... 15 A3
Vik • Iceland ... 16 (1) D3
Vikbolandet • Sweden ... 125 G8
Vikeke • Norway ... 124 C5
Viken • Sweden ... 125 F11
Vikersund • Norway ... 124 B1
Vikhren • Bulgaria ... 4 K8
Vikinglandet Park L • Norway ... 98 [4]
VikingLandet • Norway ... 98 [4]
Vikna • Norway ... 16 F4
Vikos-Aóos Nat. Park Park N • Greece ... 89 [136]
Viksøyri • Norway ... 124 C4
Vila de Conde • Portugal ... 11 C3
Vila do Bispo Beach • Portugal ... 96 [100]
Vila do Bispo • Portugal ... 118 E5
Vila do Porto • Azores ... 118 B2

Vila Franca de Xira • Portugal ... 118 D2
Vila Franca do Campo Beach • São Miguel, Azores ... 96 [105]
Vila Franca do Campo • Azores ... 118 B1
Vila Nogueira de Azeitão • Portugal ... 118 D2
Vila Nova de Gaia • Portugal ... 11 C3
Vila Nova de Sales • Angola ... 23 A6
Vila Praia de Vitória Beach • Terceira, Azores ... 96 [104]
Vila Real • Portugal ... 11 D3
Vila Real [Adm] • Portugal ... 118 A1
Vila Real de Santo António Beach • Portugal ... 96 [100]
Vila Real de Santo António • Portugal ... 118 E8
Vila Velha • Brazil ... 163 C2
Vilafranca del Penèdes • Spain ... 117 D3
Vilagarcía Beach • Spain ... 96 [93]
Vilaine • France ... 114 C4
Vilamoura • Portugal ... 118 E7
Vilanova i la Geltrú Beach • Spain ... 96 [122]
Vilanova i la Geltrú • Spain ... 117 D3
Vilcabamba • Peru ... 163 B1
Vilcanota • Peru ... 163 B2
Vilcheka, Zemlya • Russian Fed. ... 126 A3
Vileyka • Belarus ... 16 N9
Vilhelmina • Sweden ... 16 I4
Vilhena • Brazil ... 51 E6
Viljandi • Estonia ... 126 B5
Vilkaviskis • Lithuania ... 126 B5
Vilkitskogo, Proliv • Russian Fed. ... 26 R2
Villa Adriana Heritage C • Italy ... 86 [146]
Villa Ahumada • Mexico ... 47 A2
Villa Altagracia • Dominican Rep. ... 159 G7
Villa Ángela • Argentina ... 52 D4
Villa Carlos • Minorca, Spain ... 117 F4
Villa Constitución • Argentina ... 163 D1
Villa de María • Argentina ... 52 C4
Villa Dolores • Argentina ... 52 C5
Villa General Roca • Argentina ... 52 C5
Villa Gesell • Argentina ... 163 D4
Villa Hayes • Paraguay ... 52 E4
Villa Hermosa • Mexico ... 47 F5
Villa Huidobro • Argentina ... 52 D5
Villa Insurgentes • Mexico ... 157 F4
Villa, la Ski • Italy ... 100 [231]
Villa, la • Italy ... 120 B2
Villa María • Argentina ... 52 D5
Villa Nueva • Argentina ... 52 C5
Villa Romana del Casale Heritage C • Sicily, Italy ... 86 [157]
Villa San Martín • Argentina ... 52 D5
Villa Unión • Mexico ... 47 D3
Villa Vásquez • Dominican Rep. ... 159 G2
Villabassa Ski • Italy ... 100 [246]
Villablino • Spain ... 11 E2
Villacañas • Spain ... 11 F2
Villach • Austria ... 119 H8
Villach del Bierzo • Spain ... 11 E2
Villafrance de los Barros • Spain ... 11 C2
Villafrance de los Barros • Spain ... 11 E2
Villaggio Cóppola • Italy ... 121 G1
Villagran • Mexico ... 47 E5
Villaguay • Argentina ... 52 E5
Villahermosa • Mexico ... 37 C4
Villalba • Spain ... 11 D1
Villalón de Campos • Spain ... 11 E2
Villandry [Château] • France ... 114 C2
Villanueva de Córdoba • Spain ... 11 G6
Villanueva de la Serena • Spain ... 11 F6
Villanueva del Río y Minas • Spain ... 11 F7
Villaputzu • Sardinia, Italy ... 12 D9
Villar del Rey • Spain ... 11 E6
Villarcayo • Spain ... 11 H2
Villard-de-Lans Ski • France ... 100 [54]
Villard-de-Lans • France ... 115 F3
Villard-Reculas Ski • France ... 100 [58]
Villarrica • Chile ... 53 B3
Villarreal de los Infantes • Spain ... 11 K5
Villarrica • Paraguay ... 52 E4
Villars-sur-Ollon Ski • Switzerland ... 100 [84]
Villars-sur-Ollon • Switzerland ... 119 G6
Villasimius • Sardinia, Italy ... 120 C4
Villavicencio • Colombia ... 51 C3
Villaviciosa • Spain ... 11 F1
Ville Platte • LA, United States ... 47 H2
Villefranche-de-Rouergue • France ... 115 G4
Villefranche-sur-Mer • France ... 115 H2
Villefranche-sur-Sâone • France ... 115 F1
Villena • Spain ... 11 J7
Villeneuve • Switzerland ... 119 G5
Villeneuve-les-Maguelonne Beach • France ... 96 [130]
Villeneuve-Loubet • France ... 115 H4
Villeneuve-sur-Lot • France ... 115 G4
Villers-la-Ville, Abbaye de • Belgium ... 109 D14
Villerupt • France ... 5 I5
Villesavin [Château] • France ... 114 C2
Villeurbanne • France ... 10 J8
Villingen-Schwenningen • Germany ... 9 D8
Villingili Beach • Maldives ... 138 F4
Villivaru • Maldives ... 138 F4
Villmanstrand • Finland ... 16 O6
Vilm • Germany ... 8 I2
Vilnius Heritage C • Lithuania ... 86 [239]
Vilnius • Lithuania ... 16 N9
Vilppula • Finland ... 128 E2
Vils • Germany ... 9 H8
Vilsbiburg • Germany ... 9 H8
Vilsburg • Germany ... 112 F4
Vilshofen • Germany ... 9 I8
Vilvoorde • Belgium ... 5 H4
Vilyuy • Russian Fed. ... 27 J4
Vimmerby • Sweden ... 125 F8
Vimperk • Czech Rep. ... 128 B3
Viña del Mar • Chile ... 52 B5
Viñales Beach • Cuba ... 158 B7
Viñales valley Heritage C • Cuba ... 84 [38]
Vinaròs • Spain ... 11 L4
Vinaròs Beach • Spain ... 96 [120]
Vinaròs • Spain ... 116 A2
Vincennes • IN, United States ... 48 D1
Vindealven • Sweden ... 16 J4
Vindelälven • Sweden ... 16 J4
Vindeby • Denmark ... 125 F9
Vindhya Range • India ... 28 C4
Vineland • NJ, United States ... 44 H6
Vineyard Haven • MA, United States ... 44 J5
Vingåker • Sweden ... 125 F9
Vingeanne • France ... 10 K6
Vinh • Vietnam ... 31 D3
Vinh Long • Vietnam ... 141 E3
Vinh Long • Vietnam ... 141 E3
Vinkovci • Croatia ... 14 F4
Vinnytsya • Ukraine ... 17 E2
Vinslöv • Sweden ... 125 F11
Vinson Massif • Antarctica ... 54 (1) GG2
Vinton • IA, United States ... 43 K5

Vipiteno • Italy ... 120 B1
Vir • Croatia ... 128 D3
Virac • Philippines ... 31 G4
Virden • MN, Canada ... 43 F2
Vire • France ... 10 E5
Vire [Riv] • France ... 114 C4
Virei • Angola ... 24 A3
Virful Curcubata • Romania ... 13 L11
Virgenes, Cabo • Argentina ... 53 C6
Virgin • United States ... 153 E1
Virgin Gorda • British Virgin Is. ... 160 B
Virgin Is. Nat. Park • US Virgin Is. ... 160 Z
Virginia • United States ... 41 K4
Virginia • MN, United States ... 43 J3
Virginia Beach • VA, United States ... 153 D11
Virginia City • NV, United States ... 152 C3
Virihaure • Sweden ... 16 I3
Virovitica • Croatia ... 128 D2
Virrat • Finland ... 125 E2
Virsbo • Sweden ... 125 F9
Virton • Belgium ... 109 D19
Virtsu • Estonia ... 126 B1
Virunga, Parc nat. des Heritage N • Dem. Rep. of Congo ... 83 [94]
Virunga, Parc nat. des Park • Dem. Rep. of Congo ... 133 [55]
Vis • Croatia ... 128 C4
Visalia • CA, United States ... 45 C3
Visayan Sea • Philippines ... 31 G4
Visby • Sweden ... 16 J8
Visby Heritage C • Sweden ... 86 [8]
Vischering Castle • Germany ... 113 [18]
Viscount Melville Sound • NU, Canada ... 38 J2
Visegrad • Bosnia-Herz. ... 14 G6
Visegrad • Bulgaria ... 15 H2
Viseu • Portugal ... 11 D4
Viseu [Adm] • Portugal ... 118 A1
Viseu de Sus • Romania ... 14 L2
Vishakhapatnam • India ... 28 D5
Vishniy Volochek • Russian Fed. ... 126 C3
Visingsö • Sweden ... 125 F3
Vislanda • Sweden ... 125 F7
Viso, Monte • Italy ... 121 E5
Visoko • Bosnia-Herz. ... 14 F6
Visselhövde • Germany ... 8 E4
Vista • CA, United States ... 45 D5
Vistonias, Ormos • Greece ... 15 G3
Vistonida, Limni • Greece ... 124 B4
Vistula • Poland ... 128 C2
Viterbo • Italy ... 121 F1
Vitet, Mont du • St Barthélemy ... 160 E
Viti Levu • Fiji Is. ... 35 (2) D2
Vitiaz Strait • Papua New Guinea ... 35 (1) D2
Vitigudino • Spain ... 11 E4
Vitim • Russian Fed. ... 27 H5
Vitim [Riv] • Russian Fed. ... 27 I5
Vitön • Svalbard ... 54 L2
Vitória • Brazil ... 163 C2
Vitória da Conquista • Brazil ... 52 H1
Vitória Gasteiz • Spain ... 11 I2
Vitorog • Bosnia-Herz. ... 14 F5
Vittangi • Sweden ... 16 K3
Vittel • France ... 9 A8
Vitteaux • Sweden ... 125 D1
Vittoria • Sicily, Italy ... 12 J4
Vittório Véneto • Italy ... 120 B4
Vittoriosa • Malta ... 123 H4
Vittsjö • Sweden ... 125 F11
Vitznau • Switzerland ... 119 G3
Viveiro • Spain ... 11 D1
Viveiro Beach • Spain ... 96 [91]
Viver • Spain ... 11 K5
Vivian • LA, United States ... 153 F1
Vizcaíno, Desierto del • Mexico ... 157 F3
Vizcaino, Sierra • Mexico ... 157 C2
Vize • Turkey ... 15 I2
Vizianagaram • India ... 28 D5
Vizinga • Russian Fed. ... 17 I2
Vlaams-Brabant • Belgium ... 109 D15
Vlaanderen • Belgium ... 5 F3
Vlaardingen • Netherlands ... 109 F3
Vladikavkaz • Russian Fed. ... 17 G6
Vladimir Heritage C • Russian Fed. ... 86 [247]
Vladimir • Russian Fed. ... 126 C4
Vladivostok • Russian Fed. ... 27 L8
Vlasic • Bosnia-Herz. ... 14 E5
Vlasotince • F.R. of Yugoslavia ... 14 H6
Vlasovo • Russian Fed. ... 27 M2
Vlieland • Netherlands ... 109 D3
Vlihada, Paralía • Crete, Greece ... 123 E4
Vlihó • Levkas, Greece ... 122 C3
Vlissingen • Netherlands ... 109 D10
Vlissingen • Netherlands ... 5 E5
Vlotho • Germany ... 111 D4
Vlkolínec Heritage C • Slovak Rep. ... 86 [178]
Vlorë • Albania ... 15 A3
Vltava • Czech Rep. ... 128 B4
Vluyn • Germany ... 111 B1
Vnukovo [Apt] • Russian Fed. ... 126 C3
Vockelabruck • Austria ... 13 C9
Vodice • Croatia ... 12 J5
Vodice • Croatia ... 128 D3
Voerde • Germany ... 111 B1
Vogar • Iceland ... 125 F6
Vogelsberg • Germany ... 112 D2
Vogelsberg • Germany ... 9 H6
Voi • Kenya ... 131 G4
Voile de la Mariée, Cascade du • Réunion ... 132 H2
Voiron • France ... 115 F3
Vojens • Denmark ... 125 F13
Vojvodina • F.R of Yugoslavia ... 14 G4
Voknavolok • Russian Fed. ... 16 P4
Volary • Czech Rep. ... 128 B3
Volborg • MT, United States ... 154 G8
Volcano • Italy • ... 12 J4
Volcano Is. • Japan ... 140 A13
Volcans, Parc des Park • Rwanda ... 133 [3]
Volda • Russian Fed. ... 17 H3
Volda • Norway ... 124 C1
Volendam • Netherlands ... 109 F2
Volga • Russian Fed. ... 17 H4
Volga, Cities of the • Russian Fed. ... 126 A10
Volga Delta • Russian Fed. ... 17 H5
Volga, Ózero • Russian Fed. ... 126 C3
Volgodonsk • Russian Fed. ... 4 T6
Volgograd • Russian Fed. ... 17 G5
Volgograd • Russian Fed. ... 17 H4
Volgogradskoye Vdkhr. • Russian Fed. ... 17 H4
Volissós • Greece ... 15 G5
Völkermarkt • Austria ... 13 D11
Volkhov • Russian Fed. ... 126 C1
Volkhov [Riv] • Russian Fed. ... 126 C1
Völklingen Heritage C • Germany ... 86 [52]
Völklingen • Germany ... 112 D3
Volksrust • South Africa ... 134 B1
Volodymyr-Volyns'kyy • Ukraine ... 13 N7

Vologda • Russian Fed. ... 126 C2
Vólos Beach • Greece ... 97 [188]
Vólos • Greece ... 122 D4
Volovets • Ukraine ... 14 K1
Volta area Heritage C • Ghana ... 85 [111]
Volta Blanche • Burkina Faso/Ghana ... 22 D2
Volta, Lake • Ghana ... 22 E3
Volta Noire • Burkina Faso/Ghana ... 22 D2
Volta Redonda • Brazil ... 163 C3
Volterra • Italy ... 121 E11
Volturno • Italy ... 121 G1
Volubilis Heritage C • Morocco ... 86 [252]
Volubilis • Morocco ... 131 D1
Volvi, Limni • Greece ... 15 E3
Volzhskiy • Russian Fed. ... 17 H4
Voma • Fiji Is. ... 35 (2) D2
Von Frank Mtn • AK, United States ... 49 K3
Vóni • Crete, Greece ... 123 E7
Vónitsa • Greece ... 122 C1
Voorburg • Netherlands ... 109 F3
Voorne Beach • Netherlands ... 96 [68]
Voorne • Netherlands ... 109 F3
Voorschoten • Netherlands ... 109 F1
Vorarlberg • Austria ... 119 H1
Vordingborg Beach • Denmark ... 96 [37]
Vordingborg • Denmark ... 125 F14
Vorë • Albania ... 15 A2
Vóries Sporádes • Greece ... 15 E4
Varingsfossen • Norway ... 124 C4
Vórios Evoïkós Kólpos • Greece ... 124 B4
Vorkuta • Russian Fed. ... 26 J4
Vorma • Norway ... 124 B2
Vormsi • Estonia ... 126 B1
Vornholz Castle • Germany ... 113 [21]
Vorogovo • Russian Fed. ... 26 P4
Voronezh • Russian Fed. ... 17 F4
Vorpommersche Boddenlandschaft, Nationalpark Park N • Germany ... 89 [58]
Vörts järv • Estonia ... 126 B2
Võru • Estonia ... 126 B2
Vosges • France ... 10 L5
Vosnesens'k • Ukraine ... 17 E5
Vosresensk • Russian Fed. ... 126 C4
Voss • Norway ... 124 C4
Vostochno Sibirskoye More • Arctic Ocean ... 54 II2
Vostochnyy Sayan • Russian Fed. ... 26 Q7
Vostok [Base] • Antarctica ... 54 (1) P2
Vostok • Kiribati ... 33 L7
Votkinsk • Russian Fed. ... 17 I3
Vouga • Portugal ... 11 C4
Voukoliés • Crete, Greece ... 123 E1
Voúla • Greece ... 122 D7
Vouliagméni Beach • Greece ... 97 [185]
Vouliagméni • Greece ... 122 D7
Voúrinos • Greece ... 15 C3
Vouvray • France ... 114 B1
Vouvray • France ... 10 G7
Vouxa, Akra • Crete, Greece ... 123 E1
Vouziers • France ... 5 H5
Voyage to the Glaciers cruise area • N. America ... 80 A2
Voyageurs Nat. Park Park N • MN, United States ... 151 [154]
Voyvozh • Russian Fed. ... 17 J2
Vrå • Denmark ... 125 F6
Vrådal • Norway ... 124 C6
Vrahási Beach • Crete, Greece ... 97 [193]
Vrahási • Crete, Greece ... 123 E7
Vrahási Beach • Crete, Greece ... 97 [178]
Vrakhiónas • Zante, Greece ... 15 B6
Vran • Bosnia-Herz. ... 14 E6
Vrangelya, Óstrov • Russian Fed. ... 27 V2
Vranica • Bosnia-Herz. ... 14 E6
Vranje • F.R. of Yugoslavia ... 14 I7
Vranov nad Topl'ou • Slovak Rep. ... 13 K9
Vrassná Beach • Greece ... 97 [193]
Vratsa • Bulgaria ... 14 K6
Vrbas • Bosnia-Herz. ... 14 E5
Vrchlabi • Czech Rep. ... 13 E7
Vredenburg • South Africa ... 134 C1
Vredendal • South Africa ... 134 C1
Vrindabam • India ... 137 C2
Vrine • Albania ... 122 B1
Vrissa Beach • Greece ... 97 [199]
Vrontismou, Moní • Crete, Greece ... 123 E6
Vrsac • F.R. of Yugoslavia ... 14 I4
Vryburg • South Africa ... 134 A1
Vryheid • South Africa ... 134 B1
Vsetín • Czech Rep. ... 13 G8
Vukovar • F.R. of Yugoslavia ... 14 G4
Vuktyl • Russian Fed. ... 17 J2
Vukuzakhe • South Africa ... 134 B1
Vulcan • AL, United States ... 48 B4
Vulcano • Italy ... 100 D2
Vulkaneifel • Germany ... 112 E1
Vulture • Italy ... 12 J8
Vung Tao • Vietnam ... 141 E4
Vuntut Nat. Park Park N • YT, Canada ... 156 [2]
Vuoatti • Finland ... 16 A5
Vuollerim • Sweden ... 16 K3
Vuotso • Finland ... 17 D1
Vyatka • Russian Fed. ... 17 I3
Vyatka [Riv] • Russian Fed. ... 17 I3
Vyatko-Chepetsk • Russian Fed. ... 17 H3
Vyazemskiy • Russian Fed. ... 29 I1
Vyazma • Russian Fed. ... 126 C3
Vyborg • Russian Fed. ... 17 E1
Vychegda • Russian Fed. ... 17 I2
Vyksa • Russian Fed. ... 17 G3
Vylkove • Ukraine ... 14 Q4
Vym • Russian Fed. ... 17 I2
Vynnykiv • Ukraine ... 13 N8
Vynohradiv • Ukraine ... 13 M9
Vyrnwy, Lake • United Kingdom ... 104 C4
Vyshniy Volochek • Russian Fed. ... 126 C3
Vyskov • Czech Rep. ... 13 F8
Vyškovskoye • Ukraine ... 14 K1
Vysokaye • Belarus ... 13 M5
Vysoké Tatry Nat. Park Park N • Slovak Rep. ... 89 [100]
Vysoké Tatry Nat. Park • Slovak Rep. ... 128 C2
Vyšší Brod • Czech Rep. ... 128 B4
Vytegra • Russian Fed. ... 17 F2
Vyvenka • Russian Fed. ... 27 S4

Waddan • Libya ... 21 C2
Waddan, Jabal • Libya ... 21 C2
Waddeneilanden • Netherlands ... 5 H1
Waddeneilanden • Netherlands ... 109 D3
Waddeneilanden • Netherlands ... 109 D3
Waddinxveen • Netherlands ... 109 F3
Waddell, Grosser • Austria ... 119 H1
Waddington, Mt • BC, Canada ... 155 C3
Wadebridge • United Kingdom ... 104 F4
Wadena • MN, United States ... 43 I3
Wadi • India ... 138 D2
Wadi ar Ru'ays • Libya ... 21 C2
Wadowice • Poland ... 128 C3
Wadsworth • OH, United States ... 44 E5
Wagendrift Nature Reserve • South Africa ... 134 B3
Wageningen • Netherlands ... 5 I3
Wager Bay • NU, Canada ... 39 N3
Wagga Wagga • NS, Australia ... 144 C1
Wagin • WA, Australia ... 34 C6
Waging • Germany ... 112 F4
Wagner See • Germany ... 112 F4
Wagon Mound • NM, United States ... 46 G3
Wagoner • OK, United States ... 46 H5
Wagrain Ski • Austria ... 100 [176]
Wagrain • Austria ... 119 H4
Wagrowiec • Poland ... 13 G5
Wah • Pakistan ... 18 J3
Wah Wah Mtns • UT, United States ... 45 F2
Waha • Libya ... 21 C2
Wahai • Indonesia ... 32 (1) D3
Wahat al Kufrah • Libya ... 21 D3
Wãhãt, El • Egypt ... 20 D2
Wãhãt Jalu • Libya ... 21 E3
Wahat Salimah • Sudan ... 21 E3
Wahat Salimah • Sudan ... 154 G5
Wahn [Apt] • Germany ... 112 D1
Wahoo • NE, United States ... 46 G2
Wahpeton • ND, United States ... 43 H3
Waialeale • HI, United States ... 154 G2
Waialeale • HI, United States ... 154 G2
Waianae • HI, United States ... 47 K8
Waianae Range • HI, United States ... 154 G5
Waiau • New Zealand ... 145 G3
Waiamu • Indonesia ... 32 (1) D3
Waigeo • Indonesia ... 32 (1) D3
Waihi • New Zealand ... 35 F3
Waihi Beach • New Zealand ... 145 F2
Waikaremoana, Lake • New Zealand ... 145 F4
Waikato [Adm] • New Zealand ... 145 E1
Waikato [Riv] • New Zealand ... 145 E4
Waikawa • New Zealand ... 145 G4
Waikiki • HI, United States ... 47 K8
Waikouaiti • New Zealand ... 35 F4
Wailua Falls • HI, United States ... 154 G1
Wailuku • HI, United States ... 154 G3
Wailua River State Park • HI, United States ... 154 G1
Waimanalo Beach • HI, United States ... 154 G6
Waimangu Volcanic Valley • New Zealand ... 145 F2
Waimate • New Zealand ... 35 C7
Waimea • Kauai, HI, United States ... 154 G2
Waimea • Hawaii, HI, United States ... 154 G8
Waimea • HI, United States ... 154 G1
Waimea Canyon State Park • HI, United States ... 154 G2
Waingapu • Indonesia ... 32 (1) B4
Wainganga • India ... 28 D4
Waini • New Zealand ... 145 F1
Wainuiomata • New Zealand ... 145 F1
Wainwright • AL, Canada ... 38 I6
Waiotapu • New Zealand ... 145 F2
Waiouru • New Zealand ... 145 F1
Waipahu • HI, United States ... 47 K8
Waipara • New Zealand ... 145 F4
Waipio • HI, United States ... 154 G8
Waipukurau • New Zealand ... 145 F4
Wairakei Thermal Valley • New Zealand ... 145 F2
Wairoa • New Zealand ... 145 F4
Waitaki • New Zealand ... 145 C6
Waitara • New Zealand ... 35 E3
Waitemata • New Zealand ... 145 F1
Waitomo Caves • New Zealand ... 35 E3
Waiuku • New Zealand ... 35 E3
Wajima • Japan ... 30 I6
Wajir • Kenya ... 131 G2
Wak, Ei • Kenya ... 23 G3
Wakasa-wan • Japan ... 30 H7
Wakatipu, Lake • New Zealand ... 145 C6
Wakayama • Japan ... 140 B3
Wakayama [Adm] • Japan ... 140 A8
Wake • Marshall Is. ... 33 H4
Wake • Marshall Is. ... 46 F3
Wakefield • United Kingdom ... 104 D5
Wakhan • Afghanistan ... 18 J2
Wakkanai • Japan ... 30 K2
Wakkerstroom • South Africa ... 134 B1
Wakulla Springs • FL, United States ... 154 H2
Walachia • Romania ... 13 F7
Walbrzych • Poland ... 13 F6
Walchensee • Germany ... 112 F7
Walcott • WY, United States ... 42 L6
Walcz • Poland ... 13 F4
Wald im Oberpinzgau Ski • Austria ... 100 [147]
Walden • NY, United States ... 44 H5
Walden • CO, United States ... 45 I1
Waldkirch • Germany ... 112 D8
Waldkrappen • Germany ... 112 D3
Waldo • FL, United States ... 49 B3
Waldshut • Germany ... 112 D8
Walensee • Switzerland ... 119 G3
Wales • United Kingdom ... 7
Wales I. • NU, Canada ... 39 N3
Wales I. • Belgium ... 98 [49]
Walbli • Belgium ... 109 D15
Walker • MN, United States ... 43 I3
Walker • MN, United States ... 44 C4
Walker Lake • NV, United States ... 152 C4
Walkerston • QL, Australia ... 144 B3
Wall • SD, United States ... 43 E5
Walla Walla • WA, United States ... 42 F4
Wallaceburg • OT, Canada ... 44 D4
Wallasey • United Kingdom ... 7 I8
Wallblake [Apt] • Anguilla ... 160 C
Wallis, Is de •
Wallis & Futuna • Pacific Ocean ... 161 Q
Wallis & Futuna ... 35 (2) E1
Wallowa • OR, United States ... 42 G4
Wallowa Mtns • OR, United States ... 152 B4

Walnut Creek • CA, United States ... 45 A3
Walsall • United Kingdom ... 104 D2
Walsenburg • CO, United States ... 46 C4
Walsertal, Grosser • Austria ... 119 H1
Walsrode • Germany ... 8 E4
Walt Disney World Int. Sports Complex • FL, United States ... 151 C1
Walt Disney World Resort Complex • FL, United States ... 151 C1
Walshausen • Germany ... 9 F6
Walton Heath • United Kingdom ... 104 E3
Waltrop • Germany ... 111 B2
Walvis Bay • Angola ... 19 F8
Walvis Bay • Namibia ... 24 A4
Wamba • Nigeria ... 22 F3
Wamba • Kenya ... 23 F3
Wamba • Dem. Rep. of Congo ... 23 D3
Wamba • Dem. Rep. of Congo ... 23 B5
Wamena • KS, United States ... 46 G3
Wamena • Indonesia ... 35 (1) B1
Wami • Tanzania ... 23 F3
Wan Chai • Hong Kong, China ... 139 B6
Wan Hsa-la • Myanmar ... 142 B1
Wan Zhi • China ... 139 C1
Wanaka • New Zealand ... 145 G2
Wanaka, Lake • New Zealand ... 145 G2
Wanapa • Bonaire ... 160 W
Wanapiri • Indonesia ... 32 (1) E3
Wanapitei Lake • OT, Canada ... 44 E2
Wanditz • Germany ... 111 C2
Wandlitzer See • Germany ... 111 C2
Wang • Thailand ... 142 B3
Wang Phetburi Mtn • Thailand ... 142 C3
Wang Takhrai • Thailand ... 142 B2
Wang Takhrai Gardens • Thailand ... 142 F3
Wanganui [Riv] • New Zealand ... 145 F3
Wanganui • New Zealand ... 145 F1
Wangaratta • VI, Australia ... 144 C3
Wangen • Germany ... 8 E3
Wangerooge • Germany ... 8 C3
Wangerooge Spa • Germany ... 113 [c12]
Wangpanyang • China ... 139 E3
Wangqing • China ... 30 E2
Wanne-Eickel [Area] • Germany ... 111 A2
Wanneperveen • Netherlands ... 109 D8
Wannsee (Berlin) • Germany ... 111 C2
Wanshan Qundao • Zhuhai, China ... 139 B4
Wanxian • China ... 29 D4
Wanzai • Zhuhai, China ... 139 B1
Wapakoneta • OH, United States ... 44 D5
Wappapello Lake • MO, United States ... 46 J4
Warangal • India ... 138 D2
Waratah Bay • VI, Australia ... 144 C3
Warburg • Germany ... 8 E5
Warburton • SA, Australia ... 34 G5
Warburton Mission • WA, Australia ... 34 E5
Warburton Range • WA, Australia ... 34 E5
Ward • New Zealand ... 35 F3
Wardija Point • Malta ... 123 H1
Wareham • United Kingdom ... 104 E5
Waremme • Belgium ... 5 I4
Waren • Germany ... 8 H3
Waren • Indonesia ... 32 (1) E3
Warendorf • Germany ... 5 K3
Warendorf • Germany ... 8 C5
Wargla • Algeria ... 20 G2
Warkworth • New Zealand ... 35 E3
Warkworth Beach • United Kingdom ... 101 [19]
Warm Springs • NV, United States ... 45 D2
Warm Springs • GA, United States ... 48 E4
Warmbad • South Africa ... 24 C4
Warminster • United Kingdom ... 104 F3
Warminster • PA, United States ... 44 H5
Warnemünde • Germany ... 8 H2
Warnemünde Beach • Germany ... 96 [33]
Warner Brothers Movie World Park L • Germany ... 98 [56]
Warner Brothers Movie World • QL, Australia ... 144 B6
Warner Mtns • United States ... 48 F4
Warner Robins • GA, United States ... 48 F4
Warner Valley • OR, United States ... 152 B3
Warnow • Germany ... 8 H3
Waroona • WA, Australia ... 34 C6
Warrego • NS/QL, Australia ... 34 I5
Warren • MT, United States ... 42 K4
Warren • MI, United States ... 44 D4
Warren • OH, United States ... 44 E5
Warren • AR, United States ... 46 I6
Warren • PA, United States ... 153 D1
Warrensburg • MO, United States ... 46 H4
Warrenton • OR, United States ... 42 D3
Warrenton • GA, United States ... 48 F4
Warri • Nigeria ... 22 F3
Warrington • United Kingdom ... 7 J8
Warrington • FL, United States ... 49 C5
Warstein • Germany ... 5 L3
Warszawa • Poland ... 13 J5
Warszawa Heritage C • Poland ... 86 [162]
Warta • Poland ... 13 H6
Wartberg • South Africa ... 24 C6
Wartburg Heritage C • Germany ... 86 [44]
Wartburg Castle • Germany ... 113 [181]
Wartburg • TN, United States ... 48 E2
Warth • Austria ... 119 H5
Waru • Indonesia ... 32 (1) D3
Warwick • United Kingdom ... 104 C2
Warwick • RI, United States ... 44 J5
Warwick Long Bay • Bermuda ... 159 J3
Warwickshire • United Kingdom ... 104 D2
Wasalandia Park L • Finland ... 98 [10]
Wasatch Range • ID/UT, United States ... 42 K5
Wasco • CA, United States ... 45 C4
Waseca • MN, United States ... 43 J4
Wash, The • United Kingdom ... 7 M9
Washago • OT, Canada ... 155 D5
Washburn • ND, United States ... 43 F3
Washburn • WI, United States ... 43 K2
Washington • United Kingdom ... 7 J5
Washington • PA, United States ... 44 E5
Washington • NC, United States ... 153 D11
Washington • MO, United States ... 46 J3
Washington • IN, United States ... 48 D1
Washington • NC, United States ... 48 I3
Washington [Adm] • United States ... 152 B1
Washington Court House • OH, United States ... 44 D6
Washington Crossing State Hist. Park • PA, United States ... 153 D6
Washington DC • United States ... 151 D15
Washington • WI, United States ... 44 B3
Washington, Mt • NH, United States ... 44 J3
Washington Mon. Park N • DC, United States ... 151 [289]
Washington, Mt • OR, United States ... 152 B3
Walney I. Beach • United Kingdom ... 101 [242]
Walnut Canyon Nat. Mon. Park N • AZ, United States ... 150 [106]
Walnut Canyon Nat. Mon. • AZ, United States ... 153 E1
Washington National [Apt] • VA, United States ... 153 D9

Washington/Slagbaai Nat. Park •
Bonaire .... 160 W
Washita Battlefield Nat. Hist. Site
Park N • OK, United States .. 150 [145]
Wasilków • Poland 13 M4
Wasilla • AK, United States 49 L3
Wasior • Indonesia 32 (1) D3
Waspám • Nicaragua 37 E5
Wassaw I. • GA, United States ... 48 G5
Wassenaar • Netherlands 109 F1
Wasserburg • Germany 112 F4
Wast Water • United Kingdom ... 104 C3
Wat Phra That Doi Suthep •
Thailand 142 B1
Watampone • Indonesia 32 (1) B3
Watarrka Nat. Park •
NT, Australia 145 D3
Water Cay • Bahamas 158 B2
Water Cay • Turks & Caicos Is. .. 158 C1
Water I. • US Virgin Is. .... 160 Z
Water Mania • United States 151 C11
Waterbury • CT, United States .. 153 D7
Wateree Lake •
SC, United States 48 G3
Waterford • Ireland 7 E9
Waterford [Adm] • Ireland 108 A2
Waterland • Netherlands 109 F1
Waterloo • Belgium 5 H4
Waterloo • IA, United States 43 J5
Waterloo • NY, United States 44 G4
Waterloo • OT, Canada 44 E4
Waterloo [Battlefield] •
Belgium 109 D14
Watermouth Castle •
United Kingdom 104 F2
Waterport • NY, United States ... 153 D1
Waterton Lakes Nat. Park •
AL, Canada 155 C4
Waterton Lakes Nat. Park Park N •
AL, Canada .... 156 [18]
Waterton-Glacier Int. Peace Park
Heritage N • Canada/United States 82 [5]
Waterton-Glacier Int. Peace Park •
Canada/United States 155 C4
Watertown • SD, United States .. 43 H4
Watertown • NY, United States .. 44 H4
Waterville • ME, United States .. 108 C7
Waterville • ME, United States ... 44 K3
Waterville Valley Ski •
NH, United States .... 149 [220]
Watervliet • NY, United States .. 44 I4
Waterways • AL, Canada 38 I5
Watford • United Kingdom 104 E1
Watford City •
ND, United States 43 E3
Watheroo • WA, Australia 34 C6
Watkins Glen •
NY, United States 153 D2
Watonga • OK, United States 46 F5
Watrous • SA, Canada 38 J6
Watsa • Dem. Rep. of Congo 23 D3
Watseka • IL, United States 44 B5
Watsi Kengo •
Dem. Rep. of Congo 22 H5
Watson Lake • YT, Canada 38 F4
Watsonville • CA, United States .. 45 B3
Wattenscheid (Bochum) • Germany 111 B2
Watts Bar Lake •
TN, United States 48 E3
Watumu Marine Game Reserve •
Kenya 131 G5
Watumu Marine Nat. Park • Kenya 131 G5
Watzmann • Germany 112 F8
Wau • Papua New Guinea 35 (1) D2
Waukara, Gunung • Indonesia 32 (1) A3
Waukegan • IL, United States 44 B4
Waupun • WI, United States 43 L5
Waurika • OK, United States 154 J1
Wausau • WI, United States 43 L4
Wauseon • OH, United States ... 44 C5
Wauwatosa • WI, United States .. 44 A4
Waverly • IA, United States 43 J5
Waverly • TN, United States 48 D2
Wavre • Belgium 5 H4
Wavre • Belgium 109 D15
Waw • Sudan 23 D2
Waw al Kabir • Libya 21 B2
Waw an Namus • Libya 21 B2
Wawa • OT, Canada 39 O7
Waxahachie • TX, United States .. 47 F1
Waxahachie • TX, United States.. 154 J1
Way of St James Heritage C •
France .... 86 [83]
Way of St James Heritage C •
Spain .... 86 [95]
Wayabula • Indonesia 32 (1) C2
Waycross • GA, United States ... 154 H3
Wayland • MO, United States 46 J2
Wayne • NE, United States 43 H5
Waynesboro • VA, United States .. 44 F6
Waynesboro • PA, United States . 44 G6
Waynesboro • MS, United States . 48 C5
Waynesville • NC, United States . 48 F3
Waynoka • OK, United States ... 46 F4
Waza, Parc nat. de Park •
Cameroon .... 133 [41]
Wé • New Caledonia 35 (2) B3
We • Indonesia 143 G1
Weald, The • United Kingdom .. 104 E3
Wear • United Kingdom 7 J7
Weatherford • OK, United States . 46 F5
Weatherford • TX, United States . 154 J1
Weaverville • CA, United States . 42 D6
Webster • SD, United States 43 H4
Webster City •
IA, United States 43 J5
Webster Springs •
WV, United States 44 E6
Weda • Indonesia 32 (1) C2
Weddell Sea • Antarctica 54 (1) A2
Wedding (Berlin) • Germany ... 111 C2
Wedel • Germany 8 E3
Week/ Wachee Spring •
FL, United States 154 H5
Weeren Game Reserve •
South Africa 134 B3
Weener • Germany 8 C3
Weerribben, Nat. Park •
Netherlands 109 D7
Weert • Netherlands 5 I3
Weesenstein Castle • Germany 113 [188]
Weesp • Netherlands 109 F2
Weggis • Switzerland 119 G3
Wei He • China 29 D4
Wei He • China 29 F3
Weichsel • Poland 13 H4
Weidelsburg Castle • Germany 113 [36]
Weiden • Germany 9 H7
Weifeng • China 29 F3
Weikersheim Castle • Germany 113 [91]
Weilburg • Germany 112 E2
Weilburg Castle • Germany ... 113 [42]
Weiler-Simmerberg • Germany . 112 F5
Weilheim • Germany 9 G8
Weimar • Germany 9 F6
Weimar Heritage C • Germany 86 [42-43]
Weingarten • Germany 112 F5
Weinheim • Germany 9 D7
Weinsberg • Germany 9 E7
Weipa • QL, Australia 34 H2
Weir Farm Nat. Hist. Site Park N •
CT, United States .... 151 [324]
Weir Farm Nat. Hist. Site •
CT, United States 153 D7
Weirton • WV, United States ... 44 E5

Weiser • ID, United States 42 G4
Weiss Lake • AL, United States .. 48 E3
Weisse Elster • Germany 9 H5
Weissenburg • France 112 D6
Weissenburg Castle • Germany . 113 [144]
Weissenburg in Bayern • Germany 9 F7
Weissenfels • Germany 9 G5
Weissenhorn • Germany 112 F2
Weissensee (Berlin) • Germany . 111 C2
Weissenstein Castle • Germany . 113 [164]
Weisswasser • Germany 8 J5
Wejherowo • Poland 13 H3
Welbourn Hill • SA, Australia ... 34 F5
Welch • WV, United States 48 G2
Welch Village Ski •
MN, United States .... 149 [123]
Welchman Hall Gully • Barbados . 161 O
Welden • Germany 112 F2
Weldiya • Ethiopia 23 F1
Welel • Ethiopia 23 E2
Weleri • Java, Indonesia 143 J3
Welkom • South Africa 24 D5
Welland • United Kingdom 7 L9
Welland • OT, Canada 39 P8
Welland • OT, Canada 44 F4
Welland Canal • OT, Canada ... 155 B9
Wellesley Is. • QL, Australia 33 E7
Wellingborough • United Kingdom . 7 L9
Wellington • NS, Australia 34 I6
Wellington • New Zealand 35 E5
Wellington • CO, United States .. 46 C2
Wellington • KS, United States .. 46 G4
Wellington • TX, United States .. 46 E5
Wellington [Adm] • New Zealand . 145 E2
Wellington, I. • Chile 53 A5
Wells • United Kingdom 104 F3
Wells • NV, United States 152 C2
Wells Gray Prov. Park •
BC, Canada 155 C4
Wells-next-the-Sea •
United Kingdom 5 D2
Wellsboro • PA, United States .. 153 D1
Wellsford • New Zealand 35 E3
Wellston • ND, United States ... 44 D6
Wellsville • NY, United States .. 153 D1
Wels • Austria 13 C9
Welschnofen [Apt] • Netherlands 109 D11
Welschnofen • Italy 120 B3
Welsh castles Heritage C •
United Kingdom .... 86 [16]
Welshpool • United Kingdom .. 104 D1
Welwyn Garden City •
United Kingdom 5 C3
Wembley • South Africa 134 B3
Wembley Stadium •
United Kingdom 104 E1
Wembury Old Mill •
United Kingdom 104 F5
Wemyss Bay • United Kingdom 106 B2
Wenatchee • WA, United States . 152 B1
Wenchi • Ghana 22 D3
Wendelstein • Germany 112 F7
Wendover • UT, United States .. 152 C2
Wendujne • Belgium 109 E2
Wengen • Switzerland 119 G3
Wenlock • QL, Australia 34 H2
Wenlock Edge • United Kingdom . 104 D1
Wenquan • China 28 F2
Wenshan • China 29 C6
Wenshan • China 31 C2
Wentworth • NS, Australia 34 H6
Wenzhou • China 29 G5
Werda • Botswana 24 C5
Werden (Essen) • Germany 111 B1
Werder • Germany 111 C3
Werfenweng Ski • Austria ... 100 [180]
Wermelskirchen • Germany ... 111 B4
Werneck Castle • Germany ... 113 [176]
Werneuchen • Germany 111 C2
Wernigerode • Germany 8 F5
Werra • Germany 9 E7
Werris Creek • NS, Australia 34 I5
Wertach • Germany 112 F2
Wertheim • Germany 9 E7
Wertheim Castle • Germany ... 113 [89]
Werther • Germany 111 B1
Weser • Germany 8 E4
Weser • Germany 8 E5
Wesergebirge • Germany 8 E5
Weslaco • TX, United States 47 F4
Wesleyville • NF, Canada 156 D4
Wessel, Cape • NT, Australia ... 34 G2
Wessel Is. • NT, Australia 34 G2
West Africa cruise area •
Africa 81 A5
West Allis • WI, United States ... 44 A4
West Angle Bay Beach •
United Kingdom .... 101 [172]
West Bali Nat. Park •
Bali, Indonesia 143 H1
West Bay • Cayman Is. 159 E3
West Bend • WI, United States .. 44 A4
West Bengal • India 28 E4
West Branch Delaware •
NY, United States 153 D2
West Branch Susquehanna •
PA, United States 153 D5
West Bromwich • United Kingdom 104 D2
West Caicos •
Turks & Caicos Is. 158 C1
West Cape • New Zealand ... 33 H10
West Cape • New Zealand 145 G3
West Chester •
PA, United States 44 H6
West Coast • New Zealand 145 E3
West Coast Nat. Park •
South Africa 134 C1
West Country • United Kingdom . 104 F
West Des Moines •
IA, United States 46 I2
West Edmonton Mall Park L •
AL, Canada .... 156 [C]
West End • Bahamas 158 B2
West End • Cayman Is. 159 E2
West End • Anguilla .... 160 C
West End Point •
Little Cayman, Cayman Is. 159 E1
West End Point •
Cayman Brac, Cayman Is. 159 E2
West Falkland • Falkland Is. 53 D6
West Fargo • ND, United States . 43 H3
West Frankfort •
IL, United States 48 C2
West Grand Lake •
ME, United States 44 K3
West Hamlin • WV, United States . 48 F1
West Hartford •
CT, United States 44 I5
West Haven • CT, United States . 44 I5
West Hawk Lake • MN, Canada . 43 I2
West Helena • AR, United States . 46 J5
West Jordan • UT, United States . 45 G1
West Kirby Beach •
United Kingdom .... 101 [237]
West Lafayette •
IN, United States 44 B5
West Lake • China 139 C3
West Liberty •
KY, United States 48 F2
West Lothian • United Kingdom 104 B4
West Memphis •
AR, United States 46 J5
West Midland Safari Park •
United Kingdom 104 D1
West Monroe • LA, United States . 47 H1
West Nicholson • Zimbabwe ... 130 C3
West Palm Beach •
FL, United States 154 H6

West Pensacola •
FL, United States 48 D5
West Plains • MO, United States . 46 J4
West Point • Falkland Is. 81 A10
West Point • NE, United States .. 46 G2
West Point • MS, United States .. 48 C4
West Point • NY, United States .. 153 D7
West Point Lake •
AL/GA, United States 48 E4
West Poplar • SA, Canada 42 L2
West Sand Spit •
Turks & Caicos Is. 158 C1
West Seneca • NY, United States . 44 F4
West Siberian Plain •
Russian Fed. 26 M5
West Thumb • WY, United States . 42 J4
West Union • OH, United States . 44 D6
West Valley City •
UT, United States 42 I6
West Virginia • United States ... 41 J4
West Vlaanderen • Netherlands . 109 D13
West Wittering Beach •
United Kingdom .... 101 [89]
West Wyalong • NS, Australia ... 144 C1
West Yellowstone •
MT, United States 42 J4
Westbrook • ME, United States .. 44 J4
Westeinderplassen • Netherlands . 109 F1
Westende-Bad • Belgium 109 E1
Westendorf Ski • Austria ... 100 [151]
Westendorf • Austria 119 H6
Westerland • Germany 8 D2
Westerland, Sylt Spa • Germany 113 [c2]
Westerly • RI, United States 44 J5
Western • NU, Canada 38 J3
Western Australia • Australia ... 34 D5
Western, Bukit •
Penang, Malaysia 141 F1
Western Cape • South Africa ... 134 C6
Western Desert • Egypt 21 E3
Western Lakeland • Finland ... 125 E2
WESTERN SAHARA • Africa 20 C4
Westernport • MD, United States . 44 F6
Westerschelde • Netherlands 5 G3
Westerschouwen • Netherlands .. 5 G3
Westerstede • Germany 8 C3
Westerville • OH, United States .. 44 D5
Westerwald • Germany 112 D2
Westerwinkel Castle • Germany . 113 [20]
Westfield • MA, United States ... 44 I4
Westhope • ND, United States ... 43 F2
Westkapelle • Netherlands 5 G3
Westland • Netherlands 109 F3
Westland Lake • OT, Canada ... 44 D4
Westliche Karwendelspitze •
Austria/Germany 112 F7
Westminster • United Kingdom . 104 C4
Westminster • CO, United States . 46 C3
Westmoreland •
TN, United States 48 D2
Westmorland • United Kingdom 104 C4
Weston • Malaysia 32 F1
Weston • WV, United States 44 E6
Weston-super-Mare Beach •
United Kingdom .... 101 [155]
Weston-super-Mare •
United Kingdom 104 F3
Westport • New Zealand 35 C5
Westport • Ireland 108 C1
Westport House • Ireland 42 C3
Westport House • Ireland 108 C1
Westray • United Kingdom ...... 160 X
Westree • OT, Canada 44 E2
Westville • IN, United States 44 B5
Westward Ho! • United Kingdom 104 F2
Westwego • LA, United States ... 48 B6
Westwego • LA, United States .. 153 F4
Westwood • NJ, United States .. 153 D7
Wet'n'Wild • FL, Australia 144 B6
Wet'n'Wild • FL, United States . 151 C2
Wetar • Indonesia 32 (1) D4
Wetaskiwin • AL, Canada 38 I6
Wethersfield •
CT, United States 153 D7
Wetter • Germany 5 L4
Wetter • Germany 111 B2
Wetteren • Belgium 5 G3
Wettin Castle • Germany ..... 113 [211]
Wetumpka • AL, United States .. 48 D4
Wetzlar • Germany 112 D2
Wewak • Papua New Guinea 35 (1) C1
Wexford • Ireland 7 F9
Wexford [Adm] • Ireland 108 A2
Weyburn • SA, Canada 38 K7
Weymouth Beach • United Kingdom 101 [109]
Weymouth • United Kingdom .. 104 F6
Weymouth • MA, United States . 44 J4
Weza State Forest •
South Africa 134 B5
Whakapapa • New Zealand ... 145 F4
Whakatane • New Zealand 145 F2
Whale Coast • South Africa 134 C6
Whampoa • China 139 B1
Whanganui Nat. Park •
New Zealand 145 E4
Whangarei • New Zealand 35 E2
Wharton • TX, United States 47 F3
Wheat Ridge • CO, United States . 46 C3
Wheatland • WY, United States .. 43 A5
Wheaton • IL, United States 44 A5
Wheaton • MD, United States .. 153 D6
Wheeler Lake •
AL, United States 48 D3
Wheeler Peak •
NM, United States 46 C4
Wheeler Peak •
NV, United States 152 C4
Wheeling • WV, United States ... 44 E5
Whiddy I. • Ireland 108 C7
Whim Greathouse Museum •
US Virgin Is. .... 160 Z
Whipsnade Zoo • United Kingdom 104 E1
Whiskeytown-Shasta-Trinity Nat. Recreation
Area Park N • CA, United States . 150 [39]
Whistler • BC, Canada 155 C3
Whistler & Blackcomb Ski •
BC, Canada .... 149 [2]
Whitburn Beach • United Kingdom 101 [23-24]
Whitby • United Kingdom 7 L7
Whitby Beach • United Kingdom 101 [28]
Whitby • Turks & Caicos Is. 158 C1
Whitby • OT, Canada 155 B9
Whitchurch-Stouffville •
OT, Canada 44 F3
White • SD, United States 43 H4
White • CO/UT, United States ... 45 H1
White • AR/MO, United States .. 46 H4
White • AR, United States 46 J5
White Bay • NF, Canada 156 D3
White Bear Lake •
MN, United States 43 J4
White Butte • ND, United States . 43 E3
White Horse Hills •
United Kingdom 5 B3
White House, The Park N •
DC, United States .... 151 [290]
White I. • New Zealand 145 F2
White I. • New Zealand 39 O3
White Lake • NT/WA, Australia .. 34 E4
White Lake • WA, United States . 153 F3
White Mtn Peak •
CA, United States 45 C3
White Nile • Sudan 38 B3
White Oak Lake •
AR, United States 46 I6
White Otter Lake • OT, Canada . 43 J2

White Pass Village Ski •
United States .... 149 [52]
White Plains •
NY, United States 153 D7
White Plains •
NM, United States 153 D7
White River • YT, Canada 38 C4
White River • SD, United States . 38 K8
White River • OT, Canada 44 C1
White River Junction •
VT, United States 44 I4
White River Plateau •
CO, United States 45 I2
White Rock • BC, Canada 42 D2
White Salmon •
WA, United States 42 E4
White Sands Nat. Mon. Park N •
NM, United States .... 150 [119]
White Sands Nat. Mon. •
NM, United States 153 E4
White Sea • Russian Fed. 17 F1
White Settlement •
TX, United States 47 F1
White Sulphur Springs •
MT, United States 42 J3
White Sulphur Springs •
WV, United States 48 G2
White Umfolozi • South Africa .. 134 B2
Whitecap Mtns Ski •
United States .... 149 [128]
Whiteface Mtn Ski •
NY, United States .... 149 [196]
Whitefish • MT, United States .. 42 H2
Whitefish Bay •
WI, United States 44 B4
Whitefish Bay •
MI, United States 44 C2
Whitefish Point •
MI, United States 44 C2
Whitehall • NY, United States ... 44 D6
Whitehall • OH, United States .. 44 I4
Whitehaven • United Kingdom .. 104 C3
Whitehorse • YT, Canada 38 D4
Whitehouse • Jamaica 159 F3
Whiteman Range •
Papua New Guinea 35 (1) D2
Whitemark • TS, Australia 34 I8
Whitesand Bay • United Kingdom 104 F5
Whitesboro • TX, United States . 46 H5
Whitetail Ski •
PA, United States .... 149 [172]
Whitetail • PA, United States .. 153 D9
Whiteville • NC, United States .. 48 H3
Whitewater • WI, United States . 43 L5
Whitewater Lake • OT, Canada . 43 L1
Whitewood • SA, Canada 43 E1
Whitman Mission Nat. Hist. Site Park N •
WA, United States .... 150 [30]
Whitman Mission Nat. Hist. Site •
WA, United States 152 B2
Whitmore Village •
HI, United States 154 G5
Whitney, Lake •
TX, United States 47 F2
Whitney, Mt • CA, United States . 152 C4
Whitsunday Group •
QL, Australia 144 A4
Whitsunday I. • QL, Australia .. 144 B1
Whittier • AK, United States 49 L3
Wholdaia Lake • NT, Canada ... 38 K4
Whyalla • SA, Australia 34 G6
Wiang Ko Sai Nat. Park •
Thailand 142 B4
Wichita • KS, United States 46 G4
Wichita Falls •
TX, United States 47 F2
Wick • United Kingdom 6 I3
Wickenburg • AZ, United States . 45 G4
Wickiup Reservoir •
OR, United States 42 E5
Wicklow • Ireland 108 B4
Wicklow [Adm] • Ireland 108 B4
Wicklow Head • Ireland 108 B4
Wicklow Mtns • Ireland 108 B4
Wicklow Mtns Nat. Park Park N •
Ireland .... 89 [41]
Widgiemooltha • WA, Australia . 34 D6
Widyan, Al • Iraq/Saudi Arabia . 18 D3
Wiehl • Germany 112 E2
Wiefelstede • Germany 8 D3
Wieliczka Heritage C • Poland . 86 [164]
Wieliczka • Poland 128 C4
Wielun • Poland 13 H6
Wien • Austria 13 F9
Wien Heritage C • Austria .... 86 [127]
Wien [Adm] • Austria 119 F4
Wiener Becken • Austria 13 F10
Wiener Neustadt • Austria 13 F10
Wieprz • Poland 13 J6
Wieringermeer • Netherlands .. 109 D3
Wies Heritage C • Germany .... 86 [58]
Wiesbaden • Germany 112 E4
Wiese • Germany 10 M6
Wieskirche • Germany 112 F6
Wiesloch • Germany 5 L5
Wiesmoor • Germany 8 C3
Wieżyca • Poland 13 H3
Wigan • United Kingdom 112 E1
Wiggins • MS, United States ... 153 F4
Wight, Isle of • United Kingdom . 7 K11
Wigierski Nat. Park Park N •
Poland .... 89 [92]
Wigtown • United Kingdom 7 H7
Wigtown Bay • United Kingdom . 7 H7
Wil • Switzerland 9 E9
Wilbur • WA, United States 42 F3
Wilcannia • NS, Australia 34 H6
Wild Coast • South Africa 134 A2
Wild Mtn Ski •
United States .... 149 [120]
Wild Zone Park L • OT, Canada . 156 [K]
Wildau • Germany 111 C4
Wildbad Kreuth • Germany 112 F7
Wildcat Mtn Ski •
United States .... 149 [227]
Wildenbruch • Germany 111 C3
Wildenburg Castle • Germany . 113 [172]
Wildenstein Castle • Germany . 113 [111]
Wilderness Nat. Lake Area •
South Africa 134 C6
Wilderswil bei Interlaken Ski •
Switzerland .... 100 [102]
Wildeshausen • Germany 8 D4
Wildhaus • Switzerland 119 G3
Wildschönau Ski • Austria .... 100 [148]
Wildspitze • Austria 119 H6
Wildwood • NJ, United States . 153 D10
Wilfrath • Germany 111 B3
Wilhelmshaven • Germany 8 D3
Wilhelmshaven Spa • Germany 113 [c6]
Wilhelmshöhe, Kassel Castle •
Germany .... 113 [34]
Wilhelmsthal Castle • Germany 113 [33]
Wilkes Land • Antarctica 54 (1) R2
Wilkesboro • NC, United States . 48 G2
Wilkins Strait • Antarctica 54 (1) A4
Willamette • OR, United States . 152 B3
Willamette Pass Ski •
OR, United States .... 149 [56]
Willamette Pass •
OR, United States 42 E5
Willandra Lakes Heritage N •
Australia .... 83 [147]
Willandra Lakes Heritage C •
Australia .... 85 [210]
Willapa Bay • WA, United States . 152 B1

Willeroo • NT, Australia 34 F3
Willet • OT, Canada 43 L1
William H. Bramble [Apt] •
Montserrat .... 161 H
William Howard Taft Nat. Hist. Site
Park N • OH, United States .... 151 [180]
Williamatic • CT, United States . 44 I5
Williams • CA, United States 42 D7
Williams • AZ, United States ... 153 E1
Williams Lake • BC, Canada 155 C3
Williamsburg •
KY, United States 48 E2
Williamsburg •
VA, United States 153 D11
Williamson • WV, United States . 48 F2
Williamsport •
PA, United States 153 D5
Williamston • NC, United States . 48 I3
Willich • Germany 111 B3
Willingen Spa • Germany .... 113 [k4]
Willis Group • CL, Australia 34 J3
Williston • South Africa 134 C2
Williston • ND, United States ... 43 E2
Williston • FL, United States ... 154 H4
Williston K, United States 89 B3
Williston Lake • BC, Canada ... 155 C1
Willits • CA, United States 42 D7
Willmar • MN, United States ... 43 I4
Willow Creek •
CA, United States 42 D6
Willowmore • South Africa 134 C3
Willows • CA, United States ... 42 D7
Wills, Lake • WA, Australia 34 E4
Wilmersdorf (Berlin) • Germany . 111 C3
Wilmington • OH, United States . 44 D6
Wilmington • NC, United States . 44 I3
Wilmington • DE, United States . 153 D10
Wilmot Mtn Ski •
WI, United States .... 149 [135]
Wilnsdorf • Germany 9 D6
Wilok • Poland 13 K8
Wilpattu Nat. Park • Sri Lanka 138 D15
Wilson • NC, United States 48 I3
Wilson Bluff • Antarctica 54 (1) A1
Wilson, Cape • NU, Canada 39 O3
Wilson Lake • KS, United States . 46 F3
Wilson Lake • AL, United States . 48 D3
Wilson, Mt • CO, United States . 46 C3
Wilson's Creek Nat. Battlefield Park N •
MO, United States .... 151 [173]
Wilsons Promontory •
VI, Australia 144 C3
Wiltz • Luxembourg 109 D20
Wiluna • WA, Australia 34 D5
Wimbledon • United Kingdom .. 104 E1
Wincanton • United Kingdom .. 104 F3
Winchelsea Beach •
United Kingdom .... 101 [60]
Winchester • United Kingdom 7 K10
Winchester • IN, United States .. 44 C5
Winchester • VA, United States . 44 F6
Winchester • OT, Canada 44 H3
Winchester • TN, United States . 48 D3
Winchester • KY, United States . 48 E1
Wind • WY, United States 43 A5
Wind Cave Nat. Park Park N •
United States .... 150 [151]
Wind Mtn • NM, United States .. 47 B1
Wind River Range •
WY, United States 42 K5
Windeck • Germany 9 D6
Windemin, Pointe • Vanuatu . 35 (2) B2
Winder • GA, United States 48 F3
Windermere • United Kingdom . 104 C4
Windermere [Lake] •
United Kingdom 104 C4
Windermere Lake • OT, Canada . 44 D2
Windhoek • Namibia 24 B4
Window Rock • AZ, United States . 153 E2
Windows of the World •
Shenzhen, China 139 B3
Windrush • United Kingdom ... 104 E1
Windsor • United Kingdom 104 E1
Windsor • OT, Canada 39 O8
Windsor • IL, United States 44 A6
Windsor • OT, Canada 44 I4
Windsor • QU, Canada 44 I3
Windsor • NS, Canada 156 D7
Windwardside • Saba .... 161 F
Winfield • KS, United States 46 G4
Wingham • OT, Canada 44 E4
Winisk • OT, Canada 39 N5
Winisk Lake • OT, Canada 39 N6
Winisk [Riv] • OT, Canada 39 N5
Winkler • MN, Canada 43 H2
Winneba • Ghana 22 D3
Winnebago, Lake •
WI, United States 43 L5
Winnemucca • NV, United States . 152 C2
Winner • SD, United States 43 G5
Winnfield • LA, United States .. 153 F1
Winnibigoshish, Lake •
MN, United States 43 I3
Winningen • Germany 112 E1
Winnipeg • MN, Canada 38 L6
Winnipeg Beach • MN, Canada . 43 H1
Winnipeg, Lake • MN, Canada . 38 L6
Winnipeg [Riv] • MN/OT, Canada . 38 L6
Winnipegosis • MN, Canada 38 L6
Winnipegosis, Lake •
MN, Canada 38 K6
Winnipesaukee, Lake •
NH, United States 44 J4
Winona • MN, United States ... 43 K4
Winona • MO, United States ... 46 J4
Winona • MS, United States ... 48 C4
Winschoten • Netherlands 5 K1
Winsen • Germany 8 E4
Winsen • Germany 8 F3
Winslow • Kiribati 33 J6
Winslow • AZ, United States .. 153 E2
Winston-Salem •
NC, United States 48 G2
Winter Gardens •
FL, United States 151 C1
Winter Harbour • NT/NU, Canada . 38 I2
Winter Haven •
FL, United States 154 H5
Winter Park Ski •
CO, United States .... 149 [99]
Winter Park • FL, United States . 151 C2
Winterberg • Germany 9 D5
Winterberge • South Africa 134 C4
Wintergreen Ski • AL, Canada . 149 [48]
Wintergreen •
WV, United States .... 149 [163]
Wintergreen • VA, United States . 153 D11
Winterset • IA, United States ... 46 H2
Winterswijk • Netherlands 109 D8
Winterthur • Switzerland 9 D9
Winton • New Zealand 145 G4
Winton Heights • Bahamas 158 B3
Wipperfürth • Germany 111 B4
Wirrulyarrayi Aboriginal Land •
NT, Australia 145 D1
Wisbech • United Kingdom 7 M9
Wischhafen • Germany 41 I2
Wisconsin • United States 43 L5
Wisconsin Dells •
WI, United States 43 L5
Wisconsin [Riv] •
WI, United States 43 L5
Wisconsin Rapids •
WI, United States 43 L4
Wisdom • MT, United States ... 42 I4

Wiseman • AK, United States ... 49 K2
Wiseman's Bridge Beach •
United Kingdom .... 101 [161]
Wisła • Poland 128 C3
Wisła [Riv] • Poland 13 K6
Wisłany, Zalev •
Poland/Russian Fed. 13 I3
Wiślica • Poland 128 C2
Wisłoka • Poland 13 K8
Wismar • Germany 8 G3
Wisp Ski • MD, United States . 149 [168]
Wisseler See Beach • Germany . 96 [36]
Witbank • South Africa 24 D5
Witjira Nat. Park •
SA, Australia 145 D4
Witney • United Kingdom 7 K10
Witten • Germany 111 B2
Wittenberg • Germany 8 H5
Wittenberg Heritage C • Germany 86 [41]
Wittenberge • Germany 8 G3
Wittingen • Germany 8 F4
Wittlich • Germany 112 E3
Wittmund • Germany 8 C3
Wittstock • Germany 8 H3
Witu • Namibia 24 B4
Witwatersrand • South Africa .. 24 D5
Wloclawek • Poland 13 I5
Wlodawa • Poland 13 M6
Wodonga • VI, Australia 144 C3
Wodzisław Śląski • Poland 128 C1
Woerden • Netherlands 109 F4
Wokam • Indonesia 32 (1) D4
Woking • United Kingdom 104 E1
Wolds, The • United Kingdom .. 5 C1
Wolf • Galapagos Is. 51 (1) A1
Wolf Creek • OR, United States . 42 D5
Wolf Creek • MT, United States . 42 I3
Wolf Point • MT, United States . 43 D2
Wolf Trap Farm Park Park N •
VA, United States .... 151 [257]
Wolf, Volcán • Galapagos Is. .. 51 (1) A2
Wolfe I. • OT, Canada 44 G3
Wolfegg • Germany 112 F5
Wolfen • Germany 8 H5
Wolfenbüttel • Germany 8 F4
Wolfenbüttel Castle • Germany . 113 [7]
Wolfhagen • Germany 9 E5
Wolfratshausen • Germany 112 F3
Wolfsberg • Austria 13 D11
Wolfsburg • Germany 8 F4
Wolgast • Germany 8 I2
Wolin • Poland 13 D4
Woliński Nat. Park Park N •
Poland .... 89 [89]
Wolkenstein Ski • Italy .... 100 [238]
Wolkenstein in Gröden • Italy .. 120 B1
Wollaston, I. • Chile 53 C7
Wollaston Lake • SA, Canada ... 38 K5
Wollaston Peninsula •
NU, Canada 38 H3
Wolomin • Poland 13 K5
Wolvega • Netherlands 5 I2
Wolverhampton • United Kingdom 104 D2
Wolverton • United Kingdom 7 L9
Wolwefontein • South Africa .. 134 C3
Women's Rights Nat. Hist. Park N •
NY, United States .... 151 [305]
Women's Rights Nat. Hist. Park •
NY, United States 153 D2
Wondersorejo • Indonesia 143 H1
Wonju • Rep. of Korea 30 E6
Wonobo • Java, Indonesia 143 J7
Wonsan • D.P.R. of Korea 30 D5
Wonthaggi • VI, Australia 144 C3
Wood Buffalo Nat.Park Heritage N •
AL/NT, Canada .... 82 [3]
Wood Buffalo Nat. Park Park N •
AL, Canada .... 156 [14]
Wood River • IL, United States .. 46 J3
Woodbridge • United Kingdom .. 5 E2
Woodbridge • VA, United States . 44 G6
Woodbridge Bay • Dominica ... 80 B11
Woodbridge Bay • Dominica ... 161 M
Woodburn • OR, United States . 42 D4
Woodhall Mtn •
MS, United States 48 C3
Woodhouse Reef Dive • Red Sea 135 B1
Woodland • CA, United States .. 45 B2
Woodland Park •
CO, United States 46 C3
Woodlands Bay • Montserrat ... 161 H
Woodlands New Town • Singapore 141 H1
Woodlark • Papua New Guinea 35 (1) D2
Woodroffe, Mt • SA, Australia .. 145 D3
Woods Hole • MA, United States 153 D8
Woodstock • United Kingdom 5 B2
Woodstock • OH, United States . 44 E6
Woodstock • IL, United States .. 44 A4
Woodstock • OT, Canada 44 E4
Woodstock • NB, Canada 44 L2
Woodstock • NY, United States . 153 D6
Woodstock • GA, United States . 153 F4
Woodville • TX, United States .. 153 F4
Woodward • OK, United States . 46 F4
Wookey Hole • United Kingdom 104 F3
Woolacombe Beach •
United Kingdom .... 101 [151]
Woollongong • NS, Australia .. 144 C2
Woomera • SA, Australia 34 G6
Woonsocket • SD, United States . 43 G4
Woonsocket • RI, United States . 153 D4
Wooramel • WA, Australia 34 B5
Wooster • OH, United States ... 44 D5
Worcester • South Africa 134 C5
Worcester • MA, United States . 153 D4
Worcestershire • United Kingdom 104 D2
Wordsworth House •
United Kingdom 104 C1
Workington • United Kingdom . 104 C1
Worksop • United Kingdom 7 K8
Worland • WY, United States ... 42 L4
World's View • Zimbabwe 130 C3
Wörlitz Castle • Germany .... 113 [214]
Wormerveer • Netherlands 109 F2
Worms • Germany 5 L5
Wörth • Germany 112 F5
Worthing Beach • United Kingdom 101 [86]
Worthing • United Kingdom ... 104 E3
Worthington • MN, United States 43 I5
Worthington • OH, United States 44 D5
Worthsee • Germany 112 F3
Wosi • Indonesia 32 (1) C2
Wowoni • Indonesia 32 (1) B3
Woy Woy • NS, Australia 34 J6
Wrangel I. • Russian Fed. 27 V2
Wrangell • AK, United States ... 49 O4
Wrangell, Cape •
AK, United States 49 D5
Wrangell, Mt •
AK, United States 49 M3
Wrangell Mtns •
AK, United States 38 C4
Wrangell-St Elias Nat. Park •
AK, United States 49 M3
Wrangell-St Elias Nat. Park & Preserve
Heritage N • AK, United States . 82 [12]
Wrangell-St Elias Nat. Park & Preserve
Park N • AK, United States .... 150 [12]
Wrath, Cape • United Kingdom . 6 H3
Wray • CO, United States 46 D2
Wrekin, The • United Kingdom . 104 D1
Wrexham • United Kingdom 7 J8

Wright

Wright • WY, United States ... 43 D5
Wright Brothers Nat. Mem. Park N • NC, United States ... 151 [245]
Wright Patman Lake • TX, United States ... 46 H6
Wrightson, Mt • AZ, United States ... 45 G6
Wrigley • NT, Canada ... 38 G4
Wrka • Poland ... 13 J5
Wroclaw • Poland ... 13 F6
Wronki • Poland ... 13 F5
Wrzesnia • Poland ... 13 G5
Wschowa • Poland ... 13 F6
Wu Jiang • China ... 29 D5
Wu Xia • China ... 29 D4
Wuakesha • WI, United States ... 44 A4
Wudangshan Heritage C • China ... 85 [171]
Wudaoliang • China ... 28 F1
Wudu • China ... 29 C4
Wuhan • China ... 29 E4
Wuhu • China ... 139 C1
Wujiang • China ... 139 C2
Wukari • Nigeria ... 22 F3
Wuliang Shan • China ... 29 C6
Wulingyuan Heritage N • China ... 83 [126]
Wulur • Indonesia ... 32 (1) I4
Würzburg Castle • Germany ... 113 [143]
Wum • Cameroon ... 22 G3
Wümme • Germany ... 5 M1
Wun Rog • Sudan ... 23 D2
Wunsiedel • Germany ... 9 H6
Wunstorf • Germany ... 8 E4
Wupatki Nat. Mon. Park N • AZ, United States ... 150 [104]
Wupatki Nat. Mon. • AZ, United States ... 153 E1
Wupper • Germany ... 111 B4
Wuppertal • Germany ... 111 B4
Würm • Germany ... 112 F3
Wurno • Nigeria ... 22 F2
Würzburg • Germany ... 9 E7
Würzburg Heritage C • Germany ... 86 [56]
Wurzen • Germany ... 8 H5
Wushaoling • China ... 29 C3
Wusheng Guan • China ... 29 E4
Wusong • China ... 81 A8
Wustermark • Germany ... 111 C1
Wutach • Germany ... 9 D9
Wutai Shan • China ... 29 E3
Wutong Shan • China ... 139 B4
Wuwei • China ... 29 C3
Wuxi • China ... 139 C2
Wuyi Shan • China ... 29 F5
Wuyi Shan Heritage N • China ... 83 [127]
Wuyi Shan Heritage C • China ... 85 [177]
Wuyiling • China ... 29 F2
Wuyuan • China ... 29 D2
Wuyuanzhen • China ... 139 C4
Wuzhi Shan • China ... 31 D3
Wyandotte • MI, United States ... 44 D4
Wyandra • QL, Australia ... 144 B5
Wye • United Kingdom ... 104 D3
Wye Valley • United Kingdom ... 104 D3
Wyk, Föhr Spa • Germany ... 113 [c3]
Wyndham • WA, Australia ... 34 E3
Wyndham • New Zealand ... 145 G4
Wyndmere • ND, United States ... 43 H3
Wynne • AR, United States ... 46 J5
Wynyard • TS, Australia ... 34 I8
Wynyard • SA, Canada ... 38 K6
Wyoming • United States ... 40 E3
Wyoming • MI, United States ... 44 C4
Wyre Forest • United Kingdom ... 104 D1
Wysoczyna Ciechanowska • Poland ... 13 J4
Wyszków • Poland ... 13 K5
Wytheville • VA, United States ... 48 G2
Wyżyna Krakowsko-Częstochowsk • Poland ... 13 I7
Wyżyna Lubelska • Poland ... 13 L6
Wyżyna Lubelska • Poland ... 13 M6

Xabia Beach • Spain ... 96 [118]
Xabia • Spain ... 117 C2
Xaghra • Malta ... 123 H1
Xai-Xai • Mozambique ... 24 E4
Xainza • China ... 28 E2
Xalapa • Mexico ... 157 G2
Xangongo • Angola ... 24 B3
Xanten • Germany ... 109 D12
Xanten • Germany ... 111 B1
Xánthi • Greece ... 122 D1
Xanthos • Turkey ... 122 D9
Xanthos-Letoon Heritage C • Turkey ... 86 [222]
Xanxerê • Brazil ... 52 F4
Xapuri • Brazil ... 51 D6
Xàtiva • Spain ... 11 K5
Xcalak • Mexico ... 157 H4
Xcaret • Mexico ... 157 H2
Xelha • Mexico ... 157 H2
Xenia • OH, United States ... 44 D6
Xeraco Beach • Spain ... 96 [119]
Xewkija • Malta ... 123 H1
Xi Hu • China ... 139 C3
Xi'an • China ... 29 D3
Xi'an Heritage C • China ... 85 [170]
Xiaguan • China ... 29 C5
Xiamen • China ... 29 F6
Xiang Jiang • China ... 29 E4
Xiangfan • China ... 29 E4
Xianggang • China ... 29 E6
Xiangshan • China ... 139 C4
Xiangtan • China ... 29 E5
Xiangzhou • Zhuhai, China ... 139 B3
Xiannumiao • China ... 139 C1
Xianqouan He • China ... 28 C2
Xianxia Ling • China ... 29 F5
Xiao Hinggan Ling • China ... 27 K7
Xiaobole Shan • China ... 27 J6
Xiaolan • China ... 139 B3
Xiaomeisha Beach Resort • Shenzhen, China ... 139 B4
Xiaoshan • China ... 139 C4
Xiapu • China ... 31 F1
Xichang • China ... 29 C5
Xigazê • China ... 28 E3
Xijir Ulan Hu • China ... 28 E2
Xili Lake Resort • Shenzhen, China ... 139 B3
Xilókastro • Greece ... 15 C6
Xilókastro Beach • Greece ... 97 [178]
Xilxes Beach • Spain ... 96 [120]
Ximiao • China ... 29 C2
Xingtai • China ... 29 E3
Xingu • Brazil ... 51 G5
Xingxingxia • China ... 29 C2
Xingyi • China ... 31 C2
Xining • China ... 29 C3
Xinjiang Uygur Zizhiqu • China ... 26 N10
Xinxian • China ... 29 E3
Xinxiang • China ... 29 E3
Xinyang • China ... 29 E4
Xinzo de Lima • Spain ... 11 D2
Xiongyuecheng • China ... 30 B4
Xiró • Greece ... 15 E5
Xisha Qundao • South China Sea ... 31 E3
Xisha Qundao • South China Sea ... 139 A7
Xitianmu Shan • China ... 139 C3
Xiuyan • China ... 30 B4
Xixabangma Feng • China ... 28 E3
Xizang Zizhiqu • China ... 28 E2
Xkichmook • Mexico ... 157 H1

Xlacah • Mexico ... 157 H2
Xlendi • Malta ... 123 H1
Xlendi Bay • Malta ... 123 H1
Xochicalco Heritage C • Mexico ... 157 G4
Xochicalco • Mexico ... 157 G4
Xochimilco Heritage C • Mexico ... 84 [22]
Xpuhil • Mexico ... 157 H3
Xuan Loc • Vietnam ... 141 E2
Xuanhua • China ... 29 F2
Xuanwei • China ... 29 C5
Xuanzhou • China ... 139 C3
Xuefeng Shan • China ... 29 D5
Xun Jiang • China ... 29 E6
Xupu • China ... 31 E1
Xuwen • China ... 29 E6
Xuzhou • China ... 29 F4
Xylóskalo • Crete, Greece ... 123 E5

Ya Men • China ... 139 B3
Ya'an • China ... 29 C4
Yabelo • Ethiopia ... 23 F3
Yablonovyy Khrebet • Russian Fed. ... 27 H6
Yablunyts'kyy • Ukraine ... 14 L1
Yabu, Laem • Ko Phuket, Thailand ... 142 E1
Yabulu • QL, Australia ... 144 B1
Yachats • OR, United States ... 42 C4
Yacuma • Bolivia ... 52 C1
Yadè, Massif du • Cameroon/Central African Rep. ... 22 H3
Yaeyama-shoto • Japan ... 29 G6
Yafo • Israel ... 135 A5
Yafran • Libya ... 21 B1
Yagoua • Cameroon ... 22 H2
Yagradagzê Shan • China ... 28 F2
Yai, Khao • Ko Samui, Thailand ... 142 D1
Yai, Laem • Ko Samui, Thailand ... 142 D1
Yaiza Beach • Lanzarote, Canary Is. ... 96 [111]
Yaiza • Lanzarote, Canary Is. ... 117 E3
Yakacik • Turkey ... 123 G4
Yakima • WA, United States ... 152 B1
Yako • Burkina Faso ... 22 D2
Yaku • Japan ... 30 F9
Yaku-shima Heritage N • Japan ... 83 [130]
Yakumo • Japan ... 30 K3
Yakutat • AK, United States ... 49 N4
Yakutat Bay • AK, United States ... 38 C5
Yakutia • Russian Fed. ... 27 H3
Yakutsk • Russian Fed. ... 27 K4
Yala • Thailand ... 31 B5
Yala Nat. Park • Sri Lanka ... 138 D16
Yalgoo • WA, Australia ... 34 C5
Yalinga • Central African Rep. ... 23 C2
Yaloké • Central African Rep. ... 22 H3
Yalong Jiang • China ... 29 C4
Yalongxue Shan • China ... 29 C5
Yalova • Turkey ... 122 D3
Yalpuh, Ozero • Ukraine ... 14 F6
Yalta • Ukraine ... 17 E6
Yalu • China/D.P.R. of Korea ... 30 D4
Yalutorovsk • Russian Fed. ... 26 K6
Yamagata • Japan ... 30 K5
Yamagata [Adm] • Japan ... 140 A4
Yamaguchi • Japan ... 30 F7
Yamaguchi [Adm] • Japan ... 140 A7
Yamal Peninsula • Russian Fed. ... 126 A3
Yamal, Poluostrov • Russian Fed. ... 26 K3
Yamanashi [Adm] • Japan ... 140 C1
Yamarovka • Russian Fed. ... 27 H6
Yamaska Prov. Park • QU, Canada ... 155 B8
Yamato-Koriyama • Japan ... 140 B2
Yambol • Sudan ... 23 D3
Yambol • Bulgaria ... 128 E3
Yamdena • Indonesia ... 32 (1) D4
Yamma Yamma, Lake • QL, Australia ... 34 H5
Yamoussoukro • Côte d'Ivoire ... 22 C3
Yampa • CO/UT, United States ... 45 H1
Yamsay Mtn • OR, United States ... 42 E5
Yamsk • Russian Fed. ... 27 P5
Yamuna • India ... 137 C7
Yamzho Yumco • China ... 28 F3
Yan'an • China ... 29 D3
Yana • Russian Fed. ... 27 M2
Yanam • India ... 138 D4
Yanbu • Saudi Arabia ... 18 C5
Yanchang • China ... 29 E3
Yancheng • China ... 29 G4
Yangambi • Dem. Rep. of Congo ... 23 C3
Yangiyul • Uzbekistan ... 18 I1
Yangjiang • China ... 29 E6
Yangon • Myanmar ... 31 B3
Yangquan • China ... 29 E3
Yangtze • China ... 29 F4
Yangtze Gorges • China ... 139 A7
Yangzhou • China ... 139 C1
Yanji • China ... 29 H2
Yankari Nat. Park Park • Nigeria ... 133 [B3]
Yankee Harbour • Antarctica ... 81 A10
Yankton • SD, United States ... 43 H5
Yano-Indigirskaya Nizmennost • Russian Fed. ... 27 N2
Yanqi • China ... 26 O9
Yanskiy Zaliv • Russian Fed. ... 27 M2
Yantai • China ... 29 G3
Yantian • Shenzhen, China ... 139 B4
Yantra • Bulgaria ... 128 E3
Yao • Chad ... 22 H2
Yao • Japan ... 140 B4
Yaoundé • Cameroon ... 22 G4
Yap • Fed. States of Micronesia ... 25 B8
Yap • Fed. States of Micronesia ... 106 I1
Yapen • Indonesia ... 32 (1) E3
Yapu • Myanmar ... 31 B4
Yaque del Norte • Dominican Rep. ... 159 G2
Yaque del Sur • Dominican Rep. ... 159 G7
Yaqui • Mexico ... 157 F2
Yar-Sale • Russian Fed. ... 26 L4
Yaraka • QL, Australia ... 34 H4
Yaransk • Russian Fed. ... 17 H3
Yardimci Burun • Turkey ... 123 E4
Yariga • Japan ... 30 I6
Yarim • Yemen ... 18 D7
Yarkand • China ... 18 K2
Yarkant • China ... 127 D2
Yarkant He • China ... 26 M10
Yarlung Zangbo Jiang • China ... 28 E3
Yarmouth • United Kingdom ... 106 D7
Yaroslavl' • Russian Fed. ... 126 C2
Yartsevo • Russian Fed. ... 26 P5
Yarumal • Colombia ... 51 B2
Yasawa Group • Fiji Is. ... 35 (3) Z2
Yashi • Nigeria ... 22 F2
Yass • NS, Australia ... 144 C2
Yatagan • Turkey ... 122 D4
Yateritas • Cuba ... 158 D8
Yates Center • KS, United States ... 46 H4
Yatsushiro • Japan ... 30 F8
Yatta Plateau • Kenya ... 131 G4
Yau Ma Tei • Hong Kong, China ... 139 B6
Yauco • Peru ... 163 B3
Yauco • Puerto Rico ... 159 H3
Yauyos • Peru ... 163 B1

Yavari • Brazil/Peru ... 51 C4
Yavero • Peru ... 163 B2
Yavoriv • Ukraine ... 13 M8
Yawatahama • Japan ... 37 C4
Yaxchilan • Mexico ... 18 F3
Yazd • Iran ... 18 F3
Yazoo • MS, United States ... 153 F2
Yazoo City • MS, United States ... 153 F2
Ydre • Sweden ... 125 F8
Ye • Myanmar ... 31 B3
Ye-u • Myanmar ... 31 B3
Yebbi Bou • Chad ... 20 I4
Yecheng • China ... 28 C1
Yecla • Spain ... 117 C1
Yedi Burun • Turkey ... 15 J7
Yefremov • Russian Fed. ... 17 F4
Yeha • Eritrea ... 21 G5
Yeji • Ghana ... 22 D3
Yekaterinburg • Russian Fed. ... 26 J6
Yelabuga • Mexico ... 157 G1
Yelizovo • Russian Fed. ... 27 Q6
Yell • United Kingdom ... 6 K1
Yellow Mountains • China ... 139 C1
Yellow Sea • Asia ... 29 G3
Yellowhead Pass • AL/BC, Canada ... 155 C2
Yellowknife • NT, Canada ... 38 I4
Yellowknife [Riv] • NT, Canada ... 38 I4
Yellowstone Lake • WY, United States ... 42 J4
Yellowstone Nat. Park Heritage N • WY, United States ... 82 [15]
Yellowstone Nat. Park Park N • WY, United States ... 150 [72]
Yellowstone Nat. Park • WY, United States ... 42 J4
Yelwa • Nigeria ... 22 E2
YEMEN • Asia ... 18 D7
Yenakiyeve • Ukraine ... 17 G5
Yenice • Turkey ... 15 I4
Yenierenköy • Cyprus ... 123 J2
Yenifoça • Turkey ... 15 H5
Yenisey • Russian Fed. ... 26 O5
Yeniseyskiy Kryazh • Russian Fed. ... 26 P5
Yeniseyskiy Zaliv • Russian Fed. ... 26 N3
Yeo Lake • WA, Australia ... 34 D5
Yeovil • United Kingdom ... 104 F3
Yeppoon • QL, Australia ... 144 B4
Yerbogachen • Russian Fed. ... 27 G4
Yercaud • India ... 138 D7
Yercaud Hill Sta • India ... 138 E2
Yercpótamos • Crete, Greece ... 123 F7
Yerevan • Armenia ... 18 D1
Yerington • NV, United States ... 45 C2
Yerköprü • Turkey ... 123 G3
Yermasóyia Beach • Cyprus ... 97 [218]
Yermasóyia • Cyprus ... 123 J3
Yermo • CA, United States ... 45 A4
Yermolayevo • Russian Fed. ... 26 I7
Yeroskipos • Cyprus ... 123 J3
Yerres • France ... 5 G6
Yershov • Russian Fed. ... 51 B6
Yerwa • Nigeria ... 22 H2
Yesa, Embalse de • Spain ... 11 J2
Yesilbag • Turkey ... 123 F3
Yesilhisar • Turkey ... 123 G2
Yesilköy • Turkey ... 15 J3
Yesilova • Turkey ... 123 F1
Yessey • Russian Fed. ... 26 R4
Yeu, Î. d' • France ... 11 I6
Yevlakh • France ... 10 C7
Yevpatoriya • Russian Fed. ... 17 D5
Yeysk • Russian Fed. ... 17 F5
Yi • Uruguay ... 163 D2
Yi Xian • China ... 139 C3
Yialousa • Cyprus ... 123 J2
Yibin • China ... 29 C5
Yibug Caka • China ... 28 E2
Yichang • China ... 29 E4
Yichun • China ... 29 E4
Yidu • China ... 29 E4
Yilan • China ... 27 K7
Yilan • China ... 123 F2
Yilanlikale • Turkey ... 123 G4
Yildiz Daglari • Turkey ... 15 I2
Yinchuan • China ... 29 D3
Yingde • China ... 29 E6
Yingkou • China ... 29 G2
Yining • China ... 26 N9
Yirga 'Alem • China ... 29 F1
Yishun New Town • Singapore ... 141 H2
Yixing • China ... 139 C1
Yiyang • China ... 29 E5
Yläne • Finland ... 125 E3
Ylikitka • Finland ... 16 I3
Ylitornio • Finland ... 16 I3
Ylivieska • Finland ... 16 M4
Ylöjärvi • Finland ... 125 D3
Yngaren • Sweden ... 47 F3
Yoakum • TX, United States ... 47 F3
Yoakum • TX, United States ... 154 J5
Yodo-gawa • Japan ... 140 B2
Yogan, Cerro • Chile ... 53 C6
Yogyakarta • Java, Indonesia ... 143 J7
Yogyakarta [Adm] • Java, Indonesia ... 143 J7
Yoho Nat. Park • BC, Canada ... 155 C4
Yoho Nat. Park Park N • BC, Canada ... 156 [12]
Yoju • Rep. of Korea ... 30 D6
Yokadouma • Cameroon ... 22 H4
Yokkaichi • Japan ... 30 I7
Yoko • Cameroon ... 22 G3
Yokote-jima • Japan ... 140 A11
Yokohama • Japan ... 140 C2
Yokohama-Hakkeijima Sea Paradise • Japan ... 140 C2
Yokosuka • Japan ... 140 C4
Yokote • Japan ... 30 K5
Yola • Nigeria ... 22 G3
Yom • Thailand ... 142 B2
Yonago • Japan ... 30 G7
Yonaguni-jima • Japan ... 140 A10
Yongan • D.P.R. of Korea ... 30 E4
Yongdok • Rep. of Korea ... 30 E6
Yonghung • D.P.R. of Korea ... 30 D5
Yongju • Rep. of Korea ... 30 E6
Yonkers • NY, United States ... 153 H1
Yonne • France ... 10 I5
Yonne [Riv] • France ... 7 K8
Yonori Land • Japan ... 140 C2

Yorktown • VA, United States ... 153 D11
Yoro Gorge • Japan ... 140 C4
Yoron-jima • Japan ... 140 A10
Yorton • SA, Canada ... 38 K6
Yosemite Nat. Park Heritage N • CA, United States ... 82 [12]
Yosemite Nat. Park Park N • CA, United States ... 150 [49]
Yosemite Nat. Park • CA, United States ... 152 C3
Yoshino-Kumano Nat. Park • Japan ... 140 B4
Yoshinoyama • Japan ... 140 B4
Yoshkar Ola • Russian Fed. ... 17 H3
Yosu • Rep. of Korea ... 30 D7
You Jiang • China ... 29 D6
Youghal • Ireland ... 104 C2
Youghal Beach • Ireland ... 96 [59]
Young I., St Vincent & Gren. ... 161 Q
Youngstown • NU, Canada ... 39 N4
Youngstown • OH, United States ... 44 E5
Youngstown • NY, United States ... 153 D1
Youshashan • China ... 26 P10
Youyang • China ... 29 D5
Yow Beach • Ko Samui, Thailand ... 142 D2
Ypres • Belgium ... 109 D13
Ypsilanti • MI, United States ... 44 D4
Yreka • CA, United States ... 42 D6
Yrghyz • Kazakstan ... 18 H1
Yrghyz [Riv] • Kazakstan ... 26 J8
Ystad • Sweden ... 97 [13]
Ystad Beach • Sweden ... 125 F8
Ysyk Köl [Lake] • Kyrgyzstan ... 26 M9
Ysyk Köl [Lake] • Kyrgyzstan ... 124 C3
Ytre Sula • Norway ... 124 C3
Ytre Arna • Norway ... 29 C6
Yuan Jiang • China ... 29 C6
Yuanling • China ... 29 D5
Yuantouzhu • China ... 139 C1
Yuba City • CA, United States ... 45 B2
Yucatán [Adm] • Mexico ... 37 D3
Yucatan Basin • West Indies ... 160 A6
Yucatán Channel • Mexico ... 37 D3
Yucatán, Peninsula de • Mexico ... 157 H1
Yucca House Nat. Mon. Park N • CO, United States ... 150 [92]
Yudoma • Russian Fed. ... 27 M5
Yuen Long • Hong Kong, China ... 139 B6
Yuendumu • NT, Australia ... 145 D1
Yuendumu Aboriginal Land • NT, Australia ... 145 D1
Yueyang • China ... 29 E5
Yugo-Tala • Russian Fed. ... 27 P3
YUGOSLAVIA, FEDERAL REPUBLIC OF • Europe ... 14 H5
Yuhang • China ... 139 C4
Yukagirskoye Ploskogorye • Russian Fed. ... 27 N3
Yukon • OK, United States ... 46 G5
Yukon Flats • AK, United States ... 38 B3
Yukon Plateau • YT, Canada ... 38 D4
Yukon [Riv] • United/Canada ... 49 J3
Yukon Territory • Canada ... 38 D4
Yukon-Charley Rivers Nat. Preserve Park N • AK, United States ... 150 [6]
Yulara • NT, Australia ... 145 D3
Yulin • Shaanxi, China ... 29 D3
Yulin • Guangxi, China ... 31 E2
Yulin Jiao • China ... 25 M8
Yulongxue Shan • China ... 31 C1
Yuma • CO, United States ... 46 D2
Yuma • AZ, United States ... 153 E3
Yumari • Venezuela ... 51 D3
Yumen • China ... 29 B3
Yumurtalik • Turkey ... 123 G4
Yun-Gun-Gui Gaoyuian • China ... 31 C1
Yuna • Dominican Rep. ... 159 G3
Yunak • Turkey ... 15 M5
Yunan • China ... 139 A6
Yungas • Bolivia ... 52 D2
Yunkai Dashan • China ... 31 E2
Yunkanjini Aboriginal Land • NT, Australia ... 145 D1
Yunzhong Shan • China ... 29 E3
Yurga • Russian Fed. ... 26 N6
Yurimaguas • Peru ... 51 B5
Yurungkax He • China ... 28 C1
Yushan • Taiwan ... 29 G6
Yushkozero • Russian Fed. ... 16 O4
Yushu • China ... 29 B4
Yutian • China ... 31 C2
Yuxi • China ... 29 C5
Yuxikou • China ... 139 C1
Yuyao • China ... 139 C4
Yuzawa • Japan ... 30 K5
Yvelines • France ... 115 E3
Yverdon-les-Bains • Switzerland ... 119 C2
Yvetot • France ... 10 F4
Yvoir • Belgium ... 109 D15

Za Qu • China ... 28 G2
Zaanse Schans • Netherlands ... 109 F2
Zaanstad • Netherlands ... 109 F2
Zabargad • Egypt ... 21 G3
Zabargad I. Dive • Red Sea ... 135 B2
Zabid • Yemen ... 18 D7
Zabid Heritage C • Yemen ... 85 [120]
Zabkowice Slaskie • Poland ... 13 F7
Zabolotiv • Ukraine ... 14 M1
Zabrze • Poland ... 128 C1
Zacatecas Heritage C • Mexico ... 84 [15]
Zacatecas • Mexico ... 157 F3
Zacatecas [Adm] • Mexico ... 37 (1) B1
Zachodnio-Beskidy • Poland ... 128 C1
Zadar • Croatia ... 128 D3
Zadetkyi Kyun • Myanmar ... 31 B4
Zadi • Angola ... 23 B5
Zafra • Spain ... 11 E6
Zagan • Poland ... 13 E6
Zagazig, El • Egypt ... 21 F2
Zaghouan • Tunisia ... 131 E2
Zagóra • Greece ... 122 D4
Zagora • Morocco ... 131 D6
Zagora • Greece ... 122 D4
Zagreb • Croatia ... 128 D1
Zagreb • Croatia ... 13 F10
Zagros, Kuhha-ye • Iran ... 18 E2
Zaground Beach • Greece ... 97 [188]
Zagunao • China ... 29 C4
Zagyva • Hungary ... 13 J10
Zaháro • Greece ... 122 C5
Zaháro Beach • Greece ... 97 [180]
Zahedan • Iran ... 18 H4
Zahrada Cech • Czech Rep. ... 128 B4
Záhony • Hungary ... 13 L9
Zajecar • F.R. of Yugoslavia ... 14 J6
Zakamensk • Russian Fed. ... 27 G6
Zakataly • Azerbaijan ... 17 H6
Zákinthos [I.] • Greece ... 15 B6
Zakopane • Poland ... 128 C4
Zákros • Crete, Greece ... 123 E8

Zala • Hungary ... 13 G11
Zalaegerszeg • Hungary ... 13 F11
Zalau • Romania ... 14 L2
Zalim • Saudi Arabia ... 18 D5
Zalingei • Sudan ... 21 E4
Zallaca • Spain ... 90 A16
Zaltan • Libya ... 21 C2
Zambezi • Africa ... 24 C2
Zambezi • Zambia ... 24 C2
Zambezi [Riv] • Zambia ... 24 D2
Zambezi Nat. Park Park • Zimbabwe ... 133 [111]
ZAMBIA • Africa ... 24 D2
Zamboanga • Philippines ... 31 G5
Zamboanga Peninsula • Philippines ... 31 G5
Zambrów • Poland ... 13 L5
Zamek Bonerów • Poland ... 128 C1
Zamek Krysztopor • Poland ... 128 C2
Zamek Lubomirskich • Poland ... 128 C4
Zamora • Spain ... 11 F3
Zamosc • Poland ... 13 M7
Zamosc Heritage C • Poland ... 86 [163]
Zamzam • Libya ... 21 B1
Zandvoort • Netherlands ... 109 F1
Zandvoort, Auto Circuit • Netherlands ... 109 F1
Zanesville • OH, United States ... 44 D6
Zanjan • Iran ... 18 E2
Zante Beach • Zante, Greece ... 97 [172]
Zante • Greece ... 122 C3
Zanthus • WA, Australia ... 34 D6
Zanzibar • Tanzania ... 130 B2
Zanzibar I. • Tanzania ... 130 B2
Zanzibar • Tanzania ... 130 B2
Zaouiatallaz • Algeria ... 20 G4
Zaozernyy • Russian Fed. ... 26 P6
Západné Karpaty • Europe ... 13 I8
Zapadno Dvina • Russian Fed. ... 126 C3
Zapadno Sibirskaya Ravnina • Russian Fed. ... 26 M5
Zapadnyy Sayan • Russian Fed. ... 26 D7
Zapala • Argentina ... 53 C3
Zapata • TX, United States ... 47 E4
Zapata, Peninsula de • Cuba ... 158 D2
Zapican • Uruguay ... 163 D2
Zapolyarnyy • Russian Fed. ... 17 E1
Zaporizhzhya • Ukraine ... 17 F5
Zara • Croatia ... 90 A14
Zarafshon • Uzbekistan ... 18 I2
Zaragoza • Spain ... 11 K3
Zaragoza • Colombia ... 51 C2
Zaragoza • Mexico ... 47 A2
Zárate • Argentina ... 18 H3
Zárate • Argentina ... 163 D1
Zarautz • Spain ... 11 I1
Zarca • Venezuela ... 51 D2
Zarco, Baia do • Madeira ... 118 C2
Zarechensk • Russian Fed. ... 16 P3
Zaria • Nigeria ... 22 F3
Zarnesti • Romania ... 14 M4
Zarqa, Az • Jordan ... 21 G1
Zary • Poland ... 13 E6
Zarzaitine • Algeria ... 20 G3
Zarzis • Tunisia ... 131 E6
Zatec • Czech Rep. ... 128 B2
Zaventem [Apt] • Belgium ... 109 D14
Zawiah • Libya ... 21 B2
Zawiercie • Poland ... 128 C1
Zaysan • Kazakstan ... 26 N8
Zaysan Köli • Kazakstan ... 26 N8
Zayü • China ... 29 B5
Zdunska Wola • Poland ... 13 H6
Zealand • Denmark ... 125 F10
Zebbug • Malta ... 123 H4
Zeebrugge • Belgium ... 109 D13
Zeeland • Netherlands ... 109 D10
Zeeland • St Eustatius ... 161 F
Zehdenick • Germany ... 8 I3
Zehlendorf (Berlin) • Germany ... 111 C3
Zeil, Mt • NT, Australia ... 145 D1
Zeist • Netherlands ... 109 F1
Zeitz • Germany ... 9 H5
Zelená Hora Heritage C • Czech Rep. ... 86 [175]
Zelenoborskiy • Russian Fed. ... 16 P3
Zelenodolsk • Russian Fed. ... 17 H3
Zelenogradsk • Russian Fed. ... 13 J3
Zelezná Rudá • Czech Rep. ... 128 A3
Zell • Baden-Württemberg, Germany ... 112 D6
Zell • Rheinland-Pfalz, Germany ... 112 D2
Zell am See Ski • Austria ... 100 [165]
Zell am See • Austria ... 119 H4
Zell am Ziller Ski • Austria ... 100 [144]
Zell am Ziller • Austria ... 119 H7
Zelzate • Belgium ... 123 G2
Zemaitija Nat. Park Park N • Lithuania ... 89 [145]
Zemaitija Nat. Park • Lithuania ... 126 B3
Zembra • Tunisia ... 131 E2
Zembretta • Tunisia ... 131 E2
Zemgale • Latvia ... 126 B4
Zemun • F.R. of Yugoslavia ... 11 L9
Zempoala • Mexico ... 37 B4
Zemst Beach • Belgium ... 96 [73]
Zemst • Belgium ... 109 D14
Zengfeng • China ... 30 E3
Zenica • Bosnia-Herz. ... 128 D2
Zennor • United Kingdom ... 104 F4
Zepce • Bosnia-Herz. ... 128 D2
Zepernick • Germany ... 111 C2
Zerbst • Germany ... 8 H5
Zermatt Ski • Switzerland ... 100 [92]
Zermatt • Switzerland ... 119 G6
Zernabatim Beach • Goa, India ... 137 B2
Zernez • Switzerland ... 119 G4
Zernsdorf • Germany ... 111 C4
Zestienhoven [Apt] • Netherlands ... 109 F3
Zetel • Germany ... 5 K1
Zeulenroda • Germany ... 9 G6
Zeuthen • Germany ... 111 C4
Zeven • Germany ... 8 E3
Zevenaar • Netherlands ... 5 J3
Zeya • Russian Fed. ... 27 K6
Zeya [Riv] • Russian Fed. ... 27 K6
Zeytindag • Turkey ... 15 I5
Zeze • Portugal ... 11 C5
Zgierz • Poland ... 13 I6
Zgorzelec • Poland ... 13 E6
Zhambyl • Kazakstan ... 26 L9
Zhanagazaly • Kazakstan ... 26 J8
Zhangbei • China ... 29 E2
Zhanggu • China ... 29 C4
Zhanggung Cave • China ... 139 C1
Zhangjiakou • China ... 29 F2
Zhangmutou • China ... 139 B2
Zhangping • China ... 29 C3
Zhangwu • China ... 29 G2
Zhangye • China ... 29 C3
Zhangzhou • China ... 29 F6
Zhanyi • China ... 29 C5
Zhaotong • China ... 29 C5
Zhaoqing • China ... 29 E6
Zhaoyuan • Kazakstan ... 28 D2
Zhejiang • China ... 139 A8
Zhelezndorozhnyy • Russian Fed. ... 17 J2
Zhem • Kazakstan ... 26 I8
Zhen Jiang • China ... 139 C1
Zhengzhou • China ... 29 E4
Zhenjiang • China ... 139 C1
Zhenlai • China ... 29 G2
Zhenyuan • China ... 31 D1
Zhetiqara • Kazakstan ... 26 J7

Zhezqazghan • Kazakstan ... 26 K8
Zhi Qu • China ... 28 G2
Zhigalovo • Russian Fed. ... 27 G6
Zhigansk • Russian Fed. ... 27 J3
Zhijiang • China ... 29 D5
Zhitomir • Ukraine ... 14 D4
Zhob • Pakistan ... 28 A2
Zhongba • China ... 28 D3
Zhongdian • China ... 29 B5
Zhongning • China ... 29 D3
Zhongshan Qundao • South China Sea ... 139 A8
Zhongshan • China ... 139 B1
Zhongsha Qundao • South China Sea ... 31 E4
Zhosaly • Kazakstan ... 26 J8
Zhoukoudian Heritage C • China ... 85 [168]
Zhoukouzhen • China ... 29 E4
Zhoushan • China ... 139 C4
Zhoushan Dao • China ... 139 C4
Zhoushan Qundao • China ... 139 C4
Zhu Jiang • China ... 139 B2
Zhuanghe • China ... 30 B5
Zhuhai Holiday Resort • China ... 139 B1
Zhuhai, China ... 139 B1
Zhuhai Special Economic Zone • China ... 139 B1
Zhuji • China ... 139 C4
Zhujing • China ... 139 C4
Zhuzhou • China ... 29 E5
Zhytomyr • Ukraine ... 13 N6
Zibo • China ... 29 F3
Zicavo • Corsica, France ... 115 L4
Ziegenhals • Germany ... 111 C4
Zielona Góra • Poland ... 13 E6
Zierikzee • Netherlands ... 5 G3
Zigong • China ... 29 C5
Zigui • China ... 29 D4
Ziguinchor • Senegal ... 22 A2
Zihuatanejo • Mexico ... 157 G3
Zijin Shan • China ... 139 C1
Zijing Shan • China ... 29 E3
Zijpe Beach • Netherlands ... 96 [67]
Zilina • Slovak Rep. ... 13 H8
Zillah • Libya ... 21 C2
Zillertal • Austria ... 119 H7
Zillertaler Alpen • Austria/Italy ... 119 H7
Zima • Russian Fed. ... 27 F6
Zimba • Zambia ... 24 D3
ZIMBABWE • Africa ... 130 C
Zimnicea • Romania ... 128 E1
Zinal • Switzerland ... 119 G6
Zinder • Niger ... 20 G6
Zingst • Germany ... 8 H2
Zingst Beach • Germany ... 96 [32]
Zingst Spa • Germany ... 113 [c23]
Zinnowitz Beach • Germany ... 97 [30]
Zion Nat. Park Park N • UT, United States ... 150 [78]
Zion Nat. Park • UT, United States ... 45 F3
Zipaquirá • Colombia ... 51 C3
Zippori • Israel ... 135 A4
Zirje • Croatia ... 128 D3
Zirkel, Mt • CO, United States ... 45 I1
Zirndorf • Germany ... 9 F7
Zittau • Germany ... 9 K5
Ziway, Lake • Ethiopia ... 23 F2
Ziyaraiyali • Maldives ... 138 F2
Ziyang • Kazakstan ... 26 N8
Zlatá Koruna • Czech Rep. ... 128 B4
Zlaté Moravce • Slovak Rep. ... 13 H9
Zlatijata • Bulgaria ... 14 K6
Zlatni Pyasutsi • Bulgaria ... 128 E4
Zlatograd • Bulgaria ... 15 G2
Zlatoust • Russian Fed. ... 26 I6
Zleby • Czech Rep. ... 128 B2
Zlín • Czech Rep. ... 13 G8
Zlocieniec • Poland ... 13 F4
Zlotów • Poland ... 13 G4
Zmeyinka • Ukraine ... 17 E5
Znin • Poland ... 13 G5
Znojmo • Czech Rep. ... 128 B4
Zoetermeer • Netherlands ... 109 F1
Zoldo Alto Ski • Italy ... 100 [228]
Zoldo Alto • Italy ... 120 B4
Zomba • Malawi ... 24 E3
Zonári, Akra • Rhodes, Greece ... 122 D12
Zongo • Dem. Rep. of Congo ... 22 H4
Zongshan Hot Springs • China ... 139 B1
Zonguldak • Turkey ... 15 M2
Zonhoven Beach • Belgium ... 96 [72]
Zonhoven • Belgium ... 109 D15
Zonnebeke (Battlefield) • Belgium ... 109 D13
Zons • Germany ... 111 B3
Zoologischer Garten Berlin • Germany ... 111 C2
Zoomarine Park L • Portugal ... 98 [79]
Zoorama • France ... 115 G1
Zorzor • Liberia ... 22 C3
Zossen • Germany ... 111 C4
Zouar • Chad ... 21 C3
Zourât • Mauritania ... 20 C4
Zrenjanin • F.R. of Yugoslavia ... 14 H4
Zrinska Gora • Croatia ... 128 D3
Zuancheng • China ... 139 C3
Zuari Estuary • Goa, India ... 137 B1
Zufar • Oman ... 25 G8
Zug Ski • Austria ... 100 [130]
Zug • Switzerland ... 119 G3
Zuger See • Switzerland ... 119 G3
Zugspitze • Austria/Germany ... 112 F6
Zuid-Beveland • Netherlands ... 109 D10
Zuid-Holland • Netherlands ... 109 D6
Zújar, Embalse del • Spain ... 11 F6
Zülpich • Germany ... 112 D1
Zululand • South Africa ... 134 B2/B4
Zumaia Beach • Spain ... 96 [87]
Zumbo • Mozambique ... 24 E3
Zuni • NM, United States ... 153 E2
Zunyi • China ... 29 D5
Zuoz • Switzerland ... 119 G4
Zuqar, Jabal • Yemen ... 21 H5
Zürich • Switzerland ... 9 D9
Zürichsee • Switzerland ... 119 G3
Zurmi • Nigeria ... 20 G6
Zurrieq • Malta ... 123 H4
Zürs Ski • Austria ... 100 [131]
Zürs • Austria ... 119 H5
Zuru • Nigeria ... 22 F2
Zusmarshausen • Germany ... 112 F2
Zut • Croatia ... 128 D3
Zutphen • Netherlands ... 109 D8
Zuurberg Nat. Park • South Africa ... 134 C8
Zuwarah • Libya ... 21 B1
Zvezda • Czech Rep. ... 128 B4
Zvishavane • Zimbabwe ... 130 C4
Zvishtov • Bulgaria ... 14 M6
Zvolen • Slovak Rep. ... 13 I9
Zweibrücken • Germany ... 112 D3
Zweisel • Germany ... 9 J7
Zweisimmen Ski • Switzerland ... 100 [88]
Zwettl • Austria ... 119 J2
Zwickau • Germany ... 9 H6
Zwickauer Mulde • Germany ... 9 H6
Zwijndrecht • Netherlands ... 109 F2
Zwinger Castle • Germany ... 113 [83]
Zwinger Castle • Germany ... 113 [195]
Zwolle • Netherlands ... 109 D8
Zyrardów • Poland ... 13 J5
Zyryan • Kazakstan ... 26 N8
Zyryanka • Russian Fed. ... 27 P3
Żywiec • Poland ... 128 C3

WORLD

EUROPE AND THE MEDITERRANEAN

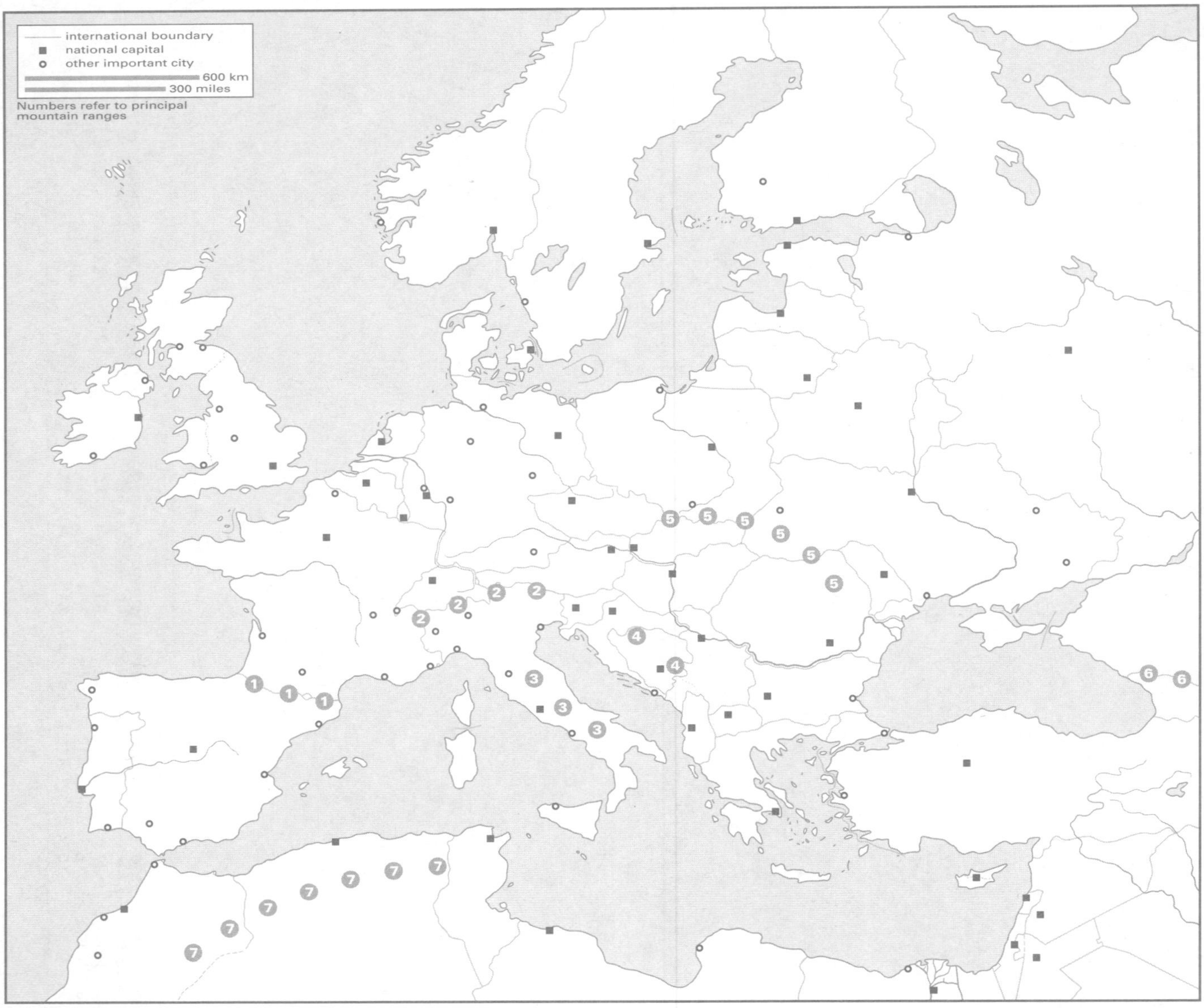

international boundary
■ national capital
○ other important city

‒‒‒‒‒‒‒ 600 km
‒‒‒‒‒‒‒ 300 miles

Numbers refer to principal
mountain ranges

THE FORMER SOVIET UNION

international boundary
■ national capital
○ other important city

See Europe map above

BRITISH ISLES

international boundary
geographical county boundary (UK),
regional boundary (Ireland)
national capital
capital of constituent parts of UK
other important city/town
100 kilometres
50 miles

Letters refer to English Tourist Council regions

CHANNEL IS.

NETHERLANDS

international boundary
provincial boundary
national capital
provincial capital
other important city/town
80 km
40 miles

BELGIUM AND LUXEMBOURG

international boundary
provincial boundary
national capital
provincial capital
other important city/town
80 km
40 miles

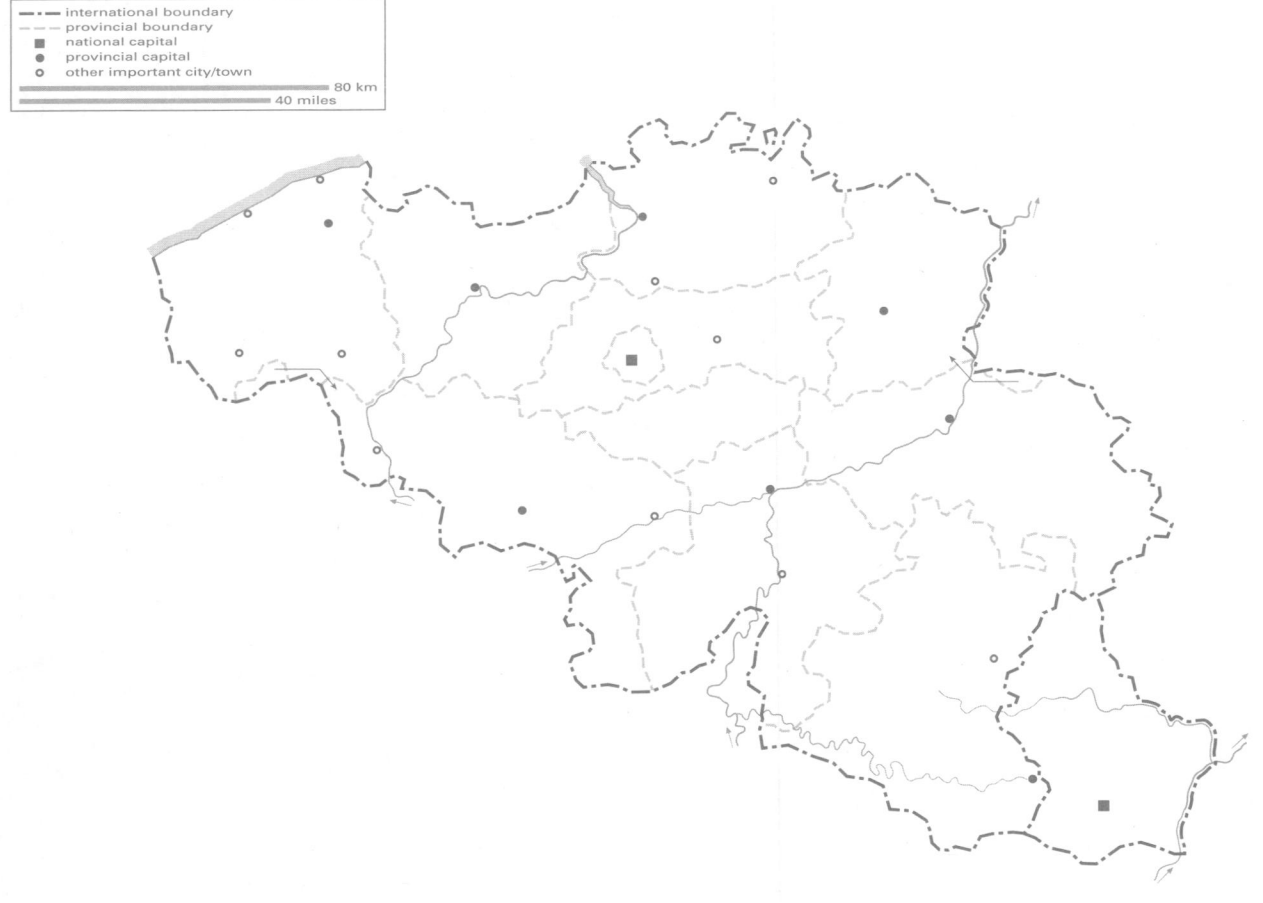

GERMANY

FRANCE

--·-- international boundary
-- -- regional boundary
■ national capital
● regional capital
○ other important city/town

200 km
100 miles

60 kilometres
30 miles

SPAIN AND PORTUGAL

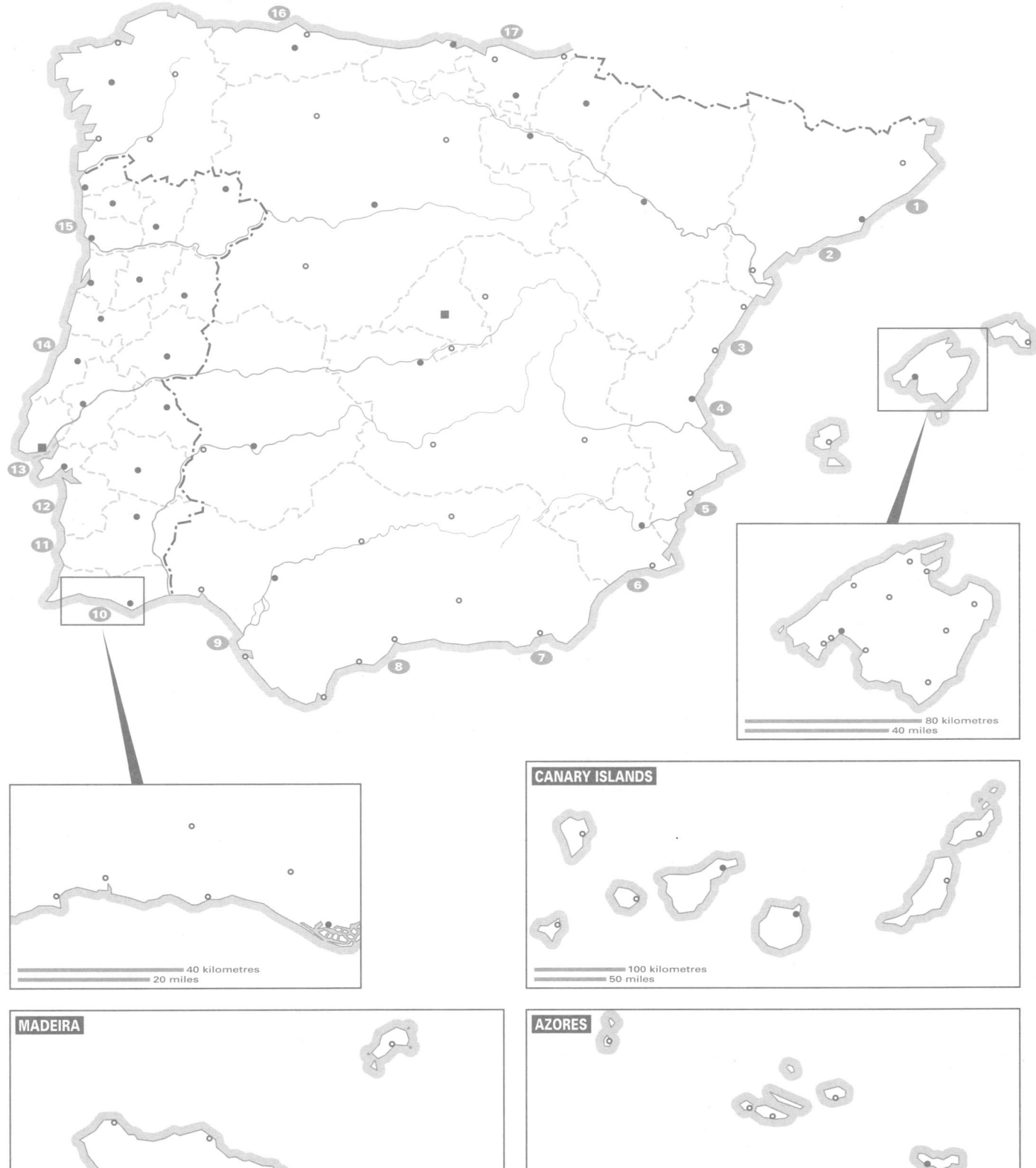

international boundary
autonomous community boundary (Spain)
district boundary (Portugal)
national capital
autonomous community capital (Spain)
district capital (Portugal)
other important city/town

200 km
100 miles

Numbers refer to Spanish and Portuguese 'Costas'

80 kilometres
40 miles

40 kilometres
20 miles

CANARY ISLANDS

100 kilometres
50 miles

MADEIRA

40 km
20 miles

AZORES

200 kilometres
100 miles

SWITZERLAND

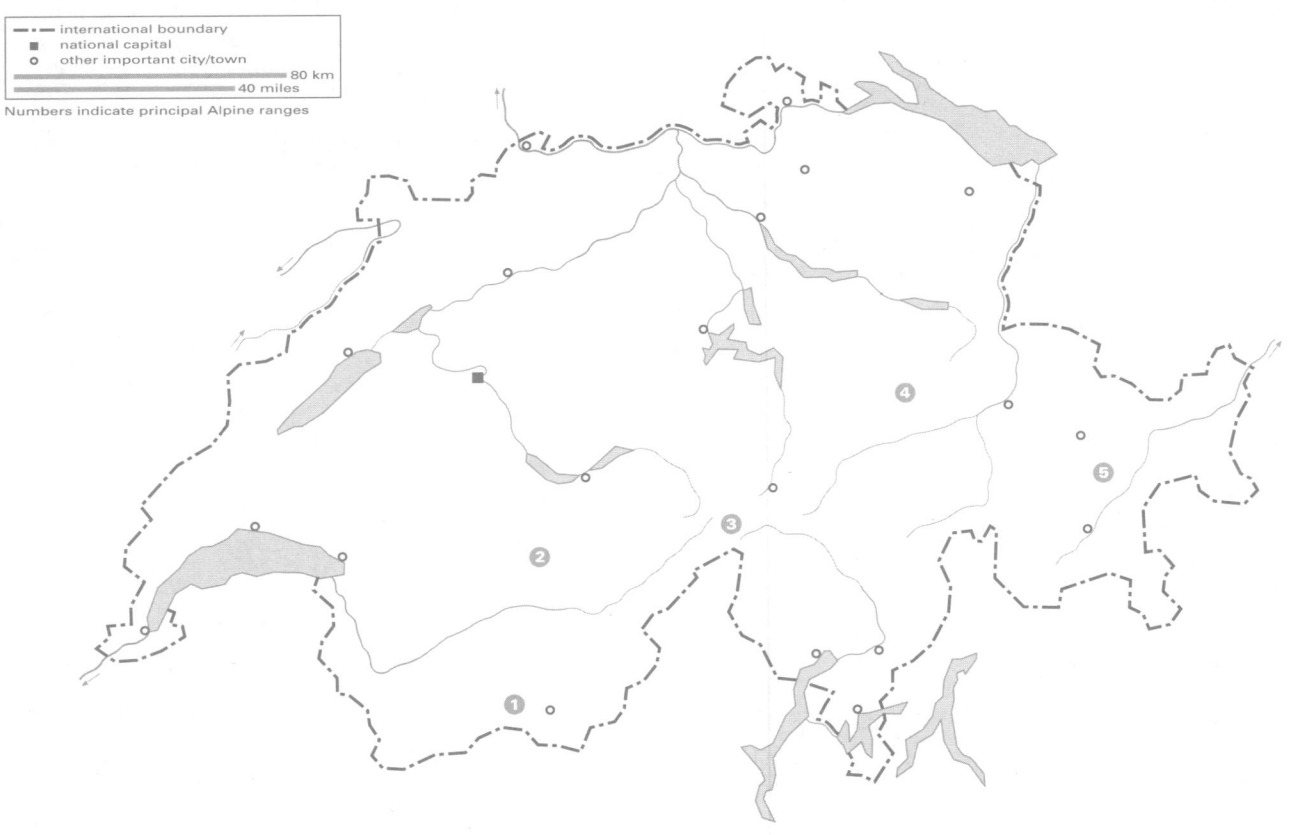

international boundary
national capital
other important city/town

80 km
40 miles

Numbers indicate principal Alpine ranges

AUSTRIA

international boundary
Land boundary
national capital
Land capital
other important city/town

100 km
50 miles

Numbers indicate principal Alpine ranges

ITALY

international boundary
regional boundary
■ national capital
● regional capital
○ other important city/town

200 km
100 miles

GREECE AND WESTERN TURKEY

international boundary
national capital
other important city/town
200 km
100 miles

TURKEY

international boundary
national capital
other important city/town
400 km
200 miles

SCANDINAVIA

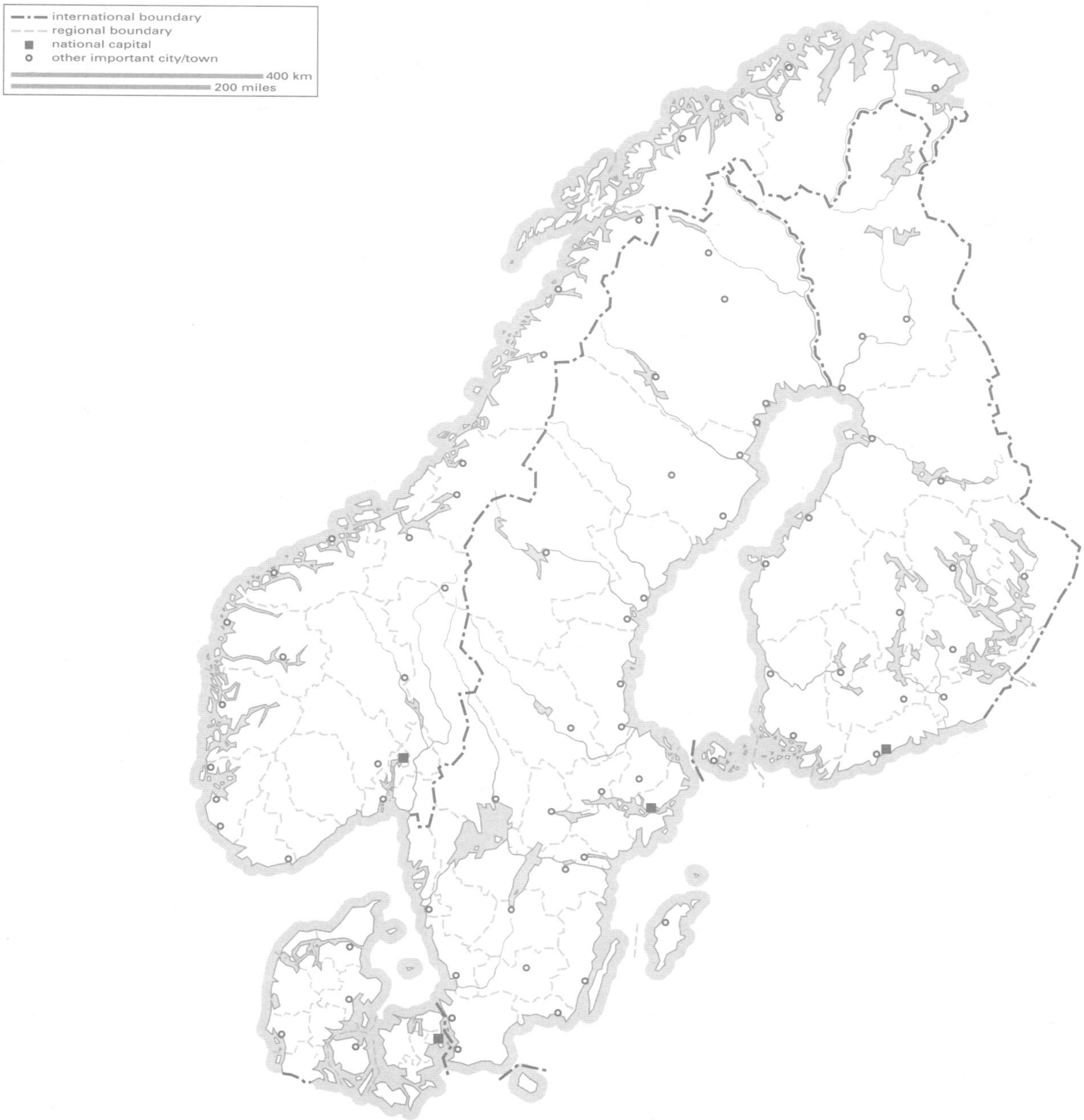

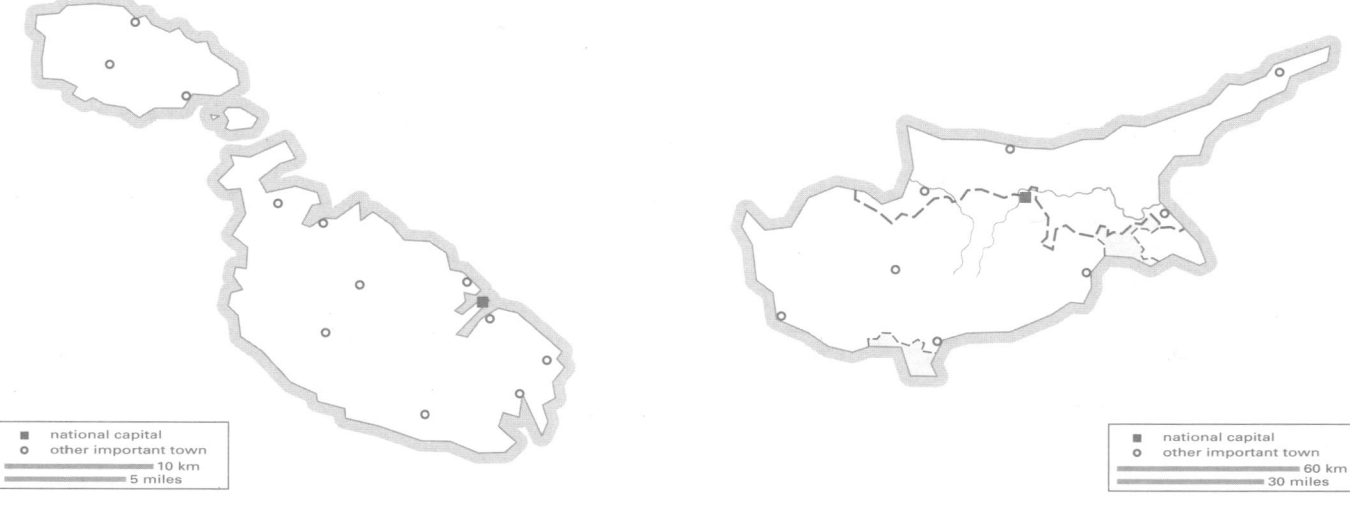

MALTA

CYPRUS

AFRICA

international boundary
■ national capital
○ other important city

SOUTH AFRICA

─·─·─ international boundary
─ ─ ─ provincial boundary
■ national capital
● provincial capital
○ other important city/town
▬▬▬ 600 km
▬▬▬ 300 miles

INDIA

–·–·–	international boundary
– – –	state/union territory boundary
■	national capital
●	state capital
○	other important city/town

800 km
400 miles

CHINA

–·–·–	international boundary
– – –	province/autonomous region boundary
■	national capital
●	province/autonomous region capital
○	other important city/town

1000 km
500 miles

AUSTRALIA

state/territory boundary
national capital
state/territory capital
other important city/town

1000 km
500 miles

CANADA

international boundary
province/territory boundary
national capital
province/territory capital
other important city/town

1000 km
500 miles

UNITED STATES

international boundary
state boundary
national capital
state capital
other important city/town

800 km
400 miles

1000 km
500 miles

300 km
150 miles

MEXICO

international boundary
state boundary
national capital
state capital
other important city/town

500 km
250 miles

THE CARIBBEAN

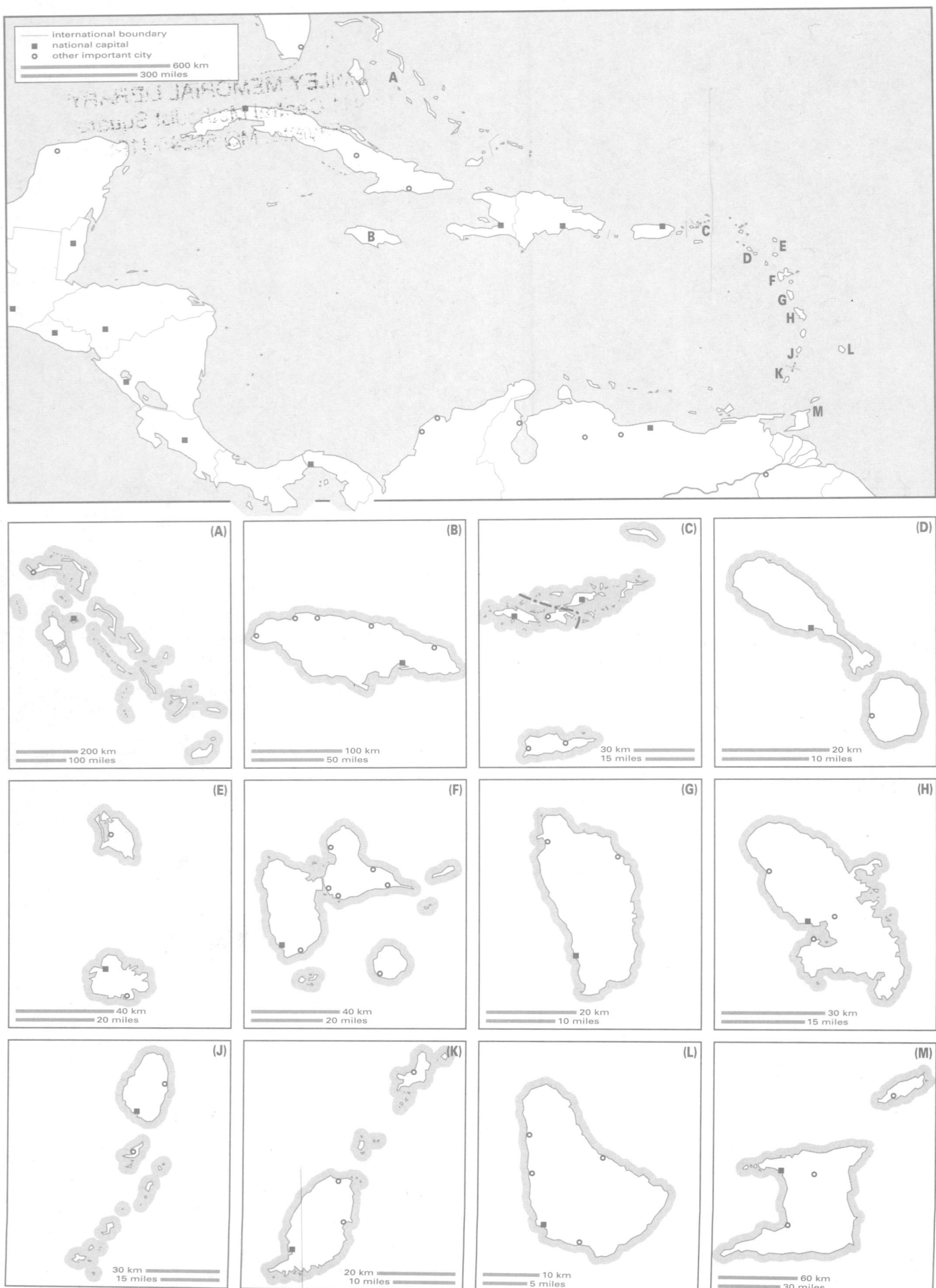

Legend:
- — international boundary
- ■ national capital
- ○ other important city
- 600 km
- 300 miles

Map labels: A, B, C, D, E, F, G, H, J, K, L, M

(A) 200 km / 100 miles

(B) 100 km / 50 miles

(C) 30 km / 15 miles

(D) 20 km / 10 miles

(E) 40 km / 20 miles

(F) 40 km / 20 miles

(G) 20 km / 10 miles

(H) 30 km / 15 miles

(J) 30 km / 15 miles

(K) 20 km / 10 miles

(L) 10 km / 5 miles

(M) 60 km / 30 miles